PEARSON ALWAYS LEARNING

Economics and Finance of Higher Education

ASHE Reader Series

Edited by
John C. Weidman

Associate Editors
John L. Yeager
Laurie Cohen
Linda Theresa DeAngelo
Kristin M. DeLuca
Michael G. Gunzenhauser
W. James Jacob
Maureen W. McClure
Stewart E. Sutin

Series Editor
Jerlando F.L. Jackson, University of Wisconsin

Cover photo courtesy of the University of Pittsburgh.

Pearson Learning Solutions, 501 Boylston Street, Suite 900, Boston, MA 02116
A Pearson Education Company
www.pearsoned.com

Printed in the United States of America

47 2022

000200010271810096

JH/VP

ISBN 10: 1-269-91294-1
ISBN 13: 978-1-269-91294-5

TABLE OF CONTENTS

Advisory Board

In seeking advice on specific readings to include in this edition of the Reader, assessments and recommendations were sought from higher education scholars and practitioners. In consultation with the editors, the following people provided feedback on at least one of the sections:

Valarie L. Avalone, Monroe Community College, USA
Sheng Yao Cheng, National Chung Cheng University, Taiwan
Jane Crisler, University of Wisconsin Colleges, USA
Mark P. Curchack, Arcadia University, USA
William P. Fenstermacher, Kaludis Consulting, USA
Deborah Greene, Georgia Institute of Technology, USA
Jake Julia, Northwestern University, USA
Donna Kidd, George Mason University, USA
Wanhua Ma, Peking University, China
Ka Ho Mok, Hong Kong Institute of Education, China
Daniel Morris, College of Southern Nevada, USA
Joseph L. Murray, Bucknell University, USA
Najeeb Shafiq, University of Pittsburgh, USA
Charles Tegen, Clemson University, USA
Ed Valeau, Hartnell Community College and ELS Group, USA

ACKNOWLEDGMENTS

The editors acknowledge the assistance of Veysel Gokbel, a doctoral student in the Department of Administrative and Policy Studies, School of Education, University of Pittsburgh, with collection and preparation of materials for submission to the publisher.

Grateful acknowledgment is made to the following sources for permission to reprint material copyrighted or controlled by them:

Section I Economics and Finance of Higher Education

"On the Meaning of Markets in Higher Education," by William E. Becker and Robert K. Toutkoushian, reprinted from *Higher Education: Handbook of Theory and Research* 28 (2013), by permission of Springer Science & Business Media.

"The For-Profit Postsecondary School Sector: Nimble Critters or Agile Predators?" by David J. Deming, Claudia Goldin, and Lawrence F. Katz, reprinted from the *Journal of Economic Perspectives* 26, no. 1 (2012), American Economic Association.

"Accounting for Higher Education Accountability: Political Origins of State Performance Funding for Higher Education," by Kevin J. Dougherty et al., reprinted from *Teachers College Record* 115, no. 1 (2013), by permission of Columbia University.

"Financial Aid Policy: Lessons from Research," by Susan Dynarski and Judith Scott-Clayton, reprinted from *Future of Children* 23, no. 1 (2013), by permission of the Woodrow Wilson School of Public and International Affairs at Princeton University and the Brookings Institution.

"American Higher Education in Transition," by Ronald G. Ehrenberg, reprinted from *Journal of Economic Perspectives* 26, no. 1 (2012), American Economic Association.

"The Financial Aid Picture: Realism, Surrealism, or Cubism?" by Donald E. Heller, reprinted from *Higher Education: Handbook of Theory and Research* 26 (2011), by permission of Springer Science & Business Media.

"Economic Models and Policy Analysis in Higher Education: A Diagrammatic Exposition," by Michael B. Paulsen and Robert K. Toutkoushian, reprinted from *Higher Education: Handbook of Theory and Research* 23 (2008), by permission of Springer Science & Business Media.

Section II Economic Outcomes of Higher Education

"From 'Financial Considerations' to 'Poverty': Towards a Reconceptualisation of the Role of Finances in Higher Education Student Drop Out," by Mignonne Breier, reprinted from *Higher Education* 60, no. 6 (December 2010), by permission of Springer Science & Business Media.

"College Student Engagement and Early Career Earnings: Differences by Gender, Race/Ethnicity, and Academic Preparation," by Shouping Hu and Gregory C. Wolniak, reprinted from the *Review of Higher Education* 36, no. 2 (2013), by permission of Johns Hopkins University Press.

"Toward a Greater Understanding of the Effects of State Merit Aid Programs: Examining Existing Evidence and Exploring Future Research Direction," by Shouping Hu, Matthew Tengrove, and Liang Zhang, reprinted from *Higher Education: Handbook of Theory and Research* 27 (2012), by permission of Springer Science & Business Media.

"Influences on Labor Market Outcomes of African American College Graduates: A National Study," by Terrell L. Strayhorn, reprinted from the *Journal of Higher Education* 79, no. 1 (2008), by permission of Ohio State University Press.

"Post-Baccalaureate Wage Growth within Four Years of Graduation: The Effects of College Quality and College Major," by Scott L. Thomas and Liang Zhang, reprinted from *Research in Higher Education* 26, no. 46 (2005), by permission of Springer Science & Business Media.

"Term-Time Employment and the Academic Performance of Undergraduates," by Michael Wenz and Wei-Choun Yu, reprinted from the *Journal of Educational Finance* 35, no. 4 (2010), by permission of the Journal of Educational Finance, Inc.

Section III Government Financing of Higher Education

"Maintenance of State Effort for Higher Education: 'Barriers to Equal Educational Opportunity in Addressing the Rising Costs of a College Education'," by F. King Alexander, reprinted from the *Journal of Educational Finance* 36, no. 4 (2011), by permission of the Journal of Educational Finance, Inc.

"Student Loans: Do College Students Borrow Too Much — Or Not Enough?" by Christopher Avery and Sarah Turner, reprinted from the *Journal of Economic Perspectives* 26, no. 1 (2012), American Economic Association.

"The Roles of Public Higher Education Expenditure and the Privatization of the Higher Education on U.S. States Economic Growth," by Bradley R. Curs, Bornali Bhandari, and Christina Steiger, reprinted from the *Journal of Economic Perspectives* 36, no. 4 (spring 2011), American Economic Association.

"Transfer Access from Community Colleges and the Distribution of Elite Higher Education," by Alicia C. Dowd, John J. Cheslock, and Tatiana Melguizo, reprinted from the *Journal of Higher Education* 79, no. 4 (July-August 2008), by permission of the Ohio State University Press.

"Toward a More Complete Understanding of the Role of Financial Aid in Promoting College Enrollment: The Importance of Context," by Laura W. Perna (2010), reprinted from *Higher Education: Handbook of Theory and Research* 25 (2010), by permission of Springer Science & Business Media.

"State Support of Higher Education: Data, Measures, Findings, and Directions for Future Research," by David A. Tandberg and Casey Griffith, reprinted from *Higher Education: Handbook of Theory and Research* 28 (2013), by permission of Springer Science & Business Media.

Section IV Institutional Resources and Financial Management

"Community College Student Success: What Institutional Characteristics Make a Difference?" by Juan Carlos Calcagno et al., reprinted from *Economics of Education Review* 27, no. 6 (2008), by permission of Elsevier B.V.

"Budget Systems Used in Allocating Resources to Libraries," by Mott Linn, reprinted from *Bottom Line: Managing Library Finances* 20, no. 1 (2007), by permission of Emerald Group Publishing Ltd.

"Towards Decentralized and Goal-oriented Models of Institutional Resource Allocation: The Spanish Case," by Maria Jose Gonzalez Lopez, reprinted from *Higher Education* 51, no. 4 (2006), by permission of Springer Science & Business Media.

"Resource Allocation in Public Research Universities," by Jose L. Santos (2007), reprinted from the *Review of Higher Education* 30, no. 2 (2007), by permission of Johns Hopkins University Press.

"Funding Historically Black Colleges and Universities: Progress Toward Equality?" by G. Thomas Sav, reprinted from the *Journal of Educational Finance* 35, no. 3 (2010), by permission of the Journal of Educational Finance, Inc.

"Models of Institutional Resource Allocation: Mission, Market, and Gender," by Cindy S. Volk, Sheila Slaughter, and Scott L. Thomas (2001), reprinted from the *Journal of Higher Education* 72, no. 4 (July-August 2001), by permission of Ohio State University Press.

Section V Higher Education Expenditures

"National Models for College Costs and Prices," by Alisa F. Cunningham and Jamie P. Merisotis, reprinted from *Planning for Higher Education* 30, no. 3 (2002), by permission of the Society for College and University Planning.

"Budget Development Process for Community Colleges," by Daniel Derrico, reprinted from *Increasing Effectiveness of the Community College Financial Model: A Global Perspective for the Global Economy*, edited by Stuart E. Sutin et al. (2011), by permission of Palgrave Macmillan.

"The High Cost of Building a Better University," by Donald J. Guckert and Jeri Ripley King (2003), reprinted from *Planning for Higher Education* 32, no. 2 (2003), by permission of the Society for College and University Planning.

"Do Costs Differ Between For-Profit and Not-for-Profit Producers of Higher Education?" by David N. Laband and Bernard F. Lentz, reprinted from *Research in Higher Education* 45, no. 4 (June 2004), by permission of Springer Science & Business Media.

"Understanding the Cost of Public Higher Education: In the Case of Higher Education Costs, Diametrically Opposed Views Have Persisted Over Time. Why?" by Peter McPherson and David Shulenburger, reprinted from *Planning for Higher Education* 38, no. 3 (April-June 2010), by permission of the Society for College and University Planning.

"The Cost of Excellence: The Financial Implications of Institutional Rankings," by Steve O. Michael, reprinted from the *International Journal of Educational Management* 19, no. 5 (2005), by permission of Emerald Group Publishing Ltd.

"Understanding Higher Education Costs," by Michael F. Middaugh, reprinted from *Planning for Higher Education* 33, no. 3 (2005), by permission of the Society for College and University Planning.

Section VI Strategic Planning and Resource Allocation

"Integrating Risk Management and Strategic Planning: Integrated Risk Management and Strategic Planning Leverages the Benefits of Both Processes and Makes Them Mutually Reinforcing," by Francis K. Achampong, reprinted from *Planning for Higher Education* 38, no. 2 (2010), by permission of the Society for College and University Planning.

"Aligning Values with Resources and Assessment Results," by Marilee J. Bresciani, reprinted from *Academic Leader* 26, no. 7 (2010), by permission of Magna Publications.

"Financial Planning: Strategies and Lessons Learned," by Paul T. Brinkman and Anthony W. Morgan, reprinted from *Planning for Higher Education* 38, no. 3 (2010), by permission of the Society for College and University Planning.

"'Incentives for Managed Growth': A Case Study of Incentives-Based Planning and Budgeting in a Large Public Research University," by James C. Hearn et al., reprinted from the *Journal of Higher Education* 77, no. 2 (March-April 2006), by permission of Ohio State University Press.

"Funding, Resource Allocation, and Performance in Higher Education Systems," by Ingo Liefner, reprinted from *Higher Education* 46, no. 4, by permission of Spring Science and Business Media.

"Linking Strategic Planning, Priorities, Resource Allocation, and Assessment," by Brenda S. Trettel and John L. Yeager, reprinted from *Increasing Effectiveness of the Community College Financial Model: A Global Perspective for the Global Economy*, edited by Stewart E. Sutin et al. (2011), by permission of Palgrave Macmillan.

Section VII Ethics and Higher Education Financing

"Why Act for the Public Good? Four Answers," by C. Daniel Batson, reprinted from *Personality and Social Psychology Bulletin* 20, no. 5 (October 1994), by permission of Sage Publications.

"Ethical Behavior in Higher Educational Institutions: The Role of the Code of Conduct," by Zabihollah Rezaee, Robert C. Elmore, and Joseph Z. Szendi, reprinted from *Journal of Business Ethics* 30, no. 2 (March 2001), by permission of Springer Science & Business Media.

"The Normative Structure of College and University Fundraising Behaviors," by Timothy C. Caboni, reprinted from the *Journal of Higher Education* 81, no. 3 (May-June 2010), by permission of Ohio State University Press.

"Revenue Generation and Its Consequences for Academic Capital, Values and Autonomy: Insights from Canada," by Julia Antonia Eastman, reprinted from *Higher Education Management & Policy* 19, no. 3 (2007), by permission of the Organization for Economic Cooperation & Development.

"Diversity, College Costs, and Postsecondary Opportunity: An Examination of the Financial Nexus between College Choice and Persistence for African Americans and Whites" by Edward P. St. John, Michael B. Paulsen, and Deborah Faye Carter, reprinted from *Journal of Higher Education* 76, no. 5 (2005), by permission of Ohio State University Press.

"Neoliberalism, Corporate Culture, and the Promise of Higher Education" by Henry A. Giroux, reprinted from *Harvard Educational Review* 72, no. 4 (winter 2002), by permission of Harvard Education Publishing Group.

"Academic Capitalism and Academic Culture: A Case Study," by Pilar Mendoza and Joseph B. Berger, reprinted from *Education Policy Analysis Archives* 16 (2008), by permission of the authors.

Section VIII International Financing of Higher Education

"Access to Higher Education in Egypt: Examining Trends by University Sector," by Elizabeth Buckner, reprinted from *Comparative Education Review* 57, no. 3 (2013), by permission of Chicago University Press.

"Financing Schemes for Higher Education" by Elena Del Rey and Maria Racionero, reprinted from *European Journal of Political Economy* 26, no. 1 (March 2010), by permission of Elsevier B.V.

"Making Higher Education Finance Work for Africa," by Shantayanan Devarajan, Celestin Monga, and Tertius Zongo, reprinted from *Journal of African Economies* 20, no. 3 (2011), by permission of Oxford Journals.

"Cost Sharing in Higher Education in Kenya: Examining the Undesired Policy Outcomes," by Mary S. Ngolovoi, reprinted from *Higher Education Policy* 23, no. 3 (2010), by permission of Oxford University Press.

"Internationalization as a Response to Globalization: Radical Shifts in University Environments," by Nelly P. Stromquist, reprinted from *Higher Education* 53, no. 1 (January 2007), by permission of Springer Science & Business Media.

"The Equity Challenge in China's Higher Education Finance Policy," by Fengshou Sun and Armando Barrientos, reprinted from *Higher Education Policy* 22 (June 2009), by permission of Palgrave Macmillan.

Introduction to the ASHE Reader on Economics and Finance of Higher Education

John C. Weidman and John L. Yeager
University of Pittsburgh

Since the 2001 publication of the Second Edition of *The ASHE Reader on Finance in Higher Education*, there has been a large increase in the amount of research and scholarly publication on issues of higher education finance. This is not surprising, given the pattern of decreased public funding and increased student cost over this period. Strategic planning and its relationship to budgeting under growing financial constraints have also been of continuing interest among both higher education scholars and practitioners.

What has changed, however, is the greater inclusion of explicitly economic perspectives in publications dealing with various aspects of postsecondary education. This is observable in chapters published in *Higher Education: Handbook of Theory and Research* (Springer), an annual sponsored in part by the Association for the Study of Higher Education (ASHE), as well as the *Journal of Education Finance*, including a special issue in 2011 (Vol. 36, No. 4). Volume 132 (2006) of *New Directions for Institutional Research* (Jossey-Bass) dealt entirely with contributions of economics to understanding higher education.

Along with the foregoing, scholars who identify themselves primarily as economists are also publishing more on the economics of higher education. This is reflected in an issue on Postsecondary Education in the United States published in *The Future of Children* (Vol. 23, No. 1, 2013). This periodical is published by the Center for the Future of Children, run jointly by the Princeton University School of Public and International Affairs and the Brookings Institution (http://www.futureofchildren.org). A symposium on higher education was also included in the *Journal of Economic Perspectives* (Vol. 26, No. 1, 2012), a publication of the American Economic Association.

Because of these changing publication patterns, the editorial team decided it was appropriate to add the word "Economics" to the title of this book. Consequently, the title has been changed from the *ASHE Reader on Finance in Higher Education (Second Edition)* to the present *ASHE Reader on Economics and Finance of Higher Education.*

The editorial team decided to include primarily work that has been published since 2001, but a few "classics" have also been retained. There is a mix of scholarly and practitioner-oriented publications, depending on the focus of the particular section. As is always the case with a reader, not every deserving article or chapter can be included due to space and budget constraints. For instance, both reviewers and editors recommended several articles from both the *Journal of Education Finance* and *Journal of Higher Education Policy & Management*, but permission costs to include them were prohibitive. The following are selected sources that were highly recommended but could not be included:

Additional Recommended Readings

Baldwin, J. N. & McCracken, W. A. III. (2013). Justifying the ivory tower: Higher education and state economic growth. *Journal of Education Finance, 81*(3), 181–209.

Bernasconi, Andrés. 2007. Constitutional prospects for the implementation of funding and governance reforms in Latin American higher education. *Journal of Education Policy, 22* (5), 509–529.

Brinkman, P. T. & Morgan, A. W. (1997). Changing fiscal strategies for planning. In M. W. Peterson, D. D. Dill and L. A. Mets (Eds.), *Planning and Management for a Changing Environment*. San Francisco: Jossey-Bass.

Chapman, B. (2006). Income contingent loans for higher education: international reforms. In E. A. Hanushek and F. Welch (Eds.), *Handbook on the Economics of Education, Vol. 2* (pp. 1435–1503). Amsterdam, Netherlands: North-Holland.

Cheslock, J. J., & Hughes, R. P. (2011). Differences across states in higher education finance policy. *Journal of Education Finance, 36*(4), 369–393.

Del Rey, E., & Racionero, M. (2012). Voting on income-contingent loans for higher education. *Economic Record, 88*, 38–50.

Delaney, J. A., & Doyle, W. R. (2011). State spending on higher education: Testing the balance wheel over time. *Journal of Education Finance, 36*(4), 343–368.

Eckwert, B., & Zilcha, I. (2012). Private investment in higher education: Comparing alternative funding schemes. *Economica, 79*(313), 76–96.

Jarzabkowski, P. (2002). Centralised or decentralised? Strategic implications of resource allocation models. *Higher Education Quarterly, 56*(1), 5.

Jones, Dennis P. (1993). Strategic Budgeting. In Vandament, W. E. & Jones, D. P. (Eds.), *Financial Management: Progress and Challenges*. San Francisco: Jossey-Bass.

Leach, L. (2013). Participation and equity in higher education: Are we going back to the future? *Oxford Review of Education, 39*(2), 267–286.

Lebeau, Y., Stumpf, R., Brown, R., Lucchesi, M. A. S., Kwiek, M. 2012. Who shall pay for the public good? Comparative trends in the funding crisis of public higher education. *Compare, 42*(1), 137–157.

Marcucci, P., Johnstone, D. B, & Ngolovoi, M. (2008). Higher educational cost-sharing, dual-track tuition fees, and higher educational access: The East African experience. *Peabody Journal of Education, 83*(1), 101–116.

Mohrman, K. M., Ma, W. M., & Baker, D. B. (2008). The research university in transition: The emerging global model. *Higher Education Policy, 21*(1), 5–27.

Mok, K. H. (2009). The growing importance of the privateness in education: Challenges for higher education governance in China. *Compare, 39*(1), 35–49.

Morphew, C. C. & Baker, D. B. (2004). The cost of prestige: Do new research I universities incur higher administrative costs? *Review of Higher Education, 27*(3): 365–384.

Nkrumah-Young, K. K., Huisman, J. & Powell, P. (2008). The impact of funding policies on higher education in Jamaica. *Comparative Education, 44*(2), 215–227.

Oduoza, C. F. 2009. Reflections on costing, pricing and income measurement at UK higher education institutions. *Journal of Higher Education Policy & Management, 31*(2), 133–147.

Taylor, J., Machado, M.D. & Peterson, M.W. (2008). Leadership and strategic management: Keys to institutional priorities and planning. *European Journal of Education, 43*(3): 369–386.

Toutkoushian, R. K., Shafiq, M. N. & Trivette, M. J. (2013). Accounting for risk of non-completion in private and social rates of return to higher education. *Journal of Education Finance, 39*(1), 73–95. [Recipient of the Outstanding Article Award from the Journal of Education Finance at the 2014 National Education Finance Conference (NEFC)]

Trostel, P. A. (2010). The impact of new college graduates on intrastate labor markets. *Journal of Education Finance, 36*(2), 186–213.

Zierdt, G. L. (2009). Responsibility-centred budgeting: An emerging trend in higher education budget reform. *Journal of Higher Education Policy & Management, 31*(4), 345–353.

SECTION I

ECONOMICS AND FINANCE OF HIGHER EDUCATION

Introduction to Section I

Maureen W. McClure and John C. Weidman
University of Pittsburgh

Becker and Toutkoushian ("On the Meaning of Markets in Higher Education") explore the highly contested terrain of higher education, markets, and their terrain. Setting ground rules for the debate, they review the different ways in which markets and systems are defined and used. They argue that the U.S. higher education "industry" is composed not of a single, but multiple markets, some for students and others for resources. Market segmentation ensures that the structure of the University of Phoenix can't threaten institutions like Harvard. Finally, in this topsy-turvy, complicated world they found that sometimes competition drives prices (and occasionally quality) up, not down.

According to Deming, Goldin, and Katz ("The For-Profit Postsecondary School Sector: Nimble Critters or Agile Predators?"), for-profit postsecondary schools are rooted in the vocational schools and correspondence schools of the past. Today they represent about 9% of total college enrollment but garner a much greater share of Pell grant funding. They disproportionately serve older students, women, minorities, and the poor. Some of these institutions are less stable financially. For example, at about the time this article was written, the University of Phoenix peaked in 2010 with enrollments pushing 600,000 students, but by 2013 enrollments had declined by 60% to about 269,000. Using data from the 2004 to 2009 Beginning Postsecondary Students (BPS) Longitudinal Study, these authors find that, in the shorter term, those taking certificate or associate degree programs do better than their counterparts attending community colleges or other public or private non-profit institutions in terms of retention. In the longer term these students don't place as well and default more often on their loans.

Dougherty et al. ("Accounting for Higher Education Accountability: Political Origins of State Performance Funding for Higher Education") address the politically charged origins of higher education performance funding using three political science theories: advocacy coalition frameworks (ACF), political entrepreneurship, and policy diffusion. They examined eight states, six with performance funding laws, and two without. Successful states had strong direct support from Republican legislators and higher education officials. They also had strong indirect support from strong business communities committed to market-based solutions that equated effectiveness and fairness. Performance funding unified Republicans around improved quality in college graduates and lower state spending on higher education that kept taxes down. States learned both from other states across the country and from national consultants. Key political drivers identified included technical feasibility, budgetary realities, values acceptability, and a lack of backlash from government officials and the public.

Dynarski and Scott-Clayton ("Financial Aid Policy: Lessons from Research") review the research on financial aid, which has become ubiquitous across higher education institutions (HEIs) in the U.S. Of significant concern is the lack of available research on the effectiveness of student loans, even though their consequences increasingly are felt throughout the economy. More research is available on grant aid; suggesting, for example, that scholarships requiring a pre-defined level of academic achievement that are awarded to students who have already decided to enroll produce better outcomes (e.g., persistence to degree) than awards with "no strings attached."

Ehrenberg ("American Higher Education in Transition") analyzes major shifts in higher education created by increasing economic pressures across a wide variety of institutions. Faculty composition is changing, as greater increases in non-tenured faculty may result in shifts toward less politically challenging research. Resource allocation is shifting resources away from instruction toward other areas of the budget, particularly toward student services and institutional aid. Pedagogy is shifting toward greater technology use, and differential tuitions are being used to "tax" programs with greater enrollments or better career incomes. These changes are contested for many reasons.

Heller's chapter ("The Financial Aid Picture: Realism, Surrealism, or Cubism?") presents both a policy history of financial aid for higher education and an analysis of its trends. Federal aid, supported by a committed bureaucracy, has largely remained need-based, supporting public goals for equality of opportunity by narrowly targeting poor and minority students. State aid, however, has shifted away from similar goals over the past twenty years. Some states shifted toward merit-based scholarships in the 1990s and early 2000s, but since then most aid programs suffered cutbacks during the recent economic downturns. Institutional aid has tended to shift away from needs-based aid toward aid that supports enrollment management. While a few elite and influential institutions have begun to shift back toward needs-based policies, there are only a small number of them.

Paulsen and Toutkoushian ("Economic Models and Policy Analysis in Higher Education: A Diagrammatic Exposition") give the reader a crash course in micro-economics in order to demonstrate how economic thinking can be applied to many areas of human behavior, not just finance. Building on an assumption of rational behavior, education policy is framed in terms of how students invest in human capital, including knowledge, skills, talents, and attitudes. Returns to human capital investments result in increases in students' productive capacities that can be traded for wages in labor markets. They discuss how opportunities and constraints can alter policy decision-making, and argue for its usefulness in evaluation. Limits to economic behavior approaches, they point out, can be seen in issues such as student access—where sociological approaches may better suffice.

CHAPTER 1

ON THE MEANING OF MARKETS IN HIGHER EDUCATION

WILLIAM E. BECKER AND ROBERT K. TOUTKOUSHIAN

Introduction

There is significant and growing interest around the globe in understanding and evaluating the way in which institutions of higher education (henceforth, IHE) are organized and compete with each other. Governments at national and state levels focus attention on encouraging citizens to acquire postsecondary degrees as a means to increase both the private benefits to individuals and the positive externalities that spill over to citizens within their domains (McMahon, 2009). Education is also seen by some nations as a means to foster economic growth and thus better enable them to compete with each other (Arimoto, 1997; Dill, 1997a; Marginson, 1997).

There are many different approaches that governments use for providing higher education services to consumers. Some nations (and states) have mature higher education systems that offer a substantial range of choices for students, whereas other nations/states have fewer options for students and force many of them to look outside their geographic boundaries for postsecondary education. In addition to differences in the number of suppliers in the industry, nations vary in terms of the types of institutions available to students. The United States in particular is known for its relatively wide breadth of postsecondary options for consumers, which include 2-year community colleges; 4-year baccalaureate institutions that range in size from several hundred to more than 50,000 students; institutions that focus significant attention not only on instruction but also research; and institutions that specialize in engineering, liberal arts, and so on. In other nations, however, postsecondary industries tend to be more uniform but are quickly becoming more diverse as well.

Different philosophies have also been taken with regard to how a nation manages its higher education system. It was common in the past for nations to rely on a centralized management model in which the government made decisions regarding which students could receive a postsecondary education, how students were distributed among institutions, and which colleges and universities were permitted to operate (Jongbloed, 2003). However, increasingly, nations have moved toward decentralized management models where students are free to select whether and where to go for postsecondary education and training, and institutions are permitted to compete directly for students and other resources (Teixeira, Jongboed, Amaral, & Dill, 2004; Williams, 1997). The hope is that through decentralization, the higher education sector will become more efficient in the production of higher education services and lead to subsequent gains in the standard of living.

In academic circles and higher education policy discussions, it is common to hear the word "market" used in conjunction with "higher education," in varying and sometimes even negative contexts. Whereas some nations have encouraged institutions to more actively compete with each other in the hopes of the benefits that would accompany this shift, some academics have raised concerns with this movement. The notions of "commercialization" and "academic capitalism" (Bok, 2003; Leslie & Slaughter, 1997), for example, hold that due to reductions in relative government support for higher education, colleges and universities in the United States have been forced to deliberately engage in more activities that have the potential to raise revenues and that this shift is altering the nature of academe. Will pursuing profitable partnerships with corporations change the type of research and perhaps teaching that occurs on college campuses? Winston (1999, 2000, 2003) has further argued that there is an increasing stratification among postsecondary institutions as they seek to maximize their prestige through donative resources, leading to a "positional arms race" in academe. As institutions compete for the best students and the gap between the elite and other institutions increases, what will this mean for educational opportunities for students?

Confusion also exists in discussions on this topic due to the fact that, as noted by Leslie and Johnson (1974, p. 5), ". . . the term 'market' is not only complex but is also subject to varying interpretations and definitions." A number of studies use "market" to represent the privatization of a nation's higher education system and increased reliance on competition among suppliers to set prices and allocate students. To illustrate, Brunner (1997) uses the terms "market" and "system" interchangeably to refer to the lack of central direction of higher education by the Chilean national government. Similarly, Robert Reich, now a professor of social and economic policy at the University of California Berkeley and previously a labor secretary in President Clinton's administration in the United States, opined that "Higher education in the United States is coming to resemble any other kind of personal service industry . . . higher education products . . . are sold on the market, there is a kind of marketisation that has set in" (Reich, 2004).

Although many economists have pointed to the potential efficiency gains that are thought to accompany increased reliance on the free market to make pricing and allocation decisions in product and labor markets, not all academics and policymakers view this shift as a positive development. Dill and Soo (2004), for example, argue that "The worldwide adoption of market-based policies for higher education such as common degree frameworks . . . could foster an international 'arms race' among universities . . . " (p. 67). As another example, Massy (2004) wrote of the higher education market in the United States as an allocation system in which the government was not in charge and decentralized decision making on both the demand and supply side results in less than satisfactory results because markets cannot discipline price without information on quality. Implicit in this statement is that there is a well-defined national market for higher education goods and services.

The phrase "market for higher education" has also been used at times to describe the broad collection of postsecondary providers within a nation or region. Studies in this area may focus attention on the number and types of colleges and universities that exist within a nation. The source of confusion here is that the set of higher education providers within a nation more properly represent the higher education industry or sector for a country, as opposed to a specific higher education market where a group of buyers (students) and sellers (institutions) come together to set prices and allocate services and where colleges compete with each other for customers. Due to reasons we will explain, it is likely the case that a nation's higher education industry is comprised of a number of separate markets as opposed to only a single market.

There is considerable confusion as to whether, and how, colleges and universities compete in a market or markets. Which institutions, divisions within an institution, or individuals are included in a market? If there is not a single market in the higher education industry, then are there well-defined submarkets, and if so how should they be identified? The approach used by economists to examine the market for any good or service relies on specific attributes of the potential suppliers of the good/service and their customers. A higher education market represents a group of institutions for which the breaks in the chain of substitution are relatively clear between the institutions, but where the product or service is still sufficiently similar (in terms of function, appearance, quality, and the like) to not require classifying these providers into different markets. In antitrust hearings and legal proceedings, as well as in individual institution's advertising and promotion efforts, the definition of a market and who participates in that market (either as rivals, potential rivals, input suppliers or buyers) is critical (see, e.g., Scheffman & Spiller, 1987).

In contrast to antitrust issues that require well-defined markets, consider the comments made by Charles Miller, the chairman of the US Commission on the Future of Higher Education, in "Colloquy," *The Chronicle of Higher Education's* online forum (Selingo, 2006). Miller was interviewed about his Commission's final report, which urged that the US higher education system be overhauled, including making universities more innovative and more accountable to the public. In this interview, Miller was reminded that he had said "we do not actually have a market system in higher education" and was asked what he would call the competition between different universities for students. He acknowledged the existence of this competition but continued to say, "however I think competition does not automatically make a market system." Although competition between amateur tennis players does not make a market, competition between like universities (suppliers of similar products and services, for a price) for students (demanders of the products and services, at a price) does. Whether students pay the full cost of production or have some portion of cost paid for by others is irrelevant to the existence of a market. Competition between the sellers of close substitute goods or services takes place in a market. A market may thus be thought of as a group of firms that are in close competition with each other. The two concepts are, in fact, inextricably linked when it comes to exchange.

It has also been suggested that there is too little competition in higher education markets due to the high market power held by a small number of prestigious institutions (Epple, Romano, & Sieg, 2006; Leslie & Johnson, 1974). Perhaps the best illustration of this view is the 1991 antitrust case that was brought against Massachusetts Institute of Technology (MIT) and the eight Ivy League institutions in the United States for collusive behavior. The US Justice Department accused MIT and the Ivy League institutions of price fixing in the allocation of financial aid and setting of tuition. The schools argued that their cooperative behavior was aimed at helping needy students with financial aid and did not affect price. Nevertheless, all but MIT signed a consent decree agreeing to stop the cooperative behavior. In the 1992 trial, *USA v. Brown University, et al.*, 805 F. Sup. 288 (E.D.Pa. 1992), MIT was found guilty of price fixing. Following this conviction, the US Congress passed the Higher Education Act of 1992 that enabled schools to cooperate in the assignment of need-based aid. In 1993, the Third Circuit overturned the MIT guilty verdict, *USA v. Brown University, et al.*, 9 F.3d 658 (3rd Cir. 1993), and the government dropped all inquiries into the matter of cooperation among "the overlap" schools in assigning need-based aid. As reported in Bamberger and Carlton (1999) and Carlton, Bamberger and Epstein (1995), Carlton gave expert testimony that the schools' cooperation did not raise prices, concluding that there were no grounds for the application of antitrust against these nonprofits in the absence of adverse price and output effects. Subsequently, Netz (1999) "found that a need-only financial aid policy significantly increases the price paid (tuition) by non-needy students; increases the average price paid by students who receive financial aid; and substantially increases earnings from tuition." Readers are also referred to Salop and White (1991) and Carlson and Shepherd (1992) for more discussion of this case.

Concerns about collusive behavior in academic markets still persist nearly twenty years after the MIT case. Miller went on to say that it was "possible to argue that among certain sets of institutions we have the equivalent of an oligopoly, where there may be competition within a group of institutions, but that set of institutions has powerful advantages over other sets of institutions"(Selingo, 2006). Miller acknowledged in his comments, perhaps unwittingly, that many distinct markets do exist in higher education and that it is entirely feasible that different groups of institutions can be delineated into economically meaningful and separate markets. But he then argued that higher education is heavily subsidized and regulated, lacks transparency, and that no penalties are incurred for poor performance; therefore, "it would be difficult to describe this as a market system." Miller's range of comments demonstrates the perils of failure to understand the characteristics of markets as used by economists. Informed public policy debate is not enhanced, for example, by confusing the term "market system," which describes the way a nation's economy is organized (capitalist, socialist, etc.), with the term "market," which describes a much narrower grouping of institutions into clusters of close competitors.

If antitrust legislation and the efforts of public policymakers to regulate or influence higher education institutions were not sufficient reasons to look at markets, the possibility of a connection between pricing and competition could provide a compelling reason for campus policymakers to refine their understandings of the extent to which markets exist among colleges and universities. Hoxby (1997), for example, found that increased competition between IHE from 1940 to 1991 explained real tuition increases of approximately 50% for selective private colleges in the United States. Outside of the USA, the British government has significantly cut funding to universities, with yet another new fee structure scheduled for the 2012 class, further shifting the funding burden from the state to the student, with increased competition for those students not just in the United

Kingdom but within the European Union and the rest of the world. As Great Britain and the rest of Europe move more and more toward a market-driven postsecondary system through the Bologna Process, institutional managers and politicians alike will learn that competition for students (being both consumers of and part of the education process) will drive up cost and perhaps quality as well, if Hoxby's results can be generalized.

At the same time, there is debate within the literature whether it is appropriate to even apply the notion of markets from the private sector to postsecondary institutions in the first place (Breneman, 1981; Leslie & Johnson, 1974; Winston, 1997). On the one hand, a number of researchers (Astin, 1993; Borden & Bottrill, 1994; Cave, Hanney, & Kogan, 1991; Toutkoushian & Danielson, 2002) have used the production analogy of firms to describe the operations of colleges and universities. It may also be argued, however, that colleges are so different from firms that the concept of markets is irrelevant for higher education.

It is important to properly define what is meant by "markets and higher education" in order to better inform policy analysis. If the intent of higher education policy is to alter the behavior of students and institutions in a specific market, then it is crucial that policymakers begin by defining which market they are trying to affect. There are instances where a policy, such as not allowing for-profit colleges to receive federal student aid, would clearly have effects on for-profit institutions and their students but have little or no effect on major research universities given that they compete in different markets for students. Or, if the State of Georgia changed the parameters of its HOPE Scholarship program, it is important for policymakers to know which institutions, in addition to the four-year public institutions in the state, would possibly be affected by the change. Would it also include out-of-state public institutions and private institutions within the State of Georgia? And if so, would it affect all private institutions or only certain private institutions?

In this chapter, we provide a review of the ways in which the concept of markets has been—and could be—applied to higher education.[1] We first summarize the ways in which markets and higher education have been described by academics and policymakers in the sizable literature on this topic. Following this section, we provide an overview of the economist's textbook definition and perspective on markets as they apply to firms in the for-profit world. These ideas are then used to consider how economists would conceptualize the different markets that exist in higher education. We focus on the attributes of markets in higher education (specifically, how higher education services are priced and bundled for consumers) and then turn to a more detailed exploration of the various markets that exist within the higher education industry in the United States. We further examine how to identify the specific markets within higher education and the resulting implications for policymakers. Through this discussion, we will argue that a nation's higher education system should rightfully be thought of not as a single market, but rather a series of separate markets for students and resources, with segmented markets within these groups. Although much of our discussion will focus on the higher education industry in the United States, we also provide illustrations of how these concepts play out in the higher education industries in other nations as well.

Literature Review on Markets and Higher Education

Even a cursory perusal of the literature will reveal that there have been many books, journal articles, and commentaries published on the general topic of markets and higher education. Books such as *Universities in the Marketplace: The Commercialization of Higher Education* (Bok, 2003), *Markets in Higher Education: Rhetoric or Reality?* (Teixeira, Jongbloed, Dill, & Amaral, 2004), *Higher Education as Competitive Enterprise: When Markets Matter* (Zemsky, Shaman, & Schapiro, 2001), and *The Global Market for Higher Education* (Mazzarol & Soutar, 2001), combined with numerous articles in peer-reviewed journals on markets and higher education, give the impression that the topic of markets in higher education is well understood by academic education specialists and policymakers alike. As we argue in the Introduction, however, we believe that this is not the case.

The phenomenon of competition between colleges and universities in the United States can be traced back to the nineteenth century, when the nation began to seriously challenge the notion that higher education should be reserved for the elite in society and/or the religious indoctrination of citizens. With the passage of the Morrill Act of 1862, the United States greatly expanded the supply of publicly supported institutions that would alter the shape of the higher education industry by providing direct competition with private colleges and universities for students and resources. Nations around the world would later embrace the same concept through what is often referred to as the "massification of higher education" (Guri-Rosenblit, Šebková, & Teichler, 2007; Teichler, 1998; Yorke, 2003). The higher education industry in the United States would later experience additional increases in demand in the twentieth century due to the Servicemen's Readjustment Act of 1944 (commonly referred to as the G. I. Bill) and population shifts due to the baby boomer generation. As the number of higher education suppliers increased, it led to more pressure for all institutions to attract students in sufficient numbers to fulfill their respective missions.

Academic discussions of the role of markets in higher education industries can be traced back at least to 1918, when the economist Thorstein Veblen produced a compelling critique on higher education in the United States in the early twentieth century in his book *The higher learning in America: A memorandum on the conduct of universities by business men*. Veblen (1918) observed that even at the turn of the twentieth century, colleges and universities were acting in ways similar to that of firms in competitive markets:

> The fact that the universities are assumed to be irreconcilable competitors, both in the popular apprehension as evidenced by the maneuvers of their several directors, is too notorious to be denied... (1918, p. 89)

Even though Veblen acknowledged that IHE at the time competed for students and resources, he struggled to explain why competition in higher education was necessary. He attributed the competition to the "habits of thought" of businessmen, which he saw as an encroachment on the traditional domain of IHE. Interestingly, Veblen (1918) made a careful distinction between the "modern university" (where scholarly inquiry occurred) and "lower and professional schools" (where training of students occurred), which is similar to later descriptions of the bifurcation of our current sectors of the higher education industry into 2- and 4-year institutions.

Since the publication of Veblen's book, a number of academics have agreed with his observation that to some degree, colleges and universities do, in fact, compete with each other. Outside of the United States, there have also been studies that have examined the presence of competition between colleges and universities in many nations including Australia (Marginson, 1997; Meek & Wood, 1997), Great Britain (Gibbs, 2001; Glennerster, 1991; Williams, 1997), Spain (Mora, 1997), Japan (Arimoto, 1997; Yonezawa, 1998), Korea (Kim & Lee, 2006), the Netherlands (van Vught, 1997), Chile (Brunner, 1993), and Argentina (Rozada & Menendez, 2002). Glennerster (1991, p. 1273), for example, noted that "Selective institutions become the norm and competition between institutions to provide the best or most appropriate courses has always been a feature of higher and further education . . . Such is the case for treating post school education as any market commodity."

Academics have observed that colleges and universities compete with each other in a number of ways. Not only do postsecondary institutions try to obtain the best and brightest students, but they also must compete for other resources, including faculty, research funding, state support, and private donations. The prestige of an institution is affected not only by the academic quality of the students enrolled but also the faculty members employed (Dill, 1997b; Jongbloed, 2003; Leslie & Slaughter, 1997). Brewer, Gates and Goldman (2002) argued that IHE compete in four different revenue markets: student enrollments, research funding, public fiscal support (i.e., state and federal appropriations), and private giving. Depending on the market structure, it could be the case that an institution competes with one set of institutions in the market for students and with another set of institutions in the market for faculty.

The notion of competitive markets and colleges adopting businesslike behavior has not been embraced by all as a positive development for higher education. Some have argued that postsecondary institutions enjoy considerable market power and use this power to affect how they set prices for students (Carlton et al., 1995; Epple et al., 2006; Geiger, 2004; Leslie & Johnson, 1974; Leslie & Slaughter, 1997). Massy's (1989) model of higher education, for example, implicitly assumes that each institution is a separate monopoly that can raise prices at will to cover costs without ramifications. Even if higher education markets could be construed as having some degree of competition, concern would exist that if there is not a sufficient amount of competition, colleges may be able to collude to set prices as evidenced in the MIT case previously discussed.

Others have argued that the notion of truly free markets does not apply to higher education in that even in higher education markets that are competitive, governments usually provide some level of intervention and oversight (Dill, 1997b; Glennerster, 1991; Jongbloed, 2003). Jongbloed (p. 111), for example, observed that ". . . in reality a true market for higher education does not exist in many countries. This is because government policies effectively prevent such a market from forming." This description certainly applies to the higher education industry in the United States, where individual states often explicitly control the number of public institutions in the market, the degrees they can offer, and the prices they can charge. Some have used the phrase "quasi-markets" to describe a higher education industry when there is some freedom among suppliers, but governments are not totally divorced from the operations of the market (Glennerster, 1991; Marginson, 1997; Massy, 2004; Teixeira, Jongbloed, et al., 2004; Williams, 1997).

The shift toward applying free market principles to higher education has raised concerns that there could be negative ramifications for the nature of higher education services. Gibbs (2001), for example, argues that market mechanisms may be problematic in higher education if they lead IHE to emphasize degree production over encouraging critical thinking and other skills that are more difficult to quantify. Similarly, the work of Slaughter and Leslie (1997), Rhoades and Slaughter (1997, 2004), Slaughter and Rhoades (2009), Bok (2003), Glenna, Lacy, Welsh and Biscotti (2007), and others holds that as colleges and universities increasingly pursue extramural funding and partnerships with industry in the name of competition, it may divert attention away from more traditional academic inquiry. Pugsley (2004) has opined that the adoption of free market principles by higher education has led to discrimination against various groups of students, and others have gone so far as to decry the "McDonaldization of higher education" (Hayes & Wynyard, 2002; Ritzer, 1998). Even most critics, however, would certainly acknowledge that some degree of competition exists between colleges and universities across the globe.

The concept of the market has been used in a variety of ways throughout the literature. The ambiguity in how the term "market" is defined and used in these studies contributes to the confusion surrounding this topic. Based on our review, it appears as though these studies of markets and higher education can be generally grouped into one of three categories: (1) studies that examine the trend toward deregulation of higher education industries by nations, (2) studies that seek to describe the structure of higher education industry within a specific region (typically a nation), and (3) studies that analyze the ways in which institutions compete with each other. We will examine each of these in turn.

Deregulation of Higher Education Industries

The largest segment of the literature on markets and higher education focuses on the global trend toward reducing the role of government in making decisions about who should go to college, where they should go to college, and how decisions about college pricing and supply are made. Studies in this line of inquiry include Glennerster (1991), Jongbloed (2003), Dill (1997a, 1997b), Brunner (1997), Meek and Wood (1997), Williams (1997), and many others. To these authors, the term "market" refers to the notion of allowing the free (competitive) market to set prices and output and allocate the supply of students across institutions.

The introduction of competitive markets into higher education has been driven by a number of factors. Going back to Adam Smith's seminal book *The Wealth of Nations* (1776), and more contemporary economists including F. A. Hayek's *The Road to Serfdom* (1944), *The Fatal Conceit: The Errors of Socialism* (1988), Milton Friedman's *Capitalism and Freedom* (1962), and many others, the field of economics has a long tradition of advocating in favor of competitive markets as a means to achieve the efficient allocation of resources. The fact that the United States, with its capitalist economic system and competitive higher education industry, saw substantial economic growth in the twenty-first century certainly provided an incentive for other nations to try and replicate its approach to reap similar benefits.

Milton Friedman (1955, 1962) in particular has had a profound influence on the use of competitive markets, rather than governments, to organize and operate markets within education in the United States. The deregulation movement in higher education outside of the United States has coincided with the political changes that occurred in much of eastern Europe in the early 1990s (Williams, 1997; Friedman, 2005). Thomas Friedman in *The World Is Flat: A Brief History of the Twenty-First Century* (2005) observed that world economic systems have become more interconnected in recent years, which has led to increased competition among nations. As nations across the globe adopted capitalistic economic systems, it was natural to conclude that their educational systems could likewise benefit from becoming more competitive.

The decentralization of higher education and decline in the share of costs covered by state governments have led to greater competition among IHE for other sources of revenue. The concepts of "academic capitalism" (Rhoades & Slaughter, 1997, 2004; Slaughter & Leslie, 1997; Slaughter & Rhoades, 2009) and "commercialization of higher education" (Bok, 2003) refer to how colleges have increasingly sought out new partnerships with industry and opportunities to secure revenues from students and state governments. The concern expressed with this phenomenon is that by focusing more attention on revenue generation, IHE may be changing the nature of what they do in ways that go against the pure pursuit of knowledge. Slaughter and Leslie (1997) argued that between 1970 and 1995, national policy in Australia, Canada, the United Kingdom, and the United States promoted a shift in higher education from basic curiosity-driven inquiry to the formation of academic capitalism, in which the pursuit of external moneys was the driving force. The emergence of academic capitalism is traced to "the growth of global markets, the development of national policies that target faculty-applied research, the decline of the block grant as a vehicle for state support for higher education, and the accompanying increase in faculty engagement with the market" (p. 11). Slaughter and Leslie, and more recently Rhoades and Slaughter (2004), do not differentiate between capitalism (which is usually associated with private ownership of resources and entrepreneurship) and markets as defined by Marshall (1920) nearly 100 years ago.

Descriptions of Higher Education Industries

Other studies have attempted to explain how institutions within a nation's higher education system can be categorized. It is recognized in these works that not all colleges are the same with regard to ownership (public versus private), profit status, level of educational degree offered, and involvement in producing research. It is important to note, however, that groupings of institutions by these types of characteristics do not coincide with what economists would describe as a market where a set of institutions directly compete with each other for students and resources.

Among the earliest efforts to develop meaningful groupings of institutions within the higher education industry in the United States was the classification scheme created by The Carnegie Commission on Higher Education [CCHE] (1973). The Carnegie Commission developed its first set of categories based on the level of highest degree offered, amount of federal funding received for sponsored research, and the number of degrees awarded by level. This resulted in groupings of institutions such as "Research I," "Research II," "Doctoral I," and so on. Of particular concern to the Carnegie Commission is that some institutions began to view the categories as having normative value with more research-oriented categories considered more prestigious than teaching-oriented categories. Some colleges increasingly sought ways to move up in the Carnegie classifications from, say, a Doctoral I institution to a Research II institution, as part of the research drift occurring within the higher education industry (Dill & Soo, 2004; Massy, 2004). To reduce this strategic behavior by institutions, as well as provide a richer description of the types of institutions within the higher education industry, the Carnegie Commission has made several modifications to their classification scheme over the years. The 2010 classification scheme groups institutions according to their instructional programs, enrollment profiles, size, and settings.

There seems to be no shortage in the number of organizations that have developed their own categorizations of institutions of higher education in the United States. The American Association of University Professors (AAUP), for example, groups institutions into categories based on highest degree offered and the number of degrees conferred. The College and University Personnel Association (CUPA) likewise has produced their own groups of colleges and universities based on public/private status, research intensity, and selected other criteria. *US News and World Report* ranks colleges and universities within a number of groupings, including whether an institution primarily competes for students on a national or regional basis. It is important to note that many of the institutions within the categories developed by these organizations do not directly compete with each other for the majority of students they enroll, and thus the groupings should not be viewed as markets within the higher education industry.

Finally, Zemsky et al. (2001) offered a different type of classification scheme that begins to connect categories of institutions to the concept of markets. They created a "seven segment market taxonomy" (also see Zemsky, Shaman, & Ianozzi, 1997) where institutions were grouped according to their selectivity, graduation rates, and enrollment patterns of students (national, regional, within state, and local). Although the taxonomy did not identify specific markets, it represented an important step toward recognizing how institutions compete with each other.

Competition in Higher Education Markets

One limitation with the aforementioned categorization schemes developed by various organizations is that they are largely atheoretical in that little justification is often given for the choice of criteria for grouping institutions. In contrast, some academics have focused on the reasons why institutions may differ from each other. Most notable in this strand of literature is the work by Gordon Winston. Winston (1999, 2000, 2003) argued that the uneven level of donative resources (subsidies) received by institutions has created a hierarchical stratification of colleges and universities. Institutions with high levels of donative resources are better able to compete for top students, which in turn enables them to raise their prestige. Despite the importance of Winston's work for helping to better understand the nature of differences across institutions, the resulting hierarchy does not necessarily correspond with distinct markets for students and resources. For example, institutions within the same decile group of donative resources may have similar financial and pricing structures but may rarely compete for the same students if they are located in different geographic regions.

There have been several efforts to apply economic-like concepts of markets to higher education. The article "The market model and higher education" by Leslie and Johnson (1974) is one of the first in this strand of literature. Leslie and Johnson suggested that the higher education industry consists of a number of markets and that for a number of reasons, the perfectly competitive market structure does not apply to higher education markets. They further discussed economic concepts of markets such as the homogeneity of higher education services and barriers to entry and exit. Jongbloed (2003) described eight conditions for a market which in some ways overlap the traditional criteria examined by economists. He also observed that ". . . there is not a single higher education market but rather a multitude of markets" (2003, p. 111) and argued that government involvement in higher education markets was an important constraint on the competitive actions of institutions. Other studies that have examined the structure of higher education markets include Breneman (1981), Dill and Sporn (1995), Dill (1997a), Rothschild and White (1993, 1995), and Epple et al. (2006).

Brewer et al. (2002) provide perhaps the most thorough examination to date of the ways in which postsecondary institutions in the United States compete with each other. The authors developed their own typology of postsecondary institutions based on the extent to which institutions can be grouped according to their primary strategy in higher education markets. In their framework, reputation and prestige are "assets that allow institutions of higher education to convey nonprice information to customers" (2001, p. 27). Unlike other writers who often use these terms interchangeably, Brewer et al. asserted that there is an important distinction between an institution's reputation and prestige that affects how it competes for students and resources. The authors used the term "reputation" to refer to whether an IHE is known for delivering high-quality services to their customers, such as the success of students in earning a degree or finding a job in their field of study. Graduation and job placement rates would be considered indicators of whether an institution has been successful in improving its reputation. In contrast, prestige is meant to capture whether an institution has acquired assets that are consistent with the perception of providing a high-quality education. Prestige is a more intangible construct than reputation and may include the quality of students who enroll, the production process used for education, and even the look and feel of a campus. Possible indicators of prestige might include institutional rankings in *US News and World Report* and average SAT scores of incoming freshmen.

Using this distinction, Brewer et al. (2002) placed institutions into the following strategic categories: prestigious, prestige-seeking, and reputation-based. Prestigious institutions are those that have already achieved a high level of prestige. Prestige-seeking institutions are those that have made investments to raise their prestige, but they are not yet viewed as prestigious relative to the leading institutions. Those institutions that are neither prestigious nor actively trying to acquire prestige are described as reputation-based institutions.

Finally, there have been a few attempts to model the ways in which colleges interact and compete with each other. Early work by James (1978, 1986) and James and Neuberger (1981) attempted to describe university behavior by assuming that institutions functioned as price takers, whereas Leslie and Johnson (1974), Massy (2004), Epple et al. (2006) and others countered that colleges exerted considerable market power and influence over prices. Rothschild and White (1993, 1995) outlined a theoretical model to explain how colleges and universities compete for students using price and nonprice means. An important feature of their model was the recognition that in education, students are both inputs and outputs from production. Rothschild and White (1993) dichotomize postsecondary education into "graduate education and research" and "undergraduate education," wrongfully implying that research is not associated with undergraduate education and teaching is not associated with graduate education. They then go on to dismiss the idea that undergraduate education subsidizes graduate education and research with the argument that an industry with joint undergraduate and graduate production at some institutions and single undergraduate production at others would not be sustainable; that we observe this industry implies that there are no subsidies. Despite the validity of their argument (if A, then B; thus, not B implies not A), Rothschild and White's premise (A) is a compound event: if institutions of higher education faced the same regulations, and if they all produced the same undergraduate product, and if students and their parents had accurate information, and if firms were free to enter, and if undergraduate education subsidizes graduate education, then undergraduate institutions and joint graduate and undergraduate institutions would not coexist. Existence of the different types of producers implies only that at least one of the many premises is wrong. Curiously, in discussing the issue of subsidies, Rothschild and White never address the issues and evidence advanced by critics such as Anderson (1992) as to which one of the many premises is wrong.

Economic Concept of Markets

What, exactly, is a market? Economists have adopted a fairly consistent approach to answering this question dating back at least to Marshall (1920), although as noted by Leslie and Johnson (1974, p. 5), ". . . while it is a relatively simple matter to describe a potential market it is considerably more difficult and often impossible to specify exactly who is and who is not a part of that market." Virtually every introductory-level microeconomics textbook devotes multiple chapters to defining the relevant market for goods and services, market participants and how they interact, and the structure of the market. Despite having general agreement about the purpose of a market and the main characteristics of a market, even economics textbooks can gloss over some of the finer details about defining a market that can have important implications for how to conceptualize markets in higher education.

Defining a market is a purposive exercise—it is done not for its own sake, but to serve the broader purpose of providing the analytical basis on which the behavior of one or more suppliers can be analyzed. In other words, the act of defining a market is a focusing device that seeks to identify the key players and their interactive strategies that determine the environment we seek to assess and, presumably, improve through the development of appropriate policies. The institutions that make up a market will exercise some meaningful constraint on each other, whereas those not assigned to this market will have no tangible immediate competitive impact on these institutions. Competitive processes within markets can be studied to assess whether institutions and markets are achieving true economic efficiency (reflecting an allocation of goods and services that provides the greatest benefits at the least cost), and if they are not, what market incentives or government regulatory intervention initiatives could be used to encourage more competitive behavior that will lead to greater benefits from society's scarce resources.

Characteristics of Markets

Economists begin by describing a market as the place where buyers and sellers come together to exchange a particular good or service.[2] The market may be a specific physical location (such as the Mall of America in Bloomington, Minnesota) or a geographic region (such as a 60-mile radius around Athens, Georgia). The different goods or services produced by suppliers in the market must be viewed by consumers as being reasonable substitutes for each other. For example, a single market would not be said to exist for cameras and pizza because consumers would not typically view these as even imperfect substitutes for each other. In contrast, one could define the fast-food market for a geographic area as consisting of restaurants that supply a variety of foods such as hamburgers and tacos, which may not be exactly the same, but are still substitute goods for many consumers who are looking to purchase dinner within a specific price range.

Markets are also separated by economists into either markets for goods and services made by organizations ("product markets") or markets for resources such as labor that are used to produce goods and services ("resource markets"). Ford Motor Company is a supplier in the product market for automobiles, a demander in the labor market for engineers and technicians, and a demander in markets for steel, rubber, glass, and other resources needed to produce automobiles. This distinction is particularly important for identifying markets in the higher education industry due to the multiproduct nature of colleges and universities and their need to compete for resources from multiple groups including state and federal governments and donors.

An important feature of markets is the geographic span over which the market exists. The geographic span relates to how far customers will travel to purchase the good or service. Does the behavior of hotels in one city directly affect the conduct of those in another? If not, then there is no competition between them so they cannot be said to operate in the same analytical market. For example, are hotels in New York City in the same market as hotels in Sydney, Australia? Do travelers see them as close substitutes? Clearly not business travelers, who may not have a choice of where to conduct their work. Leisure travelers who have already chosen their destination will likewise define the geographic scope of their market in terms of only hotels that are in the vicinity of their destination. In contrast, for a world convention, large five-star hotels in these two cities could well be competing with each other in the same international market for an association's business for the "customer" is not as place bound as in the prior two examples. To illustrate, in the United States, there are only a few cities with the five-star hotel capacity to cater to very large conferences such as the annual meeting of the American Economic Association, which in 2005 and 2006 attracted well over 8,000 registrations each year and used 5,122 and 5,688 hotel rooms, respectively, on the peak conference night. Only a few cities have sufficient hotel space to host such a large conference, so the market for conferences with this number of people would only include a small number of cities over a rather large geographic span.

The geographic span of a market is also influenced by the size of the purchase and the frequency with which consumers purchase the product. The geographic market would be determined by how far buyers would be prepared to travel in order to think that they had found the best deal—a benefit-cost trade-off for them. The span for large and infrequent purchases (such as an automobile) is probably larger than the span for the market for groceries, where purchases are done more frequently and each purchase is a smaller portion of the consumer's budget. Supermarkets will generally compete in a narrow geographical span, the boundaries of which will usually be determined by the location of major roads, the presence of shopping malls, and the travel time preferences of consumers. For new car sellers located in a specific area, and who for whatever reason are the subject of a search that needs to be conducted within the confines of a defined market, it would be necessary to discover what other dealers in which other locations constrained the activities of the sellers in question and which dealers were seen by buyers as offering a substitute product, after allowing for search costs. Similarly, postsecondary education can be viewed as a relatively large and infrequent purchase, which helps explain why students are often willing to travel hundreds if not thousands of miles in order to use the service.

Industry Versus Market

As may be apparent in our use throughout this chapter, an important distinction should be made between an industry and a market. An industry, as used by economists, refers to the collection of all organizations that supply a specific good or service. For higher education, the broadest definition of the higher education industry would consist of all postsecondary institutions around the globe. It is also common to speak of an industry within a nation, such as the higher education industry in the United States. Within an industry, there may be a number of organizations that make the same product and yet do not directly compete with each other in the product or resource markets in question. As a simple illustration, the hotel industry can be thought of as consisting of all suppliers of hotel rooms within the United States. However, the Holiday Inn in Indianapolis would likely not view itself as competing with the Marriott in San Diego for most customers on any given evening. In this way, the two hotels are in the same industry but compete in different product markets.

A second distinction between an industry and a market is that a market consists of both buyers and sellers, whereas an industry is defined in terms of sellers producing similar products using similar inputs, technology, and production processes. That is, the term "industry" focuses only on the supply side, whereas Leslie and Johnson (1974, p. 5) note that ". . . there are two distinct parts or sides to any market: the producer's side and the consumer's side. Thus, in discussing a market for a particular commodity both sides of the market must be discussed." We could talk about the US bread industry in an economically meaningful way if we wanted to analyze bread-making technology, the optimum size of baking ovens, the types of bread and yeast products, and the best types of flour to use. But it would not be correct to talk about the US bread market in the same way, because all American bread manufacturers do not compete with each other for the same groups of buyers. Perishability, transport costs, and local taste preferences all mean that there will exist a large number of quite small geographic markets for bread, each of which may exhibit quite different patterns of competitive interaction and require different analytical assessments of their behavior. Unfortunately, even economists do not always distinguish between these two concepts. For example, in the principles-level microeconomics textbook by McEachern (1994), the author explicitly states that the terms "industry" and "market" will be used interchangeably. It is therefore not surprising that noneconomists have also struggled to understand the difference between these two terms as well.

On the demand side, customers help to define a market in a variety of ways. First, customers differ in their abilities to pay for a good or service. Generally, wealthier consumers will have a wider range of suppliers from which to choose within an industry, whereas less well-to-do consumers would have more limited choices. It is common for consumers with different income levels to participate in different product markets for goods and services such as restaurants, automobiles, housing, wine, sailboats, and even higher education. Second, the personal characteristics of consumers may affect the markets in which they choose to participate. For example, within the music industry, younger consumers may have different tastes than older consumers in the sets of music groups that they would consider close substitutes for each other. Other personal characteristics of consumers, such as their gender and race/ethnicity, can also influence the specific product markets within an industry in which they choose to participate.

Market Structures

Economic textbooks devote significant attention to the concept of market structure, which can be thought of as ". . . all of the characteristics of a market that influence the behavior of buyers and sellers when they come together to trade" (Lieberman & Hall, 2000, p. 172). These characteristics include the number of buyers and sellers in the market, the barriers to entry and exit from the market, and the homogeneity of the good or service being produced. All of these characteristics are helpful when thinking about the various markets that exist in higher education.

The number of sellers in a market is affected by the presence of barriers to entry or exit. These barriers represent how difficult it is for new suppliers to enter a market when conditions are favorable or how easy it is for suppliers to leave a market in less lucrative times. Barriers to entry in a market may be due to the presence of large fixed costs to enter the market. For example, a supplier wishing to enter the market for electricity provision would have to spend a large amount of money to create a power plant and accompanying infrastructure to deliver electricity to consumers. Governments can also be another barrier to entry if they impose laws or regulations on markets that make it more difficult—or even impossible—for new suppliers to enter the market. Similarly, in some markets, it is not easy for suppliers to leave due to government regulations or high expenses that would be incurred from closing. Not surprisingly, markets where there are low barriers to entry or exit tend to have more suppliers, and vice versa.

The number of suppliers in a market is important in that as the number increases, holding all else constant, each supplier would normally have less market power, or ability to impact the prices charged for the good or service through their actions. At the extreme, if there was only one supplier in the market (a monopolist), then the supplier (monopolist) would not have to worry about losing customers to another supplier if they were to increase the price for the good or service, and the price they charge becomes the going price in the market. In contrast, if the market consists of many suppliers and each has a very small share of the total market output, then the pricing decisions of one supplier may have a negligible or no effect on the overall price set in the market.

The homogeneity of a product relates to the similarity of the goods or services produced by suppliers, and hence the degree of substitutability across suppliers. If the goods or services in a market are exactly the same (homogeneous), then consumers know that they can obtain the same exact product from any supplier in the market. Thus, the goods and services produced by suppliers are said to be perfect substitutes for each other. In contrast, a market with heterogeneous goods or services is one where the goods/services are similar, but not identical, across suppliers. It is important to note that the homogeneity of goods or services is defined by how similar they are in the minds of consumers and not necessarily whether there are real or tangible differences between products. If supplier A can convince consumers that their product is different from that made by supplier B, then the products in the market are heterogeneous even though in reality they may be exactly the same.

In most cases, markets consist of products that have some degree of perceived heterogeneity. The 2001 Nobel Memorial Prize in Economics recipient and former senior vice president and chief economist of the World Bank, Joseph Stiglitz (1987), wrote:

> Markets in which commodities are completely homogeneous—with respect to location and the date as well as other characteristics—are almost inherently sufficiently thin so that the postulate of perfect competition is inapplicable. Markets that are sufficiently 'thick' to be competitive are almost always nonhomogeneous. (p. 25)

What Stiglitz is saying, in the former case, is that in order to have perfectly homogeneous products, the market may well be very narrowly characterized, as with a single product or single seller. In the latter case, he is acknowledging that competition can take place in terms of many variables, including product quality, ingredients, and style, so that in a competitive market (speaking in the real world sense of the term "competitive"), the products of rival sellers are unlikely to be homogeneous.

If products can be different from each other and yet be considered part of the same market, then at what point would two goods/services be so different that they are actually in separate markets? Where to draw this product boundary between markets is often difficult to determine and can be controversial. The product boundary of a market, in fact, indicates which products of rival institutions are seen as substitutes in the minds of buyers. These substitutes do not have to be perfect. To illustrate, do the five-star hotels close to Central Park in New York City compete for guests with the two-star hotels on the outskirts? If the Holiday Inn at LaGuardia Airport lowers its nightly rate by a few dollars, will the Plaza on Central Park be forced to lower its rate? Highly doubtful! Thus, they operate in different markets. But where does one draw the line? The key is that ideally, those hotels classified within the same market will constrain each other (in terms of price, services, and amenities), whereas those that are not included in the market will not be regarded by travelers as offering a substitute product at going market prices, either now or within the planning horizon of the firm in question.

Taken together, economists have used these concepts to define several market structures that serve as standards by which existing markets may be compared and contrasted. At one extreme of the range of market structures is the notion of a perfectly competitive market, in which there are no barriers to entry/exit, there are a large number of buyers and sellers each with a small share of the market's output, and each seller produces a homogeneous product. In this market structure, suppliers have no ability to raise the market price through their actions given that consumers can find the same exact good or service at other suppliers for a lower price. The perfectly competitive market structure is admittedly a theoretical construct that is difficult, if not impossible, to find parallels to in existing markets.

At the other extreme of the spectrum of market structures is a monopolistic market. In this market structure, there is only one seller of the good or service and (obviously) significant barriers to entry. The good or service provided by the firm in a monopolistic market is very heterogeneous in that there are no close substitutes for it. Accordingly, the firm in a monopolistic market has significant influence over the market price for the good/service and the quantity of the good/service that is available to consumers. This market structure is also a theoretical construct in that it is hard to find many examples in the real world where pure monopolies exist. However, there have been instances where governments have established a monopoly for a specific good or service, such as the government-imposed monopoly that existed for years for local telephone services provided by AT&T. It may also be the case that local monopolies exist for goods/services that are narrow in geographic span, such as for water and electricity in a given town. These firms may function as if they were monopolists for they are the only supplier in the relevant geographic span, even though their respective industries may consist of many firms. Despite the fact that K-12 public schools are sometimes described by critics as being local monopolies, it is important to note that there are other competitors within the region including private schools, charter schools, magnet schools, and even homeschooling.

Between these two extremes are market structures known as monopolistic competition and oligopoly. In a monopolistically competitive market, there are low barriers to entry (and hence a large number of suppliers), but the goods or services are not identical across suppliers. In this market, firms attempt to differentiate their product from those of their rivals and may compete on both price and nonprice features (such as the quality of service). A fast-food market is typically used as an example of a monopolistically competitive market because there are many suppliers within a geographic span, it is relatively easy to enter and exit the market, and the products are substitutable, but not identical across suppliers.

In contrast, an oligopolistic market consists of a small number of firms that typically produce a relatively homogeneous product. These markets have high barriers to entry due to either large start-up costs or government regulations. Firms can be tempted to engage in collusive behavior to minimize price competition, as was seen during the 1970s with the cartel of oil-producing nations in the Middle East. As discussed earlier in this chapter, allegations were raised in the 1990s that MIT and the Ivy League institutions in the United States were operating as if they were an oligopoly and colluding to fix prices by making similar financial aid offers to students. Other examples of oligopolistic markets outside of academe may include television services (cable and satellite providers) and air transportation.

Product Differentiation

As can be seen from this discussion, product differentiation is an important dimension in defining the market for a good or service. Suppliers can differentiate their product in a number of ways, the most obvious of which is to make physical changes to the good or service that make it different from, and yet substitutable for, those produced by other suppliers in a market. Advertising is often viewed as a way for firms to convince consumers that their product is different from, and better than, the products made by rivals in the market. Regardless of how it is achieved, the supplier's hope is that through differentiating its product, it may be able to increase its market power and charge a higher price for their particular good or service. In the extreme, if the level of product differentiation becomes large enough, the market may become segmented into several submarkets with suppliers of higher-quality goods/services competing in a separate product market from suppliers of lower-quality (but similar) goods/services. For example, the market for automobiles in a given geographic region may be thought of as a series of submarkets, in that consumers who are looking to purchase a higher-quality (and more expensive) automobile will primarily consider suppliers such as Lexus, BMW, and Mercedes-Benz, whereas other consumers who are looking for more affordable automobiles will participate in a separate submarket of firms such as Ford and Chevrolet. If all automobiles were perceived by consumers to be perfect substitutes for each other, then such market segmentation would not exist.

Product differentiation is related to the ease at which consumers can acquire information about the quality of the goods and services produced by suppliers. The model of a perfectly competitive market assumes that consumers have access to complete information about the products being sold by suppliers in the market. However, if consumers have difficulty in determining how comparable goods and services are within a market, then it creates opportunities for suppliers to convince consumers that their products are in fact different and thus deserving of a higher price. The requirement of consumers having perfect information about products within a given market is very difficult, if not impossible, to realize in practice due to the time and cost that is needed to obtain this information. As a result, consumers often form impressions of products based on indicators of quality such as ratings by other entities such as *Consumer Reports*.

In the absence of good information, consumers may also rely on the price charged by the supplier as an indicator of quality, with a higher price suggesting to them that more/better resources went into its production and thus the resulting good or service is also better. In part, elite liberal arts colleges differentiate themselves from perceived lesser institutions by their higher tuition (price). To lower their price would give the wrong signal to those seeking an elite higher education. Note that this pricing signal would not exist if students and their parents (consumers) had perfect information about the products sold by colleges (suppliers).

Markets can be affected by how easy it is for consumers to learn what prices suppliers are charging for the good or service. The model of a perfectly competitive market assumes that consumers have full knowledge of the prices being charged by all firms. As the products in this market structure are perfect substitutes for each other, a supplier cannot get away with charging a higher price than others because consumers can get the same exact product at any number of other suppliers in the market and they know what prices other suppliers are charging.

The assumption that consumers have full knowledge of all prices within a market can be difficult to achieve in practice. It is typically the case that acquiring information about prices is a time-intensive and thus costly activity. The expansion of the Internet has certainly made it easier for consumers in many product markets to compare prices and products across suppliers. Searching and comparing prices and products still requires time and effort, however, and the comparison may be incomplete if it does not include all suppliers in a specific market.

Pricing information can be more difficult for customers to obtain in markets where firms engage in frequent price discounting. Even though consumers can find information on the manufacturer suggested retail price for virtually any brand of automobile across dealerships within a designated geographic area, the actual net price that they would pay depends on the extent to which a specific dealership (and perhaps salesperson within a dealership) is willing to negotiate with buyers for a lower price. Such information is not readily available to consumers. A similar process of price discounting occurs in higher education product markets, where students can observe the same posted tuition and fee rates for an institution but may end up paying different prices due to the fact that they are given varying amounts of financial aid for criteria such as their ability to pay and their academic performance.

Another important feature of some markets is that consumers actually purchase a bundle of (complementary) goods or services as opposed to a single product. To illustrate, when a person buys a house, the person is not only paying for the physical attributes of the house, such as its square footage, number of bathrooms, and acreage, but also access to attributes of the neighborhood where the house is located. These attributes might include the quality of the public school to which residents are assigned, the availability of parks and playgrounds, the safety of the neighborhood, and even the perceived beauty of the view from the house. Accordingly, these attributes (complementary goods) can affect the price that consumers would be willing to pay for the house. Or as the old adage goes in real estate, the three most important factors in the price of a house are location, location, and location. Similarly, when a person goes to a restaurant, he or she is not only paying for the food consumed but also for the amenities that go along with the dining experience, such as the ambiance of the dining room, the quality of service, and other attributes. This notion of bundling certainly applies to higher education markets, where students are not only purchasing instructional services but also access to features of the campus and town that provide utility to the student.

Finally, products may differ depending on whether the consumer derives short-term ("consumptive") or long-term ("investment") benefits from purchasing them (Brewer et al., 2002). The majority of goods and services are primarily consumptive in nature, in that the purchaser obtains benefits near the time of consumption from the good or service in question. In other situations, however, the consumer does not receive the benefits until some point in the future. For example, individuals who purchase an exercise plan may not receive any benefits at the time that they use the plan, but still purchase the plan in the hope they will derive benefits in the future due to improvements in their health and fitness. Viewed in this way, the consumer is purchasing the good or service as an investment in much the same way that an individual purchases a mutual fund in the hope that it will be worth more in the future. As we explain in the next section, this applies to higher education product markets because higher education services provide both consumptive and investment benefits to students.

Attributes of Higher Education Markets

We now apply the economic framework from the previous section to discuss how economists would conceptualize markets within the higher education industry in the United States. In short, we assert that (1) IHE compete in a variety of product and resource markets, (2) the higher education industry consists of a series of different product markets within degree levels and fields of study, and (3) the product markets share characteristics with both an oligopolistic and monopolistically competitive market structures.

Before delving into the details of product markets in higher education, we need to consider the claim that markets are meaningless in higher education in that colleges and universities are not the same as firms in the for-profit world. The argument goes that due to the fact that most traditional colleges and universities are not-for-profit, are highly subsidized, and have a low risk of failure, they do not have to compete with each other in the same way as do firms in the for-profit sector.

A free market starts with the notion that there are many identical and independent firms, each with the objective of maximizing profits subject to constraints and many independent potential buyers who are seeking to maximize utility subject to income and wealth constraints. However, the majority of degree-granting postsecondary institutions are not set up as profit-maximizing entities to benefit the equity capital shareholders. Gordon Winston (1999, 2000, 2003), possibly more than any other economist, has articulated how IHE differ from the textbook idea of profit-motivated firms operating in a competitive free market.

What is the main objective of postsecondary institutions, then, if it is not profit maximization? Winston asserts that a primary objective of IHE is to build prestige and attempt to advance up the hierarchy. But which hierarchy? From unknown to known? On what scale? From a local student body to an international mix? From the bottom of the sports world to the final four? From a liberal arts college to a university with multiple colleges including professional medicine and law schools? From undergraduate teaching institutions to well-recognized graduate schools producing Nobel Laureate-level research? Postsecondary institutions have different objectives at different times in their history. The only thing that appears safe to say is that profit maximization for the benefit of equity shareholders is not typically one of them, but yet this is a cornerstone of analysis in the typical market setting.

Unlike most firms in the for-profit world, colleges and universities are highly subsidized organizations. IHE receive subsidies from a number of different entities, including governments (federal, state, local), private donors, philanthropic groups, and others. Winston (1999) and Toutkoushian (2001a) have shown that a sizable fraction of the cost of providing higher education services is subsidized by various entities. This remains true in the twenty-first century even though increasingly larger portions of the cost of higher education services are being paid by consumers. Grants and state appropriations make it possible for both private and public institutions of higher education to sell their products for less than cost, which is a highly unique attribute not seen in most other markets.

Another way in which colleges and universities differ from traditional for-profit firms is that there is a very low risk of failure. Data from IPEDS show that in 2010–2011, for example, only twenty (20) degree-granting postsecondary institutions closed their doors and all of these institutions were private (National Center for Education Statistics [NCES], 2011). Public institutions enjoy some degree of protection from failure by state governments or coordinating and governing boards. The fact that there have been few college closings even in years when there has been significant economic downturns in the United States that have led to cuts in appropriations for many institutions shows that the risk of failure is low relative to what firms in many other industries face. If this is true, then the argument goes that colleges do not have to worry about competing for customers as they most likely will be able to survive regardless of their success in attracting students and securing resources.

The way in which colleges and universities provide higher education services is likewise different from the traditional industrial process in which labor and raw material inputs are turned into finished good (outputs). Students are consumers of educational services provided, inputs into that process, and they are also one dimension of output. As a result, the supply side and demand side of higher education markets are not "distinct" as asserted by Leslie and Johnson (1974) because (as will be discussed in more detail) students are both consumers and inputs to the educational process. Demand and supply curves cannot be identified as distinct functions. In comparison to an automobile factory, the steel in a car does not care how it is handled but as inputs and outputs, students do. The car producers have to cover their costs with sales revenue but universities and colleges have endowments and state funds on which they can draw to subsidize the educational process. As inputs, the attributes of the student are important to production so institutions buy or subsidize desired students. Grants and state appropriations make it possible for both private and public institutions of higher education to sell their products for less than cost, which is a highly unique attribute not seen in other markets.

It is the case that producers of luxury items want the availability of their wares to appear limited and to be seen with the beautiful people. These producers are willing to provide incentives (subsidies) to encourage use by opinion and fashion makers. Similarly, but to a larger extent, prestigious colleges and universities do the same thing. For example, Harvard, Princeton, Stanford, and other highly selective universities could greatly increase their respective tuition and fees and likely still have students clamoring to get in (at least in the short run). They do not do this for they want to select what each considers the most appropriate attributes for the activities and images they each wish to project. At the same time, they cannot lower their prices too much because price is an indication of quality.

As we will discuss in what follows, highly selective private colleges in the United States are notorious for maintaining high sticker or list prices and then providing discounts in the form of grants, scholarships, merit aid, and the like to attract desirable students. In economics this is known as the "efficiency wage hypothesis," which states that wages can be determined by more than simply supply and demand. To get the best workers (students), firms (colleges) pay their employees (enrolling students) more than the market-clearing wage (market-clearing financial aid). Because workers are paid more than the equilibrium wage, there will be lines of applicants looking to get these jobs. Thus, the existence of "efficiency wages" is a sign of market failure.

The importance or role of multidimensionality in higher education appears lost on many critics. In a *Wall Street Journal* review of Andrew Rosen's book *Change.edu: Rebooting for the New Talent Economy* (2011), for example, Riley (2012) argues that research universities and even liberal arts colleges are attempting to please too many constituents, which Rosen and Riley call customers in a market place: students, parents, taxpayers, alumni, sports fans, and the list goes on.[3] According to Riley, "this mix of financial imperatives can lead colleges to focus too little on what students are learning in the classroom. Money and effort, instead, go to moving up the prestige ladder, often by enhancing 'selectivity.'" Riley then cites Rosen's claim (in a chapter titled "Harvard Envy") that under "the existing rules of higher education, a college is defined as 'better' by turning away more potential students—no different than a nightclub that's 'hot' in that its system of bouncers and velvet ropes leaves a critical mass of people on the outside, noses pressed to the glass."

How diverse constituents operating in many different markets result in a single measure of quality (entering-class selectivity) is never made clear by Riley or Rosen; it is only asserted. Their solution to confusion over the many purposes of higher education, however, is the single-purpose profit motive driven by student tuition. According to them, for-profit institutions have largely opted out of the prestige game. These schools are not looking to turn away students. Their professors are engaged exclusively in teaching, not research. No one has tenure, so incompetence means dismissal. Teaching is quality-controlled and student performance strictly measured.

Although Rosen meant his comments to be derogatory, in some respects, highly selective institutions of higher education share much in common with the idea of hot nightclubs, which Rosen does not recognize in his emphasis on selection as a negative attribute. Student groupings (peer effects) are important in education: bright and highly motivated students want to be with other bright and highly motivated students just as socially adept and attractive dancers in a nightclub want to be with similar club goers. Also keep in mind that students are an input and output of the educational process and dancers are an input and output of the nightclub scene. In any given evening, the hot night club might be able to earn higher profits by letting more dancers, in but in the longer run, profits might fall as the quality of the experience is deteriorated. Similarly, highly select colleges and universities may be able to make greater profits by admitting more students but in the longer term the quality of education may be deteriorated. College admission committees provide a screening function just as bouncers do but based on different criteria.

We acknowledge and accept that these are important differences between postsecondary institutions and traditional firms in the for-profit world, but also believe that it is appropriate to characterize IHE as competing with each other in markets. Postsecondary institutions must generate sufficient revenues to meet expenditures and run their operations, and tuition revenue remains an important source of funding for virtually all institutions. Even not-for-profit institutions must generate sufficient revenues to cover their operational costs, and thus competing for students (and the revenue they bring) is necessary for colleges and universities. IHE must likewise compete with other state agencies for appropriations and compete with other organizations for donations from individuals. In addition, based on the hierarchical nature of markets where enrolling high-quality students lead to institutional prestige, many colleges compete with each other not only for the number of customers but also for the best customers in the market.

We assert as have others before us (Brewer et al., 2002; Jongbloed, 2003; Leslie & Johnson, 1974; Meek & Wood, 1997; Rothschild & White, 1993) that colleges and universities participate in separate markets for students and resources. Though we focus here on competition among IHE for students, there is also competition between IHE for state funding, private funding, faculty, and so on. The markets for full-time, tenure-eligible faculty are usually national in geographic scope for most 4-year institutions. Within the labor supply of faculty, individuals who are more oriented toward research will more often choose to supply their services in the labor markets at Doctor- and Master-degree-granting institutions, whereas other individuals will gravitate toward the labor market at Bachelor-granting institutions. In contrast, the faculty labor market for 2-year institutions tends to be more regional/local in geographic span, as is true for the nontenure track labor markets for 4-year institutions. The market for sponsored research is best described as national in geographic span, with Doctor- and Master-degree-granting institutions across the country competing for research funding from the federal government and private agencies.

Postsecondary institutions offer a number of different services that may be useful for grouping them into product markets. First, colleges provide a mix of services in the general areas of instruction, research, and public service. The mission of a college or university will dictate the extent to which it chooses to provide services in each of these areas. The vast majority of institutions of higher education provide some form of instructional services; however, there are exceptions where an institution may be established solely for the purpose of producing research. Likewise, although many institutions engage in some level of public service activities that are aimed at benefitting the institution's local, state, or national communities, these activities tend to be a small portion of an IHE's overall activity. There is, however, significant variability across institutions with regard to their involvement in research, with many institutions doing little if any research, whereas other institutions devote significant attention to this activity.

The variation in research activity is often tied to the types of academic degrees offered to students. It is usually the case that institutions that have chosen to offer higher-level (graduate) degrees are also more involved in producing research due to the need to integrate research with teaching in the preparation of graduate students (Becker & Kennedy, 2006). Universities that focus on research are more expensive to maintain than are teaching-oriented institutions, but it has been asserted that they are critical to economic growth. Romer (1990) defines innovation as an improvement in the instructions for mixing raw materials. He argues that advances in technology are the primary source of economic growth in that the creation of new instructions can occur without bound and these instructions can be used over and over again at next to no additional cost. They are nonrival, meaning one person's use of the instructions does not rival or preclude its use by another. Although improvements in the instructions by which resources are mixed can occur by chance, Romer argues that innovation is the result of intentional actions taken by people who respond to market incentives. For an innovation to be profitable, the owner must be able to exclude or prevent others from using it freely. Growth requires the input of an excludable but nonrival good.

To Romer, the basic skills (reading, writing, and arithmetic), machine skills (keyboard entry, monitoring instruments, filling out forms), and the like that are associated with rote or repetitive education are tied to the individual. Such human capital is a rival input because the person who possesses this ability cannot be in more than one place at the same time nor can this person solve many problems at once. This ability is also bounded by the population; it is embedded in physical objects. It cannot account for unbounded growth in per capita output for its accumulation must involve diminishing returns. In contrast, a new design, piece of software, or mathematical model is nonrival; once the design, software, and model have been created, they can be used as often as desired by as many people as would like at little to no cost. They are not closely tied to any physical object. Education that contributes to the creation of these new ways of mixing raw materials can lead to unbounded growth. But the rivalrous skills associated with teachers who are not also engaged in creating knowledge are not sufficient for unbounded growth.

For the remainder of this chapter, we focus on the product markets for instruction. For illustrative purposes, we begin by assuming that product markets in higher education are first bounded by field of study within each degree level, such as the market for a Master's degree in economics, as depicted in Fig. 1.1. This categorization is drawn from how customers (students) identify the suppliers (institutions) they would consider for higher education services. In academe, students begin by selecting the type of degree they will pursue, either an Associate's, Bachelor's, Master's, or Doctor's degree. Students then or concurrently identify institutions that award the desired degree in the field of study (or major) in which they would like to specialize. From this subset of institutions, students might then choose the specific market of institutions after taking into account other considerations such as their desired geographic span, academic skills, ability to pay for college, and personal characteristics.

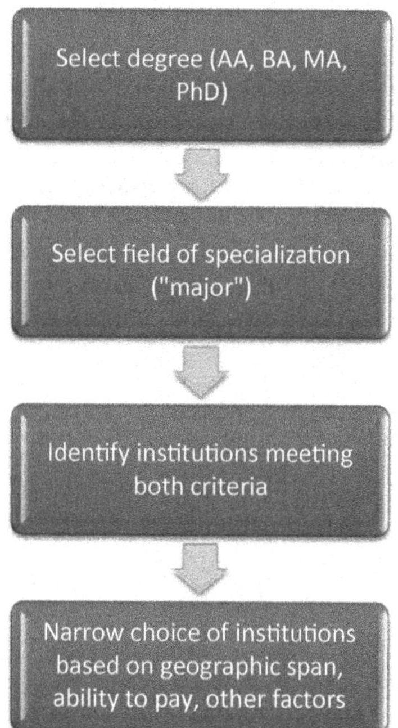

Figure 1.1 Depiction of process for students to identify higher education market.

The connection between markets, degrees, and fields of study is very important at the graduate degree levels due to the fact that these degree programs primarily require students to take courses in their chosen field of study. Institutions that have chosen to offer Master's and Doctor's degrees may opt to only offer them in specific subject areas, and thus not all institutions that award Doctor's degrees will, for example, award a Doctor's degree in sociology. At the Associate's and Bachelor's degree levels, however, it is not always clear whether the appropriate definition of markets should include the field of study. From the perspective of students seeking an Associate's or Bachelor's degree, many of them either do not know what major they will choose when they decide to enroll in college or they may change majors during college. In this case, they may be more interested in the services at an institution as a whole rather than the services within a specific major. Institutions also compete with each other to some extent at the aggregate (institutional) level as well as the field level. Many institutions do not set specific enrollment targets by field of study and instead make strategic decisions to influence the size and quality of all incoming students regardless of major. Nonetheless, the aggregate level is ultimately affected by the institution's ability to compete for students with other institutions that offer the same major and degree within a designated geographic span.

On the supply side of product markets, an IHE has to decide which degrees to offer and in which fields to do so. These decisions are influenced by the mission of the institution, the markets in which they would like to compete, and any rules or regulations at the state level that might restrict their ability to move into specific markets. In some states, a public IHE would have to get approval from a state board or commission before being allowed to start a new degree program.

Table 1.1 shows the distribution of colleges and universities in the United States in 2010–2011 by highest degree offered, broken down by control and profit status from the Integrated Postsecondary Education Data System (IPEDS). As shown, there are almost 4,600 degree-granting institutions in the higher education industry in the United States. Of these institutions, approximately one-third focus mainly on Associate's degrees and thus are said to be in the 2-year sector, and the remaining institutions concentrate on degrees at higher levels and are considered to be part of the 4-year sector. The distribution becomes much more complex when IHE are further broken down by both degree level and field of study. For example, out of almost 1,000 institutions that award a

TABLE 1.1

Breakdown of Institutions of Higher Education in the United States by Highest Degree Awarded, 2010–2011

	Institutional control			
Highest degree awarded	**Public**	**Private not-for-profit**	**Private for-profit**	**Total**
Associate's degree	978	87	664	1,729
Bachelor's degree	132	381	373	886
Master's degree	226	595	225	1,046
Doctor's Degree	320	567	51	938
Grand total (2- and 4-year)	1,656	1,630	1,313	4,599
Subtotals:				
Bachelor's and higher	678	1,543	649	2,870
Master's and higher	546	1,162	276	1,984

Source: Table 4 from NCES Tables Library. US Department of Education, National Center for Education Statistics, Integrated Postsecondary Education Data System (IPEDS), Fall 2010, Institutional Characteristics component

Notes: Only includes institutions that qualify for Title IV and grant degrees

Doctor's degree, only 139 of them offer a Doctor's degree in economics (http://www.aeaweb.org/gradstudents/Schools.php).

It is important to note how the industry is divided by institutional control. The total number of suppliers is fairly evenly split between public, private not-for-profit, and private for-profit institutions. As public institutions are on average much larger than private institutions, they award most of the degrees in the product market for instruction. Public institutions comprise a large share of institutions in Associate's degree markets, whereas private not-for-profit institutions are more likely to be found in the 4-year sectors. Private, for-profit institutions are highly concentrated in the Associate's and Bachelor's degree markets, with little (but growing) involvement in the markets for graduate degrees.

There are three complications that must be addressed to determine the number of suppliers in the industry at each degree level. The first complication is that some institutions in the 4-year sector also offer Associate's degrees. Therefore, a number of institutions in the 4-year sector compete with institutions in the 2-year sector for students seeking an Associate's degree. The second complication is that most institutions that offer Master's degrees also offer Bachelor's degrees, and most Doctor-granting institutions award both Bachelor's and Master's degrees. According to our calculations using IPEDS data for Title IV degree-granting institutions, in the fall of 2010, there were 3,162 institutions that award Associate's degrees, 2,609 institutions that award Bachelor's degrees, and 1,968 institutions that award Master's degrees. As noted earlier, the relevant markets within each degree level are much smaller than this once institutions are broken down by field of study and geographic span and other factors are also taken into account.

Table 1.2 provides an overview of some of the key attributes of the segments of the higher education industry by degree levels. As noted in Table 1.1, the number of suppliers in the segments of the higher education industry declines by level of degree. The number of customers, as represented by degrees conferred, also varies by degree level, with the largest number of students receiving Bachelor's degrees followed by Associate's, Master's, and then Doctor's degrees. With regard to ownership, the suppliers are a mix of public and private institutions, with Associate markets consisting of mostly public (and increasingly private for-profit) institutions and graduate markets consisting of private and public not-for-profit institutions. The degree levels of the higher education industry vary in terms of whether there are hierarchies of suppliers based on their prestige. At

TABLE 1.2

General Characteristics of Suppliers in US Higher Education Industry by Degree Level

Characteristic	Associate's Degree	Bachelor's Degree	Master's Degree	Doctor's Degree
Number of providers	Many (~3,200)	Many (~2,600)	Many (~2,000)	Some (~1,000)
Number of degrees awarded in 2009–2010	849,000	1,650,000	693,000	159,000
Ownership	Public and private	Public and private	Public and private	Public and private
Profit status	Majority are not-for-profit, but many for-profit	Majority are not-for-profit	Majority are not-for-profit	Almost all are not-for-profit
Hierarchical nature of industry	Very little hierarchy based on prestige	Substantial hierarchy based on prestige	Some hierarchy based on prestige	Some hierarchy based on prestige
Residential status of customers	Few students are in residence; many attend part-time	Most students are in residence; many attend full-time	Most students (but fewer than Bachelor's degree) are in residence; many attend full-time	Most students (but fewer than Bachelor's degree) are in residence; many attend full-time

the Associate level, there is very little hierarchy based on prestige, whereas prestige is a significant factor at the Bachelor's and graduate degree levels. Finally, only a small minority of students seeking an Associate's degree will live on campus and attend college full-time. In contrast, the majority of traditional students pursuing a Bachelor's degree will live on or in close proximity to campus. Graduate students also tend to live on or near campus, but they may be more likely than Bachelor's degree-seeking students to attend college part-time due to outside commitments such as work.

The hierarchical nature of the markets for Bachelor's degrees by institutional prestige is not unique to the higher education industry in the United States. In Australia, the long-established so-called "sandstone" universities (the original universities in each capital city) belong to what is referred to as the "Group of Eight." Another group of five relatively new universities (one in each of the five mainland states) that have grown from business-, technology-, and engineering-based origins is known as the ATN Group (Australian Technology Network). The two groups differ in reputation, history, and course offerings but compete with each other for research grants and, to a limited (but increasing) extent, for students willing to move interstate for tertiary studies. However, the competition for students is largely confined within the borders of the home state, among the different tertiary institutions located therein. A discussion of the changing picture of higher education in Australia is provided by Harman (2006). As with the United Kingdom, national policy is aimed at rewarding institutions for specific measured outcomes. This action can be seen as an attempt to solve a principal-agent problem (difficulties that arise under conditions of incomplete and asymmetric information), but it has nothing to do with what markets might produce if universities were left to their own devices.

Pricing in Higher Education Markets

The manner in which colleges and universities set prices for instructional services has puzzled many academics, policymakers, and students and their families. The price for attending college in the United States in 2012 (including tuition, fees, and room and board) can exceed $60,000/year at private not-for-profit institutions and $30,000/year at public institutions. Accordingly, it is not surprising that many stakeholders are concerned that the high price of going to college is severely restricting the postsecondary choices of many students.

Winston (1999) describes the price of higher education services as being the difference between the cost of providing the service and the level of subsidies (or donative resources) that the institution has been able to secure. This framework is important for it shows that the price charged to customers is only a fraction of the cost of providing the service. Institutions that are more successful at obtaining subsidies (through private donations, state appropriations, research funding, and so on) are thus able to charge lower net prices and build excess demand for their services. It is the excess demand that enables colleges and universities to then become more selective in which customers they choose to serve, which in turn raises their prestige within the higher education industry.

In addition to the connection between subsidies and pricing, there are several other important facets with regard to how prices are set in postsecondary education, as detailed in Table 1.3. Recall that one of the conditions of perfectly competitive markets is that consumers have full knowledge of the prices set by all suppliers within the market. This condition certainly does not apply to higher education markets for several reasons. Despite the fact that posted tuition and fees for each institution can be readily obtained from the Internet and various publications and college guidebooks, a substantial portion of students seeking a Bachelor's, Master's, or Doctor's degree pay different net prices due to financial aid (McPherson & Schapiro, 1998). Institutions may reduce the price charged

TABLE 1.3

Pricing Characteristics in US Markets for Students by Degree Level

Characteristic	Associate's Degree	Bachelor's Degree	Master's Degree	Doctor's Degree
Variations in posted tuition	Lower than for B.A., M.A., Ph.D. markets	Large variations by public/private status, prestige of institution, level of subsidies	Some variations by public/private status, level of subsidies	Some variations by public/private status, level of subsidies
Price discounting	Some discounts for financial need	Substantial discounts for financial need, student ability (merit), and special student attributes	Substantial discounts for financial need, some discounts for student ability (merit); some discounts for graduate assistantships	Substantial discounts for financial need, student ability (merit); more discounts for graduate assistantships
Consumer information on prices	Easy to find posted prices, some difficulty finding net prices	Easy to find posted prices, more difficulty than AA finding net prices	Easy to find posted prices, some difficulty finding net prices	Easy to find posted prices, some difficulty finding net prices
Segmented pricing	Most students pay same posted price	Two-tiered pricing in public institutions for resident and nonresident students	Two-tiered pricing in public institutions for resident and nonresident students	Two-tiered pricing in public institutions for resident and nonresident students

to some students seeking a Bachelor's degree by giving them grants or scholarships due to financial need, academic merit, or special characteristics (such as a basketball scholarship). It is also common for graduate students to receive financial aid for need and merit, as well as assistantships for providing teaching or research services to the institution. In contrast, Associate level institutions focus primarily on price discounts for financial need. According to the College Board, in 2011–2012, a full-time undergraduate student received, on average, $5,750 in grant aid and federal tax benefits at public 4-year institutions; $15,530 at private 4-year institutions; and $3,770 at 2-year institutions (College Board [CB], 2011). Even though the practice of price discounting is common across private and public institutions, consumers rarely know the exact amount of discounts they can expect at the time that they are making postsecondary choices; they must first apply to the institution and then be offered admission before they can see the true price that they would be charged.

The pricing of higher education services is affected by two additional factors. First, with a few exceptions, institutions set the same price for all fields of study even though they compete in separate markets. A student who wants to receive a Bachelor's degree in a high-paying field such as finance would pay the same tuition rate as another student who is seeking a Bachelor's degree in a lower-paying field such as history. In another industry, the firm would be able to set different prices for each market in response to supply and demand conditions. Second, prices are usually set for the entire year, even if market conditions change in the interim. This is due to the fact that consumers purchase higher education services at one or two points in time during the year. In contrast, in a local market for gasoline where consumers make frequent purchases, if a gasoline station were to lower its price to help attract more customers, other gasoline stations would be able to quickly match or exceed the price drop to help maintain their market shares.

Bundling of Higher Education Services

As noted earlier, students are purchasing a bundle of services when they enroll in a postsecondary institution. Universities do not produce a single output and students do not buy a single product from them. In addition to instructional services at the undergraduate or graduate level, institutions provide a range of noninstructional services and benefits. Students pay for the entire bundle of goods and services when they shell out tuition money. We break down the bundle of services into five categories as summarized in Table 1.4. The first category ("instructional services") relates to the

TABLE 1.4

Description of Bundle of Services Students Receive from Higher Education

Category	Description
Instructional services	Services that are directly connected to the quality of student instruction and learning. Includes classes taken, curriculum and pedagogy, research opportunities, quality of teaching, and quality of peers
Academic support services	Services that complement or enhance the instructional services received by students. Includes the library facilities and computing infrastructure at the institution
Student services	Services that help students become acclimated and succeed in college. Includes tutoring, counseling, academic advising, and job placement services
Extracurricular opportunities	Services that relate to opportunities for students to participate in on-campus activities from which they derive consumptive value. Includes intramural athletics, formal and informal socializing, and clubs
Locational attributes	Services that relate to the attractiveness of the institution's location (both campus and town) for students. Includes the quality of food and housing, the aesthetic beauty of the campus and town, and access to entertainment from athletic and cultural events

quality of education that students receive at the institution. This quality will be influenced by the structure of the degree program, the content of courses, the quality of teaching, and any effects that peers have on student learning. The second category for academic support includes all services provided by the institution that are meant to support the teaching mission of the institution. Although wireless Internet service and library materials are not part of an institution's instructional services, they can certainly facilitate student learning. Student services represent those services that institutions provide to improve a student's emotional and physical development outside of the classroom and in turn help them succeed academically. These services might include access to tutoring, counseling, and assistance with academic and career planning. By and large, these three types of services are all provided by institutions in varying quantities and are focused on the investment benefits from higher education.

The last two categories—extracurricular opportunities and locational attributes—are more difficult to define and clearly delineate from each other. They are unique in that they focus on the consumptive benefits of higher education because students value these services due to the immediate utility gained from them as opposed to the future benefits they may derive from them. We use the term "extracurricular opportunities" to refer to services in which students may be active participants, such as joining an intramural team, a club, the marching band, a fraternity or sorority, or even informal opportunities to form friendships with other students. The final category ("locational attributes") is intended to capture benefits to students that are connected with the location of the institution and the town/city where the college resides. These attributes would not only include the scenic beauty of the campus and town but also the availability of entertainment and the quality of food and housing in the immediate area for students.

The breakdown of the bundle of higher education services is helpful as it enables us to better understand the range of attributes that students consider when making decisions in higher education markets. The tendency of many academics and policymakers is to focus on the instructional services portion of the bundle when thinking about what colleges should do. They fail to consider that the customers in the market also value the consumptive benefits from college when making enrollment decisions, and thus colleges must provide complementary services in order to compete with other institutions for students. In short, the reason colleges and universities spend considerable sums of money in activities such as developing athletic facilities, improving the landscaping on campus, expanding the menu of food options for students, and adding wireless Internet and other features to dormitories is that these services provide consumptive value to students which in turn may increase their demand.

The bundle of services that students are buying in higher education product markets differs by the type of degree they are pursuing. The noninstructional aspects of higher education services are arguably most important in Bachelor's degree markets where students may focus considerable attention on the amenities that go along with their instructional experiences. Students seeking a Bachelor's degree will often live on or near campus and are at an age where social benefits tend to be very important to them. In contrast, graduate students tend to be older and less interested in the noninstructional services that go along with their education. Students seeking an Associate's degree are likewise on average more focused on the instructional services in part because the majority of them do not reside on campus and thus do not look to the institution to provide as many supplemental benefits. Accordingly, 2-year institutions have opted to specialize primarily in delivering instructional services and do not spend considerable resources on amenities and noninstructional services such as creating football teams. As outlined in Becker and Andrews (2004), public community colleges with no research mission have thrived under the belief that a faculty devoted to research is not essential to performing the less-expensive teaching function. In the Master's and Doctor's degree markets, students will likely place less weight than Bachelor-seeking students on the consumptive value from going to college. However, as the majority of institutions that award Master's and Doctor's degrees also award Bachelor's degrees, graduate students usually find that suppliers offer them the same kinds of noninstructional services as they would to students seeking a Bachelor's degree.

Higher Education Markets by Degree Level

We are now in a position to provide a more complete description of the types of product markets for instruction that exist within the four main degree levels. For each degree level, we discuss the geographic span of markets; the focus, breadth, bundling, and homogeneity of services; the barriers to entry and exit; and the characteristics of students. These points are summarized in Table 1.5. Together, these attributes provide a fuller picture of how economists would conceptualize markets within the higher education industry. The reader should keep in mind that each of the degree levels contains separate markets defined by field of study and then the type of student within each combination of degree and field.

Geographic Span of Markets by Degree Level

The geographic span will tend to be smallest for Associate's degree markets and largest for Doctor's degree markets. Given that students seeking Associate's degrees usually do not reside at the institution, the Associate's degree markets are more properly defined by institutions that are within commuting distance of students. Students who participate in Master's and Doctor's degree markets, on the other hand, normally move to and live on or near campus and thus would consider institutions in a much larger geographic span (national or perhaps regional). There are thus fewer markets for graduate degrees than there are for Associate's degrees.

The geographic spans of Bachelor's degree markets fall in between these two cases. There are prestigious and highly selective universities who draw interest from academically talented students from around the nation (and the world) and do not have any particular regional appeal to students. Institutions in this market, such as Harvard, Princeton, Dartmouth, and Stanford, compete with each other in national markets for high-ability students. Other institutions offering Bachelor's degrees in specific fields primarily compete with other suppliers in the same geographic region. This occurs even though they enroll students from outside their primary region, provided that they tend to get the majority of student demand from within their immediate geographic area.

Public institutions often have a high degree of competition with other public institutions in the same state, even when they have substantial differences in prestige and mission. The competition is driven in part by proximity to consumers as well as the fact that they enjoy substantial price advantages for state residents due to appropriations from the state government. It is often the case that the state's most prestigious, research-oriented public institution will share significant numbers of resident applicants at the Bachelor's degree level with their teaching-focused institutions. Public institutions also operate in separate markets for resident and nonresident students at the Bachelor's degree level. This bifurcation is due to the importance given to enrolling sufficient numbers of in-state students and the additional revenue that can be gained from charging higher prices to out-of-state students. In fact, some public institutions set separate enrollment targets for in-state and out-of-state students.

Getz and Siegfried (1991, p. 12) called readers' attention to the fact that in the United States, higher education is relatively decentralized, with 50 separate state regimes and hundreds of private institutions run by self-perpetuating boards of trustees. Following Bok (1986), they argued that this decentralization has encouraged competition that is not associated with government-imposed fixed prices and quality mix. At the highest level, public and private institutions compete for the same students at different prices and turn out students that are equally demanded by employers. Decentralization and competition have resulted in the United States having a less monolithic higher education establishment as reflected in Fallows (1990, pp. 17–18) observation that only two (Kennedy and Bush) of the then seven American presidents since 1960 graduated from elite private institutions, whereas all Japanese leaders graduated from a single college, the University of Tokyo, which also accounts for a third of all presidents of large corporations, 60% of senior government officials, and all postwar prime ministers but enrolls only 1% of the population (Rohlen, 1983, pp. 88–91).

In contrast to this view that the education and imprimatur from the elite colleges and universities differ little from the others, Bound, Hershbein and Long (2009) claim that increasing demand

TABLE 1.5

Characteristics of US Markets for Instructional Services by Degree Level

Characteristic	Associate's Degree	Bachelor's Degree	Master's Degree	Doctor's Degree
Geographic scope of markets	Within commuting distance of a student's home	National for high-ability students; regional for other students; separate markets in public IHE for in-state and out-of-state students	National for high-ability students; regional for nontraditional students	National for the majority of traditional students; regional for nontraditional students
Focus of service	Instruction	Instruction	Instruction and some research	Instruction and substantial research
Breadth of service	Take courses in a range of subjects plus major	Take courses in a range of subjects plus major	Take courses in one field of study	Take courses in one field of study
Bundling of service	Instruction, academic and support services; some extracurricular and locational	Substantial bundling of instruction, academic and support services, many extracurricular and locational	Some bundling of instruction, academic and support services; some extracurriculars and locational	Some bundling of instruction, academic and support services; some extracurriculars and locational
Homogeneity of service	Some heterogeneity: service varies by courses in program, quality of courses	Considerable heterogeneity: service varies by program content, course quality, nonclassroom attributes, prestige of degree from supplier	Some heterogeneity: less variation in degree content, still have variations in prestige from supplier	Some heterogeneity: less variation in degree content, still have variations in prestige from supplier
Barriers to entry	Fixed costs and government regulation, lower barriers than for B.A., M.A., Ph.D.	Fixed costs and government regulation; higher barriers than AA due to costs of nonclassroom attributes	Fixed costs and government regulation; lower barriers than B.A. Incur fixed and variable costs for research	Some barriers from fixed costs and government regulation. Incur added fixed and variable costs for research
Student characteristics	Lower academic ability; looking for career preparation and skills	Substantial variation in student academic ability; looking for general knowledge as well as career preparation	Above-average academic ability; looking for general knowledge as well as career preparation	High academic ability; looking for general knowledge as well as career preparation

for admission to these highly selective schools is likely related to the notion that the institution a student attends has become increasingly important, citing the findings of Hoxby and Long (1999) that nearly half of the explained growth in the widening income distribution among college-educated workers is associated with the increasing concentration of peer and financial resources at more selective colleges and universities relative to other institutions. As emphasized by Hoxby (2009), Bachelor's degree markets have shifted from regional in focus to national. Also, as more workers become college educated, employers may view the average college-educated worker as less productive than in the past. Under this signaling type of framework, a degree from an elite college is alleged to become even more valuable in the future.

Focus and Breadth of Markets by Degree Level

With regard to the focus of service, the markets for Master's and Doctor's degrees combine aspects of research and instruction, in that an important part of a graduate student's education involves learning how to conduct research within a specific field of study. In contrast, at the Associate's degree level (and largely the Bachelor's degree level), the focus of the service is on instruction and not research.

The breadth of instructional services varies by degree level as well. Students seeking an Associate's or Bachelor's degree are paying for not only instruction in their primary subject of choice but also for instruction in other subjects that are needed as part of their general education requirements for the degree. In contrast, instruction at the graduate levels is focused almost exclusively on the student's main field of study.

Bundling of Services in Markets by Degree Level

The bundling of services occurs in different ways across the markets by degree levels. There is arguably the largest amount of bundling in Bachelor's degree markets, where students are not only purchasing instruction across a wide range of subjects but also academic and student services to help them succeed, as well as consumptive benefits from extracurricular opportunities and locational attributes. Students in Associate's degree markets also purchase bundles of instructional and noninstructional services. However, given that students in these markets do not usually reside on or near campus, there is less emphasis placed on extracurricular opportunities and locational attributes that generate consumptive benefits. Similarly, on average, the consumptive benefits derived from extracurricular opportunities and locational attributes in graduate markets are likely to be lower than in Bachelor's degree markets.

Homogeneity of Service in Markets by Degree Level

Within the product markets for Bachelor's degrees, it is safe to say that there is a fair amount of product differentiation—both real and perceived—among suppliers. First, the courses required for students to obtain a Bachelor's degree within a specific major can vary across institutions. A student who earned a Bachelor's degree in sociology from College A likely received a different service from another student who received a Bachelor's degree in sociology from College B. Note that different course requirements across institutions apply not only to courses within the student's major but also for the general education and elective requirements needed for completing a Bachelor's degree. Viewed in this way, it is very difficult to envision two colleges providing the same exact set of courses for students who want to earn a Bachelor's degree in a given major. In graduate degree markets, the instructional services are also heterogeneous but arguably less than in Bachelor's degree markets for students who only take courses within their field of study.

Product differentiation across colleges and universities expands as one also considers other ways in which the services are delivered by colleges. The quality of each class can be affected by a number of factors, including the curriculum used for the course, the spillover benefits from interactions with peers, and the faculty member's ability to help students learn the material. For example, even though almost every college offers a course in introductory statistics, the specific content of the course can differ from institution to institution, and even from section to section within the same institution.

Higher education services can be perceived by customers to differ in ways beyond tangible differences in programs of study and course content. Prospective college students learn quickly in the college search process that it is difficult to obtain information about the factors discussed above, which makes it challenging to compare the quality of services offered by providers. As in other industries where this occurs, students often turn to indicators to estimate the likely quality of the service they would receive at different institutions. The growth of college rankings such as those produced by *US News and World Report* reflects the interest among students in finding information about the relative quality of suppliers within the higher education industry. Students also rely on the decisions of other consumers to provide information about the likely quality of services at various institutions, with the notion being that the quality of education is "better" at College A than at College B if more high-ability students have chosen to attend College A.

Barriers to Entry in Markets by Degree Level

The barriers to entry and exit from higher education markets depend on the type of services rendered by the institution. The barriers to entry are highest for those providers who offer more traditional postsecondary education services for consumers (students) living on or near campus and pursuing a Bachelor's, Master's, or Doctor's degree. For these providers, there can be substantial fixed costs for starting a 4-year, comprehensive college or university that would make it difficult for new potential institutions to enter the market. In addition, the number and scope of public (state supported) institutions that may operate within a state's boundaries can be controlled by either the state government, higher education coordinating board, or public university system. At a minimum, such constraints would make it very difficult for new publicly supported institutions to enter the postsecondary markets in many states. As the fixed costs are likely to be smaller for 2-year colleges and/or colleges that provide services online to students, the barriers to entry and exit would be lower in markets comprised of these types of institutions. Barriers to entry also exist in graduate markets due to government regulations and expenditures needed to develop the research infrastructure to provide graduate degrees in selected fields. However, due to the fact that graduate programs are usually added by institutions that already offer Bachelor's degrees, many of the fixed costs associated with starting an institution would not apply to graduate degree programs.

Characteristics of Students in Markets by Degree Level

There are a number of differences in the types of students participating in markets within the four degree levels. Students in Associate's degree markets will likely be lower in ability and more homogeneous than are students who opt for Bachelor's degree markets. When combined with the lack of hierarchy of Associate institutions by prestige and their use of open admissions policies, there is little sorting of students across institutions in Associate's degree markets by academic ability. Students within graduate degree markets tend to be more homogeneous than students in Bachelor's degree markets as they are typically drawn from the upper portion of the student ability distribution. There will be some sorting of students across institutions in graduate markets due to the hierarchy of graduate programs by prestige. In contrast, Bachelor's degree markets in the USA consist of a wide range of students by academic ability, and higher-ability students seek to enroll in more-prestigious institutions.

Structures of Markets by Degree Levels

It is worth considering which of the four market structures discussed earlier (perfect competition, monopolistic competition, oligopoly, monopoly) apply best to the product markets for instructional services in higher education. In short, higher education markets are not exactly the same as any of the four structures, but they do have some similarities with these structures that are helpful for understanding how colleges behave in their respective markets.

First, it is clear that higher education markets are not perfectly competitive. This stems from the fact that higher education services are not homogeneous, there are substantial barriers to entry and exit, and consumers do not have perfect information about the prices charged by colleges and the quality of their respective services. Likewise, higher education markets cannot be characterized as monopolistic as there is certainly some degree of substitutability across IHE within every market. Even a highly prestigious institution such as Harvard, for example, has competitors such as Princeton and Stanford that are viewed by many consumers as fairly close substitutes within relevant markets.

An argument can be made, however, that the most prestigious and highly selective institutions in the United States operate in oligopolistic markets for Bachelor's degrees by field. These institutions are relatively few in number, compete at the national level for the best students, and have similar profiles of students, finances, and so forth. The institutions within a market can be thought of as the ideal collusive group (or the hypothetical monopolist test, as it is often now called in legal work); that is, in the minds of buyers, they are all essentially substitutable for each other, but products outside the group are seen to offer no relevant substitution possibilities. In other words, acting as a group, the institutions in a market could raise prices in small but nevertheless significant and nontransitory ways and not lose buyers to a rival's product. To the extent that Harvard, Yale, and like Ivy League institutions could jointly raise tuition and fees without altering their attractiveness to both domestic and foreign students, they would constitute a unique market. The oligopoly market structure may also be a fitting model for the best students at the Master's and Doctor's degree levels within specific fields, in that there are relatively few suppliers with high prestige that offer degrees within fields of study.

Perhaps the best description of market structures in higher education is that they are mixtures of monopolistic competition and oligopoly. Some higher education markets are similar to monopolistic competition in that the service offered by suppliers is very heterogeneous, and for those students who have large geographic spans to consider, there may be many suppliers offering Bachelor's degrees within their field of study. At the same time, markets may resemble oligopolies for there are notable barriers to entry and exit in higher education, and markets defined at the regional level (such as the market for Bachelor's degrees in history in the State of Indiana or the market for an Associate's degree in nursing within 60 miles of Ames, Iowa) may have relatively few suppliers.

Issues in Identifying Markets in Higher Education

The prior discussion laid out in general terms how economists would characterize the various markets that exist within higher education. However, it leaves open the question as to how to determine which institutions are in which markets. Identifying specific markets usually involves either obtaining information on which suppliers react to price and product changes by other firms or using decisions of consumers to see which suppliers they consider.

The traditional approach used in economics for identifying markets is to determine how potential competitors react to changes in price and services of another supplier. For example, consider the following three institutions: Ivy Tech Community College (Bloomington, IN), Indiana University (Bloomington, IN), and Harvard University (Cambridge, MA). Ivy Tech is a 2-year public institution with open enrollment, offering many remedial courses that do not count toward a degree and a range of Associate's degrees in fields such as nursing and business administration. Indiana University is a 4-year public institution offering a full range of Bachelor's, Master's, and Doctor's degree programs. It is relatively selective and draws students from Indiana and around the world. Harvard University is a highly selective, 4-year private institution that also offers a wide range of degree programs and competes on a national level for the very top students. Changes in the tuition rate charged at Ivy Tech will likely not cause Harvard to also change its tuition, and it is easy to see that they are in different product markets.

More interesting from an analytical policy perspective, however, would be to ask under what conditions would Ivy Tech and Indiana University (both located in Bloomington, Indiana) be considered to compete in the same market, and what are the consequences of viewing them as such? For example, Indiana University offers a Bachelor of Science in Nursing degree, which may be viewed by some students as a substitute for Ivy Tech's Associate of Science in Nursing degree in that both degrees are viable options for many entry-level nursing positions. Or would an introductory statistics class taught at Ivy Tech in the summer be a substitute for the same class taught at Indiana University for those students living near Bloomington who want to take an introductory statistics course in the summer? Ultimately, it may be a matter of subjective judgment and not an absolute as to where to draw the appropriate product-market boundary. Nevertheless, the task must be carried out, even if done with reservations.

The discussion above highlights the fact that the extent to which institutions compete with each other in markets cannot be neatly drawn along traditional categories of institutions. In the United States, we often find public institutions competing with private institutions and institutions of different prestige levels competing with each other for students. In fact, the work of Dale and Krueger (2002) suggests students who are accepted by the elite privates but who elect to attend a major state institution do better in later life. That is, the big major state university like Indiana University may, indeed, be part of the same market in which the high sticker-priced private institutions are alleged to form a relatively tight oligopoly. An interesting market-related policy question is whether the major state universities can continue to compete with the private universities as state legislatures decree that credits from local community colleges, regional universities, and the like be accepted by their state-subsidized research universities. Or at the very least for some students, they may be considered as acceptable substitutes.

One way to conceptualize this issue draws on our earlier explanation of the bundling of instructional services. Recall that when students select an institution, they are taking into account the expected benefits from instruction, academic support, student services, extracurricular opportunities, and locational attributes. To put it another way, the expected utility for a student from choosing a given institution depends on the expected utility from the anticipated investment benefits (gross benefits minus costs) and consumptive benefits. Holding all else constant, students would expect higher utility from attending institutions with either greater gross benefits, lower costs of attendance, or more consumptive benefits.

The bundling of services presents opportunities for institutions of varying prestige levels to compete with each other. If more-prestigious institutions on average have higher expected gross benefits (e.g., a Bachelor's degree from Harvard will result in higher salaries than a Bachelor's degree from Valdosta State), then this provides an obvious advantage for prestigious institutions in competing for students. This does not, however, mean that less-prestigious institutions cannot successfully compete with more-prestigious ones. If less-prestigious institutions charge lower prices than more-prestigious ones, for example, then this may offset some of the lower utility students would receive from choosing the less-prestigious institution. Or less-prestigious institutions may offer students better extracurricular opportunities and/or locational attributes that enable them to provide more utility to students and therefore become more competitive with more-prestigious institutions.

Competition between different types of institutions is also facilitated by two additional factors. First, given that students often do not know the true price that they would have to pay at different institutions, they may end up applying to some colleges that are ultimately out of their price range. In particular, the fact that private institutions have long engaged in substantial price discounting through merit- and need-based scholarships may lead some prospective students to apply for admission in the hope of receiving enough financial aid to make attendance possible. Second, students usually apply to a range of institutions as there is no guarantee that they will be accepted by their top choice. This is different from most product markets where consumers know that they can acquire the good/service as long as they have the ability to pay for it. In contrast, higher education markets are more similar to markets for spouses, where both parties have to accept the other in order for a transaction to occur. As a result, students will normally apply to several institutions that differ in terms of prestige and selectivity. The University of Georgia, for example, may be both an "aspirational" choice for lower-ability students and a "safety school" for higher-ability students.

Universities in the same analytical market will compete with each other for inputs on the demand side—for intake students, resources (including faculty, government funding, endowments, and other funding sources), capacity, and political influence—as well as on the supply side, for available classroom seats, graduating students, research output, athletic programs, and other services. Under such conditions of interdependence, what one institution does can result in a competitive reaction from another if they operate in the same market. If no such response occurs within a meaningful time period (which may be long in higher education markets), then the nonresponding institution must feel that it is not constrained by the institution that initiated the new strategy and thus feels it will not lose buyers. So, if the University of South Australia lowers its fees or makes its product (whatever that might be) more readily available, we would expect Indiana University to respond in kind only if the two universities were in the same market. Although institutions do compete with each other over geographical space, the extent of the competitive constraints will diminish with distance, if for no other reason than the fact that a student's search and transaction costs will increase with distance. Thus, even in Australia, it is likely that the University of South Australia, located in Adelaide, would not operate in the same market for the intake of undergraduate students as the University of Sydney, located some 1,500 km (950 miles) away. It would, however, compete for entering students with the two other universities in Adelaide.

With more than 4,000 degree-granting institutions from which to choose in the United States, as well as institutions in other nations, how can students begin to isolate the set of institutions that fall within their desired market? Students now have a range of tools that they can use to help identify institutions that fall within the market of which they are interested. The College Navigator (http://nces.ed.gov/collegenavigator/) is an online search engine created by the National Center for Education Statistics. Students can use the search engine to not only identify institutions that offer degrees in specific subject areas but also restrict their search to institutions within specific geographic spans, price ranges, and other criteria. Table 1.6 provides an illustration of how the College Navigator can help students identify the relevant market. In this example, the student lives in Athens, GA, and would like to pursue a Bachelor's degree in business. According to College Navigator, there are more than 500 institutions that offer a Bachelor's degree in business across the United States. If the student narrowed the search down to only institutions within 200 miles of Athens, the number of institutions in the market fell to 148. The student could continue to narrow down the scope of the market by restricting the search to institutions where the tuition was below $25,000/year ($n$ = 123) and where the acceptance rate was also below 70% (n = 62).

The growth of for-profit and distance education providers of higher education services introduces more complexity into the topic of markets. To illustrate, the University of Phoenix may move into a new geographic area and award degrees in the same subjects as regional private or public institutions. However, it is unlikely that the degrees from the University of Phoenix would be viewed

TABLE 1.6

Example of Market Search Results using College Navigator

Search	Description	Number of Institutions Meeting Criteria
(A)	All institutions offering Bachelor's degree in business	n = 500+
(B)	Same as (A), but within 200 miles of Athens, GA	n = 148
(C)	Same as (B), but with tuition below $25,000/year	n = 123
(D)	Same as (C), but with acceptance rate below 70%	n = 62

Notes: Data obtained from the College Navigator search engine (http://nces.ed.gov/collegenavigator/)

as substitutable for degrees from Stanford or from a highly selective public university such as the University of Michigan by the students who are considering attending these prestigious resident campus institutions. At the same time, nontraditional students in the region may well consider the services to be substitutes. Thus, in this case, it would be a mistake for the regional public college to ignore the entry of the University of Phoenix into the market, but it would be a mistake of equal magnitude for the likes of Stanford to respond to the moves of the University of Phoenix. Clearly, given the purposive nature of market definition—where a market is defined by the nature of the reasons for examining it—there will rarely be one consistent or "right" definition of the relevant market for any one policy, antitrust, regulation, or commercial issue. The criteria to be used are arguable, and the empirical measurement techniques are debatable, such that it is rare, certainly in a contested legal situation, to reach agreement as to what the precise boundaries of the relevant market are for the issue in question (Church & Ware, 2000; Keyte & Stoll, 2004). But this does not refute the need to be aware that markets do exist and that their boundaries must be considered prior to creating or assessing policy or analyzing the behavior of buyers, sellers, or input suppliers in the relevant market.

It could be argued that this formal process of market definition is extremely difficult and unnecessary and is likely to lead to artificially or inaccurately defined markets that do not correctly reveal the true or relevant area of constraints. This leads to the proposition that markets be allowed to reveal themselves through the actions of suppliers and demanders. The analyst or observer should not seek to impose an artificial market construct that does not coincide with commercial or regulatory reality. Rather, the observations should be made of what institutions and consumers actually do—which other institutions are targeted by their conduct, which other institutions (both current as well as potential rivals) they respond to, and which customers they particularly seek to attract (by way of, e.g., advertising, sponsorships, trade fairs, product endorsements). This is a more commercially realistic way in which to identify the true area of close competition, rather than the more academic process of formally identifying the various market boundaries through economic measurements or through abstract thought processes relating to the measurement of demand-side and supply-side substitution possibilities.

The mere fact that a market has been defined through the use of objective economic processes (though reasonable economists, using the same objective evaluators, may still emerge with different market boundaries, depending on how they weight or interpret the results) does not mean that each institution and product assigned into the market is homogeneous. Far from it! Institutions in the same market could be big or small, use different technologies or marketing techniques, be differently organized, or have different corporate goals. Within a market, there could be distinct hierarchies or groups of institutions defined by different organizational, operational, or size factors, yet all of which compete to sell products that are seen by buyers as either actually or potentially highly substitutable. Restaurants in a city provide a good example of this situation. Differences in cooking styles, seating capacities, ambiences, wine lists, price ranges, locations, and so on all mean that the restaurant market, if it exists in this broad characterization, might consist of many different strategic groups or submarkets, but they all seek to appeal to a wide range of diners and do compete, at least at the margin, especially within a given price bracket or food type or geographic span. To repeat an earlier point, if a state legislature decrees that credits earned at in-state community colleges are to be fully transferable to the state's research universities, then at least, for these courses and the students who take them, both types of institutions could be viewed as belonging to the same market.

Similarly, it can be difficult to use changes in prices in higher education to identify which colleges compete with each other. Institutions typically change their prices only once each year, and price changes can be affected by changes in state appropriations and other factors in addition to responses to competitors. Institutions have become much more sophisticated over time in using data on potential students as a way to identify who they compete with in their markets. Many colleges in the United States now have offices of "enrollment management" that are set up to find potential markets of students and analyze how to recruit them in light of competition from other institutions. Institutions may also exploit information from the Census Bureau using geocoding software to identify neighborhoods where the socioeconomic characteristics of families are consistent with the types of students that the institution seeks to attract.

Students can reveal the markets they are considering through their early indicators of demand for higher education. If a student applies to a group of five institutions, for example, then it suggests that these are the institutions that the student considers to be competitors for the service she is seeking. Similarly, given that students are usually required to submit standardized test scores when applying for admission to Bachelor's degree programs, they can reveal their initial choice set of institutions through the colleges to which they send their standardized test scores from either the Scholastic Aptitude Test (SAT) or the American College Testing (ACT) exam (Toutkoushian, 2001b). Institutions that share a large number of applicants or SAT score senders might therefore be thought of as competitors for students. It is now common for institutions to obtain such data and track information on those institutions with whom they compete most heavily for students.

To illustrate, Table 1.7 provides data on the overlap of SAT score submissions by high school seniors in the State of New Hampshire to a set of designated institutions in a particular year (1996). These high school seniors were at the point where they were considering pursuing either an Associate's degree or a Bachelor's degree; however, the majority of students were most likely interested in a Bachelor's degree given that they have taken the SAT and that the test is only required for Bachelor's degree programs in the region. The four columns correspond to the four public institutions in the state with residential campuses: the University of New Hampshire's main campus at Durham (UNH-D), Keene State College (KSC), Plymouth State University (PSU), and the University of New Hampshire's branch campus at Manchester (UNH-M). Among these four institutions, UNH-D offers the fullest range of graduate degrees and is the most research intensive and prestigious. KSC and PSU focus on Bachelor's degree programs and a limited number of Master's degree programs. Finally, UNH-M specializes in Associate's and some Bachelor's degree programs.

For each of these institutions, we calculated the percentage of New Hampshire seniors who submitted their SAT scores to each institution as well a group of seven other institutions that are in

TABLE 1.7

Overlap of SAT Senders for New Hampshire Students, 1996

Category	Institution	UNH-D (%)	KSC (%)	PSU (%)	UNH-M (%)
New Hampshire public institutions	University of New Hampshire (Durham campus)—UNH-D	—	65	67	43
	Keene State College (KSC)	24	—	54	31
	Plymouth State University (PSU)	22	49	—	29
	University of New Hampshire (Manchester campus)—UNH-M	4	8	8	—
New Hampshire private institutions	Franklin Pierce College	2	6	5	6
	Dartmouth College	9	5	4	6
New England private institutions	Boston University	12	5	5	6
	Boston College	9	3	3	4
	Northeastern University	11	6	7	7
New England public institutions	University of Vermont	12	6	6	4
	University of Massachusetts	8	6	5	5

Notes: Data were obtained from the College Board. Values represent the percentage of students who submitted their SAT scores to both institutions in 1996

close proximity to the four public institutions in New Hampshire. These other institutions are broken down into three groups: (1) private institutions in New Hampshire, (2) private institutions in New England, and (3) public flagship institutions in New England. The figure 65% in the first row of the column for KSC shows, for example, that 65% of the students who submitted their SAT scores to Keene State College also submitted their SAT scores to UNH-D.

Several interesting findings regarding competition among the institutions emerge from these data on SAT overlaps. Note first that despite the significant differences among the four public institutions in New Hampshire, they experience a high degree of overlap in SAT submissions, with approximately two-thirds of the SAT senders to the state colleges (KSC and PSU) also sending their test scores to the state's public flagship research institution (UNH-D). Similarly, there is a high degree of overlap between the two UNH campuses, even though UNH-M has a more limited range of degree programs as compared to the main campus in Durham. Even though UNH-D is considered to be a research-oriented institution, it shares more SAT senders with the teaching-oriented public institutions in the state than it does with other research-oriented public institutions in the region such as the University of Vermont and the University of Massachusetts at Amherst. At the same time, UNH-D has more SAT overlap with the research-focused institutions in the region that is true for KSC, PSU, and UNH-M, as would be expected.

Policy Analysis and Markets in Higher Education

Finally, we end with some thoughts on the connection between properly defining markets in higher education and policy analysis. Higher education policies come in many forms, from state and federal laws and regulations to institution-specific initiatives. Because higher education markets by definition consist of IHE that directly compete with each other and are thus interconnected, policies that target one or more institutions in a market will likely have an influence on all of the other institutions within the same market.

Before embarking on any form of economic or policy analysis of market failure, behavior, incentives, inefficiencies, innovation, or restructuring, it is crucial to first ensure that all of the participants in the market have been correctly identified, including not only the rival sellers but also buyers, suppliers, and current or potential rivals to the incumbents. This involves problematic empirical issues such as identifying potential entrants, when they are likely to enter and at what scale, and identifying goods that are close enough substitutes in either demand or supply to constrain the operations of the institution in question and at what prices.

Markets can be defined too narrowly, in which case some competing institutions will be excluded from consideration, and the institutions assigned to a market will be thought to have more market power and fewer constraints on their behavior than is actually the case. If, on the other hand, markets are defined too broadly, then it is likely that they will be found to be more competitive than they really are and that policy action may be misdirected in the form of failing to act to remedy a deficiency in the market's performance. This problem of getting the breadth of market definition right applies to all three market dimensions.

Although, conceptually, a market is a simple economic construct—a collection of buyers and sellers of close substitute products—in practice, it can be difficult to define its boundaries with any great precision and without great controversy. But it is within markets that economic activity takes place, and it is this activity we want to be conducted to ensure the optimum allocation of resources, both private and public. Therefore, it is important that all those who seek to influence resource allocation in higher education—government policymakers, academics, university decision-makers—realize that a one-size- fits-all policy perspective might not produce the best results throughout the variety of distinct markets that constitute the higher education sector. For example, markets can only be shown to be "efficient" (reflecting an allocation of goods and services that provide the greatest benefits at the least cost) if potential like sellers and like buyers can be defined and the influences on them can be accurately identified.

In an overview such as this, we cannot hope to cover all of the issues that could arise in any empirical or policy situation that calls for market definition. We put forward the following checklist as illustrative of the kinds of practical problems that will confront researchers who need to define markets for postsecondary education:

- Start with the program, institution, or group that is the subject of the inquiry, keeping in mind the purpose of the inquiry.
- Seek to identify the closest substitute from the perspective of the relevant buyers or sellers and assess whether and by how much this constrains the actions of the original party. Keep adding rival institutions until no further substitution appears to be acceptable, such that a group of institutions has been identified that faces no effective constraints from those outside the group. In this process, it is essential to identify the nature and extent of the constraints that are being assessed.
- As part of this process, consider geographic substitution, taking into account the extra costs that might be involved.
- Take care to include in the assessment any constraints offered by potential entrants into the market, as long as this entry is currently a real enough threat to constrain the institution(s) in question.
- Consider also the influence of suppliers to the institution.

Market delineation is far from an exact science. It is frequently a matter of great contention in antitrust cases. But this does not obviate the need to provide the definition that best informs those who must make policy judgments about how best to shape the operation of the market through appropriate policy instruments and changes.

Concluding Thoughts

The concept of markets and competition between colleges and universities within markets is now a global phenomenon. As institutions struggle to acquire financial resources to compete in these markets, they will surely look to innovative ways of extending their market power and reaching new customers. This framework can be used to consider how higher education markets are likely to change in the future. For example, what will the role of research be in the future of higher education? We have seen a gradual ratcheting up of research activities at many postsecondary institutions in the United States as they search for ways to increase their prestige and ranking within the industry. A similar shift has occurred in higher education industries around the globe, as evidenced by the growth of international rankings schemes that focus on bibliometric measures of research output (Shin, Toutkoushian, & Teichler, 2011).

The fact that graduate markets have substantial fixed costs and high variable costs has served to limit the size of these markets. Nonetheless, research is a necessary component of educational services at the graduate degree levels and is likely to have benefits at the undergraduate level as well. Becker and Andrews (2004) provided examples to show that higher education involves much more than the teaching of traditional doctrine. It is the academic inquiry that elevates higher education above mere training. They argued that at a research university, instruction has the potential to be enhanced as it can be made a part of an integrated and aggressive campaign of inquiry. Active researchers can engage students in the challenging ideas, questions, and methods of inquiry at the forefront of their disciplines, whereas docents can be expected only to teach that which they have been taught or learned from textbooks. They called attention to the fact that research is expensive and that public community colleges with no research mission have thrived under the belief that a faculty devoted to research is not essential to performing the less-expensive teaching function. A contextual updating of Gresham's law (inferior currency drives out superior currency) might suggest that the less-expensive educational practices of community colleges will force out the more expensive, full-time, tenured faculty members teaching at the research universities. As Becker and Andrews demonstrated, there is evidence of this happening with both public research and doctoral institutions increasing the proportions of both part-time and full-time faculty members with non-tenure track appointments. Following the community college model, universities are increasingly looking to part-time and nontenure track docent-type appointments to teach in undergraduate baccalaureate programs. Unfortunately, Gresham's law in this context is just as deficient in assessing effects as it is for monetary policy.

What types of institutions appear to be best positioned to compete in higher education markets in the future? Clearly, those that have been successful at attaining prestige have been able to use this to generate excess demand for their services and in turn become even more prestigious and successful in higher education markets. Some less-prestigious institutions (mainly public) have achieved success through a combination of lower prices and better extracurricular opportunities and locational attributes. It is not hard to see, however, why the less-prestigious private institutions have had the most difficulty competing in markets in recent years. They cannot rely on the same level of donative resources as prestigious private institutions or state-supported public institutions. As a result, their prices tend to be high and the investment return lower than for many other suppliers in the market. At the same time, they still have to compete with other institutions for faculty.

Finally, the growth of the for-profit sector and accompanying distance education providers has raised questions with regard to how this will affect the markets for higher education. By allowing students to consume higher education services from many different locations, distance education providers can alter the geographic span of existing higher education markets. Berret (2012) reported on a Harvard University conference on teaching where Clayton M. Christensen, a professor of business administration at the Harvard Business School, described how new businesses often enter the bottom of a market and claim untapped customers whom they reach through some new technological advance. Eventually, they move up in their market and overtake the dominant player. He said that higher education once was immune to market forces until the spread of online learning, "which will allow lower-cost providers to extend into the higher reaches of the marketplace."

Given our understanding of markets, however, it is extremely difficult to envision how a provider such as the University of Phoenix with its open enrollment and for-profit mentality could ever move up in prestige to threaten highly selective institutions such as Harvard University. Despite the fact that online institutions may enjoy cost advantages over their more-prestigious counterparts and offer degree programs in similar subject areas, they will likely always compete in separate markets for the vast majority of customers. In particular, the hierarchical nature of Bachelor's degree markets and corresponding differences in investment returns have a strong effect on the specific markets where high-ability students choose to participate. Distance education services will also provide fewer academic support and student services than residential institutions and place less emphasis on consumptive benefits, which will limit their attractiveness to students in higher education markets.

It is our hope that this chapter is helpful in distinguishing between the many ways in which academics, policymakers, and stakeholders have applied the term "market" to higher education. Debate is certain to continue as to whether the application of business practices is beneficial or harmful to higher education. Nonetheless, it is crucial for all involved to understand that there are many different markets within the higher education industry and that it can be extremely challenging to identify precisely which institutions are in which markets.

Notes

1. The ideas presented in this chapter are extensions of some of the ideas presented in Becker and Round (2009).
2. As economists, we do not attempt to address the idea that there is "market space" for the various things produced by institutions of higher education as one might find in marketing courses offered by business schools but rather focus on the general concept of a market as the interaction of buyers and sellers as treated in an economics course.
3. Andrew S. Rosen is chief executive of Kaplan Inc., which is one of if not the largest for-profit postsecondary education providers in the world. Naomi Schaefer Riley is the author of *The Faculty Lounges: And Other Reasons Why You Won't Get the College Education You Pay For* (2011).

References

Anderson, M. (1992). *Impostors in the temple*. New York: Simon and Schuster.

Arimoto, A. (1997). Market and higher education in Japan. *Higher Education Policy, 10*, 199–210.

Astin, A. (1993). *What matters in college: Four critical years revisited*. San Francisco: Jossey-Bass.

Bamberger, G., & Carlton, D. (1999). Antitrust and higher education: MIT financial aid. In J. Kwoka Jr. & L. White (Eds.), *The antitrust revolution: Economics, competition, and policy*. New York: Oxford University Press.

Becker, W., & Andrews, M. (Eds.). (2004). *The scholarship of teaching and learning in higher education: Contributions of research universities*. Bloomington, IN: Indiana University Press.

Becker, W., & Kennedy, P. (2006, January). The influence of teaching on research in economics. *Southern Economic Journal*, 72 (3), 747–759.

Becker, W., & Round, D. (2009). *'The' market for higher education: Does it really exist?* (IZA Discussion Paper No. 4092). Available at SSRN: http://ssrn.com/abstract=1373326

Berret, D. (2012, February 5). Harvard conference seeks to Jolt University Teaching, *The Chronicle of Higher Education*, http://online.wsj.com/article/SB10001424052970204879004577110970031199712.html?KEYWORDS =The+University+of+Adam+Smith#printMode

Bok, D. (1986). *Higher learning*. Cambridge, MA: Harvard University Press.

Bok, D. (2003). *Universities in the marketplace: The commercialization of higher education*. Princeton, NJ: Princeton University Press.

Borden, V., & Bottrill, K. (1994). Performance indicators: History, definitions, and methods. *New Directions for Institutional Research*, 82, 5–22.

Bound, J., Hershbein, B., & Long, B. (2009). Playing the admissions game: Student reactions to increasing college competition. *Journal of Economic Perspectives*, 23, 119–146.

Breneman, D. (1981). Strategies for the 1980s. In J. Mingle (Ed.), *Challenges of retrenchment*. San Francisco: Jossey-Bass.

Brewer, D., Gates, S., & Goldman, C. (2002). *In pursuit of prestige: Strategy and competition in U.S. higher education*. New Brunswick, NJ: Transaction Publishers.

Brunner, J. (1993). Chile's higher education—Between market and state. *Higher Education*, 25, 35–43.

Brunner, J. (1997). From state to market coordination: The Chilean case. *Higher Education Policy*, 10, 225–237.

Carlson, D., & Shepherd, G. (1992). Cartel on campus: The economics and law of academic institutions' financial aid price-fixing. *Oregon Law Review*, 71, 563–629.

Carlton, D., Bamberger, G., & Epstein, R. (1995). Antitrust and higher education: Was there a conspiracy to restrict financial aid? *The Rand Journal of Economics*, 26, 131–147.

Cave, M., Hanney, S., & Kogan, M. (1991). *The use of performance indicators in higher education: A critical analysis of developing practice* (2nd ed.). London: Jessica Kingsley.

Church, J., & Ware, R. (2000). *Industrial organization: A strategic approach*. Boston, MA: Irwin McGraw Hill.

College Board. (2011). *Trends in college pricing 2011*. New York: The College Board. Paper downloaded on June 18,2012, from http://trends.collegeboard.org/downloads/College_ Pricing_2011.pdf

Dale, S., & Krueger, A. (2002). Estimating the payoff to attending a more selective college: An application of selection on observables and unobservables. *Quarterly Journal of Economics*, 117, 1491–1527.

Dill, D. (1997a). Markets and higher education: An introduction. *Higher Education Policy*, 10, 163–166.

Dill, D. (1997b). Higher education markets and public policy. *Higher Education Policy*, 10, 167–185.

Dill, D., & Soo, M. (2004). Transparency and quality in higher education markets. In P. Teixeira, B. Jongbloed, D. Dill, & A. Amaral (Eds.), *Markets in higher education: Rhetoric or reality* (pp. 61–85). Dordrecht, The Netherlands: Kluwer.

Dill, D., & Sporn, B. (1995). The implications of a postindustrial environment for the university: An introduction. In D. Dill & B. Sporn (Eds.), *Emerging patterns of social demand and university reform: Through a glass darkly* (pp. 1–19). Oxford: Pergamon Press.

Epple, D., Romano, R., & Sieg, H. (2006). Admission, tuition, and financial aid policies in the market for higher education. *Econometrica*, 74, 885–928.

Fallows, J. (1990, March 1). Wake Up, America! *New York Review of Books*, 17–18.

Friedman, M. (1955). The role of government in education. *Economics and the Public Interest*, 2, 85–107.

Friedman, M. (1962). *Capitalism and freedom*. Chicago: University of Chicago Press.

Friedman, T. (2005). *The world is flat: A brief history of the twenty-first century*. New York: Farrar, Strauss and Giroux.

Geiger, R. (2004). Market coordination of higher education: The United States. In P. Teixeira, B. Jongboed, D. Dill, & A. Amaral (Eds.), *Markets in higher education: Rhetoric or reality?* (pp. 161–183). Dordrecht, The Netherlands: Kluwer.

Getz, M., & Siegfried, J. (1991). Costs and productivity in American colleges and universities. In C. Clotfelter, R. Ehrenberg, M. Getz, & J. Siegfried (Eds.), *Economic challenges in higher education, Part III* (pp. 259–392). Chicago: The University of Chicago Press.

Gibbs, P. (2001). Higher education as a market: A problem or solution? *Studies in Higher Education*, 26, 85–94.

Glenna, L., Lacy, W., Welsh, R., & Biscotti, D. (2007). University administrators, agricultural biotechnology, and academic capitalism: Defining the public good to promote university-industry relationships. *The Sociological Quarterly*, 48, 141–163.

Glennerster, H. (1991). Quasi-markets for education? *The Economic Journal, 101*, 1268–1276.

Guri-Rosenblit, S., Šebková, H., & Teichler, U. (2007). Massification and diversity of higher education systems: Interplay of complex dimensions. *Higher Education Policy, 20*, 373–389.

Harman, G. (2006). Adjustment of Australian academics to the new commercial university environment. *Higher Education Policy, 19*, 153–172.

Hayek, F. (1944). *The road to serfdom*. Chicago: The University of Chicago Press.

Hayek, F. (1988). *The fatal conceit: The errors of socialism*. Chicago: The University of Chicago Press.

Hayes, D., & Wynyard, R. (Eds.). (2002). *The McDonaldization of higher education*. Westport, CT: Bergin & Garvey.

Hoxby, C. (1997, December). *How the changing market structure of U.S. higher education explains college tuition* (NBER Working Paper No. 6323). Cambridge, MA: National Bureau of Economic Research.

Hoxby, C. (2009). The changing selectivity of American colleges. *Journal of Economic Perspectives*, 23, 95–118.

Hoxby, C., & Long, B. (1999). *Explaining rising income and wage inequality among the college-educated* (NBER Working Paper No. 6873). Cambridge, MA: National Bureau of Economic Research.

James, E. (1978). Product mix and cost disaggregation: A reinterpretation of the economics of higher education. *Journal of Human Resources*, 12, 157–186.

James, E. (1986). Cross-subsidization in higher education: Does it prevent private choice and public policy? In D. Levy (Ed.), *Private education: Studies in choice and public policy* (pp. 237–257). New York: Oxford University Press.

James, E., & Neuberger, E. (1981). The university department as a nonprofit labor cooperative. *Public Choice, 36*, 585–612.

Jongbloed, B. (2003). Marketisation in higher education, Clark's triangle and the essential ingredients of markets. *Higher Education Quarterly*, 57, 110–135.

Keyte, J., & Stoll, N. (2004). Markets? We don't need no stinking markets! The FTC and market definition. *The Antitrust Bulletin, 49*, 593–632.

Kim, S., & Lee, J. (2006). Changing facets of Korean higher education: Market competition and the role of the state. *Higher Education, 52*, 557–587.

Leslie, L., & Johnson, G. (1974). The market model and higher education. *Journal of Higher Education, 45*, 1–20.

Leslie, L., & Slaughter, S. (1997). The development and current status of market mechanisms in United States postsecondary education. *Higher Education Policy, 10*, 239–252.

Lieberman, M., & Hall, R. (2000). *Introduction to economics*. Cincinnati, OH: South-Western Publishing Company.

Marginson, S. (1997). Competition and contestability in Australian higher education, 1987–1997. *Australian Universities Review*, 40, 5–14.

Marshall, A. (1920). *Principles of economics* (8th ed.). New York: Macmillan.

Massy, W. (1989). *A strategy for productivity improvements in college and university academic departments*. Stanford, CA: Stanford University.

Massy, W. (2004). Markets in higher education: Do they promote internal efficiency? In P. Teixeira, B. Jongbloed, D. Dill, & A. Amaral (Eds.), *Markets in Higher Education: Rhetoric or Reality?* Dordrecht, The Netherlands: Kluwer Publishers.

Mazzarol, T., & Soutar, G. (2001). *The global market for higher education: Sustainable competitive strategies for the new millennium*. Cheltenham, UK: Edward Elgar.

McEachern, W. (1994). *Microeconomics: A contemporary introduction* (3rd ed.). Cincinnati, OH: South-Western Publishing Company.

McMahon, W. (2009). *Higher learning, greater good: The private and social benefits of higher education*. Baltimore: Johns Hopkins University Press.

McPherson, M., & Schapiro, M. (1998). *The student aid game: Meeting need and rewarding talent in American higher education*. Princeton, NJ: Princeton University Press.

Meek, L., & Wood, F. (1997). The market as a new steering strategy for Australian higher education. *Higher Education Policy*, 10, 253–274.

Mora, J. (1997). Market trends in Spanish higher education. *Higher Education Policy*, 10, 187–198.

National Center for Education Statistics. (2011). *Digest of education statistics 2011*. Washington, DC: Institute of Education Sciences.

Netz, J. (1999, March). *Non-profits and Price-fixing: The case of the Ivy League*. Retrieved March 3, 2008, from the Applied Economics Consulting Web site: http://www.applecon.com/publications/ivy.pdf

Pugsley, L. (2004). *The university challenge: Higher education markets and social stratification*. Burlington, VT: Ashgate Publishing Company.

Reich, R. (2004, March 24). Higher Education 'Market' Warning. *The Higher Education Policy Institute Lecture*. Retrieved March 3, 2008, from BBC News at http://news.bbc.co.uk/1/hi/education/3564531.stm#transcript

Rhoades, G., & Slaughter, S. (1997). Academic capitalism, managed professionals, and supplyside higher education. *Social Text*, 51, 9–38.

Rhoades, G., & Slaughter, S. (2004). *Academic capitalism and the new economy*. Baltimore: John Hopkins University Press.

Riley, N. (2011). *The faculty lounges: And other reasons why you won't get the college education you pay for*. Chicago: Ivan R. Dee.

Riley, N. (2012, February 6). The University of Adam Smith. *Wall Street Journal*. http://online. wsj.com/article/SB10001424052970204879004577110970031199712.html?KEYWORDS= The+University+of+Adam+Smith

Ritzer, G. (1998). *The McDonaldization thesis: Explorations and extensions*. London/Thousand Oaks, CA: Sage.

Rohlen, T. (1983). *Japan's high schools*. Berkeley, CA: University of California Press.

Romer, P. (1990). Endogenous technological growth. *Journal of Political Economy*, 99, S71–S102.

Rosen, A. (2011). *Change.edu: Rebooting for the new talent economy*. New York: Kaplan Publishing.

Rothschild, M., & White, L. (1993). The university in the marketplace: Some insights and some puzzles. In C. Clotfelter & M. Rothschild (Eds.), *Studies of supply and demand in higher education* (pp. 11–42). Chicago: The University of Chicago Press.

Rothschild, M., & White, L. (1995). The analytics of the pricing of higher education and other services in which the customers and inputs. *Journal of Political Economy*, 103, 573–586.

Rozada, M., & Menendez, A. (2002). Public university in Argentina: Subsidizing the rich? *Economics of Education Review*, 21, 341–351.

Salop, S., & White, L. (1991). Antitrust goes to college. *Journal of Economic Perspectives*, 5, 193–202.

Scheffman, D., & Spiller, P. (1987). Geographic market definitions under the U.S. Department of Justice merger guidelines. *Journal of Law and Economics*, 30, 123–147.

Selingo, J. (2006, August 30). The Commission's Report: Landmark or Footnote Charles Miller (Guest). *The Chronicle of Higher Education's online Live Discussion*. http://web.archive.org/web/20090210073258/http://chronicle.com/colloquy/2006/09/spellings/

Shin, J., Toutkoushian, R., & Teichler, U. (Eds.). (2011). *University rankings: Theoretical basis, methodology and impacts on global higher education*. Dordrecht, The Netherlands: Springer.

Slaughter, S., & Leslie, L. (1997). *Academic capitalism: Politics, policies and the entrepreneurial university*. Baltimore: John Hopkins University Press.

Slaughter, S., & Rhoades, G. (2009). *Academic capitalism and the new economy: Markets, state, and higher education*. Baltimore: Johns Hopkins University Press.

Smith, A. (1776). *The wealth of nations*. New York: Barnes & Noble Books.

Stiglitz, J. (1987). The cause and consequences of the dependence of quality and price. *Journal of Economic Literature*, 25, 1–48.

Teichler, U. (1998). Massification: A challenge for institutions of higher education. *Tertiary Education and Management*, 4, 17–27.

Teixeira, P., Jongboed, B., Amaral, A., & Dill, D. (2004). Introduction. In P. Teixeira, B. Jongboed, D. Dill, & A. Amaral (Eds.), *Markets in higher education: Rhetoric or reality?* Dordrecht, The Netherlands: Kluwer.

Teixeira, P., Jongbloed, B., Dill, D., & Amaral, A. (Eds.). (2004). *Markets in higher education: Rhetoric or reality?* Dordrecht, The Netherlands: Kluwer.

The Carnegie Commission on Higher Education. (1973). *The purposes and performance of higher education in the United States: Approaching the year 2000.* New York: McGraw-Hill.

Toutkoushian, R. (2001a). Trends in revenues and expenditures in public and private higher education. In M. Paulsen & J. Smart (Eds.), *The finance of higher education: Theory, research, policy & practice* (pp. 11–38). New York: Agathon Press.

Toutkoushian, R. (2001b). Do parental income and educational attainment affect the initial choices of New Hampshire's college-bound students? *Economics of Education Review*, 20, 245–262.

Toutkoushian, R., & Danielson, C. (2002). Using performance indicators to evaluate decentralized budgeting systems and institutional performance. In D. Priest, W. Becker, D. Hossler, & E. St. John (Eds.), *Incentive-based budgeting systems in public universities* (pp. 205–226). Northampton, MA: Edward Elgar Publishing.

van Vught, F. (1997). Combining planning and the market: An analysis of the government strategy towards higher education in the Netherlands. *Higher Education Policy*, 10, 211–224.

Veblen, T. (1918). *The higher learning in America: A memorandum on the conduct of universities by business men.* New York: B. W. Huebsch.

Williams, G. (1997). The market route to mass higher education: British experience 1979–1996. *Higher Education Policy*, 10, 275–289.

Winston, G. (1997). Why can't a college be more like a firm? *Change*, 29 (5), 32–38.

Winston, G. (1999). Subsidies, hierarchy and peers: The awkward economics of higher education. *Journal of Economic Perspectives*, 13, 13–36.

Winston, G. (2000). *Economic stratification and hierarchy among US colleges and universities* (Discussion Paper 58, Williams Project on the Economics of Higher Education). Williamstown, MA; Williams College.

Winston, G. (2003). *Toward a theory of tuition: Prices, peer wages, and competition in higher education* (Discussion Paper No. 65). Williamstown, MA: Williams Project on the Economics of Williams College. http://sites.williams.edu/wpehe/files/2011/06/DP-65.pdf

Yonezawa, A. (1998). Further privatization in Japanese higher education? *International Higher Education*, 13, 20–22.

Yorke, M. (2003). Formative assessment in higher education: Moves towards theory and the enhancement of pedagogic practice. *Higher Education*, 45, 477–501.

Zemsky, R., Shaman, S., & Ianozzi, M. (1997, November/December). In search of strategic perspective: A tool for mapping the market in postsecondary education. *Change*, 29, 23–38.

Zemsky, R., Shaman, S., & Schapiro, D. (Eds.) (2001). *Higher education as competitive enterprise: When markets matter* (New Directions for Institutional Research, Number 111). San Francisco: Jossey-Bass, Inc.

CHAPTER 2

THE FOR-PROFIT POSTSECONDARY SCHOOL SECTOR: NIMBLE CRITTERS OR AGILE PREDATORS?

DAVID J. DEMING, CLAUDIA GOLDIN, AND LAWRENCE F. KATZ

Private for-profit institutions have become an increasingly visible part the U.S. higher education sector. Within that sector, they are today the most diverse institutions by program and size, have been the fastest growing, have the highest fraction of nontraditional students, and obtain the greatest proportion of their total revenue from federal student aid (loan and grant) programs. They are, as well, the subjects of high-profile investigations and are facing major regulatory changes.

Today's for-profit postsecondary schools were preceded a century ago by a group of proprietary schools that were also responding to an explosion in demand for technical, vocational, and applied subjects. Business, managerial, and secretarial skills were in great demand in the late nineteenth and early twentieth centuries, and a multitude of proprietary institutions emerged that taught accounting, management, real estate, stenography, and typing. The numbers and enrollments of these institutions were greatly reduced when public high schools expanded and increased their offerings in the business and vocational areas. But many survived and morphed into some of the current for-profits, such as Blair College (established 1897; now part of Everest College), Bryant and Stratton College (1854), Gibbs College (1911), Globe University (1885), Rasmussen College (1900), and Strayer University (1892).

Distance learning, known today as online education, also has an interesting past in "correspondence courses" that were offered by many universities beginning in the late nineteenth century including some of the most prestigious, such as the University of Chicago and the University of Wisconsin (Watkins 1991). Online education is today's most rapidly growing part of higher education. Walden University, founded in 1970 and today one the largest for-profit online institutions, pioneered online studies to allow working professionals to earn further degrees.

In this article, we describe the schools, students, and programs in the for-profit higher education sector, its phenomenal recent growth, and its relationship to the federal and state governments. As a starting point, for-profit postsecondary enrollments have grown considerably during the past several decades, particularly in degree programs and at large national providers with substantial online offerings. Fall enrollment in for-profit degree-granting institutions grew by more than 100-fold from 18,333 in 1970 to 1.85 million in 2009. During that same time period, total fall enrollment in all degree-granting institutions increased 2.4-fold from 8.58 million in 1970 to 20.43 million in 2009 (U.S. Department of Education, NECS, 2010, *Digest*, table 197). Thus, for-profit enrollment increased from 0.2 percent to 9.1 percent of total enrollment in degree-granting schools from 1970 to 2009. For-profit institutions for many decades also have accounted for the vast majority of enrollments in non-degree-granting postsecondary schools (those offering shorter certificate programs), both overall and among such schools eligible for federal (Title IV) student financial aid.

Figure 2.1 highlights the rise of for-profits in the enrollments of Title IV–eligible (degree and non-degree-granting) higher education institutions since 2000, a period when enrollment in the for-profit sector tripled while enrollment for the rest of higher education increased by just 22 percent. The solid dark line shows that the fraction of fall enrollments accounted for by the for-profits increased from 4.3 percent in 2000 to 10.7 percent in 2009. For the descriptive data presented here, we rely extensively on the Integrated Postsecondary Education Data System (IPEDS) of the

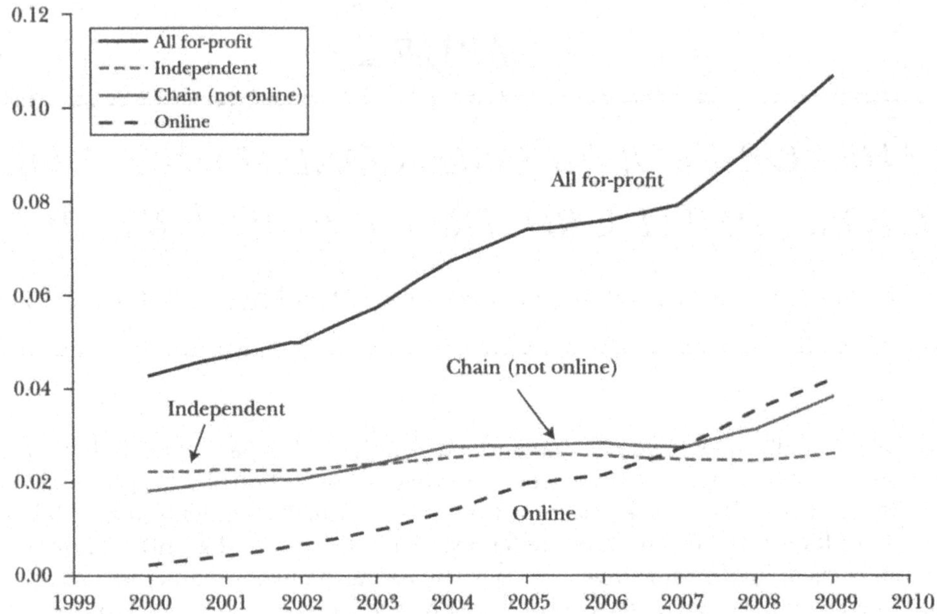

Figure 2.1 For-profit institution share of total Title IV fall enrollment: total and by school type, 2000 to 2009.

Source: Integrated Postsecondary Education Data System (IPEDS).

Notes: A for-profit institution is classified as "online" if it has the word online in its name or if not more than 33 percent of the school's students are from one U.S. state. The "chain (not-online)" category covers all other for-profit institutions that operate in more than one state or have more than five campus branches within a single state. The "independent" category includes for-profits that operate in only one state and have fewer than five campus branches.

U.S. Department of Education, which is an annual survey of all postsecondary institutions that participate in the federal student financial aid programs.[1]

Under the solid dark line in Figure 2.1, the growth of the for-profit sector is broken down into "independent" schools, online institutions, and for-profit "chains." We must first define these terms, because these categories are not designated in the official IPEDS data. "Independent" schools are defined here as those operating in no more than one state and having no more than five campus branches. A "chain" is a for-profit institution that operates in more than one state or has more than five campus branches within a single state. A for-profit is designated as online if it has the word "online" in its name or, more commonly, if no more than 33 percent of the school's students are from one U.S. state. All online institutions are considered to be chains because they serve students in multiple geographic markets. Independent schools showed little increase in their share of overall enrollments in higher education from 2000 to 2009; chains with largely in-person enrollment showed a doubling over this period; and online institutions, typically part of national publicly traded companies, increased from almost nothing to become the largest part of the sector. Indeed, almost 90 percent of the increase in for-profit enrollments during the last decade occurred because of the expansion of for-profit chains.

The rapid growth of the for-profits from 2000 to 2009 is illustrated in various ways in Figure 2.2. The for-profit share of enrollments (unduplicated headcount) over a 12-month period increased from 5 percent in 2001 to 13 percent in 2009. The 12-month enrollment measure better captures enrollments in for-profits than the standard fall enrollment measure because it includes students in less-conventional and short programs entered throughout the year.

For-profits have expanded their enrollment share more rapidly for women than for men, and they play an increasingly large role in the higher education of older students. The for-profit

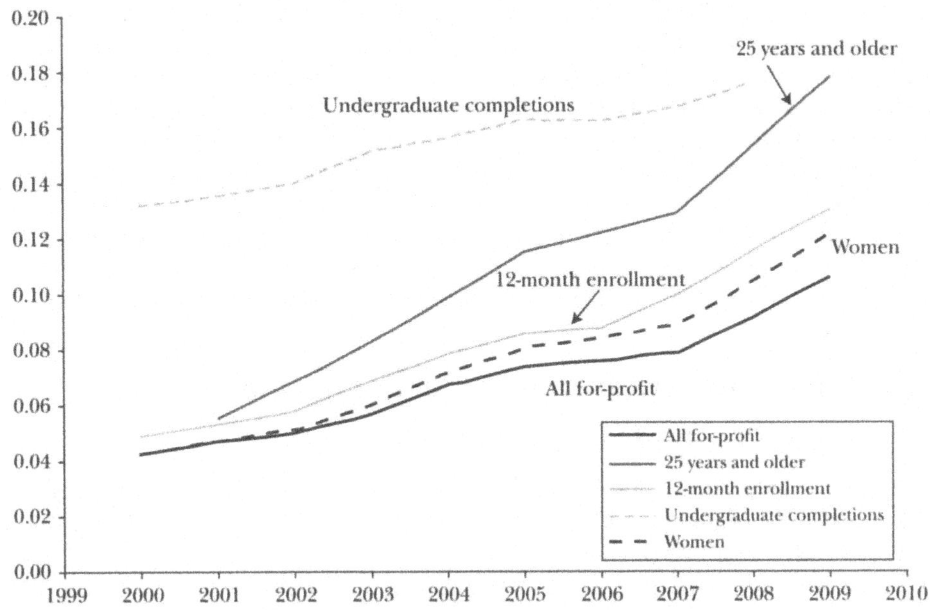

Figure 2.2 For-profit share of enrollments and undergraduate completions: 2000 to 2009.

Source: Integrated Postsecondary Education Data System (IPEDS).

Notes: "All for-profit" is fall enrollment, that is enrollment at the beginning of the academic year; "12-month enrollment" = unduplicated enrollment during the entire year; "25 years and older" = fall enrollment of those 25 years and older; "women" = female fall enrollment; "undergraduate completions" = all undergraduate completions (certificates + associate's degrees + bachelor's degrees). The series for "25 years and older" is for the odd-numbered years and the even-numbered years are interpolated from those.

enrollment share of students 25 years and older expanded from around 6 percent in 2001 to 18 percent in 2009. Undergraduate completions from for-profit institutions grew from 13 percent of the total in 2000 to almost 18 percent in 2008. The fraction of completions is considerably larger than that for enrollments because more than half of for-profit completions are certificates and most certificate programs are no more than one year.

For-profit enrollments and completions in recent years have been growing most rapidly in longer degree programs. In the last decade, the for-profits increased their share of completers in all types of undergraduate programs, but more so for AAs (associates' degrees) and BAs (bachelor's degrees) than for certificates. They produced about 39 percent of certificates in 2000 and 42 percent in 2008. For-profit AAs were 13 percent of all AAs in 2000 but 18 percent in 2008; BAs were less than 2 percent of all in 2000 but were 5 percent of all BAs in 2008 (U.S. Department of Education, NECS, 2010, *Digest*, table 195).

The current incarnation of the for-profit sector is big business; its largest providers are major, profitable, publicly traded corporations (Bennett, Lucchesi, and Vedder 2010). They appear to be nimble critters that train nontraditional learners for jobs in fast-growing areas, such as health care and information technology. On the other side, most of them depend on U.S. government student aid for the vast bulk of their revenues. Default rates on the loans taken out by their students vastly exceed those of other institutions of higher education, and audit studies have shown that some for-profits have engaged in highly aggressive and even borderline fraudulent recruiting techniques (U.S. Government Accountability Office 2010).

Are the for-profits nimble critters or agile predators? Using the 2001 to 2009 Beginning Post secondary Students (BPS) Longitudinal Study, we assess outcomes of a recent cohort of first-time undergraduates who attended for-profits relative to comparable students who attended community colleges or other public or private nonprofit institutions. We find that relative to community colleges and other public and private nonprofits, for-profits educate a larger fraction of minority, disadvantaged, and older students, and they have greater success at retaining students in their first year and getting them to complete shorter degree and nondegree programs at the certificate and AA levels. But we also find that for-profits leave students with far larger student loan debt burdens. For-profit students end up with higher unemployment and "idleness" rates and lower earnings from employment six years after entering programs than do comparable students from other schools. Not surprisingly, for-profit students have trouble paying off their student loans and have far greater default rates. And for-profit students self-report lower satisfaction with their courses of study and are less likely to consider their education and loans worth the price-tag relative to similarly-situated students who went to public and private nonprofit institutions.

What is the For-Profit Postsecondary School Sector?

Apollo and the Lesser For-Profit Deities: A Diverse Sector

The for-profit postsecondary school sector, at its simplest level, is a group of institutions that give post-high school degrees or credentials and for which some of the legal "nondistribution requirements" that potentially constrain private nonprofit schools do not bind. For example, for-profit institutions can enter the equity market and have few constraints on the amounts they can legally pay their top managers. In practice, only the largest players in this market raise substantial capital in organized equity markets, and they tend to pay their top executives mega-salaries that exceed those of presidents at the public and nonprofit private universities. Among the for-profits, Andrew Clark, chief executive officer of Bridgepoint Education, Inc., received more than $20 million in 2009, while Charles Edelstein, co-chief executive officer of the Apollo Group, Inc., earned more than $11 million.[2]

For-profit sector institutions are a varied group. For-profit schools offer doctorates but also nondegree courses, and their programs run the gamut from health care, business, and computers to cosmetology, massage, and dog grooming. The sector contains the largest schools by enrollment in the United States and also some of the smallest. For example, the University of Phoenix Online campus enrolled over 532,000 students, and Kaplan University enrolled 96,000 during the 2008–2009 academic year. Taken together, the largest 15 institutions account for almost 60 percent of for-profit enrollments (Bennett, Lucchesi, and Vedder 2010, table 1). But tabulations from the IPEDS also indicate that the median Title IV-eligible, for-profit institution had a Fall 2008 enrollment of 172 students as compared with 3,713 for the median community college (two-year public institution), 7,145 for the median four-year public university, and 1,149 for the median four-year, private not-for-profit school.

The for-profit sector has become in many people's minds synonymous with the large for-profit chains that have rapidly expanded their presence in the BA and graduate education markets, especially the Apollo Group, which owns the University of Phoenix. But even though the big players in this sector do account for the majority of for-profit enrollments, another important part of the sector consists of career colleges that focus on a wide range of shorter AA and certificate programs. Completions in the for-profit sector are still dominated by certificate programs, and 55 percent of the certificates granted by the for-profits are awarded by the 1,700 or so independent career colleges and institutes. Our tabulations from the IPEDS indicate that certificates account for 54 percent of the degrees and awards conferred by for-profits in 2008–2009.

There are several important commonalities across this mixed group. The for-profit sector offers almost no general education and liberal arts programs. For-profit programs typically are not meant to prepare students to continue to another form of higher education, as is the case with most community colleges. Rather, the for-profits almost always offer training for a vocation or trade. In that sense, they are "career colleges." In addition, virtually all the for-profits require that admitted students have a high school diploma or another secondary school credential such as a GED. Their ability to obtain federal (Title IV) financial aid for their students is typically contingent on their admitting primarily students who have already completed secondary school. However, beyond requiring a high school degree, for-profit institutions are almost always nonselective and open admissions.

For-profit higher education is more likely to flourish in providing vocational programs that lead to certification and early job placement—programs that have clear short-run outcomes that can serve to build institutional reputation in the labor market. But the for-profits are likely to be in a far less advantageous position where external benefits (and subsidies from donors and government) are important and where the qualities of inputs and outputs are difficult to verify (Winston 1999). For-profits also have been successful at designing programs to attract nontraditional students who may not be well-served by public institutions (Breneman, Pusser, and Turner 2006).

What is Title IV Eligibility?

The for-profit sector that we analyze here includes almost exclusively those that are termed "Title IV eligible." Because for-profits often cater to independent students and those from low-income families who finance college through Pell grants and federal student loans, they have an intricate relationship with the federal government to ensure they maintain eligibility to receive Title IV federal student aid. The for-profits, like public institutions of higher education, receive an extremely large fraction of their revenues from government sources.

Title IV eligibility is granted by the U.S. Department of Education and requires that the institution be accredited by at least one of their approved accrediting agencies, be registered by one of the states, and meet other standards on a continued basis. Some of these standards concern the length of programs and some concern students and their federal loan repayment activity. A Title IV–eligible, private for-profit school must either provide training for gainful employment in a recognized occupation or provide a program leading to a baccalaureate degree in the liberal arts (U.S. Department of Education 2011a). Our discussion excludes non–Title IV, for-profit schools, about which little has been known because the U.S. Department of Education does not track them. Virtually all degrees are granted by Title IV-eligible institutions, but programs that are less than two years in length that grant certificates (also diplomas) often are found at non-Title IV institutions. For an analysis of the importance of the non–Title IV group of for-profit schools using state registration data, see Cellini and Goldin (forthcoming). Because virtually all degree-granting institutions are Title IV–eligible, the undercount from limiting the analysis to Title IV schools impacts only the nondegree (typically certificate) programs in institutions without any degree program.

For-Profit Programs

The for-profits loom large in the production of degrees and certificates in certain programs. For-profits produce 18 percent of all associate's degrees, but they produce 33 percent of the AAs granted in business, management, and marketing, 51 percent in computer and information sciences, 23 percent in the health professions, and 34 percent in security and protective services. In the public and nonprofit private sectors, an AA degree is often the gateway to a four-year college and, in consequence, 38 percent of these AA programs are in general studies and liberal arts programs. In the for-profits, a mere 2.4 percent are in general studies and liberal arts.

Although 5 percent of all BAs are granted by for-profit institutions, 12 percent of all BAs in business, management, and marketing are. Other large for-profit BA programs are in communications (52 percent of all BAs in communications are granted by for-profits), computer and information sciences (27 percent), and personal and culinary services (42 percent).

Certain programs are highly concentrated in the for-profit degree categories. Among AA degrees just two program groups—business, management, and marketing, and the health professions account for 52 percent of all degrees. In the BA group, the business program produces almost 50 percent of the total. Among certificates granted in the Title IV for-profit sector, health professions—and personal and culinary services account for 78 percent of certificate completers (U.S. Department of Education, NCES, 2009, tables 37 and 40; authors' tabulations from the IPEDS).

Who Are the Students?

The for-profit sector disproportionately serves older students, women, African Americans, Hispanics, and those with low incomes. Table 2.1 looks at the characteristics of students in various types of

TABLE 2.1

Student Characteristics from the BPS and IPEDS for For-Profits, Two-Year Public Colleges, and Four-Year (Nonprofit) Colleges

	Student Characteristics by IPEDS Institution Type, 2009/2010			
	For-Profit Institutions	2-year Public Colleges	4-year Public Colleges	4-year Private Nonprofit Colleges
Female	0.651	0.570	0.552	0.576
African-American	0.221	0.136	0.109	0.104
Hispanic	0.150	0.157	0.105	0.093
Full-time	0.579	0.410	0.733	0.742
Age 25 years and over	0.651	0.404	0.306	0.392
Federal loans per student	11,415	759	3,512	5,769
Pell Grant per student	2,370	773	738	632
Tuition (in-state)	13,103	2,510	5,096	24,470
Number of institutions	2,995	1,595	690	1,589

	BPS 2004–2009 Sample Characteristics		
	For-Profit Institutions	Community Colleges	4-year Public and Nonprofit Colleges
Female	0.659	0.564	0.558
African-American	0.248	0.140	0.141
Hispanic	0.264	0.159	0.103
Age	24.4	23.8	19.5
Single parent	0.288	0.124	0.030
Delayed enrollment after high school	0.576	0.481	0.142
High school diploma	0.754	0.852	0.947
GED	0.172	0.095	0.022
Mother high school dropout	0.224	0.137	0.055
2003 family income if a dependent	36,854	60,039	76,509
2003 family income if independent	17,282	31,742	78,664
Enrolled full-time	0.809	0.460	0.903
Worked while enrolled, 2003–2004	0.635	0.755	0.499
Enrolled in a certificate program	0.551	0.072	0.015
Enrolled in an AA program	0.326	0.774	0.061
Enrolled in an BA program	0.106	0	0.891
Expects to earn a BA	0.643	0.799	0.980
Sample size (unweighted)	1,950	5,970	8,760

Sources: BPS:04/09, or Beginning Postsecondary Students Longitudinal Study data for 2003-2004 first-time beginning postsecondary students in their first, third, and sixth years since entering an undergraduate institution, through 2009; and Integrated Postsecondary Education Data System (IPEDS) data.

Notes: Community colleges include two-year public and private nonprofit institutions. Unweighted sample sizes in the BPS data are rounded to the nearest 10. The IPEDS tabulations cover the (undergraduate and graduate) enrollments of Title IV institutions in Fall 2009. The BPS tabulations cover beginning postsecondary students entering a Title IV institution in the 2003-2004 academic year.

institutions of higher education. African Americans account for 13 percent of all students in higher education, but they are 22 percent of those in the for-profit sector. Hispanics are 11.5 percent of all students but are 15 percent of those in the for-profit sector. Women are 65 percent of those in the for-profit sector. For-profit students are older: about 65 percent are 25 years and older, whereas just 31 percent of those at four-year public colleges are, and 40 percent of those at two-year colleges are.

Using the Beginning Postsecondary Students longitudinal survey data for students entering postsecondary school during the 2003–2004 academic year, we can get a more detailed picture of for-profit students relative to those at other colleges. Because the BPS surveys only first-time undergraduates, the results are somewhat different from the IPEDS, which surveys institutions about all students. But the storyline remains the same.

Compared with those in community colleges (almost entirely two-year public schools), for-profit students are disproportionately single parents, have much lower family incomes, and are almost twice as likely to have a General Equivalency Degree (GED). Among for-profit students in the Beginning Postsecondary Students data, 55 percent are in certificate programs and just 11 percent are enrolled in a BA program. Similarly, among all for-profit students in the IPEDS, certificates are 54 percent of all completions or degrees conferred, and associates are 22.5 percent (U.S. Department of Education, NECS 2010, Digest, table 195). The BA group is just 13 percent but is the fastest-growing degree group among the for-profits. Postgraduate programs, primarily master's degrees, account for the remaining 10.5 percent.[3]

The Business Model of the For-Profit Sector

For-profit chains led by online institutions experienced phenomenal growth in the past several decades. The growth has been largely due to an extension of a business model that has emphasized the special client base of the for-profits combined with the ability to "clone" successful programs using web technology and the standardization of curriculum for traditional in-person courses. In this section, we turn to the financial and business aspects of the for-profits. For more detail on the business strategies of for-profit colleges, the interested reader might start with Breneman, Pusser, and Turner (2006) and Hentschke (2010).

The expansion of the chains (including online institutions) accounts for 87 percent of the increase in fall enrollment during the past decade. The increase in online enrollment alone accounts for 54 percent of the total. The rise of the chains is responsible, as well, for 80 percent of the increase in federal loan and grant volumes of the for-profits. For-profit chains and online programs also benefit from economies of scale in advertising and recruitment costs.

Client Base and Recruiting

The Title IV-eligible, for-profit sector receives the majority of its revenues from federal financial aid programs in the form of loans and grants to their students. For-profits appeal to older individuals who are simultaneously employed and in school or taking care of family members. Some of the for-profits offer services, such as child care, to deter enrollees from dropping out, especially during the period when the student can get a refund and to minimize the institution's dropout rate to maintain accreditation (for example, Rosenbaum, Deil-Amien, and Person 2006). The for-profits are attractive to nontraditional students, many of whom are low income, require financial aid, and need help filling out aid forms. For-profits often give generous transfer credit to students who began their BAs at other institutions.

For-profit institutions devote substantial resources to sales and marketing. Advertising in 2009, as demonstrated in one study of 13 large national chains, was around 11 percent of revenue. Sales and marketing (including advertising) for this group was around 24 percent of revenue. In consequence, the average new student recruit costs one of the large national chains about $4,000 (Steinerman, Volshteyn, and McGarrett 2011).[4] Annual tuition at for-profit institutions was about $16,000 for a BA program, $15,000 for an AA program, and $13,000 for a certificate program in 2010–11, as compared to average undergraduate tuition of about $7,000 at public four-year institutions for in-state students and $16,000 for out-of-state students, and $22,000 for private nonprofit schools (Knapp, Kelley-Reid, and Ginder 2011, table 3).

Responsiveness to Markets

For-profits cater to the expanding market of nontraditional students, develop curriculum and teaching practices to be able to provide identical programs at multiple locations and at convenient times, and offer highly-structured programs to make timely completion feasible (Hentschke 2010). For-profits are attuned to the marketplace and are quick to open new schools, hire faculty, and add programs in growing fields and localities. For example, Turner (2006) finds that change in for-profit college enrollments are more positively correlated with changes in state college-age populations than are changes in public sector college enrollments.

For-profits are less encumbered than public and nonprofit schools by physical plant, alumni, and tenured faculty. Take the expanding health profession fields, for example. Enrollment in programs involving the health professions doubled from 2000 to 2009. In the for-profit sector, it tripled, whereas in all other postsecondary institutions it increased by 1.4 times. In consequence, the fraction of enrollment in the allied health fields in the for-profits increased from 35 percent to 52 percent, as illustrated in Figure 2.3. The increase in such enrollments at the national and regional chains accounts for almost the entire 17 percentage point increase.

Looking more closely at these programs, the for-profits have rapidly entered the growing fields of medical assisting, phlebotomy, x-ray and ultrasound technicians, practical nursing, and even registered nursing. The total number of AA degrees in the health professions doubled during the past decade, but degrees in this area from for-profits quadrupled, with degrees from the large for-profit chains rising by a multiple of six. A similar pattern arises for certificates in the health professions,

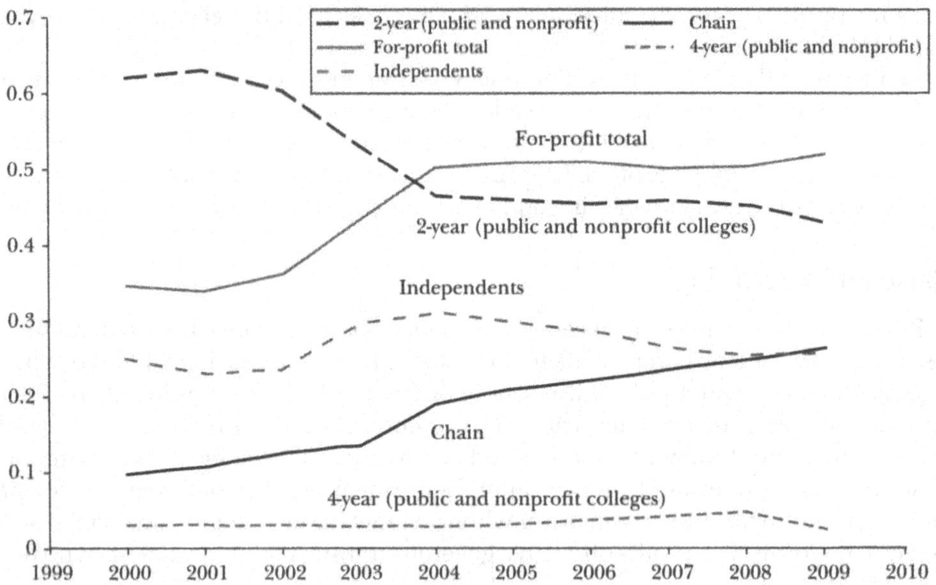

Figure 2.3 Enrollment in allied health fields by type of institution.

Source: Integrated Postsecondary Education Data System (IPEDS).

Note: "4-year (public and nonprofit colleges)" = public and private nonprofit four-year institutions; "2-year (public and nonprofit colleges)" = two year public (community colleges) and two-year private nonprofit colleges; "independents" = for-profit independent (non-chain) institutions; "chain" = for-profit institutions with "online" in the school name or that operate in more than one state or that have more than five campus branches in a single state.

where for-profit national and regional chains more than tripled their awards from 2000 to 2009 at a time when the public sector only more than doubled theirs.

Online Education

Online education fits many of the features of the for-profit business model. For example, it attracts older students who need to combine work with schooling and appeals to students who do not want to learn on the academic calendar. (There is even a popular advertisement: "Earn your college degree in your pajamas.") Much of the growth of for-profits during the last decade has been in schools emphasizing online programs, as seen in Figure 2.1.

Some of this increase was due to U.S. Department of Education regulatory changes. Prior to 1998, a Title IV-eligible institution could not have more than half of its enrollment in distance education. Then in 1998, the Higher Education Act authorized the U.S. Department of Education to grant waivers to promote new advances in distance education. By the early 2000s many of the larger chains were granted waivers, and the limit on share of enrollment in distance education was dropped. The regulatory change in 2005 spurred the growth of dedicated online institutions. By 2007–2008, 12 percent of undergraduates and 25 percent of graduate students at for-profits took their entire program through distance education as compared with less than 3 percent for undergraduates and 8 percent for graduate students at public and private nonprofit institutions combined (U.S. Department of Education, NCES, 2011, tables A-43-1 and A-43-2).

Federal Student Financial Aid

Federal student financial aid is the lifeblood of for-profit higher education. Federal grants and loans received under Title IV of the Higher Education Act accounted for 73.7 percent of the revenues of Title IV-eligible, private for-profit higher education institutions in 2008–09 (based on data in U.S. Department of Education, Federal Student Aid Data Center 2011). Under current regulations, for-profit schools can derive no more than 90 percent of their revenue from Title IV financial aid sources to maintain Title IV eligibility, and the constraint comes close to binding for many for-profits. In fact, 30 percent of for-profit institutions, including many of the largest national chains such as the University of Phoenix and Kaplan University, received more than 80 percent of their revenues from federal Title IV student aid in 2008–2009. These Title IV revenue figures actually understate the importance of federal student aid to for-profit institutions since they do not include military educational benefits provided to veterans and active service members, which do not count towards the limit of 90 percent federal Title IV student aid revenues. The for-profits have, in consequence, actively recruited military benefit recipients—veterans, service members, and their family members—especially under the Post-9/11 GI Bill of 2008. For-profits accounted for 36.5 percent of the benefits paid under the Post-9/11 GI Bill during the first year of the program (Health, Education, Labor and Pensions Committee 2010, p. 4).

For-profit institutions receive a disproportionate share of federal Title IV student financial aid both because they have higher tuition and fees than public institutions and because they attract large numbers of students who are financially independent or come from low-income families. For-profits accounted for 24 percent of Pell grant disbursements and 26 percent of federal student loan disbursements in 2008–2009 even though they enrolled 12 percent of the students (authors' tabulations from the IPEDS and NSLDS). Half of undergraduates at for-profit schools received Pell grants, as compared with 25 percent at public and private nonprofit institutions combined.

The sharp increase in the enrollments at for-profit schools has been accompanied by a rapid rise in their share of federal student financial aid from 2000 to 2010, as shown in Figure 2.4. The for-profit share of Pell grants increased over the last decade from 13 to 25 percent and their share of total federal student loans (both subsidized and unsubsidized loans) increased from 11 percent in 2000 to 26 percent in 2009 before dipping to 23 percent in 2010.[5]

Of course, public sector institutions receive direct taxpayer support largely from state government appropriations, enabling tuition and fees to be lower than they otherwise would be. If

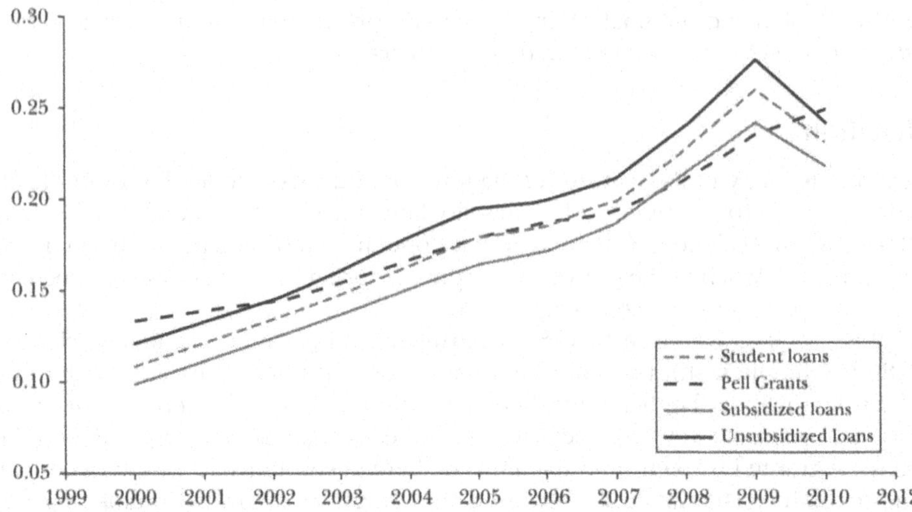

Figure 2.4 For-profit share of federal financial aid (Pell Grants and student loans): 2000 to 2010.

Source: National Student Loan Data System (NSLDS).

Note: Student loans include subsidized and unsubsidized federal student loans under the Federal Family Education Loan (FFEL) and Direct Loan Programs.

federal student loans to students at for-profits are repaid, taxpayer costs are actually lower to finance education in for-profits than in public sector institutions. But the comparison is not quite apples-to-apples. The rationale for subsidies to public institutions and private nonprofit schools is that they produce research with potentially large spillover benefits and that they educate students in the liberal arts and other fields that may improve civil society and generate external benefits. Also, loans to students attending for-profits often do not get repaid.

Default Rates

Students from for-profit institutions have higher default rates on federal student loans than students in other sectors. And the default rates of for-profits have risen substantially during the last five years.[6]

The two-year "cohort default rate" measures the percentage of borrowers who enter repayment of federal student loans (by leaving a program through graduation or dropping out) during a fiscal year and default prior to the end of the next fiscal year. An institution loses Title IV eligibility if its two-year cohort default rate exceeds 25 percent for three consecutive years or is 40 percent in any one year. The two-year cohort default rate of for-profit institutions was 11.6 percent for fiscal year 2008 as compared with 6 percent for public institutions and 4 percent for private nonprofits. The U.S. Department of Education is moving to a three-year cohort default rate standard for maintaining Title IV eligibility in fiscal year 2012. Three-year cohort default rates for fiscal year 2008 were 24.9 percent for for-profits, 7.6 percent for private nonprofits, and 10.8 percent for public institutions (Steinerman, Volshteyn, and McGarrett 2011). The sharp increase in default rates from a two- to a three-year window may, to some extent, reflect incentives for institutions to minimize defaults within the current two-year regulatory window. Thus, three-year default rates also are likely to provide a more realistic indicator of long-run loan repayment rates than the two-year default rates.[7]

We examine the role of student demographics, financial aid take-up, and institutional characteristics (degree types, distance education, remedial course offerings, and student services) in explaining the higher federal student loan default rates of for-profit institutions. Figure 2.5 graphs (regression-adjusted) differences in three-year cohort default rates by type of institution. The differences are computed from regressions of default rates on institution type (with public four-year

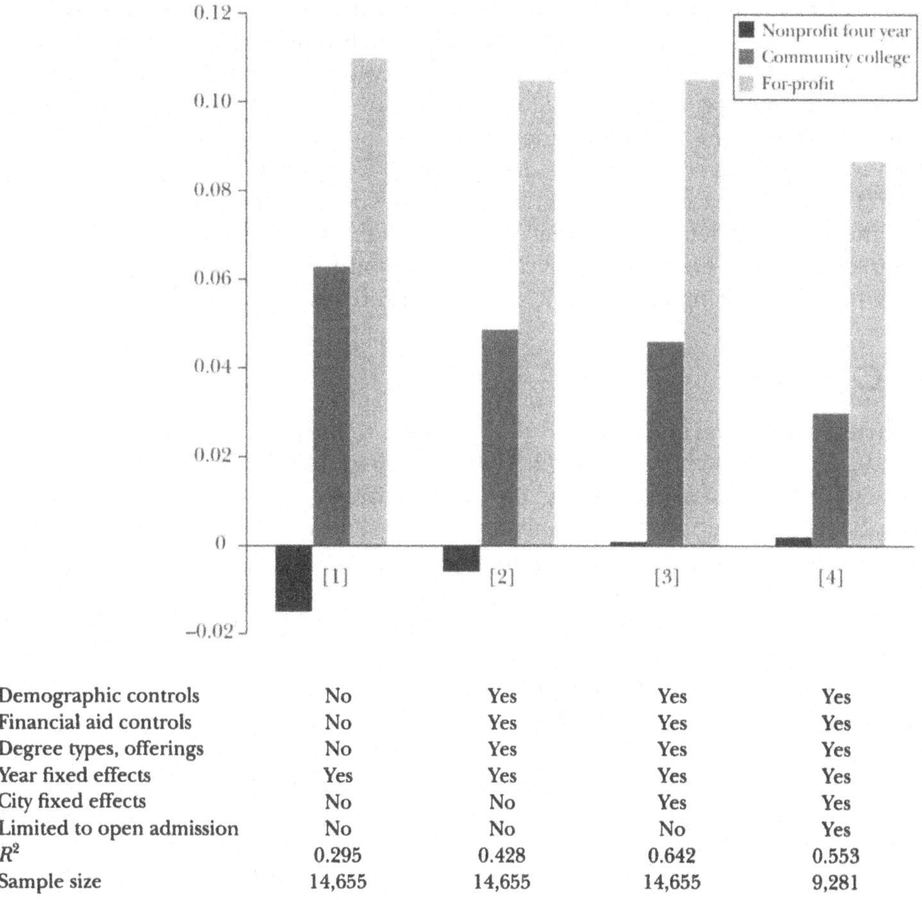

	[1]	[2]	[3]	[4]
Demographic controls	No	Yes	Yes	Yes
Financial aid controls	No	Yes	Yes	Yes
Degree types, offerings	No	Yes	Yes	Yes
Year fixed effects	Yes	Yes	Yes	Yes
City fixed effects	No	No	Yes	Yes
Limited to open admission	No	No	No	Yes
R^2	0.295	0.428	0.642	0.553
Sample size	14,655	14,655	14,655	9,281

Figure 2.5 Differences in three-year cohort default rate by type of institution: 2005 to 2008.

Source: National Student Loan Data System (NSLDS) and Integrated Postsecondary Education Data System (IPEDS).

Note: Each bar gives the coefficient on a type of institution from a regression where the dependent variable is the three-year cohort default rate for an institution-year observation and the omitted group is four-year public institutions. The sample covers institution-year observations for the fiscal years 2005 to 2008. Demographic controls are fractions part-time, 25 years and older, female, African American, and Hispanic. Financial aid controls are the number of recipients of Pell grants and subsidized and unsubsidized federal loans, total yearly disbursement amounts for each, and total loans and Pell grants per enrollee. Degree types and offerings are indicators for distance education, remedial course offerings, whether the institution offers assistance with job placement, whether it offers part-time employment services for enrolled students, the highest award or degree offered by the institution, and whether it has open admissions. Standard errors are clustered by institution.

institutions as the base group) including year dummies plus successive additions of controls for student and institution characteristics, geography, and school selectivity for pooled institution-year data covering the 2005 to 2008 fiscal years.

The raw default rates and those regression-adjusted for institutional and student characteristics are highest for the for-profit schools, followed by community colleges and then four-year public and nonprofit institutions. The unadjusted 11 percentage point higher three-year cohort default rates for for-profits (column 1) relative to the base group of four-year public institutions is reduced slightly to 10.5 percentage points with the addition of detailed controls for student demographics, institutional characteristics, and city fixed effects (columns 2 and 3) despite the fact that these controls explain a substantial fraction of the cross-institution variation in default rates. The addition of the covariates modestly expands the for-profit default rate gap relative to community colleges.

The for-profit default rate is 8.7 percentage points higher than that for four-year publics and nonprofits and 5.7 percentage points higher than for community colleges even when the sample is limited to nonselective (open admission) institutions (column 4). Higher three-year cohort default rates are apparent for all segments of the for-profit sector, including independent schools, regional chains, national chains, and largely online institutions. National chains have higher default rates and online institutions lower default rates relative to all for-profits.

For-profit institutions account for a large and rising share of federal financial aid. For-profit students have much higher default rates than those at other schools even adjusting for differences in student characteristics. In the most recent data, they account for 47 percent of defaults. In addition, default rates have been rising particularly for the for-profit chains.

Student Outcomes

The large increase in federal student aid dollars flowing to for-profits has attracted substantial scrutiny about the quality of their programs and whether they provide students with sufficient skills to enable them to thrive in the labor market and be able to pay off their student debts (for example, Baum 2011). Simple comparisons of student outcomes between the for-profits and other institutions may be misleading: after all, the for-profits disproportionately attract minority, older, independent, and disadvantaged students. Thus, we assess student outcomes of the for-profits relative to other higher education institutions after adjusting for observable differences in students who have attended different types of schools.

The recent and rapid growth of for-profit colleges means that most of the standard individual-level longitudinal data sets do not identify those who went to for-profit institutions or do not have large enough samples of for-profit students for a meaningful analysis. To overcome these constraints we use the most recent cohort of the Beginning Postsecondary Students Longitudinal Study, known as BPS:04/09. A sample of 2003–2004 first-time beginning postsecondary students are followed, in their first, third, and sixth years since entering an undergraduate institution, up through 2009. Because it covers a recent cohort, a significant fraction of the sample initially enrolled in a for-profit institution. The BPS has detailed student background variables, low attrition rates, and an oversample of students at for-profit institutions yielding approximately 1,950 students starting at for-profits out of a total of about 16,680 students in our main sample.[8]

The Beginning Postsecondary Students data is representative of first-time postsecondary students (those starting an undergraduate program with no previous postsecondary schooling). But because a large fraction of students in for-profit institutions are older, nontraditional students returning to higher-education, they will not be picked up in this sample. Thus, our analysis estimates the for-profit school treatment effect (relative to other types of institutions) for first-time postsecondary students but not for the large group of returning students.

The outcome variables in the Beginning Postsecondary Students data are divided into two major groups. Those concerning college costs and financial aid are given in Table 2.2, and those regarding student persistence, educational attainment, employment, earnings, and satisfaction with the program are in Table 2.3. The raw data, given in columns 1–3 of Tables 2.2 and 2.3, reveal that beginning postsecondary students at for-profits accumulate larger student debt burdens, are more likely to default on their student loans, have poorer employment outcomes five years after entering postsecondary school, and are less likely to be satisfied with their course of study than students starting at public or private nonprofit schools. The short-run (one-year) dropout rate is slightly lower for starting for-profit students than those starting in a community college. For-profit students in certificate and AA programs have higher completion rates than community college students. In contrast, BA completion rates of for-profit students are much lower than of those starting in four-year public and nonprofit schools.

Using the Beginning Postsecondary Students data, we assess whether the raw mean student outcome differences have been overstated because for-profit students differ from those in the public and the private nonprofit sectors (as was demonstrated in the bottom panel of Table 2.1). To do this,

TABLE 2.2

Differences in College Costs and Financial Aid between For-Profit Institutions and Other Schools for First-Time Undergraduates: 2004/2009 Beginning Postsecondary Students Longitudinal Study

	Beginning Postsecondary Students (Full Sample)				
	Dependent Variable Means			For-Profit Institution Impact	
Dependent Variables	4-year Public and Nonprofits (1)	2-year and Public Nonprofits (2)	For-Profits (3)	OLS (4)	Matching (5)
College costs and financial aid, 2003–2004					
Applied for aid (share)	0.895	0.749	0.986	0.094 (0.010)	0.072 (0.011)
Title IV loan and grant aid ($)	3,837	1,022	6,852	4,439 (183)	3,417 (164)
Tuition ($)	9,230	1,269	8,434	5,632 (173)	5,108 (201)
Net tuition minus grants ($)	5,183	734	5,573	4,521 (157)	4,418 (158)
Pell grant ($)	0.285	0.294	0.790	0.190 (0.014)	0.061 (0.020)
Pell grant amount ($)	771	633	2,149	557 (48)	180 (68)
Financial aid through 2009					
Cumulative Pell grant ($)	2,923	2,399	4,084	–170 (146)	–852 (223)
Cumulative Title IV borrowing ($)	8,702	3,502	7,699	3,960 (421)	2,239 (381)
Title IV loan balance in 2009 ($)	8,024	3,306	7,460	4,071 (460)	2,242 (401)
Repaid any amount on loan, conditional on a student loan (share)	0.642	0.640	0.529	–0.093 (0.029)	–0.040 (0.046)
Defaulted on loan, conditional on a student loan (share)	0.035	0.056	0.188	0.067 (0.018)	0.082 (0.018)
Sample size	8,760	5,970	1,950		

Source: BPS:04/09 Restricted-Use Data File. BPS:04/09 is Beginning Postsecondary Students Longitudinal Study data for 2003-2004 first-time beginning postsecondary students in their first, third, and sixth years since entering an undergraduate institution, through 2009.

Notes: The ordinary least squares (OLS) column reports coefficient estimates (robust standard errors) for a for-profit institution dummy variable in regressions for each dependent variable, estimates that include the following covariates: dummy variables for race, sex, citizenship, born in the United States, parents born in the United States, English as the native language, household size, distance of school from home, lives with parents, marital status, single parenthood, independent student, number of kids, use of child care, maternal and paternal education categories, high school diploma, GED receipt, delayed enrollment after high school, certificate or degree program, degree expectations, region, and on or off-campus residence; and second-order polynomials in age, prior income (own for independent students and family for dependent students), household income percent of the poverty line, expected family contribution from the FAFSA (Free Application for Federal Student Aid), individual adjusted gross income from tax returns and government transfers. Each number in the "Matching "column represents the average treatment on the treated estimate (standard error) for going to a for-profit institution using from nearest neighbor (propensity score) matching with replacement and excluding observations outside of common support. The same covariates used in the ordinary least squares regressions were used for the matching models. The ordinary least squares and matching model estimates use the BPS sampling weights. Unweighted sample sizes are rounded to the nearest 10.

TABLE 2.3

Differences in Student Outcomes between For-Profit Institutions and Other Schools for First-Time Undergraduates: 2004/2009 Beginning Postsecondary Students Longitudinal Study

	Beginning Postsecondary Students (Full Sample)				
	Dependent Variable Means			For-Profit Institution Impact	
Dependent Variables	4-year Public and Nonprofits (1)	2-year and Public Nonprofits (2)	For-Profits (3)	OLS (4)	Matching (5)
Persistence and educational attainment					
Left school in 2003–2004 (share)	0.062	0.233	0.212	–0.046 (0.016)	–0.051 (0.018)
Attained certificate (if enrolled in certificate program; share)	—	0.424	0.537	0.086 (0.036)	0.046 (0.034)
Attained AA (if enrolled in AA program; share)	—	0.224	0.284	0.041 (0.028)	0.019 (0.029)
Attained AA or more (if enrolled in AA program; share)	—	0.283	0.291	–0.006 (0.028)	–0.016 (0.030)
Attained BA (if enrolled in BA program; share)	0.658	—	0.262	–0.115 (0.045)	–0.194 (0.052)
Idle (not employed, not enrolled) at 2009 survey (share)	0.106	0.133	0.236	0.052 (0.017)	0.058 (0.017)
Enrolled in 2009 (share)	0.271	0.389	0.216	–0.114 (0.018)	–0.080 (0.019)
Employment and earnings (for those no longer enrolled in 2009)					
Any job in 2009 (share)	0.839	0.784	0.706	–0.028 (0.021)	–0.031 (0.022)
Earnings from work in 2009 ($)	28,613	24,795	19,950	–1,771 (931)	–1,936 (950)
Earnings from work in 2009, conditional on employment ($)	34,080	31,622	28,243	–1,355 (934)	-243 (937)
Unemployed and seeking work (share)	0.121	0.148	0.232	0.048 (0.019)	0.067 (0.020)
Unemployed 3 months or more after leaving school (share)	0.238	0.259	0.404	0.077 (0.022)	0.084 (0.023)
Earnings less than gainful employment standard (share)	0.135	0.046	0.271	0.194 (0.019)	0.147 (0.017)
Course content and job and school satisfaction					
Remedial coursework in 2003–2004 (share)	0.181	0.289	0.076	–0.180 (0.015)	–0.187 (0.017)
Left school because dissatisfied (2003-2004) (share)	0.012	0.024	0.081	0.043 (0.009)	0.048 (0.009)
Left school because dissatisfied (2003-2006) (share)	0.032	0.051	0.117	0.052 (0.013)	0.053 (0.011)
Education was worth the cost (share)	0.802	0.821	0.648	-0.204 (0.019)	-0.179 (0.017)

Loans were a worthwhile investment (share)	0.836	0.803	0.664	-0.143 (0.022)	-0.121 (0.024)
Satisfied with major or program (share)	0.860	0.871	0.789	-0.097 (0.017)	-0.065 (0.015)
Satisfied with current job, (employed, not enrolled; share)	0.772	0.764	0.752	-0.011 (0.025)	-0.032 (0.023
Sample size	8,760	5,970	1,950		

Source and Notes: See Table 2.2.

we adjust the raw outcomes for differences in baseline observables between for-profit students and others using two methods.

The first method is a standard ordinary least squares regression of student outcomes on a rich set of covariates of student baseline characteristics at entry into college (listed in the table notes), and a dummy variable for starting postsecondary schooling in a for-profit institution. The alternative method is a matching approach, which takes students starting in for-profits as the treatment group and students starting in public and private nonprofit schools as the control group. We compare the outcomes of the for-profit students to the control group members who are observably comparable to for-profit students. More specifically, we estimate the average treatment-on-treated effect of starting in a for-profit institution using nearest neighbor (propensity score) matching models with replacement excluding observations outside of common support.[9] For educational attainment outcomes, the estimation samples are separated into the subgroups of students initially enrolled in each type of program (certificate, AA, BA).

The ordinary least squares results are shown in column 4 for the full sample and those for the matching estimator are in column 5 of Tables 2.2 and 2.3. The ordinary least squares and matching approaches produce qualitatively and quantitatively similar estimates for almost every outcome considered.

Our conclusions with regard to the relative performance of students starting in for-profit institutions are mixed. For-profit students have a higher probability of staying with a program through its first year. Early persistence translates into a higher probability of obtaining a degree or certificate in a one- or two-year program. The ordinary least squares estimates indicate that certificate seekers starting at for-profits are almost 9 percentage points more likely to gain a certificate than community college students. Although for-profit students seeking an AA are somewhat more likely than community college students to attain an AA degree, they are less likely to continue to higher-level college courses and to gain a BA degree. The matching estimates indicate that the for-profit advantage in completing certificate and AA programs is more modest and less statistically significant than the ordinary least squares estimates.

Students in for-profit institutions are also much less likely to report taking remedial courses in their first year in postsecondary school than students in other institutions. The greater ability of for-profit students to take courses they consider directly relevant and not languish in remedial courses may play a role in their greater first-year retention rates.[10]

For the longer undergraduate programs, such as BA, for-profits do not fare as well as four-year public and private nonprofit institutions. The ordinary least squares estimate implies a 12 percentage point completion deficit and the matching model implies a 19 percentage point deficit for students starting BA programs at for-profits. The control group of students in the full range of public and private nonprofit four-year schools is probably less comparable in the case of BA students than for certificate and AA programs. But even when the sample is restricted to students starting in nonselective schools, a statistically significant deficit of almost 5 percentage points remains.

Also, for-profits leave students with considerably higher debt, even conditional on a rich set of observables. For-profit students face higher sticker-price tuition and pay higher net tuition (tuition plus fees minus grants) than comparable students at other institutions. Students who began at a for-profit school default on their loans at higher rates than other students conditional on controls for demographics, academic preparation, and pre-enrollment family resources. For-profit students have substantially higher default rates even when comparing students across school types with similar cumulative debt burdens. For example, the default rate by 2009 for the BPS:04/09 students with $5,001 to $10,000 in cumulative federal student loans is 26 percent for students from for-profits versus 10 percent for those from community colleges and 7 percent for those from four-year public and nonprofit schools; and for those with $10,001 to $20,000 in debt, the default rate among for-profit students is 16 percent versus a 3 percent rate for community college students and 2 percent rate for other four-year college students.

Although the vast majority of students from for-profits express satisfaction with their course of study and programs, they report significantly lower satisfaction than observably similar students starting in public and nonprofit schools. Students who began in for-profit colleges are also less likely to state that their education was worth the amount they paid and are less apt to think their student loans were a worthwhile investment. Even though the for-profits have higher short-run retention of students, their students are more likely to leave their certificate or degree programs before completion because of dissatisfaction with the program.

In terms of economic outcomes in the medium-run, for-profit students are more likely to be idle (that is, not working and no longer enrolled in school) six years after starting college. Among the students who left school by the 2009 wave of the BPS survey, those from for-profits are more likely to be unemployed and to have experienced substantial unemployment (more than three months) since leaving school. For-profit students no longer enrolled in 2009 have earnings from work in 2009 that are $1,800 to $2,000 lower (or 8 to 9 percent of their predicted mean earnings) than had they gone to another type of institution.[11] Some of the earnings reduction is due to lower rates of employment. Once we condition on employment, for-profit students have modestly lower earnings and slightly lower job satisfaction, but neither difference is statistically significant.

For-profit schools, therefore, do better in terms of first-year retention and the completion of shorter certificate and degree programs. But their first-time postsecondary students wind up with higher debt burdens, experience greater unemployment after leaving school and, if anything, have lower earnings six years after starting college than observationally similar students from public and nonprofit institutions. Not surprisingly, for-profits students end up with higher student loan default rates and are less satisfied with their college experiences.

Lower satisfaction with the programs may provide an additional psychological factor accounting for the high default rates of for-profit students, even for those with modest absolute student debt levels. In fact, students in this dataset from for-profits with less than $2,500 in federal student loan debt had a default rate of 20 percent by 2009 as compared with 12 percent for students from community colleges and 4 percent for those from four-year public and nonprofit institutions. These patterns are troubling since the consequences of federal student loan default cannot be escaped through bankruptcy and can adversely impact an individual's credit rating and future access to credit, not to mention result in wage garnishment, harassment by private collection agencies, and tax refund offsets.

Although we have used the detailed background covariates in the Beginning Postsecondary Students survey data to make comparisons between individuals who are as similar as can be observed, we do not have quasi-experimental variation concerning who goes to which type of higher-education institution. Thus, one needs to be cautious in providing a causal interpretation of the estimated for-profit school treatment effects in Tables 2.2 and 2.3 since the potential problem of selection bias from nonrandom sorting on unobservables remains. Furthermore, our comparison of the medium-term outcomes for beginning postsecondary students starting at for-profits versus comparable students starting at other higher-education institutions does not directly provide information on whether attendance at a for-profit college (or, for that matter, attendance at public or private, nonprofit colleges) is a worthwhile (private or social) investment.

Nimble Critters or Agile Predators?

The U.S. economy has experienced a substantial increase in the pecuniary returns to postsecondary education since 1980, particularly for BA and higher degrees (Autor, Katz, and Kearney 2008;

Goldin and Katz 2008). At the same time, state budgetary difficulties have constrained the expansion of public sector higher education; for example, Cellini (2009) provides compelling evidence from California on how public sector funding constraints on community colleges increased the rate of entry of for-profit colleges. In the meantime, federal and state financial aid for students going to for-profit institutions has become more available and generous (for example, Cellini 2010). Based on these factors, and others discussed in this paper, the for-profit postsecondary school sector became the fastest growing part of U.S. higher education from the 1990s through 2010. Increased regulatory scrutiny and adverse publicity from Congressional hearings, investigative reporting, and Government Accountability Office (GAO) audits have led to a substantial slowdown in the growth of for-profit enrollments in 2011 and actual declines in new students at many of the larger national chains (Steinerman, Volshteyn, and McGarrett 2011; Fain 2011).

Evaluating the successes and failures of U.S. for-profit higher education must go beyond mean outcomes and consider the distribution of labor market effects and financial default rates. For many, the for-profits have been a success. They have played a critical role in expanding the supply of skilled workers in an era of tight state budgets and stagnating state appropriations to public sector schools. They have provided educational services to underserved populations. Their innovative use of web services has further allowed them to accommodate nontraditional students. Their disproportionate share of federal student grants and loans has enabled them to provide skills to disadvantaged populations. Short-run retention is high and the for-profits do an admirable job of graduating students from shorter certificate programs. The vast majority of their students are satisfied with their programs.

But the for-profits also charge higher tuition and fees than public sector alternatives, and their students are more likely to end up unemployed and with substantial debts. Students who attended a for-profit have much higher default and nonrepayment rates on federal student loans than do observationally similar students who attended a public or private nonprofit institution.

The U.S. Department of Education (2011b) has recently sought to address this issue of the high default rate on loans to students at for-profit institutions by passing "Gainful Employment" regulations, which will require most for-profit programs and certificate programs at public and nonprofit institutions to pass at least one of three metrics to remain Title IV-eligible: 1) at least 35 percent of former students repaying their loans ("repaying" defined as reducing their loan by at least $1 over the course of a year); 2) annual loan payments not exceeding 30 percent of a typical graduate's discretionary income; or 3) annual loan payments not exceeding 12 percent of a typical graduate's earnings.

How these rules will work in practice, as students and for-profit institutions adjust to their presence, remains to be seen. The former students of for-profit institutions have comparable (but slightly lower) earnings, combined with substantially higher loan burdens, relative to other school leavers, suggesting that some for-profit institutions may face challenges meeting the new Gainful Employment standards. As one example, consider the rule that the debt burden (annual federal student loan yearly payments) should not exceed 12 percent of annual earnings for a typical graduate. In fact we find (conditional on observables), in Table 2.3 for the Beginning Postsecondary Students data, that for-profit students would have had a 15 to 19 percentage point lower rate of meeting the recently enacted Gainful Employment earnings threshold in 2008 (four to five years after starting) than would students from other types of institutions.

In effect, the Gainful Employment rule seeks to hold the for-profits more accountable and put a greater burden on the schools, rather than only on the students who have difficulties in repaying their loans. The new regulations will also require institutions to disclose their program costs, as well as completion, placement, and loan repayment rates. These regulations will increase transparency but may be insufficient to contain an agile predator. A reality check by a third party might be needed before a student is allowed to take out a loan.

The for-profits have taken a large burden of increased enrollment in higher education off the public sector. The high default rates of their students on federal loans, however, increase their cost to the taxpayer. Regulating for-profit colleges is tricky business. The challenge is to rein in the agile predators while not stifling the innovation of these nimble critters.

Acknowledgments

We gratefully acknowledge the superb research assistance of Tanya Avilova, Jason Poulos, and Bernie Ziprich. We are grateful to Stephanie Cellini and the Editors for helpful comments. The research reported here was supported by the Institute of Education Sciences, U.S. Department of Education, through Grant R305C1 10011 to Teachers College , Columbia University. The opinions expressed are those of the authors and do not represent views of the Institute or the U.S. Department of Education.

Notes

1. An online Appendix available with this paper at (http://e-jep.org) provides the details of our processing of the micro IPEDS data, linkage of the IPEDS institution-year data to financial aid to data from the National Student Loan Data System, and construction of an institution-level panel data set for 2000 to 2009.
2. In higher education, nonprofits and publics are not that far behind in pay, just below the very top of the for-profit scale. In 2006/07, before the stock market decline, the highest paid university president was Gordon Gee at Vanderbilt who earned slightly more than $2 million in total compensation. A bit lower down the scale, the tenth highest-paid CEO at a for-profit was Wallace Boston, Jr., CEO of American Public Education, with $961,000, while number 10 among the presidents of public institutions on the list was Jack Varsalona at Wilmington University who earned $974,000. After the stock market drop, earnings in 2008/09 for presidents at public and nonprofit private universities were far lower. The data on for-profit CEO pay is from *Chronicle of Higher Education* (2010); data on public and nonprofit president's pay is from Gibson (2009).
3. We should note that the comparison between enrollments in the Beginning Postsecondary Students data and completions in the IPEDS is generally not valid when programs vary in length. But because BPS surveys a cohort, the comparison has greater validity.
4. The large national chains in the study are American Public Education, Apollo Group, Bridgepoint Education, Capella Education, Career Education, Corinthian Colleges, DeVry Inc., Education Management, Grand Canyon Education, ITT Educational Services, Lincoln Education, Strayer Education, and Universal Technical Institute.
5. The slight decline in the for-profit share of loans in 2010 may reflect the shift from the Federal Family Education Loan program with bank lending under federal guarantees to the Direct Loan program where the federal government makes the loans directly to students.
6. Current default rates at for-profits, however, remain lower than in the late 1980s and early 1990s before the 1992 amendments to the Higher Education Act that tightened institutional eligibility for Title IV funds and removed many nondegree proprietary schools with very high default rates from the Title IV financial aid programs (Bennett, Lucchesi, and Vedder 2010).
7. Furthermore, since federal Stafford loans have an initial 6-month grace period and can be up to 360 days delinquent before being considered in default, the two-year default rates typically cover a much shorter window in which a recorded default is possible.
8. We use the sampling weights from the Beginning Postsecondary Students data in all our analyses to account for the variation in sampling rates among different student subgroups. The attrition rates from the BPS:04/09 by the final 2009 survey round are relatively balanced by starting institution at 6.4 percent for students from for-profits, 10.9 percent for community college students, and 10.7 percent for students from four-year public and nonprofit schools. The differences in attrition rate by starting institution type are small and not statistically significant after conditioning on baseline covariates. Unweighted sample sizes are rounded to the nearest 10.
9. We implement the nearest-neighbor matching estimator in STATA using the routines developed by Becker and Ichino (2002).
10. See Rosenbaum, Deil-Amien, and Person (2006) for rich case study evidence of the roles of clearer program paths, more relevant courses, and student services in better retention and short program completion rates for students in for-profit schools relative to community colleges. Rutschow and Schneider (2011) summarize recent evidence from interventions designed to improve students' progress through remedial courses at community colleges.

11. In slight contrast, Cellini and Chaudhary (2011) find similar weekly earnings gains of around 6 percent to attending a two-year AA program at a private or public two-year college and of 15 to 17 percent (or 8 percent per year of education) to completing an AA degree at private postsecondary institutions (largely for-profit schools) and at public institutions (largely community colleges) using an individual fixed effects strategy of comparing earnings before and after college using workers under 30 years old in the 1997 National Longitudinal Survey of Youth. Cellini and Chaudhary likely understate the relative economic returns to going to a public two-year college relative to a private for-profit institution by dropping from their sample the students who continued beyond an AA to get a BA or more.

References

Autor, David H., Lawrence F. Katz, and Melissa S. Kearney. 2008. "Trends in U.S. Wage Inequality: Revising the Revisionists." *Review of Economics and Statistics* 90(2): 300–323.

Baum, Sandy. 2011. "Drowning in Debt: Financial Outcomes of Students in For-Profit Colleges." Testimony to the U.S. Senate Committee on Health, Education, Labor and Pensions, June 7.

Becker, Sascha O., and Andrea Ichino. 2002. "Estimation of Average Treatment Effects based on Propensity Scores." *STATA Journal* 2(4): 358–77.

Bennett, Daniel L., Adam R. Lucchesi, and Richard K. Vedder. 2010. "For-Profit Higher Education: Growth, Innovation, and Regulation." A Policy Paper from the Center for College Affordability and Productivity, July, http://heartland.org/sites/all/modules/custom/heartland_migration/files/pdfs/29010.pdf.

Breneman, David W., Brian Pusser, and Sarah E. Turner, eds. 2006. *Earnings from Learning: The Rise of For-Profit Universities*. Albany, NY: State University of New York Press.

Cellini, Stephanie Riegg. 2009. "Crowded Colleges and College Crowd-Out: The Impact of Public Subsidies on the TwoYear College Market." *American Economic Journal: Economic Policy* 1(2): 1–30.

Cellini, Stephanie Riegg. 2010. "Financial Aid and For-Profit Colleges: Does Aid Encourage Entry?" *Journal of Policy Analysis and Management* 29(3): 526–52.

Cellini, Stephanie Riegg, and Latika Chaudhary. 2011. "The Labor Market Returns to a Private Two-Year College Education." http://home.gwu.edu/~scellini/Index/Research_files/Cellini%26Chaudhary_Returns_Aprill 1.pdf.

Cellini, Stephanie Riegg, and Claudia Goldin. Forthcoming. "Does Federal Student Aid Raise Tuition?: New Evidence on For-Profit Colleges" NBER Working Paper.

Chronicle of Higher Education. 2010. "CEO Compensation at Publicly Traded HigherEducation Companies." June. 23. http://chronicle.com/article/Graphic-CEO-Compensation-at/66017/.

Fain, Paul. 2011. "Enrollments Tumble at For-Profit Colleges." *Inside Higher Ed*, November 11. http://www.insidehighered.com/news/201 1/11/11/enrollments-tumble-profit-colleges.

Gibson, Ellen. 2009. "College Campuses Debate Administrators' Lofty Pay." *Bloomberg Business Week*, February 16. http://www.businessweek.com/bwdaily/dnflash/content/feb2009/db20090216_614557.htm?chan=top+news_top+news+index-(-ftemp_news+ % 2B+analysis.

Goldin, Claudia, and Lawrence F. Katz. 2008. *The Race between Education and Technology*. Cambridge, MA: Belknap Press, Harvard University Press.

Health, Education, Labor and Pensions Committee, U.S. Senate. 2010. "Benefiting Whom? For-Profit Education Companies and the Growth of Military Educational Benefits." December 8. http://harkin.senate.gov/documents/pdf/4eb02b5a4610f.pdf.

Hentschke, Guilbert C. 2010. "Innovations in Business Models and Organizational Cultures: The For-Profit Sector." Unpublished paper, USC Rossier School of Education, June.

Knapp, Laura G., Janice Kelley-Reid, and Scott A. Ginder. 2011. *Postsecondary Institutions and Price of Attendance in the United States: 2010–11: Degrees and Other Awards Conferred: 2009–10, and 12-Month Enrollment: 2009–10. First Look.* NCES 2011-250. Washington, D.C: U.S. Department of Education. http://nces.ed.gov/pubs2011/2011250.pdf.

Rosenbaum, James E., Regina Deil-Amien, and Ann E. Person. 2006. *After Admission: From College Access to College Success*. New York: Russell Sage Foundation Press.

Rutschow, Elizabeth Zachry, and Emily Schneider. 2011. *Unlocking the Gate: What We Know About Improving Developmental Education*. New York: Manpower Demonstration Research Corporation.

Steinerman, Andrew, Jeffrey Volshteyn, and Molly McGarrett 2011. *Education Services Data Book*. September. J.P. Morgan, North American Equity Research, Business and Education Services.

Turner, Sarah E. 2006. "For-Profit Colleges in the Context of the Market for Higher Education." In *Earnings from Learning: The Rise of For-Profit Universities*, edited by D. Breneman, B. Pusser, and S. Turner, 51–68. Albany: State University of New York Press.

U.S. Department of Education. 2011a. 2011–2 *Federal Student Aid Handbook, Vol. 2, School Eligibility and Operations*, http://ifap.ed.gov/fsahandbook/1112FSAHbkVo2.html.

U.S. Department of Education. 2011b. "Additional Background on the Gainful Employment Regulations." Go to: http://www.ed.gov/news/press-releases/gainful-employment-regulations, click on "Supplemental Information."

U.S. Department of Education, Federal Student Aid Data Center. 2011. *Proprietary School 90/10 Revenue Percentages, Report for 2009–2010 Award Year*. Available at http://federalstudentaid.ed.gov/datacenter/proprietary.html.

U.S. Department of Education, National Center for Education Statistics (NCES). 2010. *Digest of Education Statistics: 2010*. http://nces.ed.gov/programs/digest/.

U.S. Department of Education. National Center for Education Statistics (NCES). 2011. *The Condition of Education 2011*. http://nces.ed.gov/programs/coe/.

U.S. Department of Education, National Center for Education Statistics (NCES), Integrated Postsecondary Education Data System (IPEDS). 2009. IPEDS Fall 2009 Compendium Tables, http://nces.ed.gov/das/library/tables_listings/fall2009.asp.

U.S. Government Accountability Office. 2010. "For-Profit Colleges: Undercover Testing Finds Colleges Encouraged Fraud and Engaged in Deceptive and Questionable Marketing Practices." GAO-10-948T, August 4. http://www.gao.gov/products/GAO-1 0-948T.

Watkins, Barbara L. 1991. "A Quite Radical Idea: The Invention and Elaboration of Collegiate Correspondence Study." In *The Foundations of American Distance Education: A Century of Collegiate Correspondence Study*, edited by Barbara L. Watkins and Stephen J. Wright, 1–35. Dubuque, IA: Kendall/Hunt.

Winston, Gordon C. 1999. "For-Profit Higher Education: Godzilla or Chicken Little?" *Change* 31(1): 12–19.

CHAPTER 3

ACCOUNTING FOR HIGHER EDUCATION ACCOUNTABILITY: POLITICAL ORIGINS OF STATE PERFORMANCE FUNDING FOR HIGHER EDUCATION

KEVIN J. DOUGHERTY, REBECCA S. NATOW, RACHEL H. BORK, SOSANYA M. JONES, *AND* BLANCA E. VEGA
TEACHERS COLLEGE, COLUMBIA UNIVERSITY

Background/Context: Performance funding finances public higher education institutions based on outcomes such as retention, course and degree completion, and job placement rather than inputs such as enrollments. One of the mysteries of state performance funding for higher education is that despite great interest in it for over 30 years, only half of all states have ever adopted it.

Purpose/Objective/Research Question/Focus of Study: This study examines the political forces that have driven the development of performance funding in some states but not others. To do this, the authors draw on theories of policy origins such as the advocacy coalition framework, the policy entrepreneurship perspective, and policy diffusion theory.

Research Design: This study contrasts the experiences of six states that established performance funding for higher education (Florida, Illinois, Missouri, South Carolina, Tennessee, and Washington) and two that have not (California and Nevada). These states differ considerably in their performance funding programs, higher education governance arrangements, and political and socioeconomic characteristics.

Data Collection and Analysis: Our study is qualitative, drawing on documentary records and extensive interviews with higher education officials, legislators and staff, governors and advisors, business leaders, and other actors.

Findings and Results: Our study finds that many of the actors and motives cited by the prevailing perspective on the origins of performance funding did operate in the six states that have established performance funding, including state legislators (particularly Republicans), governors, and business people pursuing performance funding in the name of greater effectiveness and efficiency for higher education. However, the prevailing perspective misses the major role of state higher education coordinating boards and individual higher education institutions (particularly community colleges) that pursued performance funding to secure new funds in an era of greater tax resistance and criticism of higher education. Our findings further move beyond the prevailing explanation by examining how policy entrepreneurs mobilized support for performance funding by finding ideological common ground among different groups, identifying policies that those groups could support, and taking advantage of political openings to put performance funding onto the decision agenda of state elected officials.

Conclusions and Recommendations: This examination of the origins of performance funding policies sheds light on factors that facilitate and frustrate the development of such policies. For example, our research highlights the important role of higher education opposition and the presence of certain political structures and political values in frustrating the development of performance funding.

Performance funding is a method of financing public education institutions based on outcomes such as retention, course and degree completion, and job placement, not on inputs such as enrollments. The principal rationale for this type of funding has been its ability to prod institutions toward greater effectiveness and efficiency, particularly during a time of increasing demands on higher education and increasingly straitened state finances (Burke, 2002a; Dougherty & Hong, 2006; Layzell, 1999; Ruppert, 1995).

One of the mysteries of state performance funding is that it is not more widespread. Although there has been great interest in it for over 30 years, only half of all states have ever created a performance funding program for higher education (Dougherty & Reid, 2007; McLendon, Hearn, & Deaton, 2006). This reality inspires the question, What forces have driven the development of performance funding in many states but not others? What accounts for these differences?

The variable origins of state performance funding programs are of interest for a number of reasons. First, an analysis of the political sources of performance funding sheds light on its prospects in states that do not have performance funding now but are considering it. From an examination of why performance funding arose in some states but not others, one can glean indications of what might facilitate or frustrate the development of performance funding in states without it. Second, there is evidence that the political origins of programs affect their later success and sustainability (Racine, 2006; Scheirer, 2005; Shediac-Rizkallah & Bone, 1998). An important predictor of the later demise of performance funding is the breadth of the coalition initially supporting it, particularly whether the coalition included higher education institutions (Dougherty, Natow, & Vega, 2012). Moreover, as we explore, it is noteworthy how little concern was expressed in the states we studied about the possible impacts of performance funding on equality of higher education opportunity. The weakness of equity concerns and the lack of involvement of equity-oriented actors—particularly representatives of the minority and low-income communities—not only make it less likely that performance funding will serve egalitarian goals but also weaken performance funding when it comes under fiscal or political pressure (Dougherty et al., 2012).

This article examines both the origins of state performance funding in six states (Florida, Illinois, Missouri, South Carolina, Tennessee, and Washington) and the lack of its development in another two states (California and Nevada). Our analysis of the political origins of state performance funding systems draws on three perspectives on policy origins: the advocacy coalition framework, the policy entrepreneurship perspective, and policy diffusion models. Used together, they powerfully illuminate many features of the politics of performance funding for higher education at the state level.

Reasons for the Rise of State Performance Funding

The Prevailing Explanation

A number of authors have offered explanations for why states have enacted performance accountability (Alexander, 2000; Burke, 2002a; McLendon et al., 2006; Rhoades & Sporn, 2002; Ruppert, 1995; Slaughter & Leslie, 1997; Zumeta, 2001). In the 1990s, state governments faced a revenue and cost squeeze because of the coincidence of an economic slowdown and rapidly rising costs of higher education and other governmental programs. The economic recession caused state government revenues to grow much more slowly than before and in some states even to drop (Alexander; Burke, 2002a; Rhoades & Sporn, 2002; Ruppert; Slaughter & Leslie, 1997; Zumeta, 2001). At the same time, state governments were facing rapidly escalating costs of higher education. Enrollments were growing because of the baby boom echo and a belief that individual and collective economic futures required higher levels of college-going. Moreover, the per capita costs of operating higher education institutions were expanding faster than the general rate of inflation (Alexander, 2000; Rhoades & Sporn, 2002; Ruppert, 1995; Zumeta, 2001). Meanwhile, outside higher education, state governments were facing rapidly rising demands for spending on K–12 education, prisons, and health care (Alexander, 2000; Burke, 2002a; Zumeta, 2001; see also Breneman & Finney, 1997; Callan, 2002; Kane, Orszag, & Gunter, 2003).

Even if these factors were not enough, the argument goes, state elected officials also faced strong demands from the general public and business for greater efficiency and lower costs of higher education. In the case of the general public, rapidly rising tuitions—caused by growing costs of college operation and a dropping share of state revenues—were causing great distress to students and their parents (Zumeta, 2001). At the same time, business associations pushed for greater efficiency on the part of higher education to improve the quality of college graduates, to lower the cost of government provision of higher education, and to keep down taxes (Burke, 2002a; Zumeta, 2001).

The translation of these pressures into performance funding demands on higher education was aided by several factors. In the 1990s, Republicans greatly increased their share of state legislative seats, a shift found to be a strong predictor of whether states enacted performance funding, as Republican legislators brought a heightened regard for business interests and a greater interest in market-based solutions to government administration (McLendon et al., 2006).

In addition, higher education's standard operating procedures were increasingly questioned. More and more policy-makers, opinion leaders, and even ordinary citizens were coming to see higher education as inefficient (characterized by out-of-control spending, underworked faculty, and administrative bloat), applying weak admission and academic standards (with affirmative action often targeted as the source), and favoring research at the expense of teaching (Alexander, 2000; Ruppert, 1995; Zumeta, 2001). Finally, traditional approaches to higher education accountability (e.g., accreditation, peer review, student choice) were increasingly considered ineffective (Alexander, 2000).

At the same time, higher education was seen as able to absorb cuts. Colleges could increase class sizes, hire more part-time instructors, and run their operations more efficiently. And they could raise more funds through tuition increases and private fund-raising (Callan, 2002; Zumeta, 2001).

Performance funding also became more feasible because states were much better able to gather data on institutional performance and tie funding to it. State capacity to gather and analyze data had increased greatly because of the revolution in information technology (Zumeta, 2001).

In addition to these dynamic factors was a more stable, structural element. There is evidence that states without consolidated governing boards have been significantly more likely to adopt performance funding than states with other governance arrangements. A possible explanation is that consolidated governing boards tend to be oriented to the desires of administrators and faculty and therefore resist performance funding in favor of less restrictive forms of performance accountability, such as performance budgeting (McLendon et al., 2006).

Moving Past the Prevailing Perspective

As we will show, our findings support but also go beyond the claims of the prevailing explanation of the rise of performance funding. Our analysis of the origins of performance funding in six states and its nondevelopment in two states finds that several factors posited by the prevailing perspective were at work in propelling performance funding. However, we also identify a variety of actors and motives—particularly in opposition to performance funding—that the prevailing perspective does not address. Our analysis further uncovers how the extent and form of support for and opposition to performance funding are shaped by a state's constitutional structure and basic social-cultural beliefs. Finally, our research points to the importance of policy learning and political opportunities (policy windows or external shocks) in fostering the rise of performance funding. We come to all these findings by applying theoretical approaches to policy origins that have typically not been used by the prevailing studies of the origins of performance funding.

Theoretical Perspectives

Treated as complementary rather than mutually exclusive explanations, the advocacy coalition framework, policy entrepreneurship perspective, and policy diffusion analysis together powerfully illuminate different facets of the origins of performance funding policies. As we show next, each of these perspectives illuminates different facets of the origins of policies and addresses limitations in the other theories.[1]

The Advocacy Coalition Framework

According to the advocacy coalition framework (ACF), policy change takes place within a "policy subsystem" of individuals, interest groups, and government agencies that interact regularly over a long period of time (at least a decade) to formulate and implement policies within a particular policy domain. These actors regard this domain as a major area of interest and have specialized subunits dealing with that domain (Sabatier, 1993; Sabatier & Jenkins-Smith, 1999; Sabatier & Weible, 2007). Within a policy subsystem, various "advocacy coalitions" promote different issues and solutions to problems. The coalitions are broad in membership and may include elected officials, government agency personnel, interest group members, and researchers who focus on a particular policy area (Sabatier, 1993; Sabatier & Jenkins-Smith, 1999; Sabatier & Weible, 2007).

According to the ACF, advocacy coalitions cohere primarily around the belief structures of their members. The most basic or "deep core" beliefs concern the nature of society and humanity, fundamental social values, the appropriate role of government, and the importance of different social groups. Not as powerful but particularly important to coalition formation are "policy core beliefs," which reflect coalition members' deep core beliefs as applied to specific policy areas. Policy core beliefs typically involve views about how serious a problem is, what has caused it, and what the most appropriate solutions to the problem are. Finally, coalition members have certain "secondary aspects" to their beliefs, which concern their preferences for the specific forms that policies should take, such as the amount of state spending on a particular program (Sabatier, 1993; Sabatier & Jenkins-Smith, 1999; Sabatier & Weible, 2007).

Policy evolution occurs in a variety of contexts, some of which are "relatively stable" and others of which are "dynamic" (Sabatier, 1993; Sabatier & Jenkins-Smith, 1999; Sabatier & Weible, 2007). The more "stable" contexts include the constitutional provisions under which a subsystem operates, the fundamental social-cultural beliefs of a polity, and the long-term resources available to a society. These characteristics shape the types of advocacy coalitions likely to form and the political resources they can deploy. "Dynamic" contexts include economic swings, changes in partisan control of government, big changes in public sentiment, and significant policy events taking place in other, similar subsystems. Such dynamic contexts provide a "shock" that may provoke a policy change by causing the dominant coalition to lose political resources or to change its beliefs (Sabatier, 1993; Sabatier & Jenkins-Smith, 1999; Sabatier & Weible, 2007). Another mechanism through which policy change takes place is policy learning: Advocacy coalition members gain increased knowledge about policies and surrounding contexts, which causes them to modify some of their beliefs, typically their secondary beliefs (Jenkins-Smith & Sabatier, 1993; Sabatier & Jenkins-Smith, 1999; Sabatier & Weible, 2007).

Although the ACF provides a very useful lens through which to view the evolution of performance funding policies, the framework lacks a detailed analysis of how and why advocacy coalitions arise and develop their policy stances. It also lacks sufficient analysis of how the "shocks" described earlier result in policy change. Moreover, the analysis of policy learning is focused on internal influences; it ignores the role of external influences highlighted by policy diffusion theory. Complementing the ACF with the policy entrepreneurship perspective and policy diffusion theory can resolve these shortcomings.

The Policy Entrepreneurship Perspective

The policy entrepreneurship perspective (Kingdon, 1995; Mintrom & Norman, 2009; Mintrom & Vergari, 1996; Roberts & King, 1996)[2] sheds light on the details of the political dynamics among policy actors that the ACF does not fully address (Mintrom & Vergari, 1996). At the forefront of this perspective is the policy entrepreneur, who takes the initiative to promote particular policy problems, identify solutions, and assemble a coalition of advocates for these solutions.

The policy entrepreneurship perspective fills a theoretical weakness of the ACF by clarifying how advocacy coalitions are created. The policy entrepreneurship perspective draws attention to the role of policy entrepreneurs who identify and mobilize political supporters by investigating their beliefs and trying to find points of agreement (Mintrom & Norman, 2009; see also Mintrom & Vergari, 1996).

The policy entrepreneurship perspective also addresses another shortcoming of the ACF: a lack of clarity on how political events (what the ACF refers to as "shocks") advance policy change. According to policy entrepreneurship theory, policy entrepreneurs provide the key mediation. External shocks in and of themselves do not necessarily cause political change. For political events to create policy change, they must be observed and interpreted by policy entrepreneurs who see the shocks as an opening to draw attention to particular problems and possible policy solutions (Kingdon, 1995; Mintrom & Norman, 2009; Mintrom & Vergari, 1996).

Policy entrepreneurs also play an important role in identifying and promoting public policy proposals. To be politically viable, policy proposals need to be technically effective, fiscally realistic, ideologically acceptable, and unlikely to provoke a backlash (Kingdon, 1995; Mintrom & Norman, 2009; Mintrom & Vergari, 1996). Policy entrepreneurs play an important role in winnowing down possible solutions to a short list of politically viable policy proposals that they can try to insert into the political process.

But where do these policy ideas come from? Policy entrepreneurship theory points to the role of policy networks spanning political jurisdictions (Mintrom & Norman, 2009). This point is powerfully amplified by policy diffusion theory.

The Policy Diffusion Perspective

The policy diffusion perspective has long emphasized that state policy makers often get policy ideas from other states. States copy policy innovations from each other under the impetus of learning from each other about what works, competing with each other for economic advantage, or conforming to national or regional cultural standards of what marks a progressive state government (F. S. Berry & Berry, 2007; McLendon, Heller, & Young, 2005; Walker, 1969).[3] This aspect of policy diffusion theory buttresses the ACF and the policy entrepreneurship perspective by providing an explanation of the sources of particular policy designs. Specifically, policy diffusion theory suggests that policy learning often occurs across state boundaries, with state policy makers often designing policies based on what other states have already done.

The main focus of the policy diffusion perspective has been on the example of neighboring states (F. S. Berry & Berry, 2007; McLendon et al., 2005, 2006). However, there is increasing attention to the role of national professional and state government associations that can diffuse policy understandings among states that are not geographically contiguous (Balla, 2001; F. S. Berry & Berry, 2007; McLendon et al., 2005; see also Walker, 1969).

Together, these three perspectives illuminate different facets of the development of performance funding for higher education at the state level and lead us to findings that are significantly at variance with those of the prevailing perspective. The ACF explains how performance funding policies are supported and opposed by "advocacy coalitions" that form within policy subsystems around common beliefs, how policy subsystems are shaped by fundamental features of state polities, and how policy change occurs through policy learning and external shocks to policy subsystems. The policy entrepreneurship perspective fills a theoretical weakness of the ACF by clarifying how advocacy coalitions are created, drawing attention to the role of policy entrepreneurs who identify and mobilize political supporters by analyzing their beliefs and finding points of agreement, identifying policy solutions, and taking advantage of external shocks. Policy diffusion theory further explains where ideas for policy solutions come from, pointing to the example of other states and the role of cross-state policy organizations and policy networks.

Research Methods

To explore the political factors that led to the development of performance funding in some states but not in others, this study examined six states that established performance funding (Florida, Illinois, Missouri, South Carolina, Tennessee, and Washington) and two that did not (California and Nevada). Our analysis is based on interviews in each state and examination of public agency reports, newspaper articles, and the academic research literature on those states.

The Choice of the States that Developed Performance Funding

About half of all U.S. states have established performance funding for higher education, since Tennessee led the way in 1979 (Burke & Minassians, 2003; Dougherty & Reid, 2007; McLendon et al., 2006). Because this is an intensive qualitative study, we could not study all of them. Thus, we selected six states that established performance funding and fit a number of selection criteria (see Table 3.1). First, we wanted states that differ on a wide variety of measures to capture a broad range of possible forces at work in the origins of performance funding. More specifically, we sought states that differ considerably in their performance funding systems (date of establishment, duration of existence, higher education sectors covered, amount of funds involved), higher education governance arrangements, and political and socioeconomic characteristics (political culture, gubernatorial powers, legislative professionalism, degree of party competition, population, wealth, and level of education). Second, we wanted the states to be dispersed across the country, given the powerful effect that regionalism has on state political processes and policy-making in the United States (Gray, 2004).[4] Third, the states should be dispersed temporally, in terms of when they started their performance funding systems. We did not want to have our sample too concentrated in any one period and therefore subject to the same period effects.[5] Temporal variation should allow for differences in economic and ideological circumstances that might affect which groups, motives, and political openings led to the establishment of performance funding. Finally, we wanted states that had established broad-based performance funding programs rather than narrow ones that did not represent the variety of outcomes that have been sought by performance funding.[6]

The application of these principles resulted in our selection of these six states: Florida, Illinois, Missouri, South Carolina, Tennessee, and Washington. Tennessee was of interest because it was the first state to establish performance funding and did so in the 1970s. Florida and Missouri enacted performance funding in the early 1990s. We selected Florida because it established two different performance funding systems, which promised to give us a particularly wide window on the factors giving rise to performance funding. We chose Missouri because it developed a performance funding system that attracted national attention for its careful design. Consequently, the demise of Missouri's system in 2002 surprised many observers. South Carolina, Washington, and Illinois established their systems in the late 1990s. We selected South Carolina because it was the first to legislate that 100% of state appropriations to public higher education institutions be based on their performance.[7] Washington afforded us the opportunity to examine the development of performance funding systems in two different decades: It established one system in 1997, relinquished it two years later, and then established a new one in 2007. Finally, Illinois provided a Midwestern counterpoint to Florida. Its performance funding program also applied only to community colleges but differed from Florida's in when it was established. Moreover, Illinois differs from Florida in its higher education governance and political and socioeconomic characteristics. As Table 3.1 makes clear, our six states vary systematically in the characteristics of their performance funding systems, their state governance arrangements, and political and socioeconomic characteristics.

Characteristics of the Performance Funding Programs

The first six dimensions involved characteristics of the performance funding programs established. First, the states differed in when the policy was first established. Tennessee initiated its program in 1979, Missouri and Florida in the early 1990s (1993 and 1994), and the other three states in the late 1990s (South Carolina in 1996, Washington in 1997, and Illinois in 1998). However, Washington also

TABLE 3.1

Characteristics of States

Characteristic	Tennessee	Missouri	Florida	South Carolina	Washington	Illinois	California	Nevada
1–6. Characteristics of the Performance Funding (PF) System								
1. Year PF established	1979	1993	1994	1996	1997, 2007	1998	Never est.	Never est.
2. If PF terminated, year of termination		2002	Suspended 2008	2003	1999	2002		
3. Duration of PF system if given up		9 years		7 years	2 years	4 years		
4. If PF system was reestablished, year done					2007			
5. Public higher education sectors covered	2 and 4 years	2 and 4 years	2 years only	2 and 4 years	2 and 4 years (1997–1999); 2 years only (2007–)	2 years only		
6. Peak in PF share of state public higher education funding	4.4% (FY 2005)	1.6% (FY 1999)	6.6% (FY 2001)	38% (FY 1999)	1.2% (FY 1999)	0.4% (FY 2001)		
7. State Higher Education Governance Structure at the Time of Enactment of Performance Funding								
* State governing board for all public higher education								X
* State coordinating board for all public higher education in the state	X	X	X	X	X	X	X	
* Public universities: Governing board for all public universities			X					

(continued)

TABLE 3.1

Characteristics of States *(continued)*

Characteristic	Tennessee	Missouri	Florida	South Carolina	Washington	Illinois	California	Nevada
* Public universities: Governing boards for each public university or university system in state	X (U of Tennessee 5 campuses)	X		X	X	X	X	
* Public 2-year colleges: Governing board for all public 2-year colleges	X (all public 2-year colleges & non-UT universities)			X				
* Public 2-year colleges: Coordinating board for all public 2-year colleges			X		X	X	X	
* Public 2-year colleges: Governing board for each public 2-year college		X						
8–14. Characteristics of the Political and Socioeconomic Systems								
8. Political culture: Conservative ideology	39.3%	35.5%	31.9%	39.1%	31.2%	29.2%	27.9%	34.8%
9. Gubernatorial powers (2002)	3.9	3.2	3.4	3.1	3.2	4.1	3.4	3.0
10. Legislative professionalism (2000)	32d	15th	10th	30th	14th	11th	1st	23d
11. Party competition index (1999–2003)	0.924	0.968	0.802	0.935	0.943	0.981	0.818	0.915
12. Population (2000)	5,689,000	5,597,000	15,983,000	4,012,000	5,894,000	12,420,000	33,872,000	1,998,000
13. Personal income per capita (2000)	$26,099	$27,243	$28,511	$24,426	$31,780	$32,187	$32,466	$30,438

14. Persons 25 years and older with bachelor's degree or more (2000)	22.0%	26.2%	22.8%	19.0%	28.6%	27.1%	27.5%	19.3%

Sources

1. Burke & Minassians (2003); McLendon et al. (2006); authors' interviews.

2. Burke & Minassians (2003); Dougherty et al. (2012).

6. See Dougherty, Natow, Hare, and Vega (2010) for derivation of these percentages.

7. McGuinness (1994). The governance structures are circa 1994 for all the states except Tennessee, for which the information is circa 1975.

8. Erikson, Wright, & McIver (2005). Figures are percentage of adults identifying as conservatives. Data are derived from CBS/*New York Times* polls for 1996–2003. For an alternative approach, see W. D. Berry, Ringquist, Fording, and Hanson (1998).

9. Beyle (2004). Average of 5-point scale applied to six items: number of separately elected executive branch officials; tenure potential of governor; governor's appointment powers; governor's budget power; governor's veto power; and gubernatorial party control of legislature. Average for 50 states is 3.5.

10. Hamm & Moncrief (2004). Squire's index based on state legislative salary, number of permanent staff, and length of legislative session.

11. Bibby & Holbrook (2004). Ranney interparty competition index: 0.5 to 1.0 scale, with higher number meaning higher competition. Average for 50 states is 0.871.

12. U.S. Bureau of the Census (2005).

13. U.S. Bureau of the Census (2005). Figures are in current dollars. U.S. average is $29,847.

14. U.S. Bureau of the Census (2005). Average for the United States is 25.6%.

affords us a look at forces at work in the 2000s: After letting its performance funding program lapse in 1999, it created a new one in 2007.

The states also differ in how long performance funding operated. Tennessee and Florida have retained performance funding to this day.[8] Missouri kept its performance funding system for 9 years and South Carolina for 7 years before relinquishing it. However, Illinois and Washington dropped theirs after 4 years and 2 years, respectively.[9] States that have retained performance funding for a long time may well have different constellations of support and opposition to performance funding than states whose performance funding did not last long.

The states also differ in terms of which sectors of public higher education were subject to performance funding. The systems in Florida, Illinois, and Washington (post-2007) applied only to community colleges. However, those in Missouri, South Carolina, Tennessee, and Washington (1997–1999) applied to all of public higher education. Given the differing social roles and political resources of community colleges and state universities, this difference should produce different patterns of support and opposition from higher education institutions.

In addition, the states vary considerably in the proportion of state higher education appropriations consisting of performance funding. It accounted for a much larger share of the state appropriation for higher education in South Carolina, Florida, and Tennessee than in Illinois, Missouri, and Washington. In fact, South Carolina's system had aimed originally at having 100% of state funding for higher education institutions be allocated on a performance basis (authors' interviews; Burke, 2002b).

Higher Education Governance

The six states also differ in their higher education governance arrangements. State governance structures for higher education have been found to affect a range of state higher education policy-making initiatives (McLendon, 2003; McLendon et al., 2006). Our six states differ considerably in the higher education governance structures they had in place at the time they adopted performance funding. Tennessee's system was rather strongly centralized, with a strong statewide coordinating board, a governing board for the University of Tennessee's five campuses, and a governing board for all other public universities and public two-year colleges. Missouri's system was at the other pole in degree of centralization: It did not have any governing boards or coordinating boards covering all public universities or public community colleges and only a weak coordinating board for all public higher education. Meanwhile, the other four states with performance funding fell somewhere in between in their degree of centralization (McGuinness, 1994, 2003).

Characteristics of the Political and Socioeconomic Systems

Our six states also differ considerably on a variety of characteristics of the political system that have been shown to affect state policy-making, including what policies are favored in states and which political groups get mobilized (Gray, 2004). First, the six states differ greatly in state political ideology. Tennessee and South Carolina have considerably more conservative electorates than do Illinois and Washington, with the other states falling in between (Erikson et al., 2005).

The differences in political culture are accompanied by variations in political structure and functioning. Illinois and Tennessee are above average in the institutional powers of the governor, whereas the other four states are a little below average (Beyle, 2004). On legislative professionalism, Illinois, Florida, Washington, and Missouri are above average, whereas South Carolina and Tennessee are below average (Hamm & Moncrief, 2004). The states also differ in degree of party competition. Florida is much less competitive than the other states (Bibby & Holbrook, 2004).[10]

Finally, the states differ considerably in their social characteristics: population, income, and education. For example, among our six states, Illinois and South Carolina are the polar opposites in population size, per capita income, and proportion of adults with a baccalaureate degree or higher. Illinois is well above the U.S. average in population size per state, per capita income, and proportion of college-educated adults, whereas South Carolina is well below (U.S. Bureau of the Census, 2005). A long-standing finding in the state policy literature is that state socioeconomic characteristics are strongly associated with differences in public policy (F. S. Berry & Berry, 2007; McLendon et al., 2005).

The Choice of the States that Did Not Develop Performance Funding

To better understand the sociopolitical forces behind the development of performance funding, we also analyzed two states that have not adopted this type of funding. They provide an important counterpoint to the cases in which performance funding was established, giving us greater confidence that we are actually isolating the factors that led to the establishment of performance funding.

The two states we examined are California and Nevada. We chose two states where some effort was made to establish performance funding, because it is much harder to determine the causes of lack of a policy when there has been no apparent effort whatsoever to create it. California interested us because a very clear effort was made to establish performance funding. In summer 2010, the state legislature considered and failed to pass a proposal to establish performance funding for community colleges on the basis of course completions, an up-and-coming form of performance funding that is receiving a lot of attention.[11]

Nevada is of interest for two reasons. First, it provides a "quieter" case of performance funding absence than California. Although the idea of performance funding has been raised in Nevada, it was never brought to formal legislative consideration. The state is of additional interest because it has a consolidated governing board for all public higher education institutions (McGuinness, 2003), a feature that has been identified in multivariate analyses as a significant predictor of why states do not enact performance funding (McLendon et al., 2006). We wished to examine how having such a board might have been a factor in why Nevada—as with several other states with consolidated governing boards (Alaska, Hawaii, Montana, North Dakota, Rhode Island, and Utah; McGuinness, 2003)—has not developed performance funding.

Beyond differing in their higher education governance arrangements,[12] California and Nevada differ greatly in their governmental systems, state political culture, and social characteristics. California's governor is more powerful and its legislature more professionalized than Nevada's. California's population is much larger and more politically liberal, educated, and wealthy (see Table 3.1). These differences should allow us to capture a variety of forces at work in leading these two states to not adopt performance funding.

Data Gathering and Analysis

For purposes of data triangulation, our analysis is based on extensive interviews with a wide variety of actors in each state and a thorough examination of other data sources. These sources include public agency reports, newspaper articles, and academic research studies in the form of books, journal articles, and doctoral dissertations.

Table 3.2 presents the number and types of interviews that we conducted with various types of political actors: state and local higher education officials, state legislators and their staff, governors and their advisors, business leaders, academics, consultants, and other observers of policy-making on performance funding in these eight states.[13]

State governors, legislators, and their advisors were chosen because of their central position in state government. Even if performance funding was initiated by a state higher education board, it would still require gubernatorial and legislative acquiescence to having state appropriations be distributed on the basis of performance indicators.

State and local higher education officials were chosen because they would have an immediate interest in performance funding either as initiators or implementers, or both. The state higher education officials we interviewed were top administrators of state governing or coordinating boards

TABLE 3.2

Interviewees in Each State

Interviewee Category	CA	FL	IL	MO	NV	SC	TN	WA
State higher education officials	5	10	8	4	4	5	7	v6
Higher education institution officials	7	8	10	4	5	7	6	5
Legislators and staff	1	3	2	5	1	4	2	6
Governors and advisors	2	3	3	3	1	1	3	2
Other state government officials		1						
Business leaders	2	2	1	2	1	3	1	1
Other (consultants, researchers, other)	4		1	2	1	5	5	2
Total	21	27	25	20	13	25	24	22

for higher education. The local higher education officials were presidents and senior administrators of public universities and community colleges.

Business officials were of interest because of business' longstanding advocacy of greater use of business methods in government operations and its increasing demand in the 1980s and 1990s for more emphasis on performance accountability in education (Business Roundtable, 1999; Fosler, 1990; Waddock, 1994). These concerns would make them likely supporters of state performance funding. In each state, we interviewed a number of top business people, typically including the president, top lobbyist, or chair of the education commission for the main business association in the state.

The interviews were semistructured. We used a standard protocol but adapted it to the circumstances of a particular interviewee and to content that emerged in the course of the interview. All interviewees spoke with the understanding of confidentiality.

Almost all the interviews were transcribed,[14] entered into the NVivo qualitative data analysis software system, and coded within the NVivo program. We also entered into NVivo and coded our documentary materials if they were in a format that allowed it. We had developed an initial list of codes focused on the content of performance funding systems, actors, beliefs, and motives supportive of or opposed to performance funding, events expected to affect the likelihood of performance funding agenda setting and adoption, and properties of the sociopolitical system that would affect the formation and actions of political groups. However, we added and altered codes as necessary as we proceeded with data collection and analysis.

To analyze the data, we ran inquiries in NVivo to find references in the data to key coding categories, such as actors, beliefs, and contextual events. Based on these references, we constructed analytic tables comparing perceptions of the same actor, motive, event, or context by different interviewees or data sources. When we found major discrepancies, we conducted additional interviews to resolve these differences.

Support and Opposition in States With Performance Funding

In this section, we analyze the advocacy coalitions supporting and opposing the establishment of performance funding in six states.[15] As the advocacy coalition framework holds, these coalitions can span actors both inside and outside government, and they can be fruitfully described in terms of the beliefs that unite a coalition and separate it from others.

Supporters

Performance funding varied considerably in its breadth of support across our six states that established it (see Table 3.3). Florida had the broadest support, with three different advocacy coalitions—encompassing the governor, legislative leaders, state higher education board officials, business, and community college presidents—that supported performance funding. Narrower bases of support were present in Missouri, South Carolina, and Washington in 1997: legislators, the governor (weakly), and either the state coordinating board or business. Illinois, Tennessee, and Washington (in 2007) had the narrowest coalitions: the state community college or higher education board and the heads of individual colleges.

In all six states that established performance funding, state officials were the main proponents. In Florida, South Carolina, and Washington (1997), state legislators, particularly Republicans, were the leaders.[16] Meanwhile, officials of a state higher education coordinating board played the leading role in Illinois, Missouri, Tennessee, and Washington (2007) and a major supporting role in Florida.

TABLE 3.3

Leading Supporters and Their Beliefs in the Six States With Performance Funding

						WA	
Supporters and Their Beliefs	**TN**	**MO**	**FL**	**SC**	**IL**	**1997**	**2007**
Supporter Category							
Legislators		X	X	X		X	
State higher education board officials	X	X	X		X		X
Governor		X	X	X		X	
Local (institutional) officials	X CC & 4-year		X CC		X CC		X CC
Business (direct)			X	X		X	
Business (indirect)		X	X	X		X	
Supporters' Beliefs and Motives							
Need to secure more funds for higher education	X	X	X		X		
Need to increase higher education efficiency		X	X	X			X
Need to increase government efficiency			X	X			X
Need to increase quality of higher education	X	X			X		X
Need to increase accountability				X	X		
Need to increase legitimacy of higher education	X		X		X		
Need to meet labor training needs of business				X			X
Need to preempt bad performance funding	X				X		X

Governors were openly supportive in four states (Florida, Missouri, South Carolina, and Washington), but played a significant role in only the first two states.

Florida provides a good example of legislators playing a leading role, drawing together a coalition in support of performance funding. When the state enacted two performance funding systems (performance incentive funding in 1996[17] and the Workforce Education Development Fund in 1997), state senators were in the lead. Two state senators—a Republican and a Democrat—drew together a group of legislative staffers and state and local community college officials to design the state's two performance funding systems (authors' interviews, FL 1, 7, 9, 10, 19, 20; also see Holcombe, 1997; Tyree & Hellmich, 1995). A community college president noted the leading role played by state Senator George Kirkpatrick (D-Gainesville):

> My sense is that without George Kirkpatrick pushing, prodding, pulling, whatever he had to do, [legislative] staff would not have had near the interest in this topic, nor would we . . . it takes the leadership of an individual oftentimes to make that happen, and Senator Kirkpatrick was the individual who really, really challenged us all to stop talking about performance funding and do something about it.

Tennessee, meanwhile, provides a good example of state higher education coordinating boards leading the effort to establish performance funding, often working in concert with heads of individual public colleges and universities (authors' interviews, TN 1, 2, 3, 4, 5, 8, 10, 12; see also Bogue, 2002; Folger, 1989). A former state-level higher education official stated, "This policy was not shoved down our throats by a legislature. It was not imposed in any way. It was something that [the Tennessee Higher Education Commission] developed from within" (authors' interview, TN 2). Beginning in 1974, the Tennessee Higher Education Commission (THEC) engaged in a 5-year effort to develop a performance funding system (authors' interviews, TN 1, 3, 4, 10; see also Banta, Rudolph, Van Dyke, & Fisher, 1996; Bogue, 1980, 2002; Folger, 1989; Levy, 1986).

As noted, the leading state officials were joined in supporting and even designing performance funding systems by the heads of public colleges and universities in Florida, Illinois, Tennessee, and Washington (in 2007). This support was concentrated in the community colleges.[18] Except in Tennessee, the state universities were much less favorable toward and even opposed to performance funding (see the discussion that follows).

Another important group supportive of performance funding was the business community. Business supported performance funding in a direct and organized fashion in South Carolina, Washington, and Florida. For example, in South Carolina, a group of business leaders lobbied hard for performance funding for higher education, working closely with legislative activists to secure and then design the performance funding system. A consultant familiar with South Carolina noted,

> the business community was very, very heavily pushing for this. This was very close to the days of TQM [total quality management] and performance management, CQI [continuous quality management]. They thought that this was really a step in the direction of modern management and would result in better data systems and more accountable management. So a lot of it was the business community pushing on that.

In addition to its direct participation, business also played an important indirect role. In South Carolina, Washington, Florida, and Missouri, business concerns about government efficiency strongly shaped the politics of performance funding by making performance funding an attractive policy for higher education in the eyes of state officials insofar as it would seem to please business.[19] A prominent state legislator in Missouri noted this indirect power of business:

> You've got [a] group of people looking for money. . . . You've got this maybe coincidental group of conservative business entities who has a resistance to additional funding . . . they want to talk about things like accountability. . . . So you know, performance-based funding was just kind of brought to us by consultants as a way to pacify various conservative groups.

Supporters' Beliefs and Motives

The ACF emphasizes the important role of shared policy core beliefs in uniting the various members of an advocacy coalition (Sabatier & Weible, 2007). The main beliefs tying together the supporters of performance funding were beliefs in the importance of finding new means to secure additional funds for higher education in a time of fiscal stringency and in the importance of increasing the efficiency of government generally and higher education specifically. In addition, there was more scattered belief in the importance of increasing the quality and accountability of higher education, meeting the workforce needs of business, and preventing performance funding from being imposed on higher education without higher education institutions having a hand in designing it.

For legislators, governors, and business, the main belief was in the importance of increasing the efficiency of government and higher education and in the utility of market or business-oriented methods such as performance funding in making government agencies operate more efficiently. This belief can be clearly seen in Florida, Missouri, South Carolina, and Washington. For example, a South Carolina business person who was a prime advocate of performance funding commented,

> We were concerned about the spiraling costs of higher education at that time. . . . The ratio of students to faculty was steadily increasing. There was a huge increase in administration and staff as compared to the number of teachers. . . . I remember they [the universities] talked about how they were short of funding, and I went to one institution and took picture of gold flush valves on the toilets. . . . It's a minor thing, but damn it put the money in the classrooms. The students needed computers and the professors needed computers.

However, for state and local higher education officials who supported performance funding, the driving belief was in the importance of finding new means of securing additional funds for higher education institutions in a time of fiscal stringency. Performance funding particularly recommended itself as a means of securing new funds because it couched requests for new funding in terms that resonated with current concerns about limited government revenues and the utility of businesslike methods in government. For example, a state higher education official in Missouri argued,

> It's not very dramatic to get up and talk about how many library books you have or the input measurements. A person sitting on the appropriations committee [is interested in] how many are graduating and what kind of citizens that you are producing and things of that type. . . . I just thought [performance funding] was a creative way to try to tell our message in a little more measurable way and put a little meat on the message so it wouldn't just be high rhetoric that tells how wonderful it is if you will support higher education and how much of a difference it will make in our economy and economic development and blah, blah, blah.

Opponents

There was discernible opposition to performance funding in four of the six states (Florida, Missouri, South Carolina, and Washington) that established performance funding. Opposition came primarily from the state universities (see Table 3.4) but, except to a degree in Florida and Washington, it was not mobilized. Instead, institutional opposition was primarily expressed by lack of enthusiasm and foot dragging rather than by any sharp attack on performance funding or higher education accountability.

Opponents' Beliefs and Motives

The main beliefs driving opponents were that performance funding was an excuse to keep down the regular state funding for higher education, that it undercut the autonomy of higher education institutions, and that the performance funding programs proposed did not sufficiently recognize different institutional missions. The first belief was evident in Florida, Missouri, and South Carolina,

TABLE 3.4

Opponents and Their Beliefs in the Six States With Performance Funding

Opponents and Their Beliefs	TN	MO	FL	SC	IL	WA
Category of Opponent						
State universities		X Inactive*	X	X inactive		X 1997
Community colleges				X Inactive		
State coordinating board				X Inactive		
Opponents' Beliefs and Motives						
PF undercuts higher education autonomy		X				X 1997
PF excuses cutting regular funding for higher education		X	X	X		
PF system does not distinguish enough among institutions		X				X 1997
PF raises institutional costs		X				
PF does not work well			X	X		
PF will lead to closing institutions				X		
PF duplicates accreditation system						X 1997

* Inactive opposition was expressed in the form of lack of enthusiasm and "foot-dragging" rather than by sharp attacks on performance funding or higher education accountability.

where institutions expressed a fear that performance funding would provide state officials with an excuse to cut back on the regular state funding of higher education. An official of the university board of regents in Florida explained why the board opposed performance funding: "So when you ask, 'Were the universities looking forward to it?' the answer I think is no, because first of all the universities saw it as punitive in nature and as a mechanism whereby there would be excuses to take funding away rather than having funding added."

The belief that performance funding undercut the autonomy of higher education institutions was present in Missouri and Washington. Institutions thought they knew how best to run themselves and resented performance indicators that were perceived as affecting what courses should be offered and how they should be taught. For example, a university official in Missouri observed, "Initially, the University of Missouri opposed it mainly on the basis that . . . the funding was based on a general education competency test and on major field exams. . . . A lot of people felt that we should not let politicians and the legislature get involved in what we teach."

Finally, higher education institutions in Missouri and Washington criticized the performance funding programs in those states as failing to tailor performance indicators to institutional missions. Indicators were perceived as not making sufficient distinctions among research universities, other state four-year institutions, and community colleges. According to a former higher education official in Washington State:

> Institutions were very diverse, very different, had different missions, for example. Our community college system versus the four-year system, and inside the four-year system, there are the research universities and the state universities. So they didn't see that being a very fair comparison. And that internally, it would not be really of much use for them in helping to manage the institution. So there was much resistance to it.

Support and Opposition in States that Did Not Establish Performance Funding

The primary reason for the lack of performance funding in California and Nevada has been the absence of the champions that played important roles in the development of performance funding in the other states that we examined: legislators, the governor, the state higher education coordinating or governing board (absent as a supporter in California, though not Nevada), and state higher education institutions (particularly the community colleges).[20] Lying behind this absence of support for performance funding were certain fundamental characteristics of the California and Nevada state polities, particularly the constitutional autonomy of the University of California and the Nevada Board of Regents, and state political cultures that value the autonomy of higher education and immunity from strong intervention by state elected officials.

Weakness of Support

Nevada

The Nevada Board of Regents raised the idea of performance funding in 2001 and 2004 but was unable to get much support (authors' interviews, NV 1, 3, 4, 7, 10; Nevada Committee to Study the Funding of Higher Education, 2000; Nevada Legislative Committee to Evaluate Higher Education Programs, 2004). In 2001, for example, at the suggestion of the board of regents, the interim Nevada Legislative Committee to Study the Funding of Higher Education recommended unanimously that a performance funding pool be created for the state higher education system, amounting to as much as 2% of the regular state appropriation in additional funding (Nevada Committee to Study the Funding of Higher Education, 2001, p. 40). The governor endorsed this recommendation and submitted a request for $3 million in FY 2002–2003 for performance funding (Nevada Legislative Counsel Bureau, 2001, p. 67). However, this budget proposal got little attention from the legislature and was not enacted (authors' interviews). In explaining the lack of legislative support, a leading observer of the state's higher education policymaking process noted,

> Without doubt this lack of stomach for big change within the legislature was almost certainly affected by Senator William Raggio's disinterest in substantially changing the higher education funding formula. Senator Raggio, who was perhaps the most powerful, effective, and highly regarded member of the Nevada legislature during the last decade, was also considered the father of the existing funding formula and remained steadfastly committed to its sustainability.

California

Meanwhile, the California Postsecondary Education Commission and the system governing boards for the University of California, California State University, and community colleges have not supported performance funding (authors' interviews, CA 1, 2, 10, 11, 12). In fact, a 2010 bill (SB 1143) to create a performance funding system for the state community colleges was supported primarily by a coalition consisting only of some local chambers of commerce (but not the state chamber), a few community colleges, some legislators, and some researchers (authors' interviews, CA 1, 2, 4, 10, 11, 17).

Explanations for the Weak Support in California and Nevada

The ACF posits that "relatively stable" characteristics of a polity—including the "constitutional structure" of the government and "fundamental socio-cultural values" of the society—influence the characteristics of policy subsystems and the advocacy coalitions that form within them (Sabatier, 1993, pp. 20–22; Sabatier & Jenkins-Smith, 1999, pp. 120–122; Sabatier & Weible, 2007, pp. 190–193). We can clearly see these two stable contextual factors at work in causing the weaker support for performance funding in California and Nevada compared with the other six states. In explaining the absence of the usual supporters of performance funding in California and Nevada, we note that both states have a state political culture of higher education immunity from strong intervention by state elected officials. Even when state elected officials have the authority to do so, they are reluctant to impose policies on state higher education institutions (authors' interviews, CA 12, 14, 15, 18, 19; NV 7, 12; see also Hutchens, 2007). This culture is related in turn to the presence in Nevada of a consolidated governing board, and in California of the University of California's constitutional autonomy from much state supervision, the state's celebrated Master Plan,[21] and powerful governing boards for the University of California and the California State University.

California

In California, the Board of Regents of the University of California is constitutionally endowed with "full powers of organization and government" over the institutions under its control (Hutchens, 2007). A state university faculty leader noted:

> Under the California Constitution, the University of California has autonomy, which means that the state legislature cannot tell us to do something. They can request us to do something. They frequently pass legislation that applies to the other segments of public higher education at the California State University System and the community college system. . . . [B]ut they cannot tell the University of California to do something because we are actually an arm of the state and so we're an independent body from the legislature, although we depend upon them for part of our budget.

A leading outside observer of California's higher education policymaking noted,

> Many of the legislators love to hate [the University of California], but they can't take it on. It's such an important institution in the state. It's constitutionally autonomous. . . . California State University System is considered to be the people's university, and it's had exceptionally strong leadership. . . . And part of what has prevented the recent performance funding and budgeting discussions from catching on at the state level is that . . . they [the presidents of UC and CSU] sort of preempted the state thinking about what it should be doing.

In addition to the preceding reasons, California legislators kept silent on performance funding because of term limits. Term limits encourage elected government officials to pick initiatives that will "leave their mark" in a short time and that are not conceptually difficult, unlike performance funding. A community college president commented:

> It's very difficult to have leadership in the legislature on issues that are as complex as this because of the nature of the legislature and term limits and the turnover that we experience in the legislature. It's very difficult for somebody to have enough knowledge and understanding of how this works to be able to persist in moving something like this to the legislature.

Also deterring legislative interest in performance funding may have been the strong Democratic presence in both the California Senate and House for the past 50 years. Across the nation, Democratic state legislators are typically less supportive of performance funding than are Republicans (Dougherty, Natow, Hare, Jones, & Vega, 2011; McLendon et al., 2006).

Nevada

In Nevada, the State Board of Regents also enjoys a substantial degree of autonomy from the rest of state government (authors' interviews, NV 7, 12). A former state executive branch official noted:

> You've got to remember the university system is not part of the executive branch of government except that they are included in our budgeting process. . . . The chancellor is hired by the Board of Regents; the Board of Regents [members] are elected by the public. They can basically tell a governor to pound sand if that's what they intend to do.

Interest in performance funding in Nevada also has been undercut by an economy that is not high skills based and therefore does not demand that higher education play a major role in job preparation and technological innovation (authors' interviews, NV 5, 7, 13). As a university official noted, "The biggest industries in the state being gaming and mining . . . those are sort of industries that don't require an educated labor force." Moreover, interest in pursuing performance funding has been hampered by the limited professionalization of the Nevada legislature, which restricts its capacity to develop complex new policies (authors' interview, NV 4). Nevada has a less professionalized legislature than four of the six states that developed performance funding (see Table 3.1). A university official observed,

> What that really translates to, I think, is a lack of interest on the part of the legislature. It's a really difficult undertaking of the legislative session because it is every two years. And a state that has grown like Topsy and has all kinds of problems that need addressing and there has been a constitutional amendment limiting the length of the biennial session to 120 days, actual days, start to finish. . . . It's a citizen's legislature. . . . These are all people who, when the legislative session is over, go back to work wherever they are.

Opposition

Unlike Nevada, California saw a decided effort to legislatively enact performance funding for community colleges and concerted opposition to this effort. The performance funding provisions of SB 1143 (2010) were vociferously opposed by the California state community college system and the Community College League of California, a group representing community college presidents and trustees; (authors' interviews, CA 1, 2, 10, 11).[22] This vocal and unified opposition by the community colleges was fateful because the support for performance funding was weak. Moreover, as mentioned, community college officials have been among the more important supporters of performance funding in Florida, Illinois, and Washington State (in 2007).

State community college officials and local community college trustees, senior administrators, and faculty were unified in their opposition by the belief that the performance funding system proposed in SB 1143 was punitive and failed to pay enough attention to the unique missions and populations of different community colleges. The bill was viewed as punitive because of a pervading perception that it would greatly reduce funding for the community colleges. Although proponents denied that claim, several opponents argued that the bill would reduce funding by as much as 20% (authors' interviews, CA 1, 2). The second major criticism was that in its original form, SB 1143 would have created incentives for institutions with many disadvantaged students to cut difficult courses and to become more selective in admissions in order to ensure favorable course completion rates (authors' interviews, CA 7, 9, 10, 11). A state community college leader noted,

> One of the big concerns with performance-based funding is the concept of "creaming." You easily can increase rates, transfer rates, graduation rates, if you reduce the denominator. So if you want to go from having a 50% success to a 70% success rate, well you just take fewer of the students that have a statistically lower chance of succeeding. And anybody can tell you exactly who those students are in their campus or colleges.

Coalitions and Policy Solutions in the States With Performance Funding

Having described the advocacy coalitions for and against performance funding in our eight states, we turn to an examination of how the supportive coalitions were formed and how they identified performance funding as a policy solution to be pursued. Policy entrepreneurship theory is very helpful here because it highlights the role of policy entrepreneurs who foster awareness of particular policy problems, offer particular solutions to those problems, and assemble coalitions of advocates to secure the adoption of those solutions (Kingdon, 1995; Mintrom & Norman, 2009; Mintrom & Vergari, 1996).

Coalition Formation

Typically, a well connected and energetic policy entrepreneur catalyzed the formation of an advocacy coalition. In Florida, Senator George Kirkpatrick took the lead in calling meetings in which legislators, state community college officials, and local community college presidents worked out a common understanding of performance funding (authors' interviews, FL 1, 7, 9, 10, 19, 20; also see Holcombe, 1997; Tyree & Hellmich, 1995). As a veteran legislative staffer noted,

> [Senator] George Kirkpatrick . . . kind of got it going with our committee and the education subcommittee of our appropriations committee. The man who was the executive director of the community college system at that time was a former senator. . . and he worked with Kirkpatrick and we got a group of about five community college presidents to work with us. And we would meet periodically, once a month maybe once every two months. And we would sit down and hammer the process out and how we were going to do it and how it was going to work.

In Tennessee, the THEC created a protracted planning process involving university governing board staff members, staff from colleges and universities, academic and financial specialists, and members of the education and finance committees of the state legislature to work out the details of the performance funding system and in the process arrive at a common understanding of its purposes and content (authors' interviews, TN 1, 2, 3, 4, 10; see also Banta et al., 1996; Bogue, 1980, 2002; Bogue & Troutt, 1977; Folger, 1989; Levy, 1986; Serban, 1997). A leading official at the THEC described the process:

> We took five years to pilot test and develop allegiance to it. . . . This policy was not shoved down our throats by a legislature. It was not imposed in any way. It was something that we developed from within. . . . We had actually two planning committees, a state committee that had political board and campus representation, and then we had an external committee representative of policy scholars in higher ed around the country . . . we awarded 10 pilot programs to institutions around the state . . . that gave us a chance to watch campuses develop the criteria and finally we settled on five indicators.

Key to creating an effective advocacy coalition was working out a design for performance funding that would secure the support of the higher education institutions. Hence, the THEC invited the state's public higher education institutions to submit proposals to develop "a set of performance indicators reflecting the identity of an institution" and "provide at least some very tentative thinking about how performance on indicators might be rewarded through the appropriation process" (quoted in Levy, 1986). The commission received proposals from 19 of the 21 public institutions and approved 12 of them. As the pilot projects were implemented, THEC staff visited the campuses to observe and provide advice for the projects (Bogue, 1980; Bogue & Troutt, 1977; Levy). In the process, the commission staff learned of the importance to institutions of performance indicators that were tailored to institutional missions. The commission also found out how important it was to institutions to have a funding system that would not lead institutions to receive, if they performed poorly, less funding than they would on an enrollment basis (Bogue & Troutt).

Similarly, in Illinois, the Illinois Community College Board used an advisory committee on a performance-based incentive system as the vehicle to mobilize the support of local community colleges. The committee was composed of local community college officials (presidents and other administrators, faculty members, and students) and several staff members of the Illinois Community College Board (including two vice presidents) and was advised by several prominent national consultants. In 1997, the committee held three hearings across the state and received feedback from community college presidents on its draft report. This feedback shaped the details of the performance funding system that was recommended in the committee's final report in May 1998, including what performance indicators should be used, how they should be measured, and what weights should be attached to each (Illinois Community College Board, 1998a).

In Missouri, the Commissioner of Higher Education, Charles McClain (1989–1995), was the key policy entrepreneur (Serban, 1997; Stein, 2002; Stein & Fajen, 1995). In 1991, McClain testified before the legislature, urging the importance of linking funding with results (Stein, 2002). He also served on the Missouri Business and Education Partnership Commission, which in its 1991 report called for performance funding (Aguillard, 1991a; Missouri Business and Education Partnership Commission, 1991). Finally, McClain led the Missouri Coordinating Board for Higher Education to form in 1992 the Task Force on Critical Choices, composed of chairs of all public college and university boards, to work out the details of a performance funding system (Missouri Coordinating Board for Higher Education, 1992; Naughton, 2004; Serban, 1997; Stein, 2002; Stein & Fajen, 1995).

South Carolina provides a cautionary note on the process of coalition formation and the costs of failing to secure the support of higher education institutions. The state's performance funding proposal emerged out of a joint legislative committee (JLC) that was given the task of conducting a comprehensive review of public higher education. The committee comprised eight legislators and four business leaders and was chaired by Senator Nikki Setzler (D-Aiken-Lexington-Saluda Counties), the main advocate for performance funding in the state. Members of the higher education community were not allowed to formally participate; they could attend meetings of the JLC but could not speak unless called on (authors' interviews, SC 3, 14, 21; see also Trombley, 1998). The proposal that emerged out of the JLC pleased the legislators and business people involved but not the higher education institutions. Although they were not vocal in their opposition, fearing political backlash, they were quite unhappy with the performance funding plan. This lack of support was a major cause of the later abandonment of performance funding in South Carolina (Dougherty et al., 2011).

Identification of Policy Solutions

Any given problem can be solved in a wide variety of ways. What shapes which potential solutions get careful consideration, whereas others are ignored?

Feasibility and Acceptability Criteria

Policy entrepreneurship theory stresses that the policy solutions that get serious attention from the policy community typically have to meet conditions of technical feasibility, budgetary reality, values acceptability, and lack of backlash from government officials and the public (Kingdon, 1995). For several of our states, the sense of technical feasibility was secured by the seeming success of other states—particularly Tennessee—with performance funding. As we discuss next, this points to evidence of the impact of cross-state diffusion of policy ideas.

Budgetary acceptability was secured by keeping the cost of performance funding down. Typically, it involved only a small increment to state funding for higher education, usually about 1%–2% percent (see Table 3.1). Sometimes the performance funding program did not involve any new funds but rather reserved a certain portion of existing funds and subjected their disbursement to performance outcomes. This was the case in South Carolina, Washington (1997–1999), and Florida (the Workforce Development Education Fund).[23]

Finally, values acceptability was secured by the fact that performance funding was tied to the neoliberal discourse that government operations—including higher education—should be increasingly subject to market control (Osborne & Gaebler, 1992; Slaughter & Leslie, 1997). Making this connection all the more attractive was the growing ascendancy of Republicans in state legislatures. Compared with Democrats, they typically were stronger supporters of performance funding and other businesslike solutions to government management, and the greater the Republican share of state legislative seats, the greater the likelihood that a state would enact performance funding

(McLendon et al., 2006). A state higher education official in Washington described the thinking of leading Republican advocates of performance funding in that state:

> They were believers in accountability in general. Not solely in higher education, but across the spectrum of governmental activities, and funding. They were proponents of smaller government, and fiscal restraint. And I think they were also believers in the notion that we tend to get more of what the funding structure responds to, so what is incentivized and measured and funded, we tend to get more of and less of other things. . . . And there was a lot of talk, in the early 90s and going forward, about reinventing and reengineering government and focusing on outcomes and data related to that as opposed to inputs.

Policy Diffusion and Policy Learning

Policy entrepreneurs in our six states drew on a variety of sources for the idea of performance funding and for particular features of it. Table 3.5 indicates these various sources as they were mentioned in our interviews or cited in state documents. We distinguish between external sources, as highlighted by policy diffusion theory (F. S. Berry & Berry, 2007; McLendon et al., 2005), and internal sources, such as the policy learning highlighted by the Advocacy Coalition Framework (Jenkins-Smith & Sabatier, 1993; Sabatier & Weible, 2007).

One of the key external sources highlighted by policy diffusion theory is the example of other states. We frequently came across references to the experiences of other states—particularly Tennessee and Florida—in interviews or documents (authors' interviews, FL 1a, 5, 14; IL 3, 5, 7, 8, 12; SC 2, 3; and WA 17, 22).[24] For example, when the idea of performance funding was first broached in Illinois, it was justified by reference to the experiences of other states:

> As society calls for greater accountability of the public and private sectors, many states indicate they are studying how to include an element in the budgetary process for performance-based funding. Florida, Tennessee, Missouri, and Ohio already have a component in their funding formulas for performance-based funding. (Illinois Council of Community College Presidents, 1995, pp. 17, 25)

South Carolina's example also influenced developments in Illinois, but in a cautionary way. As a leading Illinois state community college official noted:

> South Carolina stands out because [performance funding] was enacted there by their legislature, and they had, I don't remember 26, or 56 [laughter] or so . . . indicators, and you know, many of them, particularly at that time, were just impossible. Many of them were determined, as I recall, by the legislature itself, rather than by the educational system. And so, I think that was one of the driving forces: that we felt that if we stepped forward with it, then we were able to determine what those measures were going to be, and that they were ones that we felt comfortable with having the data, or being able to eventually have the data to be able to support it.

TABLE 3.5

Sources of Ideas for Performance Funding

						WA	
Idea Sources	**TN**	**MO**	**FL**	**SC**	**IL**	**1997**	**2007**
External Sources							
Other states			X	X	X	X	
State policy organizations			X	X			
Outside experts	X	X	X		X		X
Internal Sources							
Policy learning	X		X	X			X

State government associations comprised another external source of policy ideas (McLendon et al., 2005). Interviewees in two states (Florida and South Carolina)[25] mentioned that activists were influenced by personal contact with, and publications produced by, organizations such as the Southern Regional Education Board and the National Conference of State Legislatures that held discussions about performance funding or even recommended it (authors' interviews, FL 2a, 6b, 8, 14, 18; MO 1a, 10; SC 4, 6, 9, 14; WA 2; also see F. S. Berry & Flowers, 1999).[26] A high-ranking state higher education official in Florida noted:

> [Southern] legislators get together two or three times a year . . . and then there is a national meeting of state legislators. They share good and bad ideas, so it becomes sort of a copycat thing. So I can remember [in the] late 80s, the Florida legislature coming back from one of these meetings saying we need to put in place a performance funding system.

A third external source consisted of outside consultants, who were influential in at least five of our states. For example, the deliberations of the Illinois Advisory Committee on a Performance Based Incentive System were aided by an outside consultant who worked closely with the director of the advisory committee. A member of that committee noted:

> We brought in [a consultant] . . . she was working with several states at the time . . . and she was terrific. . . . We developed a set of principles to start with. . . . I think her experience in other states helped us in formulating those principles.

Furthermore, the National Center for Higher Education Management Systems (NCHEMS) was influential in Missouri. A Missouri state official noted that "NCHEMS historically had a consulting relationship on and off in Missouri." NCHEMS consultants evaluated an early proposal for the state's performance funding system, helped frame the effort to get state approval, and later did a midcourse evaluation of the system (NCHEMS, 2004; authors' interviews, MO 1a, 2, 10; also see FL 8 and WA 2).

In addition to the external sources of ideas mentioned earlier, performance funding programs were also shaped by internal sources of ideas, which is the focus of the "policy-oriented learning" described by the ACF (Jenkins-Smith & Sabatier, 1993; Sabatier & Weible, 2007). Among the four states where we saw evidence of policy learning,[27] Florida is particularly striking for the steady evolution of thinking about accountability on the part of state policy makers (F. S. Berry & Flowers, 1999; Bradley & Flowers, 2001; Easterling, 1999; Office of Program Policy Analysis and Government Accountability, 1997; Wright et al., 2002; Yancey, 2002). In 1977, the legislature mandated (Ch. 77-352, § 4) that every budget request include workload and other performance indicators (Easterling, 1999). In the 1980s, Democratic governor Bob Graham and other state officials started calling for public colleges and universities to publicly report their performance (authors' interview, FL 14). Moreover, the state passed legislation in 1984 requiring vocational programs to demonstrate a training-related placement rate of 70% in order to ensure continued funding (Pfeiffer, 1998). By 1991, the state developed a performance reporting system (Florida Statutes, 1991, § 240.324) that mandated certain specific indicators that later became the core of the performance funding systems established in 1996 and 1997 (Bell, 2005; Florida State Board for Community Colleges, 1998; Wright et al, 2002; Yancey, 2002).

Agenda Setting: Policy Windows and External Shocks

The policy entrepreneurship perspective stresses that a primary role of policy entrepreneurs is seizing political openings to get policy solutions onto the government's decision agenda (Kingdon, 1995; Mintrom & Norman, 2009; Mintrom & Vergari, 1996). These political openings—known as policy windows for the policy entrepreneurship approach (Kingdon, 1995) and external shocks for the ACF (Sabatier & Weible, 2007)—take such forms as changes in which party controls government, spillovers from other policy subsystems, major shifts in popular opinion, or dramatic intensification of problems. But external shocks do not necessarily cause political change. They must be recognized and interpreted by policy entrepreneurs who then frame them for policy makers in such a way as to draw attention to problems and policies of concern to the policy entrepreneurs. Table 3.6 indicates the incidence of political openings across our six states.

Change in Party Control of Government

In all the states except Tennessee, a change in control of the government, principally involving Republican capture of another house of the legislature or of the governorship, provided an important opening for advancing the idea of performance funding. For example, in Washington state, the 1996 elections brought Republican control of the House of Representatives. The new Republican majority in the state legislature (like the Republican majority that came to power in the U.S. Congress in 1994) favored less government spending, lower taxes, and greater government accountability (authors' interviews, WA 5, 9, 23; also see Modie, 1996; Shukovsky, 1997). A higher education insider described the Republican controlled legislature of the mid-1990s: "[We] . . . had a lot of conversation at the time in the state about how government should run like a business and a lot of businesses were embracing these kinds of performance metrics."

Changes in Popular Opinion

Another political opening involved the spread of an antitax mood in Florida, Missouri, Tennessee, and Washington that made it expedient to defend more spending for higher education by tying it to increased accountability. For example, in Missouri, a constitutional amendment passed by referendum in 1980 (the Hancock Amendment) put a limit on how much the state can raise taxes (Hembree, 2004). This antitax mood was then underscored by the failure of a referendum proposal (Proposition B) in 1991 to sharply increase spending on both higher education and K–12 education by raising taxes (Aguillard, 1991b, 1991c, 1991d; Serban, 1997; Stein, 2002; Stein & Fajen, 1995). The failure of Proposition B by a 2-to-1 margin of the general electorate led state officials and many higher education officials to conclude that higher education could not expect to get additional state funding unless it could strikingly demonstrate that it was improving its efficiency and

TABLE 3.6

Political Openings in the Six States With Performance Funding

						WA	
Policy Opening	**TN**	**MO**	**FL**	**SC**	**IL**	**1997**	**2007**
Change in party control of legislature			X GOP	X GOP	X GOP	X GOP	
Change in party control of governorship		X Dem		X GOP			
Growing antitax mood	X	X	X			X	
Spillover from other policy subsystems	X						X
Economic recession			X				
Economic prosperity							X

effectiveness. The interim chancellor of St. Louis Community College and a former supervisor of St. Louis County argued,

> Missouri citizens are convinced that they are not getting full value for their educational tax dollars; and until Missouri education gets its act together and our citizens become convinced that we are doing our job efficiently and effectively, we will not work our way out of our present predicament, as I see it. (cited in Thomson, 1991)

This perception provided a political opening for performance funding proposals.

Policy Spillover

A third political opening was provided by spillover from other policy subsystems. In Tennessee and Washington, accountability efforts in K–12 provided a rationale for performance funding in higher education. For example, a former Tennessee state-level higher education official explained, "State legislators were starting to impose required assessments and measurements on the [elementary and secondary] schools with very little involvement and engagement from people on the firing line, teachers. We didn't want that to happen [to higher education]." Thus, the Higher Education Commission took it upon itself to develop an accountability system that would be acceptable to the higher education community.

Summary and Conclusions

This article examines what forces have driven the development of performance funding and how those forces differ across states. This question has been prompted by the fact that, despite the great interest in performance funding over the last 30 years, only half of all states have enacted performance funding for higher education. The article examined both the origins of state performance funding in six states (Florida, Illinois, Missouri, South Carolina, Tennessee, and Washington) and the lack of such development in another two (California and Nevada).

Our explanation for the rise of performance funding in six states (and its lack in another two) agrees with several elements of the prevailing perspective on the origins of performance funding, but we also provide new findings. We did find that many of the actors and motives cited by the prevailing perspective operated in our six states, including state legislators (particularly Republicans), governors, and business people pursuing performance funding in the name of greater effectiveness and efficiency for higher education. However, we also found that the prevailing perspective misses the key advocacy role of state higher education coordinating boards and individual higher education institutions (particularly community colleges) that pursued performance funding to secure new funds in an era of greater tax resistance and criticism of the effectiveness and efficiency of higher education. And it misses the opposition of state universities to performance funding, which was the case in four states.

We further move beyond the prevailing explanation by identifying features of the politics of performance funding that the prevailing perspective missed but are highlighted by the application of the ACF, policy entrepreneurship perspective, and policy diffusion theory. One feature is how the supporters of performance funding constituted advocacy coalitions that shared common beliefs and acted in concert. Another is that those coalitions were constructed by policy entrepreneurs who found ideological common ground among different groups, identified policies that those groups could support, and took advantage of political openings to put performance funding onto the decision agenda of state elected officials. Ideas for these policies came from both policy learning based on previous policy-making in a state and external sources such as programs in other states,[28] discussions by cross-state professional associations, and suggestions from circuit-riding external consultants. Finally, we point to the role of basic social-cultural values and state government's constitutional and legal framework in explaining the absence of performance funding in California and Nevada.

Policy Implications

Our research indicates that performance funding is most likely to be established when it secures the support not only of state elected officials and, less so, of the business community, but also of higher education officials. In five of the six states where it was established, higher education officials (particularly state board officials) were important supporters (and in four cases, the main policy entrepreneurs). Moreover, in one of the two states where performance funding was not established, state and local higher education officials were key opponents. Furthermore, even when performance funding did pass but higher education institutions were opposed, as in Washington and South Carolina, this opposition later proved fateful. The opposition of higher education officials is a major reason that these states later abandoned performance funding (Dougherty et al., 2011, 2012). This finding indicates that advocates of performance funding have to think about carefully cultivating the support of higher education officials at both the state and local levels. Their participation in designing a proposed performance funding program can greatly aid its odds of being established and partially immunize it against later criticism by higher education institutions.

One of the surprising features of the politics of performance funding in the states examined is how little concern has been expressed about the possible impacts of performance funding on equality of higher education opportunity. Except in California, we saw little discussion in our case study states about how performance funding might enhance (or damage) access to and success in higher education for underserved populations, whether low-income students, students of color, or older students. Performance accountability systems could enhance the prospects of such students by making access to and success in college for disadvantaged students important performance indicators (Dougherty, Hare, & Natow, 2009). Conversely, performance funding could damage the prospects of these students to the degree that it rewards higher course completion and graduation rates but does not bar colleges from raising both rates simply by becoming more selective in admissions (Dougherty & Hong, 2006; Dougherty & Reddy, 2011). We are struck that this danger was brought up only in California because it carries an important policy implication. Performance funding advocates should be making every possible effort to enlist the support of equity oriented actors—particularly representatives of the minority and low-income communities—to ensure that performance funding reflects their concerns in its mission and its measures. Doing so will not only make performance funding more likely to serve egalitarian goals but also provide an important source of support when it comes under fiscal or political pressure (Dougherty et al., 2012).

An important issue that may arise in the future politics of performance funding is the question of its effectiveness. Until now, much of the state-level discussion about the impacts of performance funding has been largely favorable and surprisingly unmarked by extensive consideration of research evidence on the impacts of performance funding.[29] At it happens, the still quite limited research literature on these impacts raises questions about whether performance funding does indeed lead to significant changes in institutional performance, and, even if it does, whether it also causes significant unintended consequences such as weakened academic standards and lesser institutional commitment to access for disadvantaged students (Dougherty & Hong, 2006; Dougherty & Reddy, 2011). These issues have not been prominently raised in state-level political decision-making on performance funding (with the notable exception of California). However, one wonders whether attention to and controversy over the effectiveness and unintended impacts of performance funding may arise in the future. Such discussion might strongly affect the likelihood of enacting performance funding and, in any case, the shape it will take.[30]

Research Implications

Our case studies allowed us to examine, in depth and across a wide variety of states, the actors, motives, and political forces involved in state enactment of performance funding. Yet there is room for more research. We excluded from our analysis states with performance funding programs that are quite narrow, using only one performance indicator. It would be useful to have studies of the political origins of those programs to determine if they are substantially different from those of the states we studied. In addition, as new states enact performance funding programs, it will be important to analyze whether their political origins involve advocacy coalitions, motives, and agenda-setting conditions somewhat different from the ones we found. The bad economic times that states face now may well spell different political origins for performance funding.

Our research also carries important implications for the policy theories on which it draws. When used together, the advocacy coalition, policy entrepreneurship, and policy diffusion perspectives powerfully illuminate key features of the political origins (or nonorigins) of performance funding in our eight states. However, our research also points to certain limitations in these perspectives and suggests ways in which they can be further developed. The ACF and the policy entrepreneurship perspective focus on the direct exercise of political power by government officials and mobilized interest groups and ignore indirect, nonparticipatory exercises of power (Dougherty, 1994; Gaventa, 1980; Lukes, 2005; Murphy, 1982). Yet, as we have seen, even when business has not directly called for performance funding for higher education, it has nonetheless exerted considerable indirect influence over its development by advocating greater accountability of government agencies through the application of market controls and business methods. Even when higher education and performance funding have not been the objects of business attention, this business call for greater government accountability has provided an ideological context that makes performance funding for higher education an attractive option for government officials.[31] In addition, our findings suggest that policy diffusion theory should focus not just on the influence of other states, particularly adjacent states. Policy entrepreneurs and policy makers clearly attend to the examples of distant states, not just neighboring states, as demonstrated by the impact on Illinois's policy-making of the example of performance funding in Florida, Tennessee, and South Carolina. Moreover, policy entrepreneurs and policy makers are also shaped by their involvement in cross-state and national professional associations and policy organizations (Balla, 2001; McLendon et al., 2005).[32]

Acknowledgments

We thank the Lumina Foundation for its financial support of this research. The views expressed here are solely the authors'. Thanks to the following for their comments on various parts of this work: Brenda Albright, Trudy Bers, E. Grady Bogue, Steven Brint, Patrick Callan, L. Fred Carter, Edward Cisek, Stephen DesJardins, William Doyle, Peter Ewell, Charles Fitzsimons, David Longanecker, Virginia McMillan, Jane Nichols, Michael Shealy, Nancy Shulock, Dorothy Shipps, Robert B. Stein, Beth Stevens, Patricia Windham, and Jan Yoshiwara. We also wish to thank the anonymous reviewers for *Teachers College Record*. Needless to say, all remaining errors are the responsibility of the authors. We also are grateful to Wendy Schwartz, Betsy Yoon, and Amy Mazzariello for their able editing of this paper and its antecedents.

Notes

1. See Mintrom and Vergari (1996); Meijerink (2005); and Dougherty, Nienhusser, and Vega (2010) for other examples of analyses that combine these theories, particularly the advocacy coalition framework and the policy entrepreneurship perspective.
2. This perspective has its foundation in Kingdon's (1995) "multiple streams" theory and Roberts and King's (1996) policy entrepreneurship approach. Though drawing heavily on Kingdon, Mintrom did not follow him in stressing the independence of the three streams of problems (recognition of problems as public issues), policies (generation of solutions that are politically acceptable), and politics (political opportunities for action). Mintrom analyzed how policy entrepreneurs often sit astride these streams, simultaneously promoting particular problems, offering certain solutions to them, and watching for and even creating political openings to set the agenda for governmental action on those problems and solutions (compare Mintrom & Vergari, 1996, with Kingdon, 1995; and Zahariadis, 2007).
3. These mechanisms resemble the mimetic, coercive, and normative forms of isomorphism identified by DiMaggio and Powell (1983/1991) in their study of the dynamics of organizational change within organizational fields.

4. We excluded a number of states in order to have a good regional dispersion among our cases. For example, we did not select North Carolina because we did not want to overbalance our analysis with states from the Southeast. We selected Florida and South Carolina instead for reasons stated in the main text. Similarly, we excluded Arkansas because we had a greater interest in two other nearby states (Missouri and Illinois) and omitted Oregon because we had selected Washington. The main text provides our reasons for selecting Missouri, Illinois, and Washington.
5. We excluded several states in order to have a good dispersion among our cases in the timing of performance funding enactment. For example, Arkansas and Colorado began their performance funding systems in the early 1990s, but we already had good representation for that period (Florida and Missouri). Minnesota and New Jersey established their systems in the late 1990s, but we had good representation at that time as well (Illinois, South Carolina, and Washington).
6. We excluded a number of states because their performance funding systems were quite narrow: Kentucky (whose 2000–2006 system focused only on retention); Ohio (whose Success Challenge system, established in 1995, only rewarded universities for the number of students graduating in four years); and Texas (whose system, established in 2007, only rewards universities for baccalaureate graduates) (authors' interviews; Kentucky Council on Postsecondary Education, 2002; Moden & Williford, 2002).
7. This is now becoming more common. In 2009 and 2010, respectively, Ohio and Tennessee moved to put their entire state formula-based funding for higher education on a performance basis (Petrick, 2010; Tennessee Higher Education Commission, 2011; see also Dougherty & Natow, 2011).
8. Florida established two performance funding systems: Performance-Based Budgeting, which was suspended in 2008, and the Workforce Development Education Fund, which ended in 2002 (Dougherty et al., 2012).
9. Washington dropped performance funding in 1999 but then reestablished it for community colleges alone 8 years later in 2007 (Dougherty et al., 2011).
10. These are all variables that have been found to be associated with differences in state policy-making (Berry & Berry, 2007; McLendon et al., 2006). However, we should note that McLendon et al. (2006) found that these factors do not help predict interstate differences in adoption of performance funding.
11. SB 1143 originally included a provision for performance funding on the basis of course completions. However, the version of the bill that finally passed did not have any provisions for performance funding and only called for the board of governors of the California community colleges to "adopt a plan for promoting and improving student success within the California Community Colleges and . . . establish a taskforce to examine best practices within the community colleges and effective models throughout the nation for accomplishing student success" (California Legislative Counsel, 2010).
12. California has a much less centralized governance system, with three system boards for the University of California, California State University, and community colleges, and a weak state coordinating board (McGuinness, 2003).
13. Some of our interviews in Florida and Illinois were conducted as part of a study funded by the Sloan Foundation (Dougherty & Hong, 2006). We thank the foundation for its support of that research.
14. A few were not transcribed because either the interviewee asked to not be recorded, or our tape recorder failed. In these cases, we relied on handwritten notes.
15. Our discussion here is synoptic, focusing on general patterns across the states case studied. For full detail on each of the cases discussed, see Dougherty et al. (2011).
16. Conservative Democrats also tended to support performance funding, but on the whole, Republicans were more supportive (see McLendon et al., 2006).
17. The performance incentive funding system was later folded into the performance-based budgeting system established in 1994 (Wright, Dallet, & Copa, 2002).
18. The three states in which community colleges actively supported the enactment of performance funding (Florida, Illinois, and Washington in 2007) are also characterized by more liberal state political cultures, more professionalized state legislatures, larger populations, and higher incomes. It is possible that all these factors predispose community colleges to be more active politically and to be better able to get the ear of state legislators.
19. For more on this indirect, nonparticipatory form of business power, see Dougherty (1994).
20. For a more comprehensive discussion of California and Nevada, see Dougherty et al. (2011).
21. Issued in 1960, the Master Plan for Higher Education assigned distinct roles to the University of California, the California State University system, and the community colleges (Douglass, 2010).
22. This may be changing. There is evidence that California state and local community college leaders are considering the development of a performance funding system, although one less sweeping than that proposed in SB 1143 (authors' interviews, CA 10, 11).

23. Ironically, although this "hold back" feature made it easier to enact performance programs in those states, it also played an important role in the later repudiation of those programs (Dougherty et al., 2012).
24. The four states where references were made to the experiences of other states (Florida, Illinois, South Carolina, and Washington in 2007) tended to have, with the exception of South Carolina, more professionalized legislatures than the other states in our sample.
25. It is noteworthy that both states were the top two among our six states in the proportion of state funding for higher education that is allocated on the basis of performance. Their ranking raises the questions of whether the influence of national policy organizations emboldens states to adopt more radical forms of performance funding.
26. This finding accords with the suggestion of McLendon et al. (2005) that state governmental associations may be important conduits of interstate communication about the "acceptability, desirability, and feasibility of new policy ideas" (p. 388; see also Balla, 2001).
27. Among our sample of six states, these four states tend to be higher in the proportion of state higher education funds allocated on the basis of performance and lower in the degree of party competition and of centralized higher education governance structures.
28. Our respondents were mentioning not just neighboring states but states across the country. Hence, our finding does not necessarily disagree with the finding of McLendon et al. (2006) about the lack of significant impact of policy developments in neighboring states on adoption of performance funding.
29. In that sense, the politics of performance funding has involved a very strong aspect of symbolic element in which expressive goals may be as important as instrumental goals (Edelman, 1964; Yanow, 1996).
30. The current recession might provoke an increase in performance funding enactments as states try to cope with declining revenues by securing greater efficiencies from higher education. Certainly, this announced aim has accompanied recent efforts in various states to establish performance funding (Harnisch, 2011). However, the recession may also impede the establishment of performance funding insofar as higher education institutions oppose it as coming at the expense of regular state funding. This sentiment played an important role in the demise of several performance funding programs during the recession of the early 2000s (Dougherty et al., 2012).
31. The advocacy coalition framework does have the makings of an analysis of this nonparticipatory, third-dimensional power in its acknowledgement of the powerful role of basic sociocultural values in shaping political subsystems. However, this possibility is hamstrung by the fact that the ACF does not acknowledge that those sociocultural values may not be consensually held or in the general interest, but rather may enshrine the values of particular sociopolitical groups and therefore advance their interests.
32. It would be very useful to have the policy diffusion literature enriched by many studies on the policy positions and political influence of national educational policy organizations such as the National Conference of State Legislatures, National Governors Association, Education Commission of the States, Southern Regional Education Board, Western Interstate Commission on Higher Education, National Center of Higher Education Management Systems, State Higher Education Executive Officers, and Council of Chief State School Officers.

References

Aguillard, D. (1991a, January 16). State universities panel urges 50% funding increase. *St. Louis Post-Dispatch*, p. 8D.

Aguillard, D. (1991b, May 18). Tax hike to go before voters: $385 million plan passed to aid colleges, schools. *St. Louis Post-Dispatch*, p. 1A.

Aguillard, D. (1991c, May 19). Education bill goes beyond finances, officials say. *St. Louis Post-Dispatch*, p. 8A.

Aguillard, D. (1991d, May 29). "Missions," money could make colleges model for U.S. *St. Louis Post-Dispatch*, p. 1C.

Alexander, F. K. (2000). The changing face of accountability: Monitoring and assessing institutional performance in higher education. *Journal of Higher Education*, 71(4), 411–431.

Balla, S. J. (2001). Interstate professional associations and the diffusion of policy innovations. *American Politics Research*, 29(3), 221–245.

Banta, T. W., Rudolph, L. B., Van Dyke, J., & Fisher, H. S. (1996). Performance funding comes of age in Tennessee. *Journal of Higher Education*, 67(1), 23–45.

Bell, D. (2005). *Changing organizational stories: The effects of performance-based funding on three community colleges in Florida* (Doctoral dissertation). Available from ProQuest Dissertations and Theses database. (UMI No. 3210509)

Berry, F. S., & Berry, W. D. (2007). Innovation and diffusion models in policy research. In P. A. Sabatier (Ed.), *Theories of the policy process* (2nd ed., pp. 223–260). Boulder, CO: Westview Press.

Berry, F. S., & Flowers, G. (1999). Public entrepreneurs in the policy process: Performance-based budgeting reform in Florida. *Journal of Public Budgeting, Accounting, and Financial Management*, 11(4), 578–617.

Berry, W. D., Ringquist, E. J., Fording, R. C., & Hanson, R. L. (1998). Measuring citizen and government ideology in the American states, 1960–1993. *American Journal of Political Science*, 42(1), 327–348.

Beyle, T. (2004). The governors. In V. Gray & R. L. Hanson (Eds.), *Politics in the American states* (pp. 194–231). Washington, DC: CQ Press.

Bibby, J. F., & Holbrook, T. M. (2004). Parties and elections. In V. Gray & R. L. Hanson (Eds.), *Politics in the American states* (pp. 62–99). Washington, DC: CQ Press.

Bogue, E. G. (1980, March). *Recognizing and rewarding instructional performance with state fiscal policy*. Paper presented at the annual meeting of the Association for the Study of Higher Education, Washington, DC.

Bogue, E. G. (2002). Twenty years of performance funding in Tennessee: A case study of policy intent and effectiveness. In J. C. Burke (Ed.), *Funding public colleges and universities: Popularity, problems, and prospects* (pp. 85–105). Albany, NY: Rockefeller Institute Press.

Bogue, E. G., & Troutt, W. E. (1977). *Allocation of state funds on a performance criterion: Acting on the possible while awaiting perfection*. Paper presented at the Association for Institutional Research Forum.

Bradley, R. B., & Flowers, G. (2001). Getting to results in Florida. In D. W. Forsythe (Ed.), *Quicker, better, cheaper? Managing performance in American government* (pp. 365–416). Albany, NY: Rockefeller Institute Press.

Breneman, D. W., & Finney, J. E. (1997). The changing landscape: Higher education finance in the 1990s. In P. M. Callan & J. E. Finney (Eds., with K. R. Bracco & W. R. Doyle), *Public and private financing of higher education* (pp. 30–59). Phoenix, AZ: American Council of Education and Oryx Press.

Burke, J. C. (Ed.) (2002a). *Funding public colleges and universities: Popularity, problems, and prospects*. Albany, NY: SUNY Press.

Burke, J. C. (2002b). Performance funding in South Carolina: From fringe to mainstream. In J. C. Burke (Ed.), *Funding public colleges and universities: Popularity, problems, and prospects* (pp. 195–219). Albany, NY: Rockefeller Institute Press.

Burke, J. C., & Minassians, H. (2003). *Performance reporting: "Real" accountability or "accountability lite": Seventh annual survey 2003*. Albany: State University of New York, Nelson A. Rockefeller Institute of Government.

Business Roundtable. (1999). *Transforming education policy: Assessing 10 years of progress in the states*. Washington, DC: Author.

California Legislative Counsel. (2010). SB 1143. Retrieved from http://www.leginfo.ca.gov/cgi-bin/postquery?bill_number=sb_1143&sess=PREV&house=B&author=liu

Callan, P. M. (2002). *Coping with recession* (Report No. 02-2). San Jose, CA: National Center for Public Policy and Higher Education.

DiMaggio, P. J., & Powell, W. W. (1991). The iron cage revisited: Institutional isomorphism and collective rationality in organizational fields. *American Sociological Review*, 48, 147–160. (Original work published 1983)

Dougherty, K. J. (1994). *The contradictory college: The conflicting origins, impacts, and futures of the community college*. Albany: State University of New York Press.

Dougherty, K. J., Hare, R., & Natow, R. S. (2009, November). *Performance accountability systems for community colleges: Lessons for the voluntary framework of accountability for community colleges*. Report to the College Board. New York, NY: Columbia University, Teachers College, Community College Research Center. Retrieved from http://ccrc.tc.columbia.edu/Publication.asp?UID=728

Dougherty, K. J., & Hong, E. (2006). Performance accountability as imperfect panacea: The community college experience. In T. Bailey & V. S. Morest (Eds.), *Defending the community college equity agenda* (pp. 51–86). Baltimore, MD: Johns Hopkins University Press.

Dougherty, K. J., & Natow, R. S. (2011). *Incremental and non-incremental change in long-lasting systems of performance funding: The cases of Florida and Tennessee*. New York, NY: Columbia University, Teachers College, Community College Research Center.

Dougherty, K. J., Natow, R. S., Hare, R. J., Jones, S., & Vega, B. E. (2011). *The politics of performance funding in eight states: Origins, demise, and change*. New York, NY: Columbia University, Teachers College, Community College Research Center. Retrieved from http://ccrc.tc.columbia.edu/Publication.asp?UID=875

Dougherty, K. J., Natow, R. S., Hare, R. J., & Vega, B. E. (2010). *The political origins of state-level performance funding for higher education: The cases of Florida, Illinois, Missouri, South Carolina, Tennessee, and Washington* (CCRC Working Paper No. 22). New York, NY: Community College Research Center, Teachers College, Columbia University.

Dougherty, K. J., Natow, R. S., & Vega, B. E. (2012). Popular but unstable: Explaining why state performance funding systems in the United States often do not persist. *Teachers College Record, 114*(3). Retrieved from http://www.tcrecord.org ID Number: 16313

Dougherty, K. J., Nienhusser, H. K., & Vega, B. E. (2010). Undocumented immigrants and state higher education policy: The contrasting politics of in-state tuition eligibility in Texas and Arizona. *Review of Higher Education*, 34(1), 123–173.

Dougherty, K. J., & Reddy, V. (2011). *The impacts of state performance funding systems on higher education institutions: Literature review and policy responses*. New York, NY: Columbia University, Teachers College, Community College Research Center. http://ccrc.tc.columbia.edu/Publication.asp?uid=1004

Dougherty, K. J., & Reid, M. (2007). *Fifty states of Achieving the Dream: State policies to enhance access to and success in community colleges across the United States*. New York, NY: Columbia University, Teachers College, Community College Research Center. Retrieved from http://ccrc.tc.columbia.edu/Publication.asp?uid=504

Douglass, J. (2010, May). *From chaos to order and back? A revisionist reflection on the California master plan for higher education @50 and thoughts about its future* (Research and Occasional Paper Series 7.10). Berkeley: University of California, Center for the Study of Higher Education.

Easterling, C. N. (1999). Performance budgeting in Florida: To muddle or not to muddle, that is the question. *Journal of Public Budgeting, Accounting, and Financial Management*, 11(4), 559–577.

Edelman, M. (1964). *The symbolic uses of politics*. Urbana: University of Illinois Press.

Erikson, R. S., Wright, G. C., & McIver, J. P. (2005). *Public opinion in the states: A quarter century of change and stability*. New York, NY: Columbia University, Department of Government.

Florida State Board for Community Colleges. (1998). *The Florida community college accountability plan at year four: A report for South Florida Community College*. Tallahassee: Author.

Folger, J. (1989, November). Designing state incentive programs that work in higher education. In R. O. Berdahl & B. A. Holland (Eds.), *Developing state fiscal incentives to improve higher education: Proceedings from a national invitational conference* (pp. 44–66). Denver, CO, and College Park, MD: National Center for Postsecondary Governance and Finance.

Fosler, R. S. (1990). *The business role in state education reform*. Washington, DC: Business Roundtable.

Gaventa, J. (1980). *Power and powerlessness in an Appalachian valley*. Champaign: University of Illinois Press.

Gray, V. (2004). The socioeconomic and political context of states. In V. Gray & R. L. Hanson (Eds.), *Politics in the American states* (8th ed., pp. 1–30). Washington, DC: CQ Press.

Hamm, K. E., & Moncrief, G. F. (2004). Legislative politics in the states. In V. Gray & R. L. Hanson (Eds.), *Politics in the American states* (pp. 157–193). Washington, DC: CQ Press.

Harnisch, T. L. (2011). *Performance-based funding: A re-emerging strategy in public higher education financing*. Higher Education Policy Brief. Washington, DC: American Association of State Colleges and Universities.

Hembree, R. (2004). *The Hancock Amendment: Missouri's tax limitation measure*. Report 49-2004. Columbia: University of Missouri, Truman School of Public Affairs, Missouri Legislative Academy.

Holcombe, W. N. (1997). Florida's community colleges: Reflections and projections. *Community College Journal of Research and Practice*, 21, 351–363.

Hutchens, N. (2007). *A comparative legal analysis of state constitutional autonomy provisions for public colleges and universities* (Unpublished doctoral dissertation). University of Arizona, Tucson, AZ.

Illinois Community College Board. (1998a, May). *Report of the advisory committee on a performance based incentive system*. Springfield: Author.

Illinois Council of Community College Presidents. (1995). *Operational funding of community colleges in Illinois: A new look*. Springfield: Illinois Community College Board.

Jenkins-Smith, H. C., & Sabatier, P. A. (1993). The dynamics of policy-oriented learning. In P. A. Sabatier & H. C. Jenkins-Smith (Eds.), *Policy change and learning: An advocacy coalition approach* (pp. 41–56). Boulder, CO: Westview Press.

Kane, T. J., Orszag, P. R., & Gunter, D. L. (2003). *State fiscal constraints and higher education spending: The role of Medicaid and the business cycle.* Washington, DC: Brookings Institution.

Kentucky Council on Postsecondary Education. (2002). *Enrollment growth and retention program guidelines.* Lexington: Author.

Kingdon, J. (1995). *Agendas, alternatives, and public policies* (2nd ed.). New York, NY: Longman.

Layzell, D. (1999). Linking performance to funding outcomes at the state level for public institutions of higher education. *Research in Higher Education, 40*(2), 233–246.

Levy, R. A. (1986). Development of performance funding criteria by the Tennessee Higher Education Commission. In T. W. Banta (Ed.), *Performance funding in higher education: A critical analysis of Tennessee's experience* (pp. 13–26). Boulder, CO: National Center for Higher Education Management Systems. (ERIC Document Reproduction Service No. ED310655)

Lukes, S. (2005). *Power: A radical view* (2nd ed.) New York, NY: Palgrave Macmillan.

McGuinness, A. C. (1994). *State postsecondary education structures handbook, 1994.* Denver, CO: Education Commission of the States. (ERIC Document Reproduction Service No. ED375787)

McGuinness, A. C. (2003). *Models of postsecondary education coordination and governance in the States.* Denver, CO: Education Commission of the States.

McLendon, M. K. (2003). State governance reform of higher education: Patterns, trends, and theories of the public policy process. In J. Smart (Ed.), *Higher education: Handbook of theory and research* (Vol. 18, pp. 57–144). New York, NY: Kluwer.

McLendon, M. K., Hearn, J. C., & Deaton, R. (2006). Called to account: Analyzing the origins and spread of state performance-accountability policies for higher education. *Educational Evaluation and Policy Analysis, 28*(1), 1–24.

McLendon, M. K., Heller, D. E., & Young, S. P. (2005). State postsecondary policy innovation: Politics, competition, and the interstate migration of policy ideas. *Journal of Higher Education, 76*(4), 363–400.

Meijerink, S. (2005, December). Understanding policy stability and change. *Journal of European Public Policy, 12*, 1060–1077.

Mintrom, M., & Norman, P. (2009). Policy entrepreneurship and policy change. *Policy Studies Journal, 37*(4), 649–667.

Mintrom, M., & Vergari, S. (1996). Advocacy coalitions, policy entrepreneurs, and policy changes. *Policy Studies Journal, 24*(3), 420–434.

Missouri Business and Education Partnership Commission. (1991). *Report of the Missouri Business and Education Partnership Commission.* Jefferson City: Author.

Missouri Coordinating Board for Higher Education, Task Force on Critical Choices for Higher Education. (1992). *Suggested statewide public policy initiatives and goals: A report to the Coordinating Board for Higher Education.* Jefferson City: Missouri Coordinating Board for Higher Education.

Moden, G. O., & Williford, A. M. (2002). Ohio's challenge: A clash of performance funding and base budgeting. In J. C. Burke (Ed.), *Funding public colleges and universities for performance* (pp. 169–194). Albany, NY: State University of New York Press.

Modie, N. (1996, November 6). Both houses of the legislature headed for Republican control. *Seattle-Post Intelligencer*, p. A9.

Murphy, R. (1982). Power and authority in the sociology of education. *Theory and Society*, 11, 179–203.

National Center for Higher Education Management Systems. (2004). *Report to the Nevada Committee to Evaluate Higher Education Programs.* Boulder, CO: Author.

Naughton, B. A. (2004). *The efficacy of state higher education accountability programs* (Doctoral dissertation). Retrieved from ProQuest Dissertations and Theses database. (Digital Dissertations AAT 3145567)

Nevada Committee to Study the Funding of Higher Education. (2000). *Minutes for meeting of June 8, 2000.* Carson City, NV: Legislative Counsel Bureau. Retrieved from http://www.leg.state.nv.us/Session/70th1999/Interim/Studies/EdFunding/Minutes/IM-EdFunding-20000608-2384.html

Nevada Committee to Study the Funding of Higher Education. (2001). *Report* (Bulletin No. 01-4). Carson City, NV: Legislative Counsel Bureau. Retrieved from http://www.leg.state.nv.us/Session/70th1999/interim/Studies/EdFunding/Overview.htm

Nevada Legislative Committee to Evaluate Higher Education Programs. (2004, June 17). *Minutes of the Committee to Evaluate Higher Education Programs* (Assembly Bill 203-2003 Session). Carson City, NV: Legislative Counsel Bureau.

Nevada Legislative Counsel Bureau. (2001). *2001 fiscal report*. Carson City: Author. Retrieved from http://www.leg.state.nv.us/Division/fiscal/Fiscal%20Report/2001/2001FiscalReport.cfm

Office of Program Policy Analysis and Government Accountability. (1997). *Performance based program budgeting in context: History and comparison* (OPPAGA 96-077A). Tallahassee, FL: Author.

Osborne, D. E., & Gaebler, T. (1992). *Reinventing government: How entrepreneurial government is transforming the public sector*. New York, NY: Plume.

Petrick, R. (2010, February 9). *Funding based on course completions: The Ohio model (v. 1.0)*. Presentation to the Texas Higher Education Coordinating Board, Austin, TX.

Pfeiffer, J. J. (1998). From performance reporting to performance-based funding: Florida's experiences in workforce development performance measurement. *New Directions for Community Colleges*, 104, 17–28.

Racine, D. P. (2006). Reliable effectiveness: A theory of sustaining and replicating worthwhile innovation. *Administration and Policy in Mental Health and Mental Health Services Research*, 33, 356–387.

Rhoades, G., & Sporn, B. (2002). Quality assurance in Europe and the U.S.: Professional and political economic framing of higher education policy. *Higher Education*, 43(3), 355–390.

Roberts, N. C., & King, P. J. (1996). *Transforming public policy: Dynamics of policy entrepreneurship and innovation*. San Francisco, CA: Jossey-Bass.

Ruppert, S. (1995). Roots and realities of state-level performance indicator systems. *New Directions for Higher Education*, 91, 11–23.

Sabatier, P. A. (1993). Policy change over a decade or more. In P. A. Sabatier & H. Jenkins-Smith (Eds.), *Policy change and learning: An advocacy coalition approach* (pp. 13–40). Boulder, CO: Westview Press.

Sabatier, P. A., & Jenkins-Smith, H. C. (1999). The advocacy coalition framework: An assessment. In P. A. Sabatier (Ed.), *Theories of the policy process* (pp. 117–166). Boulder, CO: Westview Press.

Sabatier, P. A., & Weible, C. (2007). The advocacy coalition framework: Innovations and clarifications. In P. A. Sabatier (Ed.), *Theories of the policy process* (2nd ed., pp. 189–222). Boulder, CO: Westview Press.

Scheirer, M. A. (2005). Is sustainability possible? A review and commentary on empirical studies of program sustainability. *American Journal of Evaluation*, 26(3), 320–347.

Serban, A. M. (1997). *Performance funding for higher education: A comparative analysis* (Doctoral dissertation). State University of New York at Albany. Retrieved from ProQuest Dissertations and Theses database. (UMI No. 9809292)

Shediac-Rizkallah, M. C., & Bone, L. R. (1998). Planning for the sustainability of community- based health programs: Conceptual frameworks and future directions for research, practice, and policy. *Health Education Research*, 13(1), 87–108.

Shukovsky, P. (1997, April 24). State support for schools falls. *Seattle Post-Intelligencer*, p. B1. Slaughter, S., & Leslie, L. (1997). *Academic capitalism*. Baltimore, MD: Johns Hopkins University Press.

Stein, R. B. (2002). Integrating budget, assessment and accountability policies: Missouri's experiment with performance funding. In J. C. Burke (Ed.), *Funding public colleges and universities for performance: Popularity, problems, and prospects* (pp. 107–132). Albany: State University of New York Press,

Stein, R. B., & Fajen, A. L. (1995). Missouri's Funding for Results initiative. *New Directions for Higher Education, 1995*(1), 77–90.

Tennessee Higher Education Commission. (2011). *Outcomes based formula explanation*. Nashville: Author. Retrieved from http://www.state.tn.us/thec/complete_college_tn/ccta_files/outcomes_based_ff/Outcomes_Based_Formula_Explanation.pdf

Thomson, S. C. (1991, December 13). Ashcroft still wants parts of Proposition B. *St. Louis Post-Dispatch*, p. 10A.

Trombley, W. (1998). Performance-based budgeting: South Carolina's new plan mired in detail and confusion. *National Cross Talk*, 6(1).

Tyree, L. W., & Hellmich, D. M. (1995). Florida's continuing accountability experiment. *Community College Journal*, 65(7), 16–20.

United States Bureau of the Census. (2005). *Statistical abstract of the United States, 2004-2005*. Washington, DC: Government Printing Office.

Waddock, S. (1994). *Business and education reform: The fourth wave* (Report Number 1091-94-RR). New York, NY: The Conference Board.

Walker, J. L. (1969). The diffusion of innovations among the American states. *American Political Science Review*, 63(3), 880–899.

Wright, D. L., Dallet, P. H., & Copa, J. C. (2002). Ready, fire, aim: Performance funding policies for postsecondary education in Florida. In J. C. Burke (Ed.), *Funding public colleges and universities: Popularity, problems, and prospects* (pp. 137–168). Albany, NY: SUNY Press.

Yancey, G. W. (2002). *Fiscal equity change in the Florida community college system during the first five years after the implementation of performance funding* (Doctoral dissertation). Available from ProQuest Dissertations and Theses database. (UMI No. 3084064)

Yanow, D. (1996). *How does a policy mean? Interpreting policy and organizational actions*. Washington, DC: Georgetown University Press.

Zahariadis, N. (2007). The multiple streams perspective: Structure, limitations, prospects. In P. Sabatier (Ed.), *Theories of the policy process* (2nd ed., pp. 65–92). Boulder, CO: Westview Press.

Zumeta, W. (2001). Public policy and accountability in higher education: Lessons from the past and present for the new millennium. In D. E. Heller (Ed.), *The states and public higher education policy: Affordability, access, and accountability* (pp. 155–197). Baltimore, MD: Johns Hopkins University Press.

CHAPTER 4

FINANCIAL AID POLICY: LESSONS FROM RESEARCH

SUSAN DYNARSKI AND JUDITH SCOTT-CLAYTON

In the nearly fifty years since the adoption of the Higher Education Act of 1965, financial aid programs have grown in scale, expanded in scope, and multiplied in form. As a result, financial aid has become the norm among college enrollees. Aid now flows not only to traditional college students but also to part-time students, older students, and students who never graduated from high school. Today aid is available not only to low-income students but also to middle- and even high-income families, in the form of grants, subsidized loans, and tax credits. The increasing size and complexity of the nation's student aid system has generated questions about effectiveness, heightened confusion among students and parents, and raised concerns about how program rules may interact. In this article, Susan Dynarski and Judith Scott-Clayton review what is known, and just as important, what is not known, about how well various student aid programs work.

The evidence, the authors write, clearly shows that lowering costs can improve college access and completion. But this general rule is not without exception. First, they note, the complexity of program eligibility and delivery appears to moderate the impact of aid on college enrollment and persistence after enrollment. Second, for students who have already decided to enroll, grants that tie financial aid to academic achievement appear to boost college outcomes such as persistence more than do grants with no strings attached. Third, compared with grant aid, relatively little rigorous research has been conducted on the effectiveness of student loans. The paucity of evidence on student loans is particularly problematic both because they represent a large share of student aid overall and because their low cost (relative to grant aid) makes them an attractive option for policy makers.

Future research is likely to focus on several issues: the importance of program design and delivery, whether there are unanticipated interactions between programs, and to what extent program effects vary across different types of students. The results of this evidence will be critical, the authors say, as politicians look for ways to control spending.

On November 8, 1965, President Lyndon Johnson signed into law the Higher Education Act of 1965, which firmly established the federal government as the primary provider of financial aid for college. In his remarks that day at Southwestern Texas State College, his alma mater, President Johnson said, "To thousands of young men and women, this act means the path of knowledge is open to all that have the determination to walk it.... It means that a high school senior anywhere in this great land of ours can apply to any college or any university in any of the 50 states and not be turned away because his family is poor."[1]

In the nearly fifty years that have passed since the Higher Education Act was adopted, college enrollment has expanded dramatically and average aid per student has grown even faster (Figure 4.1).[2] Full-time-equivalent undergraduate enrollment more than doubled, from about 6.2 million in 1971–72 to 14.2 million in 2010–11, while average aid per student more than tripled, from $3,437 to $12,455 (in constant 2010 dollars).[3] The increase in aid per student is driven primarily by the expanding reach of the federal programs, which now flow to a more diverse range of students than was anticipated when the programs were conceived. The early programs were squarely focused on "traditional" students—young, recent high school graduates enrolled in college on a

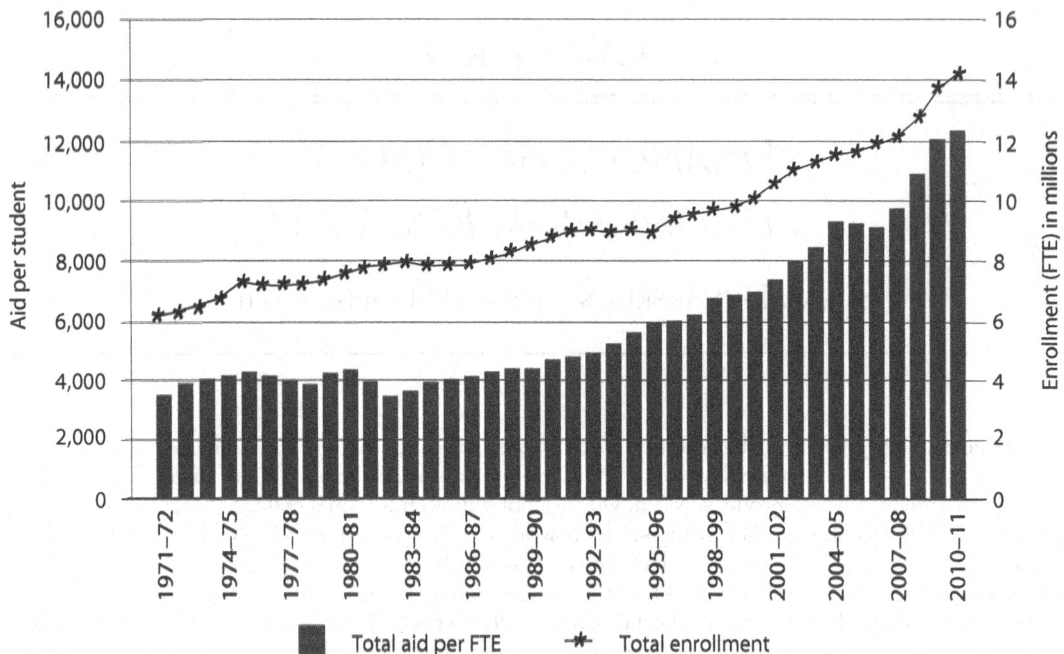

Figure 4.1 Trends in undergraduate enrollment and aid per student, 1971–2010.

Source: College Board, *Trends in Student Aid* 2011, table 3A (1990–91 though 2010–11), and authors' calculations from table 3 (1971–72 through 1989–90).

Notes: Enrollment is measured in full-time equivalent (FTE) undergraduates. Aid is per undergraduate FTE student (including nonrecipients) and includes undergraduate grant aid from all sources, loans from all sources, federal work-study, and federal tax benefits.

full-time basis. Federal aid was also focused on students with fairly low incomes. Government aid for students was delivered primarily by the U.S. Department of Education.[4]

On all of these dimensions, student aid has undergone a transformation. Aid now flows not only to traditional college students, but also to part-time students, older students, and students without a traditional high school diploma. Today, aid is available not only to low-income students but also to middle-class (and even high-income) families, in the form of subsidized loans and tax credits. And government aid is provided not only by the U.S. Department of Education but also by the U.S. Department of Treasury and by state governments. Several other forms of government support, including work-study programs, and private aid are also available. Altogether, aid to undergraduate students totaled nearly $190 billion in the 2010–11 school year, with the majority of aid ($147 billion) coming from government sources.

The growing magnitude of government expenditures on student aid has justified growing interest in its effectiveness. Policy makers and taxpayers want to know the returns on their enormous investment: does student aid really influence educational outcomes? Or does it simply subsidize students for doing what they would have done anyway? The increasing variety in the forms taken by aid, in the students who receive it, and in the agents who deliver it has made a simple answer to the question of aid effectiveness increasingly difficult to give.

Forty years ago, the main question asked about student aid was "Does it work?"—with "it" generally meaning Pell Grants and "work" generally referring to increases in initial college enrollment. Now, to understand the effectiveness of student aid, one needs to consider the wide array of grants, loans, and tax benefits administered by multiple agencies and levels of government. But to the extent that the form, design, and delivery of aid matter—as all evidence indicates they do—it may be difficult to extrapolate the effects of one program to another. Similarly, as college enrollments have risen, policy makers increasingly ask not just whether aid increases initial enrollment, but also whether it increases persistence, performance, and completion, as well as whether it affects choices about where to attend, what to study, and what to do after graduation. Thus, asking whether aid "works" now depends on both the program and the outcome examined. In some cases, researchers do not have definitive answers, but can only make educated guesses about effectiveness based on related evidence from similar programs.

Moreover, students today are a much more heterogeneous group than they were forty years ago, and the effect of a given program may vary by student characteristics such as income, age, and family status. Whether aid "works" may depend on who is receiving the aid and what outcomes they aim to achieve through postsecondary education. Coaxing an eighteen-year-old high school graduate into enrolling full-time at a four-year college is a very different task from encouraging a thirty-five-year-old displaced worker to enroll in a part-time certificate program to strengthen her job skills. The same form of federal aid—Pell Grants—funds both types of schooling for both populations, yet it may well be that Pell Grants are more effective in one case than the other. Where the evidence allows, we discuss heterogeneity in the effects of programs across groups of students who differ in age, income, or educational background, but in most cases the available evidence focuses only on average program effects.

Finally, the explosion in the variety and reach of student aid implies that the environment in which students and families make their decisions is increasingly complex. With dozens of tax and aid programs available, two-thirds of students are now eligible for some sort of discount on their college costs.[5] For these students, the net price of college (tuition and fees less any grant aid) differs from its sticker price. In fact, despite steadily rising tuition prices, net prices were *lower* in 2010–2011 than they were in 2005–2006.[6] It is tuition prices, however, that make headlines, in part because they are so much easier to communicate than net price. With the proliferation of aid and tax programs, families cannot easily know in advance how much college costs. Misperceptions about the real cost may be particularly consequential for first-generation college students, whose families have no experience with the aid system. Research shows that students are often unaware of the aid for which they are eligible and that they estimate tuition costs to be two to three times higher than the true levels.[7] If families do not know about a price subsidy, they cannot respond to it.

In this article, we describe the evolution of student aid over the past few decades, focusing on the largest programs and providing a broad overview of the rest. We then discuss whether these programs increase college enrollment, persistence, and completion (the central measures of effectiveness about which we have the most evidence), noting impacts on other outcomes where available. We first spend some time laying out the methodological challenges facing researchers in this arena, in part to explain why the evidence is sometimes so thin. We then offer some lessons about student aid policy that we believe are supported by the existing evidence. We close with a discussion of the remaining gaps in knowledge about the effectiveness of student aid.

The Changing Landscape of Financial Aid

The major programs that subsidize college costs for undergraduates are listed in table 4.1, together with the totals for each program (adjusted for inflation and expressed in 2010 dollars) for selected years between 1990 and 2010. The federal loan programs and the Pell Grant were the two largest sources of aid for college throughout this period. Loans grew more rapidly than grants: loan volume was five times higher in 2010 than in 1990, while Pell volume was four times higher. Grants from colleges were the third largest source of aid; they more than tripled over this period. The education tax benefits came on the scene in the late 1990s and are now a major source of funding for college. The reasons for the particularly large increase in the federal aid programs between 2005–06 and 2010–11 are discussed in detail in the next section.

The federal programs established in Title IV of the Higher Education Act of 1965 are known collectively as "Title IV aid" and include the precursors to Pell Grants, Stafford Loans, and Federal Work-Study. Title IV aid also includes a variety of smaller programs that have waxed and waned over the years. The following discussion focuses on the largest sources of government aid shown in table 4.1: Pell Grants, federal loans, education tax benefits, and state grant programs.

TABLE 4.1

Support for Undergraduate Students by Source, 1990–91 to 2010–11 (Billions of 2010 Constant Dollars)

Year	1990–91	2000–01	2010–11
Federal programs			
Total federal grants	$10.9	$13.5	$47.8
Pell Grants	8.3	10.0	34.8
Veterans	1.1	1.9	10.0
Other grants	1.5	1.6	3.1
Total federal loans	$14.0	$29.9	$70.0
Subsidized Stafford	10.3	14.4	28.4
Unsubsidized Stafford	0.0	9.7	30.3
PLUS (parent) loans	1.4	4.7	10.4
Other federal loans	2.3	1.2	0.8
Federal work-study	$1.2	$1.1	$1.0
Education tax credits	0.0	4.9	18.8
State grant programs	$3.0	$5.9	$9.1
Grants from colleges	8.1	15.3	29.7
Private and employer grants	2.6	5.1	6.6
Nonfederal loans	0.0	4.4	6.5
Total support for undergraduate students	$39.8	$80.1	$189.6
Total nonloan aid	$25.7	$45.7	$113.1

Source: Education Tax Credit data from Internal Revenue Service, *Statistics of Income* (2000, 2005, 2010), Table 3.3. All other components from College Board, Trends in Student Aid 2011, Table 1A.

Notes: Components may not sum to totals because of rounding. Federal loan dollars reflect disbursements beginning in 1995–96. Before then, the data reflect gross loan commitments. Figures for 2010–11 are preliminary estimates.

The Pell Grant

The Higher Education Act of 1965 established the Educational Opportunity Grant Program, which allocated funds directly to colleges that committed to identifying and recruiting students with "exceptional financial need."[8] In 1972, the program was split into the Supplemental Educational Opportunity Grant (SEOG) program, a relatively small program that delivered funds directly to colleges, and the Basic Educational Opportunity Grant (BEOG) program, which delivered funds directly to students. The BEOG program, renamed the Pell Grant in 1980 after Senator Claiborne Pell of Rhode Island, expanded eligibility to students attending part-time, as well as to those in vocational education or community colleges. Between 1972 and 1992, college enrollments rose by 44 percent, but the number of Pell Grant recipients grew twentyfold as a result of these more generous eligibility criteria.[9] Many of these new Pell recipients were adults returning to school: the proportion of recipients classified as independent (age twenty-four or older, married, or with children of their own) grew over this period from just 13 percent to 60 percent, where it remains today.[10] As noted in the article in this issue by Sandy Baum and her colleagues, the proportion of Pell recipients who are over age thirty has tripled over the past thirty years, from 8 percent in the late 1970s to 24 percent in 2009–10.[11]

While there is no explicit income limit on Pell receipt, the vast majority of recipients have family incomes below $50,000, which in 2010 was slightly above the median of U.S. household incomes.[12] The definition of who is "needy" under the Pell rules has occasionally shifted, sweeping into Pell eligibility students from the middle of the income distribution. Some of these shifts resulted from explicit efforts to open the program to a wider range of incomes: the Middle Income Student Assistance Act of 1978, as its name suggests, expanded eligibility for Pell Grants to middle-income families. More subtly, changes in the maximum Pell Grant award (the usual focus of legislative debates over Title IV funding) mechanically change the Pell phase-out range as well.[13] That means that under the current formula, it is impossible to increase the average grant without also expanding eligibility further up the income distribution. This dynamic has been clear in recent years, when the Pell maximum rose substantially, from $4,689 in 2008–09 to $5,550 in 2010–11 (in constant 2010 dollars). Over the same period, during which median family incomes were dropping, the share of Pell recipients with income over $50,000 rose from 6 percent to 9 percent.[14]

Figure 4.2 shows changes over time in the number of Pell recipients and the average Pell award among recipients. Adjusting for inflation, the average Pell Grant was flat or decreasing for most of the period between 1976–77 and 1995–96, but large increases since 2008 have raised the average Pell award to a historic high of $3,828. Even these large recent increases, however, have barely kept pace with rising tuition prices: the "purchasing power" of the Pell actually declined slightly from 33 percent of public four-year tuition in 2008–09 to 32 percent in 2011–12.[15]

In 2008, legislation was passed that increased the maximum grant and expanded summer awards. These changes, combined with higher college enrollments and weak economic conditions that pushed more families into Pell eligibility, drove Pell expenditures to record levels. Pell volume increased by more than 90 percent between 2008–09 and 2010–11, with the number of recipients

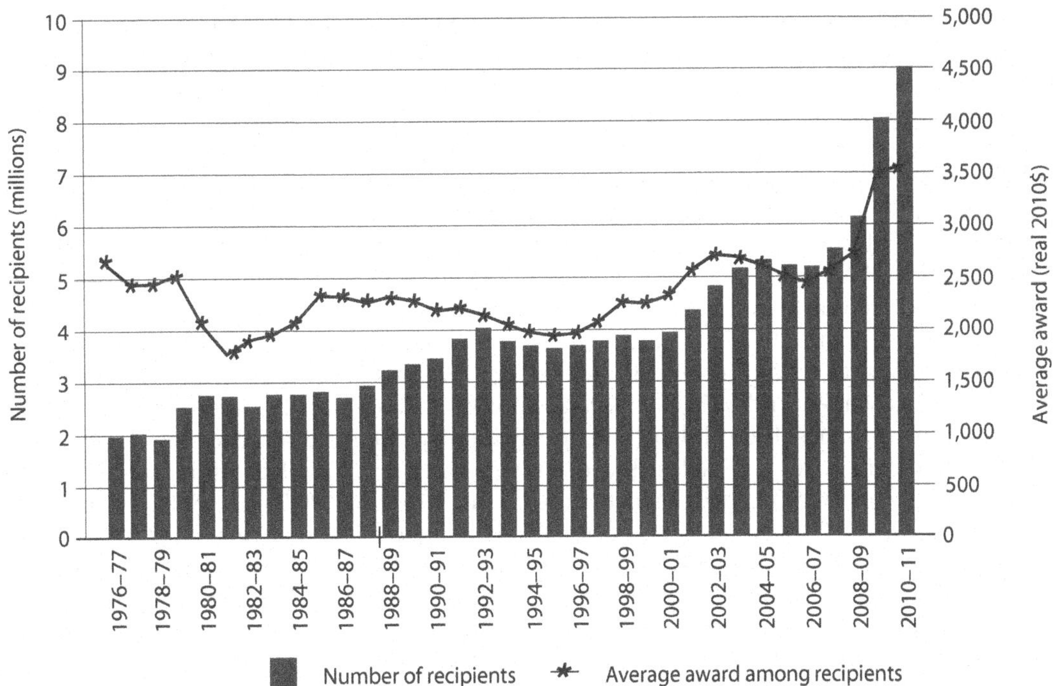

Figure 4.2 Number of Pell recipients and average aid award, 1976–77 to 2010–11.

Source: College Board, *Trends in Student Aid* (2011), figure 134A, and U.S. Department of Education, *Pell End of Year Report*, 2009–10 (2011).

Notes: Enrollment is measured in full-time equivalent (FTE) undergraduates. Aid is per undergraduate FTE student (including nonrecipients) and includes undergraduate grant aid from all sources, loans from all sources, federal work-study, and federal tax benefits. Aid is measured in 2010 constant dollars.

rising from 6.2 million to 9.1 million and the average grant among recipients increasing from $2,945 to $3,828.[16]

Federal Loans

The Stafford Loan, the largest student loan program, was named after Vermont senator and education advocate Robert T. Stafford in 1988, but it dates to 1965, when the guaranteed student loan program was introduced. In the original program, the government paid the interest on these loans during college, loans were limited to low-income students, and loan volume was only a third of grant volume. The first spike in loan volume followed enactment of the Middle Income Student Assistance Act of 1978, which opened eligibility for subsidized loans to all undergraduates, regardless of need.[17] Loan volume exploded, as families seeking cheap credit—interest rates on mortgages hovered around 15 percent at the time—flooded into the student loan program. The need requirement on subsidized loans was reinstated in 1981 to contain ballooning costs.

Changes to the loan program in 1992 resulted in a sharp uptick in volume and unabated growth over the following twenty years. In 1992, an unsubsidized version of Stafford Loans was created, open to all students regardless of need. The government does not pay the interest on unsubsidized Stafford Loans while students are enrolled, but both subsidized and unsubsidized Stafford Loans offer interest rates, forbearance protections, and flexible repayment options that make them substantially more appealing than private student loans. Dependent students are allowed to borrow $31,000 in federal loans over the course of their undergraduate career. For those deemed sufficiently needy, $23,000 of this total can take the form of subsidized loans. A student cannot take out this full amount in a single year; there are also annual limits on borrowing (of $2,625 to $7,500 depending upon the student's undergraduate standing).

Starting in 1992, parents also were allowed to borrow up to the full cost of attendance, including room and board for full-time students, through PLUS loans, which had been established in 1980 (before 1992, these loans were capped at $4,000). These loans are open to the parents of all college students, regardless of need. Unlike Stafford Loans, PLUS loans require a credit check. Parents are responsible for loan payments, which begin immediately. Over half of college loans initiated each year are now through the unsubsidized Stafford Loan and PLUS programs.[18]

Rising levels of student debt have raised fears among some commentators of a "higher education bubble" that may be exposing taxpayers to higher-than-recognized default risks, akin to the housing bubble that preceded the financial crisis of 2008.[19] The aggregate volume of outstanding student loans (both federal and private) surpassed $1 trillion in late 2011. This figure, which has received considerable press attention, nonetheless should be viewed in the context of an expanding population of current and former college students.[20] On a per-student basis, average loan debt at graduation has been virtually flat over the past decade.[21] Between 2000 and 2009, the share of graduates with loans has remained stable at 65 percent, and the average cumulative debt among borrowers has held steady at around $25,000.[22] Ninety percent of students who receive bachelor's degrees graduate with less than $40,000 of debt, and approximately one-third borrow nothing at all.[23]

Compared with other graduates, those with more than $40,000 in undergraduate debt are 20 percentage points more likely to have attended schools costing $20,000 or more a year (including room and board), and 20 percentage points less likely to have attended a public institution. Ten percent attended a private for-profit institution, compared with only 1 percent of their lesser-borrowing peers. News articles tend to focus on the most extreme cases, such as graduates with $100,000 in debt. However, only 0.1 percent of college entrants, and 0.3 percent of bachelor's degree recipients, accumulate more than $100,000 in undergraduate student debt.[24]

Tax Benefits for Education

In the late 1990s, the federal government began using the tax code to subsidize college costs. The largest and most expensive of these programs were the Hope and Lifetime Learning Credits, which allowed families of college students to offset their educational costs with tax credits of up to $1,500 a year.[25] These programs primarily benefited middle- and upper-income families, for several reasons.

The credits were not refundable, meaning that low-income families with no tax liability would not benefit even if they otherwise qualified for the credit. Further, eligible tuition expenses were reduced by any grant aid; as a result, a student who attended the typical two-year college and was poor enough to receive the maximum Pell Grant received no tax credit. Finally, the income cut-offs for eligibility for the subsidies were set so high that less than 10 percent of filing households exceeded them.[26]

In 2009, the Hope Credit was expanded and renamed the American Opportunity Tax Credit (AOTC).[27] The maximum benefit was raised to $2,500, with $1,000 refundable. Eligible expenses were expanded to include course-related books and supplies. Families were allowed to claim the credit for four years of undergraduate education instead of only two. The maximum benefit under the Lifetime Learning Credit was also raised, to $2,000. Spending on the AOTC was nearly $19 billion in 2010, compared with $35 billion for the Pell program.[28] A key disadvantage of the tax credits is that they are not delivered at the time of enrollment, but up to eighteen months later, when a family files its taxes for the relevant calendar year. This delay may limit the ability of the tax benefit to influence enrollment or persistence, because low-income individuals who most need the assistance may not be able to wait that long for the money.

Other tax breaks are available for current or former college students. Since 2002, families not claiming one of the education tax credits have been able to deduct up to $4,000 in tuition fees from income (even if they do not itemize). Although the benefit officially expired at the end of 2011, it has been retroactively reinstated in the past and may yet be resurrected.[29] Additionally, up to $2,500 in interest on student loans is deductible from taxable income, for households with incomes up to $75,000 (single) or $150,000 (married). The federal Coverdell Education Savings Account and state 529 programs allow annual, after-tax contributions (up to $2,000 a year for the Coverdell; the more generous contribution limits and state tax treatment of the 529 vary by state); earnings on the accounts are untaxed if withdrawals are used for educational expenses.[30] The benefits of these accounts rise sharply with income, because those with the highest marginal tax rates have the most capital income to shelter from taxation.[31] These additional deductions have little to no value for low-income families, who often take the standard deduction rather than itemize and who face relatively low marginal tax rates.

Finally, while children are generally considered independent for tax purposes after age eighteen, the age limit is extended to twenty-three if the child is enrolled in school. This tax break allows families to save up to several thousand dollars a year for each child enrolled in college because parents can claim a dependent exemption for the student (thus reducing their taxable income) or qualify for the Earned Income Tax Credit (a refundable credit for low-income families).[32]

State Grant Programs

Traditionally, states have helped to keep college affordable by subsidizing public colleges, which in turn charge lower tuition prices than they would without these subsidies. In recent years, state support for higher education has decreased and shifted from subsidizing institutions toward subsidizing students. In 2010–11, state and local appropriations per full-time-equivalent (FTE) student at public colleges averaged $7,200, down 13 percent from $8,300 in 1980–81 (figures in constant 2010 dollars).[33] Just in the past decade, the share of institutional revenues coming from state and local appropriations has fallen from 56 percent to 42 percent at public, four-year colleges.[34] One potential explanation is that states strapped by costs of prisons, Medicaid, and K-12 education see postsecondary education as the one place they can shift cost to users.[35]

In addition to charging artificially low prices to all students, states also offer scholarships to individual students. States have more than doubled their expenditures on grant aid since 1980 (from $285 to $640 per FTE).[36] Still, the increases in state grant aid have not been large enough to make up for the decline in institutional subsidies. Most of these state grants are small-scale programs. But, beginning in the early 1990s, more than a dozen states established broad-based "merit aid" programs, the best-known of which is Georgia's HOPE scholarship. These programs typically award full tuition and fees at state public universities (or in some cases, an equivalent voucher to attend a private school) to residents who maintain a minimum grade point average (GPA) in high school and college. Many require a GPA of 3.0, not a particularly high threshold—in 1999, 40 percent of high school seniors met this standard.[37] These programs now represent more than a quarter of all state grant aid nationwide and are the primary source of state aid in several states.

How Do Students Apply for Aid?

To apply for Title IV aid, students must complete the Free Application for Federal Student Aid (FAFSA). This form, which most students now complete online, is also required for many state and institutional aid programs (some institutions also require more detailed additional information). The form requests information about students' own income and savings, their parents' income and savings, their receipt of various other types of governmental assistance, and the amounts of other income and liabilities (such as education tax credits claimed, child support paid or received, and other "money received or paid on your behalf").[38] This information is based upon the preceding tax year (for example, 2011 for students entering college during the 2012–13 academic year), meaning that high school students would not be able to file a FAFSA until at least January of their senior year, or after taxes are filed.

Once the FAFSA is filed, the information is processed under one of eight formulas, depending upon family income, whether a student is classified as dependent or independent, whether the student has children, whether anyone in the household received benefits from another federal means-tested program, and what type of federal income tax form the family is required to use.[39] The output of this process is an "expected family contribution" (EFC), which is provided to both the students and the schools to which they have applied. While integral to aid eligibility, the EFC can be difficult to interpret: it is described to students as "*not* the amount of money that your family must provide [but rather] an index that colleges use to determine how much financial aid you would receive if you were to attend their school."[40] Before 2008, the EFC was the only information on federal aid that students received upon completing the FAFSA; online applicants now also receive an estimate of their Pell eligibility.

Schools use the EFC (and potentially other information from the FAFSA or additional institutional aid application forms) to determine students' eligibility for federal, state, and institutional aid. Students must wait for schools to admit them and present them with details of their aid package. Different schools may offer the same student different amounts of aid. For example, colleges are not required to offer students the maximum Stafford Loans for which they are eligible.

Complexity, delay, and lack of transparency in the aid process mean that students and their families have little idea how much aid they will receive until after they have applied to college, which students may never do if they think they cannot afford to go. The lack of information about available aid is acute: a recent national survey of 600 Americans aged twenty-six to thirty-four found that fewer than three in ten individuals without a college degree had any idea what a FAFSA was.[41] Although the U.S. Department of Education has taken steps to simplify the application process in recent years—by promoting the online application (which enables students to skip questions that do not apply to them), for example, and facilitating links with income tax data (which is required for the FAFSA but can be provided directly from the Internal Revenue Service)—the process remains daunting to many students and families.[42]

Complexity, delay, and lack of transparency in the aid process mean that students and their families have little idea how much aid they will receive until after they have applied to college, which students may never do if they think they cannot afford to go. A recent national survey of 600 Americans aged twenty-six to thirty-four found that fewer than three in ten individuals without a college degree had any idea what a FAFSA was.

Federal tax benefits are distributed in an entirely separate process, through the annual filing of income tax returns. Colleges provide documentation directly to the IRS of a student's enrollment and tuition payments. A disadvantage of the education tax benefits is that they are distributed only after costs are incurred; on the other hand, for many families the income tax form is easier to complete than the FAFSA.

Challenges in Evaluating the Effectiveness of Financial Aid

The theory behind student aid is straightforward: more people will buy a product (college) when its price (tuition) is lower. Price drops, demand increases: that is a lesson taught in any introductory economics course. While Econ 101 clearly predicts that financial aid should increase schooling, the magnitude of the impact is an empirical question. And because aid is offered to students on the basis of characteristics that may independently affect college enrollment and completion rates, such as income or academic performance in high school, the effect of the aid can be difficult to untangle from the effect of these other factors.

Take the example of Pell Grants, which flow primarily to students from families with income below $50,000. Students from such families are less likely to attend college in the first place, for myriad reasons: they disproportionately attended lower-quality high schools, have weaker academic skills, and are less likely to have parents who went to college.[43] Those who are eligible for a Pell Grant have lower college attendance rates than those who are ineligible, but that does not imply that Pell Grants actually lower college attendance. Those who are eligible for Pell Grants are simply less likely to go to college for reasons other than their Pell eligibility.

Now take the example of state merit-based scholarships. Many states use these grants as a tool to attract high-achieving students. Students eligible for these scholarships are very likely to go to college, given their very strong academic skills. In this case, a comparison of eligible and ineligible students would overstate the effect of aid. Those who are eligible for merit scholarships are likely to go to college for reasons other than their scholarship eligibility.

Researchers typically use statistical methods that are more sophisticated than the previous paragraphs would imply. But the same problem plagues the more technical studies: those who are eligible for aid tend to be quite different from those who are not. In theory, researchers can use statistical tools to control for any important differences between aid recipients and nonrecipients, but in practice such research is difficult. Why? First, complete data on relevant characteristics is rarely available. For example, parental wealth affects schooling decisions, both directly and through eligibility for aid, but comprehensive measures of parental (and extended family) wealth are rarely revealed in survey data, especially among adults who have completed their education. Second, and even more fundamentally, students who do receive aid may differ from those who do not on other, *unobservable* dimensions. As an example, imagine that a sample of first-year Pell Grant recipients could be matched to other first-year students at the same school, with similar age, race, gender, family income, and so on. The question would remain: if these students appear so similar in all of their other characteristics, including family income, which is the primary determinant of Pell Grant eligibility, why did some receive a grant while others did not? Several explanations for this difference may be possible, but most of them will suggest some important unobservable difference between the groups. For example, it may be that the recipients were more committed to a significant period of enrollment, compared with individuals of similar income and ability who did not apply.

The ideal solution is a randomized, controlled trial, in which aid amounts are randomly assigned to a pool of potential college students, who are then followed for a certain period of time to compare outcomes between those receiving more and those receiving less assistance. The randomized trial is the gold standard of research methods in medicine and is increasingly used in the social sciences. Randomized trials have been used to evaluate the effect of job training programs on employment rates, the effect of smaller classes on test scores, and the effect of Head Start on children's emotional and intellectual development. The Education Sciences Reform Act of 2002 elevated the randomized trial as the preferred method for evaluation, especially for research funded by the U.S. Department of Education. Several randomized trials in financial aid are discussed later in this article.

Many policy-relevant questions about aid have yet to be addressed with a randomized trial, however. The next best approach is "quasi-experimental," in which the researcher identifies a source of naturally occurring but idiosyncratic variation in access to aid. When researchers can identify a group that has access to a program and a group that does not for reasons that are, if not explicitly random, at least unrelated to expected outcomes between the groups, then a comparison of outcomes for these two groups can yield causal estimates of aid effectiveness.

Financial aid eligibility rules have themselves proved to be a rich source of such plausibly random variation. For example, many aid programs have sharp cutoffs for eligibility, with those above specific levels of income or below certain grade point averages being ineligible. Students directly above and below these sharp breaks are likely to be very similar, but the aid that they are offered is quite different. In a regression-discontinuity analysis, researchers compare the schooling decisions of individuals just above and just below these cutoffs and attribute any difference to the causal effect of the difference in aid eligibility. Another quasi-experimental approach exploits sharp changes in aid eligibility. When a program is introduced (or eliminated) for one group but not another, researchers can compare changes in outcomes before and after the policy change across the two groups. Susan Dynarski used this method—known as a "difference-in-difference" approach—to examine the effect of the Social Security student benefit program; we discuss this study below.[44]

Lessons from the Research on Financial Aid Effectiveness

We draw four major lessons from the research on financial aid effectiveness, drawing primarily on experimental and quasi-experimental analyses. The rigor of these two approaches does not come without cost. In many cases, running an experiment or identifying a naturally occurring quasi-experiment means narrowing the analysis to a subset of treated and untreated individuals, potentially limiting the ability to generalize the results to other groups. Thus, we also place the findings from the most rigorous studies in the context of the broader nonexperimental literature, where such literature is available.

Lesson 1: Money Matters for College Access

The first lesson, grounded in more than thirty years of research, is that money matters for college access. As predicted by economic theory, when students know that they will receive a discount, enrollment rates increase. In 1988, Larry Leslie and Paul Brinkman reviewed several dozen nonexperimental studies and concluded that a $1,000 decrease in net price was associated with a 3- to 5-percentage-point increase in college attendance.[45]

Susan Dynarski examined the elimination of the Social Security Student Benefit (SSSB) program, using a difference-in-difference analysis. From 1965 to 1982, the Social Security Administration paid for millions of students to go to college. Under the SSSB program, the children of deceased, disabled, or retired Social Security beneficiaries received monthly payments while in college. At the program's peak, 12 percent of young full-time college students were receiving these benefits. In 1981, Congress voted to eliminate the program. Except for the introduction of the Pell Grant program in the early 1970s, and the various GI Bills, elimination of this program is the largest and sharpest change in grant aid for college that has ever occurred in the United States. Dynarksi found that college attendance among the affected group fell by more than a third after the grant program ended, suggesting that the availability of grant aid does in fact increase college enrollment rates above what they would be otherwise.

Several quasi-experimental studies of large state merit aid programs have also found significant positive impacts on enrollment, as did a regression-discontinuity study of the Tuition Assistance Program in the District of Columbia and two separate studies of the mid-century GI Bills. Taken together, the quasi-experimental evidence suggests that an additional $1,000 of grant aid may increase college enrollment by 4 percentage points.[46]

Grant assistance affects not only whether students attend college but also where they choose to go. For students applying to an elite East Coast institution who also applied for financial aid, an additional 10 percent in grant aid increased the probability of matriculation by 8.6 percent.[47] This estimate was obtained using a regression-discontinuity design, in which students were ranked according to the strength of their application, and the matriculation rate of students just below discrete aid-eligibility cutoffs was compared with the rate of those just above the cutoff.

Like grant aid, federal tax benefits provide money for college that never needs to be repaid. Evidence regarding the enrollment effects of the tax benefits is limited to just two studies. An early study using a difference-in-difference approach—comparing financially eligible and ineligible families before and after the introduction of the Hope and Lifetime Learning tax credits—found no evidence that the benefits influenced likelihood of enrollment.[48] A more recent study used a similar difference-in-difference strategy, but included more recent years of data in its analysis and also took advantage of more accurate data on income eligibility.[49] This study found effects of roughly the same magnitude as has been found for grant assistance: the probability of college enrollment rose by 3 percentage points for every $1,000 of tax-based aid. It is possible that earlier analysis simply could not discern a true effect because some families were incorrectly classified as eligible or ineligible in the data, watering down the estimated difference between groups. Or it is possible that the credits became more effective over time as awareness about them increased among eligible families.

Until recently much of the financial aid literature focused on college entry, rather than outcomes after enrollment. Several recent studies suggest that financial aid can also improve persistence and completion.[50] These studies, however, generally examine grant programs with specific academic achievement requirements for scholarship renewal. The results of these academic incentive grants do not necessarily generalize to grant programs with no strings attached, a caveat discussed under Lesson 3.

Lesson 2: Program Complexity Undermines Aid Effectiveness

While we conclude that aid matters for college enrollment, that does not imply that all aid programs are equally effective. For example, the programs discussed above that have clearly demonstrated positive impacts on college enrollment tend to have simple, easy-to-understand eligibility rules and application procedures. The eligibility and application rules for Pell Grants—the nation's largest grant program—are comparatively complex, requiring students to submit to the lengthy and burdensome FAFSA process for determining their eligibility.

A recent experimental study provides dramatic evidence that the complexity of the financial aid application process can itself become a significant barrier to college access.[51] In the experiment, low-income families who visited a tax-preparation center were randomly assigned to one of three groups: a "full treatment" group that received both personalized information about eligibility for financial aid as well as personal assistance with completing and submitting the FAFSA; an "information-only" group that received personalized information about financial aid eligibility but no application assistance; and a control group that received a brochure with general information about college costs, financial aid, and the value of going to college. The full treatment, which took less than ten minutes and cost less than $100 per participant, increased immediate college entry rates by 8 percentage points (24 percent) for high school seniors and 1.5 percentage points (16 percent) among independent participants with no previous college experience. After three years, participants in the full-treatment group had accumulated significantly more time in college than the control group. They also were much more likely to have received a Pell Grant.

A recent experimental study provides dramatic evidence that the complexity of the financial aid application process can itself become a significant barrier to college access.

This experimental evidence, which demonstrates the importance of program design and delivery, may help explain why studies have found less conclusive evidence regarding the enrollment impact of Pell Grants than for aid programs with simpler eligibility and application procedures. The broadest quasi-experimental study of Pell Grants used a difference-in-difference approach to compare trends in college enrollment before and after increases in Pell Grant funding, between students who became eligible for increased funding and those who remained ineligible throughout the period. Consistent with previous nonexperimental findings, this study found no detectable effect of the introduction of Pell Grants on college enrollments for eligible (low-income) populations.[52]

Other studies have found evidence of Pell impacts for specific subsets of the population: one study found that Pell Grants increased enrollment of older "nontraditional" students, while a study by Bettinger, described in the next section, found suggestive evidence that the grants contributed to student persistence, at least among students who had already enrolled in college.[53] Both findings are consistent with a story in which information and experience with bureaucracy is important: older individuals may have learned about the Pell program over time, and continuing students may learn about the program once they enroll in school. Those who have recently graduated from high school but not yet enrolled may be the least informed and least equipped to figure out the process.

This limited evidence on the impact of Pell Grants is not definitive; the U.S. Department of Education recently initiated a randomized trial to study the effect of further expansions of the Pell Grant, which may help to resolve this uncertainty. But at a minimum, the FAFSA experiment has only heightened existing concerns that complexity and confusion surrounding the Pell eligibility and application process may be obscuring its benefits and dampening its impact among the individuals who need it most—those who are on the fence about college for financial reasons.[54]

Lesson 3: Academic Incentives Appear to Augment Aid Effectiveness, Particularly after Enrollment

A third emerging lesson from the literature is that achievement incentives appear to increase effectiveness, particularly when the focus is on improving college performance and completion (as opposed to simply access). Two randomized experiments have examined the results of linking financial aid to specific GPA or credit accumulation requirements. A study by the social policy research organization MDRC examined a sample of low-income, primarily minority, female enrollees at two community colleges in Louisiana and found that performance-based scholarships increased GPAs and persistence.[55] On the basis of these findings, MDRC initiated replication studies examining variations of this intervention in six other states; early indicators appear to reinforce the findings of the initial study.[56] An experiment at a large college in Canada found that a performance-based scholarship did in fact increase GPAs, though only for females who received academic support services in addition to the financial incentive.[57] While the lack of significant impacts for the full sample may be surprising, again there is suggestive evidence that program complexity may undermine effectiveness: a subsequent experiment with cash incentives at the same Canadian institution again found no effects overall, but did find some significant positive effects for those students receiving grades above the minimum threshold established for the incentive, with larger effects on grade outcomes for students who could correctly describe the program's rules.[58]

To the extent that performance-based scholarships encourage students to devote more time and energy to their studies, an important question is whether the student may be driven purely by the relaxation of financial constraints, rather than by the performance incentives per se. A quasi-experimental study by Judith Scott-Clayton examines this question, in the context of West Virginia's PROMISE scholarship, which at the time provided free tuition and fees for up to four years to academically eligible students as long as they maintained a minimum GPA and course load in college.[59] The scholarship increased five-year graduation rates by 4 percentage points and on-time graduation rates by nearly 7 percentage points. Moreover, the achievement incentives were an important mechanism driving these increases. The scholarship increased GPAs and credits completed in the first three years of college, but in the fourth and final year of the scholarship—while students are still receiving the money but no longer face the achievement incentives—the program's effect nearly disappeared.

In contrast, several studies of pure grants (with weak or no achievement incentives) have found less conclusive evidence of positive effects on persistence and graduation rates. Two quasi-experimental studies found suggestive but inconclusive evidence that pure grant aid improves college persistence and completion.[60] In contrast, a regression-discontinuity study of the Gates Millennium Scholarship found no evidence that the grants increased college retention or credit accumulation for its highly qualified, low-income minority participants (although it did reduce student employment and student loan debt).[61]

The most rigorous and broadly relevant evidence on the post-enrollment effects of grant aid comes from a randomized evaluation of the Wisconsin Scholars Grant, a privately run scholarship program that provided $3,500 grants to Pell-eligible students already enrolled at public universities in Wisconsin. The study found no effects on persistence, grade point averages, or credit accumulation after three years for the full sample.[62] However, for a subset of students entering college with a high risk of dropout (based on high school achievement and other background characteristics), the effects seemed to be more positive.

Academic incentives may improve not only performance after college entry but college preparation and initial enrollment as well. For example, a study of the introduction of Tennessee's state merit aid program, which provided large college scholarships to students with minimum high school GPA and SAT/ACT test scores, found that the scholarship significantly improved high school achievement as measured by ACT test scores (the increases in test scores were too large to be explained simply by increases in retesting).[63] A similar study of a program in Texas that paid eleventh- and twelfth-grade students and teachers for earning passing scores on Advanced Placement (AP) exams found that the policy not only improved AP exam scores but increased college enrollment rates as well as college academic performance, even for those students who would have gone to college anyway.[64]

Lesson 4: Evidence on the Effect of Loans Is Limited but Suggests Design Is Important

A fourth lesson is that even though loans are unpopular, they are a critical element in college financing, and their design might be significantly improved to minimize students' repayment risks and better communicate both risks and protections upfront. Very little rigorous research has examined how the availability of student loans affects college enrollment, performance, or completion. Susan Dynarski found suggestive, but ultimately inconclusive evidence that student loan expansions in the United States in the early 1990s led to increased college attendance.[65] Donald Heller reviewed the nonexperimental literature on whether loans increase college access and concluded that the findings "can at best be described as mixed."[66] In part, this mixed picture may reflect inconsistencies in some researchers' choice of the counterfactual: the studies may be comparing $1 of loans with $1 of grants, $1 of work-study, or no aid at all. Based on the nonexperimental evidence, Heller concluded that college enrollments are not as sensitive to loans as to grants. This is unsurprising given that loans are not worth as much to students. Nonetheless, because they also cost the government only a few cents on the dollar to provide, it remains an open question whether loans provide bigger, smaller, or the same "bang for the buck" as grant aid does.[67]

More rigorous evidence from a dramatic policy change at one selective northeastern university suggests that students' career choices, if not their enrollment decisions, are influenced by levels of student debt. Jesse Rothstein and Cecilia Rouse examined the consequences of this institution's decision to replace loans in students' financial aid packages with increased institutional grant aid.[68] In two stages, the university in 1998 eliminated student loans for incoming students from low-income families and then eliminated loans for all students receiving aid in 2001. Students in cohorts that entered after the policy was fully implemented not only graduated with about $11,000 less in debt than cohorts that entered before the policy change but also were significantly more likely to take jobs in nonprofit and public service sectors.

Debt aversion may be one important explanation for why loans do not appear to affect access as much as grants do: some students simply dislike being in debt, even when that debt enables an investment with high average returns. An experiment analyzed by Erica Field found strong evidence that students (in this case, students admitted to law school) are debt averse.[69] Admitted students at one school were randomly assigned to receive either a public service scholarship that would convert to a loan if students did not pursue public service after graduation, or a loan that would be forgiven if students decided to pursue public service after graduation. The two treatments were financially equivalent, yet framing the program as a "loan that would be forgiven if you pursue public service" was much less effective in inducing students to public service than a "grant that will convert to a loan if you do *not* pursue public service." Like the FAFSA simplification study, Field's findings provide further evidence that the details of program design and marketing can be critical.

Given the widespread reliance on student loans, a more interesting question than whether they increase college enrollment and completion at all is whether some types of loans are more effective than others. Are there ways to make loans more attractive and less risky for students, without drastically increasing costs? For example, the cost of a loan program is greatly affected by the interest rate that is charged and whether interest accrues while students are still enrolled in school. Yet evidence from other contexts indicates that individuals do not give such details as much weight as they should when making savings and borrowing decisions.[70] Similarly, with income-contingent repayment schemes, it is unclear whether students making decisions about borrowing are even aware of how their eventual payments will be calculated. If loan schemes cannot be made more comprehensible to students, any subsidies incorporated into loan programs to make them more appealing to low-income students may be ineffectual. A student's decision to enroll and persist may be more influenced by an aid package that includes an upfront grant and an unsubsidized loan, rather than a package of equal cost to the government that includes only subsidized loans.

Conclusion

The major shifts in the financial aid landscape documented in this paper have three critical implications for aid policy. First, student aid is no longer just for poor students. Forty years ago, student aid consisted almost solely of federal grants for low-income students. Today, colleges and states, as well as the federal government, provide grants, tax benefits, and loans to families with incomes well up the income distribution.[71] In fact, the majority of students now receive financial aid of one kind or another: two-thirds of full-time college students get some form of grant aid, and many of the remainder receive federal tax credits and other forms of assistance. The aggregate amount of student aid distributed—including all forms of aid at the federal, state, and institutional level—added up to nearly $13,000 a student in 2010–11. The volume of aid distributed and number of students affected make it more critical than ever to understand whether and how aid affects college enrollment, performance, and completion.

Second, the "sticker price" of college now diverges substantially from the net price most families face. Sticker prices have climbed steadily for decades. But net prices in all sectors were actually lower in 2009–10 than they were in 2005–06. The net price of a private four-year college declined by 2 percent between 2005 and 2009, and the net price for a public four-year college declined by 13 percent over this period. For public two-year institutions, average net prices dropped to negative $810, meaning the average student received more in grant aid than he or she was charged in tuition and fees.[72] The difference between sticker prices and net prices is even larger for low-income students, who qualify for the Pell Grant, which has grown increasingly generous in recent years. This divergence implies that individual students will find it harder than ever to estimate how much going to college will cost them.

Third, the increasing scope and diversity of financial aid programs implies increased complexity—both for students trying to estimate their college costs and for policy makers trying to ensure coherence across programs. The proliferation of programs, each well-intentioned, has created a system that makes it difficult for families—especially "first-generation" families in which neither parent has attended college—to know just how affordable college can be. Calculating the net price of college for a given family requires understanding their finances as well as the rules of the Pell Grant, student loans, the tuition tax credits, state grant programs, and aid offered by individual colleges. Evidence suggests that students are quite poor at estimating net prices.[73] A symptom of the general confusion is that some aid goes unclaimed: the Government Accountability Office recently calculated that 14 percent of families eligible for an education tax benefit failed to claim it.[74] Forty percent of filers who used the tuition tax deduction would have been better off claiming one of the tax credits instead.

The complexity of the student aid landscape can lead to unexpected interactions between programs. For example, Susan Dynarski found that, for families on the margin of getting more financial aid, putting money in a tax-advantaged Coverdell Savings Account led to substantial decreases in Title IV aid eligibility. In other words, the Title IV rules not only undid the tax incentive for saving but actually left a family worse off than if it had not saved at all. This collision between tax and aid policy was corrected with subsequent legislation, but there will almost certainly be more such collisions given the proliferation of aid and tax programs.

Another example of unintended interactions regards the relationship between federal aid and colleges' own tuition pricing and financial aid decisions. Some policy makers, most notably former U.S. Secretary of Education William Bennett, have raised the concern that even if financial aid lowers prices for some students, it might enable institutions to raise tuition costs overall. Some evidence supports the so-called "Bennett Hypothesis" in the for-profit sector: Stephanie Cellini and Claudia Goldin find that proprietary schools that are eligible to receive federal Title IV aid (via eligible students who enroll) charge significantly more than similar institutions that must rely on students who can pay full price.[75] But other research finds little evidence of these effects at the public institutions attended by the majority of students.[76] More subtly, recent quasi-experimental work by Lesley Turner compared financial aid packages for students just above and below Pell Grant eligibility thresholds and found that selective nonprofit institutions claw back up to two-thirds of Pell Grant awards through reductions in institutional grant aid. However, at the public institutions most Pell recipients attend, the claw-back rate is near zero.[77]

The majority of students now receive financial aid of one kind or another: two-thirds of full-time college students get some form of grant aid, and many of the remainder receive federal tax credits and other forms of assistance.

Researchers have learned an enormous amount about the effect of aid on student behavior in recent years, as the quantity and quality of research on this topic has exploded. Aid can matter, with simple, well-designed programs producing large increases in college attendance and completion. Evidence shows that the complexity of eligibility and application procedures can undermine aid effectiveness. A recent randomized trial showed that a massive simplification of the federal aid application process produced substantial increases in college attendance, further bolstering the conclusion that design matters. It also appears that pairing grants with academic requirements can bolster the impact of financial aid on college performance and completion. Both experimental and quasi-experimental studies suggest that dollars with strings attached produce larger effects than dollars alone.

In contrast, disappointingly little evidence is available on the effects of one method that students increasingly use to pay for college: loans. Loans are likely to remain a key component of student aid packages, yet almost no evidence exists about their effects on college enrollment and completion. Finally, as both the types of aid and the types of aid recipients continue to expand and to become more diverse, more research is likely to focus on the importance of program design and delivery, whether there are unanticipated interactions between programs, and to what extent program effects vary across different types of students.

As state and federal budgets face increasing pressures and politicians look for ways to control spending, financial aid programs will be vulnerable to cutbacks if evidence is lacking on their effectiveness, and even those programs with documented positive effects may be asked to do more with less. Fortunately, more may be known about the effects of financial aid than about any other interventions aimed at increasing postsecondary attainment. No longer is it necessary to ask the question, "Does aid work?"—for the research definitively shows that it can. But the evidence also suggests that some programs work better than others, and because of the magnitude of government investment as well as the numbers of individuals affected by student aid, the stakes have never been higher for understanding what aid programs work best and why.

Notes

1. Lyndon Baines Johnson, "Remarks at Southwest Texas State College Upon Signing the Higher Education Act of 1965," November 8, 1965. Archived online by Gerhard Peters and John T. Woolley, *The American Presidency Project* (www.presidency.ucsb.edu/ws/?pid=27356).
2. Sandy Baum and Kathleen Payea, *Trends in Student Aid 2011* (New York: The College Board, 2011), tables 3 and 3A. Before 1990, the original College Board data combined data on both graduate and undergraduate aid and enrollment. For 1971–72 through 1989–90, we adjusted the aggregate enrollment estimates downward by 13 percent and the average aid estimates downward by 11 percent (based on the undergraduate-to-total ratios, which have been relatively stable over time, from later years in which both series are available) to make them comparable with the undergraduate-only data for subsequent years.
3. Full-time-equivalent statistics count two half-time students the same as one full-time student; the number of individual students enrolled surpassed 20 million by 2009.
4. Before 1980, the department was known as the Department of Health, Education, and Welfare.
5. Sandy Baum and Jennifer Ma, *Trends in College Pricing 2011* (New York: The College Board 2011).
6. Ibid., table 7.
7. Laura J. Horn, Xianglei Chen, and Chris Chapman, *Getting Ready to Pay for College: What Students and Their Parents Know about the Cost of College Tuition and What They Are Doing to Find Out* (Washington: National Center for Education Statistics, 2003); Stanley Ikenberry and Terry Hartle, *Too Little Knowledge Is a Dangerous Thing: What the Public Thinks about Paying for College* (Washington: American Council on Education, 1998). Also see the review by Judith Scott-Clayton, "Information Constraints and Financial Aid Policy," Working Paper 17811 (Cambridge, Mass: National Bureau of Economic Research, 2012).
8. Lawrence E. Gladieux and Arthur M. Hauptman, *The College Aid Quandary: Access, Quality, and the Federal Role* (Washington: Brookings Institution Press, 1995), p. 15.
9. Numbers of Pell Grant recipients over time come from Baum and Payea, *Trends in Student Aid 2011* (see note 2), table 8. Enrollments over time come from National Center for Education Statistics, *Digest of Education Statistics 2009* (U.S. Department of Education, 2010), table 197.
10. Baum and Payea, *Trends in Student Aid 2011* (see note 2), table 8.
11. Sandy Baum, Charles Kurose, and Michael McPherson, "An Overview of American *Higher Education*," Future of Children 23, no. 1 (Spring 2013).
12. Bureau of the Census, "Regions—All Races by Median and Mean Income 1975–2010" (www.census.gov/hhes/www/income/data/historical/household/2010/H06AR_2010.xls), table H-6.
13. Essentially, Pell Grants are calculated by subtracting a family's expected family contribution, which rises with income, from the maximum award.
14. U.S. Department of Education, "Federal Pell Grant Program Data Books: 2000-01–2009-10" (dependent students) (www2.ed.gov/finaid/prof/resources/data/pell-historical/hist-4.html).
15. Baum and Payea, *Trends in Student Aid 2011* (see note 2), figures 13A and 13C.
16. Ibid.
17. FinAid.org, "History of Student Financial Aid" (www.finaid.org/educators/history.phtml).
18. Baum and Ma, *Trends in College Pricing 2011* (see note 5), figure 3.
19. See, for example, Antony Davies and James R. Harrison, "Why the Education Bubble Will Be Worse than the Housing Bubble," *USNews.com*, June 12, 2012.
20. Rohit Chopra, "Too Big to Fail: Student Debt Hits a Trillion" (Washington: Consumer Financial Protection Bureau, March 21, 2012 (www.consumerfinance.gov/blog/ too-big-to-fail-student-debt-hits-a-trillion/).
21. Note that cumulative debt figures cited in the press as "record highs" typically fail to adjust previous years' figures for inflation.
22. Data for 2000 come from National Center for Education Statistics, *Debt Burden: A Comparison of 1992–93 and 1999–2000 Bachelor's Degree Recipients a Year after Graduating* (U.S. Department of Education, 2005). Data for 2009 come from National Center for Education Statistics, *QuickStats: BPS: 2009 Beginning Postsecondary Students Database* (http://nces.ed.gov/datalab/quickstats/).
23. Authors' computations using National Center for Education Statistics, *QuickStats: BPS: 2001 Beginning Postsecondary Students Database and BPS: 2009 Beginning Postsecondary Students Database* (http://nces.ed.gov/datalab/quickstats/).

24. National Center for Education Statistics, *QuickStats: BPS: 2009 Beginning Postsecondary Students Database* (http://nces.ed.gov/datalab/quickstats/).
25. Families may claim an American Opportunity Tax Credit for each eligible student in the household, while only one Lifetime Learning Credit may be claimed per household. Only one credit can be claimed per student. See Internal Revenue Service, *Tax Benefits for Education: For Use in Preparing 2011 Returns*, Publication 970 (Department of the Treasury, 2001).
26. Susan M. Dynarski, "Hope for Whom? Financial Aid for the Middle Class and Its Impact on College Attendance." *National Tax Journal* 53, no. 3 (2000): 629–61.
27. The American Opportunity Tax Credit modifies the Hope and Lifetime Learning Credits through December 2012, when the modifications were scheduled to expire.
28. Margot Crandall-Hollick, "The American Opportunity Tax Credit: Overview, Analysis, and Policy Options," Congressional Research Service Report R42561 (Government Printing Office, 2012).
29. The benefit was originally set to expire in 2005, but in 2006 it was extended to cover 2006 and 2007; in 2008, it was extended to cover 2008 and 2009; and in 2010, it was extended to cover 2010 and 2011. For 2011, the income limit for this benefit was $80,000 for single filers or $160,000 for joint returns.
30. State cumulative contribution limits range from $146,000 to $305,000; a typical state allows an annual contribution of $10,000 for married filers. See FinAid.org, "FinAid: Saving for College: Section 529 Plans" (www.finaid.org/savings/529plans.phtml#Contributions); FinAid.org, "History of Student Financial Aid" (www.finaid.org/educators/history.phtml).
31. Susan M. Dynarski, "Who Benefits from the College Saving Incentives? Income, Educational Expectations and the Value of the 529 and Coverdell." *National Tax Journal* 57, no. 2 (2004): 359–83.
32. Government Accountability Office, "Improved Tax Information Could Help Families Pay for College," GAO-12-560 (Government Printing Office, 2012).
33. Baum and Ma, *Trends in College Pricing, 2011* (see note 5), figure 10b.
34. Ibid, figure 12a.
35. Thomas J. Kane and Peter R. Orszag, "Funding Restrictions at Public Universities: Effects and Policy Implications," working paper (Washington: Brookings Institution, 2003).
36. Need-based state grants per full-time-equivalent undergraduate student grew from $211 in 1969–70 to $464 in 2009–10 (constant 2010 dollars), while merit-based grants per FTE undergraduate grew from $0 in 1969–70 to $176 in 2009–10. Baum and Payea, *Trends in Student Aid 2011* (see note 2), figure 15A.
37. Susan M. Dynarski, "The New Merit Aid," in *College Choices: The Economics of Where to Go, When to Go, and How to Pay for It*, edited by Caroline M. Hoxby (University of Chicago Press and the National Bureau of Economic Research, 2004), pp. 63–100.
38. See the 2012–13 FAFSA On The Web Worksheet (http://www.fafsa.ed.gov/fotw1213/pdf/fafsaws13c.pdf).
39. The choice of formula and the formulas themselves are not computed by the student for obvious reasons, nor are they made accessible to students and their families. But enterprising individuals could find copies of the thirty-six-page formula guide online. (http://studentaid.ed.gov/sites/default/files/2012-13-efc-forumula.pdf).
40. Edicsweb.ed.gov, "2012–2013 Student Aid Report" (edicsweb.ed.gov/edics_files_web/04703/Att_2012-2013%20Student%20Aid%20Report.pdf).
41. Jean Johnson, Jon Rochkind, and Amber Ott, *One Degree of Separation: How Young Americans Who Don't Finish College See Their Chances for Success* (San Francisco: Public Agenda, 2011).
42. Susan M. Dynarski and Judith Scott-Clayton, "The Cost of Complexity in Federal Student Aid: Lessons from Optimal Tax Theory and Behavioral Economics," *National Tax Journal* 59, no. 2 (2006): 319–56; Susan M. Dynarski and Mark Wiederspan, "Student Aid Simplification: Looking Back and Looking Ahead," National Tax Journal 65, no. 1 (2012): 211–34.
43. Martha Bailey and Susan M. Dynarski, "Inequality in Postsecondary Attainment," in *Whither Opportunity: Rising Inequality, Schools, and Children's Life Chances*, edited by Greg Duncan and Richard Murnane (New York: Russell Sage Foundation, 2011), pp. 117–32.
44. Susan M. Dynarski, "Does Aid Matter? Measuring the Effect of Student Aid on College Attendance and Completion," *American Economic Review* 93, no. 1 (2003): 278–88.
45. Larry Leslie and Paul Brinkman, *The Economic Value of Higher Education* (New York: Macmillan, 1988).
46. For a detailed review, see David Deming and Susan M. Dynarski, "Into College, Out of Poverty? Policies to Increase the Postsecondary Attainment of the Poor," Working Paper 15387 (Cambridge, Mass: National Bureau of Economic Research, 2009). The following studies find enrollment effects ranging from 3 to 6 percentage points per $1,000 of aid: Neil Seftor and Sarah Turner, "Back to School: Federal Student Aid Policy and Adult College Enrollment," *Journal of Human Resources* 37, no. 2 (2002): 336–52;

Thomas J. Kane, "A Quasi-Experimental Estimate of the Impact of Financial Aid on College-Going," Working Paper 9703 (Cambridge, Mass.: National Bureau of Economic Research, 2003); Thomas J. Kane, "Evaluating the Impact of the D.C. Tuition Assistance Grant Program," Journal of Human Resources 42, no. 3 (2007): 555–82; Katharine Abraham and Melissa Clark, "Financial Aid and Students' College Decisions: Evidence from the District of Columbia Tuition Assistance Grant Program," *Journal of Human Resources* (Summer 2006): 578–610; Dynarski, "Hope for Whom? (see note 26); Dynarski, "The New Merit Aid" (see note 37); Christopher Cornwell, David Mustard, and Deepa Sridhar, "The Enrollment Effects of Merit-Based Financial Aid: Evidence from Georgia's HOPE Scholarship," *Journal of Labor Economics* 24 (2006): 761–86; Marcus Stanley, "College Education and the Mid-Century G.I. Bills," *Quarterly Journal of Economics* 118, no. 2 (2003): 671–708; John Bound and Sarah Turner, "Going to War and Going to College: Did World War II and the G.I. Bill Increase Educational Attainment for Returning Veterans?" *Journal of Labor Economics* 20, no. 4 (2002): 784–815.

47. Wilbert van der Klaauw, "Estimating the Effect of Financial Aid Offers on College Enrollment: A Regression-Discontinuity Approach." *International Economic Review* 43, no. 4 (2002): 1249–87.
48. Bridget T. Long, "The Impact of Federal Tax Credits for Higher Education Expenses," in *College Choices: The Economics of Where To Go, When To Go, and How To Pay for It*, edited by Hoxby, pp. 101–68.
49. Nicholas Turner, "The Effect of Tax-Based Federal Student Aid on College Enrollment," *National Tax Journal* 64, no. 3 (2011): 839–62.
50. Susan M. Dynarski, "Building the Stock of College-Educated Labor," *Journal of Human Resources* 43, no. 3 (2008): 576–610; Lashawn Richburg-Hayes and others, *Rewarding Persistence: Effects of a Performance-Based Scholarship Program for Low-Income Parents* (New York: MDRC, 2009); Reshma Patel and Lashawn Richburg-Hayes, *Performance-Based Scholarships: Emerging Findings from a National Demonstration* (New York: MDRC, 2012). Judith Scott-Clayton, "On Money and Motivation: A Quasi-Experimental Analysis of Financial Incentives for College Achievement," *Journal of Human Resources* 46, no. 3 (2011): 614–46.
51. Eric Bettinger and others, "The Role of Application Assistance and Information in College Decisions: Results from the H&R Block FAFSA Experiment," *Quarterly Journal of Economics* (forthcoming, 2012).
52. Thomas J. Kane, "Lessons From the Largest School Voucher Program Ever: Two Decades of Experience with Pell Grants," in *Who Chooses? Who Loses? Culture, Institutions and the Unequal Effects of School Choice*, edited by Bruce Fuller, Richard F. Elmore, and Gary Orfield (Teachers College Press, 1996); W. Lee Hansen, "The Impact of Student Financial Aid on Access," in *The Crisis In Higher Education*, edited by Joseph Froomkin (New York: Academy of Political Science, 1983), pp. 84–96.
53. Seftor and Turner, "Back to School" (see note 46); Eric Bettinger, "How Financial Aid Affects Persistence," in *College Choices: The Economics of Where to Go, When to Go, and How to Pay for It*, edited by Hoxby, pp. 207–38.
54. Dynarski and Scott-Clayton, "The Cost of Complexity in Federal Student Aid" (see note 42).
55. Richburg-Hayes and others, *Rewarding Persistence* (see note 50).
56. Patel and Richburg-Hayes, *Performance-Based Scholarships* (see note 50).
57. Joshua D. Angrist, Daniel Lang, and Philip Oreopoulos, "Incentives and Services for College Achievement: Evidence from a Randomized Trial," *American Economic Journal: Applied Economics* 1, no. 1 (2009): 136–63.
58. Joshua Angrist, Philip Oreopoulos, and Tyler Williams, "When Opportunity Knocks, Who Answers? New Evidence on College Achievement Awards," Working Paper 16643 (Cambridge, Mass.: National Bureau of Economic Research, 2010). Even for the sample of students who understood program rules, there was no impact on average GPA, but there were significant impacts on the number of courses in which students received a grade above 70 (out of 100).
59. Scott-Clayton, "On Money and Motivation" (see note 50). Since the time of the study, West Virginia has capped the value of the scholarship so that it no longer guarantees free tuition, but provides a fixed-dollar award.
60. A study by Eric Bettinger used discontinuities in the Pell Grant formula to estimate the effects of Pell Grant size on college persistence (conditional on enrollment). See Bettinger, "How Financial Aid Affects Persistence" (see note 53). Similarly, Dynarski's study of the SSSB program found positive, but statistically insignificant effects on completed years of schooling. See Dynarski, "Does Aid Matter?" (see note 44).
61. Stephen L. DesJardins and Brian P. McCall, "The Impact of the Gates Millennium Scholars Program on Selected Outcomes of Low-Income Minority Students: A Regression Discontinuity Analysis" (University of Michigan, 2008). Also see Stephen L. DesJardins and others, "A Quasi-Experimental Investigation of How the Gates Millennium Scholars Program Is Related to College Students' Time Use and Activities," *Educational Evaluation and Policy Analysis* 32, no. 4 (2010): 456–75.

62. Sara Goldrick-Rab and others, "Conditional Cash Transfers and College Persistence: Evidence from a Randomized Need-Based Grant Program," Discussion Paper 1393-11 (University of Wisconsin, 2011).
63. Amanda Pallais, "Taking a Chance on College: Is the Tennessee Education Lottery Scholarship a Winner?" *Journal of Human Resources* 44, no. 1 (2009): 199–222.
64. C. Kirabo Jackson, "A Little Now for a Lot Later: An Evaluation of a Texas Advanced Placement Incentive Program," *Journal of Human Resources* 45, no. 3 (2010): 591–639.
65. Susan M. Dynarski, "Loans, Liquidity and Schooling Decisions" (Harvard University, 2005).
66. Donald E. Heller, "The Impact of Loans on Student Access," in *The Effectiveness of Student Aid Policies: What the Research Tells Us*, edited by Sandy Baum, Michael McPherson, and Patricia Steele (New York: The College Board, 2008), pp. 39–68.
67. U.S. Government Accountability Office, "Challenges in Estimating Federal Subsidy Costs," GAO-05-874 (Government Printing Office, September 29, 2005). This report estimated that subsidized Stafford Loans cost just four cents per dollar of loans disbursed through the federal direct loan program, while unsubsidized Stafford Loans provided a net gain to the government of nearly six cents for every dollar disbursed.
68. Jesse Rothstein and Cecilia Rouse, "Constrained after College: Student Loans and Early-Career Occupational Choices," *Journal of Public Economics* 95, no. 1–2 (2011): 149–63.
69. Erica Field, "Educational Debt Burden and Career Choice: Evidence from a Financial Aid Experiment at NYU Law School," *American Economic Journal: Applied Economics* 1, no. 1 (2009): 1–21.
70. Shlomo Benartzi and Richard H. Thaler, "Heuristics and Biases in Retirement Savings Behavior," *Journal of Economic Perspectives* 21, no. 3 (2007): 81–104.
71. Baum and Ma, *Trends in College Pricing 2011*(see note 5).
72. Ibid.
73. Christopher Avery and Thomas J. Kane, "Student Perceptions of College Opportunities: The Boston COACH Program," in *College Choices: The Economics of Where To Go, When To Go, and How To Pay for It*, edited by Hoxby, pp. 355–94.
74. U.S. Government Accountability Office, *Higher Education: Improved Tax Information Could Help Families Pay for College*, Report to the Committee on Finance, U.S. Senate, GAO-12-560 (Government Printing Office, 2012).
75. Stephanie Riegg Cellini and Claudia Goldin, "Does Federal Student Aid Raise Tuition? New Evidence on For-Profit Colleges," Working Paper 17827 (Cambridge, Mass.: National Bureau of Economic Research).
76. Larry Singell and Joe Stone, "For Whom the Pell Tolls: The Response of University Tuition to Federal Grants-in-Aid," *Economics of Education Review* 26 (2007): 285–95; Michael McPherson and Morton Schapiro, *Keeping College Affordable: Government and Educational Opportunity* (Washington: Brookings Institution, 1991).
77. Lesley J. Turner, "The Incidence of Student Financial Aid: Evidence from the Pell Grant Program" (Columbia University, Department of Economics, January 2012).

CHAPTER 5

AMERICAN HIGHER EDUCATION IN TRANSITION

RONALD G. EHRENBERG

American higher education is in transition along many dimensions: tuition levels, faculty composition, expenditure allocation, pedagogy, technology, and more.

During the last three decades, at private four-year academic institutions, undergraduate tuition levels increased each year on average by 3.5 percent more than the rate of inflation. The comparable increases for public four-year and public two-year institutions were 5.1 percent and 3.5 percent, respectively (Baum and Ma 2011, Figure 4). Tuition increases in private higher education have been associated over this period with increased real expenditures per student. In public higher education, as I detail below, at best, tuition increases have helped to compensate for reductions in state support (Desrouchers, Lenihan, and Wellman 2010).

The forces that cause private and public tuitions to increase at rates that exceed the rate of inflation have been extensively discussed in Ehrenberg (2002, 2006, 2007, 2010) and Archibald and Feldman (2011). They include the aspirations of academic institutions to be the very best they can be in every dimension of their activity. Also important are student and parent perceptions that where one goes to college is almost as important as whether one goes to college and the belief that higher-priced selective private institutions confer unique educational and economic advantages on their students; this leads higher-priced, selective private institutions to have long lines of applicants and only limited market forces to limit their tuition increases, which in turn provides cover for less-selective institutions to raise their tuition levels.[1] Higher education is also driven by published rankings, such as those of *U.S. News and World Report*, which are based partially on institutions' expenditures per student. Finally, the growth of technology can lead to improvements in the quality of higher education but often comes at a high cost. For public institutions, add to these pressures the cutbacks in state support.

Even as undergraduate tuition levels and spending per student are increasing, the nature of faculty positions has changed dramatically during the last 30 to 40 years. The percentage of faculty nationwide that is full-time has declined from almost 80 percent since 1970, to 51.3 percent in 2007, and the vast majority of part-time faculty members do not have Ph.D.s (Snyder and Dillow 2010, tables 249, 253). The percentage of full-time faculty not on tenure track has more than doubled between 1975 and 2007, increasing from 18.6 percent to 37.2 percent (AAUP Fact Sheet, n.d.). Of course, this change raises the question of whether, or how much, different types of undergraduates benefit from being taught by full-time tenured or tenure-track faculty.

Part of the reason for a rise in tuition at the same time as what appears to be a decline in spending on faculty is that the *tuition discount rate*—the share of each tuition dollar that institutions returned to their undergraduate students in the form of need-based or merit grant aid—increased substantially at private four-year institutions. For example, the average tuition discount rate for first-time, full-time, first-year students at private four-year institutions reached 42 percent in fall 2008; in fall 1990, the comparable figure was 26.7 percent (National Association of College and University Business Officers 2009, 2010). In short, much of the increase in tuition revenues at private colleges and universities has been plowed back into undergraduate aid; at all but a handful of the very wealthiest private institutions, the vast majority of undergraduate financial aid dollars come from tuition revenue.[2] The wealthiest and most selective private institutions of higher education dramatically increased the generosity of their financial aid policies for several reasons: relatively small fractions of their students were coming from lower-income and lower-middle-income families (Supiano and Fuller 2011), and the institutions wanted to attract these students; a combination of rapid growth rates in their endowments during much of the period and relatively low endowment spending rates led to pressure from the U.S. Congress for them to increase endowment spending on financial aid; and, after the financial collapse in 2008, the decline in family incomes and asset levels meant dramatic increases in the financial need of their applicants. Other less-selective private institutions, which face highly salient competition from lower-priced public institutions, also faced a dramatic need to increase grant aid and offer tuition discounts both to fill all their seats and to achieve desired class composition in terms of student selectivity and other characteristics.[3]

In public higher education, tuition increases in recent decades have barely offset a long-run decline in state appropriations per full-time equivalent student. State appropriations per full-time equivalent student at public higher educational institutions averaged $6,454 in fiscal year 2010; at its peak in fiscal year 1987, the comparable number (in constant dollars) was $7,993 (State Higher Education Executive Officers 2011, figure 3), translating into a decline of 19 percent over the period. Even if one leaves out the "Great Recession," real state appropriations per full-time equivalent student were still lower in fiscal year 2008 than they were 20 years earlier. Overall, the sum of net tuition revenue and state appropriations per full-time equivalent student at the publics was roughly the same in real terms in fiscal year 2010 as it was in fiscal year 1987.

In addition, academic institutions have changed how they allocate their resources. The share of institutional expenditures going to faculty salaries and benefits in both public and private institutions has fallen relative to the share going to nonfaculty uses like student services, academic support, and institutional support (Desrochers, Lenihan, and Wellman 2010). This change has been accompanied by changing modes of instruction, together with different uses of technology—and in a number of schools by charging differential tuition across students.

This paper discusses these changes in faculty composition, expenditure allocation, pedagogy, technology, and differential tuition, how they are distributed across higher education sectors, and their implications. I conclude with some speculations about the future of American education.

The Changing Nature of the Faculty

The composition of the faculty in institutions of higher education has evolved in two ways: Ph.D.s have become more widespread among the full-time faculty across all types of institutions, but there has been a move away from full-time and tenure-track jobs.

On the spread of Ph.D.s, the best historical data is collected annually by the American Mathematical Society (and is available at http://www.ams.org/profession/data/annual-survey/annual-survey). Between 1967 and 2009, the share of full-time mathematics faculty with a Ph.D. remained constant at about 90 percent at departments that offered doctoral degrees, but rose from 40 to 80 percent at those whose highest degree offered was a master's degree and from 30 to 70 percent at departments whose highest degree offered was a bachelor's degree, with most of the increase in the latter two types of institutions occurring by the mid-1980s (Ehrenberg 2011, Figure 4.1). Assuming that mathematics was typical of many other academic disciplines, a growing supply of Ph.D.s allowed the bachelor's and master's institutions to increase the shares of their full-time faculty members with Ph.D.s.

Columns A of Table 5.1 present information on the percentages of full-time faculty members that are not on tenure tracks, by institutional type, for 1995, 2001, and 2007. In this table, and several others that follow, institutions classified as "associate's" typically offer two-year degrees as the highest degree; those classified as "bachelor's" offer primarily bachelor's degrees; those classified as "master's" typically offer undergraduate and master's degrees; and those classified as "doctoral" typically offer a wide range of undergraduate and graduate degrees including doctoral degrees. The data are for a set of 2,606 institutions that reported information to the Integrated Postsecondary Education Data System (IPEDS) *Fall Staff Surveys* in all of the years.

TABLE 5.1

Changing Faculty Types

	Full-Time, Non-Tenure-Track Faculty as a Percentage of all Full-Time Faculty (A)			Part-Time Faculty as a Percentage of All Faculty (B)		
Category (Sample Size)	**1995**	**2001**	**2007**	**1995**	**2001**	**2007**
Associate's						
Public (899)	38.4	39.4	43.1	64.7	67.0	68.9
Private not-for-profit (51)	74.3	75.4	82.5	52.3	50.4	56.1
Private for-profit (101)	98.7	90.0	97.7	49.0	51.0	57.7
Bachelor's						
Public (139)	17.1	22.9	23.4	39.6	42.2	43.7
Private not-for-profit (497)	22.2	26.9	30.8	33.1	37.4	41.7
Private for-profit (33)	79.6	91.9	90.6	57.9	64.9	78.6
Master's						
Public (261)	12.7	17.6	20.6	29.3	37.0	40.3
Private not-for-profit (332)	25.1	28.6	33.6	50.8	53.3	59.5
Private for-profit (17)	71.6	85.2	93.7	62.2	70.8	89.7
Doctoral						
Public doctoral (166)	24.4	32.1	35.2	19.7	22.5	24.0
Private not-for-profit (106)	18.2	35.4	46.2	32.2	34.9	31.7
Public doctoral (166)	24.4	32.1	35.2	19.7	22.5	24.0

Source: Author's calculations based on data for 2,606 institutions that reported information to the Integrated Postsecondary Education Data System (IPEDS) Fall Staff Surveys in all of the years.

Note: In this table, and several others that follow, institutions classified as "associate's" typically offer two-year degrees as the highest degree; those classified as "bachelor's" offer primarily bachelor's degrees; those classified as "master's" typically offer undergraduate and master's degrees; and those classified as "doctoral" typically offer a wide range of undergraduate and graduate degrees including doctoral degrees.

During the period, the percentages of full-time faculty members that were not on tenure tracks increased at all categories of institutions, with the largest absolute increase occurring at private not-for-profit doctoral institutions. As the research intensity of doctoral institutions increased over time, more of the undergraduate instruction at these institutions is being undertaken by full-time, non-tenure-track faculty. I will discuss this pattern further below. The percentages of full-time faculty members not on tenure tracks are very high at all categories of for-profit institutions.

Columns B of Table 5.1 present similar information on the percentages of all faculty members who are part-time. The part-time percentage grew at all categories of institutions, save for the private, not-for-profit doctoral institutions. In many categories the growth was relatively modest over the time frame shown here, with the greatest growth occurring in the growing for-profit higher education sector. The vast majority of part-time faculty do not have doctoral degrees (Ehrenberg 2011, table 4.4).

Data on the changes that have occurred specifically in departments of economics are more limited. The American Economic Association's annual survey of economics departments collects information on faculty types and data for a matched sample of 59 institutions offering Ph.D.s and 86 institutions where bachelor's degrees are the highest offered. Data for academic years 1998–99 and 2008–2009 appear in Scott and Siegfried (2009). During this ten-year period, the percentages of full-time faculty that were not on tenure tracks in the AEA sample increased from 4.3 to 8.7 percent in the economics departments of Ph.D. institutions, and from 7.5 to 13.8 percent in economics departments of the bachelor's institutions; the percentages of faculty that were part-time increased at the same institutions from 3.9 to 7.9 and from 6.5 to 11.9 percent, respectively (Scott and Siegfried, table 5, panel C).

To confirm these results, which after all are based on a limited number of institutions, I put a couple of research assistants to work in February 2011 looking at the web pages of the faculty employed at institutions ranked by *U.S. News & World Reports*: in particular, the top 83 ranked Ph.D. programs in economics, the economics departments at the top 189 national liberal arts colleges, and the economics departments at the top 107 regional master's institutions.[4] They calculated the number of full-time faculty members that are tenured or on tenure track, the number of full-time faculty that are not on tenure track, and the number of fulltime faculty that are visitors at each institution. In these calculations, instructors, lecturers, senior lecturers, clinical professors, professors of practice, and visiting instructors were counted as "not on tenure track." A separate tabulation looked at faculty with visiting professorial titles, because, especially at the major doctoral universities and selective liberal arts colleges, visitors may be tenured or on tenure tracks at other institutions. The research assistants then summarized the numbers over all of the departments in a category and computed the means (weighted by faculty size) across departments of the percentages of full-time faculty that are not on tenure track, excluding visitors other than visiting instructors. They also calculated the percentages of all full-time faculty that are visitors with professorial rank. These percentages appear in Table 5.2.[5]

TABLE 5.2

Full-Time Faculty in Economics Departments that Are Non-Tenure-Track or Visitors with Professorial Titles

(for top Ph.D. programs in economics, and top national liberal arts colleges and regional master's institutions as defined by U.S. News & World Report*)*

	Non-Tenure-Track		Visitors with Professorial Titles	
	Mean Percentage	(Mean Percentages Weighted by Faculty Size)	Mean Percentage	(Mean Percentages Weighted by Faculty Size)
Top 83 Ph.D. programs in economics	13.8	(15.0)	9.2	(9.5)
a) Top 25	13.1	(13.9)	15.9	(16.0)
b) Rank 27–50	15.4	(16.6)	5.9	(6.1)
c) Rank 54–83	13.0	(18.7)	6.4	(5.2)
Economics departments at the top 189 national liberal arts colleges	6.0	(6.5)	4.8	(6.6)
a) Top 50	6.6	(7.3)	11.6	(10.3)
b) Rank 51–100	5.7	(5.1)	3.8	(4.4)
c) Rank 101–189	5.8	(6.3)	1.0	(0.8)
Economics departments at the top 107 regional master's institutions	8.3	(11.8)	3.0	(3.6)

Source: Author's calculations from faculty data on departmental web pages in February 2011.

Notes: Faculty classified as non-tenure-track include lecturers, instructors, visiting lecturers, visiting instructors and faculty with titles such as professor of practice or clinical professor. Percentage "Non-tenure-track" are: Non-tenure-track faculty / (Tenured or tenure-track faculty + Non-tenure-track faculty). Percentage "Visitors with professorial titles" are: Visitors with professorial titles / (Tenured or tenure-track faculty + Non-tenure-track faculty).

The mean percentage of full-time economics faculty (excluding visitors with professorial ranks) that are *not* on tenure tracks is 13.8 percent for the top 83 Ph.D. programs, while the weighted (by faculty size) mean is 15.0 percent; both of these measures are higher than the comparable implied percentage found by Scott and Siegfried (2009). The mean percentage of full-time visiting faculty in these departments is around 9 percent. Visiting professors make up a much greater share (around 16 percent) of the faculty at top 25 ranked economics departments, probably because tenured and tenure-track faculty from other leading departments often visit for research purposes.

The percentage of full-time economics faculty that are not on tenure tracks at top liberal arts colleges is around 6 percent; somewhat lower than Scott and Siegfried (2009) found. Visiting faculty members are much more prevalent in economics departments at the top 50 liberal arts colleges than they are at the other national liberal arts colleges. Finally, the mean percentage of full-time economics faculty members that are not on tenure tracks at top regional master's institutions is 8.3 percent and the weighted mean is 11.8 percent. Visiting professors are scarcer at these master's institutions relative to the other categories of institutions.

A final source of data on economics faculty comes from the annual reports of the Committee on the Status of Women in the Economics Profession (CSWEP). These reports provide data for a larger sample of Ph.D.-granting departments and liberal arts colleges than the AEA data, because of the persistence of CSWEP members in making contacts at each department. For example, the 2010 CSWEP report was based on data from 121 Ph.D.-granting institutions and 97 liberal arts institutions. The CSWEP data indicate that the percentage of full-time faculty that were not on tenure tracks at economics departments rose from 10.8 to 20.0 at the Ph.D. institutions and from 15.0 to 16.4 at the liberal arts institutions between 2005 and 2010.[6] Some care must be used in interpreting these numbers because the responding institutions vary between the two years and the CSWEP data do not separate out visiting faculty and other non-tenure-track faculty. But they do confirm that the usage of full-time, non-tenure-track faculty has been increasing at the doctoral universities. In these data, 33 percent of the non-tenure-track faculty in economics were female at the Ph.D. institutions in 2010; the comparable female share of tenure-track assistant professors at these institutions was 27.6 percent. I will speculate below that the greater share of non-tenure-track faculty members that is female is due to the difficulty that some female economists face in trying to combine tenure-track research careers and families at research universities.

Does the Falling Proportion of Tenured and Tenure-Track Faculty Matter?

A traditional argument for the importance of a tenure system for faculty is based upon academic freedom. Absent tenure, and the job security it provides, faculty members may be reluctant to pursue research on controversial issues. The importance of this rationale for tenure was brought home to me personally in the late 1970s when several trustees at my own institution challenged my promotion to professor because they disagreed with testimony I had given in a regulatory proceeding in the state of New York (as described in Ehrenberg 2002, p. 127). The Cornell Trustees shortly thereafter took the position, repeatedly affirmed, that the final decisions on tenure are to be made by the President and Provost of Cornell, with the Trustees only pro forma approving the decisions.

Economists have developed other arguments in support of tenure systems. One is that because a tenure system provides senior faculty with job security, they have an incentive to share their expertise with junior colleagues and students without creating competitors who will challenge their position; in this way, tenure facilitates the intergenerational transmission and expansion of knowledge (Stigler 1984). Another is that a tenure system can be thought of as an implicit long-term contract model, or a winner-take-all tournament model, and that both of these models can provide incentives for all faculty members to work harder (in the case of the contract model throughout the career; in the case of the tournament model, during the years prior to tenure and then to full professor) than would otherwise be the case (Lazear 1979; Rosen and Lazear 1981). In addition, a traditional labor economics argument holds that tenure is a desirable job characteristic and, in the absence of a tenure system, academic institutions would have to pay higher salaries to attract faculty. Indeed, in Ehrenberg, Pieper, and Willis (1999), my coauthors and I found that, ceteris paribus, economics departments that offer lower probabilities of tenure have to pay higher starting salaries to attract new faculty. A final argument is that if it is desirable for academics to specialize in their research in certain narrow subject areas, they need the reassurance of a reasonable probability of receiving tenure, because otherwise their specialization puts them at risk of having few alternative career options.

However, these arguments taken as a group seem to apply more to the role of faculty in research and institutional governance, rather than teaching. Is anything lost if undergraduate students are largely taught by adjuncts or full-time, non-tenure-track faculty, while a smaller number of tenure-track faculty focus on research and graduate education? After all, undergraduate students in most courses are typically being taught material that is far inside the research frontier. Does a more costly reliance on tenured and tenure-track faculty bring corresponding benefits for undergraduate education?

Only recently have economists and other social scientists begun to address this issue. While the results have been mixed, the existing research does suggest that a greater presence of tenured and tenure-track faculty will enhance undergraduate student outcomes. For example, in Ehrenberg and Zhang (2005), my coauthor and I used institutional-level panel data and found that—holding constant other variables including the socioeconomic backgrounds and test scores of entering students, and controlling for institutional fixed effects—when a four-year academic institution increases its use of either full-time, non-tenure-track faculty or part-time faculty, its undergraduate students' first-year persistence rates and graduation rates decrease. Using a similar methodology, Jacoby (2006) found that public two-year colleges that relied more heavily on part-time faculty had lower graduation rates, while Eagan and Jaeger (2009) and Jaeger and Eagan (2009) found that increased exposure of two-year college students to part-time faculty reduced the likelihood of the students transferring to four-year colleges or completing their associate's degrees. Finally, Bettinger and Long (2007) found that students attending Ohio public four-year colleges that take "adjunct heavy" first-year class schedules are less likely to persist in college after their first year; Jaeger and Eagan (2011) found a similar result for public two-year college students within a single state system.

In contrast, Bettinger and Long (2010) showed that having an adjunct as an instructor in an introductory class in some professional fields increases the likelihood that a student will take additional classes in the field, while Hoffman and Oreopoulos (2009) found that the tenure/tenure-track status and full-time/part-time status of a faculty member has no impact, on average, on student outcomes at a major Canadian research university. Of course, the costs of any increased use of non-tenure-track faculty on graduation and persistence rates must also be balanced against the financial savings from doing so. In Ehrenberg and Zhang (2005), we found, for example, that a 10 point increase in the percentage of full-time faculty not in tenure-track positions was associated with a 4.4 percentage point reduction in graduation rates at public master's-level institutions. As Table 5.3 indicates, the difference in average salaries between full-time lecturers and assistant professors at these institutions was over $10,000 a year in 2009–2010.

Given that many non-tenure-track faculty members are dedicated teachers and can devote themselves fully to undergraduate education because they face lesser research expectations, why might they be associated with lower student outcomes than their tenured and tenure-track faculty colleagues? One likely reason is that adjunct faculty appointments are often ad hoc in nature and instructors trying to eke out a living from this type of work must take on higher teaching loads, perhaps spread in across multiple institutions within an urban area, which leaves them little time and often no place to meet students outside of class.[7] Adjunct faculty in this difficult situation are also less likely to be up-to-date on their department's curriculum and may be less prepared to advise students. Non-tenure-track faculty who are full time will often have higher teaching loads than the teaching loads for the tenure-track faculty, which may also leave them with less time to work with individual students outside of class or to keep up with new developments in their field in a way that might encourage students to persist.

The increased pressure for faculty at major research universities to specialize in research has led the doctoral institutions to make greater use of full-time, non-tenure-track faculty in undergraduate education, especially at private universities (as shown earlier in Table 5.1). On the supply side, the relatively poor academic labor market conditions that currently confront new Ph.D.s, coupled with the large and growing salary differentials between major private research universities and virtually all other categories of academic institutions (Ehrenberg 2003), have made full-time, non-tenure-track teaching positions at the private doctoral universities an increasingly attractive alternative for new Ph.D.s.

This increased usage of full-time, non-tenure-track teaching positions has brought some efforts to improve the status of such faculty. While teaching loads of these faculty are often higher than those of their tenure-track colleagues (in part because the teaching loads of the latter have declined over time), teaching loads for the non-tenure-track faculty at the private doctoral universities are often lower—or at least no higher—than they would be if they were employed at other academic institutions in tenure-track positions.[8] For example, a fall 2003 survey found that while full-time instructional faculty and staff at public and private doctoral institutions spent an average of about 8 hours per week in the classroom, those at public and private master's programs spent about 11 hours per week in the classroom, and those at public two-year institutions spent 18 hours per week in the classroom (National Center for Education Statistics, 2005).

Table 5.3 presents data for 2009–2010 on average faculty salaries for assistant professors and lecturers (all departments), by institution type and form of control, from a salary survey done by the American Association of University Professors. The private data are for non-church-related institutions. The average salary of lecturers at private doctoral universities is about $21,500 less than the average salary of assistant professors at those universities; however, it is only slightly lower than the average salary of assistant professors at public doctoral and private master's institutions and is higher than those of assistant professors at public master's, public and private bachelor's, and two-year colleges. These data suggest that the financial costs of accepting a lecturer position at a private doctoral university, if any, may not be that high relative to accepting an assistant professor position at most other types of academic institution, at least in the short-run. Furthermore, these non-tenure-track jobs need not come without a degree of job security. Conversations that I have had with economists at several private doctoral universities, who are either employed in non-tenure-track positions or are chairs of departments that hire such faculty, suggest that many of these positions now often offer "rolling multiyear contracts." For example, a lecturer may teach under a three-year contract that can be extended annually for a year if performance is satisfactory. Moreover, positions for non-tenure-track faculty members often have low or no research expectations, while offering an opportunity to teach at a major university with bright students and high-quality colleagues.

TABLE 5.3

Average Faculty Salary, by Rank and Institution Type in 2009–2010

Institution/Rank	Assistant Professor	Lecturer	Lecturer at Private Doc./Asst. Prof. in Category	Lecturer at Public Doc./Asst. Prof. in Category
Private doctoral	83,573	61,860	0.74	0.62
Public doctoral	68,718	52,529	0.90	0.76
Private master's	63,003	55,272	0.98	0.83
Public master's	59,959	49,796	1.03	0.88
Private bachelor's	58,762	58,167	1.05	0.89
Public bachelor's	57,001	50,628	1.09	0.92
Two-year colleges	53,757	52,681	1.15	0.98

Source: American Association of University Professors, 2010, *The Annual Report on the Economic Status of the Profession: 2009–2010*, table 4. Available at: http://www.aaup.org/AAUP/pubsres/research/compensation.htm.

The data in Table 5.3 indicate that the average salary of lecturers at public doctoral universities is lower than the average salary of assistant professors in all categories of institutions. However, because of the lower teaching loads that the public doctoral institutions offer, jobs at such institutions may be attractive to new Ph.D.s given the current conditions of the academic labor market. Such programs also can attract high-quality, non-tenure-track faculty. Given the access of both public and private doctoral institutions to high-quality, non-tenure-track faculty, it should not be surprising that in Ehrenberg and Zhang (2005) we found that the expansion of full-time, non-tenure-track positions at doctoral universities had a smaller effect on undergraduate students' persistence and graduation rates than it had at the public master's-level institutions.

The data cited above from the Committee on the Status of Women in the Economics Profession (CSWEP) indicate that the average share of non-tenure-track faculty that is female at Ph.D. departments of economics is greater than the average share of assistant professors that is female at these same departments. A considerable body of research has noted the underrepresentation of females, relative to their share of new Ph.D.s, in tenure-track positions in science and engineering fields at research universities. A study by the National Research Council (2010) found that this underrepresentation is largely because female Ph.D.s are not applying for these positions at the same rate as their male counterparts. One obvious possible reason for this is that female scientists in their child-bearing years face a more difficult challenge than their male colleagues in striking a work–life balance (Mason and Goulden 2004). As a result, many research universities are adopting policies to alter the workplace and faculty culture to accommodate family issues (see for example, the UC Family Friendly Edge project, at http://ucfamilyedge.berkeley.edu).

Why Is a Declining Share of Resources Going to Instruction?

The share of academic resources going to instructional expenditures has declined at all categories of public and private not-for-profit institutions. On average, instructional expenditures per full-time-equivalent student—primarily faculty salary and benefits—increased by 1.07 percent a year above the rate of increase in the Consumer Price Index during the fiscal years 1987–2008, as shown in the bottom row of Table 5.4. In contrast, average real expenditures per full-time-equivalent student grew at more rapid annual rates for most other categories of institutional expenditures. These reallocations of funds away from instruction have been a major factor driving the shift away from full-time tenure and tenure-track faculty.

Why did these budget reallocations occur? The funding of higher education institutions comes from a variety of sources—and funds provided for some activities cannot be transferred to other activities.[9] For example, the "public service" category includes separately budgeted funds for non-instructional services to external groups, such as cooperative extension activities, public broadcasting, and externally funded conferences. These activities are supported largely by targeted state appropriations, external grants, and targeted fundraising, and these funds cannot be used to support instructional activities.

Similarly, the research category includes sponsored research, which grew substantially during the period. Funds provided by external sponsors for research cannot be used for instruction. Moreover, during this period the share of academic research supported out of institutional funds grew dramatically, due to limitations established by the Office of Management and Budget in 1991 on "federal indirect cost rates" or "facilities and administration charges" (the "mark-up" allowed on the direct costs of research when universities are reimbursed through government research grants); growing requirements by the federal government for matching funds in grant proposals; and the growing cost of providing start-up funding for new scientists and engineers, which often is not recoverable in indirect cost rates (Ehrenberg, Rizzo, and Jakubson 2007). As a result, the percentage of academic institutions' total cost of research that is paid for by the institutions themselves out of institutional funds grew from about 12 percent in fiscal year 1976 to over 20 percent in fiscal year 2008 (Berdahl 2009). Increases in the institutional resources that academic institutions devote to research are associated, ceteris paribus, with increases in student/faculty ratios and with some

TABLE 5.4

Annual Average Percentage Real Changes in Expenditures per Full-Time Equivalent Student: FY1987–2008

	N	Instruction	Student Services	Academic Support	Research	Public Service	Institutional Support	Operations and Maintenance	Auxiliary
Public doctoral	151	0.87	1.64	1.39	2.89	2.13	1.35	0.79	0.46
Private doctoral	103	1.87	3.13	2.87	2.35	2.83	2.60	1.05	1.42
Public master's	227	0.72	1.82	1.49	2.80	2.81	1.27	0.70	0.06
Private master's	327	1.55	2.66	2.13	2.18	0.75	1.57	–0.33	0.11
Private bachelor's	461	1.70	3.05	2.17	2.95	1.26	1.76	–0.23	0.52
Public 2-year	739	0.67	1.57	1.14	0.06	1.00	1.42	0.76	0.42
All public	1,192	0.75	1.66	1.22	2.74	1.69	1.39	0.77	0.37
All private	891	1.67	2.94	2.22	2.39	1.40	1.79	–0.12	0.49
All	2,083	1.07	2.16	1.62	2.63	1.66	1.57	0.51	0.40

Source: Author's calculations from Integrated Postsecondary Education Data System (IPEDS) data as cleaned by the Delta Cost Project (http://www.deltacostproject.org). Public bachelor's institutions are excluded from this table because of the relatively small number of them that reported data in both years.

Note: Institutions classified as "master's" typically offer undergraduate and master's degrees; and those classified as "doctoral" typically offer a wide range of undergraduate and graduate degrees including doctoral degrees.

substitution of full-time lecturers for professorial rank faculty (Ehrenberg, Rizzo, and Jakubson 2007). In addition, the growing use of part-time faculty at doctoral institutions, holding constant the use of full-time faculty, has been shown to be associated with increased external research and development expenditures at an institution; using adjuncts at doctoral universities to reduce the teaching loads of full-time faculty allows the full-time faculty to generate more external research funding (Zhang and Ehrenberg 2010).

"Student service expenditures" include costs of admissions, registrar activities, and activities whose primary purpose is to contribute to students' emotional and physical well-being and to their development outside of the classroom. Examples include student activities, cultural events, student newspapers, intramural athletics, student organizations, supplementary instruction (such as tutoring), and student records. Intercollegiate athletics and student health services *may* also be included in this category of expenses, except when they are operated as self-supporting auxiliary enterprises.[10] The annual growth rates of student service expenditures are roughly double those of the annual growth rates of instructional expenditures for every category of academic institutions.

These expenditures are viewed by some critics as discretionary "frills" that make no direct contribution to students' persistence in and graduation from college. In Webber and Ehrenberg (2010), we showed, however, that they do positively influence both first-year persistence rates and graduation rates of undergraduate students at four-year academic institutions. Moreover, as one might expect, these expenditures have greater effects at institutions that enroll a greater share of students who are disadvantaged, as measured by either their average entrance test scores or the levels of Pell Grant dollars that they receive. Indeed, our simulations suggest that at institutions whose graduation rates were below the mean in the sample, reallocating some resources from instruction to student services would lead, on average, to an increase in graduation rates; a similar reallocation was shown not to increase graduation rates at institutions whose graduation rates were initially at or above the mean. At least for a subset of higher education institutions, the more rapid growth of student service expenditures over the period may not be symptomatic of waste.

"Academic support expenditures" are for the activities and services that support instruction, research, and public service, including libraries, museums, and academic computing. The more rapid growth rate of expenditures in this category happens in part because, while the corporate world often adopts technology to cut costs, in the academic world, technology has often been adopted by academic institutions to enhance student learning and provide students with tools they will need to compete in the job market (Archibald and Feldman 2011). Another factor in this category is the growing costs of libraries; inflation rates for library materials have, for a long time, far exceeded the general rate of inflation, and the proliferation of electronic journals have increased, rather than decreased library costs (Ehrenberg 2002, chap. 14). The Association of Research Libraries (2009, table 2) reports that between 1986 and 2006, the average price of a serial purchased by research libraries increased by 5.3 percent a year; the average annual increase in the Consumer Price Index was 3.05 percent during the same period.

"Institutional support expenditures" include legal, finance, audit, human resources, budget, alumni affairs and development, audit and risk management, and public relations costs of the university. A dramatic proliferation of government regulations and reporting requirements, as well as a cap of 26 percent in the administrative cost component of federal indirect cost rates, has substantially increased the costs borne by academic institutions in this category. Higher education institutions regularly plead for regulatory relief and an easing of reporting requirements in a variety of areas, including human subjects, animal research, effort reporting, financial reporting, conflict of interest, and hazardous materials (Association of American Universities 2011).

Higher education institutions have increasingly devoted more resources to alumni affairs and development activities, seeking to enhance flows of giving from alumni, other individuals, corporations, and foundations. From fiscal years 1989 to 2009, voluntary support to higher education institutions per student grew, on average, by about 2.3 percent a year in real terms (Council for Aid to Education 2010, table 2). These funds support current operations, capital projects, and the endowment—so not all giving shows up in current operating budgets. While the costs of generating gifts varies widely, a widely cited 1990 study found that the mean cost over all academic institutions was in the range of 15 to 17 cents per dollar raised in the late 1980s (Council for Advancement and Support of Education, 1990). A new study is underway; the results from its pilot study of a relatively small number of institutions indicate that while the costs per dollar raised continue to vary across institutions, on average they remain similar to the earlier study.[11] If the costs per dollar raised remained roughly constant over the period, academic institutions' investments in fund-raising clearly also contributed to the increase in institutional support expenditures.

Expenditures on auxiliary enterprises are typically supported primarily by user fees: for example, hospitals, campus stores, residence halls, and food service all receive very little support from institutions' operating budgets. These expenditures, as well as those on operations and maintenance, grew at slower rates than instructional expenditures. Kaiser and Davis (1996) estimated that American higher education institutions had $26 billion dollars of accumulated deferred maintenance in 1995, of which $5.7 billion were urgent needs, so the slow growth of operations and maintenance expenditures may portend longer-run problems. Private conversations that I have had with James A. Kadamus, Vice President of Sightlines, a facility asset advisory firm that has the largest verified academic institution facilities database in the country, also suggests that this may well be the case. Academic institutions, in particular public institutions, have large aging facilities structures; recently, funding for maintenance of these facilities has not kept up with needs. And the additions of new facilities increases operating and maintenance needs, often without full thought in advance about where operating and maintenance funds will come from. Only a rare institution firmly commits not to increase the total square footage of facilities on the campus. However, the Ohio State University took this step in June 2010, when the Board of Trustees adopted a framework for capital facilities that called for adding to academic space only as replacements for existing facilities.

The explanations I have provided for the decreasing share of academic budgets going to instruction does not mean that I believe that academic institutions have always carefully controlled their administrative costs. They have not! Political scientist Benjamin Ginsberg (2011) argues that the growth of administration is largely due to the growth of a class of professional administrators who seek to "feather their own nests"; the result is the expansion of the bureaucracy and the declining role of the faculty in academic governance. However, the financial meltdown and deep recession that started in 2008 caused many colleges and universities to address their administrative cost levels. A number of the more wealthy public and private universities hired outside consultants to advise them how to restructure their administrative services (Keller 2010). The consultants' recommendations commonly fell into several main categories; reducing the layers of administration; increasing the number of direct reports each administrator supervises; centralizing procurement at large institutions and systems of institutions to achieve price concessions from suppliers; achieving efficiencies in information technology; and reorganizing the delivery of support services, such as finance, communications, and human resources. At Cornell, for example, we expect to achieve savings of $75–85 million a year on our Ithaca campus by fiscal year 2015 from these efforts (see http://asp.dpb.cornell.edu), which represents more than 5 percent of Cornell's operating budget once one removes external research funding. Continual efforts to reduce both administrative and other costs will be necessary if academia is to have any hope of reducing rates of tuition increases.

Changing Modes of Instruction, Technology, and the For-Profit Sector

The financial pressures being placed on academic institutions, along with demands to increase access and to support students in persisting to the completion of a degree, are forcing institutions to reexamine how they educate students. Institutions are reexamining the prevailing "lecture/discussion" format. Many institutions, in particular those in the for-profit sector, are seeking to use technology to improve learning outcomes *and* to reduce the cost of instruction, especially in remedial and introductory classes. Several evaluation studies suggest online education can be as effective as regular classroom contacts, especially for mature students, and that a blend of online and face-to face instruction is often more effective than online instruction alone (Means, Toyama, Murphy, Bakia, and Jones 2009). These efforts may well have substantial effects on costs and on the nature of the academic workforce in the future.

One prominent illustration of this point is the work of the National Center for Academic Transformation (NCAT), which has led efforts to use information technology to improve learning outcomes and reduce costs. The NCAT website (at http://www.thencat.org/) lists over 30 large introductory courses that have been redesigned with its help, in quantitative, social science, humanities, and professional fields at a wide range of academic institutions, and provides links to descriptions of each redesign. The NCAT efforts tend to focus on replacing lectures with interactive computer-based learning resources such as tutorials, exercises, and frequent low-stakes quizzes, as well as individual and small group activities. Other points of emphasis include designing classes around mastering a series of learning objectives, and providing on-demand help, often in computer labs or online, staffed by a mixture of faculty, graduate assistants, peer tutors, or course assistants. Some of the cost reduction comes from a reduced reliance on costly full-time faculty and graduate assistants and an increased use of less-costly peer tutors and course assistants, who do things such as troubleshooting technical questions, monitoring student performance, and alerting the instructor to difficulties with teaching materials. This process may also enable institutions to leverage their best teachers more effectively.

Despite the successes of the classes reworked under the guidance of the National Center for Academic Transformation, dissemination of this model within and across institutions has been slow. There are numerous reasons: faculty skepticism about the usefulness of NCAT's approaches (in the face of the evidence); concerns about infringement on academic freedom in making decisions about how to teach; the unwillingness of some faculty to invest in new teaching methods; departmental concerns that the benefits of cost reduction will not accrue to them and that they will lose faculty positions; the difficulty of obtaining funds for required capital investments; and the need for stable leadership at departmental, college, university, and system levels committed to changing modes of instruction (Miller 2010).

A second example of innovative technology-based pedagogy comes from the Open Learning Initiative at Carnegie Mellon University (at http://oli.web.cmu.edu/openlearning/initiative). This project has designed more than a dozen classes in introductory subjects—in primarily mathematics and science fields—that make use of advances in cognitive knowledge about how learning occurs and that use technology to create intelligent tutoring systems, virtual laboratory simulations, and frequent opportunities for assessment. The Open Learning Initiative has made these classes freely available on its webpage. An evaluation of an introductory statistics class taught at Carnegie Mellon showed that when a hybrid model that combined online learning with classroom instruction was used, students learned as much or more than they did in classes using traditional instructional methods and in half the time (Lovett, Meyer, and Thille 2008). Other evaluations have confirmed the effectiveness of the Open Learning Initiative approach for other classes and for students at large public universities and community colleges (Thille and Smith 2011).

The activities of both the National Center for Academic Transformation and the Open Learning Initiative suggest that technology can be used to improve educational outcomes and reduce the time (per student) spent by faculty in introductory-level classes at institutions ranging from community colleges to doctoral institutions. These initiatives appear less likely to influence methods of instruction in specialized upper-level elective classes. Their activities also suggest that the comparison that one should be making is not between lecture classes taught by adjuncts and those taught by tenured professors (as many of the studies I cited earlier implicitly did), but between the various different ways of organizing and staffing a course and the traditional lecture/discussion format.

More specifically, how has teaching of economics changed? National surveys have been conducted of the teaching methods used by academic economists in their classrooms in 1995, 2000, 2005, and 2010 (Watts and Becker 2008; Watts and Schauer 2011). While these surveys offer some evidence of increased use of Power-Point displays, instructors putting class notes online, increased use of computer lab assignments in econometrics classes, and increased use of classroom experiments in introductory economics classes, the surveys also suggest that "chalk and talk" remains the dominant teaching method in economics (Watts and Schauer 2011).

However, response rates to the surveys have not been high: the 2010 survey had a response rate of only 10.5 percent. Thus, the surveys may not be capturing innovations in teaching economics. For example, there is an Open Learning Initiative introductory economics class developed by John Miller at Carnegie Mellon University that is associated with a textbook based in experimental economics (Bergstrom and Miller 1999). An innovation from the private sector involves Aplia, an educational technology company founded in 2000 by Paul Romer, which offers online homework assignments (with immediate grading), math and graphing tutorials, articles from news sources, real-time online market experiments, and course management systems. Currently, Aplia offers course support for introductory and intermediate microeconomics and macroeconomics, as well as courses in money, banking, and financial institutions; international economics; and advanced placement economics. Many of these classes are integrated with leading textbooks in the field.[12] Lyssa Vanderbeck, Director of Program Management at Aplia, reported that about 147,000 students in over 4,900 economics courses used Aplia during the fall of 2010 (e-mail communication to me, June 1, 2011).

As demonstrated in Table 5.1, the growing for-profit higher education sector has been the leading sector in using part-time and full-time, non-tenure-track faculty. A growing number of institutions in this sector have also been in the forefront of attempting to use technology to improve educational outcomes and developing new methods of recruiting, training, and assessing faculty members. For example, the University of Phoenix, the largest for-profit, offers associate's, bachelor's, master's, and doctoral programs in primarily professional fields to primarily working adults. The vast majority of its faculty members are practicing professionals and part-time faculty. The University of Phoenix puts them through extensive orientation and training programs. About two-thirds of these faculty have master's degrees and one-third, doctoral degrees. Curricula are developed by experts and are fairly standardized. Extensive use is made of technology to facilitate student learning, including placing course materials online, using online tutors, and having students conduct their own online self-assessments of learning. Faculty members are evaluated both by feedback from students and from assessments of how well students have mastered the subject matter. As is common with most for-profits, University of Phoenix offers classes at times and places that are most convenient for students, especially working adults.

Institutions that compete most directly with the for-profits, in particular community colleges and comprehensive public universities, will increasingly face pressure to emulate the educational model of the for-profits: in particular, they will face pressure to expand their use of part-time faculty further and to consider evaluating faculty members based more upon student outcomes. At least so far, efforts by traditional academic institutions to embed student learning outcomes in course evaluations are few and far between. Examples of efforts to embed learning outcomes in course evaluations include those of the IDEA Center (at http://www.ideacenter.org) and the Student Assessment of Learning Gains (at http://www.salgsite.org).

Differential Tuition

American colleges and universities have historically charged the same tuition levels for all of their undergraduate majors (with the exception perhaps of laboratory fees). However, as Hoenack and Weiler (1975) and Siegfried and Round (1997) pointed out, an academic institution might plausibly seek to charge different tuition levels for different majors based upon the costs of providing an education in each major and the income-earning prospects that it offers. Indeed, a growing number of public institutions are adopting differential tuitions by college or major, or by year of enrollment. To gauge how prevalent this trend has become, from November 2010 to March 2011 my research assistants pored through the web pages of virtually all public academic institutions that grant bachelor's degrees searching for information on differential tuitions. Table 5.5 summarizes their findings. The percentage of public institutions with differential tuitions in 2010–2011 was highest, at 42 percent, at the doctoral institutions. If one further narrows the doctoral category to flagship doctoral institutions, the percentage increases to over half.

Differential tuition for these institutions is typically by college or by major, although a smaller percentage of them have differential tuition by year of enrollment, with upper-level students being charged more per credit hour than lower-level students. At the public master's institutions, differential tuition is almost always by college or major. In contrast, at the public bachelor's institutions,

TABLE 5.5

Percentages of Four-Year Public Institutions with Differential Undergraduate Tuition in 2010–2011

	Doctoral	Master's	Bachelor's
Number of institutions	172	271	120
Percent with any differential tuition	42	18	30
Percent with differential tuition by college or major	40	17	23
Percent with differential tuition by year enrolled	10	4	23

Source: Author's calculations from search of institutional web pages during the January to March 2011 period.

Note: Institutions classified as "associate's" typically offer two-year degrees as the highest degree; those classified as "bachelor's" offer primarily bachelor's degrees; those classified as "master's" typically offer undergraduate and master's degrees; and those classified as "doctoral" typically offer a wide range of undergraduate and graduate degrees including doctoral degrees. Bachelor's institutions exclude public colleges that offer some bachelor's degrees but that primarily offer associate's degrees.

when differential tuition policies arise they are equally likely to be by college or major as by year of enrollment.

The most common programs for which differential tuition charges occur are business, engineering, and nursing. Examples of differential tuition charges in 2010–2011 that were obtained from institutional web pages include a $75 per engineering course fee at the University of Maine (a 9.4 percent increase over the in-state tuition of $801 for a three credit course), a $400 per credit hour additional tuition for business classes at Arizona State University (a 72 percent increase over the in-state per credit hour tuition of $557), and a $460 per semester nursing program fee at the University of Kentucky (a 10.7 percent increase over the in-state lower-division semester tuition of $4,305).

The possible consequences of differential tuition policies have not been empirically examined. Does differential tuition by major influence students' choice of major? Do higher tuition levels for upper-level students affect ultimate graduation rates? If such effects exist, are they larger for students from lower-income families? How might differential tuition charges interact with state and institutional financial aid policies?

Looking to the Future

Many faculty members will bemoan the decline of a golden age of American higher education, with its heavy reliance on tenured and tenure-track faculty. However, higher education is not immune to economic forces. The pressures that public and private colleges and universities face to expand enrollment, to increase graduation rates, and to limit future cost increases will likely only exacerbate the decline in full-time tenured and tenure-track faculty. Increasingly, academic leaders realize that how we teach our students must change, especially for remedial and introductory-level classes, and that technology must be employed to improve learning outcomes and reduce the per student costs of delivering instruction (Stripling 2011).

I am not noted for my ability to forecast the future, but I conclude with some personal speculations. The wealthy private and flagship public research universities and the leading private liberal arts colleges are in a world of their own. They will have access to the resources necessary to maintain full-time tenured and tenure-track faculty. They will increasingly employ technology in introductory-level classes in an effort to expand active learning and reduce costs, but in their case much of the cost savings will be directed to enhancing the quality of upper-division classes and furthering the research enterprise.

At research universities, the use of full-time, non-tenure-track faculty will likely continue and increase. For at least some new Ph.D.s, the combination of the pay levels at these institutions, their relatively low teaching loads (compared to other types of institutions), the low or nonexistent research demands, the possibility of rolling multiyear contracts, and the attractions of working at a large university will suffice to keep these non-tenure-track positions attractive. One result of this shift will be to free up more of the time of tenured and tenure-track faculty for research.

At the public and private regional doctoral universities, the public and private comprehensives, the other liberal arts colleges, and the two-year colleges, an ever-increasing share of faculty will not have doctoral degrees and will not be full-time on tenure-track lines. The use of technology and people in nonfaculty positions (like student assistants) to reduce costs and increase learning in remedial and introductory-level classes will likely occur much more rapidly at these institutions.

For all academic institutions, pressures for accountability surely will increase; academic institutions are increasingly being asked to provide information on assessing student learning outcomes as part of the accreditation process. Recent research by Arum and Roksa (2011) that concluded very little learning occurs in higher education for a large proportion of American students surely will add to these pressures. As such, one might expect to see an increased focus, especially in remedial and introductory classes, on evaluating faculty, at least partially, by their students' outcomes, as the for-profits do. This will put additional stresses on faculty/administration relations and faculty governance, especially at public campuses where collective bargaining contracts may specify faculty evaluation processes.

Few students who enter a Ph.D. program do so for the promise of financial rewards: other professional schools and alternate careers often promise higher annual earnings. Instead, students considering a Ph.D., especially those not considering degrees in science and engineering fields, have historically done so with the dreams of becoming a tenured faculty member and then pursuing a combination of research and teaching while participating in the governance of an academic institution. However, obtaining a Ph.D. has already become a less-attractive option in many fields, given the lengthening periods of time to complete the degree and the low levels of tenure-track hiring in the academic job market in recent years. Between 1979 and 2009, at U.S. universities, the share of new doctorates awarded to U.S citizens and permanent residents (among recipients with known nationalities) fell from 88 to 69 percent. By 2009, less than 40 percent of the new doctorates in economics were awarded to U.S. citizens or permanent residents (*2009 Survey of Earned Doctorates*, tables 16 and 19, available at http://www.nsf.gov/statistics/nsf11306/).

The share of faculty positions that are not on the tenure-track, and perhaps not full-time either, along with the high fraction of such positions staffed by faculty without a doctorate, will likely further discourage American college students from going on for Ph.D. study. Moreover, as the share of full-time tenured and tenure-track faculty dwindle, this group will inevitably play a lesser role in the governance of the institutions of higher education.

Acknowledgments

Financial support for the Cornell Higher Education Research Institute (CHERI) is provided by the Andrew W. Mellon Foundation and I am grateful to the Foundation for its support. Raj Kannappan, Andrew Key, Kristy Parkinson, Mirinda Martin, Douglas Webber, and Kenneth Whelan, all graduate and undergraduate research assistants at CHERI, assisted me in obtaining some of the data used in the paper, and I am also grateful for their help. Extraordinarily helpful comments on earlier drafts were provided by Charles Clotfelter, Gary Fethke, Daniel Hamermesh, Philip Lewis, and John Siegfried, as well as from the JEP editors. In places, this paper draws on Ehrenberg (2011).

Notes

1. That selective institutions provide students with unique advantages is disputed, with most studies, including Brewer, Eide, and Ehrenberg (1999), finding it to be true, while two other studies, Dale and Kruger (2002, 2011), offer contrary evidence.

2. A different, but important, question is how the *net tuition cost* paid by the average student has changed over time. In addition to institutional grant aid, net tuition calculations adjust posted tuition rates for federal, state, and other private grant aid and for tax credits for educational expenses. The College Board reports that while average tuition levels at public and private not-for-profit four-year institutions grew by average annual rates of 7.0 and 5.3 percent, respectively, during the 1990–91 to 2011–12 period, *net tuition* at the two types of institutions grew at lower annual rates of 4.1 and 3.4 percent, respectively, during the period. Average tuition levels grew at average annual rate of 0.6 percent per year at public two-year colleges during the period, but net tuition actually declined at them, largely due to increases in the generosity of the federal Pell Grant program (unpublished data from the College Board provided by Sandy Baum). For comparison purposes, the average annual rate of increase in the Consumer Price Index during the 1990 to 2010 period was about 2.7 percent.
3. While tuition levels rose in percentage terms by more at the four-year publics than they did at the four-year privates during the period, because tuition levels were so much lower at the publics at the start of the period, dollar increases in tuition were much larger at the privates, and the difference between public and private tuition levels (in real terms) increased during the period.
4. Some of the departments at master's institutions are departments of "economics and . . ." In these cases, wherever possible, the tabulations were limited to faculty who were teaching economics.
5. These calculations may understate the percentage of non-tenure-track faculty because some faculty with professorial ranks may not be on tenure tracks in these departments. Departmental web pages did not uniformly list all part-time faculty members so we could not tabulate information for this group.
6. Author's calculations from data in Tables 3 and 4 of the 2010 and Tables 2 and 5 of the 2005 CSWEP reports, available on the web at http://www.aeaweb.org/committees/cswep/annual_reports.php.
7. Zhang and Liu (2010) show that four-year academic institutions in urban areas make more use of part-time faculty than other four-year institutions.
8. The American Economic Association collects information on average yearly course loads for new assistant professors in economics departments in its annual *Universal Academic Questionnaire* and reports this information annually in its *American Economic Review* Papers and Proceedings (May) issue. The number of respondents to these questions is small, and the respondents vary over time. The responses (with sample sizes in parentheses) were, for academic year 1999–2000: Ph.D. institutions, 3.5 (30); master's institutions, 5.6 (11); and bachelor's institutions, 5.8 (38). For academic year 2009–2010, they were: Ph.D. institutions, 2.9 (35); master's institutions, 6.3(10); and bachelor's institutions 5.6 (32). The greatest reduction in course load was at the Ph.D. institutions. Charles Scott and John Siegfried provided me with information on ten departments at Ph.D. institutions that reported information for both 2010–11 and 2000–01, and the mean course load for new faculty at these departments fell during the ten-year period from 3.27 to 3.0 courses a year.
9. Appendix Table A1, available online with this paper at http://e-jep.org, illustrates how the sources of funds vary across categories of public and private not-for-profit academic institutions.
10. In the sample upon which Table 5.4 is based, over half of the institutions included varsity athletics in student service expenditures. The percentage that did so was over 80 percent for the private bachelor's and master's institutions and slightly more than 20 percent for the public doctoral institutions. "Public doctoral" is the only category of institutions in which more than a majority of the institutions (over 70 percent in our sample) included varsity athletics under auxiliary expenditures.
11. Private correspondence from Rae Goldsmith, Vice President for Advancement Resources, Council for Advancement and Support of Education (CASE).
12. The Aplia website is at http://aplia.com/economics. An example of Aplia's active learning materials are the active learning problem sets for principles of economics developed by Byron Brown of Michigan State University that are used by him in both his regular classroom and online teaching at http://www.bus.msu.edu/econ/brown/pim.

References

American Association of University Professors (AAUP). N.d. "Trends in Faculty Status, 1975–2007." AAUP Fact Sheet. http://www.aaup2.org/research/TrendsinFacultyStatus2007.pdf.

American Association of University Professors (AAUP). 2010. *The Annual Report on the Economic Status of the Profession: 2009–2010*, table 4. Available at: http://www.aaup.org/AAUP/pubsres/research/compensation.htm.

Archibald, Robert B., and David H. Feldman. 2011. *Why Does College Cost So Much?* New York: Oxford University Press.

Arum, Richard, and Josipa Roksa. 2011. *Academically Adrift: Limited Learning on American Campuses*. Chicago: University of Chicago Press.

Association of American Universities. 2011. "Regulatory and Financial Reform of Federal Research Policy: Recommendations to the NRC Committee on Research Universities." January 21, Available at: http://www.aau.edu/publications/reports.aspx?id=6900.

Association of Research Libraries. 2009. *ARL Statistics: 2007–2008*. Washington, DC: Association of Research Libraries.

Baum, Sandy, and Jennifer Ma. 2010. *Trends in College Pricing 2010*. New York: College Board.

Berdahl, Robert M. 2009. "Thoughts on the Current Status of American Research Universities: A Presentation to the National Academy's Board on Higher Education and Work Force." November 16. Available at: http://aau.edu/research/statement_speech.aspx?id=6898.

Bergstrom, Theodore, and James Miller. 1999. *Experiments with Economic Principles: Microeconomics*. New York: McGraw-Hill.

Bettinger, Eric P., and Bridget Terry Long. 2007. "The Increased Use of Adjunct Instructors at Public Universities: Are We Hurting Students?" In *What's Happening to Public Higher Education*, edited by Ronald G. Ehrenberg, 51–70. Baltimore: Johns Hopkins University Press.

Bettinger, Eric. P., and Bridget Terry Long. 2010. "Does Cheaper Mean Better: The Impact of Using Adjunct Instructors on Student Outcomes." *Review of Economics and Statistics* 92(3): 598–630.

Brewer, Dominic J., Eric R. Eide, and Ronald G. Ehrenberg. 1999. "Does It Pay to Attend an Elite Private College? Cross-Cohort Evidence of the Effects of College Type on Earnings." *Journal of Human Resources* 34(1): 104–23.

Council for Advancement and Support of Education. 1990. *Expenditures in Fund Raising, Alumni Relations, and Other Constituent (Public) Relations*. Washington, DC: Council for Advancement and Support of Education.

Council for Aid to Education. 2010. *2009 Voluntary Support of Higher Education*. New York: Council for Aid to Education.

Dale, Stacy, and Alan B. Krueger. 2002. "Estimating the Payoff to Attending a More Selective College: An Application of Selection on Observables and Unobservables." *Quarterly Journal of Economics* 117(4): 1491–1527.

Dale, Stacy, and Alan B. Krueger. 2011. "Estimating the Returns to College Selectivity over the Career Using Administrative Earnings Data." NBER Working Paper 17159.

Desrochers, Donna M., Colleen M. Lenihan, Jane V. Wellman. 2010. *Trends in College Spending: 1998–2008*. Washington, DC: Delta Cost Project. Available at: http://www.deltacostproject.org/analyses/index.asp.

Eagan, M. Kevin, and Audrey J. Jaeger. 2009. "Effects of Exposure to Part-Time Faculty on Community College Transfer." *Research in Higher Education* 50(2): 168–88.

Ehrenberg, Ronald G. 2002. *Tuition Rising: Why College Costs So Much*. Cambridge, MA: Harvard University Press.

Ehrenberg, Ronald G. 2003. "Studying Ourselves: The Academic Labor Market." *Journal of Labor Economics* 21(2): 267–87.

Ehrenberg, Ronald G. 2006. "The Perfect Storm and the Privatization of Public Higher Education." *Change* 38(1): 46–53.

Ehrenberg, Ronald G., ed. 2007. *What's Happening to Public Higher Education? The Shifting Financial Burden*. Baltimore: Johns Hopkins University Press.

Ehrenberg, Ronald G. 2010. "The Economics of Tuition and Fees in American Higher Education." In Vol. 2 of *The International Encyclopedia of Education* 3rd edition, edited by Barry McGraw, Penelope Peterson, and Eva Baker, 229–34. Oxford, UK: Elsevier.

Ehrenberg, Ronald G. 2011. "Rethinking the Professoriate." In *Reinventing Higher Education: The Promise of Innovation*, edited by Ben Wildavsky, Andrew Kelly, and Kevin Carey, 101–28. Cambridge, MA: Harvard Education Press.

Ehrenberg, Ronald G., Paul J. Pieper, and Rachel A. Willis. 1999. "Do Economics Departments with Lower Tenure Probabilities Pay Higher Faculty Salaries?" *Review of Economics and Statistics* 80(4): 503–12.

Ehrenberg, Ronald G., Michael J. Rizzo, and George H. Jakubson. 2007. "Who Bears the Growing Cost of Science at Universities?" In *Science and the University*, edited by Paula E. Stephan and Ronald G. Ehrenberg, 19–35. Madison: University of Wisconsin Press.

Ehrenberg, Ronald G., and Liang Zhang. 2005. "Do Tenured and Tenure-Track Faculty Matter?" *Journal of Human Resources* 40(3): 647–59.

Ginsberg, Benjamin. 2011 *The Fall of the Faculty; The Rise of the All-Administrative University and Why It Matters.* New York: Oxford University.

Hoenack, Stephen A., and William C. Weiler. 1975. "Cost-Related Tuition Policies and University Enrollments." *Journal of Human Resources* 10(3): 332–60.

Hoffman, Florian, and Phillip Oreopoulos. 2009. "Professor Quality and Student Achievement." *Review of Economics and Statistics* 91(1): 83–92.

Jacoby, Daniel. 2006. "Effects of Part-Time Faculty Employment on Community College Graduation Rates." *Journal of Higher Education* 77(6): 1081–1103.

Jaeger, Audrey J., and M. Kevin Eagan. 2009. "Unintended Consequences: Examining the Effect of Part-Time Faculty Members on Associate's Degree Completion." *Community College Review* 36(1): 167–94.

Jaeger, Audrey J., and M. Kevin Eagan. 2011. "Examining Retention and Contingent Faculty Use in a State System of Higher Education." *Education Policy* 25(3): 507–37.

Kaiser, Henry H., and Jerry Davis. 1996. *A Foundation to Uphold: A Study of Facilities Conditions at U.S. Colleges and Universities.* Alexandria, VA: APPA, Association of Higher Education Facilities Officers.

Keller, Josh. 2010. "Universities Can Save Millions by Cutting Administrative Waste, Panelists Say." *Chronicle of Higher Education,* July 25. http://chronicle.com/article/Universities-Can-Save-Millions/123686/.

Lazear, Edward. 1979. "Why Is There Mandatory Retirement?" *Journal of Political Economy* 87(6): 1261–84.

Lovett, Marsha, Oded Meyer, and Candace Thille. 2008. "The Open Learning Initiative: Measuring the Effectiveness of OLI Statistics Courses in Accelerating Student Learning." *Journal of Interactive Media in Education,* no. 14, JIME Special Issue: Researching Open Content in Education. http://jime.open.ac.uk/2008/14.

Mason, Mary Ann, and Mark Goulden. 2004. "Do Babies Matter (Part II)? Closing the Baby Gap." *Academe* 90(6): 11–16.

Means, Barbara, Yukie Toyama, Robert Murphy, Marianne Bakia, and Karla Jones. 2009. *Evaluation of Evidence-Based Practices in Online Learning: A Meta-Analysis and Review of Online Learning Studies.* Washington, DC: U.S. Department of Education.

Miller, Ben. 2010. "The Course of Innovation: Using Technology to Transform Higher Education." Education Sector Reports. May 18. http://www.educationsector.org/publications/course-innovation-using-technology-transform-higher-education.

National Association of College and University Business Officers. 2009. "Newly Released NACUBO Tuition Discounting Study Survey Report Shows Rates Remain Stable." http://www.nacubo.org/Research/Research_News/Newly_Released_NACUBO_Tuition_Discounting_Survey_Report_Shows_Rates_Remain_Stable.html.

National Association of College and University Business Officers. 2010. *2009 NACUBO Tuition Discounting Study of Independent Institutions.* Washington, DC: National Association of College and University Business Officers.

National Center for Education Statistics. 2005. Table 21 of *2004 National Study of Postsecondary Faculty (NSOPF:04): Background Characteristics, Work Activities, and Compensation of Instructional Faculty and Staff: Fall 2003.* December. http://nces.ed.gov/pubs2006/2006176.pdf.

National Research Council. 2010. *Gender Differences at Critical Transitions in the Careers of Science, Engineering and Mathematics Faculty.* Washington, DC: National Academy Press.

Rosen, Sherwin, and Edward Lazear. 1981. "Rank Order Tournaments as Optimal Labor Contracts." *Journal of Political Economy* 89(5): 841–64.

Scott, Charles, and John Siegfried. 2009. "American Economic Association Universal Academic Questionnaire Summary Statistics." *American Economic Review* 99(2): 641–45.

Siegfried, John, and David Round. 1997. "Differential Fees for Degree Courses in Australian Universities." In *Funding Higher Education: Performance and Diversity,* edited by Jonathan Pincus, and Paul Miller, 45–62. Canberra: Department of Employment, Education, Training, and Youth Affairs.

Snyder, Thomas D, and Sally A. Dillow. 2010. *Digest of Education Statistics 2009.* NCES 2010-13. Washington, DC: U.S. Department of Education.

State Higher Education Executive Officers. 2011. *State Higher Education Finance: FY 2010.* Boulder: SHEEO.

Stigler, George. 1984. "An Academic Episode." In *The Intellectual and the Marketplace.* Edited by George Stigler, 1–9. Cambridge, MA: Harvard University Press.

Stripling, Jack. 2011. "Governing Boards Turn to Technology to Reinvent the University." *Chronicle of Higher Education,* April 5.

Supiano, Beckie, and Andrea Fuller. 2011. "Elite Colleges Fail to Gain More Students on Pell Grants." *Chronicle of Higher Education*, March 27.

Thille, Candace, and Joel Smith. 2011 "Cold Rolled Steel and Knowledge: What Can Higher Education Learn About Productivity?" *Change* 43(2): 21–27.

Watts, Michael, and William E. Becker. 2008. "A Little More than Chalk and Talk: Results from a Third National Survey of Teaching Methods in Undergraduate Economics Courses." *Journal of Economic Education* 39(3): 273–86.

Watts, Michael, and Georg Schaeur. 2011. "Teaching and Assessment Methods in Undergraduate Economics: A Fourth National Quinquennial Survey." *Journal of Economic Education* 42(3): 294–309.

Webber, Douglas A., and Ronald G. Ehrenberg. 2010. "Do Expenditures Other than Instructional Expenditures Affect Graduation and Persistence Rates in American Higher Education?" *Economics of Education Review* 29(6): 947–58.

Zhang, Liang, and Ronald G. Ehrenberg. 2010. "Faculty Employment and R&D Expenditures at Research Universities." *Economics of Education Review* 29(3): 329–37.

Zhang, Liang, and Xiangmin Liu. 2010. "Faculty Employment at 4-Year Colleges and Universities." *Economics of Education Review* 29(4): 543–52.

CHAPTER 6

THE FINANCIAL AID PICTURE: REALISM, SURREALISM, OR CUBISM?

DONALD E. HELLER

Introduction

Financial assistance for students to attend college has existed almost as long as higher education in the United States. Holtschneider (1997) describes how the earliest colonial colleges offered assistance to those students deemed unable to pay for the cost of education themselves. As public colleges and universities developed in the nineteenth century, they too offered means-tested financial assistance to select students. Heller (2002a) described how from the beginning, the University of Virginia—generally considered to be the first true public university—offered free tuition to poor students from the Commonwealth of Virginia.

Over the ensuing centuries, financial aid from both institutional sources and publicly funded sources has grown and changed. A number of articles, including chapters in previous volumes of the handbook, have described and analyzed these policies. Many of these sources have focused on the federal role in funding higher education, an interesting proposition given that the US Constitution is silent on a federal role for education at any level. Gladieux and Wolanin (1976) describe the history of the federal government's role in providing financial assistance to students and institutions, including a detailed analysis of the creation of the Higher Education Act of 1965 and the important 1972 reauthorization (described in Section "A Brief History of Financial Aid"). Hearn (1993) describes the "paradox" of federal support for financial aid, noting that it "defies the ideals of logical policy development and implementation as described in the classic texts" (p. 95).

As federal student aid policy began to drift away from the primary goal of aiding poorer students as operationalized in the Higher Education Act of 1965, by the late 1970s and early 1980s, new analyses focused on the impact this change had on college access and equity. Fitzgerald and Delaney (2002), Gladieux (2002), and Hearn and Holdsworth (2004) chart the initiatives aimed at middle-class families during this era along with an emphasis on student loans over grants, a policy shift that has been shown to be detrimental to the college access and attainment interests of poorer students. St. John (2003) analyzes these trends as well and offers up a policy prescription to refocus the student financing system on its initial goals of equalizing educational opportunity.

Other analyses have focused on the role of states in financing student aid. Heller (2002b) and Hauptman (2001) documented historical shifts in student financing policy, some of which paralleled federal changes toward advantaging middle-income students, through the development of higher tuition policies and merit aid programs. Mumper (1996, 1998, 2001) analyzes how fiscal demands on states have caused them to shift resources away from higher education toward such priorities as K-12 education, corrections, and health needs, which has resulted in reduced affordability and access for lower-income students. Zumeta (1997) describes how states have expanded efforts at aiding private higher education institutions, often at the expense of the public sector.

Institutional financial aid, and its impact on access, affordability, and student success, has also received the scrutiny of researchers. Economists and college presidents Michael McPherson and Morton Owen Schapiro (1991, 1998, 2002) have been at the forefront of this research. Their work has tracked how institutions have used their own financial aid resources throughout history, how this has changed, and how these changes have interacted with state and federal student financing policies.

In this chapter, I draw on the work of many of these scholars along with my own research to describe how changes in the last three decades have altered financial aid and how it is provided to students today. The chapter opens with a brief history of aid provided by the federal and state governments, as well as that awarded by colleges and universities themselves.[1] Then I provide an overview of the current state of funding for financial aid in the nation. Finally, I use the metaphor of three distinct art movements—Realism, Surrealism, and Cubism—to analyze how the financial aid picture in the country has evolved and its current status.

A Brief History of Financial Aid

Federal Financial Aid

The passage of the Servicemen's Readjustment Act of 1944, usually referred to as the "GI Bill," is often noted as the federal government's first large-scale foray into providing financial assistance for individual college students. As I noted in Chapter 5 of Volume 17 of the Handbook (Heller, 2002a), however, the legislation was not motivated by equity or egalitarian considerations, but more as a means of ensuring that the returning veterans were not plunged into an American society that was adjusting from the economic boom of the war effort to a post-war civilian economy (for more on the GI Bill see Bennett, 1996; Greenberg, 1997).

The GI Bill was a smashing success, with college enrollments in the country increasing from 1.5 million in 1939–1940, immediately before World War II, to 2.4 million 10 years later, and 3.6 million 10 years after that, in 1959–1960 (National Center for Education Statistics, 2010b, Table 188). Much of this enrollment growth can be attributed to veterans taking advantage of their GI Bill benefits.

Even though the GI Bill was motivated more by economic considerations than by equity or egalitarianism, the federal government had examined the need for financial support for poor students to attend college. In July of 1946, President Harry Truman appointed the President's Commission on Higher Education (known as the Truman Commission), chaired by George Zook, president of the American Council on Education, the primary lobbying and advocacy group for higher education. The questions President Truman charged the commission with investigating included, "ways and means of expanding educational opportunities for all able young people" (President's Commission on Higher Education, 1947, no page). Over the course of approximately a year and a half, the commission held seven public meetings, met with representatives of higher education institutions across the country, and reviewed documents from both institutions and the federal government (Hutcheson, 2002). In December 1947, the members of the commission transmitted their final report, *Higher Education for American Democracy*, to President Truman (President's Commission on Higher Education, 1947).

Among the key findings of the commission, articulated in the first volume of its report, was that economic barriers were prohibiting many youth from attending postsecondary education:

> By allowing the opportunity for higher education to depend so largely on the individual's economic status, we are not only denying to millions of young people the chance in life to which they are entitled; we are also depriving the Nation of a vast amount of potential leadership and potential social competence which it sorely needs. (p. 29)

It is interesting to note that the language used here by the commission refers not just to the potential losses for society as a whole, but also for the opportunity lost by individual students. Thus, the commission acknowledged both the social and private benefits of attending postsecondary education.

The goal the commission established to address this finding was clear and unambiguous:

> The American people should set as their ultimate goal an educational system in which at no level—high school, college, graduate school, or professional school—will a qualified individual in any part of the country encounter an insuperable economic barrier to the attainment of the kind of education suited to his aptitudes and interests. (p. 36)

Among the specific recommendations the commission made were

> 2. The time has come to make education through the fourteenth grade available in the same way that high school education is now available. This means that tuition-free education should be available in public institutions to all youth for the traditional freshman and sophomore years or for the traditional 2-year junior college course. . .
>
> 3. The time has come to provide financial assistance to competent students in the tenth through fourteenth grades who would not be able to continue their education without such assistance. . . .
>
> 4. The time has come to reverse the present tendency of increasing tuition and other student fees in the senior college beyond the fourteenth year, and in both graduate and professional schools, by lowering tuition costs in publicly controlled colleges and by aiding deserving students through inaugurating a program of scholarships and fellowships. (pp. 37–38)

In many ways, these are stunning recommendations, and they foreshadow by decades later federal initiatives to address the issue of postsecondary educational opportunity. The notion that education through the 14th year (i.e., the first 2 years of college, whether at a community college or a 4-year institution) should be free is an issue later promoted by President Bill Clinton when he introduced the HOPE and Lifetime Learning tax credits for college during his second term in office. The call for the development of financial assistance, through scholarships and fellowships, presages Title IV of the Higher Education Act of 1965, Pub. L. No. 89–329, 1965 (see below). The urge to lower tuition increases foreshadows the congressional attention paid to the problem of rising tuition prices over the years, most noticeably during the first decade of the current century (see, for example, Burd, 2003).

However, even with the strong rhetoric contained in the Truman Commission's report, the federal government did not respond with any major initiatives on financial assistance for college until passage of the National Defense Education Act in 1958. This act, known as NDEA, was spurred by the Soviet Union's launch of the Sputnik satellite the year before. Concerned that the United States was losing ground to the Soviets in science and technology fields, Congress passed the NDEA and President Dwight Eisenhower signed it into law. The preamble to the legislation echoed some of the earlier language of the Truman Commission, stating

> The security of the nation requires the fullest development of the mental resources and technical skills of its young men and women . . . . the nation requires . . . . that the federal government give assistance for programs which are important to the nation's defense. (quoted in Mumper, 1996, p. 76)

The focus is not so much on equity for the individual as it is on the development of human capital for the nation and, in particular, in areas deemed critical to national security.

The key portion of the NDEA related to financial assistance for college was the creation of the National Defense Student Loan program. This was a pool of capital that the federal government provided to colleges, which they would in turn loan to students to be repaid after the student graduated from college. The loans were to be focused on those students majoring in fields that were determined to be important in helping the nation beat back the Soviet threat. The NDEA was a fairly limited program, however, and had little impact on equalizing postsecondary educational opportunity.

The first major federal initiative to implement the key recommendations of the Truman Commission with respect to financial assistance for college students was the Higher Education Act (HEA) of 1965. Passed as part of President Lyndon Johnson's Great Society, the HEA, through Title IV of the act, introduced a series of financial assistance programs that would be made available for the first time to a broad array of college students (as opposed to targeted programs such as the GI Bill or NDEA). President Johnson, when he signed the bill into law at his alma mater, Southwest Texas State University (later renamed the University of Texas San Marcos) in November 1965, said, "The President's signature upon this legislation passed by this Congress will swing open a new door for the young people of America. For them, and for this entire land of ours, it is the most important door that will ever open—the door to education. And this legislation is the key which unlocks it" (quoted in Heller, 2007b, p. 2).

The introduction to Title IV of the act states

> It is the purpose of this part to provide, through institutions of higher education, educational opportunity grants to assist in making available benefits of higher education to qualified high school graduates of exceptional financial need, who for lack of financial means of their own or of their families would be unable to obtain such benefits without such aid. ("Higher Education Act of 1965," § 401)

This language echoes that of the Truman Commission, yet it took almost two decades after that commission issued its report before Congress responded with legislation to codify many of the programs articulated there.

Title IV of the HEA authorized three new student aid programs. The first created Educational Opportunity Grants (EOG), available to students with financial need as determined by the college the student attended. The second program, Guaranteed Student Loans (GSL), focused on addressing the capital constraints faced by college students. The GSL program provided incentives to banks to loan money to college students by subsidizing the interest rate, guaranteeing the loans against default, and providing an in-school subsidy so that students would not have to begin repayment of the loans until a year after they left college. The third program, College Work Study, provided subsidies to colleges which paid students to work in on-campus jobs.

The early years of the Title IV programs had little impact on access to college. The EOG program was not well-funded, and the decision to allow the colleges to make the awards meant that there was little predictability in awards for poor students who were contemplating attending college. It was not until the 1972 reauthorization of HEA that Congress addressed the limitations of the EOG program, which had been acknowledged as having yet had little impact on educational opportunity for lower-income students. It restructured the EOG into a new program, the Basic Educational Opportunity Grant (BEOG) program (later renamed the Pell Grant program in 1980, after Senator Claiborne Pell, one of the key backers of the creation of the BEOG program), and funded it at a level to better meet student needs. The primary change to the program was to target the funding on financially needy students, administered through the Office of Education in the Department of Health, Education, and Welfare, rather than providing the funds directly to institutions.

The shifting of grants under Title IV of the Higher Education Act from institution to students helped introduce more of a market model of student aid, where students could use the portability of their BEOG grants to attend any accredited college or university in the United States. In addition to portability, the BEOG program also established on an annual basis an identified and fixed grant maximum, so that students could have an idea of how much federal aid they would qualify for. This provided more predictability for students, regardless of where they chose to go to college, and with the increase in funding, the program began to have more impact on college access. Mumper (1996) stated, "Title IV of the HEA was unquestionably the largest single development in the federal effort to remove college price barriers" (p. 80). Few analysts would dispute this claim, even though the value of the Title IV aid—as measured against college prices—has eroded over time. Figure 6.1 shows the relationship between the maximum Pell Grant award each year (as measured in constant dollars) and the proportion of the cost of attendance (tuition, mandatory fees, room and board charges) covered by that grant at the average-priced public and private 4-year institution in the country.

In the early years of the program, Pell Grants were limited to no more than 50% of the student's cost of attendance, a limit raised to 60% in 1985 and then eliminated in 1993. In the 1979–1980 academic year, the maximum Pell Grant was $5,416 (in 2008 dollars), and it would cover 50% of the cost of attending an average, public 4-year college or university (for an in-state student) that year.[2] The same grant covered 37% of the cost at the typical private 4-year institution.

The purchasing power of the Pell Grant, both in absolute terms and compared to tuition prices, has eroded over the years. The maximum Pell Grant award in 2009–2010 was $5,350, still below the level of 1979 (in constant dollars). The student receiving the maximum Pell award received only 35% of the cost of attending a public 4-year institution and 15% at a private institution in the 2009–2010 academic year.

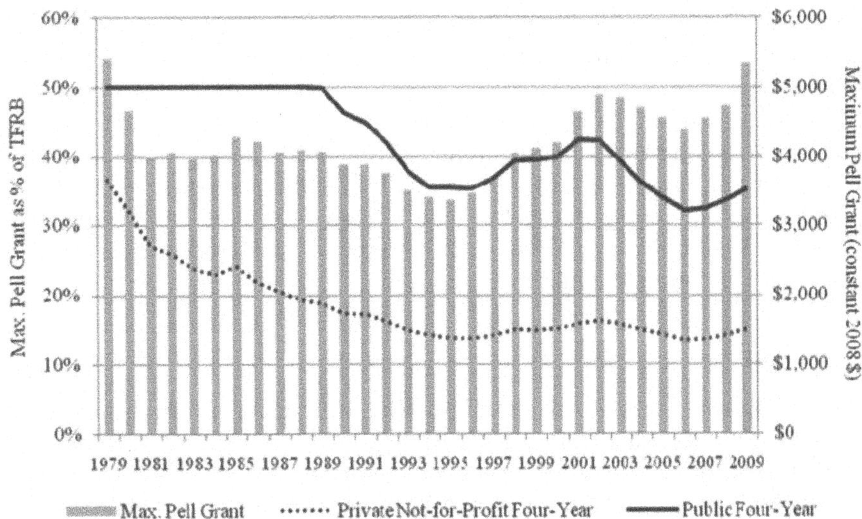

Figure 6.1 Maximum Pell Grant and maximum Pell Grant as a percent of average cost of tuition, fees, room and board charges.

Source: Author's calculations from College Board (2009a, 2009b).

Unlike the Pell Grant program, which was subject to the annual appropriation limits established by Congress, the Guaranteed Student Loan Program (later named the Stafford Loan Program, after Senator Robert Stafford of Vermont, one of the champions of the program) was structured as an entitlement. Congress was more willing to provide funding for student loans, particularly in the period beginning during the Reagan administration when changes in federal budget rules pushed student loans "off-budget" or not subject to agreements on aggregate federal spending limits. Thus, the use of federal loans grew, spurred on also by the introduction of the Parent Loan for Undergraduate Students in the 1980 reauthorization of HEA and unsubsidized Stafford loans in the 1992 reauthorization.

The late 1970s saw an important shift away from a fairly narrow focus on the needs of poor students with Congress' passage and President Jimmy Carter's signing into law of the Middle Income Student Assistance Act (MISAA). In response to pressure from middle-class voters, who felt they were being squeezed between rising college prices and federal (and state) student aid policies that remained targeted at these poorer students, this legislation liberalized the means-testing of the Pell Grant program, opening it up to more middle-income students, and it removed means-testing for subsidized Guaranteed Student Loans (St. John, 2003).

Hearn (1993) described MISAA as a "striking defeat" (p. 113) for those who had been attempting to keep the federal Title IV programs focused on providing grant aid to financially needy students:

> The stated goals of the MISAA legislation were to promote educational choice and persistence, as well as access, for both lower and middle-income students. As it turned out, upper-income students and families also benefitted substantially from the MISAA legislation. In this sense, MISAA was a clear departure from the coalition's need-base dogma in that it instituted a substantially more liberal definition of "need" for the federal aid programs. (p. 113)

The long-term impact of MISAA, however, was muted by subsequent changes after the election of President Ronald Reagan in 1980. Reagan's efforts to scale back the size of the federal government (which included an unsuccessful attempt at eliminating the Department of Education as a cabinet-level agency) resulted in the rolling back of most of the provisions of MISAA in the 1982 amendments to the Higher Education Act (Parsons, 1997).

The most recent federal program to introduce a new funding stream for higher education students was the introduction of the HOPE and Lifetime Learning tax credits in 1998. Introduced by President Clinton as part of his reelection campaign in 1996, Congress included them in the

Taxpayer Relief Act of 1997 and President Clinton signed the legislation into law. Students or their parents can utilize the tax credits to offset part of their tuition costs each year, within limits established in the federal tax code.

Figure 6.2 summarizes total federal outlays for these three forms of financial aid over the last three decades, shown in constant (inflation-adjusted) dollars.[3] Funding for federal grants has been relatively flat, increasing from $19.4 billion in the 1979–1980 academic year to $24.8 billion in 2008–2009. In contrast, borrowing under the federal loan programs has skyrocketed, increasing from $12.4 billion to $84.0 billion, or 577%, in 2008–2009. The tax credits, first introduced in 1998, have grown from $4.0 billion to $6.8 billion.[4]

State Financial Aid[5]

A handful of states operated a relatively small number of financial aid programs at the time Congress passed the Higher Education Act of 1965. By the end of that decade, 19 states had appropriated approximately $200 million in grant aid for college students (Fenske & Boyd, 1981). In 1972, the Higher Education Act was reauthorized introducing the Basic Educational Opportunity Grants and the State Student Incentive Grant (SSIG) program. The SSIG program, later renamed Leveraging Educational Assistance Partnerships (LEAP), provided matching grants from the federal government to states to encourage them to develop their own need-based grant programs.

In response to SSIG, state appropriations for grants increased to 36 states and $423 million in 1974 and to every state and the District of Columbia for a total of $800 million just 5 years later (Heller, 2002a). A 1975 survey conducted by the National Association of State Scholarship Programs commented that "Growth represented in '74–75 and '75–76 . . . . is a response to the new SSIG Program which permits up to a $1,500 annual student award (equal shares of $750 Federal/State) in this new form of State/Federal partnership" (Boyd, 1975, p. 2). This amount of $1,500 was not trivial; the maximum Pell Grant award in 1975–1976 was $1,400, so a student receiving a state grant in this amount would more than double her grant funding from public sources.

As I pointed out in an earlier contribution to this series, however, it is hard to pin the overall responsibility for increases in state grant spending on the federal government's development of the SSIG/LEAP program (Heller, 2002a). During the ensuing almost 35 years, funding for state grants has far outstripped funding for SSIG/LEAP. The latter program has seen its funding increase 242%, rising from $19 million in 1974–1975 to $65 million in 2007–2008 (measured in current dollars). In contrast, funding for need-based grants in the states has grown 1,248%, from

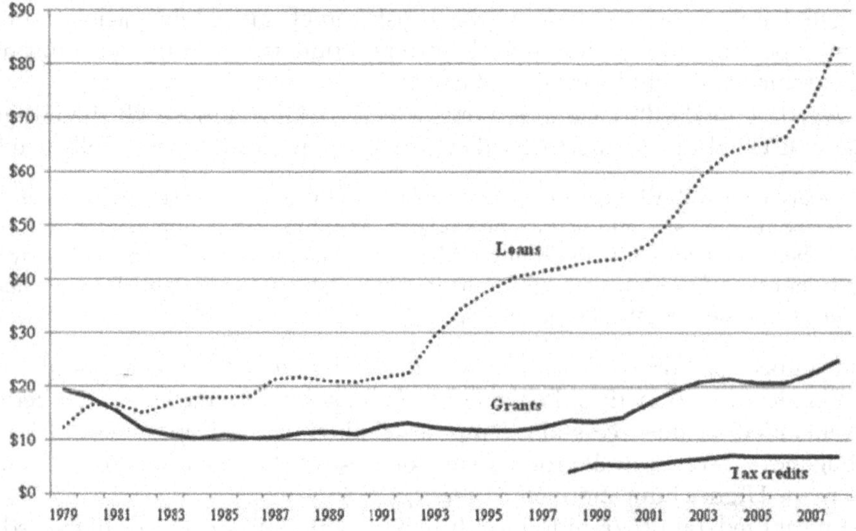

Figure 6.2 Federal outlays for financial aid programs in billions (constant 2008 dollars).
Source: College Board (2009a, 2009b).

$423 million to $5.7 billion during this same period. As I pointed out in Chapter 5 of Volume 17 of the Handbook (Heller, 2002a), "It is hard to demonstrate a linkage between the level of funding for SSIG/LEAP and the actions states took to expand their own grant programs to the extent they did" (p. 231), at least after the initial impetus provided by passage of SSIG in the 1972 reauthorization of HEA.

Besides the large growth in states' need-based grant programs, the other major development in state financial aid has been the creation of grant programs based on criteria other than financial need. In the early years, these were often very specialized and targeted programs, such as those that offered grants to widows or orphans of police officers or firefighters killed in the line of duty. However, the creation of the HOPE Scholarship program by Georgia Governor Zell Miller in 1993 was a watershed in the growth of what are generally referred to as "non-need" grant programs.

The HOPE (an acronym for "Helping Outstanding Pupils Educationally") program is funded from Georgia's lottery revenues and awards its grants based on the grade point average earned by high school students. When first introduced in 1993, the program had an income cap of $66,000, but the program proved to be so popular, and lottery sales grew so quickly, that the income cap was raised to $100,000 in the second year and eliminated entirely after that (see Cornwell & Mustard, 2002, for more on the history of HOPE). The political popularity of merit-based programs like HOPE spurred other states to develop similar programs, most using comparable measures of academic merit based on either high school grades, standardized test scores (such as the SAT or ACT), or a combination of the two. Fourteen states now have similar, broad-based merit aid programs (Heller & Marin, 2004).

Figure 6.3 shows the growth of state funding for both need-based and non-need grants for undergraduate students since 1981. As can be seen, before the development of Georgia HOPE in 1993, funding for grants awarded without means-testing was relatively flat across the nation. It was not until that program was implemented and others followed that funding for non-need-based programs began to grow at a substantial rate. In 1992–1993, the last year before Georgia HOPE, grants awarded without consideration of financial need by states represented 10% of the $2.2 billion total; by 2007–2008, non-need-based grants represented 28% of the $7.9 billion awarded by the states to undergraduates. Since 1992, funding for need-based grants increased 193%, while funding for non-need grants increased 955%. The need and non-need-based student financial assistance together represented almost 10% of the $80.7 billion provided in state support for higher education in total (Illinois State University Center for the Study of Education Policy, 2010).

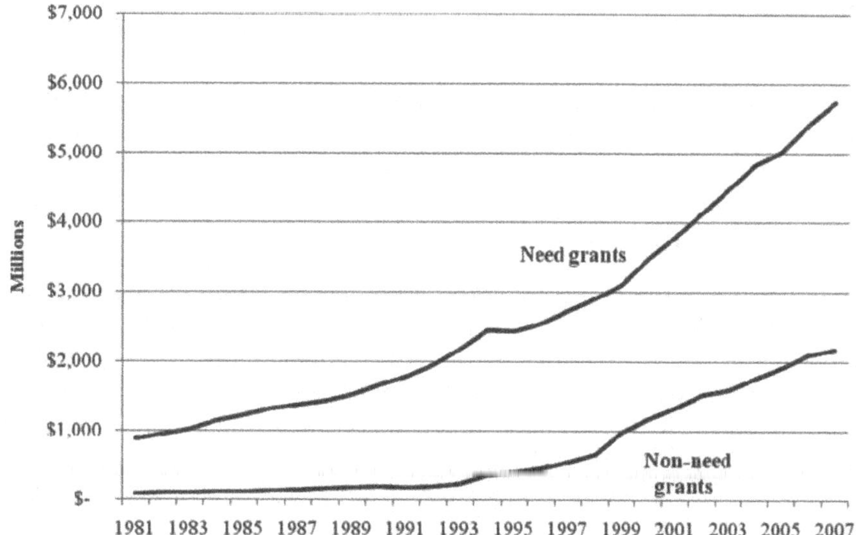

Figure 6.3 State funding for grants for undergraduate students (current dollars).
Source: National Association of State Scholarship and Grant Programs, various years

Institutional Financial Aid

As noted in the introduction to this chapter, colleges and universities have awarded scholarships and other student financial assistance since the colonial era. Holtschneider (1997) described one college's efforts at ensuring affordability this way:

> As affordable as the founders had tried to make the new college [Harvard College], they discovered a cohort of candidates eager to attend the college but unable to afford its charges. To assist these young men, scholarships were sought from wealthy friends back in England. These scholarships closely resembled the scholarships many of the founders themselves had observed or received as students in the colleges of Cambridge and Oxford. A few college jobs were instituted as well, helping a few needy students to pay their living expenses. Almost from the beginning, then, Harvard College had created financial assistance structures for its students that both attempted to keep the institutional [sic] affordable for a broad range of Massachusetts residents, and offered additional financial help to a few students who could not raise the necessary funds themselves. (pp. 3–4)

Note that Harvard offered not just scholarships to needy students, but also an early version of work study—jobs on campus as a means for students to work their way through college.

It was not just private colleges that offered scholarships, but also their public counterparts, even though they attempted to maintain policies of low tuition charges in their earliest days. The University of Virginia, founded by Thomas Jefferson, had provisions for free tuition for poor students in the Commonwealth, and Iowa State University offered 50 scholarships of free tuition when it opened in 1855 (Brubacher & Rudy, 1976; Sears, 1923).

Over the years, both public and private colleges developed financial assistance programs that focused on both students with financial need and those who were deemed academically meritorious. Lemann (1999) describes how Harvard's decision to introduce scholarships based on merit in the 1930s helped lead to the creation of the Scholastic Aptitude Test as a mechanism for identifying high-achieving public school students.

There have been few detailed studies analyzing the amount of financial aid provided by institutions throughout history. However, in 1987 the US Department of Education began a national survey representative of all college students, the National Postsecondary Student Aid Study (NPSAS), to gather data on the tuition and other charges faced by students along with how they were financing their college educations. Conducted every 3 or 4 years since that time, the NPSAS surveys provide detailed data on the topic of student financing of higher education.

The data from the 1987–1988 survey (Fig. 6.4) show that students in private 4-year colleges and universities were more than twice as likely to receive institutional grant assistance than were their counterparts in public institutions and approximately four times more likely to receive grants than community college students. The most recent survey shows that the proportion of students receiving institutional grants has increased in every sector.

In the 1987–1988 academic year, higher education institutions awarded a total of $3.1 billion in institutional grant aid to undergraduates; two decades later, this amount had grown 560% to $20.7 billion (author's calculations from National Center for Education Statistics, 2010c, 2010d).

The Current Status of Financial Aid

Having provided a history of the financial support provided to students, I now present an overview of the current status of that support. Unless otherwise indicated, the source of the estimates in this section is the author's calculations of data from the National Postsecondary Student Aid Study (NPSAS) for the 2007–2008 academic year (National Center for Education Statistics, 2010d).

Undergraduate students in the 2007–2008 academic year received $130 billion in financial assistance to help pay for college. Figure 6.5 shows the amounts and sources of that aid. Half of the aid was in the form of loans, 43% was grants, and the remaining 7% was from tax benefits or work study.

Federal grant aid is predominantly in the Pell Grant program; 78% of the federal grants awarded were from the Pell program, with the remainder in other federal grants including Supplemental Educational Opportunity Grants as well as veterans' and active duty military grants. The Pell

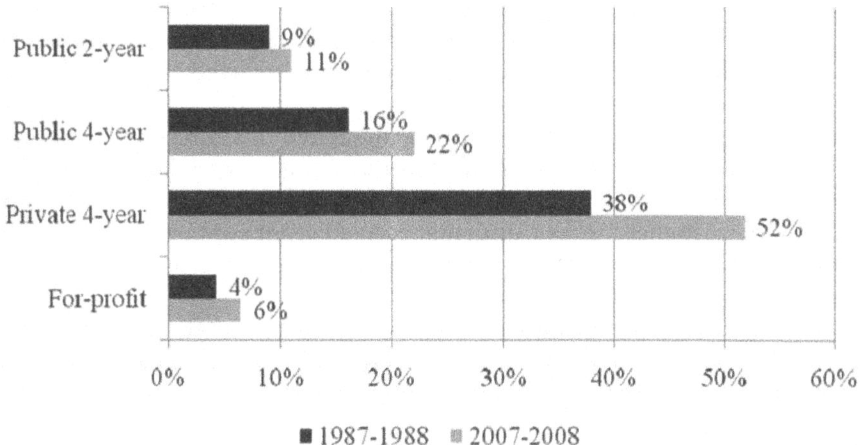

Figure 6.4 Proportion of undergraduates in 4-year institutions receiving institutional grants, by sector.
Source: Author's calculations from National Center for Education Statistics (2010c, 2010d)

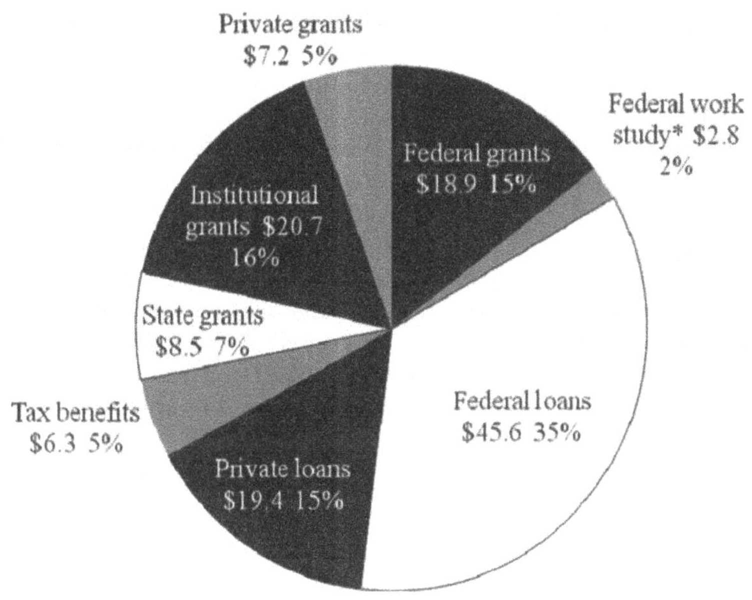

Figure 6.5 Financial aid to undergraduate students by source, 2007–2008.
*Includes institutional matching funds.

program is highly targeted at students from low- and moderate-income families; 90% of dependent Pell Grant recipients (i.e., those under the age of 24, unmarried, and not military veterans) had parents with family incomes below $47,000 in 2006.[6] In contrast, the 90th percentile for all dependent students that year was an income level of approximately $150,000. It is important to note that over half, 58%, of all Pell recipients, however, were independent students.

Approximately one-third of all undergraduates borrowed in the federal loan programs in 2007–2008 (including those with parents who borrowed through the Parental Loan for Undergraduate Students program), totaling $45 billion in borrowing. Fourteen percent of students reported also borrowing from private (non-federal) lenders.[7] A recent report from the College Board (2010) examined the cumulative debt levels of students completing bachelor's degree programs in 2007–2008. Approximately two-thirds of all bachelor's recipients had borrowed money to pay for college at some point in their undergraduate career; for those who borrowed, the median cumulative amount at graduation was $20,000.[8] One-quarter of all graduating students reported they borrowed a total exceeding $30,500, a level the report designated as a "high debt level." The proportion with high debt levels varied quite a bit by sector, however. Among students graduating with bachelor's degrees from public colleges and universities, only 12% incurred a high debt level. In private, not-for-profit institutions, 24% had a high debt level. And in the proprietary, for-profit sector, 53% of the students graduated with cumulative borrowing above this threshold. Twenty-four percent of independent students overall had debt above this level, a rate twice that of dependent students.

Figure 6.6 shows the distribution of state and institutional dollars awarded by type, need or non-need grants. Approximately 16% of students received grant support from their states and 20% from the institutions they attended. Thirty percent of all state grant dollars and 55% of institutional grants were awarded without consideration of financial need.

The awarding of these different forms of aid varies across income groups. To examine this, I divided all dependent students in the NPSAS survey for 2007–2008 into income quartiles, based on their parents' income in 2006. The income groups are as follows:

- Lower income: ≤$37,888
- Lower-middle income: $37,889–$67,754
- Upper-middle income: $67,755–$105,240
- Upper income: ≥$105,241

Figure 6.7 shows the proportion of students in each income group receiving different forms of grant aid. As noted earlier, federal grants are well-targeted on students from the lower and lower-middle income groups. Two-thirds of students from the bottom income quartile received a federal grant (mostly Pell Grants), while 21% of those in the lower-middle income group received federal grant aid; only 1% of students from above the median received federal grants.

State need-based grants, because of income means-testing, are also awarded predominantly to students from below the income median. However, means-testing of state grants is not as targeted as federal grants, as approximately 7% of students from the upper-middle income group and 3% of those in the upper-income group received a state need-based grant. Grants awarded by states without income means-testing are much more evenly distributed across the income categories, with 7–8% of each of the four quartiles receiving this form of grant.

Colleges and universities, in awarding grants from their own resources, can use whatever rules they want. Thus, institutional need-based grants, even though they are means-tested, are distributed

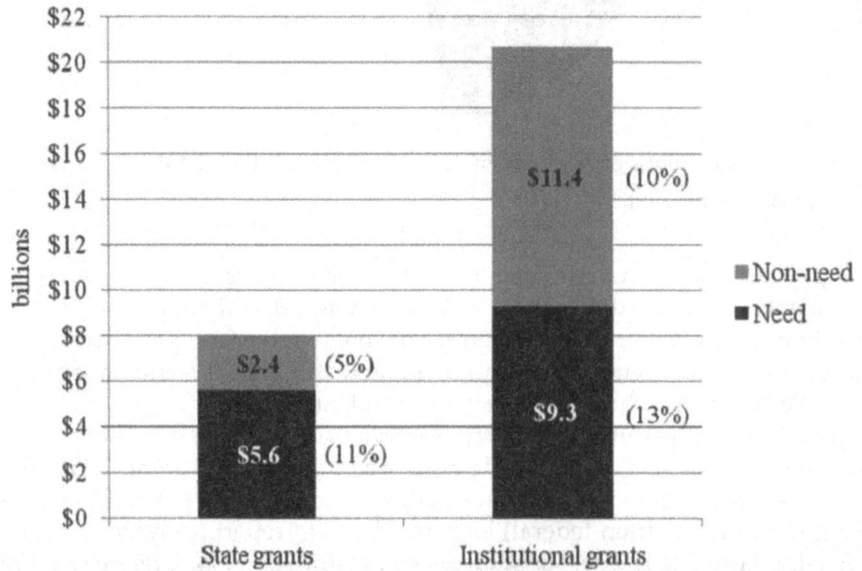

Figure 6.6 State and institutional grants to undergraduate students by type, 2007–2008.

Note: The proportion of all students who received each form of grant is shown in parentheses.

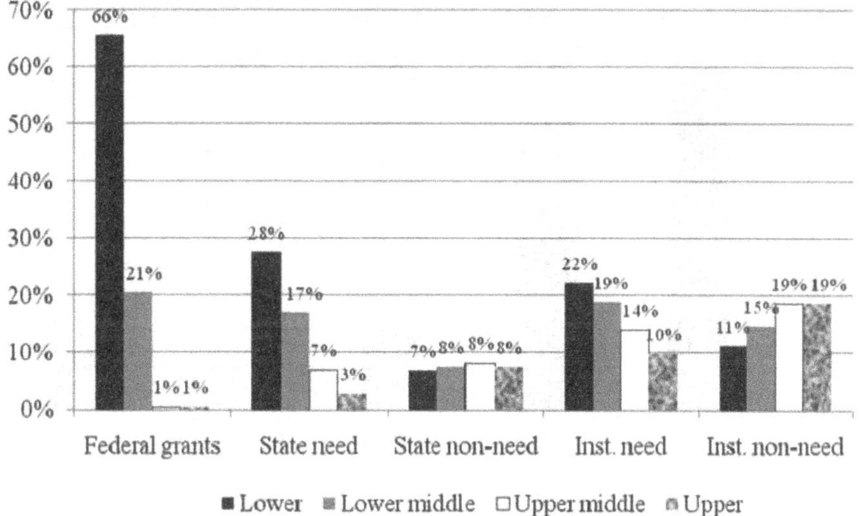

Figure 6.7 Proportion of dependent students receiving grant aid, by type and income quartile.

further up the income ladder than are either federal or state need-based grants. Many institutions have more liberal definitions of financial need than do the federal or state governments. For example, in 2007 Harvard University announced that it would begin awarding need-based grants to students from families with incomes up to $180,000 (a level that placed a family in the top 5% of all earners in that year); Yale quickly followed suit, announcing it would give need-based aid to students from families with incomes up to $200,000 ("Colleges and sticker shock," 2008; Hoover, 2007). Thus, even those institutional grants based on need tend to be awarded to students further up the income ladder than are publicly funded grants, where means-testing is much tighter.[9]

The impact of this difference can be seen in Fig. 6.7. Fourteen percent and 10% of upper-middle and upper-income students, respectively, received institutional need-based grants. While these are smaller proportions than the bottom half of the income distribution, this is still a large proportion of grants awarded based on financial need to these wealthier students. Institutional non-need grants are even more skewed toward the higher-income groups, with those students from families above the median income more likely to have received an institutional non-need award than students from below the median.

The distribution of the total amount of grant aid among the four income groups is shown in Fig. 6.8. Eighty-four percent of all federal grant dollars were awarded to dependent students from the bottom income quartile, and 15% went to the lower-middle income group; a total of only 1% of the grant aid went to those students from families above the median. State need-based grant dollars are still targeted predominantly to the bottom half of the income distribution, but one-third (as opposed to 15% of federal grant dollars) went to students in the lower-middle income group. Approximately one in six state need-based dollars went to students in the top half of the income distribution. In contrast, 56% of state non-need grant dollars went to students from the top half of the income distribution, indicative of the relationship between income and the type of academic measure used in awarding these grants (see Heller & Marin, 2002, 2004, for more on this relationship).

Institutional grants, both those awarded based on financial need and those awarded without means-testing, are more skewed toward higher-income students. Forty-five percent of all institutional need-based grants were awarded to students from incomes above the median of $67,754, and 63% of all institutional grant dollars awarded without considering financial need went to students in the upper two income quartiles. Figure 6.8 also shows that the total amount of grants awarded by institutions, $18.4 billion, was approximately one-third greater than the sum of the grants awarded by the federal and state governments.

Figure 6.9 provides information on the proportion of dependent students in each income group who borrowed from the major loan programs. Students from the bottom three income groups borrowed from the federal loan programs—including Perkins loans, subsidized Stafford loans,

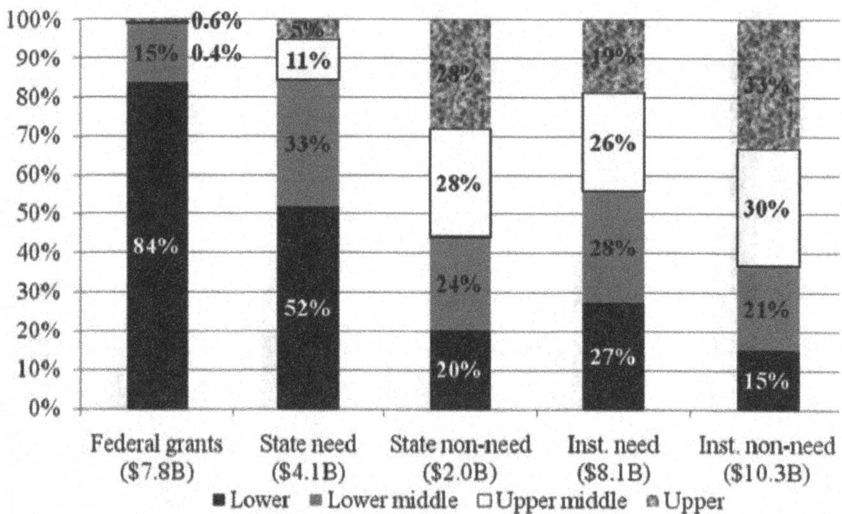

Figure 6.8 Distribution of total grant aid awarded to dependent students, by type and income quartile.

Note: Total amount of aid awarded of each type is shown in parentheses.

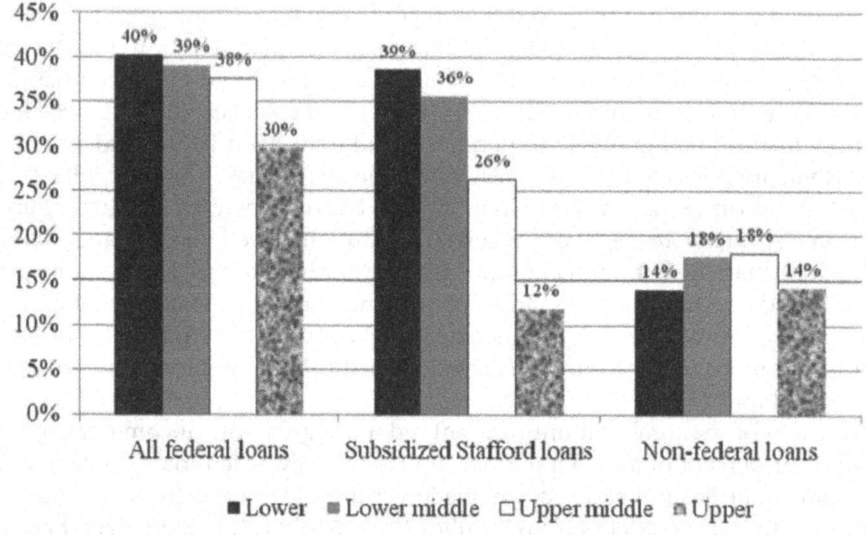

Figure 6.9 Proportion of dependent students borrowing for college, by type and income quartile.

unsubsidized Stafford loans, and parent PLUS loans—at similar rates. Students from the top income group were somewhat less likely to borrow in one or more of the federal programs.

Because of the means-testing applied to the subsidized Stafford loan program, students from the bottom half of the income distribution were more likely to borrow in this program, with 39% of the lower-income group and 36% of the lower-middle group using this source of loan aid. Only one-quarter of students in the upper-middle income group and 12% of the students in the top income quartile qualified for and availed themselves of subsidized Stafford loans.

Figure 6.9 also shows that middle-income students were slightly more likely to take out non-federal loans to help pay for college, with approximately 18% of the two middle-income groups taking out private loans. Approximately one in seven students from the bottom and top income quartiles borrowed from non-federal sources.

Figure 6.10 shows the distribution of loan dollars in each program by income quartile. The total amount of federal loans is approximately equally distributed among the four income quartiles, while borrowing in the federal subsidized Stafford program is more concentrated among the

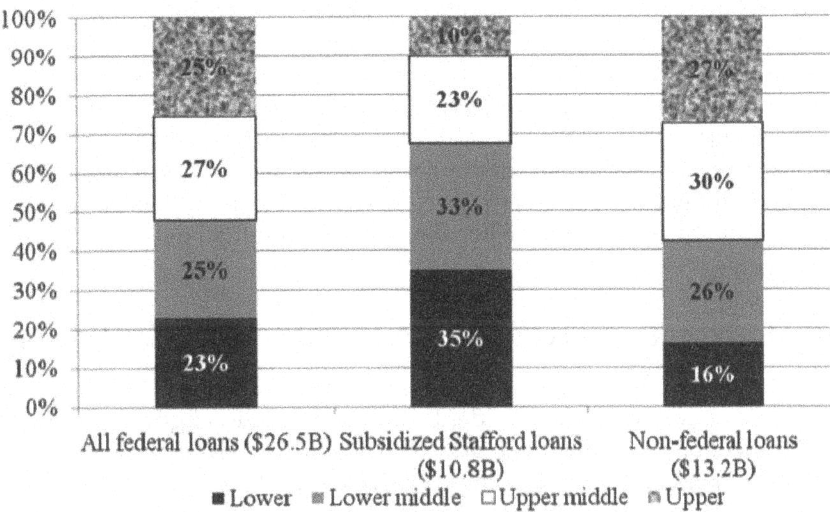

Figure 6.10 Distribution of total student loan borrowing by dependent students, by type and income quartile.

Note: Total amount borrowed in each loan program is shown in parentheses.

bottom half of the income distribution, with approximately two-thirds of all dollars in this program borrowed by students in these two income groups.

One interesting pattern in the loan data is that while students from the bottom and top income groups were just about as likely to take out non-federal loans, the amount borrowed by the top income quartile was much greater (27% of the $13.2 billion total, or $3.6 billion) than that of the lowest income group ($2.1 billion, or 16% of the total). This indicates that students from the top income group borrowed greater amounts from private lenders.

Financial Aid and the Metaphor of the Three Art Movements

The Three Movements

In this section I draw on three art movements from the last century as metaphors for analyzing how student financial aid has evolved over time. I start with a description of each of the three movements and then use each movement to describe different aspects of the financial aid system in the United States today.

The first is *Realism*. Chilvers, Osborne, and Farr (1988) describe Realism as

> . . . . implying a desire to depict things accurately and objectively. Often, however, the term carries with it the suggestion of the rejection of conventionally beautiful suspects or idealization in favor of a more down-to-earth approach, often with a stress on low life or the activities of the common man. . . . In this sense art is called "Realist" when the materials or objects from which the work is constructed are presented for exactly what they are and are known to be. (pp. 411–412)

Realism was a repudiation of the idyllic portrayal of subjects, an attempt to use art to portray the everyday person, rather than the upper class or bourgeois subjects often dominating the works of impressionist artists of the nineteenth and early twentieth centuries.

The second is *Surrealism,* which was a movement ". . . . originating in France and flourishing in the 1920s and 1930s, characterized by a fascination with the bizarre, the incongruous, and the irrational" (Chilvers et al., 1988, p. 482). Another author describes Surrealism as developing

> . . . in two directions: pure fantasy, and the elaborate reconstruction of a dream-world . . . . The second took the form of highly detailed likenesses of objects, straight or distorted, or three-dimensional abstractions, in a fantastic and unexpected juxtaposition, or in a setting of a hallucinatory kind . . . . (Murray & Murray, 1989, pp. 407–408)

Irrationality and the juxtaposition of disparate sentiments or thoughts are common traits of Surrealism.

The third movement is *Cubism*. Moffat (2010) wrote, "Cubist painters were not bound to copying form, texture, colour, and space; instead, they presented a new reality in paintings that depicted radically fragmented objects, whose several sides were seen simultaneously" (p. 1). Another author noted that "the disintegrated image of the natural object gradually took on a more and more abstract geometrical shape, until finally the geometrical shapes are so remotely related to the original form of the object that they seem almost to have been invented rather than derived . . ." (Alfred H. Barr, 1936, quoted in Robbins, 1988, p. 280).

The Three Art Movements as a Lens for Understanding Financial Aid Today

Just as Realism is a focus on "the common man" (Chilvers et al., 1988, p. 411), so are certain financial aid programs focused on working class students. Pell Grants, the largest federal grant program, represent 82% of all federal grant aid awarded to undergraduate students (College Board, 2009b). Forty-five years after their creation in the Higher Education Act of 1965, they are still targeted at students of "exceptional financial need" as described in the preamble to Title IV ("Higher Education Act of 1965," §401). Two-thirds of students from the bottom income quartile of all dependent undergraduates in 2007–2008 received a Pell Grant, and 84% of all Pell dollars awarded to dependent students went to this group, with only 15% going to students in the second income quartile (Fig. 6.8).[10]

An important trend in the Pell Grant program, one that likely was unforeseen by congressional backers and President Johnson when the program was first created, has been the growth in awards to independent students. By federal rules, students are considered dependent students unless they fall into one or more of the following categories:

- Age 24 or older on December 31 of the academic year
- Enrolled in a graduate or professional program beyond a bachelor's degree
- Married
- Orphan or ward of the court
- Have legal dependents other than a spouse
- A veteran of the US Armed Forces
- US Armed Forces active duty personnel (National Center for Education Statistics, 2010d)

In 2007–2008, 58% of Pell Grant recipients were independent students, and they received 54% of all the Pell dollars (author's calculations from National Center for Education Statistics, 2010d). In 1975–1976, 30% of Pell recipients were independent, a proportion that rose as high as 62% in 1992–1993 (College Board, 2009b).

In the 1992 reauthorization of the Higher Education Act, regulations regarding student loan defaults were changed, resulting in hundreds of proprietary (for-profit) institutions being removed from the Title IV programs (Cervantes et al., 2005). As the proprietary sector serves many of the independent students, this helped to decrease the proportion of independent students receiving Pell Grants. While 47% of all undergraduate students in 2007–2008 were independent, 76% of those in the proprietary sector were (author's calculations from National Center for Education Statistics, 2010d).

Congress and presidential administrations have kept the Pell Grant program focused on its original, highly targeted purposes as articulated in the Higher Education Act. Even as other Title IV programs were changed or added, along with other funding provisions outside of the Higher Education Act, the Pell program remained highly targeted on helping financially needy students attend college.

For example, in the 1976 reauthorization of the Higher Education Act—the first after Congress created the Basic Educational Opportunity Grants (the predecessor to Pell) in 1972—eligibility rules for the BEOG grants were liberalized, thus opening up the program to more students (Mumper, 1996). Even with this change, however, the program was still targeted at those students well below the median income in the country.

In 1978, Congress passed and President Jimmy Carter signed into law the Middle Income Student Assistance Act (MISAA). This legislation arose out of concerns that the middle class was struggling to pay for college; these students received little assistance from the federal government because the BEOG grants were only available to poorer students and some middle-income students did not even qualify for federal subsidized loans (Cervantes et al., 2005). In response, MISAA eliminated the income cap on these loans, opening them up to middle- and even upper-income students, but made few changes to the means-testing associated with the BEOG program. Three years later, in response to the rising cost of the federal loan programs, Congress reinstated an income ceiling on subsidized loans.

Tax credits to offset the cost of tuition had been proposed many times over the years, yet Congress had resisted them. It was not until President Bill Clinton pledged to make the first 2 years of college all but free (echoing one of the recommendations of the Truman Commission 50 years earlier) during his reelection campaign that Congress implemented a series of tax credits through passage of the Taxpayer Relief Act of 1997 (Fitzgerald & Delaney, 2002). This legislation created the HOPE and Lifetime Learning Tax Credits, with the former providing up to $1,500 per year for the first 2 years of postsecondary education and the latter up to $2,000 annually for subsequent years. This was an initiative, like MISAA, that was clearly targeted at the middle class and beyond. The tax credits had an income cap well into what most people would consider to be the upper classes, making it a benefit to many students who would not qualify for federal means-tested Title IV aid. In addition, the tax credits were non-refundable, meaning that they would only benefit families who had a large enough tax liability to be able to claim the credit. Research has confirmed that the credits largely benefit middle- and upper-income students (Long, 2003). Even this $40 billion influx of funds into higher education was done, however, without touching the targeting of the Pell Grant program.

The main failure of the Pell Grant program to meet the needs of the working class has not been one of structure, but rather inadequate funding. Throughout the regular reauthorizations of the Higher Education Act as well as other changes in federal law, the eligibility requirements for Pell have remained firmly to the benefit of "the common man." Even in the debates regarding the affordability of college for the middle class—as articulated during passage of MISAA as well as in more recent discussions revolving around rising college prices—Congress has resisted restructuring Pell to reach up into what the artists who were part of the Realism movement in painting would have described as the bourgeoisie.

As shown in Fig. 6.1, the maximum Pell Grant award has been largely flat, once inflation is taken into account. The maximum Pell award in 2009–2010 was $66 below the level of 1979–1980 in constant dollars. As tuition prices have risen, the purchasing power of Pell has declined, even after the 50% and later 60% award caps were removed.

Given these funding shortfalls, does Pell still meet its original intent of helping the common man (and today, woman, of course) to overcome the financial barriers of attending college and persisting through to attain a degree once enrolled? Certainly by itself it does not today fulfill this goal, but as noted in the earlier sections, Pell-eligible students receive assistance from other quarters.

Many of the state-operated need-based grant programs, for example, were created with similar purposes to the Pell program, and their creation was spurred on at least in part by the federal State Student Incentive Grant program. While these state programs are means-tested, they suffer from two limitations. First, they are not nearly as universal as Pell; as noted earlier, while two-thirds of dependent students in the bottom income quartile received a Pell award in 2007–2008, only 28% of students in this group received a state need-based grant (Fig. 6.7). Second, they are not as narrowly targeted on poorer students as is the Pell program. While all Pell awards go to dependent students from below the median income, 16% of state need-based grants go to students above median, with 5% of the total going to students from families with incomes above $105,240. Both Pell and state need-based grants provide, on average, similar levels of support to students who receive them (approximately $2,750 for each in 2007–2008).

Even with this assistance from the federal and state governments, however, poorer students face large financial barriers to attending college. Using data from the 2007–2008 NPSAS survey, Fig. 6.11 shows the average unmet need before institutional grant assistance, by income quartile for

- students in public, 4-year institutions paying in-state (resident) tuition;
- students in public, 4-year institutions paying out-of-state (non-resident) tuition; and
- students in private, 4-year institutions.

"Unmet need" is calculated as follows:

Unmet need = cost of attendance – (effective family contribution + federal grants + state grants).

In other words, this is the amount of money the student must obtain—through loans, work earnings, private grants and scholarships, or institutional grants—in order to meet the cost of attending the institution.

Figure 6.11 shows that students in the bottom income quartile attending a public institution in their home state faced unmet need of over $10,000 per year, with students in the second income quartile facing approximately two-thirds that level. Students in the upper two income groups have negative unmet need (i.e., they had resources including their families' contribution and any federal or state grant aid received *in excess* of the cost of attendance at their institution). For students in the highest income quartile, this negative unmet need was $21,000 above the cost of attendance.

Lower-income students attending public institutions outside of their home state faced even larger levels of unmet need. For students in the bottom half of the income distribution, the unmet need was approximately $10,000 greater than for in-state students in public institutions. Upper-middle income students faced unmet need of approximately $6,800. In private institutions, students in the bottom two quartiles faced unmet need of $25,000 or greater, while upper-middle income students had unmet need of $17,500. In both types of institutions, students in the top income quartile had more than enough resources to cover the cost of attendance.

Figure 6.12 shows the levels of unmet need students faced *after* institutional grant assistance is included. By comparing Figs. 6.11 and 6.12, one can see the impact of institutional grant aid. For example, in-state students in the bottom income quartile in public institutions saw their unmet need reduced from $10,152 to $8,815, or 13% on average, through assistance they received from the institutions they attended. Students in the second income quartile saw a similar 16% decrease in

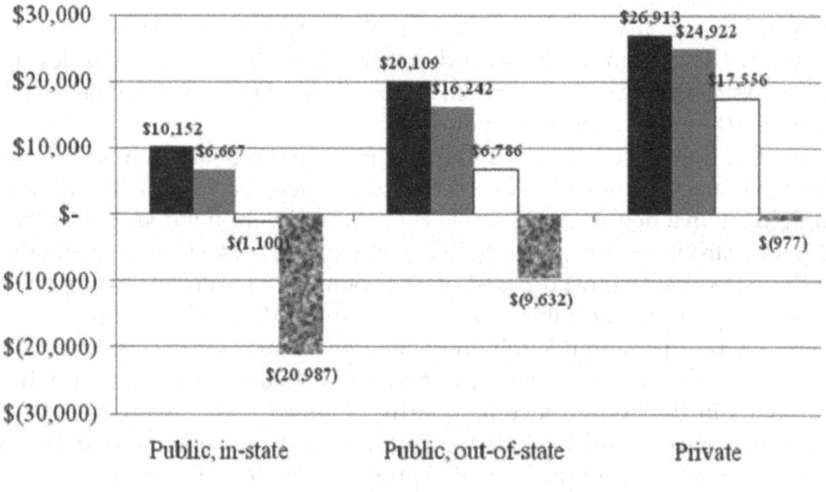

Figure 6.11 Average unmet need after state and federal grants, by institution type and income quartile.

Note: Full-time, dependent students in 4-year institutions (excludes veterans and military grants).

Source: Heller, Cheslock, Hughes, and Frick Cardelle (2010).

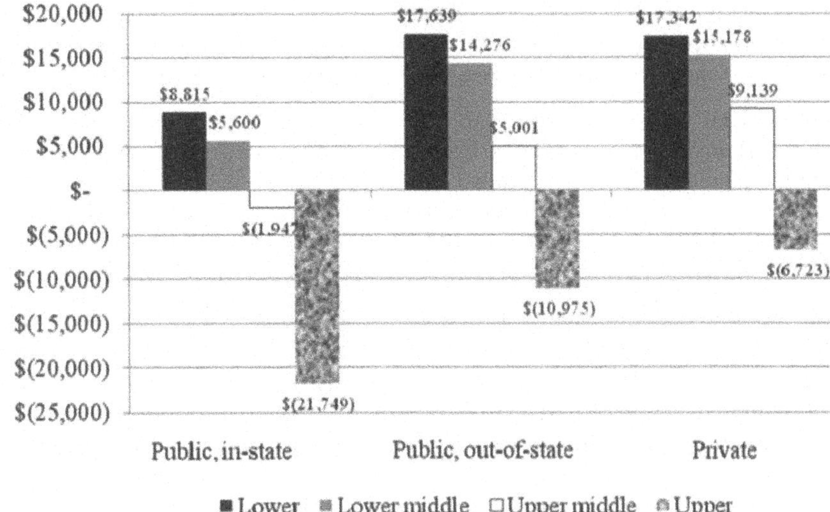

Figure 6.12 Average unmet need after state, federal, and institutional grants, by institution type and income quartile.

Note: Full-time, dependent students in 4-year institutions (excludes veterans and military grants).

Source: Heller et al. (2010)

their level of unmet need. Even with this reduction, however, both groups still faced unmet need in excess of $5,000 per year in order to attend college. Students from families above the median income received additional grant aid from their institutions, even though they already had enough resources to meet the cost of attendance.

The other categories of students and institutions saw similar changes. Out-of-state students in the bottom half of the income distribution attending public institutions saw a 12% reduction in their unmet need after institutional grants were applied. Students in private institutions saw the largest drop in their unmet need—36 and 39%, respectively, for students in the lowest and lower-middle income groups. Students from the upper-middle income group saw an even larger reduction in their unmet need in private institutions, seeing their unmet need cut almost in half. And students in the top income quartile gained, on average, an additional $5,745 in institutional grant assistance, even though they already had enough resources to meet the cost of attendance at the private institution they were attending. These larger percentages are reflective of the fact that private institutions, on average, discount tuition at higher rates than do public institutions (Davis, 2003; Heller, 2008; Lapovsky & Hubbell, 2003; National Association of College and University Business Officers, 2010; Redd, 2000).

It is important to note that Figs. 6.11 and 6.12 represent averages only for those students actually enrolled in college that year. They do not measure the impact of unmet need on students who *did not* attend college (or attended a community college or proprietary institution) because the financial barriers were so great.

Thus, even after the application of federal and state grant aid—the majority of which has remained focused on "the common man," as recommended by the Truman Commission and the Higher Education Act of 1965—students from working class families still face large financial barriers to attending and persisting through higher education. The impact of these barriers on the college access, persistence, and degree attainment of low- and moderate-income families has been well documented in the work of the federal Advisory Committee on Student Financial Assistance (ACSFA). The ACSFA is an independent agency created by Congress in the 1986 reauthorization of the Higher Education Act to advise it and the Secretary of Education on federal student aid policy.

Over the last decade, the Advisory Committee has published a series of reports analyzing the effects the policy shifts noted in the previous section have had on postsecondary education equity (2001, 2002, 2006). For example, the most recent ACSFA (2006) report noted that

> As in recent decades, financial barriers are a major factor in preventing large numbers of college-qualified students from earning a bachelor's degree, particularly those from low- and moderate-income families. . . . We have failed to take accurate account of the impact of price barriers on our lowest income students, especially those who have prepared and planned for college. During the 1990s, between nearly 1 million and 1.6 million bachelor's degrees were lost among college-qualified high school graduates from low- and moderate-income families.

The work of the Advisory Committee has focused on separating out losses in college access and degree attainment that are caused by differences in academic preparation, versus those caused by the financial barriers of rising tuition prices and inadequate need-based grant aid.

Besides publishing its own research, the ACSFA has also commissioned papers to examine the differences in the impact on college participation of inadequate academic preparation as compared to financial barriers (Becker, 2004; Heller, 2004). These analyses helped to refute some official reports of the US Department of Education that concluded that financial barriers were playing little or no role in contributing to the gaps in participation.

Other aspects of the financial aid system can best be described as characterized by the Surrealism descriptors of "bizarre, incongruous, irrational, and pure fantasy." As described earlier, in late 2007 and early 2008 a number of colleges and universities implemented new institutional grant programs that were described as need-based but moved the eligibility for these programs way up the income ladder. Harvard, for example, trumpeted its initiative—designed to reach families with incomes up to $180,000 per year—with the headline, "Harvard announces sweeping middle-income initiative" (2007). Yet, an income of $180,000 can hardly be described as "middle income"—at the time Harvard introduced its policy, an income at that echelon would place a family in about the top 5% of all families (Heller, 2007a).

Harvard described its new program as the "Zero to 10% Standard":

> Families with incomes above $120,000 and below $180,000 and with assets typical for these income levels will be asked to pay 10 percent of their incomes. For those with incomes below $120,000, the family contribution percentage will decline steadily from 10%, reaching zero for those with incomes at $60,000 and below.

Thus, a student from a family with an income of $180,000 (and "typical assets") would have to pay only $18,000 toward the cost of her education, which in the year the program took effect, 2008–2009, totaled $50,250 (National Center for Education Statistics, 2010a). That same student, however, would have had an Expected Family Contribution of approximately $50,000 under either the federal methodology or institutional methodology, well in excess of the amount Harvard would ask the student to contribute.[11]

Other universities quickly joined Harvard in expanding institutional aid to students from families of similar means. A week later, Swarthmore College, followed by the University of Pennsylvania a few days after that, followed suit (Boccella, 2007; Hardy, 2007). A little over a month later, Yale announced its initiative, upping the ante by extending the income eligibility up to $200,000 (Yale University Office of Public Affairs, 2008). In the examples given in Yale's announcement, a student from a family making $180,000 would be expected to pay anywhere from $14,150 to $25,550 toward the $51,400 cost of the education, an amount well below the calculated Expected Family Contribution.

The rhetoric used in many of these announcements focused on the problem of what many have described as "middle class affordability" (Baird, 2006;McPherson, 2004; Roth, 2001). While many of these institutions had previously implemented institutional aid policies guaranteeing that certain students could attend without incurring loan debt, most of these programs were targeted at families with incomes up to $60,000—right about at the median income in the nation and a level that most observers would agree falls smack-dab in the definition of "middle class." By expanding the income cap of these programs up to levels as high as $180,000 or even $200,000 and describing them as a "sweeping middle-income initiative," is it unfair to characterize the efforts as "bizarre" or "pure fantasy?"

Colleges and universities are not the only entities, however, that have expanded what had traditionally been characterized as "need-based" aid well into the highest income echelons of the nation. As described earlier, 14 states have developed broad-based merit scholarship programs that award grants to students based on academic criteria without consideration of financial need; as shown in Fig. 6.8, these awards go disproportionately to students in the higher-income groups. While 16% of states' need-based grant dollars went to students from above the median income, 56% of the merit grants went to students in this group.

Two studies of the impact of state merit scholarships that I co-edited for The Civil Rights Project at Harvard University found that all of these programs, because of the merit criteria used in the awards, tend to funnel the benefits disproportionately to upper-income families (Heller & Marin, 2002, 2004). One study in the first volume that analyzed the impact of Georgia HOPE found that

> Overall, the primary role of the scholarship has been to influence where, not whether high-school students attend college, but only a small fraction of HOPE expenditures affects college-going behavior at all. Over the first 5 years of the program, we estimate that HOPE raised total freshmen enrollment by about 3,800 students, which accounts for only about 4 percent of all freshmen awards during this period. *This indicates that 96 percent of HOPE expenditures had no impact on expanding college access in the state.* (Cornwell & Mustard, 2002, p. 71, emphasis added)

The most recent data on Georgia HOPE indicate that the state is spending approximately half a billion dollars on the program (National Association of State Student Grant & Aid Programs, 2009). The estimate of Cornwell and Mustard, then, would indicate that the state is only getting $20 million worth of increased college access for its expenditures; the remaining $480 million is subsidizing students who would have attended college somewhere even without the HOPE scholarship. This seems an irrational use of public resources, akin to providing food stamps to families who have more than enough of their own resources to feed themselves.

The fact that HOPE apparently has had little impact on college access is in conflict with the original intent of the program's founder, former Georgia Governor Zell Miller. Miller proposed the program, to be funded by a new lottery in the state, when he was first running for the governor's office in 1990:

> In an effort to increase the percentage of Georgia high school graduates who attend college, Mr. Miller said he would establish a scholarship fund "to assist any high school student who achieves a grade-point average of a certain level, who enrolls at an accredited college or university in Georgia, and whose family meets a certain income requirement." He did not spell out income or grade-point average requirements. (Sherman, 1991, p. A1)

When the program was first implemented in 1993, the income cap of $66,000 was more than twice the median income in the state of $31,148 (U.S. Census Bureau, 2010b). As noted earlier, the sale of lottery tickets exceeded the initial estimates, however, so eligibility for the scholarships was expanded by raising the income cap to $100,000 in the second year. By the third year, the income cap was eliminated entirely, thus pushing more awards even higher up the income ladder.

The distributional impact of the HOPE program was skewed even further toward higher-income students by the initial design, which effectively excluded students who were eligible for Pell Grants from participating. It required them to utilize their Pell awards to offset tuition costs before a HOPE scholarship could be awarded, a design referred to by one observer as "a kind of reverse means testing" (Callan, 2001, p. 88). Because the HOPE scholarship could be used only for tuition costs and not for other components of the cost of attendance (such as room, board, books, or transportation expenses) and because the maximum Pell award exceeded the cost of public college or university tuition in the state, Pell-eligible students received little or no HOPE scholarship dollars (the state has since rescinded this restriction). Since the introduction of the HOPE program, Georgia has reduced funding for its need-based grant program by 72% (National Association of State Scholarship and Grant Programs, various years).

It is not a stretch to think of the design of state financial aid programs like these as complying with the description of Surrealism as "irrational." While many of these merit aid programs have articulated goals of increasing college access, staunching the brain drain of educated labor out of the state and encouraging students to work hard in school, the policy evidence that they accomplish any of these goals is very thin at best (Heller, 2002c). This may be a reason why the spread of these programs, which was very rapid in the decade after Georgia HOPE was first launched, has since slowed.

The final art movement to be applied as a way of understanding the current status of the nation's financial aid system is Cubism. As noted earlier, this movement was characterized by "shapes . . . . so remotely related to the original form of the object that they seem almost to have been invented rather than derived" and "a new reality in paintings that depicted radically fragmented objects." Both the Truman Commission in 1947 and the Higher Education Act of 1965 emphasized the purpose of financial aid as helping students from families with inadequate resources to be able to afford to attend college. States, in the development of their own grant programs following creation of the federal State Student Incentive Grant program in the 1972 reauthorization of the Higher Education Act, also emphasized college access as a goal. Institutions, too, historically have focused their aid on helping address access for low- and moderate-income students.

As one reviews the higher education landscape today, it is easy to characterize the system as having "shapes . . . . so remotely related to the original form of the object that they seem almost to have been invented rather than derived." Many financial aid programs today have little in common with their original purpose. While the federal government has remained focused on using means-testing in the awarding of grant aid, state grant programs have moved more toward substituting merit criteria for financial need, and institutional grant programs have followed suit. Figure 6.13 shows the change between 1995 and 2007 in the proportion of state and institutional grants awarded without consideration of financial need. The proportion of state grants has increased from 14% in 1995 to 30% in 2007. For institutions, the proportion has increased from 35 to 55% during the same time period.

The financial aid system can also be characterized as fragmented, especially from the perspective of students trying to gather information about financial aid. Students, particularly those from first-generation and low-income families, have difficulty getting adequate and timely information about the financial aid for which they may qualify and desperately need (Advisory Committee on Student Financial Assistance, 2005; McDonough & Calderone, 2006; Perna, 2006). Typically, students do not have the information necessary to calculate their net cost of college (after taking into account financial aid) until they receive a financial aid offer from a university during the spring of

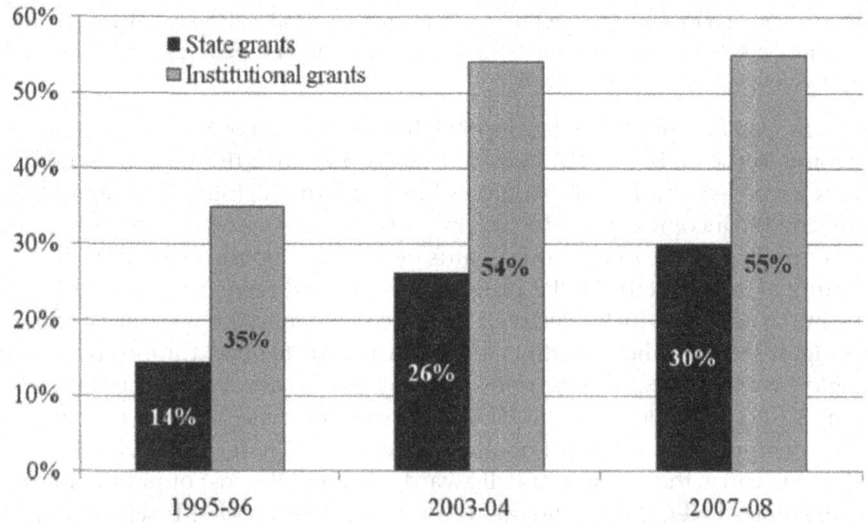

Figure 6.13 Proportion of total grant aid awarded to undergraduates without means-testing.

Source: Heller (2006), author's calculations from National Center for Education Statistics (2010d).

their final year in high school. If students base their college enrollment plans on the sticker price of college rather than the net price after aid, they are more likely to conclude they cannot afford to attend.

There is no one place for students to go to obtain their eligibility for all the different forms of financial aid for which they may qualify. Some websites, including one provided by the US Department of Education (see note 9), allow students to calculate an estimate of their Expected Family Contribution and likely eligibility for a Pell Grant, but it is difficult today for most students to estimate their eligibility for state and institutional grants. The latest reauthorization of the Higher Education Act, also known as the Higher Education Opportunity Act of 2008, has a provision (Section 111) requiring institutions to make available on their websites a "net price calculator," which will allow students to estimate what their true net cost will be. This requirement has not gone into effect, however, so it is too early to determine just how useful this information will be for students. Since many colleges package institutional aid for students on an individual basis, particularly merit aid, it is unclear how accurate the "estimates" will be.

The financial aid system is also fragmented from the perspective of public policy. The federal government has responsibility for the Title IV grant, loan, and work study programs, as well as other programs such as tax credits, regulations regarding private student loans, and a small number of undergraduate fellowship programs in other agencies. The states each develop their own grant programs, often multiple programs per state, in addition to some states that have loans. Generally the decisions about structure and funding for these programs are made in isolation of the federal financial aid programs, subject to the political and fiscal pressures in each of the states.

Colleges and universities do have to comply with state and federal regulations when awarding aid from those programs, but they have great latitude in decisions on awarding their own institutional aid. As described earlier, they can use their own criteria for determining which students are financially needy and for how much institutional aid they should qualify, independent of the dictates of federal methodology. The awarding of merit-based institutional grants is entirely at the discretion of each college and university.

The result of this disconnect between the various aid programs is that they often work at cross-purposes. While some, such as the federal Pell Grant program and state need-based programs, are primarily focused on promoting access for low- and moderate-income students, others—such as state and institutional merit grants—have more of an impact on the college choice decisions of students who are already committed to attending postsecondary education.

Conclusion

Examining the financial aid system through the lens of these three art movements—Realism, Surrealism, and Cubism—allows one to see the strengths and weaknesses of the various parts of the system and how those components do or do not help achieve some of the historical objectives the nation has had with respect to college participation. In contrast to many other countries around the world, the United States has always had, and likely will continue to have, a more decentralized higher education system with authority distributed among the federal government, the 50 states, and the over 6,000 institutions of postsecondary learning. This devolution of authority, which is often cited as one of the contributors to the quality of the American system, also means that addressing issues of public policy and higher education is a more challenging task than elsewhere.

Parts of the financial aid system, such as the federal Title IV programs, have remained largely consistent with the earlier objectives of promoting access to college for groups who have historically been underrepresented. As described earlier, these groups—including racial minority students and those from low-income families—would be considered in concert with Realism's focus on "the common man." Just as Realism sought to bring commoners out from the shadows and into the forefront as subjects in paintings, the Title IV programs have focused on bringing these same individuals into the forefront of higher education by providing them with access to postsecondary education that a generation or two ago was largely reserved for more privileged sectors of society.

The question remains of why federal financial aid has remained largely committed to the purposes articulated in the Higher Education Act over 45 years ago, while state and institutional aid has drifted toward the pursuit of other goals. Hearn (1993) examined what he described as the "paradox" of the growth in federal student aid, in light of the fact that traditional policy theory finds little rationale for the support it has enjoyed. Sociologist Theda Skocpol (1991), for example, has written about the trade-off between highly targeted social programs, which have the benefit of maximizing the use of public resources, and more universal programs that are a less-efficient use of resources but may garner more widespread political support.

One possible explanation Hearn (1993) posits is what he describes as "entrenched governmental bureaucracies":

> entrenched governmental bureaucracies, supported by the institutionalization over time of certain policies associated with those bureaucracies, maintained enough structural and procedural weight to deflect and defuse reform. (p. 124)

The longstanding support for Pell Grants, for example—which are highly targeted at individuals whom most would agree are not particularly empowered in the political process—by this explanation would be because they have became entrenched first in the Office of Education and later in the Department of Education. The Pell Grant program itself has rarely been examined by Congress or presidential administrations with the possibility of shutting it down or making radical structural changes; rather, the debates have generally been over levels of funding. This is in contrast to other Department of Education postsecondary programs, such as the TRIO programs or the SSIG/LEAP program, which have faced being eliminated in the past (Selingo, 2005).

The federal Title IV programs have not been immune from pressures for broadening their scope. As described earlier, the Middle Income Student Assistance Act in the late 1970s was a direct effort to widen the narrow targeting of both Pell Grants and subsidized student loans in order to make them available further up the income ladder. While this effort was initially successful, the changes were rolled back a few years later and both programs returned to their more narrowly targeted beneficiaries.

In contrast to the federal Title IV programs, other parts of the financial aid system—particularly state and institutional grants—have changed quite a bit over time toward the pursuit of very different goals. I have shown how some of these changes can fairly be described as incongruous, irrational, fragmented—descriptors of the Surrealism and Cubism movements—and at best be remotely related to much of financial aid's original purposes.

Why then have state and institutional aid programs—which began originally with largely similar goals of promoting access and equity—changed so much in comparison to the federal Title IV programs? To answer this question requires an examination of the two entities separately.

State grant programs are publicly funded and controlled, as are the Title IV programs, and many came about as a result of the State Student Incentive Grant program passed as part of the 1972 amendments to the Higher Education Act. They are the province of each of the states, however, and decisions regarding their structure, targeting, and funding levels are made by state legislatures and governors. Each of the states is a laboratory for innovation, with postsecondary policies subject to the local political culture (McLendon, Heller, & Young, 2005). State governments are subject to more rapid change in control and political orientation due to factors such as gubernatorial and legislative term limits, and therefore, new policies—including in the postsecondary financing domain—are more likely to be implemented (McLendon, Deaton, & Hearn, 2007).

Institutional financial aid programs enjoy a mix of governance control. In private colleges and universities, decisions about these programs are the domain of the leadership (boards and administration) of the individual institution. These institutions have responded to the competitive higher education marketplace by more frequently using their student aid programs for the enrollment management purposes outlined earlier, rather than for promoting educational equity and access for historically underserved populations (McPherson & Schapiro, 1998, 2002). This shift has caused their structure to deviate from the historical patterns and from the purposes that still bind the federal Title IV programs.

Like their private counterparts, most public colleges and universities also generally control their own student aid programs. Depending upon the state, though, these programs may also be governed at least in part by state regulations that limit the autonomy of institutional decision-making. The trend in recent years, however, is more toward devolution of authority from the states to individual public colleges and universities or systems (MacTaggart, 1998;McLendon, 2003). As this has occurred, public colleges and universities look and act more like their private counterparts, using student aid to pursue narrow institutional interests at the expense of public goals such as educational equity and improving access.

What does the future hold for the trends described in this chapter? The role of financial aid in promoting educational equity is still very much at the forefront of federal higher education policy. The Spellings Commission—a review panel formed by former Secretary of Education Margaret Spellings during the Bush administration—clearly articulated the notion that the country was far from having achieved the goals outlined by President Lyndon Johnson when he signed the Higher Education Act into law in 1965. The Commission stated

> Too few Americans prepare for, participate in, and complete higher education—especially those underserved and nontraditional groups who make up an ever-greater proportion of the population . . . . We found that access to higher education in the United States is *unduly limited by the complex interplay of inadequate preparation, lack of information about college opportunities, and persistent financial barriers* (U.S. Department of Education, 2006, p. 8, emphasis in the original).

To address the financial barriers, the Commission called for "providing significant increases in aid to low-income students" (p. 17), a recommendation many were surprised to see coming from a panel formed by a Republican administration. President Obama's higher education agenda has focused on similar efforts, including more spending on Pell Grants and increased funding for community colleges, the entry point to postsecondary education for many low-income and minority students (Field, 2009).

Are the student aid trends in the states and among higher education institutions that have been so divergent from federal policy likely to be reversed or even abated? There are some promising trends, such as the approximately 30 institutions that have made strong financial aid commitments to students from low- and moderate-income families (The Project on Student Debt, 2008). But this group represents a very small and elite sector of higher education, and evidence indicates that the majority of institutions with substantial financial aid programs are still focusing their resources on meeting institutional enrollment management goals. The development of state merit grant programs, which was so prominent in the late 1990s and early 2000s, appears to have slowed in recent years. But funding for states' need-based grants, which generally mirror the purposes of federal Pell Grants, is still very much at the whim of fiscal conditions in most states and generally suffers during economic downturns.

While there are some continuing commitments to equal opportunity goals, the political landscape in the nation has shifted from the days of President Lyndon Johnson's Great Society, when a number of government programs designed to address the underclass of American society were put into place. It is hard to imagine the country returning to an era when equality of opportunity will be the almost universal goal of financial aid programs.

Acknowledgments

The author wishes to acknowledge the invaluable research assistance of Rachel Frick Cardelle in the preparation of this work.

Notes

1. This chapter does not discuss financial aid provided from private sources such as philanthropic organizations or sources like tuition assistance from employers. In addition, the focus is on financial aid for undergraduate students.

2. Congress set maximum *authorized* awards for the program, but the *actual* maximum grant award was established by the annual appropriations established by Congress.
3. The grants category is for all types of federal grants, which includes, besides Pell Grants, programs such as veterans' and active duty military grants. In 2008–2009, Pell Grants represented almost three-quarters of the total of federal grants.
4. The federal College Work Study program has remained small relative to the other programs, and its funding has decreased over the years from $1.8 billion in 1979–1980 to $1.2 billion in 2008–2009.
5. Parts of this section have been adapted from Heller (2002a).
6. Eligibility for means-tested financial aid is based on income in the year prior to attending college, so for students in the 2007–2008 NPSAS survey, income data from 2006 are used.
7. The credit crisis and recession that began in 2008 had a large impact on the private student loan markets, with many lenders leaving the market. The College Board (2009b) reported that overall (graduate and undergraduate combined) borrowing from private lenders, which had been growing steadily over the prior decade, dropped by half between 2007–2008 and 2008–2009, from $23.8 to $11.9 billion.
8. This total is only for the borrowing incurred by the student and excludes parent PLUS loans or other borrowing by parents such as through home equity loans.
9. An income in this level would not qualify students for federal means-tested grants or most state need-based grant programs. Students and parents can estimate their eligibility for need-based federal grants and loans at http://www.fafsa4caster.ed.gov/F4CApp/index/index.jsf or http://www.finaid.org/calculators/finaidestimate.phtml
10. It should be noted here that students attending college come from families that overall have slightly higher incomes than the population at large. While the NPSAS sample has a median income of $67,754, all families in the United States with at least one child under the age of 18 had a median income of $56,788 in 2006 (U.S. Census Bureau, 2010a).
11. Federal methodology is the formula used by the US Department of Education in assessing eligibility for Title IV student aid. Institutional methodology is the more liberal formula used by some institutions in determining need that uses a broader definition of student and family income and assets, which generally results in a higher Expected Family Contribution.

References

Advisory Committee on Student Financial Assistance (2001). *Access denied: Restoring the nation's commitment to equal educational opportunity*. Washington, DC: U.S. Department of Education.

Advisory Committee on Student Financial Assistance (2002). *Empty promises: The myth of college access in America*. Washington, DC: U.S. Department of Education.

Advisory Committee on Student Financial Assistance (2005). *The student aid gauntlet: Making access to college simple and certain*. Washington, DC: U.S. Department of Education.

Advisory Committee on Student Financial Assistance (2006). *Mortgaging our future: How financial barriers to college undercut America's global competitiveness*. Washington, DC: U.S. Department of Education.

Baird, K. (2006). The political economy of college prepaid tuition plans. *The Review of Higher Education*, 29(2), 141–166.

Barr, A. H., Jr. (1936). *Cubism and abstract art*. New York: The Museum of Modern Art.

Becker, W. E. (2004). Omitted variables and sample selection in studies of college-going decisions. In E. P. St. John (Ed.), *Public policy and college access: Investigating the federal and state roles in equalizing postsecondary opportunity, Readings on equal education* (Vol. 19, pp. 65–86). New York: AMS Press, Inc.

Bennett, M. J. (1996). *When dreams came true: The GI Bill and the making of modern America*. Washington, DC: Brassey's.

Boccella, K. (2007, December 18). Penn offers expanded aid package to students; buoyed by a healthy endowment, it will replace loans with outright grants for many middle-class families starting next year. *The Philadelphia Inquirer*, p. B01.

Boyd, J. D. (1975). *State/territory funded scholarship/grant programs to undergraduate students with financial need to attend public or private post-secondary educational institutions. Seventh annual survey, 1975–1976 academic year*. Deerfield, IL: Illinois State Scholarship Commission.

Brubacher, J. S.,& Rudy,W. (1976). *Higher education in transition: A history of American colleges and universities, 1636–1976* (3rd ed.). New York: Harper and Row Publishers.

Burd, S. (2003, October 24). Republic introduces bill to penalize colleges for tuition increases. *The Chronicle of Higher Education*, p. A26.

Callan, P. M. (2001). Reframing access and opportunity: Problematic state and federal higher education policy in the 1990s. In D. E. Heller (Ed.), *The states and public higher education policy: Affordability, access, and accountability* (pp. 83–99). Baltimore: The Johns Hopkins University Press.

Cervantes, A., Creusere, M., McMillion, R., McQueen, C., Short, M., Steiner, M., et al. (2005). *Higher education act: Forty years of opportunity*. Round Rock, TX: TG Research and Analytical Services.

Chilvers, I., Osborne, H., & Farr, D. (1988). *The Oxford dictionary of art*. Oxford: Oxford University Press.

College Board (2009a). *Trends in college pricing, 2009*. Washington, DC: Author.

College Board (2009b). *Trends in student aid, 2009*. Washington, DC: Author.

College Board (2010). *Who borrows most? Bachelor's degree recipients with high levels of student debt*. Washington, DC: Author.

Colleges and sticker shock (2008, January 26). Chicago Tribune, p. 22.

Cornwell, C., & Mustard, D. (2002). Race and the effects of Georgia's HOPE scholarship. In D. E. Heller & P. Marin (Eds.), *Who should we help? The negative social consequences of merit scholarships* (pp. 57–72). Cambridge, MA: The Civil Rights Project at Harvard University.

Davis, J. S. (2003). *Unintended consequences of tuition discounting*. Indianapolis, IN: New Agenda Series, Lumina Foundation for Education.

Fenske, R. H., & Boyd, J. D. (1981). *State need-based college scholarship and grant programs: A study of their development*, 1969–1980. New York: College Entrance Examination Board.

Field, K. (2009, August 17). On higher-education spending, the White House and Congress agree, to a point. *The Chronicle of Higher Education*, Retrieved June 14, 2010 from http://chronicle.com/article/On-Education-Spending-the-/48007/

Fitzgerald, B. K., & Delaney, J. A. (2002). Educational opportunity in America. In D. E. Heller (Ed.), *Condition of access: Higher education for lower income students* (pp. 3–24). Westport, CT: Praeger Publishers (ACE/Praeger Series on Higher Education).

Gladieux, L. E. (2002). Federal student aid in historical perspective. In D. E. Heller (Ed.), *Condition of access: Higher education for lower income students* (pp. 45–58). Westport, CT: Praeger Publishers (ACE/Praeger Series on Higher Education).

Gladieux, L. E., & Wolanin, T. (1976). *Congress and the colleges: The national politics of higher education*. Lexington, MA: Lexington Books.

Greenberg, M. (1997). *The GI bill: The law that changed America*. New York: Lickle Publishing.

Hardy, D. (2007, December 13). No-loan plan at Swarthmore; College joins Harvard, Princeton and others in extending financial aid. *The Philadelphia Inquirer*, p. A01.

Harvard announces sweeping middle-income initiative. (2007). Retrieved March 31, 2010, from http://news.harvard.edu/gazette/story/2007/12/harvard-announces-sweeping-middle-incomeinitiative/

Hauptman, A. (2001). Reforming the ways in which states finance higher education. In D. E. Heller (Ed.), *The states and public higher education policy: Affordability, access, and accountability* (pp. 64–80). Baltimore: The Johns Hopkins University Press.

Hearn, J. C. (1993). The paradox of growth in federal aid for college students, 1965-1990. In J. C. Smart (Ed.), *Higher education: Handbook of theory and research* (Vol. 9, pp. 94–153). New York: Agathon Press.

Hearn, J. C., & Holdsworth, J. M. (2004). Federal student aid: The shift from grants to loans. In E. P. St. John & M. D. Parsons (Eds.), *Public funding of higher education: Changing contexts and new rationales* (pp. 40–59). Baltimore: Johns Hopkins University Press.

Heller, D. E. (2002a). The policy shift in state financial aid programs. In J. C. Smart (Ed.), *Higher education: Handbook of theory and research* (Vol. 17, pp. 221–261). New York: Agathon Press.

Heller, D. E. (2002b). State aid and student access: The changing picture. In D. E. Heller (Ed.), *Condition of access: Higher education for lower income students* (pp. 59–72). Westport, CT: Praeger Publishers (ACE/Praeger Series on Higher Education).

Heller, D. E. (2002c). State merit scholarship programs: An introduction. In D. E. Heller & P. Marin (Eds.), *Who should we help? The negative social consequences of merit scholarships* (pp. 15–23). Cambridge, MA: The Civil Rights Project at Harvard University.

Heller, D. E. (2004). NCES research on college participation: A critical analysis. In E. P. St. John (Ed.), *Public policy and college access: Investigating the federal and state roles in equalizing postsecondary opportunity. Readings on equal education* (Vol. 19, pp. 29–64). New York: AMS Press, Inc.

Heller, D. E. (2006). *Merit aid and college access*. Madison, WI: Wisconsin Center for the Advancement of Postsecondary Education, University of Wisconsin.

Heller, D. E. (2007a, December 17). How Harvard foils its own good intentions. *The Chronicle of Higher Education*.

Heller, D. E. (2007b). *Testimony before the committee on appropriations, subcommittee on labor, health and human services, education, and related agencies, February 15, 2007*. Washington, DC: U.S. Congress.

Heller, D. E. (2008). *Financial aid and admission: Tuition discounting, merit aid, and need-aware admissions*. Arlington, VA: The National Association for College Admission Counseling.

Heller, D. E., Cheslock, J., Hughes, R., & Frick Cardelle, R. (2010). *Institutional selectivity, family finances, and the distribution of grant aid: Findings from NPSAS:08*. Paper presented at the 27th Annual Student Financial Aid Research Network Conference, San Diego, CA.

Heller, D. E., & Marin, P. (Eds.). (2002). *Who should we help? The negative social consequences of merit scholarships*. Cambridge, MA: The Civil Rights Project at Harvard University.

Heller, D. E., & Marin, P. (Eds.). (2004). *State merit scholarship programs and racial inequality*. Cambridge, MA: The Civil Rights Project at Harvard University.

Higher Education Act of 1965, Pub. L. No. 89–329 (1965).

Holtschneider, D. H. (1997). *Institutional aid to New England college students: 1740-1800* (Unpublished doctoral dissertation, Harvard University, Cambridge, MA, 1997).

Hoover, E. (2007, December 21). Harvard's new aid policy raises the stakes. *The Chronicle of Higher Education*, p. A4.

Hutcheson, P. (2002). The 1947 President's commission on higher education and the national rhetoric on higher education policy. *History of Higher Education Annual*, 22, 91–109.

Illinois State University Center for the Study of Education Policy. (2010). State fiscal support for higher education, by state (Grapevine, Table 1). Retrieved April 10, from http://www.grapevine.ilstu.edu/tables/FY10/Revised_Feb10/GPV10_Table1_revised.xls

Lapovsky, L., & Hubbell, L. L. (2003). Tuition discounting continues to grow. *NACUBO Business Officer*, 36(9), 20–27.

Lemann, N. (1999). *The big test: The secret history of the American meritocracy*. New York: Farrar, Straus and Giroux.

Long, B. T. (2003). *The impact of federal tax credits for higher education expenses (No. Working Paper 9553)*. Cambridge, MA: National Bureau of Economic Research.

MacTaggart, T. J. (1998). *Seeking excellence through independence: Liberating colleges and universities from excessive regulation*. San Francisco: Jossey-Bass Publishers.

McDonough, P. M., & Calderone, S. (2006). The meaning of money: Perceptual differences between college counselors and low-income families about college costs and financial aid. *American Behavioral Scientist*, 49(12), 1703–1718.

McLendon, M. K. (2003). Setting the governmental agenda for state decentralization of higher education. *The Journal of Higher Education*, 74(5), 479–515.

McLendon, M. K., Deaton, R., & Hearn, J. C. (2007). The enactment of reforms in state governance of higher education: Testing the political instability hypothesis. *The Journal of Higher Education*, 78(6), 645–675.

McLendon, M. K., Heller, D. E., & Young, S. P. (2005). State postsecondary policy innovation: Politics, competition, and the interstate migration of policy ideas. *The Journal of Higher Education*, 76(4), 363–400.

McPherson, M. (2004). Comment on "The impact of federal tax credits for higher education expenses". In C. Hoxby (Ed.), *College choices: The economics of where to go, when to go, and how to pay for it*. Chicago: University of Chicago Press.

McPherson, M. S., & Schapiro, M. O. (1991). *Keeping college affordable: Government and educational opportunity*. Washington, DC: The Brookings Institution.

McPherson, M. S., & Schapiro, M. O. (1998). *The student aid game: Meeting need and rewarding talent in American higher education*. Princeton, NJ: Princeton University Press.

McPherson, M. S., & Schapiro, M. O. (2002). Changing patterns of institutional aid: Impact on access and education policy. In D. E. Heller (Ed.), *Condition of access: Higher education for lower income students* (pp. 73–94). Westport, CT: Praeger Publishers (ACE/Praeger Series on Higher Education).

Moffat, C. A. (2010). Cubism. Retrieved April 5, from http://www.arthistoryarchive.com/ arthistory/cubism/

Mumper, M. (1996). *Removing college price barriers: What government has done and why it hasn't worked.* Albany, NY: State University of New York Press.

Mumper, M. (1998). State efforts to keep public colleges affordable in the face of fiscal stress. In J. C. Smart (Ed.), *Higher education: Handbook of theory and research* (Vol. 13, pp. 148–180). New York: Agathon Press.

Mumper, M. (2001). The paradox of college prices: Five stories with no clear lesson. In D. E. Heller (Ed.), *The states and public higher education policy: Affordability, access, and accountability* (pp. 39–63). Baltimore: The Johns Hopkins University Press.

Murray, P., & Murray, L. (1989). *The Penguin dictionary of art and artists* (6th ed.). London: Penguin Books.

National Association of College and University Business Officers. (2010). *2009 tuition discounting study report.* Washington, DC: Author.

National Association of State Scholarship and Grant Programs. (various years). *NASSGP/NASSGAP annual survey report.* Deerfield, IL; Harrisburg, PA; Albany, NY: Illinois State Scholarship Commission; Pennsylvania Higher Education Assistance Agency; and New York State Higher Education Services Corporation.

National Association of State Student Grant & Aid Programs. (2009). *NASSGAP 39th annual survey report on state-sponsored student financial aid 2007–2008 academic year.* Washington, DC: Author.

National Center for Education Statistics. (2010a). College Navigator. Retrieved April 2, 2010, from http://nces.ed.gov/collegenavigator/

National Center for Education Statistics. (2010b). *Digest of education statistics, 2009* (No. NCES 2010-2013). Washington, DC: U.S. Department of Education.

National Center for Education Statistics. (2010c). National Postsecondary Student Aid Study 1987–1988 data analysis system. Retrieved April 15, from http://nces.ed.gov/dasol/

National Center for Education Statistics. (2010d). National Postsecondary Student Aid Study 2007–2008 data analysis system. Retrieved April 15, from http://nces.ed.gov/dasol/

Parsons, M. D. (1997). *Power and politics: Federal higher education policymaking in the 1990s.* Albany, NY: State University of New York Press.

Perna, L. (2006). Understanding the relationship between information about college prices and financial aid and students' college-related behaviors. *American Behavioral Scientist,* 49(12), 1620–1635.

President's Commission on Higher Education. (1947). *Higher education for American democracy.* New York: Harper and Brothers.

Redd, K. E. (2000). *Discounting toward disaster: Tuition discounting, college finances, and enrollments of low-income undergraduates.* Indianapolis, IN: USA Group Foundation.

Robbins, D. (1988). Abbreviated historiography of Cubism. *Art Journal,* 47(4), 277–283.

Roth, A. (2001, January 19). Who benefits from states' college-savings plans? *The Chronicle of Higher Education,* p. B13.

Sears, J. B. (1923, January). Our theory of free higher education. *Educational Review,* 65, 27–34.

Selingo, J. (2005, February 18). Bush budget takes aim at student aid and research. *The Chronicle of Higher Education,* p. A1.

Sherman, M. (1991, November 14). Miller reveals lottery plans for education; He anticipates easy referendum passage. *The Atlanta Journal and Constitution,* p. A1.

Skocpol, T. (1991). *Universal appeal.* The Brookings Review, 9(3), 28–33.

St. John, E. P. (2003). *Refinancing the college dream: Access, equal opportunity, and justice for taxpayers.* Baltimore: Johns Hopkins University Press.

The Project on Student Debt. (2008). *Comparison and analysis of financial aid pledges: How much would families actually have to pay?* Oakland, CA: Author.

U.S. Census Bureau. (2010a). Presence and number of related children under 18 Years old— Families, all races by median and mean Income: 1947 to 2008 Retrieved March 20, 2010, from http://www.census.gov/hhes/www/income/histinc/f09AR.xls

U.S. Census Bureau. (2010b). Small area income and poverty estimates: State and county data: 1989, 1993, 1995–2008. Retrieved May 10, 2010, from http://www.census.gov/did/www/saipe/data/statecounty/index.html

U.S. Department of Education (2006). *A test of leadership: Charting the future of U.S. higher education.* Washington, DC: Author.

Yale University Office of Public Affairs. (2008). Yale cuts costs for families and students. Retrieved April 5, 2010, from http://opa.yale.edu/news/article.aspx?id=2320

Zumeta, W. (1997). State policy and private higher education: Past, present and future. In J. C. Smart (Ed.), *Higher education: Handbook of theory and research* (Vol. 12, pp. 43–106). New York: Agathon Press.

CHAPTER 7

ECONOMIC MODELS AND POLICY ANALYSIS IN HIGHER EDUCATION: A DIAGRAMMATIC EXPOSITION

MICHAEL B. PAULSEN AND ROBERT K. TOUTKOUSHIAN

Introduction

Policy analysis is a term that is used very often in education circles and seems to have multiple meanings depending on the background of the person using the phrase and the context in which it is used. Generally speaking, a *policy* is "a definite course or method of action selected from among alternatives and in light of given conditions to guide and determine present and future decisions" (Merriam-Webster Dictionary, 2007), and an *educational policy* is "a specification of principles and actions, related to educational issues, which are followed or which should be followed and which are designed to bring about desired goals" (Trowler, 2003, p. 95). Who are the policy makers in higher education? For the postsecondary setting, policy makers would include entities and individuals who enact these laws and rules, including academic departments, colleges, institutions, and local, state, and national governments. The goal of educational policies is to lead to desired changes in behavior for participants within the education system. For example, a state-level educational policy may be implemented to help increase the percentage of high school students who go on to pursue a postsecondary education. The goal of this policy is to change the behavior of some high school students who may not be likely to attend college following graduation. As another example, an academic department may design policies to increase the quality of instruction given to undergraduate students. Here, the policy maker (academic department administration) is seeking to alter the actions of faculty in such a way that will lead to gains in instructional quality.

Educational policy analysis focuses on how one should evaluate the effectiveness of alternative educational policies when choosing between them. The analysis of policy in higher education—an interdisciplinary field of study—is richly informed by a diverse set of disciplines including sociology, psychology, political science, history, philosophy and more. One other discipline that has great potential to help us understand the higher education enterprise and to productively inform policy analysis in higher education is *economics*. Non-economists often associate economics with money, profit and other business-related phenomena and often equate economics with professional fields such as business, accounting or finance. Unfortunately, this perspective greatly limits and substantially narrows the view of many non-economists regarding the usefulness of economics for policy analysis in higher education. In terms of both structure and methodology, the discipline of economics is a social and behavioral science and has much more in common with sociology, psychology and political science than with accounting, finance and business fields (Paulsen & Toutkoushian, 2006b; Toutkoushian & Paulsen, 2006).

Economics is comprised of highly generalizable frameworks that are designed to analyze how *incentives* affect the *behavior* of decision makers who are in pursuit of goals. Most higher education policies represent elements of incentive structures—or changes in those incentive structures—that influence the behavior of individuals or institutions. For example, a state need-based grant to a student who is undecided about whether or not to pursue higher education changes the incentive structure this student faces by expanding the student's income *constraint*. For many students, this change in their income constraint will affect their decision-making and change their college-going behavior. This is very important for policy analysis in higher education because there are countless higher education policies that can be readily conceptualized in terms of tangible or intangible elements of incentive structures, and economics provides productive analytical frameworks for understanding, evaluating, and measuring the effectiveness of such policies.

Economists have a unique approach to looking at educational policy issues. They begin by identifying the decision makers for a given problem, the constraints those decision makers face, and the goals and objectives they want to pursue. This information, together with a series of behavioral and simplifying assumptions, is used to develop a conceptual model of the underlying process being studied. Economists then use the model to determine the allocation of resources that lead to the maximization of the goal given the constraints faced by the policy maker. More importantly, the model can shed light on how changes in one or more facets of the problem can affect this point of maximization. This is generally referred to by economists as comparative statics. Comparative statics prove to be very useful for educational policy analysis because they allow the economist to predict how policies might affect the outcome of interest. To economists, the analysis of educational policies is crucial because of the numerous policies that might be enacted to address specific issues, and the limited resources that policy makers have at their disposal to do this. Choosing an ineffective or less effective policy leads to an opportunity cost in that another action could have been taken that would have been more effective at reaching the intended goal.

In this chapter, we seek to provide the reader with a detailed explanation and one substantial illustration of how economists approach educational policy analysis, and how this can be useful for understanding and improving higher education. Our presentation is primarily intended for those higher education scholars, administrators and practitioners who are not trained in economists. Toward this end, we have minimized our use of mathematical notation and maximized our use of diagrammatic representations of all economic models, with each diagram and model accompanied by substantial and detailed narrative explanation. In the first half of this chapter, we focus on explaining how economists develop and use models in their work, and how economists use these models to examine educational policies. In the second half of this chapter, we explore the use of human capital theory—the theoretical framework from economics that is the most widely-used for the analysis of higher education policies—and a model of the market for investment in higher education to provide a detailed illustration of how economic theories, models, and methods can be and have been applied to educational policies in the realm of student access to postsecondary education. We conclude with a discussion of some of the measurement issues encountered when trying to analyze educational policies and factors such as data limitations and self selection that impose limitations on what can be done to analyze the effectiveness of alternative educational policies.

General Economic Approach to Educational Policy

In this first section, we focus on providing the reader with a general description of the approach that economists use to examine educational policies. This approach can be applied to many different problems within higher education, including student access to higher education, faculty compensation and time allocation, student retention, and educational productivity, to name but a few. We encourage those readers interested in more detailed and in-depth explanations of the general microeconomic concepts, models and methods presented in this chapter to consult some of the fine microeconomic textbooks available at the introductory level—such as Mankiw (2007) or McEachern (2006)—or intermediate-level—such as Pindyck and Rubinfeld (2005) or Frank (2003). Additional explanations of many of these concepts that are directed towards institutional researchers can be found in Toutkoushian and Paulsen (2006).

Economic Models

Economists rely heavily on the use of theoretical models to conduct their work in educational policy. A model by definition is meant to be a simplified depiction of reality, so that one can focus on a few important factors rather than all of the complexities of a given problem. An education model begins by identifying the decision maker of interest (such as a student, faculty member, or administrator), the goal or objective that they are trying to attain, and the constraints that they face in doing so. For example, a model that looks at whether or not students go on to college would begin by identifying students (and perhaps their families) as the decision maker. The presumed goal of students is to make decisions that will maximize their happiness, or utility. Students face constraints, however, in that they only have limited financial resources to be able to pay for college and limited time to allocate among competing uses of their time. The economic model would be designed to describe in a relatively simple fashion how students allocate their time and income so as to maximize their utility, and what the implications would be for whether or not they choose to go to college. Essentially, a student would opt to go to college if doing so allowed him/her to obtain more lifetime utility than would be true by not going to college.

A typical model might posit that a decision maker such as a student receives utility from different combinations of two goods or services. The utility that individuals receive from these goods and services can and does vary across individuals. This means, for example, that two high school students could receive different amounts of satisfaction from going to college and using their remaining money for other goods and services. The utility from different combinations of goods/services is usually represented graphically in the form of an indifference curve. An indifference curve shows all of the combinations of two goods and services that would give a decision maker the same level of utility, making them "indifferent" between the choices. This is illustrated graphically in Fig. 7.1, where each indifference curve shows the combinations of two goods (labeled X and Y) that yield the same satisfaction level. Each decision maker is presumed to have an infinite number of such curves, with greater combinations of X and Y yielding more utility. The decision maker would prefer to reach the highest indifference curve possible because in doing so they will have increased their satisfaction.

While the indifference curves represent the goal that the decision maker is trying to achieve (in this case, maximizing utility), there are typically one or more constraints imposed on decision makers that limit the satisfaction they can attain. These are most often in the form of constraints on the amount of financial resources that can be spent, or the amount of time that can be used. A budget constraint is a way of graphically representing the choices available to a decision maker for allocating the resource in question. Figure 7.1 depicts a typical budget constraint, where the points of intersection on each axis indicate the maximum amount of a good or service that could be consumed if all of the financial resources were spent on that particular commodity. These points are derived by dividing the total financial resources of the decision maker by the price of each good. This also means that the position and slope of the budget line is fully determined by the decision maker's level of financial resources and the prices of the two goods being measured. Any point along the budget constraint is viewed as an efficient use of resources because all of the resources are being expended for goods X and Y. Likewise, all points to the right of the budget constraint are unattainable given the current prices of the goods X and Y and available income.

The problem for the decision maker, from the point of view of an economist, becomes how to maximize their goal or objective given the constraints that they face. This can be seen graphically in Fig. 7.1. The optimal point, which is referred to as the equilibrium, is found where the indifference curve is tangent to the budget line (point A). At this point, the decision maker is obtaining as much utility as possible given the level of resources and prices of the two goods or services. Any other point along the budget line, such as point B, would be efficient but result in a lower level of utility to the decision maker. Therefore, the decision maker could become happier by reallocating resources away from good Y and towards good X until point A is reached. While the decision maker would prefer to choose any combination along the indifference curve "utility = 300," as noted earlier these combinations are unattainable with the current level of resources and prices.

Alternatives for Educational Policy

The economist's view of educational policy analysis uses a theoretical model such as the one described above to ask the question: what policy can be enacted that would lead to a desired change

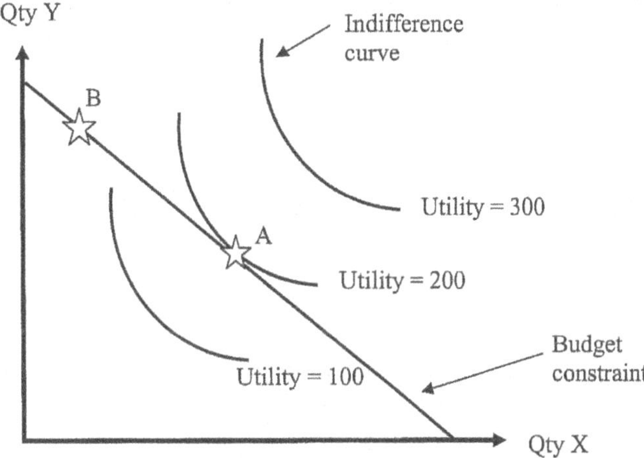

Figure 7.1 Optimization.

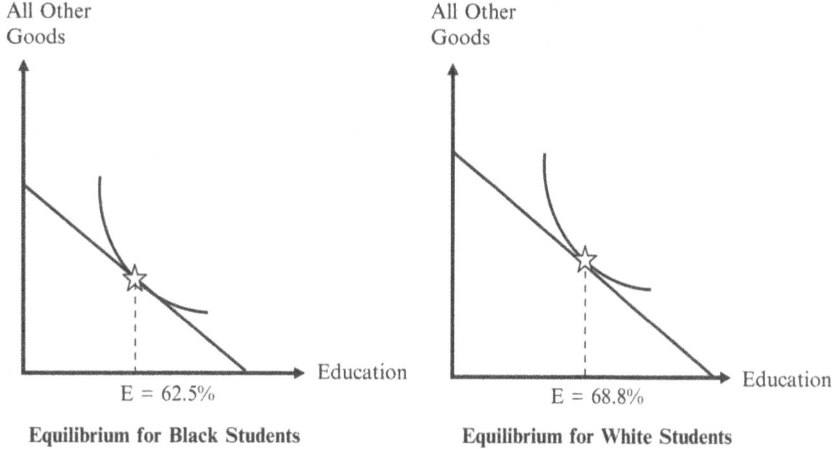

Figure 7.2 Different equilibria by race.

in equilibrium? To illustrate, in 2004 62.5% of black non-Hispanic high school graduates and 68.8% of white non-Hispanic high school graduates entered college within 12 months of graduation (National Center for Education Statistics, 2005, Table 181). Policy makers may therefore be interested in understanding why this difference in the college-going rates between students of different races has occurred and what might be done to help eliminate the gap. Figure 7.2 shows how these college-going rates might be expressed using the framework of indifference curves and budget constraints.

This framework also makes clear that the difference in college-going rates must be attributed to one or more of the following three explanations. The first is that white students have a higher preference than black students for education. Thus, holding ability to pay constant, white students would be more willing than black students to trade other goods and services for education. If true, then the entire set of indifference curves for white students is shifted more towards education, leading to an equilibrium point that has more consumption of education. This is depicted graphically in Fig. 7.3. Only the indifference curves for each group that are tangent to the budget line are shown here. It is assumed here that both white and black students have the same exact budget lines, meaning that they have the same levels of financial resources for education and face the same prices for education. Accordingly, the gap in college-going rates is due exclusively to different preferences between the groups for higher education.

A second possible cause for the difference in college-going rates is that on average white students have more financial resources (income, wealth) than black students. As a result, the budget

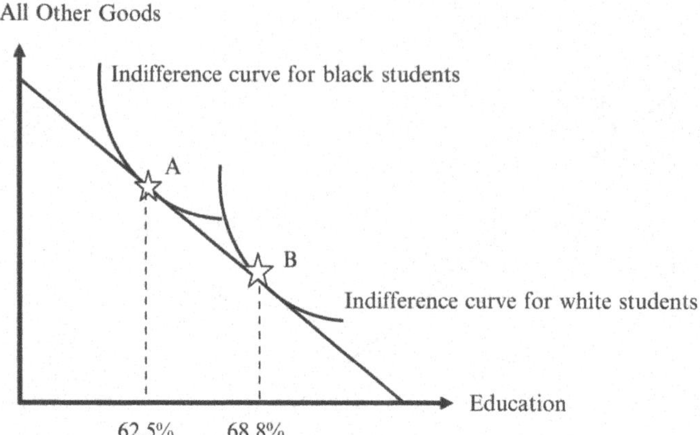

Figure 7.3 Effects of different preferences for higher education.

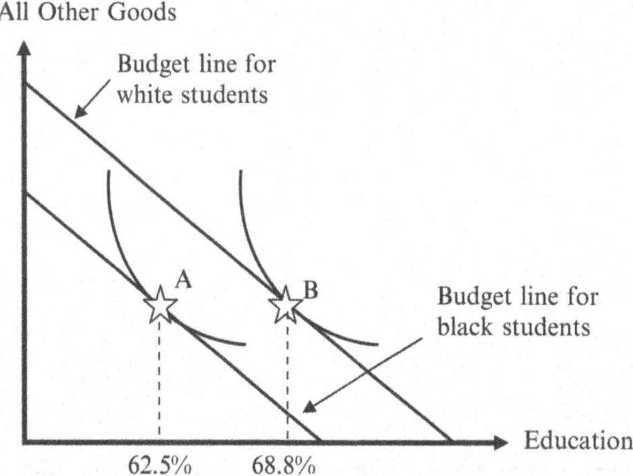

Figure 7.4 Effects of different budget constraints for higher education.

line for white students would be greater than (or to the right of) the budget line for black students, enabling white students to purchase more education and perhaps all other goods than black students. This is shown in Fig. 7.4. Note that it is assumed here that white and black students have the same indifference curves (i.e., they have the same preferences for education versus all other goods), and they face the same relative prices for education versus all other goods (i.e., their budget constraints are parallel). As a result, the different college-going rates are not due to different preferences for college, but rather different amounts of resources that could be used to pay for college.

Finally, a third potential explanation is that the relative price of education is lower for white students than it is for black students. This would enable white students to purchase more education than black students can purchase given their income. Graphically, this would cause the budget line for white students to pivot outward, and would lead to an equilibrium that contains more education for white students than for black students (Fig. 7.5). In this figure, we assume that white and black students have the same indifference curves and the same amount of financial resources, and therefore the difference in college-going rates is fully attributable to the different prices that they face. Of course, it is also possible that any combination of these three explanations hold at the same time. For example, in comparison to black students, white students could have a higher preference for education and have more financial resources to acquire education.

The focus of economists who study educational policy is not so much with understanding the reasons why decision makers are at a given equilibrium point as it is with designing policies that would lead to desired changes in equilibria. The policy maker's action plan is intended to alter

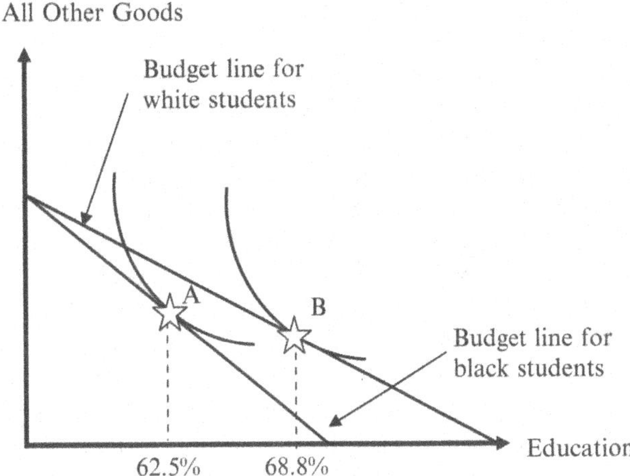

Figure 7.5 Effects of different prices for higher education.

the behavior of decision makers in a particular way, regardless of the reason that the current equilibrium condition has emerged. The framework described here shows that there are three general ways in which an equilibrium can be altered: (1) change the preferences of the decision maker; (2) change the decision maker's level of financial resources; and/or (3) change the relative prices faced by the decision maker. As shown in Figs. 7.3 through 7.5, a policy that can accomplish any of these would lead to predicted changes in equilibria.

Returning to the previous example, the difference in college-going rates between white and black students could, in theory, be reduced by either shifting the preferences of black students more towards education, increasing the level of financial resources for black students, or reducing the price of education for black students. Policy makers might attempt to alter preferences by publicizing the advantages of going to college (or the disadvantages of not going to college), or introducing support programs at pre-collegiate levels that would make it more appealing for black students to want to pursue a postsecondary education. In fact, there are many examples of initiatives such as Project Opportunity (College Entrance Examination Board, 1971), the federal TRIO programs, and private initiatives such as I Have a Dream (Fenske et al., 1997) that could be viewed as attempts to shift the indifference curves of black students towards education.

However, among the three options for changing equilibriums, economists usually focus their attention on educational policies that affect the constraints faced by decision makers rather than their preferences. Economists certainly acknowledge that changing preferences could change the equilibrium point, and that preferences of decision makers can and do shift over time. However, this approach is not often used by economists who are involved in educational policy analysis because the field of economics has relatively little to contribute to our understanding of how the preferences of decision makers are formed. This approach is best informed by the work of the behavioral sciences, such as sociology, psychology, and others that provide insights into how students' preferences are formed.[1] Therefore, economic models typically take preferences as given and develop optimization models that are independent of how they are formed.

Educational policies that alter either the location or slope of the budget line can lead to the same changes in behavior without affecting the preferences of the decision maker. An economist knows with certainty that an income supplement to students will lead to an outward shift in the student's budget line, all else equal. Likewise, a policy such as increased state appropriations to institutions of higher education that reduces the tuition paid by a group of students would cause the budget line for these students to pivot outward. In each case, the policy maker has a high level of control over the magnitude of the change in the constraint that results from the policy. For this reason, these types of policies are often referred to as "policy levers." The identification of such policy levers, and the prediction, analysis, and evaluation of the effects of the use of policy levers constitute the most common applications of economic models to policy analysis.

The economic model of optimal decision making also shows that policies could be implemented that actually force decision makers to choose non-equilibrium positions along their budget constraint. Such policies might include minimum teaching and service loads for faculty, and compulsory attendance for students. In Fig. 7.6, for example, a student who was free to choose how to allocate her resources between education and all other goods would want to choose a point such as A. However, if policy makers sought to increase the amount of education that she obtained, they could implement a policy requiring students to attend college, increasing her educational attainment to point B. The problem with this policy, from the perspective of the student, is that it has led to a reduction in her utility or satisfaction. The fact that she faces a budget constraint means that the policy has forced her to forego some consumption that would have given her more enjoyment than did the additional education.

In contrast, the policies that alter the decision maker's budget constraint in some way still allow the decision maker the freedom to act as they see fit and to maximize their utility. To shift the budget line, an educational policy maker might advocate plans to provide income supplements to students and their families, or create tax advantages for the families of students that effectively increase their disposable income. The income supplement or tax advantage would cause the entire budget line to shift to the right, enabling students to purchase more education and all other goods. Finally, a policy could be implemented that would instead reduce the price of education. This may be achieved through an explicit price discount made by the institution or a commitment from the institution, state, or other entity to cover a percentage of all education completed by the student. Other examples of price decreases for students would include reductions in the interest rate charged on student loans, and the enactment of reciprocity agreements between states to charge in-state tuition rates to each other's residents.

Another means of affecting the constraints for decision makers is through what are known as in-kind subsidies. Generally speaking, an in-kind subsidy is a benefit that can be used for only a specific purpose. To illustrate, suppose that a state provided low-income students with a $4,000 stipend that could only be used to pay for college. This is similar to a policy that would give low-income students an additional $4,000 in income, except that the income supplement can only be used to purchase education. This would lead to a discontinuous shift in the budget line as shown in Fig. 7.7. The dashed line (C,A,B) now represents the budget constraint faced by the student. The student can consume up to $4,000 in education without reducing the income available to consume all other goods and services, and therefore this segment of the budget constraint would be a horizontal line. After this point, however, additional dollars spent on education would reduce the amount of income left for purchasing other goods and services. Most forms of financial aid given to students would be characterized as in-kind subsidies because they cover a stipulated amount of the price of education as compared to a percentage discount per credit hour or year.

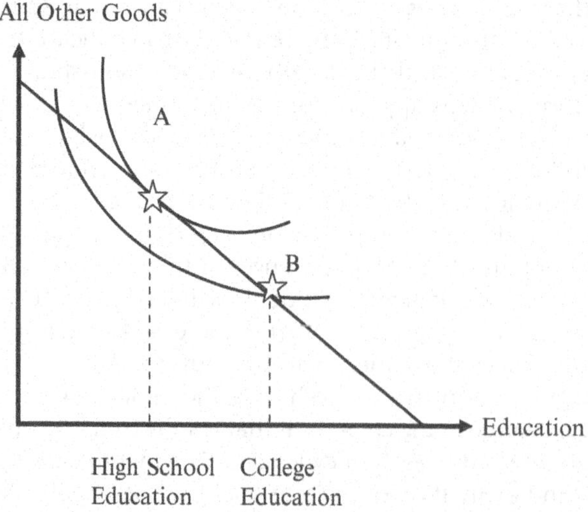

Figure 7.6 Effects of choosing a non-equilibrium point.

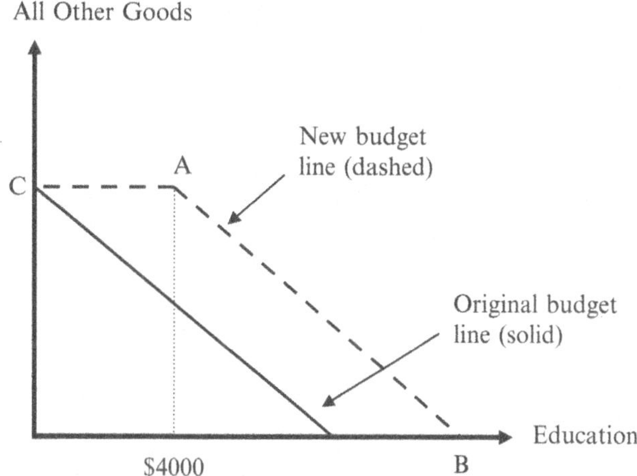

Figure 7.7 Effects of $4,000 in-kind subsidy for education.

In-kind subsidies such as this may be preferred by some policy makers because the subsidy can only be used for the purpose intended by the donor. In contrast to an in-kind subsidy, a $4,000 income subsidy could be used for many purposes aside from higher education, raising concerns that an income subsidy would be less likely to lead to a desired increase in college attendance. From the perspective of the decision maker, however, an in-kind subsidy is typically less favorable than an equivalent income subsidy. This arises because the possibility exists that a decision maker's new optimum point is along the horizontal segment (C,A), in which case the decision maker would have received more utility with an income subsidy of the same amount. Decision makers who would find new equilibrium points along the segment (A,B), however, are indifferent between receiving an in-kind versus an income subsidy because they would reach the same point regardless of the form of the policy. In this example, the student's family would have spent at least $4,000 on education, and thus can use the subsidy to free up the same amount for spending on other goods and services. Accordingly, the in-kind subsidy functions as an income subsidy for them.

This general approach to policy—targeting action plans towards the constraints faced by decision makers—can be used in a wide range of higher education applications. There are many different decision makers within higher education, each with their own set of objectives and constraints. Academic departments, for example, can be viewed as decision makers because they must choose how to allocate limited faculty to meet its research, teaching, and service commitments. If university policy makers are concerned that faculty in a department are not spending enough time teaching undergraduate students, they may consider a range of action plans that could increase this quantity. The university might achieve this goal through increasing the budget for an academic unit (a rightward shift in the budget line), thus enabling them to hire more faculty and use them to teach undergraduate students and carry out the other mission aspects of the department. An in-kind subsidy could also be provided to the department by providing them with funding to hire only faculty such as adjunct or clinical faculty who would specialize in teaching. Or the institution could focus on "price" by covering a percentage of the salary for only those faculty who specialize in teaching. All of these policies would be designed to affect the decision maker's constraints in the hopes of changing behavior in a manner intended by the policy maker. These would differ from policies where the institution attempts to shift the department's preferences towards instruction without altering the income or prices that they face.

Faculty members are another example of decision makers in higher education, in that they have some discretion over how they allocate their time between competing activities. In this instance, time and not income is the relevant constraint faced by the decision maker. In Fig. 7.8 we show an example of the constraint faced by a faculty member between allocating her time between teaching and research. For simplicity, we assume that the individual has a time constraint of 40 hours per week to allocate between these two activities. In equilibrium, she currently spends 15 hours/week in research and 25 hours/week in teaching given her preferences between teaching and research.

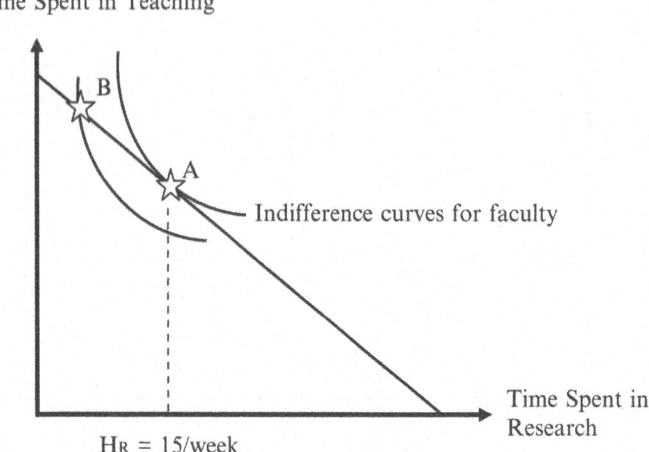

Figure 7.8 Depiction of time allocation problem for faculty.

The policy maker—in this case, the academic department, the institution, or the state—could design plans that would be intended to entice the faculty member to change her time allocation in ways that are more in line with the preferences of policy makers. Suppose that the department's administration simply asked the faculty member to increase the amount of time that she spent in teaching. To the individual faculty member, such an increase would be problematic for two reasons. First, it would lead her to choose a time allocation that was not optimal from her point of view. She would have a lower level of utility at point B, for example, than she would at point A, and thus the policy leads to a reduction in utility. Second, due to the time constraint of 40 hours/week, there would be an opportunity cost of increasing her time devoted to teaching because she would have to forego some of her time spent in research activities. Policies aimed at extolling the virtues of teaching would be viewed by economists as attempts to shift her preferences away from research and towards teaching. These policies may or may not be effective in doing so, and the institution would have difficulty determining if the action plan did indeed change preferences in the intended direction.

Alternatively, economists would normally focus on policies that would affect the constraints faced by the faculty member. The department could shift her time constraint outward to the right by reducing her service commitments because she would now have more discretionary time for both teaching and research. However, there is the risk that with the reduced service load, the faculty member would opt to only spend more time in research. If the time release from service was in exchange for the faculty member teaching an additional course, then this would be viewed as an in-kind subsidy because the additional time could not be used for research. Likewise, the department could provide additional teaching assistants to the faculty member, which would reduce the number of hours she needed to teach each course, and thus lower the "price" that she faced for teaching each course. All of these policies could lead to new equilibrium time allocations that may be in the direction intended by policy makers. However, the faculty reward system has a complex structure and institutions do not have full control over the reward system. For example, incentives or rewards related to opportunities for consulting and more attractive positions at other institutions provide extra-institutional sources of rewards for faculty that could mitigate or offset institutional efforts to adjust intra-institutional reward structures to promote desired changes in faculty behavior.

Using Economic Models for Access-Related Policy Analysis in Higher Education

Economic theories, models and their diagrammatic forms give perspective or provide frameworks for policy analysis in higher education. Some of the most prominent examples of such theories or models would include the theory of consumer behavior, human capital theory, the market model of demand and supply—including related concepts such as elasticity of demand—and microeconomic theories of the firm. This section will begin by identifying a specific policy problem or area and consider some types of "policy levers" that are relevant to the policy problem areas. For example, *access* to higher education is an important and critical policy problem area in higher education, and relevant policy levers would include federal grants and loans for students, state need-based or merit-based grants to students, and state and local appropriations to institutions.

Economic theories and models are the sources economists use to identify policy levers for addressing particular policy problems. For example, if access to higher education is the policy problem, then a key question for economists to ask would be "What policies would rearrange incentives to stimulate behavior by individuals and/or institutions that would promote access to higher education?" Policy levers can arise from federal, state, and institutional levels of policymaking. And the effective policy levers are those that use changes in "incentives" to stimulate changes in individual or institutional behavior that, in turn, promote improvements in a policy problem area like access. For economists, policy analysis is about analyzing how changing specific constraints faced by individuals and institutions alters their behavior and decision-making and moves them from one equilibrium position to another.

In this section we present and examine economic theories and models—in diagrammatic form—to illustrate the usefulness of economic theories and models as frameworks for identifying policy levers and predicting the effects of policy levers—at the federal, state, and institutional levels—on the behavior of individuals and institutions. More specifically, we articulate and illustrate—with diagrams and narrative explanation—how economic models provide a useful theoretical format for policy analysis by identifying policy levers with the potential to change behavior in ways that promote access to, and participation in, higher education. We conceptualize a student's decision about whether or not to attend college—which can be viewed as the first in a sequence of college-going decisions students make (St. John, 2003)—as an "access" decision and we view policies affecting this decision as access policies (Perna, 2006).

Human Capital Theory: A Framework for Analyzing Demand-Side and Supply-Side Policies to Promote Students' Access to and Investment in Higher Education

The most prominent of the theoretical frameworks used by economists and other social scientists to analyze students' college-going decision-making behavior relative to their access to, or participation in, higher education is *human capital theory*. The origins of modern human capital theory are often attributed to the pioneering work of Theodore Schultz (1961) and Gary Becker (1962). However, economists have further developed and refined this theory to the degree that it is now an established branch of labor economics (see, e.g., Ehrenberg & Smith, 2006), it serves as the starting point for many modern studies of investment in education and other forms of human capital (see, e.g., Avery & Hoxby, 2004), and it constitutes an important component of other theoretical structures in economics such as theories of economic growth and development (see, e.g., Cohn & Geske, 1990).[2]

Human capital theory views students' decisions to attend college as investments in higher education—an important form of human capital. Economists conceptualize human capital as a set of knowledge, skills, attitudes, abilities and talents that, when embodied in individuals, serve to enhance their productive capacities, and can therefore, be rented to employers in exchange for earnings over the life cycle. Investments in higher education—or other forms of human capital such as health care, on-the-job training, or job search—constitute additions to an individual's existing stock of human capital (Becker, 1993; Belfield, 2000; Ehrenberg & Smith, 2006; Johnes, 1993; Thurow, 1970; Woodhall, 1995). Economists view educational investment decision-makers, whether households or individuals, as seeking to maximize their utility subject to budget constraints. In utility functions, human capital investment is typically specified to affect utility directly or indirectly through its effects on other arguments in the utility function such as income or consumption (see, e.g., Becker, 1993; Belfield, 2000; Card, 1999; Checchi, 2006; McMahon, 1984; Thurow, 1970).

One straightforward specification is to assume that students allocate the resources available to them, as defined by their budget constraint, between investments in education and consumption expenditures on all other goods in order to maximize their utility across the life cycle (DesJardins

& Toutkoushian, 2005; Paulsen & Toutkoushian, 2006b). This format assumes students engage in "constrained optimization" behavior by seeking to maximize their utility—based on their individual preferences for various combinations of higher education and other goods acquired through investment and consumption decisions—subject to the limits of their time and budget constraints. Human capital theory assumes that students engage in *rational behavior*. In brief, individuals are behaving rationally if each individual makes choices about allocating the resources in their own unique budget constraint between higher education and other goods in ways that maximize their utility in accordance with their own unique and subjective preferences (DesJardins & Toutkoushian, 2005; Paulsen & Toutkoushian, 2006b).[3]

Human capital theory assumes that, in order to maximize their utility, when students make college-related investment decisions they compare the expected benefits with the expected costs of college (Carnoy, 1995; Checchi, 2006; Ehrenberg & Smith, 2006; Kaufman & Hotchkiss, 2000; McConnell et al., 2003; McMahon & Wagner, 1982; Paulsen, 2001a; Psacharopoulos, 1973). The earnings differential between college graduates and high school graduates—which continues to increase throughout most of the working life span (Murphy and Welch, 1989, 1992; McMahon & Wagner, 1982)—is quite substantial in magnitude (College Board, 2006a) and constitutes the primary monetary benefit that students expect to receive because of their investment in higher education. The primary monetary costs that students expect to pay for their investment in college include direct, out-of-pocket costs such as tuition and fees, books and supplies, commuting, and incremental living costs, as well as indirect opportunity costs due to the earnings foregone while attending college (Arai, 1998; Becker, 1993; Belfield, 2000; Checchi, 2006; Palacios, 2004).

Figure 7.9 portrays the most important monetary benefits and costs associated with the college-going investment decision for a recent high school graduate. Two possible earnings streams appear in the figure. The CC line portrays the expected earnings stream for a recent high school graduate who attends college without delay, incurs direct costs while attending college, does not work while attending college, and graduates in four years. This earnings stream is negative during the college years when the student is not working and the direct costs of college are incurred. After college graduation, the CC line continues at a positive level of earnings which rises at a substantial rate throughout the lifespan. The HH line portrays the expected earnings stream for a recent high

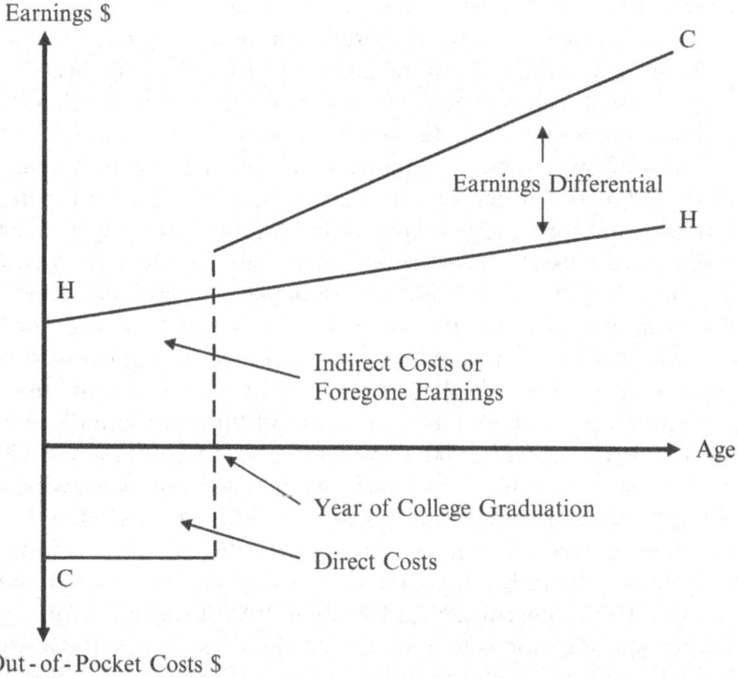

Figure 7.9 Benefits, costs and investment in higher education.

school graduate who enters the workforce by taking a full-time job instead of going to college. This earnings stream is assumed to start immediately at a positive level and not increase as fast as the CC line over the lifespan.

The most important monetary benefit of college attendance is represented by the *earnings differential*, where the CC line exceeds the HH line by increasing amounts across a typical 43-year post-college work life (i.e., 65–22 = 43 years). In order to acquire these monetary benefits, each student compares them to the expected costs of college attendance. The two most important monetary costs of college are represented as the *direct costs* which comprise the out-of-pocket expenses for tuition and fees, books, commuting, and living costs related to college attendance, and the *indirect costs* or *foregone earnings* which equals the income a college student could have earned by entering the workforce with their high school diploma instead of going to college.

As noted previously, human capital theory assumes that when students decide whether or not to attend college they compare the expected utility of going to college with the expected utility from not going to college. In general, attending college would be perceived as a worthwhile investment when the expected utility from going to college exceeds the expected utility of not going to college. Economists describe the expected utility of each choice as being affected by the costs and benefits of each choice. For higher education, the cost includes the direct and indirect costs of acquiring a higher education, and the benefit is the future income stream that students expect they will realize if they pursue a postsecondary education.[4] Accordingly, the investment in human capital model usually focuses on the costs and benefits of each choice and not the utility of each choice. Because the comparative statics of the investment in human capital model are the same regardless of whether one examines the costs and benefits of each choice or the utilities of the costs and benefits of each choice, the analysis of educational policies would not be affected by this simplification.

Even this stylized presentation of the human capital model provides a useful general framework for identifying policy levers and predicting the effects of policy levers—at the federal, state, or institutional, levels—on the students' decisions regarding whether or not to participate in college. In broad terms, the human capital model indicates that policies that either decrease the expected costs of college or increase the expected benefits of college would increase the likelihood that a student would choose to attend college. Research on the effects of each of the primary components of expected benefits and expected costs on student enrollment decisions has generated consistent findings in support of the key elements of the human capital model. For example, research has shown that the likelihood that a student will invest in college is positively related to the earnings differential between college and high school graduates (see, e.g., Averett & Burton, 1996; Freeman, 1976; Kane, 1999; Murphy & Welch, 1992; Paulsen & Pogue, 1988; Rouse, 1994; Rumberger, 1984). In addition, research has consistently shown that students' enrollment decisions are negatively related to the direct costs of college attendance, such as tuition and fees, books and living costs (Avery & Hoxby, 2004; Heller, 1997, 1999; Kane, 1995, 1999; Leslie & Brinkman, 1988; McPherson & Schapiro, 1991; Paulsen, 1998, 2000; Paulsen & Pogue, 1988; Paulsen & St. John, 2002; Rouse, 1994). Finally, research has consistently indicated that students' enrollment decisions are also negatively related to the indirect costs or foregone earnings (i.e., opportunity costs) of college (Heller, 1999; Kane, 1995, 1999; Long, 2004; Paulsen, 1990; Rouse, 1994).

A more precise algebraic presentation of the human capital model portrays students' college-going decision-making in terms of the present value method and the internal rate of return method. The expected benefits of higher education accrue and the expected costs are incurred over time, so that attention to the time value of money is important for a more precise derivation and statement of the criterion for identifying a profitable or worthwhile human capital investment decision. Using the present-value approach, a student would view an investment in higher education as profitable when the present discounted value (PDV) of the benefits of college—expressed in Equation (1) as the earnings differential between college and high school graduates ($E_t^C - E_t^H$)—exceeds the present discounted value (PDV) of the direct costs (C_t), plus the indirect costs or foregone earnings (E_t^H) during college.

$$\sum_{t=5}^{T} \frac{E_t^C - E_t^H}{(1+i)^t} > \sum_{t=1}^{4} \frac{C_t}{(1+i)^t} + \sum_{t=1}^{4} \frac{E_t^H}{(1+i)^t} \tag{1}$$

The symbol (i) in Equation (1) represents the market rate of interest used to discount the value of future streams of costs and benefits, while the symbol (r) in Equation (2) represents the *internal rate of return* on the investment, which equals the interest rate that equates the PDV of the benefits of college and the PDV of the costs of college.

$$\sum_{t=5}^{T} \frac{E_t^C - E_t^H}{(1+r)^t} = \sum_{t=1}^{4} \frac{C_t}{(1+r)^t} + \sum_{t=1}^{4} \frac{E_t^H}{(1+r)^t} \tag{2}$$

Using both the internal rate of return (r) and the market rate of interest (i), the following criterion indicates whether or not an investment in college would be profitable: the investment would be profitable when the internal rate of return (r) exceeds the market rate of interest (i) (Arai, 1998; Carnoy, 1995; Checchi, 2006; Cohn & Geske, 1990; Ehrenberg & Smith, 2006; Johnes, 1993; Kaufman & Hotchkiss, 2000; McConnell et al., 2003; McMahon & Wagner, 1982; Paulsen, 2001a).

This algebraic portrayal of the higher education investment decision in the human capital model provides a more refined framework for identifying policy levers—at the federal, state, institutional, or private levels—that can be used to influence students' decisions regarding whether or not to participate in college. For example, policies that provide subsidies to students—such as financial aid in the form of grants, scholarships, or loans from governmental, institutional or private sources—could serve to expand the budget constraints faced by students by providing them with increased funding to pay for the out-of-pocket or direct costs of college (C_t). Those students who experience such positive changes in their budget constraints would, all else equal, be more likely to choose to attend college and invest more in higher education (see, e.g., Catsiapis, 1987).

Even though the diagrammatic and algebraic portrayals of the human capital models presented above provide useful insights for identifying and predicting the effects of various policy levers on students' decisions about whether or not, and how much, to participate in higher education, there is a more comprehensive, complex and policy-specific diagrammatic presentation of the human capital model that is the most productive and revealing framework for identifying policy levers and predicting the effects of policy levers—at the federal, state, institutional, or private levels—on the students' decisions regarding whether or not to participate in college. This is the model of supply and demand in the market for funds to invest in higher education. It reveals and clarifies, for representative individuals or groups, both broad categories and specific types of policy levers that are available to influence both supply-side and demand-side factors affecting the college-going decision-making of students and their families.

This model of supply and demand in the market for funds to invest in higher education was developed by Nobel laureate Gary Becker (1967, 1975, 1993); Jacob Mincer applied the model in his study of the distribution of labor incomes (1993); and Walter McMahon estimated the coefficients of the equations for the *demand* for investment in higher education and for the *supply* of funds to invest in higher education, in a series of studies, estimating the equations separately for samples of whites, blacks, males, females, and students from all race and gender groupings in the lowest income quartile (1976, 1984, 1991). This comprehensive, theoretically-sound, empirically-supported model is useful for policy analysis in higher education for the following reasons: it serves as a very productive framework for explaining why some students, or groups of students, are more advantaged and others are more disadvantaged in the market for funds to invest in higher education; it provides, for representative individuals or groups, a useful framework for identifying specific types of policy levers—on both the supply-side and the demand-side of the market—that coincide with constraints faced by students and their families when making college-going decisions; and it provides an analytical structure for predicting the effects of policies that change constraints in ways that enable and prompt students to invest in higher education and participate in college.

The notions of *marginalism* and the method of *marginal analysis* are central concepts from microeconomics and constitute important foundational elements for constructing the logic of problems relating to educational policy (Frank, 2003; Paulsen & Toutkoushian, 2006b; Pindyck & Rubinfeld, 2005). For example, human capital theory assumes that when students consider whether or not to invest in an additional unit of education—such as one year, or two years, or four years of college—they compare expected benefits to expected costs in order to make informed and utility-maximizing decisions. Economists view such decision-making challenges as exercises in constrained optimization—i.e., students choosing in ways that will maximize their satisfaction or utility subject to relevant budget and time constraints. Economists view a student's decision regarding whether or not to invest in a college education as decision-making "at the margin." In other words, because marginal is a synonym for "incremental" or "additional," when a student is considering whether or not to invest in an additional unit of education, he or she will compare the "marginal" benefits with the "marginal" costs of such a decision. As long as the marginal benefit of an option exceeds the marginal cost, the decision maker would find it to his or her advantage to pursue the option, and vice versa.

Based on the framework of the human capital model portrayed in Fig. 7.9, and the precise expression of the investment decision criterion as expressed in Equations (1) and (2), we know that it would be profitable for a student to invest in higher education as long as the internal rate of return (r) exceeds the market rate of interest (i). This investment criterion is completely consistent with marginal analysis, because the internal rate of return (r) reflects the marginal benefit (MB) of an additional unit of investment in higher education in percentage terms (i.e., MB = r), and the market rate of interest (i) represents the marginal cost (MC) of an additional unit of investment in higher education in percentage terms (i.e., MC = i) (see, e.g., Becker, 1993; McMahon, 1984; Mincer, 1993; Paulsen, 2001a). In the model of supply and demand in the market for funds to invest in higher education constructed below, MB will be defined as the "marginal rate of return" on each additional dollar invested in higher education and the MC will be defined as the "marginal interest cost" for each additional dollar invested in higher education.[5]

The presentation of this model of human capital theory is informed by the original work of Becker (1975, 1993), the applications by Mincer (1993), and the empirical studies of McMahon (1976, 1984, 1991); as well as by the nature of its presentation and explanation in a number of textbooks and related scholarly work in labor economics and the economics of education (see, e.g., Arai, 1998; Card, 1999; Kaufman & Hotchkiss, 2000; McConnell et al., 2003; Paulsen & Smart, 2001). In order to construct the overall framework of the model, the supply side will be presented first, followed by the demand side, and a combination of demand and supply that helps portray the meaning of reaching equilibrium for individuals and groups in the market for funds to invest in higher education. Then, the overall framework is used to identify policy levers that can be used to change constraints faced by students in ways that promote changes in the behavior of individual students or groups of students and increase their likelihood of participation in higher education.

Figure 7.10 presents the supply of funds in the model of the market for funds to invest in higher education. The supply curve illustrates the dollar amounts ($) of different types of funds available at different levels of marginal interest cost (i) for a representative individual student or group of students. In order to fully illustrate the different quantities and different types of funds available at different levels of marginal interest cost, we use a stair-step format to portray the supply of funds. In subsequent analyses, however, we also present supply of funds curves in their more common and simpler upward-sloping format. For the given supply curve in Fig. 7.10 (S), $0\$_1$ dollars of "grant" funds are available at zero marginal interest cost (i.e., i = 0). From the perspective of students, grants are the least costly and most desirable source of funds and this "grants" category includes sources of funding referred to as grants, scholarships, and private gifts from federal, state, institutional or private sources—including students' parents. Only a small portion of all students are in a position to finance all the costs of their higher education from zero-marginal-interest-cost grant or gift sources and most of those individuals are students from relatively high-income households. The relative availability of zero-marginal-interest-cost grants is an important source of a substantial amount of segmentation in the market regarding the supply of funds for students. The primary reason for this market segmentation is due to the substantial variation in the family incomes and wealth of college-bound students and the concomitant variation in students' receipts of gifts from parents to finance none, some, or all of their higher education. In many instances, policies that result in grants for students from federal, state and institutional sources instead of parental or other family sources—e.g., Pell grants—are intended to address the inequities that arise from this market segmentation due to the unequal distribution of family income and wealth in the nation.

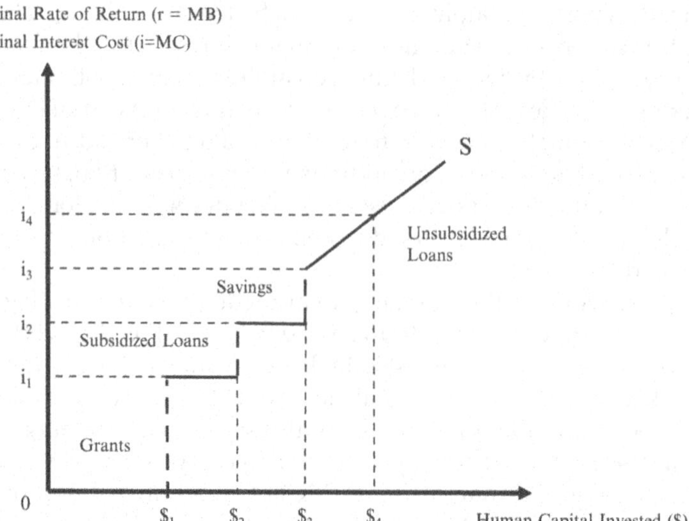

Figure 7.10 The supply of funds for investment in higher education.

Once funds at a marginal interest cost of zero are exhausted, students must turn to types of funds available at various non-zero marginal interest costs to finance their education. The category of funds with the second-lowest marginal interest cost is subsidized student loans (e.g., subsidized Stafford loans). In Fig. 7.10, $\$_1\$_2$ dollars of subsidized loans are available at a non-zero marginal interest costs of i_1. Subsidized Stafford loans, along with Pell grants, of course, were designed to increase the availability of zero-or-low-interest-cost funds for low-income students, thereby expanding their budget constraints to enable and promote their participation in higher education (Mumper, 1996; St. John, 1994, 2003). Next, $\$_2\$_3$ dollars of funds are available to students who are able to draw upon their own savings, such as earnings from summer jobs and the like. When students use their own savings to finance college investment, they give up the chance to earn interest income on the balance of those funds in an interest-earning asset, such as a savings account. The marginal interest cost of these funds is the rate at which students forego interest income on their savings, indicated in Fig. 7.10 as i_2. Finally, once funds from grants, subsidized loans, and savings are exhausted, students turn to unsubsidized loans, available at increasingly higher marginal interest costs equal to or greater than i_3 or i_4.[6] The shift in federal policy away from grants—with a marginal interest cost of zero—and towards loans with marginal interest costs ranging from a minimum of i_1 to a maximum reaching higher than i_4 has necessarily resulted in an increase in the average marginal interest cost of funds for many students—especially those eligible for federal need-based grants (College Board, 2006b; St. John, 2003).

The demand for investment in higher education is presented in Fig. 7.11. The demand curve (D) illustrates the relationship between the amounts of dollars invested in higher education ($) and the marginal rate of return (r) on each additional dollar invested in higher education. As explained above, the marginal rate of return equals the internal rate of return (r) from Equation (2). The demand for investment in higher education is downward-sloping for several reasons. For each additional investment a student makes in higher education, the number of years over which the student can benefit from the college-high school earnings differential decreases, the direct (tuition) and indirect (foregone earnings) costs increase, and a student's future earnings and productivity increase at a diminishing rate because additional human capital is being added to limited mental, physical, and temporal capacities of an individual—i.e., the law of diminishing returns in the production of human capital is in effect. This pattern is clearly illustrated in Fig. 7.11. Reading from the demand curve (D), when the amount invested is only $\$_1$, the marginal rate of return on the last dollar invested equals r_3, but when the amount invested reaches $\$_2$ and $\$_3$, then the marginal rates of return decrease to r_2 and r_1, respectively.

Figure 7.12 illustrates the equilibrium and optimal level of investment in higher education for a representative individual or group of individuals facing the demand and supply conditions

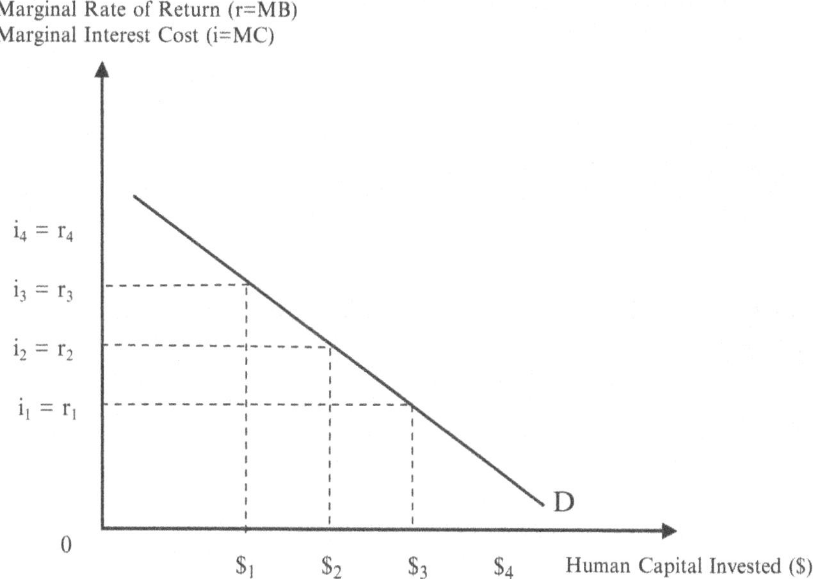

Figure 7.11 The demand for investment in higher education.

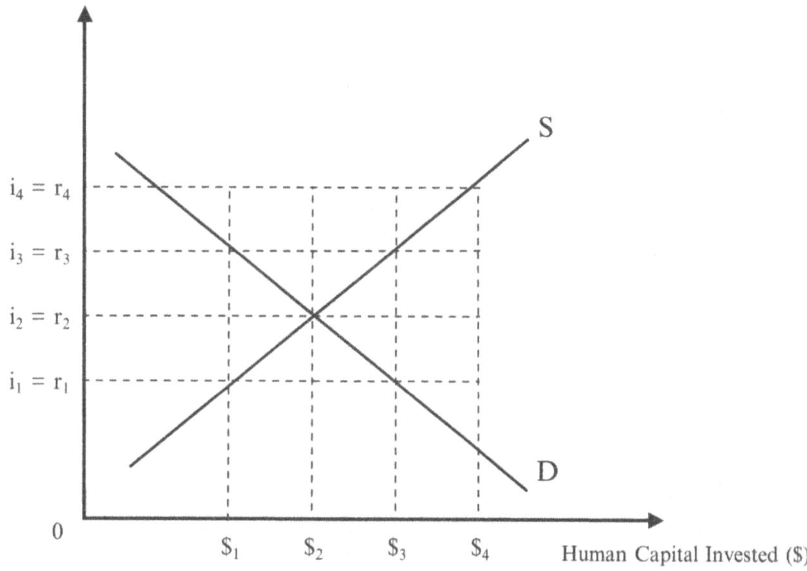

Figure 7.12 Supply, demand, and the equilibrium level of investment in higher education.

presented in the figure. In order to maximize utility subject to her budget constraint, a student should continue to invest in higher education as long as the marginal rate of return (MB = r) exceeds the marginal interest cost (MC = i) of an additional unit of investment. In Fig. 7.12, for each amount of dollars invested ($)—i.e., the horizontal coordinate of each point on the demand curve—the marginal rate of return from the last dollar invested (r) is read as the vertical coordinate off the demand curve corresponding to a particular level of investment ($), while the marginal interest cost of the last dollar invested (i) is read as the vertical coordinate off the supply curve corresponding to a particular level of funds for investment ($)—i.e., the horizontal coordinate of each point on the supply curve. As shown in Fig. 7.12, when the amount invested in higher education equals $\$_1$, the demand curve indicates that the marginal rate of return is r_3, and the supply curve indicates that the marginal interest cost is only i_1. Because r_3 exceeds i_1, increased investment in higher education would clearly be profitable for the student. The marginal rate of return continues to exceed the marginal interest cost of funds until the level of investment reaches $\$_2$, where the marginal rate of return equals the marginal interest cost of funds for the last dollar invested, which means $\$_2$ would be the equilibrium level of investment and the amount of investment that would maximize the student's utility subject to a budget constraint (Arai, 1998; Kaufman & Hotchkiss, 2000; McConnell et al., 2003; McMahon, 1984; Paulsen, 2001a).

Supply, Demand, and Policy Levers in the Market for Funds to Invest in Higher Education

In this section we present specifications for the supply and demand functions that include arguments defining the relevant supply-side or demand-side conditions or constraints faced by representative individuals or groups in the market for investment in higher education. In order to develop the most useful and straightforward specifications for supply and demand functions, the particular supply and demand specifications presented and used in this analytical model are informed by, but not identical to, the original specifications of Becker (1967, 1975, 1993), the specification and empirical estimation of the supply and demand functions by McMahon (1976, 1984, 1991), as well as by additional research on factors influencing the rates of return (see, e.g., Card, 1999) and factors influencing students' likelihood of participation in and/or level of investment in higher education (see, e.g., Ellwood & Kane, 2000).

Using this approach, the supply function in Equation (3) is consistent with Becker's original conceptualization of inter-individual or inter-group differences in supply conditions as representing *constraints* on the "opportunities" students have to access funds for investment in higher education—manifested as differences between supply curves in the marginal interest cost (i) at which various amounts of funds ($) are available (1975, 1993).

Supply Function:

$$S_{\$} = f(i, Y, G, L) \tag{3}$$

Where

i = the marginal interest cost of each additional dollar invested

Y = disposable income of the student's family

G = grants, which includes sources of funding referred to as grants, scholarships, or gifts from federal, state, institutional or private sources

L = loans available to lower and middle income students through a means test

All arguments besides "i" in the supply function represent shift parameters that change the position of the overall supply curve. Therefore, the shift parameters constitute a set of potentially fruitful policy levers that could effectively change supply conditions and constraints in ways that expand students' opportunities to invest in college (i.e., supply-side constraints) and thereby promote access to higher education.

Figure 7.13 presents two different supply curves in the market for funds to invest in higher education. Each supply curve represents a set of supply conditions or *constraints* faced by a representative individual or group of individuals in the market. These conditions or constraints can make some students more *advantaged* and others more *disadvantaged* in the market for funds to invest in higher education. It is evident from Fig. 7.13 that the marginal interest costs (i) at which various dollar amounts of funds are available clearly present a more advantaged set of supply conditions or constraints for those individuals or groups who face supply curve S_2 compared to those who face supply curve S_1 in the market for funds to invest in higher education. For example, supply curve S_1 starts with a horizontal portion from 0 to $\$_1$ and continues with a upward-sloping portion from its horizontal intercept at $1 to S_1, and supply curve S_2 starts with a horizontal portion from 0 to $(\$_3 + \$_4)/2$ and continues with a upward-sloping portion from its horizontal intercept at $(\$_3 + \$_4)/2$

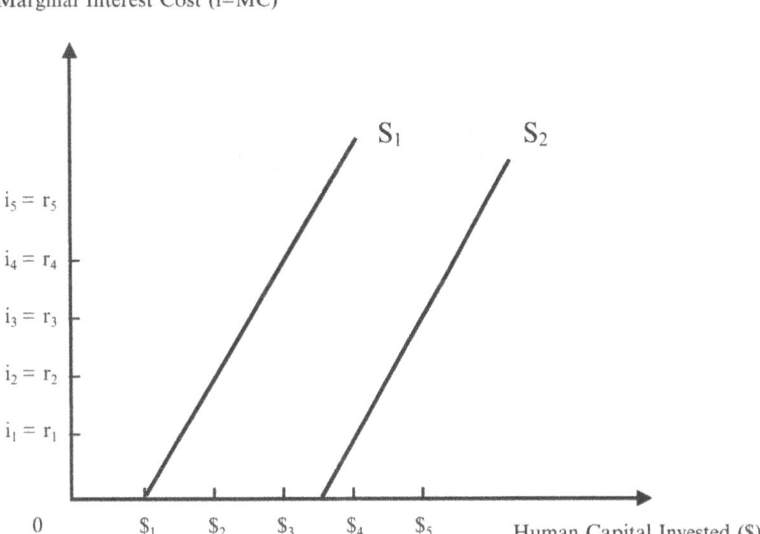

Figure 7.13 Supply conditions and advantage and disadvantage in the market for investment in higher education.

to S_2. The horizontal portion of each of the two supply curves, S_1 and S_2, indicates the amount of funds available to a student from zero-interest-cost sources, such as grants, scholarships, and gifts from federal, state, institutional and private sources, including parents.

One of the most prominent determinants of the position of the supply curve of funds to invest in higher education is family income (Y in Equation (3)) and/or wealth (Becker, 1967, 1975, 1993; McMahon, 1976, 1984, 1991). Many students from moderately to very wealthy families have access to zero-interest-cost funding for college from their parents in amounts that are often sufficient to cover a portion, if not all, of the costs of college attendance. More specifically, Ellwood and Kane (2000) estimate that parents of students from the top income quartile pay $4,083 more of their children's college costs at public institutions and $8,420 more at private institutions than those in the lowest income quartile. In terms of the supply curves in Fig. 7.13, inter-family differences in income and wealth could be responsible for a substantial share of the difference in the horizontal intercepts of S_1 and S_2 and the amounts of zero-interest-cost funds available—i.e., 0 to $\$_1$ versus 0 to $(\$_3 + \$_4)/2$ under the two sets of supply conditions. There is broad support in the literature for the hypothesis that family income has a positive effect on enrollment (Ellwood & Kane, 2000; Hossler et al., 1999; Kane, 1999; Perna, 2000), and that gaps in participation rates between income groups are both substantial and persistent (see, e.g., Mumper & Freeman, 2005; Thomas & Perna, 2004).

We are currently in a period of increasing rather than decreasing gaps in income between higher and lower income classes; therefore equalizing access to higher education—where more investment in higher education leads to greater future income—could be a potentially productive long-term method to achieve a more equal distribution of income. Many economists and other policy analysts have contended that the existence of substantial positive externalities arising from investment in higher education constitutes a compelling rationale to prompt government to intervene in the market for investment in higher education with grants for students that are intended to expand students' budget constraints and promote greater participation and investment in higher education (Baum, 2004; Breneman & Nelson, 1981; Paulsen, 2001b; Paulsen & Toutkoushian, 2006a). The greatest challenge in this regard is based on the ongoing, but only moderately successful, efforts of economists and other policy analysts to identify the nature, and measure the magnitudes, of all the sources of positive externalities due to investment in higher education (Baum & Payea, 2004; Bowen, 1977; Fatima & Paulsen, 2004; Institute for Higher Education Policy, 2005; Paulsen & Fatima, 2007). The primary sources of zero-marginal-interest-cost grants to students have included federal need-based and state need-based grant programs, as well as a rapidly increasing pool of state merit-based grants for all merit-eligible students regardless of need (College Board, 2006b; Heller, 2006; Mumper & Freeman, 2005).

The demand function in Equation (4) is also consistent with Becker's original conceptualization of differences in demand functions as representing constraints on the "capacities" students have to benefit from investments in human capital—manifested as differences between demand curves in the marginal rates of return (r) for various amounts invested ($) (1967, 1975, 1993). All arguments besides "r" in the demand function represent shift parameters that change the position of the overall demand function. Therefore, the shift parameters constitute a set of potentially fruitful policy levers that could effectively change demand conditions and constraints in ways that expand students' capacities to benefit from those investments (i.e., demand-side constraints), thereby promoting access to higher education.
Demand Function:

$$D_{\$} = f(r, A, FB, SQ) \qquad (4)^7$$

where

r = the marginal rate of return for each additional dollar invested

A = ability as measured by test scores or school grades

FB = family background, such as parents' education, income, occupation

SQ = school quality measured by indicators of school resources such as pupil-teacher ratios, teacher salaries, or length of school year (see, e.g., Card & Krueger, 1992)

Figure 7.14 presents two different demand curves in the market for funds to invest in higher education. Each demand curve represents a set of demand conditions or constraints faced by a representative individual or group of individuals in the market. These conditions or constraints can make some students more advantaged and others more disadvantaged in the market for funds to invest in higher education. The marginal rates of return (r) corresponding to various dollar amounts invested in higher education clearly present a more advantaged set of demand conditions or constraints for those individuals or groups who face demand curve D_2 compared to those who face demand curve D_1 in the market for investment in higher education. For example, in Fig. 7.14, for a representative individual or group whose demand conditions or constrains are portrayed along

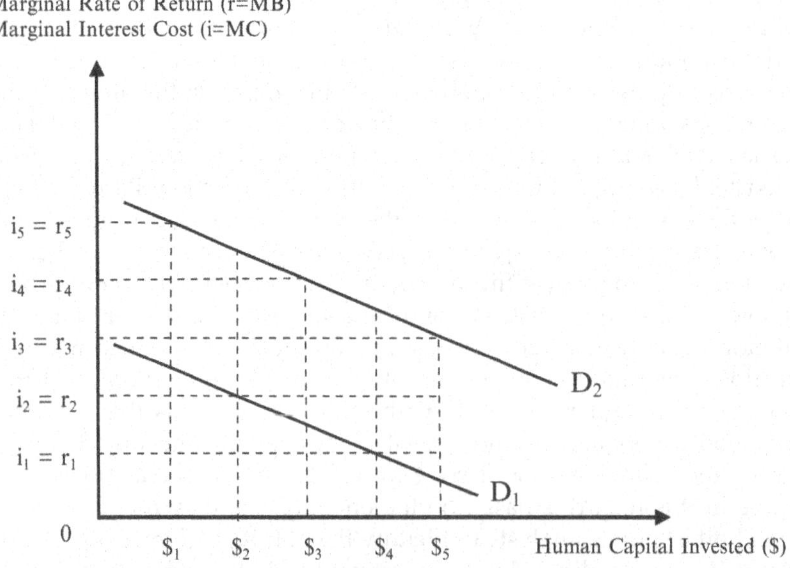

Figure 7.14 Demand, advantage and disadvantage in the market for investment in higher education.

demand curve D_1, when the amount invested is $\$_2$, the marginal rate of return on the last dollar invested equals only r_2. However, for a representative individual or group whose demand conditions or constrains are portrayed along demand curve D_2, when the same amount is invested ($\$_2$), the marginal rate of return on the last dollar invested is much higher at $(r_4 + r_5)/2$. Similar vertical differences in the marginal rates of return between the two demand curves can be observed for each amount of dollars invested.

One of the most prominent determinants of the rates of return to education, and therefore, the position of the demand curve for investment in higher education is student ability (A in Equation 4) (Arai, 1998; Becker, 1993; Card, 1999; Cipillone, 1995; Leslie & Brinkman, 1988; McMahon, 1976, 1984, 1991; Monks, 2000; Taubman & Wales, 1974; Woodhall, 1995). Students of higher ability tend to have higher rates of return than those of lower ability. Therefore, all else equal, D_2 would illustrate the demand for investment in higher education for students with higher ability and D_1 would represent the demand for investment in higher education for students with lower ability. The positive correlation between ability and earnings has been explained in a number of understandable ways. For example, some economists explain the differences in rates of returns between different demand curves in terms of interpersonal differences in ability, broadly conceived. Becker (1993) explains that higher demand curves represent higher rates of returns because "persons who produce more human capital from a given expenditure [on human capital] have more capacity or 'ability' " (p. 124), and Mincer (1993) concurs that "differences in levels of demand curves represent individual differences in productivities, or abilities" (p. 56). Other economists have argued that an individual's ability is related to a form of initial "pre-school" or "pre-existing" endowment of human capital that can be subsequently used to more productively acquire additional human capital (Cipillone, 1995; Thurow, 1970). Initial endowments of human capital can directly affect the level of education a student attains, the learning that occurs during schooling, and the earnings and rates of return that occur subsequent to that schooling.

Economists and other social scientists have also found measures of family background—particularly parental education, as well as parental income or occupation—to be related, either directly or indirectly through mediating variables, to rates of return to education and therefore, to the position of the demand curve for investment in higher education (FB in Equation 4) (Behrman et al., 1992; Card, 1999; Jencks, 1972, 1979; Korenman & Winship, 2000; McMahon, 1976, 1984, 1991; Sewell & Hauser, 1976; Taubman & Wales, 1974). Therefore, all else equal, D_2 would illustrate the demand for investment in higher education for students with more advantaged family backgrounds and D_1 would represent the demand for investment in higher education for students with less advantaged family backgrounds.

There are a number of reasons that those from more advantaged family backgrounds tend to have higher rates of return to educational investments. As one example, McMahon (1984) offers this explanation for including mother's education as his measure of family background in his investment demand function: "The hypothesis is that home investments in children, when the mother has more education, raises the IQ or ability of the child...and also, especially if the mother has been to college, shifts the utility function toward greater farsightedness. Both imply larger investment in education." (p. 82). This "farsightedness" of college-educated parents is quite important and refers to the greater likelihood that college-educated parents are well aware of the benefits of college, well-informed about the nature and extent of such benefits and all of the arrangements, resources and efforts that are necessary to acquire them, and therefore place a high value on the benefits of college—most of which would accrue in the future. As a result, college-educated parents would be more willing to forgo present consumption for future benefits from investment in college and accordingly would use a smaller rate to discount future earnings and would expect higher rates of return to investments. When children have the opportunities to inherit or adopt this information and these values, insights, beliefs, and perspectives from their parents, they acquire an early form of human capital—produced in the home or family environment—that can enhance their propensity for educational investment, as well as the productivity and fruitfulness of their investment, both in terms of the quantity and quality of the education they acquire and their subsequent earnings in the job market throughout their careers.

Another important determinant of rates of return, and therefore, the position of the demand curve for investment in higher education is school quality (SQ in Equation 4) (Altonji & Dunn, 1996; Card, 1999; Card & Krueger, 1992, 1996). Students who acquire pre-college education at schools with higher levels of resources—as measured by pupil-teacher ratios, teacher salaries or another indicator of school expenditures per pupil—tend to have higher rates of return than those who attend pre-college schools with fewer resources. Therefore, all else equal, D2 would illustrate the demand for investment in higher education for students who acquire precollege education at schools with greater resources and D1 would represent the demand for investment in higher education for students who acquire pre-college education at schools with fewer resources. According to Card and Krueger (1996), the "most plausible theoretical explanation for a link between school quality and earnings is that—other things being equal—students acquire more skills if they attend higher quality schools (i.e., schools with more generous resources)" (p. 165).

In this section, we examine the ways in which demand and supply curves—for individuals or groups who are advantaged or disadvantaged in the market—interact to generate a variety of possible equilibrium levels of investment under various supply and demand conditions and constraints. Figure 7.15 combines sets of different supply curves and different demand curves for individuals and/or groups of individuals in the market for funds to invest in higher education. Each supply curve and each demand curve represents a set of supply or demand conditions or constraints faced by a representative individual or group of individuals in the market. These conditions or constraints can make some students more advantaged and others more disadvantaged in the market for funds to invest in higher education. In this context, we can analyze the effects of changes in the shift parameters in the supply and demand functions as policy levers to expand students' constraints and change individual behavior in favor of more investment in higher education, thereby promoting access.

In Fig. 7.15, we first consider representative individuals or groups of individuals who are relatively less advantaged on both the supply and demand sides of the market. In other words, students who are not from advantaged family backgrounds, do not have high ability endowments, and did not attend high-quality pre-college schools are best portrayed by demand curve D_1. If these students are also not from higher-income families and qualify for only need-based grants with limited purchasing power in terms of covering the direct costs of college, their conditions and constraints are best represented by supply curve S_1. In order to maximize their utility students should invest in units of higher education ($) as long as the marginal rate of return exceeds the marginal interest cost of funds required for such investment. For those facing supply and demand conditions S_1 and D_1,

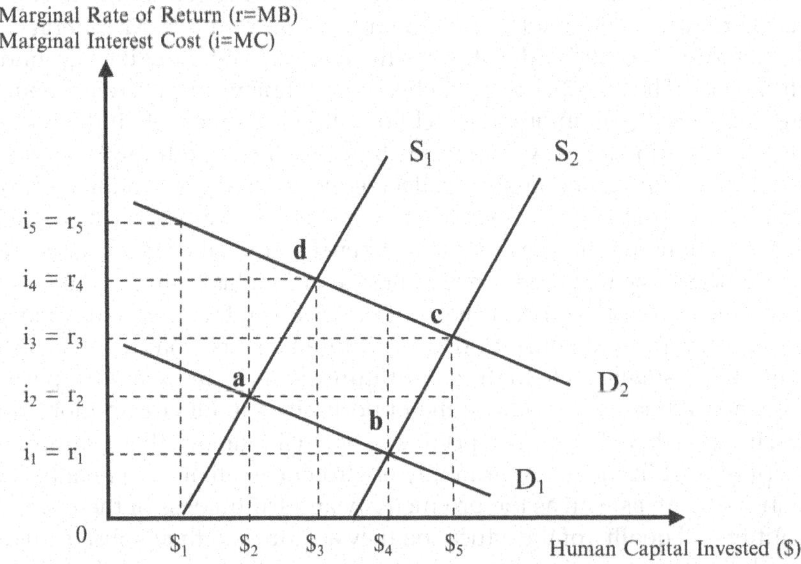

Figure 7.15 Supply, demand, advantage and disadvantage in the market for investment in higher education.

investment would be worthwhile for dollar amounts from 0 up to $\$_2$—i.e., r > i until dollars invested reaches $\$_2$ at point "a". All else equal, point "a" is the optimal and equilibrium level of investment in higher education for students with supply and demand constraints S_1 and D_1.

As noted in a previous section, the primary determinant of differences in supply conditions like those represented by S_1 and S_2 is differences in family incomes. And family incomes, of course, are private sources of zero-marginal-interest-cost funds, usually gifts to children, to pay for college. For lower-income students, supply-side policies can help address their relative disadvantage in the supply of funds for investment by providing public sources of zero-marginal-interest-cost funds in the form of federal and state need-based grants. Substantial increases in need-based grants would expand lower-income students' budget constraints, shifting them from a supply constraint indicated by S_1 to one better represented by S_2. Such policies could help address, at least in part, the different availabilities of zero-marginal-interest-cost funds between higher- and lower-income students. If these policy changes move lower-income students from S_1 to S_2 (along D_1), a new equilibrium and optimal level of investment would occur at point "b" where S_2 intersects D_1 and where $\$_4$ dollars are invested in higher education. As illustrated in Fig. 7.15, for all investment amounts from 0 to $\$_4$ the marginal rate of return exceeds the marginal interest cost of funds, making $\$_4$ the new equilibrium level of investment.

Research indicates that, as predicted by the model, increases in grants are positively related to greater enrollment and investment in higher education (see, e.g., Catsiapis, 1987), and research has demonstrated the positive enrollment effects of need-based grants from federal sources (Leslie & Brinkman, 1988; Manski & Wise, 1983; McPherson & Schapiro, 1991; Dynarski, 2003) and need-based grants from state sources (Ellwood & Kane, 2000; Heller, 1999; Kane, 1999). State merit-based grants have also become popular in recent years and their availability could also help students move from a supply constraint like S_1 to one like S_2. However, increases in these funds would provide additional zero-marginal-interest-cost funds—usually as an entitlement—for students who are merit-eligible regardless of financial need. Nevertheless, research does indicate that merit grant programs also promote greater participation and investment in higher education (see, e.g., Dynarski, 2004).

We next consider representative individuals from lower-income students—who continue to be the focus of our access-based concern—in an initial equilibrium in their investment decision-making at point "b" in Fig. 7.15, where the optimal, and utility-maximizing, level of investment in higher education is $4 dollars. In this instance, at point "b" students are relatively less advantaged on the demand side of the market as illustrated by their demand constraints on demand curve D_1, but are relatively more advantaged on the supply side of the market as illustrated by their supply constraints on supply curve S_2. In other words, demand curve D_1 portrays students who do not have high ability endowments, are not from advantaged family backgrounds, and did not attend high-quality pre-college schools. We assume that the supply-side policies discussed in the previous section were implemented and that the effects of such policies were, as illustrated in Fig. 7.15, to move the lower-income students—previously in equilibrium at point "a" and facing supply conditions S_1—to point "b" where their new supply constraints are reflected by supply curve S_2. Their somewhat more advantaged supply constraints on S_2 reflect the fact that the supply-side policies (increased grants) discussed in a previous section were effectively implemented and these students have already been the recipients of a substantially increased volume of need-based federal or state grants, and possibly also of some state merit-based grants as well.

As noted in a previous section, the primary determinants of differences in demand conditions—and perceived rates of return to educational investment—like those represented by D_1 and D_2 are differences in students' ability, family background, and pre-college school quality. Each of these determinants of rates of returns—and therefore, of the position of the two demand curves—reveal policy levers that could use demand-side policies to promote changes in the behavior and decision-making of lower-income students that lead to increases in their participation and investment in higher education, thereby addressing the access problem. Although increasing the innate or genetic ability endowments of potential students is not within the grasp of policymakers, policies to promote academic achievement and gains in academic achievement in pre-college schooling do provide accessible policy levers based on demand-side policies in the market for investment in higher education. For example, research on the "achievement model" (see, e.g., Jencks & Phillips, 1999) now provides convincing evidence that academic achievement and gains in academic achievement, as measured by test scores on cognitive tests of knowledge and skills—such as ACT or SAT math, verbal or content area scores—are significantly and positively related to students' subsequent earnings. In other words, this evidence indicates that differences in measured academic achievement or gains in academic achievement in school positively affect the earnings, and therefore, the rates of return on educational investments for students. Academic achievement is, of course, an important predictor of college participation, particularly among lower-income students; and there are many types of pre-college preparation programs that can help improve students' academic achievement (see, e.g., Perna, 2005).

Clearly, changing today's students' family backgrounds so they are more "advantaged," such as by increasing the share of today's students whose parents are college-educated, is not within the grasp of policymakers. However, there are policy levers, based on demand-side policies in the market for investment in higher education, that are available to provide alternative opportunities for today's youth to acquire some of the knowledge, information, values, insights, beliefs, and perspectives about the costs and benefits of college, the preparatory steps and efforts required to get to college and be successful there, that a family background with college-educated parents could provide. Providing adequate funding for the TRIO programs (Fenske et al., 1997) and funding to support state-level efforts like Indiana's highly successful postsecondary encouragement experiment (Hossler & Schmit, 1995) and the COACH mentoring program in Boston's public schools (Avery & Kane, 2004) serve as excellent examples of such policies.[8] Unlike many of the other policies considered in our analysis, these demand-side policies do not affect, and are not intended to affect, students' financial constraints; instead, they are targeted to influence how students form their college-going preferences, and therefore, their expected rates of return to investments in college.

The third set of policy levers we consider is also based on demand-side policies in the market for investment in higher education. These policies require increased funding to provide more resources in elementary and secondary schools. Most research on the effects of school resources on students' future earnings has identified specific targets for policy, such as raising teacher salaries and lowering pupil-teacher ratios, both of which would enhance school resources and increase the rates of return to schooling for students in the system (Card, 1999, 2001). For example, Card and Krueger (1996) conducted a meta-analysis of a group of studies of the effect of school resources and students' future earnings. They examined 25 estimates of the effect of school resources on earnings and converted them to comparable elasticites. Their findings showed that all estimated elasticities were positive and nearly all were statistically significant.

Each of the three sets of demand-side policies discussed above can help address the relative disadvantage of the lower-income students on whom our analyses is focused, in terms of the demand for investment in higher education, by increasing the rates of return to further schooling for these students. Policies such as those discussed above—i.e., increasing pre-college academic preparation programs, postsecondary encouragement and information dissemination programs, and per-pupil resources in schools—would increase the rates of return to higher education among lower-income students. This would mean that for each amount of dollars invested in higher education, rates of return would be higher than before the policy changes. This is portrayed diagrammatically in terms of a higher demand curve, because a higher demand curve represents an expansion in the demand-side constraints—i.e., constraints on what students' future earnings would be—for lower-income students.

In terms of Fig. 7.15, students' initial equilibrium position is at point "b" where D_1 and S_2 intersect. But this expansion in the demand-side constraints would shift students from a demand constraint indicated by D_1 to one better represented by D_2. If the demand-side policy changes move these lower-income students from D_1 to D_2 (along S_2), a new equilibrium and optimal level of investment would occur at point "c" where S_2 intersects D_2 and where $\$_5$ dollars are invested in higher education. For all investment amounts from 0 to $\$_5$ the marginal rate of return exceeds the marginal interest cost of funds, making $\$_5$ the new equilibrium and utility-maximizing level of investment. The equilibrium level of investment in higher education at the higher level of $\$_5$ is the result of identifying and using policy levers on both the supply-side and the demand-side to implement policies that alter the constraints faced by lower-income students in ways that make them relatively more advantaged in this market, increasing their willingness and ability to invest more in higher education, which directly addresses the access problem.

Research indicates that, as predicted by the model, increases in funding for precollege academic preparation programs, postsecondary encouragement and information dissemination programs, and per-pupil resources in schools are positively related to greater levels of enrollment and investment in higher education (Card, 1999; Card & Krueger, 1996; Ellwood & Kane, 2000; Hossler & Schmit, 1995; Hossler et al., 1999; Jencks & Phillips, 1999; Perna, 2005; Perna & Titus, 2005).

This economic model of the market for funds to invest in higher education is particularly effective at distinguishing between the effects of various types of policy levers on access to higher education. As an example, we use the model next to compare the effects of increases in the supply of grant funds versus loan funds on the higher education participation and investment decisions of students who differ in how advantaged they are in the market in terms of their expected rates of return to investment in higher education. One supply-side policy that is extensively used to help improve access to higher education is to expand the available supply of non-zero marginal-interest-cost funds such as subsidized student loans. In the previous analysis of the effects of increases in the supply of grants to students, the entire supply of funds curve shifted to the right, because grants constitute a zero-marginal-interest-cost funding. An increase in zero-marginal-interest-cost funding, by definition, shifts the horizontal intercept—i.e., the value of \$ when i = 0—to the right. However, an increase in the supply of non-zero marginal-interest-cost funds does not shift the horizontal intercept; instead it shifts the supply of funds rightward at the appropriate non-zero marginal-interest cost corresponding to the source of increased funds. In the case of an increase in subsidized student loans, the supply curve will shift rightward at the level of the marginal-interest cost of acquiring additional dollars of subsidized student loans.

In order to fully illustrate the effects of an increase in subsidized loans on the supply constraints and investment in higher education, in Fig. 7.16 we return to the stair-step format (as used in Fig. 7.10) for presenting the supply of funds curves. Figure 7.16 presents two supply curves and two demand curves. As explained previously, students who are not from advantaged family backgrounds, do not have high ability endowments, and did not attend high-quality pre-college schools are best portrayed by demand curve D_1 and tend to have lower rates of return on investments in higher education than the more advantaged students facing demand constraints D_2. The initial supply of funds curve (S_1) indicates that $0\$_1$ dollars of grants are available at zero-marginal-interest-cost (0), $\$_1\$_2$ dollars of subsidized loan funds are available at marginal interest cost i_1, $\$_2\$_3$ dollars of

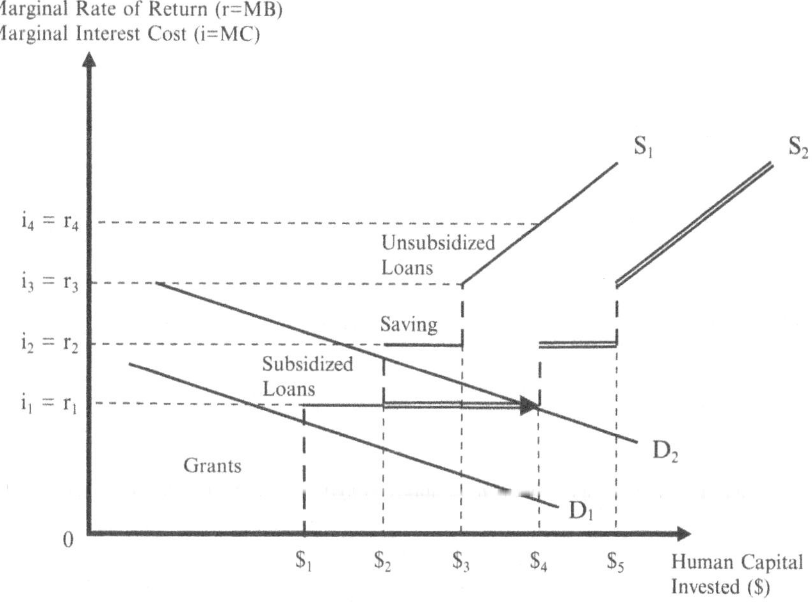

Figure 7.16 Supply, demand and investment in higher education: effects of increased supply of subsidized loan funds.

savings funds are available at marginal interest cost i_2, and unsubsidized loans are available at marginal interest costs equal to or greater than i_3. It would be worthwhile for students to keep investing dollars in higher education as long as the marginal rate of return equals or exceeds the marginal interest cost of funds. Therefore, faced with the supply constraints represented by supply curve S_1, students with demand constraints represented by D_1 will invest $\$_1$ dollars, while students with demand constraints represented by D_2 will invest $\$_2$ dollars.

Next, consider a supply-side policy change in this context. A substantial increase in available subsidized student loan funds (e.g., subsidized Stafford loans) would result in a shift in the supply of funds from S_1 to S_2. Because there is no change in the quantity of zero-marginal-interest-cost grant funds available, the horizontal intercept of the new supply curve S_2 remains at $\$_1$ dollars, exactly the same as for S_1. The shift in the supply of funds takes place only because of a substantial increase in available subsidized student loan funds. These funds are available at the marginal interest cost of i_1; therefore, the total dollars of these funds available increases from $\$_1\$_2$ dollars with supply S_1 to $\$_1\$_4$ dollars after the shift to supply S_2. The increase in the volume of subsidized student loan funds is represented by the double-lined arrow extending from $\$_2$ to $\$_4$. This increase in loan funds will stimulate greater investment in higher education for some students, but not for others. For students facing demand constraints represented by D_2, the marginal rate of return now exceeds the marginal interest cost of funds for levels of investment up to $\$_4$ dollars, and these students will increase their investment and achieve a new equilibrium and optimal level of investment where S_2 intersects D_2 and where $\$_4$ dollars are invested in higher education. However, students facing the more restrictive demand constraints represented by D_1 will not increase their investment as a result of the increase in available subsidized student loan funds. For every level of investment beyond $\$_1$, the marginal interest cost of funds exceeds the marginal rate of return on investment. As a result, no increase in investment would be worthwhile for students facing demand D_1.

In Fig. 7.17, we use stair-step supply of funds curves to more fully illustrate the model's predicted effects of increases in grants funds on investment in higher education. As in Fig. 7.16, there are two supply curves and two demand curves. Once again, students who are from advantaged family backgrounds, have high ability endowments, and attended high-quality pre-college schools are best portrayed by demand curve D_2 and tend to have higher rates of return on investments in higher education than their less advantaged counterparts facing demand constraints D_1. Given the supply constraints represented by supply curve S_1, the initial equilibrium and optimal level

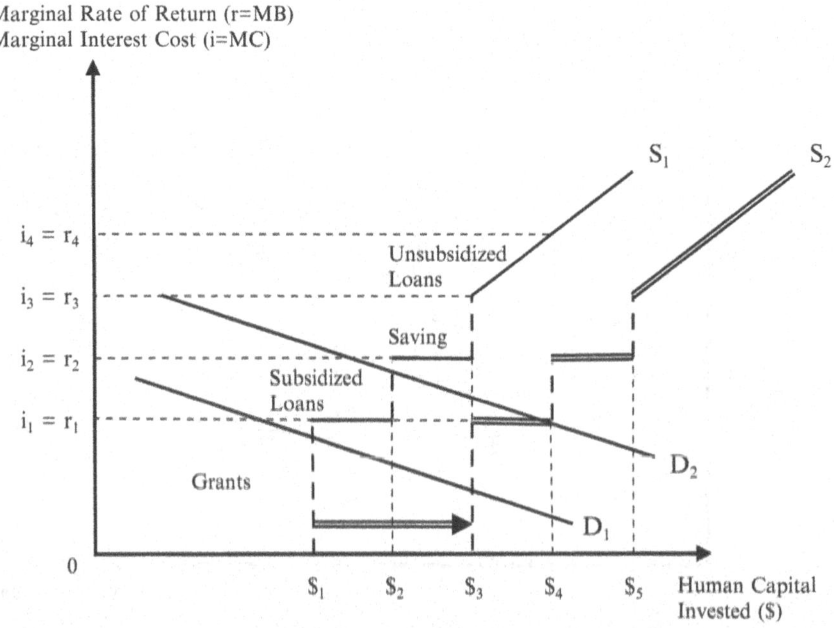

Figure 7.17 Supply, demand and investment in higher education: effects of increased supply of grant funds.

of investment for students with demand constraints represented by D_1 is $\$_1$ dollars, while the initial equilibrium and optimal level of investment for students with the less restrictive demand constraints on D_2 is $\$_2$ dollars.

Next, we assume that a substantial increase in grant funds shifts the supply curve from S_1 to S_2. Because this increase in supply is exclusively due to an increase in zero-marginal-interest-cost grant funds, the shift in supply is represented by a rightward movement in the horizontal intercept of the supply of funds curve, as indicated by the double-line arrow. The horizontal intercept of S_1 was at $\$_1$ dollars of zero-marginal-interest-cost funds, while the horizontal intercept of S_2 is at $\$_3$ dollars of zero-marginal-interest-cost funds. The only difference between the two supply of funds curves is that an additional $\$_1\$_3$ funds are now available at zero-marginal-interest cost. The total amount of zero-marginal-interest-cost funds available has increased from $0\$_1$ to $0\$_3$; however, the quantities of each type of the less-desirable non-zero marginal-interest-cost funds (subsidized loans, savings, and unsubsidized loans) available on S_2 are the same as were available on S_1. Unlike the increase in supply due to more subsidized loan funds—which would stimulate investment in higher education for some relatively more advantaged students, but not for some of their less advantaged counterparts—this increase in supply due to more grants will stimulate greater participation and investment in higher education among both more and less advantaged students. More specifically, for students facing demand constraints of D_2, the marginal rate of return now exceeds the marginal interest cost of funds for levels of investment up to $\$_4$ dollars, and these students will increase their investment up to a new equilibrium and optimal level of investment $\$_4$ dollars, where S_2 intersects D_2. In parallel fashion, for students facing demand constraints of D_1, the marginal rate of return now exceeds the marginal interest cost of funds for levels of investment up to $\$_3$ dollars, and these students will increase their investment up to a new equilibrium and optimal level of $\$_3$ dollars, where S_2 intersects D_1.

In summary, an increase in grants—i.e., an increase in zero-marginal-interest-cost funds—increases the horizontal intercept of the supply curve and stimulates more investment in higher education among both students facing relatively more advantaged and students facing relatively less advantaged demand-side conditions or constraints. However, as show in Fig. 7.16, increases in supply of funds due only to increases in subsidized student loan funds produces an increase in the supply of funds only at the non-zero-marginal-interest costs of i_1. Therefore, this supply-side policy will have different effects on students facing different demand-side constraints. Students who are relatively more advantaged in the market for investment in higher education will increase their investment, while those students who are not from advantaged family backgrounds, do not have high ability endowments, and did not attend high-quality pre-college schools are less likely to find additional investment worthwhile. This analytical result is consistent with existing theory and research. Expansion in subsidized loans is certainly a possible and a popular supply-side policy. However, the subsidy value of loans has been estimated to be only one-half of the subsidy value of grants (Leslie & Brinkman, 1988; McPherson & Schapiro, 1991), and research demonstrates that students' enrollment decisions are more responsive to grant aid than to loan aid (Heller, 1997).

Measuring the Effectiveness of Educational Policies

As the phrase implies, "policy analysis" focuses on how to determine the effectiveness of specific educational policies. This work involves using theory to draw inferences about the likely effect of an educational policy on decision makers, as described in the previous sections, as well as using inferential methods to test whether specific policies led to the changes that were predicted by theory. This is a crucial part of policy work to economists because an ineffective policy is a wasted opportunity to apply fixed resources to their most highly valued use. Policy makers are always faced with constrained resources that limit the range of things that they can do to help improve education. Accordingly, if a policy was implemented that proved to be ineffective, then the resources could have been used in a more constructive manner and therefore an education stakeholder (students, parents, society) experience losses. It is imperative that educators and policy makers find ways to evaluate the likely impact of their policies when making decisions about them, either prior to or after implementation.

Conceptual models such as those described above are indispensable to economists for conducting this type of work. These models enable researchers to make estimates regarding how specific policies will affect the behavior of the decision maker. Economists refer to these conjectures as comparative statics. The strength of economic analysis and the use of models lies not in their ability to explain how the decision makers arrived at the present equilibrium, but rather in their ability to predict how a change in some facet of the model might affect the equilibrium. Many of these changes can be framed in terms of educational policies. For example, economic models are useful for predicting how an increase in financial aid would affect the number of students choosing to go on to college. The educational policy in this example is to increase financial aid for students, and the theoretical model would show the predicted impact of this policy on the likelihood of targeted students choosing to go to college.

The cornerstone of policy analysis, however, involves finding ways to document whether a specific policy has proven to be effective. This usually takes the form of quantitative studies that look for evidence of relationships between the policy and the actions of the decision maker. A conceptual model serves as a guide to the researcher of the possible factors that should be relevant for inclusion in the quantitative analysis. In the earlier example where policy makers were interested in increasing the rate at which black students go to college, for example, a researcher might conduct a quantitative study to determine if differences across students in their family income level or financial aid affect whether or not they go to college. Thus, the theoretical model of college-going behavior would be useful in identifying the variables that should be used in such a study. Researchers would then have a theoretical basis for focusing on these factors to determine if and how they affect a student's interest in going to college.

There is also a direct connection between comparative statics and the research methods used by economists for educational policy analysis. Multiple regression models and their counterparts such as logistic regression and hierarchical linear modeling (HLM) typically estimate models of the form:

$$Y = X\beta + P\alpha + \varepsilon \qquad (5)$$

where

Y = dependent variable of interest

X = set of control variables that the theoretical model suggest might have an impact on Y with weights β

P = policy-related variables that are recommended by the theoretical model with weights α, and

ε = random error term.

The policy variables could be either direct measures of whether the policy was enacted ($P = 1$ if yes, $P = 0$ otherwise), or indirect measures of the policy such as the family income level or amount of higher education spending. The estimated coefficients for the variables in X and P are referred to as partial effects because they show the predicted change in the dependent variable due to a one-unit change in the explanatory variable, holding all other variables constant. Of course, this is precisely what is meant by the notion of comparative statics. Viewed in this way, the estimates for the coefficients (α) can be used to test the theoretical predictions of the effects of specific educational policies on decision makers.

Although the model and description of the approach to educational policy analysis seems straightforward, there are a number of challenges that researchers face when attempting to analyze specific policies. First, researchers always encounter data limitations in their work. These limitations may mean that several key variables that are predicted from the theoretical model to be important for the study cannot be measured. For example, a researcher who is studying the effects of income subsidies on how students make decisions about whether to go to college may have information on family income but not family wealth. Data limitations may also affect the way in which specific factors can be measured and used in an analysis. Surveys of students may, for instance, collect data on family income in groups such as less than \$20,000, \$20,000 but under \$40,000, and so on, and financial aid data on students may be aggregated by purpose (need-based, merit-based). Likewise, the sampling design used in the analysis will impact the surveyed population and hence the degree to which the results can be applied to other settings.

Second, it should be acknowledged that the findings from quantitative studies are probabilistic in nature rather than definitive. This is due to the reliance on drawing samples from larger populations and using the results from the samples to draw inferences about what would have been found had the entire population been examined. This sampling error is inevitable in quantitative studies and is the reason why researchers use predefined significance levels when drawing conclusions about the effects of policies on the actions of decision makers. Data limitations impose yet another source of error into quantitative studies.

Summary and Discussion

In this chapter, we provided an overview of the way in which economists approach the analysis and evaluation of educational policies, and a more complete explanation of how this works with regard to the problem of access to higher education. The focus on using constraints to alter the behavior of decision makers is drawn from the emphasis on comparative statics in economics and the use of policy levers that provide policy makers with tools that are reliable and testable. At the same time, we point out that educational policy analysts can also draw from other disciplines to target policies on the way that decision makers form preferences. With regard to access to higher education, for example, informing students of the potential benefits and costs of pursuing a higher education should always be an important component of an overall strategy to raise the college-going rate of students. However, these policies are best informed by disciplines such as sociology, psychology, and others that can yield insights into how preferences are formed. This highlights the fact that the solutions to many important policy problems in higher education require a multidisciplinary approach, and economics can make a valuable contribution to research and policy analysis in higher education through its unique theoretical and empirical perspectives on policy problems.

The wide range of entities that are involved with educational policy certainly add to the difficulty of making policies that are effective and efficient in their use of resources. Proposed policies will often be critiqued by students, parents, teachers, administrators, taxpayers, town officials, and state/local politicians, to name a few. To economists, each of these entities have objectives or goals that they are trying to reach, and will consider the likely impact of a policy on how it affects the achievement of their goals. Often policies are not Pareto optimal—i.e., socially efficient—because a policy may benefit one group and harm another. For example, increases in state appropriations to public institutions certainly benefit those students and their families who attend in-state public institutions, but they take funding away from other state uses or from taxpayers if state taxes are raised to increase the appropriations. State appropriations do constitute a potentially effective policy lever. However, because such subsidies are given to institutions and not to students, it is uncertain how much of the appropriations will be used to actually reduce the price charged to students. There are also political considerations to almost any policy proposal, whether they are for elected officials or governing boards of institutions of higher education. These instances highlight the importance of having good, empirically-based information about the likely impacts of educational policies so that deliberations can be more productive.

One area of research that promises to grow in importance with regard to educational policy analysis is the problem of *self-section* in educational policy studies. There are many instances in education where policies such as financial aid or postsecondary encouragement programs are not implemented in a random fashion across decision makers. If decision makers are allowed to choose whether or not they are subjected to an educational policy, and this policy is affected by unobservable characteristics of the decision maker, then the estimated effect of the program will be biased using standard statistical approaches such as regression analysis. The federal government has become a strong advocate for the use of randomized experiments (the so-called "gold standard" for educational research) where a group of subjects are randomly assigned to a specific treatment (policy) and their outcomes are compared to subjects who were not assigned to the treatment (US Department of Education, 2003). The emphasis on randomized experiments in funding decisions for federal grants has led to concerns among educators who point out that it is very difficult in many situations in education to implement a true randomized experiment. Analysts are therefore often forced to try to infer unbiased effects of policies using data that were generated without a random assignment. A number of approaches have emerged for accomplishing this, including instrumental variables (Heckman, 1979, 1990; Card, 1995), regression discontinuity (Battistin & Rettore, 2002; Hahn et al., 2001), propensity score matching (Heckman et al., 1998; Dehejia & Wahba, 2002), and natural experiments. Each of these approaches has its advantages and disadvantages, and whether one can be applied to a given policy depends on the nature of the policy and the information available to the analyst. This promises to be a topic of growing importance in educational policy analysis as researchers struggle to find better ways of evaluating the true impacts of alternative policies and meet federal requirements for the use of more rigorous research methodologies.

Conclusion

It is a common, but understandable, mistake for individuals who are not trained in economics to associate economics with money, business, profit and related phenomena, and to equate economics with fields of study such as business, finance, or accounting. However, this perspective substantially limits an individual's impression of the usefulness of economics for higher education policy analysis. In this chapter we have tried to explain and illustrate—using diagrams, detailed narration, and minimal mathematical notation—how economists analyze the behavior of individuals, groups and institutions engaged in decision-making processes by identifying the decision makers, considering the goals of the decision makers, and examining the constraints that the decision makers face in pursuit of their preferred goals. Because of its focus on the behavior of individuals, groups and institutions, economics is appropriately viewed as a social and behavioral science (Paulsen & Toutkoushian, 2006b; Toutkoushian & Paulsen, 2006). For example, many higher education policies influence individual behavior by affecting the constraints that student decision-makers face—such as income constraints, information constraints, and time constraints—as they pursue their goals. In this context, economics provides analytical frameworks that are particularly useful for understanding, evaluating, and measuring the effectiveness of higher education policies.

In the first half of this chapter, we explained how economists develop and utilize generalizable models of decision making to analyze higher education policies. In the second half of the chapter, we provided a detailed explanation and illustration of how human capital theory—the most widely-used theoretical framework from the economics of education—and a model of the market for investment in higher education can be and have been applied to the analysis of higher education policies in the policy problem area of student access to postsecondary education. We hope that, in combination, these two major parts of our chapter will serve as a useful introduction to economics for higher education scholars, administrators, and other practitioners who are not trained in economics, but would like to understand how certain theoretical frameworks and models from the discipline of economics can be effectively used to analyze higher education policy.

Acknowledgments

The authors would like to thank John Cheslock, Steve DesJardins, Don Hossler and Laura Perna for their helpful comments on earlier drafts of this manuscript. Any errors or omissions, however,are the responsibility of the authors.

Notes

1. This is true of traditional economics and economists. However, in the emerging field of behavioral economics, economists explicitly acknowledge and utilize the many natural connections between psychology—particularly cognitive and social psychology—and economic phenomena. Behavioral economists draw extensively on the social, cognitive, motivational, and emotional phenomena in their analysis of individual and group decision-making and in their examination of anomalies in the marketplace. For more information, interested readers should consult the volume by Camerer et al. (2003).
2. Human capital theory has received consistent empirical support for over 45 years and has provided insightful explanations of individual and institutional behavior, including decisions about investment in higher education. A central tenet of human capital theory is that education increases an individu-

al's productivity, and therefore leads to higher future earnings. Alternative perspectives on the relation between educational attainment and earnings have emerged over the years, such as the screening hypothesis (e.g., Spence, 1973), job competition model (e.g., Thurow, 1975), dual labor market hypothesis (e.g. Doeringer and Piore, 1971), and social class approach (e.g., Bowles and Gintis, 1976). A thorough analysis of these contributions is beyond the scope of this chapter; however, each approach offers an important perspective and should be studied in conjunction with human capital theory.

3. The meaning of the rational behavior assumption is very important but it is often misunderstood and applied in ways that are misleadingly restrictive. Each individual's preferences for different combinations of higher education and other goods, or the values she assigns to them, are by definition, highly subjective, idiosyncratic and unique to each individual. Preferences for various combinations of higher education and other goods vary considerably across individuals, because the formation of preferences is uniquely shaped by each individual's distinctive experiences, access to information, values, attitudes, and beliefs, which in turn are influenced by individual differences in home, school and community environments. Budget constraints also vary substantially across individuals, particularly due to differences in incomes and the prices of higher education and other goods and services for different individuals and households. Therefore, *rational behavior* means that two individuals with identical budget constraints would choose different amounts of higher education and other goods if they have different preferences; and two individuals with identical preferences would make different choices because they face different budget constraints. Paulsen and Toutkoushian (2006b) offer a brief, accessible explanation of what economists mean by rational behavior, and DesJardins and Toutkoushian (2005) provide a comprehensive treatment of the subject.
4. In a more complete analysis (see, e.g., McMahon and Wagner, 1982), this model would also include non-monetary costs and benefits as well, such as the psychic costs of college related to the time and effort associated with studying or the improvement in one's health, expansion of one's ability to enjoy non-market activities, and the consumption benefits of the college experience. Any examination of the well-known problems of identification and measurement of non-market costs and benefits, while posing an important challenge in the context of human capital theory, is beyond the scope of this chapter.
5. The marginal rate of return (r) is the yield or expected net economic payoff to an investment, defined as the "value of the (discounted lifetime) gains due to an individual's education expressed as a percentage of the (discounted) costs to the individual of acquiring that education" (Johnes, 1993, p. 28). The market rate of interest (i)—defined in this model as the marginal interest cost from an additional dollar of investment in higher education—equals "either the rate at which interest income could have been earned if the individual's funds had not been spent on college or the rate at which interest costs would have to be paid to acquire the funds necessary to make the college investment" (Paulsen, 2001a, p. 60).
6. As indicated, we assume that the decision-making unit in our analysis of the market for investment in higher education is the individual student. But this analysis can also be done using the family, or some combination of the student and the family, as the relevant decision-making unit. The analytical framework is highly generalizable and works equally well with the student or the family as the relevant decision-making unit. However, when the decision-making unit is the family, then one feature of the supply of funds curve must be interpreted differently. When the family is the decision-making unit, then family income and parental contributions to their children's education are no longer viewed as a source of zero-marginal-interest-cost funds. Instead, when a family uses "savings" from its income as a source of funds to pay for higher education, these savings have opportunity costs, and the opportunity costs are measured in terms of the marginal interest rate (i_2 in Fig. 7.10) at which the family's savings could have earned interest income if it had not been spent on investment in higher education (see, e.g., McMahon, 1984).
7. A careful study of the issues of measurement, specification, endogeneity, and selection bias in the estimation of rates of return to education is beyond the scope of this chapter. We encourage readers to consult the recent reviews of this literature by Ashenfelter and Rouse (2000) and Card (1999). Another specification of the demand for human capital could include an indicator of college quality (see, e.g., Dale and Krueger, 1999; Monks, 2000; Zhang and Thomas, 2005); however, this is not included in Equation (4) because our analysis focuses on the access decision of students regarding whether or not to attend college, but *not* the student choice of which college to attend.
8. This discussion of the effects of students' family backgrounds, such as their parents' educational attainment, on students' future earnings and rates of return to education is akin to the excellent conceptual and empirical work of sociologists interested in the access problem. A thorough examination of the invaluable contributions of educational sociologists to our understanding of the nature and complex-

ity of the issues of access and equity in college-going is beyond the scope of this chapter. However, we encourage readers to consult the following work to explore this vibrant literature, particularly regarding the constructs of habitus and symbolic capital such as cultural and social capital (Bourdieu, 1977a, b; Bourdieu and Passeron, 1990; Coleman, 1988; Horvat, 2001; Lamont and Lareau, 1988; Massey et al., 2003; McDonough, 1997).

References

Altonji, J. G., & Dunn, T. A. (1996). Using siblings to estimate the effect of school quality on wages. *Review of Economics and Statistics* 78 (4): 665–671.

Arai, K. (1998). *The economics of education: An analysis of college-going behavior*. New York: Springer.

Ashenfelter, O., & Rouse, C. (2000). Schooling, intelligence and income in America. In K. Arrow, S. Bowles, and S. Durlauf (eds.), *Meritocracy and economic inequality* (pp. 89–117). Princeton, NJ: Princeton University Press.

Averett, S. L., & Burton, M. L. (1996). College attendance and the wage premium: Differences by gender. *Economics of Education Review* 15 (1): 37–49.

Avery, C., & Hoxby, C. M. (2004). Do and should financial aid packages affect students' college choices? In C. M. Hoxby (ed.), *College choices: The economics of where to go, when to go, and how to pay for it* (pp. 239–302). Chicago, IL: University of Chicago Press.

Avery, C., & Kane, T. J. (2004). Student perceptions of college opportunities: The Boston COACH Program. In C. M. Hoxby (ed.), College choices: The economics of where to go, when to go, and how to pay for it (pp. 355–394). Chicago, IL: University of Chicago Press.

Battistin, E., & Rettore, E. (2002). Testing for programme effects in a regression discontinuity design with imperfect compliance. *Journal of the Royal Statistical Society* A 165 (1): 1–19.

Baum, S. (2004). *A primer on economics for financial aid professionals*. New York: The College Board.

Baum, S., & Payea, K. (2004). *Education pays 2004: The benefits of higher education for individuals and society*. Washington, DC: The College Board.

Becker, G. A. (1967). *Human capital and the personal distribution of income*. Ann Arbor, MI: University of Michigan Press.

Becker, G. S. (1962). Investment in human capital: A theoretical analysis. *Journal of Political Economy* 70 (Supplement): 9–49.

Becker, G. S. (1975). *Human capital: A theoretical and empirical analysis with special reference to education* (2nd ed.). New York: Columbia University Press.

Becker, G. S. (1993). *Human capital: A theoretical and empirical analysis with special reference to education* (3rd ed.). Chicago, IL: University of Chicago Press.

Behrman, J. R., Kletzer, L. G., McPherson, M. S., & Schapiro, M. O. (1992). *The college investment decision: Direct and indirect effects of family background on choice of postsecondary enrollment and quality*. Discussion Paper Series No. 18. Williamstown, MA: Williams Project on the Economics of Higher Education.

Belfield, C. R. (2000). *Economic principles for education: Theory and evidence*. Northampton, MA: Edward Elgar.

Bourdieu, P. (1977a). *Cultural reproduction and social reproduction. In J. Karabel & A. H. Halsey (eds.), Power and ideology in education* (pp. 487–511). New York: Oxford University Press.

Bourdieu, P. (1977b). *Outline of a theory of practice*. Cambridge: University Press.

Bourdieu, P., & Passeron, J.-C. (1990). Reproduction in education, society, and culture. Beverly Hills, CA: Sage.

Bowen, H. R. (1977). *Investment in learning: The individual and social value of American higher education*. San Francisco, CA: Jossey-Bass.

Bowles, S., & Gintis, H. (1976). *Schooling in capitalist America: Educational reform and the contradictions of economic life*. New York: Basic Books.

Breneman, D. W., & Nelson, S. C. (1981). *Financing community colleges: An economic perspective*. Washington, DC: The Brookings Institution.

Camerer, C. F., Loewenstein, G., & Rabin, M. (2003). *Advances in behavioral economics*. Princeton, NJ: Princeton University Press.

Card, D. (1995). Using geographic variation in college proximity to estimate the return to schooling. In L. Christophides, E. Grant, & R. Swidinsky (eds.), *Aspects of labor market behavior: Essays in honor of John Vanderkamp*. Toronto, ON: University of Toronto Press.

Card, D. (1999). The causal effect of education on earnings. In O. Ashenfelter & D. Card (eds.), *Handbook of labor economics* (Volume 3A) (pp. 1801–1863). Amsterdam, The Netherlands/New York: Elsevier.

Card, D. (2001). Estimating the return to schooling: Progress on some persistent econometric problems. Econometrica 69(5): 1127–1160.

Card, D., & Krueger, A. (1992). Does school quality matter? Returns to education and the characteristics of public schools in the United States. *Journal of Political Economy* 100 (1): 1–40.

Card, D., & Krueger, A. (1996). The economic return to school quality. In W. Becker & W. Baumol (eds.), *Assessing educational practices: The contribution of economics*. New York: Russell Sage Foundation.

Carnoy, M. (1995). Rates of return to education. In M. Carnoy (ed.), *International encyclopedia of economics of education* (2nd ed.). Tarrytown, NY: Elsevier.

Checchi, D. (2006). *The economics of education: Human capital, family background and inequality*. New York: Cambridge University Press.

Cipillone, P. (1995). Education and earnings. In M. Carnoy (ed.), *International encyclopedia of economics of education* (2nd ed.). Tarrytown, NY: Elsevier.

Cohn, E., & Geske, T. (1990). *The economics of education* (3rd ed.). New York: Pergamon.

Catsiapis, G. (1987). A model of educational investment decisions. *Review of Economics and Statistics* 69: 33–41.

Coleman, J. S. (1988). Social capital in the creation of human capital. *American Journal of Sociology* 94 (Supplement): 95–120.

College Entrance Examination Board (1971). *The college choices of thirty black project opportunity students*. Atlanta, GA: College Entrance Examination Board. ED 062914.

College Board, The (2006a). *Trends in college pricing 2006*. Washington, DC: The College Board.

College Board, The (2006b). *Trends in student aid 2006*. Washington, DC: The College Board.

Dale, S. B., & Krueger, A. B. (1999). *Estimating the payoff to attending a more selective college: An application of selection and unobservables*. Cambridge, MA: National Bureau of Economic Research Working Paper No. W7322.

Dehejia, R., & Wahba, S. (2002). Propensity score-matching methods for nonexperimental causal studies. *The Review of Economics and Statistics* 84 (1): 151–161.

DesJardins, S. L., & Toutkoushian, R. K. (2005). Are students really rational? The development of rational thought and its application to student choice. In J. C. Smart (ed.), *Higher education: Handbook of theory and research* (Volume 20) (pp. 191–240). Dordrecht, The Netherlands: Kluwer.

Doeringer, P. B., & Piore, M. J. (1971). *Internal labor markets and manpower analysis*. Lexington, MA: D. C. Heath.

Dynarski, S. (2003). Does aid matter? Measuring the effect of student aid on college attendance and completion. *American Economic Review* 93 (1): 279–288.

Dynarski, S. (2004). The new merit aid. In C. M. Hoxby (ed.), *College choices: The economics of where to go, when to go, and how to pay for it* (pp. 63–100). Chicago, IL: University of Chicago Press.

Ehrenberg, R. G., & Smith, R. S. (2006). *Modern labor economics: Theory and public policy* (9th ed.). New York: Pearson.

Ellwood, D. T., & Kane, T. J. (2000). Who is getting a college education? Family background and the growing gaps in enrollment. In S. Danziger & J. Waldfogel (eds.), *Securing the future: Investing in children from birth to college* (pp. 283–324). New York: Russell Sage Foundation.

Fatima, N., & Paulsen, M. B. (2004). Higher education and state workforce productivity in the 1990s. *Thought and Action: NEA Higher Education Journal* 20 (1): 75–94.

Fenske, R. H., Geranios, C. A, Keller, J. E., & Moore, D. E. (1997). *Early intervention programs: Opening the door to higher education*. ASHE-ERIC Higher Education Report No. 6. Washington, DC: The George Washington University.

Frank, R. (2003). *Microeconomics and behavior*. New York: McGraw-Hill Irwin.

Freeman, R. B. (1976). *The overeducated American*. New York: Academic.

Hahn, J., Todd, P., & Van der Klaauw, W. (2001). Identification and estimation of treatment effects with a regression-discontinuity design. *Econometrica* 69 (3): 201–209.

Heckman, J. (1979). Sample selection bias as a specification error. *Econometrica* 47: 153–167.

Heckman, J. (1990). Varieties of selection bias. *American Economic Review* 80: 313–318.

Heckman, J., Ichimura, H., & Todd, P. (1998). Matching as an econometric evaluation estimator. *Review of Economic Studies* 65: 261–294.

Heller, D. E. (1997). Student price response in higher education: An update to Leslie and Brinkman. *Journal of Higher Education* 68: 624–659.

Heller, D. E. (1999). The effects of tuition and state financial aid on public college enrollment. *Review of Higher Education* 23 (1): 65–89.

Heller, D. E. (2006). State support of higher education: Past, present, and future. In D. M. Priest & E. P. St. John (eds.), *Privatization and public universities*. Bloomington, IN: Indiana University Press.

Horvat, E. M. (2001). Understanding equity and access in higher education: The potential contribution of Pierre Bourdieu. In J. C. Smart (ed.), *Higher education: Handbook of theory and research* (Volume 16). New York: Agathon.

Hossler, D., & Schmit, J. (1995). The Indiana postsecondary-encouragement experiment. In E. P. St. John (ed.), *Rethinking tuition and student aid strategies*. New Directions for Higher Education No. 89. San Francisco, CA: Jossey-Bass.

Hossler, D., Schmit, J., & Vesper, N. (1999). *Going to college: How social, economic, and educational factors influence the decisions students make*. Baltimore, MD: Johns Hopkins University Press.

Institute for Higher Education Policy. (2005). *The investment payoff: A fifty-state analysis of the public and private benefits of higher education*. Washington, DC: Institute for Higher Education Policy.

Jencks, C. (1972). *Inequality: A reassessment of the effect of family and schools in America*. New York: Basic Books.

Jencks, C. (1979). *Who gets ahead? The determinants of economic success in America*. New York: Basic Books.

Jencks, C., & Phillips, M. (1999). Aptitude or achievement: Why do test scores predict education attainment and earnings? In S. E. Mayer & P. E. Peterson (eds.), *Earning and learning: How schools matter*. Washington, DC: Brookings Institution Press.

Johnes, G. (1993). *The economics of education*. New York: St. Martin's.

Kane, T. J. (1995). *Rising public college tuition and college entry: How well do public subsidies promote access to college?* Cambridge, MA: National Bureau of Economic Research Working Paper No. 5164.

Kane, T. J. (1999). *The price of admission: Rethinking how Americans pay for college*. Washington, DC: Brookings Institution Press.

Kaufman, B. E., & Hotchkiss, J. L. (2000). *The economics of labor markets* (5th ed.). New York: Harcourt.

Korenman, S., & Winship, C. (2000). A reanalysis of *The Bell Curve*: Intelligence, family background and schooling. In K. Arrow, S. Bowles, & S. Durlauf (eds.), *Meritocracy and economic inequality* (pp. 137–178). Princeton, NJ: Princeton University Press.

Lamont, M., & Lareau, A. (1988). Cultural capital: Allusions, gaps and glissandos in recent theoretical developments. *Sociological Theory* 6: 153–168.

Leslie, L. L., & Brinkman, P. T. (1988). *The economic value of higher education*. New York: American Council on Education/MacMillan.

Long, B. T. (2004). How have college decisions changed over time? An application of the conditional logistic choice model. *Journal of Econometrics* 121: 271–296.

Mankiw, G. (2007). *Principles of microeconomics, 4th Edition*. Cincinnati, OH: South-Western Publishing.

Manski, C. F., & Wise, D. (1983). *College choice in America*. Cambridge, MA: Harvard University Press.

Massey, D. S., Charles, C. Z., Lundy, G. F., & Fischer, M. J. (2003). *The source of the river: The social origins of freshmen at America's selective colleges and universities*. Princeton, NJ: Princeton University Press.

McConnell, C. R., Brue, S. L., & MacPherson, D. A. (2003). *Contemporary labor economics* (6th ed.), New York: McGraw-Hill.

McDonough, P. M. (1997). *Choosing colleges: How social class and schools structure opportunity*. Albany, NY: State University of New York Press.

McEachern, W. (2006). *Microeconomics: A contemporary introduction (with InfoTrac), 7th Edition*. Cincinnati, OH: South-Western Publishing.

McMahon, W. W. (1976). Influences on investment by blacks in higher education. *American Economic Review* 66 (2): 320–324.

McMahon, W. W. (1984). Why families invest in education. In S. Sudman & M. A. Spaeth (eds.), *The collection and analysis of economic and consumer behavior data: In memory of Robert Ferber* (pp. 75–91). Urbana, IL: Bureau of Economic and Business Research, University of Illinois.

McMahon, W. W. (1991). Improving higher education through increased efficiency. In D. H. Finifter, R. G. Baldwin, & J. R. Thelin (eds.), *The uneasy public policy triangle in higher education: Quality, diversity, and budgetary efficiency* (pp. 143–161). New York: ACE/Macmillan.

McMahon, W. W., & Wagner, A. P. (1982). The monetary returns to education as partial social efficiency criteria. In W. W. McMahon & T. G. Geske (eds.), Financing education: Overcoming inefficiency and inequity. Urbana, IL: University of Illinois Press.

McPherson, M. S., & Schapiro, M. O. (1991). *Keeping college affordable: Government and educational opportunity.* Washington, DC: The Brookings Institution.

Merriam-Webster Dictionary (2007). Retrieved July 25, 2007, from http://www.m-w.com/dictionary/policy.

Mincer, J. (1993). The distribution of labor incomes: A survey. In J. Mincer (ed.), *Studies in human capital: Collected essays of Jacob Mincer.* Brookfield, VT: Edward Elgar.

Monks, J. (2000). The returns to individual and college characteristics: Evidence from the National Longitudinal Survey of Youth. *Economics of Education Review* 19: 279–289.

Mumper, M. (1996). *Removing college price barriers.* Albany, NY: SUNY.

Mumper, M., & Freeman, M. L. (2005). The causes and consequences of public college tuition inflation. In J. C. Smart (ed.), *Higher education: Handbook of theory and research* (Volume 20) (pp. 307–361). Dordrecht, The Netherlands: Springer.

Murphy, K. M., & Welch, F. (1989). Wage premiums for college graduates: Recent growth and possible explanations. *Educational Researcher* 18 (4): 17–26.

Murphy, K. M., & Welch, F. (1992). The structure of wages. *Quarterly Journal of Economics* 107 (1): 285–326.

National Center for Education Statistics. (2005). *Digest of education statistics 2005.* Washington, DC: US Department of Education.

Palacios, M. (2004). *Investing in human capital: A capital markets approach to student funding.* Cambridge, UK: Cambridge University Press.

Paulsen, M. (1990). *College choice: Understanding student enrollment behavior.* Report No. ASHE-ERIC Higher Education Report No. 6. Washington, DC: George Washington University, School of Education and Human Development.

Paulsen, M. B. (1998). Recent research on the economics of attending college: Returns on investment and responsiveness to price. *Research in Higher Edu*cation 39 (4): 471–489.

Paulsen, M. B. (2000). Economic perspectives on rising college tuition: A theoretical and empirical exploration. In J. C. Smart (ed.), *Higher education: Handbook of theory and research* (Volume 15) (pp. 39–104). New York: Agathon.

Paulsen, M. B. (2001a). The economics of human capital and investment in higher education. In M. B. Paulsen & J. C. Smart (eds.), *The finance of higher education: Theory, research, policy, and practice.* (pp. 55–94). New York: Agathon.

Paulsen, M. B. (2001b). The economics of the public sector: The nature and role of public policy in the finance of higher education. In M. B. Paulsen & J. C. Smart (eds.), *The finance of higher education: Theory, research, policy, and practice* (pp. 95–132). New York: Agathon.

Paulsen, M. B., & Fatima, N. (2007). Higher education and growth in state workforce productivity, 1980–2000: Evidence of the public benefits of college. In P. B. Richards (ed.), Global issues in higher education (pp. 37–56). F. Columbus (ed.), *Higher education research perspectives.* New York: Nova Science Publishers.

Paulsen, M. B., & Pogue, T. F. (1988). Higher education enrollment: The interaction of labor market conditions, curriculum and selectivity. *Economics of Education Review* 7 (3): 275–290.

Paulsen, M. B., & Smart, J. C. (eds.) (2001). *The finance of higher education: Theory, research, policy, and practice.* New York: Agathon.

Paulsen, M. B., & St. John, E. P. (2002). Social class and college costs: Examining the financial nexus between college choice and persistence. *Journal of Higher Education* 73: 189–236.

Paulsen, M. B., & Toutkoushian, R. K. (2006a). Economics and IR: Expanding the connections and applications. In R. K. Toutkoushian & M. B. Paulsen (eds.), *Applying economics to institutional research.* New Directions for Institutional Research No. 132 (pp. 95–104). San Francisco, CA: Jossey-Bass.

Paulsen, M. B., & Toutkoushian, R. K. (2006b). Overview of economic concepts, models and methods for institutional research. In R. K. Toutkoushian & M. B. Paulsen (eds.), *Applying economics to institutional research.* New Directions for Institutional Research No. 132 (pp. 5–24). San Francisco, CA: Jossey-Bass.

Perna, L. W. (2000). Differences in the decision to enroll in college among African Americans, Hispanics, and Whites. *Journal of Higher Education* 71: 117–141.

Perna, L. W. (2005). The key to college access: A college preparatory curriculum. In W. G. Tierney, Z. B. Corwin, & J. E. Colyar (eds.), *Preparing for college: Nine elements of effective outreach* (pp. 113–134). Albany, NY: State University of New York Press.

Perna, L. W. (2006). Studying college access and choice: A proposed conceptual model. In J. C. Smart (ed.), *Higher education: Handbook of theory and research* (Volume 21) (pp. 99–157). Dordrecht, The Netherlands: Springer.

Perna, L. W., & Titus, M. (2005). The relationship between parental involvement as social capital and college enrollment: An examination of racial/ethnic group differences. *Journal of Higher Education* 76 (5): 485–518.

Pindyck, R. S., & Rubinfeld, D. L. (2005). *Microeconomics, 5th Edition*. Upper Saddle River, NJ: Prentice-Hall.

Psacharopoulos, G. (1973). *Returns to education: An international comparison*. Amsterdam, The Netherlands: Elsevier/Jossey-Bass.

Rouse, C. E. (1994). What to do after high school: The two-year versus four-year college enrollment decision. In R. G. Ehrenberg (ed.), *Choices and consequences: Contemporary policy issues in education* (pp. 59–88). New York: IRL.

Rumberger, R. W. (1984). The changing economic benefits of college graduates. *Economics of Education Review* 3: 3–11.

Schultz, T. W. (1961). Investment in human capital. *American Economic Review* 51: 1–17.

Sewell, W. H., & Hauser, R. M. (1976). Causes and consequences of higher education: models of the status attainment process. In W. H. Sewell, R. M. Hauser, & D. L. Featherman (eds.), *Schooling and achievement in American society*. New York: Academic.

Spence, D. (1973). Job market signaling. *Quarterly Journal of Economics* 87: 355–374.

St. John, E. P. (1994). *Prices, productivity, and investment: Assessing financial strategies in higher education*. ASHE-ERIC Higher Education Report No. 3. Washington, DC: The George Washington University, School of Education and Human Development.

St. John, E. P. (2003). *Refinancing the college dream: Access, equal opportunity, and justice for taxpayers*. Baltimore, MD: Johns Hopkins University Press.

Taubman, P., & Wales, T. (1974). *Higher education and earnings: College as an investment and a screening device*. New York: McGraw-Hill.

Thomas, S. L., & Perna, L. W. (2004). The opportunity agenda: A reexamination of postsecondary reward and opportunity. In J. C. Smart (ed.), *Higher education: Handbook of theory and research* (Volume 19) (pp. 43–84). Dordrecht, The Netherlands: Kluwer.

Thurow, L. (1970). *Investment in human capital*. Belmont, CA: Wadsworth.

Thurow, L. C. (1975). *Generating inequality: Mechanisms of distribution in the U.S. economy*. New York: Basic Books.

Toutkoushian, R., & Paulsen, M. (eds.) (2006). *Applying economics to institutional research*. New Directions for Institutional Research, no. 132. San Francisco, CA: Jossey-Bass.

Trowler, P. (2003). *Education policy* (2nd ed.). London: Routledge.

US Department of Education (2003). *Identifying and implementing educational practices supported by rigorous evidence: A user friendly guide*. Washington, DC: US Department of Education.

Woodhall, M. (1995). Human capital concepts. In M. Carnoy (ed.), *International encyclopedia of economics of education* (2nd ed.). Tarrytown, NY: Elsevier.

Zhang, L., & Thomas, S. L. (2005). Investments in human capital: Sources of variation in the return to college quality. In J. C. Smart (ed.), *Higher education: Handbook of theory and research* (Volume 20) (pp. 241–306). Dordrecht, The Netherlands: Springer.

SECTION II

ECONOMIC OUTCOMES OF HIGHER EDUCATION

INTRODUCTION TO SECTION II

JOHN C. WEIDMAN AND LINDA THERESA DEANGELO
UNIVERSITY OF PITTSBURGH

In this section, we focus on the financial benefits of college attendance, with particular attention to early career outcomes for graduates. Consideration is given to aspects of the college experience (especially those related to retention) that are important as well as the longer term economic consequences for students from diverse backgrounds who attend different types of higher education institutions.

Breier ("From 'Financial Considerations' to 'Poverty:' Towards a Reconceptualization of the Role of Finances in Higher Education Student Drop Out") customizes Tinto's classic model on student attrition to help explain conditions of extreme poverty and racial privilege in South Africa. Finding that financial considerations were a much deeper driver of withdrawal decisions than suggested by other leading researchers, she also discovered that many poor students were also hopeful, seeing their withdrawal as a temporary situation. Despite growing economic pressures created by limited state budgets and family means, some students from extreme poverty were successful, perhaps due to greater social capital.

Hu and Wolniak ("College Student Engagement and Early Career Earnings: Differences by Gender, Race/Ethnicity, and Academic Preparation") used longitudinal data from the 2001 cohort of applicants to the Gates Millennium Scholars (GMS) program, examining scaled measures of academic and social engagement in relation to labor market earnings to test whether the economic value of student engagement among high-achieving students of color differs by student background characteristics. Results confirm that academic and social engagement during college had differential effects on early career earnings. Findings suggest conditional effects of student engagement on labor market outcomes, providing evidence for individual and institutional decisions and theory-building related to the lasting influence of student engagement in college.

Hu, Trengove, and Zhang ("Toward a Greater Understanding of the Effects of State Merit Aid Programs: Examining Existing Evidence and Exploring Future Research Direction") review and synthesize the existing literature and research on the effects of state merit aid programs on such educational outcomes as college choice and access, degree attainment, migration, student academic preparation, major choice (especially STEM fields), student persistence, and degree attainment. The authors describe how various theoretical perspectives from economics, sociology, and psychology can be used to enhance understanding of more general underlying patterns. They also identify areas not covered adequately by current research.

Using data from the NCES Baccalaureate and Beyond Longitudinal Survey, Strayhorn ("Influences on Labor Market Outcomes of African American College Graduates: A National Study") studied the impact of students' traits, postsecondary experiences, and post-BA experiences on labor market outcomes of Black college graduates, comparing those who attended HBCUs (Historically Black Colleges and Universities) with those who did not. Overall, HBCU graduates and non-HBCU graduates differed significantly on post-BA annual earnings (advantage to non-HBCU graduates) but did not differ in terms of occupational status and job satisfaction.

Thomas and Zhang ("Post-Baccalaureate Wage Growth within Four Years of Graduation: The Effects of College Quality and College Major") examine the impact of college quality and academic major on the earnings of a nationally representative sample of baccalaureate recipients, extending previous work in this area by analyzing the magnitude of change in the influence of these factors at two points in the early career of these graduates. Their results demonstrate that, despite significant variation, graduates from higher quality colleges enjoy a greater rate of growth in earnings during their early career. They also show that growth in earnings varies significantly by the graduates' major field of study (advantage to business, engineering, and health). Wage growth for women (negative) and racial minorities (no effect) are also examined.

Wenz and Yu ("Term-Time Employment and the Academic Performance of Undergraduates") present a framework for evaluating undergraduate students' decisions to engage in term-time employment in order to finance higher education. The authors examine the impact of work on academic achievement and find that employment has modest negative effects on student grades. Using a unique custom dataset based on students at a traditional regional state university, Wenz and Yu find that students who work for primarily financial reasons earn lower grades than students who work for career-specific skills but higher grades than those students motivated by a desire for general work experience.

CHAPTER 8

From 'Financial Considerations' to 'Poverty': Towards a Reconceptualisation of the Role of Finances in Higher Education Student Drop out

MIGNONNE BREIER
UNIVERSITY OF CAPE TOWN

While the role of financial considerations in higher education student dropout is being recognized increasingly, the dominant international literature fails to reflect the extent of socio-economic deprivation among students in countries where many people live below the poverty datum line. This article draws on a study of student retention and graduate destination at seven HE institutions in South Africa, focusing on the University of the Western Cape which caters for a large proportion of impoverished students. The study found many students left before completing a qualification because they were too poor to stay. A model of student departure is presented which draws on the very influential work of Vincent Tinto but also allows for greater emphasis than he did on students' ability to pay (real or perceptual) and demarcates the times in the academic calendar when finances present their greatest challenge to retention. The model also invites consideration of the national and international factors which impact on the social/economic/political milieu in which students' persist-or-depart decisions are made.

Introduction

International research on student retention in higher education presents a wide range of reasons why students might leave a higher education institution without completing a qualification and generally argues that students are affected by a combination of factors rather than one factor alone. The literature is vast and this article will not attempt to portray the range but will concentrate instead on the work of Vincent Tinto whose writings on student retention and departure since the 1970s, have acquired 'paradigmatic status' (Braxton et al. 2004). The article provides an outline of Tinto's theories of the role of student finance in higher education attrition before presenting the findings of a South African study which challenges the terminology, and thereby perhaps also the central thrust, of Tinto's approach. The paper ends with alternative models of student departure that show the importance of finances as well as national and international contexts.

Tinto's Theories on Student Finances and Critiques

Tinto is one of the most prolific writers in the field of higher education and credited with bringing theory to the field. In Tinto (1993) he presents a longitudinal model of student dropout (Fig. 8.1) that focuses on the concept of integration. He explains:

> Individual departure from institutions can be viewed as arising out of a longitudinal process of interactions between an individual with given attributes, skills, financial resources, prior educational experiences, and dispositions (intentions and commitments) and other members of the academic and social systems of the institution. The individual's experience in those systems, as indicated by his/her intellectual (academic) and social (personal) integration, continually modifies his or her intentions and commitments.' (Tinto 1993: 114–115).

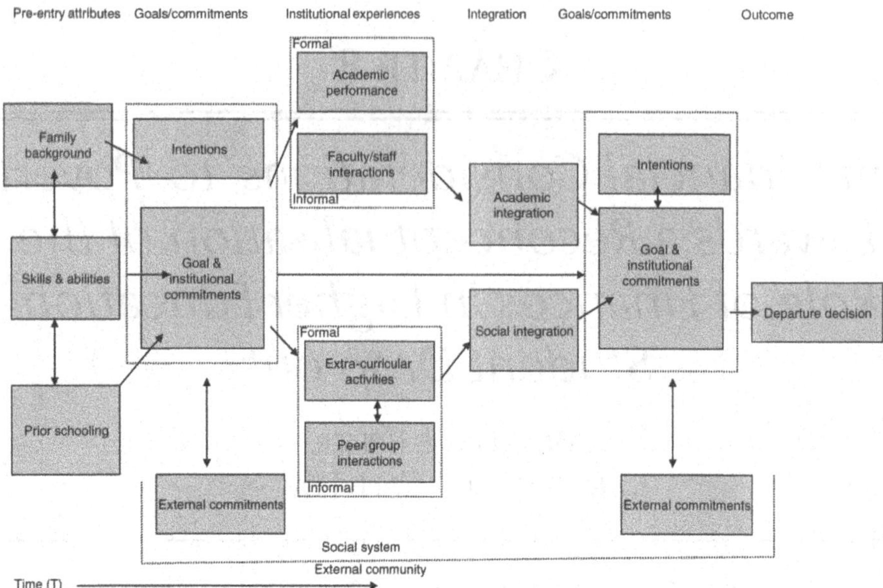

Figure 8.1 Tinto's longitudinal model of student departure.
Source: (Tinto 1993:114).

Tinto's arguments have been criticized for their emphasis on the individual and neglect of external factors including social, political and economic forces and the role of institutions themselves. Koen (2007) notes that many students in South Africa in the 1980s dropped out of university to participate in the political struggle against apartheid. Ben-Tsur (2007) considers the effect of compulsory military service on student retention in Israel. Goldrick-Rab (2006) explores social class differences. Abramson and Jones (2003: 148) point to the importance of institutional culture and urge institutions to 'accept the new realities of growth and diversity' and also recognize that study is only one aspect of a student's life.

Of greater concern, from the point of view of this article, is Tinto's relative lack of emphasis on financial reasons for drop out. Tinto (1993) asserts that 'financial considerations' are 'important to the continued persistence of some students, most notably those from working-class and disadvantaged backgrounds' but 'tend to be of secondary importance to the decisions of most other students' (1993: 88).

He says that financial considerations are felt most keenly at the point where the student is deciding whether to attend, where to attend and whether part or full time. Secondly, 'although students frequently cite finances as reasons for withdrawing, their true reasons often reflect other forces not associated with finances, such as dissatisfaction with the institution.'

> Their citing of financial reasons for leaving is simply another way of stating their view that the benefits of continued attendance do not outweigh the costs of doing so. Conversely, when students are satisfied with their institutional experience, they often are willing to accept considerable economic hardships in order to continue. For them the benefits of attendance more than justify costs. (1993: 88).

Tinto does concede that short-term fluctuations in finances can and do cause a number of students to withdraw from college and financial aid programmes, work study programmes in particular, can in certain situations 'help prevent departure by enabling students to overcome temporary financial difficulties (1993: 179).

Critiques of Tinto's views on finances, suggest that the issue is more important and more complex than he suggests, very context- (country-) specific and affected by national and institutional budgets for student support and perceived as well as actual experiences of financial hardship among students.

St. John et al. (2000) have developed models to explain how finances interact with other factors that influence college persistence. In this view *perceptions of ability to pay* are important influences on choice of college as well as subsequent integration processes.

Yorke (1999) and Thomas (2002) have shown that in the UK changes in student funding have put greater financial pressures and stress on students, particularly those from low-income groups. Other UK studies point to the importance of the student's knowledge of the extent of financial demands of higher education study *before* they enter a programme. Lack of information can cause students both to avoid higher education (Mangan et al. 2010) or to enter higher education without full appreciation of the financial implications (Yorke 1999).

It is also widely recognized, however, that some students do persist and achieve their qualifications despite financial hardship. Thomas (2002: 423) states '. . . many students cope with poverty, high levels of debt and significant burdens of paid work to successfully complete their courses of study'. Thomas attributes this trend to 'institutional habitus', particularly the 'willingness of institutions to embrace and value diversity' (2002: 439).

All the studies quoted above refer to countries that are highly developed and generally prosperous. The question arises whether the same trends apply to developing countries. The following analysis of student drop out in South Africa indicates the extreme importance of financial considerations in such contexts.

Student Drop Out in South Africa

South Africa is regarded as a middle income country in general but it is also one of the most unequal in the world, with a Gini coefficient in some surveys estimated to be as high as 0.72 (Stats SA 2007). There are pockets of extreme wealth and a significant middle class, but the majority of the population is very poor, with the extent of poverty still mirroring the patterns of racial discrimination under apartheid when the National Party government privileged whites and discriminated against Indians/Asians, Coloureds and Africans, in that order of severity.[1] Africans achieved the worst quality and least financed education and were—and still are—the poorest (despite a rapidly growing elite), followed by Coloureds.[2]

Post apartheid policies in all aspects of South African society are geared towards more equitable representation of blacks[3] and higher education is no exception. However, although there have been very large increases in the numbers of blacks attending HE institutions, graduation rates, of Africans and coloureds in particular, remain low. The Department of Education (2005) has estimated that 30% of students drop out in their first year of study and only about one quarter of those who start studying for a 3 year degree in any given year actually achieve the qualification in the specified period.

The study to which this paper refers was conducted by the Human Sciences Research Council (HSRC) in South Africa and aimed to contribute to an understanding of the throughput and drop-out trends. (See Letseka et al. 2009a, for a full report).

Methodology

The HSRC research included a postal questionnaire survey of 20,353 persons from selected fields and at selected institutions who left their institutions in 2002 without achieving a qualification (referred to here as the 'leavers') and 14,195 who graduated in the same year (the 'graduates'): a total of 34,548. The overall response rate was 16%. Of the graduates 2,163 responded (making a response rate of 15%). Of the leavers 3,328 responded (response rate of 16%). The fields included Science, Engineering and Technology (SET), Education (Ed), Humanities (HSS) and Business, Commerce and Management (BCM). The institutions included the practically-oriented technikons, Peninsula Technikon (now Cape Peninsula University of Technology) and Pretoria Technikon (now Tswane University of Technology), as well as the universities, of the Witwatersrand (Wits), Stellenbosch (US), Fort Hare (UFH), North (now University of Limpopo) and Western Cape (UWC).[4] These institutions are also distinguished in the study by their racial categorisation and financial favour or disadvantage under apartheid. Wits, US and Pretoria Tech are regarded as historically white and advantaged institutions (abbreviated as HWI and HAI) and UFH, UN, UWC and Pentech historically black and disadvantaged (HBI/HDI).

In addition to the questionnaire data, the study also used institutional statistics, reports and documents and qualitative data derived from semi-structured interviews with senior members of academic staff and of management at the seven public HEIs.

Reasons for Premature Departure

The questionnaire for leavers asked respondents: 'To what extent did the following factors affect your leaving of the institution?' and then listed 31 possible factors on a Likert scale of 1–5, with 1 signifying 'Not at all' and 5 'To a very large extent'. Respondents were asked to mark one box for each item.

Table 8.1 analyses the three major reasons at each of the seven institutions and shows that financial reasons were prioritized at all the historically black institutions, where respondents were mainly from poor backgrounds with parents/guardians with little formal education.

Academic reasons were only prioritised at Stellenbosch and Wits, both historically white institutions with relatively high admission criteria and (arguably) academic standards. These universities also had higher proportions of respondents from relatively affluent and well-educated homes.[5]

The Case of a Historically Disadvantaged Institution[6]

At the University of the Western Cape it has long been a matter of concern that many students leave the institution without completing their qualifications, a trend which is often attributed to the institution's admission and financial policies. The University was established in 1960 in the heart of apartheid for coloureds only. In the late 1980s it set out to become the 'intellectual home of the left' with a virtually open admissions policy and among the lowest student fees in the country. There was a large influx of African students, mainly from the impoverished Eastern Cape where many had received very poor quality schooling. Enrolments overall increased from a total of 10,661 in 1988 to 13,568 in 1998 while the numbers of African students grew from 1,398 to 6,267 in the same period, and their proportions from 13 to 58% (Cooper and Subotzky 2001). During this period the

TABLE 8.1

Three Major Reasons for Leaving Prematurely in 2002

Factor	Historically Disadvantaged Institutions				Historically Advantaged Institutions		
	Fort Hare	North	UWC	Pentech	Stellenbosch	Witwatersrand	Pretoria
1	Financial (1)	Financial (1)	Financial (1)	Financial (1)	Academic	Academic	Financial (1)
2	Financial (2) Admin	Admin	Academic	Academic	Lost interest	Financial (1)	Academic
3	Career guidance	Financial (2) Academic	Financial (2)	Social	Financial (1)	Admin Lost interest	Financial (2)

Source: Letseka et al. (2009b: 35)

Financial (1) = I did not have funds to pay for my studies; Financial (2) = I could not afford to spend 3 or 4 years on continuous study, so I left, planning to return at a later point; Academic = I was failing some or all of my courses, and realized I was unlikely to pass at the end of the year; Admin = I was frustrated by the way the institution's administration dealt with students; Lost interest = I lost interest in the programme I was studying; Career guidance = The institution did not have adequate career guidance and counseling facilities; Social = I had a very active social life university accrued massive debt as many students were unable to pay fees. It also became clear that many of the students were under-prepared for university study. Koen (2007) asserts that over the period 1993–1999 more than 7,600 students did not complete their qualifications at UWC because they were excluded for financial and academic reasons. About one-third were excluded on academic grounds and the remaining two-thirds, roughly 5,000 students, for not paying their fees. In addition to these 'forced exclusions', many undergraduate and postgraduate students also left voluntarily despite being in good academic standing (2007: 11).

By 2000, student enrolments had dropped again, largely because of the transformation of the historically white Eastern Cape universities which enabled many African students to study closer to home. UWC relaxed its admission polices once again, by admitting students with senior certificate but without exemption under particular conditions (called the 'Senate discretionary' students). By the year 2002, which is the focus of the HSRC study, these students were due to graduate.[7] By this time, however, student numbers were above 10,000 again and growing and the university was tightening its academic criteria again. Higher education policy had come to reflect the growing realization that physical access did not necessarily mean 'epistemological access' (Morrow 1993; UWC 2000). Universities had an obligation to ensure success as well as access. A new funding formula that rewards throughput and completion rather than student numbers per se was on the horizon (it was introduced in 2004.). It was now extremely important for UWC to attract academically able students and ensure they graduate in minimum time to remain a financially viable institution. Despite a number of efforts across the university to ensure academic success and to support financially needy students, student drop out remained a major problem, to the extent that the university management asked the HSRC to include UWC in the study.

Reasons for Departure from UWC

In the year 2002, a total of 10,265 students were studying at UWC for the qualifications targeted in the HSRC study. Of these 1,327 (13%) graduated and 7,113 (69%) continued with their studies in 2003, while 1,825 (18%) dropped out either during or at the end of 2002. The HSRC sent questionnaires to all in these targeted fields who either graduated or left without achieving a qualification. Of the graduates, 246 (19%) responded and of the leavers 257 (14%) responded. The case study also included analysis of institutional reports and documents and interviews with 21 academics and administrators.

The study indicated that nearly a decade after democracy, and despite the establishment of a National Student Financial Aid Scheme, students were still being excluded on financial grounds. Asked if they had been excluded from UWC in or after 2002, 159 respondents (68% of the total) said they had been: 63 (27% of total) for financial reasons; 53 (23%) for financial and academic reasons and 43 (18%) for academic reasons. When these findings were presented to the management of the university, they insisted that the university will not allow any student to leave prematurely for financial reasons if they are in good academic standing. It would find the funds to meet their costs. However, this policy is not publicized lest it will be abused and the study suggested that many students do not make use of it.

When presented with a range of factors which might have contributed to their leaving the university and asked to rate these from 1 ('not at all') to 5 ('to a very large extent'), leaver respondents gave the highest value by far to 'I did not have funds to pay for my studies'. This option yielded a mean score of 3.8 and was rated highest by Africans. Coloureds also indicated they could not afford to pay for their studies, but they also suggested more strongly than any other group, that they planned to return later. Indians rated academic reasons most highly and Whites were most concerned by the way the administration dealt with students. (They gave the same high rating to 'Culturally I did not "fit" at the institution' but this factor was not rated highly by the other groups and is not reflected in Table 8.2 because it achieved a low overall score. Bear in mind that Indians and whites, in particular, are minority groups at UWC and even together formed only a very small percentage of the UWC survey population (9% of graduates and 2% of leavers,) and similar proportions of the survey respondents.

TABLE 8.2

Factors that Contributed to Leaving UWC in 2002, By Order of Importance Within Race

Factor	African	Col	In	White	Aggregated Mean Score
I did not have the funds to pay for my studies	3.9	3.7	2.7	2.5	3.8
I was failing some or all of my courses and realized I was unlikely to pass at the end of the year	2.8	2.7	3.7	1.5	2.8
I could not afford to spend 3 or 4 years on continuous study, so I left, planning to return to my studies at a later point	2.5	3.1	2.7	2.5	2.7
I was frustrated by the way the institution's administration dealt with students	2.5	2.7	3.0	3.0	2.6
I lost interest in the programme I was studying	2.4	2.2	3.3	2.0	2.4

The Views of Academics and Administrators at UWC

While the responses in the survey are obviously perceptions, there was sufficient other evidence in the study to suggest that they were grounded in reality. All the 21 UWC academics and administrators who were interviewed for the Student Pathways Study mentioned poverty as a major reason why students leave UWC prematurely. For some it was the single greatest issue. Administrators pointed out that although many students receive funding from the National Student Financial Aid Scheme (NSFAS), a number of factors make that funding insufficient to cover all their needs. Firstly although NSFAS allocations are announced at the end of the preceding year, the first tranche to institutions is only released on 1 April, which is the beginning of the government's fiscal year. Many institutions, particularly the HBUs, experience cash flow problems in the first quarter of the year and consequently demand an upfront payment from students (DoE 2005). At UWC non-resident students were required to pay R3,000 and resident students R3,500, at the time of the interviews, which equates to the monthly income of the greatest proportion of the leavers' parents/guardians.[8]

Staff in the financial aid office also reported that this payment caused a great deal of distress for some students. Although there was a (NSFAS defined) means test to establish whether a student qualifies for NSFAS funding, there was no test to determine whether a student had the means to pay the upfront amount. Some students genuinely did not have the money to pay even the R580 portion of this amount which was for registration.

A dean quoted examples of excellent matriculants who would not have been able to come to the university and others who were already students and had passed all their courses that would not have been able to return had he (the dean) not been able to obtain for them the R580 fee, through pleading their case to the Student Financial Aid Office.

The second major concern is the amount of the NSFAS loan/bursary itself. Because the demand for financial aid is far greater than the supply, institutions tend to give students less than the full amount they need, so that NSFAS can spread the available support as far as possible. The 90,000 odd students nationally who were receiving NSFAS aid at the time of the survey were being funded at only 75 to 80% of the amount needed, as determined by the means test (Department of Education (DoE) 2005: 29). At UWC, even the fullest loan/bursary was unlikely to cover more than fees, accommodation and food. The extras which a student needs—tampons, toothpaste and other toiletries; photocopying, printing and other study-related expenses; transport etc.—must come from alternative sources of income. Some students are also expected to support other family members. The senior manager who identified 'under preparedness' as one of two major reasons for drop-out, said the anxiety experienced by students who were struggling to sustain themselves from one-month to the next was the other major reason.

Several interviewees spoke of students who were so poor they often went hungry. One said that because of the stigma associated with 'food insecurity' they often tried to conceal this fact. Students who wished to be supportive had to be careful not to offend the dignity of the hungry person when offering to share their food. It was easier for poor students to ask to share other items—toiletries, for example—than to admit they had no food.

Socio-economic Background of Graduates

Although poverty appeared to be a major reason for drop out, the graduates were just as likely to come from poor homes as the leavers. According to the responses, both groups had the same proportion of fathers/male guardians (8%) who were unemployed, while the proportion with mothers or female guardians who were unemployed was only slightly lower among graduates than among leavers (23% compared with 25%). The percentage of leavers' fathers with tertiary education (13%) and of mothers (10%) was almost the same as that of the graduates (13 and 11% respectively). In both groups, 15% of fathers and 13% of mothers had no formal education at all.

Analysis of responses on questions about parental income also showed the graduates had little advantage over the leavers. In both groups a fair proportion of fathers/male guardians (13% for leavers and 11% for graduates) and an even higher proportion of mothers/female guardians (24 and 28% respectively) had no income at all.

In both groups, the most frequent income category was under R3,200 (41% of leavers' fathers and 39% of graduates' fathers, against 53% of leavers' mothers and 45% of graduates' mothers). High proportions of respondents (particularly leavers) did not know their father's income: 25% of leaver respondents compared with 20% of graduates. This finding, combined with the high proportion of leavers who did not know their father's type of employment, indicates a possible absence of a father figure in the homes of the leavers.

Despite largely similar socio-economic backgrounds, there were nonetheless substantial differences in the *current* financial circumstances of leavers and graduates. A greater proportion of leavers than graduates were still relying on their parents for some financial support and leavers were less likely than the graduates to have a bursary or job, part-time or otherwise. (This trend confirms the importance of work-study programmes, which Tinto (1993) also argues.)

It was notable that the leavers tended to have poorer results in the school-leaving 'Senior Certificate' examination, than the graduates. About 61% had entered UWC without 'exemption. This means they had not obtained the combination of subjects and grades normally required for admission to university. Only 39% had attained a Senior Certificate with exemption compared with 62% of the graduates.[9] This finding also confirmed what academics at UWC said in interviews: matric exemption is the best available indicator of future success (second only to a foreign matric). The leavers also had higher failure rates than graduates in the three Senior Certificate subjects which are regarded as important indicators of potential for higher education study (English, Mathematics and Physical Science).

It is likely that there were other less tangible differences. Academics and administrators said some students were just as impoverished as others, but had been brought up in such a way that they were more motivated, resilient and focused.

There was also a question of 'fit' with the institutional and student cultures. UWC has traditionally accommodated a majority of Coloured students with distinct, Afrikaans speaking Cape cultures (although there were higher proportions of Africans in the mid to late nineties.). Administrators tend to be Coloured and academics are more likely to be white or Coloured. African lecturers are few and far between and tend to be from other African countries. In this context it is likely that many students have difficulty integrating into institutional and student cultures, depending on their personal backgrounds. However, the survey showed institutional factors were relatively low on the list of factors for leaving the institution overall. It was one of the two most important reasons for white departure and fairly highly rated by Indians. However, as noted earlier, these groups formed a very small percentage of the survey population and responses and these findings should be viewed with caution.

Another reason for dropout that was mentioned by several of the senior staff members was HIV/AIDS. They spoke of students who had told them they were leaving because their parents had died of HIV/AIDS and their siblings needed their support, or because they were HIV positive themselves and had lost interest in their studies. It is strange, given the very high prevalence of HIV among young adults in South Africa,[10] that very few of the leaver responses indicated that their own ill health, or that of their relatives, had anything to do with their early departure. It is possible that this low level of response arises because the leavers who might report on HIV/AIDS related factors in leaving have no time to respond to surveys. This contrast might also be related to the stigma attached to the disease and would support the experience of the HIV/AIDS programme on campus which has found that even the students attending support groups and receiving assistance from that programme are not prepared to disclose their status, primarily because they fear the information might leak back to their communities. It is also possible that the effects of HIV/AIDS on a student can present themselves most prominently in financial problems. The sparsity of respondents may also have been influenced by the fact that the questionnaire did not mention HIV/AIDS specifically but referred rather to 'ill health'.

Diary

The research indicated that there are certain times of the South African academic year when the potential to drop out is highest. Finances are most critically felt when choosing the institution (UWC's fees remain among the lowest in the country) traveling to university, paying the upfront fee on arrival, half the annual fee by April, and the final fee by the end of the year, to ensure the release of their results.

Academic considerations, which are integrally related to issues of race and poverty in South Africa, are inevitably felt as soon as lectures start with summative effects in June and December.

Cultural factors are also likely to impact from time of arrival at the university and social integration will depend to a large extent on whether—and how soon—the student makes friends. At all stages the student's progress will be affected by his/her health, including nutrition and HIV status.

The following figure provides an overview of most likely points of departure in an academic year, which could be applied to any higher education institution with poor students. The figure shows upward progression towards the goal of completion of a particular year of study, with arrows indicating the potential drop out points.

While Fig. 8.2 provides specific details of the drop out crunch points, Figs. 8.3 and 8.4 present increasingly abstract depictions of the trends. Fig. 8.3 represents the 'diary' of Fig. 8.2 and Fig. 8.4 shows the 'diary' in national and international context.

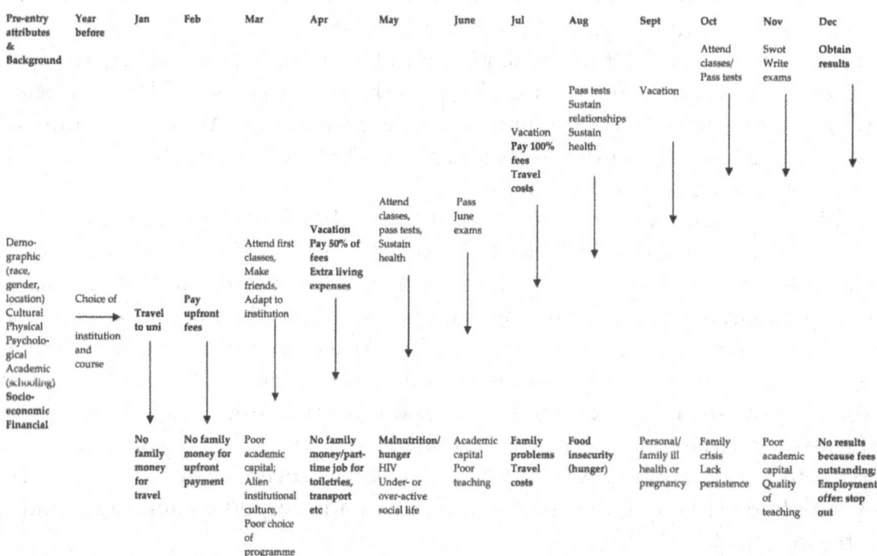

Figure 8.2 A university diary of potential drop out.

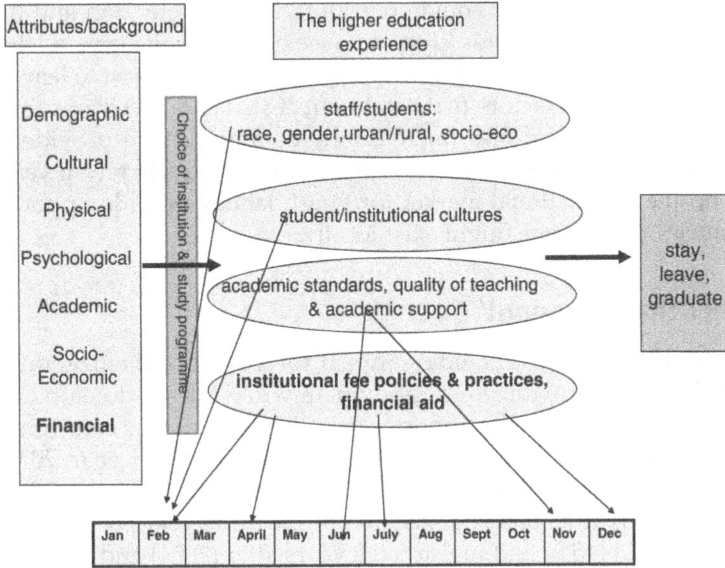

Figure 8.3 Personal and institutional factors affecting premature departure.

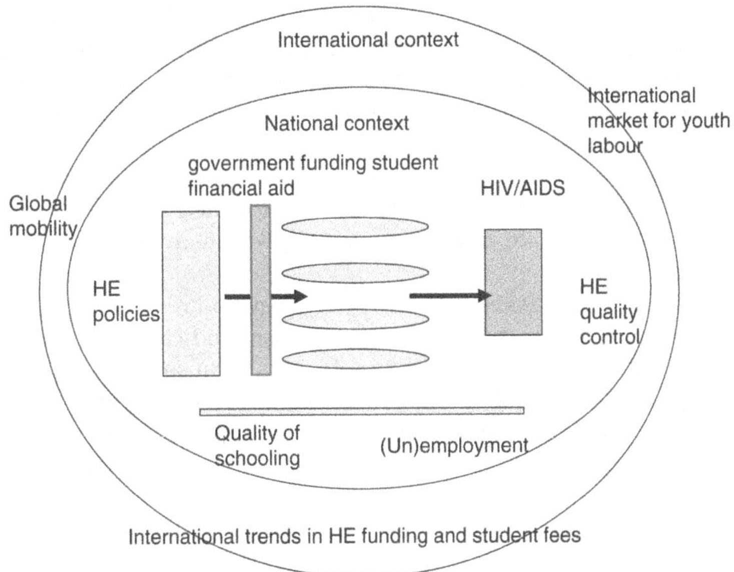

Figure 8.4 Student departure in national and international context.

The models allow for greater emphasis on financial reasons as a cause of departure than is evident in Tinto's model but also allow for many of the factors to which he attributes attrition or retention. The fact that students at UWC from poor backgrounds could be graduates as well as leavers indicates the importance of other factors:, family values, personal attitudes, demographic and cultural "fit" as well as the state of current finances.

While Figs. 8.2 and 8.3 concentrate on possible trends within a particular institution, Fig. 8.4 tries to place those trends within a national and international context. It shows that at national level, the quality of schooling is central to the development of academic capital, HE funding policies and their implementation (including those policies instituted under apartheid) affect the financial standing of particular institutions and consequently their ability to absorb debt or disburse student aid; HE quality control affects the standards of education in HE institutions; while ability of NSFAS to support needy students is dependent, mainly, on government funding and, to a less extent, international donors. Unemployment could contribute to both retention and drop out. The availability of jobs provides opportunities for 'stop out' (see below), while lack of jobs can mean, contradictorily, both the inability to finance one's studies and also little reason to leave.

There are also international factors that might affect students' decisions to stay or leave. International trends in the charging of fees (increasingly common) have provided the milieu within which South African universities have consistently raised their fees in recent years, with impunity.[11] Global mobility and the international market for youth labour provide opportunities for employment in other countries where none might exist locally.

'Stop Out' Rather than 'Dropout'

During interviews at UWC, some academics argued for a reconceptualization of 'dropout' to recognize favourably those who are forced to 'stop out' a while (mostly to earn money) but intend to return (Walters and Koetsier 2006). The importance of this pattern was confirmed in the survey.

Asked whether they intended returning to their studies in a later year, 207 leavers (85% of the 244 respondents who answered this question) said 'yes'. A total of 95 respondents provided a year of registration. Of these, six (6%) had re-registered in the same year,) 33 (35% of the 95) had registered the following year, 43 (45%) had registered 2 years after (2004) and 13 (14%) in 2005.

A total of 105 respondents indicated the institution at which they had re-registered. Of these, 33 (31%) said UWC, 16 (15%) UNISA, 11 (10%) Cape Technikon, 11 (10%) other public universities, seven (7%) other technikons and 27 (26%) 'other private institution'.[12]

Further analysis indicates that students changed their academic focus on re-registering. A total of 101 gave details of the programme for which they had re-registered. Of these 62 (62%) had re-registered for a diploma or certificate and 38 (38%) for a degree. Of these 58% had re-registered for an undergraduate diploma or certificate, 34% for an undergraduate degree, 4% for postgraduate qualifications, 5% for diplomas of unknown status.

Yet, out of 239 leaver respondents who answered the question 'What qualification were you studying towards when you left in/after 2002?', 35% indicated they were studying towards an undergraduate diploma or certificate, 57% for an undergraduate degree and 11% for a postgraduate qualification.

The leaver questionnaire also asked returnees why they had resumed their studies and allowed them to provide more than one response. Their responses indicated the importance of financial factors. Of the 185 ticks, 27% indicated that they returned because funds had been made available to them, either through NSFAS, another financial institution, their relatives or because they had worked and saved. 31% had realized they needed the qualification to become more employable or to earn more; 19% had been persuaded by family or other significant persons to return and 9% were able to do so because the institution's policies admitted them either as mature or Senate Discretionary students, 14% indicated there were other reasons for their return.

Conclusion

One of the most influential and dominant voices in the literature on student attrition is that of Vincent Tinto. This article takes issue with his approach to student finance as a reason for student drop out. It confirms some aspects of his views: that finances are felt most strongly by the lower socio-economic groups; that they influence choice of institution; that sudden unexpected demands can lead to premature departure; and that work study programmes can help poor students. However, the general thrust of his argument—indicated by the relative lack of attention to the topic and the euphemistic terms such as 'financial considerations'—is not appropriate for a developing context where students come from backgrounds of extreme poverty.

The quantitative and qualitative research on which this article is based suggests that finances play a *very important* role for those in the lower socio-economic groups, not only in choice of institution and study programme, but also in leading to premature departure after registration, either because of unexpected financial demands or because the student underestimated the full cost of higher education. In South Africa, the latter is often the case because the government-funded aid scheme funds only partial costs, in an attempt to provide funding to as many needy students as possible. Family finances, which in South Africa are inextricably associated with racial privilege or disadvantage, also determine the type of school which the student was able to attend and the quality of tuition.

Nonetheless the study also indicated that some students from socio-economically disadvantaged backgrounds do succeed in graduating in time. Further qualitative research is necessary to determine reasons for this. The study suggests that social capital and personal habitus, as conceptualized in Bourdieu (1986) and Bourdieu and Passeron(1990) respectively, might be important factors.

Alternative models of student departure are presented which emphasise the importance of finances, while not discounting other psychological and physical factors, and which show the points in a financial year when students are likely to feel greatest pressure to drop out, as well as the potential reasons, and also locates these issues within national and international contexts. Institutions could use such models to customize the manner and timing of their own financial support for needy students.

It is likely that financial considerations are also playing a much more important role in developed countries than before, due to the international credit crunch and changing (increasingly market-oriented) approaches to student funding. Financial considerations in such countries might appear to be insignificant in comparision with those experienced in developing countries. But in a generally affluent context, they might nonetheless still be reasons for dropout.

Acknowledgments

I wish to acknowledge the role of Moeketsi Letseka who co-ordinated the HSRC study and Mariette Visser who managed the data and developed the raw tables on which much of my analysis in this paper is based. I am also grateful to Pieter Le Roux and Tim Dunne for commenting on early drafts of this paper. However, the analysis in this paper, including the narrative, tables and figures, is ultimately my own and I accept sole responsibility for any imperfections or misinterpretations.

Notes

1. The racial terminology in this paper is commonly used in higher education in South Africa to monitor progress towards equity.
2. According to StatsSA (2007), Africans formed 79.0% of the SA population in 2007, Coloureds 9.0%, Indian/Asians 2.6% and whites 9.6%.
3. The term 'black' is used in this paper to signify all groups other than white.
4 Pentech and UWC were established originally for Coloureds only.
5. The HSRC study included an analysis of the socio-economic status of respondents in terms of education and income levels of parents/guardians.
6. See Breier et al. (2007)' and Breier (2009).
7. It is possible that the UWC's dropout rates are better today than they were in 2002 because the university might have more academically able students. However, the cost of living has increased substantially and financial pressures are as likely as ever—or more so—to be reasons for premature departure.
8. Exchange rate at time of the survey (2005): 11.3 ZAR to 1 GBP; 7.8 ZAR to 1 EUR; 6.0 ZAR to 1 USD.
9. In South Africa, a student who attains a 'Senior Certificate' with a 'matric exemption' has achieved the required number and combination of subjects and grades to be admitted to a university.
10. Shisana et al. (2005).
11. See HESA (2008).
12. Percentages do not add to 100% due to rounding.

References

Abramson, M., & Jones, P. (2003). Tinto's model revisited. In L. Thomas, M. Cooper, & J. Quinn (Eds.), *Improving completion rates among disadvantaged students*. Stoke-on-Trent, UK, and Sterling, USA: Trentham Books.

Ben-Tsur, D. (2007). Affairs of state and student retention: An exploratory study of the factors that impact student retention in a politically turbulent region. *British Journal of Sociology of Education*, 28(3), 317–332.

Bourdieu, P. (1986). The forms of capital. In J. Richardson (Ed.), *Handbook of theory and research for the sociology of education*. New York: Greenwood Press.

Bourdieu, P., & Passeron, J.-C. (1990). *Reproduction in education, society and culture*. London: Sage Publications.

Braxton, J. M., Hirschy, A. S., & McClendon, S. A. (2004). *Understanding and reducing college student departure*. AHSE-ERIC higher education report, 30(3). California: Jossey-Bass.

Breier, M. (2009). Dropout or stopout at the University of the Western Cape? In M. Letseka, M. Cosser, M. Breier, & M. Visser (Eds.), *Student retention and graduate destination: Higher education and labour market access and success*. Cape Town: HSRC Press.

Breier, M., Visser, M., & Letseka, M. (2007). *Pathways through higher education to the labour market: factor's affecting student retention, graduation, and destination: Case study report University of the Western Cape*. Unpublished report prepared for the Student Pathways Study of the Human Sciences Research Council, 21 June 2007.

Cooper, D., & Subotzky, G. (2001). *The skewed revolution*. Bellville, South Africa: Education Policy Unit, University of the Western Cape.

Department of Education (DoE). (2005). *Student enrolment planning in Public Higher Education*. Pretoria: Department of Education.

DesJardins, S. L., Ahlburg, D. A., & McCall, B. P. (2006). The effects of interrupted enrollment on graduation from college: Racial, income and ability differences. *Economics of Education Review*, 25(6), 575–590.

Goldrick-Rab, S. (2006). Following their every move: an investigation of social-class differences in college pathways. *Sociology of Education*, 79(1), 61–80.

HESA (Higher Education South Africa) (2008). Tuition Fees: Higher education institutions in South Africa. Report of HESA task team. www.hesa.ac.za.

Koen, C. (2007). *Postgraduate student retention and success: A South African case study*. HSRC Monograph, Cape Town: HSRC Press.

Letseka, M., Cosser, M., Breier, M., & Visser, M. (2009a). *Student retention and graduate destination: Higher education and labour market access and success*. Cape Town: HSRC Press.

Letseka, M., Breier, M., & Visser, M. (2009b). Poverty, race and student achievement in seven higher education institutions. In M. Letseka, M. Cosser, M. Breier, & M. Visser (Eds.), *Student retention and graduate destination: Higher education and labour market access and success*. Cape Town: HSRC Press.

Mangan, J., Hughes, A., & Slack, K., (2010) Student finance, information and decision making. *Higher Education*, doi:10.1007/s10734-010-9309-7....

Morrow, W. (1993). A Picture Holds Us Captive. In S. Pendlebury, L. Hudson, Y. Shalem, & D. Bensusan (Eds.), *Kenton-on-broederstroom 1992 conference proceedings*. Johannesburg: University of the Witwatersrand Education Department.

Shisana, O., Rehle, T., Simbayi, L., Parker, W., Zuma, K., Bhana, A., et al. (2005). *South African national HIV prevalence, HIV incidence, behaviour and communication survey, 2005*. Cape Town: HSRC Press.

St. John, E. P., Cabrera, A. F., Nora, A., & Asker, E. H. (2000). Economic influences on persistence reconsidered. In J. M. Braxton (Ed.), *Reworking the student departure puzzle*. Nashville, US: Vanderbilt University Press.

Statistics South Africa (2007) Community Survey 2007. Revised edition. Statistical Release P0301. 24 October 2007. Pretoria: Statistics South Africa. http://www.statssa.gov.za/community_new/content.asp Accessed 28 February 2010.

Thomas, L. (2002). Student retention in higher education: The role of institutional habitus. *Journal of Education Policy*, 17(4), 423–442.

Tinto, V. (1993). *Leaving college: Rethinking the causes and cures of student attrition* (2nd ed.). Chicago and London: The University of Chicago Press.

University of the Western Cape (2000). Strategic Plan 2001–2005. 21 November 2000. Unpublished document.

Walters, S., & Koetsier, J. (2006). Working adults learning in South African higher education. *Perspectives in Education*, 24(3), 97–108.

Yorke, M. (1999). *Leaving early: Undergraduate non-completion in higher education*. London, UK: Falmer Press.

CHAPTER 9

COLLEGE STUDENT ENGAGEMENT AND EARLY CAREER EARNINGS: DIFFERENCES BY GENDER, RACE/ETHNICITY, AND ACADEMIC PREPARATION

SHOUPING HU AND GREGORY C. WOLNIAK

Background

The quality of undergraduate education in the United States has constantly undergone scrutiny, while heightened skepticism and calls for higher education reform have recently intensified along with dissatisfaction about the current status of higher education (Arum & Roksa, 2011; National Commission on the Future of Higher Education, 2006). Promoting student engagement in educationally purposeful activities has been advocated as an effective way to transform undergraduate education (National Survey of Student Engagement, 2004, 2005). Strong empirical evidence points to the promise of reform strategies centered around student engagement as the higher education literature unequivocally indicates that what matters most in student learning and personal development is what the students do in college (Astin, 1993; National Survey of Student Engagement, 2004, 2005; Pascarella & Terenzini, 1991, 2005). The concept of student engagement has historical roots in Astin's theory of involvement (1999), as well as the concept of "quality of effort" put forth by Pace (1979) and Pascarella (1985). These concepts are theoretically and empirically associated with Chickering and Gamson's (1987) *Seven Principles for Good Practice in Undergraduate Education*, including: (a) student-faculty contact, (b) cooperation among students, (c) active learning, (d) prompt feedback, (e) time on task, (f) communication of high expectations, and (g) respect of diverse talents and ways of learning.

Student engagement is an integral part of a quality education and plays an important role in many desirable college outcomes such as student learning, academic performance, and persistence (Astin, 1993; Hu & Kuh, 2003; Kuh, Cruce, Shoup, Kinzie, & Gonyea, 2008; Pascarella & Terenzini, 1991, 2005). However, little is known about the relationship between student engagement and career or occupational outcomes following college. Given the prominent role of earnings in job satisfaction, socioeconomic status, and individual well-being, as well as evidence suggesting the ability to make more money and get a better job is a priority in students' decisions to attend college (Astin, 1993), the lack of empirical evidence on the economic and career impacts of the college experience presents a void in our understanding of these important relationships.

Recent work by Hu and Wolniak (2010) demonstrated significant relationships between measures of student engagement and labor market earnings following college. In this study, we sought to extend Hu and Wolniak's (2010) earnings model of student engagement by focusing on student sub-populations. Across a vast array of postsecondary outcomes, evidence increasingly points to the fact that the effects of college and models of student development are not equally applicable to all students. Summarizing their extensive review of the college impact literature, Pascarella and Terenzini (2005) pointed to the increasing diversity in the college-going population to encourage greater attention to conditional effects; this approach offers the possibility of uncovering whether "any given college experience may have a different effect on different kinds of students" (p. 626).

It appears that the socioeconomic outcomes of college are highly conditional, while economic and sociological perspectives suggest that academic and social engagement, as well as subsequent labor market earnings, vary by student backgrounds (Knox, Lindsay, & Kolb, 1993; Pascarella & Terenzini, 2005; Thomas, 2003; Tinto, 1975). By focusing on the interactions between academic and social dimensions of student engagement and students' ascribed and achieved characteristics prior to college, we examine whether the economic impacts of college are moderated by (or conditional on) student characteristics at college entry. In the sections below we provide an overview of the theory and existing evidence that inform this study, followed by methods, results, and a discussion of the findings.

Theoretical Perspectives

In order to examine college student engagement in relation to postsecondary outcomes, we draw on economic and sociological perspectives related to human and social capital. These two perspectives are particularly relevant because student engagement in college activities has the feature of engagement in both the academic and social dimensions of campus life (Tinto, 1975, 1993).

Human capital is considered to be a set of skills that individuals acquire through education, training, and other means that improve health, productivity, and therefore labor market earnings (Becker, 1994). In formalizing human capital theory, Becker (1994) applies the assumptions that schooling results in greater earnings and productivity because it provides "knowledge, skills, and a way of analyzing problems" (p. 19), and that individuals respond rationally to expected benefits and costs. Human capital theory therefore lends itself to understanding the earnings effects of postsecondary education by grounding educational experiences in the language of productivity-enhancement and investment returns (Becker, 1994; Paulsen, 2001). Job-related earnings following college provide a signal of the productive capabilities of students once they enter the labor market.

A positive relationship between student engagement during college and subsequent earnings would provide evidence of (a) the economic value tied to specific student behaviors, and (b) a policy rationale for promoting the kinds of educational programs and academic structures that facilitate purposeful involvement among students. Given the evidence suggesting a positive relationship between student engagement and student learning (Carini, Kuh, & Klein, 2006; Hu & Kuh, 2003; Kuh, Cruce, Shoup, Kinzie, & Gonyea, 2008; Pascarella & Terenzini, 1991, 2005), it is reasonable to expect that student engagement could be related to productivity in the labor market and, therefore, earnings. That is, student engagement in college could lead to attaining the kind of "knowledge, skills, and a way of analyzing problems" (Becker, 1994, p. 19) that accompany economic value in the labor market.

In addition to the human capital development that may result from engagement during college, sociological perspectives on student development add to our understanding of the overall impacts of student activities. Defined as social relations and the resources available through social networks (Coleman, 1988; Lin, 1999), social capital is central to understanding the impacts of the student experience and the college environment in relation to a variety of student-centered college outcomes. The extent to which students have access to social capital is largely related to the socioeconomic status of their families and to parent, peer, and friendship networks. Such social ties influence students' educational and career choices, and contribute to their ability to achieve desirable educational outcomes. Similarly, the theory of peer influence suggests that academic outcomes are partially determined by the social environment accompanying the educational process (Hallinan, 1982; Sewell, Haller, & Portes, 1969), Further, models of student socialization suggest that students' values, aspirations, and educational choices are affected by the institutional context and interactions with a variety of different social agents, such as students, faculty, and staff (Weidman, 1989). Student engagement in college therefore has the potential to influence outcomes in the labor market directly through the accumulation of social capital and indirectly through its effects on educational and career decision-making.

Evidence of Engagement's Conditional Effects

The role of background characteristics such as gender, race/ethnicity, and academic achievement are commonly used in studies of status attainment and economic attainment (Coleman, Hoffer, & Kilgore, 1982; Sewell, Haller, & Ohlendorf, 1970). Researchers have also demonstrated that background factors exert strong direct and indirect influences on educational and economic outcomes

(Coleman, Hoffer, & Kilgore, 1982; Hearn, 1988, 1991; Karen, 1991; Sewell, Haller, & Ohlendorf, 1970), and that individual characteristics can influence the interrelationship between inputs and related outcomes.

Economic research has found that the rates of return on education vary significantly for students of different gender, race/ethnicity, and socioeconomic status (Perna, 2005). An earlier study (Thomas, 2000) recommends examining postsecondary earnings premiums by different subpopulations of students. Among college-educated individuals, studies have shown that minority groups earn significantly less than their White counterparts, and this pattern may be worsened by economic characteristics such as the minority representation in a given labor market sector (Tienda & Lii, 1987).

Research on college students has also indicated that the relationship between student experiences and a host of outcomes varies by student backgrounds. In a study on student behavioral outcomes, Nora, Cabrera, Hagedorn, and Pascarella (1996) found that student academic and social experiences in college had different effects on student college outcomes by ethnic and gender groups. Group differences were also identified by Cabrera, Nora, Terenzini, Pascarella, and Hagedorn's (1999) study of student persistence and were further discussed in the work by Rendón, Jalomo, and Nora (2000).

Other college impact studies have identified conditional effects based on students' demographic, socioeconomic, and academic backgrounds. For example, Sax, Bryant, and Harper (2005) found that student-faculty interactions are related to a wide range of college outcomes such as GPA and satisfaction but that men and women report different results. Kim and Sax (2009) further found different effects of student-faculty interaction on a set of college outcomes based on student race/ethnicity, social class, and first-generation status. Carini, Kuh, and Klein (2006) found that students with the lowest SAT scores benefited more from student engagement than those with highest SAT scores; they claim that this finding somewhat "dovetails with some recent research" (p. 23), while cautioning that measurement issues in survey research could have contributed to their findings. In a study examining the relationship between student engagement and success in college, Kuh et al. (2008) found that student engagement in educationally purposeful activities can benefit all students but tend to carry greater benefit for low-ability students and students of color.

Existing theory and empirical evidence suggest that gender, race/ethnicity, and academic preparation play a substantial role in understanding the effects of student engagement on many important college outcomes, and researchers have encouraged increased analysis of gender and racial/ethnic-related conditional effects across many types of student-centered college outcomes (Pascarella & Terenzini, 2005; Reason, Terenzini, & Domingo, 2006). Building on past evidence and drawing on perspectives based on human capital and social capital, we hypothesize that the influence which student engagement exerts on professional and career outcomes is moderated by ascribed and achieved characteristics at college entry.

Purpose and Research Question

The purpose of this study is to examine whether student background characteristics moderate the relationship between student engagement in college activities and labor market earnings in the years immediately following college. Building on past research and extending Hu and Wolniak's (2010) earnings model of student engagement, we focus on student sub-populations to examine if the early career economic impacts of student engagement are conditional rather than general.

The research question guiding this study is: Are the relationships between measures of student engagement and earnings moderated by students' gender, race/ethnicity, and academic preparation?

Method

Data

To address our research question, we sought data containing information on college student engagement and post-college labor market earnings, and we identified data fitting this unique criterion based on the longitudinal surveys of the 2001 cohort of applicants to the Gates Millennium Scholars (GMS) program. The longitudinal and tracking component of the GMS project was designed and conducted by NORC at the University of Chicago with support from the Bill & Melinda Gates Foundation (Lodato Nichols, Zimowski, Lodato, & Ghadialy, 2004).

NORC administered three waves of surveys to the 2001 GMS cohort, comprised of freshmen entering college in the 2001–2002 academic year. The initial data were collected through a base-year survey focused on student backgrounds and college choices. The first follow-up survey, conducted in 2004, gathered information on a wide range of student experiences during college. The final wave of data was gathered in 2006 with a second followup survey to collect information on several facets of post-college outcomes roughly five years after the GMS applicants had completed high school. The information on student engagement in college activities that we examine was collected as part of the first follow-up survey, and information on individual earnings originated from the second follow-up survey.

Applying the same standards and survey procedures used in the national surveys conducted by the National Center of Educational Statistics (NCES), NORC surveyed all GMS recipients and representative samples of nonrecipients. The general patterns showed that female students had higher response rates than their male counterparts, and that Asian Americans had the highest response rates, while American Indians had the lowest (NORC, 2003, 2006). Response rates for all waves were above 50%, and NORC derived weighting strategies to compensate for survey nonresponse and study attrition that adjusted for differences between the survey respondents and the overall population of 2001 GMS applicants (Kuo et al., 2006; NORC, 2003, 2006).

The analytic sample for our study included students who had graduated from college at the time of the second follow-up survey, mirroring other studies of labor market earnings (e.g., Thomas, 2000, 2003). We used the longitudinal panel weights for all analyses because we drew the variables in the models from each of the three survey waves. The total sample consisted of 1,278 respondents, including GMS scholarship award recipients and nonrecipients. The sample reflects the full population of GMS scholars and nonrecipients in the 2001 cohort in terms of gender and racial/ethnic compositions (Kuo et al., 2006; NORC, 2003, 2006).

Altogether, the sample was predominately female (74% female, 26% male) and was distributed across four racial/ethnic minority groups, including African Americans (37%), Hispanic Americans (25%), Asian/Pacific Islanders (30%), and American Indian/Alaskan Natives (8%). Among all the students, 15% were in the low-SAT/ACT group, 34% high-SAT/ACT group, and 51% middle-range SAT/ACT group. Students in the middle-range group had SAT scores of 990–1,230, and students in the low- and high- SAT/ACT groups had scores of below 990 and above 1,230 respectively.

The NORC data set for the GMS program is a uniquely constructed and rich source of information enabling the examination of student engagement in college activities in relation to early career earnings among students of different gender, race/ethnicity, and academic preparation. While our analyses were designed to address the research question centered on the relationships between student engagement in college activities, early career labor market earnings, and the moderating effect of student background characteristics, it is important to note that the focus of this study was not to evaluate the GMS program and our results should not be interpreted as an indication of GMS program effects.

Variables

The dependent variable was the natural log of annual earnings as reported by college graduates. Annual earnings were collected from survey questions asking non-enrolled college graduates to indicate the amount of income earned at their current job as well as the job's pay scale (e.g., annually, monthly, weekly, etc.), which we then converted to an annual basis for comparability.

Independent variables included an indicator of GMS scholarship award status (recipient = 1, nonrecipient applicant = 0) to control for the potential influence of GMS program selection on student earnings. Based on the literature of the impact of college on students' labor market outcomes (Pascarella & Terenzini, 1991, 2005) and Hu and Wolniak's (2010) recent study, we included four groups of variables in the analytic models to account for the influence of student backgrounds, institutional characteristics, major fields, and student engagement. The description and coding strategy for all variables are presented in Table 9.1, and we analyzed the overall sample according to the following student characteristics: gender (female as the reference group), race/ethnicity (Asian Americans as the reference group), SAT/ACT scores (middle-SAT/ACT as the reference

TABLE 9.1

Description and Coding of Variables

Variables	Description and Coding
Log of annual income	Natural log of graduates' annual income five years after high school graduation.
GMS recipients	Recipient of GMS scholarship (Yes = 1, No = 0)
Male	A dummy variable (Yes = 1, No = 0)
African American	A dummy variable (Yes = 1, No = 0)
American Indian	A dummy variable (Yes = 1, No = 0)
Hispanic American	A dummy variable (Yes = 1, No = 0)
Asian American	Reference group
Parental education of bachelor or above	A dummy variable (Yes = 1, No = 0)
Low-SAT/ACT	A dummy variable (Yes = 1, No = 0)
Middle-SAT/ACT	Reference group
High-SAT/ACT	A dummy variable (Yes = 1, No = 0)
Number of AP exams	The number of AP exams students have taken: 0 (none), 1 (one), 2 (two), 3 (three), and 4 (four and more)
Low selectivity	A dummy variable (Yes = 1, No = 0); Selectivity no higher than 2 on *Barron's* (2001)
Middle selectivity	Reference group; Selectivity at 3 or 4 on *Barron's* (2001)
High selectivity	A dummy variable (Yes = 1, No = 0); Selectivity higher than 4 on *Barron's* (2001)
Public institution	A dummy variable (Yes = 1, No = 0)
STEM major[a]	A dummy variable (Yes = 1, No = 0)
Academic engagement scale	Summation of response ranging from 1 (less than once a month) to 6 (four or more times a week) on these items: (1) Work with other students on school work outside of class (2) Discuss ideas from your readings or classes with students outside of class (3) Discuss ideas from your readings or classes with faculty outside of class (4) Work harder than you thought to meet an instructor's expectations
Social engagement scale	Summation of responses ranging from 1 (never) to 5 (very often) on these items: (1) Participate in events sponsored by a fraternity or sorority (2) Participate in residence hall activities (3) Participate in events or activities sponsored by groups reflecting your own cultural heritage (4) Participate in community service activities

Note: [a]STEM major fields include biology, engineering, computer science, science, and math. Non-STEM major fields include social sciences, humanities, education, professional, and others.

group), parental educational level, and the number of Advanced Placement (AP) exams students have taken.

The full analytic model included a host of other variables shown in the literature to be important for understanding college impacts (Pascarella & Terenzini, 2005). Concerning the institutions student attended, we included measures of institutional control (private as the reference group) and selectivity (based on *Barron's Profile of American Colleges*, 2001) converted into three categories (low selectivity for a Barron's rating of 1 or 2, middle selectivity for ratings of 3 or 4, and high selectivity for ratings of 5 or 6; middle selectivity was the reference group).

The variables indicating major fields of study were biology, engineering, computer science, math, and science fields, grouped into a single category of STEM fields. In addition, students in social science, humanities, education, and professional fields were classified as non-STEM students (reference group). We used the variables described here mainly as control variables so that the relationship between student engagement and early career earnings could be reliably estimated without the confounding influence of college major.

We included eight student engagement measures in the analysis representing two engagement scales resulting from factor analysis (Table 9.2). The wording of the engagement measures was similar, but not identical, to that in the NSSE survey (National Survey of Student Engagement, 2004, 2005), resulting in a four-item scale measuring student academic engagement, with survey response options ranging from 1 (less than once a month) to 6 (four or more times a week). The four academic engagement items included: (a) Work with other students on school work outside of class; (b) Discuss ideas from your readings or classes with students outside of class; (c) Discuss ideas from your readings or classes with faculty outside of class; and (d) Work harder than you thought to meet an instructor's expectations.

The additional four-item scale constructed to measure student social/community engagement contained response options ranging from 1 (never) to 5 (very often), and included: (a) Participate in events sponsored by a fraternity or sorority, (b) Participate in residence hall activities, (c) Participate in events or activities sponsored by groups reflecting your own cultural heritage, and (d) Participate in community service activities. Alpha reliabilities ranged from .75 for academic engagement scale to .78 for social engagement scale, indicating acceptable psychometric property of scale reliability.

TABLE 9.2

Factor Loadings and Reliability for Scaled Measures of Engagement

	Factor Loading	Reliability (Alpha)
Academic Engagement		0.75
Work with other students on school work outside of class	0.779	
Discuss ideas from readings or classes with students outside of class	0.814	
Discuss ideas from readings or classes with faculty outside of class	0.767	
Work harder than thought to meet an instructor's expectations	0.549	
Social Engagement		0.78
Participate in events sponsored by a fraternity or sorority	0.627	
Participate in residence hall activities	0.632	
Participate in events by groups reflecting own cultural heritage	0.748	
Participate in community service activities	0.753	

Analysis

Using multiple regression techniques, our analysis consisted of two stages that addressed whether the effects of student engagement on early career earnings are conditional on selected student characteristics. Across all analyses, we applied a variation on the standard log-linear Mincerian (Mincer, 1974) earnings function which corrects for positively skewed earnings distributions and allows unstandardized regression coefficients to approximate percent of differences, or proportional changes, in earnings due to incremental changes in predictor variables (Björklund & Kjellström, 2002; Rosenfeld & Kalleberg, 1990).

Our first analytic stage was a preliminary examination of whether annual labor market earnings were influenced by interactions between levels of engagement (academic and social) and gender, racial/ethnic minority group, and academic preparation (based on SAT/ACT scores). In this step, we regressed the natural log of annual earnings on student background characteristics, major fields, institutional characteristics, and scaled engagement measures, followed by interaction (cross-product) terms. Following Pedhauzer's (1982) well-established approach, if the addition of an interaction term simultaneously improved model fit (a statistically significant increase in R^2) while also having a significant net effect, we then moved on to the second analytic stage in which we disaggregated our sample by gender, race/ethnicity, and level of precollege academic preparation. We then used disaggregated subpopulations to estimate earnings models for different groups. When one of the background variables was used to disaggregate the sample, all other measures of student characteristics remained in the model as control variables.

It is worth noting that the results from the use of interaction (cross-product) terms are informative on what variables significantly moderate the relationship between student engagement and early career earnings, while the findings from the disaggregated sample can tell whether scaled student engagement measures are significantly related to earnings for different student subpopulations. Together, these analyses illustrate a more comprehensive picture about the relative role of engagement measures (from the general model with interaction terms) and direct contributions of such engagement on early career earnings across different populations (from the conditional model).

Results

We began our analysis by examining the mean values of scaled measures of academic and social engagement, as well as annual income across the overall analytic sample (N = 1,278) by gender, race/ethnicity, and categories of precollege academic preparation. (Additional descriptive statistics appear in the Appendix.) Results from this descriptive analysis are shown in Table 9.3, indicating several important trends to consider when interpreting the multivariate results. In particular, we identified statistically significant gender differences in the mean values of academic engagement, social engagement, and annual income. Compared to their female counterparts, males were, on average, more engaged academically and enjoyed higher annual earnings in the labor market ($31,101 vs. $25,822) but were less socially engaged.

In terms of racial/ethnic minority group, we found statistically significant differences in average levels of both academic and social engagement, while annual income did not differ significantly by racial/ethnic groups. Across all racial/ethnic minority groups, Hispanics reported the highest average levels of engagement in academic activities, and African Americans reported the highest levels of social engagement. A pattern that prompts concern emerged among American Indians in our sample who showed low levels of both academic and social engagement. With respect to academic preparation, there were significant differences in social engagement and annual income, but not in academic engagement. Interestingly, students in the high-SAT/ACT group had the lowest levels of engagement in social activities and students in the low-SAT/ACT group had the lowest early career earnings ($23,178 vs. $28,367 for the middle-SAT/ACT group and $27,917 for the high-SAT/ACT group).

Building on the examination of group means, our first stage of analysis involved running multiple regressions with interaction (cross-product) terms to establish evidence of group differences

TABLE 9.3

The Scaled Measures of Engagement and Early Career Annual Earnings

	N	Academic Engagement		Social Engagement		Log Earnings ($\$_{2006}$)	
	(%)	Mean	S.D.	Mean	S.D.	Mean	S.D.
Full Sample	1,278 (100%)	15.475	4.524	11.008	3.639	10.207 ($27,092)	0.608
Gender							
Male	331 (25.9%)	16.882	3.921	10.564	2.814	10.345 ($31,101)	0.615
Female	947 (74.1%)	14.983	4.618	11.164	3.876	10.159 ($25,822)	0.599
Sig		***		***		***	
Race/Ethnicity							
African American	478 (37.4%)	15.492	4.802	11.896	3.575	10.195 ($26,769)	0.527
American Indian	100 (7.8%)	14.163	4.623	8.862	2.403	10.108 ($24,538)	0.672
Hispanic	324 (25.4%)	15.782	4.420	10.890	3.680	10.181 ($26,396)	0.529
Asian American	376 (29.4%)	15.538	4.166	10.555	3.633	10.270 ($28,853)	0.734
Sig.		*		***			
Academic Preparation							
Low SAT/ACT	263 (20.6%)	15.735	4.433	11.504	4.535	10.051 ($23,178)	0.404
Middle SAT/ACT	652 (51.0%)	15.438	4.721	11.206	3.413	10.253 ($28,367)	0.690
High SAT/ACT	363 (28.4%)	15.352	4.222	10.294	3.180	10.237 ($27,917)	0.555
Sig.				***		***	

Note: Statistical significance of group mean differences: $^*p < 0.05$, $^{**}p < 0.01$, $^{***}p < 0.001$.

in the relationship between measures of engagement and log annual earnings. The results from this analytic stage indicate that the inclusion of interaction terms significantly improved the variance explained in the regression model and that several interaction terms were statistically significant. Specifically, gender, race/ethnicity, and academic preparation significantly moderated the relationship between student engagement and early career earnings (Baron & Kenny, 1986). These results provided the empirical basis for disaggregating the sample by gender, racial/ethnic minority group, and precollege levels of academic preparation.

Running separate multiple regression models on disaggregated samples based on students' gender, race/ethnicity, and academic preparation yielded evidence that academic engagement had a positive net effect on early career earnings among males, but no net effect among females. (See Table 9.4.) Social engagement positively influenced subsequent labor market earnings for females but had no discernable effect for males in the presence of the model's control variables. This finding points to existing gender differences in the impact of academic and social engagement on early

TABLE 9.4

Total and Conditional Model Estimates of the Relationship between Engagement and Annual Earnings ($\log_{\$2006}$)

Total and Conditional Models	Model R^2	Estimated Effect of Academic Engagement			Estimated Effect of Social Engagement		
		B	Beta	Sig	B	Beta	Sig
Total Sample Population (N = 1,278)	0.094***	0.005	0.036		0.019	0.111	***
Gender Conditional Models							
Female (n = 947)	0.072***	–0.002	–0.016		0.024	0.153	***
Male (n = 331)	0.271***	0.048	0.307	***##	–0.025	–0.113	###
Race/Ethnicity Conditional Models							
African American (n = 475)	0.222***	0.011	0.098		0.012	0.096	*†
American Indian (n = 100)	0.591***	0.079	0.544	***†	–0.172	–0.616	***†††
Hispanic (n = 324)	0.212***	0.024	0.203	***	0.007	0.052	†
Asian American (n = 376)	0.176***	0.012	0.068		0.086	0.424	***
SAT/ACT Conditional Models							
Low (n = 263)	0.270***	–0.039	–0.427	***^^^	–0.004	–0.050	
Middle (n = 652)	0.114***	0.025	0.170	***	0.019	0.096	*
High (n = 363)	0.200***	0.004	0.028	^	0.019	0.107	*

Note: In addition to the academic and social engagement scales, the regression models were specified to contain the variables shown in Table 9.1. *$p < 0.05$, **$p < 0.01$, ***$p < 0.001$

Estimated effect is significantly different from females, # $p < 0.05$, ## $p < 0.01$, ### $p < 0.001$.

† Estimated effect is significantly different from Asian Americans, † $p < 0.05$, †† $p < 0.01$, ††† $p < 0.001$.

^ Estimated effect is significantly different from the middle SAT/ACT achievers, ^ $p < 0.05$, ^^ $p < 0.01$, ^^^ $p < 0.001$.

career earnings, where academic engagement appears to have greater explanatory power among men and social engagement has greater explanatory power among women.

The results of examining disaggregated samples based on racial/ethnic minority groups show that academic engagement has a positive and statistically significant impact on earnings among American Indian and Hispanic students, but no net effect among African Americans or Asian Americans. Social engagement had a positive and significant impact on earnings among African American and Asian American students. Alternatively, all other factors being equal, American Indian students who were more socially engaged during college experienced lower annual earnings once they were in the labor market, such that social engagement had a negative effect on earnings among American Indians. Academic engagement had a significant influence on the earnings of American Indian students, but not for their Asian American or African American counterparts. Social engagement had a positive role in determining early career earnings among African American and an even more pronounced positive influence among Asian Americans.

Focusing on the models run on samples disaggregated by precollege academic preparation, we found that academic engagement and social engagement were both positive predictors of early career earnings for students in the middle-SAT/ACT group, while social engagement had a positive influence on earnings among the most academically prepared students (e.g., those in the high-SAT/ACT group). Interestingly, after controlling for all the other variables in the model, academic engagement was significantly and negatively associated with early career earnings for the least academically prepared students (e.g., the low-SAT/ACT group). Thus, it appears that academic engagement has a negative influence on earnings among the low-SAT/ACT group, a positive influence among middle-SAT/ACT scorers, and an insignificant influence among students who achieved the highest SAT/ACT scores. Social engagement did not have a substantially different role for students in three groups but was statistically significant for students in high-SAT/ACT group.

Limitations

There are four limitations in this study. First, because the outcome in this study is early career earnings, results may differ when considering longer-term earnings; subsequent follow-up surveys by the Gates Foundation could facilitate examination of longer-term socio-economic outcomes.

Second, the data did not contain sufficient information to differentiate the employment type of college graduates, which can be an important indicator of career attainment and earnings for college graduates.

Third, even though we included a number of institution-level variables (e.g., institutional selectivity, control, etc.) as covariates in our multivariate models, it is possible that additional institutional characteristics are confounding the results and could be added to the analysis.

Finally, earnings models and labor market studies suggest controlling for local labor market conditions based on geographic regions and occupations. While we recognize the importance of such measures in modeling earnings, our interest in this study was mainly on the effects of engagement on early career earnings. To examine the overall influences of student engagement on early career earnings while maintaining the parsimony of our models, we decided not to include additional state or regional variables in our analyses. When interpreting the results of our analyses, it is important to consider that student engagement in college may have influenced students' occupational choices and in turn affect their earning power in the labor market.

It is also worthwhile to consider the generalizability of findings from this study to the broad higher education sector. The GMS scholars are a group of high-achieving low-income minority students selected according to the criteria determined by the Gates Foundation, and the nonrecipients were also applicants to the GMS programs with comparable qualifications. Scholars and nonrecipient applicants are therefore different from the general college student population. However, the racial/ethnic composition of our sample approximately reflects the national population of students of color who graduated from four-year institutions within a six-year time frame. Based on the national composition of undergraduates who enrolled in a four-year institution and who graduated within six years of entering college across all racial/ethnic groups, 57% were female and 43% were male. Among non-White graduates, 36% were classified as Black non-Hispanic, 29% Hispanic, 34% Asian or Pacific Islander, and 1% American Indian or Alaska Native. Thus, while it is important to recognize that the analytic sample used in this study is disproportionally female in comparison to the broader postsecondary system, the racial/ethnic make-up mirrors the national composition of college graduates (IPEDS, 2011). We hope this study can start a conversation on the long-term effects of the college experience and that more datasets containing rich information on student engagement and labor market outcomes will emerge to further strengthen inquiry in this direction.

Conclusions and Implications

The results from this study show that student academic and social engagement play distinct roles in determining the early career earnings that are conditional on students' gender, race/ethnicity, and precollege academic preparation. At least two conclusions stem from these findings.

First, it appears that the effects of student engagement on earnings in the early stages of students' careers depend on the nature or type of engagement in which students participate. In other words, engagement in the form of academic activities influences earnings differently than engagement in social activities. Researchers have long conceptualized that students in college must navigate both the academic and social systems in order to achieve successful educational outcomes (Tinto, 1993). Our findings substantiate the distinctive role of student engagement across both academic and social systems as reflected in the influence that both types of activities exert on earnings in the years immediately following college. It is therefore critical to differentiate academic engagement and social engagement when explaining career and labor market outcomes.

Second, the effects of academic engagement and social engagement vary by students' gender, race/ethnicity, and academic preparations. Given the ever-growing body of evidence showing that college impact models differ across a range of individual background characteristics (Pascarella & Terenzini, 2001, 2005), our findings add support for examining conditional models when explaining post-college outcomes. In particular, our findings indicate that the earnings effects of engagement are conditional on gender, such that men disproportionately experience an earnings benefit from being academically engaged during college while women uniquely benefit from social engagement during college.

Among students with lower levels of academic preparation, engagement during college appears to have little influence on early career earnings. This finding marks a dramatic deviation from past research using non-labor market outcomes (Carini, Kuh, & Klein, 2006; Kuh et al, 2009), where students with the lowest SAT scores were found to benefit more from student engagement than those with higher SAT scores. As the researchers acknowledged (Carini, Kuh, & Klein, 2006), it may be that a ceiling effect confounded previous studies based on student GPAs or self-reported learning outcomes, whereas earnings in labor market do not have that limitation. Nevertheless, this is an interesting contrast that warrants recognition and further investigation.

In summary, by focusing on differences in students' background characteristics, our study adds to the field's understanding of the influence that academic engagement and social engagement have on early career earnings. As past studies have demonstrated (Cabrera, Nora, Terenzini, Pascarella, & Hagedorn, 1999; Nora, Cabrera, Hagedorn, & Pascarella, 1996; Pascarella & Terenzini, 2005; Reason, Terenzini, & Domingo, 2006), characteristics such as gender, race/ethnicity, and other ascribed and achieved qualities can moderate the impacts of college, and the effects of college experiences are often conditional rather than general. It is increasingly important for educational policy and practice to take into consideration the diversity of today's college students so that programs and interventions may be designed in a manner that may translate desirable program effects to students of different backgrounds. It appears that this concept holds true for labor market outcomes in the years immediately following college. As researchers put forth more efforts toward understanding the economic implications of student engagement (Hu & Wolniak, 2010), it is increasingly important to consider the extent to which student engagement is conditional on specific student characteristics as a way to understand how distinct facets of the college experience may serve to compensate for, or possibly reinforce, precollege differences. The kinds of conditional effects uncovered in this study may contribute to an improved understanding of student engagement from both human capital and social capital perspectives.

Students identify the ability to make more money and the ability to get a better job as the two most important issues in their decision to enter college (Astin, 1993), and it is essential to recognize that labor market earnings provide a signal of occupational skill development. However, earnings are only one of many desirable college outcomes that students and the society as a whole are concerned about. We should therefore also consider the role of student academic and social engagement on other desirable outcomes when shaping educational policy and practice. With future studies, we encourage scholars to consider the underlying mechanisms by which student engagement may influence the formation of career dispositions, occupational preferences, job searching, and vocational decision-making.

Implications for future research include building on our findings by examining how academic and social dimensions of student engagement may contribute to the accumulation of human capital and social capital across the broad college-going population and how students from different backgrounds use such forms of capital when making career decisions. For instance, our findings suggest that American Indian students who are more engaged in social activities tend to earn less in the labor market after college graduation. It is possible that such students who are more socially engaged on campus are more committed to social issues and thus choose careers with more service orientation but lower financial returns. While our data did not support an exploration of this possibility, it is a topic worthy of further investigation.

Concerns over the quality of undergraduate education occupy a prominent role in the current educational and political dialogue, and emerging research empirically questions the amount of learning that is taking place on campuses nationwide (Arum & Roksa, 2011; Pascarella, Blaich, Martin, & Hanson, 2011). Together these trends are fueling calls for accountability in higher education and demanding that our colleges and universities provide all students with a quality education that translates into productive careers and lasting professional development.

Labor market earning is one measure of occupational productivity and economic success, and our findings contribute new evidence on the broad value of college student engagement across diverse student populations. The relationships between student engagement and early career earnings that we have demonstrated among students of color—and the implications these findings have for research, policy, and practice—may contribute to the development of social theories that explain racial/ethnic differences. Ultimately, this study provides new evidence to improve our broad understanding of how the academic and social engagement of students of color translates into economic success once they enter the labor market. It may also contribute to the dialogue surrounding the broad value of the college student experience.

APPENDIX

Sample Composition by Gender, Race/Ethnicity, and Academic Preparation

Variables	Full Sample	Percent Gender		Percent Race/Ethnicity				Percent Academic Preparation		
		Men	Women	African American	American Indian	Hispanic	Asian American	Low	Middle	High
GMS Recipients	25.2%	27.9%	24.3%	21.3%	57.3%	33.3%	14.8%	24.3%	21.9%	31.8%
Male (female = 0)	25.9%	100.0%	0.0%	15.2%	28.9%	33.7%	32.0%	12.0%	26.7%	34.6%
African American	37.4%	21.9%	42.8%	100.0%	0.0%	0.0%	0.0%	42.3%	29.1%	12.3%
American Indian	7.8%	8.8%	7.5%	0.0%	100.0%	0.0%	0.0%	13.4%	8.1%	3.3%
Hispanic	25.3%	33.0%	22.7%	0.0%	0.0%	100.0%	0.0%	23.6%	24.8%	27.5%
Asian American	29.5%	36.3%	44.4%	0.0%	0.0%	0.0%	100.0%	20.7%	38.0%	56.9%
Parental education of bachelor or above	31.5%	27.4%	32.9%	31.4%	46.4%	22.7%	35.3%	32.6%	27.6%	37.8%
Low-SAT/ACT	20.6%	9.5%	24.5%	23.7%	35.1%	19.2%	14.0%	100.0%	0.0%	0.0%
Middle-SAT/ACT	51.0%	52.6%	50.4%	66.9%	52.9%	49.9%	31.2%	0.0%	100.0%	0.0%
High-SAT/ACT	28.4%	37.9%	25.1%	9.4%	12.0%	30.9%	54.8%	0.0%	0.0%	100.0%
Low selectivity	10.5%	11.7%	10.1%	14.8%	13.3%	10.0%	4.8%	28.2%	7.8%	2.5%
Middle selectivity	45.5%	43.6%	46.1%	57.3%	58.4%	40.9%	30.9%	61.7%	54.3%	17.9%
High selectivity	44.0%	44.7%	43.8%	27.9%	28.3%	49.1%	64.3%	10.1%	37.9%	79.6%
Public institution (private institution = 0)	56.9%	65.7%	53.4%	57.1%	67.8%	48.9%	60.5%	76.9%	54.8%	45.9%
STEM major (non-STEM = 0)	37.3%	49.4%	33.0%	39.5%	22.5%	26.9%	47.3%	37.1%	36.0%	39.7%
Total	100.0% (*N*=1,278)	25.9% (*n*=331)	74.1% (*n*=947)	37.4% (*n*=478)	7.8% (*n*=100)	25.4% (*n*=324)	29.4% (*n*=376)	20.6% (*n*=263)	51.0% (*n*=652)	28.4% (*n*=363)

References

Arum, R., & Roksa, J. (2011). *Academically adrift: Limited learning on college campuses*. Chicago: University of Chicago Press.

Astin, A. W. (1993). *What matters in college: Four critical years revisited*. San Francisco: Jossey-Bass.

Astin, A. W. (1999). Student involvement: A developmental theory for higher education. *Journal of College Student Development*, 40, 518–529.

Baron, R., & Kenny, D. (1986). The moderator-mediator distinction in social psychological research: Conceptual, strategic, and statistical considerations. *Journal of Personality and Social Psychology*, 51, 1173–1182.

Barron's Profiles of American Colleges. (2001). Hauppage, NY: Barron's Educational Series.

Becker, G. S. (1994). *Human capital: A theoretical and empirical analysis with special reference to education* (3rd ed.). Chicago: University of Chicago Press.

Björklund, A., & Kjellström, C. (2002). Estimating the return to investments in education: How useful is the standard Mincerian equation? *Economics of Education Review*, 21, 195–210.

Cabrera, A. F., Nora, A., Terenzini, P. T., Pascarella, E. T., & Hagedorn, L. S. (1999). Campus racial climates and the adjustment of students to college: A comparison between White students and African American students. *Journal of Higher Education*, 70, 134–160.

Carini, R. M., Kuh, G. D., & Klein, S. P. (2006). Student engagement and student learning: Testing the linkages. *Research in Higher Education*, 47, 1–32.

Chickering, A. W., & Gamson, Z. (1987). Seven principles of good practice in undergraduate education. *American Association of Higher Education Bulletin*, 39, 3–7.

Coleman, J. (1988). Social capital in the creation of human capital. *American Journal of Sociology*, 94, S95–S120.

Coleman, J., Hoffer, T., & Kilgore, S. (1982). *High school achievement: Catholic, public, and private schools compared*. New York: Basic Books.

Hallinan, M. T. (1982). The peer influence process. *Studies in Educational Evaluation*, 7, 285–306.

Hearn, J. C. (1988). Attendance at higher-cost colleges: Ascribed, socioeconomic, and academic influences on student enrollment patterns. *Economics of Education Review*, 7, 65–76.

Hearn, J. C. (1991). Academic and nonacademic influences on the college destinations of 1980 high school graduates. *Sociology of Education*, 64, 158–171.

Hu, S., & Kuh, G. D. (2003). Maximizing what students get out of college: Testing a learning productivity model. *Journal of College Student Development*, 44, 185–203.

Hu, S., & Wolniak, G. (2010). Initial evidence of the influence of college student engagement on early career earnings. *Research in Higher Education*, 51, 750–766.

IPEDS Data Center. (2011). Retrieved on March 30, 2011, from http://nces.ed.gov/ipeds/datacenter).

Karen, D. (1991). The politics of class, race, and gender: Access to higher education in the United States, 1960–1986. *American Journal of Education*, 99, 208–237.

Kim, Y. K., & Sax, L. J. (2009). Student-faculty interaction in research universities: Differences by student gender, race, social class, and first-generation status. *Research in Higher Education*, 50, 437–459.

Knox, W. E., Lindsay, P., & Kolb, M. N. (1993). *Does college make a difference? Long-term changes in activities and attitudes*. Westport, CT: Greenwood Press.

Kuh, G. D., Cruce, T. M., Shoup, R., Kinzie, J., & Gonyea, R. M. (2008). Unmasking the effects of student engagement on first-year college grades and persistence. *Journal of Higher Education*, 79, 540–563.

Kuo, V., Wilds, D., Garcia, P. B., Trent, W. T., Nichols, L., Bronwyn, Z., et al. (2006). *The Gates Millennium Scholars research program: A conceptual framework*. Chicago: National Opinion Research Center at the University of Chicago.

Lodato Nichols, B., Zimowski, M., Lodato, R. M., & Ghadialy, R. (2004). The survey of diverse students. In E. P. St. John (Ed.), *Improving access and college success for diverse students: Studies of the Gates Millennium Scholars Program* (pp. 23–44). *Readings on equal education*, Vol. 20. New York: AMS Press.

Lin, N. (1999). Social networks and status attainment. *Annual Review of Sociology*, 25, 467–487.

Mincer, J. (1974). *Schooling, experience, and earnings*. New York: National Bureau of Economic Research.

National Commission on the Future of Higher Education (2006). *A test of leadership: Charting the future of U.S. higher education*. Washington, DC: US Department of Education.

National Opinion Research Center (2003). *Gates Millennium Scholars tracking and longitudinal study: Year 1 final report*. Chicago: The National Opinion Research Center (NORC) at the University of Chicago.

National Opinion Research Center (2006). *The inaugural cohort of the Gates Millennium Scholars: The first few years after high school*. Chicago: The National Opinion Research Center (NORC) at the University of Chicago.

National Survey of Student Engagement. (2004). *Student engagement: Pathways to collegiate success*. Bloomington: Indiana University Center for Postsecondary Research.

National Survey of Student Engagement. (2005). *Student engagement: Exploring different dimensions of student engagement*. Bloomington: Indiana University Center for Postsecondary Research.

Nora, A., Cabrera, A. F., Hagedorn, L., & Pascarella, E. T. (1996). Differential impacts of academic and social experiences on college-related behavioral outcomes across different ethnic and gender groups at four-year institutions. *Research in Higher Education*, 37, 427–452.

NORC. See National Opinion Research Center.

Pace, R. C. (1979). *Measuring outcomes of college*. San Francisco: Jossey-Bass.

Pascarella, E. T. (1985). College environmental influences on learning and cognitive development: A critical review and synthesis. In J. C. Smart (Ed.), *Higher education: Handbook of theory and research* (Vol. 1., pp. 1–62). New York: Agathon.

Pascarella, E. T., Blaich, C., Martin, G. L., & Hanson, J. M. (2011). How robust are the findings of *Academically Adrift? Change: The Magazine of Higher Learning*, 43, 20–24.

Pascarella, E. T., & Terenzini, P. T. (1991). *How college affects students: Findings and insights from twenty years of research*. San Francisco: Jossey-Bass.

Pascarella, E. T., & Terenzini, P. T. (2005). *How college affects students: A third decade of research*. San Francisco: Jossey-Bass.

Paulsen, M. B. (2001). The economics of human capital and investment in higher education. In M. B. Paulsen & J. C. Smart (Eds.), *The finance of higher education: Theory, research, policy, and practice* (pp. 55–94). New York: Agathon Press.

Pedhazur, E. J. (1982). *Multiple regression in behavioral research: Explanation and prediction*. New York: Holt, Rinehart and Winston.

Perna, L. W. (2005). The benefits of higher education: Sex, racial/ethnic, and socioeconomic group differences. *Review of Higher Education*, 29(1), 23–52.

Reason, R. D., Terenzini, P. T., & Domingo, R. J. (2006). First things first: Developing academic competence in the first year of college. *Research in Higher Education*, 47, 149–175.

Rendón, L. I., Jalomo, R. E., & Nora, A. (2000). Theoretical considerations in the study of minority student retention. In J. Braxton (Ed.), *Rethinking the student departure puzzle: New theory and research on college student retention* (pp. 127–156). Nashville, TN: Vanderbilt University Press.

Rosenfeld, R. A., & Kalleberg, A. L. (1990). A cross-national comparison of the gender gap in income. *American Journal of Sociology*, 96, 69–106.

Sax, L. J., Bryant, A. N., & Harper, C. E. (2005). The differential effects of student-faculty interaction on college outcomes for women and men. *Journal of College Student Development*, 46, 642–659.

Sewell, W. H., Haller, A. O., & Ohlendorf, G. W. (1970). The educational and early occupational status attainment process: Replication and revision. *American Sociological Review*, 35, 1014–1027.

Sewell, W. H., Haller, A. O., & Portes, A. (1969). The educational and early occupational attainment process. *American Sociological Review*, 34, 82–92.

Thomas, S. (2000). Deferred costs and economic returns to college major, quality, and performance. *Research in Higher Education*, 41, 281–313.

Thomas, S. (2003). Longer-term economic effects of college selectivity and control. *Research in Higher Education*, 44, 263–299.

Tienda, M., & Lii, D. (1987). Minority concentration and earnings inequality: Blacks, Hispanics, and Asians compared. *American Journal of Sociology*, 93, 141–165.

Tinto, V. (1975). Drop out from higher education: A theoretical synthesis of recent research. *Review of Educational Research*, 63, 89–125.

Tinto, V. (1993). *Leaving college: Rethinking causes and cures of student attrition* (2nd ed.). Chicago: The University of Chicago Press.

Weidman, J. C. (1989). Undergraduate socialization: A conceptual approach. In J. C. Smart (Ed.), *Higher education: Handbook of theory and research* (pp. 289–322). New York: Agathon Press.

CHAPTER 10

TOWARD A GREATER UNDERSTANDING OF THE EFFECTS OF STATE MERIT AID PROGRAMS: EXAMINING EXISTING EVIDENCE AND EXPLORING FUTURE RESEARCH DIRECTION

SHOUPING HU, MATTHEW TRENGOVE AND LIANG ZHANG

Introduction

Government-sponsored financial aid programs in the United States were traditionally intended to eliminate financial barriers for student participation in higher education so that equal educational opportunity could be achieved (Heller and Marin 2002; St. John 2003). This type of program has been known as need-based financial aid program. Federal student financial assistance programs, along with various financial aid programs in states, are the backbone of need-based financial aid programs in higher education (Advisory Committee on Student Financial Assistance 2001, 2002, 2010; St. John 2003). At the federal level, Pell grants and other student financial assistance programs that including grants, loans, and work study have historically functioned as a financial supporting system to help eliminate financial barriers for students so that they can realize their college dreams (St. John 2003). The federal goals in student financial assistance are multifaceted, but the paramount feature is the commitment to equalize educational opportunities for all students (McPherson and Shapiro 1998; St. John 2003). At the state level, a combination of financial appropriations to institutions and direct financial aid to students is the way that states finance higher education. States help achieve college affordability by lowering college tuition pricing through providing financial support to higher education institutions (Hearn and Longanecker 1985). States also, rather common than not, provide direct financial assistance to individual students. Such financial aid support policies have historically been based on the need of students, mirroring the federal commitment to equalizing educational opportunities (Doyle 2008; Hearn and Longanecker 1985).

However, the political landscape has changed dramatically in the financial aid policy arena. At the federal level, the historical financial commitment has been wavering due to both financial and political realities (Hearn 1993; St. John 2003). The purchasing power of Pell grants, the cornerstone of the federal student financial assistance system, has not kept up with the increase of college costs, and the installation of federal tax credits signaled a shift in the focus of federal financial assistance away from the neediest student (Advisory Committee on Student Financial Assistance 2001, 2002, 2010; Long 2004). Still, one of the most dramatic changes came in the state financial aid arena with the emergence and prevalence of state merit aid programs (Doyle 2006). Since the inception of Georgia's HOPE scholarship program in 1993, state-sponsored broad-based merit aid programs, where student academic achievement and performance are key factors in program eligibility, have been enacted in many states across the country (Cohen-Vogel et al. 2008; Heller and Marin 2002). The distinctive feature of broad-based state merit aid programs is the use of academic criteria in determining financial aid award eligibility. Some of those programs can have high academic criterion. For example, programs in Missouri, Mississippi, New Jersey, and Washington set their eligibility criterion roughly at the 90th percentile of standardized test scores. Most programs, however, have modest eligibility criterion of 3.0 grade point average (GPA) and/or 20–22 ACT, roughly corresponding to 48th and 62nd percentile in the distribution of ACT scores (Delaney and Ness 2009). Student financial need, which has been a key factor in determining need-based financial aid, has relatively minor role or no role in the broad-based state merit aid programs. Statistics show that the percentage of state financial aid based on merit has been trending upward while need-based aid has experienced a downward trend (Fig. 10.1).

Even though not the first state merit aid program, Georgia's HOPE scholarships program is arguably one of the most visible such programs in the United States. Georgia began offering HOPE scholarships in 1993, designing the program in such a way that the scholarship would cover 100% of the tuition and fees at public state colleges for high school graduates with a 3.0 GPA. The program would allow students attending in-state postsecondary institutions to receive enough funding to cover tuition, book expenses, and fees at all public postsecondary institutions, while students attending private universities would receive funding comparable to that provided to students attending public programs (Cornwell et al. 2006b). A minimal college GPA of 3.0 is required for students to maintain their HOPE scholarship. Student financial need was initially a consideration in the HOPE scholarship program when family income cap was used in scholarship qualification. Such requirement was removed from the HOPE scholarship program in two years (Dynarski 2004).

The state of Florida is another early state that adopted state-sponsored merit aid program. After observing the HOPE scholarship program in neighboring Georgia and voters' discontent with the use of state lottery proceeds, Florida legislature created and funded the Bright Futures Scholarship program in 1997, somewhat mirroring Georgia's HOPE scholarship program. The two previously existing programs in the state, Florida Academic Scholars Award (FAS) for students on academic tracks and Florida Gold Seal Vocational Scholars Award (GSV) for students on vocational tracks, were integrated into the newly created Bright Futures program with the addition of Florida Medallion Scholars Award (FMS), also for students on academic tracks. The FAS awards cover 100% of tuition and have some allowance for fees and college-related expenses while requiring 3.5 GPA on 15 college preparatory credits in high school and SAT at 1,270 or ACT at 28 for initial qualification and 3.0 GPA on all postsecondary work attempted for renewal. The FMS awards cover 75% of tuition and required fees while requiring 3.0 GPA on 15 college preparatory credits and SAT at 970 or ACT at 20 for initial qualification and 2.75 GPA on all postsecondary work for renewal. The GSV awards are similar to FMS award but toward students in vocational tracks (Florida Department of Education 2010). No financial need is considered in the Bright Futures program.

Both Georgia's HOPE Scholarship program and Florida's Bright Futures Scholarship program have the trait of being simple and straightforward. That is, as long as students have met the qualification of academic performance and file an application for the scholarship program, they are qualified for the generous financial assistance for their college tuition and related expenses. They are the two largest state merit aid programs and received most of the attention in research and policy conversation on state merit aid programs.

Many other states have adopted merit aid programs, and we described the program features of those programs in Table 10.1. In addition to the variation in program eligibility criteria, some

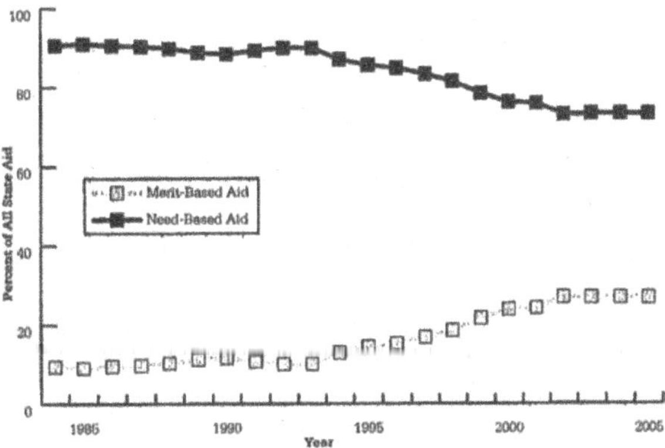

Figure 10.1 Percentage of all state aid based on merit or need.

Source: Doyle (2008). Used with author's permission.

TABLE 10.1

Description of State Merit Aid Programs

State	Program	Start Year	Funding Sources	Initial Eligibility Criteria	Renewal Requirements	Award Amount	Others
Alaska	University of Alaska scholars award	1999	Land leases & sales	Top 10% of high school class in their junior year	Must maintain a 12 credit hour schedule and a minimum collegiate GPA of 2.5	$2,750 at University of Alaska	Enrolled at University of Alaska campuses
Delaware	Diamond State	1987	General revenues	Upper quartile of class and a combined score of SAT of 1,800	Cumulative GPA of 3.0 renewed each year with a three-year limitation	$1,250 per year	Scholarship attending regionally accredited colleges in any state
	B. Bradford Barnes Memorial Scholarship	1989				Full tuition, fees, room, board and books	Enrolled at The University of Delaware
	Herman M., Holloway, Sr. Memorial Scholarship	1995		Upper half of class and a combined SAT of at least 1,350		Full tuition, fees, room, board and books	Enrolled at Delaware State University
	Charles L. Hebner Memorial Scholarship	2000				Full tuition, fees, room, board and books	Enrolled at either University of Delaware or Delaware State University majoring in humanities or social sciences
Florida	Bright Futures Scholarships	1997	Lottery	Three-tiered awards with both GPA and ACT requirements:	Collegiate GPA 1. FAS = 3.0 2. FMS = 2.75 3. GSV = 2.75	FAS = 100% tuition and required fees. FMS & GVS = 75% tuition and required fees	

				1. Florida Academic Scholars (FAS) HSGPA 3.5 & SAT/ ACT 1270/28 2. Florida Medallion Scholars (FMS) HSGPA 3.0 SAT/ ACT 970/20 3. Florida Gold Seal Vocational Scholars Award (GSV) HSGPA 3.0			
Georgia	Helping Outstanding Pupils Educationally (HOPE)	1993	Lottery	1. High school graduate = 3.0 GPA 2. Home school graduate = 3.0 GPA 3. Graduates from ineligible high school/ home study program, or receiving a GED, must score in the national composite 85th percentile or higher on the SAT or ACT tests. 4. Graduates from an ineligible high school or an ineligible home study program, who earn a 3.0 grade point average on 30 semester hours or 45 quarter hours of college degree-level coursework, can be compensated for their first 30 semester hours or 45 quarter hours *after* they are taken.	Collegiate GPA 3.0	HOPE award amounts are based upon a per hour rate at the institution the student is attending (varies according to the institution)	Full-time students enrolled in private schools will receive: $1,800 per semester, or $1,200 per quarter, Half-time students enrolled in private institutions will receive $900 per semester, $600 per quarter

(continued)

TABLE 10.1

Description of State Merit Aid Programs *(continued)*

State	Program	Start Year	Funding Sources	Initial Eligibility Criteria	Renewal Requirements	Award Amount	Others
				5. Students who earn a 3.0 grade point average at the college level on degree coursework after attempting 30, 60, or 90 semesters hours or 45, 90, or 135 quarter hours, regardless of high school graduation status.			
Kentucky	Educational Excellence Scholarship (KEES)	1998	Lottery	Awards are based on sliding scale of HS GPA (2.5–4.0) for each year in high school grades 9–12 and earn a bonus based on ACT score (15–36)	If collegiate GPA = 3.0 +, your full award will be renewed. If collegiate GPA = 2.5–3.0 your college must verify that you are on track to graduate. If yes—your award amount will be reduced by 50%. If no—you will become ineligible until you meet above standards	GPA for each year of high school: 2.5 = $125, 4.0 = $500; ACT bonus: 15 = $36, 28 + = $500	
Louisiana	Tuition Opportunity Program for Students (TOPS)	1998	General revenues	Three-tiered awards with both GPA and ACT requirements: 1. Honors—3.0 GPA & 27 ACT 2. Performance—3.0 GPA & 23 ACT 3. Opportunity—2.5 GPA & 20 ACT	Three-tiered awards with the following requirements: 1. GPA = 3.0 & has earned 24 credit hours 2. GPA = 3.0 & has earned 24 credit hours 3. GPA = 2.5 & has earned 24 credit hours	Three-tiered awards with both GPA and ACT requirements: 1. Full tuition + $800 per year 2. Full tuition + $400 per year 3. Full tuition	

Massachusetts	John and Abigail Adams Scholarship Program	2006	General revenues	Students must score "advanced" on either mathematics or language arts section of the grade 10 MCAS test and score in the proficient or advanced category on the second subject. Have a combined MCAS score on these assessments that ranks in the top 25% in their school district.	GPA of at least 3.0	Full tuition	
Michigan	Merit Award Scholarship	2000	Tobacco settlement	"Acceptable" score on all four components of MEAP test assessment, or "acceptable" score on two tests & 24 ACT		One-time awards: $2,500, in-state institutions (public or private); $1,000, out-of-state public or private institutions	Eligibility for the Michigan Merit Award has now expired for all students unless they have served or are currently serving in the military
Mississippi	Eminent Scholars Program	1995	General revenues	Has a minimum GPA of 3.5 & 29 ACT or 1,280 on the SAT. Students may also be a national merit or national achievement finalist or semi-finalist	Minimum GPA of 3.5 & enrolled in at least 12 credit hours per semester	Tuition and fees up to $2,500 per year	
Missouri	Higher Education Academic Scholarship Program (Bright Flight)	1997	General revenues	Top 5% of all Missouri ACT or SAT test takers in the state qualify for the award	GPA of 2.5	$2,000	

(continued)

TABLE 10.1

Description of State Merit Aid Programs *(continued)*

State	Program	Start Year	Funding Sources	Initial Eligibility Criteria	Renewal Requirements	Award Amount	Others
Nevada	Millennium Scholarship	1999	Tobacco lawsuit	3.25 GPA and have completed a core curriculum of 14 units of English (4), Math (including Algebra II) (4), Natural Science (3) and Social Science and History courses (3)	Maintain a GPA of 2.6 (1st yr) and a GPA of 2.75 during the 2nd, 3rd, and 4th yrs	Variable rates ranging from $40 to $80 per credit hour depending on institution type; maximum annual awards: $2,500 (four-year institutions), $1,250 (two-year institutions)	University students enrolled in 12 credit hours would be eligible to receive a maximum of $960 ($80 × 12 credits). Community college students enrolled in 9 semester credit hours would be eligible to receive $360 ($40 × 9 credits), up to a total of 12 credits per term maximum
New Mexico	Lottery Success Scholarship	1996	Lottery	College GPA 2.5 after first 12 credit hours	Maintain a GPA of 2.5	Full tuition	
North Carolina	Education Lottery Scholarship (ELS)	2005	Lottery	• Eligibility is determined based on the same criteria as the Federal Pell Grant with one exception; students not eligible for the Federal Pell Grant with an estimated family contribution of $5,000 or less will be eligible for an Education Lottery Scholarship. Students who have earned baccalaureate (four-year) college degrees are ineligible • Enroll for at least six credit hours per semester • Meet the satisfactory academic progress requirements of the institution	Meet satisfactory progress requirements of the institution	Grants will range from $100 to $3,400 for the year	

South Carolina	South Carolina has three awards: 1. Legislative Incentive for Future Excellence (LIFE). 2. Palmetto Fellows. 3. Hope Scholarship	2004	General revenues	Three-tiered awards with both GPA and SAT/ACT requirements: 1. Score of 1,100+ on SAT I or 24 + on ACT earn a cumulative of at least 3.0 GPR and rank in the top 30% of the graduating class. 2. Score 1,200+ on the SAT (27 + on the ACT) and earn a minimum 3.5 cumulative GPA and rank in the top 6% of the class at the end of either the sophomore or the junior year or score at least 1,400 on the SAT (32+ on the ACT) and earn a minimum 4.00 cumulative GPA (junior year) 3. Earn a minimum 3.0 cumulative GPA and cannot be recipients of the Palmetto Fellows Scholarship, LIFE Scholarship, or Lottery Tuition Assistance	Three-tiered awards	Three-tiered awards with both GPA and ACT requirements: 1. Up to $5,000/yr + $300 for books. 2. $6,700 (1st year) and $7,500 (2nd, 3rd, 4th yrs), $300 book allowance 3. $2,800 and a $300 book allowance

(continued)

TABLE 10.1

Description of State Merit Aid Programs *(continued)*

State	Program	Start Year	Funding Sources	Initial Eligibility Criteria	Renewal Requirements	Award Amount	Others
Tennessee	Education Lottery Scholarship Program (TELS)	2004	Lottery	Three-tiered awards with different GPA, ACT, and income requirements: 1. *Tennessee HOPE Scholarship* = High school and home school graduates must have a minimum of a 980 SAT (21 ACT), or a 3.0 GPA, GED applicants must have a minimum of a 980 SAT (21 ACT) 2. *Aspire Award* = 3.0 GPA or 21 ACT & AGI ≤ \$36 k 3. *Tennessee HOPE Access Grant* = a GPA of 2.75–2.99 GPA & 860–970 SAT (18 ACT) & AGI ≤ \$36k	Must have a cumulative GPA of 2.75 after 24 and 48 hours. After 72 students may retain the award by either: Keeping a GPA of 3.0 or above, or achieving a cumulative GPA of 2.75–2.99 *and* a semester GPA of at least 3.0 in the preceding term for which the student will receive the award as a full-time enrolled student	1. \$4,000 (4 yr) & \$2,000 (2 yr) 2. \$1,500 3. \$2,750 (4 yr) or \$1,250 (2 yr)	
West Virginia	Providing Real Opportunities for Maximizing In-State Student Excellence (PROMISE)	2005	Video lottery and state general appropriations	3.0 GPA and a 1,020 SAT (22 ACT) with at least a 20 in all subsections and have completed a core curriculum of 14 units of English (4), Math (4), Natural Science (3), and Social Sciences (4)	Minimum 3.0 GPA throughout their collegiate career	Pays tuition and mandatory fees at any public college or \$4,752 to a private college	

Sources: Delaney (2007), Doyle (2006), Dynarski (2004), Heller (2002, 2004), Zhang and Ness (2010) and various websites

programs are more generous than others. Some states (e.g., Tennessee, Georgia, and South Carolina) spend more than $1,000 per undergraduate student on merit aid award while others (e.g., Arkansas, Colorado, Maryland, and Mississippi) spend less than $25 per undergraduate student. In light of the wide range of variation in some key features in state merit aid programs, it is important to consider specific state contexts and program characteristics when evaluating the impact of these programs. It is worth noting that the current literature on state merit aid programs does not agree on the number of states that have a merit aid program. This is in part due to the fact that these state programs were implemented in different points of time. Most importantly, there has been no agreed-upon criterion for such programs.

State merit aid programs are among one of the most visible policy initiatives in state higher education policy arena. The embedded policy values in such programs make the discourses of such programs spirited and sometimes contentious, perhaps also served as one of the reasons that make such programs highly visible and politically popular by and large. As calls for evidence-based policy making permeate, it is time to assemble both conceptual and empirical evidence related to the effects of state merit aid programs (Brewer et al. 2010; Krathwohl 1998).

Purposes and Guiding Questions

Because of the contentious nature of conversation surrounding state merit aid programs, it is important for policy researchers and scholars to provide conceptually solid explanation on how merit aid programs can affect educational outcomes and generate rigorous empirical evidence to demonstrate the effects of such programs. Moreover, researchers and scholars should periodically reexamine their own work and think more critically about the implications of their research. Thus, the purposes of this chapter are multifaceted. First, we synthesize the existing literature and research on the effects of state merit aid programs on educational outcomes in the policy states and individual student decisions in higher education. The following two questions guide the organization of the evidence: Do merit aid programs serve the interests of policy states? How do merit aid programs affect student decisions and related outcomes? Second, we consider the broad context facing American higher education and broaden the conversation of the role of state merit aid programs from a national perspective. The question that guides our critique is: do state merit aid programs help achieve the national educational attainment goal and national interest in international competitiveness? Third, given the nature of state merit aid programs as high-profile policy initiatives and the heightened emphasis on the rigor of policy research, we discuss the theories that can help us understand how merit aid programs could affect student outcomes in higher education. Specifically, what can we learn from existing theories on whether and how state merit aid programs may affect educational outcomes? Fourth, to improve our understanding of the effects of state merit aid programs, inquiry methods certainly are critical to the credibility and trustworthiness of research findings. Thus, we discuss the methodological issues related to research on state merit aid programs. The guiding question is: how different inquiry methods can help us understand the effects of state merit programs? Finally, we explore the areas that more research can be valuable and propose the directions for future research related to state merit aid programs. That is, which topical areas could be fruitful for researchers and scholars to further explore in order to help develop a greater understanding of the effects of state merit aid programs?

Effects on Educational Outcomes in Policy States

Commonly mentioned purposes of state merit aid programs are: (1) Promoting college access to the residents in the state; (2) Retaining the best and brightest students in the state; and (3) Incentivizing students to work harder for academic excellence (Cohen-Vogel et al. 2008; Heller 2004). To assess whether state merit aid programs achieve such goals, researchers and scholars can provide answers by analyzing aggregate data, among which the most important are data from the Integrated Postsecondary Education Data System (IPEDS) or US Census data. Research in this area has primarily focused on three state-level outcomes: college enrollment, college degree attainment, and migration of college students.

Effects on College Enrollment

Since state merit aid programs are still relatively recent policy innovations, much of the research on enrollment effects has been limited either to single-state studies most often of Georgia's HOPE program or to studies of the southeast region. In studying college enrollment, one must make distinctions between college enrollment in a merit aid state and college enrollment of residents from that state. If we take Georgia as an example, the former consists of all students who are enrolled at postsecondary institutions in Georgia regardless of their states of residence, while the latter includes all Georgia resident students who are enrolled at any postsecondary institution in the United States. Although studies along this line have shown large and significant effects of merit aid programs on both measures of college enrollment, their differences are important as they have different policy implications.

Treating Georgia's HOPE program as a natural experiment, Cornwell et al. (2006b) compared college enrollment data from IPEDS between 1988 and 1997 (i.e., 5 years before and after the policy implementation) in the state of Georgia with those in other states of the Southern Regional Educational Board. Their difference-in-difference estimates suggest that the HOPE increased total freshmen enrollment by about 6% following the adoption of the program. It is noteworthy that this 6% growth in freshmen enrollment does not represent the net gain of college enrollment by Georgia residents because it includes those students who would have attended out-of-state institutions without the merit aid. In fact, their subsequent analyses using IPEDS freshmen migration data suggest that the majority of this increase is due to reduced out-migration of resident students from Georgia.

Dynarski (2000) used data from October Current Population Survey from 1989 to 1997 to estimate the net gain of college enrollment by Georgia residents. Since CPS data provided information on an individual's state of residence but not on where he or she attended college, estimates based on these data represented the effect of HOPE on college enrollment for Georgia residents, regardless of the location of college enrollment. Again, using difference-in-difference technique to compare college enrollment by Georgia residents with those by residents from other states, this study found roughly a 7–8% enrollment increase by Georgia residents as a result of the HOPE Scholarship program. Dynarski (2004) expanded this early analysis in an evaluation of the effect of state merit aid programs in seven states; the results showed that these programs typically increased the college enrollment by 5–7%.

Despite the difference in the definition of college enrollment, studies along this line have shown large and significant effects of merit aid programs on college enrollment. Furthermore, these studies have also shown that the largest enrollment growth has occurred at public four-year institutions. In fact, Dynarski (2004) suggested that Georgia's HOPE scholarship "appears to push more students out of two-year, public institutions than it pulls in" (p. 79), resulting in a net drop of student enrollment in two-year institutions, while the enrollment in four-year institutions increases. This pattern reflects that merit aid programs can have effects on student choice of institutions for college education.

Effects on College Degree Attainment

Growth in college enrollment is important because college participation is the critical first step in college education; however, increased college enrollment in those merit aid states does not guarantee improved degree attainment. On one hand, the average six-year college graduation rate at all four-year colleges and universities in the United States is slightly over 50%. Many merit aid students lose their financial support while in college, especially in science, engineering, and computing fields where maintaining good academic standing is challenging (Dee and Jackson 1999). On the other hand, these merit aid programs might improve student persistence through college. Consequently, the impact of these merit aid programs on college degree attainment could be higher or lower than on college enrollment. Without degree attainment, college education in the form of college credits still matters, but much less so (Jaeger and Page 1996; Kane and Rouse 1995). Perhaps for this reason, the focus of public policies in higher education has shifted in recent years from college participation to college persistence and degree attainment.

Similarly, in studying college enrollment, one must make distinctions between degree production by postsecondary institutions in a merit aid state and degree attainment of residents from that state. If we take Georgia as an example, degrees awarded by postsecondary institutions located in Georgia could be obtained by both Georgia residents and nonresident students who attend colleges in Georgia. Similarly, residents of Georgia may obtain their college degrees from postsecondary institutions in Georgia or elsewhere in the United States.

Treating Georgia's HOPE program and Florida's Bright Future program as natural experiments, Zhang (2011) compared degree completion data from IPEDS in these two states and with those in other states of the SREB. Results suggest that the HOPE program increased four-year degree production at Georgia institutions by about 3–4% and at Florida institutions by about 11%. Considering that the increase in freshmen enrollment in Georgia is estimated at about 6% (Cornwell et al. 2006b) and in Florida at more than 20% (Zhang and Ness 2010), it appears that the increase in degree production is lower than the increases of freshmen enrollment. More importantly, the growth has occurred in both STEM and non-STEM disciplines. In Georgia, the number of STEM degrees has increased by about 5–7% and non-STEM degrees by 1–4%, depending on comparison groups and model specifications. The growth is even larger in Florida, with about 10–13% for STEM degrees and 11–13% for non-STEM degrees. Both the public and private sectors have experienced growth in the number of STEM degrees conferred, although the growth is uneven. The positive effect of state merit aid programs on STEM degree production is consistent with the effect of these programs on enrollment and the academic quality of students who are attending in-state institutions. Since data on degree production by institutions are not available by status of residence, it is difficult to know whether these merit aid programs have increased or decreased overall STEM degree production by their resident students. However, at least from a state perspective, these merit aid programs are quite effective in retaining the best and bright and improving their degree production in both STEM and non-STEM fields.

Dynarski (2008) used data from the 2000 Census 1% public use microdata sample (PUMS) to examine the impact of state merit aid programs on degree attainment by their residents. Because an individual's residence state could change over time and could be a function of these programs, state of birth was used as the identification strategy. After comparing similar age cohorts between merit aid states (Arkansas and Georgia) and the rest of the United States, Dynarski (2008) found that the share of the population with college degrees (including both associate and bachelor degrees) who were born in these two states increased by 2.98 percentage points after implementation of these policies. This is a quite large increase considering that the base share of college attainment in these two states before policy implementation is about 27%.

Effects on Migration of College Students

Because one of the main policy goals for these merit aid states has been to retain the best and brightest students to attend in-state colleges and universities with the hope that they will enter the state's workforce after college graduation, it is important to evaluate whether these programs have been successful in stemming the brain drain. From a national perspective, because the net gain of college enrollment for those merit aid states is a function of both increased college enrollment in their home states and (presumably) decreased college enrollment of their resident students in other states, it is important to examine to what extent these programs are successful in boosting the net college enrollment. For example, if these programs increase college enrollment in their home states simply by reducing the out-migration of their resident students, these programs will not improve college attainment from a national perspective.

Empirical evidence on student migration suggests that these programs have been quite successful in stanching the brain drain from those merit aid states. Dynarski (2004) found that immediately after the establishment of these programs, enrollment in border state colleges, defined as postsecondary institutions located near the border in neighboring states, was reduced by 3.4%. Cornwell et al. (2006b) also found strong evidence of HOPE reducing the migration of Georgia high school graduates to out-of-state institutions. Using the IPEDS data and examining the unique effects of state merit aid programs and the combined effects of merit aid with other state policies, Orsuwan and Heck (2009) found that state merit aid programs affect first-year college student interstate migration in a way that students in states with merit aid programs are less likely to migrate out.

In a more recent study, Zhang and Ness (2010) conducted a systematic analysis on the effect of merit aid programs on student migration in 14 merit aid states. They distinguished stayers who attended colleges in their home states and leavers who attended colleges elsewhere. Their results suggested that state merit aid programs indeed stanched the migration of the best and brightest students to other states. In the aggregate and on average, the implementation of state merit aid programs boosted resident college enrollment in these states by about 10% and decreased the number of resident students from these states who attend out-of-state institutions by about 10%. However, there was a great deal of variation across states and across types of institutions. These variations appeared to be related to differences in eligibility criteria and award amount across states. In addition, it appears that the largest increased stayer enrollment and decreased leaver enrollment have occurred in research and doctoral institutions, suggesting that these programs have been quite successful in retaining the best and brightest students in state.

Results in Zhang and Ness (2010) provide an important tool to simulate the impact of merit aid programs on different enrollment types. For example, a typical state has 70% resident enrollment and 30% nonresident enrollment. After the introduction of merit-based aid program, the resident enrollment increases by about 10%, from 70 to 77. At the same time, student out-migration decreases by 10%, from 30 to 27. In other words, although the college enrollment in this policy state has increased by 7 percentage points (assuming that the nonresident enrollment at this state does not change), the net increase of college enrollment of its residents only increases by 4 percentage points because about 3 percentage points in college enrollment is due to reduced out-migration.

These studies deal solely with student migration for postsecondary education enrollment and do not address where students will reside upon graduating from college. However, many state merit aid programs explicitly aim to enhance the state's workforce as a means to generate economic development. Although it is unclear whether these state merit aid programs encourage college graduates to stay in their home states or not, limited empirical evidence in this area suggests that students attending college in-state are more likely to remain in-state post graduation than students who attend college out-of-state are to return to their home state. For example, Perry (2001) uses Baccalaureate and Beyond data and finds that 84% of students attending college in-state remain in the state after graduation compared to 64% of students attending out-of-state institutions who return to their home state. In another study that tracks students 10 and 20 years post graduation, Groen (2004) finds a roughly 10 percentage point increase of home state residence post graduation among students attending in-state colleges as compared to students attending college elsewhere.

Effects on Educational Outcomes for Students

To understand the effects of merit aid programs on individual students, we utilize the "choice construct" proposed by St. John et al. (2001) to organize the empirical evidence. The student choice construct starts with two core propositions: (1) Students make their educational choices within the situated contexts of their life experiences, including their family lives, community members, schools, and dreams, which all influence their choices; (2) There is a sequence in student choice process, where initial choices influencing subsequent decisions. Specifically, the choice sequence in understanding policy effects on individual students include the critical junctures in student educational attainment process: Academic preparation for college, educational aspiration to go to college, opportunity to attend college (access), the choice of college to attend, choice of major field of study in college, persistence and graduation from college, and possibly the decision for graduate education and choice of occupations after graduation.

The majority of the research on financial aid awards has consistently indicated that financial aid subsidies improve college attendance, persistence, and degree completion rates (Heller 1997; Hu and St. John 2001; Leslie and Brinkman 1987; St. John 2003) with cost and preparation being two of the most common and critical barriers to college degree attainment identified by previous research (Cornwell et al. 2006b; St. John 2003). Furthermore, financial aid awards can help students to "upgrade" their college choice options (Hoxby 2004; Hu and Hossler 2000). That is, students who received financial aid awards are more likely to attend higher priced or more selective colleges and universities (Hoxby 2004; Hu and Hossler 2000; McPherson and Shapiro 1998). Most of the research on how state merit aid programs affect individual student outcomes is, not surprisingly, from the studies on Georgia's HOPE program and Florida's Bright Futures programs and a few others.

Effects on Student Academic Preparation

Some researchers found that state merit aid programs improved student performance in K-12 education and increased student motivation to improve academic preparation (Henry and Rubenstein 2002). Research conducted by Harkreader et al. (2008) suggested that while low-income and minority high school graduates in Florida were overall less likely to receive a Bright Futures scholarship, or take preparatory courses, the test scores of individuals in these groups did improve with each successive graduation cohort. This was measured by the percentage of students taking college prep classes increased from 53.5% in 1997 to 67.2% in 2001. Similarly, the overall percentage of students eligible to receive a Bright Futures Scholarship increased from 20.1% in 1997 to 29.3% in 2001 (Harkreader et al. 2008). Similar findings have been reported in Cornwell and Mustard (2002) which reported that the SAT scores of college freshmen had risen by approximately 35 points over a 10-year period (1988–1998) bringing Georgia's average SAT scores into alignment with the national average.

Henry et al. (2004) discovered increases in levels of student performance on both individual student SAT scores and high school GPAs. They also found that students receiving HOPE scholarships outperform their peers in several significant ways with performance boosts found even among borderline HOPE scholars, by earning an average 50 more credits, than their peers, over a four-year period (Henry et al. 2004). These findings were a major factor in Tennessee's decision to lower the standards and enabling "less qualified" students earning a GPA of 2.75 to have access to HOPE Access grants when it established its HOPE scholarship program in 2003 (Heller and Marin 2004). Later studies by Cornwell and Mustard (2006) found that the requirements of HOPE scholarships have encouraged students to withdraw from courses in which they perform poorly lowering the likelihood of a full load program by 9.3%, and shift to more summer courses (Cornwell and Mustard 2006); and while there has been considerable debate on this issue over how these changes initiated by merit-based aid programs have affected student "college experiences," the end results are generally positive with students showing higher levels of persistence, earning more college credits, and maintaining higher college GPA's (Henry et al. 2004).

Some worry about the uneven qualification rates for state merit aid programs given that low-income and minority students are less likely to take college preparatory courses and have lower college completion rates (Heller and Marin 2002), which means that the programs are more likely to support the academic efforts of wealthy, White and middle-upper class families. This issue is exasperated by the fact that African Americans as a group score lower on the SAT, putting them at a disadvantage when seeking admission to top universities as the SAT scores are one of the main criteria for admission to these institutions (Cornwell and Mustard 2003). These positions are supported by the fact that merit-based programs have regressive effects, meaning that scholastic funding from lottery programs that are disproportionately supported by low-income groups (Binder et al. 2002; Dynarski 2004).

The side effect of increasing SAT scores and student GPAs is that merit-based scholarship programs are facing an increasing number of qualified students applying for these scholarships, which has outpaced the states' ability to fund these programs. In terms of the dollars disbursed and students served, Cornwell and Mustard (2001) found that the HOPE scholarship program in Georgia was roughly twice as large as the need-based federal Pell Grant funding allocated in the state. While the actual number of HOPE awards has been evenly divided between HOPE scholarships and HOPE grants, HOPE scholarships account for nearly 80% of all aid disbursed—and given the differential tuition costs between four- and two-year institutions with four-year public institutions absorbing 77% of all scholarship aid and private colleges accounting for 12.5% of aid—this leaves very little for community colleges (Cornwell and Mustard 2001).

Effects on Student Access

Another issue commonly addressed when describing merit aid programs is the desire to improve college access, which is defined by a process where traditionally disadvantaged students are given an increasing opportunities to obtain higher education. Statistical reports indicate that only 29% of citizens aged 25 to 29 years old, had completed four or more years of college in 2002. Thus, there are strong theoretical and policy rationales to examine how merit aid programs affect educational outcomes for students of different background characteristics. Statistics presented by researchers indicates that a majority of the students benefiting from merit aid programs are White, upper-middle-class students, given the high eligibility requirements for merit aid programs (Heller and Marin 2002).

Even though there are quite forceful arguments about the possible unequal effects of state merit aid programs on the probability of receiving merit aid scholarships, the examination on the effects of state merit aid programs on educational decisions for students of different backgrounds is still scarce. Binder et al. (2002) found New Mexico's program had somewhat stronger positive effects on access and persistence of Native American students. A study based on student perception in Tennessee indicates that students from disadvantaged groups tend to consider merit aid programs had larger effects on their opportunity to enroll in colleges and universities (Ness 2008).

Dynarski (2004) used aggregate data to examine the enrollment effects of state merit aid programs on students of different backgrounds. She found that even though state merit aid programs tend to narrow the enrollment gaps in Florida, Arkansas, and Mississippi, Georgia's HOPE program appears to be an outliner whereby the program enlarged the enrollment gaps between White students and African-American and Hispanic students. However, Cornwell and Mustard (2002) found that after Georgia's HOPE scholarship program was established, the percentage of African-American students enrolling in public, four-year institutions rose by 21% and 16% at private colleges between 1993 and 1997, exceeding the gains of White enrollments, of 5% and 12%. During a recent study examining the effects of HOPE scholarships on enrollment by race, they found that the scholarship increased White enrollment by only about 3.6% but boosted the enrollment of African-American students by about 15% (Cornwell and Mustard 2006). It is worth noting that Dynarski (2004) and Cornwell and Mustard (2002, 2006) used different types of data (state administrative data vs. Census data) and examined different aspects of the effects of the HOPE program. As Dynarski (2002) suggested, her study was about any student from Georgia enrolled in any college, while Cornwell and Mustard (2002, 2006) examined student enrollment in Georgia's colleges and universities. Thus, HOPE program may have sizeable effects on student migration across the state border in the way that minority students tend to more likely attend in-state colleges due to the HOPE program.

Some researchers were worried that Georgia's higher education system may become less diverse as a significant portion (45%) of all African-American students is enrolled in one of the state's HBCUs (Cornwell and Mustard 2006). This becomes an issue because any enrollment gains that have occurred since the HOPE scholarship program was initiated primarily occurred at less selective institutions (like the HBCUs) and not at the flagship institutions like Georgia Tech or the University of Georgia (Cornwell and Mustard 2002). This is because increases in SAT math (9.4 points) and verbal scores (14.3 points) encouraged the top institutions to become more selective with their applicants, exacerbating the stratification of enrollment by student quality (Cornwell and Mustard 2006). Some suggested that the primary role of Georgia's HOPE Scholarship has been to influence where, not whether, students attend college because 96% of the students would have enrolled in college without the program (Cornwell and Mustard 2003).

Effects on Student College Choice

College choice on the other hand refers to the increased opportunity of all students to attend the institution they select. On this issue, merit aid scholarship programs have had a significant effect, with multiple studies finding that students are more likely to attend a four-year university program rather than a two-year college when receiving a scholarship (Cornwell et al. 2006b; Doyle 2010). The choice of college, or which colleges are viable options, has become an important yet largely shadowed topic in public policy discourse in the United States. In a book on the economics of college choices, Hoxby (2004) argued that future public policies could have more substantial effects on educational outcomes if the focus of the policy is on where students go to college and who goes where to college. She contended that although college access has historical policy significance, the current status in American higher education leaves little room for policy makers to have substantial impact in the area of college access. Instead, the college choices made by a diverse student population can be an area for policymakers to play a significant role that can help broaden postsecondary opportunities for individual students and level the playground for students of different backgrounds in choosing their college destinations (Hoxby 2004).

Research findings suggest that merit-based scholarships offer students with more potential career opportunities as empirical research has indicated that attending different types of colleges confers different benefits to students (Zhang 2005). Furthermore, attending different types of postsecondary institutions (i.e., institutional selectivity) can also influence students' eventual success in college (Melguizo 2008, 2010). Therefore the proliferation of merit-based scholarships, may force states to compete against each another to retain/obtain the "best" students by using these scholarships to motivate institutions that may be less attractive to them if not for the scholarships (Cornwell and Mustard 2006).

The size and scope of the merit-based scholarships have had a pronounced effect on student attendance patterns, further increasing the likelihood that students will enroll in an in-state institution. For example, the state of Florida provided $ 346 million in Bright Futures Scholarships to over 149,000 students in the 2006–2007 fiscal year (Florida Department of Education 2008). As a result, the overall percentage of Florida high school graduates enrolling in out-of-state institutions has declined from 9.8% in 1997 to 7.2% in 2001 (Harkreader et al. 2008). Similar results were outlined in Dynarski's study (2004) finding that immediately after the establishment of Georgia's HOPE scholarship program, enrollment in border state colleges, defined as postsecondary institutions located near the border in neighboring states was reduced by 3.4%. In addition to affecting student choice of in-state versus out-of-state institutions, state merit aid can also affect students' choice of different types of institutions. For example, Dynarski (2004) found that students appear to be more likely to attend four-year institutions in Georgia after the implementation of the HOPE scholarship program. In a study on New Mexico's merit aid program, Binder et al. (2002) also found that New Mexico's program affect student's choice of colleges in the way that students were more likely to attend in-state institutions and more likely to go to four-year institutions, even though the program did not appear to generate additional college enrollment.

Effects on Choice of STEM Fields

There is only limited indirect evidence on the effects of merit aid programs on students' STEM educational decisions (Cornwell et al. 2005, 2006a; Hu 2008; St. John and Hu 2006b). Economists treat student choice as an investment decision by which students consider both the costs and benefits associated with their choice (Becker 1994; Leslie and Brinkman 1988; Montmarquette et al. 2002; St. John 2003). Merit aid programs then could affect student decisions by affecting the costs of college education for the aid recipients. As Delaney (2007) suggested, merit aid scholarships provided subsidies for students to choose "high-risk" fields such as the STEM fields. As a result, merit aid could help increase the likelihood of choosing STEM fields by students. However, some scholars suggest otherwise, particularly in the literature related to college grading practices (Hu 2005; Johnson 2003). After reviewing the literature on college grading practices, Hu (2005) suggested that merit aid programs based on college grades could function as financial disincentives for students to choose degree programs in STEM fields due to the fact that grading policies in STEM fields tend to be more stringent. For example, a study of Georgia's student-record data indicated that freshmen and sophomores completed roughly 1.2 fewer math and science core-curriculum credits than their peers (Cornwell and Mustard 2006). Essentially, students could be encouraged to withdraw from the more difficult courses if they are performing poorly, in order to fulfill the GPA requirements of the scholarship program. By necessity students who withdraw must increase their summer course when grades are generally higher, "even though the typical summer-school enrollee has a lower SAT score and high school GPA" (Cornwell and Mustard 2006, p. 36). In addition, Cornwell and Mustard (2006) present evidence that suggests HOPE scholarship programs have increased the likelihood of a typical freshman choosing an education major by 1.2%, with the percentages for women and White students being even higher. The scholarship's influence on declared majors is potentially costly because earnings are so closely tied to that choice (Cornwell and Mustard 2006). Research conducted by Cornwell et al. (2005, 2006a) and Hu (2008) provided some evidence that the renewal rules of merit aid programs could affect student choice and course load requirements of college major. However, from the limited literature, it is still inconclusive how merit aid programs could affect individual decisions in STEM education.

Using data from the state of Florida, Hu (2008) found that receiving a Bright Futures award was associated with higher level of probability to be enrolled in a baccalaureate degree program in science and engineering, but there was a significant drop in student enrollment in science and engineering baccalaureate degree programs after the implementation of the Bright Futures program, as indicated in the comparison of student data from the two time periods before and after the program. In combination, these findings on the one hand suggest that the financial aid such as the Bright Futures could function as price subsidies on students and could encourage students to choose more "risky" fields such as the STEM, consistent with findings from other studies on merit aid programs (Delaney 2007; St. John and Hu 2006b). This can be part of the reasons that aid recipients were more likely to enroll in the STEM degree programs. On the other hand, because college grades in all fields are treated equally in the merit aid award renewal criteria, there is a negative influence on all students in their decisions to enroll in the STEM programs, aid recipients and nonrecipients alike. This possibility can be illustrated in Fig. 10.2. Other researchers also found some evidence that students did adopt some strategies to protect their eligibility to merit aid scholarships. In another study on Florida's students, Zhang et al. (2006) found that students strategize their college load and major fields to manipulate college GPAs to remain eligible to merit aid scholarship, and this phenomenon is more pronounced to students whose college grades are close to the eligibility cut-off point.

Effects on Student Persistence

In the public policy arena, student persistence has almost become synonymous with student success (Kuh et al. 2007). A dozen state merit aid programs have eligibility criteria that are lenient enough that more than 30% of high school seniors qualify (Dynarski 2008), but to help students benefit fully from postsecondary opportunity, college access alone cannot accomplish it because the economic benefits of college education largely depend on student degree completion (Jaeger and Page 1996; Pascarella and Terenzini 2005). That is, "access" to postsecondary education does not necessarily coincide with student persistence, especially given that the college graduation rate has been just around 50% for decades in the United States (Kuh et al. 2005). As a result one question that is common in the minds of public policy makers and institutional administrators is: How can the educational system effectively promote student success in college?

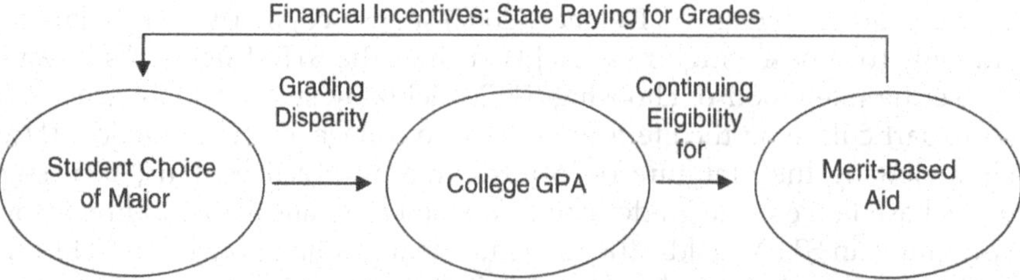

Figure 10.2 Possible mechanism that merit-based aid could affect student choice of major fields.
Source: Hu (2008).

Cornwell et al. (2005) found that students were actually less likely to complete a full course load at the University of Georgia after the HOPE scholarship program was initiated. Similarly, Scott-Clayton (2009) found that merit aid recipients in West Virginia were nearly 25% more likely to complete 30 credits during their freshman year. Using the 2000 Census data, Dynarski (2008) estimated the impact of the HOPE scholarship on persistence rate indirectly and found that the program reduced the dropout rate by 3–5 percentage points.

As previously described, research of merit-based aid programs have concluded with the findings that cost and preparation are the two most critical barriers affecting college persistence (Cornwell et al. 2006a, b; St. John 2003). The size and scope of these awards provide many students with the necessary funding to ensure their pursuit of a college degree is not limited by financial risk or instability, given that research has consistently indicated that financial aid subsidies improve college attendance, persistence, and degree completion rates (Heller 1997; Hu and St. John 2001; Leslie and Brinkman 1987; St. John 2003), as students enrolled in these programs face higher levels of persistence, earning more college credits, and maintaining higher college GPAs when compared with their peers (Henry et al. 2004).

State Merit Aid Programs and National Interests

In the public policy arena related to higher education, educational attainment in general and degree production in Science, Technology, Engineering, and Mathematics (commonly known as the STEM fields) in particular are undoubtedly two of the most important issues. The arrival of age of knowledge economy has made college education a necessity toward decent employment in a new economy. Meanwhile, as globalization in the world economy is deepening and international competition is intensifying, the quantity and quality of human capital in the fields of STEM has become necessary for Americans to maintain its historical edge in a new world order (Clotfelter 2010). It is with this understanding that we think it is not only useful but also necessary to broaden the perspectives in discussing the effects of state merit aid programs. Even though state merit aid programs are policies and programs initiated and sponsored by the states, the examination of such programs have to be based on broader perspectives. Granted, it is important to understand merit aid programs from the policy perspectives, and the interests, of the states, it is also valuable and important to consider the implications for the country as a whole in achieving its educational attainment goal and the goal of training a workforce with strong STEM preparation.

State Merit Aid Programs and Educational Attainment

The landscape of American higher education is changing dramatically as an increasingly diverse population gets ready to go to college. Meanwhile, the intensified global competition demands more Americans to acquire higher level of education. While it is critical to provide access to higher education for American citizens, it is also important to recognize the importance of the choice of college and success in college. The United States has been leading the world in percentage of population with more than a high school education mostly throughout the twentieth century, but can no longer claim this distinction. The statistics from the Organization for Economic Cooperation and Development (OECD) show the United States is trailing several other countries in the percentage of population ages 25–34 having attained "tertiary" education (2005). It has now become a clear policy priority related to higher education in the United States to ensure more students graduate from college. President Obama—as well as some prominent foundations including the Lumina Foundation for Education and the Bill & Melinda Gates Foundation (Ashburn 2010; Gonzalez 2010; Hebel 2009)—has repeatedly called for a dramatic increase of college degree completion rates to meet the need of economic development and international competition.

Because the primary interest of state merit aid programs is to meet the needs of the states, it is not surprising that many evaluative studies focused on whether such programs meet the state policy goals in retaining the best and brightest students (Zhang and Ness 2010). However, given the need to increase the number of college graduates in the United States as a national goal, it is important to examine the efficacy of the policy from a national perspective as well. That is, it is important to evaluate state merit aid programs from both the state and national perspectives.

To better understand the impact of state merit aid programs, two different yet related outcomes can be adopted: The degree production in the state that adopted the policy and educational decisions of individual students. The former outcome has direct policy implications to the state and the latter outcome has implication to the individual student and ultimately the country as a whole. For policy makers in a state that adopts a merit aid program, they are more concerned about the gain or loss of talents to their state. That is, they are interested in whether the adoption of the merit aid program affects the degree production for the state. If merit aid programs can help retain students attending in-state colleges, as some research suggests (Zhang and Ness 2010), it is a beneficial policy to the state. However, from a national perspective, such an outcome might have limited significance if the policy effect is only about student redistribution across state borders. To see whether such a policy has any impact in meeting the national goal, it is more important to understand whether the adoption of merit aid programs by the states affects the decision of individual students in their choice of college (other than in-state versus out-of-state) and eventual attainment of college degrees. Interstate migration of students has little bearing on the overall degree production in the country whereas individual student decisions related to college choice and persistence do. Unfortunately, there is a lack of explicit consideration of state merit aid policy from the national perspective. Most of the research to date is to evaluate the loss or gain of talent from the state perspectives, mostly using aggregated data (Zhang and Ness 2010). While it is certainly a valuable undertaking, it does not help to develop a comprehensive understanding of such programs, particularly from a national perspective. What is called for is a comprehensive analysis of state aggregated data and student record data to deepen our understanding of the effects of state merit aid programs in meeting the needs of the states and the nation.

State Merit Aid Programs in STEM Workforce Preparation

For over a half century, the United States has led the way in scientific discoveries and the application of new knowledge to scientific advancement, as well as in business and industry worldwide (Geiger 2004). However, in the last few years, other countries have caught up to and have eventually surpassed the United States in the international rankings. The 2006 Science and Engineering Indicators (National Science Board 2006) show the US ranking on several indicators has been matched or surpassed by other countries.

The state of undergraduate education in the STEM fields is also in decline. The United States ranks 32nd out of 90 countries in the number of natural science and engineering degrees per 100 degrees awarded among 24-year olds—with just 6 out of 100 students completing such degrees (National Science Board 2006). These figures are complicated by the fact that there are more women than men in college. Clearly, more students, especially women and minorities, must be encouraged to seek degrees in the STEM fields in order for the United States to maintain a competitive edge with the rest of the world. International competition has intensified with the coming of the age of globalization, and science and engineering education is essential to a sustainable national economic development and global competitiveness (National Commission on the Future of Higher Education 2006; National Science Board 2006).

State merit aid programs provide strong financial incentives to eligible students in the form of scholarship awards. The awards are based on student academic achievement and performance in the initial qualification stage and eventual renewal considerations, as well as a student's decision to stay in state or pursue education in another state. Such financial incentive and eligibility criteria, along with the disparity in college grading practices across the major fields (Hu 2005; Sabot and Wakeman-Linn 1991), could conceivably influence student decisions on whether or not to choose the STEM fields and persist in those fields in college. However, there has been little effort to examine such influences. With the increasing popularity of merit aid programs in state policy arena (Cohen-Vogel et al. 2008), it is critical to examine whether and to what extent state merit aid programs could affect the outcomes in STEM fields for individual students and the state and the country as a whole.

To understand the impact of state merit aid programs, two different yet related outcomes in STEM education can be adopted to develop a better policy perspective: The STEM degree production in the states that have adopted the policy and the educational decisions of individual students. The former outcome has direct policy implications to the state, and the latter outcome has implications to individual students and ultimately the country as a whole.

For policymakers in a state that adopts a merit aid program, they are more concerned about the gain or loss of talents to their state. In terms of STEM education outcomes, they would be interested in knowing whether the adoption of the merit aid program affects the STEM degree production in the state. Studies on the HOPE program indicated that HOPE helped increase student enrollment and reduce student migration to out-of-state colleges and universities (Cornwell et al. 2006a, b; Dynarski 2000, 2004). Because students with higher-level academic preparation are more likely to choose STEM fields than counterparts with lower academic preparation (Xie and Shauman 2003), merit aid programs could help increase STEM degree production in the state by retaining high-performing students. However, whether it is a net gain or loss of STEM talents by the state also depends on the choice of and degree attainment in the STEM fields by individual students who would not have left their home state even without the merit aid program. Therefore, the outcome of degree production in the STEM fields in the state is a combination of student redistribution across state borders and individual student choices of STEM fields.

From a national perspective, it is more important to understand whether the adoption of merit aid programs by the states affects the decisions of individual students in their choice of STEM majors and eventual attainment of STEM degrees. Interstate migration of students has little bearing on the overall STEM degree production in the country, whereas individual student decisions related to STEM fields do. Thus, there are two aspects in understanding the effects of merit aid programs on STEM education outcomes: (1) The "redistribution" aspect—that merit aid programs could affect student decisions of obtaining college education in-state or out-of- state, which could subsequently influence the STEM education outcomes for the state; and (2) The "choice" aspect—that merit aid programs could affect individual choice of STEM fields and eventual degree attainment. For the state, if there are more students choosing to attain STEM degrees, whether through "redistribution" or "choice," merit aid programs benefit the state in STEM degree production. For the country as a whole, the "choice" aspect has much more bearing, while the "redistribution" aspect has little consequence. Whether the interests of the states and the country as a whole converge or diverge depends on the policy effects on student STEM educational outcomes.

Summary

State merit aid programs in general do not have very complicated policy configurations. However, because of the policy values embedded in those programs and the competition of policy values such as equity, efficiency, excellence, and fraternity in American society (Fowler 2000), the conversations surrounding those programs are intense and contentious. Also, because those programs are initiated and financed by states, the examination of the effects of those programs tended to be focused on state interests. Even though it makes sense to evaluate the "gains" and "losses" from the standpoint of the policy states, such types of studies essentially pit one state's interests against others. In other words, it is about an "arms race" of talents among states. Such phenomenon clearly has policy importance to the states, but the implications for individual students and the country as a whole are unclear. Perhaps such programs instead have some "externality" from student redistribution among different types of higher education institutions (McPherson and Schapiro 1994) because most of the talents would concentrate in a limited number of highly prestigious colleges and universities if without such programs, but tangible evidence beyond state interests is close to nonexistent.

We argue that a comprehensive understanding of the effects of state merit aid programs should consider a wide range of outcomes from the perspectives of the states, individual students, and the country as a whole. The educational outcomes for the policy states will likely depend on the effects of state merit aid programs on student migration across state borders and their eventual decisions and the effects of such programs on individual decisions for those students who would have stayed in state regardless of state merit aid programs. It is useful to differentiate those effects and distill clearer policy implications for individual students, states, and the country as a whole.

Theoretical Issues in Studying the Effects of State Merit Aid Programs

The key feature of state merit aid programs is financial awards to students who demonstrate merits as reflected in academic achievement in course work, performance in academic assessment, and/or standardized tests such as SAT or ACT (Table 10.1). The states expect that such a mechanism can incentivize students to put more effort into academic work and achieve academic excellence, can help retain the best and brightest students in state, and can promote higher education opportunity for state residents (Heller 2004; Zhang and Ness 2010). That is, central to state policy goals is to use financial awards to improve student educational performance and attainment and to increase the stock of college-educated labor force for the state. In the following section, we review the common theoretical perspectives used by researchers in dealing with state merit aid programs and some other potential useful theories overlooked in studying those programs.

Economic Perspective

Economics as a discipline has exerted enormous influence on research in higher education, especially on studies of college choice and persistence. The economic demand theory and human capital theory are the foundations of economic modeling on student postsecondary decisions (Chen 2008; Hossler et al. 2009; Perna 2006, 2010).

The economic demand theory suggested that the quantity of a good or service an individual demands is a function of the monetary income of the individual, the price of the good or service, prices of alternative good or service, and individual tastes or preferences. Human capital theory, on the other hand, provided the basis for considering higher education as an investment, by which educational recipients would enjoy economic returns from their investment in education. The concurrent views coming from human capital and student demand theories for student postsecondary education are as follows: (1) higher education is a wise investment for individuals because college graduates can earn enough to offset the expense of attending college in addition to the forgone earnings due to the delayed entrance into the labor market, that is, the opportunity costs; and (2) student demand for higher education is related to college tuition prices and financial aid because tuition prices and financial aid ultimately influence student utility maximization.

Although there remain some controversies over the effectiveness of student financial aid, existing literature provides relatively sound evidence that financial aid can encourage college access and persistence in higher education, and the effects vary depending on student backgrounds and the configuration of the financial aid programs (Chen 2008; St. John et al. 2011; Perna 2006). Like many other financial supports to students, state merit aid awards provide financial assistance to students which can change the costs students face when selecting educational programs, which in turn can alter student educational decisions. Not surprisingly, the economic perspectives have been used in existing literature in guiding the studies. Typically from those perspectives, state merit aid awards are considered as financial incentives that could affect student college decisions (Cornwell et al. 2006a, b; Dynarski 2004).

Sociological Perspectives

Sociological perspectives have demonstrated strong powers in explaining phenomena in higher education. Researchers in higher education have used the social capital perspective by Coleman (1988) and cultural capital perspective by Bourdieu (1986), among some other theoretical perspectives, to examine student educational participation and attainment. Both social capital and cultural capital perspectives could help understand who may be more likely to receive merit aid scholarships and why. The niche of those theoretical perspectives in understanding the effects of state merit aid programs, though, needs further exploration. Still, some sociological perspectives may be relevant in the research on the effects of state merit aid programs.

Sociological perspectives on social stratification and inequality in educational opportunity have been used in the discourse of merit aid programs. Those perspectives were mostly adopted in the discussion on the unequal distribution of state merit aid scholarship among students of different backgrounds such as income and racial/ethnic backgrounds (Heller and Marin 2002). As mentioned before, state merit aid programs consider student academic achievement and performance as a key factor in scholarship eligibility. Such a consideration could have differential effects on students of different socioeconomic and racial/ethnic backgrounds because students from low-income and minority backgrounds tend to achieve lower academically (Heller and Marin 2002, 2004). This situation could be exacerbated when the funds from state lottery proceeds are used in state merit aid programs as individuals of disadvantaged backgrounds disproportionately contributed to such funds (Heller and Marin 2002, 2004). Thus, state merit aid programs were considered "a particularly regressive form of redistribution" (Dynarski 2004, p. 93).

Another prominent sociological theory that can be useful in understanding state merit aid programs is the status attainment model (Blau and Duncan 1967). However, existing literature on state merit aid programs has not paid sufficient attention to it. The status attainment model viewed social mobility as a process of status attainment developing through the person's life history. The process is an interactive one between social environment and individual student characteristics (Hossler et al. 1998), and finally determines the outcome such as educational or occupational attainment.

The logical model proposed by Blau and Duncan (1967) dealt with the interactions among four factors: family background, educational attainment, early occupational status, and current occupational status. They linked current occupational status with family background, educational attainment, and early occupational status, but also emphasized that each phase of later attainment was a function of previous attainment. Alexander and Eckland (1975) expanded the basic status attainment model by including student academic ability and educational plans. The basic status attainment model was also expanded when attainment was viewed as a dynamic process that traces an individual's movement through the most crucial educational decision points. College access and persistence are among the critical decision points in the chain of the student status attainment process, where family background variables, academic ability, and individual aspirations potentially have influence.

The underlying interpretive views from status attainment models, however, are somewhat different. The critical theorists, such as Bowles and Gintis (1976) and Karabel (1972), argued that educational institutions are structured to serve the interests of the ruling class. Student educational decisions, therefore, are understood not as isolated individual events but as part of a larger process of social stratification, through which the existing educational and social inequalities were perpetuated. Another school of thought advanced the idea of meritocracy in status attainment (Sewell and Hauser 1975). From this view, differences in educational attainment mirrored the differences in individual skills and abilities rather than social status per se, and the social origins of students largely had indirect effects on student attainment mediated by student academic ability and achievement.

The status attainment model is relevant in understanding the role of state merit aid programs in student academic preparation and postsecondary participation. The key concept is academic achievement and whether the financial awards based on academic achievement can mitigate or exacerbate the inequality in postsecondary opportunity. The end outcome of educational attainment for students of different backgrounds likely depends on how different students respond to the financial incentives in their academic effort and educational decisions. However, little research exists on the effects of state merit aid programs on academic effort and achievement by students of different backgrounds.

Psychological Perspectives

Higher education literature on student educational attainment has traditionally been based on the sociological and economic perspectives to understand student decisions regarding higher education. Recent literature synthesis shows a trend toward more multidisciplinary effort. In a synthesis to examine whether financial aid affects student college decisions, Goldrick-Rab et al. (2009) explored some new theories that are pertinent to the understanding of how financial aid may affect student success in college. In particular, they introduced several aspects that should be considered in understanding the role of merit aid student decisions: differences in individual expected returns from education and the importance of time horizon, and the role of risk aversion and loss aversion in individual decision-making process.

Goldrick-Rab et al. (2009) suggested that students from different backgrounds may have very different expected return from their college education, and they could also use different time horizon to calculate the benefits from higher education investment. Thus, even though the interventions are similar, the decision responses could vary largely due to the way individuals make cost-benefit analysis. This reasoning can have implications to state merit aid awards on student decisions, as applicable in research on the effects of other financial aid programs. Moreover, given the risk that students can lose their merit aid awards due to the eligibility criteria based on continuous academic performance, the perspectives of risk aversion and loss aversion become highly relevant in understanding how state merit aid awards could affect student educational decisions. This is particularly true in understanding student choice of course work and major fields. One example is the finding by Dee and Jackson (1999) that students in the disciplines of science, engineering, and computing are more likely to lose their HOPE scholarship in Georgia, a phenomenon that is consistent with the argument by Hu (2005) in his analysis of college grading practices. Thus, the risks of losing merit aid scholarship are not the same for students in different disciplines, and it is reasonable to expect that students would take this into the consideration of their educational decisions (Goldrick-Rab et al. 2009).

Summary

The three theoretical perspectives provide conceptual arguments about the possible effects of state merit aid programs on student educational achievement and attainment. Furthermore, they also offer some insights about some possible unintended consequences given the high stakes embedded in the state merit aid programs where financial awards are contingent upon student continuous academic performance as measured by student GPAs, which could alter student choices as different decisions may imply different risks. Researchers on state merit aid programs can use those theories to frame their studies, and can also explore the utility of other theoretical perspectives such as social capital and cultural capital to understand the effects of merit aid programs.

Methodological Considerations in Evaluating the Effects of State Merit Aid Programs

Educational research could be more valuable if researchers can provide rigorous evidence to demonstrate the causal effects of policies and programs (Brewer et al. 2010). To obtain a "causal" estimate of the effect of state merit aid programs, one would then calculate the difference in the average outcome for students who receive the treatment versus the same students if they had not received the treatment (the counterfactual). Given that students are not randomly assigned into those programs, researchers have been using different quasi-experimental methods to evaluate these program effects. Two commonly used techniques in this area, namely, difference-indifferences (DD) and regression discontinuity (RD) can help remedy the inferential problems encountered when trying to establish causal effects using observational data (Schneider et al. 2007). In addition, researchers may also benefit from using other research perspectives, including qualitative approaches, to enrich the understanding of the effects of merit aid programs.

Difference-in-Differences (DD)

The DD approach is by far one of the most widely used approaches to evaluate the effects of state merit aid programs. This approach has been used by economists analyzing aggregate data from IPEDS and Census (Dynarski 2004; Zhang and Ness 2010) and state or institutional administrative data (Binder et al. 2002; Cornwell et al. 2006b).

The DD technique is a variation of fixed effects panel data models (Zhang 2010). Since the work by Ashenfelter and Card (1985), the use of DD technique has been increasingly popular, especially in program and policy evaluation research (e.g., Cornwell et al. 2006b; Dynarski 2000). In the simplest set-up, suppose two states are observed for two time periods, with one of the states exposed to a treatment (i.e., the merit aid program) in the second period but not in the first period, while the other not exposed to any treatment in either period. The change between the two periods for the first state (i.e., the treatment group) represents both policy and time effects; and the change between the two periods for the second state (i.e., the control group) represents the time effect. Assuming the time effect is the same for both treatment and control groups, the difference between the above two differences would provide an estimate for the policy effects.

The DD technique is based on two indispensable assumptions. First, there are no other variables/policies that might have affected the outcome variable in the treatment group. Otherwise, the DD estimate will include both the effect of the policy of interest and other variables. If there are time-varying factors that might have affected the outcome, one could control those factors in the empirical model. Second, the time effect is group-invariant. No group-specific factors other than the policy of interest have led to different time trends across groups. Selection of comparable states (i.e., the control group) is crucial because the difference between the before and after period in the comparable states is substituted for the difference between the before and after period in the policy state. In empirical research, different sets of comparable states have been used to check the robustness of DD estimates (e.g., Doyle 2006; Hearn and Griswold 1994; Zhang and Ness 2010).

Regression Discontinuity

A substantial quantity of literature is developed which is centered around the use of RD to examine postsecondary access and educational attainment (Bettinger 2004; Lesik 2006; Trochim 1984; van der Klaauw 2002). RD is a useful technique for situations in which there are specific, measurable criteria for eligibility into a program (van der Klaauw 2002). This is the case for merit aid programs. It is worthwhile to note that the RD design assumes that the students whose eligibility scores are close to the cut-off threshold are very similar, akin to being randomly assigned around this threshold. If we take college persistence as an example, the RD design answers whether the students who are slightly above the eligibility threshold (thus receiving merit aid) are more likely to persist into the next year than those who are slightly below the threshold, holding all other factors constant.

In employing the RD design in quasi-experimental study, one has to attend to the differences of a "sharp" RD design versus a "fuzzy" design. In a "sharp" RD design, the prediction of treated versus untreated is perfect based on test scores. Results from this sharp design can be interpreted as intent-to-treat (ITT) effects, which estimates the effect of providing someone the treatment, regardless whether they choose to participate or not. This certainly might not be the case with a large program such as the Bright Futures. To address the potential issue of noncompliance, a fuzzy RD design is required. This can be accomplished by using an instrumental variable (IV) in the first stage to predict the probability of being treated and then using the predicted probability in the second stage to estimate the effect of actual treatment on the treated. It is noteworthy that different student test scores should be used for different outcome variables. For example, high school GPA and SAT/ACT will be used to examine the effect of a merit aid program on college choice, while college GPA will be used to estimate the effect of such a program on subsequent college persistence and degree completion.

Since the identification of RD technique is based on the difference between the groups above and below the threshold, choosing appropriate bandwidth for RD design becomes critical because it involves balancing between precision and bias. Using a larger bandwidth yields more observations, thus more precise estimates. However, the local linear functional form becomes less accurate with a large bandwidth, leading to biased estimates. Fan and Gijbels (1996) developed an optimal bandwidth in the case of local linear regression.

Another issue related to evaluating the effects of a merit aid program on educational outcome is the potential problem of "gaming" for qualifying for the awards. For example, if college GPA is used in determining the eligibility for students to renew their merit awards, it is possible that faculty members would give out qualifying grades to students who could have not received such grades. In this case, some cautions should be taken to address such a potential problem. McCrary (2008) suggests that if the manipulation is monotonic, that is, if the merit aid program induces changes of the assignment variable in one direction (in this particular case, to make students more likely to qualify for the aid), a discontinuity in the density of the assignment variable would raise the question whether its value has been manipulated. This can be done by examining the distribution of observations around the cut-off point. In addition, one has to check whether individuals on either side of the cut-off point are observationally similar. If the manipulation systematically favors certain students (e.g., from certain area and high schools, with certain individual characteristics), one would detect an imbalance of observed covariates at the cut-off point. The alternative is to conduct the regression discontinuity analysis treating these covariates as outcome variables (van der Klaauw 2008).

Although RD is a highly desirable approach to evaluate the effects of state merit aid programs, it is surprising to see few researchers studying state merit aid programs actually used this approach. With the availability of state administrative data on student longitudinal records, RD would be a highly valuable approach for researchers to evaluate the effects of state merit aid programs on student educational decisions and progression in higher education.

Other Research Approaches

Using aggregate data at institutional level or state level can help understand policy effects from a macroperspective, and using student-level data can help understand how such programs affect educational outcomes from a microperspective. It is not surprising that most of policy studies have used existing data to examine the effects of state merit aid programs on a wide range of outcomes including college enrollment and the production of college-educated workforce. However, there are limitations with the use of existing data such as the IPEDS, Census, and state administrative data sets. The data elements there essentially deal with the factual information while do not have measures on student attitudinal aspects, which are important in student decision-making process (Clotfelter and Rothschild 1993).

The use of longitudinal survey of students could help "unpack" the underlying decision process of individual students and shed light on the mechanism for state merit aid programs affecting desirable outcomes. In particular, the threads of survey questions on student attitudes and values and experiences in the academic, social, and financial dimensions can be very valuable. Measures on student attitudes and values can improve the accuracy of modeling on student educational decisions, whereas measures on student experiences can help examine the potential mediating variables in understanding the effects of merit aid on student educational decisions.

Another potential beneficial research approach studying the effects of state merit aid program is the use of qualitative inquiry method. Very few studies on state merit aid program used qualitative methods, with a recent exception of Perna and Steele (2011). Qualitative research approach can help shed new light on effects of state merit aid programs, particularly some unintended consequences. For instance, Perna and Steele (2011) uncovered some unintended consequences of state merit aid programs as reflected in grade inflation and student choice of less rigorous course work due to the concern of losing merit aid scholarships. Qualitative approach can also provide insights about the roles of parents, students, teachers, and others may play in student educational decisions in merit-aid environments.

Future Direction in Studying State Merit Aid Programs

State merit aid programs have been enacted in around one-third of the states as of now. Researchers in various disciplines have devoted considerable amount of time and energy in studying those programs. Such research effort has generated useful literature base related to the effects of state merit aid programs. Future research effort on the following areas, whether using quantitative or qualitative approaches or a combination, can further advance the understanding of the effects of state merit aid programs.

Attending to the Missing Links in Student Educational Decision Sequence

There is clearly a need to evaluate the effects of various state merit aid programs on educational outcomes such as academic achievement and student access and success in higher education. It is also important to expand the outcomes of interest so that a better understanding of such programs can be developed. First, can merit aid programs affect student educational aspirations? Student education aspiration has long been considered as one of the important juncture in student educational decision sequence (St. John et al. 2001). Abundant research literature shows that student educational aspiration is among one of the most important determinants for student college access and success (Hossler and Stage 1992; Hossler et al. 1998). Previous research on student financial aid indicated that financial aid availability can help remove student concerns on college affordability and enhance student educational aspirations (Hossler et al. 1989; Hossler and Stage 1992; St. John and Hu 2006a).

Another important aspect is to examine whether merit aid programs affect student college experiences and learning outcomes. Higher education literature has consistently pointed to the importance of student experiences in student learning and personal development outcomes (Astin 1993; Pascarella and Terenzini 1991, 2005). Given the increasing use of surveys on college students by colleges and universities such as participation in the National Survey of Student Engagement (NSSE) and Collegiate Learning Assessment (CLA) programs, it is now possible to conduct studies examining whether merit aid programs could affect student experiences in college and outcomes from college. Can merit aid programs affect student effort on academic work? Can merit aid scholarships affect student academic and social experiences and learning outcomes? Answers to those questions can not only provide answers directly related to the fundamental argument that state merit aid programs can induce students to put forth more effort in the learning process but also have important implications in educational reform aiming to improve the quality of both K-12 and postsecondary education.

Finally, as more and more states develop state longitudinal data systems and enhance capacity to link student record data with information regarding college graduates in the labor market (such as Unemployment Insurance), the opportunity to examine longer-term effects of state merit aid programs is also feasible. One logical question is whether students who received state merit aid scholarships eventually work in the policy states. Another question is the economic returns of state merit aid scholarships to individual students, the states, and the country. The benefits of higher education to individuals and the society have long been the driving force in policy debate on investing in higher education (McMahon 2009), and rigorous evidence of the effects of state merit aid programs on individual in the labor market and the society would certainly enrich the conversation on state merit aid programs.

Recognizing Policy Dynamics and the Complication of Policy Effects

Most of the time, evaluative studies on public policy do not pay sufficient attention to the interactivity of various policy actors and tend to simplify the connection (or lack thereof) between policy intervention and outcomes of interest. This is clearly the case in examining the effects of state merit aid programs. A common tendency is to compare the outcomes before and after the implementation of programs, or compare outcomes for those who receive policy interventions to those who do not. What is missing is the consideration of possible responses by colleges and universities in reaction to state merit aid programs and the potential complication of such possible reactivity to outcomes under study.

Some researchers have paid attention to this phenomenon. For example, Dynarski (2004) and Long (2004) found that colleges and universities tend to raise the costs of attendance for students in response to the implementation of state merit aid programs so that they can capture the additional revenues from such programs, either through increase in tuition fees or increased charges on other education-related costs. This is a very important phenomenon to consider given the increasing concerns on college costs and prices and college affordability problems for many Americans. This reactivity may or may not directly exert financial burdens to individual students due to the configuration of state merit aid programs, but if it does have linkage to college pricing behavior, it could affect the financial context for higher education and influence student educational decisions in a still unknown way. Future studies explicitly considering this phenomenon can help shed light on this possibility.

Studying Conditional Effects of Merit Aid Programs

As much as it is important to understand the general effects of merit aid programs on degree production and educational decisions of the individuals, it is also critical to examine whether the effects are different for students of different gender or racial/ethnic background for a number of reasons. Existing statistics indicate that among 25- to 29-year-olds in 2002, only 29% had completed four or more years of college. Perhaps more striking element of these statistics is the racial divide as 36% of this group were White; 18% were non-Hispanic Blacks; and Hispanics accounted for only 9% of the graduates. For the same age group, only 45% of whites, 26% of non-Hispanic blacks, and 15% of Hispanics had completed at least an associate's degree (National Center for Educational Statistics 2004).

Differential effects of a state program on educational outcomes for students from different backgrounds could have implications from an equity perspective, but more importantly, the changing demographics in the United States make it critical to have more traditionally disadvantaged students to succeed and obtain college degrees. Across a vast array of postsecondary outcomes, evidence increasingly points to the fact that the effects of programs and practices are not equally applicable to all students. For instance, Pascarella and Terenzini (2005) pointed to the increasing diversity in the college-going population to encourage greater attention examining conditional effects of policies and programs on students from different backgrounds. Researchers have repeatedly called for increased analysis of gender and racial/ethnic-related conditional effects across many types of college outcomes including student educational attainment (Pascarella and Terenzini 2005; Reason et al. 2006; Tinto 1993). This call is certainly relevant in studying a large-scale state policy initiative like merit aid programs. Can state merit aid programs affect the sequence of educational outcomes differentially for students of different backgrounds? How do the eligibility criteria and award generosity play a role in moderating those effects? Answers to those questions can provide critical information on the social consequences of state merit aid programs and also could shed light on potential remedies.

Comparing the Effects of Merit Aid to Need-Based Aid and Other Policy Interventions

Attention to educational attainment has never been in shortage, even though the accomplishments have been less than satisfactory. Various policy interventions and programs have been in place aiming to improve educational attainment (Kazis et al. 2004).

Higher education has very complicated "objective" functions, among which maximizing educational attainment for all and minimizing the attainment gaps among students of different characteristics are both important (St. John 2003; Hu 2005). In addition, program efficiency is an important consideration, which has become even more critical given the financial difficulties and scarce resources available. However, it has some policy relevance to compare the effects of merit aid programs with other policy interventions. The comparison between merit aid programs to need-based programs and other programs can be an interesting and useful direction for policy researchers. How do the effects of merit aid programs compare to need-based financial aid programs and other interventions such as early encouragement program or outreach programs on college access, choice, and success? There is just not much information to gather to answer questions like this yet, but it is important for policy makers to know the answer to make evidence-based policy decisions.

Conclusions

In an age of scarce public resources and increasing need to promote postsecondary education opportunity to all students while minimizing the disparity of such opportunity for students of different backgrounds, it is valuable to carefully examine the effects of public policies that involve resource allocation at the magnitude of state-sponsored merit aid programs on college degree production in the state and individual student college choices, persistence, and degree completion, as well as educational outcomes in the STEM fields. At the same time, the financial difficulties facing many states, coupled with the increasing tuition pricing in higher education, have forced state policy makers to reprioritize and rethink about strategies related to merit aid programs. In this context, it is important to analyze both the conceptual and empirical evidences regarding the effects of merit aid programs on individual students, states, and the country as a whole. Our analysis in this chapter generated some promising findings of state merit aid programs on educational outcomes that have strong policy implications. It also exposes the areas that further efforts are warranted to develop a greater understanding of state merit aid programs. The future of research on merit aid programs is bright. There remain some challenges and opportunities as well, as identified in this chapter.

Acknowledgments

This chapter was prepared with financial support from the Institute of Education Sciences, US Department of Education, through Grant # R305A110609 to Shouping Hu at Florida State University and Liang Zhang at Penn State University. The opinions expressed are those of the authors and do not represent views of the Institute or the US Department of Education. The authors would like to thank Laura Perna for her helpful feedback.

References

Advisory Committee on Student Financial Assistance. (2001). *Access denied: Restoring the nation's commitment to equal educational opportunity*. Washington: Author.

Advisory Committee on Student Financial Assistance. (2002). *Empty promise: The myths of college access in America*. Washington: Author.

Advisory Committee on Student Financial Assistance. (2010). *The rising price of inequality: How inadequate grant aid limits college access and persistence*. Washington: Author.

Alexander, K. L., & Eckland, B. K. (1975). Basic attainment processes: A replication and extension. *Sociology of Education*, 48, 457–495.

Ashburn, E. (2010, August 8). Gates' millions: Can big bucks turn students into graduates? *Chronicle of Higher Education*, Daily News.

Ashenfelter, O. A., & Card, D. (1985). Using the longitudinal structure of earnings to estimate the effect of training programs. *The Review of Economics and Statistics*, 67, 648–660.

Astin, A. W. (1993). *What matters in college: Four critical years revisited*. San Francisco: Jossey-Bass.

Becker, G. S. (1994). *Human capital: A theoretical and empirical analysis with special reference to education*. Chicago: University of Chicago Press.

Bettinger, E. (2004). How financial aid affects persistence. In C. Hoxby (Ed.), *College choices: The economics of where to go, when to go, and how to pay for it* (pp. 207–238). Chicago: University of Chicago Press.

Binder, M., Ganderton, P. T., & Hutchens, K. (2002). Incentive effects of New Mexico's merit-based state scholarship program: Who responds and how? In D. Heller & P. Marin (Eds.), *Who should we help? The negative social consequences of merit scholarships* (pp. 42–56). Cambridge: Harvard Civil Rights Project.

Blau, P. M., & Duncan, O. D. (1967). *The American occupational structure*. New York: Wiley.

Bourdieu, P. (1986). The forms of capital. In J. G. Richardson (Ed.), *Handbook of theory and research for the sociology of education* (pp. 241–258). New York: Greenwood Press.

Bowles, S., & Gintis, H. (1976). *Schooling in capitalist America: Educational reform and the contradictions of economic life*. New York: Basic Books.

Brewer, D. J., Fuller, B., & Loeb S. (2010). *Editor's introduction. Educational Evaluation and Policy Analysis*, 32, 3–4.

Chen, R. (2008). Financial aid and student dropout in higher education: A heterogeneous research approach. In J. C. Smart (Ed.), *Higher education: Handbook of theory and research* (Vol. 23, pp. 209–239). New York: Springer.

Clotfelter, C. T. (2010). *American universities in a global market*. Chicago: University of Chicago Press.

Clotfelter, C. T, & Rothschild, M. (Eds.). (1993). *Studies of supply and demand in higher education*. Chicago: University of Chicago Press.

Cohen-Vogel, L., Ingle, K., Albee, A., & Spence, M. (2008). The "spread" of merit-based college aid: Politics, policy consortia and interstate competition. Educational Policy, 22, 339–362.

Coleman, J. S. (1988). Social capital in the creation of human capital. American Journal of Sociology, 94(Suppl.), 95–120.

Cornwell, C. M., & Mustard, D. B. (2001). HOPE scholarship affects where, not whether, students attend college. Public policy research series (Vol. 2, no. 10.). Athens: Carl Vinson Institute of Government, University of Georgia.

Cornwell, C. M., & Mustard, D. B. (2002). HOPE, the brain drain, and diversity: The impact of the scholarship on high achievers and African Americans. Policy Notes, 3(4), 1–2.

Cornwell, C. M., & Mustard, D. B. (2003). Georgia's HOPE scholarship program: Enrollment gains and lottery finance. Insights on Southern Poverty, 1(3), 5–8.

Cornwell, C. M., & Mustard, D. B. (2006). Evaluating HOPE-style merit scholarships. Federal Reserve Bank of Cleveland Innovation in Education Conference Proceedings, Cleveland, OH.

Cornwell, C. M., Lee, K. H., & Mustard, D. B. (2005). Student responses to merit scholarship retention rules. The Journal of Human Resources, 40(4), 895–917.

Cornwell, C. M., Lee, K. H., & Mustard, D. B. (2006a). The effects of state-sponsored merit scholarships on course selection and major choice in college. IZA Discussion Paper #1953. Bonn, Germany: Institute for the Study of Labor.

Cornwell, C. M., Mustard, D. B., & Sridhar, D. J. (2006b). The enrollment effects of merit-based financial aid. Journal of Labor Economics, 24(4), 761–786.

Dee, T. S., & Jackson, L. A. (1999). Who loses HOPE? Attrition from Georgia's college scholarship program. Southern Economic Journal, 66(2), 379–390.

Delaney, J. A. (2007). The academic consequences of state merit aid: The case of Kentucky. Doctoral dissertation. Stanford: Stanford University.

Delaney, J. A., & Ness, E. (2009, November). A state-level merit aid typology. Paper presented at the annual meeting of the Association for the Study of Higher Education (ASHE), Vancouver, Canada.

Doyle, W. R. (2006). Adoption of merit-based student grant programs: An event history analysis. Educational Evaluation and Policy Analysis, 28, 259–285.

Doyle, W. R. (2008). Access, choice, and excellence: The competing goals of state financial aid programs. In S. Baum, M. McPherson, & P. Steele (Eds.), The effectiveness of student aid policies: What the research tells us (pp. 159–188). New York: College Board.

Doyle, W. R. (2010). Does merit-based aid "crowd out" need-based aid? Research in Higher Education, 51(5), 397–415.

Dynarski, S. (2000). Hope for whom? Financial aid for the middle class and its impact on college attendance. National Tax Journal, 53(3), 629–661.

Dynarski, S. (2004). The new merit aid. In C. M. Hoxby (Ed.), College choices: The economics of where to go, when to go, and how to pay for it (pp. 63–100). Chicago: University of Chicago Press.

Dynarski, S. (2008). Building the stock of college-educated labor. Journal of Human Resources, 43, 576–610.

Fan, J., & Gijbels, I. (1996). Local polynomial modeling and its applications. London: Chapman and Hall.

Florida Department of Education. (2008). Annual report to the commissioner (2007–08). Tallahassee: Office of Student Financial Assistance.

Florida Department of Education. (2010). Florida Bright Futures Scholarship program fact sheet. Tallahassee: Florida Department of Education.

Fowler, F. C. (2000). Policy studies for educational leaders: An introduction. Upper Saddle River: Merrill.

Geiger, R. L. (2004). Research and relevant knowledge: American research universities since World War II. Piscataway: Transaction Publishers.

Goldrick-Rab, S., Harris, D. N., & Trostel, P. A. (2009). Why financial aid matters (or does not) for college success: Toward a new interdisciplinary perspective. In J. C. Smart (Ed.), Higher education: Handbook of theory and research (Vol. 25, pp. 1–45). New York: Agathon.

Gonzalez, J. (2010, August 9). In Texas speech, Obama renews his educational goals for the nation. Chronicle of Higher Education, Daily News.

Groen, J. A. (2004). The effect of college location on migration of college-educated labor. Journal of Econometrics, 121(1–2), 125–142.

Harkreader, S., Hughes, J. Hicks-Tozzi, M., & Vanlandingham, G.,(2008). The impact of Florida's Bright Futures Scholarship Program on high school performance and college enrollment. Journal of Student Financial Aid, 38(1), 5–16.

Hearn, J. C. (1993). The paradox of growth in federal aid for college students: 1965–1990. In J. C. Smart (Ed.), Higher education: Handbook of theory and research. New York: Agathon.

Hearn, J. C., & Longanecker, D. (1985). Enrollment effects of alternative postsecondary pricing policies. Journal of Higher Education, 56, 485–508.

Hearn, J. C., & Griswold, C. P. (1994). State-level centralization and policy innovation in U.S. postsecondary education. Educational Evaluation and Policy Analysis, 16(2), 161–190.

Hebel, S. (2009). Lumina's leader sets lofty goals for fund's role in policy debates. Chronicle of Higher Education, 55(34), A1–A12.

Heller, D. E. (1997). Student price response in higher education: An update of Leslie and Brinkman. Journal of Higher Education, 68(6), 624–659.

Heller, D. E. (2002). State merit scholarship programs: An introduction. In D. E. Heller & P. Marin (Eds.), Who should we help? The negative social consequences of merit scholarships (pp. 15–23). Cambridge, MA: Harvard Civil Rights Project.

Heller, D. E. (2004) State merit scholarship programs: An overview. In D. E. Heller & P. Marin (Eds.) State merit scholarship programs and racial inequality. Cambridge: Harvard Civil Rights Project.

Heller, D. E., & Marin, P. (Eds.). (2002). Who should we help? The negative social consequences of merit aid scholarships. Cambridge: Harvard Civil Rights Project.

Heller, D. E., & Marin, P. (2004). State merit scholarship programs and racial inequality. Cambridge: Harvard Civil Rights Project.

Henry, G. T., & Rubenstein, R. (2002). Paying for grades: Impact of merit-based financial aid on educational quality. Journal of Policy Analysis and Management, 21, 93–109.

Henry, G. T., Rubenstein, R., & Bugler, D. T. (2004). Is HOPE enough: Impacts of receiving and losing merit-based financial aid. Educational Policy, 18, 686–709.

Hossler, D., & Stage, F. K. (1992). Family and high school experience influences on the postsecondary educational plans of ninth-grade students. American Educational Research Journal, 29(2), 425–451.

Hossler, D., Braxton, J., & Coopersmith, G. (1989). Understanding student college choice. In J. Smart (Ed.), Higher education: Handbook of theory and research (Vol. 5, pp. 231–288). New York: Agathon Press.

Hossler, D., Schmit, J., & Vesper, N. (1998). Going to college: How social, economic, and educational factors influence the decisions students make. Baltimore: Johns Hopkins University Press.

Hossler, D., Ziskin, M., Gross, J. P. K., Kim, S., & Cekic, O. (2009). Student aid and its role in encouraging persistence. In J. C. Smart (Ed.), Higher education: Handbook of theory and research (Vol. 24, pp. 389–425). New York: Springer.

Hoxby, C. M. (2004). College choices: The economics of where to go, when to go, and how to pay for it. Chicago: The University of Chicago Press.

Hu, S. (2005). Beyond grade inflation: Grading problems in higher education. San Francisco: Jossey-Bass.

Hu, S. (2008, May). Merit-based aid and student enrollment in baccalaureate degree programs in science and engineering: An examination of Florida's Bright Futures program. Paper presented at the annual forum of the Association for Institutional Research, Seattle, WA.

Hu, S., & Hossler, D. (2000). Willingness to pay and preference for private institutions. Research in Higher Education, 41, 685–701.

Hu, S., & St. John, E. P. (2001). Student persistence in a public higher education system: Understanding racial/ethnic differences. Journal of Higher Education, 72, 265–286.

Jaeger, D. A., & Page, M. E. (1996). Degrees matter: New evidence on sheepskin effects in the returns to education. The Review of Economics and Statistics, 78(4), 733–740.

Johnson, V. E. (2003). Grade inflation: A crisis in college education. New York: Springer.

Kane, T. J., & Rouse, C. E. (1995). Labor-market returns to two- and four-year colleges. American Economic Review, 85(3), 600–614.

Karabel, J. (1972). Community college and social stratification. Harvard Educational Review, 42, 521–562.

Kazis, R., Vargas, J., & Hoffman, N. (Eds.) (2004). Double the numbers: Increasing postsecondary credentials for underrepresented youth. Cambridge: Harvard Education Press.

Krathwohl, D. R. (1998). Methods of educational & social science research: An integrated approach (2nd ed.). Longman.

Kuh, G. D., Kinzie, J., Schuh, J. H., & Whitt, E. J. (2005). Student success in college: Creating conditions that matter. San Francisco: Jossey-Bass.

Kuh, G. D., Kinzie, J., Buckley, J., Bridges, B., Hayek, J. (2007). Piecing together the student success puzzle: Research, propositions, and recommendations. ASHE Higher Education Report, 32(5). San Francisco: Jossey-Bass.

Lesik, S. A. (2006). Applying the regression discontinuity design to infer causality with nonrandom assignment. Review of Higher Education, 30, 1–19.

Leslie, L. L., & Brinkman, P. T. (1987). Student price response in higher education: The student demand studies. Journal of Higher Education, 58(2), 181–204.

Leslie, L. L., & Brinkman, P. T. (1988). The economic value of higher education. New York: Macmillan.

Long, B. T. (2004). How do financial aid policies affect colleges? The institutional impact of the Georgia HOPE scholarship. Journal of Human Resources, 39(3), 1045–1066.

McCrary, J. (2008). Manipulation of the running variable in the regression discontinuity design: A density test. Journal of Econometrics, 142(2): 698–714.

McMahon, W. W. (2009). Higher Learning, greater good: The private and social benefits of higher education. Baltimore: Johns Hopkins University Press.

McPherson, M. S., & Schapiro, M. O. (1994). Merit aid: Students, institutions, and society. New York: College Board.

McPherson, M. S., & Shapiro, M. O. (1998). The student aid game: Meeting need and rewarding talent in American higher education. Princeton: Princeton University Press.

Melguizo, T. (2008). Quality matters: Assessing the impact of attending more selective institutions on college completion rates of minorities. Research in Higher Education, 49, 214–236.

Melguizo, T. (2010). Are students of color more likely to graduate from college if they attend more selective institutions? Evidence from a cohort of recipients and nonrecipients of the Gates Millennium Scholarship Program. Educational Evaluation and Policy Analysis, 32, 230–248.

Montmarquette, C., Cannings, K., & Mahseredjian, S. (2002). How do young people choose college majors? Economics of Education Review, 21, 543–556.

National Center for Education Statistics. (2004). Digest of education statistics. Washington: Authors.

National Commission on the Future of Higher Education. (2006). A test of leadership: Charting the future of U.S. higher education. Washington: US Department of Education.

National Science Board. (2006). Science and engineering indicators 2006 (Vol. 1 No. NSB 06–01). Arlington: National Science Foundation.

Ness, E. (2008). Eligibility effects on college access: Under-represented student perceptions of Tennessee's merit aid program. Research in Higher Education, 49, 569–588.

Organisation for Economic Cooperation and Development. (2005). Education at a glance: OECD indicators. Paris: Author.

Orsuwan, M., & Heck, R. H. (2009). Merit-based student aid and freshman interstate college migration: Testing a dynamic model of policy change. Research in Higher Education, 50, 24–51.

Pascarella, E. T., & Terenzini, P. T. (1991). How college affects students: Findings and insights from 20 years of research. San Francisco: Jossey-Bass.

Pascarella, E. T., & Terenzini, P. T. (2005). How college affects students: A third decade of research. San Francisco: Jossey-Bass.

Perna, L. W. (2006). Toward a more complete understanding of the role of financial aid in promoting college enrollment: The importance of context. In J. C. Smart (Ed.), Higher education: Handbook of theory and research (Vol. 21, pp. 99–157). New York: Springer.

Perna, L. W. (2010). Studying college access and choice: A proposed conceptual model. In J. C. Smart (Ed.), Higher education: Handbook of theory and research (Vol. 25, pp. 129–179). New York: Springer.

Perna, L. W., & Steele, P. (2011). The role of context in understanding the contributions of financial aid to college opportunity. Teachers College Record, 113, 895–933.

Perry, K. K. (2001). Where college students live after they graduate. Washington: U.S. Department of Education.

Reason, R. D., Terenzini, P. T., & Domingo, R. J. (2006). First things first: Developing academic competence in the first year of college. Research in Higher Education, 47, 149–175.

Sabot, R., & Wakeman-Linn, J. (1991). Grade inflation and course choice. Journal of Economic Perspectives, 5, 159–171.

Schneider, B., Carnoy, M., Kilpatrick, J., Schmidt, W., & Shavelson, R. (2007). Estimating causal effects using experimental and observational designs. Washington: American Educational Research Association.

Scott-Clayton, J. (2009). On money and motivation: A quasi-experimental analysis of financial incentives for college achievement. Working paper. New York: Columbia University.

Sewell, W., & Hauser, R. (1975). Education, occupation, and earnings: Achievement in early career. New York: Academic.

St. John, E. P. (2003). Refinancing the college dream: Access, equal opportunity, and justice for taxpayers. Baltimore: Johns Hopkins University Press.

St. John, E. P., & Hu, S. (2006a). The impact of guarantees on financial aid on college enrollment: An evaluation of the Washington State Achievers Program. In E. P. St. John (Ed.), Public policy and educational opportunity: School reforms, postsecondary encouragement, and sate policies on postsecondary education. Reading on equal education (pp. 213–257). New York: AMS Press.

St. John, E. P., & Hu, S. (2006b, April). State financial policies and student choice of college and major field: A national study of high-achieving low-income students of color. Paper presented at the annual meeting of the American Educational Research Association in San Francisco, CA.

St. John, E. P., Asker, E., & Hu, S. (2001). The role of finances in student choice: A review of theory and research. In M. B. Paulsen & J. C. Smart (Eds.), The finance of higher education: Theory, research, policy, and practice (pp. 419–438). New York: Agathon.

St. John, E. P., Hu, S., & Fisher, A. F. (2011). Breaking through the access barrier: Academic capital formation informing policy in higher education. New York: Routledge.

Tinto, V. (1993). Leaving college: Rethinking the causes and cures of student attrition (2nd. Ed.). Chicago: The University of Chicago Press.

Trochim, W. (1984). Research design for program evaluation: The regression discontinuity approach. Newbury Park: Sage.

van der Klaauw, W. (2002). Estimating the effect of financial aid offers on college enrollment: A regression-discontinuity approach. International Economic Review, 43, 1249–1287.

van der Klaauw, W. (2008). Breaking the link between poverty and low student achievement: An evaluation of Title I. Journal of Econometrics, 142(2), 731–756.

Xie, Y., & Shauman, K. A. (2003). Women in science. Cambridge: Harvard University Press.

Zhang, L. (2005). Does quality pay? Benefits of attending a high-cost, prestigious college. New York: Routledge.

Zhang, L. (2010). The use of panel data methods in higher education policy studies. In Smart, J. (Ed.), Higher education: Handbook of theory and research (Vol. 25, pp. 309–347). The Netherlands: Springer.

Zhang, L. (2011). Does merit-based aid affect degree production in STEM fields? Evidence from Georgia and Florida. Journal of Higher Education, 82(4), 389–415.

Zhang, L., & Ness, E. (2010). Does state merit-based aid stem brain drain. Educational Evaluation and Policy Analysis, 32, 143–165.

Zhang, G., Min, Y. K., Frillman, S. A., Anderson, T. J., & Ohland, M. W. (2006). Student strategies for protecting merit-based scholarships: Grades, courseload, and major choice. Proceedings of the 2006 IEEE/ASEE Frontiers in Education Annual Conference. San Diego.

CHAPTER 11

INFLUENCES ON LABOR MARKET OUTCOMES OF AFRICAN AMERICAN COLLEGE GRADUATES: A NATIONAL STUDY

TERRELL L. STRAYHORN

Much of the research on the effects of college suggests that earning a bachelor's degree significantly influences one's economic success and labor market outcomes such as earnings, job security, and prestige of one's occupation (Ehrenberg & Rothstein, 1994). For example, several studies provide evidence to support the belief that college graduates earn higher annual salaries than do high school graduates (Pascarella & Terenzini, 1991, 2005; Smart, 1986; Smart & Pascarella, 1986) and are less likely to face periods of unemployment. A report from the U.S. Department of Education (2000) indicates that bachelor's degree (BA) recipients earned between 1.4 and 1.8 times more than those with only a high school diploma or its equivalent in 1988. Approximately 10 years later, BA recipients earned between 1.6 and 2 times more than those who graduated from high school only. Taken together, these results suggest that receiving a BA yields a substantial increase in earnings over one's lifetime. In fact, reports in the popular press suggest that college graduates earn approximately $1 million dollars more than nongraduates over their lifetime (Day & Newburger, 2002).

However, a segment of this body of research provides evidence of differences in the labor market outcomes of African American college graduates (Allen, 1992; Constantine, 1995; Sagen, Dallam, & Laverty, 1997; Thomas, 2000). The weight of the evidence suggests that African American college graduates are at a disadvantage with respect to post-graduate earnings and occupational status. Despite some progress, still today the Black unemployment rate is more than two times that of White Americans, and Black families earn only 58% as much income as White families. Perhaps an even more dramatic depiction of the current situation is reflected in national net worth comparisons: "In 2001, the typical Black household had a net worth of just $19,000 (including home equity) compared with $121,000 for Whites" (Muhammad, Davis, Lui, & Leondar Wright, 2004, p. 1). Although the evidence is quite clear that African Americans face significant disadvantages with respect to labor market outcomes, it is less clear just why this is the case. That is, the causal mechanism underlying this disadvantage is difficult to ascertain but an important and necessary piece of the puzzle.

As a result, some studies have examined the influence of race on economic or labor market outcomes (Hoffman, 1984; Pascarella, Smart, & Stoecker, 1989; Phelan & Phelan, 1983). For example, researchers have shown that African Americans, as a whole, earn lower annual salaries than any other racial group (National Center for Education Statistics [NCES], 2001). Moreover, other studies provide evidence that African Americans reported lower job satisfaction than did their White counterparts (Phelan & Phelan, 1983) and reported lower scores on job satisfaction than did other racial groups (Mau & Kopischke, 2001).

Perhaps the largest single body of research on the labor market outcomes of African American college graduates concerns the impact of attending a historically Black college or university (HBCU) (Allen, 1992; Constantine, 1994, 1995; Ehrenberg & Rothstein, 1994; Fitzgerald, 2000; London, 1998; Solnick, 1990; Thomas, 2000). Findings concerning the net impact of graduating from an HBCU on African American college graduates' economic success are mixed. For example, Ehrenberg and

Rothstein analyzed national data and found that attending an HBCU had a statistically nonsignificant effect on subsequent occupational status and earnings, controlling for gender, SAT scores, high school rank, educational attainment, and a number of other confounding influences. On the other hand, Constantine studied African Americans at four-year institutions and found that attendance at an HBCU versus a predominately White institution (PWI) had a statistically significant positive effect on graduates' earnings, controlling for a battery of individual level characteristics such as high school achievement and gender. More evidence is needed to substantiate the net impact of HBCU graduation on the post-BA labor market outcomes of African American college graduates. This is the gap addressed by this study.

In sum, several major themes were found in the literature. First, college graduates reap significant economic benefits or private returns on their investments in higher education (Day & Newburger, 2002; Ehrenberg & Rothstein, 1994; NCES, 2000). However, African American college graduates still face significant disadvantages with respect to post-BA earnings and occupational status. A limited number of studies also examined job satisfaction for African American college graduates (Mau & Kopischke, 2001; Phelan & Phelan, 1983) and found similar conclusions. While the weight of evidence provides clear and compelling information about the economic disparities of African American college graduates, much less is known about the underlying causal mechanism and those factors that influence their post-BA labor market outcomes.

One possible factor that has received a relatively significant amount of research attention is the impact of graduating from an HBCU. The weight of evidence is inconsistent in suggesting that, net of other influences, graduating from an HBCU has a significant, positive impact on subsequent earnings and other labor market outcomes. Some studies support this conclusion (Constantine, 1994, 1995), while others provide little to no support (Ehrenberg & Rothstein, 1994; London, 1998). Indeed, some research has shown that HBCU graduates face a statistically significant disadvantage in subsequent earnings (Thomas, 2000). Given these equivocal findings, estimates of the net impact of HBCU graduation on post-BA labor market outcomes of African American college graduates are obscured and in need of additional empirical testing.

Thus, the purpose of this study was to estimate the effects of factors that influence the post-BA earnings, occupational status, and job satisfaction of African American college graduates. These factors include background traits, precollege characteristics, institutional characteristics, college experiences, and post-BA experiences. Specifically, this analysis centered on the relationship between graduating from an HBCU and one's subsequent economic outcomes (e.g., earnings, occupational status, and job satisfaction). Using data from the NCES' *Baccalaureate and Beyond Longitudinal Survey* (B&B: 1993/1997; Green, Myers, Veldman, & Pedlow, 1999), this study sought to determine the impact of students' traits, postsecondary experiences, and post-BA experiences on labor market outcomes of Black college graduates. Specifically, the following research questions guided this investigation:

1. Do HBCU graduates and non-HBCU graduates differ on three measures of labor market outcomes (e.g., salary, occupational status, and job satisfaction)?
2. What is the net effect of attending an HBCU on the post-baccalaureate earnings of African American college graduates?
3. What is the net effect of attending an HBCU on the occupational status of African American college graduates?
4. What is the net effect of attending an HBCU on the job satisfaction level of African American college graduates?
5. Are the effects of HBCU attendance conditional on the basis of gender?

This analysis differs from prior research studies in several ways. First, prior research consists largely of single-institution or small student samples (Constantine, 1994, 1995); samples from a single employment sector (Solnick, 1990); and even single states (Johnson, 1982). This analysis was based on nationally representative data drawn from a large-scale survey of students from multiple institutions and across various academic majors. Second, previous studies tend to examine the outcomes of college using simple correlational or "flat" analytical techniques without statistical controls. The absence of statistical controls proves problematic (Keith, 2006), thus potentially biasing the estimates of the effects upward by not accounting for the confounding influences of other independent variables. In this analysis, an extensive array of statistical controls for potentially confounding variables was included to isolate the net impact of HBCU graduation on labor market outcomes. Finally, this investigation employed a theoretical framework to establish relationships among the variables and to guide the selection of variables (and proxies) included in the statistical model. In part, this allows one to test the power of an expanded, hierarchical model in explaining labor market outcomes of recent African American college graduates.

Theoretical Framework

This study of the effects of college on African American students' labor market outcomes was guided by a number of theoretical explanations. First, this study was informed by human capital theory (Becker, 1993; Schultz, 1971). Human capital suggests that an individual makes investments in education or training, thereby gaining additional skills and knowledge that are often associated with increased likelihood of occupational attainment and economic success. Broadly conceived, human capital refers to the information, knowledge, skills, and abilities of an individual that can be exchanged in the labor market for returns such as salary, financial rewards, and jobs. In short, the more education an individual attains, the more human capital one accumulates and then the more an individual gains with respect to outcomes.

Occupational attainment research has also shown that other factors influence economic outcomes of college graduates. College major has been found to play a significant role in predicting after-college outcomes of graduates. Graduates in science and engineering fields earn higher salaries than those who major in social sciences and humanities. Other findings support this conclusion and highlight the way in which college major impacts post-BA earnings and other measures of labor market success, including job satisfaction (Bisconti & Solomon, 1977; Johnson, 1982; Pascarella & Terenzini, 2005; Smart, 1986). These relationships are also substantiated by findings from studies on the effects of college attendance on socioeconomic attainment (Astin, 1977, 1993; Pascarella & Terenzini, 1991; Terenzini & Wright, 1987).

Continuing with this line of thought, grade point average (GPA) was expected to be related to economic outcomes of college graduates such as annual earnings. Findings suggest that college grades have a positive effect on income and that the effect is stronger for African Americans than for Whites (Pascarella & Smart, 1990). Other researchers have studied the effect of background traits and grades on labor market outcomes and found that grades also influence post-BA job satisfaction (Johnson, 1982).

This study employed an integrated model that expands traditional econometric models that are typically applied in economic analysis by including measures of social and cultural capital. Like human capital, social and cultural capital are resources that can be invested to enhance profitability (Bourdieu & Passeron, 1977), increase productivity (Coleman, 1988), and facilitate upward mobility (DiMaggio & Mohr, 1985; Lamont & Lareau, 1988). Social capital takes the form of information-sharing networks as well as social norms, values, and expected behaviors (Coleman, 1988). Social capital also refers to the way in which those connections are maintained (Morrow, 1999). Cultural capital, on the other hand, is the system of beliefs, tastes, and preferences derived from one's parents (or guardians) that ultimately define an individual's class status (Bourdieu & Passeron, 1977; McDonough, 1997).

One way social and cultural capital may influence one's economic and labor market outcomes is through the provision of knowledge and information about college, jobs, and career options (Bourdieu & Passeron, 1977; McDonough, 1997). In this model, proxies for the availability of information about college, job, and career choices include type of high school attended, family income, and college selectivity. Previous studies set the precedent for using such factors (McPherson & Winston, 1993; Perna, 1998, 2004; Trusheim & Crouse, 1981; Zhang, 2005). Also, I control for geographic region of undergraduate college because regional differences may reflect variations in salary and the presence of an HBCU (Constantine, 2000; McDonough, Antonio, & Trent, 1995).

Social and cultural capital may also refer to one's values and preferences for education, such as one's values about obtaining a college degree (DiMaggio & Mohr, 1985; McDonough, 1997). In this analysis, proxies for the value placed on education include students' educational expectations and parental educational attainment. Given previous findings that suggest differences between the influence of mother's and father's educational background for African Americans (Maple & Stage, 1991; Strayhorn, McCall, & Jennings, 2006), two separate measures were included to reflect the educational attainment of each parent. Including such measures allowed me to test whether social and cultural capital variables increase the predictive power of a typical econometric outcome model.

In sum, theoretical explanations and empirical research findings provide support for the influence of earning a BA degree on labor market outcomes such as annual earnings and job satisfaction (Becker, 1993; Bisconti & Solomon, 1977; Geske, 1996; NCES, 2000; Smart, 1986). Findings also provide evidence to suggest that this relationship is mediated by factors such as college major (Bisconti & Solomon, 1977; Johnson, 1982; Pascarella & Terenzini, 2005; Smart, 1986), college grades (Johnson, 1982; Pascarella & Smart, 1990), and race (Hoffman, 1984; Mau & Kopischke, 2001; Pascarella et al., 1989; Phelan & Phelan, 1983). Finally, sociocultural explanations also posit how background and environmental factors relate to economic outcomes such as salary and occupational status (Cole man, 1988; DiMaggio & Mohr, 1985; Lamont & Lareau, 1988; Paulsen, 2001). Prior research has shown that expanded econometric models that include measures of human, social, and cultural capital are improved over traditional economic models when explaining college student decisions and outcomes such as enrollment in college (Perna, 2000), pursuit of graduate study (Perna, 2004), and graduate student persistence (Strayhorn, 2005). Therefore, it seems plausible that an expanded model may also be more useful when studying post-BA labor market outcomes.

Thus, another purpose of this study was to explore this hypothesis: Do measures of human, social, and cultural capital add to the power of statistical models to explain variance in post-BA outcomes?

Method

Data Source

Data were drawn from the National Center for Education Statistics' *Baccalaureate & Beyond Longitudinal Study* (B&B:93/97). The B&B study follows baccalaureate degree completers over time to provide information on work experiences after college and post-BA outcomes such as earnings. Using NPSAS:93 as the base year, the B&B:93/97 Longitudinal Study follows baccalaureate degree completers beyond their undergraduate graduation (U. S. Department of Education, 1999). This is particularly useful for studying the effect of college on post-BA labor market outcomes such as annual earnings. In addition, given the maximum economic return is associated with graduating from college (Murphy & Welch, 1989; Rupert, Schweitzer, Serverance-Lossin, & Turner, 1996; Turner & Bowen, 1990), this data source was most appropriate as it provides information on a national sample of college graduates.

The follow-up surveys provide a unique opportunity to gather information concerning delayed entry into graduate education, graduate school aspirations, persistence, and the interaction between work and education experiences beyond obtaining a bachelor's degree (U. S. Department of Education, 1999). The first-year follow-up (B&B:93/94) surveys BA recipients one year after receiving their college degree, while the second follow-up (B&B:93/97) elicits information about participants four to five years after graduation. These data were deemed appropriate for this investigation and have been used in previous studies to explore the decision to enroll in college (Perna, 2000, 2004) and graduate student persistence (Strayhorn, 2005).

From the NPSAS:93 sampling criteria, 16,316 baccalaureate degree recipients were identified. All those who completed the NPSAS interview and for which NPSAS parent data were available were retained. The total sample included 11,192 cases that were retained for future rounds, including the second follow-up. The present study used data drawn from the B&B:93/97 second follow-up study. For the second follow-up, the total sample consisted of 9,274 respondents, 83% of the original sample. For this analysis, the sample was restricted to African American students only. The weighted sample size was 71,831. The majority were female (67%), and 33% graduated from an HBCU while 67% did not. Table 11.1 presents additional information to describe the sample.

TABLE 11.1

Description of Sample

Characteristic/Variable	%
Father's Educational Attainment	
Not HS graduate or equivalent	8.0
HS graduate or equivalent	30.2
Some postsecondary, less than 2 years	8.6
2 years of postsecondary, less than BA	13.6
Bachelor's degree	21.0
Advanced degree	18.6
Mother's Educational Attainment	
Not HS graduate or equivalent	6.4
HS graduate or equivalent	33.6
Some postsecondary, less than 2 years	24.8
2 years of postsecondary, less than BA	8.1
Bachelor's degree	17.0
Advanced degree	10.1
Gender	
Male	33.3
Female	66.7
HBCU Graduate	
No	67.0
Yes	33.0
Graduate School Enrollment	
No	69.4
Yes	30.6

Note: HS = high school. BA = bachelor's degree. HBCU = historically Black college or university.

Variables

The dependent variables in this study are measures of labor market success—namely, annual earnings, occupational status attainment, and job satisfaction. Specifically, one dependent variable measured the annual salary (in dollars) of recent college graduates as reported on the B&B survey. Occupational status attainment (dependent variable 2) was measured by converting each individual's occupational code to a measure of occupational status attainment as defined by Duncan (1961) and later revised by Featherman and Stevens (1982). That is, each occupational code was assigned a socioeconomic index based on extensive research on occupational status (see Featherman & Stevens, 1982, for a full discussion of the socioeconomic index). These variables are consistent with techniques used in previous studies (Ehrenberg & Rothstein, 1994; Lin & Vogt, 1996; Smart, 1986; Trusheim & Crouse, 1981).

For the purposes of this study, job satisfaction (dependent variable 3) was defined as the degree of pleasure or happiness derived by employees from their work, work relations, and work-related factors such as salary, fringe benefits, working conditions, opportunity for advancement, and job security, to name a few (Fisher, 2000; Mau & Kopischke, 2001; Price & Mueller, 1986). Theoretically speaking, job satisfaction is based on the degree of congruence between an individual's skills and aspirations and the perceived or actual nature of the job (Bretz & Judge, 1994). Job satisfaction was measured using nine variables from the B&B:93/97 database. Similar variables were used in previous research and were deemed appropriate for the current analysis (Mau & Kopischke, 2001).

The independent variables consist of five sets of predictors. The first set includes background traits and precollege characteristics. These include race, gender, age, family income, mother's educational attainment, father's educational attainment, type of high school attended, precollege ability as measured by college entrance exam scores, and educational aspirations. Educational aspirations were measured using four categories ranging from less than BA to advanced degree. Parental educational attainment was measured by six categories: less than high school; high school; some postsecondary education, less than BA; bachelor's degree; and advanced degree.

The second and third set of predictors included institutional characteristics and academic factors, respectively. Institutional characteristics were measured by whether one graduated from an HBCU, college selectivity defined as the mean value of SAT/ACT scores, and institutional control. Academic variables included college GPA, attained associate's degree, and major. Major was operationalized using a set of four dichotomous variables indicating whether one's major was classified as specialized hard, specialized soft, broad professional, or general liberal arts. This conceptualization was also used in Sagen, Dallam, and Laverty's 1997 study. Finally, nonacademic experiences and post-BA experiences were included in the model. Nonacademic experiences refer to the hours worked per week, while post-BA experiences include participation in graduate education and marital status. Precedent for using these variables to estimate the net impacts of college attendance on student-level outcomes was set in previous studies (Ehrenberg & Rothstein, 1994; Lin & Vogt, 1996; Pascarella & Smart, 1990).

Data Analysis

Several analytical procedures were used to investigate the research questions. First, descriptive statistics were computed to characterize the sample and to distinguish those who graduated from HBCUs from those who did not. Independent sample *t*-tests were used to determine differences between these groups on selected background and precollege characteristics, institutional characteristics, and experiences. Finally, hierarchical linear regression techniques were used to measure the influence of such factors on three measures of labor market outcomes—namely, annual earnings, occupational status attainment, and job satisfaction. Independent variables were entered into the model proceeding from precollege and background traits, to college experiences (academic and non-academic) and institutional factors, to post-BA experiences. The independent variable of interest, whether a student graduated from an HBCU, was entered in the last and final model. This statistical design permitted the use of a rigorous set of statistical controls and isolated the "net effect" of individual sets of predictors on the dependent variable(s) under study.

Weighting and Technical Issues

While the instruments used for both the NPSAS and the B&B surveys were found to be reliable through field testing and follow-up studies, adjustments must be made to compensate for "unequal probability of selection into the B&B sample and to adjust for non-response" (U.S. Department of Education, 1999, p. 108). Due to the complex sampling design, appropriate sampling weights must be applied when approximating the population of the 1992–1993 bachelor's degree recipients in the longitudinal sample. The B&B:93/97 panel weight is appropriate for this purpose and was applied to provide national probability estimates adjusted for differential rates of selection and nonresponse. To "minimize the influence of sample sizes on standard errors while also correcting for the oversampling of some groups, each case is weighted by the panel weight divided by the average weight for the sample [the relative weight]" (Perna, 2004, p. 492).

All statistical analyses were conducted using *AM software* (version 0.06.03 beta) provided by the American Institutes of Research (2002), which is appropriate for use with weighted data from complex samples. In addition, due to the nested nature of these data, a more rigorous threshold of statistical significance was used to interpret the results where possible (Thomas & Heck, 2001). Despite these adjustments, there are several limitations that should be discussed before presenting the findings from this analysis.

Limitations

Missing Data

Some analyses in this study are limited by the magnitude of missing data. Variables with the largest share of missing data are those pertaining to family income, salary, and age, though all variables in the study were missing less than 10% of cases. In some cases, listwise deletion would reduce the analytic sample significantly and possibly result in a sample that is not representative of the population of 1992–93 bachelor's degree recipients.

While researchers disagree about the minimum number of cases that is required per independent variable, most generally agree that larger samples will generate more stable parameter estimates and more accurate χ^2 distributions (Peng, So, Stage, & St. John, 2002). To avoid the substantial reduction in sample size that would occur during listwise deletion of missing data and to account for the tendency of cases to be missing data for more than one independent variable, I took several steps to reduce the number of missing cases (Cohen & Cohen, 1983). First, mean scores were imputed for cases that were missing data on continuous independent variables. While these data were imputed to minimize the effects of missing data, this procedure may result in an underestimation of standard errors by 10–20% and increase the chances of making a type-1 error. Therefore, a more rigorous threshold of statistical significance was used when interpreting such results.

Some cases were missing data on scale variables. In this case, I used trend equations (Thomas & Heck, 2001) to impute values for the missing cases. Trend equations act much like regression equations and predict missing values using data provided on valid cases in the sample. Predicted values were imputed for all missing cases on scale items, except when missing values constituted no more than 1% of all cases.

It is important to note that imputation of mean values in place of missing observations was used only for continuous independent variables, while trend calculations were used to impute values for missing observations on scale items. Missing cases for the dependent variables were excluded from the analysis, as recommended by others (Galloway, 2004; Perna, 2004).

Results

Descriptive statistics suggest that the sample of 1993 African American bachelor's degree recipients were majority female (67%), and the average age at the time of graduation was 26.25 years (SD = 7.82). Black graduates' average SAT scores (M = 897.32; SD = 164.23) reflect the national average for African Americans at that time (College Board, n.d.). For those who did not take the SAT, average ACT scores were computed (M = 20.89; SD = 3.51). On average, participants worked 19.24 hours per week while enrolled (SD = 15.05). Results suggest that the sample is sufficiently representative of the population. Table 11.2 presents means and standard deviations for all independent and dependent variables included in this analysis.

Differences in Earnings, Occupational Status Attainment, and Job Satisfaction of HBCU and non-HBCU Graduates

An independent sample t test was conducted to determine differences between HBCU and non-HBCU graduates with respect to annual earnings. HBCU and non-HBCU graduates differed significantly in terms of annual earnings, $t(384.28) = 3.36, p < 0.01$. That is, HBCU graduates reported lower salaries (M = 27,910; SD = 15,144) than did their counterparts who graduated from non-HBCU institutions (M = 32,317, SD= 15,145).

TABLE 11.2

Mean and Standard Deviations of Independent and Dependent Variables

Independent Variables	M	SD
Gender	0.67	0.47
Age	26.25	7.82
Family income	$39,159.12	$10,031.90
Mom's level of education	3.08	1.48
Dad's level of education	3.19	1.63
Type of high school	1.30	0.75
Marital status	4.04	2.35
Education aspirations	4.06	1.36
GPA	273.22	56.38
Hours worked	19.24	15.05
ACT Score	20.89	3.51
SAT Score	897.32	164.23
Control	1.41	0.53
Associate's degree	0.11	0.32
Attend graduate school	0.31	0.46
Attend HBCU	0.33	0.47
Annual salary	$30,842.62	$14,849.69
SEI	58.48	22.82
Satisfaction	20.82	3.70
Weighted N	71,831	

Note: GPA = grade point average. HBCU = historically Black college or university. SEI = socioeconomic index.

Independent sample t tests were conducted to test for differences between HBCU and non-HBCU graduates in their post-BA occupational status attainment level (as measured by the socioeconomic index, or SEI) and their level of job satisfaction. The tests were not significant, $t(478.19) = -1.76$, $p = 0.07$ and $t(421.89) = .11$, $p = 0.91$, respectively. Though HBCU graduates rank higher with respect to SEI ($M = 60.62$, $SD = 21.38$) than do non-HBCU graduates ($M = 57.40$, $SD = 23.47$), the difference does not reach the level of statistical significance. Even smaller differences are observed for job satisfaction. Table 11.3 presents a summary of these findings.

Relationship of Factors with Earnings

Exploratory correlation analyses reveal a number of important relationships between the independent and dependent variables. Still, correlation results suggest low to modest relationships. On the one hand, this indicates that multicollinearity is not a problem for this research investigation. On the other, it shows that variables are loosely related and may not be sufficiently related to explain a significant proportion of variance. Table 11.4 presents a summary of the correlation analysis.

Hierarchical multiple regression techniques were used to investigate the relationship between background and precollege characteristics, college variables, post-BA experiences, and annual earnings. That is, a sequential multiple regression was ordered in such a way as to examine the

TABLE 11.3

Differences between HBCU and non-HBCU Graduates on Selected Variables

Variable/Group	n[a]	M	SD	t
ACT score				
Non-HBCU	47,863	20.27	3.73	3.23*
HBCU	23,968	21.20	3.36	
SAT score				
Non-HBCU	47,863	888.34	175.99	0.96
HBCU	23,968	901.82	158.02	
Age				
Non-HBCU	47,863	26.56	8.22	1.52
HBCU	23,968	25.64	6.94	
Aspirations				
Non-HBCU	47,863	.32	.47	0.76
HBCU	23,968	.29	.45	
Satisfaction				
Non-HBCU	47,863	20.83	3.64	0.11
HBCU	23,968	20.79	3.83	
Salary				
Non-HBCU	47,863	$27,910.33	805.59	3.36*
HBCU	23,968	$32,317.38	1036.94	

Note: HBCU = historically Black college or university.
[a] Weighted sample sizes are shown in table; adjusted weighted sample sizes were used to conduct analyses.
*$p < .01$

relationship between all of the independent factors (including measures of human, social, and cultural capital) and a measure of labor market outcome, annual earnings. The regression model that included only background and precollege variables (step 1) was significant, $F(8,441) = 3.801$, $p < 0.01$. The sample correlation coefficient was 0.25, indicating that approximately 6% of the variance in annual earnings can be accounted for by the linear combination of background and precollege measures. Based on these results, background and precollege characteristics appear to be significant, albeit modest, predictors of earnings.

After adding the college experiences factors and post-BA variables, including both social and cultural capital measures, the regression model was found to be significant again, $F(18,431) = 2.626$, $p < 0.01$. The sample correlation coefficient was 0.31, indicating that approximately 9% of the variance in earnings can be explained by the linear combination of independent and control variables. Based on these findings, these factors appear to be significant predictors of annual earnings, as college experiences and post-BA experiences add significantly to the power of the model, $\Delta R^2 = 0.03$.

The final hierarchical model consisted of all independent factors that were entered previously in order to test the relationship between HBCU attendance and post-BA annual earnings. The final model was found to be significant overall, $F(19,430) = 2.764$, $p < 0.01$. The sample correlation coefficient was 0.33, indicating that 11% of the variance in earnings can be accounted for by the combination of all predictor variables. Model change statistics indicate that the final model is a significant improvement over the previous models, $\Delta R^2 = 0.01$, $\Delta F(1,430) = 4.832$, $p < 0.05$.

Finally, results suggest that several independent variables are significant predictors of the criterion variable, annual earnings. Relative beta weight comparisons suggest that gender, age, hours worked while enrolled, and HBCU attendance have the strongest significant influence on earnings. Results from the final model are reported in Table 11.5.

TABLE 11.4

Correlations among Selected Independent and Dependent Variables

	1	2	3	4	5	6	7	8	9	10	11	12	13
1. Gender													
2. Age	–0.01												
3. Family income	–0.11*	0.10*											
4. Mom's education	–0.08	–0.27*	0.16*										
5. Dad's education	–0.11*	–0.21*	0.15*	0.49*									
6. GPA	–0.00	0.07	–0.05	–0.02	0.00								
7. Post-BA enrollment	0.06	–0.07	–0.07	0.02	0.04	0.17*							
8. ACT score	–0.07	0.10*	0.06	0.05	0.03	0.11*	–0.00						
9. SAT score	–0.05	0.21*	0.16*	0.01	0.05	0.09*	–0.07	–0.03					
10. Associate's degree	–0.04	0.17*	0.01	–0.08*	–0.14*	0.00	0.02	0.07	0.08*				
11. Annual salary	–0.12*	0.17*	0.04	–0.00	–0.01	–0.06	0.02	0.11*	0.12*	0.07			
12. SEI	–0.20*	0.06	0.02	0.02	–0.03	0.08	–0.01	0.00	–0.03	0.01	0.25*		
13. Job satisfaction	0.10*	0.05	0.01	–0.01	–0.03	–0.03	0.12*	0.01	–0.04	–0.02	0.16*	0.03	

Note: GPA = grade point average. BA = bachelor's degree. SEI = socioeconomic index.
* $p < 0.05$.

TABLE 11.5

Summary of Model Predicting Earnings from Background, Precollege, College, and Related Variables

Variable	*B*	*SE B*	β	*t*	*p*
(Constant)	15150.553	7582.899		1.998	0.046
Gender	−3483.387	1500.155	−0.111	−2.322	0.021
Age	293.527	109.787	0.155	2.674	0.008
Dad's education	145.316	499.848	0.016	0.291	0.771
Mother's education	360.502	543.802	0.036	0.663	0.508
Marital status	539.645	330.378	0.085	1.633	0.103
High school type	933.340	967.027	0.047	0.965	0.335
Family SES	0.027	0.071	0.018	0.381	0.037
Educational aspirations	−897.538	508.842	−0.082	−1.764	0.078
College GPA	−16.947	13.332	−0.064	−1.271	0.204
Hours worked	99.581	49.845	0.101	1.998	0.046
ACT score	306.316	202.841	0.072	1.510	0.132
SAT score	7.290	4.453	0.081	1.637	0.102
Institutional control	4.155	1414.103	0.000	0.003	0.998
Associate's degree	892.067	2235.150	0.019	0.399	0.690
Specialized hard major	2023.249	2215.064	0.048	0.913	0.362
Broad professional major	1815.524	1829.132	0.054	0.993	0.321
General liberal arts major	−1438.208	1954.938	−0.040	−0.736	0.462
Attend graduate school	1227.685	1558.460	0.038	0.788	0.431
Graduate from HBCU	−3404.102	1548.662	−0.108	−2.198	0.028
R	0.33				
R^2	0.11				

Note: SES = socioeconomic status. GPA = grade point average. HBCU = historically Black college or university.

Relationship of Factors with Occupational Status Attainment or Socioeconomic Index (SEI)

Hierarchical multiple regression analyses were conducted to evaluate the relationship between all independent and control variables included in the model and another labor market outcome, occupational status attainment as measured by Duncan's SEI. The regression model was significant, $F(18,539) = 3.521$, $p < 0.01$. The sample correlation coefficient was 0.32, indicating that approximately 10.5% of the variance in the individual's occupational status attainment level can be accounted for by the combination of independent variables.

A second analysis was conducted to evaluate whether the indicator for graduating from an HBCU predicted one's occupational status attainment level over and above the previous model including background, precollege, college, and post-BA experiences. Adding the HBCU variable accounted for a statistically significant proportion of the SEI variance after controlling for the effects of all previously entered variables in the model, $\Delta R^2 = 0.007$, $F(1,538) = 4.300$, $p < 0.01$. The sample correlation coefficient was 0.34, indicating that approximately 12% of the variance in SEI scores can be accounted for by the variables in the model.

Results suggest that one's aspirations, academic major, attending graduate school, and graduating from an HBCU are significant predictors of occupational status. Results from the final regression model are reported in Table 11.6.

TABLE 11.6

Summary of Model Predicting Occupational Status Attainment (SEI) from Background, Precollege, College, and Related Variables

Variable	*B*	*SE B*	β	*t*	*p*
(Constant)	47.527	10.398		4.571	0.000
Gender	3.748	2.057	0.077	1.822	0.069
Age	0.060	0.151	0.021	0.402	0.688
Dad's education	–0.812	0.685	–0.058	–1.185	0.236
Mother's education	–0.072	0.746	–0.005	–0.096	0.924
Marital status	–0.472	0.453	–0.049	–1.041	0.298
High school type	2.671	1.326	0.088	2.014	0.044
Family SES	0.000	0.000	0.060	1.383	0.167
Educational aspirations	1.607	0.698	0.096	2.303	0.022
College GPA	–0.014	0.018	–0.035	–0.764	0.445
Hours worked	–0.039	0.068	–0.026	–0.567	0.571
ACT score	0.257	0.278	0.040	0.924	0.356
SAT score	–0.004	0.006	–0.031	–0.707	0.480
Institutional control	0.498	1.939	0.012	0.257	0.797
Associate's degree	–0.792	3.065	–0.011	–0.259	0.796
Specialized hard major	0.469	3.037	0.007	0.155	0.877
Broad professional major	–12.293	2.508	–0.240	–4.901	0.000
General liberal arts major	–5.454	2.681	–0.098	–2.034	0.042
Attend graduate school	5.688	2.137	0.115	2.661	0.008
Graduate from HBCU	4.403	2.124	0.091	2.074	0.039
R	0.34				
R^2	0.12				

Note: SES = socioeconomic status. GPA = grade point average. HBCU = historically Black college or university.

Relationship of Factors with Job Satisfaction

Hierarchical or sequential multiple regression analyses were conducted to evaluate the relationship between background characteristics, precollege and college variables, post-BA experiences, and the level of job satisfaction reported by participants. The regression equation was significant, $F(18,540) = 2.331, p < 0.01$. The sample multiple correlation coefficient was 0.27, indicating that approximately 7% of the variance in job satisfaction can be accounted for by the combination of independent factors.

A second analysis was conducted to estimate the net impact of graduating from an HBCU on one's job satisfaction level. Adding the HBCU variable to the model did not add significantly to the power of the model already containing a number of control variables and measures of social and cultural capital. That is, graduating from an HBCU had a statistically nonsignificant net effect on job satisfaction, $F(1,537) = .210, p > .05$.

Findings suggest that gender, marital status, and college GPA have a statistically significant relationship with job satisfaction for African American college graduates. Results are summarized in Table 11.7

Conditional Effects of HBCU Attendance

To test for conditional effects of HBCU attendance on the basis of gender, a cross-product term was added to each statistical model. Results suggest that HBCU attendance does not have differential

TABLE 11.7

Summary of Model Predicting Job Satisfaction from Background, Precollege, College, and Related Variables

Variable	*B*	*SE B*	β	*t*	*p*
(Constant)	20.669	1.722		12.000	0.000
Gender	−1.775	0.341	−0.226	−5.208	0.000
Age	0.040	0.025	0.086	1.624	0.105
Dad's education	−0.161	0.114	−0.071	−1.420	0.156
Mother's education	0.146	0.124	0.059	1.186	0.236
Marital status	0.147	0.075	0.093	1.962	0.050
High school type	0.010	0.220	0.002	0.046	0.964
Family SES	0.024	0.000	0.007	0.150	0.881
Educational aspirations	0.028	0.116	0.010	0.240	0.810
College GPA	0.007	0.003	0.102	2.207	0.028
Hours worked	0.014	0.011	0.059	1.280	0.201
ACT score	−0.026	0.046	−0.025	−0.564	0.573
SAT score	−0.002	0.001	−0.068	−1.517	0.130
Institutional control	−0.326	0.321	−0.047	−1.015	0.310
Associate's degree	0.012	0.508	0.001	0.024	0.981
Specialized hard major	0.019	0.503	0.002	0.037	0.971
Broad professional major	−0.337	0.415	−0.041	−0.811	0.418
General liberal arts major	−0.339	0.444	−0.038	−0.764	0.445
Attend graduate school	−0.257	0.354	−0.032	−0.726	0.468
Graduate from HBCU	0.091	0.352	0.012	0.258	0.797
R	0.27				
R^2	0.07				

Note: SES = socioeconomic status. GPA = grade point average. HBCU = historically Black college or university.

effects on salary, occupational status, or job satisfaction depending on the sex of the student. That is, the addition of interaction terms to the models did not lead to a statistically significant increase in the model's parameters. Therefore, these results will not be explicated further.

According to tolerance statistics, multicollinearity was not a problem for this investigation as the correlations between the independent and dependent variables are moderate to trivial and largely statistically nonsignificant. Moreover, correlations among independent variables were not a cause for concern.

Discussion

This study employed a hierarchical design with statistical controls for potentially confounding characteristics to estimate the net impact of attending an HBCU on three measures of labor market outcomes using a national sample of African American college graduates. Specifically, this longitudinal analysis examined the influence of attending an HBCU on African American graduates' earnings, occupational status or socioeconomic index, and job satisfaction after college. Findings suggest a number of important conclusions. Overall, HBCU graduates and non-HBCU graduates differed significantly on post-BA annual earnings but did not differ in terms of occupational status and job satisfaction. Still, a number of other important relationships should be highlighted.

Differences in Earnings of HBCU and non-HBCU Graduates

Attending an HBCU was associated with lower levels of annual salary for African American graduates. Such results are consistent with findings reported by Ehrenberg and Rothstein (1994), Thomas (2000), and Fitzgerald (2000). However, they challenge conclusions drawn in Constantine's (1995) study that suggest attendance at an HBCU may exert a positive influence on subsequent wages.

While the results of this study present compelling evidence of the impact of HBCU attendance on annual earnings, far less is revealed about the causal mechanism underlying this phenomenon. On the other hand, the results of this study suggest that HBCU attendance may be part of the causal mechanism underlying differences in earnings between African Americans and other racial/ethnic groups (see Phelan & Phelan, 1983; NCES, 2001). By including African Americans only (who represent the largest proportion of HBCU students), this study sought to isolate the true, net effect of HBCU attendance on earnings and to advance this line of inquiry by adjusting the estimates of effects downward by accounting for potentially confounding variables.

These findings are important for a number of constituent groups in higher education. Families and students should consider this evidence when making college choices. Yet, caution should be exercised when interpreting the finding that relates to the impact of HBCU attendance on earnings. Previous research provides compelling evidence of the positive effects of attending an HBCU on outcomes for African American students, such as racial ideology (Cokley, 1999), racial identity (McCowen & Alston, 1998), and even racial uplift (Brown & Freeman, 2002; Hirt, Strayhorn, Amelink, & Bennett, 2006). Though evidence about the impact of attending an HBCU on economic success is inconsistent (Pascarella & Terenzini, 2005), prior studies suggest that attending HBCUs has a positive net impact on cognitive and affective outcomes such as knowledge acquisition, intellectual development, academic and social self-concepts (Berger & Milem, 2000), and persistence for African American collegians. Indeed, results from the present study suggest that HBCU attendance has a negative net impact on future earnings and may provide evidence of employers' preferences for non-HBCU graduates rather than an actual negative "effect" that HBCUs confer upon their students. The research literature provides rather consistent and compelling information about the nurturing environments that Black institutions engender (Allen, 1992; Bonner & Bailey, 2006; Hirt et al., 2006).

Of course, there is an obvious alternative hypothesis to explain the differences found relative to the effects of college on earnings. Prior reports indicate that HBCUs tend to offer degrees in some areas (i.e., humanities and social sciences) more than in others (i.e., engineering, medicine, business). To the extent that the effect of HBCU attendance on earnings is related to one's academic major, there may be less cause for concern about employers' perceptions. Still because the B&B data do not contain additional information on major offerings of schools (particularly HBCUs) and specific in formation about coursework, we cannot determine the extent to which such factors may have accounted for the differences observed in this study.

Differences in Occupational Status of HBCU and non-HBCU Graduates

This study also provides evidence of the net effect of graduating from an HBCU on one's occupational status. For example, in this analysis, graduating from an HBCU was associated with higher levels of occupational status. These results suggest that African American college graduates who have similar educational and personal histories, who are the same with respect to age, and who share similar levels of social and cultural capital are more likely to achieve high status occupations if they graduated from an HBCU.

On the one hand, these findings are somewhat consistent with those found in earlier research (Ehrenberg & Rothstein, 1994; London, 1998) and may also reflect prior conclusions that HBCUs tend to foster educational climates that engender African American college student success (Watson et al., 2002). On the other, that African Americans who attend HBCUs achieve higher occupational statuses than those who do not attend such institutions lends support to the continuing significance of HBCUs. Despite the fact that predominately White institutions educate (not necessarily graduate) most Black college students today, HBCUs still award a large majority of all BAs earned by

African Americans. This is particularly true in high status career fields such as law, medicine, and science (Brown & Freeman, 2002). Findings from this study may reflect that HBCUs continue to produce "the vast majority of black professionals and those whom the black community and society in general have acknowledged as 'black leaders'" (Barthelemy, 1984, p. 14).

Relationships of Independent Variable with Earnings

The evidence also suggests that those who graduated from HBCUs had higher levels of educational aspirations than those who did not attend such institutions. It is also interesting to note that educational aspirations of those who attended HBCUs exceeded the overall B&B sample average including students from other racial/ethnic groups (M = 4.02, SD = 1.07). These estimates are consistent with previous research (Cole, Barber, Bolyard, & Linders, 1999; Pascarella & Terenzini, 2005), and they also provide compelling information about the differences between the educational aspirations of African Americans and students from other groups. However, despite their high aspirations, Black students graduate at lower rates (Nettles & Perna, 1997) and earn less money than their non-Black counterparts. That is, despite their "high hopes," African Americans tend to earn less.

The analysis shows that earnings are a function of age; these findings are consistent with Zhang's conclusion that "salary is a concave function of age" (2005, p. 322). In this study, controlling for all other factors, predicted earnings are significantly, positively influenced by one's age. For example, a one-unit increase in age is associated with a 293.5-unit increase in earnings. For example, if an individual who is younger (received BA at 20 years old) earns approximately $15,000 per year, one who is older (received BA at 25 years old) is predicted to earn much more. This may reflect additional compensation for years of experience, but additional investigation is warranted. Previous studies suggest that there is a tipping point in the effect of age on earnings (Cain, Freeman, & Hansen, 1973; Taubman, 1975). Future research might explore this topic more closely and focus on whether the relationship between age and earnings is mediated by time.

Family income is associated with higher earnings, although the estimated effect is rather small. A one-unit increase in family income is associated with a 0.028 increase in annual earnings. Prior research indicates that socioeconomic factors significantly influence educational outcomes and labor market success (Mare, 1980). Results of this study regarding socioeconomic factors generally support prior conclusions and critical views of American education. For example, socioeconomic factors such as family income and parent's level of education continue to influence earnings, enrollment in graduate school, and type of graduate school selected (Zhang, 2005). This proves both theoretically promising and practically problematic as it provides empirical evidence of the (a) importance of sociocultural capital in theory and (b) the continuing disparities between those who "have" and those who "have not."

Annual earnings vary across academic majors. For example, predicted early career earnings of graduates majoring in humanities and social sciences are among the lowest of all academic majors. However, the predicted earnings of graduates in STEM-related (science, technology, engineering, and math) and other fields are significantly higher, with more money going to those in engineering and health. Such results are consistent with findings reported by Thomas (2000) and Fitzgerald (2000).

Though the variable indicating participation in graduate education was statistically nonsignificant, the direction of the relationship between this variable and post-BA earnings is curious and therefore noteworthy. The graduate education variable had a positive, nonsignificant influence on earnings. This may make sense given that graduate education is an integral part of human capital accumulation as it enhances one's knowledge, skills, and abilities, thereby leading to additional economic benefits. However, students in graduate school typically earn less as they "forego" the wages that could be earned in exchange for additional education. In this analysis, one who enrolled in graduate school after 1993 is predicted to earn more than those who did not participate in graduate education. Any increase in post-BA earnings is likely due to those who had enough time to start and finish a master's (or graduate) program before the 1997 follow-up survey. Such individuals could have attained jobs that allow them to reap the economic benefits of additional education.

Use of Sociocultural Variables in Economic Models

Another contribution of this research to the extant body of literature relates to its theoretical and conceptual underpinnings. Researchers (DeYoung, 1989) posit that human capital theory is limited in its ability to explain some differences in labor market experiences. In like fashion, Youn (1988) demonstrated the value of applying structural approaches to the study of labor markets. With this in mind, an integrated econometric model was developed for this study including measures of human, social, and cultural capital. Results suggest that adding sociocultural capital measures to a traditional econometric framework adds significantly to the power of the model to explain variance in labor market outcomes. This evidence is a valuable offering to the growing body of research on the use of social and cultural capital terms in higher education studies. Likewise, it provides information that might prove useful to educational researchers and policy analysts. For example, sociocultural capital indicators such as family income, high school type, and marital status were significant predictors in at least one of the three models presented in this study. Findings suggest that social capital, as measured by these variables, may be a way for African Americans to acquire the cultural capital necessary not only to succeed in college (Pascarella et al., 2004) but also to achieve labor market success.

Although adjustments would improve the overall predictability of the model by enhancing the accuracy of its estimates, more important conclusions from this study point to the relative importance of the model's main components and its theoretical basis. Future studies would benefit from the use of an integrated econometric model like that employed here and else where (Perna, 2000, 2004). Additional variables can be extracted from prevailing sociocultural explanations of the inequalities experienced by African Americans (Carter, 2005) and included in future conceptualizations.

Overall, this model explained less than half of the variance in earnings, occupational status, and job satisfaction. While this is not a particularly powerful association, these lower estimates are quite consistent with the conclusions from previous analyses. As Pascarella and Terenzini (2005) put it:

> Unless one is willing to accept the view that two-thirds or more of the earnings differences among college graduates are attributable to luck, it seems reasonable to conclude that a number of important influences on earnings [and other measures] are not taken into account. (p. 471)

These findings have implications for future practice, policy, and theory.

Implications

This study was significant for several higher education constituents. One group that might benefit from the results of this study includes those who work in career services. The results of this study provide career services professionals with data about the relationship between college major, college experiences, and post-BA earnings. Counselors might use these results when advising students about their career choice options.

Major policy implications can be derived from these conclusions. First, the results of this study suggest that HBCU graduates are at a disadvantage with respect to post-BA earnings. This may be due to employers' preferences or individual differences (although a number of them are controlled for in this study). Still, other factors shaped by historical segregationist policies and court decisions might limit the opportunity of HBCU graduates to garner equal pay. Therefore, interventions that specifically address past and current effects of racial discrimination are still needed to achieve equality of opportunity and parity in income.

Finally, the study has implications for future theory. To date, economic or labor market theory has focused on how human capital investments translate into monetary returns such as earnings. The current study offered insight into the ability of social and cultural capital measures to explain labor market differentials. These data might be used to expand existing labor market theory to include information about individual's values, tastes, and preferences, especially their aspirations or values toward education.

Directions for Future Research

To extend this line of inquiry, research might study the differential impact of personological variables and institutional variables on important outcomes for students after they leave college, including earnings, occupational status, and job satisfaction. Future research might identify the linkages, if any, among personality traits, background characteristics, educational investments, and variables like those examined in the present study. Research along these lines will advance our knowledge about the way in which multiple levels of influences (i.e., personal, institutional, environmental) impact student outcomes.

There are other areas for future research that could clarify and extend the results of the current study. Here, I analyzed data to measure the influence of graduating from an HBCU on labor market success of African American college graduates. In light of the fact that a large majority of African American students begin at two-year colleges, future research might measure the net effect of attending a two-year college on earnings of community college graduates or those who transfer and subsequently graduate from four-year institutions.

The evidence suggests that those who graduate from an HBCU had higher levels of educational aspirations than did non-HBCU students. Interestingly, high aspirations did not translate into higher earnings. Future research studies might center on understanding the causal mechanism underlying this relationship. Additionally, researchers might explore whether high aspirations result in higher attainment rates or increased productivity over time using longitudinal designs.

In this analysis, no significant difference was observed in the job satisfaction levels of HBCU and non-HBCU African American graduates. Quite simply, this means that African American graduates do not differ in their job satisfaction levels on the basis of the type of institution attended. However, African Americans are less often found among the higher occupational status categories relative to the general population (Nettles & Perna, 1997) and typically report lower levels of satisfaction when compared to other racial/ethnic groups. Future studies might explore this issue more deeply to compare African Americans to other racial/ethnic groups such as White and Hispanic students.

Conclusions

This study improves upon prior labor market outcomes research by modeling the impact of attending an HBCU on post-BA earnings, occupational status, and job satisfaction levels of Black college graduates only, thereby correcting for potential bias that may occur when this relationship is modeled for individuals from all racial/ethnic groups. In doing so, I was able to model the net effect of HBCU attendance on post-BA outcomes while controlling for an extensive array of potentially confounding variables. In short, attending an HBCU exerts a negative net effect on post-BA earnings. These findings raise questions about issues of equity and diversity in America.

In addition, this analysis explored the nexus between background traits, precollege characteristics, college experiences, post-BA experiences, and labor market outcomes. This investigation was placed within the broad context of postsecondary access, attainment, and opportunities. Specifically, I explored the interactions between precollege factors, college experiences (including academic and nonacademic factors), and post-BA experiences (such as graduate enrollment) and found that these factors work in tandem. That is, these factors converge in different ways to influence labor market outcomes of African American college graduates.

Cuyjet said, "Logic dictates that if opportunities and resources were available equally and freely to all U.S. residents, the proportional distribution of representatives of various ethnic cultures would be spread across economic levels, throughout occupations, across educational levels" (2006, p. 9). Yet, to the contrary, data from this investigation suggest that HBCU attendance and other variables (e.g., gender) have an influence on post-BA outcomes such as earnings and occupational status. It goes beyond the limits of this article to determine whether this issue of inequity is evidence of institutional discrimination or racism. However, this study provides evidence that can be used to form a persuasive argument about the need to examine closely these forms of social pathology. Indeed, more information is needed to unravel this complex issue.

Acknowledgments

The author wishes to thank Dr. Elchanan Cohn and two anonymous reviewers for their guidance on this manuscript.

References

Allen, W. R. (1992). The color of success: African American college students outcomes at predominately White and historically Black public colleges and universities. *Harvard Educational Review*, 62(1), 26–44.

American Institutes for Research. (2002). *AM software* (version 0.06.03 beta) [Computer software]. Washington, DC: Author

Astin, A. W. (1977). *Four critical years: Effects of college on beliefs, attitudes, and knowledge*. San Francisco: Jossey-Bass.

Astin, A. W. (1993). *What matters in college: Four critical years revisited*. San Francisco: Jossey-Bass.

Barthelemy, S. J. (1984). The role of Black colleges in nurturing leadership. In A. M. Garibaldi (Ed.), *Black colleges and universities: Challenges for the future* (pp. 14–26). New York: Praeger.

Becker, G. S. (1993). *Human capital: A theoretical and empirical analysis with special reference to education*. Chicago: University of Chicago Press.

Berger, J. B., & Milem, J. F. (2000). Exploring the impact of historically Black colleges in promoting the development of undergraduates' self-concept. *Journal of College Student Development*, 41(4), 381–394.

Bisconti, A. S., & Solomon, L. C. (1977). *Job satisfaction after college: The graduates' viewpoint*. Bethlehem, PA: CPC Foundation.

Bonner, F. A., II, & Bailey, K. W. (2006). Enhancing the academic climate for African American men. In M. J. Cuyjet (Ed.), *African American men in college* (pp. 24–46). San Francisco: Jossey-Bass.

Bourdieu, P., & Passeron, J. C. (1977). Reproduction in education, society, and culture. Beverly Hills, CA: Sage.

Bretz, R. D., & Judge, T. A. (1994). Person-organization fit and the theory of work adjustment: Implications for satisfaction, tenure, and career success. *Journal of Vocational Behavior*, 44, 32–54.

Brown, M. C, & Freeman, K. A. (Eds.). (2002). Research on historically Black colleges. *The Review of Higher Education*, 25(3), 237–368.

Cain, G. G., Freeman, R. B., & Hansen, W. L. (1973). *Labor market analysis of engineers and technical workers*. Baltimore: Johns Hopkins University Press.

Carter, P. L. (2005). *Keepin' it real: School success beyond Black and White*. New York: Oxford University Press.

Cohen, J., & Cohen, P. (1983). *Applied multiple regression for the behavioral sciences*. Hillsdale, NJ: Erlbaum Associates.

Cokley, K. O. (1999). Reconceptualizing the impact of college racial composition on African American students' racial identity. *Journal of College Student Development*, 40, 235–246.

Cole, S., Barber, E., Bolyard, M., & Linders, A. (1999). *Increasing faculty diversity: The occupational choices of high achieving minority students* (Report to the Council of Ivy Group Presidents). Stony Brook: State University of New York, Department of Sociology.

Coleman, J. S. (1988). Social capital in the creation of human capital. *American Journal of Sociology*, 94(Suppl.), 95–120.

College Board, (n.d.). Mean SAT scores for college-bound seniors, 1972–1997. Retrieved November 14, 2005, from http://www.collegeboard.com/sat/cbsenior/yrl997/nat/72-97.html

Constantine, J. M. (1994). The "added value" of historically Black colleges and universities. *Academe*, 80, 12–17.

Constantine, J. M. (1995). The effects of attending historically Black colleges and universities on future wages of Black students. *Industrial and Labor Relations Review*, 48(3), 531–546.

Constantine, J. M. (2000). Black colleges and beyond: An analysis of labor market experiences of Black college students. *Review of African American Education*, 1(1), 83–102.

Cuyjet, M. J. (Ed.). (2006). *African American men in college*. San Francisco: Jossey-Bass.

Day, J. C, & Newburger, E. C. (2002). *The big payoff: Educational attainment and synthetic estimates of work-life earnings* (Current Population Reports, Special Studies, P23-210). Washington, DC: Commerce Department, Economics and Statistics Administration, Census Bureau.

De Young, A. J. (1989). *Economics and American education: A historical and critical overview of the impact of economic theories on schooling in the United States*. White Plains, NY: Longman.

DiMaggio, P., & Mohr, J. (1985). Cultural capital, educational attainment, and marital selection. *American Journal of Sociology*, 90, 1231–1261.

Duncan, O. D. (1961). A socioeconomic index for all occupations. In A. J. Reiss (Ed.), *Occupations and social status* (pp. 109–138). New York: The Free Press.

Ehrenberg, R. G., & Rothstein, D. S. (1994). Do historically Black institutions of higher educations confer unique advantages on Black students? An initial analysis. In R. G. Ehrenberg (Ed.), *Choices and consequences: Contemporary policy issues in education* (pp. 89–137). Ithaca, NY: ILR Press.

Featherman, D. L., & Stevens, G. (1982). A revised socioeconomic index or occupational status: Application in analysis of sex differences in attainment. In R. M. Hauser, D. Mechanic, A. O. Haller, & T. S. Hauser (Eds.), *Social structure and behavior* (pp. 141–181). New York: Academic Press.

Fisher, C. D. (2000). Mood and emotions while working: Missing pieces of job satisfaction? *Journal of Organizational Behavior*, 21, 185–202.

Fitzgerald, R. (2000). *College quality and the earnings of recent college graduates* (Research Development Report No. NCES 2000-043). Washington, DC: U.S. Department of Education, National Center for Education Statistics.

Galloway, F. J. (2004). *A methodological primer for conducting quantitative research in postsecondary education at Lumina Foundation for Education.* Retrieved November 27, 2004, from www.luminafoundation.org/research/researchersgalloway.pdf

Geske, T. (1996). The value of investments in higher education: Capturing the full return. In D. S. Honeyman, J. L. Wattenbarger & K. C. Westbrook (Eds.), *A struggle to survive: Funding higher education in the next century* (pp. 29–48). California: Corwin Press.

Green, P., Myers, S., Veldman, C, & Pedlow, S. (1999). *Baccalaureate and Beyond Longitudinal Study: 1993/97 second follow-up methodology report* (NCES 1999-159). Washington, DC: U.S. Department of Education, Office of Educational Research and Improvement.

Hirt, J. B., Strayhorn, T. L., Amelink, C. T., & Bennett, B. R. (2006). The nature of student affairs work at historically Black colleges and universities. *Journal of College Student Development*, 47(6), 661–676.

Hoffman, S. D. (1984). Black-White differences in returns to higher education: Evidence from the 1970s. *Economics of Education Review*, 3, 13–21.

Johnson, R. B. (1982). *Factors related to the postbaccalaureate careers of Black graduates of selected four-year institutions in Alabama.* Atlanta, GA: Southern Education Foundation.

Keith, T. Z. (2006). *Multiple regression and beyond.* Boston, MA: Pearson.

Lamont, M., & Lareau, A. (1988). Cultural capital: Allusions, gaps, and glissandos in recent theoretical developments. *Sociological Theory*, 6, 153–168.

Lin, Y, & Vogt, W. P. (1996). Occupational outcomes for students earning two-year college degrees. *Journal of Higher Education*, 67, 446–475.

London, C. (1998, April). *A pilot study on the career advancement of Black graduates of predominately Black versus predominately White colleges.* Paper presented at the annual meeting of the People of Color in Predominately White Institutions, Lincoln, NE.

Maple, S. A., & Stage, F. K. (1991). Influences on the choice of math/science major by gender and ethnicity. *American Educational Research Journal*, 28, 37–60.

Mare, R. (1980). Social background and school continuation decisions. *Journal of the American Statistical Association*, 75, 295–305.

Mau, W., & Kopischke, A. (2001). Job search methods, job search outcomes, and job satisfaction of college graduates: A comparison of race and sex. *Journal of Employment Counseling*, 38, 141–149.

McCowen, C, & Alston, R. (1998). Racial identity, African self-consciousness, and career decision making in African American women. *Journal of Multicultural Counseling and Development*, 26, 28–38.

McDonough, P. M. (1997). *Choosing colleges: How social class and schools structure opportunity.* Albany, NY: State University of New York Press.

McDonough, P. M., Antonio, A., & Trent, J. (1995, April). *Black students, Black colleges: An African American college choice model.* Paper presented at the American Educational Research Association, San Francisco, CA.

McPherson, M. S., & Winston, G. C. (1993). The economics of cost, price, and quality in U. S. higher education. In M. S. McPherson, M. O. Shapiro & G. C. Winston (Eds.), *Paying the piper: Productivity, incentives, and financing in U.S. higher education* (pp. 3–13). Ann Arbor, MI: University of Michigan Press.

Morrow, V. (1999). Conceptualizing social capital in relation to the well-being of children and young people: A critical review. *Sociological Review*, 47, 744–765.

Muhammad, D., Davis, A., Lui, M., & Leondar-Wright, B. (2004). *The state of the dream 2004: Enduring disparities in Black and White*. Boston, MA: United for a Fair Economy.

Murphy, K., & Welch, F. (1989, May). Wage premiums for college graduates: Recent growth and possible explanations. *Educational Researcher*, 18, 17–26.

National Center for Education Statistics. (2000). College quality and the earnings of recent college graduates. Washington, DC: U.S. Department of Education.

National Center for Education Statistics. (2001). *From bachelor's degree to work: Major field of study and employment outcomes of 1992–93 bachelor's degree recipients who did not enroll in graduate education by 1997*. Washington, DC: U.S. Department of Education.

Nettles, M. T., & Perna, L. W (1997). *The African American education data book: Higher and adult education*. Fairfax, VA: Frederick D. Patterson Research Institute.

Pascarella, E. T., & Smart, J. C. (1990). Is the effect of grades on early career income general or conditional? *Review of Higher Education*, 14, 83–99.

Pascarella, E. T, Smart, J. C, & Stoecker, J. (1989). College race and the early status attainment of Black students. *Journal of Higher Education*, 60, 82–107.

Pascarella, E. T, & Terenzini, P. T. (1991). *How college affects students: Findings and insights from twenty years of research*. San Francisco: Jossey-Bass.

Pascarella, E. T, & Terenzini, P. T. (2005). *How college affects students: A third decade of research* (Vol. 2). San Francisco: Jossey-Bass.

Paulsen, M. B. (2001). The economics of human capital and investment in higher education. In M. B. Paulsen & J. C. Smart (Eds.), *The finance of higher education: Theory, research, policy, and practice* (pp. 55–94). New York: Agathon.

Peng, C. J., So, T.-S. H., Stage, F. K., & St. John, E. P. (2002). The use and interpretation of logistic regression in higher education journals. *Research in Higher Education*, 43, 259–294.

Perna, L. W. (1998). Does financial aid help students to attend higher priced colleges? *Journal of Student Financial Aid*, 28(1), 19–38.

Perna, L. W. (2000). Differences in the decision to enroll in college among African Americans, Hispanics, and Whites. *Journal of Higher Education*, 71, 117–141.

Perna, L. W. (2004). Understanding the decision to enroll in graduate school: Sex and racial/ethnic group differences. *Journal of Higher Education*, 75(5), 487–527.

Phelan, T. J., & Phelan, J. C. (1983, November). *A comparative study of college impacts on human outcomes*. Paper presented at the annual meeting of the Association for the Study of Higher Education, Washington, DC.

Price, J. L., & Mueller, C. W. (1986). *Handbook of organizational measurement*. Marsh field, MA: Pitman.

Rupert, P., Schweitzer, M., Serverance-Lossin, E., & Turner, E. (1996). Earnings, education, and experience. *Economic Review*, 32(4), 2–12.

Sagen, H., Dallam, J., & Laverty, J. (1997). *Effects of career preparation experiences on the initial employment success of college graduates*. Unpublished manuscript, University of Iowa, Iowa City.

Schultz, T. W. (1971). *Investment in human capital: The role of education and of research*. New York: McMillan.

Smart, J. C. (1986). College effects on occupational status attainment. *Research in Higher Education*, 24, 47–72.

Smart, J. C, & Pascarella, E. T. (1986). Socioeconomic achievements of former college students. *Journal of Higher Education*, 57, 529–549.

Solnick, L. M. (1990). Black college attendance and job success of Black college graduates. *Economics of Education Review*, 9, 135–148.

Strayhorn, T. L. (2005). More than money matters: An integrated model of graduate student persistence (Doctoral dissertation, Virginia Tech University, 2005). *Dissertation Abstracts International*, A66(2), 519.

Strayhorn, T. L., McCall, F. C, & Jennings, K. (2006, February). *Reversing the plight of African American male college students*. Paper presented at the annual meeting of the National Association of Student Affairs Professionals (NASAP), Hampton, VA.

Taubman, P. J. (1975). *Sources of inequality in earnings*. Amsterdam: North-Holland.

Terenzini, P. T., & Wright, T. (1987). Influences on students' academic growth during four years of college. *Research in Higher Education*, 26, 161–179.

Thomas, S. L. (2000). Deferred costs and economic returns to college major, quality, and performance. *Research in Higher Education*, 41, 281–313.

Thomas, S. L., & Heck, R. H. (2001). Analysis of large-scale secondary data in higher education research: Potential perils associated with complex sampling designs. *Research in Higher Education,* 42(5), 517–540.

Trusheim, D., & Crouse, J. (1981). Effects of college prestige on men's occupational status and income. *Research in Higher Education,* 14, 283–304.

Turner, S., & Bowen, W G. (1990). The flight from the arts and sciences: Trends in degrees conferred. *Science,* 250(4980), 517–522.

U.S. Department of Education. (1999). *Baccalaureate and Beyond Longitudinal Study: 1993/1997 Second Follow-up Methodology Report (NCES 99-159).* Washington, DC: National Center for Education Statistics.

U.S. Department of Education. (2000). *The condition of education.* Washington, DC: U.S. Government Printing Office.

Watson, L. W, Terrell, M. C, Wright, D. J., Bonner, E, Cuyjet, M. J., Gold, J. M., et al. (2002). *How minority students experience college: Implications for planning and policy.* Sterling, VA: Stylus.

Youn, T. I. K. (1988). Studies of academic markets and careers: An historical perspective. In D. W. Breneman & T. I. K. Youn (Eds.), *Academic labor markets and careers* (pp. 8–27). New York: Falmer.

Zhang, L. (2005). Advance to graduate education: The effect of college quality and under graduate majors. *The Review of Higher Education,* 28(3), 313–338.

CHAPTER 12

POST-BACCALAUREATE WAGE GROWTH WITHIN 4 YEARS OF GRADUATION: THE EFFECTS OF COLLEGE QUALITY AND COLLEGE MAJOR

SCOTT L. THOMAS AND LIANG ZHANG

This paper examines the impact of college quality and academic major on the earnings of a nationally representative sample of baccalaureate recipients. We extend previous work in this area by analyzing the magnitude of change in the influence of these factors at two points in the early career of these graduates. Our results demonstrate that, despite significant variation, graduates from higher quality colleges enjoy a greater rate of growth in earnings during their early career. We also show that growth in earnings varies significantly by the graduates' major field of study. Wage growth for women and racial minorities is also examined.

Introduction

The purpose of this study is to examine the rate of wage growth among early career college graduates that can be attributed to college quality and academic major. After first revisiting earlier estimates of economic returns to the baccalaureate degree (with especial focus on differences relating to major field of study and institutional quality) we compare changes in early career earnings reported by a nationally representative group of baccalaureate recipients receiving degrees in 1993. Most work on economic returns has focused on the modest returns to college quality at discrete points in time (usually 1–5 years after graduation) and very little is known about the ways in which institutional factors such as "quality" or "prestige" influence the wage growth of college graduates in the early stages of their careers. This analysis extends previous research in this area by providing a detailed examination of changes in the earnings of graduates from colleges of different quality and academic majors across a 4-year window in the early career.

Our research builds on earlier work by Thomas (2000, 2003) and Rumberger and Thomas (1993) that examined initial earnings of college graduates. Among other contributions, this earlier work provided more rigorous insight to the economic returns to the baccalaureate and used institutional characteristics to explain significant differences in the earnings of graduates from different types of colleges. Consistent with most work preceding it, this more recent research documented a modest earnings return to college selectivity after controlling for academic major, performance, and a host of background factors. The findings from Thomas' (2000, 2003) earlier studies are particularly important for our analysis. Key to the present examination is a substantively important shift in findings across these two earlier studies. Namely, the economic returns to college quality in Thomas' (2000) study were existent but quite small when observed only 1 year after graduation. In contrast, the impact of college quality on earnings was found to be substantially, but not uniformly, larger when examined 3 years further into the career span of these graduates. These observations prompt a key question that we address in this paper: How do college quality and academic major systematically impact earnings at different points in one's early career, net of other relevant influences?

We begin from the premise that graduates from different colleges and academic majors may have different earnings trajectories over their careers. While a great deal is known about the earnings trajectories of particular occupations (and we often draw on this knowledge to make inferences about the earnings trajectories of graduates from particular academic majors) we know very little about how these wage trajectories may be impacted by the colleges from which students graduate. Due to the lack of available longitudinal data, most work on economic returns to college quality has focused on these returns at discrete points in time.

Because nationally representative longitudinal data on labor market outcomes of distinct cohorts of college graduates are still a recent phenomenon, there is little data allowing the comparison of earnings at different points in the career path. Our knowledge about changes in earnings related to college quality and academic major is based on findings from numerous studies examining earnings of college graduates at discrete points in time. Many studies on this subject examine the 1986 earnings for the well-known NLS-72 cohort, a span of about 10 years after college graduation (e.g., James, Alsalam, Conaty, and To, 1989). Others employ data from HS & B (e.g., Brewer and Ehrenberg, 1996) or data from non-governmental sources such as the Cooperative Institutional Research Program (e.g., Smart, 1988). Few studies have employed samples representative of college graduates and none have used statistical designs that allow for the systematic assessment of changes in effects over time.[1] So while Brewer, Eide, and Ehrenberg (1999) note a trend of increasing impact of college quality during the early stage of graduates' careers, no systematic analysis of potential changes in this impact over time has been conducted.

We cast our inquiry in terms of the relative earnings gap between graduates from lower and higher quality colleges. Given that graduates from low-quality colleges earn less than those from high-quality colleges, we would expect that the absolute earnings gap (in actual dollar terms) widens over time, assuming that all graduates share the same growth rate. If this pattern can be borne out empirically, one could conclude that, in real dollars, college quality has a more powerful influence on earnings at the end of one's career relative to the early years (e.g., a 12% premium on $80,000 is considerably greater than a 12% premium on $30,000). But perhaps there is more to the story. What if the data were to show that the earnings of graduates from high-quality institutions grow at a faster pace than those from low-quality institutions? This would result in a widening *relative earning gap* among graduates from colleges of different quality and powerfully differentiate calculations of the longer-term return on investment implicit in the human capital framework.

If earnings partially reflect one's occupational position, this widening earnings gap would probably suggest quite different career paths among graduates from colleges of varying quality. If the influence of college quality on earnings varies over the career span, the relatively small effect of college quality on earnings usually examined at the early stage of graduates' career could be valid but prove problematic as an indicator of the effect over one's lifetime.

Perspectives

A close look at the corpus of work on the private benefits of higher education that has developed in this area over the last 40 years shows that at least two primary factors influence the magnitude of the wage premium that is associated with college attendance. First, research consistently shows that academic major has a substantial impact on the earnings of college graduates (Berger, 1988; Eide, 1994; Grogger and Eide, 1995; James et al., 1989; Rumberger, 1984; Rumberger and Thomas, 1993; Thomas, 2000). This finding is important because the choice of academic major has minimal implications for direct costs borne by the student. While there are a number of constraints on such choices (e.g., academic preparation or capacity within the major at any institution) there is little if any additional direct investment cost in a student's choice of major field of study.

A second factor shown to impact earnings is the perceived "quality" of the baccalaureate granting institution (Brewer et al., 1999; Fox, 1993; James and Alsalam, 1993; Mueller, 1988; Rumberger and Thomas, 1993; Sewell and Hauser, 1975; Smart, 1988; Solmon, 1973, 1975; Thomas, 2000; Trusheim and Crouse, 1981). While institutional "quality" and "prestige" are difficult concepts to operationalize, the findings are remarkably consistent across a large number of studies: Graduates from more prestigious, more selective, and higher academic quality colleges enjoy small but significant wage premiums relative to peers graduating from less academically distinctive institutions.

Unlike the choice of academic major, students' choice of institution is often constrained by their ability to pay—a reality central to human capital theory. Other characteristics such as academic performance are also known to positively impact the salaries of college graduates (James et al., 1989; Jones and Jackson, 1990; Rumberger and Thomas, 1993; Thomas, 2000, 2003; Wise, 1975), but the two largest drivers of post-baccalaureate earnings are student choice of academic major and institutional type. In short, all else being equal, students graduating in higher demand majors (e.g., engineering and business) from higher quality institutions (where quality is usually measured by a single index of institutional selectivity) tend to command higher salaries than their peers from lower quality colleges and/or alternate academic majors.

While a large body of empirical work provides strong support for these conclusions, there exists considerable controversy over the mechanisms by which these advantages manifest themselves in enhanced earnings. The controversy centers on whether these advantages result from genuine improvements in human capital (Becker, 1993; Schultz, 1961)—where one might assume that more prestigious institutions provide greater opportunities for improvement—or whether credentials from more prestigious institutions send signals to employers about a graduate's capabilities (Spence, 1974). While this is not an either/or proposition, both of these possibilities have been explored over the years. The vast majority of studies in this area employ the human capital framework. In its simplest form, human capital theory asserts that the labor market rewards investments individuals make in themselves (e.g., their education or training) and these investments lead to higher salaries (Becker, 1993).

In most early work examining the returns to improvements in human capital conceptualizations were usually confined to investments in the quantity of education (i.e., years of schooling). Subsequent work expanded this conceptualization to incorporate both the quantity and quality of education experiences presumed to improve one's stock of human capital. High-quality colleges, which usually possess quality academic faculty, capable and motivated students, large libraries, well-equipped laboratories, and so on, would appear to provide their students with better resources for human capital improvement than low-quality colleges. The quality component has thus come to be a central feature of econometric work in this area.

Students and their families often make great financial sacrifices to attend higher prestige institutions—sacrifices often predicated on the belief that such "investment" will pay off in the post-graduation labor market. This highlights the importance of accurate knowledge about the returns to college at different junctures in graduates' lives. Thomas (2000, 2003) reported that over half the graduates in the sub-sample he analyzed reported borrowing to pay for costs associated with their undergraduate education. This proportion varied across majors from 48% in the social sciences to over 63% in engineering. Of those borrowing, average total debt across majors ranged from $9458 for graduates in education to $12,845 for graduates in health fields. Among borrowers, this translated into first-year earnings to total educational debt ratios as small as .43 (engineering) and as large as .62 (humanities).[2] Students attending more prestigious schools paid higher tuition prices than their counterparts attending less prestigious schools—real costs that resulted in higher levels of indebtedness that persisted years after graduation. These findings point to the economic stakes involved with decisions about students' choice of college and academic major—decisions often made on the basis of very limited information about the true longer-term payoff to particular types of colleges.

So to the degree that the human capital framework can guide inquiries in this area, we would expect individuals to be willing to bear a greater economic burden to attend colleges that are believed to subsequently confer greater labor market rewards. But while much of the previous work in this area is built on the premise that college quality may significantly influence earnings, the bulk of these studies have demonstrated only a relatively small effect.

This study provides comparisons of growth in early career earnings attributable to academic major and college quality. This examination of early career earnings shifts related to students' choices of institution and major advances our understanding of the economic returns to the baccalaureate degree by providing a more complete picture of the extent to which wages grow or stagnate for graduates from different academic majors and types of institutions.

Methods and Data

Our analysis draws on data from individual college graduates and on data from the colleges conferring their degrees. The individual level data come from the 1997 follow-up of the Baccalaureate and Beyond study (B & B:93/97). The B & B: 93/97 is part of a national longitudinal study designed to provide information concerning education and work experiences after completion of the bachelor's degree (National Center for Education Statistics, 1999). The second follow-up survey was administered to over 10,000 baccalaureate recipients who received a degree in 1992 or 1993. The restricted B & B: 93/97 data set is used to enable the connection of students and institutions. All analyses reported in this paper have been weighted by the B & B: 93/97 panel weight, normalized on the final sample.

College-level data come from two sources: the Integrated Postsecondary Education Data System 1992–1993 (IPEDS) and the 1994 edition of Barron's *Profiles of American Colleges*. Institutional control (i.e., public vs. private) is extracted from IPEDS. College selectivity data is from Barron's *Profiles of American Colleges*. The Barron's ratings categorize institutions into six selectivity groups on the basis of entering students' class rank, high school grade point average, average SAT scores, and the percentage of applicants admitted (see Fox, 1993). In this analysis, we follow the conventional approach by collapsing six institutional categories into three based on a rating of most competitive or highly competitive (with Barron's rating of 5 or 4), very competitive or competitive (with Barron's rating of 3 or 2), and less competitive or non-competitive (with Barron's rating of 1 or 0).[3] Different categorizations can be used in order to single out the effect of the specific classes of institutions. Since perceptions of public and private institutions are quite different, we further distinguish between privately and publicly controlled institutions in each group, yielding six college types: highly selective privates, highly selective publics, middle selective privates, middle selective publics, low selective privates, and low selective publics.

Recent research has employed model based approaches (e.g., multilevel modeling) to address problems associated with analyzing data collected through complex sample designs and to bring empirical models into closer congruence with inherently multilevel theoretical models being used (e.g., Rumberger and Thomas, 1993; Thomas, 2000, 2003). While the increasing use of these more refined techniques is encouraging, in this analysis we chose to use more traditional OLS and GLS estimates for two practical reasons. First, the multilevel model yields similar results at discrete points in time.[4] Second, the multilevel model is difficult to implement when comparing differences at multiple points in time [see Heck and Thomas (2000) for a complete consideration of these modeling issues].

As in all studies of this type, our estimates are subject to bias resulting from self-selection of graduates into their respective colleges and majors (see Brewer and Ehrenberg, 1996; Heckman, 1979, 1980; Stolzenberg and Relles, 1997). Since the models developed in this paper include a large number of variables typically associated with selection bias [intellectual ability, family socioeconomic background, etc. (see Karabel and Astin, 1975)] and the technique being used allows for the independent control of these variables, we do not expect there to be a large bias in the estimates reported here.[5]

Our main goal is to determine if substantively and statistically significant differences exist in the economic return to various factors being modeled, especially college quality and academic major, across two points in time, net of other factors included in our models. In other words, we test the degree to which there is a significant change in the salary determination structure (i.e., the combination of effects of independent variables on how much one earns at any given point in time) across the two points in time. We then attempt to isolate the role played by college quality among the factors that initiated the observed structural change. In effect, we estimate separate models of earnings determination at two points in time.

$$Y_{i97} = X_{i97}\beta_{97} + \varepsilon_{i97} \quad (1)$$

$$Y_{i94} = X_{i94}\beta_{94} + \varepsilon_{i94} \quad (2)$$

where Y_{i97} and Y_{i94} represent log annual salary in 1997 (roughly 4 years after graduation) and in 1994 (roughly 1 year after graduation) respectively, and X_{i97} and X_{i94} represent vectors of exogenous variables capturing graduates' demographic characteristics, family background, academic experiences, labor market experiences, and college characteristics at these two points in time respectively. Treating the two models separately yields estimates of β_{97}, and β_{94}, and their variance terms. Assuming the error terms of these estimates are not correlated between the two models, we can construct the difference between these two estimates ($\beta_{97} - \beta_{94}$) and the estimated variance of these differences ($Est{:}Asy{:}Var(\hat{\beta}_{97}) + Est{:}Asy{:}Var(\hat{\beta}_{94})$) Based on these estimates, we can test whether each independent variable has different effect on earnings between 1994 and 1997.

While intuitively appealing, this approach makes a strong assumption about the independence of the error terms between Model 1 and Model 2. An easy way to understand this is to rewrite the models as:

$$Y_{i97} = X_{i97}\beta_{97} + \theta_i + \mu_{i97} \tag{3}$$

$$Y_{i94} = X_{i94}\beta_{94} + \theta_i + \mu_{i94} \tag{4}$$

Eq. (3) and Eq. (4) assume that the error terms in Eq. (1) and Eq. (2) are composed of two components: an individual specific time-invariant term θ_i and time-variant terms μ_{i97} and μ_{i94}. Clearly, the existence of time-invariant component creates the correlation between the error terms in Eq. (1) and Eq. (2). Ignoring this correlation will have two immediate consequences in our analyses. First, the OLS estimation of Eq. (1) and Eq. (2) will be inefficient. Second, the variance of $\beta_{97} - \beta_{94}$ is incorrect since the covariance between β_{97} and β_{94} is ignored. Thus GLS proves a more appropriate estimation strategy—an approach that allows the incorporation of the error structure directly into the analysis.[6] Effectively, we will estimate the following system of equations:

$$\begin{bmatrix} Y_{i97} \\ Y_{i94} \end{bmatrix} = \begin{bmatrix} X_{i97} & 0 \\ 0 & X_{i94} \end{bmatrix} \begin{bmatrix} \beta_{97} \\ \beta_{94} \end{bmatrix} + \begin{bmatrix} \varepsilon_{i97} \\ \varepsilon_{i94} \end{bmatrix} \tag{5}$$

Zellner's seemingly unrelated regression estimator (Zellner, 1962, 1963; Zellner and Huang, 1962) is used to estimate this system of equations along with the asymptotically efficient, feasible generalized least-squares algorithm (Greene, 2000).

There are two points that warrant mention with regard to the specification of our models. First, the specification of each of the models in our analysis is informed by the long line of related research using very similar specifications. Models used in previous research have not attended to the potential for endogeneity of variables included nor do we attempt to address this issue here. We did however run several variations of our models to determine the impact of potentially endogenous relationships such as that between academic major and labor market experiences. In no case did the systematic inclusion or removal of such variables alter the statistical or substantive significance of our main findings.

Second, some of the variables included in our models are modestly intercorrelated. The threat of problematic multicollinearity was assessed using traditional indicators (i.e., VIF and Condition Indices, see Ethington, Thomas, and Pike, 2002). For each model we determined that none of these intercorrelations were sufficiently strong to necessitate the removal of variables or adjustments to our models.[7]

The sample of students used in the study is divided into two overlapping subsets. The first subset is based on the B & B: 93/94 sample (the first B & B follow-up 1–2 years after graduation) students who (1) received bachelor's degrees during the period between July 1992 and June 1993 (2) were working full-time, as of April 1994, earning between $1,000 and $500,000 per year, (3) were not enrolled in school full-time, and (4) had institutional-level data available. This results in a 1994 sample of 4,961 graduates from 512 colleges. The second subset of students is based on the B & B: 93/97 sample (the second B & B follow-up 4–5 years after graduation). Using the exact criteria as described for the first subset, the second subset (1997) is limited to 3,965 students from 500 institutions. The union of these two samples, those employed at both time periods and meeting the criteria described above, is used for the current analysis. Table 12.1 contains descriptive statistics for the

TABLE 12.1

Descriptive Statistics of Variables

Variable	1997 Sample Mean	1997 Sample Std. Dev.	1994 Sample Mean	1994 Sample Std. Dev.
Log earnings	10.3610	0.4790	10.0009	0.4532
Institutional Characteristics				
Low-quality, public institution	0.1472	0.3543	0.1472	0.3543
Middle-quality, public institution	0.4722	0.4993	0.4722	0.4993
High-quality, public institution	0.0498	0.2176	0.0498	0.2176
Low-quality, private institution	0.0559	0.2298	0.0559	0.2298
Middle-quality, private institution	0.2076	0.4056	0.2076	0.4056
High-quality, private institution	0.0673	0.2506	0.0673	0.2506
Historically black colleges and institutions	0.0249	0.1558	0.0249	0.1558
Demographic Characteristics				
Female	0.5098	0.5000	0.5098	0.5000
White	0.8526	0.3546	0.8526	0.3546
Indian American	0.0051	0.0713	0.0051	0.0713
Asian	0.0340	0.1813	0.0340	0.1813
Black	0.0619	0.2410	0.0619	0.2410
Hispanic	0.0422	0.2012	0.0422	0.2012
Family Background				
Family income (in $10,000)	4.7184	4.7549	4.7184	4.7549
First generation college graduate	0.5088	0.5000	0.5088	0.5000
Academic Background				
Merged SAT/ACT quartile	1.9709	1.3475	1.9709	1.3475
Business major	0.3123	0.4635	0.3123	0.4635
Engineering major	0.0655	0.2474	0.0655	0.2474
Health major	0.0564	0.2308	0.0564	0.2308
Public affair major	0.0356	0.1854	0.0356	0.1854
Biological science major	0.0238	0.1525	0.0238	0.1525
Math science major	0.0558	0.2296	0.0558	0.2296
Social science major	0.0865	0.2811	0.0865	0.2811
History major	0.0145	0.1194	0.0145	0.1194
Humanity major	0.0695	0.2543	0.0695	0.2543
Psychology major	0.0314	0.1744	0.0314	0.1744
Education	0.1046	0.3061	0.1046	0.3061
Other major	0.1442	0.3514	0.1442	0.3514
Labor Market				
Age	29.9570	6.3686	26.9570	6.3686
Age squared/100	9.3797	4.8483	7.6723	4.4690

Tenure	2.9385	3.4330	1.6370	3.2939
Tenure squared/100	0.2042	0.7073	0.1353	0.6312
Number of hours per week	45.5920	8.9755	43.7847	8.4673
N	2990		2990	

final overlapping sample of these 2,990 students. This table displays 1994 and 1997 values for each of the variables used in the models. The variables are broken out into several different conceptual categories that include institutional characteristics, demographic characteristics, family background, educational experiences, and labor market experiences.

Results

The results of our analysis are presented in Table 12.2. The estimated effect of college quality in 1994 earnings equation (1–2 years after graduation) confirms Thomas' (2000) earlier findings. Net of all other variables in the model, the effects of college quality are small though statistically significant. For example, relative to graduates from low-quality public institutions (the comparison group in each model), graduates from high-quality public colleges enjoy a roughly 9% earnings advantage [see the log coefficient value of .0911 in the middle column (1994) of Table 12.2]. This earnings advantage is about 7% for graduates from high-quality private institutions relative to those from low-quality public colleges. Graduating from a middle-quality college provides even smaller earnings advantages (for example, Table 12.2 also shows that graduates from middle quality public institutions in 1994 enjoyed 4.68% advantage over their peers from lower quality public colleges, or roughly one-half the advantage of those graduating from high quality public institutions). Thus it appears that, on average, while graduating from a high-quality college yields an earnings advantage immediately after college graduation, such advantages are considerably smaller than those reported in other studies.

While the wage returns to college quality are relatively small immediately after graduation, larger differences do emerge several years later. The results in column 1 of Table 12.2 (1997) show that graduates from high-quality public and private colleges enjoy a more than 20% earnings advantage relative to graduates from public low-quality colleges (log coefficients of .1976 and .2043, respectively). Graduating from a middle-quality college also yields a considerable earnings advantage in 1997. Consider that the relative earnings advantages of graduates from middle-quality colleges over those from low-quality public colleges is about 11–12% in 1997, while this advantage is only 5–6% in 1994. Interestingly, the estimated effect of low-quality private colleges relative to low-quality public colleges is negative in 1994 and positive in 1997, although both are non-significant.

Testing the hypothesis that there are no differences in returns to sector and selectivity between 1994 and 1997, the last column of Table 12.2 suggests that significant wage growth attributable to college quality occurred among graduates from high-quality public and private institutions. For example, the estimated effect of graduating from a high-quality private institution is .0723 in 1994 and .2043 in 1997, representing a .1320 (see the "Differences" coefficient in column 3 of Table 12.2) increase in the estimated effect in 1997. In other words, the wage gap between graduates from high-quality private colleges and those from low-quality public institutions has almost tripled between 1994 and 1997 (a 7% gap in 1994 vs. a 20% gap in 1997). This increase in the wage gap is statistically significant with a t value of 3.19 (see the "Differences" t value in column 3 of Table 12.2). Similarly, the wage gap between graduates from high-quality and low-quality public institutions has increased from about 9% to 20%, suggesting that the wage gap has more than doubled between 1994 and 1997. The estimated effects of middle-quality institutions have also increased more than 5% points in 1997 compared with 1994. So while Thomas' (2003) analysis suggested that, on average, earnings of graduates from all types of colleges grew significantly between

TABLE 12.2

SUR Estimation of Earnings Equations in 1994 and in 1997 (absolute *t* included)

	1997		1994		Differences	
Variable	**Coeff.**	***t***	**Coeff.**	***t***	**Coeff.**	***t***
Constant	8.6744	39.93	8.2379	47.90	0.4366	1.94
Institutional Characteristics						
Middle-quality, public institution	0.1059***	4.53	0.0468*	2.20	0.0591*	2.34
High-quality, public institution	0.1976***	4.82	0.0911*	2.44	0.1066*	2.40
Low-quality, private institution	0.0528	1.35	–0.0010	0.03	0.0537	1.26
Middle-quality, private institution	0.1227***	4.58	0.0661**	2.71	0.0566	1.95
High-quality, private institution	0.2043***	5.35	0.0723*	2.08	0.1320***	3.19
Historically black colleges and institutions	–0.1159*	2.00	–0.1033*	1.96	–0.0126	0.20
Demographic Characteristics						
Female	–0.1099***	6.63	–0.0613***	4.05	–0.0486*	2.69
Indian American	0.1461	1.36	0.1112	1.13	0.0349	0.30
Asian	0.1005*	2.34	0.0531	1.36	0.0474	1.02
Black	–0.0397	1.05	0.0357	1.04	–0.0754	1.85
Hispanic	0.0445	1.15	0.0929**	2.63	–0.0483	1.15
Family Background						
Family income (in $10,000)	0.0066***	3.74	0.0060***	3.75	0.0006	0.30
First generation college graduate	–0.0408*	2.45	–0.0042	0.28	–0.0366*	2.03
Academic Background						
Merged SAT/ACT quartile	0.0039	0.46	0.0206**	2.67	–0.0167	1.82
Business major	0.2845***	10.12	0.2070***	8.05	0.0775*	2.54
Engineering major	0.4284***	10.70	0.4011***	11.00	0.0273	0.63
Health major	0.4430***	11.00	0.4374***	11.92	0.0057	0.13
Public affairs major	0.1377**	2.89	0.1205**	2.77	0.0172	0.33
Biological science major	0.0676	1.21	0.0775	1.53	–0.0099	0.16
Math science major	0.4149***	10.12	0.2594***	6.93	0.1556***	3.50
Social science major	0.2186***	6.10	0.0925**	2.83	0.1262***	3.25
History major	–0.2322***	3.37	–0.0144	0.23	–0.2178**	2.92
Humanities major	0.1377***	3.62	0.0628	1.81	0.0749	1.81
Psychology major	0.1131*	2.28	0.0325	0.72	0.0806	1.50
Other major	0.1467***	4.66	0.1012***	3.52	0.0455	1.33
Labor Market						
Age	0.0478***	4.17	0.0450***	4.58	0.0029	0.24
Age squared/100	–0.0563***	3.81	–0.0459***	3.38	–0.0104	0.64
Tenure	0.0096	1.92	0.0340***	6.14	–0.0243***	3.45
Tenure squared/100	0.0059	0.25	–0.0681*	2.46	0.0740*	2.17
Number of hours per week	0.0101***	12.10	0.0136***	16.83	–0.0035***	3.21
Number of observations	2990		2990			
F statistic	11.61		22.97			

$*p < .05$, $**p < .01$, $***p < .001$.

these two time periods, those graduates from highly selective private institutions enjoyed the greatest wage growth across this window. This confirms that different pictures emerge when examining returns to college quality at different post-graduation time periods.

Other, non-college differences are also revealed in Table 12.2. The results point to the changing nature of returns associated with a number of individual level characteristics. These individual level changes include widening wage gap between male and female graduates and increasing earnings penalty for first-generation graduates. College graduates from majors in the fields of business, math/science, and the social sciences have enjoyed an increasing return relative to graduates in education. In contrast, graduates from history fall further behind during this period.

Educational experiences have important impacts on earnings at both time periods. Graduates from fields in business, math/science, and the social sciences enjoyed significant increases in their net advantage over peers graduating from education related majors. These majors started out with large earnings premiums and continued to enjoy high growth momentum. In contrast, history majors started with similar earnings with education majors but lost ground over time. Also interesting are those majors displaying a relatively stable earnings advantage over education majors. These include graduates from health and engineering who started out with large earnings advantages over graduates from most other majors while the earnings trajectory emerging over time is relatively flat. Thus we see distinct shifts in earnings emerge among graduates from different academic majors. Focusing on either point in time independently disguises the important dynamic of the role of college major in earnings determination over time.

Demographic variables were also tightly bound to earnings in both 1994 and 1997. Race and gender have significant impacts on earnings during at least one of the time periods under consideration. Consistent with earlier findings, women experience a significant earnings penalty: about 6% in 1994 and 11% in 1997. The difference between these two estimated effects is statistically significant and suggests that the gender gap in earnings is actually increasing over the time period considered. Other things being equal, there do not appear to be large earnings gaps between racial groups, although Hispanics (in 1994) and Asians (in 1997) enjoy a slight earnings premium on average. Notably, the incomes of blacks, net of all other variables in the model, were statistically indistinguishable from those of whites. None of these effects were found to have shifted across the two time periods. Family background plays a significant role in earnings at both time points. Family income is shown to be positively related to earnings in both 1994 and 1997 with no significant shift between the two periods. First generation college graduates, on the other hand, experience a small but increasing earnings penalty across this window.

Consistent with the large literature in labor economics, earnings are found to be a concave function of both age and job tenure in most cases. From a human capital perspective, this could largely be explained by the accumulation and depreciation of general and specific human capital (Becker, 1993). Human capital theory suggests that, if individuals invest their time and resources in general human capital optimally over their lifetime, they will tend to undertake most of the investment at younger ages, suggesting a concave age-earnings profile (Ehrenberg and Smith, 2003). Similarly, individuals acquire firm-specific human capital faster early in their tenure.

The number of hours worked per week has a significant impact on earnings in both time periods but this had much less of an impact in 1997 than it did in 1994. This is somewhat intuitive as the number of hours worked per week has a larger impact in determining earnings at the beginning of one's career than at later points in time after the graduate has been able to actually demonstrate the value of more important characteristics such as productivity. In essence, the valuation of a worker's contribution can be based more on the employer's perception of quality rather than quantity of hours worked alone. It is therefore not surprising to us that this effect starts to wane in the later time period.

Discussion

College Quality

The real impact of college quality has long been a controversial issue in higher education and economics research. Findings from studies of these effects are not totally unequivocal. Some studies, for example, demonstrate substantial economic benefits associated with attending high-quality colleges. Brewer et al. (1999) provide an outstanding overview of such results. After controlling for gender, race/ethnicity, family size, parents' education, test scores, and part-time job status, they found that students who attended private elite institutions enjoyed a relatively large salary premium. This finding was echoed by Thomas (2003) who also found substantial economic benefits associated with graduating from high-quality colleges, 5 years after college graduation. In contrast, other studies have indicated either statistically nonsignificant or even negative effects of college quality on earnings. For example, Dale and Krueger (1999) found that college quality had either non-significant or negative effects on earnings after controlling for some salient, confounding variables.

The results of our study have shed new light on this controversy by illuminating the potentially changing pattern of this influence over time. Our findings serve to demonstrate that at least some of the controversy about the effect of college quality may be an artifact of the post-graduation time periods on which different studies have focused. Our findings are also consistent with the possibility that college quality does not have an important effect on earnings in the early career whereas its stronger effects may emerge eventually emerge over the years.

Academic Major

Many studies have demonstrated that academic major field of study yields one of the largest influences on post-graduation earning (e.g., Berger, 1988; Griffen and Alexander, 1978; James et al. 1989; Rumberger, 1984; Rumberger and Thomas, 1993; Thomas, 2000). Our results are consistent with this long line of work showing that fields of study such as business, engineering, and health have a very large positive effect on graduates' earnings.

This previous work has not systematically evidenced the potential for the change in this effect over time, however. While relative earnings advantages associated with most academic major areas remain stable across these two time periods, when compared with the earnings of education graduates, our results highlight significant divergences in advantages realized by graduates from business, math and science, social science, and history. While two points in time do not constitute a base from which we are comfortable arguing that these divergences represent true long-term earnings trajectories, what is clear is that shifts in these areas can serve to obscure the real benefits associated with specific majors when these are assessed at discrete points in time.

Gender

The increase in the wage gap between men and women is noteworthy. Between 1994 and 1997 relative penalty faced by women almost doubled (from 6% to 11%). A rich literature exists documenting this gap and its underlying dynamics. Both human capital theory and occupational crowding theory dominate this literature (Borjas, 1996; England, 1982, 1992; MacPherson and Hirch, 1995). Human capital explanations center on women's tendency to choose occupations with work schedules that better conform to daily schedules, longer term workforce intentions, and the pursuit of occupations in which a deterioration of skills through disuse will have little effect. Occupational crowding explanations focus on a general socialization which emphasizes distinct categories of "men's work" and "women's work." "Female" occupations are fewer in number and result in a surplus of women workers willing to fill them. This surplus, in turn, leads to a general depression of women's wages.

Of most interest in our analysis of this gap is that it increases between the two time periods we examine. This growth could be explained by men being promoted at a faster rate than women and/or by wage growth in female dominated occupations being lower than that enjoyed by men in male dominated occupations. This growing gap concerns us because it challenges the notion that evidence of gender discrimination is more of an artifact of a less enlightened past than it is the existence of blatant wage discrimination against women. Hecker (1998) shows that the gap between older college educated women and men is greater than that observed among 25–34 year old women and men with comparable credentials. The decrease in the gap observed by Hecker corresponds with a significant shift in the 1980s by women who increasingly majored in areas leading to traditionally male dominated occupations such as business, computer science, and engineering. Despite this shift, women are still significantly less likely to major in areas that have historically been dominated by men (Eide, 1994). Our results, taken in this context, encourage the more pessimistic view that the larger gender gap Hecker (1998) observed among older women is at least in part a function of women's less pronounced opportunities for wage growth across their career spans.

Race

Like gender, race and ethnicity also figure into patterns of economic status. Farley (1980) shows that the average black family's income was less than 60% of that of the average white family during that period. A more recent study by Kominski and Adams (1994) suggests that, in 1993, earnings among 25–34 year old black males were only 83% of that of white males in the same age range. Similar to explanations of the gender gap in earnings, educational attainment has been identified as a primary factor of this considerable earnings gap between racial groups. For example, the Kominski and Adams study shows the proportion of 25–29 year old black males who are college graduates to be only half that of white males in the same age range (12.6% relative to 24.4%).

Considering the influential impact of college education on earnings, we would reasonably expect that earnings differences by race should be much smaller, if not eliminated entirely, among college graduates. Indeed, our results are consistent with that expectation in that they do not reveal a significant earnings gap between white and black graduates after controlling for college quality. The lack of a significant black–white earnings gap is consistent with recent evidence of similar patterns in academic major between whites and blacks (Simpson, 2001). Unlike the uneven distribution of men and women across academic majors—a distribution presumed to affect occupational attainment and earnings—the distribution of blacks and whites across majors is generally similar.[8]

The lack of a significant black–white earnings gap is consistent with human capital theory and with changes in the subscription patterns to academic majors. While statistically non-significant, the switch in the direction of the black coefficient between our 1994 and 1997 models warrants further observation, however. Although relative parity exists between blacks and whites within academic majors (enabling greater occupational mobility for blacks) recent work suggests an increase within occupation wage disparities between blacks and whites in the private sector (Grodsky and Pager, 2001). This shift in our earnings coefficients for blacks may be the result of such within occupation wage disparity between blacks and whites.

Theoretical Perspectives

These observations encourage further consideration of the ongoing debate over the role of college credentials as signals to employers (e.g., Spence, 1974) or as genuine value-added in terms of human capital development (Becker, 1993). Clearly, many of our findings are consistent with the human capital framework. But these results suggest that other frameworks can also provide important insights to the dynamics defining the relationship between baccalaureate education, occupational attainment, and earnings. For example, to the degree that baccalaureate credentials are signals to prospective employers, these signals contain messages about social class background, race, and gender—dimensions on which the workforce is powerfully stratified and reproduced (Bourdieu and Passeron, 1977). A more comprehensive understanding of these differences and the influences defining them requires the thoughtful consideration of multiple theoretical frames.

Potential Biases

Patterns of baccalaureate attainment shade our findings and conclusions in important ways. Ignored in this analysis are those students starting college but not completing the requirements for the baccalaureate and those students opting to continue on to obtain graduate degrees. Both of these alternative outcomes have significant implications for the relationship between college quality, race, gender, occupational status, and earnings. Blacks and Hispanics enrolling in college are less likely to complete requirements for a baccalaureate degree by age 25–29 (Mortenson, 2003) and are therefore at a proportional disadvantage in terms of access to higher earning occupations. On the other side of the baccalaureate, race and family background are known to influence attendance in programs leading to graduate degrees (Eide and Waehrer, 1998; Mullen, Goyette, and Soares, 2003), credentials that confer significant occupational and earnings advantages. Eide and Waehrer (1998) show that many higher quality colleges serve as staging grounds for students to gain entry into prestigious graduate programs. Thus the economic benefit of graduating from such institutions is in the signal sent to potential employers and the option value resulting from the signals sent to potential graduate programs. The true effects of college quality are likely understated here as a result of our exclusive focus on terminal baccalaureate recipients.

Summary

The results of this study are the first to confirm that, net of other salient influences, the effects of college quality actually increase in the early period of graduates' careers. While conclusions about wage growth attributable to college quality have been based on the results of separate studies—often using different samples and model specifications—our results are based on a longitudinal sample, one that is nationally representative of college graduates as opposed to secondary school students, employees of a large corporation, or some other, less appropriate population. We also show significant earnings shifts for graduates from a number of academic fields of study. While earnings growth was observed among graduates from every field except the biological sciences (no real wage growth) and history (a statistically significant decline in wage growth) relative to majors in education, graduates with majors in business, engineering, and math fields enjoyed earnings increases greater than those observed among education graduates. An increasing gender gap and relatively little racial disparity in earnings and growth were also shown.

A number of policy issues emerge from this analysis. Our demonstration of time-variant wage returns attributable to college quality may inform future considerations of the longer-term impacts of education related investments and indebtedness associated with college costs. From the student or family point of view, the results of this study may serve to provide a better framework for understanding the magnitude of the college payoff as well as its timing. A longer-term view such as this may thereby importantly influence decisions of college choice and financing. The results of this approach and analysis should encourage scholars to focus on other periods of graduates' earning years in an effort to understand the stabilizing or destabilizing effects of the various types of college experiences on lifetime earnings and to examine the many nonpecuniary labor market benefits (e.g., benefits packages) that constitute the total economic payoff to college.

Acknowledgments

This research was supported by a grant from the American Educational Research Association which receives funds for its AERA Grants Program from the National Science Foundation and the U.S. Department of Education's National Center for Education Statistics of the Institute of Education Sciences under NSF Grant #REC-9980573. Opinions reflect those of the authors and do not necessarily reflect those of the granting agencies. We are indebted to two anonymous reviewers for their insightful comments and criticism of an earlier draft of this paper.

Notes

1. It is noteworthy here that the B & B is representative of baccalaureate recipients whereas most surveys such as HS & B, NLS-72, and NELS-88 are not.
2. The debt to annualized earnings ratios used in this earlier work were calculated by dividing a graduate's total outstanding education related debt by his or her annualized salary. Debt-to-earning ratios exceeding 1.0 indicate that outstanding education-related debt exceeds annual income, 1.0 indicates that debt is equal to annualized income, and ratios less than 1.0 indicate that debt is less than the graduate's annualized income.
3. College "quality" has been operationalized in many different ways over the years (e.g., Carnegie Classification system, mean or median SAT score of entering freshmen class, tuition and fees, per FTE edu-

cational expenditure, Gourman ratings, and recently Barron's ratings). We suggest, as have others, that selectivity is a key component of institutional quality (Hansmann, 1999; Winston, 1996, 1997; Winston and Yen, 1995; Winston and Zimmerman, 2004). Not only is selectivity tightly correlated with other measures of quality such as student/faculty ratios, endowment per student, expenditure per student, etc., but it also importantly informs students' educational and social experiences on campus (Hansmann, 1999).

4. We used both OLS and HLM in estimating the model for our dataset. These two methods yield very similar coefficient estimates. Regression results are available upon request from the authors.
5. Adjustments for sample selection bias are theoretically important (Heckman, 1979) but have yielded little substantive difference in the interpretation of college effects (see Brewer et al., 1999 as an example). In the current analysis, a standard Heckman type model is also estimated. It turns out that the selection terms (λ) are not significant in the second stage wage equations, and that the unconditional earnings differentials which take self-selection into account are similar to the conditional earnings differentials which do not.
6. To test the correlation between the error terms across these two equations, the likelihood ratio statistic $\lambda_{LR} = T\left(\sum_{i=1}^{M} \log \hat{\sigma}_i^2 - \log|\hat{\Sigma}|\right)$, where $\hat{\Sigma}$ is the estimated variance structure. For detailed discussion of seemingly unrelated regression (SUR), see Greene (2000).
7. Condition Index values and VIF scores were evaluated at 30 and 5, respectively. Estimates from models without the squared terms (age and tenure) fell well within these limits. While, as expected, estimates of the age and tenure parameters exceeded these limits when their squared terms were included, other parameters in the model were relatively unchanged. Results of these tests and alternative specifications are available from the authors upon request.
8. Simpson's (2001) findings diverge from those of authors examining this issue in the 1980s. Trent (1984) and Thomas (1985) demonstrate different patterns in academic major for blacks and whites in this earlier time period.

References

Becker, G. S. (1993). Human Capital: *A Theoretical and Empirical Analysis with Specific Reference to Education* (3rd Ed.), Chicago: The University of Chicago Press.

Berger, M. (1988). Predicted future earnings and choice of college major. *Industrial and Labor Relations Review* 41: 418–429.

Borjas, G. (1996). *Labor Economics*. New York: McGraw-Hill.

Bourdieu, P., and Passeron, J. (1977). *Reproduction in Education, Society, and Culture*. London: Sage.

Brewer, D., and Ehrenberg, R. (1996). Does it pay to attend an elite private college? Evidence from the senior class of 1980. *Research in Labor Economics* 15: 239–272.

Brewer, D., Eide, E., and Ehrenberg, R. (1999). Does it pay to attend an elite private college? Cross cohort evidence on the effects of college type on earnings. *Journal of Human Resources* 34: 104–123.

Dale, S. B., and Krueger, A. (1999). *Estimating the Payoff to Attending a More Selective College*. Working Paper No. 409, Industrial Relations Section. Princeton University.

Ehrenberg, R. G., and Smith, R. S. (2003). *Modern Labor Economics: Theory and Public Policy* (8th Ed.), Boston: Addison Wesley.

Eide, E. (1994). College major choice and changes in the gender wage gap. *Contemporary Economic Policy* 7: 55–64.

Eide, E., and Waehrer, G. (1998). The role of the option value of college attendance in college major choice. *Economics of Education Review* 17: 73–82.

England, P. (1982). The failure of human capital theory to explain occupational sex segregation. *Journal of Human Resources* 17: 358–70.

England, P. (1992). *Comparable Worth: Theories and Evidence*. New York: Aldine De Gruyter.

Ethington, C. A., Thomas, S. L., and Pike, G. (2002). Regression as it should be. Back to the basics. In: Smart, J. (ed.), *Higher Education: Handbook of Theory and Research*, VOl. XVII. New York: Agathon Press, pp. 263–294.

Farley, R. (1980). The long road: Blacks and Whites in America. *American Demographics* 2: 11–17.

Fox, M. (1993). Is it a good investment to attend an elite private college? *Economics of Education Review* 12: 137–151.

Greene, W. H. (2000). *Econometric Analysis* (4th Ed.), Upper Saddle River, NJ: Prentice Hall.

Griffin, L., and Alexander, K. (1978). Schooling and socioeconomic attainments: High school and college influences. *American Journal of Sociology* 84: 319–347.

Grodsky, E., and Pager, D. (2001). The structure of disadvantage: Individual and occupational determinants of the black–white wage gap. *American Sociological Review* 66: 542–567.

Grogger, J., and Eide, E. (1995). Changes in college skills and the rise in the college wage premium. *Journal of Human Resources*, 30: 280–310.

Hansmann, H. (1999). Higher education as an associative good. *The Forum for the Future of Higher Education*, Available online: http://www.educause.edu/ir/library/pdf/ffp9901s.pdf.

Heck, R. H., and Thomas, S. L. (2000). *An Introduction to Multilevel Modeling*. Mahwah, NJ: Lawrence Erlbaum.

Hecker, D. (1998). Earnings of college graduates: Women compared with men. *Monthly Labor Review* 121: 62–71.

Heckman, J. (1979). Sample selection bias as a specification error. Econometrica 47: 153–161.

Heckman, J. (1980). Addendum to sample selection bias as a specification error. In: Stormsdorfer, E., and Farkas, G. (eds.), *Evaluation Studies Review Annual*. Beverly Hills, CA: Sage, pp. 153–161.

James, E., and Alsalam, N. (1993). College choice, academic achievement and future earnings. In: Hoffman, E. P. (ed.), *Essays on the Economics of Education*. Kalamazoo MI: W.E. Upjohn Institute for Employment Research, pp. 111–137.

James, E., Alsalam, N., Conaty, J., and To, D. (1989). College quality and future earnings: Where should you send your child to college? *American Economic Review* 79: 247–252.

Jones, E., and Jackson, J. (1990). College grades and labor market rewards. *Journal of Human Resources* 25: 253–266.

Karabel, J., and Astin, A. (1975). Social class, academic ability, and college quality. *Social Forces* 53: 381–398.

Kominski, R., and Adams, A. (1994). *Educational Attainment in the United States: March 1993 and 1992 (Current Population Reports, Population Characteristics P20–476)*. Washington, DC: Government Printing Office.

MacPherson, D., and Hirsch, B. (1995). Wages and gender composition: Why do women's jobs pay less? *Journal of Labor Economics* 13: 426–71.

Mortenson, T. (2003). Undergraduate degree completion by age 25–29 for those who enter college 1947–2002 (Report no. 137). *Postsecondary Education Opportunity*, Available online: http://www.postsecondary.org

Mueller, R. (1988). The impact of college selectivity on income for men and women. *Research in Higher Education* 29: 175–191.

Mullen, A., Goyette, K., and Soares, J. (2003). Who goes to graduate school? Social and academic correlates of educational continuation after college. *Sociology of Education* 76: 143–169.

National Center for Education Statistics (1999). *Baccalaureate and Beyond Longitudinal Study: 1993/97 Second Follow-up Methodology Report, NCES 99–159*. Washington, DC: U.S. Department of Education.

Rumberger, R. (1984). The changing economic benefits of college graduates. *Economics of Education Review* 3: 3–11.

Rumberger, R., and Thomas, S. (1993). The economic returns to college quality, major, and performance. *Economics of Education Review* 12: 1–19.

Schultz, T. W. (1961). Education and economic growth. In: Henry, N. B. (ed.), *Social Forces Influenceing American Education*. Chicago: University of Chicago Press.

Sewell, W. H., and Hauser, R. M. (1975). Education, Occupation, and Earnings: *Achievement in the Early Career*. New York: Academic Press.

Simpson, J. (2001). Segregated by subject: racial differences in the factors influencing academic major between Euro-Americans, Asian-Americans, and Latino-, African-, and Native Americans. *The Journal of Higher Education* 72: 63–100.

Smart, J. (1988). College influences on graduates income levels. *Research in Higher Education* 29: 41–59.

Solmon, L. (1973). The definition and impact of college quality. In: Solmon, L., and Taubman, P. (eds.), *Does College Matter?* New York: Academic Press.

Solmon, L. (1975). The definition of college quality and its impact on earnings. *Exploring Economic Research* 2: 537–588.

Spence, M. (1974). *Market signaling*. Cambridge, MA: Harvard University Press.

Stolzenberg, R., and Relles, D. (1997). Tools for intuition about sample selection bias and its correction. *American Sociological Review* 62: 494–507.

Thomas, G. (1994). *Black College Students and Factors Influencing Their Major Field Choice.* Baltimore, MD: Center for Social Organization of Schools at Johns Hopkins University.

Thomas, S. L. (2000). Deferred costs and economic returns to college quality, major, and academic performance. *Research in Higher Education* 41: 281–313.

Thomas, S. L. (2003). Longer-term economic effects of college selectivity and control. *Research in Higher Education* 44: 263–299.

Trent, W. (1984). Equity considerations in higher education: Race and sex differences in degree attainment and major fields from 1976 through 1981. *American Journal of Education* 92: 280–305.

Trusheim, D., and Crouse, J. (1981). Effects of college prestige on men's occupational status and income. *Research in Higher Education* 14: 283–304.

Winston, G. (1996). *The Economic Structure of Higher Education: Subsidies, Customer-inputs, and Hierarchy.* (Report no. 40). Williams Project on the Economics of Higher Education. Williamstown, MA: Williams College.

Winston, G. (1997). Why can't a college be more like a firm? *Change* 29: 32–39.

Winston, G., and Yen, I. C. (1995). *Costs, Prices, Subsidies, and Aid in U.S. Higher Education.* (Report no. 32). Williams Project on the Economics of Higher Education. Williamstown, MA: Williams College.

Winston, G., and Zimmerman, D. (2004). Peer Effects in Higher Education. In: Hoxby, C. (ed.), *College Decisions: How Students Actually Make Them and How They Could.* Chicago: University of Chicago Press for the NBER.

Wise, D. (1975). Academic achievement and job performance. *American Economics Review* 65: 350–366.

Zellner, A. (1962). An efficient method of estimating seemingly unrelated regressions and tests for aggregation bias. *Journal of the American Statistical Society* 57: 348–368.

Zellner, A. (1963). Estimators for seemingly unrelated regression equations: Some exact finite sample results. *Journal of the American Statistical Society* 58: 977–992.

Zellner, A., and Huang, D. S. (1962). Further properties of efficient estimators for seemingly unrelated regression equations. *International Economic Review* 3: 300–313.

CHAPTER 13

TERM-TIME EMPLOYMENT AND THE ACADEMIC PERFORMANCE OF UNDERGRADUATES

MICHAEL WENZ AND WEI-CHOUN YU

This article outlines a framework for evaluating the decision of undergraduate students to engage in term-time employment as a method of financing higher education. We then examine the impact of work on academic achievement and find that employment has modest negative effects on student grades, with a grade point average (GPA) falling by 0.007 points per work hour. We use a unique custom dataset based on students at a traditional regional state university that provides information on student motivations and allows us to directly address some of the endogeneity problems that affect existing literature. We find that students who work for primarily financial reasons earn lower grades than students who work for career-specific skills but higher grades than those students motivated by a desire for general work experience.

Introduction

Graduating high school seniors are presented with a choice to either enter the work force or attend college, and more and more their decision has been to do some of each. Nearly half of all four-year college students were employed in October 2006, an increase from about one third in 1970 (U.S. Department of Education 2008). The allocation of time between work and study has potentially important implications for their earnings profiles in the future. With the increasing role of employment in education finance, comparing the rates of return of employment-financed education to loan-financed education can provide important insights for students and policymakers. Term-time employment offsets some of the opportunity cost associated with attending college and may provide additional human capital in the form of on-the-job training, but it also may distract students from their studies, leading to lower levels of learning, longer time to degree, lower graduation probability, and a less attractive GPA to present to potential employers upon graduation. This study examines the effect of term-time employment on academic performance for students at Winona State University—a regional state university in Minnesota made up primarily of traditional students who come directly from high school, live on or near campus but away from their parents, and take a full-time course load with an eye toward graduation in four years. We carefully distinguish between students who work primarily to finance their education and those who work primarily for other reasons.

This project makes use of survey data on students over the years 2004–2008 and finds that an increase in work hours has negative effects on GPA. These findings are robust to a number of specifications and controls, including variations in work hours for the same individual. Our research design allows us to make two significant improvements over previous research that struggle to address endogeneity bias in the work-school decision. We use a differencing model to control for individual-specific characteristics that influence the decision to work. We also surveyed students about their motivations to work in an effort to disentangle those students who are working with an eye toward increasing their stock of human capital from those who are working for other reasons. An examination of students' motivations for work shows that students who work in order to gain skills specific to their desired career path perform better in the classroom than students who work for other reasons.

This study begins with a review of the existing literature on the relationship between schooling, experience, and earnings and on the link between term-time employment and academic performance. The second section describes the survey instrument and data, and the third section presents the empirical model and results. The final section concludes and suggests some implications for understanding earnings profiles and investments in human capital.

Literature Review

The human capital earnings function most commonly presented in the literature takes the form of what has come to be known as the Mincerian equation, which expresses earnings as a function of schooling, experience, and the square of experience (Mincer 1974). The standard form of the human capital earnings function is:

$$ln\ (\text{Earnings}) = a + b\ \text{Schooling} + c\ \text{Experience} + d\ \text{Experience}^2 + \varepsilon \qquad (1)$$

This specification is frequently augmented to estimate compensating differentials or rates of return to different kinds of investments in human capital. Often, schooling is represented as years of schooling, and experience is represented as working years since the completion of schooling (see Card 1999). Yet, introducing overlap between work and schooling confounds the traditional approach. Additionally, simply using years of schooling fails to account for differences in school quality and academic performance. To date, little work has been done exploring how term-time employment affects earnings profiles and the measured rate of return to schooling.

This study focuses on one piece of that puzzle—namely how term-time employment affects student academic performance. Term-time employment potentially enters the earnings function in three places. First, it impacts experience directly, providing some on-the-job training, either skill-based or general. Second, it affects the amount of learning and human capital accumulation done by students who choose to allocate some of their time to labor-market activities. Third, it might affect students' grades, which provide signals to prospective employers. Working students may study less, earn lower grades, or choose a less demanding major, so simply using years of schooling or degree status may not accurately capture the dimensions of schooling that influence future earnings. It should be noted that the decision to work may be optimal in spite of its deleterious effects. The experience gained may boost future earnings, and the part-time earnings will offset some of the cost of foregone earnings associated with attending college. It may also lengthen the time to degree. Barry Chiswick (1998) discusses how an inability to account for these issues will influence the interpretation of the estimated return to schooling in the basic human capital earnings function.

Figure 13.1 illustrates three representative earnings profiles—no college, college without employment, and college with employment. Working during college offsets some of the earnings difference between full-time workers and full-time students. It may also lengthen the time to permanent attachment to the labor force, increase the starting wage, and affect the slope of the earnings profile into the future.[1] If we define the employment-financed earnings profile as E(t) and the loan-financed profile as L(t), the decision to finance education is based on the following rule. If:

$$\int_{18}^{T} \frac{E(t) - L(t)}{r(t)}\, dt > 0 \qquad (2)$$

where 18 is the age at which students enter college, T is the age at which earnings desist, and $r(t)$ is the (potentially time varying) discount rate, then employment-financed education is the optimal decision. Note that the left hand side of equation (2) represents the discounted difference in the earnings streams.

Despite the important link between term-time employment and schooling and labor-market outcomes, little work has been done to examine the link between term-time employment and academic performance of undergraduates. Prior studies fall into two broad categories—(1) national studies based on longitudinal data in the National Longitudinal Survey of Youth (NLSY) (Ehrenberg and Sherman 1987; Kalenkoski and Pabilonia 2010) and (2) studies based on a single school

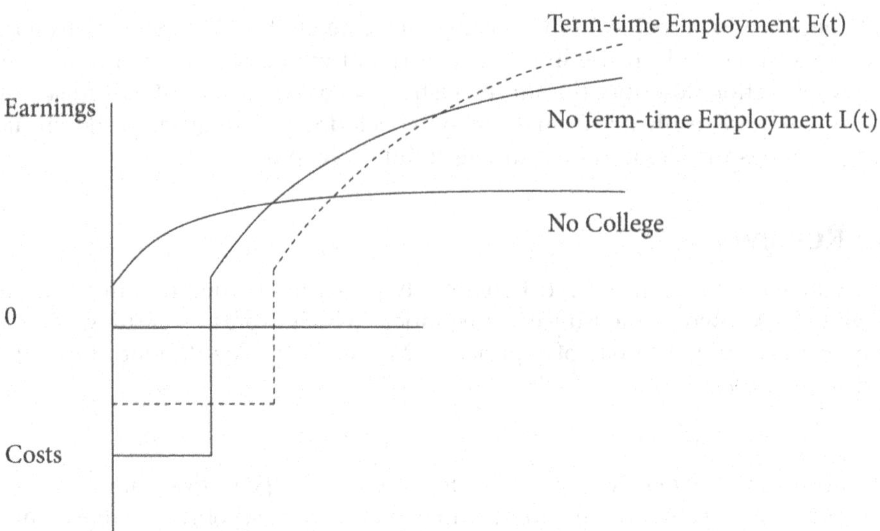

Figure 13.1 Alternative earnings profiles.

(Stinebrickner and Stinebrickner 2003) or small group of schools (Callender 2008). Each of the national surveys suggest a negative relationship between employment and GPA. The advantages of a national dataset are the ability to generalize to a broader group of students, yet previous studies are not able to distinguish between differences in universities. Focusing on a smaller population results in some loss of generality, but eliminates the problem of trying to measure differences in the relationship between work and academic performance from across a heterogeneous set of colleges, and also allows for a richer set of control variables. Stinebrickner and Stinebrickner (2003) focus their study on students at Berea College—a small liberal arts college targeted to low-income students and with a mandatory work-study program. They find a negative impact of work hours on GPA, and are careful to discuss sources of bias in Ordinary Least Squares (OLS) estimates, particularly bias related to the endogeneity of the work-study decision. The concern is that students who see themselves as having a low probability of graduation or a low motivation to earn good grades will find it more important to engage in term-time employment, or perhaps that able students who can sufficiently take care of their study will engage in term-time employment. The authors suggest that the bias is likely to be smaller with data that contains information on worker motivation. The survey data used in our study is aimed directly at bridging this gap. In a broader survey on schools in the UK, Callender (2008) finds a negative relationship between student employment and student performance, but does little to address the potential endogeneity problem.

This study departs in a number of ways from previous studies. First, we focus our study on Winona State University, a traditional college and one that is representative of a wider class of U.S. universities than the unique Berea College. We also make use of a detailed dataset that allows us to exploit variations in an individual's work hours and employment status throughout their academic career. Presumably, most of the unobservable characteristics of a particular student that influence both work and academic performance will remain the same across time. Additionally, we address the concerns noted in Stinebrickner and Stinebrickner (2003) about understanding student motivations for employment by directly surveying students about their motivations.

Data

This study focuses on students who attended Winona State University, a public university located on two campuses in Southeastern Minnesota, between 2004 and 2008. Winona State students are primarily traditional students, particularly at the main campus located in Winona. In the fall of 2007, 7,472 students were enrolled at the main campus, and an additional 788 were enrolled in Rochester.

Full-time students comprised 92% of the student body, 95% of students have parents who reside outside Winona, 99% of the students entered Winona State at age 21 or younger, with 98% entering prior to age 20. Thirty-three percent of students live in campus housing, and more than 99% of the student body come from four states—Minnesota, Illinois, Wisconsin, and Iowa. Eighty eight percent of students identify themselves as Caucasian, and the other ethnicities make up less than 2% of the student body. The student population is 61% female. While the relative homogeneity of the population makes a generalization of these results inappropriate for more diverse student bodies, Winona State is representative of a mid-sized state university serving traditional students. U.S. News and World Report classifies Winona State as a comprehensive, regional public master's university, alongside schools like Missouri State University, University of Colorado at Colorado Springs, Western Carolina University, and SUNY-Fredonia (U.S. News and World Report 2009).

Each February, Winona State holds an assessment day in lieu of regularly scheduled classes, and as part of the assessment day, they administer a survey to the students. The survey is voluntary, and not completely random, but the university offers incentives to participate and participation rates are fairly high. In the spring of 2008, 3,632 students completed the survey, which is slightly less than half the student body, and response rates range between 45% and 55% throughout the period of study. The survey asks a number of questions of each student, and their responses are matched with information from the admissions office on a number of characteristics. For the past four years, the university has collected data on hours worked and self-reported hours spent studying. In 2008, a number of questions were added to the survey, including whether the respondent receives course credit for their employment, whether they work on campus or off campus, and how many hours they study per week. Additionally, students who worked were asked to rate the importance of a number of factors on their decision to work. The admissions office provided data on GPA, high school rank, ACT scores, self-reported parental income and work status, permanent zip code, credit hours attempted and earned, and major field of study.

The dataset contains information on the surveys administered in February 2005, 2006, 2007, and 2008 for students who initially enrolled in the Fall of 2004 or later. A change in computer systems at Winona State made it difficult to obtain a full set of control variables for students who enrolled prior to 2004, and no employment data exists for records prior to 2004 in any case. While an overwhelming majority of students at Winona State are traditional students, there are some who are commuters or local residents enrolled as part time. Rather than confound the results with nonrepresentative students, a subset of students were dropped from the analysis. Students who were older than 20 years of age when they entered Winona State and students who indicated they worked more than 30 hours per week were dropped from the analysis. Observations with missing data for hours worked were also dropped from the sample. There are also a number of missing responses for parental income, ACT scores, and high school class rank that reduces the usable sample. This resulted in a panel that included 6,992 observations on 4,140 individuals. Descriptive statistics are provided in Table 13.1. The dataset contains 935 responses to the 2005 survey, 1,637 responses to the 2006 survey, 2,219 responses to the 2007 survey, and 2,201 responses to the 2008 survey.

The mean GPA was 3.07, and the mean hours worked was 14.4. 49% of students in the sample engaged in term-time employment. On average, students who worked carried a 3.12 GPA, while non-workers carried a 3.03 GPA. The average student reported studying 15 hours per week, with workers reporting 15.2 hours and non-workers reporting 14.9 hours. There are very few differences in the characteristics of workers versus non-workers. Workers are somewhat more likely to be liberal arts majors, and somewhat less likely to be education majors. The incoming high school class rank was the 71st percentile for workers, compared with the 69th percentile for non-workers. Mean Composite ACT scores were 22.8 for both groups. Workers self-reported lower parental incomes than non-workers $69,671 for the former and $82,806 for the latter. Just 3% of workers earned credit for their employment, and 21% held an on-campus job.

Table 13.2 reports the results of the survey administered to employed students in February 2008 regarding their motivations for work. They were asked in five separate questions to rate the importance of five factors on their decision to work by choosing one of four categories—not important,

TABLE 13.1

Winona State University Student Sample Characteristics and Means

	All	Non-Workers	Workers
Number of Respondents	6992	3593	3399
GPA	3.07 (0.77)	3.03 (0.78)	3.12 (0.76)
High School Rank	70.34 (19.15)	69.49 (19.77)	71.23 (18.44)
ACT Composite	22.79 (3.05)	22.78 (3.02)	22.80 (3.08)
Work Hours	7.01 (8.79)		14.42 (7.21)
Cumulative Credit Hours	99.04 (37.11)	92.24 (37.07)	106.23 (35.78)
Study Hours	15.06 (9.99)	14.91 (10.05)	15.23 (9.94)
Parental Income	$76,328.71 (39,266.72)	$82,806.00 (39,937.92)	$69,670.51 (37,420.72)
Parental Work Status			
Both Work	85.0%	84.8%	85.3%
Mother Only Works	4.8%	4.5%	5.1%
Father Only Works	9.4%	10.0%	8.9%
Neither Works	0.7%	0.8%	0.7%
Work for Credit (2008 respondents)			3.1%
Work on Campus (2008 respondents)			21.3%
Primary Major			
Business	15.6%	15.1%	16.1%
Education	14.5%	13.3%	15.7%
Liberal Arts	28.1%	26.2%	30.2%
Nursing & Health Sciences	20.3%	23.0%	17.4%
Science & Engineering	17.4%	17.0%	17.7%
Undeclared	4.2%	5.7%	2.9%
Multiple Majors	20.9%	19.5%	22.4%

In parenthesis are standard deviations

somewhat unimportant, somewhat important, or very important. These categories were assigned values from 1 to 4. The factors were earning money to pay tuition, earning spending money, developing skills specific to their future career, gaining general work experience, and making friends. Fifty-four percent of respondents indicated that earning money to pay tuition was very important, the highest rate in the survey, while just 16% said the same about making friends. In general, the motivation for spending money has the highest mean (3.28) and lowest variation (0.83) while the motivation for making friends has the lowest mean (2.50).

TABLE 13.2

Student Survey Response Percentages on Motivations for Work

	Motivating Factors				
Response	**Pay Tuition**	**Spending Money**	**Gain Specific Skills**	**Gain General Experience**	**Make Friends**
Very Important	54.03%	46.67%	35.93%	40.11%	15.91%
Somewhat Important	25.08%	40.00%	33.72%	41.21%	38.75%
Somewhat Unimportant	6.79%	7.77%	15.65%	10.31%	25.27%
Not Important At All	14.09%	5.56%	14.71%	8.36%	20.08%
Mean	3.19	3.28	2.91	3.13	2.50
Standard Deviation	1.07	0.83	1.05	0.91	0.98
Sample Size	2356	2355	2352	2356	2351

Each motivation was asked as a separate question.
Mean and Standard deviation are computed based on the assigned values (Very important = 4; Somewhat important = 3; Somewhat unimportant = 2; Not important at all = 1)

Econometric Analysis

The following analysis examines the effect of term-time employment on student GPAs, which is first modeled as a function of employment characteristics, student quality, and a number of control variables:

$$GPA = f(\mathbf{W}, \mathbf{Q}, \mathbf{Z}) \tag{3}$$

W represents a vector of employment characteristics, including the number of hours worked, whether the work is for course credit, and whether the work is on campus or off campus. The vector **Q** includes the student's comprehensive ACT score and high school class percentile rank as measures of student quality. The control variables included in **Z** include the number of hours enrolled, the number of hours previously acquired, field of study, family characteristics, and year-fixed effects. Results of OLS (Model 1) and Tobit regressions (Model 2) are presented in Table 13.3. The Tobit regressions account for the bounded nature of the dependent variable,[2] since GPA is constrained between zero and four. For interpretation purposes, average marginal effects are included in Table 13.3 as well. The marginal effects reported represent the average impact on GPA of an incremental change in the explanatory variable for each observation in the dataset. True marginal effects vary with changes in the levels of the explanatory variables.

As expected, the quality of the student as measured by high school rank and composite ACT score is positively related with GPA at 1% significance level. One extra point on the ACT composite predicts approximately extra 0.03 points in GPA, and one percentile higher in class rank adds approximately 0.01 points in GPA. We included college fixed effects to control for college-specific differences in grading standards and found that the field of study matters as well. Education, Liberal Arts, and Nursing and Health Sciences majors receive significantly higher grades than undecideds, Business, and Science and Engineering majors. Studying helps as well, with one additional hour of studying per week leading to a 0.006 point increase in GPA. Students' cumulative credit hours have a significantly positive effect on GPA (0.004 points). This may result from student improvement, easier grading standards in upper-division courses, or selection bias associated with low achievers leaving the university at higher rates than high achievers. Female students earn higher GPA than males by 0.04 points. Students with both parents working earn somewhat lower grades than

TABLE 13.3

Regression Estimates of Student Employment Effects on Grade Point Average

	Model 1	Model 2	
Variable	**OLS Estimates**	**Tobit Estimates**	**Marginal Effect**
Intercept	0.78552** (0.09)	0.41825** (0.11)	
Work Hours	–0.00722** (0.00)	–0.00860** (0.00)	–0.0073
Dummy for Work Status	0.06737* (0.03)	0.08269* (0.03)	0.0698
Dummy for Work for Credit	0.04639 (0.05)	0.04921 (0.05)	0.0416
Dummy for Work On–Campus job	0.13175** (0.02)	0.15280** (0.03)	0.1290
High School Rank	0.01423** (0.00)	0.01596** (0.00)	0.0135
ACT Composite	0.03186** (0.00)	0.04285** (0.00)	0.0362
Dummy for Business Major	0.08745 (0.07)	0.06730 (0.07)	0.0568
Dummy for Education Major	0.40572** (0.07)	0.43692** (0.07)	0.3690
Dummy for Liberal Arts	0.17995** (0.06)	0.17506* (0.07)	0.1478
Dummy for Nursing & Health	0.32923** (0.06)	0.33282** (0.07)	0.2811
Dummy for Science & Engineering	0.03907 (0.07)	0.01646 (0.08)	0.0139
Number of Majors, Undecided=0	0.00553 (0.02)	0.01482 (0.02)	0.0125
Cumulative Credit Hours	0.00357** (0.00)	0.00395** (0.00)	0.0033
Female Dummy	0.04258* (0.02)	0.04849* (0.02)	0.0409
Study Hours	0.0063** (0.00)	0.00790** (0.00)	0.0067
Both Parents Work	–0.04647 (0.29)	–0.07166* (0.033)	–0.0605
Only Mother Works	–0.0154 (0.05)	–0.03866 (0.05)	–0.0326
Neither Parent Works	0.12914 (0.10)	0.11007 (0.11)	0.0930
Parental Income	2.77E–07 (0.00)	1.75E–07 (0.00)	0.0000
Year 2005 Dummy	–0.28568** (0.04)	–0.32117** (0.04)	–0.2712

Year 2006 Dummy	−0.1787** (0.03)	−0.20761** (0.03)	−0.1753
Year 2007 Dummy	−0.07148** (0.02)	−0.08539** (0.02)	−0.0721
Sigma		0.648482 (0.01)	
N	5029	5029	
R^2	0.3112		
Log Likelihood		−4920	

In parenthesis are standard errors.
*Indicates parameter estimate is statistically significant at a 95% confidence interval.
**Indicates parameter estimate is statistically significant at a 99% confidence interval.

students with just fathers working, but family income was not found to impact grade point averages at all.

The model also included year-fixed effects to control for unobserved differences across years and found that there was significant variation from year to year in GPAs. The external environment was generally stable over the sample period 2004–2008, though tuition increased at an annual rate of about 7% per year over the sample period. There was a small increase in the number of students participating in the Innovation Work Study program, from 28 to 55 over the period, but otherwise the university financial aid policy was substantively unchanged. We are unable to identify which students who held campus jobs were part of the Innovation Work Study program. The Innovation Work Study program essentially gives faculty and staff some increased latitude in designing work-study positions, but did not increase the amount of funding or change the pool of eligible students. It may have had an affect on student outcomes, perhaps by increasing the connection between paid work and coursework, but the small number of students affected suggest that this effect should be small.

The labor-market variables had significant impacts on academic performance. Off-campus employment was associated with a 0.07 point increase in GPA and on-campus employment was associated with a 0.20 point increase in GPA. This difference between on- and off-campus employment is consistent with the findings of Ehrenberg and Sherman (1987). However, each additional hour of employment reduced GPA by 0.007 points. Earlier studies (Ehrenberg and Sherman 1987; Stinebrickner and Stinebrickner 2003) find a nonlinear effect of hours worked on GPA, with marginal increases at low work hours leading to higher grades, but increases in work hours beyond some level leading to GPA declines. We did not find this pattern in our data. There are two competing explanations for the positive effect of workforce participation, yet negative effect of increasing work hours. The first explanation is that students who work are better students on some unobserved dimension, but working more hours lowers their academic performance. The second possibility is that the act of working causes a level increase in GPA, perhaps by forcing the student to engage in better time management or organization, but that each additional hour of work makes it more difficult to maintain their academic performance. These two competing explanations are examined in detail. Working for course credit did not significantly impact student GPA.

The next step was to estimate the same equation but including measures to capture the students motivation for work. Since data on student motivation is only available for 2008, observations from earlier periods were dropped from the analysis. Table 13.4 presents the results of OLS (Model 3) and Tobit (Model 4) models. In general, the results are similar to the results of Model 1 and Model 2. The positive impact of employment status on GPA is not statistically significant when motivations are included. This is consistent with the hypothesis that more able students may be driven to choose work. However, the effect of an additional hour worked was to reduce grades by about 0.007 to 0.008 points. Only two motivational factors were found to influence GPA. Students who reported working for specific skills relevant to their future career earned higher grades by about 0.04 points, while students who reported working for general experience earned about 0.05 points lower grades.

TABLE 13.4

Regression Estimates of Student Employment Effects on Grade Point Average Including Motivations for Work

Variable	Model 3 OLS Estimates	Model 4 Tobit Estimates	Marginal Effect
Intercept	1.120501**	0.752733**	
	(0.16)	(0.19)	
Work Hours	–0.00758**	–0.008771**	–0.0071
	(0.00)	(0.00)	
Dummy for Work Status	0.05495	0.064715	0.0524
	(0.06)	(0.07)	
Dummy for Work for Credit	0.07625	0.080112	0.0649
	(0.09)	(0.10)	
Dummy for Work On-Campus job	0.15785**	0.186858**	0.1514
	(0.04)	(0.05)	
High School Rank	0.01460**	0.016823**	0.0136
	(0.00)	(0.00)	
ACT Composite	0.02616**	0.037191**	0.0301
	(0.00)	(0.01)	
Dummy for Business Major	–0.01044	–0.016589	–0.0134
	(0.09)	(0.11)	
Dummy for Education Major	0.35062**	0.413858**	0.3354
	(0.10)	(0.11)	
Dummy for Liberal Arts	0.09182	0.093182	0.0755
	(0.09)	(0.10)	
Dummy for Nursing & Health Sciences	0.17575	0.179916	0.1458
	(0.09)	(0.10)	
Dummy for Science & Engineering	–0.10063	–0.108047	–0.0876
	(0.10)	(0.08)	
Number of Majors, Undecided=0	–0.01798	–0.019639	–0.0159
	(0.03)	(0.04)	
Cumulative Credit Hours	0.00387**	0.004333**	0.0035
	(0.00)	(0.00)	
Female Dummy	0.08118*	0.102568*	0.0831
	(0.04)	(0.04)	
Study Hours	0.00593**	0.007917**	0.0064
	(0.00)	(0.00)	
Both Parents Work	–0.10128	–0.145040*	–0.1175
	(0.05)	(0.06)	
Only Mother Works	–0.09345	–0.161572	–0.1309
	(0.09)	(0.10)	
Neither Parent Works	0.02668	0.051549	–0.0418
	(0.19)	(0.21)	
Parental Income	0.0000	3.96E-07	0.0000
	(0.00)	(0.00)	
Work for Experience	–0.06435**	–0.072846*	–0.0590
	(0.02)	(0.03)	

Work for Paying Tuition	−0.01559 (0.02)	−0.020579 (0.02)	−0.0167
Work for Skills	0.04794* (0.02)	0.061624** (0.02)	0.0499
Work for Spending	0.00502 (0.02)	0.001393 (0.02)	−0.0011
Work for Making Friends	−0.00634 (0.02)	−0.011542 (0.02)	−0.0094
Sigma		0.716191** (0.01)	
N	1846	1846	
R^2	.2898		
Log Likelihood		−1953	

In parenthesis are standard errors.
*Indicates parameter estimate is statistically significant at a 95% confidence interval.
**Indicates parameter estimate is statistically significant at a 99% confidence interval.

From the results, we can conjecture that there are two distinct groups of students that work. Students seeking career specific skills achieve higher GPAs, while students seeking general work experience obtain lower GPAs. The former may view work as a complement to schooling in the human capital earnings function and positively self select into employment. The latter group may view work as a substitute for schooling and, thus, negatively self select into employment. Interestingly, the importance of earning for tuition or spending had no influence on grades, even though they were the factors most often indicated to be important or very important.

In an additional effort to disentangle whether joining the work force had a positive causal relationship with GPA or whether it was simply a matter of more talented students choosing to work, two differenced models were estimated to check the robustness of our results. The models are given in equation (3).

$$GPA_t - GPA_{t-1} = f(\mathbf{W_t} - \mathbf{W_{t-1}}, \mathbf{Q}, \mathbf{Z}) \tag{4}$$

Using first differences eliminates unobservable time-invariant individual specific differences and allows for an examination of how grades change for individuals as they adjust their own working behaviors. The results of the differenced models are presented in Table 13.5. The dependent variable is the change in GPA. The model includes all individuals who provided data on work hours in two consecutive years between the 2005 and 2008 surveys. The independent variables of interest are the change in work status in Model 5 and the change in work hours in Model 6. The change in work status takes the value of 1=Began Work, 0=No Change, and -1=Stopped Work. Separating the two allows the model to capture whether increasing work effort or choosing to work is responsible for changes in GPA.

The results in Model 5 indicate that a change in work status from no work to work leads to a 0.05 point reduction in GPA for an individual. This is consistent with the hypothesis that the people who choose to work are different on some unobserved characteristic from students with similar observed characteristics who choose not to work, and that the unobserved characteristic contributes to higher grades. Model 6 shows that each additional hour of work for people who changed their work hours from one year to the next lowers grades by about 0.004 points. In both of these equations, the other explanatory variables are not statistically significant, suggesting that the effects of a change in working behavior are consistent across wide ranges of the explanatory variables.

Conclusions and Implications

Understanding the link between term-time employment and academic performance has a great deal of value to educators and incoming students. The decision to work or not while attending college

TABLE 13.5

Regression Estimates of Student Employment Effects on Grade Point Averages, Using First Differences

Variable	Model 5 First Differences On Work Status	Model 6 First Differences On Work Hours
Intercept	0.37127 (0.21)	0.38361 (0.21)
Work Hours		–0.00367** 0.00
Dummy for Work Status	–0.0526* (0.03)	
Dummy for Work for Credit	–0.07536 (0.06)	–0.0727 (0.06)
Dummy for Work On-Campus job	0.03225 (0.03)	0.02863 (0.03)
High School Rank	–0.00125 (0.00)	–0.00126 (0.00)
ACT Composite	–0.00472 (0.00)	–0.00484 (0.00)
Dummy for Business	–0.09522 (0.18)	–0.10264 (0.18)
Dummy for Education	0.06213 (0.18)	0.05625 (0.18)
Dummy for Liberal Arts	–0.02045 (0.18)	–0.02637 (0.18)
Dummy for Nursing & Health Sciences	–0.05428 (0.18)	–0.06169 (0.18)
Dummy for Science & Engineering	–0.12188 (0.18)	–0.13021 (0.18)
Number of Majors, Undecided=0	0.00764 (0.03)	0.00684 (0.03)
Cumulative Credit Hours	–0.00052516 (0.00)	–0.00052632 (0.00)
Female Dummy	0.04985 (0.03)	0.04993 (0.03)
Study Hours	0.00074714 (0.00)	0.00082383 (0.00)
Both Parents Work	–0.02179 (0.05)	–0.01843 (0.05)
Only Mother Works	–0.00743 (0.07)	–0.00582 (0.07)
Neither Parent Works	–0.12237 (0.16)	–0.11249 (0.16)
Parental Income	1.28178E-08 (0.00)	–6.2265E-09 (0.00)
Year 2005 Dummy		

Year 2006 Dummy	0.0305	0.0305
	(0.04)	(0.04)
Year 2007 Dummy	0.00311	0.00261
	(0.03)	(0.03)
N	1993	1993
R^2	0.0224	0.0236

In parenthesis are standard errors.
*Indicates parameter estimate is statistically significant at a 95% confidence interval.
**Indicates parameter estimate is statistically significant at a 99% confidence interval.

plays a key role in human capital formation during the critical transition period between full-time study and fulltime employment. This article examines the link between term-time employment and academic performance at Winona State University—a primarily traditional regional public university. Our specialized focus limits the ability to draw conclusions between work and academic performance at, for instance, small liberal arts colleges or large urban commuter schools. Further study at other types of institutions is necessary for a complete picture of the link between work and academic performance. However, Winona State University serves as a good representative of the traditional four-year, in-residence state university.

The empirical analysis in this article suggests that term-time employment has a modest but statistically significant negative effect on student performance. Cross-sectional estimates suggest that one additional hour of work reduces student GPA by 0.007 points. However, the cross-sectional model suggests that choosing to work at all is associated with higher grades. To remove individual-specific unobserved characteristics from the data, the model was reestimated using first differences. The new model suggested that a person who increased their work hours by one would see approximately 0.004 point decline in GPA.

For university administrators and policymakers, one important finding is that on-campus employment does not have as detrimental an effect on GPA as off-campus employment. This suggests that universities may gain by finding ways to move some students from off-campus to on-campus employment. The negative impact of increased work hours also suggests that universities may benefit from managing the amount of time students are permitted to work in on-campus employment. Taken together, this suggests that spreading on-campus employment across more students working fewer hours may help boost academic performance for a significant number of students. Additionally, work motivation matters to some degree. Our evidence suggests that workers who view term employment as a complement for schooling to accumulate broader human capital have better academic performance, while workers who view term employment as a substitute for schooling have worse academic performance. This suggests that there may be value in integrating work study positions with the academic curriculum.

Understanding the link between term-time employment and academic performance is a first step toward answering the question of whether working during college is a wise decision. Future research is necessary to understand the effect that the work experience has on earnings profiles and the effect that the lower grades have on earnings profiles. Armed with that information, it would be possible and desirable to compute a rate of return to term-time employment.

Acknowledgements

The authors thank Hyesung Park, Jeffrey Spors, and Susan Hatfield for their assistance with the data. Barry Chiswick, Shane Murphy, Basit Zafar, and seminar participants at the Illinois Economic Association and Midwest Economic Association provided helpful comments. Wenz acknowledges support from the Winona State University Faculty Development Small Grants Program. Any errors are our own.

Notes

1. Hotz and others (2002) estimate the return to working during school with a primary focus on work during high school based on an examination of different earnings profiles.
2. See William Greene 1993 for a full discussion of Tobit regression.

References

Callender, Claire. "The Impact of Term-Time Employment on Higher Education Student's Academic Attainment and Achievement." *Journal of Education Policy* 23, No. 4 (2008): 359–377.

Card, David. "The Causal Effect of Education on Earnings." *In Handbook of Labor Economics, vol. 3*, edited by David Card and Orley Ashenfelter, 1801–1863. Elsevier Science, 1999.

Chiswick, Barry R. "Interpreting the Coefficient on Schooling in the Human Capital Earnings Function." *Journal of Educational Planning and Administration* 12, No. 2 (April 1998): 123–130.

Ehrenberg, Ronald G, and Daniel R Sherman. "Employment While in College, Academic Achievement, and Postcollege Outcomes: A Summary of Results." *The Journal of Human Resources* 22, No. 1 (1987): 1–23.

Greene, William H. *Econometric Analysis*. New York: Macmillan, 1993.

Hotz, V. Joseph, Lixin Colin Xu, Marta Tienda, and Avner Ahituv. "Are There Returns to the Wages of Young Men from Working While in School?" *Review of Economics and Statistics* 84, No. 2 (2002): 221–236.

Kalenkoski, Charlene M., and Sabrina W. Pabilonia. "Parental Transfers, Student Achievement, and the Labor Supply of College Students." *Journal of Population Economics* 23, No. 2 (2010): 469–496.

Mincer, Jacob. *Schooling, Experience, and Earnings*. New York: Columbia University Press, 1974.

Stinebrickner, Ralph, and Todd R Stinebrickner. "Working During School and Academic Performance." *Journal of Labor Economics* 21, No. 2 (2003): 473–491.

U.S. Department of Education. *Digest of Education Statistics*. 2008. http://nces.ed.gov/programs/digest (accessed July 21, 2009).

U.S. News and World Report. Best Colleges 2010. 2009. http://colleges.usnews.rankingsandreviews.com/best-colleges (accessed August 28, 2009).

SECTION III

GOVERNMENT FINANCING OF HIGHER EDUCATION

Introduction to Section III

Maureen W. McClure and John C. Weidman
University of Pittsburgh

According to Alexander ("Maintenance of State Effort for Higher Education: Barriers to Equal Educational Opportunity in Addressing the Rising Costs of a College Education"), federal and state governments should aid needy students by expanding public access to higher education, and not by providing private choices. States need "maintenance of state tax effort" measures: a) to ensure federal monies are used to supplement not supplant state tax efforts; and b) to protect higher education from increasingly unstable state funding allocations. Withdrawals of federal and state investments in higher education are primary drivers of increased tuition. These drivers may also be more than one-way relationships. Current federal government regulations are allowing states to increasingly shift the costs of economic opportunity onto the very families who need it most.

Avery and Turner ("Student Loans: Do College Students Borrow Too Much or Not Enough?") clearly reject the argument that students are borrowing too much money for college. Investments in college have to be compared in terms of career earnings. What are viable alternative choices, such as not attending college? Their research claims that despite the problems, college borrowing can pay off even more than in the past. They refer to college as a major capital investment with both risks and rewards, and suggest ways to reduce risks. These include careful investigation of the employability of different occupations, both in terms of salaries and chances of being hired. In addition they ask students to reflect on their own strengths to see where they would best fit. The authors encourage students to take their investments seriously, understanding that they are complicated and not easily understood.

Curs, Bhandari, and Steiger ("The Roles of Public Higher Education Expenditure and the Privatization of the Higher Education on U.S. States Economic Growth") challenge earlier work that found negative correlations between state investments in higher education and state-level economic growth. First, it supported research that indicated the presence of private higher education institutions negatively biased the results, as states with small private sectors showed less negative results. Second, it extended existing research by successfully testing the hypothesis that states with larger percentages of students in public institutions would offset the negative bias and show positive results.

Does higher education reproduce class structures, generation after generation? Dowd, Cheslock, and Melguizo ("Transfer Access from Community Colleges and the Distribution of Elite Higher Education") argue that it does. And it is not getting better. Rich kids go to elite schools and poor kids go to community colleges. And almost never do the twain meet, even though elite institutions can benefit from greater diversity in the exchanges of ideas. This is important research, given that European students now face greater lifetime social mobility than those in the U.S. The American Dream is clearly in jeopardy, and HEIs are right at the center of the problem. Access to elite higher education, they argue, has to move away from the marketplace and into more merit-based opportunities for selection. Democracy in the U.S. depends on it.

Perna's work ("Toward a More Complete Understanding of the Role of Financial Aid in Promoting College Enrollment: The Importance of Context") focuses on the critical importance of context in understanding the limits to educational access and financial aid. Most research assumes that the value of the concrete dollar amounts of aid is self-evident. Her research explores how students filter their problems of academic preparation for college, its access, and financial aid through their own personal and community experience. She argues that responses to aid policies are not self-evident, so they should not be standardized. Rather, both students' perceptions and expectations need to be taken into account in the design of institutional policies because they are likely to influence decision-making in complex, multivalent ways.

Tandberg and Griffith ("State Support of Higher Education: Data, Measures, Findings, and Directions for Future Research") turn a critical eye to contemporary explanations of state support for higher education through a comparative analysis of data sources, policy analysis measures, theories, related methods, literature, and findings. They provide a comprehensive and thoughtful crash course for researchers new to the area. Concurrently, they also design a generalized meta-analysis for more experienced researchers looking for a solid map of this new and rapidly changing field. It is not only an excellent policy analysis research reference in its own right, it also models the good practice of interdisciplinary methods in comparative analyses, with a special emphasis on political science and political economy.

CHAPTER 14

*MAINTENANCE OF STATE EFFORT FOR HIGHER EDUCATION: "BARRIERS TO EQUAL EDUCATIONAL OPPORTUNITY IN ADDRESSING THE RISING COSTS OF A COLLEGE EDUCATION"**

F. KING ALEXANDER

A Maintenance of Effort (MOE) provision for higher education was first adopted in the Higher Education Opportunity Act of 2008 and was included as a requirement for states to participate in the American Recovery and Reinvestment Act of 2009 (ARRA). The information below was presented before the U.S. House of Representatives Committee on Education and Labor on November 1, 2007 supporting the enactment of the maintenance of effort statutory language.

Introduction

Nearly four years ago in a hearing before the House Education and Workforce Committee on 21st Century Competitiveness, I stressed to the former Chairman and other Committee members a number of important issues including the introduction of the "net tuition" concept which has since been taken very seriously by this Committee. This Committee has also acted to address the critical issue that was raised regarding dangers of simply monitoring percentage growth without considering actual dollar increases which substantially disadvantages those colleges and universities that have endeavored to keep costs low. I also made the point then that by simply making new reporting requirements instead of developing new policy strategies to provide incentives for institutional effectiveness, we are missing a crucial opportunity to reform the current system of higher education.

On these important points, these comments are focused and particularly address two distinct areas—both of which have significant ramifications for collegiate costs and equal opportunity—(1) accountability and transparency, and (2) college costs, state appropriations, and "maintenance of state tax effort." In these areas, the attempt is to describe the existing problems and then offer policy recommendations that would help remedy some of the primary concerns of taxpayers and policymakers.

Improving Accountability and Transparency

The California State University System (CSU) commends and supports the efforts of this committee to require that higher education become more transparent and accountable to students, parents, and taxpayers. The marketplace for education, or any market for that matter, cannot function

---

*Testimony before the House Committee on Education and Labor, U.S. House of Representatives, U.S. Congress, November 1, 2007.

effectively or efficiently without adequate information. The California State University, Long Beach, and the CSU System have taken these legislative and public concerns very seriously and created the most transparent and accountable measurement strategy in the nation. This method is known as the California State University Voluntary System of Accountability (CSU VSA) which augments the national public university Voluntary System of Accountability (VSA). The CSU VSA is an important addition to the national VSA and adds numerous measurement categories designed to indicate the role that the 23 public universities in the CSU are playing when addressing a series of "Public Good" domains. This information will be made available for policymakers and taxpayers throughout California and the nation, in addition to the institution—specific information resulting from the national VSA. While the national public university VSA was developed primarily to address student and parental concerns regarding the lack of substantive institutional student learning information, the CSU VSA was developed to address additional concerns that are of value to the general public-at-large.

Both the American Association of State Colleges and Universities (AASCU) and the National Association of State Universities and Land-Grant Colleges (NASULGC) advance the VSA template for public discussion. This reporting system will make additional information available to parents and students regarding student specific actual college costs, financial aid results, community service participation, as well as numerous standardized test results that assess value-added learning growth both inside and outside of the classroom. We fully endorse the public university VSA, and California State, Long Beach, will be among one of the first pilot institutions to provide the necessary information for reporting purposes. The CSU System will, in addition, set forth what is called a "public good" measurement system to provide more clarity and transparency, especially for categories that are not included in the national VSA or the model adopted by the private higher education sector.

In addition to the national VSA, the augmented CSU VSA (see Appendix A), addresses four important "public good" categories that are either de-emphasized or not included in the other measurement systems. It is planned that this information—which has already been collected from each of the 23 universities in the Cal State system—will be made available for public discussion. The categories include:

Average Undergraduate Student Debt

- Average amount in debt of graduating seniors
- Proportion of graduating seniors in debt

Degrees Granted

- Degrees Granted in High Demand Fields
- Race/Ethnicity of Undergraduate Degree Recipients

Economic Diversity: Access and Completion

- Undergraduate Pell Grant Eligibility (enrollment and percentage enrolled)
- Undergraduate Pell Grant Recipients five-year Average (enrollment and percentage)
- Undergraduate Degrees Awarded to Pell Grant Students (Degrees and Percentage)

Actual "Net Tuition and Fees" Paid by an Average Student when Compared to the Posted Sticker Price

As indicated in Appendix A, it is anticipated that the federal government will also consider these items when developing new reporting requirements for colleges and universities. However, unfortunately, at this time many institutions refuse to make economic diversity data available to consumers, taxpayers, and other constituencies.

Recommendations for More Effective Accountability and Transparency

A. In addition to the current reporting of graduation rates, the federal government should collect and distribute aggregate graduate numbers and economic diversity characteristics of enrolled and graduating students. This reporting can be accomplished by requiring and publishing Pell Grant eligibility access and completion data in aggregate numbers and percentages. Also, existing graduation rate reporting should be disaggregated using federal financial aid receipt (Pell Grant eligibility) as a proxy for income so that policymakers can better understand risk categories in order to support timely and successful graduation.

B. The federal government should require that an average "net tuition and fees" be calculated by each institution and made available to students, parents, and taxpayers. This average net tuition should reflect the average cost versus the sticker price per full-time student—not simply aided student. Sticker prices do not reflect the actual cost of higher education. Using "sticker prices" distorts and creates a flow of misinformation to consumers and students further confusing the economic realities of college attendance. If the federal government is to help improve the efficiency of the marketplace of higher education, it can contribute materially by collecting, calculating, and distributing actual program cost information by types of institutions. Such information can then be used to develop a more viable basis for the allocation of federal subsidies. This initiative would simplify federal policies while not penalizing states that continue to publicly support higher education and encourage institutions to keep costs down.

C. The federal government should require colleges and universities to collect and distribute average student undergraduate debt amounts and the percentage of seniors graduating with student loan debt. Consumer information about student debt loads is currently very difficult to obtain for most people.

D. The federal government should require that federal agencies collect and pay closer attention to institution specific expenditure trends when making policy-based determinations. Understanding institutional expenditure trends is essential for determining which colleges and universities have actually increased their costs to serve more students, more needy students, or simply to maximize the prestige of the institution.

College Costs, State Appropriations, and "Maintenance of State Tax Effort"

In addressing the issue of college and university tuition and fee growth, it is obvious that the higher education costs have differing effects on parents, students, and institutions. This fact is evidenced in numerous congressionally mandated studies of college costs and prices, showing drastic variations in average tuition and fee growth between private and public universities during the last two decades. Public perception of rising tuition costs has been shaped by a number of reasons, including geographic location and the media which is heavily influenced by high cost institutions in the northeastern region of the U.S. Importantly, a misunderstanding is fueled by an overall lack of information in the academic marketplace that prevents students and parents from distinguishing real net costs from "sticker prices." For example, students and families pay college tuition in dollars, not in percentages—yet, the vast majority of public discourse by policymakers and the media dwell on college cost increases reflected simply as percentage growth. In fact, if you analyze actual tuition and fee dollar increases, instead of tuition and fee percentage growth, you will discover that many of the public universities with the largest percentage increases over the last few years are the very institutions that are the most affordable and accessible. A small dollar increase may well be reflected in a relatively large percentage increase at lower tuition institutions. This is especially true in lower cost/high tax effort states like California, Hawaii, North Carolina, West Virginia, and Kentucky which have sought to keep student tuition and fees at a reasonable level in exchange for maintaining above-average state tax support. These low tuition states remain low cost in an effort to ensure widespread access and affordability. It should also be noted that these same states are among the lowest in the nation in average student loan debt per graduate.

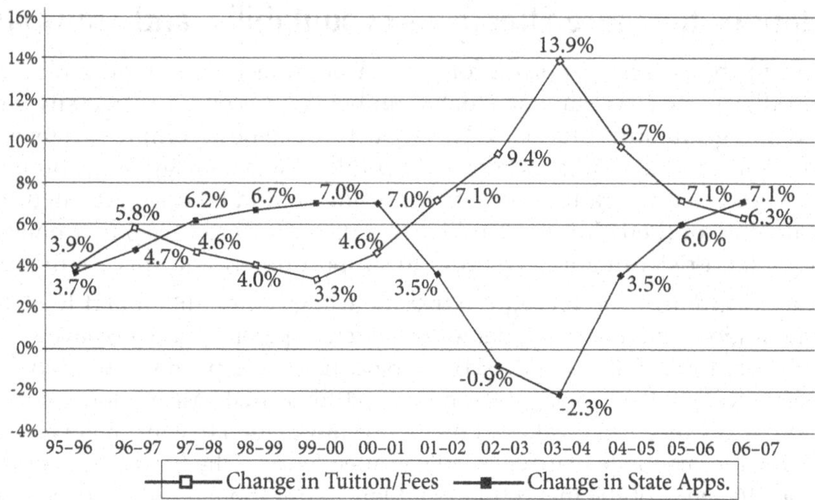

Figure 14.1 Change in resident undergraduate tuition and state appropriations, public colleges and universities, academic years 1995–1996 to 2006–2007.

Source: The College Board, Trends in College Pricing, 1995–2006 and Center for the Study of Education Policy, Illinois State University, Grapevine.

Furthermore, it is obvious that as state appropriations slide downward, student tuition and fees must rise. The interlocking relationship between public institutions, tuition and fee policies, and state appropriations is an area that seems to be pervasively misunderstood by taxpayers and policymakers. Over the last decade, studies have highlighted the instability of state appropriations and the effects of state policy on public institutional tuition changes. In a recent congressionally mandated NCES study on college costs and prices, it was shown that state general fund appropriations was by far the most significant factor in determining public college and university resident tuition rates. This is especially evident when reviewing overall public college and university tuition and fee changes when compared to state appropriation changes during the last decade. As shown in Figure 14.1, the most influential reason for increases in public college and university costs is the drastic fluctuations of state appropriations. Therefore, it should be a federal imperative to ensure that states maintain their public support of higher education. This "maintenance of fiscal effort" is a necessary part of the federal-state partnership to ensure that states continue their current level of support. A "maintenance of effort" federal-state partnership would make it more difficult for states to further reduce their fiscal responsibility to public colleges and universities by shifting the increasing costs of higher education to students, and ultimately, federal tuition-based programs.

In the case of the State of California, the dependent relationship between state appropriations and student tuition and fees was never more apparent than when the state budget was developed in recent years. State legislators and the Governor made a conscience decision to increase funding for higher education by approximately 6.5% to alleviate the need for a student fee increase while still allowing the CSU to expand by 25,000 additional students. The result was that student tuition and fees did not increase during that year.

It is also important to point out that state legislatures do not allow, in most cases, public institutions to set their own tuition and fees. Currently, there are only 14 states that allow individual institutions such prerogative.

College Costs and Equal Opportunity Recommendations

A. Thirty-five years ago, the original Pell Grant legislative proposal called for the creation of a companion program that would grant additional funds to the institutions that served Pell Grant recipients. The program was premised on the well-recognized fact that it costs more to educate lower-income students at all levels. The original legislation recommended the creation of "cost of education" allowances to be allocated directly to institutions. These grants were to accompany the Pell Grant recipients to their respective college or university. This proposal emphasized the benefit to the individual as opposed to the institution by recommending that the Department of Education create "cost of attendance" allocations in the amount of $2,500 per Pell Grant eligible student. This plan provided additional assistance to institutions serving needy students. To ensure that these funds were properly devoted to student enrichment, the proposal required that federal funds be used to support campus-based academic and student-service programs that primarily assist lower-income students. This program would have created important fiscal incentives for institutions to enroll lower-income students. However, this part of the original plan was never enacted.

Currently, there are no federal incentives of this kind in place and as a result, many high-priced private and public institutions have seen their enrollments of lower-income students stagnate and even decline. These proposed incentives would foster greater fiscal collaboration among federal and state governments and institutions. This would also promote greater college access for lower-income students, support retention efforts, and reward higher completion rates. As part of this partnership, this recommendation calls for the creation of a "state maintenance of effort" provision to ensure that states do not reduce their commitment to public higher education. These federal incentives would not only provide invaluable support to those institutions serving the neediest students, but would ensure sustainability of state funding at federally supported levels. To accomplish this, the federal government should require that states maintain current levels of state support in the form of average per student appropriation or an expected level of fiscal tax effort, which would be defined at the federal level. If states do not abide by this provision and use these federal funds to "supplant" existing state support, then the amount of the federal institutional grant can be reduced or withheld pending.

B. Limits, so long as such, are tied to the sticker prices established by the individual institutions. Rather, any increases in federal loan limits should be based on the actual costs incurred by the institutions in the provision of the educational programs. If the current system that incorporates sticker pricing remains in place when aggregate loan limits are expanded, this will result in even higher sticker prices in the years to come on many college campuses. This trend also would further generate more public backlash against all higher education institutions—not just the institutions that have escalated their pricing. By simply expanding the aggregate loan limits without making additional formulaic changes, the federal government would ultimately drive more students toward higher amounts of student loan debt.

   Institutionally, the expansion of the aggregate loan limits would primarily advantage public and private wealthy institutions that charge significantly higher tuition rates over the lower cost, less affluent public universities, and community colleges. Instead, the federal government should direct institutions to provide adequate student loan counseling and assistance that encourages students to use all federally supported loan opportunities. Currently, numerous studies indicate that students who have been increasingly turning to additional private loans to pay for college have not fully maximized the existing federal loan programs. Federal loan programs and their subsidies should be focused on expanding access instead of providing choice. By not expanding the aggregate loan, it limits the federal government by putting more pressure on the wealthy institutions to better control their sticker pricing and expenditures.

C. The federal government should require that all colleges and universities, that receive federal direct student aid, enroll at least a given percentage of Pell Grant eligible students or demonstrate that the institution is making progress toward this goal. Institutions with less than the prescribed percentage of Pell Grant eligible students would face federal direct student aid reductions.

Conclusion

In summary, the important issues regarding the enhancement of institutional accountability and transparency, the determination of actual college costs, and the role of the federal government in "state maintenance of effort" in supporting higher education have been described. Obviously, some of these recommendations require a significant overhaul in our national higher education agenda by requiring a much more strategic partnership between the federal government and our state governments, and the timeline for this reauthorization is very short and soon upon us. However, I believe that these kinds of national conversations are necessary to reform our current higher education fiscal system, especially if we are going to promote equal and affordable education opportunities.

APPENDIX A

California State University (CSU: VSA)

The information provided in this section addresses many important institutional contributions to California. This small collection of data is designed to ensure that many of our public universities are recognized for their societal contributions as well as demonstrating greater accountability to individual students, parents and the public-at-large.

"Public Good" Contributions

Degrees Granted 2005–06	
Total Degrees Awarded	
Bachelor's	5,912
Master's	1,581
Doctoral	—
Total	7,493
Undergraduate Degrees in High Demand Fields	
Nursing	165
Engineering	347
Elementary/Secondary education	446
Accountancy	163
Health-related fields	290
Race/Ethnicity of Undergraduate Degree Recipients	
African American/Black	293
American Indian/Alaskan Native	35
Asian/Pacific Islander	1,054
Mexican American	1,291
White, Non-Latino	2,148
International	328
Other/Ethnicity Unknown	763

Economic Diversity: Access & Completion	
Undergraduate Pell Grant Eligibility (2006–07) Avg.	
Total undergraduate enrollment	28,700
Undergraduate Pell grant recipients	9,384
Percentage of undergraduate enrollment	32%
Undergraduate Degrees Awarded to Pell Grant Eligible Students (2006–07)	
Awarded degrees	1,384
Percentage of graduates	24%

"Net Tuition & Fees"—Average Undergraduate Tuition and Fees Per CSULB Student	
Actual Net Tuition & Fees Paid by Students	
Full Year/Full Time (2 semesters: 7 or more units)	
Listed price	$2,864
Actual price paid per student	$1,698

Average Undergraduate Student Loan Debt	
Average Student Loan Debt (2006)	
CSULB	$6,319
State average	$17,270
National average	$18,126
Proportion of Graduates with Debt (2006)	
CSULB	29%
State average	47%
National average	67%
Undergraduate Pell Grant Recipients 5 year	
Fall undergraduate enrollment	26,914
Pell grant recipients	9,302
% of Pell grant recipients	34%

CHAPTER 15

STUDENT LOANS: DO COLLEGE STUDENTS BORROW TOO MUCH—OR NOT ENOUGH?

CHRISTOPHER AVERY AND SARAH TURNER

Total student loan debt rose to over $800 billion in June 2010, overtaking total credit card debt outstanding for the first time. By the time this article sees print, the continually updated Student Loan Debt Clock (at http://www.finaid.org/loans/studentloandebtclock.phtml) will show an accumulated total of roughly $1 trillion. New federal student loans for higher education amounted to $97 billion in 2009–2010: $66.8 billion to undergraduates and $31 billion to graduate students. Borrowing to finance educational expenditures has been increasing—more than quadrupling in real dollars since the early 1990s—as shown in Figure 15.1. The sheer magnitude of these figures has led to increased public commentary on the level of student borrowing.

On the one side, it has become fashionable to suggest that we are in the midst of an "education bubble" (for example, Schumpeter Blog 2011). As Surowiecki (2011) summarizes, "[Y]ou can't flip a college degree the way you can flip a stock, or even a home. But what bubble believers are really saying is that young people today are radically overestimating the economic value of going

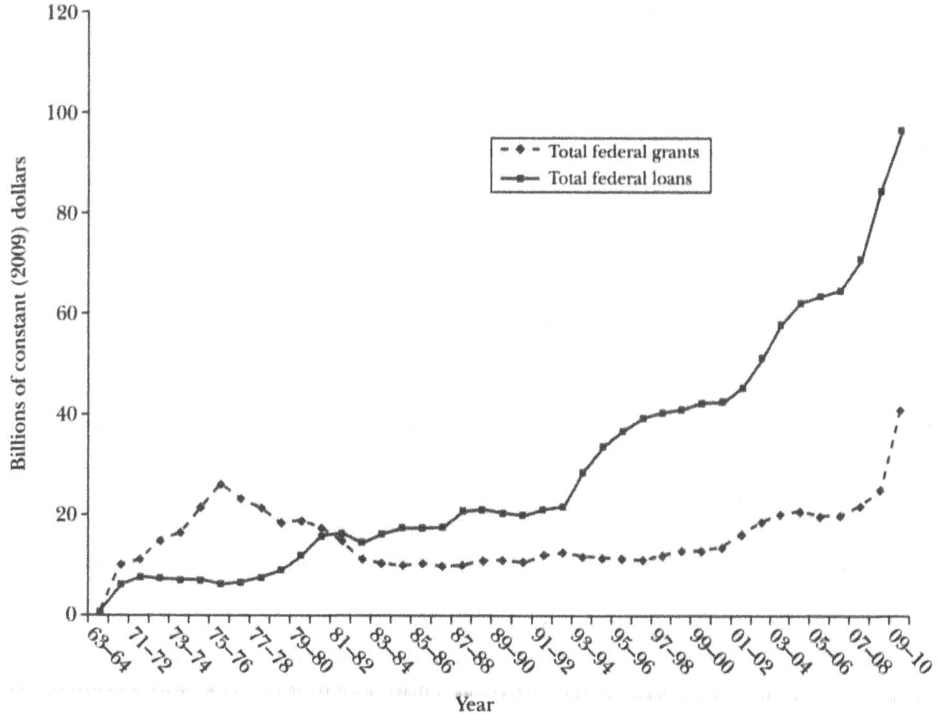

Figure 15.1 Trends in federal grant and loan aid.
Source: College Board, *Trends in Student Aid,* 2010.

to college, and that many of them would be better off doing something else with their time and money." Similarly, Kamenetz (2006) argues that a combination of wage declines in entry-level jobs and increases in college tuition have placed many high school graduates in a no-win position, pressuring them to take on unmanageable levels of financial risk in the form of student loans. Of course, the depressed job market during the Great Recession and its aftermath has only strengthened such concerns, and added others. Rothstein and Rouse (2011) provide evidence that high debt burdens make students less likely to choose a lower-paying career, like becoming a teacher. Gicheva (2011) suggests that additional student debt of $10,000 decreases the long-term probability of marriage by 7 percentage points. A 2010 poll found that 85 percent of college graduates were planning to move back home after graduation (Dickler 2010). Newspaper stories tell of students who finish their undergraduate degree with $100,000 or more in debt (Leiber 2010).

On the other side, the earnings premium for a college degree relative to a high school degree nearly doubled in the last three decades (Goldin and Katz 2008). Further, there is no particular evidence this earnings premium has declined as a result of the Great Recession, as the alternative to a weak labor market for college graduates today is a much weaker labor market for those without a college degree. In November 2011, data from the Bureau of Labor Statistics website shows that the unemployment rate for college graduates (including those with advanced degrees) was 4.4 percent, while high school graduates faced an unemployment rate of 8.5 percent and those with collegiate attainment less than a BA faced an unemployment rate of 7.6 percent. While the fraction of college-educated workers in the labor force has increased considerably in recent decades, current projections suggest the education level of the labor force will increase little, if at all, in the early twenty-first century (Ellwood 2001; see also Goldin and Katz 2008).

Concurrent with the recent and dramatic increase in the college earnings premium, overall undergraduate enrollment in college has increased from 10.5 million in 1980 to 17.6 million in 2009, while the annual volume of federal loans has increased more rapidly from 2.3 million loans in 1980 to 10.9 million loans in 2009 (Institute of Education Sciences 2010; see data at http://www2.ed.gov/finaid/prof/resources/data/opeloanvol.html). In theory, federal student loans can help to overcome a problem of social underinvestment in capital markets that was described by Milton Friedman in his 1962 *Capitalism and Freedom*:

> This underinvestment in human capital presumably reflects an imperfection in the capital market: investment in human beings cannot be financed on the same terms or with the same ease as investment in physical capital. It is easy to see why there would be such a difference. If a fixed money loan is made to finance investment in physical capital, the lender can get some security for his loan in the form of a mortgage or residual claim to the physical asset itself, and he can count on realizing at least part of his investment in case of necessity by selling the physical asset. If he makes a comparable loan to increase the earning power of a human being, he clearly cannot get any comparable security; in a non-slave state, the individual embodying the investment cannot be bought and sold. But even if he could, the security would not be comparable. The productivity of the physical capital does not—or at least generally does not—depend on the co-operativeness of the original borrower.

In this perspective, student loans can potentially improve the efficiency of the economy by raising the supply of college-educated workers in the labor market. Moreover, because credit constraints are most likely to affect students from low-income families, student loans can reduce both educational and income inequality among those in the same generation and between generations. Higher levels of federal student loans may also reduce supply constraints generated by declining state-level support for public colleges and universities, reducing the extent to which collegiate attainment is deterred by insufficient educational offerings.

So are college students borrowing too much or too little?[1] The question turns on the source of the college wage premium and on the magnitude of that wage premium for the marginal college student. The college experience provides graduates with skills and social networks, and a college degree may serve as a signal of ability to employers. These factors suggest a causal link between collegiate attainment and future wages. But it is also possible that students who choose to go to college would still be unusually successful if they entered the workforce directly upon high school graduation—that is, the college wage premium could result primarily from self-selection.

At the individual level, the choice of how much to borrow requires substantial information about expected collegiate attainment and the future path of earnings under alternative educational attainment scenarios. The connection between educational attainment and career success has been sufficiently well-publicized that even disadvantaged students from urban public schools tend to produce relatively accurate estimates of average wages at age 25 for those with and without a college degree (Avery and Kane 2004; Rouse 2004; see also Dominitz and Manski 1996). Yet, it is far from clear that young people are able to estimate *their own* future earnings accurately and take into account the extent to which there may be systematic differences between expectations and realizations. Manski (1993) emphasizes the importance of understanding how youth form expectations about future earnings and whether they condition on ability, in predicting their educational attainment and their own returns to education. Moreover, on the cost side, researchers have documented that students often misunderstand financial aid packages, fail to understand the much greater cost of consumer loans (such as credit card debt) relative to student loans, and miscalculate the trade-off between academic study and market work (Long 2004; Burdman 2005; Somers, Woodhouse, and Cofer 2004; King 2002; St. John 2004; Warwick and Mansfield 2000). Information constraints may lead to underborrowing if students do not avail themselves of borrowing opportunities, or to overborrowing if students overestimate the return to education.

Our focus in this paper is to move the discussion of student loans away from anecdote and to establish a framework for considering the use of student loans in the optimal financing of collegiate investments. We begin by providing a brief summary of the institutional framework and broad trends associated with U.S. student lending. The next section turns to the consideration of an analytic frame-work for determining how much a student should be willing to borrow and how this sum has likely changed over time. We will emphasize considerations of uncertainty and heterogeneity: even if the return to college is favorable on average, it need not be favorable for all agents. In our terminology, uncertainty is unknown, while heterogeneity represents difference among agents in their personal returns to college—including nonmonetary returns—that are known (or knowable) to them. We then look to available—albeit limited—evidence to assess which types of students are likely to be borrowing too much or too little.

Borrowing for College

Federal Student Lending Programs

There are currently four major federal sources of loans for higher education: subsidized Stafford loans, the unsubsidized Stafford loans, the Parent Loans for Undergraduates (PLUS) program, and the Perkins loans program. We provide a brief overview of these programs, along with a comparison to private sector loans for higher education.

The Higher Education Act of 1965 created the Stafford loan program, which has long been by far the largest federal student loan program. Federal student loans were initially means tested and have traditionally featured favorable terms for students from poor families through the subsidized Stafford Loan program. These loans offer three substantive advantages over private market loans: 1) subsidized interest rates; 2) deferral of repayment while student is enrolled at least half-time in college; and 3) subsidies for interest payments while a student is enrolled at least half-time in college. These subsidized Stafford loans rose from about $15 billion in 1990 to $20 billion in 2000, before jumping to $35 billion in 2009 (all in constant 2009 dollars).

In 1992, Congress created an unsubsidized Stafford program for borrowers ineligible for the means-tested subsidized Stafford loans. In 2011–12, for example, subsidized Stafford loans carry an interest rate of 3.4 percent, but the unsubsidized Stafford loans carry an interest rate of 6.8 percent. Annual new loans in the unsubsidized Stafford program had already reached $15 billion by 2000, but since then have leaped to almost $45 billion in 2009. In addition, the federal government introduced a student loan program for parents in 1980 called Parent Loans for Undergraduate Students Program (PLUS). This program loaned about $2 billion in 1990 and $5 billion in 2000, before rising to $12 billion in 2009.

Finally, the 1958 National Defense Education Act created the National Defense Student Loan Program (NDSL) which is now known as the Federal Perkins Loan Program. Perkins loan funds have been distributed by the federal government to collegiate institutions, with institutions in turn allocating funds on the basis of financial need. In the 2009–10 academic year, about 520,000 students from 1,800 institutions received Perkins loans, averaging $2,125, so total spending on the program is a little over $1 billion. The Perkins program is set to expire in 2012, limiting new loans to any funds available from repayments.

Overall, in 2009, subsidized Stafford loans accounted for about 43 percent of federal loan volume, with unsubsidized Stafford loans accounting for 40 percent and PLUS loans for 16 percent. However, it is naturally important to remember that federal lending for higher education is not a comprehensive measure of total lending for that purpose. For example, the growth in federal student loans may overstate the true increase in borrowing for students to attend college if the increase in Stafford loans supplanted other types of loans—like home equity loans in some cases—used previously to pay for college costs.

Starting in the mid-1990s, there has also been a dramatic increase in private sector loans that can be explicitly linked to higher education, driven in part by increased demand for such loans and in part by financial services sector innovations such as greater securitization of student loans through asset-backed securities. While private sector loans were about $1.5 billion (constant 2009 dollars) in 1995–96, they grew to $21.8 billion by 2007–2008, representing about 20 percent of all loan funds distributed (College Board 2010a). Because these loans generally carry somewhat higher interest rates than federal loans, students typically take these loans after exhausting other sources of credit. Mazzeo (2007) reviewed private student loan offerings and noted that many of these loans are marketed as supplements to Stafford loans. Mazzeo also suggests that some parents may prefer private lending options over PLUS loans, because the private loans are made in the student's name. Because private lenders have a greater capacity to discriminate among borrowers by their choice of collegiate investments, higher-ability students and students enrolled in the most remunerative degree programs will be offered more credit by private lenders (Lochner and Monge-Naranjo 2011). In the wake of the financial crisis of 2008 and 2009—and its effects on the market for securitized loans in general—private sector student loans have returned to their historical level of about 7 percent of the market.

Shifting from borrowing to repayment, conventional student loans carry monthly payments over a 10-year horizon. With federal loans, students can choose from among alternative repayment options, which may increase the duration of the loan to 25 years, and graduated payments, with payments increasing every two years (see Krueger and Bowen, 1993, for discussion of income-contingent repayment plans).

Student Borrowing

To be eligible for federal loan options, a student must complete the Free Application for Federal Student Aid (FAFSA) form (available at http://federalstudentaid.ed.gov). This application qualifies students for federal student aid programs authorized under Title IV of the Higher Education Act, including both direct loan programs and Pell grants. Eligibility for student loans is restricted to U.S. citizens, permanent residents, and eligible noncitizens (like those granted asylum) with high school degrees or who have passed the General Educational Development (GED) test. Eligibility for subsidized government loans is further restricted to students with demonstrated unmet financial need—or those students for whom cost of attendance minus grant aid minus the "Expected Family Contribution" (calculated through analysis of income and assets) is positive. This level of unmet need serves as a cap on the amount that a student will be permitted to borrow through federal loan programs and is the total cost of attendance less any grant aid (federal, state, or institutional). Economic models predict that students will exhaust borrowing from the lowest cost of capital first (subsidized loans, if the student is eligible), followed by unsubsidized government loans and private loans, though such a pattern does not always hold in the data.

Table 15.1 provides summary statistics for undergraduate borrowing from federal programs over the past 20 years. During this time, the total volume of federal loans has expanded several-fold, but average loan levels per student borrower were largely constant in real terms. That is, the

TABLE 15.1

Percentage of All Undergraduate Borrowing, by Student and Institution Characteristics

	1989–90	1992–93	1995–96	1999–2000	2003–04	2007–08
Percent of undergraduates borrowing						
Total	**19%**	**19%**	**25%**	**27%**	**32%**	**35%**
Type of institution						
Public 4-year	19%	23%	37%	39%	43%	41%
Private nonprofit 4-year	31%	34%	47%	49%	53%	54%
Public 2-year	4%	6%	4%	5%	8%	10%
For-profit	63%	47%	59%	74%	76%	88%
Dependency status						
Dependent	18%	20%	31%	34%	36%	36%
Independent	19%	17%	19%	21%	28%	33%

Source: The information in the table is taken from Table 1.1 of *Trends in Undergraduate Stafford Loan Borrowing: 1989–90 to 2007–08* (Wei 2010). The table is based on data from U.S. Department of Education, National Center for Education Statistics, and 1989–90, 1992–93, 1995–96, 1999–2000, 2003–04, and 2007–08 National Postsecondary Student Aid Studies (NPSAS:90, NPSAS:93, NPSAS:96, NPSAS:2000, NPSAS:04, NPSAS:08).

Note: This table includes both subsidized and unsubsidized borrowing from the Stafford program.

increase in loans disbursed by the federal government is largely due to an expansion in the number of borrowers over time. In addition to an increase in the number of students enrolling in college over time, the proportion of undergraduates who take out student loans has increased, rising from about 19 percent in 1989–90 to about 35 percent in 2007–2008. As shown in Table 15.1, this increase in borrowing has been somewhat larger among dependent undergraduate students than independent students.[2] Students who begin at two-year public institutions are the least likely to borrow (about 10 percent in 2007–2008) and borrow the lowest average amounts (conditional on borrowing at all). Students at for-profit institutions are the most likely to borrow (88 percent).

This variation in borrowing by type of institution is a function of both the revenue structure of colleges and universities and the extent to which institutions draw students with a high degree of financial need. For-profit institutions depend largely on student tuition and fees and receive about three-quarters of their funding through federal Title IV loans and grants (as Deming, Goldin, and Katz discuss in their paper in this symposium).

There is a structural reason that average federal loan levels per student have been fairly constant in real terms over time: borrowing under the federal loan programs is limited by both cost of attendance (less grant aid) and nominal loan limits associated with the Stafford, Perkins, and PLUS program. For the Stafford program, annual loan limits are defined in terms of year of study and independent status, rising from $3,500 per year for first-year undergraduates to $8,500 for graduate students. The loan limits associated with the Stafford program bind in many cases, with borrowers often clustered at the maximum loan level. For two decades from 1987 to 2007, loan limits remained fixed in nominal terms: for example, first-year students were limited to borrowing $2,625 from the subsidized Stafford program. In addition to annual limits, there are lifetime limits on subsidized Stafford ($23,000) and unsubsidized Stafford ($31,000 for dependents and $57,500 for independent). With rapid increases in college costs during the 1990s and unchanging loan limits, the share of undergraduate borrowers reaching loan limits increased from 1989–90 until 2007 when loan limits were increased. In 1989–90, 42 percent of subsidized Stafford borrowers were at the maximum, while 17.8 percent of all Stafford borrowers were at the maximum; by 2003–2004, these numbers had risen to 50.3 and 50.6 percent for subsidized Stafford borrowers and all student borrowers, respectively. With Stafford loan limits raised in 2007, the percentage at the maximum for subsidized and unsubsidized Stafford loans fell to 42.4 and 44.1 percent, respectively, in 2007–2008 (Wei 2010).

College as an Investment

The decision as to whether to invest in one's human capital in the form of education requires that an individual compare the present discounted value of benefits—among which are the gains in future earnings as a result of education—to the present discounted value of costs, including tuition, fees, and foregone wages.[3] In this section, we consider the question of the extent to which the monetary returns from college have exceeded the costs over recent decades for an average student. (For discussion of the nonmonetary returns to college—for example, conditioning on wage levels, the extent to which higher educational attainment predicts higher job satisfaction, see the article by Oreopoulos and Salvanes in the Winter 2011 issue of this journal.) In the next section, we focus on uncertainty and heterogeneity across students.

Suppose that two students graduate from high school simultaneously in June 2009, and that one completes college in four years and subsequently earns wages equal to the average for college graduates at each age, while the other enters the job market immediately and earns wages equal to the average for high school graduates at each age. Based on data from the 2009 Current Population Survey, the gap in average earnings between college graduates and high school graduates starts at $7,000 at age 22 ($28,200 for college graduates versus $21,000 for high school graduates), grows steadily from age 22 to 42 and then levels off at later ages. Though at the point of college graduation the fictitious college graduate would be more than $100,000 behind the high school graduate in the present discounted value of net income, the college graduate overtakes the high school graduate at age 34.

With this example, we want to emphasize that we are not making a causal statement about the magnitude of the returns to education. Such a comparison would rest critically on the assumption that the counterfactual wage distribution for someone earning the average college wage is the average wage of high school graduates. However, at least some of the characteristics that lead a person to select college may also be relevant to their income-earning abilities after college, and observed wages will reflect selection into different levels of education. In addition, changes in earnings streams over time may reflect compositional shifts in the characteristics of individuals with different levels of educational attainment. Later in the paper, we will delve further into these issues of heterogeneity and their implications for the choices of individuals.

In a present discounted value calculation with a 3 percent yearly discount rate, by age 64 the college graduate would have compiled a total of approximately $1.2 million in earnings net of tuition at age 64 as opposed to approximately $780,000 in total earnings for the high school graduate. Of course, this calculation of the average life-time benefit to a college degree requires a number of assumptions: the discount rate, years of work, growth rate of earnings over the life course, labor force participation, and so forth. But, given the large difference in outcomes between the two fictitious students in this example, the qualitative comparison between them is clearly robust to plausible changes in underlying assumptions. In particular, the comparison is robust to adjustments for the effect of self-selection. For instance, if we assume that half of the difference in wages between a college graduate and a high school graduate is due to self-selection,[4] then the lifetime earnings for the college graduate decline to $925,000 and the college graduate would not overtake the high school graduate until age 42. The present discounted value only becomes the same for the high school graduate and the college graduate if we attribute about 75 percent of the difference in observed earnings to self-selection. This seems like an implausibly large effect given the connection between college graduation and many lucrative career paths.

Figure 15.2 compares the average lifetime earnings for a college graduate relative to a high school graduate for men and women from 1965 to 2008. The annual values reflect what a man or woman would expect to earn working full time, full year over a career of 42 years, with a discount rate of 3 percent, assuming the college graduate delayed the start of earnings for four years while in school. We calculate the expectation formed in any given year by assuming that the future high school and college graduates will have the future earnings at each age equal to the average earnings of high school and college graduates (respectively) presently observed at each age: thus, the expectation in, say, 1980 is formed based on data across ages for 1980, and so on for each year. The present discounted value of earnings for high school graduates has remained mostly flat (particularly for men). At the same time, the present discounted value of the earnings for a college graduate have

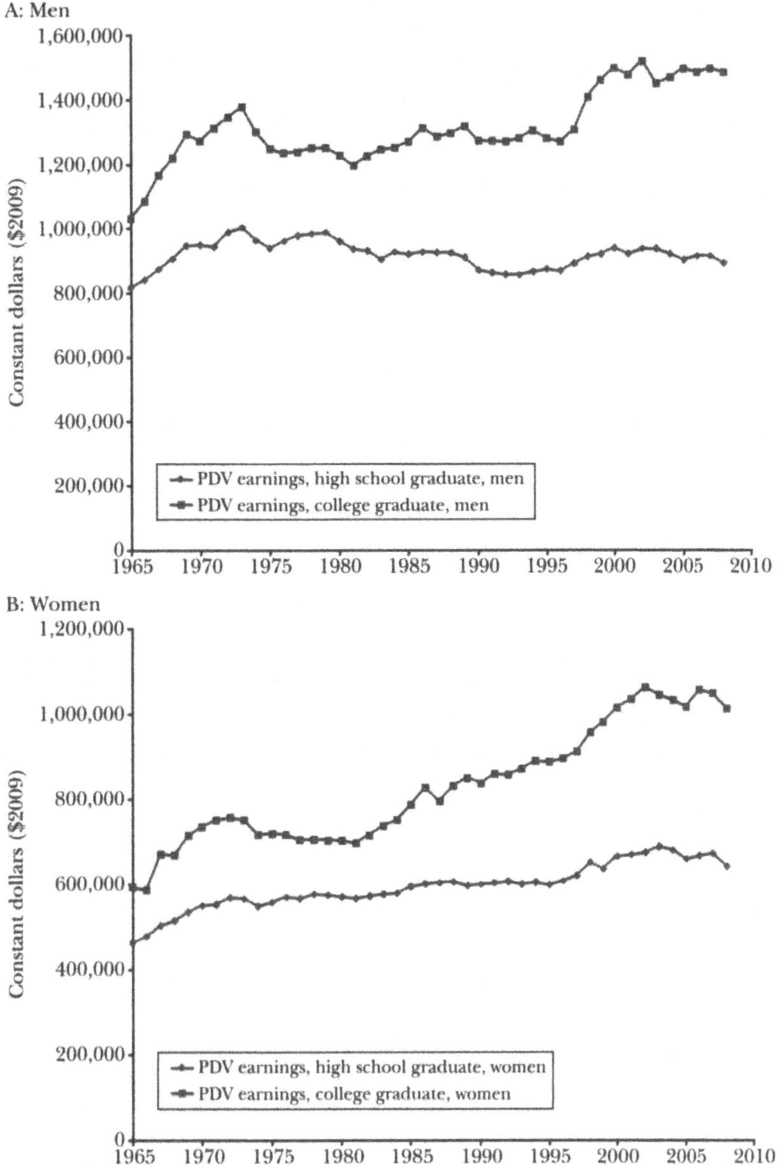

Figure 15.2 Trends in the present discounted value (PDV) of high school and college earnings net of tuition.

Notes: Expected earnings are calculated from the March Current Population Survey files for full-time, full-year workers using sample weights, assuming 42 years of work experience per person. Results for college-educated workers are net of four years of tuition and fees associated with appropriate year-specific values for public universities.

risen markedly between 1981 and 2008, rising from $1.2 to $1.5 million for men and from $720,000 to $1.1 million for women.[5]

Figure 15.3 makes clear that the lifetime earnings increment, on average, of a college degree receipt relative to a high school degree has grown markedly over the last three decades for men and women. These earnings increments are shown in comparison to the discounted value of tuition expenditures over four years (the on-time degree completion for a full-time student) over time in recent years. Thus, even as the present discounted value of tuition for four years at a private college (which would be the most expensive option) has increased over the interval from about $50,000 to $122,000 (all in constant 2008 dollars), average benefits of college completion in terms of future earnings have increased

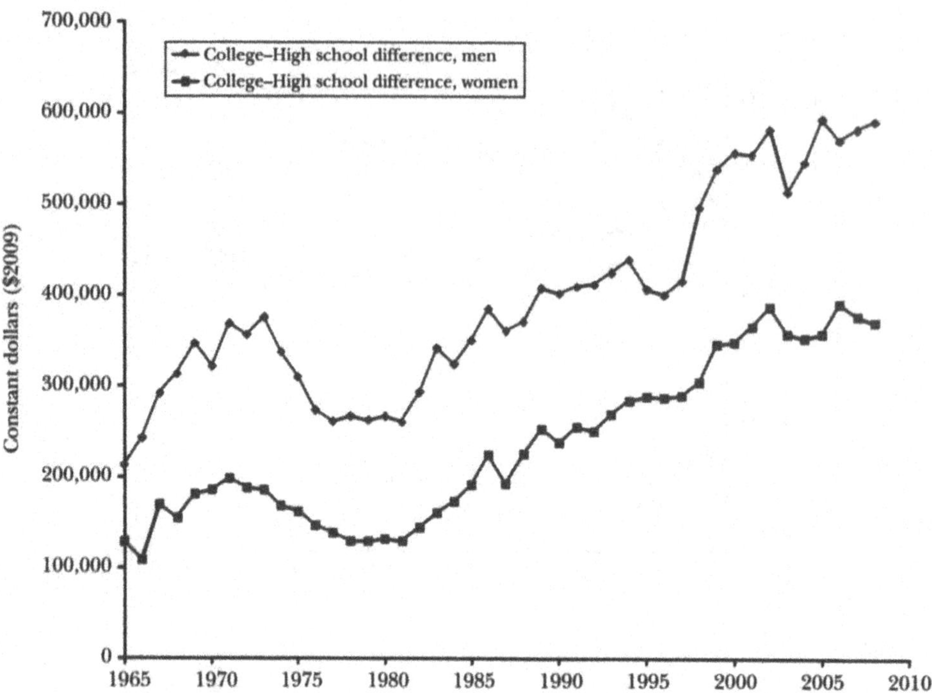

Figure 15.3 Present discounted value of college degree net of tuition, 1965–2010.

Source: These calculations are based on data from the March Current Population Survey files for full-time, full-year workers using sample weight.

Notes: College–High school difference represents the difference between the present discounted value of the average expected earnings of a college graduate (assuming that earnings begin four years after college entrance and the student pays tuition for four years) and the stream of earnings for a high school graduate. See Figure 15.2 for earnings calculations.

more rapidly. To be sure, the average net price of college is somewhat below these figures, because grant-based financial aid from government and institutions reduces the price paid by students below the sticker price.[6]

One natural conjecture is that a risk of recession should affect how students invest in a college education, but the direction of this effect is not clear. On one side, the opportunity cost of attending college in terms of foregone wages is lower during a recession, which should tend to increase college attendance during recessions; on the other side, there is a negative effect on wages for those who graduate from college during a recession that can persist as long as ten years (Kahn 2010), which might tend to discourage college attendance in a recession. Figure 15.3 indicates, however, that the estimated present discounted value of a four-year college degree has increased fairly steadily over the past 30 years through both booms and busts. Further, the comparisons in the figure are based on the average difference in wages for full-time workers with and without BA degrees, but the unemployment rate for college graduates tends to be substantially lower than that for high school graduates in a recession. For that reason, Figure 15.3 may understate the financial return to a college degree during a recession.[7]

The message is clear: expected lifetime earnings associated with a college degree have increased markedly over time. As the investment value of a college degree rises, it is natural to think of individuals increasing their willingness to borrow to achieve these higher returns.

Of course, a number of factors also affect realized student borrowing which may well diverge from willingness to borrow. For example, the direct cost of college represented by tuition charges has increased markedly in both the public and private sectors, which will tend to increase demand for borrowing among those students who do not receive commensurate increases in financial aid. In addition, a decline in family resources generated by adverse shocks to parental income or assets could contribute to increased student borrowing. On the other side, a student might react to greater availability of student loans by rationally deciding to borrow more to allow for consumption smoothing, leading to higher debt levels. In addition, low-income students often receive grant-based aid (including federal Pell grants as well as institutional awards) which reduce the expected cost of college and reduce pressure to borrow. These sorts of differences across households raise the broader issue that even if increased borrowing makes sense on average, there can be considerable variation in realized borrowing, even among students with similar expected gains from collegiate attainment.

Uncertainty and Heterogeneity across Individuals

To this point, we have focused on the college investment and borrowing decisions on average; however, substantial variation in expected returns at the time of college entry for individuals may lead to different conclusions about the investment value of college and the associated level of borrowing. First, ultimate educational attainment varies considerably: some students will start but not complete college, while others will go on to complete graduate degrees that can pave the way to lucrative careers. Second, choice of occupations varies considerably, some with higher and some with lower average wages, among those students who achieve a given level of educational attainment. Third, substantial dispersion in wages exists even conditional on educational attainment and (broad) choice of occupation. In this section, we discuss these three factors, and the implications for the expected financial returns to college for a given student. As students make borrowing decisions, a central question is the extent to which they can accurately predict these determinants of future earnings. If students can accurately predict these determinants of future earnings, we would expect borrowing to vary substantially with these outcomes.

Collegiate Attainment

Only 55 percent of dependent students who anticipate completing a BA degree actually do so within six years of graduating high school, while more than one-third of them do not complete any postsecondary degree within six years. Similarly, more than half of dependent students who anticipate completing an associate's degree do not do so within six years of graduating high school (authors' tabulations, Beginning Postsecondary Study 2004:2009). Table 15.2 shows expected degree completion, realized degree completion, and the associated distribution of borrowing. One particularly negative outcome emerges: among students who anticipate completing a BA degree, 51.3 percent will end up with no degree and an average of $7,413 in student loans ($14,457 conditional on having borrowed at all).

To some degree, differences in educational outcomes across the set of college freshmen can be predicted by factors that are observable at the time of college entry. Not surprisingly, Bound, Lovenheim, and Turner (2010) show substantial differences in degree completion rates conditional on student achievement. In addition, graduation rates and expected future earnings may differ among colleges and universities, perhaps because U.S. colleges and universities differ widely in available resources. Tabulations specific to this paper show that among students beginning at four-year colleges, private for-profit colleges have dramatically lower average graduation rates (16 percent) for dependent students than do public (63 percent) or private not-for-profit (68 percent) colleges. In addition, there is substantial variation in graduation rates within each college category, with more-selective colleges typically having higher graduation rates.[8]

A student's computation of the expected financial return to entering college should incorporate the conditional probability of not completing college given all known factors, including that student's past achievement and the historical graduation rates for the college chosen. These adjustments would have more effect in reducing the expected value of attending higher education for students with lower achievement levels and especially for those attending colleges—such as private for-profit colleges—with very low documented graduation rates.

Choice of College Major and Career

One widely cited story about a student struggling with an unusual amount of debt is the case of a 26 year-old graduate from New York University with $97,000 in loans referenced in a May 2010 *New*

TABLE 15.2

Expected Degree Completion, Realized Degree Completion, and Borrowing

	Expected Attainment			
	No Degree	**Certificate**	**AA**	**BA**
Distribution by expected attainment	3.6%	4.0%	13.0%	79.4%
Realized attainment				
No degree	66.2%	51.9%	62.0%	38.0%
Certificate	7.0%	31.9%	9.1%	2.1%
AA	4.9%	5.5%	21.5%	7.5%
BA	21.9%	10.8%	7.3%	52.4%
Percentage with student loans				
No degree	35.6%	37.0%	39.2%	51.3%
Certificate	22.0%	29.8%	47.9%	43.8%
AA	4.6%	35.1%	54.7%	55.6%
BA	66.3%	42.8%	65.4%	63.7%
Average student loans (unconditional)				
No degree	$4,475	$4,128	$4,222	$7,413
Certificate	$1,618	$2,788	$4,794	$5,113
AA	$7,651	$3,565	$8,544	$9,564
BA	$22,183	$9,658	$16,645	$15,562
Average student loans among borrowers				
No degree	$12,571	$11,160	$10,758	$14,457
Certificate	$7,367	$9,361	$10,008	$11,666
AA	$14,006	$10,149	$15,609	$17,194
BA	$33,480	$22,582	$25,465	$24,437

Source: Authors' tabulations from Beginning Postsecondary Survey (BPS) 2004:2009, including survey results in 2008–09 for students who entered any four-year college or public two-year college in 2003–2004.

Note: AA is Associate's degree; BA is Bachelor's degree.

York Times story (Leiber 2010). With an inter-disciplinary degree in religious and women's studies—which are fields of study with quite low expected earnings—one is left to wonder how this student's expectations about future earnings aligned with her borrowing decisions, both at the start of her college career and as she settled on her choice of major. Plainly, the student's prospects of paying the loan back are somewhat limited with a $22/hour job working for a photographer. Could this student have predicted the divergence between her earnings and her capacity to repay the loan? In practice, there are substantial differences in the expected lifetime earnings by choice of major.

Figure 15.4 shows the present discounted value of predicted lifetime earnings associated with different fields of specialization for men with exactly a BA. The estimates are based on a regression with the log of annual earnings as the dependent variable, and dummy variables for undergraduate major, post-baccalaureate degree attainment, job experience, race, and gender as explanatory variables. Not surprisingly, students who have chosen a technical field—in the broad categories of computer science, engineering, and math—tend to earn more than the average and more than those with education or humanities undergraduate concentrations. There is a substantial economics literature on the return to different undergraduate specializations including Paglin and Rufolo (1990), Grogger and Eide (1995), and dynamic models like Arcidiacono, Hotz, and Kang (2010). There are also more accessible publications available through public policy and career services sources (like

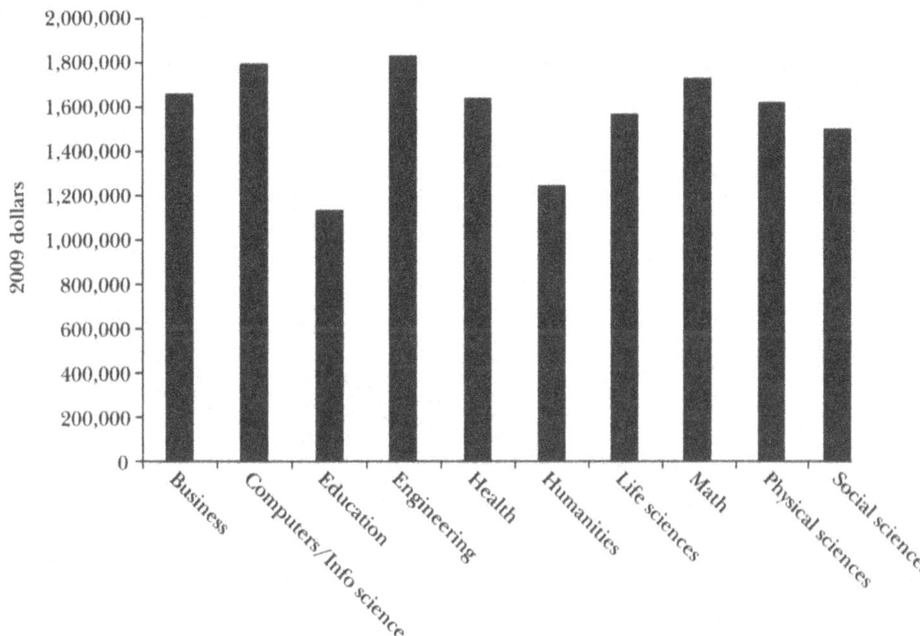

Figure 15.4 Expected lifetime earnings by undergraduate major, 2008.

Source: Authors using data from the American Community Survey (2009).

Note: Based on regression of log annual earnings on dummy variables for undergraduate major, post-baccalaureate degree attainment, a quartic in experience, and indicators for race and gender using data from the American Community Survey (2009) with sample weights.

Carnevale, Strohl, and Melton 2011), although it is not clear that students use this information when selecting a college major and choosing how much to borrow for college.

If students enter college with knowledge of their intended major, we would expect to see systematic differences in borrowing by field of study in relation to the expected earnings by field of study. Of course, some students enter college with no specific choice of major or career field in mind, while others may change their majors while enrolled in college, which in either case makes it difficult to take this factor into account in advance.

Collegiate Investment and the Increased Dispersion in Earnings and Attainment

As the average earnings of college graduates has increased, so too has the variance in earnings, and gains have been disproportionately concentrated among graduates with professional degrees and those with earnings outcomes in the top deciles (Acemoglu and Autor 2010; Lindley and Machin 2011). Annual differences in earnings among college graduates are magnified over the life course and, in turn, have a substantial impact on the expected return to a collegiate investment.

Figure 15.5 presents the distributions of lifetime earnings for different levels of postsecondary attainment for men in 1978, which is approximately the trough in the return to a college education, and 2008. (See the online Appendix available with this paper at http://ejep.org for a similar figure for women, a group for whom participation in the labor market changed substantially during this time.) In both years, distribution of lifetime earnings for those with graduate degrees dominates the distribution for those with BA degrees, which in turn dominates the distribution for those completing some college, which in turn dominates the distribution for high school graduates. The difference in outcomes across these distributions widens markedly at the top part of the distribution beyond about the 80th percentile.

Figure 15.5 suggests two conspicuous changes from 1978 to 2008. First, differences in earnings between different postsecondary outcomes are more pronounced in 2008 than in 1978, with especially large gaps in 2008 between graduate degree recipients and BA degree recipients, and separately for BA degree recipients and those completing less than a BA degree. Secondly, within each

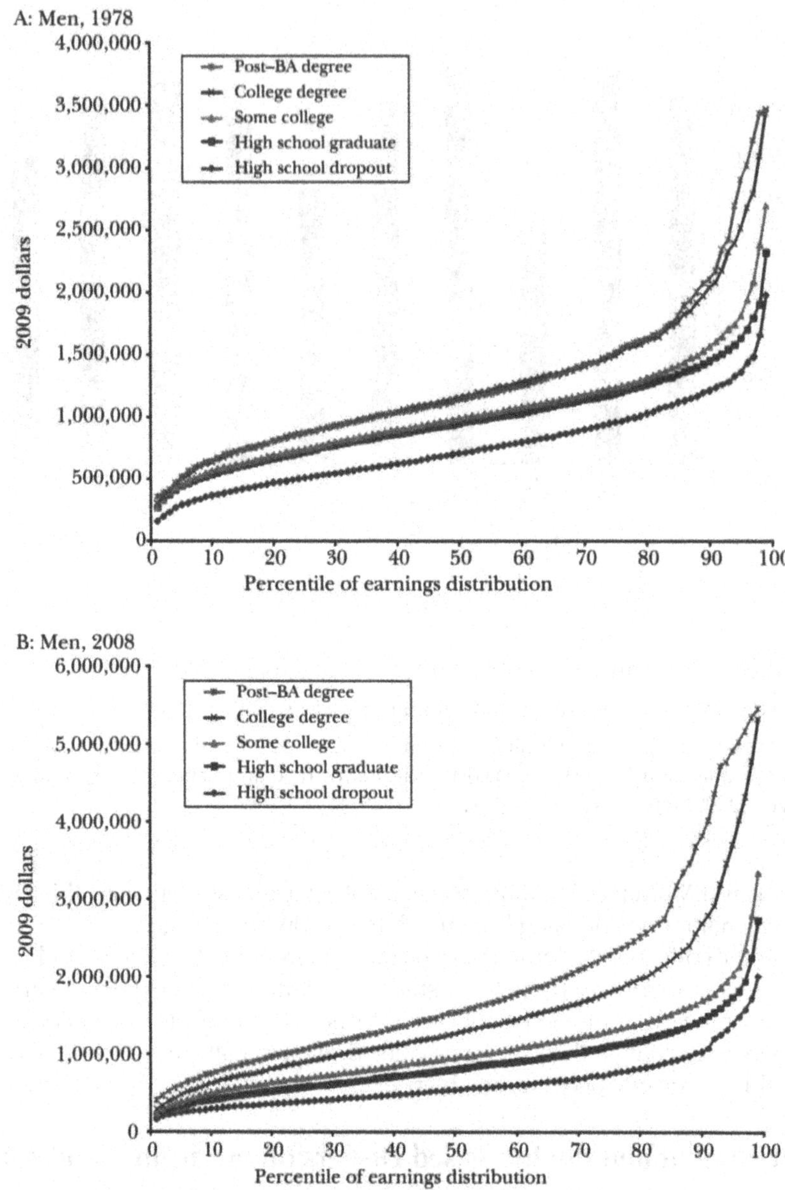

Figure 15.5 Distribution of present discounted value of career earnings, men.

Source: Data are from the 1979 and 2009 annual files of the March CPS and are limited to full-time, full-year workers.

Note: Percentiles of age-specific earnings profiles in each year are discounted to generate the expected value of lifetime earnings assuming a discount rate of 3 percent.

education group, the difference between the median and the top of the distribution is much larger in 2008 than in 1978. To illustrate, the difference in expected lifetime earnings between a male college graduate at the 90th percentile and a male college graduate at the median rises from $963,149 in 1978 to $2,287,067 in 2008. For those who complete a graduate degree and find themselves in the top part of the distribution, the difference in earnings in 2008 relative to 1978 is extraordinary—on the order of $1.7 million over a lifetime for a man at the 90th percentile. For those who attend college and do not receive a degree, outcomes are notably stagnant, particularly in the lowest two-thirds of the distribution. Among men, those who have attended college but not received a BA degree are actually somewhat worse off over the life course in 2008 relative to 1978, while women in this situation are only modestly better off in 2008 than in 1978.

As we consider the increased observed variance in earnings within postsecondary outcomes, a key question is whether individuals are able to predict their position in the earnings distribution at the start of college and as they are making within-college borrowing decisions. If individuals have such information, we would expect borrowing to increase with an individual's place in the earnings distribution. Alternatively, the increase in the variance in earnings over time may reflect increased uncertainty about the economic outcomes associated with any educational trajectory.

While the relative importance of heterogeneity and uncertainty provide one framework for considering differences in collegiate investments and borrowing, it may be that student borrowing and investment decisions are also affected by imperfect information. If students systematically misperceive the likelihood of collegiate attainment or expected earnings, they may make "mistakes" in borrowing too much (or too little).

Implications for Borrowing and Collegiate Investments

How does the variation in the likelihood of completing a degree, choice of major, or where one will end up on the income distribution affect the decision to invest in a college education and, in turn, the decision to borrow for college? If individuals can make accurate predictions about whether they will complete college and what they would earn conditional on attaining a college degree, then most of the variation in lifetime earnings outcomes can be attributed to heterogeneity that is observable at the time of the decision—differences in individual aptitude or preparation, choice of college, and so forth. If, instead, individual characteristics that are observable at the time of college enrollment provide little information about future educational attainment and subsequent labor market outcomes, then an individual's best estimate of the financial return to enrolling in college, and how much to borrow, must be based on a probabilistic assessment of earnings, which may encompass a wide range of outcomes. In effect, are realized differences in earnings a result of heterogeneity or uncertainty?[9]

To illustrate the implications of these two different cases, consider hypothetical scenarios based on the correlation between a student's rank order in the distribution of career earnings for college graduates (assuming that this student attends and graduates from college) and that student's rank order in the distribution for high school graduates (assuming instead that the student does not go to college). At one extreme, an individual would have the same position in the rank order distribution of earnings at each degree level—so that someone at the 80th percentile of the high school distribution could expect to be at the 80th percentile of the collegiate distribution. At the other extreme, the correlation between an individual's position in the high school distribution and the college distribution is zero, which means that the best estimate of the outcome will be the earnings outcome for the person at the median of the college distribution. An intermediate case is the assumption of a correlation coefficient between postsecondary and college outcomes on the order of 0.75.[10]

How do these projections differ across the three decades from 1978 to 2008, given the appreciable gains at the very top of the collegiate wage distribution? Table 15.3 presents estimates under the three alternative assumptions of the high school-college correlation in rank ($p = 0, 0.75, 1$); the top panel shows the expected present value of net lifetime earnings of a college graduate and the bottom panel shows the expected differential between collegiate and high school earnings. Assuming perfect correlation between high school rank and college rank produces the distributions with the steepest upward trajectories—increasing earnings. To illustrate, a man at the 90th percentile of the high school, career-earnings distribution would be projected to have net collegiate, career earnings of \$1.8 million in 1978 (constant dollars) and \$2.3 million in 2008, while a student at the 10th percentile of the high school distribution would be projected to have career earnings of \$603,624 in 1978 and the slightly lower outcome of \$570,865 in 2008. As uncertainty increases, or the correlation coefficient decreases, projected career earnings "flatten" across the baseline distribution. With a weaker correlation, a greater share of the distribution (and, at the extreme, the entire distribution) is expected to benefit from the rise in the return to collegiate attainment between 1978 and 2008, with this increase particularly large for women. In essence, with substantial uncertainty and rising benefits to college, more people would be expected to "give college a try," though as a result of this uncertainty, some college graduates would be expected to achieve smaller gains to college attainment than the values indicated in Table 15.3.

TABLE 15.3

Projected Net Lifetime Earnings with a College Degree, and College–High School Differential, Alternative Assumptions, 1978 and 2008

Percentile of Earnings Distribution	1978			2008		
	$\rho = 1$	$\rho = .75$	$\rho = 0$	$\rho = 1$	$\rho = .75$	$\rho = 0$
Expected PDV collegiate earnings						
Women						
10	378,180	492,778	579,126	436,140	588,301	901,908
25	492,775	564,747	579,126	603,199	697,208	901,908
50	646,042	646,042	579,126	840,787	840,787	901,908
75	824,934	736,132	579,126	1,154,114	996,244	901,908
90	1,012,494	824,934	579,126	1,571,831	1,195,242	901,908
95	1,162,783	869,542	579,126	1,929,559	1,274,998	901,908
99	1,418,246	930,391	579,126	3,337,826	1,470,333	901,908
Men						
10	603,625	838,579	1,138,378	570,865	786,540	1,261,489
25	810,516	926,495	1,138,378	795,659	941,104	1,261,489
50	1,072,293	1,072,293	1,138,378	1,143,475	1,143,475	1,261,489
75	1,372,471	1,217,483	1,138,378	1,639,365	1,413,594	1,261,489
90	1,814,302	1,366,319	1,138,378	2,357,862	1,734,813	1,261,489
95	2,172,964	1,440,285	1,138,378	3,337,949	1,871,475	1,261,489
99	3,095,903	1,552,359	1,138,378	5,031,368	2,278,956	1,261,489
Percentile of High School Wage Distribution	**1978**			**2008**		
	$\rho = 1$	$\rho = .75$	$\rho = 0$	$\rho = 1$	$\rho = .75$	$\rho = 0$
Expected net returns (Coll–HS)						
Women						
10	134,813	249,411	335,759	203,784	355,945	669,552
25	167,899	239,871	254,250	305,930	399,938	604,639
50	221,041	221,041	154,125	439,393	439,393	500,514
75	273,940	185,138	28,132	644,108	486,238	391,902
90	296,916	109,356	–136,452	886,685	510,096	216,762
95	322,090	28,849	–261,567	1,108,659	454,099	81,008
99	292,183	–195,673	–546,937	2,327,401	459,908	–108,517
Men						
10	235,318	470,272	770,070	277,920	493,595	968,544
25	298,880	414,859	626,742	408,338	553,783	874,169
50	361,800	361,800	427,885	607,035	607,035	725,050
75	410,767	255,779	176,674	896,534	670,763	518,658
90	599,569	151,586	–76,355	1,326,780	703,732	230,408
95	813,152	80,473	–221,434	1,941,625	475,151	–134,834
99	1,116,979	–426,564	–840,546	3,024,145	271,733	–745,734

Source: Authors.

Yet this initial presentation assumes that high school graduates considering college essentially can uniformly expect to receive the earnings drawn from the distribution of all collegiate outcomes, including graduate attainment (where changes in returns have been the greatest in the last three decades). This estimate is surely an extreme upper bound for the students currently in the high school graduate pool.

Additional Factors

Two additional factors may have important implications for the financial costs and gains of enrolling in college: risk aversion and option value. Since enrolling in college can be viewed as a lottery with substantial probability of amassing debt but earning no degree, risk aversion would likely reduce the attractiveness of borrowing to enroll in college. At the same time, students can anticipate a flow of new information about costs (for example, time and effort required to complete a degree) and benefits (likely job placement and salaries) of college while enrolled. Since it is possible to drop out at any time, this flow of information induces an option value to initial college enrollment. Indeed, Stange (forthcoming) estimates that 14 percent of the (positive) expected return to college enrollment can be attributed to this option value (see also Stinebrickner and Stinebrickner 2009).

One important implication of the option value of enrolling in college is that even assuming optimal enrollment decisions by students based only on the financial implications of college (excluding, for example, the consumption value of attending college), we should still expect to see some students dropping out. George Stigler once commented, "If you never miss a plane, you're spending too much time at the airport." Similarly, if no one dropped out of college, we could likely conclude that more students should be enrolling.

Do Students Make Optimal Use of Loans in Financing College?

While it is too early to assess the extent to which early twenty-first century student borrowers as a group will face oppressive long-term burdens from their student debt, a look at student outcomes six years after college enrollment provides some indication of whether it is likely that the current generation is part of a "debt bubble." Table 15.4 presents total accumulated student borrowing six years after college entrance by type of first institution.

Table 15.4 also highlights the widespread variation in borrowing levels. Borrowing among students at the median is relatively modest: zero for students beginning at community colleges, $6,000 for students at four-year public colleges, and $11,500 for students at private nonprofit colleges. Even at the 90th percentile, student borrowing does not exceed $40,000 outside of the for-profit sector. Examples of students who complete their undergraduate degree with more than $100,000 in debt are clearly rare: outside of the for-profit sector, less than 0.5 percent of students who received BA degrees within six years had accumulated more than $100,000 in student debt. The 90th percentile of degree recipients starting at for-profits have $100,000 in debt; so a nontrivial number of students at for-profits accumulate this much debt, but the situation is still far from the norm.

Leaving aside extreme cases, are student borrowing levels assumed by the majority of undergraduate students consistent with their capacity to repay these loans? There is little evidence to suggest that the average burden of loan repayment relative to income has increased in recent years. The most commonly referenced benchmark is that a repayment to gross income ratio of 8 percent, which is derived broadly from mortgage underwriting, is "manageable" while other analysis such as a 2003 GAO study set the benchmark at 10 percent. To put this in perspective, an individual with $20,000 in student loans could expect a monthly payment of about $212, assuming a ten-year repayment period. In order for this payment to accrue to 10 percent of income, the student would need an annual income of about $25,456, which is certainly within the range of expected early-career wages for college graduates. Overall, the mean ratio of student loan payments to income among borrowers has held steady at between 9 and 11 percent, even as loan levels have increased over time (Baum and Schwarz 2006; Baum and O'Malley 2003). Among student borrowers in repayment six years

TABLE 15.4

Borrowing Distribution after Six Years, by Degree Type and First Institution

	Type of Institution of First Enrollment			
	Public 4-Year	Private Nonprofit 4-Year	Private For-Profit 4-Year	Public 2-Year
All students beginning in 2004				
% Borrowing	61%	68%	89%	41%
Percentile of borrowers				
10th	$0	$0	$0	$0
25th	$0	$0	$6,376	$0
50th	$6,000	$11,500	$13,961	$0
75th	$19,000	$24,750	$28,863	$6,625
90th	$30,000	$40,000	$45,000	$18,000
Mean	**$11,706**	**$16,606**	**$19,726**	**$5,586**
BA recipients				
BA completion	61.5%	70.7%	14.8%	13%
% Borrowing	59%	66%	92%	69%
Percentile of borrowers				
10th	$0	$0	$12,000	$0
25th	$0	$0	$30,000	$0
50th	$7,500	$15,500	$45,000	$11,971
75th	$20,000	$27,000	$50,000	$23,265
90th	$32,405	$45,000	$100,000	$40,000
Mean	**$12,922**	**$18,700**	**$45,042**	**$15,960**

Source: Authors' tabulations based on the Beginning Postsecondary Survey 2004:2009.

after initial enrollment, the mean ratio of monthly payments to income is 10.5 percent (author's tabulations from the Beginning Postsecondary Study 2004:2009).

Table 15.4 also highlights differential levels of borrowing by first institution of attendance. In particular, the borrowing behavior among students beginning at for-profit institutions is distinctly higher at all levels of credit attainment than among students at other types of postsecondary institutions. These systematic differences in borrowing translate predictably into differences in default rates by first institution of attendance. Data from the Department of Education on the Official Cohort Default Rates for Schools (available at http://www2.ed.gov/offices/OSFAP/defaultmanagement/cdr.html#table) shows two-year cohort default rates rising from 6.7 to 8.8 percent between 2007 and 2009. At for-profit institutions, default rates are appreciably greater, reaching 15 percent over two years and 24.9 percent over three years. Student characteristics are insufficient to account for these high default rates in the for-profit sector (as discussed by Deming, Goldin, and Katz in this symposium), which suggests that students choosing to attend these institutions may be systematically borrowing too much.

Student Loans and Financial Portfolios

Even when college is a "good investment" in a net present value sense, students may finance it badly. Do students borrow the "right" amount for college? Do they borrow from the lowest cost of capital? Even if some students may borrow "too much" for college, other students may make the opposite mistake, "underborrowing" by insufficient use of student loans in financing college.

Cadena and Keys (2010) estimate that one in six full-time students at four-year institutions who are eligible for student loans do not take up such loans—thus forgoing the subsidy.[11] The most obvious explanations for this behavior are that some students are deterred by the complexity of the FAFSA form (Dynarski and Scott-Clayton 2006) or that students rationally avoid student loans as a self-control device (Cadena and Keys 2010). Another possible sign of the underuse of student loans is that a number of students are carrying more-expensive credit card debt when they could instead be borrowing through student loans. Among students who entered college in 2004, 25.5 percent of those who were still enrolled in 2006 and 37.7 percent of those who were still enrolled in 2009 reported that they had credit card debt. But between one-third and one-half of these students (45.6 percent of students with credit card debt in 2006 and 38.5 percent of students with credit card debt in 2009) had not borrowed from the Stafford loan program. Carrying credit card debt without maximizing Stafford borrowing burdens students with unnecessarily inflated interest rates—a choice that can interfere with a student's ability to finish a degree: some years back, a school administrator, John Simpson at Indiana University, said: "[W]e lose more students to credit card debt than academic failure" (Rubin 1998). Along similar lines, about half of the students who are working more than 20 hours per week while attending a public or private nonprofit four-year college have no Stafford loans at all (authors tabulations from Beginning Postsecondary Study 2004:2009). But since there is some evidence that part-time work reduces academic performance and the likelihood of attaining a degree (Stinebrickner and Stinebrickner 2003), it might be optimal for some of these students to work fewer hours and use Stafford Loans to substitute in the short- and medium-term for lost wages.

Conclusions and Further Thoughts

Enrolling in college is likely the first major capital investment that young people will make. For many students, it will be their first encounter with a formal loan. From a financial perspective, enrolling in college is equivalent to signing up for a lottery with large expected gains—indeed, the figures presented here suggest that college is, on average, a better investment today than it was a generation ago—but it is also a lottery with significant probabilities of both larger positive, and smaller or even negative, returns.

The natural advice for a high school graduate contemplating the economic consequences of investing in college is to estimate the probabilities of the long-term outcomes as precisely as possible. In particular, a student needs to focus on the probability of degree completion, the earnings differences associated with different levels of degree completion, and the choice of a field of study. Although self-knowledge is difficult, students can look at their own observed traits, and then at how students with similar traits have fared at the school they are planning to attend. For example, those who begin their studies at community colleges and for-profit colleges have particularly low college completion rates and are unlikely to realize substantial earnings gains associated with degree completion. For students at for-profit institutions, the consequences of weak outcomes are compounded by high levels of borrowing; not surprisingly, these students are unusually likely to default on loans. Perhaps the hardest risk to estimate involves the substantial and increasing variation in realized earnings within different levels of postsecondary attainment: for students who end up in the bottom part of the wage distribution (given attainment in college), debt levels are likely higher than their earnings would justify.

The claim that student borrowing is "too high" across the board can—with the possible exception of for-profit colleges—clearly be rejected. Indeed, media coverage proclaiming a "student loan bubble" or a "crisis in student borrowing" even runs the risk of inhibiting sound and rational use of credit markets to finance worthwhile investments in collegiate attainment. McPherson and Baum (2011) note that one form of cognitive bias impacting collegiate investments is attaching too much significance to extreme examples, like the few instances of undergraduate students burdened with more than $100,000 in debt with poor job prospects. Even if macroeconomic shocks were to erode the higher education earnings premium to levels not seen in three decades, collegiate attainment would remain a good investment for many potential students. Given the relatively slow rate of growth in the supply of college graduates in recent decades and modest projections for further increases in the coming decades, it is highly unlikely that the economy will experience a demand shock that will have a substantial adverse impact on the wages of college graduates.

The observation that college is a good investment for most young people still leaves a number of significant and unanswered research questions about how students make decisions about collegiate attainment and student borrowing. In the context of this paper, an especially important question would be to assess more carefully what verifiable characteristics students could observe about their own skills and attributes at the time of college entry which in turn would affect their outcomes both in higher education and in the workplace later in life. Student decisions about whether to enroll in college, where to enroll in college, what to study in college, and how to finance college are complex and highly dependent on individual circumstances. While some uncertainty will inevitably remain about the decision of whether and how to invest in higher education, it seems clear that a substantial number of students could benefit from more-tailored and individualized advice than they have been receiving.

Acknowledgments

We thank the JEP Editors and Assistant Editor for their patience and guidance and also Adrew Barr and Erin Dunlop for research assistance.

Notes

1. Our focus in this analysis is on student borrowing among undergraduates in the United States. We note that loan funding is also an important source of funding in graduate programs, particularly in professional fields, though this is not the focus of our analysis.
2. For purposes of financial aid awards, an independent student is a student who meets any one of the following: at least 24 years old; married; a graduate or professional student; a veteran; an orphan; a ward of the court; or someone with legal dependents other than a spouse.
3. With well-functioning capital markets and full opportunities to borrow, the human capital investment decision of how much education to acquire is separable from the consumption and savings choice at each moment in time conditional on expected lifetime earnings (for a formal demonstration, see Lochner and Monge-Naranjo 2011).
4. The average yearly earnings at age 22 are $21,000 for a high school graduate and $28,000 for a college graduate; attributing half of this difference to self-selection corresponds to a predicted wage of $24,500 for someone who is switched from being a high school graduate to a college graduate.
5. These estimates are similar in spirit to Census Bureau estimates produced in Day and Newburger (2002); our estimates of the total value of lifetime earnings to different educational credentials is somewhat lower owing to discounting annual earnings and subtracting expected direct costs of educational investments.
6. Data from the College Board (2010b, table 7) indicate that tuition and fees net of grant aid changed much less markedly than posted tuition or "sticker price." At private four-year institutions, average net tuition and fees (in 2010 constant dollars) decreased from $12,230 to $11,320 between 2000–01 and 2010–11, decreased at public four-year institutions from $1,990 to $1,540, and also decreased at public two-year institutions from $920 to $670.
7. At the macroeconomic level, some combination of demographic changes and sectoral shifts in employment would be more likely than a long-lived recession to reduce the financial gains from a college degree indicated in Figure 15.3. In fact, 35 years ago, in *The Overeducated American*, Richard Freeman noted the dramatic decline in the earnings of new college graduates and argued that there would be little net benefit to further increases in the supply of college graduates. Consistent with Freeman's analysis, Figure 15.3 suggests that expected financial returns to a college degree were near a long-term low for this time period towards the end of the 1970s. But our computations still indicate a clear positive value for completing college at that time. We compute average lifetime earnings in a given year by simply adding the average earnings of workers at each age in that year. As Smith and Welch (1978) note, although young (age 25 to 34) college graduates were earning relatively low wages, there remained large gaps in wages between college graduates and high school graduates at older ages throughout the 1970s. In essence, the qualitative comparisons from Figure 15.3 for the 1970s rely on the conjecture that

college graduates would continue to enjoy substantial wage gains at age 35 and beyond—a conjecture that has been borne out in subsequent years.

8. There is some debate in the literature about whether the economic benefits of attending a more-selective college can be explained entirely by selection, because more-promising students tend to attend more-selective colleges (for example, Hoxby 2001; Black, Daniel, and Smith 2005; Hoekstra 2009; Dale and Krueger 2011). But for the purpose of assessing the expected willingness to borrow, this debate is mostly immaterial—the question of interest to any particular student is "What is my expected financial gain (or loss) given that I am attending college instead of taking a full-time job" and not "What would be my expected financial gain (or loss) if I attend more-selective College *Y* rather than less-selective College *Z*?"
9. Recent work in applied econometrics including Chen (2008) and Cunha, Heckman, and Navarro (2005) addresses the challenges of measuring the extent to which the potential dispersion of earnings is attributable to individual heterogeneity or uncertainty. In general, the problem of distinguishing heterogeneity from uncertainty is complicated by the absence of clear identification without very strong functional form assumptions. Chen (2008) attributes much of the greater wage inequality among college graduates than high school graduates to relatively larger effects of heterogeneity among individuals, though she estimates that about 80 percent of potential wage inequality among college graduates is attributable to uncertainty.
10. In essence, we match the percentile of the high school distribution (*HS*) to a percentile in the college distribution as a conditional expectation which is a function of the correlation between *HS* and *C*, such that $E(C \mid HS) = (1 - \gamma)\overline{HS} + \gamma HS$ where γ is the square of the correlation coefficient and $\overline{HS}$ is the average percentile (the median). When the correlation is 0.75, gamma is equal to 0.5625, and the expected rank in the college distribution is a weighted average of the median and the observed high school rank. Expected earnings are computed as a share-weighted combination of the earnings distributions for those at the different levels of collegiate attainment from less than a BA to graduate degrees.
11. A growing number of community college students do not have access to federal Stafford loans. For students entering college in 1992–93, less than 3 percent of community college students did not have access to Stafford loans (calculated from National Longitudinal Study of 1988). For community college students entering college in 2004–2005, about 11 percent of students did not have access to loans (Educational Longitudinal Study of 2002). The Project on Student Debt report found similar numbers, and in their April 2011 report, they calculated that 9 percent of community college students do not have access to Stafford loans. One explanation for why a community college might not offer loans is that if an institution has a default rate over 25 percent for three consecutive years or if a community college has a default rate of 40 percent in one year, the institution will lose access to Title IV funds (including Pell grants). But few community colleges are near the default thresholds.

References

Acemoglu, Daron, and David Autor. 2010. "Skills, Tasks and Technologies: Implications for Employment and Earnings." Chap. 12 in *Handbook of Labor Economics,* Volume 4B, edited by Orley Ashenfelter and David Card, Amsterdam: Elsevier, North Holland.

Arcidiacono, Peter; V. Joseph Hotz, and Songman Kang. 2010. "Modeling College Major Choices using Elicited Measures of Expectations and Counterfactuals." NBER Working Paper 15729.

Avery, Christopher, and Thomas J. Kane. 2004. "Student Perceptions of College Opportunities. The Boston COACH Program." Chap. 9 in *College Choices: The Economics of Where to Go, When to Go, and How to Pay For It*, edited by Caroline M. Hoxby. University of Chicago Press.

Baum, Sandra, and Marie O'Malley. 2003. "College on Credit: How Borrowers Perceive Their Education Debt." *Journal of Student Financial Aid* 33(3): 7–21.

Baum, Sandy, and Saul Schwartz. 2006. "How Much Debt is Too Much? Defining Benchmarks for Manageable Student Debt." Commissioned by the College Board and the Project on Student Debt. http://professionals.collegeboard.com/prof download/pdf/06-0869.DebtPpr060420.pdf.

Black, Dan, Kermit Daniel, and Jeffrey Smith. 2005. "College Quality and Wages in the United States." *German Economic Review* 6(3): 415–43.

Black, Dan, and Jeffrey Smith. 2006. "Evaluating the Returns to College Quality with Multiple Proxies for Quality." Journal of Labor Economics 24(3): 701–28.

Bound, John, Michael Lovenheim, and Sarah Turner. 2010. "Why Have College Completion Rates Declined? An Analysis of Changing Student Preparation and Collegiate Resources. *American Economic Journal: Applied Economics* 2(3): 129–57.

Burdman, P. 2005. "The Student Debt Dilemma: Debt Aversion as a Barrier to College Access." Project on Student Debt, Institute for College Access and Success, Inc.

Cadena, Brian C., and Benjamin J. Keys. 2010. "Can Self-Control Explain Avoiding Free Money? Evidence from Interest-Free Loans," December. http://spot.colorado.edu/~cadenab/Research_files/cadenakeys_loans_resub.pdf.

Carnevale, Anthony, Jeff Strohl, and Micheli Melton. 2011. *What's it Worth? The Economic Value of College Majors.* Georgetown University, Center on Education and the Workforce.

Chen, Stacey. 2008. "Estimating the Variance of Wages in the Presence of Selection and Unobserved Heterogeneity." *Review of Economics and Statistics* 90(2): 275–89.

College Board, Advocacy and Policy Center. 2010a. "Trends in Student Aid: 2010." http://advocacy.collegeboard.org/sites/default/files/2010_Student_Aid_Final_Web.pdf.

College Board, Advocacy and Policy Center. 2010b. "Trends in College Pricing." http://advocacy.collegeboard.org/sites/default/files/2010_Trends_College_Pricing_Final_Web.pdf.

Cunha, Flávio, James J. Heckman, and Salvador Navarro. 2005. "Separating Uncertainty from Heterogeneity in Life Cycle Earnings." *Oxford Economic Papers* 57 (2): 191–261.

Dale, Stacy, and Alan Krueger. 2011. "Estimating the Return to College Selectivity over the Career Using Administrative Earning Data." http://www.mathematica-mpr.com/publications/PDFs/education/returntocollege.pdf.

Day, Jennifer Cheeseman, and Eric Newburger. 2002. "The Big Payoff: Educational Attainment and Synthetic Estimates of Work-Life Earnings." U.S. Census Bureau, Current Population Reports, P23-210, July, http://www.census.gov/prod/2002pubs/p23-210.pdf.

Dickler, Jessica. 2010. "Boomerang: 85% of College Graduates Move Back Home." CNNMoney, November 15. http://money.cnn.com/2010/10/14/pf/boomerang_kids_move_home/index.htm.

Dominitz Jeffrey, and Charles Manski. 1996. "Eliciting Student Expectations of the Returns to Schooling." *Journal of Human Resources* 31(1): 1–26.

Dynarski, Judith, and Judith Scott-Clayton. 2006. "The Cost of Complexity in Federal Student Aid: Lessons from Optimal Tax Theory and Behavioral Economics." NBER Working Paper 12227.

Ellwood, David. 2001. "The Sputtering Labor Force of the 21st Century. Can Social Policy Help?" Chap. 9 in *The Roaring Nineties: Can Full Employment Be Sustained?* Edited by Alan Krueger and Robert Solow. New York: Russell Sage Foundation.

Freeman, Richard. 1976. *The Overeducated American.* New York: Academic Press.

Friedman, Milton. 1962. *Capitalism and Freedom.* University of Chicago Press.

Gicheva, Dora. 2011. "Does the Student-Loan Burden Weigh into the Decision to Start a Family?" March, http://www.uncg.edu/bae/people/gicheva/Student_loans_marriageMarch11.pdf.

Goldin, Claudia, and Lawrence Katz. 2008. *The Race between Education and Technology.* Cambridge, MA: Harvard University Press.

Grogger, Jeff, and Eric Eide. 1995. "Changes in College Skills and the Rise in the College Wage Premium." *Journal of Human Resources* 30(2): 280–310.

Hoekstra, Marie. 2009. "The Effect of Attending the Flagship State University on Earnings: A Discontinuity-Based Approach." *Review of Economics and Statistics* 91 (4): 717–24.

Hoxby, Caroline. 2001. "The Return to Attending a More Selective College: 1960 to Present." Chap. 2 in *Forum Futures Exploring the Future of Higher Education, 2000 Papers,* edited by Maureen Devlin and Joel Meyerson. San Francisco: Jossey-Bass.

Institute of Education Sciences. 2011. Digest of Education Statistics: 2010 http://nces.ed.gov/programs/digest/dlO/index.asp. National Center for Education Statistics, U.S. Department of Education.

Kahn, Lisa. 2010. "The Long-Term Labor Market Consequences of Graduating from College in a Bad Economy." *Labour Economics* 17(2): 303–316.

Kamenetz, Anya. 2006. *Generation Debt.* Riverhead Books.

King, Jacqueline E. 2002. *Crucial Choices: How Students' Financial Decisions Affect Their Academic Success.* Washington, DC: American Council on Education, Center for Policy Analysis.

Krueger, Alan B., and William G. Bowen. 1993. "Policy Watch: Income-Contingent College Loans." Journal of Economic Perspectives 7 (3): 193–201.

Leiber, Ron. 2010. "Placing the Blame as Students Are Buried in Debt." *New York Times,* May 28. http://www.nytimes.com/2010/05/29/your-money/student-loans/29money.html.

Lindley, Joanne, and Stephen Machin. 2011. "Rising Wage Inequality and Postgraduate Education." CEP Discussion Papers dpl075, Center for Economic Performance, London School of Economics.

Lochner, Lance J., and Alexander MongeNaranjo. 2011. "The Nature of Credit Constraints and Human Capital." *American Economic Review* 101(6): 2487–2529.

Lochner, Lance, and Alexander MongeNaranjo. Forthcoming. "Credit Constraints in Education." *Annual Review of Economics*.

Long, Bridget 2004. "The Role of Perceptions and Information in College Access: An Exploratory Review of the Literature and Possible Data Sources." July. Report commissioned by TERI, Boston, MA.

Manski, Charles. 1993. "Adolescent Econometricians: How Do Youth Infer the Returns to Schooling?" In *Studies of Supply and Demand in Higher Education*, edited by Charles Clotfelter and Michael Rothschild, 43–57. Chicago: University of Chicago Press.

Mazzeo, Christopher. 2007. "Private Lending and Student Borrowing: A Primer." In *Footing the Tuition Bill*, edited by Frederick M. Hess. Washington, DC: AEI Press.

McPherson, Michael, and Sandra Baum. 2011. "Get Smart about College." *Wall Street Journal*, September 19.

Oreopoulos, Philip, and Kjell G. Salvanes. 2011. "Priceless: The Nonpecuniary Benefits of Schooling." *Journal of Economic Perspectives* 25(1): 159–184.

Paglin, Morton, and Anthony M. Rufolo. 1990. "Heterogeneous Human Capital, Occupational Choice, and Male-Female Earnings Differences." *Journal of Labor Economics* 8 (1): 1 23–44.

Rothstein, Jesse, and Cecilia Rouse. 2011. "Constrained after College: Student Loans and Early Career Occupational Choices." *Journal of Public Economics* 95 (1–2): 1 49–63.

Rouse, Cecelia Elena. 2004. "Low-Income Students and College Attendance: An Exploration of Income Expectations." *Social Science Quarterly* 85(5): 1299–1317.

Rubin, Bonnie Miller. 1998. "College Students Charge Right into Valley of Debt," *Chicago Tribune*, August 16. http://articles.chicagotribune.com/1998-08-16/news/9808160239_1_credit-history-college-students-credit-card.

Schumpeter Blog. 2011. "Higher Education: The Next Bubble?" *Economist*, April 13. http://www.economist.com/blogs/schumpeter/2011/04/higher_education.

Smith, James P., and Finis Welch. 1978. "The Overeducated American: A Review Article." RAND Working Paper No. P-6253. http://www.rand.org/pubs/papers/P6253.html.

Somers, Patricia, Shawn Woodhouse, and Jim Cofer. 2004. "Pushing the Boulder Uphill: The Persistence of First-Generation College Students." *NASPA Journal* 41(3): 418–35.

St. John, Edward P. 2004. "The Impact of Information and Student Aid on Persistence: A Review of Research and Discussion of Experiments." October. Report commissioned by TERI, Boston, MA. http://www.teri.org/pdf/research-studies/ReseachReport_Stlohn.pdf.

Stange, Kevin. Forthcoming. "An Empirical Examination of the Option Value of College Enrollment." *American Economic Journal: Applied Economics*.

Steven Ruggles, J. Trent Alexander, Katie Genadek, Ronald Goeken, Matthew B. Schroeder, and Matthew Sobek. 2010. Integrated Public Use Microdata Series: Version 5.0 (Machine-readable database). University of Minnesota.

Stinebrickner, Ralph, and Todd R. Stinebrickner. 2003. "Working during School and Academic Performance." *Journal of Labor Economics* 21(2): 449–72.

Stinebrickner, Todd R., and Ralph Stinebrickner. 2009. "Learning about Academic Ability and the College Drop-Out Decision." NBER Working paper 14810.

Surowiecki, James. 2011. "Debt by Degrees." *New Yorker*, November 21. http://www.newyorker.com/talk/financial/2011/11/21/111121ta_talk_surowiecki.

U.S. Department of Education. Nd. "Official Cohort Default Rates for Schools" Database. Available at: http://www2.ed.gov/offices/OSFAP/defaultmanagement/cdr.html#table.

Warwick, Jacquelyn, and Phyiis Mansfield. 2000. "Credit Card Consumers: College Students' Knowledge and Attitude." *Journal of Consumer Marketing* 17(7): 617–26.

Wei, Christina Chang. 2010. *Trends in Undergraduate Stafford Loan Borrowing: 1989–90 to 2007–08*. National Center for Education Statistics Web Tables. Washington, DC: U.S. Department of Education, http://nces.ed.gov/pubs2010/2010183.pdf.

CHAPTER 16

THE ROLES OF PUBLIC HIGHER EDUCATION EXPENDITURE AND THE PRIVATIZATION OF THE HIGHER EDUCATION ON U.S. STATES ECONOMIC GROWTH

BRADLEY R. CURS, BORNALI BHANDARI, AND CHRISTINA STEIGER

Previous empirical literature finds that government expenditure on higher education has a negative, or null, effect on U.S. economic growth rates. This empirical result may be driven by omission of an important variable—the privatization of higher education. Using state-level panel data from 1970 to 2005, this analysis investigates whether the exclusion of the privatization level of the higher education system within a state potentially biases the estimated relationship between state higher education spending and economic growth. The results indicate that the omission of the size of the private higher education system may negatively bias the estimated relationship between higher education spending and economic growth. Specifically, states with a large market share of students in private higher education institutions have a negative relationship between higher education spending and economic growth, while states with large public shares are found to have a positive relationship.

Introduction

Over the past 30 years, the value of human capital investment in the U.S. has significantly increased leading to dramatic upward pressure on tuition prices from both the demand (Heller 1997; Leslie and Brinkman 1987; Vedder 2004a) and supply (Archibald and Feldman 2006; Getz and Siegfried 1991; Massey 2003) sides. This increase in tuition levels has rekindled the debate of what is the proper public investment in human capital and what are its true effects on economic growth (Courant, McPherson, and Resch 2006; Vedder 2004a). Specifically under question is the assumption that investment in human capital through state higher education expenditure leads to substantial positive externalities. One could argue that greater public funding for education is needed to increase the productivity of labor force. Alternatively, there are arguments indicating that the cost of investing in human capital has increased to such levels that its returns no longer outweigh the costs—more precisely, at least not at the expected level or in the regions where the initial investments were made.

Endogenous economic growth theory predicts that when investments in higher education are financed through non-distortionary taxes it promotes economic growth by creating a labor force that is more productive and better able to create and absorb new technologies (Barro 1990, 2000; Barro and Sala-i-Martin 2004). However, within the endogenous growth model, the effect of productive government expenditure on growth is ambiguous if financed by distortionary taxation and is negative if unproductive government expenditure is financed by distortionary taxation (Barro 1990). Thus, without a strong understanding of the distortionary nature of individual state tax structures the hypothesized effects of higher education expenditure on economic growth is ambiguous.

Empirical evidence from country level studies generally show that expenditure into higher education is positively related to economic growth (Barro 1990, 2000; Barro and Sala-i-Martin 2004;

Romer 1990; Stokey 1991). When the relation of growth and higher education expenditure is analyzed across the U.S. there is still uncertainty as to what the true effect of state-level education spending is on economic growth. In general, cross-sectional and panel studies find a negative or insignificant relation between higher education expenditure and growth (Wang and Davis 2005; McCracken 2006; Vedder, 2004b). Studies observing a negative relation frequently posit the common hypothesis that a potential reason for this observed outcome is the inefficient allocation of public funds within the higher education sector.

Alternatively, a few researchers have found a positive relationship (Aghion et al. 2005; Evans and Karras 1994). Furthermore, micro-level studies consistently show a positive relation between higher education spending and local economic growth (Blackwell, Cobb, and Weinberg 2002; Goldstein and Renault 2004). One possible explanation is that the impact on growth will depend upon the region or state in which the investment is made (Aghion et al. 2005). In particular, Aghion et al. (2005) finds that the return to higher education spending will depend on the distance of the state from the technological frontier. A more recent theoretical model of higher education spending and growth (Arcalean and Schiopu 2010) allows for both public and private inputs in higher education, and finds that optimal public investments in all levels of education will depend on the tax environment and the size of the private education market, and on the degree of substitution between public and private inputs in education. Both Aghion et al. (2005) and Arcalean and Schiopu (2010) point to the need to allow for the effect of state heterogeneity on the return to public higher education spending in terms of its effect on state-level economic growth.

This article enters into the debate around the effects of state government expenditure on higher education and its effects on state level economic growth. We investigate whether the omission of constructs controlling for the private higher education market can cause bias in the estimated relationship between public higher education expenditure and state economic growth. The omission of the private higher education market can potentially cause negative omitted variable bias if the following two conditions are satisfied. First, do states that have large higher private higher education markets, such as Massachusetts, spend less on their public higher education systems relative to other states? Second, do these states with larger private higher education systems experience larger economic growth? If the response to both questions is affirmative, we would expect to observe a negative bias on the estimated coefficient relating public higher education spending and state economic growth.

Due to data availability issues, enrollments are used to measure the size of the education market. Our empirical evidence reveals that by omitting private higher education enrollments, it may negatively bias the estimated relationship between public higher education spending and economic growth. Specifically, states with large private higher education markets experience a negative, and significantly different from zero, effect of higher education spending on economic growth. In contrast, states with relatively small private education markets experience positive effects of public higher education spending on economic growth. Thus, these findings indicate that state level higher education system attributes may be important when analyzing the relationship between higher education expenditure and economic growth.

State Higher Education Expenditure Determinants and Impacts

For the most part, state tax effort for higher education peaked in the late 1970s for the majority of U.S. with all states being in decline since 1991 (Archibald and Feldman 2006; Tandberg 2010). Specifically, between 1977 and 2002, state support for higher education fell from $8.50 to $7.00 per $1,000 in personal income (Kane, Orszag, and Gunter 2003). The ratio of higher education expenditure at public versus private institutions declined from 70 cents to 55 cents per $1 spent between the early 1980s and late 1990s (Kane, Orszag, and Gunter 2003) which led to concerns that public higher education institutions would fall behind their private counterparts (Ehrenberg 2006). Furthermore, when state appropriations decline, the inability of less-selective public institutions to raise revenues from sources other than appropriations likely leads to greater inequality in public institution resources (Cheslock and Gianeschi 2008).

Determinants of State Higher Education Expenditure

A number of determinants have been found to be correlated with state education expenditures including economic conditions, other state expenditures, the role of the private higher education market, and state political factors. Hovey's (1999) balance wheel hypothesis states that higher education should experience greater than proportional increases in state appropriations in good economic times and greater than proportional decreases in appropriations in bad economic times. The reasoning is that higher education is an attractive expenditure for legislators during good times, and it has the ability to increase revenues through alternative mechanisms during economic downturns. Delaney and Doyle (2007) directly tested Hovey's hypothesis and found strong evidence of this nonlinear relationship between state appropriations on higher education and state expenditures. Similarly, consistent with Hovey's hypothesis, other researchers have found that states with positive economic conditions—higher levels of wealth and lower unemployment levels—tend to have higher expenditures on higher education (Goldin and Katz 1998; Kane, Orszag, and Apostlolov 2005; Koshal and Koshal 2000; Lowry 2001; Toutkoushian and Hollis 1998).

As the largest discretionary line in most state budgets, declines in state higher education support can be partially explained by increases in the need to fund other budget items such as Medicaid, K–12 education, and corrections (Kane, Orszag, and Gunter 2003; Titus 2009). Furthermore, Tandberg (2010) finds that states with a high density of non-higher education interest groups invest relatively less on higher education appropriations. Similarly, states with historically large private higher education markets are less likely to support public higher education (Goldin and Katz 1998; Lowry 2001).

As expected, state political attributes are correlated with state expenditures on higher education. States with larger proportions of democrats in legislature and in the governor's office tend to support higher education at greater levels (Archibald and Feldman 2006; Koshal and Koshal 2000; McLendon, Hearn, and Mohker 2009; McLendon, Mohker, and Doyle 2009). States with governors who retain strong budgetary powers tend to have lower higher education effort (McLendon, Hearn, and Mohker 2009; McLendon, Mohker, and Doyle 2009). States with more professional legislatures invest in higher education at higher levels (McLendon, Hearn, and Mohker 2009; Nicholson-Crotty and Meier 2003; Tandberg 2010). States which implement tax and expenditure limits or supermajority requirements for tax increases subsequently experience lower higher education appropriations effort (Archibald and Feldman 2006).

Benefits of State Higher Education Expenditure

The direct benefit of higher education expenditure on a state's citizens is increased access to higher education opportunities through lowered prices and increased educational capacity. Research finds that increased state appropriations to higher education institutions leads to increased degree production within the state, and across all types of institutions (Titus 2009; Zhang 2009). Bound and Turner (2007) find that when resources per student decline, whether through increases in the size of the college-going cohort or through declines in state support, the subsequent supply of college-educated workers declines. While research indicates that state appropriations to higher education institutions are related to increased state college graduates, Toutkoushian and Shafiq (2010) argue that when a state's ultimate goal is increasing degree production, they would be better off funding needs-based financial aid programs.

A plausible explanation for increased access to higher education due to state higher education expenditures is through the lowering of the net-price that potential students face. Generally, research finds state government funding and tuition levels at public institutions are negatively correlated (Koshal and Koshal 2000; Lowry 2001; Rizzo and Ehrenberg 2004). However, Koshal and Koshal (2000) found a two-way relationship where appropriations affect tuition but increases in tuition lead to decreases in appropriations. Rizzo and Ehrenberg (2004) find that in order for institutions to make up lost revenues, they increase both instate and out-of-state tuition levels and adjust the ratio of instate and out-of-state students in response to declines in state appropriations.

While increased access to college degrees is one benefit of state expenditure on higher education, states benefit in a number of other ways. Trostel (2009) estimated the real fiscal rate of return due to government expenditure on higher education to be greater than 10%. Specifically, he finds the decline in lifetime government spending on college graduates is roughly $10,000 larger than the governmental expenditures provided to subsidize the degree. Further, Trostel (2009) finds that the direct tax revenue increase from a college degree is roughly six times larger than the governmental expenditure for that degree.

Researchers have also attempted to identify other social benefits due to higher education attainment. Dee (2004) finds educational attainment substantially increases civic engagement through increased voter participation, support for free speech, and civic knowledge. Moretti (2004) finds that increases in college educated workers have positive spillover effects on less-educated workers in the same geographic area. These spillover effects, along with the fiscal impacts of higher education spending, would tend to support the hypothesis of a positive effect of higher education spending on state-level economic growth.

Empirical Methodology

A statistical analysis will be carried out using economic growth models. To estimate the effect of higher education expenditure on growth at a state level, a sample of 50 U.S. states between 1975 and 2005 is analyzed. The contribution of this study to the existing literature on higher education spending and state-level economic growth is in our treatment of the key explanatory variable, higher education expenditure. Typically, previous research has investigated whether total higher education expenditure affects state level economic growth. This analysis builds on previous research by investigating whether the relationship between state higher expenditure and state economic growth is moderated by the size of the private higher education market.

Following the previous U.S. state level endogenous economic growth literature (Kneller, Bleaney, and Gemmell 1999; Wang and Davis 2005) we begin by estimating the relationship between economic growth and state higher education expenditure using the following empirical model:

$$g_{it} = \alpha HEE_{it} + \phi' X_{it} + \delta_i + \varphi_t + \varepsilon_{it} \quad (1)$$

where, g_{it} is the annual growth rate of real per-capita personal income[1], HEE_{it} is the average state-level expenditure on higher education as a percentage of gross state product for the previous five years, X_{it} are time-varying state-level characteristics, and δ_i are state-level fixed effects, φ_t are time fixed effects, and ε_{it} is an idiosyncratic error term. Annual per-capital income growth rates are regressed upon the average of the previous five years of higher education expenditure to account for the fact that higher education is an investment over many years.[2]

An identical set of control variables is included across all models. The reason for their inclusion is that these are factors likely to affect the economy of a state, or serve as a burden for higher education expenditure.[3] The control variables (X_{it}) have been classified into two categories. The first category includes fiscal variables related to state-level revenues and expenditures. The state fiscal variables related to the expenditure side separate state expenditure on educational sectors from expenditure on other governmental programs. The fiscal variable on the revenues side is own government revenue as a percentage of gross state product. Including total tax revenue as a percentage of gross state product introduces multicollinearity, thus it has been omitted from the specification (Kneller, Bleaney, and Gemmell 1999).

The next group of control variables includes the sectoral composition—the size of the agricultural, mining, and manufacturing sectors as a percentage of GSP—and the size of the economy (population growth rate). All variables related to the economic composition and size of the economy are included in the model contemporaneously. The U.S. farm output grew at an average annual growth rate 1.6% between 1948 and 2008 versus a growth in total non-farm output of 3.6% for the same time period (United States Department of Agriculture [USDA] 2010). On average, this would imply that states with a higher share of agriculture would grow slowly but Barro and Sala-i-Martin (1992) point out that price changes in agriculture have been quite volatile. High agricultural prices might translate to higher growth for those states with a higher share of agriculture. Similarly, manufacturing has experienced an increase and decrease in its share during the time period of our study. Therefore, the expected signs on the shares are ambiguous. The population growth rate is expected to be positively related to economic growth as this implies growth in both the labor force and the consumption market (Becker, Glaeser, and Murphy 1999).

Research indicates that states with larger private higher education enrollments are less likely to support public higher education (Lowry 2001; Goldin and Katz 1998), thus it could be expected that the omission of a variable indicating the relative size of the public to private higher education market could lead to a negative bias in the higher education expenditure coefficient (α). Our first extension to estimation equation 1 is to include a control which measures the percentage of higher education enrollments within a state which are in the public sector ($Public_{it}$):[4]

$$g_{it} = \alpha HEE_{it} + \beta Public_{it} + \phi' X_{it} + \delta_i + \varphi_t + \varepsilon_{it} \quad (2)$$

However, this extension is unlikely to yield substantial differences in the estimated coefficient on higher education expenditure within a state fixed-effects framework. Goldin and Katz (1998) find a strong correlation between private sector enrollments per-capita between 1900 and 1998 indicating that the relative market share of public to private students is relatively stable across time. As the models are estimated with state fixed effects, it is understandable that little variation in growth rates are explained by the small changes in the compositions of students across public and private institutions within a state. To further examine these research questions, the estimating equation is further altered by including an interaction term between higher education expenditure and the share of public sector enrollments to allow for the effect of higher education expenditure to vary across states with different public versus private higher education compositions:

$$g_{it} = \alpha HEE_{it} + \beta Public_{it} + \gamma HEE_{it}{}^{*} Public_{it} + \phi' X_{it} + \delta_i + \varphi_t + \varepsilon_{it} \quad (3)$$

The coefficient on the interaction term (γ) can be interpreted as the difference in the relationship between higher education expenditure and economic growth as the ratio of public to private enrollments increase. A positive coefficient would indicate that as public enrollments shares increase within a state the relationship between state higher education expenditure and economic growth increases. Alternatively, a negative coefficient implies that the relationship becomes smaller, or more negative, as the share of public enrollments increases.

A threat to the validity of our state fixed-effects empirical growth framework is the potential that governmental expenditure may be correlated with unobserved variation in the economic growth process—that is, higher education expenditure is endogenous. It may be entirely plausible that unobserved factors that are related to economic growth are also related to governmental expenditure. Given this potential endogeneity bias, a secondary empirical estimation is employed to attempt to isolate the effect of higher education expenditure on economic growth. Specifically, a dynamic fixed-effects model is applied (Arellano and Bond 1991; Arellano and Bover 1995; Blundel and Bond 1998), which uses lagged values of the dependent variable and other independent variables as instruments for potentially endogenous variables. Furthermore, the Arellano-Bond estimator first differences the variables which removes the correlation between state-level fixed effects and the lagged dependent variable (Baum 2006).

Discussion of the Empirical Results

Table 16.1 presents the results of the estimated relationship between public expenditure on higher education and state per-capita income growth within a state fixed-effects framework. When estimating equation (1), presented in column 1, a small positive relationship between public spending on higher education and state per-capita income growth within a state is found.[5] The statistically insignificant results are similar to previous literature which finds small or insignificant relationships between public expenditure on higher education and state income growth (McCracken 2006; Vedder 2004b; Wang and Davis 2005). These findings provide a baseline case similar to prior research

TABLE 16.1

Fixed Effects Estimates of the Effect of State Spending on Higher Education on Per-Capita Income Growth

The dependent variable in all three columns is defined as the annual growth rate of per-capita income. Governmental expenditure variables are measured as the average value of the previous 5 years. Economic sector variables are measured contemporaneously. The sample period is 1975–2005.

	Growth in Per-Capita Income		
	(1)	(2)	(3)
Higher education expenditure as a percentage of GSP (previous 5 year average)	0.439 (0.883)	0.653 (1.004)	–6.192* (3.190)
Percentage of students enrolled in a public higher education institution (previous 5 year average)		–8.916 (5.573)	–23.38** (9.293)
Higher education expenditure × percentage of students in public higher education (previous 5 year average)			8.568** (3.831)
Elementary and secondary educational expenditure as a percentage of GSP (previous 5 year average)	1.159** (0.434)	1.107** (0.436)	1.019** (0.433)
Other government expenditure as a percentage of GSP (previous 5 year average)	0.279* (0.146)	0.281* (0.145)	0.261* (0.142)
State own revenue as a percentage of GSP (previous 5 year average)	–0.138 (0.1000)	–0.121 (0.0995)	–0.0958 (0.0964)
Agriculture as a percentage of GSP (contemporaneous)	0.438*** (0.0914)	0.423*** (0.0961)	0.409*** (0.102)
Mining as a percentage of GSP (contemporaneous)	0.0704 (0.0741)	0.0686 (0.0719)	0.0899 (0.0748)
Manufacturing as a percentage of GSP (contemporaneous)	0.176** (0.0718)	0.174** (0.0717)	0.172** (0.0735)
Population growth rate (contemporaneous)	0.960*** (0.178)	0.966*** (0.177)	0.944*** (0.178)
State fixed effects	Yes	Yes	Yes
Time fixed effects	Yes	Yes	Yes
Constant	88.36*** (2.246)	94.99*** (3.607)	106.5*** (6.585)
Observations	1,500	1,500	1,500
Number of states	0.560	0.563	0.565
R-squared	50	50	50

Clustered standard errors in parentheses. *** $p<0.01$, ** $p<0.05$, * $p<0.1$

to investigate the hypotheses surrounding the exclusion of the private higher education market in research into the effects of expenditure on higher education.

With respect to control variables, a few empirical patterns emerge. Expenditure on elementary and secondary education sectors is positively related to state per-capita income growth. Education and cognitive skills have consistently been shown to be related to economic growth (Hanuskek 2010) and these findings would be consistent with a model where education production functions translate stated investment in education into labor market skills (Hanuskek 2002). Consistent with the findings of Reed (2008) positive effects of contemporaneous growth are found in the agriculture and manufacturing sectors. Population growth is positively related to per-capita income growth, indicating that growth in labor force has a positive impact on growth rates. The positive sign on the share of mining is the only surprising result. For brevity, the remaining discussion focuses on the extensions to the first models surrounding public higher education expenditure. Nonetheless, the qualitative results surrounding the control variables are robust to all alternative specifications.

To investigate whether the omission of the private higher education market may be a source of bias in the public higher education expenditure coefficient equation (1) was expanded by including a measure of the percentage of students that attend public higher education institution in the state, as represented by equation (2). However, the inclusion of the public market share variable yields little effect on the coefficient of inquiry (column 2)—higher education spending. Through further examination it was revealed that there is little within state variation over time in the percentage of students attending public higher education institutions, consistent with the findings of Goldin and Katz (1998). Further, the direct effect of changes in the ratio of public to private enrollments has a positive but insignificant relationship. Given the models are estimated with state fixed effects it is understandable that little variation in growth rates are explained by the small changes in the compositions of students across public and private institutions within a state.

The second extension to the growth model includes an interaction term between public higher education expenditure and the percentage of students in the public higher education system, as represented in equation (3). The interaction term allows the effect of public higher education expenditure on economic growth to vary with the percentage of students in the public higher education system. The estimated results—as presented in column 3 of Table 16.1—are consistent with the theoretical priors. Specifically, higher education expenditure is found to have a statistically significant negative coefficient while the interaction effect between higher education expenditure and public higher education enrollment is positive and significant. This would imply that states with large private higher education sectors experience a larger negative relationship between their public higher education expenditure and state level income growth. However, as the proportion of students in public higher education institutions increases, the combined effect changes to positive at roughly a 72% ratio of public to private enrollments.

Within this data, there are significant differences across states in the percentage of students attending public versus private institutions. For the most recent time period (2005), Massachusetts has the lowest share of students in public institutions at roughly 43%. Thus, for Massachusetts a one percentage point increase in public higher education expenditure would be expected to lead to a –2.5 percentage point decrease in per-capita income growth—all else equal. At the high end of the public enrollment spectrum is Wyoming with a roughly 95% public institution share of higher education enrollments. It would be expected that a one percentage point increase in higher education spending would lead to a 1.9 percentage point increase in per-capita income. Thus, if inefficiency is a key determinant of why higher education spending and growth are typically found not to be related, it would appear that states in which the public market dominates do not face the same consequences of spending on higher education. Potential students in states like Massachusetts have the ability to choose private market substitutes if they believe that the public higher education institutions are underfunded, thus still having access to a higher education. This is not the case in states like Wyoming, where if a student did not want to attend a public institution they would have to look in another state.

Table 16.2 presents the findings when equations (1–3) are re-estimated using the Arellano-Bond dynamic fixed-effects estimator. In general, the directions of the relationships found when estimating equations (1) and (3) with respect to the relationship between higher education expenditure and state economic growth are equivalent to those of the fixed-effects model, however, the coefficients in the Arellano-Bond estimator are generally found to be statistically significant at traditional levels. Thus, in correcting for potential endogeneity problems and possible inconsistencies in estimation due to large N and small T, the re-estimation of equations (1) and (2) yield results which indicate that public expenditure on higher education is not only positive but also statistically different than zero.

TABLE 16.2

Arellano-Bond Estimates of the Effect of State Spending on Higher Education on Per-Capita Income Growth

The dependent variable in all three columns is defined as the annual growth rate of per-capita income. Governmental expenditure variables are measured as the average value of the previous 5 years. Economic sector variables are measured contemporaneously. The sample period is 1975–2005.

	Growth in Per-Capita Income		
	(1)	(2)	(3)
Lagged per-capita income	–0.0270 (0.0268)	–0.0394 (0.0263)	–0.0415 (0.0263)
Higher education expenditure as a percentage of GSP (previous 5 year average)	1.553** (0.662)	2.724*** (0.659)	–8.302* (4.698)
Percentage of students enrolled in a public higher education institution (previous 5 year average)		–20.92*** (4.220)	–41.97*** (9.859)
Higher education expenditure × percentage of students in public higher education (previous 5 year average)			12.92** (5.455)
Elementary and secondary educational expenditure as a percentage of GSP (previous 5 year average)	0.861** (0.363)	1.659*** (0.359)	1.620*** (0.359)
Other government expenditure as a percentage of GSP (previous 5 year average)	0.897*** (0.121)	0.465*** (0.123)	0.466*** (0.123)
State own revenue as a percentage of GSP (previous 5 year average)	–0.432*** (0.0810)	–0.306*** (0.0790)	–0.273*** (0.0800)
Agriculture as a percentage of GSP (contemporaneous)	0.537*** (0.0594)	0.610*** (0.0583)	0.594*** (0.0586)
Mining as a percentage of GSP (contemporaneous)	0.225*** (0.0308)	0.186*** (0.0299)	0.213*** (0.0320)
Manufacturing as a percentage of GSP (contemporaneous)	0.288*** (0.0322)	0.305*** (0.0310)	0.302*** (0.0310)
Population growth rate (contemporaneous)	0.934*** (0.104)	0.982*** (0.100)	0.945*** (0.101)
State fixed effects	Yes	Yes	Yes
Time fixed effects	Yes	Yes	Yes
Constant	82.28*** (2.776)	103.7*** (4.498)	121.2*** (8.669)
Observations	1,450	1,450	1,450
Number of states	50	50	50

Standard errors in parentheses. *** $p<0.01$, ** $p<0.05$, * $p<0.1$

Similarly, including the interaction between higher education expenditure and the share of students in public education qualitatively similar results are found between the fixed effects and the Arellano-Bond model. Specifically, the direct negative effect of higher education expenditure on economic growth increased by roughly 34%, while the interaction effect increased by over 50%. While the magnitudes of the coefficients are estimated to be larger, when state-specific growth rates are calculated, the overall magnitudes are relatively similar to the fixed-effects model. Within this framework, the relationship between higher education expenditure and economic growth turns positive at around a two-thirds ratio of public to private enrollment. Specifically, a one percentage point increase in higher education expenditure as a percentage of GSP in Massachusetts would be expected to lead to a 2.7 percentage point decrease in per-capita income growth. In contrast, the same increase in higher education expenditure in Wyoming would lead to a 4.0 percentage point increase in per-capita income growth.

An interesting finding within the Arellano-Bond model is the finding of a direct negative effect of public sector enrollment on economic growth. Thus, it appears that as the private enrollment share increases within a state, that state would be expected to experience an increase in economic growth. Given that private higher education is more expensive that public higher education, it is entirely plausible that this effect is due to the correlation between a family's ability to pay for private higher education and general economic wellbeing. Furthermore, a good private college attracts people from all over the country and so people come and spend the money inside the state—which may be thought of as *export service* which adds to the growth rate of the state.

As a test of robustness, the results are presented using growth in Gross State Product (GSP) as the dependent variable in equation (3) and in Table 16.3 as estimated through both a state fixed effects (column 1) and Arellano-Bond estimator (column 2). Although, the estimated coefficients are larger in magnitude, the relationships are qualitatively similar. For example, the point at which the relationship between higher education expenditure and growth in GSP turns positive is with a ratio of public to private enrollments of 67% for the fixed-effects estimator and 74% for the Arellano-Bond estimator.

As a second test of robustness, we added lagged five-year average higher education expenditure variables—as well as the other government expenditures—to test longer term effects of higher education expenditure. Using growth in per-capita income as the dependent variable, Table 16.3 presents the result of the re-estimation of equation (3) with added lagged expenditure variables in columns 3 (fixed effects) and 4 (Arellano-Bond). The addition of the set of lagged variables did not affect the direction of the estimated relationship between higher education expenditure—or its interaction with the public to private enrollment ration—and income growth, however, the estimates are no longer statistically significant at traditional levels. Furthermore, the signs of the estimated coefficients on the lagged variables parallel those for the first group of higher education variables. The loss in significance is probably due to multicollinearity in the system.

Conclusions and Implications

This article enters into the debate of whether public investment in higher education is an efficient use of state funds to promote economic growth. Given the high level of variation across states in the size of their private higher education systems, and the positive correlation between a strong private higher education system and state-level economic growth, it is expected that growth analyses which neglect to control for the size of the private higher education system yield negatively biased estimates of the effect of higher education spending on growth.

These results indicate that states with larger shares of students in private, as opposed to public, higher education institutions experience a statistically significant larger negative growth effect on per-capita income of public expenditure on higher education. Conversely, states with a relatively large ratio of public to private higher education enrollments experience a positive effect on per-capita income due to public expenditure on higher education. Specifically, in the final year of our sample (2005) 37 states had a ratio of public to private higher education enrollments (that is, above 72%) which would be associated with a positive relationship between public higher education expenditure and state-level economic growth as estimated through our model. Similarly, the Arellano-Bond estimates would indicate that 40 states would experience an increase in state-level economic growth—given an increase in public higher education expenditure based upon these calculations. Thus, the results would imply that the omission of the size of the private higher education system may bias the estimated relationship between higher education spending and economic growth negatively. Further, it may be more advantageous for states with small private higher

TABLE 16.3

Robustness Analysis

Governmental expenditure variables are measured as the average value of the previous 5 years (and lagged in columns 3 and 4). Economic sector variables are measured contemporaneously. The sample period is 1975–2005.

	Growth in Gross State Product		Growth in Per-Capita Income	
	Fixed Effects (1)	Arellano-Bond (2)	Fixed Effects (3)	Arellano-Bond (4)
Lagged per-capita income		0.0398 (0.0256)		0.00212 (0.0254)
Higher education expenditure as a percentage of GSP (previous 5 year average)	−14.84*** (5.469)	−40.15*** (6.260)	−3.203 (4.107)	−6.491 (5.139)
Percentage of students enrolled in a public higher education institution (previous 5 year average)	−43.76*** (14.23)	−111.5*** (13.13)	−25.02** (10.66)	−36.71*** (10.33)
Higher education expenditure × percentage of students in public higher education (previous 5 year average)	21.90*** (7.104)	54.15*** (7.330)	5.469 (5.105)	10.74* (5.851)
Higher education expenditure as a percentage of GSP (lagged 5 year average)			−0.785 (3.748)	−2.930 (3.812)
Percentage of students enrolled in a public higher education institution (lagged 5 year average)			15.73* (8.779)	8.183 (7.980)
Higher education expenditure × percentage of students in public higher education (lagged 5 year average)			0.0157 (4.448)	3.428 (4.424)
Control variables	Yes	Yes	Yes	Yes
Lagged control variables	No	No	Yes	Yes
State fixed effects	Yes	Yes	Yes	Yes
Time fixed effects	Yes	Yes	Yes	Yes
Constant	122.2*** (11.64)	163.6*** (11.16)	90.60*** (10.49)	99.52*** (9.233)
Observations	1,500	1,450	1,250	1,200
Number of states	50	50	50	50
R-squared	0.379		0.600	

Standard errors in parentheses. *** p<0.01, ** p<0.05, * p<0.1

education systems, which is a majority of states, to invest in higher education than states with large private markets.

These findings have direct implications for research and theory. Specifically, these results compliment the findings of Aghion et al. (2005), which indicate that the relationship between higher education expenditure and state economic growth is not homogenous across the varied higher education landscape of states. This finding, that the relationship between higher education expenditure and economic growth is significantly different for states with large and small private higher education markets, implies that theoretical models relating higher education expenditure to economic growth need to integrate the private higher education markets. Further extensions of empirical models that take into account the heterogeneity of state higher education systems are needed to better understand whether states are efficiently investing in their public higher education systems. In addition, future work could also control for movement of people within the U.S. especially since students educated at state colleges tend to stay within the state and contribute to the local and thereby state economy whereas students in private colleges tend to move across states.

APPENDIX A

Data Dictionary

Real Personal Income	Bureau of Economic Analysis
Higher education governmental expenditure as a percentage of GSP	US Census & Bureau of Economic Analysis
Percentage of students enrolled in a public higher education institution	National Center for Education Statistics
Elementary and secondary educational expenditure as a percentage of GSP	US Census & Bureau of Economic Analysis
Other governmental expenditure as a percentage of GSP	US Census & Bureau of Economic Analysis
State own revenue as a percentage of GSP	US Census & Bureau of Economic Analysis
Agriculture as a percentage of GSP	US Census & Bureau of Economic Analysis
Mining as a percentage of GSP	US Census & Bureau of Economic Analysis
Manufacturing as a percentage of GSP	US Census & Bureau of Economic Analysis
Population growth rate	Bureau of Economic Analysis

Acknowledgments

The authors would like to thank Joe Stone, Christine Neill, and participants of the 2010 meetings of the Western Economics Association and the 2008 meetings of the American Education Finance Association for valuable feedback on earlier versions of this article.

Notes

1. As a robustness test, the same model is tested using the Gross State Product as a dependent variable. The difference between Gross State Product and Personal Income is capital income.
2. As a robustness test, a lagged higher education expenditure variable is included—accounting for average expenditure for the period 6–10 years past—to assess longer term effects.
3. Reed (2008 and 2009) points out that there are 32 control variables that have been used in previous studies and choosing one or a few sets of control variables can change the coefficients. As a robustness test, a broader set of control variables were tested and the results were qualitatively similar.
4. Collected from the Digest of Education Statistics (http://nces.ed.gov/programs/digest/), a publication of the National Center for Education Statistics (NCES). We employ the average value over the previous five years.
5. As in any fixed-effects estimating model, the identification occurs on variation within the unit and not between the units.

References

Aghion, Philippe, Leah Boustan, Caroline Hoxby, and Jerome Vandenbussche. 2005. *Exploiting States' Mistakes to Identify the Causal Impact of Higher Education on Growth.* Cambridge, MA: Harvard University Working Paper.

Arcalean, Calin, and Iona Schiopu. 2010. "Public versus Private Investment and Growth in a Hierarchical Education System." *Journal of Economic Dynamics and Control* 34 (4): 604–622.

Archibald, Robert B., and David H. Feldman. 2006. "State Higher Education Spending and the Tax Revolt." *The Journal of Higher Education* 77 (4): 618–644.

Arellano, Manuel, and Stephen Bond. 1991. "Some Tests of Specification for Panel Data: Monte Carlo Evidence and an Application to Employment Equations." *The Review of Economic Studies* 58 (2): 277–297.

Arellano, Manuel, and Olympia Bover. 1995. "Another Look at the Instrumental Variable Estimation of Error-Components Models." *Journal of Econometrics* 68 (1): 29–51.

Barro, Robert. 1990. "Government Spending in a Simple Model of Endogenous Growth." *The Journal of Political Economy* 98 (5): 103–125.

Barro, Robert J. 2000. "Inequality and Growth in a Panel of Countries." *Journal of Economic Growth*, 5 (1): 87–120.

Barro, Robert J., and Xavier Sala-i-Martin. 1992. "Convergence". *Journal of Political Economy*. 100(2): 223–251.

Barro, Robert J., and Xavier Sala-i-Martin. 2004. *Economic Growth*. Cambridge, MA: MIT Press.

Baum, Christopher F. 2006. *An Introduction to Modern Econometrics Using Stata*. College Station, TX: Stata Press.

Becker, Gary S., Edward L. Glaeser, and Kevin M. Murphy. 1999. "Population and Economic Growth." *The American Economic Review* 89 (2): 145–149.

Blackwell, Melanie, Steven Cobb, and David Weinberg. 2002. "The Economic Impact of Educational Institutions: Issues and Methodology." *Economic Development Quarterly* 16 (1): 88–95.

Blundell, Richard, and Stephen Bond. 1998. "Initial Conditions and Moment Restrictions in Dynamic Panel Data Models." *Journal of Econometrics* 87 (1): 115–143.

Bound, John, and Sarah Turner. 2007. "Cohort Crowding: How Resources Affect Collegiate Attainment." *Journal of Public Economics* 91 (5): 877–899.

Cheslock, John J., and Matt Gianneschi. 2008. "Replacing State Appropriations with Alternative Revenue Sources: The Case of Voluntary Support." *The Journal of Higher Education* 79, (2): 208–229.

Courant, Paul, Michael McPherson, and Alexandra M. Resch. 2006. "The Public Role in Higher Education." *National Tax Journal* 59 (2): 291–318.

Dee, Thomas S. 2004. "Are there civic returns to education?" *Journal of Public Economics* 88 (9): 1697–1720.

Delaney, Jennifer A., and William R. Doyle. 2007. "The Role of Higher Education in State Budgets." In *State Postsecondary Education Research: New Methods to Inform Policy and Practice*, edited by Kathleen M. Shaw and Donald E. Heller, 55–76. Sterling, VA: Stylus.

Ehrenberg, Ronald G. 2006. "The Perfect Storm and the Privatization of Public Higher Education." *Change* 38 (1): 47–53.

Evans, Paul, and Georgios Karras. 1994. "Are Government Activities Productive? Evidence from a Panel of U.S. States." *The Review of Economics and Statistics* 76 (1): 313–344.

Getz, Malcolm, and John J. Siegfried. 1991. "Costs and Enrollments." In *Economic Challenges in Higher Education*, edited by Charles T. Clotfelter, Ronald G. Ehrenberg, Malcom Getz, and John J. Siegfried, 332–356. Chicago, IL: University of Chicago Press.

Goldin, Claudia, and Lawrence F. Katz. 1998. "The Origins of State-Level Differences in the Public Provision of Higher Education: 1890–1940." *The American Economic Review* 88 (2): 303–308.

Goldstein, Harvey A., and Catherine S. Reanult. 2004. "Contributions of Universities to Regional Economic Development: A Quasi-experimental Approach." *Regional Studies*, 38 (7): 733–746.

Hanushek, Eric. 2002. "Publicly Provided Education." In Alan J. Auerbach and Martin Feldstein (Eds.), *Handbook of Public Economics* (pp. 2045-2141). Amsterdam: North-Holland.

Hanushek, Eric. 2010."The Economic Value of Education and Cognitive Skills." In Gary Sykes, Schneider, Barbara, & Plank, David N. (Eds.), *Handbook of Education Policy Research* (pp. 39–56). New York, NY: Routledge.

Heller, Donald E. 1997. "Student Price Response in Higher Education: An Update to Leslie and Brinkman." *The Journal of Higher Education* 68 (6): 624–659.

Hovey, Harold A. 1999. *State Spending for Higher Education in the Next Decade: The Battle to Sustain Current Support*. San Jose, CA. The National Center for Public Policy and Higher Education.

Kane, Thomas J., Peter R. Orszag, and Emil Apostolov. 2005. "Higher Education Appropriations and Public Universities: Role of Medicaid and the Business Cycle." *Brookings-Wharton Papers on Urban Affairs* 2005: 99–145.

Kane, Thomas J., Peter R. Orszag, and David L. Gunter. 2003. *State fiscal constraints and higher education spending: The role of Medicaid and the business cycle*. Washington, DC: The Brookings Institute.

Kneller, Richard, Michael F. Bleaney, and Norman Gemmell. 1999. "Fiscal Policy and Growth: Evidence from OECD Countries." *Journal of Public Economics* 74 (2): 171–190.

Koshal, Rajindar K., and Manjulika Koshal. 2000. "State Appropriation and Higher Education Tuition: what is the relationship?" *Education Economics* 8 (1): 81–90.

Leslie, Larry L., and Paul T. Brinkman, 1987. "Student Price Response in Higher Education: the Student Demand Studies." *Journal of Higher Education*, 58 (2): 181–204.

Lowry, Robert C. 2001. "The Effects of State Political Interests and Campus Outputs on Public University Revenues." *Economics of Education Review* 20 (2): 105–119.

Massey, William F. 2003. *Honoring the Trust: Quality and Cost Containment in Higher Education*. Bolton, MA: Anker Publishing Company.

McCracken, Casey 2006. *Whether State Fiscal Policy Affects State Economic Growth*. Palo Alto, CA: Stanford University Department of Economics.

McLendon, Michael K., James C. Hearn, and Christine G. Mokher. 2009. "Partisans, Professionals, and Power: The Role of Political Factors in State Higher Education Funding." *The Journal of Higher Education* 80 (6): 686–713.

McLendon, Michael K., Christine G. Mokher, and William Doyle. 2009. "'Privileging' Public Research Universities: An Empirical Analysis of the Distribution of State Appropriations Across Research and Non-Research Universities." *Journal of Education Finance* 34 (4): 372–401.

Moretti, Enrico. "Estimating the Social Return to Higher Education: Evidence From Longitudinal and Repeated Cross-Sectional Data." *Journal of Econometrics* 121 (1): 175–212.

Nicholson-Crotty, Jill, and Kenneth J. Meier. 2003. "Politics, Structure, and Public Policy: The Case of Higher Education." *Educational Policy* 17 (1): 80–97.

Reed, W. Robert. 2008. "The Robust Relationship between Taxes and U.S. State Income Growth". *National Tax Journal*. 61(1): 57–80.

Reed, W. Robert. 2009. "The Determinants of U.S. State Income Growth: A Less Extreme Bounds Analysis". *Economic Inquiry*. 47(4): 685–700. October

Rizzo, Michael, and Ronald G. Ehrenberg. 2004. "Resident and Nonresident Tuition and Enrollment at Flagship State Universities." In *College Choices: The Economics of Where to Go, When to Go, and How to Pay For It*, edited by Caroline Hoxby, 303–354. Chicago, IL, University of Chicago Press.

Romer, Paul M. 1990. "Endogenous Technological Change." Journal of Political Economy 95 (5): 71–102.

Stokey, Nancy. 1991, "Human Capital, Product Quality and Growth." *Quarterly Journal of Economics* 106 (2): 587–616.

Tandberg, David A. 2010. "Politics, Interest Groups and State Funding of Public Higher Education." *Research in Higher Education* 51 (5): 416–450.

Titus, Marvin. 2009. "The Production of Bachelor's Degrees and Financial Aspects of State Higher Education Policy: A Dynamic Analysis." *Journal of Higher Education* 80 (4): 439–468.

Toutkoushian, Robert K. and Paula Hollis. 1998. "Using Panel Data to Examine Legislative Demand for Higher Education." *Education Economics* 6 (2): 141–157.

Toutkoushian, Robert K., and M. Najeeb Shafiq. 2009. "A Conceptual Analysis of State Support for Higher Education: Appropriations Versus Need-Based Financial Aid." *Research in Higher Education* 51 (1): 40–64.

Trostel, Philip A. 2009. "The Fiscal Impacts of College Attainment." *Research in Higher Education* 51 (3): 220–247.

United States Department of Agriculture. 2010. "Agricultural Productivity in the United States." Last modified May 5, 2010. http://www.ers.usda.gov/Data/AgProductivity/.

Vedder, Richard. 2004a. *Going broke by degree: Why college costs too much*. Washington, DC: The American Enterprise Institute Press.

Vedder, Richard. 2004b. "Private vs. Social Returns to Higher Education: Some New Cross-Sectional Evidence." *Journal of Labor Research* 25 (4): 677–686.

Wang, Lu, and Otto A. Davis. 2005. *The Composition of State and Local Government Expenditures and Economic Growth*. Pittsburgh, PA: Carnegie Mellon University Working Paper.

Zhang, Liang. 2009. "Does State Funding Affect Graduation Rates at Public Four-Year Colleges and Universities?" *Educational Policy* 23 (5): 714–731.

CHAPTER 17

TRANSFER ACCESS FROM COMMUNITY COLLEGES AND THE DISTRIBUTION OF ELITE HIGHER EDUCATION

ALICIA C. DOWD, JOHN J. CHESLOCK, AND TATIANA MELGUIZO

The admissions practices of the most highly selective colleges and universities of the United States are under scrutiny for their failure to enroll poor and working-class students (Douthat, 2005; Karabel, 2005; Klein, 2005). This negative attention has been spearheaded by findings reported in two important books examining the shortage of low-income students at the pinnacle of American higher education, *Equity and Excellence in Higher Education* by William Bowen, Martin Kurzweil, and Eugene Tobin (2005) and *America's Untapped Resource: Low-Income Students in Higher Education,* edited by Richard Kahlenberg (2004), as well as by research articles (e.g. Winston & Hill, 2005). In a chapter in the Kahlenberg text, for example, Carnevale and Rose reported that only 3% of freshmen entering 146 highly selective institutions in 1992 came from the lowest quartile of a socioeconomic status (SES) index and about 10% came from the entire bottom half of the SES distribution (2004, p. 106). Demonstrating a highly skewed distribution of access, nearly three fourths (74%) of students enrolled at these institutions come from the highest SES quartile.

Contributing further attention to the lack of socioeconomic diversity at elites, Thomas Mortenson of the Pell Institute for the Study of Opportunity in Higher Education began ranking prestigious schools according to their success or failure in enrolling financially needy students, as indicated by the proportion of the student body receiving federal Pell grants (Fischer, 2006a). The findings of these studies have been widely reported (see, for example, Fischer, 2006a; Gose, 2005; Hong, 2005; Selingo & Brainard, 2006), inspiring headlines such as "The chorus grows louder for class-based affirmative action" (Gose, 2005). The controversy raises substantial questions about the way in which valuable educational resources are distributed and the definitions of merit that prevail when elite institutions choose among numerous qualified candidates.

Family affluence clearly affects what type of college a student attends or whether they go to college at all. This is shown, for example, by differences in college participation by high- and low-income students with "medium-high preparedness"—in other words, those who are not at the top of their class but are well qualified for college. Only 3% of well-qualified students from high-income families did not attend college, in comparison to 13% of those from low-income families. Well-qualified students from high-income families were also much more likely to attend a high-priced college than were their low-income peers (52% vs. 20%) (Hoxby, 2000, cited in Bowen et al., 2005, p. 87).

Socioeconomic inequalities in college enrollments raise troubling issues for education in a democratic society. Providing students with the opportunity to enroll at a college appropriate for their level of academic ability, regardless of family circumstances, is a cornerstone of higher education policy (Bowen et al., 2005; Kahlenberg, 2004; St. John, 2003). Maintaining this commitment has become more challenging as per capita government funding for college operating subsidies and low-income student aid has declined (Archibald & Feldman, 2006; *Trends in Student Aid*, 2006; Weerts & Ronca, 2006). As the returns to a college degree have increased, so has demand (*Education Pays*, 2006), particularly for spots at highly selective colleges, whose graduates enjoy an even higher earnings premium than others (Eide, Brewer, & Ehrenberg, 1998). Students at elite colleges enjoy additional benefits as well, including a greater likelihood of degree completion and greater access to graduate and professional study (Carnevale & Rose, 2004). These benefits have spawned intense competition for enrollment at highly selective colleges, and the recent increases in socioeconomic inequities in access (Astin & Oseguera, 2004) suggest that upper-income students have successfully utilized their numerous advantages to win this competition.

Partly because attendance substantially increases one's chances for later success, elite institutions are important symbols of power and prestige. As a result, the representation of lower socioeconomic status and racial-ethnic minority students at all levels of postsecondary education becomes a marker of a fair and just educational system in a multicultural democracy. As Sullivan has observed, the rags-to-riches story of social mobility through hard work and self-improvement is the "archetypal American cultural narrative" (2005, p. 142). Substantial intergenerational mobility becomes more difficult when an important determinant of social position and earnings, attendance at a selective higher education institution, appears to be the near exclusive domain of more affluent groups (Labaree, 1997).

Furthermore, many are concerned that when elite colleges lack sociocultural diversity, society loses the benefits of diverse perspectives among its civic and business leaders (Bowen et al., 2005; Hurtado, 2007; Kahlenberg, 2004). The exclusion of poor, working-class, and racial-ethnic minority students from elite institutions reduces the probability that these students will enter positions of power in society. It also decreases the likelihood that graduates of elite institutions will interact with a diverse set of peers while in college.

The strength of empirical evidence showing the benefits of student body diversity at selective institutions were influential in the recent Supreme Court decisions upholding certain forms of affirmative action in admissions at the University of Michigan (Hurtado, 2007; Joint Statement of Constitutional Law Scholars, 2003). Studies of the effects of interactions in diverse student groups have indicated that, controlling statistically for incoming student predispositions and characteristics, positive interactions are "associated with increases in students' democratic sensibilities including their pluralistic orientation, interest in poverty issues, and concern for the public good" (Hurtado, 2007, p. 191). Such awareness is viewed as necessary for citizenship in a pluralistic democracy and for the production of "leadership with greater social awareness and the complex thinking skills to alleviate social problems related to the complexities of inequality" (p. 193).

Informed by these perspectives, the agenda to reduce socioeconomic inequalities in access to elite institutions supports the larger goals of increasing social mobility, improving democratic participation, and promoting the civic ideals of equal treatment and opportunity.

Responses to the SES Enrollment Gap

The research findings demonstrating a large socioeconomic enrollment gap support the contention that elite colleges must cast their nets wider in recruiting academically capable students of modest family means. Three high-profile responses—one designed to reduce economic barriers to elite college enrollment, another to provide class-based affirmative action, and the last intended tb increase transfer access—have emerged in the face of these pressures to increase socioeconomic diversity. The first, which comes from a relatively small group of affluent institutions that have announced full or significantly increased institutional aid to cover costs for low-income students at their schools (Fischer, 2006a; Wasley, 2006), is not likely to have a broad reach because only the most well-endowed institutions have the financial resources to make such a commitment.

Another limitation of this response stems from the fact that lowering costs without revising admissions practices does not necessarily lead to a significant increase in low-income student enrollment. Changes in enrollment at the University of Virginia after adoption of the "AccessUVa" program illustrate this point. Although the program essentially covers all direct costs for low-income students—removing requirements to work or take loans, as well as providing money for extra expenses—only 6% of the student body was able to take advantage of the offer in the 2005–06 academic year, and university officials reported that they expected incremental annual enrollment growth among low-income students of only 0.5% (Fischer, 2006b).

The small potential impact of "no loans" financial aid policies (and others that provide complete funding for low-income students) results from the strong correlation between income and SAT scores. In comparison to their wealthy counterparts, only a small number of poor students make it into what Bowen et al. (2005) described as the "credible applicant pool" of elite colleges. Well over half (58%) of top SAT exam scorers (i.e., those scoring above 1200) from the high school class of 1992 were students from the highest SES quartile. In comparison, a mere 4% of students from the lowest quartile achieved such high scores (Carnevale & Rose, 2004, p. 130).

In addition, even those low-income students who earn high SAT scores are frequently overlooked by elite colleges. Despite glaring socioeconomic inequities in their enrollments, approximately half of the low-income applicants with SAT scores between 1350 and 1400 in Bowen et al.'s study of 19 highly selective institutions were rejected for admission (2005, p. 181). Under need-blind admissions policies, institutions aim to demonstrate that they do not discriminate against students with financial need, but they do not take affirmative steps to enroll low-income students when applications are reviewed. Consequently, several observers have argued that elite colleges should do more to enroll poor and working-class students through the adoption of class-based affirmative action (Bowen et al., 2005; Carnevale & Rose, 2004; Kahlenberg, 2004).

Bowen et al. (2005) argued that elite colleges should place a "thumb on the scale" in favor of low-income families. They explored the implications of weighting that "thumb" in such a way as to provide an advantage equal to that accorded "legacy" students (children of alumni). They found that by doing so the colleges in their sample could increase the share of low-income students from 11% to 17% (p. 179). Similarly, Carnevale and Rose (2004) simulated the share of low-income students at the 146 elite colleges in their study who would be enrolled under a number of alternative admissions policies, including those that currently prevail, which are largely neutral in their treatment of income status. Exploring the advantages and disadvantages of class rank plans, selection from among all qualified students by lottery, and economic affirmative action, they argued that the latter provided for the most equitable outcomes and was politically feasible. Through simulation of their plan, which focused on outreach to students with SAT scores between 1000 and 1300, high school GPAs above 3.0, excellent recommendations, and a strong showing in extracurricular activities, they showed that the percentage of students from the lower two SES quartiles can be increased from 10% to 38% (p. 149). While class-based affirmative action policies do show promise, they face several obstacles. Such plans can be perceived as supplanting race-based affirmative action, even when proponents argue for both. Furthermore, institutions may not embrace such policies, fearing that the proposed admissions criteria will have a negative impact on their *U.S. News* rankings (by lowering SAT scores).

The third response to socioeconomic inequities in elite college enrollment, which is the subject of this study, calls for a fundamental reorientation of admissions policies and practices. Based on the assumption that a pool of academically able low-income students is going untapped, it involves increasing the number of students transferring from community colleges to elite colleges (Burdman, 2003; Capriccioso, 2006; Padgett, 2004; Wyner, 2006). At the institutional level, such efforts have been spearheaded by the Jack Kent Cooke Foundation's Community College Transfer Initiative (Wyner, 2006), which has stimulated the investment of nearly $50 million by the foundation and its partner institutions to institute new transfer programs (Kattner, 2006). At the state and federal level, transfer from community to four-year colleges has gained attention as a potentially cost-effective way to increase bachelor's degree attainment, not only for the poor but also for middle-class families feeling squeezed by rising college costs (Keller, 2007; U.S. Department of Education, 2006; Walters, 2006).

A longstanding policy debate, still unsettled, concerns whether community colleges democratize higher education by providing low-cost access or divert students from bachelor's degrees that they would otherwise attain if they began their studies at a four-year college (Brint & Karabel, 1989; Dougherty, 1994; Melguizo & Dowd, in press). As college enrollments become more stratified by socioeconomic status (Astin & Oseguera, 2004), the equity implications of policies that rely on transfer to efficiently provide access to the baccalaureate deserve additional scrutiny (Dowd, 2003). Competition for transfer access is likely to increase as states implement stricter four-year college admission standards (Boswell, 2004; Long, 2005). Theories of social reproduction and class conflict suggest that poor and working-class students are unlikely to prevail in an intensified struggle for educational resources that ensure upward mobility (Bourdieu, 1986; Labaree, 1997).

Purpose of the Study

This study improves our understanding of the potential impact of expanded community college transfer access to elite institutions by examining a variety of key questions using two national databases with complementary strengths. We start by estimating the number of low-income students that transfer to elite institutions from community colleges. This number is the product of answers to three questions: (1) To what extent are elite institutions currently enrolling transfer students? (2) Of those transfers, how many admitted are from community colleges? (3) Of those community college transfers, how many are from low-income family backgrounds? We answer each of these questions for elite institutions and also provide the corresponding estimates for less selective institutions for comparison. We then estimate the total number of two-year transfers at elite institutions to understand the contribution of community college transfer access in reducing the underrepresentation of low-income students at these institutions.

Our findings clearly demonstrate that elite institutions currently enroll very few community college transfers. Consequently, we investigate possible explanations for why these numbers are so low. Our examination centers on two broad questions. First, do community college transfers have the academic preparation required to succeed at highly selective institutions? To answer this question, the academic preparation of community college students is compared with that of students who enrolled directly in highly selective colleges as first-time freshmen. Second, to what extent do highly selective institutions possess characteristics, such as high attrition, that are associated with greater institutional demand for transfer students at four-year institutions? In addition to answering this question, we also investigate whether the effects of these characteristics on transfer enrollment differ between highly selective and less selective colleges.

Prior Research

To our knowledge, this study is unique in its comprehensive investigation of community college student transfer to elite institutions through analysis of two nationally representative databases. Other studies have examined collaborative relationships between elite institutions and community colleges through case study research and qualitative data analysis (Gabbard et al., 2006; Laanan, 1996; Morphew, Twombly, & Wolf-Wendel, 2001) or conducted analyses of transfer to selective and less selective colleges in individual states (Burdman, 2003; Romano, 2005; Townsend & Wilson, 2006; Wassmer, 2003) or from particular community colleges (Bers, 2002). Cheslock (2005; Dowd & Cheslock, 2006) has shown that transfer to elite private colleges and universities is at a historic low point.

By estimating the number of low-income community college students currently transferring to highly selective institutions, this study demonstrates that elite institutions are not currently utilizing the transfer route to substantially increase the representation of low-income students on their campuses. In addition, by examining the influence of student academic preparedness and the effects of institutional characteristics on transfer enrollment rates at elite institutions, this study helps specify the nature of the problem of low transfer access. Although earlier research has described the socioeconomic inequity of the distribution of elite education and the lack of students from poor and working-class backgrounds among the entering freshmen classes of the most prestigious institutions in the United States, this study fills a gap in the literature by examining the socioeconomic distribution of transfer access to elite higher education.

This article is organized into five sections including this introduction. The second section presents the conceptual framework, which draws on three perspectives informing this issue: policy perspectives concerning the equity and efficiency of education; philosophical perspectives considering the legitimate criteria for admissions to elite higher education in a democracy; and institutional fiscal perspectives that influence admissions and enrollment management decisions. The third section describes the data analyzed. The fourth section describes the methods and results of the analyses, and the results are also compared to the findings of prior studies. The final section summarizes the major conclusions of the study and considers their implications.

Conceptual Framework

Policy Perspectives: Equity and Efficiency of Education

Arguments to facilitate transfer from community colleges to elite institutions reflect concerns for educational equity and efficiency and emphasize four points. First, the distribution of quality secondary schooling is highly inequitable. For example, students from the lowest SES quintile are more likely to attend schools that do not offer advanced mathematics courses (Adelman, 2006). Many students from poor families might well have been able to gain acceptance to and succeed at elite institutions if given proper instruction and encouragement during their schooling. That lost opportunity to learn can be provided by community colleges, which focus on teaching to a greater extent than research universities and which pride themselves on being learner-centered institutions (O'Banion, 1997). Second, the number of academically prepared high school graduates who choose to start at community colleges for financial, educational, or family reasons is believed to be getting larger (Adelman, 2005; Bailey, Jenkins, & Leinbach, 2005), increasing the pool of students qualified for successful degree completion at elite institutions. Third, population growth and increased enrollment demand have stressed higher education capacity in many states. As a result, even academically successful high school graduates fail to gain entry to public colleges with competitive admissions. The education of many more students in lower-cost community colleges is efficient and desirable from the standpoint of legislatures facing structural budget deficits. However, the rationing of access to elite institutions undermines educational equity if there is no opportunity for upward mobility through a stratified educational system (Labaree, 1997).

Finally, the number of low-income students concentrated in community colleges is large and provides a ready pool of potential transfers who, by earning a bachelor's degree, would increase their own human capital, contribute to closing the socioeconomic enrollment gap in higher education, and increase overall educational attainment in the United States. Over 6 million students enrolled at community colleges during the fall 2001 semester (Phillippe & González Sullivan, 2005, p. 12). Among them were approximately 1.7 million full-time students 18 to 24 years old (p. 34), the traditional college-age group most often served by elite institutions. Recent estimates indicate that 48% of community college students who were financially dependent on their parents were from the lower half of the income distribution (less than $50,000 in 2003) (p. 54). Together, these statistics suggest the presence of over 800,000 students from the bottom half of the income distribution, the very segment of the population that is absent from elite institutions. While not all of these 800,000 students would be qualified for enrollment at a highly selective college, the estimate gives a sense of the population of students who are the focus of debate regarding transfer access to elite higher education.

The size of the low-income student population in community colleges is very large relative to the number of low-income students missing from elite institutions. Comparative estimates are available. Carnevale and Rose (2004) estimated that for the 170,000 high school graduates who entered their sample of 146 elite institutions in 1992, 17,000 (10%) were from the lower half of the SES distribution. Researchers have sought to give a sense of the magnitude of the underrepresentation of low-SES students by comparing existing enrollments to the SES population distribution. Carnevale and Rose pointed out that if the representation of this group were proportional at 50%, an additional 68,000 low-income students would have enrolled (to reach the proportional number of 85,000). Similarly, Winston and Hill (2005) estimated that at the 28 private institutions that are members of the Consortium on Financing Higher Education (COFHE), the number of low-income students would have to almost double, from 2,750 students matriculated in 2001–2002 (10% of the entering class) to 5,005 students annually, in order to reach a socioeconomic distribution proportional to the national population.

Philosophical Perspectives: Legitimate Admissions Criteria

Nonselective and selective institutions have distinct "primary democratic purposes" (Gutmann, 1987, p. 194). Places at selective institutions, which are responsible for educating political officeholders and professionals, are scarce and valuable social goods. Therefore admissions committees cannot "arbitrarily" exercise "unconstrained preferences" in deciding whom to admit and exclude (Gutmann, 1987, p. 196). In distributing scarce spaces at elite institutions, admissions committees should be held, Gutmann argues, to the principle of nondiscrimination, which creates two main tenets for judging admissions criteria: (a) the desired qualifications must be "relevant to the legitimate purpose" of the institution, and (b) "all applicants who qualify or satisfy those standards should be given equal consideration for admission" (p. 196).

The application of these principles becomes difficult when the legitimate purposes of the university are in conflict in determining admissions criteria. As places of free academic inquiry, universities also have "associational freedom" to select members who share intellectual and educational values (p. 185). This interest in establishing communal standards and a certain type of communal life may place higher value on certain student qualifications than others. The qualifications preferred for associational purposes often appear to conflict with the institution's equal consideration of students' academic qualifications, because some academically qualified students are inevitably excluded on the grounds of associational freedom.

Gutmann argues that admissions standards set to establish the quality of communal life should be subordinate to academic qualifications because elite institutions function as a gatekeeper to important political, civil, and professional offices (1987, p. 202). Therefore, universities "should be constrained to consider academic ability as a necessary or primary qualification for admission, yet free to consider as additional qualifications nonacademic characteristics that are relevant to their social purposes" (p. 202). The tension between the communal goals and the role of gatekeeper, in which institutions serve society, is exacerbated by the difficulty of measuring academic ability or other important qualities, such as "intellectual creativity, honesty, aesthetic sensibility, perseverance, motivation to help others, leadership" (p. 200). Academic ability and a person's "character" are both difficult to judge. (For other philosophical and political-economic discussions concerning the allocation of educational opportunity, see Howe, 1997; Klitgaard, 1985; McPherson & Schapiro, 1990; Rawls, 1993).

These tensions are clearly recognizable in the conflicts an admissions committee faces when evaluating the applications of community college transfer students. Gutmann's principles indicate that the activities and policies that build college communities, student classes, and cohorts within programs and majors—such as residence life requirements, orientation activities, and major field of study prerequisites—are indeed important and in some ways constitute socialization experiences with core educational value. However, a college's general education requirements and cohort-based educational programming do not in themselves trump the right of qualified transfer applicants to receive equal consideration of their academic merits. This follows even if the admission of transfer students, who by definition begin college elsewhere and do not experience the same communal activities as entering freshmen, is perceived as diminishing a strong residential or communal culture.

Fiscal Perspectives: Enrollment Management and Institutional Prestige

The enrollment of low-income transfer students can have several financial implications for an institution. While any low-income student will depress net tuition revenue more than an upper-income student because of the required need-based institutional aid, low-income transfer students may have less of an effect than low-income freshmen if they transfer in a substantial number of credits. The institution may annually allocate less financial aid because transfers will have lower total educational costs as a result of their initial attendance at a lower-priced college. In addition, for "on time" graduates, financial aid need only be offered for two years to transfers as opposed to four years for freshman entrants. Regardless of the student's family income, transfer students can have very different cost implications than students admitted as freshmen. If substantial excess capacity exists in upper-level courses, institutions may actually enroll transfers at a savings, because they are simply filling capacity that would otherwise go unused. In the absence of such capacity, however, transfer students may actually be more costly than freshman admissions, because they spend a larger share of their time in upper-level courses, which are more expensive (Cheslock, 2005).

College and universities are also driven by prestige considerations that affect institutional economics (Garvin, 1980). The impact of transfer enrollment on institutional status is ambiguous. On one hand, some may view admitted transfers as less academically qualified and their admission as a sign of lower status (Gabbard et al., 2006; Manzo, 2004). But transfer enrollment could also serve to improve prestige, due to a "blind spot" in the formulas used in many influential publications, such as the *U.S. News and World Report*, which rank higher education institutions on indicators of selectivity. These rankings are derived from institutional freshman admission rates and on the average standardized test scores of the freshman class. The fact that transfer students are typically omitted from the ranking formulas provides an opportunity for colleges to strategically decrease the size of their freshman class and replace the lost enrollment with transfer students. This would have the effect of decreasing the admissions rate and increasing the average SAT or ACT scores, both of which would lead to higher rankings and signal higher status.

Summary

The three perspectives informing our conceptual framework—policy, philosophical, and fiscal—are interrelated. Given that demand for an elite education outstrips the supply of spaces, the policy perspective argues that moving more students from community colleges to selective institutions makes a lot of sense. The inequities in precollege educational opportunities and the rising costs of college have pushed students with high academic potential to begin at community colleges, even when the two-year sector is not their first choice. As many of these students are from the lower-half of the income distribution, promoting transfer access can help alleviate the severe underrepresentation of low-income students at elite institutions and potentially can do so at a lower cost than through freshman admissions.

Gutmann's (1987) philosophical discussions of the characteristics of a legitimate admissions system in a democratic society provide a framework to argue that these potential community college transfers should, indeed, be given equal consideration for admission. Finally, the fiscal perspective emphasizes the fact that colleges face financial and prestige considerations that will deter them from enrolling community college transfers. However, that will not always be the case, as transfers can fill unused upper-level class space and, by providing increased flexibility in "crafting a class" for freshman admission, even help an institution improve its rankings in popular college guides.

Data

This study takes advantage of the strengths of two national surveys to analyze institutional- and student-level data and presents a comprehensive profile of the prevalence and predictors of transfer admissions to selective institutions in the United States, accompanied by comparative information concerning transfer to less-selective institutions. The 2003 Annual Survey of Colleges and Universities from the College Board, which is an institutional-level census sample of all colleges and universities in the United States, includes the number of transfer students admitted from two-year and four year colleges at four-year institutions in fall 2002.[1]

Highly selective institutions are defined as those ranked as "most" or "highly" competitive in the *Barron's Profile of American Colleges* 2003 or 2005 editions and are referred to as "selective" or "elite" colleges,[2] where the latter expression is in a generic manner inclusive of both colleges and universities. Taking account of fluidity in the rankings and allowing elite status to be defined by a most or highly competitive ranking in one of these two years creates a larger group of elite institutions—179 cases compared to the 146 examined by Carnevale and Rose (2004)—than those included in previous studies.[3] The estimates of transfer enrollment at institutions of lesser selectivity are based on all the other institutions with valid data for the variables included in the analyses.[4] The final analytic sample includes 892 less selective institutions.

The Department of Education's National Educational Longitudinal Study (NELS:88/2000), which is a nationally representative sample of the graduating high school class of 1992, is analyzed to obtain estimates of the proportion of low-income students among transfers to four-year colleges.[5] In addition, the precollege academic preparedness of community college transfer students is compared to that of four-year college transfers and direct entrants to selective colleges. Following Adelman (2005), community college transfer students are defined as those who (a) begin in a community college, (b) earn more than 10 credits that count toward a degree at the community college before attending a four-year college, and (c) subsequently earn more than 10 credits from four-year colleges.[6] Four-year college transfers are defined in an analogous manner, based on the completion of 10 credits at one four-year college prior to transfer to another. The sample is limited to early or on-time high school graduates and is representative of traditional-age college entrants. The affluence of a student's family is represented by a socioeconomic status (SES) index provided by the National Center for Education Statistics (NCES).[7] Students whose SES index scores fall in the two lowest quintiles of the distribution are referred to as "low-SES" and "low-income" students.

Analyses

Prevalence of Community College Transfers at Elites

The share of transfer students in a four-year college's entering class differs considerably by institutional selectivity and type. As shown in Table 17.1, typical (median) two-year and four-year combined transfer enrollment shares at selective institutions are 24% in the public sector, 8% among the private non–liberal arts colleges, and 4% at liberal arts colleges. These shares rise by slightly less than half to 33% in the less selective public sector and triple at less selective private universities (26%) and liberal arts colleges (12%), indicating that transfer is much more prevalent at less selective institutions, particularly among private institutions.

In addition to enrolling smaller shares of transfers overall, private selective institutions also have a strong preference for four-year versus two-year transfers. The median share of two-year students among transfers, only 20% at private universities and 12% at private liberal arts colleges, clearly demonstrates that community college students are in the minority among transfers at elite private institutions. The corresponding figures for less selective privates are much higher at 53% and 43%, respectively. This preference for four-year transfers is not discernible among the public elites, where at the median 57% of transfers are from two-year colleges, quite similar to the 61% observed for less selective publics.

At private selective institutions, the combination of low overall transfer enrollments and a preference for four-year-college transfers results in an extremely low number of two-year transfers. The median enrollment numbers are two students at elite private liberal arts colleges and 14 students at other elite privates (only 1% or less of new students entering in the fall semester in both cases).[8] The corresponding figures at public selective institutions are higher, a 14% enrollment share and a median two-year transfer enrollment of 371, but they are still small given the emphasis on community colleges as an access point to the baccalaureate.

Prevalence of Low-Income Community College Transfers at Elites

Based on analyses of the NELS data, the disaggregated SES distribution of two-year transfer, four-year transfer, and direct entry students to selective and less selective four-year institutions are shown in Table 17.2.[9] At selective institutions, approximately 7% of two-year transfers, 5% of four-year transfers, and 8% of direct entrants are from low-SES backgrounds, based on the combined

TABLE 17.1

Enrollment Figures, Fall 2002[a,b]

	Public				Private, Non-Liberal Arts				Private, Liberal Arts			
	Mean	**25th**	**Med.**	**75th**	**Mean**	**25th**	**Med.**	**75th**	**Mean**	**25th**	**Med.**	**75th**
Selective institutions[c]												
# Freshmen enrolled	3067	1191	3274	4235	1411	751	1104	1685	459	342	454	573
# Transfers enrolled	999	227	891	1603	186	36	84	229	24	10	20	33
# 2-yr transfers enrolled	657	121	371	1209	80	2	14	86	6	0	2	7
# 4-yr transfers enrolled	342	97	213	443	106	24	52	134	19	8	15	23
% Incoming students, transfers	24%	15%	24%	28%	10%	4%	8%	13%	6%	2%	4%	9%
% Transfers, 2-yr	58%	43%	57%	77%	27%	10%	20%	42%	18%	0%	12%	25%
% Incoming students, 2-yr transfers	16%	7%	14%	23%	4%	0%	1%	5%	1%	0%	0%	2%
N	28				48				70			
Less-selective institutions												
# Freshmen enrolled	1658	674	1327	2331	401	186	317	513	319	201	308	440
# Transfers enrolled	887	354	724	1233	149	61	97	170	47	26	44	58
# 2-yr transfers enrolled	564	176	402	761	81	26	49	92	23	8	18	31
# 4-yr transfers enrolled	323	118	243	439	68	27	45	74	24	14	21	31
% Incoming students, transfers	35%	25%	33%	44%	29%	15%	26%	39%	15%	8%	12%	18%
% Transfers, 2-yr	60%	46%	61%	74%	52%	38%	53%	65%	45%	30%	43%	60
% Incoming students, 2-yr transfers	22%	13%	20%	30%	16%	7%	13%	22%	8%	3%	5%	11%
N	267				431				95			

[a] *Source:* Analysis of the Annual Survey of Colleges of the College Board and Database, 2003–2004.

[b] 25th denotes the 25th percentile, Med. denotes the 50th percentile (i.e., median), and 75th denotes the 75th percentile.

[c] Selective institutions are those ranked as most or highly competitive in the 2003 or 2005 *Barron's Profiles of American Colleges*.

TABLE 17.2

Community College Transfers, Four-Year College Transfers and Direct Attendees at Selective and Less Selective Institutions, by Socioeconomic Status[a,b,c]

	Community College Transfer Students[d]		Four-Year College Transfer Students[e]		Direct Attendees[f]	
	Selective	Less Selective	Selective	Less Selective	Selective	Less Selective
Highest	0.51	0.27	0.71	0.44	0.65	0.33
	(0.10)	(0.03)	(0.04)	(0.03)	(0.04)	(0.02)
Second quintile	0.28	0.29	0.17	0.27	0.18	0.28
	(0.09)	(0.03)	(0.03)	(0.02)	(0.03)	(0.02)
Third quintile	0.15	0.22	0.07	0.15	0.09	0.20
	(0.05)	(0.02)	(0.02)	(0.02)	(0.02)	(0.01)
Fourth quintile	0.05	0.16	0.03	0.10	0.05	0.14
	(0.02)	(0.02)	(0.01)	(0.02)	(0.01)	(0.01)
Lowest quintile	0.02	0.06	0.02	0.04	0.03	0.06
	(0.01)	(0.01)	(0.01)	(0.01)	(0.02)	(0.01)
N	100	780	400	790	670	1,740
Total	29,070	203,200	82,230	174,470	119,170	393,440

[a]*Source:* Analysis of the National Education Longitudinal Study of 1988/2000 (NCES 2003–402).

[b]Proportions and standard errors (in parentheses) are reported. Weighted Ns reported for all with known first institution of attendance. Flags and weights: For the 1992 senior sample the g12cohrt flag was used with a correction suggested by Adelman. The weight is F4F2P2WT.

[c]Selective institutions are those ranked as most or highly competitive in the 2003 or 2005 *Barron's Profile of American Colleges.*

[d]A community college transfer is defined as a student who first attends a community college, earns more than 10 credits that count towards a degree at the community college before attending a four-year college, and subsequently earns more than 10 credits from the four-year college.

[e]A four-year college transfer is defined as a student who first attends a four-year institution, earns at least 10 credits there, and subsequently transfers to a four-year institution.

[f]A direct attendee is defined as a student who first attends a four-year institution, earns more than 10 credits there, and does not subsequently transfer to either a two-year or a four-year institution by the time of the last follow up.

enrollment shares from the two lowest quintiles (i.e., summing the bottom two quintile values in Table 17.2). The representation of poor and working-class students in the elite college student body is extremely small in all three groups of students. In contrast, the enrollment share of students from the highest SES quintile is 51% among two-year transfers, 71% among four-year transfers, and 65% among direct entrants, a significant overrepresentation in every group beyond the 20% expected for one quintile.

The community college transfer route appears to be a comparatively advantageous pathway to elite institutions for middle-income students. The shares of the second and third SES quintiles are 1.5 times larger (43% vs. 27%) among two-year transfers than direct entrants.[10] In contrast, transfer from four-year colleges to elites does not provide an enrollment boost for middle-income students. Their shares are essentially the same as those for middle-income direct entrants. The distribution of four-year transfers to elites is highly skewed in favor of affluent students in the highest quintile.

At less selective four-year colleges and universities, the low-SES share increases but is still far below proportional representation. For community college transfers, the combined share of the lowest SES quintiles rises from 7% at selective colleges to 22% at less selective institutions. This rise does not indicate that the community college transfer route is substantially more effective than other routes at enhancing socioeconomic diversity at less selective institutions. The share of students from the bottom two SES quintiles is only 2 percentage points lower (20% vs. 22%) for direct entrants than for community college transfers. As is the case for the more selective institutions, the greatest stratification by SES still occurs among four-year transfers, not surprising given the costs associated with transfer among four-year institutions. In total, these results show that low-income students have very poor transfer access to the baccalaureate, especially at the most selective institutions. Transfer serves primarily middle- and high-income students, and the most affluent students have the greatest opportunities for transfer.

Population Estimates of Community College Transfers at Elites

Population estimates based on the College Board data show that the total number of two-year transfers at elites is quite small: 22,691 at the 38 elite public universities, 4,227 at the 65 elite private universities, and 424 at the 76 elite private liberal arts colleges, for a total of 27,343.[11] By multiplying these population estimates by the proportion of low-income two-year transfers at elites (7%, as shown in the previous section), we obtain the following population estimates of low-income two-year transfers entering elite institutions in the fall of 2002: 1588 at public universities, 296 at private universities, and 30 at private colleges, for a total of 1,914.[12] The ratio of these 1,914 low-income two-year transfers and our estimated total of entering freshmen and transfers (293,803) indicates that nationally fewer than 1 in 1,000 (.0065) of the students entering elite institutions each year are low-income community college transfers.

These figures become even more striking when we limit our analysis to the sample of COFHE institutions that were the subject of prior studies of the number of low-income students at elites (e.g., Winston & Hill, 2005). These schools enroll only 287 two-year transfer students in total, and 21 of 31 schools enroll five two-year transfers or fewer. Given the 7% low-income enrollment share presented above, these figures suggest that COFHE institutions enrolled only 20 low-income community college transfers in their fall 2002 entering classes.

The magnitude of 1,914 low-income community college transfers among the entering class of elite institutions can be placed in context by Carnevale and Rose's (2004) finding that, based on the numbers expected under a proportional SES distribution, 68,000 low-income students were missing from elite college campuses. For elite institutions to achieve proportional SES enrollment strictly through community college transfer enrollment, the size of the low-income community college transfer population would need to increase enormously, by a factor of 34. Not even a hundredfold increase in the numbers of low-income community college transfers at COFHE institutions would fill the enrollment gap of 2,255 low-income students estimated by Winston and Hill (2005). These numbers clearly demonstrate the magnitude of the underrepresentation of low-income students at elite institutions and the substantial changes in transfer recruitment and admissions that would be required for those practices to contribute to socioeconomic enrollment equity at elite institutions.

Academic Preparation of Community College Transfer Students

One potential reason why elite institutions prefer transfers from four-year colleges over those from two-year colleges is differences in the academic preparation levels of the two groups. Analysis of NELS data does suggest that four-year transfers are more likely than two-year transfers to have the highest level of academic preparation.[13] Thirty-eight percent of four-year transfers earned high school GPAs in the highest quintile, while only 15% of two-year transfers had GPAs in the highest quintile. Furthermore, 37% of four-year transfers completed calculus or precalculus in high school compared to 13% of two-year transfers.

While the above figures suggest that elite institutions could more easily find academically prepared four-year transfers than academically prepared two-year transfers, they do not imply that an elite institution could not find a pool of prepared two-year transfers if the institution concentrated on this population and recruited nationally. Based on the above figures, about one in seven two-year transfers have strong high school grades and a similar share has high levels of mathematics preparation, a major predictor of college success (Adelman, 2006).[14] Furthermore, some community college students could join the "credible applicant pool" (Bowen et al., 2005) through exceptionally strong performance during their first two years of college.

Elite institutions may not feel compelled to target two-year transfers in general but could be compelled to specifically target low-income community college students in order to improve their socioeconomic diversity. Our analysis of academic preparation using NELS suggests that some academically prepared lower-income students may be available, but students from the lowest income bracket may be few in number. Among those students from the lowest SES quintile who transferred from a community college, only 8% had high school grades in the highest quintile and only 3% completed calculus or precalculus in high school.[15] These figures, however, expand to 19% and 10%, respectively, for students in the fourth quintile (20th to 40th percentiles).

Predictors of Institutional Receptivity to Transfer Enrollment

Cheslock (2005) identified a number of factors that determine the share of an institution's incoming students who are transfers (the transfer enrollment rate), but two factors were found to be the strongest and most consistent predictors: an institution's attrition rate and its share of students living on campus in residence halls. The attrition variable is influential because, through transfer admissions, institutions can replenish upper-level course enrollments and tuition revenues depleted when students drop out. The residential housing variable likely demonstrates the challenge of introducing transfers into cohorts of students who share many academic and social experiences during their first two years of college and develop an identity as a freshman class.

One would expect institutions with higher attrition rates and low campus housing rates to be particularly amenable to increasing the enrollment of transfer students. The most selective schools do not have these characteristics. In our sample of selective institutions from the College Board data, the attrition rate is 11% for public institutions and 9% for private institutions, while the corresponding figures for less selective four-year institutions are 28% and 27%. The mean campus housing rates are 88% and 97% at public and private selective institutions, respectively, compared with considerably lower rates of 62% and 78% for less selective schools.

Furthermore, the attrition rate appears to be an especially influential determinant of transfer enrollment for the selective institutions in our sample. Table 17.3 contains separate regression analyses for selective and less selective schools.[16] (See Cheslock, 2005, for a complete discussion of the variables, data sources, and analytic model.[17]) The results demonstrate that a 10 percentage point increase in attrition is associated with a 5.8 percentage point increase in the transfer enrollment rate at selective institutions, compared with an increase of only 1.3 percentage points at less selective institutions. The results for campus housing, however, are quite similar for selective and less selective institutions. The larger effect of attrition for elites is not surprising, because selective institutions can more easily adjust their enrollments in response to high attrition. Elite institutions have an ample supply of applicants, including transfers who were turned away as freshmen. Consequently, increasing the enrollment of transfer students only requires the acceptance of applicants who would otherwise have been denied. In contrast, less selective institutions must increase the number of applicants through recruitment and marketing in order to expand enrollment. They may not always be able to meet their enrollment goals for their freshman class and are less likely, faced with attrition, to have a ready supply of upper-class transfer students whose enrollment was deferred because of initial rejection of their application, a less competitive financial aid offer, or placement on an admissions waiting list.

Discussion and Implications of the Findings

The findings of this study make it clear that elite colleges are not using transfer admissions to reduce the inequitable socioeconomic composition of their student bodies, despite the disproportionate enrollment and availability of low-income students in community colleges. In a particularly striking finding, our results show that fully half of all community college transfer students from the high school graduating class of 1992 who enrolled in highly selective colleges were from the very highest SES quintile. In contrast, a mere 7% were from the two lowest quintiles combined. On a national level, the current number of low-income community college transfer students in the

TABLE 17.3

Determinants of the Fall 2002 Transfer Enrollment Rate, by Selectivity[a,b,d]

Independent Variable	Selective[c]	Less Selective
First-year attrition rate	0.5780*** (0.1996)	0.1270** (0.0567)
% Freshmen in campus housing	–0.3429*** (0.0835)	–0.2482*** (0.0275)
Number of majors	0.0002 (0.0002)	0.0001 (0.0002)
Percent of applicants accepted	–0.0296 (0.0370)	–0.0289 (0.0491)
Undergraduate enrollment (in 1,000s), logged	0.0048 (0.0149)	–0.0322*** (0.0080)
Tuition & fees (in $1,000s)	–0.0013 (0.0012)	–0.0035** (0.0014)
% of state students in two-year institutions	0.0684 (0.0536)	0.3036*** (0.0519)
Previous cohort size/current cohort size	–0.1005 (0.1905)	0.2487 (0.1843)
Public institution	0.0734 (0.0487)	0.0297 (0.0258)
Location: rural or town	–0.0094 (0.0130)	–0.0194*** (0.0069)
Liberal arts college	–0.0240* (0.0123)	–0.0766*** (0.0130)
Intercept	0.4884** (0.1881)	0.1682 (0.2067)
N	172	892
R-squared	0.6183	0.4326

[a] *Source:* Analysis of the Annual Survey of Colleges of the College Board and Database, 2003–2004.

[b] Coefficients and standard errors (in parentheses) are reported.

[c] Selective institutions are those ranked as most or highly competitive in the 2003 or 2005 *Barron's Profiles of American Colleges.*

[d] * $p<0.10$; ** $p<0.05$, *** $p<0.01$.

entering classes of elite institutions is extremely small—less than 1 in 1,000. Surprisingly, although low-income transfer students increase in numbers at less selective institutions, they are still substantially underrepresented there, with an enrollment share of only 22% for the lowest two SES quintiles. These findings suggest that community colleges do not act as effectively as we might hope as the "people's college" or "democracy's college" (Valadez, 2002) in a higher education system where transfer provides social mobility for poor and working-class students.

Our study also sheds light on why elite institutions do not typically enroll low-income community college transfer students. First, elite colleges and universities admit very few transfer students in general. This is largely because highly selective institutions have very low attrition rates, so, unlike less selective institutions, they have only a minimal need to replenish lost enrollments in upper-level classes. When elite institutions do admit transfers, the students are far more often arriving from other four-year institutions (and, again, are disproportionately from the highest SES quintile). The pool of students who can present academic credentials that place them in the "credible applicant pool," to use Bowen et al.'s (2005) expression, is much larger among the four-year college transfer population than among community college transfers.

Given these conditions, before elite institutions will begin to recruit and enroll low-income community college transfer students in greater numbers, the case must be made that they have an obligation to do so. Governed by state-level articulation agreements and higher education strategic plans, highly selective public universities in some states, such as California, Florida, Illinois, and Washington, do have a statutory obligation to enroll community college transfers. Compared to their private sector counterparts, they do enroll many more of these students (14% of the entering class versus 1% at private universities) and are clearly playing a role in providing access to the baccalaureate through transfer.[18] This share is somewhat lower than at less selective public universities, where it is 20%, and perhaps also less than what would be necessary to meet the expectations of policies that place considerable emphasis on transfer access to the baccalaureate (Boswell, 2004; Long, 2005; Manzo, 2004; *StateNotes*, 2005). Despite this emphasis, the majority of states do not have efficient and concrete articulation policies (*StateNotes*, 2005) and some agreements become compromised when high-demand colleges or majors do not accept transfer students (Gabbard et al., 2006).

Here we argue that society has a democratic interest in ensuring access to elite higher education for students who were disenfranchised in their precollege schooling and that expanding the community college transfer pathway is an appropriate way to do so. Then we outline a research agenda to deepen understanding of the most effective ways to increase transfer access for low-income students. Because transfer may in fact provide a particularly efficient way to provide such access, we focus on studies that will investigate the costs and effectiveness of transfer policies and programs.

The Democratic Imperative for Community College Transfer Access

A number of objections quickly arise against the notion that elite institutions are obligated to enroll community college transfer students. Given low attrition, for example, there is little room for transfers under current enrollment levels. Further, there is an ample supply of academically prepared low-income high school graduates available to increase the socioeconomic diversity of elite campuses (Carnevale & Rose, 2004). If more low-income students are to be admitted, enrolling them for four-years and exposing them to the full range of curricular and extracurricular benefits of an elite education makes even more sense. Moreover, in their role as gatekeepers and educators of officeholders and professionals, elite institutions have the right to set relevant academic and communal standards for admission.

However, these objections can be countered by the more fundamental point that the system for distributing the benefits of an elite college education is legitimate and nondiscriminatory only when all students meeting the academic standards receive equal consideration. Gutmann (1987) argued that applicants should not be excluded from consideration on the basis of the associational freedom of the elite college or university. According to principles of nondiscrimination, elite institutions have an obligation to evaluate the applications of all qualified applicants, including community college students. In light of the severe underrepresentation of low-income students at elite institutions, the case can also be made for special treatment of low-income community college applicants, who are among those most likely to have been disadvantaged in their precollege schooling.

Although universities are not primarily responsible for the inequities of early schooling, they do have a responsibility not to perpetuate those inequities through their admissions standards and educational practices. This responsibility can be carried out by recognizing that some students had only a "bare opportunity" (Howe, 1997) to gain a high-quality education by the end of high school. Community colleges provide a critical second chance to those students. It is essential that elite institutions accept the educational attainments of community college students as legitimate credentials for application and admission; otherwise educational inequities are perpetuated. This argument is complementary to calls for class-based affirmative action through direct outreach to low-income students in high schools as well as to affirmative action to enroll African American, Latino, and other historically disadvantaged students. The SES gaps in elite college participation are so large that colleges will need to use all strategies at their disposal to achieve an equitable distribution of access.

From a compensatory education perspective, the evaluation of applications of community college students from poor and affluent backgrounds may be subject legitimately to different evaluation criteria. Elite institutions can justify rejecting some qualified applicants to compensate other qualified applicants who were not provided an adequate opportunity to learn during their early schooling (Gutmann, 1987). The admission of lesser qualified students who meet a threshold of academic preparation is justified if the institution can bring educationally disadvantaged students to their standards and graduate them successfully. To some extent, then, the obligation of elite institutions to low-income transfer applicants hinges on their capacity to provide effective compensatory academic programming and student services. Elite colleges need not aim to compensate all who faced educational deprivation in their precollege years. Only those with the ability to benefit deserve special treatment in admissions and the provision of additional resources to ensure they succeed (Gutmann, 1987).

Gutmann (1987) also distinguishes between the academic contributions of the most academically able and the academically able. Restricting admissions to the most academically able does not necessarily enable an institution to generate the greatest academic benefit, because the most academically able are likely capable of learning on their own. In addition, an intellectually, racially and ethnically, and socioeconomically diverse group of academically able learners may well generate a more intellectually stimulating environment by bringing together students who question each others' assumptions, stereotypes, and unconscious cultural perspectives. Supporting this view, the recent Supreme Court decisions in the University of Michigan affirmative action cases (*Grutter v. Bollinger et al.* and *Gratz v. Bollinger et al.*) provide a "ringing endorsement of the value of student body diversity in promoting numerous benefits" (Joint Statement of Constitutional Law Scholars, 2003, p. 5). The Court's decisions established that keeping the paths to positions of leadership open to "all segments of American society" is a compelling democratic interest (cited in Bowen et al., 2005, p. 344, note 54).

A Research Agenda to Support Effective Transfer Access to Elites

This study demonstrates that, despite the democratic imperative to distribute access to elite higher education in an equitable manner, elite institutions are missing an important opportunity to do so. This is surprising, in a way, because expanded recruitment of community college transfer students is one of only a small number of strategies at their disposal to reduce enrollment inequities. Our study reveals several reasons for this underutilization of transfer, such as the low attrition rates at elite institutions and the effort required to identify academically prepared students. We recommend a broad-based research agenda to further improve understanding of the costs and effectiveness of transfer programs and policies.

Our study provides some suggestive evidence regarding the size of the pool of academically prepared low-income community colleges students, but this topic deserves a more extensive examination than allowed here. Such an examination would help identify the extent to which college readiness contributes to the poor transfer rates of low-income students. Researchers also need to examine the interactions between student aspirations, social expectations, and student choice and how these contribute to the number of available community college transfers, a topic not addressed in this study. This choice process is heavily influence by faculty, counselors, and other institutional "transfer" agents (Pak, Bensimon, Malcom, Marquez, & Park, 2006). Additional research into effective outreach, counseling, and academic preparation programs at community and elite colleges is needed.

Elite colleges may have difficulty examining the collegiate academic record of community college transfer applicants, who typically attend institutions with a substantially different mix of missions, pedagogy, and curricular structures than those at selective colleges. This uncertainty may partially explain the preference of elite institutions for four-year transfers over those from community colleges. Studies of those experiences at the community college that are associated with later success at elite institutions will help develop effective transfer admissions standards. Recent research has shown that elite colleges do graduate, at rates similar to direct entrants, community college transfers who had high baccalaureate aspirations at the end of high school (Melguizo & Dowd, in press). Future research should examine the links between successful bachelor's degree attainment and cognitive and noncognitive indicators of ability, such as leadership and community organizing, at the community college level.

Elite colleges may be concerned that transfers will diminish a strong residential or communal culture. Colleges have a legitimate right to define their college culture and communal values through education, residency, and cohort requirements. Program evaluation and interpretive case study research can uncover what is lost and gained in this respect when elite institutions enroll transfers in greater numbers. Elite institutions may also be concerned that increasing transfer students may require an expansion of upper-level courses, which are smaller and consequently more expensive. These costs can be examined empirically, however, to assess transfer capacity in particular courses and majors. Research into these fiscal issues may show that there are areas where transfers can be absorbed with little cost, thereby reducing fiscal barriers to expanded transfer enrollment.

Any elite institution wishing to substantially increase its enrollment of low-income community college transfer students will need to consider new recruitment, admissions, counseling, and curricular structures in order to ensure success. Case studies of successful institutions will be valuable, although relatively few instances appear to exist. A recent national study involving interviews with counselors, administrators, and faculty at highly selective institutions and community colleges demonstrates that a small number of specialized programs currently recruit and graduate community college transfers (Dowd, Bensimon, Gabbard et al., 2006; Gabbard et al., 2006). By and large, however, such efforts are nonexistent or underdeveloped at most elite colleges. Evaluation of the colleges funded by the Jack Kent Cooke Foundation's Community College Transfer Initiative is likely to shed light on the characteristics of effective strategies.

Finally, assessment strategies focused on transfer practices and policies are needed. Researchers have developed a transfer access self-assessment inventory to assist two- and four-year colleges in completing a cultural audit of transfer-oriented practices, programs, and policies (Dowd, Bensimon, & Gabbard, 2006). Assessment instruments should also be developed to conduct cost studies of the human, physical, and material resources allocated to promote transfer and to determine how effectively those resources are used.

Conclusion

Treating transfer to an elite institution as a valuable academic outcome for students who start their postsecondary education at colleges of lesser status, the results of this study demonstrate clear outcome inequities (Dowd, 2003; Howe, 1997) in transfer access for low-income community college students. That the same can be said, based on prior research by others (Bowen et al., 2005; Carnevale & Rose, 2004; Winston & Hill, 2005), about freshmen admission or, based on the results of this study, about transfer to less selective four-year colleges only compounds the problem. These socioeconomic inequities in transfer access severely undermine a higher education system where community colleges are intended to be low-cost engines of social and economic mobility. In a democracy, equitable access to elite institutions is critical to ensure public investments in higher education do not simply reproduce the existing class structure.

Acknowledgments

This work was funded as part of the Study of Economic, Informational, and Cultural Barriers to Community College Access at Selective Institutions by the Jack Kent Cooke Foundation, Lumina Foundation for Education, and the Nellie Mae Education Foundation. We would like to thank Leticia Bustillos, Rhonda Gabovitch, Nancy Ludwig, Lindsey Malcom, Amalia Márquez, Daniel Park, and Edlyn Vallejo Peña for helpful research assistance. In addition, we are grateful to three anonymous reviewers and Guilbert Hentschke who provided helpful recommendations for revisions.

Notes

1. Source of Data: the Annual Survey of Colleges of the College Board and Data Base, 2004–2005. Copyright 2003–2004. Copyright 2003. College Entrance Examination Board. All rights reserved.

   Colleges report their total number of transfer students and the proportion of those transfers enrolling from two-year and four-year colleges. The number of two-year and four-year transfers is calculated from the product of these proportions and the total number of transfers.

   The College Board does not provide a precise definition of a transfer student in its survey, so individual institutions determine which students count as transfers. The definitions used by individual institutions will differ slightly from those established by Adelman (2005) and used in our analysis of the NELS data.

   The survey does not distinguish community college transfer students from those transferring from proprietary or private nonprofit two-year colleges. However, given the relative population size of students in these two sectors (Knapp, 2003), it is reasonable to assume that about 95% of these two-year transfers were in fact community college students. In fall 2001, 95% of the more than 6,250,000 students enrolled in degree-granting two-year institutions were at public colleges. About 3.5% were at private for-profit colleges, with the remainder at private not-for-profit colleges (Knapp, 2003).

   To increase sample size, we used the most recently available data from the fall 1999 to fall 2001 period for those schools missing fall 2002 data. This imputation was used for approximately 20% of our sample. Because enrollment figures vary relatively little across corresponding years, this imputation does not introduce substantial measurement error.
2. Institutions in the most competitive bracket had a student body with an average SAT I or ACT score at or above 655 or 29, respectively. Students typically ranked in the top 20% of their class and had an average high school grade point average of B+ or higher. These institutions accept less than a third of their applicants. The equivalent values for institutions ranked as highly competitive are SAT I/ACT scores at or above 620/27, average GPA of B or higher, and an admissions rate less than or equal to 50%.
3. Several unique institutions, such as the military academies, were omitted from the sample. While all 179 institutions are used for the population estimates, smaller subsamples are used in other analyses due to missing data for key variables.
4. The sample does not include proprietary colleges or institutions that were not ranked in one of the following categories of the 2000 Carnegie Classification: Doctoral Research University, Master's College or University, Baccalaureate College, School of Engineering and Technology, or School of Business and Management.
5. The NELS:88/2000 is a complex survey sample with a stratified sampling design and unequal probabilities of selection. The findings are appropriately weighted (using the weight F4F2P2WT) for point and population estimates. Robust methods were similarly employed for variance estimation using the "svy" functions where appropriate in Stata.
6. Many students, including transfer students, attend more than one four-year institution, and often those institutions differ in terms of their institutional selectivity. Therefore, the selectivity of the institution to which a student transfers can be defined by the first, last, or most selective four-year institution attended. In this study, the institutional selectivity of a student's four-year college is represented by the most selective institution attended.
7. The index is based on the father's occupation and education, the mother's education, family income, and material possessions.
8. There are noteworthy exceptions at liberal arts colleges with special programs that serve higher numbers of community college transfers, such as the Ada Comstock Scholars at Smith College, Francis Perkins Scholars at Mt. Holyoke College (both of which are designed for older female students), and Exploring Transfer at Vassar College (Chenoweth, 1998; Geraghty, 1997).
9. While it would be desirable to observe the college readiness of students across the SES distribution and the three comparison groups, the small sample size of community college transfers to selective colleges prohibits a more disaggregated analysis with any reasonable degree of statistical precision.
10. These differences in the middle-class quintiles are not statistically significant due to imprecise estimates for the small sample of two-year transfer students. However, an alternative test using income quartiles in a larger sample of selective institutions yields statistically significant results for differences in the middle-income quartiles with substantively equivalent enrollment shares. In the alternative specification, the sample included institutions coded as selective in the NELS:88/2000 postsecondary transcripts restricted database. The number of cases of community college transfers to selective institutions increases from 99 to 877.

11. By definition, population estimates should be based on the full population of institutions, not only those reporting valid data. For the 33 institutions not included in Table 17.2 due to missing data in the variable indicating the share of two-year transfers in their entering fall cohort, the number of two-year transfers was calculated by multiplying the institution's reported number of total transfers, which typically was not missing, by the median two-year transfer enrollment share for their institutional type.
12. Four states with a large number of community college students contribute 71% of the total population of two-year college transfer students at elite institutions: Enrollments at selective institutions in California contribute 36% of the elite transfer population, while Texas, Florida, and New York each contribute 11% to 12%.
13. In this analysis, we examine all students who transfer to another four-year institution, regardless of the receiving institution's selectivity. Incorporating students who transfer to less selective institutions allows us to describe the pool of transfer students that may be available to elite institutions.
14. A GPA from the highest quintile or the completion of calculus or precalculus is not sufficient for admission at an elite institution, and some students with these characteristics may lack other credentials necessary for admission. That said, analysis of the high school GPAs and mathematics preparation of direct entrants at elite institutions indicates that a perfect record is not required for admissions at some of these institutions. Thirty-seven percent of direct entrants were admitted with a high school GPA below the top quintile, and 32% had not completed calculus or precalculus.
15. The differences in high school GPAs across SES quintiles should be viewed with caution as they are not statistically significant at conventional levels.
16. We report the results from an ordinary least squares regression (OLS). A curvilinear logistic model was also estimated to test the severity of departure from linearity in the OLS model. The results were similar across the two specifications, indicating the OLS results are robust.
17. Because of the high concentration of a large proportion of community college students in certain states, we use robust standard errors with clustering, which relaxes the assumption that the error terms are identically distributed, as well as the assumption of independence between observations in the data. This technique is an extension of the robust variance estimation developed by Huber (1967) and White (1980) that was first provided in writing by Rogers (1993).
18. Our analyses do not indicate what proportion of these transfers are low-income students. A recent national case study of transfer access at highly selective institutions suggests that highly selective public universities do not typically collect data to analyze transfer enrollment by socioeconomic status and do not typically target their transfer outreach efforts to low-income students (Gabbard et al., 2006). Furthermore, the higher tuition and housing costs (Long, 2005) and the distinct cultural emphasis on competitiveness and prestige (Dowd, Bensimon, Gabbard, et al., 2006) at highly selective research universities may depress the enrollment of low-income transfers.

References

Adelman, C. (2005). *Moving into town-and moving on: The community college in the lives of traditional-age students.* Washington, DC: U.S. Department of Education.

Adelman, C. (2006). *The toolbox revisited: Paths to degree completion from high school through college.* Washington, DC: U.S. Department of Education.

Archibald, R. B., & Feldman, D. H. (2006). State higher education spending and the tax revolt. *Journal of Higher Education, 77*(4), 618–644.

Astin, A. W., & Oseguera, L. (2004). The declining "equity" of American higher education. *Review of Higher Education, 27*(3), 321–341.

Bailey, T., Jenkins, D., & Leinbach, T. (2005). *Community college low-income and minority student completion study: Descriptive statistics from the 1992 high school cohort.* Retrieved February 27, 2006, from http://ccrc.tc.columbia.edu/

Barron's profiles of American colleges. (2003, 2005). Hauppauge, NY: Barron's Educational Series.

Bers, T. (2002). *Tracking Oakton transfers: Students last at Oakton Fall 1997–Spring 2001.* Des Plaines, IL: Oakton Community College.

Boswell, K. (2004). Bridges or barriers? Public policy and the community college transfer function. *Change, 36*(6), 22–30.

Bourdieu, P. (1986). The forms of capital. In J. G. Richardson (Ed.), *Handbook of theory and research for the sociology of education* (pp. 241–258). New York: Greenwood Press.

Bowen, W. G., Kurzweil, M. A., & Tobin, E. M. (2005). *Equity and excellence in American higher education*. Charlottesville: University of Virginia Press.

Brint, S., & Karabel, J. (1989). *The diverted dream: Community colleges and the promise of educational opportunity in America, 1900–1985*. New York: Oxford University Press.

Burdman, P. (2003). Taking an alternate route. *Black Issues in Higher Education*, 32–35.

Capriccioso, R. (2006). *$27 Million for community college pipeline*. Retrieved March 6, 2006, from http://www.insidehighered.com/news/2006/03/06/cooke

Carnevale, A. P., & Rose, S. J. (2004). Socioeconomic status, race/ethnicity, and selective college admissions. In R. D. Kahlenberg (Ed.), *America's untapped resource: Low-income students in higher education* (pp. 101–156). New York: Century Foundation Press.

Chenoweth, K. (1998, February 19). The new faces of Vassar. *Black Issues in Higher Education*, 22–24.

Cheslock, J. J. (2005). Differences between public and private institutions of higher education in the enrollment of transfer students. *Economics of Education Review*, 24, 263–274.

Dougherty, K. J. (1994). *The contradictory college: The conflicting origins, impacts, and futures of the community college*. Albany: State University of New York Press.

Douthat, R. (2005). *Does meritocracy work?* Retrieved December 28, 2005, from http://www.theatlantic.com/doc/prem/200511/college-and-meritocracy

Dowd, A. C. (2003). From access to outcome equity: Revitalizing the democratic mission of the community college. *Annals of the American Academy of Political and Social Science*, 586(March), 92–119.

Dowd, A. C., Bensimon, E. M., & Gabbard, G. (2006). *Transfer access self-assessment inventory* [assessment instrument]. Los Angeles and Boston: University of Southern California and University of Massachusetts Boston.

Dowd, A. C., Bensimon, E. M., Gabbard, G., Singleton, S., Macias, E., Dee, J., Melguizo, T., Cheslock, J., Giles, D. (2006). *Transfer access to elite colleges and universities in the United States: Threading the needle of the American dream*. Retrieved June 28, 2006, from www.jackkentcookefoundation.org

Dowd, A. C., & Cheslock, J. J. (2006). *An estimate of the two-year transfer population at elite institutions and of the effects of institutional characteristics on transfer access*. Retrieved June 28, 2006, from www.jackkentcookefoundation.org

Education pays. (2006). Retrieved February 1, 2007, from www.collegeboard.com/trends

Eide, E., Brewer, D., & Ehrenberg, R. (1998). Does it pay to attend an elite private college? Cross cohort evidence on the effects of college quality on earnings. *Economics of Education Review*, 17(4), 371–376.

Fischer, K. (2006a, May 12). *Elite colleges lag in serving the needy: The institutions with the most money do a poor job of reaching the students with the least*. Retrieved May 12, 2006, from http://chronicle.com/

Fischer, K. (2006b, May 12). Well-heeled U. of Virginia tries to balance access with prestige. *Chronicle of Higher Education*, p. A13.

Gabbard, G., Singleton, S., Macias, E., Dee, J., Bensimon, E. M., Dowd, A. C., Giles, D., Fuller, T., Parker, T., Malcom, L., Marquez, A., Park, D., Fabienke, D. (2006). *Practices supporting transfer of low-income community college transfer students to selective institutions: Case study findings*. Retrieved June 28, 2006, from www.jackkentcookefoundation.org

Garvin, D. A. (1980). *The economics of university behavior*. New York: Academic Press.

Geraghty, M. (1997, May 2). *Smith College clears the way for community college transfers*. Retrieved May 1, 2006, from http://chronicle.com/

Gose, B. (2005, February 25). The chorus grows louder for class-based affirmative action. *Chronicle of Higher Education*, p. B5.

Gratz v. Bollinger, 539 U.S. 244 (2003).

Grutter v. Bollinger, 539 U.S. 306 (2003).

Gutmann, A. (1987). Democratic education. Princeton, NJ: Princeton University Press. Hong, P. (2005, October 23). *The rich get smarter: More scholarships for wealthy students cut out the poor kids*. Los Angeles Times, p. 6.

Howe, K. R. (1997). *Understanding equal opportunity: Social justice, democracy, and schooling*. New York: Teachers College Press.

Hoxby, C. M. (2000). Testimony prepared for U.S. Senate, Committee on Governmental Affairs, hearing on the rising cost of college tuition and the effectiveness of government financial aid. In Senate Committee on Governmental Affairs, *Rising cost of college tuition and the effectiveness of government financial aid: Hearings*, 106th Cong., 2d sess., 120–128 (2000) (S. Hrg. 106–515, February 9).

Huber, P. (1967). *The behavior of maximum-likelihood estimates under non-standard conditions.* Paper presented at the Proceedings of the Fifth Berkeley Symposium on Mathematical Statistics and Probability, Berkeley, CA.

Hurtado, S. (2007). Linking diversity with the educational and civic missions of higher education. *Review of Higher Education*, 30(2), 185–196.

Joint Statement of Constitutional Law Scholars. (2003). *Reaffirming diversity: A legal analysis of the University of Michigan affirmative action cases.* Cambridge, MA: The Civil Rights Project at Harvard University.

Kahlenberg, R. D. (2004). *America's untapped resource: low-income students in higher education.* New York: Century Foundation Press.

Karabel, J. (2005). *The chosen: The hidden history of admission and exclusion at Harvard, Yale, and Princeton.* Boston: Houghton Mifflin Company.

Kattner, T. (2006, September). Six ways to increase low-income students' transfer to elite institutions. *Recruitment and Retention in Higher Education*, 20, 1–4.

Keller, J. (2007). *Virginia lawmakers consider bill to encourage students to start at a two-year college.* Retrieved January 19, 2007, from www.chronicle.com

Klein, J. M. (2005, November 4). Merit's demerits. *Chronicle of Higher Education*, p. B12.

Klitgaard, R. (1985). *Choosing elites.* New York: Basic Books.

Knapp, L. G. (2003). *Enrollment in postsecondary institutions, Fall 2001 and Financial statistics, fiscal year 2001* (E.D. Tabs No. NCES 2004–155). Washington, DC: U.S. Department of Education, National Center for Education Statistics.

Laanan, F. S. (1996). Making the transition: Understanding the adjustment process of community college transfer students. *Community College Review*, 23(4), 69–84.

Labaree, D. F. (1997). *How to succeed in school without really learning: The credentials race in American education.* New Haven, CT: Yale University Press.

Long, B. T. (2005). *State financial aid policies to enhance articulation and transfer.* Boulder, CO: Western Interstate Commission for Higher Education

Manzo, K. K. (2004). Report: Transfer barriers loom large for two-year students. *Black Issues in Higher Education*, 21(15), 6–7.

McPherson, M., & Schapiro, M. O. (1990). *Selective admission and the public interest.* New York: College Entrance Examination Board.

Melguizo, T., & Dowd, A. C. (in press). *Baccalaureate success of transfers and rising four-year college juniors.* Teachers College Record.

Morphew, C. C., Twombly, S. B., & Wolf-Wendel, L. E. (2001). Innovative linkages: Two urban community colleges and an elite private liberal arts college. *Community College Review*, 29(3), 1–21.

O'Banion, T. (1997). *A learning college for the 21st Century.* Phoenix, AZ: Oryx Press.

Padgett, T. (2004). *An Ivy stepladder.* Time, p. 61.

Pak, J., Bensimon, E. M., Malcom, L., Marquez, A., & Park, D. (2006). *The life histories of ten individuals who crossed the border between community colleges and selective four-year colleges.* Los Angeles: University of Southern California.

Phillippe, K. A., & González Sullivan, L. (2005). *National profile of community colleges: Trends and statistics.* Washington, DC: American Association of Community Colleges.

Rawls, J. (1993). *Political liberalism.* New York: Columbia University Press.

Rogers,W. (1993). Regression standard errors in clustered samples. *Stata Technical Bulletin*, 13, 19–23.

Romano, R. M. (2005). *Tracking community college transfers using National Student Clearinghouse Data.* Tallahassee, FL: Association for Institutional Research.

Selingo, J., & Brainard, J. (2006, April 6). The rich-poor gap widens for colleges and students. *Chronicle of Higher Education*, p. A1.

St. John, E. P. (2003). *Refinancing the college dream: Access, equal opportunity, and justice for taxpayers.* Baltimore: The Johns Hopkins University Press.

StateNotes: Transfer and Articulation. (2005). Retrieved May 1, 2006, from www.ecs.org/clearinghouse/23/75/2375.htm

Sullivan, P. (2005). Cultural narratives about success and the material conditions of class at the community college. *Teaching English in the Two-Year College*, 32(2), 142–160.

Townsend, B. K., & Wilson, K. (2006). "A hand hold for a little bit": Factors facilitating the success of community college transfer students to a large research university. *Journal of College Student Development*, 47(4), 439.

Trends in student aid. (2006). Retrieved February 1, 2007, from www.collegeboard.com/trends

U.S. Department of Education. (2006). *A test of leadership: Charting the future of U.S. higher education*. Washington, DC: Author.

Valadez, J. R. (2002). Transformation of the community colleges for the 21st Century. *Educational Researcher*, 31(2), 33–36.

Walters, A. K. (2006). *U of Virginia offers guarantee of admission to the state's top community-college students*. Retrieved January, 2007, from http:chronicle.com/daily

Wasley, P. (2006, March 17). *Stanford U. increases aid to cover tuition for low-income students*. Retrieved March 17, 2006, from http://chronicle.com/daily

Wassmer, R. (2003). *A quantitative study of California community college transfer rates: Policy implications and a future research agenda*. Sacramento, CA: Institute for Higher Education Leadership and Policy, California State University.

Weerts, D. J., & Ronca, J. M. (2006). Examining differences in state support for higher education: A comparative study of state appropriations for Research I universities. *Journal of Higher Education*, 77(6), 935–967.

White, H. (1980). A heteroskedasticity-consistent covariance matrix estimator and a direct test for heteroskedasticity. *Econometrica*, 48, 817–830.

Winston, G. C., & Hill, C. B. (2005). *Access to the most selective private colleges by high-ability, low-income students: are they out there?* (Discussion Paper No. 69). Williamstown, MA: Williams Project on the Economics of Higher Education.

Wyner, J. (2006, February 10). Educational equity and the transfer student. *Chronicle of Higher Education*, p. B6.

CHAPTER 18

TOWARD A MORE COMPLETE UNDERSTANDING OF THE ROLE OF FINANCIAL AID IN PROMOTING COLLEGE ENROLLMENT: THE IMPORTANCE OF CONTEXT

LAURA W. PERNA

Competing demands for public resources and demands for accountability of program effectiveness underscore the need to better understand the role of student financial aid in eliminating financial barriers to college enrollment. Although many researchers have examined the effects of student financial aid on student outcomes, gaps in knowledge persist. Based on their comprehensive review of research for the College Board's "rethinking student aid" project, Baum and McPherson (2008) concluded that more research is needed, as "many questions remain about how to develop the most effective student aid policies" (p. 6).

Through a review, synthesis, and critique of relevant prior research, this chapter argues that one reason knowledge about how student financial aid programs can best promote college enrollment is incomplete is that existing research does not devote sufficient attention to the "context" in which these programs operate or the ways that context mediates the effects of aid. Potentially relevant aspects of context include characteristics of other available financial aid programs, students and their families, the high school attended, available higher education options, and the broader economic, social, and policy environment. These aspects of context come together to define and delimit the ways financial aid may influence enrollment. Available research also provides insufficient attention to the indirect effects of aid, particularly the ways information and perceptions of financial aid may influence not only college enrollment but also college aspirations and academic preparation (Mundel, 2008). The chapter begins by explaining the need to increase educational attainment, the ways inadequate finances limit educational attainment, and the role of financial aid in addressing these financial barriers. Then the characteristics of student financial aid programs are described and what is known from existing research about the effects of financial aid on college-related behaviors is summarized. A conceptual model for understanding the ways "context" may influence the relationship between financial aid and college enrollment is proposed. Building on this framework, the chapter concludes by offering questions to guide future research, as well as recommendations for fruitful research strategies.

The Importance of Increasing Educational Attainment

Improving college enrollment and degree attainment is critical to ensuring the nation's continued economic and social prosperity as a growing share of jobs need workers with a college education. The United States Department of Labor's Bureau of Labor Statistics (BLS, 2003) projects that, on average, employment in occupations that generally require a bachelor's or associate's degree will increase faster than employment in other occupations. Jobs generally requiring a college degree comprised 29% of all jobs in 2000 and are expected to account for 42% of projected new job growth during the coming decade. BLS (2003) also predicts that 12 of the 20 fastest growing occupations typically require a bachelor's or associate's degree. Analyses of data from the Census Bureau and Current Population Survey show that 69% of white-collar office workers, the largest, fastest-growing, and among the highest-paying categories of employment, had at least some college education in 2001, up from 37% in 1973 (Carnevale & Desrochers, 2003). Moreover, although the number of frontline factory jobs declined by 21 million between 1959 and 2001, the remaining jobs in this sector are increasingly held by workers who have at least some college education (31% in 2001 versus 8% in 1973) (Carnevale & Desrochers, 2003).

Although increasingly important, educational attainment in the United States has fallen behind that of other developed nations (Baum & Ma, 2007; National Center for Public Policy and Higher Education, 2006). The educational attainment of the U.S. adult population has increased over time, as 28% of adults age 25 and older in the U.S. held at least a bachelor's degree in 2006, up from 26% in 2000 and 21% in 1990 (Baum & Ma, 2007). But, other nations are increasing the educational attainment of their populations at a faster rate (National Center for Public Policy and Higher Education, 2006). Although the quality and focus of available postsecondary education varies across nations, the rate of first-time enrollment into programs that lead to a traditional college degree (i.e., "tertiary-A programs") is now lower in the United States than in New Zealand, Sweden, Iceland, Finland, Poland, Australia, Norway, and Hungary (Organization for Economic Co-operation and Development [OECD], 2006). The OECD predicts that, because the United States is experiencing both slower enrollment and lower rates of college completion than some other nations, the share of college graduates in OECD nations produced by the United States will decline over the next decade.

Recognizing these trends, in a nationally-televised, prime-time address to a joint session of Congress on February 24, 2009, President Barack Obama presented an ambitious goal: "By 2020, America will once again have the highest proportion of college graduates in the world." Along the same lines, Lumina Foundation for Education (2009) has a goal of increasing the percentage of young adults in the United States who have attained an associate's or bachelor's degree from the current 40% to 60% by 2025. The first goal in the State Higher Education Executive Officers' (SHEEO, 2008) "national agenda for higher education" is to increase the percentage of young adults who earn at least an associate's degree to 55% by 2025, which would require producing an additional three million degrees each year between now and 2025 (SHEEO, 2008). The College Board's Commission on Access, Admissions, and Success in Higher Education (2008) embraces this goal, promising to annually report progress toward achieving it.

One Approach to Increasing Attainment: Eliminate Financial Barriers to Enrollment

One area of opportunity for raising the nation's production of degree recipients is the population of students who are academically prepared for college but do not attend. The Advisory Committee on Student Financial Assistance (2006) estimates that between 2000 and 2010 1.4–2.4 million students from low- and middle-income families will be academically qualified for college but will not complete a bachelor's degree because of insufficient financial resources.

Although inadequate academic preparation and other forces also play a role (Adelman, 1999, 2006; Perna, 2005, 2006a), data and research consistently demonstrate that money is a primary deterrent for academically-qualified students who do not enroll in college (Hahn & Price, 2008; Perna, 2006a; St. John, 2003). The positive relationship between college enrollment and family income persists even though postsecondary educational participation rates have increased since the mid-1980s regardless of family income (Baum & Ma, 2007). The magnitude of the gap has fluctuated, but over this period college enrollment rates have been at least 25–30% points lower for high school graduates in the lowest family income quintile than for those in the highest quintile (Baum & Ma, 2007). College choices are also stratified by family income, as students from lower-income families who enroll in college are relatively concentrated in public 2-year and private for-profit institutions and underrepresented at public and private 4-year doctoral-granting universities (Baum & Ma, 2007). In 2003–2004, dependent undergraduates with family incomes below $20,000 represented 26% of all dependent undergraduates attending private for-profit institutions and 16% of those attending public 2-year colleges, but only 10% of dependent undergraduates attending public and private 4-year doctoral-granting institutions (Baum & Ma, 2007).

The positive relationship between family income and college enrollment persists even after controlling for differences in academic achievement. Only 29% of 1988 eighth graders in the highest quartile of math achievement and lowest quartile of socioeconomic status had attained at least a bachelor's degree within 8 years of their scheduled high school graduation, compared with 74% of those in the highest quartile of math achievement but highest quartile of socioeconomic status (Baum & Ma, 2007). Family income is also positively related to educational attainment among students with the highest SAT scores. Among dependent undergraduates with SAT scores in the top quartile (i.e., 1,100 or higher) who first enrolled full-time in a 4-year college in 1995, only 71% of those with family incomes below $40,000, but 86% of those with family incomes above $70,000, had completed at least a bachelor's degree by 2001 (Baum & Ma, 2007).

The Role of Financial Aid in Eliminating Financial Barriers to Enrollment

Each year federal and state governments, as well as colleges and universities, foundations and other organizations, invest substantial resources in programs designed to eliminate financial barriers to college enrollment. In 2007–2008 alone, students nationwide received more than $96 billion in federally-supported financial aid, and more than $162.5 billion in aid from all sources, to offset postsecondary educational expenses (College Board, 2008a). In 2007–2008, two-thirds (66%) of all undergraduates received some type or amount of financial aid; for these recipients the average award was $9,100 (Wei et al., 2009).

The continued stratification of college opportunity even for academically qualified students despite the substantial annual investment of dollars into financial aid programs suggests that either: (1) existing financial aid resources are insufficient to meet students' entire financial need; and/or (2) existing financial aid programs are not constructed or implemented as effectively as possible.

Various indicators support the former explanation. About half of all 2003–2004 undergraduates had some amount of unmet financial need, where unmet need is defined as total price of attendance less expected family contribution and all types of financial aid; the average amount of unmet financial need for undergraduates in 2003–2004 was $5,300 (Berkner & Wei, 2006). Undergraduates with the lowest family incomes are most likely to have some amount of unmet financial need, as the share of dependent undergraduates in 2003–2004 with unmet financial need ranged from 85% for those with family incomes below $20,000 to 12% for those with family incomes of $100,000 or more (Berkner & Wei, 2006). Even at public 2-year colleges, 87% of dependent undergraduates with family incomes below $20,000 averaged $4,500 in unmet financial need (Berkner & Wei, 2006).

Despite the apparent need for additional financial aid resources, however, federal and state governments are challenged to increase their investment in student aid programs. These challenges are typically exacerbated during economic downturns. The National Bureau of Economic Research (2008) determined that the U.S. economy began a recession in December 2007, defining a recession as "a significant decline in economic activity spread across the economy, lasting more than a few months, normally visible in production, employment, real income and other indicators" (p. 1). One consequence of a recession is a decline in government revenues. A December 2008 report from the Center on Budget and Policy Priorities projected that at least 41 states will have mid-year shortfalls in their FY2009 budgets (totaling $42 billion) and projected that nearly all states will have shortfalls in FY2010 (totaling $145 billion) and FY2011 (totaling $180 billion) (McNichol & Lay, 2008).

Most states are required to balance their budgets. As a result, when faced with revenue shortfalls states must utilize reserves, raise taxes, and/or reduce expenditures. Some (e.g., National Center for Public Policy and Higher Education, 2009) have urged states and higher education institutions to avoid responding to economic shortfalls through actions that increase the financial burden of college attendance on students and their families. Nonetheless, in response to shortfalls in their FY2009 budgets, at least 26 states have implemented or are considering reductions for higher education (McNichol & Lay, 2008). State budget shortfalls typically have a disproportionately negative effect on state appropriations for public higher education institutions, as higher education has historically served as a "balance wheel" in state budgets (Hovey, 1999). State appropriations for higher education are especially vulnerable in times of revenue shortfalls, as many legislators believe that colleges and universities have access to alternative sources of revenue, including tuition and fees, and may reduce personnel expenditures and realize other cost savings more easily than other state agencies (Lasher & Sullivan, 2004).

At the same time, federal and state governments are not only experiencing revenue shortfalls but also increasingly calling for accountability in the use of available resources. The federal government now requires that "effectiveness" be considered in decisions about the funding and management of federal programs. Reflecting the perspective that "federal programs should receive taxpayer dollars only when they prove they achieve results," the U. S. Office of Management of Budget (2003) now rates federal programs as effective, moderately effective, adequate, or ineffective using the Program Assessment Rating Tool (PART). The PART evaluation produces an overall rating of effectiveness based on program performance in four areas: purpose and design (20% of total score), strategic planning (10% of total score), management (20% of total), and results and accountability (50% of total). Results and accountability must be demonstrated by measures of outcomes, outputs, and efficiency. Use of the PART ratings has been phased in, beginning with 130 federal programs for the 2003 budget and 234 programs for 2004, and will include all programs by 2008 (U.S. Office of Management and Budget, 2003). For the FY2009 budget, the Office of Management and Budget (2008, September) designated several student financial aid programs as "adequate" (e.g., Federal Family Education Loans, Federal Pell Grants, William D. Ford Direct Student Loans), meaning that these programs must "set more ambitious goals, achieve better results, improve accountability or strengthen its management practices" (U.S. Office of Management and Budget, 2009). The Federal Perkins Loan program was designated "ineffective," meaning that the program has not demonstrated "results due to a lack of clarity regarding the program's purpose or goals, poor management, or some other significant weakness" (U.S. Office of Management and Budget, 2009). Still other federal student aid programs (e.g., Byrd Honors Scholarships, Federal Work Study, Leveraging Educational Assistance Partnerships) were categorized as "results not demonstrated," meaning that these programs do not have acceptable performance goals or data to assess performance (U.S. Office of Management and Budget, 2008).

Characteristics of Student Financial Aid

A first step toward developing a more complete understanding of the effects of financial aid on students' college enrollment and how these effects may be mediated by context is to consider the complexities of available aid programs. Four relevant dimensions of student financial aid are: the source, the form of aid, goals, and eligibility criteria.

Source

Financial aid is available from many sources. In 2007–2008, about three-fourths of all student aid was awarded to undergraduates ($106.7 billion of $143.4 billion) rather than graduate or professional students; about two-thirds of this aid was awarded through federal programs (College Board, 2008a). Other providers of financial aid are colleges and universities (21% of all aid to undergraduates in 2007–2008), state governments (7%), and private organizations and employers (7%) (College Board, 2008a). In 2007–2008, 47% of all undergraduates received some type or amount of federal aid, 17.5% received some amount of state aid, and 21% received some amount of institutional aid (Wei et al., 2009).

With a few recent exceptions (e.g., Tebbs & Turner, 2006; Perna, 2008a), most research focuses on federal and state grants and federal loans with relatively little attention to understanding the effects on enrollment of scholarships from colleges and universities and other non-governmental sources (corporations, foundations, civic and community organizations and churches). Aid from these other sources may be substantial, as suggested by one electronic provider's claim of having a database of "1.3 million scholarships worth over $3 billion" (Fastweb, 2009).

Form of Aid

Student financial aid comes in many different forms, including loans, grants, work-study, and tax credits and deductions (Hearn, 2001). The annual growth rate in loans, including non-federal loans, to undergraduates has exceeded the annual growth rate in grants to undergraduates since 1991–1992 (College Board, 2008a). As a result, loans represented 49% of all aid (including non-federal loans) received by undergraduates in 2007–2008, up from about 32% in 1991–1992 (College Board, 2008a). Colleges and universities are the largest source of aid in the form of grants, as 42% of all grant aid in 2007–2008 was from colleges and universities, 31% was from federal grants (i.e., federal Pell grants and other federal grant programs), 15% was from private and employer grants, and 12% from state grants (College Board, 2008a). About 6% of all aid to undergraduates in 2007–2008 was in the form of federal education tax credits (e.g., Hope and Lifetime Learning tax credits) and tax deductions, and 1% was in the form of federal work-study (College Board, 2008a). Looked at another way, in 2007–2008, 39% of all undergraduates received student aid in the form of loans, 52% in the form of grants, 7% in the form of work-study, and 2% in the form of veterans benefits (Wei et al., 2009). The average loan amount for those who received loans ($7,100) was higher than the average grant amount for those who received grants ($4,900) (Wei et al., 2009).

Goals of Aid Programs

Student financial aid programs are designed to achieve a range of goals (Hearn, 2001; Perna, Rowan-Kenyon, Bell, Li, & Thomas, 2008). Based on his examination of federally-sponsored financial aid programs, Hearn concluded that federal aid policies lack "philosophical coherence," as reflected by the wide array of distinct goals, including promoting access for low-income students, improving college affordability for middle-income students, rewarding achievement, advancing economic development, and encouraging human capital investment. Perhaps reflecting the absence of "well-considered patterns of policy development" for federal student aid programs, Hearn also observed that taken together, federal student aid policies lack "programmatic clarity and distinctiveness." In other words, based on his review of the literature, Hearn concluded that, "instead of an array of clearly discrete programmatic efforts addressing in distinctive fashion a set of overarching policy objectives, constituents for the programs . . . confront an array of overlapping efforts with rather vaguely differentiated objectives" (p. 270).

Similarly, based on a review of programs sponsored by the federal government and five states (California, Florida, Georgia, Maryland, and Pennsylvania), another study (Perna et al., 2008) identified distinctive state approaches to college-enrollment programs. Even for just these five states, the analyses showed variations in the extent to which college-enrollment programs include attention to addressing financial barriers and/or other barriers to college, recognize the role of schools in promoting students' college enrollment, limit eligibility for aid based on financial need and/or academic achievement, and attempt to influence students' decision to enroll in college versus their choice of institution to attend or some other outcome. Along the same lines, McDonough and colleagues (2007) concluded from their review of grant programs in 11 states that state approaches to financial aid vary in ways that reflect a state's policy goals and objectives and that these variations likely have differential effects on college access and attainment.

Eligibility Criteria

Differences in program goals are manifest in part by differences in eligibility criteria, particularly the relative importance of measures of financial need and/or academic achievement. Over the past decade, the share of state financial aid awarded based on criteria other than financial need has increased substantially (College Board, 2008a). Between 1996–1997 and 2006–2007, the amount of non-need-based state grant aid awarded to undergraduates increased in constant dollars by 250%, while the amount of need-based state grant aid to undergraduates increased by only 59% (College Board, 2008a). Some states consider both financial need and academic achievement; 18% of all need-based state grant aid awarded in 2006–2007 also included academic criteria (College Board,

2008a). Although the majority of state grant aid is still need-based, and need-based state aid continues to increase annually, the faster rate of growth for merit- than need-based state aid raises concerns about the extent to which scarce public resources are being invested in ways that increase financial access for students from low-income families.

Summary of Current Knowledge Regarding the Effects of Financial Aid on College Enrollment

Others have provided outstanding reviews of research examining the effects of financial aid on college enrollment. Most notably, the Rethinking Student Financial Aid project sponsored by the College Board recently issued recommendations for reforming federal student aid along with a 220-page review entitled, "The Effectiveness of Student Aid Policies: What the Research Tells Us" (Baum, McPherson, & Steele, 2008). Several conclusions may be drawn from the Rethinking Student Aid literature reviews (Baum et al., 2008) and other relevant sources identified below.

First, the effects of student financial aid on college enrollment vary based on the type of aid. Based on their review of research examining the effectiveness of student financial aid, Baum and McPherson (2008) concluded that existing research devotes "strikingly uneven" attention to the effects on student outcomes of different types of aid programs (p. 5). Nonetheless, research consistently shows that grants promote college enrollment, especially for students from low-income families (Avery & Hoxby, 2004; Heller, 1997; Kane, 1999; Mundel, 2008). In contrast, while some studies (e.g., Avery & Hoxby, 2004) suggest that an offer of loans is positively related to enrollment net of other variables, Heller (2008) concluded that prior research generally shows loans to have minimal effect on college access and success. Although some research has examined the effects of work-study on student persistence in college (e.g., Pascarella & Terenzini, 2005; St. John, 2003), little is known about the effects of work-study on students' college enrollment. In one of the few available studies, Avery and Hoxby (2004) found that, among high-ability high school seniors nationwide, the amount of work-study offered was positively related to the likelihood of enrolling after controlling for other student and institutional characteristics. The small number of available studies suggests that federal tax policies, including tax credits, deductions for higher education expenses and student loan interest, and tax-preferred savings programs, are unrelated to postsecondary access and choice (Long, 2004b; Reschovsky, 2008).

Second, research suggests that the effects of financial aid on college enrollment depend on a student's family income and race/ethnicity (Avery & Hoxby, 2004; Heller, 1997; Kane, 1999; Mundel, 2008). Specifically, research consistently shows that changes in tuition and financial aid have a larger effect on college enrollment for students from lower-income families than higher-income families and for African Americans and Hispanics than for Whites (Avery & Hoxby, 2004; Heller, 1997; Kane, 1999; Long, 2004a). Some evidence suggests that the effects of financial aid on students' choice of institution to attend also vary by race. Kim (2004) found that, net of other variables, receiving grants was associated with a higher probability of attending the first-choice institution for Whites, and receiving loans was positively related to attendance for Asians, while neither grants nor loans were related to the likelihood of attending the first choice institution for Blacks or Hispanics (Kim, 2004).

Nonetheless, although suggesting relationships between financial aid and college enrollment, existing research has several limitations. One limitation, as noted by others (e.g., Mundel, 2008; Heller, 2008), is that, because of methodological restrictions, existing research does not determine student outcomes in absence of the aid program.

A second limitation is that most research focuses on the relationship between a specific financial aid program and one college-related outcome, without considering how the broader context of student financial aid programs may mediate this relationship. This narrow focus is consistent with the goal of understanding whether a particular program "works." However, research that does not consider the broader financial aid context may generate misleading conclusions. For example, in his review of research on the effects of loans on student outcomes, Heller (2008) recognizes the importance of considering the financial aid context when interpreting the results of available research.

Specifically, Heller concludes that, although research generally finds that loans have a limited effect on college enrollment, this finding must be interpreted in light of the availability of grant aid:

> This finding needs to be understood in the context of a financial aid landscape in which many students do not receive sufficient grant aid to pay for college. If grant aid were proportionally higher, then loans might provide more of a positive impact on college participation. But absent sufficient grant aid, simply piling on higher amounts of borrowing to students with large levels of unmet financial need may not be an effective vehicle for getting them to college (p. 49).

Similarly, Reschovsky (2008) concludes from his literature review that efforts to understand the effects of a specific federal tax policy on college outcomes are complicated by "the complex interactions among and between deductions, credits, subsidized savings plans, and direct higher education subsidy programs" (p. 76).

A third limitation is the absence of attention to the ways other aspects of context may mediate the relationship between student aid and college enrollment. Efforts to isolate the effects of a particular financial aid program on college enrollment should recognize the role of other policies aimed at promoting college enrollment. A few recent studies illustrate the ways multiple aspects of the state context come together to improve students' college enrollment. For example, in an exploration of the forces that contributed to the substantial increase in college enrollment and other college-related outcomes in Indiana over the past two decades, Erisman and Del Rios (2008) concluded that Indiana's success was driven by a commitment to, and progress toward attaining, four goals: (1) improving high school students' academic readiness for college by making the college preparatory curriculum the "default" for all high school students; (2) increasing college affordability especially for low-income students; (3) increasing the diversification of the state higher education system by expanding the role of community colleges; and (4) promoting college success by rewarding institutions for student outcomes and developing policies to facilitate transfers across institutions in the state. Efforts to improve college affordability included attention to the cost of public higher education institutions, availability of need-based state grants (i.e., Frank O'Bannon Grants), dissemination of information about the availability of financial aid (e.g., Learn More Indiana website), early commitment of financial aid and academic and social supports through the Twenty-first Century Scholars Program, and establishment of the Part-Time Grant program to promote enrollment of non-traditional students (Erisman & Del Rios, 2008).

Other analyses, using different methods, also suggest the need to consider how the state policy environment and other state characteristics may mediate the effects of any particular aid program on enrollment. Using interrupted time-series analyses of data from the Integrated Postsecondary Education Data System (IPEDS), Orsuwan and Heck (2009) found that state merit aid was inversely related to the percentage of freshmen who attended out-of-state colleges and universities. But, the magnitude of the relationship depended on other characteristics of the state, including whether the state also adopted a prepaid tuition program and tuition rates at the state's public flagship university relative to tuition at public flagship universities nationwide (Orsuwan & Heck, 2009).

A fourth limitation of available research is the failure to consider how the effects of aid may be mediated by characteristics of individual students and their families, such as what students and their families know about student aid. Existing research tends to examine the effects of actual amounts of aid on student enrollment, with little consideration of students' knowledge or perceptions of the aid. Despite the availability of financial aid, many reports document the absence of accurate knowledge of financial aid among high school students and their families (e.g., Chan & Cochrane, 2008; Grodsky & Jones, 2004; Horn, Chen & Chapman, 2003; Ikenberry & Hartle, 1998). National surveys consistently show that most adults, parents, and students are uninformed or poorly informed about college prices and financial aid (Grodsky & Jones, 2004; Horn et al., 2003; Ikenberry & Hartle, 1998). Levels of awareness and understanding of college prices and financial aid are particularly low among Latino students and parents (Immerwahr, 2003; Tomás Rivera Policy Institute, 2004).

A related limitation is that available research typically considers only the direct effects of a financial aid award on enrollment, without examining how knowledge or perceptions of financial aid may indirectly promote college enrollment. As others (e.g., Fitzgerald, 2006; Paulsen & St. John, 2002) have argued, financial aid may promote college access not only directly by reducing or eliminating financial barriers at the time of college entry but also indirectly by encouraging students to engage in other college-related behaviors, including other stages of the college-enrollment process, because they know aid will be available.

Based on their review and synthesis of prior research, Hossler and Gallagher (1987) concluded that the three stages of the college process are predisposition, search, and choice. In the first stage, students become predisposed toward or interested in attending college as they develop educational and occupational aspirations (Hossler & Gallagher, 1987; Terenzini, Cabrera, & Bernal, 2001). In the second stage, students search for information about colleges (Hossler & Gallagher, 1987; Terenzini et al., 2001). While still less frequently researched than the other two stages, researchers who have examined this stage typically operationalize "search" in terms of the sources of college-related information that students and parents use (e.g., Hossler, Schmit, & Vesper, 1999) and/or the number of colleges that students consider or to which they apply (e.g., Hossler et al., 1999; Hurtado, Inkelas, Briggs, & Rhee, 1997). In the third stage, students decide to enroll in a particular college or university. Little is known about the timing of these three stages for non-traditional enrollment. But, for "traditional" college enrollment (i.e., enrollment into college immediately after graduating from high school), predisposition typically occurs between the 7th and 10th grades, search during the 10th–12th grades, and choice during the 11th and 12th grades (Hossler et al., 1999; Terenzini et al., 2001).

Finally, existing research does not devote sufficient attention to the ways that student and family demographic and cultural characteristics may mediate the effects of aid on college enrollment. As an example, research demonstrates that responsiveness to aid varies across groups based on race/ethnicity and family income (Avery & Hoxby, 2004; Heller, 1997; Kane, 1999; Mundel, 2008), but does not explain why these differences occur. Potential explanations may include cultural differences in perceptions of aid, as well as differences across groups in access to resources that promote knowledge and understanding of financial aid.

In short, while providing a baseline of knowledge, existing research on the effects of student financial aid on college enrollment provides insufficient attention to the context in which the programs are implemented or the ways various dimensions of context may mediate the effects of aid on enrollment. Moreover, existing research does not consider the ways financial aid may indirectly promote college enrollment. Addressing the limitations of prior research requires the use of a conceptual model that explicitly considers the role of context. The following section offers a potential conceptual model.

Conceptual Framework for Understanding the Role of Context

In earlier work (Perna, 2006a), I drew on a review and synthesis of prior research to propose a multi-layered conceptual model of college enrollment. This prior work identified financial aid as one force that contributes to college enrollment but did not focus specifically on the relationship between aid and enrollment. Drawing on this earlier work as well as St. John's (2003) balanced access model, this chapter argues that the relationship between financial aid and college enrollment is mediated by various dimensions of context. Like "the student choice construct" (Paulsen & St. John, 2002; St. John, Asker, & Hu, 2001), the conceptual model assumes that college enrollment decisions reflect an individual's "situated context" and that pathways to college enrollment differ in ways that reflect the diversity in individual circumstances, as well as the ways that individual circumstances serve to define and constrain students' college opportunities.

Drawing on the economic theory of human capital, the model assumes that students make decisions about college enrollment based on an assessment of the lifetime benefits and costs of enrollment relative to alternative choices (Perna, 2006a). Consistent with this economic approach, students are assumed to make choices that maximize their utility. Reflecting sociological theoretical perspectives, the model also assumes that students' college enrollment decisions occur within multiple layers of context. The four nested contextual layers proposed in the model are: students and their families; K-12 schools; higher education institutions; and the broader societal, economic, and policy context (Perna, 2006a).

The conceptual model is designed in part to illustrate the multiple ways policymakers may intervene to promote college enrollment (Perna, 2006a). By specifying linkages between policies and college-related outcomes, St. John's (2003) balanced access model provides additional insights into the ways public policy interventions such as student financial aid shape college enrollment behavior. In his framework for assessing the influence of policy on educational opportunity, St. John identifies several key steps in the educational attainment process: K-12 attainment and achievement, postsecondary transitions and access, undergraduate and graduate student outcomes, and individual development and educational attainment. St. John's framework posits that K-12 policies pertaining to schooling and school reform (e.g., standards and testing) shape K-12 attainment and achievement, policy interventions (e.g., financial aid policy, postsecondary information, and affirmative action) shape postsecondary transitions and access, and college and university policies (e.g., financial and academic strategies) shape undergraduate and graduate student outcomes. The relationship between financial aid and college enrollment may be understood from both a macro- and micro-economic perspective. Figure 18.1 shows how the two perspectives may be considered together.

Financial Aid as a Lever for Increasing Student Demand for Higher Education (Macro-Level)

At the macro-level (i.e., a public sector finance perspective), student financial aid is conceptualized as a "lever" that may be used to intervene in the "market" for higher education with the goal of promoting college-related outcomes (Paulsen, 2001a). More specifically, student financial aid policies are designed to increase students' demand for higher education, and thus their college enrollment, by increasing the supply of resources that students have available to invest in higher education (Paulsen, 2001a).

Economists argue that government intervention in the higher education market, including intervention in the form of student financial aid, is warranted for at least four reasons (Kane, 1999; Paulsen, 2001a). First, individual participants do not capture all of the benefits that higher education produces, as the benefits "spillover" to non-participants. Because individuals make enrollment decisions based on an assessment of only the individual benefits without considering the benefits that accrue to society, the level of investment in higher education that would occur without market intervention is less than optimal (Paulsen, 2001a; Steuerle, 2001). By providing student financial aid

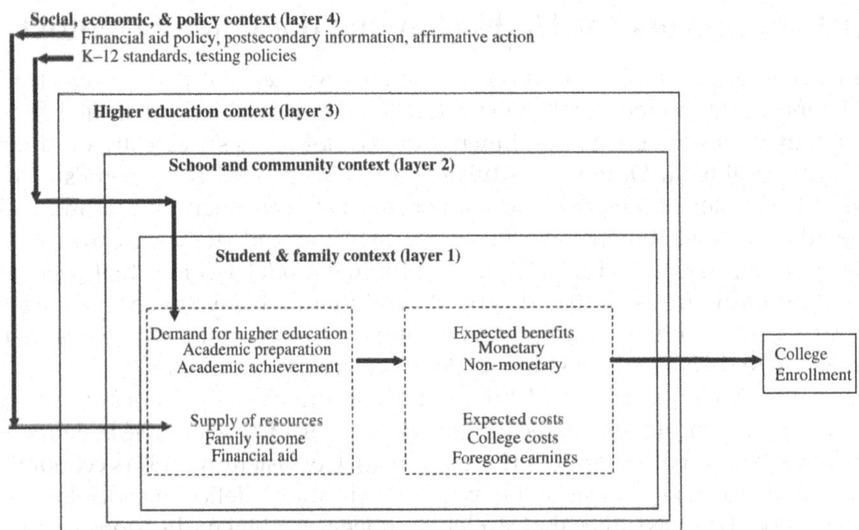

Figure 18.1 Conceptual model of student college enrollment with policy linkages.
Source: Perna et al., 2008.

to reduce the costs of enrollment to individual participants, governments attempt to address this tendency to under-invest in higher education and maximize the societal benefits of higher education (Hansen & Weisbrod, 1969). The societal benefits of higher education are well-documented (Baum & Ma, 2007; Bowen, 1997; Institute for Higher Education Policy, 1998), and include increased economic productivity, tax revenues, and community and civic engagement, as well as reduced crime rates and dependence on public welfare.

Government-sponsored financial aid programs, particularly student loan programs, are also designed to correct for a second market failure: the inability of participants to use their post-higher education level of human capital as collateral against which to borrow funds needed to pay educational prices (Kane, 1999; Paulsen, 2001a). In the absence of market intervention, private capital markets fail to provide funds students need to pay college prices, again resulting in an under-investment in higher education. Guaranteed student loan programs address this limitation by providing incentives for lenders to make funds available for students to borrow and allocating funds to students in the form of grants.

A third justification for government intervention is that individuals not only lack perfect information about college opportunities but also have differential access to such information (Kane, 1999). As with some other goods (e.g., restaurant meals, shoes), buyers of higher education are unable to obtain complete information about the "product" until they "experience" it (Winston, 1999). Potential first-generation college students, a disproportionate percentage of whom are from low-income families and are Black or Hispanic (National Center for Education Statistics, 2001), are likely to be particularly disadvantaged by this characteristic of higher education markets since they cannot rely on their parents for relevant information. Governments may address this market failure by disseminating information about the availability of financial aid programs.

Government intervention in the higher education market is also warranted when the public supports a reduction in inequities across groups (Paulsen, 2001a). Paulsen argues that public polices that increase higher education enrollment are a more efficient approach to equalizing incomes than other government interventions including direct transfers to low-income individuals or those from underrepresented racial/ethnic groups. By building human capital, student aid and other policies that promote college enrollment enable individuals to earn higher incomes throughout their lifetimes, thereby eliminating the need for the public sector to provide annual income subsidies to these individuals.

Government-sponsored student aid programs are typically designed to directly influence students' demand for college enrollment by increasing the supply of resources they have available to pay college prices (Paulsen, 2001a). One review revealed that, although the federal and state governments have distinct approaches to college-enrollment policy, 89% of all college-enrollment policies sponsored by the federal government and five selected states (California, Florida, Georgia, Maryland, and Pennsylvania) include only a financial component and are designed to impact students' college enrollment directly (Perna et al., 2008). For example, with Pell Grants the federal government aims to directly increase low-income students' college enrollment by providing need-based grants that reduce the price of attending college. Only a minority of programs include components to address other barriers to college enrollment (e.g., academic preparation and information), and relatively few programs explicitly recognize the role of high schools in implementing financial aid programs.

Financial Aid as a Mechanism for Increasing a Student's Supply of Resources (Micro-Level)

At the micro-economic level, human capital theory assumes that students decide to enroll in college by comparing the lifetime benefits and costs for all alternatives and then selecting the alternative (e.g., college, work) that maximizes the student's utility (Becker, 1993; Paulsen, 2001b). This perspective predicts that the provision of financial aid directly to students will increase the supply of resources a student and his/her family have to pay for college and consequently increase the likelihood a student will conclude the benefits of attending college outweigh the costs.

Limitations of Human Capital Theory

Nonetheless, as others have noted (e.g., Long, 2009; Paulsen, 2001b; Perna, 2006a), although conceptually appealing human capital theory alone is insufficient for completely understanding how financial aid influences students' college enrollment decisions. First, human capital models do not explain several inconsistencies in students' responses to financial aid (Long, 2009). For example, human capital models do not explain why students "react differently to various forms of financial aid and tuition changes, even if the economic value of each is the same" (Heller, 1997, p. 632). Human capital theory also does not explain why college enrollment is influenced by non-pecuniary aspects of financial aid, including whether the aid is labeled "grant" or "scholarship" or whether the grant aid is frontloaded (Avery & Hoxby, 2004).

A second limitation is that, although acknowledging differences in students' preferences for different types of aid, human capital theory does not explore how or why preferences are formed (Manski, 2009). A rational human capital investment model assumes that, even when the expected benefits and costs are the same, two individuals may make different college choices because of differences in their preferences, tolerance for risk, and uncertainty (DesJardins & Toutkoushian, 2005). But, human capital theory does not explore why preferences, tastes, and expectations differ across groups (DesJardins & Toutkoushian, 2005).

Therefore, although useful for conceptualizing the effects of costs and benefits on students' college enrollment behaviors, traditional human capital approaches alone are insufficient for understanding inconsistencies in college-enrollment decision-making or how students develop perceptions or understandings of financial aid. Drawing on other frameworks provides additional insights.

Other Theories

Both behavioral economics and psychological approaches to decision making assume that, because of informational and computational constraints on information processing capacities, individuals adopt such strategies as satisficing or bounded rationality (Hogarth, 1987; Long, 2009). Thus, because of cognitive limitations, individuals make decisions that are bounded by time and resource constraints.

Drawing on a sociological perspective, McDonough (1997) uses Bourdieu's notion of habitus to illustrate the ways that bounded rationality influences college-related decision making. This perspective assumes that college-related decisions reflect an individual's habitus, or the internalized system of thoughts, beliefs, and perceptions that is acquired from the immediate environment. Rather than consider all possible alternatives, habitus defines and limits the alternatives that are considered, how different alternatives are perceived and valued, and the choices that are made (McDonough, 1997; Paulsen & St. John, 2002). These alternatives are defined and delimited by the social, organizational, and cultural contexts in which individuals are embedded, including class-based values and the organizational habitus of high school attended (McDonough, 1997). According to McDonough, the notion of organizational habitus considers both the availability of resources and structures within a high school to promote college enrollment, as well as the underlying norms and expectations for college enrollment at a school, norms and expectations that reflect class-based values about college-going.

Other sociological theories, such as cultural and social capital, may also be useful for understanding differences in students' perceptions and use of financial aid. Consideration of cultural and social capital provides a more complete assessment of the resources that students have available from their social contexts to inform college-related decisions (McDonough, 1997). Cultural capital refers to the system of attributes, such as language skills, cultural knowledge, and mannerisms, that is derived, in part, from one's parents and that defines an individual's class status (Bourdieu, 1986; Bourdieu & Passeron, 1977). Members of the dominant class possess the most economically and symbolically valued kinds of cultural capital (Bourdieu & Passeron, 1977; McDonough, 1997). McDonough uses the notion of "entitlement" to further understand the role of cultural capital in college-going decisions. For example, students attending elite private high schools feel "entitled" to highly-selective colleges while students attending urban high schools in working-class neighborhoods feel "entitled" to community colleges (McDonough, 1997).

Social capital focuses on social networks and the ways social networks and connections are sustained (Morrow, 1999). In his comprehensive assessment of the origins and uses of social capital, Portes (1998) noted that social capital is acquired through an individual's relationships with other individuals, particularly through membership in social networks and other social structures. Coleman's (1988) approach stresses the role of social capital in communicating the norms, trust, authority, and social controls that an individual must understand and adopt in order to succeed. Whereas Coleman's perspective suggests that parents play a primary role in promoting the status attainment of their children, Bourdieu's approach describes the restrictions that structural barriers to institutional resources, in the form of differential access across racial/ethnic, gender, and other groups, impose (Dika & Singh, 2002). According to Bourdieu (1986), the amount of social capital to which an individual may gain access through social networks and relationships depends on the size of the networks as well as the amounts of economic, cultural, and social capital that individuals in the network possess.

The Importance of Context in Understanding the Effects of Aid on Enrollment

Among other conclusions, these theories and the research that tests them illustrate the ways that various aspects of "context" influence postsecondary access and choice. Students make postsecondary access and choice decisions largely determined by the norms and values embedded within a student's family and high school, as well as a broader economic, social, and policy context (Perna, 2006a). Greater attention to context may help identify the structures and processes that define and delimit students' perceptions and use of financial aid in college-enrollment decisions. These understandings, in turn, may suggest ways to improve the construction, implementation, and/or marketing of student financial aid programs to more effectively promote enrollment of all students.

Other researchers assert the benefits of considering context when examining students' college-related behaviors (e.g., Orsuwan & Heck, 2009; Tierney & Colyar, 2006). McDonough, Calderone, and Purdy (2007) argue that attention to context may be especially useful for understanding inconsistencies in students' financial aid-related decisions:

> Reinterpreting affordability as a localized, highly contextualized, deliberative process sheds potential light on why low-income students fail to claim state and federal aid even when they qualify, as well as why large-scale attempts to disseminate financial aid information, streamline the FAFSA process, and improve practitioner knowledge related to financial aid have resulted in minimal improvements to the college-financing perceptions of those most in need (pp. 5–6).

With this conceptual model as a guide, the following section suggests the ways that the student and family, school, higher education, and broader economic, social, and policy contexts may mediate the relationship between student financial aid and college enrollment.

Applying the Conceptual Model to Understanding the Ways the Effects of Aid on College Enrollment are Mediated by Context

The Student and Family Context

An emerging body of research suggests that perceptions of aid vary by race/ethnicity and family income (Cunningham & Santiago, 2008; Hahn & Price, 2008; Heller, 2008; Linsenmeier, Rosen, & Rouse, 2006; Perna, 2008b). Differences across groups in willingness to borrow are typically inferred based on students' actual use of loans. For example, using regression discontinuity and difference-in-difference analyses, Linsenmeier et al. (2006) found that an institution's decision to eliminate loans from financial aid packages for low-income students increased the likelihood of enrollment for low-income, minority students but was unrelated to the likelihood of enrollment for low-income students overall. The authors speculated that replacing loans with grants had a greater effect on enrollment for minority than non-minority applicants because minority students are more averse to debt than non-minority students.

Research also suggests that willingness to borrow varies by family income, although the nature of the relationship is ambiguous. Some descriptive (e.g., Baum & O'Malley, 2003; Perna, 2008b) and multivariate (e.g., Callender & Jackson, 2005; Linsenmeier et al., 2006) analyses find that students from low-income families are less willing than other students to borrow, while multivariate analyses (e.g., Christou & Haliassos, 2006; Eckel, Johnson, Montmarquette, & Rojas, 2007) show that students from low-income families are more likely than other students to borrow.

Several aspects of the student and family context may help explain differences across racial/ethnic and family income groups in perceptions of aid, as well as differences in the effects of aid on enrollment. One potentially relevant dimension of the student and family context pertains to social values and cultural norms about loans (Cunningham & Santiago, 2008; Heller, 2008). For example, using data from the 2004 National Postsecondary Student Aid Survey and BPS:04/06, Cunningham and Santiago (2008) found that minority students, especially Asian and Hispanic students, were more likely than other students to have at least $2,000 in unmet financial need but low loan amounts. Using focus groups to probe this finding, Cunningham and Santiago concluded that Asian and Hispanic students may be less willing to borrow, at least in part, because of cultural norms against borrowing.

A second potentially relevant dimension for understanding differences in the use and perceptions of aid may pertain to a family's prior experience with financial aid, including the experiences of parents and older children (Long, 2009; McDonough, 1997; Perna, 2008b). Consistent with cultural and social capital theories, data from one exploratory study show that students' perceptions of loans are closely related to their parents' views (Perna, 2008b).

A related dimension of the student and family context pertains to the relative roles of students and their families in paying college prices (Long, 2009; Manski, 2009; Perna, 2006b). An exploratory study suggests that some students do not apply for available scholarships (Perna, 2008a) or learn the specifics of student financial aid programs (Perna & Steele, in press) when they believe that their parents will fund the costs of their postsecondary education.

Over the past decade, the share of college costs paid by parents has declined, while the share paid by students has increased (Hearn, 2001; Stringer, Cunningham, O'Brien, & Merisotis, 1998). Although many factors (e.g., increased consumer debt, inadequate savings, slow personal growth) may contribute, one source of the decline in the share of costs covered by parents may be parents' reduced willingness to pay (Stringer et al., 1998).

Some research suggests variations across racial/ethnic and socioeconomic groups in terms of the expected distribution of college costs between parents and students. In her case study analyses of college-related decisions of students attending four high schools, McDonough (1997) found that students in high-SES families typically defer college financing decisions to their parents but that students in low-SES families generally assume responsibility for identifying ways to pay college prices and more explicitly consider college prices and financial aid in college application and enrollment decisions. Using national data and multinomial logit analyses, Steelman and Powell (1993) found that, even after controlling for parents' education, parents' marital status, number of children, and family income, African American, Hispanic, and Asian parents were more likely than White parents to perceive college costs to be the responsibility of parents rather than students. Based on their analyses, Ellwood and Kane (2000) concluded that college enrollment rates may be positively related to family income at least in part because parental willingness to pay college prices increases with family income.

Although most families want to promote their child's educational attainment, the ability of low-income and minority families to do so is often constrained by economic, social, and psychological barriers (Perna, 2004). Barriers to parental involvement may be associated with mother's employment, parents' education, family composition, child care responsibilities, language and culture, and discrimination, as well as a lack of prior experience with college-related processes (Ceja, 2001; Kerbow & Bernhardt, 1993; López, Scribner, & Mahitivanichcha, 2001; Tierney & Auerbach, 2005). In the face of these barriers, some families rely on their children to obtain college-related information (Ceja, 2001; Tomás Rivera Policy Institute, 2004; Tornatzky, Cutler, & Lee, 2002). Children are then responsible not only for acquiring and understanding information about college prices and financial aid, but also for educating their families about this information (Ceja, 2001).

School Context

A central aspect of school context that may mediate the effects of aid on enrollment is the availability of financial aid and other college-related counseling from school staff. Qualitative research illustrates that school counselors play an important role in structuring students' aspirations, plans, and readiness for college (McDonough, 1997, 2004, 2005a, 2005b). Using case study analyses of four high schools in California, McDonough (1997) identified variations across schools not only in the availability of college counseling but also in counselors' assumptions about students' other sources of college-related knowledge, "appropriate" college destinations for students attending the school, and ways to best disseminate college-related information to students.

Research also suggests the role of school counselors in shaping students' perceptions of financial aid (McDonough & Calderone, 2006; Perna, Rowan-Kenyon, Thomas, et al., 2008). Based on her review of available research, McDonough (2004) concluded that students and parents rely on school counselors as a source of information about financial aid (when counselors are available), and that students who talk with "available and trained" school counselors are more knowledgeable about college prices than other students.

Support from high school counselors may be especially important when parents do not have the knowledge, information, prior direct experience, or other resources required to adequately guide their children through college-related processes (Furstenberg, Cook, Eccles, Elder, & Sameroff, 1999; Kerbow & Bernhardt, 1993; McDonough, 1997; Tierney & Auerbach, 2005). Compared to White students and parents, African American, Hispanic, and low-income students and parents appear to be more dependent on high school personnel for information about college (Cabrera & La Nasa, 2001; Ceja, 2001; Freeman, 1997; Horn et al., 2003; Terenzini et al., 2001; Tomás Rivera Policy Institute, 2004; Tornatzky et al., 2002; U. S. GAO, 1990). However, the high schools these students typically attend are generally not equipped to provide support for college admissions-related activities to all students (McDonough, 1997; Rosenbaum, 2001). The availability of college counseling varies across schools not only in terms of actual student-to-counselor ratios, but also in terms of time devoted to college counseling, relationships between school counselors and college admissions staff, and types of counseling services offered, as well as the availability of other school structures to support college counseling, such as a school's mission and norms regarding college-going and degree of college-preparatory curricular focus (McDonough, 1997). The ability of school counselors to engage in college counseling is further limited by the need for counselors to engage in other activities including crisis intervention counseling, developmental counseling, scheduling, test administration, and discipline (Ballard & Murgatroyd, 1999; McDonough, 2005a, 2005b; NACAC, 2006; Venezia & Kirst, 2005). One exploratory study suggests that these resource constraints reduce the availability of counselors for one-on-one meetings, shift the focus of counseling to the needs of the school's "typical" or most "needy" students, and require students and their families to initiate contact with school counselors (Perna, Rowan-Kenyon, Thomas, et al., 2008).

School counselors appear to be especially unavailable and ill-equipped to talk with students about financial aid (McDonough, 2004, 2005a, 2005b). Financial aid training is typically not part of a school counselor's formal education, as college counseling has traditionally been viewed as inconsistent with a counselor's focus on students' mental health (McDonough, 2005a, 2005b). Although counselors typically provide information about financial aid as part of their duties, only one in four counselors responding to a NACAC (2006) survey felt "very prepared" to guide students' borrowing decisions. Counselors are particularly unsure about advising students about the amount to borrow, the optimal type of loan, or the consequences of failing to repay loans (NACAC, 2006).

Other research raises questions about the quality or comprehensiveness of financial aid information school counselors provide. Few counselors appear to systematically disseminate information to students about financial aid (McDonough & Calderone, 2006; Perna, 2008a, 2008b). Drawing on interviews and focus groups with 63 college counselors at urban high schools in southern California, McDonough and Calderone (2006) found that, with a few exceptions, most counselors provided no more than minimal information or assistance to students regarding college financing, most encouraged students to attend low-price institutions (e.g., community colleges) based on their assumptions about students' ability to pay, and some counselors advised students based on the assumption that African American and Latino parents are reluctant to use loans to finance college prices. Similarly, an exploratory study of the forces that contribute to college-going among students attending 15 high schools revealed that high school counselors and teachers provide a range of messages to students about loans, with some discouraging and others encouraging their use (Perna, 2008b).

Higher Education Context

Variations in both the prevalence of institutional grant aid and the criteria for awarding institutional grant aid suggest that colleges and universities may also mediate the effects of financial aid on college enrollment. The share of undergraduates receiving financial aid varies by institutional type. In 2007–2008, 48% of undergraduates attending public 2-year institutions received some type or amount of financial aid, compared with 70% of undergraduates at public 4-year colleges and universities, 87% of undergraduates at private, not-for-profit non-doctorate-granting institutions, and 98% at private for-profit, 2-year or 4-year institutions (Wei et al., 2009). Average amounts of financial aid for recipients also vary by institutional type, ranging from $3,400 at public 2-year institutions, to $10,100 at public 4-year doctorate-granting institutions, to $19,000 at private 4-year doctorate granting institutions (Wei et al., 2009). On average, private 4-year institutions award a higher share of aid to students based on financial need than public 4-year institutions. In 2006–2007, 70% of all institutional grants at private 4-year institutions were awarded based on financial need, compared with only 44% at public 4-year institutions (College Board, 2008a). Public 4-year colleges and universities also tend to devote a larger share of institutional aid to athletic awards than private 4-year colleges and universities (18% versus 6%, on average, in 2006–2007, College Board, 2008a).

Private 4-year colleges and universities charging higher tuition also tend to allocate a higher percentage of institutional grant aid based on financial need than those charging lower tuition, regardless of Carnegie classification (College Board, 2008a). For example, high-tuition private doctoral-granting institutions allocated 80% of their institutional aid based on financial need, while their low-tuition counterparts devoted just 61% (College Board, 2008a). Institutional grants tended to cover a higher percentage of published tuition and fees at lower-priced than higher-priced private institutions (e.g., 34% versus 18% at higher- and lower-priced private baccalaureate colleges) (College Board, 2008a).

Even among highly selective private colleges and universities financial aid and pricing polices vary. In an examination of financial aid records of students attending 28 highly-selective private colleges and universities, Hill, Winston, and Boyd (2005) found that, on average, net prices increased with family income; net-price as a share of median family income ranged from 49% for students in the lowest family income quintile to 21% for students in the 95th percentile of family income. But, the ratio of net price to family income varied substantially, ranging, for the lowest-income students, from 5 to 74% (Hill et al., 2005). At seven of the 28 institutions, net price represented a larger percentage of income for low-income students than for high-income students (Hill et al., 2005).

Social, Economic, and Policy Context

Many aspects of the broader social, economic, and policy context may mediate students' perceptions of aid and the effects of financial aid on enrollment. Two particularly relevant aspects of this broader context are state variations in student financial aid and changes in the characteristics of available financial aid. Variations in student financial aid across states suggest the importance of considering the characteristics of aid programs, as well as other state characteristics, when examining the effects of aid on student outcomes (Perna & Titus, 2004; Orsuwan & Heck, 2009). Changes in the characteristics of financial aid programs over time suggest limitations on the generalizability of findings from prior research (Heller, 2008; Hossler, Ziskin, Sooyeon, Osman, & Gross, 2008).

Variations in State Financial Aid

Research shows that state grant aid is positively related to college enrollment, regardless of whether the aid is awarded based on need or merit. For example, the likelihood of enrolling in any type of postsecondary education within 2 years of graduating from high school and the likelihood of attending an in-state private 4-year or in-state public 4-year college or university increase with the availability of state need-based financial aid (Kane, 1999; Perna & Titus, 2004). Using fixed-effect regression analyses of state-level data from 1992 to 2000, St. John, Musoba, and Chung (2004) found that, after controlling for state demographic and other characteristics, both need-based and non-need-based grants were positive predictors of college enrollment among high school graduates; a $1,000 increase in need-based grants was associated with an 11.5% point increase in college enrollment rates, while a $1,000 increase in non-need-based grant aid was associated with an 8.9% point increase.

Research also suggests that the effects of state merit-aid programs on enrollment vary in ways that reflect the characteristics of the aid program. For example, studies show increases in college enrollment associated with the state merit-aid program in Georgia (Cornwell, Mustard, & Sridhar, 2004; Dynarski, 2000, 2002, 2004) but not in New Mexico (Binder, Ganderton, & Hutchens, 2002). Dynarski (2004) also found that the Georgia HOPE Scholarship has a greater effect on enrollment at public 4-year institutions than at other types of institutions. In a comparison of seven state merit-aid programs, Dynarski (2004) found the largest enrollment effects in Georgia, Kentucky, Louisiana, and Mississippi and the smallest in South Carolina (where the relationship was not statistically significant). The effects of merit-aid programs on racial/ethnic gaps in enrollment also varied across states (Dynarski, 2004). Merit-aid programs in three states had larger effects on enrollment for Blacks and Hispanics than for Whites, thereby reducing racial/ethnic gaps in enrollment. In contrast, the Georgia HOPE Scholarship program had larger effects for Whites than for Blacks and Hispanics, suggesting that the program contributes to the racial/ethnic stratification of enrollment in the state (Dynarski, 2004).

Other research suggests that the effects of state aid on college enrollment may be mediated by other state characteristics. For instance, using interrupted time-series analysis of data from IPEDS, Orsuwan and Heck (2009) concluded that measures of a state's economic and political characteristics mediated the positive effects of a state merit-aid program on the out-migration of college freshmen. Out-migration was positively related to per-capita income and negatively related to the percentage of state education expenditures allocated to higher education. The reduction in out-migration associated with having a state merit-aid program was even larger in states that also had prepaid tuition programs and relatively higher rates of tuition at the state's public flagship institutions than in other states (Orsuwan & Heck, 2009).

Changes in Financial Aid Over Time

The availability and purchasing power of financial aid also likely influence the relationship between aid and enrollment. These types of changes over time stem from several sources. Some occur with the periodic reauthorization of the Higher Education Act of 1965, the authorizing legislation for federal student aid programs. For example, the 2008 reauthorization of the Higher Education Act (aka the Higher Education Opportunity Act) broadened eligibility for the federal Academic Competitiveness and Smart Grants to include students enrolled part-time and in certificate programs (Field, 2008). The 1992 reauthorization included changes that increased the amounts students could borrow and relaxed some aspects of the needs-analysis criteria. These changes led to substantial increases in borrowing and thus limit the generalizability of findings from research examining the use of loans prior to 1992 (Heller, 2008).

Changes in the purchasing power of student financial aid programs have occurred in response to changes in government resources. For example, although the Higher Education Act of 1965 authorizes the Federal Pell Grant program, the federal government must annually appropriate resources for the awards. As result, maximum and average Pell grant awards have fluctuated over the past three decades. In the past decade alone, the maximum Pell grant (in 2007 dollars) rose and fell from $3,504 in 1997–1998, to $4,626 in 2002–2003, to $4,146 in 2006–2007, and $4,310 in 2007–2008 (College Board, 2008a). As another example, in response to funding concerns, Georgia legislators tightened academic eligibility requirements for the Georgia HOPE Scholarship in 2004, effective for students entering college on or after May 1, 2007 (Fisher, 2007). Because of this change, the number of 2007 high school seniors eligible for HOPE declined by about 18,000 (Fisher, 2007).

Changes in economic conditions may restrict the availability of student aid. For example, one implication of the current credit crisis is that 130 fewer lenders offered federal student loans and 31 fewer lenders offered private loans at the start of 2008–2009 than at the start of 2007–2008 (Thomson, 2008). A second implication of the current economic recession and subsequent budget constraints is that some states are seeking to reduce expenditures by restricting the availability of state student aid programs. For example, in December 2008, New Jersey state legislators voted to reduce expenditures for two merit-based state aid programs by making eligibility requirements more restrictive (Giordano, 2008). The changes require high school students to graduate in the top 15% rather than the top 20% of their class in order to receive the NJ STARS scholarship, a program established in 2004 to cover tuition and fees at any New Jersey community college. With the revisions, the scholarship will no longer cover tuition and fees for remedial coursework. The changes also require STARS recipients to graduate from a community college with at least a 3.25 grade point average rather than a 3.0 grade point average to receive NJ STARS II, a scholarship to attend a 4-year public college or university, restrict eligibility for NJ STARS II to students with family incomes below $250,000, and limit the scholarship award from full-tuition to $6,000 per year for students with grade point averages between 3.25 and 3.49 and $7,000 for students with grade point averages above 3.49 (Giordano, 2008).

The purchasing power of financial aid also changes over time due to changes in the price of attendance. Over the past two decades, the sticker price of attending all types of colleges and universities has increased dramatically (College Board, 2008b). Between 1998–1999 and 2008–2009, average tuition and fees increased by 27% at private 4-year colleges and universities, 50% at public 4-year colleges and universities, and 15% at public 2-year colleges and universities after controlling for inflation (College Board, 2008b). The extent to which increases in financial aid have kept pace with increases in tuition has also varied over time. For example, the share of average tuition and fees at public 4-year colleges and universities that is covered by the maximum Pell grant was 50% in 1987–1988, declined to 35% in 1996–1997, rose again in the early 2000s, and fell again to 32% in 2007–2008 (College Board, 2008a).

Questions for Future Research

The proposed conceptual model suggests the ways various aspects of context mediate the relationship between financial aid and students' college-related behaviors. Considering the limitations of prior research described earlier in this chapter, the proposed conceptual model suggests at least five broad questions for future research. Addressing these questions with a conceptual model that explicitly considers the role of context will likely generate insights into how to maximize the effectiveness of available financial aid resources.

How Do Different Types of Aid Separately and Together Influence College Enrollment?

One area for future research is to better understand how different types of aid separately and together influence college enrollment. As described in the review of existing research above, one limitation of most research is the tendency to focus on isolating the effects of only grants or loans, with relatively little attention to the effects on college enrollment of other forms of aid (Baum & McPherson, 2008) or how different forms of aid interact to influence students' college-related behaviors (Orsuwan &

Heck, 2009). The "purest" forms of financial aid are grants and scholarships, i.e., funds that may be used to pay post-secondary educational expenses and do not have to be repaid. About half (50%) of all undergraduates enrolled in 2003–2004 received financial aid in the form of grants; the average amount of grant aid received was $4,000 (Berkner & Wei, 2006).

Other forms of aid, including loans, work-study, and tax credits, have "strings" attached. Unlike grants, loans need to be repaid. Moreover, even within "loans," program terms vary. In 2007–2008, 34% of all loans were federal subsidized Stafford Loans, 31% federal unsubsidized Stafford Loans, 13% federal PLUS loans (for parents of dependent undergraduates), and 23% non-federal loans (College Board, 2008a). The College Board notes that federal loans are a form of aid but non-federal loans are not, as non-federal loans include no interest subsidy and "generally have less favorable terms than federal loans" (p. 9). Unlike non-federal loans, federal Subsidized and Unsubsidized Stafford Loans include a fixed-rate of interest and allow for deferment of repayment until 6 months after graduation. Unlike Unsubsidized Stafford Loans, Subsidized Stafford Loans are awarded based on a student's financial need and include an interest "subsidy," i.e., the federal government, not the student, pays the interest while a student is enrolled at least half-time.

Federal work-study also has "strings," as students must work in designated positions in order to realize the award. A form of campus-based federal aid, eligible colleges and universities may award federal work-study to financially needy students. About 1% of all aid to undergraduates in 2007–2008 was in the form of federal work-study (College Board, 2008a). Other forms of financial aid have increased substantially over the past decade. For example, between 1997–1998 and 2007–2008, total federal grants increased in constant dollars by 79% and total federal loans increased by 70%. In contrast, over this period the total amount of federal work-study dollars awarded to undergraduates has remained virtually unchanged after controlling for inflation (College Board, 2008a).

Federal education tax credits and tuition deductions have characteristics that differentiate them from other forms of aid. Whereas other federal student aid programs (e.g., Pell grants, Stafford Loans, Federal Work-Study) are authorized and periodically reauthorized under the Higher Education Act of 1965, the federal Hope and Lifetime Learning tax credits were established as part of the federal tax code (i.e., the Taxpayer Relief Act of 1997). In 2007–2008, 6% of all aid to undergraduates was in the form of federal education tax credits and tuition deductions (College Board, 2008a). Observers point to several reasons for the absence of an enrollment effect for federal tax policies, including the delay in receiving the award (i.e., in the year after tuition expenses were paid), the failure of tax credits to cover costs of attendance other than tuition and fees (e.g., room, board, books, other educational supplies), the limitation of the credits based on tax liability (i.e., tax credits are not refundable), and the complexity of the programs and tax forms (Long, 2004b; Reschovsky, 2008).

States also offer a range of programs that are designed to increase the resources that students have to pay for college. These programs include not only state-sponsored financial aid programs, but also prepaid tuition and college savings plans, tuition reciprocity agreements with other states, and loan forgiveness programs, among others (Orsuwan & Heck, 2009). Prepaid tuition and college savings plans are tax-advantaged vehicles that encourage families to save for their children's post-secondary educational expenses, but by definition require families to have sufficient disposable income from which to save.

Given the complexity of financial aid, it is not surprising that most research tends to consider only broad categories of particular forms of aid (e.g., "grants" or "loans"). Nonetheless, in order to understand how to structure financial aid so as to maximize its impact on enrollment, future research should give greater attention to the complexities of aid, including variations in the effects of aid based on the sources, types, goals, and eligibility criteria. Future research should also consider the ways the effects of any particular financial aid program are mediated by the context for aid, including the availability and characteristics of other financial aid programs (Orsuwan & Heck, 2009). Because of the tendency to examine particular financial aid programs in isolation, little is known about how the effects of a particular financial aid program vary based on the availability of other types of financial aid (Heller, 2008; Reschovsky, 2008).

How Do Perceptions of Aid Influence Students' College-Related Decisions?

Future research should also consider how the effects of financial aid are mediated by student and family characteristics, particularly their knowledge and perceptions of aid. Rational human capital models do not assume that individuals have perfect and complete information about all alternatives, only that individuals use available information to make "reasoned" choices (DesJardins & Toutkoushian, 2005, p. 218). Despite this acknowledgement, and as described in the review of prior research above, human capital models typically consider actual amounts of grants and loans rather than students' knowledge or perceptions of financial aid (Long, 2009; Manski, 2009). Considering only actual amounts of financial aid is especially problematic since, with the exception of some state merit-aid programs (e.g., Georgia HOPE), students and their families only learn the amounts and types of financial aid they will receive after they have applied for admission and financial aid (Kane, 1999; Perna & Steele, in press).

Some evidence suggests that perceptions of loans vary across groups and that these perceptions are related to college-related behaviors. For example, although the growth of student loans suggests that the use of loans to finance postsecondary educational expenses is commonplace (College Board, 2008a), the emphasis of the U.S. financial aid system on loans may limit college opportunity for individuals who are unwilling or unable to incur this type of debt (Perna, 2008b). Although some research suggests that students' perceptions of loans vary across groups (e.g., Christie & Munro, 2003; Christou & Haliassos, 2006; ECMC Group Foundation, 2003; Linsenmeier et al., 2006), only a few studies have explored the forces that contribute to these differences (e.g., Christie & Munro, 2003; Perna, 2008b).

Some research suggests that willingness to borrow is positively related to college enrollment (Callender & Jackson, 2005; Ekstrom, 1991). Using data from the High School and Beyond longitudinal survey of 1980 high school sophomores and seniors, Ekstrom found that students who reported they would be willing to borrow to pay $1,500 in college prices that could not be covered by family or other sources of financial aid were more likely than other students to enroll in college within 4 years of graduating from high school, enroll in a 4-year than a 2-year institution, and enroll full-time than part-time even after controlling for background characteristics, educational aspirations, academic achievement, encouragement from significant others, and knowledge of college costs and financial aid. Using data from surveys of 2,000 prospective higher education students in Britain, Callendar and Jackson found that the likelihood of applying to a university increased with students' tolerance for debt even after controlling for educational achievement, social class, ethnicity, age, and mother's educational attainment. Moreover, debt aversion had a greater negative relationship to the probability of applying for admission for students from low- than high-income families (Callender & Jackson, 2005).

Although these studies suggest the importance of students' perceptions of aid, additional research is required to understand the ways these perceptions influence students' college-related behaviors. Future research should further explore students' perceptions of financial aid, the forces that influence these perceptions, and the implications of these perceptions for student outcomes. Future research should also examine how perceptions of financial aid are informed by various aspects of the context in which students are embedded, including their family background, support from school staff, the characteristics of available aid programs, and other forces including the media.

What Types of Information About Financial Aid, at What Points in Time, from What Sources, and for What Groups of Students Promote College Enrollment?

Little is known from prior research about how financial aid indirectly promotes enrollment, including how knowledge of financial aid may raise students' college-aspirations or encourage students to become academically prepared for college. Therefore, a third area for future research is to consider how financial aid—and particularly information about financial aid-influences these college-related behaviors and how the relationship between financial aid information and college-related behaviors is mediated by various aspects of context.

Various policies and practices are aimed at increasing students' and families' college-related knowledge. Among the most recent is the public service advertising campaign, KnowHow2Go campaign that was launched in January 2007 by the American Council on Education, Lumina Foundation for Education, and the Ad Council. This campaign is designed to disseminate information about the steps required to enroll in college, including how to "put your hands on some cash."

Nonetheless, as indicated in the discussion of the limitations of existing research above, despite the availability of information dissemination efforts reports consistently demonstrate that most students and parents are poorly informed (Perna, 2004). One benefit of improving knowledge of financial aid may be to reduce the number of students who enroll in college and are eligible for financial aid but do not apply. Using descriptive analyses of data from the National Postsecondary Student Aid Survey, King (2004) found that about 1.7 million low- and moderate-income undergraduates enrolled in colleges and universities nationwide in 1999–2000 had not completed the FAFSA; about half of these students were likely eligible for Pell grants. A substantial number of other undergraduates completed the FAFSA but submitted it after April 1, the preferred deadline for most state and institutional grant aid (King, 2004). Additional descriptive analyses of data from the Beginning Postsecondary Student survey suggest that many eligible students do not submit a FAFSA because of incomplete or inaccurate understandings of their eligibility for aid and submission deadlines (King, 2004).

Despite the belief that "information" about financial aid promotes college enrollment, little is known about the necessary content, timing, and/or modes of delivering messages about financial aid (Mundel & Coles, 2004; Perna, 2004). Therefore, future research should identify what types of knowledge "matter" (i.e., promote various college-enrollment behaviors), at what points in time, from which sources, for which groups of students. If "information" is to serve as an effective policy lever for increasing college access and choice, then we need to know more about whether information *can* promote changes in student behavior and what kind of information different groups of students need to have at different points in the pathway to college.

Types of Information

While descriptive data consistently illustrate gaps in knowledge about college prices and financial aid (Perna, 2004), future research should identify the types of knowledge that are important. For example, do students need to have accurate and complete knowledge of college prices and financial aid, or do they more simply need to be confident that, when it comes time to enroll, they'll be able to secure the necessary resources? One exploratory study Perna & Steele (in press) suggests that knowledge of financial aid per se may be less important in encouraging college-enrollment behaviors than the presence of family, school, and other supports and structures that engender confidence in students that they will be able to pay.

Timing of Information

Future research should also examine when students and their families need to have information about financial aid. Several recent reports call for "early" information about financial aid, asserting that students and research now tend to learn about financial aid only during the later years of high school, i.e., too late to influence other college-related behaviors (Advisory Committee on Student Financial Assistance, 2008; Perna, 2004).

Nonetheless, little is known about how the timing of information, including an early promise of aid, shapes college-related behaviors. Based on a review of available research, Schwartz (2008) concluded that little is known about the effects of early commitments of aid, due to limitations of available research. Schwartz identifies four types of financial aid programs that make an "early commitment" to students about the future availability of aid: (1) state merit-aid grant programs that award aid based on high levels of academic achievement; (2) I Have a Dream, Indiana's Twenty-first Century Scholars Program, and other programs in which students self-select to participate; (3) stakeholder grants such as the Child Trust Fund in the United Kingdom; and (4) other programs, including individual development accounts (IDAs). Research examining the effects of early commitment programs is limited by methodological issues (e.g., self-selection of students and families into these programs) and programmatic issues (e.g., limited participation in most programs of students from low-income families, limited dollar amounts of most awards).

Knowledge of financial aid is believed to be related to students' college-enrollment decisions (Perna, 2004), as research shows that students' and parents' understanding of college prices and financial aid is positively related to college expectations (Flint, 1993; Horn et al., 2003), application (Cabrera & LaNasa, 2000), enrollment (Plank & Jordan, 2001), and choice (Ekstrom, 1991), as well as such college financing strategies as students' willingness to borrow, students' use of financial aid, parental saving for college (Ekstrom, 1991; Flint, 1997), and student application for financial aid (U. S. Government Accounting Office, 1990).

Available research does not, however, establish the direction of causality between knowledge of financial aid and students' college-related behaviors (Perna, 2004). In other words, existing research does not establish whether having knowledge of financial aid causes students to engage in college-related behaviors, or whether those who engage in these behaviors acquire information and knowledge. Available research also does not establish the relationship between knowledge of aid and other college-related behaviors, including aspirations for college prior to the 11th grade, curricular choices, college search processes, or students' choice among institutions (Mundel, 2008).

Sources of Information

Future research should also consider how, and with what consequence, the effects of information about financial aid are mediated by various aspects of context—particularly the sources providing financial aid information. The proposed conceptual framework suggests that potential sources of information may include other family members (e.g., older siblings and extended family members), high school staff, peers attending the same high school, pre-college outreach programs (e.g., Upward Bound), colleges and universities, and federal and state sponsors of student financial aid. Available research includes limited attention to only some of these potential sources.

School Staff

Perhaps in response to what is known from available research, some have begun to advocate for improving the quantity and quality of college counseling by high school counselors. For example, one of the ten recommendations made by the College Board's Commission on Access, Admissions and Success in Higher Education (2008) is to increase the availability of college counseling during middle and high school by reducing student-to-counselor ratios, improving preparation and training for college and financial aid counseling, and maximizing the use of other resources to provide counseling, including local colleges and universities and community-based non-profit organizations.

As others have noted (e.g., McDonough, 2004; Mundel, 2008), although existing research suggests the importance of counselors as a source of financial aid information, more research is required to understand the ways they influence students' and families' knowledge of financial aid. As McDonough (2004) notes, although research suggests the benefits to college enrollment of timely and educated discussions between students and school counselors, little is known about school counselors' knowledge of aid.

Additional research is also required to understand how and with what consequences other school staff may be providing financial aid counseling to students. The ability of teachers to serve as a source of information about college costs and financial aid is often limited because teachers are often focused on other priorities, including reducing high school dropout rates and teen pregnancies (Immerwahr, 2003), and/or lack knowledge about college-related requirements beyond their own direct experience (Venezia, Kirst, & Antonio, 2003). Teachers also often have low educational expectations for African Americans and Hispanics (Freeman, 1997; Immerwahr, 2003). Nonetheless, in the absence of sufficient financial aid counseling from school counselors, at least some students may be relying on information from teachers (Perna, Rowan-Kenyon, Thomas, et al., 2008).

Future research should also examine how the provision of financial aid information varies based on the complexity and other characteristics of student aid programs (Mundel, 2008; Perna, 2004). One exploratory analysis suggests that, although state merit-aid programs in Florida and Georgia may have negative consequences for equity, the relative simplicity of eligibility may enable counselors and teachers to more confidently communicate with students about the availability of and criteria for receiving financial aid (Perna, Rowan-Kenyon, Thomas, et al., 2008). In three other study states (i.e., California, Maryland, and Pennsylvania), school staff did not provide extensive financial aid assistance to students at least in part because of the complexity of need-based aid application processes (Perna et al., 2008).

Higher Education Institutions

More research is needed to understand how colleges and universities affect students' understanding and use of financial aid. Variations across institutions in the presence of Pell-grant recipients suggest that the effects of aid on college enrollment depend on institutional characteristics. Using regression analyses of IPEDS data to explore this variation, Steinberg, Piraino, and Haveman (2009) found that the representation of Pell-grant recipients among undergraduates was inversely related to the institution's median SAT score at both public and private institutions. The magnitude of the relationship was substantially greater at public than private institutions. At private institutions, the percentage of Pell-grant recipients was also inversely related to the total cost of attendance.

More research is needed to understand the effects of higher education institutions' efforts to "market" financial aid on students' perceptions and use of financial aid (Mundel, 2008; Perna, 2004). Merely by their presence and geographic proximity to students' homes, higher education institutions may passively convey some information about college to students and their families (Leppel, 1994; McDonough, Antonio, & Trent, 1997). Geographic proximity may be a proxy for greater availability of information about an institution and greater knowledge of the institution among a student's family, school, and community (Leppel, 1994; McDonough et al., 1997).

Higher education institutions may actively convey information to students and their parents through targeted marketing and recruiting efforts (Chapman, 1981). Most such actions are likely only reactive, however, occurring in response to some type of initiative by the student, including taking college admissions examinations and applying for admission (Cabrera & LaNasa, 2001). Because students with low socioeconomic status are less likely than other students to apply for admission (Cabrera & La Nasa, 2001), the "reactive" ways in which higher education institutions convey information may contribute to differences across groups in knowledge of various aspects of college including financial aid.

Higher education institutions actively convey information about college prices and financial aid to students and their families through the financial aid notification process (Kane, 1999). But colleges and universities typically do not inform students and their families of their eligibility for financial aid until they have applied and been accepted for admission, applied for student financial aid, and been deemed eligible for some amount and type of aid. In other words, students and their families typically only learn about the amounts and types of financial aid that they will receive after they have made substantial investments in the college-going process (Heller, 2006). Along the same lines, some research suggests that financial aid offices of colleges and universities may influence the loan-related experiences of students who actually enroll (Wroblewski, 2007). Although mandatory entrance and exit counseling may improve borrowers' understanding of some aspects of loans (Wroblewski, 2007), such counseling comes too late to influence high school students' perceptions of loans (as only students who successfully apply for and receive admission and financial aid and decide to borrow receive entrance counseling).

Future research should examine the effects on perceptions and use of financial aid of recent efforts by some colleges and universities to replace loans with grants for students from low-income families. Most of these programs have been established by Ivy League institutions (e.g., Princeton; University of Pennsylvania), public flagship universities (e.g., University of North Carolina Chapel Hill; University of Maryland College Park), and elite private liberal arts colleges (e.g., Amherst, Davidson, and Williams Colleges), institutions with relatively small numbers of low-income students (McPherson & Shapiro, 2006). Research should not only consider the effects of these institutional aid programs on enrollment and choice for low-income students, but also examine how these effects vary based on student characteristics and other institutional characteristics. Among the potentially important institutional characteristics may be the ways that an institution communicates the availability of this aid program to prospective students.

More research is needed to understand how students' perceptions of institutional financial aid, including the lack of knowledge of need-based aid, may lead students to self-select out of particular colleges. One exploratory study suggests that at least some high school students and parents have a particularly sophisticated understanding of institutional scholarships, with some planning to attend the college that makes the best institutional aid offer (Perna, 2008a). But the findings also suggest that other parents believe that, because colleges and universities target aid to students' with the lowest family incomes and highest academic achievement, relatively few resources are available for "average" students (Perna, 2008a).

Finally, additional research is required to understand how colleges and universities may work with high schools to best inform students about the availability of student financial aid (Perna, Rowan-Kenyon, Thomas, et al., 2008). One exploratory study suggests that both schools and higher education institutions benefit from the common practice of higher education staff conducting an annual financial aid night at local high schools; schools benefit from the provision of financial aid information by local experts and colleges and universities benefit from direct access to potential applicants and their families. By working to identify other collaborative opportunities, schools and higher education institutions may not only advance their own goals but also maximize the availability of college and financial aid counseling in the context of scarce resources.

Federal, State, and Local Providers

Several recent reports argue the need to simplify, and increase the transparency of, financial aid application processes (e.g., Advisory Committee on Student Financial Assistance, 2005, 2009; Baum & McPherson, 2008; Chan & Cochrane, 2008; Commission on Access, Admissions, and Success in Higher Education, 2008; Secretary of Education's Commission on the Future of Higher Education, 2006). But little research has considered the other ways federal, state, and local providers of financial aid may promote or deter knowledge of financial aid. Future research should examine the utility of other mechanisms for disseminating information about financial aid. One potential type of intervention that warrants further consideration is the effort to match available scholarship dollars to eligible students. The Georgia Career Information System (GCIS) offers a potential model for providing students with one source for information about all available scholarship dollars and matching students to scholarship dollars (Perna, 2008a). The GCIS (2007), housed at Georgia State University, is designed to "provide current and accurate career information to schools and agencies throughout Georgia in order to help young people and adults make informed occupational and educational choices." Among other types of information, the GCIS "contains information on more than 3,567 federal, state, and independent aid programs representing about 5 billion dollars" (GCIC, 2007).

Technology

Little is known about the effects on students' and families' knowledge and use of financial aid of Internet sites or other mechanisms for disseminating information about financial aid, including financial aid workshops, required college and career counseling sessions, or one-on-one counseling sessions with college alumni and others (Porter et al., 2006). Lumina Foundation for Education (2009) urges the Obama administration to work toward the following goal: "By the 8th grade, provide all children and families with information needed to plan for college success." But Lumina goes on to note that KnowHow2Go and other public awareness campaigns alone are insufficient to ensure that students have the knowledge required to enroll in college. Lumina is now focusing on "develop[ing] a ground campaign to link youth to local resources of caring adults and organizations to help students take the steps needed, including developing stronger state and local college access networks." This action suggests a disillusionment with the potential benefits of relying on technology alone as an information source. Given the prevalence of financial aid-related Internet sites, future research should consider the ways technology, with and without other types of support, may provide financial aid information to different groups of students and families (Mundel, 2008).

How Can Financial Aid Promote College-Related Outcomes Other than College Enrollment, Particularly Students' Academic Preparation for College?

A fourth area for future research is to consider how another aspect of context—namely the characteristics of aid—may directly and indirectly promote college enrollment. More specifically, given that college enrollment and success are limited not only by insufficient financial resources but also by inadequate academic preparation (Perna, 2006a), future research should examine the ways to construct aid programs so as to both encourage academic achievement and eliminate financial barriers (McDonough, Calderone, & Purdy, 2007).

Little is known about the effects of federal efforts to use grant aid to improve college readiness, largely because these efforts are still relatively new. Established by then-president Bush in FY2006, the Academic Competitiveness Grant (ACG) and Smart Grant programs award supplemental Pell grant funds to financially needy students who complete a rigorous curricular program in high school, or major in mathematics or science in college. The number of recipients of ACG and Smart grants was higher in 2007–2008, the second year of the program, than in 2006–2007 (465,000 versus 370,000, Field, 2009). Nonetheless, the number of participants and total spending on the program were still lower than expected in 2007–2008. In 2006–2007, about $430 million was awarded to students through the two programs, substantially less than the $790 million Congress had appropriated (Field, 2009). The future of these programs is unclear as President Obama's proposed FY10 budget would allow these programs to expire after 2010 (Lederman, 2009).

Little is also known about the effects of programs with multiple eligibility criteria on student outcomes, even though state aid programs are increasingly including both academic merit and financial need criteria (McDonough et al., 2007). McDonough and colleagues underscore the policy-relevance of research that informs decisions about the criteria for awarding financial aid by stating:

> As a society, we lack a comprehensive student-aid policy that attempts to provide a threshold of financial aid that truly enables poor students to afford college while providing the appropriate proportion of aid that encourages and rewards meritorious performance (p. 24).

One goal of many merit-based state grant programs is to improve students' educational attainment by increasing their academic readiness (Doyle, 2008). Nonetheless, based on a review Doyle concluded that available research does not establish whether merit-aid programs achieve this result. Similarly, Dynarski (2004) concluded from her research review that state merit aid programs are associated with improved academic performance in high school and college, but that other forces may also explain these trends.

Some research suggests a complex relationship between state merit-aid programs and academic preparation. For example, one exploratory study suggests that Georgia's HOPE Scholarship program may motivate students to achieve the academic requirements of the state grant award (Perna & Steele, in press). By clearly communicating academic eligibility criteria, these programs may increase parents' attention to students' academic preparation (Perna & Steele, in press). This study also suggests potential negative consequences of state merit-aid programs for academic readiness, such as increasing pressure on teachers to inflate grades and encouraging students to take less-rigorous courses (i.e., where they are more likely to meet the grade point average requirement for the merit aid).

More research is needed on other potential unintended consequences of state merit-aid programs for academic preparation. Based on his review of research, Mundel (2008) speculates that, with the apparent simplicity and transparency of state merit-aid programs, some students may conclude that the academic eligibility criteria are impossible to achieve and consequently lower their educational aspirations and forgo other college-preparatory activities (Mundel, 2008). Others may conclude that financial aid is available only based on academic merit, without appropriately recognizing the availability of need-based aid (Mundel, 2008).

One commonly observed disadvantage of state merit-aid programs is that these programs disproportionately benefit students from upper-income families and others who would have attended college even without the aid (Heller, 2004; Heller & Marin, 2002). Given these well-documented challenges, the College Board's Commission on Access, Admissions and Success in Higher Education (2008) declares that "merit aid, particularly when financed publicly by regressive taxes or lotteries, has to clear a very high bar before it can justify itself as appropriate merit aid" (p. 29).

Nonetheless, recent growth in state merit aid (College Board, 2008a) and the establishment of the federal ACG and Smart Grants suggest policymakers' interest in using student aid to motivate students to become adequately academically prepared to enroll and succeed in college. Therefore, future research should further explore the ways financial aid eligibility requirements may be constructed to promote academic preparation and eliminate financial barriers while also minimizing any unintended negative consequences (McDonough et al., 2006).

Future research should also consider how other types of approaches to financial aid may also improve students' academic performance and readiness for college. One particularly promising approach may be to provide an early commitment of student financial aid. Based on his review, Harnisch (2009) notes that state-based early-commitment programs have several characteristics including targeting of middle-school students and their families; a clear and simple contract that specifies the requirements for receiving financial aid; minimum high school grade point averages and college preparatory curricular requirements; and guaranteed financial aid for college. While some research examines the effects of Indiana's Twenty-First Century Scholars on students' college-related outcomes (e.g., St. John, Musoba, Simmons, & Chung, 2002; St. John, Gross, Musoba, & Chung, 2005; St. John, Fisher, Lee, Daun-Barnett, Williams, 2008), little is known about the effects of other state-based early-commitment programs including Oklahoma's Promise, Wisconsin Covenant, and Washington College Bound Scholarship. Future research should capitalize on the variations across these programs to develop a better understanding of the implications of early-commitment programs for students' academic preparation and other college-related behaviors. These four state-based early-commitment programs vary in terms of the grade level students must make the commitment (e.g., as early as sixth grade in Indiana and as late as 10th grade in Oklahoma); maximum income (e.g., free and reduced lunch status in Indiana and no income requirement in Wisconsin); and minimum high school grade point average (ranging from 2.0 in Indiana and Washington to 2.85 in Wisconsin) (Harnisch, 2009).

How Does Financial Aid Affect College Enrollment for Adult Students, and How is the Relationship Between Aid and Enrollment for Adult Students Mediated by Various Aspects of Context?

A final area for future research is to examine the effects of financial aid on college enrollment for an under-researched population, adult students, and how aspects of context mediate this relationship. Virtually all of the research and the conceptual model presented in this chapter focus on understanding the effects of financial aid on college enrollment for traditional-age students. This focus likely reflects, at least in part, the absence of research on the role of financial aid in college-going decisions for adult students, as well as the general absence of aid programs specifically targeted toward adult students (e.g., Lapovsky, 2008). In his review, Mundel (2008) concludes that little is known about the effects of grants on college-related behaviors of students who delay college enrollment after finishing high school.

Policymakers have begun to recognize the importance of improving college-related outcomes for adult students. As an example, recommendations from the U. S. Department of Education Margaret Spellings Commission on the Future of Higher Education (2006) include ensuring that individuals have the opportunity to participate in higher education over the course of their lifetimes. Nonetheless, based on her review, Lapovsky (2008) concluded that the existing financial aid system was not developed to promote college access among adult students. She speculates that some aspects of the financial aid system may favor adult students, as suggested by the high percentage of Pell Grant awards received by financially independent students. Other aspects, however, do not, such as the emphasis of state and institutional grant aid programs on full-time enrollment; a spring deadline for applying for many state and institutional aid programs; work disincentives in the needs-analysis formula; and the diversity of personal and enrollment characteristics among adult students (Lapovsky, 2008). Additional research is required to understand the ways these and other dimensions of context influence adult students' use and perceptions of financial aid and their consequences for enrollment-related outcomes. Additional research should also consider the availability, use, and consequences of employer-provided financial aid for the enrollment of adult workers.

Recommended Strategies for Future Research

Further drawing on the limitations of prior research and the proposed conceptual model, this section offers four recommended strategies to guide future research: (1) develop research designs that will identify not just what "works" but how to improve financial aid programs; (2) recognize the contributions of multiple methodological approaches; (3) capitalize on differences among financial aid programs; and (4) recognize the contributions of multiple theoretical perspectives.

Develop Research Designs that Identify How to Improve Programs

In this era of accountability, demonstrating whether a particular financial aid program "works" is critical to a program's future funding. In its discussion of the federal PART ratings, the U.S. Office of Management and Budget (OMB, 2003) clearly articulates the value it places on such research by stating, "No program, however worthy its goal and high-minded its name, is entitled to continue perpetually unless it can demonstrate it is actually effective in solving problems" (p. 47). OMB goes on to underscore this point by stating: "What works is what matters, and achievement should determine which programs survive and which do not" (p. 53).

Certainly program effectiveness should be considered when making decisions about the allocation of scare public resources. Nonetheless, there are at least three cautions associated with relying on measures of program effectiveness to determine whether a program is a good investment. One caution pertains to the interpretation of the findings from such research. In an article in the *New England Journal of Medicine,* Henry Aaron (2008) discusses the question, "What, exactly, is wasteful health care spending?" (p. 1). Like health care, investments in education programs likely have a continuum of benefits with the magnitude varying across individuals. Even when an investment in health care—or education is labeled as "wasteful" or "ineffective," some individuals are likely benefiting. Given these benefits, whether we continue to offer these programs becomes an ethical decision (Aaron, 2008).

A second caution is that policymakers and practitioners need to know more than simply whether a program "works." Clearly more information is also needed about *how* financial aid programs work and how they may be adjusted to maximize their effects on college-related outcomes (Mundel, 2008). For example, although most research focuses on whether grants are related to college enrollment, policymakers and practitioners would also benefit from knowing how grants directly and indirectly contribute to college enrollment, as well as how grant programs may be improved so as to increase the magnitude of the enrollment benefits and/or the number of individuals who benefit (Mundel, 2008).

Finally, a consideration of the limitations of prior research in light of the conceptual model demonstrates that understanding whether a financial aid program "works" is complicated by the complexities of the contexts in which these programs operate. Other researchers have recognized these complexities (Orsuwan & Heck, 2009). For example, Stout (2008) identifies the "confounding factors" that challenge efforts to isolate the effects of the Academic Competitiveness and SMART grant programs on student outcomes, including other federal, state, and local initiatives; the complexity of the programs; and changes in student eligibility and economic conditions. Considering the role of context suggests the challenges associated with determining whether a particular program causes a particular change in student outcomes, or what student outcomes would have occurred in the absence of the program.

Recognize the Contributions of Multiple Methodological Approaches

Although existing research examining the effects of financial aid on student outcomes has important analytic and methodological limitations (Heller, 2008), no single design or study is without flaws. When selecting a research design or methodology, researchers must acknowledge that all designs have limitations (Baum & McPherson, 2008).

Given the limitations inherent in any design, as well as the complexities of the questions that should be addressed in future research, multiple methodological approaches are necessary. Taken together, findings from multiple methodological approaches will produce a more comprehensive understanding of these complex questions. In particular, researchers should consider the insights that may be gained from randomized control trials, multi-level modeling, qualitative methods, and longitudinal designs.

Randomized Control Trials

According to the federal government, the "gold standard" for research is randomized control trials (RCTs), the only design that can establish whether a particular program causes a given outcome (U.S. Office of Management and Budget, February 2008). By randomly assigning students to "treatment" and "control" groups, randomized control trials, unlike other methods, are assumed to control for all other explanations for any differences in outcomes between the two groups (besides the treatment). As others (e.g., Heller, 2008; Long, 2004c) have noted, the heavy reliance in existing research on descriptive and quasi-experimental designs necessarily limits what is known about whether financial aid causes improvements in college enrollment.

Ethical and political challenges restrict the use of randomized control trials (Baum & McPherson, 2008). OMB (2008, February) recognizes these challenges by noting that "randomized controlled trials are generally the highest quality, unbiased evaluation to demonstrate actual impact, but [should be used] only when it is appropriate and feasible to conduct such studies" (slide 40). OMB goes on to note that "a variety of quasi-experimental methods (e.g., comparison group studies) and non-experimental methods may help shed light on *how* or *why* a program is effective;" "evaluations must be appropriate for the type of program" (U. S. Office of Management and Budget, 2008, February, slide 40).

Therefore, given the potential insights gained from establishing causal relationships, researchers should consider the ways RCTs may be utilized for examining the relationship between financial aid and college enrollment. When politically and ethically feasible, RCTs may offer important insights.

Multi-level Modeling

A second fruitful approach to future research examining the effects of financial aid on college enrollment is to use multi-level modeling (e.g., hierarchical linear modeling). By explicitly considering multiple levels, multi-level modeling may be particularly useful for understanding the effects on enrollment of multiple dimensions of context.

Some existing studies suggest the insights that may be generated through multi-level modeling. For example, using multilevel modeling, Perna and Titus (2005) explore the ways the characteristics of the high school attended influence the college enrollment decisions of high school graduates. Focusing specifically on the role of parental involvement as a form of social capital, Perna and Titus operationalize aspects of the school context in terms of the extent to which the school encourages parental involvement, the volume of resources that may be accessed via social networks at the school, and the homogeneity of these social networks.

Their analyses show that, regardless of an individual student's social, economic, cultural, and human capital, the likelihood of enrolling in a 2-year or 4-year college after graduating from high school is related to the volume of resources that may be accessed through social networks at the school attended. The volume of resources is measured by such variables as the average levels of parental involvement, family income, parental education, and parental educational expectations at the school the child attends.

Multi-level modeling may also shed light on how the state context influences college enrollment. Perna and Titus (2004) use multilevel modeling to examine the effects of various types of state public policies on the type of college or university high school graduates attend after taking into account student-level predictors of enrollment. State-level variables included measures of state appropriations to higher education, tuition, availability of need-based and non-need-based student financial aid, K-12 education, and the availability of higher education in the state.

With relatively large sample sizes, high response rates, multiple data sources, national samples, and the clustering of students within high schools, the longitudinal datasets sponsored by the National Center for Education Statistics (NCES) are an important source of data for modeling effects at the student, school, and state levels (Perna & Titus, 2004, 2005). NCES is currently beginning the fourth in a series of longitudinal studies that provide data on students' transition from high school to postsecondary education. The National Longitudinal Study (NLS) of 1972 high school seniors followed students periodically through 1986. The High School and Beyond (HS&B) Study followed 1980 high school seniors through 1986 and 1980 high school sophomores through 1992. The National Educational Longitudinal Study (NELS) contains data for a cohort of students in the 8th grade (1988) when most of the students were high school sophomores (1990), high school seniors (1992), 2 years after their scheduled high school graduation (1994), and 8 years after (2000). The sample was freshened in 1990 and 1992 to ensure representative cohorts of 1990 tenth graders and 1992 twelfth-graders, respectively. The Educational Longitudinal Study 2002 (ELS) tracks the experiences of 2002 tenth graders through high school and into postsecondary education and the workforce, with data collections in 2002, 2004, and 2006. The High School Longitudinal Study (HSLS:09) will follow 2009 ninth graders forward. The HSLS will include data from about 20,000 high school students, their parents, and school staff (i.e., teachers, guidance counselors, and administrators).

Qualitative Methods

Existing knowledge of the effects of student financial aid on students' college-related outcomes is largely informed by the results of quantitative research methodologies. A small but growing body of research, however, demonstrates the insights that may also be generated from qualitative research methodologies.

As others (e.g., St. John, 2006) note, qualitative methods may be especially useful for understanding students' perceptions of financial aid and how these perceptions influence their college-related decisions. For instance, using semi-structured interviews with 49 students in the United Kingdom, Christie and Munro's (2003) qualitative study offers useful insights into how students view debt and how financial and cultural resources influence their views.

In an examination of the college pathways of five students attending one urban high school in Los Angeles, Tierney and Colyar (2006) (along with their chapter authors) demonstrate the contribution of qualitative methods to understanding the ways students' educational choices are influenced by their contexts. The authors use intensive qualitative data collection methods, including weekly meetings with each student over the course of 1 year, and "cultural biography" as a framework for identifying the ways cultural contexts influence high school students' college pathways. Colyar (2006) argues that cultural biography is an understanding of students as situated within a particular culture and social context. Together, the portraits of these five students illustrate the ways college-going processes are informed by a student's "cultural system," including their family (e.g., encouragement to be first-generation college student), school (e.g., scarcity of resources), community (e.g., poverty), and other aspects of their context (Tierney, 2006).

Longitudinal Research Designs

Longitudinal designs are especially important for understanding how information and knowledge about financial aid influence not only students' actual college enrollment but also other college-related behaviors including aspirations for college, academic preparation for college, search for and application to colleges, and choice among colleges (Long, 2009; Perna, 2004).

Longitudinal designs are especially important for understanding when students need to receive various types of financial aid information. Most agree that providing students and their families with information about college prices and financial aid early in the educational pipeline may encourage students to engage in college preparatory behaviors, such as becoming academically prepared for college (Perna, 2004; Baum & McPherson, 2008). Nonetheless, as explained in this chapter's review of prior research, existing research does not indicate whether having information causes students to engage in college-related behaviors, or whether students who would have engaged in these behaviors anyway acquire information (Long, 2009; Perna, 2004). Data that longitudinally track changes in both knowledge and behavior would help to address this knowledge gap.

Longitudinal designs are also important for addressing other questions regarding the effects of financial aid on students' college-related behaviors. For example, longitudinal designs are needed to better understand the extent to which students retain financial aid (especially merit-based aid) after enrolling and go on to successfully complete their degree programs (Perna & Steele, in press). As another example, Orsuwan and Heck (2009) demonstrate the ways that a longitudinal design (i.e., interrupted time-series analysis) may be used to examine the effects of adopting state merit-aid and prepaid tuition policies on the enrollment of freshmen in out-of-state colleges and universities.

Capitalize on Variations in Student Financial Aid

While complicating efforts to understand the effects of financial aid on college enrollment, variations in existing financial aid programs also offer an opportunity for researchers. In particular, future research might consider exploiting variations in state approaches to financial aid in order to better understand how various program characteristics influence college enrollment and choice.

Some research (e.g., Dynarski, 2004; Orsuwan & Heck, 2009; Perna & Steele, in press) suggests how differences in state approaches to financial aid may be used to better understand how different approaches influence students' perceptions about and use of financial aid. State grant programs have several different goals, including promoting access and attainment of postsecondary education for qualified students; promoting student choice among public and private institutions; encouraging students to attend in-state rather than out-of-state institutions to reduce "brain drain;" and promoting and recognizing academic achievement in high school or college (Doyle, 2008; Heller, 2004). Need-based aid programs are used to promote access, equalization funds are used to promote choice, and merit-based aid programs are used to reward academic achievement (Doyle, 2008).

States vary in the foci and magnitude of their grant aid. Two states award 100% of their aid for undergraduates based on financial need only (Rhode Island and Wyoming) while one state (Louisiana) awards virtually all aid to undergraduates based only on merit (National Association of State Scholarships and Grant Aid Programs [NASSGAP], 2007). Some states (e.g., South Carolina and Georgia) offer over $1,000 in grant aid per full-time equivalent (FTE) undergraduate student, while others (e.g., Hawaii and Wyoming) offer less than $10 per FTE (College Board, 2008a). State grant expenditures represent at least one-fifth of higher education operating expenses in South Carolina (33%), Vermont (23%), Georgia (22%), West Virginia (21%), New York (21%), Pennsylvania (20%), and Indiana (20%), but less than 1% of higher education operating expenses in North Dakota, Alabama, Arizona, Alaska, Hawaii, and Wyoming (NASSGAP, 2007).

States also vary in the ways they disseminate information about financial aid (McDonough et al., 2007), as well as the extent to which they provide other forms of support for students' college enrollment. Future research should use these variations to examine the ways that "college access marketing" campaigns influence college-related behaviors (McDonough et al., 2007), as well as how the effects of financial aid on college opportunity vary based on the availability of other resources that promote college enrollment. Perhaps the most comprehensive state-grant program, Indiana's

Twenty-first Century Scholarship program, includes early commitment of aid, activities to involve parents in college planning and preparation, and academic and social support services for students. Based on a review of data from a survey of students and state records, St. John et al. (2002) found that program participants were more likely to enroll in public 2-year, public 4-year, private, and out-of-state colleges and universities than non-participants and to remain continuously enrolled during the first year of college. Some evidence suggests that, compared to non-participants, program participants are more likely to persist from the first to second semester of their freshman year of college and to attain an associate's degree (St. John et al., 2005, 2002; St. John, Musoba, Simmons & Chung, 2004), while other research suggests that scholars are less likely than non-recipients to attain a bachelor's degree within 6 years (St. John et al., 2008). Students who take the Scholars Pledge are more likely than other students to graduate from high school with an Honors diploma (which requires completion of an advanced preparatory curriculum), suggesting that bachelor's degree attainment rates for Scholars may improve over time (St. John et al., 2008, 2002; St. John, 2003; St. John, Musoba, Simmons & Chung, 2004) conclude that the promise of the availability of financial aid for college during the 8th grade encouraged students to engage in behaviors required to prepare for college. Schultz and Mueller (2006) conclude that the available research provides "promising evidence" of the program's effectiveness for participating students, as the available research shows positive outcomes but uses a quasi-experimental rather than an experimental design.

Future research might also explore how the effects on students' college-related behaviors vary based on other aspects of financial aid, including the providers of information about aid and the extent to which use of financial aid is framed as the "norm" or "default." For example, Long (2009) speculates that students' use and knowledge of financial aid would be substantially greater if students were automatically informed of their eligibility (using IRS data for example) than when students must proactively complete the Federal Application for Federal Student Aid (FAFSA).

Recognize the Contribution of Multiple Theoretical Approaches

Finally, future research should recognize the potential contribution of multiple theoretical approaches for understanding the ways financial aid influences students' college-enrollment behaviors. As described in the conceptual framework section, no one theoretical perspective alone is sufficient. As a substantial body of research demonstrates, human capital models are useful for understanding that financial aid promotes college enrollment by increasing the resources that students and families have to pay college prices. Nonetheless, human capital models alone are insufficient for explaining inconsistencies in students' decision-making (Long, 2009) or for understanding how the relationship between student aid and enrollment-behaviors varies based on other aspects of context (Manski, 2009).

Other perspectives, including those from behavioral economics, psychology, and sociology, may be especially useful for understanding how students acquire financial aid information and develop perceptions about financial aid, how students use this information and their perceptions to make college-related decisions, and how and why these relationships may vary across groups.

Conclusion

Clearly, financial aid is a critical policy-lever for increasing postsecondary access and choice, especially for Blacks, Hispanics, low-income students, and other groups underrepresented in higher education. This chapter argues research that more explicitly examines the ways financial aid is mediated by the context in which students are situated will generate important insights not only for improving public policy and practice but also for demonstrating accountability in financial aid expenditures. This chapter also argues that no single theoretical perspective or methodological approach alone is sufficient for completely understanding all that is still unknown about the effects of financial aid on college enrollment for different groups of students. Multiple theoretical frameworks, using multiple methods, addressing multiple questions, focusing on multiple populations, and recognizing multiple dimensions of context will help to address these knowledge gaps, an important step toward maximizing the effectiveness of student financial aid programs.

Acknowledgments

I am grateful to David Mundel for the conversations we have had about some of the ideas in this paper.

References

Aaron, H. J. (2008). Waste, we know you are out there. *New England Journal of Medicine, 359*, 1865–1867.

Adelman, C. (1999). *Answers in the tool box: Academic intensity, attendance patterns, and bachelor's degree attainment*. Washington, DC: Office of Educational Research and Improvement, U.S. Department of Education.

Adelman, C. (2006). *The toolbox revisited: Paths to degree completion from high school through college*. Washington, DC: U. S. Department of Education, Office of Vocational and Adult Education.

Advisory Committee on Student Financial Assistance (2005). *The student aid gauntlet: Making access to college simple and certain*. Washington, DC: Author. Retrieved January 7, 2009 from http://www.ed.gov/about/bdscomm/list/acsfa/gauntletcorrected.pdf

Advisory Committee on Student Financial Assistance (2006). *Mortgaging our future: How financial barriers to college undercut America's global competitiveness*. Washington, DC: Author.

Advisory Committee on Student Financial Assistance (2008). *Early and often: Designing a comprehensive system of financial aid information*. Washington, DC: Author.

Advisory Committee on Student Financial Assistance (2009). *Advisory Committee on Student Financial Assistance*. Retrieved January 7, 2009 from http://www.ed.gov/about/ bdscomm/list/acsfa/edlite-index.html

Avery, C., & Hoxby, C. M. (2004). Do and should financial aid packages affect students' college choices? In C. M. Hoxby (Ed.), *College choices: The economics of where to go, when to go, and how to pay for it* (pp. 239–302). Chicago: University of Chicago Press.

Ballard, M. B., & Murgatroyd, W. (1999). Defending a vital program: School counselors define their roles. *NASPA Bulletin, 83*, 603.

Baum, S., & Ma, J. (2007). *Education pays 2007*. Washington, DC: College Board.

Baum, S., & McPherson, M. (2008). Introduction. In S. Baum, M. McPherson, & P. Steele (Eds.), *The effectiveness of student aid policies: What the research tells us* (pp. 1–7). Washington, DC: The College Board.

Baum, S., McPherson, M., & Steele, P. (Eds.) (2008). *The effectiveness of student aid policies: What the research tells us*. Washington, DC: The College Board.

Baum, S., & O'Malley, M. (2003). College on credit: How borrowers perceive their education debt. *Journal of Student Financial Aid, 33*(3), 7–19.

Becker, G. S. (1993). *Human capital: A theoretical and empirical analysis with special reference to education* (3rd ed.). Chicago: University of Chicago Press.

Berkner, L., & Wei, C. C. (2006). *Student financing of undergraduate education: 2003–2004*. Washington, DC: U.S. Department of Education, Institute of Education Sciences, National Center for Education Statistics (NCES 2006-186).

Binder, M., Ganderton, P. T., & Hutchens, K. (2002). *Incentive effects of New Mexico's merit-based state scholarship programs: Who responds and how?* Cambridge, MA: The Civil Rights Project, Harvard University.

Bourdieu, P. (1986). The forms of capital. In J. G. Richardson (Ed.), *Handbook of theory and research for the sociology of education*. New York: Greenwood Press.

Bourdieu, P., & Passeron, J. C. (1977). *Reproduction in education, society, and culture*. Beverly Hills, CA: Sage Publications.

Bowen, H. R. (1997). *Investment in learning: The individual and social value of American higher education*.

Bureau of Labor Statistics (2003). Tomorrow's Jobs. U.S. Department of Labor: Bureau of Labor Statistics, www.bls.gov/oco/oco2003.htm.

Cabrera, A. F., & La Nasa, S. M. (2000). Three critical tasks America's disadvantaged face on their path to college. In A. F. Cabrera, & S. M. La Nasa (Eds.), *Understanding the college choice of disadvantaged students* (Vol. 107, pp. 23–29). San Francisco: Jossey-Bass Publishers.

Cabrera, A. F., & La Nasa, S. M. (2001). On the path to college: Three critical tasks facing America's disadvantaged. *Research in Higher Education, 42*, 119–149.

Callender, C., & Jackson, J. (2005). Does the fear of debt deter students from higher education? *Journal of Social Policy, 34*, 509–540.

Carnevale, A. P., & Desrochers, D. M. (2003). *Standards for What? The economic roots of K-16 reform*. Princeton, NJ: Educational Testing Service.

Ceja, M. A. (2001). *Applying, choosing, and enrolling in higher education: Understanding the college choice process of first-generation Chicana students*. Unpublished doctoral dissertation, University of CA, Los Angeles

Chan, D., & Cochrane, D. F. (2008). *Paving the way: How financial aid awareness affects college access and success*. Institute for College Access and Success. Retrieved December 5, 2008 from http://projectonstudentdebt.org/fckfiles/Paving_the_Way.pdf

Chapman, D. W. (1981). A model of student college choice. *Journal of Higher Education, 52*(5), 490–505.

Christie, H., & Munro, M. (2003). The logic of loans: Students' perceptions of the costs and benefits of the student loan. *British Journal of Sociology of Education, 24*, 621–636.

Christou, C., & Haliassos, M. (2006). How do students finance human capital accumulation? The choice between borrowing and work. *Journal of Policy Modeling, 28*(1), 39–51.

Coleman, J. S. (1988). Social capital in the creation of human capital. *American Journal of Sociology, 94*(Supplement), 95–120.

College, B. (2008a). *Trends in student aid 2008*. Washington, DC: Author.

College, B. (2008b). *Trends in college pricing 2008*. Washington, DC: Author.

Colyar, J. E. (2006). Afterword: The syntax of cultural biography. In W. G. Tierney & J. E. Colyar (Eds.), *Urban high school students and the challenge of access: Many routes, difficult paths* (pp. 149–168). New York, NY: Peter Lang Publishers, Inc.

Commission on Access, Admissions, and Success in Higher Education (2008). *Coming to our senses: Education and the American future*. Washington, DC: College Board.

Cornwell, C., Mustard, D., & Sridhar, D. (2004). *The enrollment effects of merit-based financial aid: Evidence from Georgia's HOPE Scholarship program*. Athens, GA: University of Georgia, Department of Economics.

Cunningham, A. F., & Santiago, D. A. (2008). *Student aversion to borrowing: Who borrows and who doesn't*. Washington, DC: Institute for Higher Education Policy.

DesJardins, S. L., & Toutkoushian, R. K. (2005). Are students really rational? The development of rational thought and its application to student choice. In J. C. Smart (Ed.), *Higher education: Handbook of theory and research* (Vol. 20, pp. 191–240). Dordrecht, The Netherlands: Kluwer Academic Publishers.

Dika, S. L., & Singh, K. (2002). Applications of social capital in educational literature: A critical synthesis. *Review of Educational Research, 72*, 31–60.

Doyle, W. R. (2008). Access, choice, and excellence: The competing goals of state student financial aid programs. In S. Baum, M. McPherson, & P. Steele (Eds.), *The effectiveness of student aid policies: What the research tells us* (pp. 159–187). Washington, DC: The College Board.

Dynarski, S. (2000). Hope for whom? Financial aid for the middle class and its impact on college attendance. *National Tax Journal, 53*(3), 629–662.

Dynarski, S. (2002). Race, income, and the impact of merit aid. In D. E. Heller & P. Marin (Eds.), *Who should we help? The negative social consequences of merit scholarships* (pp. 73–92). Cambridge, MA: The Civil Rights Project, Harvard University.

Dynarski, S. (2004). The new merit aid. In C. M. Hoxby (Ed.), *College choices: The economics of where to go, when to go, and how to pay for it* (pp. 63–100). Chicago: University of Chicago Press.

Eckel, C. C., Johnson, C., Montmarquette, C., & Rojas, C. (2007). Debt aversion and the demand for loans for postsecondary education. *Public Finance Review, 35*(2), 233–262.

ECMC Group Foundation (2003). *Cultural barriers to incurring debt: An exploration of borrowing and impact on access to postsecondary education*. Santa Fe, NM: Author.

Ekstrom, R. (1991). *Attitudes Toward Borrowing and Participation in Post-Secondary Education*. Paper presented at the Association for the Study of Higher Education Annual Meeting.

Ellwood, D. T., & Kane, T. J. (2000). Who is getting a college education? Family background and the growing gaps in enrollment. In S. Danzinger J.Waldfogel (Eds.), *Securing the future: Investing in children from birth to college* (pp. 283–324). New York: Russell Sage Foundation.

Erisman, W., & Del Rios, M. (2008). *Creating change one step at a time: Efforts to improve college access and success in Indiana*. Washington, DC: Institute for Higher Education Policy.

Fastweb (2009). *FastWeb: About us*. Retrieved January 7, 2009 from http://www.fastweb.com/fastweb/about/index

Field, K. (2008, August 8). A bill that took longer than a bachelor's degree. *Chronicle of Higher Education, 54*(48), A1.

Field, K. (2009, January 23). New grants have more takers, but still fall short of goals. *Chronicle of Higher Education, 55*(20), A1, A22.

Fisher, K. (2007). Fewer GA students earn HOPE funds. *Chronicle of Higher Education, 53*(49), A17.

Fitzgerald, B. K. (2006). Lowering barriers to college access: Opportunities for more effective coordination of state and federal student aid policies. In. P. C. Gandara, G. Orfield, and C. L. Horn (Eds.), *Expanding opportunity in higher education: Leveraging promise*. Albany, NY: State University of New York Press.

Flint, T. (1993). Early awareness of college financial aid: Does it expand choice? *Review of Higher Education, 16*, 309–327.

Flint, T. (1997). Intergenerational effects of paying for college. *Research in Higher Education, 38*(3), 313–344.

Freeman, K. (1997). Increasing African Americans' participation in higher education: African American high-school students' perspectives. *Journal of Higher Education, 68*, 523–550.

Furstenberg, F. F., Cook, T. D., Eccles, J., Elder, G. H., & Sameroff, A. (1999). *Managing to make it: Urban families and adolescent success*. Chicago: University of Chicago Press.

Georgia Career Information Center (2007). Georgia Career Information Center. Retrieved July 1, 2007 from http://www. gcic.peachnet.edu/default.htm

Giordano, R. (2008, December 16). College-aid programs take a hit in New Jersey. *Philadelphia Inquirer*, Retrieved January 6, 2009 from http://www.philly.com/philly/news/local/36217549.html

Grodsky, E., & Jones, M. (2004). *Real and imagined barriers to college entry: Perceptions of cost*. Paper presented at the annual meeting of the American Education Research Association: San Diego, CA.

Hahn, R. D., & Price, D. (2008). *Promise lost: College-qualified students who don't enroll in college*. Washington, DC: Institute for Higher Education Policy.

Hansen, W. L., & Weisbrod, B. A. (1969). *Benefits, costs, and finance of public higher education*. Chicago: Markham Publishing Company.

Harnisch, T. L. (2009). *State early commitment programs: A contract for success?* Washington, DC: American Association of State Colleges and Universities.

Hearn, J. C. (2001). The paradox of growth in federal aid for college students, 1960–1990. In M. B. Paulsen & J. C. Smart (Eds.), *The finance of higher education, Theory, research, policy, and practice* (pp. 267–320). New York: Agathon Press.

Heller, D. E. (1997). Student price response in higher education: An update to Leslie and Brinkman. *Journal of Higher Education, 68*, 624–659.

Heller, D. E. (2004). State merit scholarship programs. In E. P. St. John (Ed.), *Public Policy and College Access: Investigating the Federal and State Roles in Equalizing Educational Opportunity, Readings on Equal Education*. Brooklyn, NY: AMS Press Inc.

Heller, D. E. (2006). Early notification of financial aid eligibility. *American Behavioral Scientist, 49*, 1719–1739.

Heller, D. E. (2008). The impact of student loans on college access. Chapter 3 In S. Baum, M. McPherson, & P. Steele (Eds.), *The effectiveness of student aid policies: What the research tells us* (pp. 39–68). Washington, DC: College Board.

Heller, D., & Marin, P. (Eds.) (2002). *Who should we help? The negative social consequences of merit scholarships*. Cambridge, MA: The Civil Rights Project at Harvard University.

Hill, C. B., Winston, G. C., & Boyd, S. A. (2005). Affordability: Family income and net prices at highly selective private colleges and universities. *Journal of Human Resources, 40*, 769–790.

Hogarth, R. M. (1987). *Judgement and choice: The psychology of decision* (2nd ed.). Chicago: John Wiley & Sons.

Horn, L. J., Chen, X., & Chapman, C. (2003). *Getting ready to pay for college: What students and their parents know about the cost of college tuition and what they are doing to find out*. Washington, DC: U.S. Department of Education, Institute of Education Sciences.

Hossler, D., & Gallagher, K. S. (1987). Studying college choice: A three-phase model and the implications for policy-makers. *College and University, 2*, 207–221.

Hossler, D., Schmit, J., & Vesper, N. (1999). *Going to college: How social, economic, and educational factors influence the decisions students make*. Baltimore: Johns Hopkins University Press.

Hossler, D., Ziskin, M., Sooyeon, K., Osman, C., & Gross, J. (2008). Student aid and its role in encouraging persistence. *The effectiveness of student aid policies: What the research tells us* (pp. 101–116). Washington, DC: College Board.

Hovey, H. (1999). State funds for higher education: Fiscal decisions and policy implications. In J. L. Yeager, M. Glenn, E. A. Potter, J. C. Weidman, & T. G. Zullo (Eds.), *ASHE Reader on finance in higher education* (2nd ed., pp. 179–198). Boston, MA: Pearson Custom Publishing.

Hurtado, S., Inkelas, K. K., Briggs, C., & Rhee, B. S. (1997). Differences in college access and choice among racial/ethnic groups: Identifying continuing barriers. *Research in Higher Education, 38*, 43–75.

Ikenberry, S., & Hartle, T. (1998). *Too little knowledge is a dangerous thing: What the public thinks and knows about paying for college.* Washington, DC: American Council on Education.

Immerwahr, J. (2003). *With diploma in hand: Hispanic high school seniors talk about their future* (Report No. National Center Report #03–2). San Jose, CA: National Center for Public Policy and Higher Education, and Public Agenda.

Institute for Higher Education Policy (1998). *Reaping the benefits: Defining the public and private value of going to college.* Washington, DC: Author.

Kane, T. (1999). *The price of admission: Rethinking how Americans pay for college.* Washington, DC: Brookings Institution Press.

Kerbow, D., & Bernhardt, A. (1993). Parental intervention in the school: The context of minority involvement. In B. Schneider, & J. S. Coleman (Eds.), *Parents, their children, and school* (pp. 115–145). Boulder, CO: Westview Press.

Kim, D. (2004). The effect of financial aid on students' college choice: Differences by racial groups. *Research in Higher Education, 45*(1), 43–70.

King, J. E. (2004). *Missed opportunities: Students who do not apply for financial aid.* Washington, DC: American Council on Education, Center for Policy Analysis.

Lapovsky, L. (2008). Rethinking student aid: Nontraditional students. In S. Baum, M. McPherson, P. Steele (Eds.), *The effectiveness of student aid policies: What the research tells us* (pp. 141–157). Washington, DC: The College Board.

Lasher, W. F., & Sullivan, C. A. (2004). Follow the money: The changing world of budgeting in higher education. In J. C. Smart (Ed.), *Higher education: Handbook of theory and research* (Vol. XIX, pp. 197–240). Springer: Netherlands.

Lederman, D. (2009, May 8). Fleshing out the federal budget. *Inside Higher Ed.* Retrieved May 29, 2009 from http://www.insidehighered.com/news/2009/05/08/budget

Leppel, K. (1994). Logit estimation of a gravity model of the college enrollment decision. *Research in Higher Education, 34*, 387–398.

Linsenmeier, D. M., Rosen, H. S., & Rouse, C. E. (2006). Financial aid packages and college enrollment decisions: An econometric case study. *Review of Economics and Statistics, 88*, 126–145.

Long, B. T. (2004a). How have college decisions changed over time? An application of the conditional logistic choice model. *Journal of Econometrics, 121*, 271–296.

Long, B. T. (2004b). The impact of federal tax credits for higher education expenses. In C. M. Hoxby (Ed.), *College choices: The economics of where to go, when to go, and how to pay for it* (pp. 101–168). Chicago: University of Chicago Press.

Long, B. T. (2004c). *The role of perceptions and information in college access: An exploration of the literature and possible data sources.* Boston, MA: The Education Resources Institute (TERI).

Long, B. T. (2009, January). *Emerging issues in postsecondary access and choice: Implications for the conceptualization and modeling of college decisions.* Paper presented at NISS/NCES Postsecondary Choice Workshop. Washington, DC.

López, G. R., Scribner, J. D., & Mahitivanichcha, K. (2001). Redefining parental involvement: Lessons from high-performing migrant-impacted schools. *American Educational Research Journal, 38*, 253–288.

Lumina Foundation for Education (2009). *Our goal.* Retrieved January 23, 2009 from www.luminafoundation.org

Manski, C. F. (2009, January). *Data collection for econometric analysis of school decisions.* Paper presented at NISS/NCES Postsecondary Choice Workshop. Washington, DC.

McDonough, P. M. (1997). *Choosing colleges: How social class and schools structure opportunity.* Albany: State University of New York Press.

McDonough, P. M. (2004). *The impact of advice on price: Evidence from research.* Boston, MA: TERI.

McDonough, P. M. (2005a). Counseling and college counseling in America's high schools. In D. A. Hawkins and J. Lautz (Eds.), *State of college admission* (pp. 107–121). Washington, DC: National Association for College Admission Counseling.

McDonough, P. M. (2005b). Counseling matters: Knowledge, assistance, and organizational commitment in college preparation. In W. G. Tierney, Z. B. Corwin, & J. E. Colyar (Eds.), *Preparing for college: Nine elements of effective outreach* (pp. 69–88). Albany, NY: State University of New York Press.

McDonough, P. M., Antonio, A. L., & Trent, J. W. (1997). Black students, Black colleges: An African American college choice model. *Journal for a Just and Caring Education, 3*, 9–36.

McDonough, P. M., & Calderone, S. (2006). The meaning of money: Perceptual differences between college counselors and low-income families about college costs and financial aid. *American Behavioral Scientist, 49*, 1703–1718.

McDonough, P. M., Calderone, S. M., & Purdy, W. C. (2007). *State grant aid and its effects on students' college choices*. Boulder, CO: Western Interstate Commission for Higher Education.

McNichol, E., & Lay, I. J. (2008, December). *State budget troubles worsen*. Retrieved January 7, 2009 from http://www.cbpp.org/9-8-08sfp.htm

McPherson, M., & Shapiro, M. O. (2006). Introduction. In M. S. McPherson and M. O. Schapiro (Eds.), *College access: Opportunity or privilege?* (pp. 3–15). New York, NY: College Board.

Morrow, V. (1999). Conceptualising social capital in relation to the well-being of children and young people: A critical review. *Sociological Review, 47*, 744–765.

Mundel, D. (2008). What do we know about the impact of grants to college students? In S. Baum, M. McPherson, & P. Steele (Eds.), *The effectiveness of student aid policies: What the research tells us* (pp. 9–38). Washington, DC: The College Board.

Mundel, D. S., & Coles, A. S. (2004). *Summary project report: An exploration of what we know about the formation and impact of perceptions of college prices, student aid, and the affordability of college-going and a prospectus for future research*. Boston, MA: TERI.

National Association for College Admissions Counselors (NACAC) (2006). *State of college admission, 2006*. Washington, DC: Author.

National Association of State Student Grant and Aid Programs (2007). *37th annual survey report on state-sponsored student financial aid: 2005–2006 academic year*. Retrieved July 25, 2007 from www.nassgap.org.

National Bureau of Economic Research (2008, December 11). *Determination of the December 2007 peak in economic activity*. Retrieved January 5, 2009 from http://www.nber.org/cycles/dec2008.pdf

National Center for Education Statistics (2001). *Digest of education statistics*. Washington, DC: Author.

National Center for Public Policy and Higher Education (2006). *Measuring up 2006*. San Jose, CA: Author.

National Center for Public Policy and Higher Education (2009). *Preserving college access and affordability in a time of crisis*. San Jose, CA: Author.

Organization for Economic Co-operation and Development (2006). Education at a Glance 2006, www.oecd.org. Table C2.1

Orsuwan, M., & Heck, R. H. (2009). Merit-based student aid and freshman interstate college migration: Testing a dynamic model of policy change. *Research in Higher Education, 50*, 24–51.

Pascarella, E. T., & Terenzini, P. T. (2005). *How college affects students, volume 2: A third decade of research*. San Francisco, CA: Jossey-Bass.

Paulsen, M. B. (2001a). The economics of the public sector: The nature and role of public policy in the finance of higher education. In M. B. Paulsen and J. C. Smart (Eds.), *The finance of higher education: Theory, research, policy, and practice* (pp. 95–132). New York: Agathon Press.

Paulsen, M. B. (2001b). The economics of human capital and investment in higher education. In M. B. Paulsen & J. C. Smart (Eds.), *The finance of higher education: Theory, research, policy, and practice* (pp. 55–94). New York: Agathon Press.

Paulsen, M., & St. John, E. P. (2002). Social class and college costs: Examining the financial nexus between college choice and persistence. *Journal of Higher Education, 73*, 189–236.

Perna, L. W. (2004). *Impact of student aid program design, operations, and marketing on the formation of family college-going plans and resulting college-going behaviors of potential students*. Boston, MA: The Education Resources Institute, Inc. (TERI).

Perna, L. W. (2005). The key to college access: A college preparatory curriculum. In W. G. Tierney, Z. B. Corwin, & J. E. Colyar (Eds.), *Preparing for College: Nine Elements of Effective Outreach* (pp. 113–134). Albany, NY: State University of New York Press.

Perna, L. W. (2006a). Studying college choice: A proposed conceptual model. In J. C. Smart (Ed.), *Higher Education: Handbook of theory and research* (Vol. XXI, pp. 99–157). New York: Springer.

Perna, L. W. (2006b). Understanding the relationship between information about college costs and financial aid and students' college-related behaviors. *American Behavioral Scientist, 49*, 1620–1635.

Perna, L. W. (2008a). High school students' perceptions of local, national, and college scholarships. *Journal of Student Financial Aid, 37,* 4–16.

Perna, L. W. (2008b). Understanding high school students' willingness to borrow to pay college prices. *Research in Higher Education, 49,* 589–606.

Perna, L. W., Rowan-Kenyon, H., Bell, A., Li, C., & Thomas, S. L. (2008). Typology of federal and state policies designed to promote college enrollment. *Journal of Higher Education, 79,* 243–267.

Perna, L. W., Rowan-Kenyon, H., Thomas, S. L., Bell, A., Anderson, R., & Li, C. (2008). The role of college counseling in shaping college opportunity: Variations across high schools. *Review of Higher Education, 31,* 131–160.

Perna, L. W., & Steele, P. (in press). Understanding the contribution of state financial aid to college opportunity: Variations across states and schools.

Perna, L. W., & Titus, M. (2004). Understanding differences in the choice of college attended: The role of state public policies. *Review of Higher Education, 27*(4), 501–525.

Perna, L. W., & Titus, M. (2005). The relationship between parental involvement as social capital and college enrollment: An examination of racial/ethnic group differences. *Journal of Higher Education, 76,* 485–518.

Plank, S. B., & Jordan, W. J. (2001). Effects of information, guidance, and actions on post-secondary destinations: A study of talent loss. *American Educational Research Journal, 38,* 947–979.

Porter, J. Y., Fossey, W. R., Davis, W. E., Burnett, M. F., Stuhlmann, J., & Suchy, P. A. (2006). Students' perceptions of factors that affect college funding decisions. *Journal of Student Financial Aid, 36*(1), 25–33.

Portes, A. (1998). Social capital: Its origins and applications in modern sociology. *Annual Review of Sociology, 24,* 1–24.

Reschovsky, A. (2008). Higher education tax policies. In S. Baum, M. McPherson, & P. Steele (Eds.), *The effectiveness of student aid policies: What the research tells us* (pp. 69–100). Washington, DC: The College Board.

Rosenbaum, J. E. (2001). *Beyond college for all: Career paths for the forgotten half.* New York: Russell Sage Foundation.

Schultz, J. L., & Mueller, D. (2006). *Effectiveness of programs to improve postsecondary education enrolment and success of underrepresented youth: A literature review.* St. Paul, MN: Wilder Research.

Schwartz, S. (2008). Early commitment of student financial aid: Perhaps a modest improvement. In S. Baum, M. McPherson, & P. Steele (Eds.), *The effectiveness of student aid policies: What the research tells us* (pp. 117–140). Washington, DC: The College Board.

St. John, E. P. (2003). *Refinancing the college dream: Access, equal opportunity, and justice for taxpayers.* Baltimore, MD: Johns Hopkins University Press.

St. John, E. P. (2006). Contending with financial inequality: Rethinking the contributions of qualitative research in the policy discourse on college access. *American Behavioral Scientist, 49,* 1604–1619.

St. John, E. P., Asker, E. H., & Hu, S. (2001). The role of finances in student choice: A review of theory and research. In M. B. Paulsen & J. C. Smart (Eds.), *The Finance of Higher Education: Theory, Research, Policy, and Practice.* New York: Agathon Press.

St. John, E. P., Fisher, A. S., Lee, M., Daun-Barnett, N., & Williams, K. (2008). *Equal opportunity in Indiana: Studies of the Twenty-first Century Scholars Program using state student unit record data systems.*

St. John, E., Gross, J. P. K., Musoba, G. D., & Chung, A. S. (2005). *A step toward college success: Assessing attainment among Indiana's Twenty-first Century Scholars.* Indianapolis, IN: Lumina Foundation for Education.

St. John, E. P., Musoba, G. D., & Chung, C. G. (2004). Academic access: The impact of state education policies. In E. P. St. John (Ed.), *Public policy and college access: Investigating the federal and state roles in equalizing postsecondary opportunity* (Vol. 19, pp. 131–152). New York: AMS Press, Inc.

St. John, E., Musoba, G., Simmons, A., & Chung, C. (2002). *Meeting the access challenge: Indiana twenty-first century scholars program* New Agenda Series. Indianapolis, IN: Lumina Foundation for Education.

St. John, E., Musoba, G., Simmons, A., Chung, C., Schmit, J., & Peng, C. (2004). Meeting the access challenge: Meeting the access challenge: An examination of Indiana's twenty-first Century Scholars Program. *Research in Higher Education, 45*(8), 829–871.

State Higher Education Executive Officers (2008, October). Second to none in attainment, discovery, and innovation: The national agenda for higher education. *Change, 40*(5), 16–23.

Steelman, L. C., & Powell, B. (1993). Doing the right thing: Race and parental locus of responsibility for funding college. *Sociology of Education, 66,* 223–244.

Steinberg, M. P., Piraino, P., & Haveman, R. (2009). Access to higher education: Exploring the variation in Pell Grant prevalence among U. S. colleges and universities. *Research in Higher Education, 32*, 235–270.

Steuerle, C. E. (2001). A principled approach to educational policy. *National Tax Journal, 54*, 351–365.

Stout, S. (2008). *Academic competitiveness grant and SMART grant programs: A proposal for ex-ante evaluation, comparing standard and Bayesian approaches.* Paper presented at the annual meeting of the American Evaluation Association, Denver, CO.

Stringer, W. L., Cunningham, A. F., O'Brien, C. T., & Merisotis, J. (1998). *It's all relative: The role of parents in college financing and enrollment.* Indianapolis, IN: Lumina Foundation for Education, New Agenda Series.

Tebbs, J., & Turner, S. (2006). The challenge of improving the representation of low-income students at flagship universities: Access UVA and the University of Virginia. In M. S. McPherson and M. O. Schapiro (Eds.), *College access: Opportunity or privilege?* (pp. 103–116). New York, NY: College Board.

Terenzini, P. T., Cabrera, A. F., & Bernal, E. M. (2001). *Swimming against the tide: The poor in American higher education.* (Report No. 2001–1). New York, NY: College Entrance Examination Board.

Thomson, S. C. (2008, Fall). The credit crisis goes to college: Upheaval in the student-loan business leaves students and parents scrambling. *National CrossTalk.* Retrieved January 5, 2009 from http://www.highereducation.org/crosstalk/index.shtml

Tierney, W. G. (2006). Introduction: Si, se puede. In W. G. Tierney & J. E. Colyar (Eds.), *Urban high school students and the challenge of access: Many routes, difficult paths* (pp. 1–5). New York, NY: Peter Lang Publishers, Inc.

Tierney, W. G., & Auerbach, S. (2005). Toward developing an untapped resource: The role of families in college preparation. In W. G. Tierney, Z. Corwin, & J. E. Colyar (Eds.), *Preparing for college: Nine elements of effective outreach.* Albany, NY: State University of New York Press.

Tierney, W. G., & Colyar, J. E. (2006). *Urban high school students and the challenge of access: Many routes, difficult paths.* New York, NY: Peter Lang Publishers, Inc.

Tomás Rivera Policy Institute at the Unversity of Southern California. (2004). *Caught in the financial aid information divide: A national survey of Latino perspectives on financial aid.* Reston, VA: The Sallie Mae Fund.

Tornatzky, L. G., Cutler, R., & Lee, J. (2002). *College knowledge: What Latino parents need to know and why they don't know it.* Claremont, CA: The Tomás Rivera Policy Institute.

U.S. Department of Education, Commission on the Future of Higher Education (2006). *A test of leadership: Charting the future of U.S. higher education.* Washington, DC: Author.

U.S. Government Accounting Office (1990). *Higher education: Gaps in parents' and students' knowledge of school costs and federal aid.* (GAO/PEMD-90–20BR). Washington, DC: Author.

U.S. Office of Management and Budget (2003). *FY2004 budget chapter introducing the PART: Rating the performance of federal program*, pp. 47–53. Retrieved January 5, 2009 from http://www.gpoaccess.gov/usbudget/fy04/pdf/budget/performance.pdf

U.S. Office of Management and Budget (2008, February). *Part 101: PART 2008 training slides.* Retrieved January 5, 2009 from http://www.whitehouse.gov/omb/ part/training/2008_training_slides.pdf

U.S. Office of Management and Budget (2008, September). *Program Assessment Rating Tool (PART): FY2009 budget, spring update.* Retrieved January 5, 2009 from http://www.whitehouse.gov/omb/expectmore/part.pdf

U.S. Office of Management and Budget (2009). *ExpectMore.gov: Expect federal programs to perform well, and better every year.* Retrieved January 5, 2009 from http://www.whitehouse.gov/omb/expectmore/index.html

Venezia, A., & Kirst, M. W. (2005). Inequitable opportunities: How current education systems and policies undermine the chances for student persistence and success in college. *Educational Policy, 19*, 293–307.

Venezia, A., Kirst, M. W., & Antonio, A. L. (2003). *Betraying the college dream: How disconnected K-12 and postsecondary education systems undermine student aspirations.* Stanford, CA: The Bridge Project.

Wei, C. C., Berkner, L., He, S., Lew, S., Cominole, M., Siegal, P., et al. (2009). *2007–2008 National Postsecondary Student Aid Study (NPSAS:08), Student financial aid estimates for 2007–2008: First look.* Washington, DC: U. S. Department of Education, National Center for Education Statistics (NCES 2009-166).

Winston, G. C. (1999). Subsidies, hierarchies, and peers: The awkward economics of higher education. *Journal of Economic Perspectives, 13*, 13–36.

Wroblewski, M. (2007). *Helping families finance college: Improved student loan disclosures and counseling.* Yonkers, NY: Consumers Union. Retrieved September 4, 2007 from http://www.consumersunion.org/pdf/CU-College.pdf

CHAPTER 19

STATE SUPPORT OF HIGHER EDUCATION: DATA, MEASURES, FINDINGS, AND DIRECTIONS FOR FUTURE RESEARCH

DAVID A. TANDBERG AND CASEY GRIFFITH

Higher education provides students with the opportunity for upward mobility and personal development. In addition, higher education delivers to states an educated workforce and citizenry as well as economic stimulation. A major factor in determining how well higher education can achieve these objectives is the fiscal resources of the institutions. In fact, there is evidence that state's higher education funding impacts both access and quality and is therefore an issue of real social importance (e.g., Kane & Orszag, 2003; Koshal & Koshal, 2000; Heller, 1999; Volkwein, 1989). In each state, public institutions receive a significant portion of their funding from state coffers. In fact, while the actual level may depend on the precise definition or data source, in 2011, states spent around $79 billion on higher education, not counting tuition and fees (Grapevine System, 2011). Yet, the importance of higher education in each state, expressed through quantity of appropriated funds, varies greatly in the United States. Additionally, measured a variety of ways, states' commitment to higher education has been shown to be fickle, and most recently, in the face of increasingly scarce resources, states have generally shown less of a financial commitment to higher education. This phenomenon is observable to the degree that many scholars, institutional leaders, and policy experts are discussing the "privatization" of public higher education. It makes sense then that state funding for higher education has received much attention in both higher education policy literature and the mainstream media.

Recent scholarly attention to the issue of what factors explain and/or predict state support of higher education has led to a flurry of new theoretical explanations and empirical findings. While much of this attention has been motivated by the recent relative decline in state support for higher education, these scholarly advances have been made possible by the introduction of new theories and empirical measures borrowed from political science and economics and new (at least to the field of higher education research) econometric techniques. Recent research has revealed the significant influence of the following: Various political factors, which, until recently, were dismissed as relatively unimportant; other state budgetary demands (i.e., Medicaid); budgetary trade-offs (where one state budgetary area is supported at the expense of another); the business cycle; income inequality; and state higher education governance structures, just to name a few (e.g., Delaney & Doyle, 2011; Doyle, 2007; McLendon, Hearn, & Mokher, 2009; Tandberg, 2010a, 2010b).

Despite the attention paid to state support of higher education in the scholarly literature, considerable confusion remains. This confusion and disagreement exists in regard to trends in state support and what factors influence state support of higher education. The source of the confusion and disagreement is the fact that empirical evaluations of state funding of higher education differ in regard to their data sources, measures (in regard to both dependent and independent variables), methods, and what time periods they cover. In addition, because of the relatively rapid progress in the last several years, it has become difficult to keep up with the many new findings. To date, there has not yet been a comprehensive evaluation of what we know and what we do not know. Such an evaluation would need to make sense of:

1. The various sources that provide data on state funding of higher education
2. The various ways state funding can be conceptualized and measured
3. The various guiding theories on determinants of state support
4. The independent variables (and categories of variables) that have been found to significantly impact state funding of higher education
5. The various methods for evaluating state funding of higher education and factors related to it
6. Any innovations in this area
7. What is left unknown and directions for future research

This chapter attempts to do just that, with an emphasis on informing the direction of future, empirical research designed to predict and explain state support of higher education. Therefore, when data sources and measures are discussed, they will be discussed from the perspective of their utility in explanatory models. Likewise, this chapter will primarily focus on studies which employ inferential statistics meant to explain state support of higher education and theories that can guide such research. Put succinctly, the ultimate goal of this chapter is to provide future researchers interested in predicting and explaining state support of higher education with the tools they need to advance the field's understanding of this important topic.

This chapter will begin with a review of the popular sources for data on state funding of higher education and then go into a discussion of the most commonly used measures of state support. The chapter begins with these discussions because it is critical to understand these details in order to make sense of the disparate findings in the literature, to properly understand state support of higher education and examine the historical trends in state support. Therefore, these first two sections will inform the remainder of the chapter. The chapter will then move on to discuss the other topics in the order listed above.

Analysis of State Higher Education Funding Data Sources

Researchers need to understand the distinctions among the various sources of data and carefully choose the source that best matches what they are trying to explain. Additionally, researchers must be clear when discussing their data why they chose their particular source and explain the relevant details regarding what constitutes the data and possible implications for the results of their study. This section will attempt to provide researchers with the information they need to accomplish both of those tasks.

Policy analysts and researchers primarily rely on five data collection efforts for measures of state funding of higher education. These sources are the National Association of State Budget Officers' (NASBO) annual *State Expenditure Reports*, the Grapevine *Annual Compilation of State Fiscal Support for Higher Education*, the State Higher Education Executive Officers' *State Higher Education Finance* (SHEF) report, the US Census, and the National Center for Education Statistics (NCES). The organizations discussed here do far more than simply collect data on state funding of higher education, and several produce rather sophisticated reports that include additional data (beyond what are discussed here) and analysis related to higher education finance. However, for the purposes of this chapter, the discussion will center specifically on the higher education funding data each organization collects.

1. NASBO's *State Expenditure Reports*: NASBO collects higher education expenditure data as part of its annual *State Expenditure Report*. The *State Expenditure Reports*, published since 1987, include state spending on all major state expenditure areas.
2. *Grapevine*: The Grapevine project was begun in 1958 by M. M. Chambers and entails an annual survey of state higher education and government officials. The *Grapevine* data is collected by The Center for the Study of Education Policy at Illinois State University.
3. *State Higher Education Finance* (SHEF) data: The SHEF data is collected by State Higher Education Executive Officers (SHEEO). SHEF builds directly on an earlier 25 year effort by Kent

Halstead and reports data from 1980. The reports include extensive data analysis with the intent of helping state policymakers answer several critical higher education finance questions related to adequacy and productivity as well as trends. Since the 2009–2010 collection year, the *SHEF* and *Grapevine* surveys have been merged, creating the State Support for Higher Education Database. This was done to streamline the data collection efforts and to minimize the burden placed on states in reporting these data. Nevertheless, the focus of the respective organizations' reports maintains many of their historic distinctions.

4. *United States Census*: Census data on state expenditures for higher education come from two surveys: (1) the Annual Survey of State and Local Government Finances and (2) the Annual Survey of State Government Finances. These data have been collected annually since 1951.[1]
5. *NCES*: NCES currently collects financial data via their Integrated Postsecondary Education Data System's (IPEDS) finance survey. This data collection effort has existed under this name since 1987. Data are available from the IPEDS website. Previous to 1987, similar data were collected via the now discontinued Higher Education General Information Survey for *The Digest of Education Statistics*. Currently, *The Digest* relies on IPEDS data.

Comparison of Data Collected

There are several state budgetary concepts that need to be understood in order to properly understand and discuss state funding of higher education and the various collections of those data. First, the difference between appropriations and expenditures needs to be understood. Appropriations include the money that the state governments have set aside for higher education. *Grapevine* and SHEF both collect data on appropriations. Expenditures, on which NASBO and the Census collect data, include the money that was actually spent on higher education. The latter of course are only available at a later date than the former. The amounts can and do vary, as mid-year changes are common (in response to budgetary demands, states may not end up giving all the promised support or ask for funds back). IPEDS collects data on funds received by the institutions and, therefore, can be understood as measuring actual state expenditures as reported by them.

Second, it is important to understand the various categories or types of state appropriations and expenditures. These are commonly broken down as follows:

- *General funds* are funds that are appropriated through the normal budgetary or appropriations process. Most often when a state-funded organization discusses their "state budget," they are referring to their general fund appropriation. These appropriations are mostly funded by broad-based taxes; however, to a greater or lesser extent (depending in the state), they may also be funded by nontax resources such as state lotteries.
- *Capital funds* may be distributed through the annual (or biennial, as the case may be) appropriations process or through a separate process. These funds go toward the specific purpose of supporting new construction; significant improvements; and the purchase of equipment, land, and existing structures. These are often funded by the tax resources of the state, bonds, and/or special state endowments.
- *Non-appropriated funds* are those funds that are designated for a specific purpose and are not distributed through the normal state budgetary or appropriations process. Examples of these types of funds include institutional support generated from receipt of lease income and oil/mineral extraction fees.
- *State grants and contracts* are nonrecurring and are entered into on an as-needed basis between the state and specific institutions for the delivery of some sort of service such as an evaluation project.

The various data collections reviewed here include all or some of these funds (several also include tuition and fees). Additionally, several of the data sources allow for the tracking of local support of higher education. The specific types of monies within these fund categories will be considered within the discussion of each data collection. This section discusses each collection in detail, examining exactly what each attempts to measure and the data each collects. Table 19.1 summarizes this information.

TABLE 19.1

Characteristics of State Higher Education Funding Data Sources

	NASBO[a]	Grapevine	SHEF	Census	NCES/IPEDS
Timeframe	Fiscal year	Fiscal year	Fiscal year	Fiscal year	Fiscal year
State endowment income included	No	Yes	Yes	Yes	No
Med/health included	Yes	Yes	No	Yes, for medical education	Yes
State governing or coordinating boards included	Assume yes	Yes	Yes	Assume yes	Yes
Tuition and fees included	Yes	No	Yes	Assume yes	Yes
Student loan programs included	Yes	No	No	No	No
Student grant aid included	Assume yes	Yes	Yes	No	Yes
Capital funding included	Yes	No	No	Yes	No
Private higher education included	Yes	Yes	Yes (delaminated only after 1999)	No	Yes
Nontax appropriated funds included	Assume yes	No before 2010; Yes after	Yes	Yes	Yes
Funding received from non-appropriated sources included	Assume yes	No before 2010; yes after	Yes	Yes	Assume yes
Funding received from Nonreccurring sources (grants, contracts, etc.) included	No (not clear)	No (not clear)	No (not clear)	Yes	Yes

Federal flow-through funds included	Yes	No	No	Yes	No
Auxiliary enterprises included	Assume no	No	No	Yes	Yes
Separately reports ARRA funds	No	Yes	Yes	No	No
Sector data provided	No	Years before 2010	No	No	Yes, by aggregating
Institution level data provided	No	Years before 2010	No	No	Yes
Unit of analysis	State governments	State governments	State and local governments	State and local governments	Institutions (data may be aggregated to the state level)
Years included	1986 to current	1961 to current	1980 to current	1951 to current	Separately: HEGIS 1966–1986; IPEDS – 1987 to current
Person/organization responsible	Chief state budget officers	State higher education finance officer	State higher education finance officer	State finance/budget officers	Higher education institutions
Appropriations or expenditures	Expenditures	State appropriations	State and local appropriations	Total expenditures	Institution's governmental revenues

[a]The lack of specificity in the reporting guidelines, and their general reporting categories, makes it difficult to precisely determine all of what is included in, or reported by the states into, the NASBO collection

National Association of State Budget Officers (NASBO)

NASBO defines state support of higher education as expenditures reflecting support for community colleges; public colleges and universities; vocational education, law, medical, veterinary, nursing, and technical schools; assistance to private colleges and universities; as well as capital construction, tuition, fees, and student loan programs. Higher education expenditures exclude federal research grants and endowments to universities.[2,3]

Fund revenue sources include:

- Sales tax
- Gaming tax
- Corporate income tax
- Personal income tax
- Other taxes and fees (depending on the state, these may include cigarette and tobacco taxes, alcoholic beverage taxes, insurance premiums, severance taxes, licenses and fees for permits, inheritance taxes, and charges for state-provided services)
- Tuition and fees and student loan programs (in most states)

NASBO breaks their expenditure data down into six categories including general fund expenditures, federal funds, other state funds, bond expenditures, state funds, and total funds. NASBO also reports state capital expenditures separately. Capital expenditures for each area are broken down into the same categories listed above. NASBO asks states for lump sum amounts for each of the categories; therefore, the data cannot be broken down any further. They define the six categories in this way:

- General fund: The predominant fund for financing a state's operations. Revenues are received from broad-based state taxes.
- Federal funds: Funds received directly from the federal government (other than research grants).
- Other state funds: Expenditures from revenue sources that are restricted by law for particular governmental functions or activities (i.e., tuition and fees and lottery supported expenditures).
- Bonds: Expenditures financed by the sale of bonds.
- State funds: General funds plus other state fund spending, excluding state spending from bond proceeds.
- Total funds: Refers to funding from all sources—the sum of general fund, federal funds, other state funds, and bonds.

Figure 19.1 below displays the amount for total funds and general funds expended for HE from 1990 to 2010. The general fund declines from 2008 through 2010 most likely occur because that category does not include federal stimulus dollars (assumed to be included in the federal funds category) and also does not include tuition and fees, both of which increased to help stabilize total institutional revenue during the most recent recession.

The NASBO *Expenditure Reports* include a table which indicates what expenditure sources were excluded by which states. For example, in calculating higher education expenditures for fiscal 2010, 11 states wholly or partially excluded tuition and fees, and 19 states wholly or partially excluded student loan programs. Additionally, other items that are wholly or partially excluded include university research grants (32 states), postsecondary vocational education (17), and assistance to private colleges or universities (22). The items excluded by various states generally, though not always, fall into the "Other State Funds" category. It is not clear from the NASBO data whether, for example, each of the 22 states that did not provide any assistance to private institutions or if some of them did but were not reporting those data. These reporting figures also vary year to year, for example, in 2009, 13 states wholly or partially excluded tuition and fees compared to the 11 in 2010 (this could

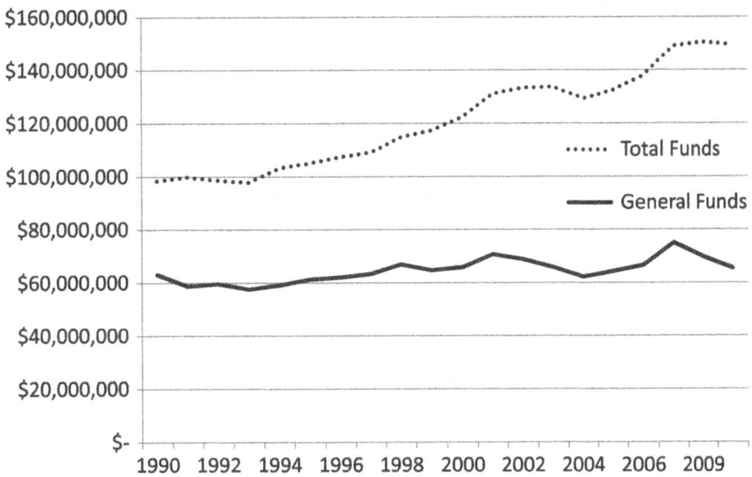

Figure 19.1 NASBO expenditures on higher education (all US states), 1990–2009.

Source: NASBO; Calculations: Author's; real dollars (thousands) adjusted by HECA [The Higher Education Cost Adjustment (HECA) is an inflation adjustment developed by SHEEO specifically for higher education. The details of HECA can be found in the SHEF reports (http://www.sheeo.org/finance/shef/SHEF_FY11.pdf)].[4]

be the result of changes in state finance practices or because states chose not to fully report in 2010). This possible variation in reporting practices may explain why there is more year-to-year variance in the NASBO data than there is in either the Grapevine, SHEF, or Census data. It also potentially makes cross-state comparisons nearly impossible.

Benefits of the NASBO data:

- The six separate categories of funds allow the researcher to isolate the expenditure areas of interest.
- Provides data on capital expenditures.
- Provides data on federal flow-through funds that can be separated from state-originated funds.
- Provides total state expenditures and expenditures by major state budgetary area, providing a single source for comparison purposes.
- Allows for yearly corrected data.

Potential drawbacks:

- The lack of consistency makes cross-state comparisons difficult, as what is reported often varies significantly by state.[5]
- Data definitions are not very detailed.
- Does not provide any local government expenditure data.
- Data are only available in PDF form.
- Data cannot be disaggregated any further than the six fund categories provided in the reports.

Grapevine

As indicated earlier, the Grapevine report draws its data from the State Support for Higher Education Database collection which asks states to report only appropriations, not actual expenditures, and report only sums appropriated for annual operating expenses (State Higher Education Executive Officers [SHEEO], 2011).

From this collection, the Grapevine report makes use of the following data elements: state support generated from taxes and those generated from nontax sources (previous to 2010 Grapevine only included appropriations from tax monies). The resulting figure is what Grapevine refers to as "state effort."[6]

The tax-generated data points include[7]:

- Sums appropriated to four-year public colleges and universities
- Sums appropriated for state aid to local public community colleges, for the operation of state-supported community colleges, and for vocational-technical two-year colleges or institutes that are predominantly for high school graduates and adult students
- Sums appropriated to statewide coordinating boards or governing boards, either for board expenses or for allocation by the board to other institutions or both
- Sums appropriated for state scholarships or other student financial aid
- Sums destined for higher education but appropriated to some other state agency (as in the case of funds intended for faculty fringe benefits that are appropriated to the state treasurer and disbursed by that office)
- Appropriations directed to private institutions of higher education at all levels

Since 2010, states are also asked to report on nontax-based funds, including:

- Funding under state auspices for appropriated nontax state support (i.e., monies from lotteries set aside for institutional support or for student assistance)
- Funding under state auspices for non-appropriated state support (e.g., monies from receipt of lease income and oil/mineral extraction fees on land set aside for public institution benefit).
- Nontax sums destined for higher education but appropriated to some other state agency.
- Interest or earnings received from state-funded endowments set aside for public sector institutions.
- Portions of multiyear appropriations from previous years.

States are asked to exclude:

- Appropriations for capital outlays and debt service
- Appropriations of sums derived from federal sources, student fees, and auxiliary enterprises

In addition, the Grapevine project does not include local tax and nontax appropriations to higher education.

Figure 19.2 displays state tax appropriations using the Grapevine data (pre-2010 data). The data is inclusive of federal stimulus funds which helped state higher education tax appropriations continue their upward trajectory, albeit at a slightly slower rate.

Benefits of the Grapevine data:

- A well-established and recognized source for state operating appropriations for higher education
- The second longest running data source for state funding of higher education
- Clear data standards and definitions
- Provides additional analysis and relevant data on their website

Potential drawbacks:

- Does not include local support of higher education.
- A significant amount of their data is only available in PDF form on their website.
- After 2010, disaggregation by institution, system level, and funding type (financial aid, etc.) is no longer possible.
- They do not provide data on state capital appropriations, federal "flow-through" money (federal dollars that are appropriated by the state to higher education), or auxiliary enterprises.
- Because they began adding nontax funds to their measure in 2010, the data from their website going forward cannot be compared to pre-2010 data.[8]

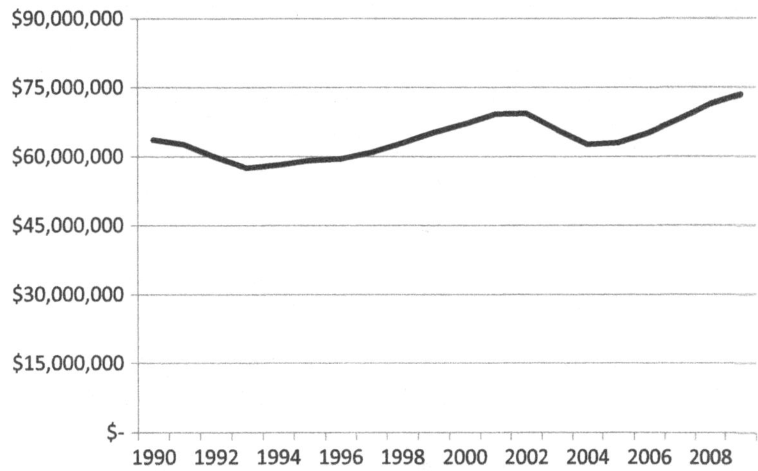

Figure 19.2 Grapevine state tax effort for higher education (tax appropriations) (all US states), 1990–2009.

Source: Grapevine; Calculations: Author's; real dollars (thousands) adjusted by HECA.

SHEEO-SHEF

The annual SHEF report generated by SHEEO utilizes the State Support for Higher Education Database and uses the Grapevine "State Effort" measure as its base. It also makes use of local tax appropriations and tuition and fee data.[9] The SHEF report breaks their data down into six primary categories:

1. State support: This measure is identical to Grapevine's "State Effort" measure (from 2010 forward).
2. Local tax appropriations: Annual appropriations from local government taxes for public higher education institution operating expenses.
3. State and local support: State support plus local tax appropriations.
4. Educational appropriations: State and local support minus spending for research, agricultural, and medical education and support for independent institutions or students attending them.
5. Net tuition revenue: The sum of gross tuition and mandatory fees minus state-funded student financial aid, institutional discounts and waivers, and medical school student tuition revenue.
6. Total educational revenue: The sum of educational appropriations and net tuition revenue excluding any tuition revenue used for capital and debt service or similar nonoperational expenses.

The SHEF reports use these appropriations and revenue data as the basis for additional analysis utilizing cost and inflation adjustments and state full-time equivalent enrollments to address questions related to adequacy and productivity.

Figure 19.3 displays the trend lines for the SHEF categories. Each category shows a decline beginning in 2008 despite the inclusion of the federal ARRA dollars (federal stimulus funds), except total education revenues which includes tuition and fees.

Benefits of the SHEF data:

- Much of the raw data is available allowing the researcher the ability to cut, combine, and analyze the data in the way he or she chooses (including or excluding tuition, private higher education, local support, ARRA funding, etc.).
- A significant amount of the data is accessible via their website in Excel format.

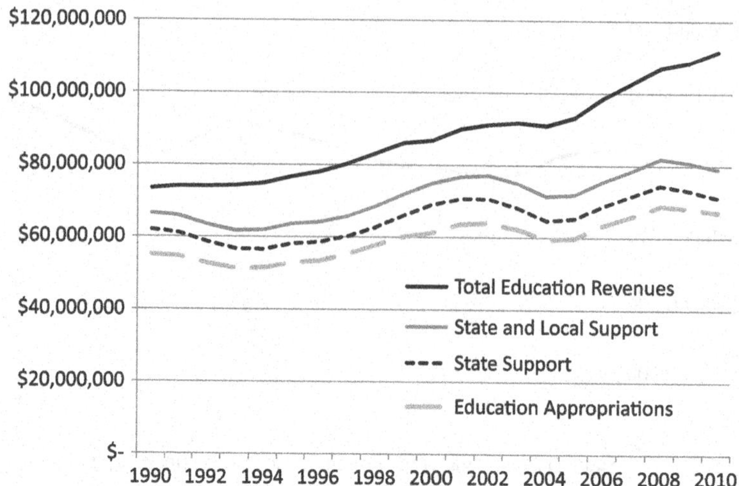

Figure 19.3 SHEF state support of higher education (all US states), 1990–2010.
Source: SHEEO; Calculations: SHEEO's and author's; real dollars (thousands) adjusted by HECA.

- The description of the data and the data definitions are clear, specific, and easily found.
- The survey instrument is provided in their annual report.
- They provide a variety of inflation and cost adjustments with their data.
- The data collection has existed for a long enough period of time such that their data standards and survey instrument have become well understood and accepted.
- The SHEF report provides researchers and policymakers with extensive and useful data analysis.

Potential drawbacks:

- They do not make their entire dataset available for download from the website.
- They do not provide institutional or system level data.
- They do not provide data on state capital appropriations, federal "flow-through" money, or auxiliary enterprises.

Census

Census data on state expenditures for higher education comes from two surveys: (1) the Annual Survey of State and Local Government Finances and (2) the Annual Survey of State Government Finances.[10] These data have been collected annually since 1951.[11]

The Census surveys define expenditures as all amounts of money paid out by a government during its fiscal year—net of recoveries and other correcting transactions. Expenditures include payments from all sources of funds, including not only current revenues but also proceeds from borrowing and prior year fund balances. Expenditures include amounts spent by all agencies, boards, commissions, or other organizations categorized as dependent on the government concerned. Excluded from the Census expenditure data are:

- Loans or other extensions of credit
- Refunds of revenues collected during the same fiscal year
- Erroneous payments and other outlays that are recovered during the same fiscal year
- Purchase of securities for investment purposes
- Payments for the retirement of debt principal (interest on debt is reported as an expenditure)
- Transfers to other agencies or funds of the same government
- Agency or private trust transactions

- Noncash transactions
- Depreciation of capital assets

Within the larger expenditure categories described above, expenditures are broken down into direct expenditures that include everything (including capital) except intergovernmental expenditures (money directed from one government office to another) and current operations expenditures, which are direct expenditures minus capital expenditures. These expenditures are reported at both the state and local levels.

Within these surveys, expenditures for higher education include those directed to degree-granting institutions operated by state or local governments that provide academic training beyond the high school (grade 12). Reported expenditures include activities for instruction, research, public service (except agricultural extension services), academic support, libraries, student services, administration, and plant maintenance. Based on examination of the data, it appears that tuition and fees are included here. Also reported as higher education expenditures are those directed to auxiliary enterprises which include dormitories, cafeterias, bookstores, athletic facilities, contests, events, student activities, lunch rooms, student health services, college unions, college stores, and the like. State expenditures on higher education auxiliary enterprises amounted to $18 billion nationally in 2008. Direct expenditures, expenditures for auxiliary enterprises and capital outlays, are separable for analysis. Likewise, local expenditures are reported separately using the categories discussed above.

Excluded expenditures include those directed to training academies or programs which do not confer college-level degrees; state vocational-technical schools which award certificates equal to less than 2 years of college; hospitals for the general public operated by universities; agricultural experiment stations, farms, and extension services; state scholarships and fellowships awarded to students; state aid to or in support of private colleges; and state administration of school building authorities.

Higher education-related capital expenditures are also collected by these surveys and are reported separately and also within the direct expenditures category. The Census defines capital outlay and project funds as: "Direct expenditures for contract or force account construction of buildings, grounds, and other improvements, and purchase of equipment, land, and existing structures. Includes amounts for additions, replacements, and major alterations to fixed works and structures. However, expenditure for repairs to such works and structures is classified as current operation expenditure."

Figure 19.4 displays the trend lines for the Census data. There is a fairly consistent trend upward progressing through the duration of the chart. The continued upward trajectory into the recession is indicative of the data including tuition and fees.

Benefits of the Census data:

- Census data collections are widely recognized and respected.
- It is the longest running collection.
- Data on higher education expenditures can be compared to data on expenditures in other areas from the same collection.
- It has long established data standards and definitions.
- Capital and auxiliary enterprise expenditures are included in the collection but are separable for analysis.
- Data are available in electronic form from their website.

Potential drawbacks:

- Aside from being able to separate out auxiliary, local, and capital expenditures, no additional disaggregation or combinations are possible.
- They do not provide institutional or system level data.
- It is not entirely clear what all is included under the category of higher education expenditures, that is, are tuition and fees included? Comparisons with the other data collections would indicate that they are. However, the inability of researchers to disaggregate tuition and fees is problematic for many analytic purposes.

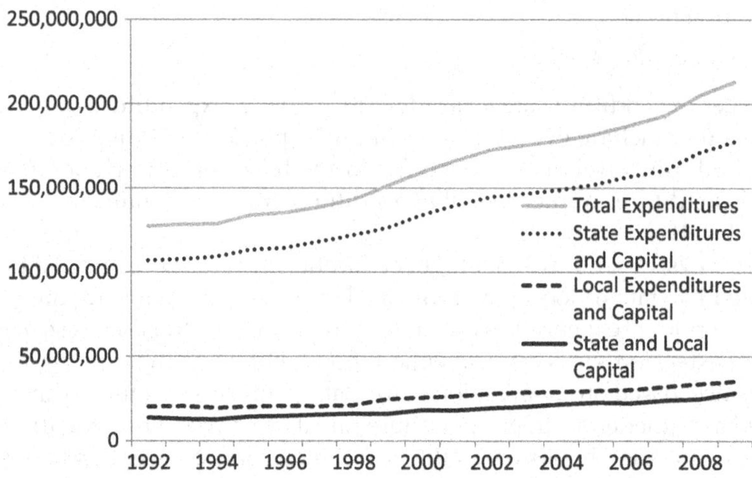

Figure 19.4 Census expenditures on higher education (all US states), 1992–2009.
Source: U.S. Census; Calculations: Author's; real dollars (thousands) adjusted by HECA.

NCES

IPEDS collects data directly from institutions through a number of surveys addressing a number of different data domains. The data are provided to researchers at the institutional level via the IPEDS website.[12] Within the IPEDS finance survey, several relevant data points are collected. These include (reported separately for state and local sources)[13]:

- Institutional revenue from state and local appropriations: Defined as amounts received by the institution through acts of a state or local legislative body for meeting current operating expenses, not for specific projects or programs. Not included are grants and contracts and capital appropriations.
- Institutional revenue from state and local operating grants and contracts: Defined as revenues that are for specific research projects or other types of programs and that are classified as operating revenues.
- Institutional revenue from state and local nonoperating grants and contracts: Defined as amounts reported as nonoperating revenues from state governmental agencies that are provided on a non-exchange basis. This excludes capital grants and gifts.
- Revenue from grants by state/local government: Grants by state/local government include expenditures for scholarships and fellowships that were funded by the state.

The finance survey includes net institutional revenue from tuition and fees defined as revenues from all tuition and fees assessed against students (net of refunds and discounts and allowances) for educational purposes. The Delta Cost Project (discussed later) uses the IPEDS data and further refines the tuition and fees revenue measure by developing a net student tuition revenue measure which is net tuition and fee revenue coming directly from students (not including Pell, federal, state, and local student aid grants). The IPEDS finance survey also collects data on revenue from capital appropriations; however, it is a single category that combines federal, state, and local sources into one.

While the IPEDS system, and the web interface they have created, provides a huge amount of institutional level data that can be aggregated by the researcher to the state and national levels, that can be an unwieldy process. Fortunately, there are at least two sources that report out the IPEDS data in more usable formats. These are *The Digest of Education Statistics*, published by NCES, and The Delta Cost Project. The *Digest* has been reporting state and local appropriations since 1962. Since 1987, it has aggregated the IPEDS data to report those appropriation amounts.

The Delta Cost Project[14] is a nonprofit, grant-supported organization whose primary mission is to bring greater attention to college spending through better data, cost metrics, and communication. One of the primary ways they are doing this is by using IPEDS data on institutional operating expenditures and revenues (like state appropriations) to develop measures of costs per student and costs per degree/certificate produced, organized into Carnegie classifications and separating public and private nonprofit institutions. The organization puts out regular reports which provide institution, state, and national level data. Additionally, The Delta Cost Project allows users to instantly download IPEDS state and local institutional revenue (appropriations and both types of grant and contracts) and expenditure data (with the Delta Cost Project's uniquely developed measures), plus a significant amount of additional institution level data, in a single, clean, and usable file.[15]

Displayed in Fig. 19.5, the NCES/IPEDS data (downloaded from the Delta Cost Project) are cut in several different ways: (1) state appropriations, which does not include grants and contracts; (2) state and local appropriations; (3) total state expenditures, which includes state appropriations plus state grants and contracts; (4) total state and local expenditures; and (5) total education expenditures which includes total state and local expenditures, net student tuition revenue (see above), and institutional revenue from state student grant aid. The first four data categories show a slight dip in 2008, which may indicate that institutions did not report stimulus funds as state appropriations or it may simply show a general agreement with the SHEF data. The data reveal that institutions more than made up for any loss in government revenue with increases in tuition and fee revenue.

Benefits of the NCES data:

- Single source for extensive institutional data (enrollment, student demographics, revenues and expenditures, program, and other data points)
- A well-established survey from a well-known source
- Clear definitions
- Ability to cut the data by system, institution, and institution type (sector, level, classification, etc.)

Potential drawbacks:

- The data can be somewhat unwieldy for state and national analyses.
- Does not separate out state and local capital revenue.
- Extensive disaggregation by state budgetary categories is not possible.

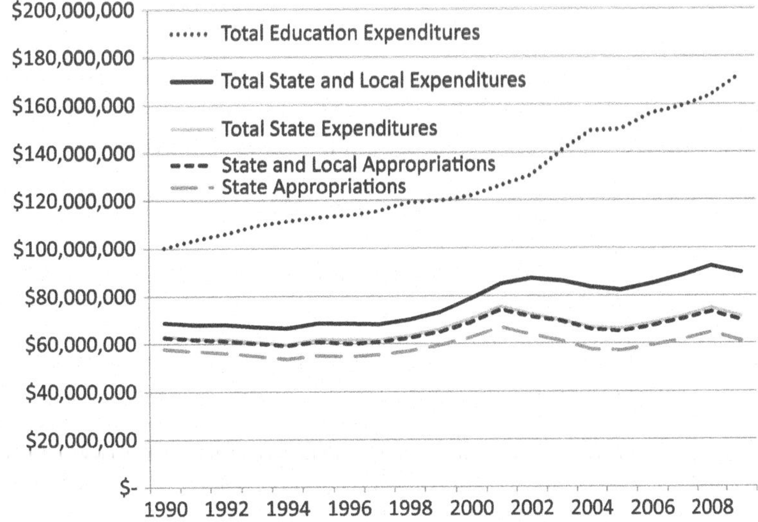

Figure 19.5 NCES expenditures on higher education (all US states), 1990–2009.

Source: NCES/Delta Cost Project; Calculations: Delta Cost Project & Author's; real dollars (thousands) adjusted by HECA.

Data Comparisons

In order to get a better sense of how the differences in what is collected by the various organizations impacts the actual data, the most comparable measures from each organization are placed in the same charts. First, the most exclusive data from each organization are compared. These data tend to isolate only state general fund appropriations or expenditures.[16] Second, the most inclusive data from each organization are compared. These tend to include all state and local appropriations and expenditures, including expenditures from tuition and fees and for capital, financial aid, and grants and contracts.[17]

The trend lines for state general fund appropriations and expenditures (Fig. 19.6) tend to display similar patterns (while the levels vary significantly resulting from the differences in what is collected by each organization) with each revealing rather dramatic fluctuations throughout the time series. The most significant difference occurs at the end of the series, with the NASBO general fund data showing a dramatic decline in 2007, the two NCES measures and the SHEF data also showing declines, and the Grapevine data showing a slight increase (including ARRA funds). The NASBO data appear somewhat more erratic than the other measures. This is most likely due to the apparent lack of consistency in the way states report their data from year to year.

Simple correlation analysis (Table 19.2) reveals that the data series are highly correlated with each other. The NASBO data is the least correlated with the other measures. This again suggests the inconsistency of the NASBO data.

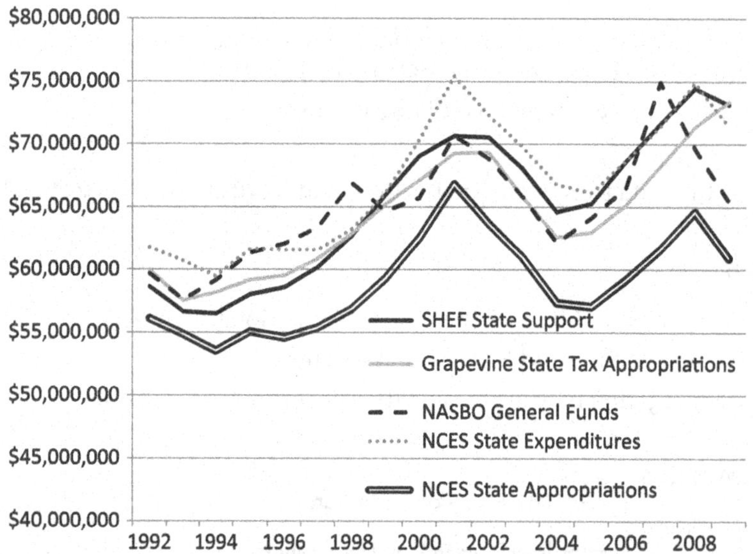

Figure 19.6 Comparison of state general fund appropriations and expenditure data sources.
Source: Grapevine, NASBO, NCES, & SHEEO; Calculations: Author's; real dollars (thousands) adjusted by HECA.

TABLE 19.2

Correlation of State General Fund Appropriations and Expenditures Data Sources

	NASBO General Fund	Grapevine Tax Appropriations	SHEF State Effort	NCES State Expenditures	NCES State Appropriations
NASBO general fund	1.000				
Grapevine tax appropriations	0.792	1.000			
SHEF state effort	0.839	0.974	1.000		
NCES state expenditures	0.808	0.896	0.905	1.000	
NCES state appropriations	0.824	0.936	0.964	0.971	1.000

Analyzing the most inclusive state higher education expenditure data reveals that again the trends are fairly consistent, with the NASBO data showing a bit more volatility than the other series (Fig. 19.7).[18] Much of the variation seen in the general fund data is smoothed, revealing how other revenue sources are used to make up for any year-to-year losses in base funding.

Predictably, these data are even more highly correlated than the general fund data, revealing almost perfect correlation (see Table 19.3). The NASBO data also correlate considerably better with this data series.

Both the various state general fund data and the various total expenditure data compared here tend to tell similar stories. However, there are important differences in the levels of funding they report and also, at times, in the patterns of support over time. These differences are a result of the way the various organizations conceptualize state funding of higher education, what they intend to collect, and how they define their specific elements. As indicated at the beginning of this section, researchers need to understand the distinctions between the various sources of data and carefully choose the source that best matches what they are trying to explain. Additionally, researchers must be clear when discussing their data why they chose their particular source and explain the relevant details regarding what constitutes the data they employ and possible implications for the results of their study.

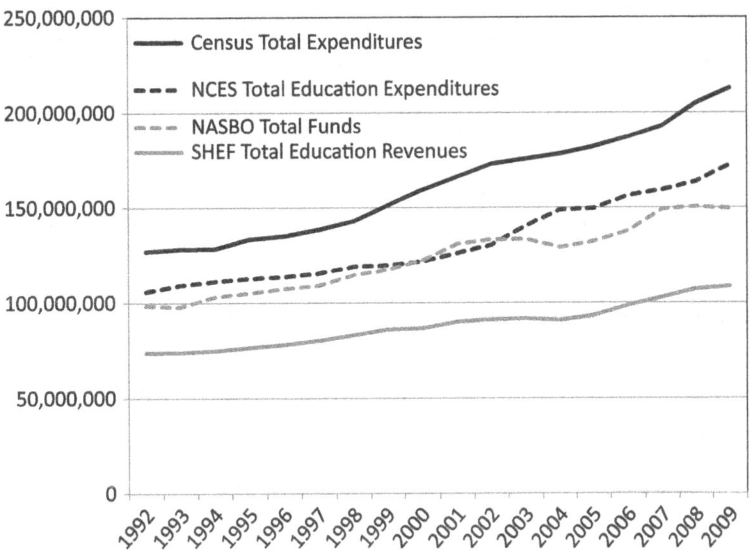

Figure 19.7 Comparison of complete measures of higher education expenditures data sources.
Source: Census, NASBO, NCES, & SHEEO; Calculations: Author's; real dollars (thousands) adjusted by HECA.

TABLE 19.3

Correlation of Complete Measures of Higher Education Expenditures Data Sources

	NASBO Total Expenditures	SHEF Total Education Revenues	Census Total Expenditures	NCES Total Education Expenditures
NASBO total expenditures	1.000			
SHEF total education revenues	.985	1.000		
Census total expenditures	.982	.988	1.000	
NCES total education expenditures	.940	.963	.975	1.000

Measures of State Support of Higher Education

Using the data sources discussed above, researchers have conceptualized state support for higher education in a number of ways and developed quantitative measures accordingly. These measures have been developed in an effort to address certain underlying concepts of interest and to create normalized measures that can be compared across the states (Trostel & Ronca, 2009). Some of the more popular ones include the natural log of actual state funding, funding per capita, funding per $1,000 of personal income, funding as a share of total state expenditures, funding per full-time equivalent student (FTE), and finally a relatively new measure of what they call "state support of higher education" developed by Trostel and Ronca. This section will evaluate each measure over-time and compare and contrast them.

When the trend lines of the various measures do not agree, it is important to remember that this variation does not indicate that some measures are more accurate than others. Rather, the measures vary because they include different elements and are meant for different purposes. Therefore, they are telling different stories. It is likewise important to indicate at the outset that the goal of this section is not to identify the one "true" measure of state support of higher education as we are not considering the measures for comparative purposes; instead, we are considering these measures for their possible utility in explanatory models.[19] When researchers attempt to explain and predict state support of higher education, they should be guided by their research questions and the underlying theory guiding their research when choosing their dependent variable. (What exactly are they trying explain?) For example, is the researcher primarily interested in the factors which predict how higher education fares in relation to other state budgetary areas? Or is the researcher interested in revealing the factors associated with the value states place on higher education relative to their state resources (e.g., appropriations in relation to state personal income)? This section will therefore endeavor to provide researchers with adequate information so that they can make informed decisions about their choice of dependent variable. Additionally, this section is meant to help set the stage for the later literature review portion, by providing more detailed information about the dependent variables employed.

All but one of the measures reviewed here involve dividing state higher education funding by a variable of interest. Trostel and Ronca (2009) divided several of the more commonly employed variables into two categories; these include what they call *ability to pay* variables and *need* variables. Ability to pay variables attempt to get at the capacity of the state to pay for (or support) higher education (i.e., state personal income). When ability to pay variables are used as a denominator under higher education funding, the result can be understood as a measure of a state's "effort" in regard to higher education (capacity for funding compared to actual funding). Need variables attempt to gauge the demand for resources (e.g., FTE enrollments or youth population). When need is used as the denominator under actual funding, the resulting figure can be understood as a measure of adequacy (need for funding relative to actual funding). Most higher education funding measures can be placed into one of these categories. The majority of the remainder of this section will use these categories as a way of examining state higher education funding measures. First, however, we will discuss a more technical issue: using the natural log of actual state funding in regression equations.

The Natural Log of State Funding of Higher Education

Often, researchers seek to predict actual state funding of higher education and include any normalizing variables as predictor variables on the right-hand side of the regression equation (e.g., Lindeen & Willis, 1975; Rabovsky, 2012; Toutkoushian & Hollis, 1998). However, state funding for higher education is not normally distributed as this histogram using the Grapevine data on all 50 states from 1976 to 2005 shows the following (Fig. 19.8).

Therefore, researchers use the natural log of their funding variable which significantly improves the normality of the distribution (Fig. 19.9).

Clearly, researchers must either take the natural log or use a normalizing variable (like one of those discussed below) before using state funding of higher education in a regression equation. The benefit of using the natural log of actual state funding is that the researcher can talk in clear terms

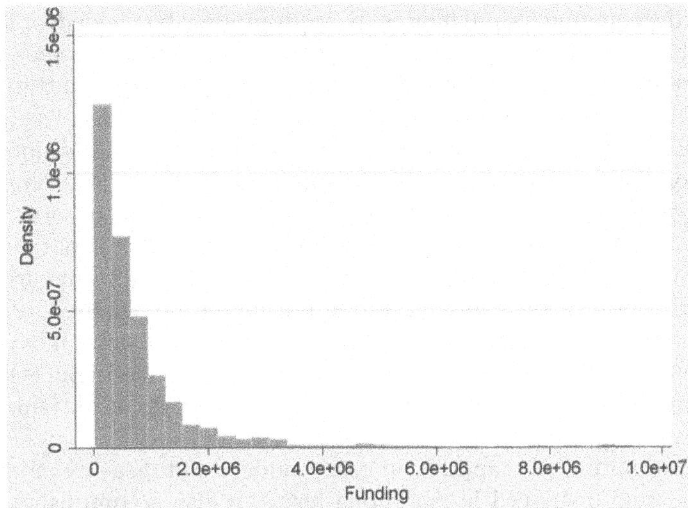

Figure 19.8 Distribution of state tax support of higher education (1976–2005, all 50 states).
Source: Grapevine; Calculations: Authors'.

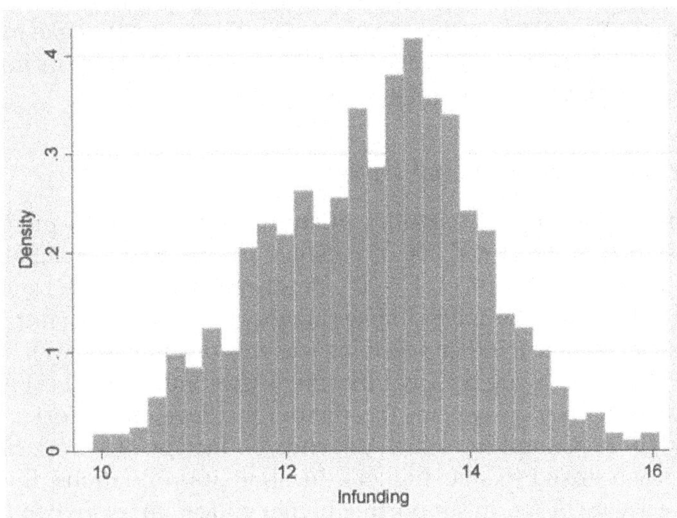

Figure 19.9 Distribution of the natural log of state tax support of higher education (1976–2005, all 50 states).
Source: Grapevine; Calculations: Authors'.

about the impact of the independent variables on state funding rather than the slightly more complex measures discussed next. The potential drawbacks of using this measure are that the logged values themselves are for the most part meaningless to the average reader; likewise, the regression coefficients can be difficult to understand and translate, and finally, the measure itself does not take into account the ability of states to pay for higher education nor the financial need of the higher education institutions as reflected by enrollments or some similar indicator. However, such factors (enrollments) can be treated as independent/explanatory variables in the regression equation, which again hearkens back to the need to reflect on the purposes of the researcher.

State Higher Education Funding per Capita

State higher education funding per capita has been employed by various researchers (i.e., Goldin & Katz, 1998; Kane, Orszag, & Gunter, 2003). It may be seen as a measure of adequacy or effort, as the denominator in the equation, population, may appropriately be viewed, at least indirectly, as an ability to pay variable or as a need variable. Seen as an effort measure, states with larger populations may have a larger tax base (taxable citizens, products, commerce, and industries) and therefore be able to direct greater resources toward higher education. In fact, Trostel and Ronca (2009) suggest that population might be viewed as an ability to pay measure. Additionally, as an adequacy measure, a larger population may mean greater demand for higher education, as states with larger populations presumably have more students and prospective students to serve.

Viewed from a national perspective, this state funding per capita is not terribly interesting, as the nation's population has been steadily increasing, and so any significant variance in the measure is driven almost entirely by changes in the funding portion of the equation, which has risen faster than the nation's population (see Fig. 19.10). However, a number of states have experienced significant population changes in the last 30 years (e.g., Arizona (+) and Michigan (–)) (US Census, 2011), and therefore, the measure becomes more meaningful at the state level, which is where most of higher education's funding comes from.

Higher education funding per capita is an easily understood measure, and people are used to seeing state financial data displayed in per capita terms. It also accomplishes the important goal of normalizing state funding for higher education for population differences. However, from the perspective of it serving as a measure of effort or adequacy, it has some limitations as states with larger populations are not necessarily wealthier and states with larger populations do not necessarily send a significant portion of their population to college. If population is something a researcher is interested in, or desires to control for in a regression equation, it may make more sense to include it as an independent variable on the right-hand side of the equation where its impact on state higher education support can be controlled for and measured directly.

State Funding per $1,000 of Personal Income

One of the more popular dependent variables in studies attempting to predict state support of higher education is state funding per $1,000 of personal income (e.g., Archibald & Feldman, 2006; Dar & Spence, 2011; McLendon, Hearn, et al., 2009; Tandberg, 2010b). Trostel and Ronca (2009) place personal income squarely within the ability to pay category of measures. In fact, those authors argue that (comparing personal income to other possible measures of ability to pay): "Income, however, is the most frequently used basis. State personal income is presumably the best measure of ability to pay. This is consistent with taxation systems throughout the developed world, which are generally based on income and/or consumption, which depends on income" (p. 221). Extending the ability to pay idea further, when linked to state higher education appropriations, this measure therefore becomes a measure of a state's *effort* in supporting higher education relative to its available tax base or wealth (Archibald & Feldman, 2006; McLendon, Hearn, et al., 2009; Mortenson, 2005).

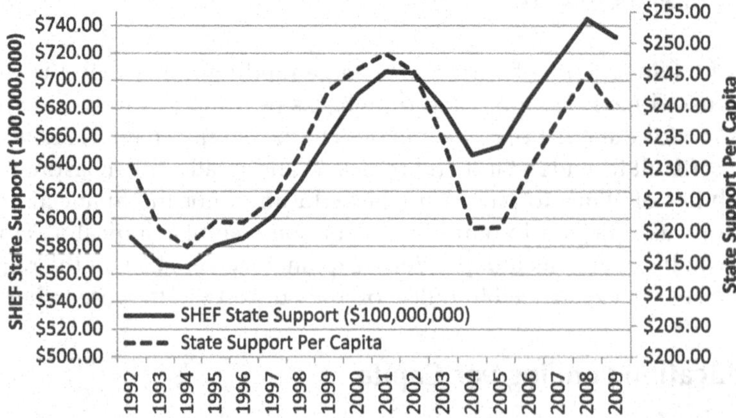

Figure 19.10 State support per capita.
Source: SHEEO, U.S. Census; Calculations: SHEEO's and Author's; real dollars (thousands).

Analyzed using this measure, state support for (or effort in regard to) higher education has been declining fairly steadily for over 30 years (see Fig. 19.11).[20] This changed in the late 2000s with personal income dipping sharply in 2008 and state tax fund appropriations for higher education increasing significantly since the mid-2000s with that upward slope only moderating slightly in 2008 (when federal stimulus funds are included).

When interpreting what a change in state funding for higher education per $1,000 of personal income means, researchers are making the assumption that the income elasticity of nominal higher education appropriations equals one, and this assumption may not be entirely accurate (Archibald & Feldman, 2006). Additionally, Archibald and Feldman point out that when this dependent variable is employed, the researcher cannot use nominal personal income as an independent variable. However, these authors argue that there is no clear rationale for why nominal income would impact state funding for higher education per $1,000 of personal income.

Researchers must be cognizant when using this measure as a dependent variable of state support for higher education (or any of the other measures discussed here) that they employ accurate language and interpret their results carefully. Once state funding of higher education is adjusted by personal income, it becomes an entirely new measure, a measure of state effort relative to its tax base. Therefore, it would not be accurate to discuss the results in regard to the independent variables' impact on state funding of higher education as that is not the dependent variable, state effort is. Likewise, the researchers should construct their arguments and interpret their results keeping in mind both sides of the equation, higher education funding and personal income, and how the two components interact.

State Higher Education Spending as a Percentage of Total State Spending

State spending on higher education relative to total state spending has been used as a dependent variable in a variety of studies in the recent past (e.g., Dar & Spence, 2011; Tandberg, 2010a).[21] Trostel and Ronca (2009) argue that total state spending ought to be categorized as an ability to pay variable, in that it highlights the total available resources for expenditure of the state. This would make higher education spending relative to total state spending a measure of higher education effort.

As Fig. 19.12 reveals, using two different data sources (Census and NASBO), state higher education spending as a percentage of total state spending has fluctuated over the past 20 years, with a significant dip in the late 1980s and early 1990s. As discussed earlier, the NASBO data again shows greater variability and more dramatic fluctuations.

There are several reasons why researchers might employ this measure as their dependent variable. First, it allows the researcher to control for general increases or decreases in state spending and therefore isolates the specific relationship each independent variable has with spending on higher education. Second, using state higher education spending as a percentage of total state spending

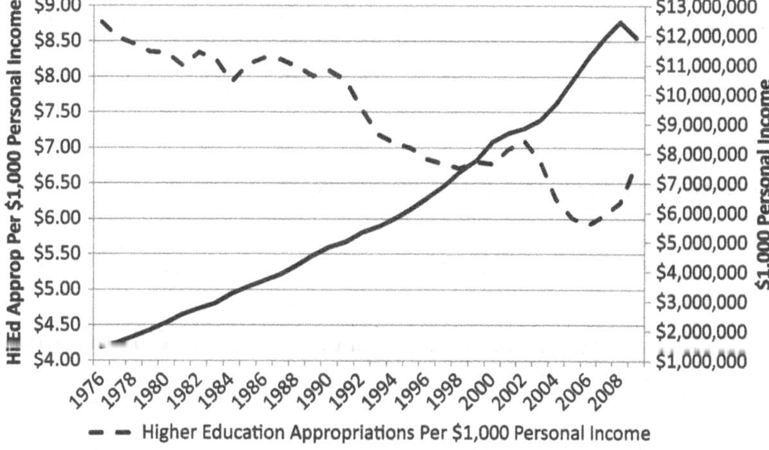

Figure 19.11 State tax fund appropriations for higher education per $1,000 of personal income.
Source: Grapevine, Bureau of Economic Analysis; Calculations: Authors'.

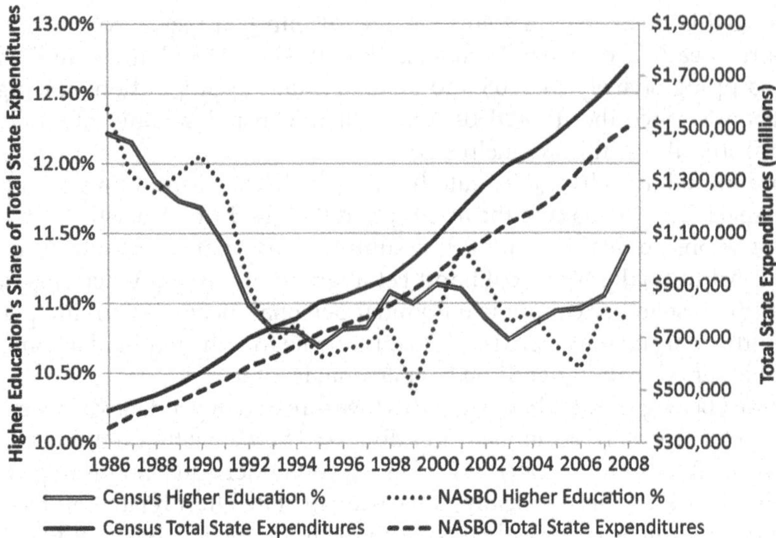

Figure 19.12 Higher education's share of total state expenditures.
Source: U.S. Census, NASBO; Calculations: Authors'.

may enable the researcher to capture different dynamics of the state budgetary process than other measures of state support of higher education. For example, states are generally required to balance their budgets. Therefore, an increase in one area often necessitates a decrease in another because of state policymakers' reluctance to increase taxes. Using this variable as the dependent variable in a regression equation may capture that tradeoff. Furthermore, the decision regarding which area gets how much funding is a political one involving give-and-take between interest groups, individual actors with their own interests and attributes, and numerous other factors. This variable may help capture that complex dynamic. In this regard, state higher education spending as a percentage of total state spending may better highlight the internal budgetary and political factors that influence the decision making of state policymakers as they decide how they will support higher education relative to other major state expenditure areas (Dar & Spence, 2011; Tandberg, 2010a).

However, Trostel and Ronca (2009) argue that, especially when used for descriptive and comparative purposes, state higher education spending as a percentage of total state spending can be a deceptive measure as it can change for reasons unrelated to state postsecondary education funding. As states increase funding in one area and nothing else changes, the percentage higher education receives will go down, even if funding for higher education remains unchanged (funding for higher education could even go up, but if funding for other areas increases more dramatically, higher education's share would go down). This is of interest to higher education researchers as a significant portion of state budgets are made up of case load-driven categories such as Medicaid, corrections, and K–12 education. Higher education is seen as discretionary and capable of generating its own revenue (i.e., tuition and fees).

State Funding of Higher Education per FTE Student

State funding of higher education per FTE has been employed as a dependent variable in a number of studies and may, in fact, be the most commonly used measure (e.g., Bailey, Rom, & Taylor, 2004; Cheslock & Gianneschi, 2008; Humphreys, 2000; Koshal & Koshal, 2000; McLendon, Mokher, & Doyle, 2009; Nicholson-Crotty & Meier, 2003; Peterson, 1976; Strathman, 1994). As displayed in Fig. 19.13, state higher education support per FTE has followed a wave pattern with reductions and then commensurate recoveries, until the 2000s where the reduction was followed by a much smaller recovery. Additionally, every successive low point in the chart is lower than the last, with the end point of the chart representing the lowest point on the trend line. The significant dip beginning around 2008 seems to be driven, along with the "Great Recession," by a rapid increase in enrollments.

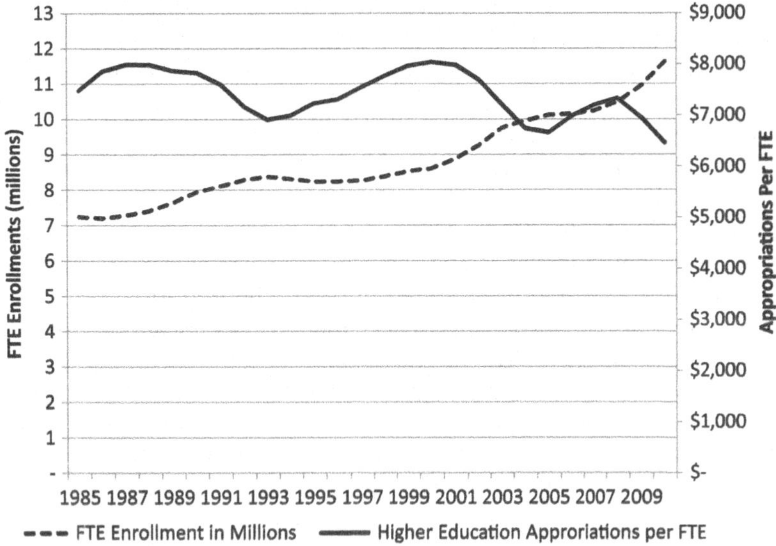

Figure 19.13 State higher education appropriations per FTE.
Source: SHEEO (SHEF's Education Appropriations and FTE measures); Calculations: Authors'.

Trostel and Ronca (2009) classify FTE enrollments as being a gauge of need for funding. Clearly, the more students, the greater the need for financial support from the state. Therefore, the combined measure of FTE enrollments and state appropriations would serve as one way of assessing adequacy. While higher education appropriations per FTE is one of the most popular dependent variables in studies of state support of higher education, Trostel and Ronca raise some concerns about its usage for descriptive time series and comparative purposes. Their primary concern is one of endogeneity. Specifically, increased state funding for higher education may drive increases in enrollments. The authors are right to be concerned about endogeneity; however, others have investigated this idea, and while there does appear to be an endogeneity problem, the direction of the effect is in the opposite direction of Trostel and Ronca's concerns, with enrollments appearing to drive funding more than funding drives enrollments. Various authors (Clotfelter, 1976; Hoenack & Pierro, 1990; Leslie & Ramey, 1986; Toutkoushian & Hollis, 1998) have found an enrollment elasticity of around 1.0 (with a range of .85–1.55). This means that a 1% increase in enrollments results in approximately a 1% increase in appropriations. This makes sense as public college and university presidents frequently use the existence of increased enrollments as a way to justify requests for increased appropriations. Additionally, state higher education funding formulas generally include enrollments as an important factor. In fact, both Leslie and Ramey (1986) and Toutkousian and Hollis (1998) found some evidence that the enrollment effect was even more pronounced in states where funding formulas are used to distribute state funds to postsecondary institutions.

As noted, Trostel and Ronca (2009) raise some important concerns about the FTE measure when used for descriptive and comparative purposes; however, it appears that, while endogeneity is inherent in the measure, the stronger relationship runs in the opposite direction to that with which they are concerned. Likewise, including enrollments as part of the dependent variable is one way of controlling for its effects. More importantly however, while Trostel and Ronca suggest an alternative measure of need, which will be discussed next, enrollment remains the only direct and immediate measure of need available to researchers.

Trostel and Ronca's (2009) "Unifying Measure of State Support for Postsecondary Education"

Trostel and Ronca (2009) address a persistent issue in the state higher education finance discussions, which is the disagreement over how to measure state support for higher education. As Longanecker (2006) reveals, and the charts above show, the levels of support and the trajectory over time vary significantly depending on how they are measured. Those who desire to show that state support for higher education has decreased have been able to find measures to support their case. Likewise, those who want to show that support has remained steady or increased have likewise been able to find measures to support their case (though, due to the recent recession and increasing enrollments, finding such measures has become increasingly difficult). In an effort to minimize such disagreements and confusion, Trostel and Ronca set out to develop a unified measure of state support for higher education and in the process correct for any deficiencies in other established measures.

As indicated earlier, Trostel and Ronca (2009) categorize the various normalizing variables into two categories: ability to pay and need. They argue that state per capita personal income is the best ability to pay measure and that the number of high school graduates over the last 4 years is the best measure for need. As previously discussed, the reason they suggest high school graduates instead of current postsecondary enrollments is primarily because of concerns about the endogeneity of state higher education funding and current enrollments.[22] The resulting index of state support for postsecondary education is a measure of need relative to ability to pay and is calculated by dividing their need-based indicator (total number of high school graduates over 4 years) by their ability-to-pay indicator (state per capita income). State funding for higher education is then divided by the result of the need relative to ability to pay equation. In the equation below, F equals state funding, i equals state per capita income, S equals state support, G equals high school graduates over the previous 4 years, t represents time, k represents state, and s represents year:

Equation 1: Unifying measure of state support for postsecondary education

$$S_{kt} = \frac{F_{kt}}{i_{kt}\sum_{s=t-4}^{t-1} G_{ks}}.$$

Source: Trostel and Ronca (2009), p. 225.

The authors suggest that the final index best captures the concept of "state support" of higher education. The majority of the article is spent justifying their use of total number of high school graduates over the previous 4 years as a proxy for need. This is appropriate as the idea is not without its own apparent weaknesses. The authors directly address various possible weaknesses with their measure and provide some data to address them. A few of the most important of them will be discussed here.[23] The authors concisely state their primary assumptions in regard to this measure in this way:

> Thus, in summary, states' number of potential traditional, four-year, in-state college students is conservatively assumed to be proportional to their total need for public support for post-secondary education (i.e., the sum of the needs from research, public service, nontraditional students, graduate education, etc.). (Trostel & Ronca, 2009, p. 225)

These assumptions are based on a variety of factors. Using national data, the authors show that the rate of students going directly from high school to college has remained fairly steady from 1992 (65.5%) to 2006 (65.8%), although it has increased since. They also show, again using national data, that the majority of students in college are undergraduate students and the proportion has only changed slightly from 1980 to 2006; that a slight majority of students enroll in four-year institutions (something that has remained fairly consistent since 1980); and that the ratio of GEDs to high school diplomas varies significantly year to year. Therefore, from a national perspective, while it is not a perfect proxy (e.g., it ignores adult students and those who enter with a GED, and around 35% of high school graduates are not entering college right away, not to mention needs for graduate education and research capacity), the authors make the case for it being a reasonable proxy and one that avoids any endogeneity issues. Further, it is the only measure that takes both need and ability to pay into consideration.

The real issue is at the state level where there are very large differences between states in rates at which students enter college immediately after college, their adult participation rates, proportion of students enrolled in private institutions, the ratio of students enrolled in two-year institutions to those enrolled in four-year institutions, their GED programs, the rate at which students stay in state or go out of state for college, etc. For example, 45.7% of high school graduates go directly to college in Alaska, and in Mississippi, the figure is 77.4%. The result of these differences is that in some states, the need will be significantly overstated by the proposed measure while in other states the

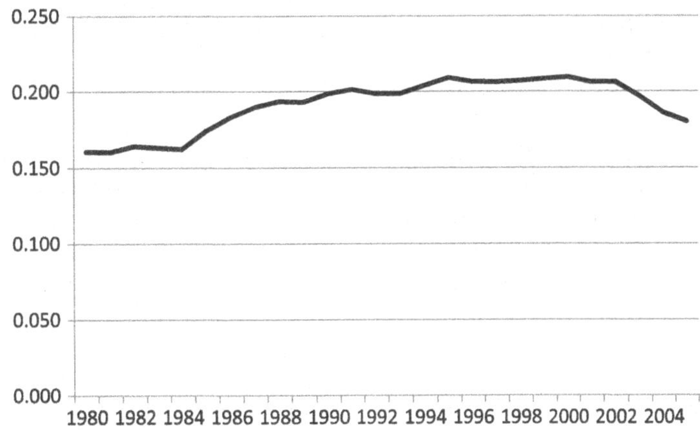

Figure 19.14 Trostel and Ronca's (2009) "Unifying Measure of State Support for Postsecondary Education."

Source: Source and Calculations: Trostel and Ronca.

need will be significantly understated. Therefore, the measure may be of limited use for cross-state comparison purposes.

Based on the Trostel and Ronca (2009) measure, state support of higher education increased fairly rapidly starting in 1983, plateaued somewhat through the 1990s and then began declining in the early 2000s. This pattern is significantly different than appears in any of the other measures. This difference is logical due to the fact that this measure is the only one to take both need and ability to pay into account (Fig. 19.14).

Similar to the choice of data source, when it comes to the measures employed, researchers ought to think carefully about the phenomenon they are interested in assessing and carefully choose the appropriate measure of state support and provide some justification for and explanation of their choice in relation to their research questions. The measures can tell dramatically different stories; therefore, it makes sense that they are impacted by different forces which can and do result in significantly different findings.

Theories and Frameworks

This chapter focuses directly on the program spending patterns of state governments and specifically analyzes state support of public higher education. In so doing, appropriations and expenditures are seen as manifestations of institutional (governmental) commitments. State spending is one important measure of the relative salience that state-level public officials accord to various social and political issues—in this case, to state public higher education (Baumgartner & Jones, 1993). In other words, patterns of spending represent the "governmental decision agendas" within the respective states (Kingdon, 1995). By analyzing appropriations and expenditures, researchers focus on the tangible distribution of public resources and not merely on the intentions of politicians and office holders, because adequate financing is a necessary precondition for any meaningful policy activity (Garand & Hendrick, 1991). As such, expenditure commitments are the targets of those who aim to influence government (e.g., parties and interest groups, as well as individual citizens). Furthermore, state budgeting has a profound effect on the ways that state governments ultimately address issues and ameliorate social problems. In short, policy spending represents a critical concept deserving of attention from political scientists and issue-specific policy scholars and analysts.

In line with Kingdon's (1984) and Baumgartner and Jones's (1993) means of conceptualizing governmental expenditures, Jacoby and Schneider (2001) define state policy priorities as "the component of governmental decision-making in which public officials allocate scarce resources, in the form of expenditures, to different program areas" (p. 545), essentially the budgetary process. Policy research has several well-developed theories to explain the policy process and policy outputs. Since appropriations decisions are processed through the same system and organization as other policy decisions, it seems natural to assume that general policy theoretical frameworks may also be applied to state budgetary research.

This section will begin by reviewing two popular ways of understanding the behavior of political actors and government behavior: the median voter theorem and new institutionalism. The review of new institutionalism will naturally lead to a discussion of two frameworks that developed out of the new institutionalism school of thought. The first was developed by Elinor Ostrom (1991, 1999) and is referred to as the institutional rational choice framework. The second takes off from Ostrom's framework and adapts it to state funding of higher education. This section will conclude with a discussion of principal-agent theory, which also has its roots in new institutionalism.

Median Voter Theorem

The median voter theorem is a widely utilized model among researchers attempting to explain elected official decision making. The theorem argues that when running for office, politicians will attempt to maximize their number of votes by committing to the policy position preferred by the median voter. Likewise elected politicians will attempt to position themselves on policy and finance issues nearest the preferences of the median voter for fear of not being reelected. From the perspective of the median voter theorem, the preference of the median voter dominates the preferences of the electorate and therefore drives the actions of popularly elected officials. Of course, the central assumption of the theorem is that the primary motivation driving politicians' behavior is a desire to be reelected (Black, 1948; Coughlin & Erekson, 1986; Downs, 1957; Holcombe, 1989).

When applying the median voter theorem to state funding of higher education, researchers face a particular challenge in that it can be difficult to determine what the median voters' preferences are in regard to higher education a priori. Nevertheless, several scholars have utilized the median voter theorem when examining state higher education funding decisions (e.g., Borcherding & Deacon, 1972; Clotfelter, 1976; Doyle, 2007; Tandberg & Ness, 2011; Toutkoushian & Hollis, 1998). Toutkoushian and Hollis use the median voter theorem as a way of establishing a theoretical link between various state economic and demographic factors (including postsecondary enrollments) and legislative demand for higher education, exhibited through state appropriations. The authors essentially make the implicit argument that, for example, since their regression analysis reveals that as state median income rises, so too does legislative demand for higher education (increased appropriations for higher education), and therefore, it can be deduced that as the income of the median voter increases, he or she prefers increased appropriations for higher education.

Doyle (2007) extends the discussion of the median voter theorem and state support of higher education further by using the theorem as a way of examining the relationship between income inequality, income redistribution, and state support of higher education. Doyle adapts a model developed by Fernandez and Rogerson (1995), which argues that, from the perspective of the median voter theorem, median voters with greater than average income will prefer lower taxes and general subsidy rates and that the opposite should hold true for median voters with less than average income. Doyle then goes on to argue that as income inequality increases (increased wealth concentration among those with greater than average income), support for increased spending on higher education should decrease. Doyle's empirical test finds support for this theory, as he finds that, holding other factors constant, increased inequality leads to lower appropriations for higher education.

Doyle (2007) argues that the median voter theorem and the results of his analysis reveal that appropriations for higher education are not driven entirely by a simple mathematical formula which takes into consideration last year's appropriation, this year's available resources, and the needs of higher education (i.e., enrollments), but are instead, at least partially, driven by elected officials attempting to maximize their reelection chances and an electorate attempting to "exclude certain parts of the population from attendance in higher education" (p. 401).

Doyle's (2007) application of the median voter theorem for higher education and the results of his study may help researchers better interpret certain results and also develop more sophisticated models. For example, it might be illuminating to interact a measure of voter turnout with income inequality. Theoretically, greater voter turnout should magnify the effect of income inequality as increased turnout should force elected officials to be even more cognizant of the desires of the electorate. The median voter theorem can help researchers understand the relationship between a host of measures of state population attributes including, for example, political ideology measures and age group shares (McLendon, Hearn, et al., 2009; Toutkoushian & Hollis, 1998; Dar, 2012). The median voter theorem, however, is not as helpful when it comes to helping researchers account for system level attributes of the political and governmental systems.

New Institutionalism

Increasingly, recent research has highlighted political institutions' influence on state budgetary practices and outputs (e.g., Alt & Lowry, 1994; Barrilleaux & Berkman, 2003; Jacoby & Schneider, 2001; Thompson & Felts, 1992; McLendon, Hearn, et al., 2009). Even some of the early foundational research on incrementalism provided some evidence of the effect of institutions on budgetary outputs (Sharkansky, 1968). Of particular interest to this study is what has been termed "new institutionalism" (March & Olsen, 1984; Shepsle, 1979, 1989). New institutionalism is more of a general perspective on social behavior than a specific theory. In fact, the perspective encompasses numerous theories, such as institutional rational choice, normative (or sociological) institutionalism, and historical institutionalism. Many other theories within policy research have been birthed or heavily influenced by new institutionalism, even though some do not have the word "institutionalism" in their names (Sabatier, 1999).

Used within the context of new institutionalism, the term "institution" is broadly defined to include the formal and informal rules, norms, and strategies of an organization; shared concepts used by actors in repetitive situations; plus the formal organizations and structures of government and public service. Even more broadly, institutions might include patterns of behavior, negative norms, and constraints (Coriat & Dosi, 1998; Ostrom, 1999). Institutionalists argue that institutions define the goals, meaning, and actions of individuals who are interacting within governments and therefore impact the decisions and outputs of governments. March and Olsen (1984), when discussing new institutionalism, succinctly assert that institutionalism "is simply an argument that the organization of political life makes a difference" (p. 747).

Shepsle (1989) explains new institutionalism in this way: "Like the rational choice theories that preceded them, and in contrast to the older institutional traditions ... these efforts are equilibrium theories. They seek to explain characteristics of social outcomes on the basis not only of agent preferences and optimizing behavior, but also on the basis of institutional features" (p. 135). In viewing institutions more widely, that is, as social constructs, and taking into account the influence that institutions have on individual preferences and actions, new institutionalism has moved away from its pure institutional (formal, legal, descriptive, and historical) roots and has become a more explanatory discipline within political science and policy research. This wide-angle view has also extended to budgetary research. Kiel and Elliott (1992) explain that a proper understanding of budgeting must consider the relationships between relevant institutional actors and other exogenous forces.

The new institutionalism perspective has recently migrated to the state higher education policy and finance literature. It has been used, often in combination with other perspectives, to explain state political actors' higher education policy decisions (e.g., Cornwell, Mustard, & Sridhar, 2006; Doyle, McLendon, & Hearn, 2010; McLendon, Deaton, & Hearn, 2007; McLendon, Hearn, & Deaton, 2006; McLendon, Heller, & Young, 2005; McLendon, Mokher, & Flores, 2011). It has also recently been used in efforts to predict state support of higher education (e.g., Dar & Spence, 2011; McLendon, Hearn, et al., 2009; Nicholson-Crotty & Meier, 2003; Rizzo, 2004; Tandberg, 2010a, 2010b; Weerts & Ronca, 2006). The new institutionalism perspective has helped scholars move away from seeing state support of higher education as being driven entirely by economic- and higher education-related factors to also being affected by various political and governmental institutions and other political characteristics of the states. As will be discussed in greater detail later, the inclusion of various political factors in predictive models of state support of higher education has been a fruitful development as many of the political variables have been proven to be significant predictors and to operate in theoretically predictable ways.

Institutional Rational Choice Framework

While there has existed significant debate about the merits of rational choice theory versus new institutionalism, there has also been convergence of the two ideas in a framework offered by Elinor Ostrom. She argues that the two schools of thought converge at key elements of the choice process. As she explains: "To offer coherent rational choice explanations of complex institutional behavior, however, requires a deep understanding of the logic of institutions and institutional choice. Thus, rational choice and institutional analysis are likely to be essential complements in the political science of the twenty-first century" (1991, pp. 242–243).

While Ostrom is not the only scholar to merge elements of rational choice theory and institutionalism (Dowding & King, 1995; Grafstein, 1992), hers is perhaps the most influential. Ostrom calls her framework institutional rational choice (IRC). IRC is a general analytic framework that stresses how various norms, rules, structures, and strategies affect the internal incentives confronting individuals. IRC argues that actions are a function of the attributes of the individuals (e.g., values and resources) and the attributes of the decision situation (Kiser & Ostrom, 1982; Ostrom, 1991, 1999). The latter is a product of institutional rules, the nature of the relevant good(s), and the attributes of the community/environment (Kiser & Ostrom, 1982; Sabatier, 1991). Rational choice institutionalism sees institutions as evolving over time as politicians seek to remake them in order to further their own interests (Geddes, 1994, 1996; North, 1990).

A central focus of the IRC is the decision situation (or action arena). The decision situation is in the "social space where individuals interact, exchange goods and services, engage in appropriation and provision activities, solve problems, or fight" (Ostrom et al., 1994, p. 28). Within the decision situation, participants "must decide among diverse actions in light of the information they possess about how actions are linked to the potential outcomes and the costs and benefits assigned to actions and outcomes" (Ostrom et al., p. 29). Institutional rational choice scholars view choice and incentives as being shaped in a significant way by the presence of rules governing the negotiations within the decision situation and also the monitoring and enforcement of consensual agreements (Ostrom, 1992).

While the IRC has received limited attention in the higher education policy literature (i.e., Richardson, Shulock, & Teranishi, 2005; Shakespeare, 2008) and in the state higher education finance literature (Tandberg, 2010a, 2010b), the framework may prove quite useful. The advantages of Ostrom's framework to those interested in learning about the factors influencing state funding decisions for higher education are that it enables the researcher to isolate the decision-making process of the political actors involved in the process and opens the process to the effect of its context, including history and culture. Likewise, the framework isolates the possible effect of the action arena or decision situation for higher education funding. For example, it brings attention to the possible motivation and attributes of those directly involved (within the decision situation) in making the appropriations decisions (e.g., legislators, governors, and perhaps state governance structure officials), those trying to influence those individuals (colleges and universities and competing interests), institutions (various norms, rules, structures, and strategies) of the decision situation (e.g., does the state use a funding formula? How professionalized is the legislature?), and the history and culture of higher education and higher education finance in each particular state. Employing the IRC forces researchers to take a much broader view of the possible factors influencing state finance of higher education, going well beyond last year's appropriation amount, enrollments, and the influence of a few economic and demographic factors.

State Fiscal Policy Framework

Tandberg (2010a, 2010b) took Ostrom's framework and adapted it using previous research on state higher education support and research on interest groups to help explain state support of higher education. This framework is displayed in Fig. 19.15. Similar to other frameworks, Tandberg's makes the assumption that the decisions of elected officials are a function of their individual attributes and the attributes of others involved in the decision process (e.g., values and resources) and also the attributes of the decision situation. The framework suggests that it is within those constraints

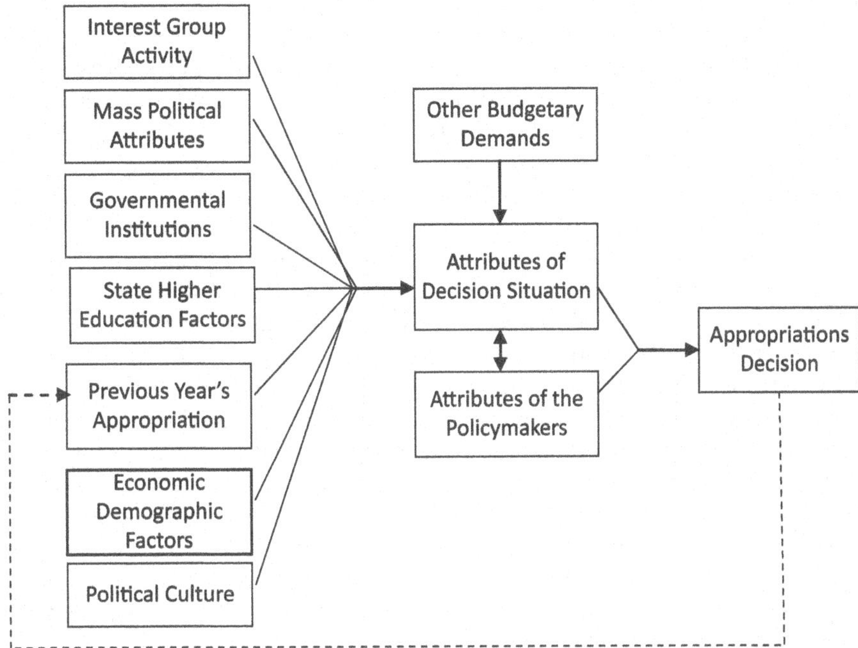

Figure 19.15 Fiscal policy framework.
Source: Tandberg 2010b, Copyright _ 2009, SAGE Publications.

that actors weigh the expected benefits and costs of their possible actions prior to making a decision. They then choose the option that best serves their interests. Borrowing from new institutionalism, the framework assumes that various norms, rules, structures, and strategies affect the internal incentives confronting state political decision makers and influence their resulting behavior. These factors are categorized in the following way: political culture, economic-demographic factors, mass political attributes, governmental institutions, and attributes of the policymakers.

The model also accounts for the influence of other state budgetary demands and the potential impact of state interest group activity (Garand & Hendrick, 1991; Gray & Lowery, 1996; Sabatier, 1999). Likewise, the model accounts for the previous year's appropriation and the influence of higher education sector factors. Finally, the model also allows for interactions to occur between various actors and influences as they converge in the attributes of the decision situation.

Tandberg (2010a, 2010b) has examined the applicability of this framework and found that individual variables fitting within each of the categories described above have significant and theoretically predictable influences on state support of higher education measured in two different ways: state tax appropriations for higher education (Grapevine) per $1,000 of personal income and share of state general fund expenditures devoted to higher education (NASBO). Among such variables are citizen political ideology, interest group activity, partisanship of the governor and the legislature, legislative professionalism, centralization of the state governance structure for higher education, income inequality in the state, institutional fundraising, and others (several of these variables will be discussed in greater detail later in the chapter). While this framework does not function as a predictive model, it can help researchers to frame their studies and think about and account for the multiple factors which influence state support of higher education.

Principal-Agent Theory

As McLendon (2003) suggests, principal-agent theory provides a useful conceptual lens through which facets of political control of the state higher education institutions and bureaucracy can be examined. In general terms, principal-agent theory helps researchers understand the relationship between two or more parties in which one party (the principal) engages another party (the agent) to perform some task or service on the behalf of the principal (Eisenhardt, 1989; Ross, 1973; Moe, 1984). Within an established principal-agent relationship, both parties are assumed to be self-interested actors, and therefore, their preferences often diverge. This results in goal conflict between the parties. Additionally, these relationships are plagued by informational asymmetries which generally favor the agent. These conditions compel the principals to invest resources in monitoring the behavior of agents in an effort to control their behavior. How the various actors manage their relationships and individual interests are primary concerns of principal-agent theorists and researchers (Moe, 1987).

Within state higher education systems, principals include elected officials (both legislative and executive) and to a greater or lesser extent (depending on the state) state-level governance structures. The agents are the public institutions themselves who have been contracted (by their state charters and their annual appropriations) to provide educational services to the state. The complex relationship between higher education institutions and state government provides theoretically and empirically rich soil for the investigation of principal-agent relationships. As McLendon (2003) explains: "Principal-agent perspectives provide a useful starting point for conceptualizing how and why elected officials seek control of state higher education agencies, how agencies respond to political control, and in what ways agency structure influences policy implementation" (p. 174). Additionally, the principal-agent perspective can shed new light on the appropriations process for higher education. Possible areas for investigation might include the following: How agency structures might influence the process or rules and levels of funding; how greater or lesser state oversight and control may impact support for higher education; how greater gubernatorial, legislative, or state governance agency power might alter state support; and how principals and agents might attempt to use, manipulate, or alter the annual appropriations process to further their own self-interest in a number of ways not limited to level of funding.

Indeed, recently, a growing number of researchers have been integrating principal-agent theory into the study of higher education policy and governance (e.g., Kivisto, 2005, 2007; Lane, 2003, 2005, 2007; Lane & Kivisto, 2008; McLendon et al. 2006; Payne, 2003; Payne & Roberts, 2004).[24] Additionally, several scholars (even if they have not cited principal-agent theory by name) have examined the impact of state-level governance structures on state support of higher education (e.g., McLendon, Hearn, et al., 2009; Tandberg, 2010a, 2010b). Nicholson-Crotty and Meier (2003) and Tandberg (2010c) further advanced these analyses by examining how state-level governance structures condition the impact that other political variables have on state support of higher education. Despite these recent endeavors, there is certainly more to be learned through the application of principal-agent theory to the appropriations process for higher education.

Literature Review

The literature on explaining and predicting state support of higher education has progressed through a series of stages as conceptual understanding, methods, and data have all advanced and improved. This section will discuss these trends and along the way highlight some of the more important studies. This section will also review some innovative findings in regard to specific independent variables.

Two studies published in the mid-1970s by several political scientists (Lindeen & Willis, 1975; Peterson, 1976) proposed relatively broad conceptualizations of the possible factors influencing state funding decisions for higher education.[25] Both studies accounted for various political, demographic, and economic factors. In both cases, they found that the economic and demographic factors have a large impact on state support measured multiple ways but perhaps more interesting is that they also found that various political variables have a significant impact on state support. These included such variables as voter turnout, measures of governmental innovation and governmental centralization, legislative conflict, interparty competition, governors' powers, and legislative professionalism. Both studies used cross-sectional data (state-level data from single years) and basic methods such as descriptive statistics, correlation analysis, and simple linear regression. Nevertheless, their findings suggested that the state budgetary process for higher education was open to be influenced by various demographic and economic factors and also various political factors. It was not until much later that the politics of state funding of higher education again received any significant attention.

Researchers' perspective took an interesting turn in the 1980s and 1990s as they abandoned the approach of Lindeen and Willis (1975) and Peterson (1976) and instead viewed factors influencing state support of higher education more narrowly. In fact, Layzell and Lyddon (1990) concluded that the only significant predictor of current state higher education appropriations were past appropriation levels. Similarly, Hossler et al. (1997)[26] found that public higher education enrollments and previous appropriation levels were the only significant predictors of current state higher education appropriations. However, cross-sectional data were utilized, which means that their sample size was at most an *n* of 50. Such a small sample size means that it would have been very difficult for any of the individual independent variables to reach statistical significance, which may have limited their findings.

Later, attention returned to the possible impact of state economic, demographic, and higher education sector variables. One of the first studies to return to this broader view of the factors influencing state support of higher education was Toutkoushian and Hollis (1998).[27] The authors employed panel data covering the year 1982–1996 for all 50 states. They also employed a fixed effects model which allowed them to isolate the impacts of state and year effects from the effect of the independent variables. Finally, for one of their models, they employed a two-stage least squares approach which allowed them to treat enrollments as endogenous and obtain accurate estimates of their elasticity with respect to appropriations. The authors found that indeed state funding of higher education is significantly impacted by various economic and demographic factors, that enrollments also affect state appropriations, and that state funding formulas generally have a significant positive impact on levels of funding. Other researchers later reported similar findings (Kane et al., 2003; Kane, Orszag, Apostolov, Inman, & Reschovsky, 2005; Okunade, 2004; Toutkoushian & Hollis, 1998). These latter studies revealed the influence of a variety of demographic-, economic-, and higher education-related variables, including unemployment levels, population size, other state budgetary demands (i.e., Medicaid), and public and private sector enrollments.

In the 2000s, attention returned to the possible influence of state-level political influences on state support of higher education (Archibald & Feldman, 2006; Lowry, 2001; Nicholson-Crotty & Meier, 2003; Rizzo, 2004; Weerts & Ronca, 2008). For example, Archibald and Feldman found democratic control of the lower chambers of state houses and of governors' offices to be positively associated with funding levels and likewise found that liberal states were more generous toward higher education. Rizzo found Republicans and unified party control of the legislature were negatively associated with the share of state education budgets allocated to public higher education. Additionally, Weerts and Ronca found that partisanship of the governor (Republican—yes/no) and the legislature (percentage of Republicans) and voter turnout were significantly associated with state support of higher education.

Most recently, three studies have significantly expanded our understanding of the role of politics and political institutions in influencing state support of higher education. Borrowing theory and measures from political science, McLendon, Hearn et al. (2009) and Tandberg (2010a, 2010b)[28] engaged in similar analyses, and their results taken together also showed that partisanship of the governor and the legislator were significantly associated with state support of higher education, but also that legislative professionalism, whether the state had term limits, gubernatorial powers, the impact of interest groups (measured a number of different ways), political ideology, the existence of a unified legislature and a consolidated state governing board for higher education, and political culture[29] all significantly impacted state support for higher education. These authors' models also included a number of economic-, demographic-, and higher education-related independent variables that were found to play a role. Finally, and most recently, research by Dar (2012) has significantly improved our understanding of political ideology and states' trend toward greater privatization of public higher education.

Independent Variables

Appendix A provides basic information on over 30 different studies meant to account for state support of higher education. There may have been additional studies published that were missed; however, this is believed to be a fairly comprehensive listing of the studies published since 1980 (plus a few published in the 1970s).[30] Researchers can use Appendix A to determine, for each of these studies, which variables have been used in past research; which independent variables have been found to be significant predictors of state support measures, the direction of the effect; and which dependent variable(s)—that is, which measures of state support for higher education—they have been associated with, the years covered and related sample information, the empirical approach, and other methods employed.

There have been many independent variables employed to explain some measure of state support of higher education. Some of those variables measure aspects of the higher education systems in the states; others measure various political attributes of, and aspects of the governmental systems in, the states; and some of the more traditional variables can be categorized as economic and demographic variables.

Of the various independent variables that have been evaluated for their possible impact on state support of higher education, this section will only focus on several key variables that fall within the political category. This area is chosen for special focus because it has only recently received significant attention, and this attention has led to important new findings that have caused researchers to reconsider state finance of higher education. The variables/factors from this political category that will be discussed are interest groups, state higher education governance structures, and legislative professionalism. All three are worth considering for inclusion in future analytic efforts and also represent areas for future theoretical and empirical development.

Interest Groups

Interest groups remain a conceptually and empirically underdeveloped concept within the larger state higher education policy and finance literature. Within political science, interest groups have been and remain a central and well-developed area of study. Political scientists have developed measures and theories which have led to significant findings in regard to the influence of interest groups on policy and finance decisions (e.g., Gray & Lowery, 1996, 2001; Nownes, 2006; Toma, Berhane, & Curl, 2006) but only recently has the higher education literature begun paying attention to this area of research (Ness, Tandberg, & McLendon, 2008).[31]

Truman (1951) defines an interest group as "any group that, on the basis of one or more shared attitudes, makes certain claims upon other groups in the society for the establishment, maintenance, or enhancement of forms of behavior that are implied by the shared attitudes" (p. 235). The members of such groups presumably establish shared attitudes, providing members a similar frame of reference for interpreting behaviors or events. In the context of American politics, Thomas and Hrebenar (2004) describe an interest group as "an association of individuals or organizations or a public or private institution that, on the basis of one or more shared concerns, attempts to influence policy in its favor" (p. 102). Interest group research generally attempts to understand interest groups, their attributes and behaviors, and the influence they have on governments and policy outcomes or outputs. Interest groups attempt to influence governmental outcomes and outputs through direct and indirect lobbying activities (Thomas & Hrebenar). While higher education is by no means the most influential lobby in the American states, as a sector, colleges and universities have become more influential over time (Nownes, Thomas, & Hrebenar, 2008; Thomas & Hrebenar, 1999, 2004), and there is reason to believe that, when it comes to issues particular to their sector (i.e., higher education appropriations), they can have a significant impact over governmental decision making (McLendon, Hearn, et al., 2009; Tandberg, 2008, 2010a, 2010b; Tandberg & Ness, 2011).

The majority of the work related to state-level interest groups and higher education policy and finance has been case study evaluations of interest group activity in one or two states (e.g., deGive & Olswang, 1999; Frost, Hearn, & Marine, 1997; Ness, 2010; Sabloff, 1997; Tandberg, 2006; Tankersley-Bankhead, 2009). There have also been a few scattered survey-based studies (e.g., Blackwell & Cistone, 1999; Ferrin, 2003, 2005). These studies have revealed insights into coalition building, interest group alliances, the relative perceived influence of various actors and interest groups, and the activities of campus-based lobbyists. Only recently have higher education scholars turned their attention to the impact these groups have on governmental decision making.

Tandberg (2008, 2010a, 2010b) borrowed a widely used measure from the political science literature developed by Gray and Lowery (1996) which they refer to as a "relative density" indicator.

Tandberg employed data provided by these authors and available in public archives to construct his measures of state interest group activity in regard to higher education. Both measures attempt to account for the wider interest group environment in the states, assume that interest groups compete for scarce resources, and assume therefore that the relative size of the higher education lobby matters. States with more interest groups may be less generous to higher education, and states with more powerful higher education lobbies may be more generous. The first measure is a higher education interest group ratio. This measure indicates the density of the higher education lobby relative to the larger interest group universe in a given state. It is a ratio that positions all higher education interest groups relative to all non-higher education interest groups. The variable is constructed by dividing the total number of state higher education institutions and registered noncollege or nonuniversity higher education interest groups by the total number of interest groups in the state minus the registered colleges and universities or other registered higher education interests groups that may lobby for higher education. The second is an interest group density measure, which attempts to measure the size of the total non-higher education lobby. It is constructed by taking the total number of registered interest groups minus the total number of registered higher education interest groups.[32]

Using his measures, Tandberg (2008, 2010a, 2010b) found that the ratio of higher education interest groups to all state-level interest groups (state higher education interest group ratio) has a positive effect on higher education appropriations per $1,000 of personal income, while the total number of non-higher education interest groups in a state has a negative effect on higher education's share of total state expenditures appropriations. McLendon, Hearn et al. (2009) also found a positive effect of the total number of higher education interest groups in a state on higher education appropriations. Most recently, Tandberg and Ness (2011) found that Tandberg's higher education interest group ratio is associated with increased state spending on higher education capital projects.

The limited extant literature on interest groups and state higher education funding decisions supports the notion that interest groups matter in significant and measurable ways. Indeed, this in an area of research ripe for further exploration and development, including, for example, the exploration of lobbying strategies of institutions and their possible impact on levels of state funding for higher education and how differences in states' interest group ecologies (the mix of interest groups in a state) might impact their generosity toward higher education.

State Higher Education Governance Structures

All states have some sort of governance structure for higher education.[33] These structures are meant to provide some level of oversight and coordination of public higher education in the various states. However, the specific structure employed and the power granted to the structure differ from state to state. McGuinness (2003) developed a state governance typology based on (in descending order) strength of control: (1) consolidated governing board, (2) regulatory coordinating board, (3) weak coordinating board, and (4) planning agency. Consolidated governing boards and regulatory coordinating boards possess direct control over the academic and fiscal affairs of campuses. Weak coordinating boards and planning agencies' authorities are limited to reviewing campus policies and making recommendations to the legislature or governor. In this second group of governance models, decision authority is less centralized, which allows individual campuses to have far more autonomy (McGuinness, 2003; McLendon et al., 2005).

A growing body of literature supports the idea that the way a state arranges its higher education governance structure can influence the higher education policies the state pursues (Doyle et al., 2010; Hearn & Griswold, 1994; McLendon et al., 2005, 2006, 2007; Zumeta, 1996). A smaller group of studies have examined the impacts of governance structures on state funding for higher education (e.g., Lowry, 2001; McLendon, Hearn, et al., 2009; Nicholson-Crotty & Meier, 2003; Tandberg, 2008, 2010a, 2010b; Tandberg & Ness, 2011). While at least a couple have not reported significant results (McLendon, Hearn, et al., 2009; Tandberg, 2010a), these analyses have tended to find distinctive connections between postsecondary governance arrangements and financing levels. For example, Tandberg's studies reveal that the existence of a consolidated governing board for higher education is negatively associated with state tax appropriations per $1,000 of personal income and with state capital expenditures for higher education but is not significantly associated with the share of total state expenditures received by higher education.

Tandberg (2010c) and Nicholson-Crotty and Meier (2003) further highlight the role of state governance structures in influencing state funding decisions for higher education by examining their conditioning effect on other political factors and those factors' influence on state appropriations decisions. Tandberg found that indeed various political measures had differing impacts on state funding decisions in regard to size and direction depending on whether a state employed a consolidated governing board or not. State higher education interest groups' impact was muted, the influence of the governor was diminished, and the influence of the legislature was magnified (among other findings) with or without such a board. Nicholson-Crotty and Meier engaged in a similar analysis which likewise revealed conditioning effects of state higher education governance structures. Further analysis of the conditioning role of state higher education governance structures and new measures of governance structures themselves are possible areas for future research.

Legislative Professionalism

One of the political variables that has the most consistent and, in fact, largest impact on state support of higher education is legislative professionalism (e.g., McLendon, Hearn, et al., 2009; Nicholson-Crotty & Meier, 2003; Peterson, 1976; Tandberg, 2008, 2010a, 2010b; Tandberg & Ness, 2011). In each of these studies, legislative professionalism has been found to have a significant and positive impact on state support of higher education measured a number of different ways. Legislative professionalism represents the degree of institutional resources in the legislature (full-time staff, session length, and member pay) (Squire, 2000). There is substantial variation across states in terms of the professionalism of their legislatures, which makes the variable quite useful for empirical analyses. Legislative professionalism has been linked with higher public spending generally (Squire & Hamm, 2005) and, as indicated earlier, has specifically been found to positively impact spending for higher education, including higher education's share of total state expenditures (Tandberg, 2010a).

Legislative professionalism has been measured in two different ways. First, and most popular, is the Squire index. This is an index of the state legislature's average member pay, average days in session, and average staff per member relative to the US Congress (Squire & Hamm, 2005). A value of 1.0 indicates a perfect resemblance to Congress and therefore a high level of professionalism, while a value close to 0.0 indicates little institutional professionalism. McLendon, Hearn et al. (2009) utilized this measure. The second, utilized by Tandberg (2008, 2010a, 2010b; Tandberg & Ness, 2011), simply uses the legislature's average pay. This approach has also been used in the political science literature for some time (e.g., Barrilleaux & Berkman, 2003; Carey, Niemi, & Powell, 2000; Fiorina, 1994). Either measure produces similar results.

The remaining question is why does legislative professionalism produce these results? We do not clearly know yet. However, Tandberg theorizes that there may be at least two possible reasons. First, more professionalized legislatures generally attract more educated members, who may be more sympathetic toward higher education and value it more highly. And second, McLendon, Hearn et al. (2009) and Tandberg (2010a), both recognize that the greater analytic ability of more professional legislatures may have something to do with the results. The basic argument is that more educated legislatures may value higher education more highly (Pascarella & Terenzini, 2005), as will legislatures with access to better information and resources, which may be more sympathetic toward higher education. Nevertheless, this is an area warranting further theoretical and analytical attention. As McLendon, Hearn et al. ask: "Why and how, precisely, does professionalism influence decision making in legislative bodies, particularly in the context of decisions about higher-education funding? Conceptually, why does professionalism seem to influence this particular kind of policy activity, i.e., state funding decisions, whereas previous studies have shown scant evidence of the effect of legislative professionalism in other areas of postsecondary policy?" (p. 700).

Methodological Advances

The most significant methodological development in the area of state finance of higher education is the creation of large-scale panel data sets and the use of fixed effects. Panel data sets greatly increase the analytical degrees of freedom by increasing the sample size. For example, a study utilizing data on all 50 states over the course of 20 years will have an n of 1,000. A simple cross-sectional study will only have an n of 50. The larger n dramatically increases the possibility of statistically significant findings. The larger n also frees the researcher to be able to include many more variables because of the increased degrees of freedom. This has led researchers to collect numerous economic-, demographic-, political-, and higher education-related variables, and the findings from these studies have significantly improved our understanding of the budgetary process.

In conjunction with the introduction of the panel data sets has come the use of fixed effects models. These models remove state-specific and time-specific effects from the coefficient estimates of the variables of interest. In other words, fixed effects allow researchers to control for unobservable characteristics about states and time that may impact state support for higher education. Generally, fixed effects are implemented within an ordinary least squares (OLS) model with the inclusion of dummy variables for state and/or time effects (Zhang, 2010; Toutkoushian & Hollis, 1998).[34] Such a model, meant to predict state support of higher education and primarily focused on examining the role of politics, might look like this:

Equation 2: OLS fixed effects model

$$y_{it} = a + b_1 p_{st} + b_2 c_{st} + \tau_t + \delta_s + v_{st}.$$

where y is the dependent variables (a measure of state support of higher education), a is the intercept coefficient, p_{st} represents the vector for various political variables, c_{st} represents the vector for various higher education and economic and demographic control variables, τ_t represents the year effects, δ_s represents the state effects, v_{st} is the pure residual, s and t are indices for individual states and time, and b_1 and b_2 represent the coefficients associated with the variables included in each vector.

Additionally, the use of interaction terms may continue to be a fruitful approach going forward. The use of interaction terms made the examination of the conditioning effect of state higher education governance structures, conducted by Tandberg (2010c) and Nicholson-Crotty and Meier (2003), possible (see above for a more detailed discussion). When an interaction term is created, the effect of two, or more, variables are not simply additive; instead, the effect of one variable depends on the value of another. Interaction terms are computed by multiplying the two main effect terms by each other. When a dummy variable for governance form is included in an interaction term (as they were in the Tandberg and Nicholson-Crotty & Meier studies), whether the results for the interaction terms are significant or not generally indicates whether there is a significant difference for states with and without a consolidated governing board for each political variable. For example, if the interaction term including budget powers of the governor and the dummy variable for higher education governance structure (coded 1 if such a board exists in a given state/year and 0 if not) is significant, then the difference between the results for different budget powers of the governor varies significantly depending upon whether a state is with or without a consolidated governing board. When employing interaction terms with a dummy variable, the final step is to split the sample based on whether each state/year has a consolidated governing board and then run two additional regressions: one including only those state/years coded 1 and one including only those state/years coded 0. This reveals the impact of the independent variables with and without the conditioning variable of interest (Tandberg).

A final methodological advance might be the use of two-stage least squares to address the possible endogeneity between various independent variables (i.e., enrollments) and state support of higher education (Toutkoushian & Hollis, 1998). Of course, there may be many other advances, and more will be developed if research in this domain continues. Indeed, the advancements in data and methods have been at the core of the recent expansion of our understanding of the factors that influence state support of higher education.

Conclusion

The data, measures, theories, literature, findings, and methods analyzed and reviewed in this chapter should provide a solid foundation for future empirical examinations of the factors associated with state support of higher education. Future researchers should be sensitive to the differences in the measures of state funding of higher education data depending on the source and its purpose. They should justify their decision in regard to their data source and provide a discussion of what the data includes and does not include. Likewise, researchers ought to think carefully about the phenomenon they are interested in assessing and carefully choose the appropriate measure of state support of higher education and provide some justification for, and explanation of, their choice. Researchers may want to consider one of the theories or frameworks reviewed here as they provide reasonable guides to, and explanations of, political decision making within a larger context and make room for the influence of politics and economic-, demographic-, and higher education system-related factors. They will also help researchers make better sense of their findings. The use of theory to guide research into the factors related to state support of higher education has, by and large, been sorely underutilized in the literature to date. Researchers also ought to carefully review and then build upon what has already been found in the literature to date. Hopefully, Appendix A will help in this regard. Researchers should consider utilizing and further investigating the three political variables discussed at length in this chapter (state interest groups, state higher education governance structures, and legislative professionalism) for there remains much to be learned about how they influence state support of higher education. Additionally, researchers ought to continue to explore research from other disciplines (e.g., public policy, public finance, political science, and economics) in order to investigate whether there are other variables of possible significance to add to the large panel data sets.

We need to learn more about the dynamics of the political decisions being made in regard to state support of higher education, and we need to arrive at better understandings and explanations for many of the relationships we have already observed. As indicated at the beginning of this chapter, state higher education funding impacts both access and quality and is therefore an issue of real social importance. Arriving at a better understanding of what drives it is critical for those who want to influence it. As Layzell and Lyddon (1990) explained in reference to state budgeting for higher education: "You have got to know the system to beat the system" (p. xix).

Acknowledgements

The authors wish to thank William M. Zumeta, Shouping Hu, and Michael B. Paulsen for their helpful suggestions and edits which greatly improved this chapter. The authors would also like to thank Andy Carlson from SHEEO, Brian Sigritz from NASBO, Allison Bell from NCES and formerly with SHEEO, Colleen Lenihan from NCES, and Jane Wellman formerly with the Delta Cost Project who all provided excellent suggestions and corrections to the first two sections of this chapter. Finally, we would like to thank Luciana Dar for her willingness to share her exceptional work with us. Of course, all errors are the responsibility of the authors alone.

APPENDIX A

Studies of State Appropriation to Higher Education[a]

	Authors	Year	Citation	Dependent Variable(s) (RE: State Support)[b]	Dependent Source	Time Period and Empirical Approach	Sample	Significant Independent Variables (+/−)
1	Archibald, R. B., & Feldman, D. H.	2006	Archibald, R. B., & Feldman, D. H. (2006). State higher education spending and the tax revolt. *Journal of Higher Education, 77*(4), 618–643	State appropriations to higher ed. per $1,000 of personal income (excluding federal and lottery funds)	Grapevine, Census, Book of the States	1961–2001 Panel data, fixed effects	47 States	Democratic Governor, + Democratic Strength, + Super Majority Requirement, + Corrections Spending, + Health Spending, + Tax and Expenditure Limits, −
2	Bailey, M. E., Rom, M. C., & Taylor, M.	2004	Bailey, M. E., Rom, M. C., & Taylor, M. (2004). State competition in higher education: A race to the top or a race to the bottom? *Economics of Governance, 5*(1), 53–75	Change in state support for higher education, annually (higher ed. exp. per state resident; higher ed. exp. FTE, CPI adjusted)	IPEDS, ICPSR, state finances	1986–1987 Panel data, two-way fixed effects	48 States	Democratic Strength, − Competition (spending between states and neighbors), − Convergence (policy measure between states and neighbors), − Personal Income per Capita, − Student Aged Pop. (18–24), + Elderly Pop. (65<), +

(continued)

APPENDIX A

Studies of State Appropriation to Higher Education *(continued)*

	Authors	Year	Citation	Dependent Variable(s) (RE: State Support)[b]	Dependent Source	Time Period and Empirical Approach	Sample	Significant Independent Variables (+/–)
3	Cheslock, J. J., & Gianneschi, M.	2008	Cheslock, J., & Gianneschi, M. (2008). Replacing state appropriations with alternative revenue sources: The case of voluntary support. *Journal of Higher Education, 79*, 208+	State appropriations per student (adjusted CPI, HEPI, FTE)	IPEDS ICPSR, state finances	1994–2004 Panel data	All public four-year institutions that offer undergraduate degrees, have a 2000 Carnegie Classification of Research/ Doctoral, Masters, or Baccalaureate, 47 states	Barron's Selectivity Ranking, + Enrollment, – Research/Doctoral Carnegie Classification, + US News Ranking, – Personal Income per Capita, + State Appropriations Previous Year, + Unemployment Rate, –
4	Coughlin, C. C., & Erekson, O. H.	1986	Coughlin, C. C., & Erekson, O. H. (1986). Determinants of state aid and voluntary support of higher education. *Economics of Education Review, 5*(2), 179–190	State appropriations per student	Halstead, *How States Compare in Financial Support of Public Higher Education,* 1983–1984	1980–1981 Cross-sectional OLS	52 Major research universities	Top Undergraduate Quality, + SAT, + Top Faculty, + Tuition, – Relative Tuition, + Per Capita State Income, + Tax Effort, + NCAA Appearance, + TV Appearances, + Basketball Winning %, +

5	Dar, L., & Franke, R.	2010	Dar, L., & Franke, R. (2010). *Revisiting the political economy of government support for higher education: Evidence from a new unifying measure for the American states.* Presented at the Annual Consortium for Higher Education Researchers, Oslo, Norway	Trostel and Ronca's (2009) "unifying measure of state support of higher education"	Trostel and Ronca (2009)	1980–2005 Panel data, fixed effects	49 States	Carnegie Classification I or II, + Private Enrollment FTE, – Tuition per FTE, – Democratic Strength, + Polarization, + State Policy Priority Score, – Personal Income per Capita, – Student Aged Pop. (18–24), + State Revenue, + Unemployment Rate, +
6	Dar, L., & Spence, M. J.	2011	Dar, L., & Spence, M. J. (2011). Partisanship, political polarization, and state budget outcomes: The case of higher education. *SSRN eLibrary,* Retrieved from http://ssrn.com/abstract=1577365	Appropriations per $1,000 in personal income, relative appropriations by share of budget	STATE GOVERNMENT FiNANCES 1900–2004—File provided by the Census Bureau Staff Grapevine/Center for the Study of Education Policy—Illinois State University http://coe.ilstu.edu/grapevine/Welcome.htm	1976–2004 Panel Data, fixed effects	49 States	Private Enrollment FTE, – Tuition per FTE, – Democratic Strength, + Polarization, + State Policy Priority Score, – Personal Income per Capita, – Student Aged Pop. (18–24), + Pop. Share of School Aged (18–24), + State Revenue, + Unemployment Rate, –
7	Delaney, J. A., & Doyle, W. R.	2007, 2011	Delaney, J. A., & Doyle, W. R. (2011). State spending on higher education: Testing the balance wheel over time. *Journal of Education Finance, 36*(4), 343–368	State appropriations for higher education (CPI adjusted) (1) Absolute levels of state funding for higher ed. (2) Year-to-year funding for Higher ed. by state and by year data evaluated by decade and business cycle	Grapevine, http://www.grapevine.ilstu.edu/historical/index.htm	1985–2004 Panel Data	49 States	Enrollment, + Private Enrollment FTE, – Share of Public, 2 year Enrollment, – Share of Private, 2 year Enrollment, – Share of Public, 4 year Enrollment, – Gross State Product, + Total Expenditure all Budget Categories other than HE, +

(continued)

APPENDIX A

Studies of State Appropriation to Higher Education *(continued)*

	Authors	Year	Citation	Dependent Variable(s) (RE: State Support)[b]	Dependent Source	Time Period and Empirical Approach	Sample	Significant Independent Variables (+/–)
8	Doyle, W. R.	2007	Doyle, W. R. (2007). The political economy of redistribution through higher education subsidies. In J. C. Smart (Ed.), *Higher education: Handbook of theory and research* (Vol. XXII, pp. 335–409). Dordrecht, The Netherlands: Springer	State tax appropriations for higher education (CPI adjusted)	Center for the Study of Education Policy, US Census Bureau, Grapevine	1985–1989 1951–2007 (no data for 1973) Panel data, two-stage least squares estimation	50 States 48 States	Private Enrollment FTE, + Student Aged Pop. (18–24), +
9	Hossler, D., Lund, J. P., Ramin, J., Westfall, S., & Irish, S.	1997	Hossler, D., Lund, J. P., Ramin, J., Westfall, S., & Irish, S. (1997). State funding for higher education: The Sisyphean Task. *The Journal of Higher Education, 68*(2), 160–190	Levels of state appropriations to public four-year institutions	Grapevine	1990, 1991, 1992, Separately CROSS-TABs, regression analyses, and exploratory factor analyses	50 States	Enrollment, + State Appropriations Previous Year, +
10	Humphreys, B. R.	2000	Humphreys, B. R. (2000). Do business cycles affect state appropriations to higher education? *Southern Economic Journal, 67*(2), 398–413	Real state appropriations for higher ed. per FTE (HEPI adjusted)	Department of Commerce, Grapevine, IPEDS	1969–1994 Panel data, fixed effects	50 States	Growth in Income, + Personal Growth in Income Expansionary Years, + Personal Growth in Income Recessionary Years, + Personal Income Expansionary Years, + Personal Income Recessionary Years, +

11	Kane, T. J., Orszag, P. R., & Gunter, D. L	2003	Kane, T. J., Orszag, P. R., & Gunter, D. L. (2003). *State fiscal constraints and higher education spending: The role of Medicaid and the business cycle.* Washington, DC: Brookings Institution	(1) Real higher education appropriations per capita ($1,000) (2) Real higher education appropriations as % of GSP	Dept. of Commerce, Grapevine, *Digest of Higher Education Statistics*	1981–2001 Panel data, two-way fixed effects (state, time) regression	48 States	Democratic Strength, + Avg. Income Tax on Wages, + Medicare Appropriations,– State Revenue, + Top Marginal Income Tax Rate, + Unemployment Rate, –
12	Knott, J., & Payne, A.	2004	Knott, J., & Payne, A. (2004). The impact of state governance structures on management and performance of public organizations: A study of higher education institutions. *Journal of Policy Analysis and Management, 23*(1), 13–30	State appropriations institution (adjusted for 1996 price indices)	CASPAR, Institute for Scientific Information	1997–1998 Panel data	48 States, comprehensive and Ph.D.-granting public universities	Medical School, + Faculty Size, + Undergrad Enrollment, + HE Governance Structure, –
13	Koshal, R. K., & Koshal, M.	2000	Koshal, R. K., & Koshal, M. (2000). State appropriation and higher education tuition: What is the relationship? *Education Economics, 8*(1), 81–89	Appropriation per FTE in a state	*The Statistical Abstract of the United States*	1990 Panel data, two-stage least squares	47 States (Nebraska excluded)	Share of Public, 2 year Enrollment, + Tuition per FTE, – Democratic Strength, + FTE Ratio to High School Grad 4 year, – Personal Income per Capita, – State Revenue, +

(continued)

APPENDIX A

Studies of State Appropriation to Higher Education *(continued)*

	Authors	Year	Citation	Dependent Variable(s) (RE: State Support)[b]	Dependent Source	Time Period and Empirical Approach	Sample	Significant Independent Variables (+/–)
14	Leslie, L. L., & Ramey, G.	1986	Leslie, L. L., & Ramey, G. (1986). State appropriations and enrollments: Does enrollment growth still pay? *The Journal of Higher Education, 57*(1), 1–19	Real (inflation adjusted) appropriations in year	Chambers's State Tax Funds for Operating Expenses of Higher Education	1965–1981 Panel Data, OLS Regression	439 Public colleges and universities: 25 research I universities, 31 research II universities, 35 doctoral-granting I, 18 doctoral-granting II, 235 comprehensive I, and 95 comprehensive II institutions (using Carnegie classifications)	Enrollment, – Research/Doctoral Carnegie Classification, –
15	Lindeen, J. W., & Willis, G. L.	1975	Lindeen, J. W., & Willis, G. L. (1975). Political, socioeconomic and demographic patterns of support for public higher education. *The Western Political Quarterly, 28*(3), 528–541	(1) Public Financial Support: Total Amount per Taxpayer; Taxpayer Effort (2) Increase in state Support. 1960–70: gross net Percentage; Net Percentage Increase	*Statistical Abstract of the United States* (1962), *Statistical Abstract of the United States* (1972), *Digest of Educational Statistics* (1971), *Ohio Basic Data Series: Higher Education* (1971)	1960–1970 Correlation analysis, OLS	48 States	Gross % Increase State Support, + Taxpayer Effort, –

16	Lowry, R. C.	2001	Lowry, R. C. (2001). The effects of state political interests and campus outputs on public university revenues. *Economics of Education Review, 20*(2), 105–119	Dollar amount of state government appropriations, grants and contracts per 100,000 voting-age residents in the state	IPEDS	1994–1995 Panel data, two-stage least squares regression (separate analyses)	All public, four-year institutions in the 50 states for which complete financial and enrollment data was available at the time (428 universities in most cases)	Graduate & Professional Enrollment, + Mean Faculty Compensation, + Medical School, + Private Enrollment FTE, – Tuition per FTE, + Undergrad, Non-resident Enrollment, + Undergrad, Resident Enrollment, + HE Governance Structure, – Local Government Funds, – Elderly Pop. (65<), – Public Service Spending, + Research Spending, +
17	McLendon, M. K., Hearn, J. C., & Mokher, C. G.	2009	McLendon, M. K., Hearn, J. C., & Mokher, C. G. (2009). Partisans, professionals, and power: The role of political factors in state higher education funding. *The Journal of Higher Education, 80*(6), 686–713	State appropriations per $1,000 of personal income (CPI adjusted 2004)	Grapevine, Postsecondary Opportunity	1984–2004 Panel Data, regression model, fixed effects	49 States (e.g., Nebraska)	Private Enrollment FTE, – Share of Public, 2 year Enrollment, + Gubernatorial Power, – HE Interest Groups, + Legislative Professionalism, + Republican Governor, – Republican Strength, – Term Limits, + Student Aged Pop. (18–24), – Elderly Pop. (65<), – Unemployment Rate, –

(continued)

APPENDIX A

Studies of State Appropriation to Higher Education *(continued)*

	Authors	Year	Citation	Dependent Variable(s) (RE: State Support)[b]	Dependent Source	Time Period and Empirical Approach	Sample	Significant Independent Variables (+/–)
18	McLendon, M. K., Mokher, C. G., & Doyle, W.	2009	McLendon, M. K., Mokher, C. G., & Doyle, W. (2009). "Privileging" public research universities: An empirical analysis of the distribution of state appropriations across research and non-research universities. *Journal of Education Finance, 34*(4), 372–401	State appropriations per FTE for each institution	IPEDS	2003–2004 Random effects model conditioned on the mean of individual-level variables	501 Institutions in 46 states, excluding institutions with missing data	Graduate & Professional Enrollment, + Proportion Completion in STEM, + Democratic Strength, + Gubernatorial Budget Powers, – Inst. Located in State Capital, + of Appropriations Comm. Members Graduating from Inst., + Term Limits, – Student Aged Pop. (18–24), –
19	Morgan, D., Kickham, K., & LaPlant, J.	2001	Morgan, D., Kickham, K., & LaPlant, J.	State and general education expenditures for	*Digest of Education Statistics*, Census	1986–1995 Panel data	49 States (e.g., Arizona)	Enrollment, + Federal Aid, – Faculty Size, +
20	Nicholson-Crotty, J., & Meier, K. J.	2003	Nicholson-Crotty, J., & Meier, K. J. (2003). Politics, structure, and public policy: The case of higher education. *Educational Policy, 17*(1), 80–97	State/local appropriations per Student	*Digest of Education*	1989–1996 Panel data, fixed effects	47 States (e.g., Nebraska, Michigan, Delaware)	Citizen Ideology (Berry Data), – HE Governance Structure, – Government Ideology, + Legislative Professionalism, –

21	Okunade, A. A.	2004	Okunade, A. A. (2004). What factors influence state appropriations for public higher education in the united states? *Journal of Education Finance, 30*(2), 123–138	Public higher education appropriation share of the total state budget	US Census	1993–1994, 1994–1995 OLS, GLS, pooled regression, Panel Data	50 States	Per Capita Enrollment, + Tuition per FTE, – Annual Expenditure per Inmate, + Debt to Expenditure Ratio, + Medicare Appropriations,–
22	Peterson, R. G.	1976	Peterson, R. G. (1976). Environmental and political determinants of state higher education appropriations policies. *The Journal of Higher Education, 47*(5), 523–542	Appropriations for both per capita and per student, for: (1) All public institutions (2) Public 4 year (3) Public 2 year	US Office of Education, US Bureau of the Census	1960, 1969 Panel data, 2 cross-sectional studies	50 States	Enrollment, + Share of Public, 2 year Enrollment, + Share of Private, 2 year Enrollment, – Share of Public, 4 year Enrollment, + Adults w/College Degree, + Hofferbert's Influence Factor Scores, + Hofferbert's Industrialization Factor Scores, – Median Yrs. School completed by Pop, +
23	Rabovsky T.	2012	Rabovsky, T. M. (2012). Accountability in higher education: Exploring impacts on state budgets and institutional spending patterns. *Journal of Public Administration Research and Theory*	State appropriations, measured in constant dollars	SHEEO	1999–2008 for stage one; 1998–2008 for stage two Panel data	50 States	Graduate & Professional Enrollment, + Graduation Rate, + % Black, + % Hispanic, – Performance Funding, + Research/Doctoral Carnegie Classification, + Selectivity, + Undergrad Enrollment, +

(continued)

APPENDIX A

Studies of State Appropriation to Higher Education *(continued)*

	Authors	Year	Citation	Dependent Variable(s) (RE: State Support)[b]	Dependent Source	Time Period and Empirical Approach	Sample	Significant Independent Variables (+/–)
24	Rizzo, M. J.	2004	Rizzo, M. J. (2004). State preferences for higher education spending: A panel data analysis, 1977–2001. *Federal Reserve Bank of Cleveland's Conference on Education and Economic Development*	(1) Share of the public general fund budget allocated to education (2) Share of the education budget allocated to higher education (3) Share of the higher education budget allocated to institutions	US Bureau of the Census, State Government Finance Files (1972–2001), IPEDS, HEGIS, NASSGAP, Grapevine	1977–2001 Panel data	50 States	Giving, – PhD/BA Degrees Awarded, – Regional Non-Resident Tuition, – Share of Public, 2 year Enrollment, + State-Based Merit Scholarship, – Assembly Seats Per Capita, – Voter Turn Out, – Court Reform State, – Crime Rate, – Gross In-Migration, – Gross Out-Migration, – Median Household Income, – Median Household Income Squared, + Student Aged Pop. (18–24), + Race Interact, + Revenue Corporate Income Tax, + Revenue from Fuels, – Revenue Income Tax. + Revenue Lottery, – School Race Ratio, – Share of GSP (Ag, Fishing, Mining), + Share of GSP (Construction, Manufacturing, Trans. and Utilities), + Share of GSP (Government), + Share of GSP (Trade), + Unemployment Rate, – Unemployment Rate Non-White, –

25	Strathman J. G.	1994	Strathman, J. G. (1994). Migration, benefit spillovers and state support of higher education. *Urban Studies, 31*(6), 913–920	State and local appropriations per FTE student	*Digest of Education Statistics, Statistical Abstract of the US Census*	1989–1990 Three-stage least squares parameter estimates	48 States	Gross Out-Migration, – Personal Income per Capita, +
26	Tandberg, D. A.	2008	Tandberg, D. A. (2008). The politics of state higher education funding. *Higher Education Review, 5*, 1	Higher education appropriation as a % of state general fund expenditures	Grapevine, Census	1971–2001 Panel data, fixed effects	50 States	Giving, – In State Tuition (lagged), – Private Enrollment FTE, + Regional Non-Resident Tuition, + Democratic Governor, + Democratic Strength, + Electoral Competition, + HE Interest Ratio, + Legislative Unity, – Appropriations to K-12, – Gross State Product, + Health (Medical CPI) Share of pop. > 65 year, – Inequality, + Medicaid, – Medicaid CPI, – Student Aged Pop. (18–24), – Elderly Pop. (65<), – Population Below PELL, – Race Interact, + Unemployment Rate, –

(continued)

APPENDIX A

Studies of State Appropriation to Higher Education *(continued)*

	Authors	Year	Citation	Dependent Variable(s) (RE: State Support)[b]	Dependent Source	Time Period and Empirical Approach	Sample	Significant Independent Variables (+/–)
27	Tandberg, D.	2010	Tandberg, D. (2010). Interest groups and governmental institutions: The politics of state funding of public higher education. *Educational Policy, 24*(5), 44	State appropriations per US$1,000 personal income	Grapevine, Postsecondary Opportunity	1976–2004 Panel data, fixed effects	50 States	Private Enrollment FTE, + Share of Public, 2 year Enrollment, – State uses Formula Funding, + Tuition Avg 4 year, – Democratic Governor, + Democratic Strength, + HE Governance Structure, – Government Ideology, + HE Interest Ratio, + Legislative Professionalism, + Legislative Unity, – Gini Coefficient, – Gross State Product, + Medicaid, – Student Aged Pop. (18–24), – Population Below PELL, + Unemployment Rate, +
28	Tandberg, D. A.	2010	Tandberg, D. A. (2010). Politics, interest groups and state funding of public higher education. *Research in Higher Education, 51*(5), 416–450	State expenditure on higher education as a % of total state expenditures	NASBO	1986–2004 Panel data, fixed effects	50 States	Private Enrollment FTE, + Tuition Avg 4 year, – Citizen Ideology (Berry Data), + Democratic Governor, – Interest Group Density, – Legislative Professionalism, + Legislative Unity, – Political Culture, + Gross State Product, –

29	Tandberg, D. A. & Ness, Eric	2011	Tandberg, D. A. & Ness, E. (2011). State capital expenditures for higher education: "Where the real politics happens." *Journal of Education Finance, 36*(4), 394–423	Natural log of state capital expenditures	NASBO	1988–2004 Panel data	50 States	Giving, + State uses Formula Funding, + Tuition Avg 4 year, – Electoral Competition, + HE Governance Structure, – Gubernatorial Budget Powers, – HE Interest Ratio, + Legislative Professionalism, + Political Culture, + Voter Turn Out, – Student Aged Pop. (18–24), –
30	Toutkoushian, R. K., & Hollis, P.	1998	Toutkoushian, R. K., & Hollis, P. (1998). Using panel data to examine legislative demand for higher education. *Education Economics, 6*(2), 141–157	Natural log of Level of appropriations for higher education in each state	Halstead data (State Profiles: Financing Public Higher Education)	1982–1996 Panel data, OLS, 2SLS, fixed effects	50 States	Mean Faculty Compensation, + Median Household Income, + Unemployment Rate, –
31	Weerts, D. J., & Ronca, J. M.	2008	Weerts, D. J., & Ronca, J. M. (2008). *Determinants of state appropriations for higher education from 1985–2005: An organizational theory analysis.* Madison, WI: Wisconsin Center for the Advanced of Postsecondary Education	First difference of the natural log of total restricted plus unrestricted state appropriations converted to 2004 dollars	US Bureau of Labor Statistics, IPEDS	1985–2004 Panel data, random effects	50 States, 1,000 institutions	Carnegie Classification, – # of Pub Inst. in State, + Republican Governor, + Voter Turn Out, + Appropriations to K-12, – Court Reform State, – Health Spending, – Personal Income per Capita, – Student Aged Pop. (18–24), – Unemployment Rate, –

[a]Findings in regard to significance and direction reflect the results for each variable from what appeared to be the final or most inclusive model in each of the associated studies

[b]Only the dependent variable(s) measuring state support of higher education are included here. Many studies also include measures of other phenomena as additional dependent variables; however, they are not included here

Notes

1. Researchers have also gathered state funding of higher education data from *The Statistical Abstracts of the United States* (the country's data book). However, since *The Statistical Abstracts* rely on other data sources for their funding figures (including recently SHEF for state funding of higher education data and NASBO for total state expenditure data), they are not discussed here.
2. The reporting instructions have remained consistent since 1990. In 1989, states were given very general guidance (i.e., to *exclude* federal research grants and to *include* tuition and fees and support for community colleges). In the first 2 years (1987 and 1988), states were asked to exclude tuition and fees and federal research grants.
3. For additional details and to view examples of NASBO's *State Expenditure Reports*, visit their website here: http://nasbo.org/
4. For example, Zumeta (1992, 1996) reported that in 1988, 21 states provided direct financial support to private colleges and universities. NASBO reports that in 1988, 20 states excluded data on funding for private colleges and universities, meaning 30 states reported those data. However, some may have reported $0s.
5. As indicated, NASBO does track which states leave out what elements, which helps when attempting to make cross-state comparisons.
6. Additional information and the Grapevine data can be found at the project website here: http://grapevine.illinoisstate.edu/
7. For those years in which American Recovery and Reinvestment Act (ARRA) dollars were provided to states to support higher education, states were asked by SSHED to report:
   - "education stabilization funds used to restore the level of state support for public higher education;
   - government services funds used for public higher education (excluding modernization, renovation, or repair); and
   - government services funds used for modernization, renovation, or repair of higher education institutions (public and private).

   Government services funds used for modernization, renovation, or repair of higher education institutions were excluded from *Grapevine* analyses."
8. Using data from the State Support for Higher Education Database and available from SHEEO, a consistent State Tax Effort measure can be constructed.
9. For additional information and for examples of the SHEF reports, please visit SHEEO's website at http://www.sheeo.org/
10. Additional details and the Census data can be found here: http://www.census.gov/govs/estimate/
11. Researchers have also gathered state funding of higher education data from *The Statistical Abstracts of the United States* (the country's data book). However, since *The Statistical Abstracts* rely on other data sources for their funding figures (including, recently, SHEF for state funding of higher education data and NASBO for total state expenditure data), they are not discussed here.
12. Additional information and the extensive IPEDS data can be found here: http://nces.ed.gov/ipeds/datacenter/
13. Institutions report data using the accounting standards they employ at their institutions (FASBE or GASBE); therefore, the categories vary slight depending on the chosen standard. The Delta Cost Project has developed a useful crosswalk to merge across the standards.
14. The full name is *The Delta Project on Postsecondary Education Costs, Productivity, and Accountability*. Additional information and the data can be found on its website found here: http://www.deltacostproject.org/
15. Starting in 2012, NCES will take over maintenance of the Delta Cost Project Database.
16. Data from the Census are not included in the comparison as the most comparable Census measure (not including auxiliary enterprises, capital, or local expenditures) indicates that there was $135 billion in state higher education expenditures in 2008. The closest of the other four sources (Grapevine) shows only $73 billion in state higher education appropriations. The difference is most likely due to the Census data including tuition- and fee-based expenditures.
17. Grapevine data are not included in the second chart because the organization does not include a complete measure of total spending for higher education.
18. As Grapevine does not include a "complete" measure of state support they are not included in this comparison.
19. If the reader is interested in comparing and contrasting state higher education support measures, the discussion provided by Trostel and Ronca (2009) and the annual SHEF reports (SHEEO, 2011) are good places to start.

20. The mid-1970s represented a high point for this measure. In 1960, the states appropriated just over $3.00 for every $1,000 of personal income.
21. Rizzo (2004) uses a similar measure(s) however his conceptualization led him to develop three dependent variables:
    1. EDShare—Education's share of total state expenditures
    2. HEShare—Higher education's share of total state education expenditures
    3. InShare—Institution's share of total state higher education expenditures
22. For a full discussion of their concerns, please see Trostel and Ronca (2009).
23. For a full discussion, please see Trostel and Ronca (2009).
24. For an extensive review of principal-agent theory and its application to higher education, see Lane and Kivisto (2008).
25. Lindeen and Willis's (1975) primary dependent variable was total expenditures per tax payer, and their data source was the precursor to the IPEDS survey, the Higher Education General Information Survey. Peterson's (1976) primary dependent variables were appropriations per capita and per student, and his data source was also the Higher Education General Information Survey.
26. Hossler et al. (1997) used levels of state appropriations to public four-year institutions. The data were from the Grapevine surveys.
27. Toutkoushian and Hollis (1998) used the natural log of state appropriation levels as their dependent variable. Their data source was the precursor of the SHEEO SHEF compilation, the *State Profiles: Financing Public Higher Education* data collected by Kent Halstead.
28. McLendon, Hearn et al. (2009) employed state tax appropriations per $1,000 of personal income as their dependent variable (Grapevine data). Tandberg (2010b) likewise used the same variable and Grapevine data. Tandberg (2010a) employed higher education's share of total state general fund expenditures as his dependent variable (NASBO data).
29. See Tandberg (2010a, 2010b) and Hero and Tolbert (1996) for details on the political culture measure.
30. We apologize for any studies we missed and for any inaccuracies in Appendix A. They were not intentional.
31. For a detailed discussion of interest groups and state higher education policy research, see Ness et al. (2008).
32. See Gray and Lowery's (various years) extensive discussions on the use of interest group density measures.
33. Michigan does not have a traditional state-level coordinating or governing agency for postsecondary education. However, the State Board of Education has very limited state postsecondary coordinating functions. While its primary responsibility is for elementary and secondary education, the board does have limited responsibility for the coordination of services for public two-year and four-year colleges and universities. Vermont likewise does not have a traditional structure. Instead, it has a voluntary state higher education coordinating system plus two system level boards (McGuinness, 2003).
34. See Zhang (2010) for a full discussion of the use of panel data in higher education research.

References

Alt, J. E., & Lowry, R. C. (1994). Divided government, fiscal institutions, and budget deficits: Evidence from the states. *The American Political Science Review, 88*(4), 811–828.

Archibald, R. B., & Feldman, D. H. (2006). State higher education spending and the tax revolt. *Journal of Higher Education, 77*(4), 618–643.

Bailey, M. E., Rom, M. C., & Taylor, M. (2004). State competition in higher education: A race to the top or a race to the bottom? *Economics of Governance, 5*(1), 53–75.

Barrilleaux, C., & Berkman, M. (2003). Do Governors matter? Budgeting rules and the politics of state policy making. *Political Research Quarterly, 56*(4), 409–417.

Baumgartner, F. R., & Jones, B. D. (1993). *Agendas and instability in American politics.* Chicago: University of Chicago Press.

Black, D. (1948). On the rationale of group decision making. *Journal of Political Economy, 56*(1), 23–34.

Blackwell, E. A., & Cistone, P. J. (1999). Power and influence in higher education: The case of Florida. *Higher Education Policy, 12*, 111–122.

Borcherding, T., & Deacon, R. (1972). The demand for the services of non-federal governments. *American Economic Review, 62*, 891–901.

Carey, J. M., Niemi, R. G., & Powell, L. W. (2000). Incumbency and the probability of reelection in state legislative elections. *Journal of Politics, 62*, 671–700.

Cheslock, J., & Gianneschi, M. (2008). Replacing state appropriations with alternative revenue sources: The case of voluntary support. *Journal of Higher Education, 79*, 208+.

Clotfelter, C. T. (1976). Public spending for higher education: An empirical test of two hypotheses. *Public Finance, 31*(2), 177–195.

Coriat, B., & Dosi, G. (1998). Learning how to govern and learning how to solve problems: On the coevolution of competences, conflict and organizational routines. In A. Chandler, P. Hagstrom, & O. Solwell (Eds.), *The dynamic firm* (pp. 103–133). Oxford, UK: Oxford University Press.

Cornwell, C., Mustard, D. B., & Sridhar, D. J. (2006). The enrollment effects of merit-based financial aid. *Journal of Labor Economics, 24*, 761–786.

Coughlin, C. C., & Erekson, O. H. (1986). Determinants of state aid and voluntary support of higher education. *Economics of Education Review, 5*(2), 179–190.

Dar, L., & Franke, R. (2010). *Revisiting the political economy of government support for higher education: Evidence from a new unifying measure for the American states.* Presented at the Annual Consortium for Higher Education Researchers, Oslo, Norway.

Dar, L., & Spence, M. J. (2011). Partisanship, political polarization, and state budget outcomes: The case of higher education. *SSRN eLibrary*, Retrieved from http://ssrn.com/abstract=1577365

Dar, L. (2012). The political dynamics of higher education policy. *The Journal of Higher Education, 83*(6), 769–794.

deGive, M. L., & Olswang, S. (1999). Coalition building to create a branch campus system. *The Review of Higher Education, 22*(3), 287–313.

Delaney, J. A., & Doyle, W. R. (2007). The role of higher education in state budgets. In D. E. Heller & K. M. Shaw (Eds.), *State postsecondary education research.* Sterling, VA: Stylus Publishing.

Delaney, J. A., & Doyle, W. R. (2011). State spending on higher education: Testing the balance wheel over time. *Journal of Education Finance, 36*(4), 343–368.

Dowding, K., & King, D. (1995). *Preferences, institutions and rational choice.* Oxford, UK: Clarendon.

Downs, A. (1957). *An economic theory of democracy.* New York: Harper.

Doyle, W. R. (2007). The political economy of redistribution through higher education subsidies. In J. C. Smart (Ed.), *Higher education: Handbook of theory and research* (Vol. XXII, pp. 335–409). Dordrecht, The Netherlands: Springer.

Doyle, W. R., McLendon, M. K., & Hearn, J. C. (2010). Why states adopted prepaid tuition and college savings programs: An event history analysis. *Research in Higher Education, 51*(7), 659–686.

Eisenhardt, K. (1989). Agency theory: An assessment and a review. *Academy of Management Review, 14*, 57–74.

Fernandez, R., & Rogerson, R. (1995). On the political economy of education subsidies. *Review of Economic Studies, 62*(2), 249–262.

Ferrin, S. E. (2003). Characteristics of in-house lobbyist in American colleges and universities. *Higher Education Policy, 16*(1), 87–108.

Ferrin, S. E. (2005). Tasks and strategies of in-house lobbyists in American colleges and universities. *International Journal of Educational Advancement, 5*(2), 180–191.

Fiorina, M. (1994). Divided government in the American States: A byproduct of legislative professionalism? *American Political Science Review, 88*, 304–316.

Frost, S. H., Hearn, J. C., & Marine, G. M. (1997). State policy and the public research university: A case study of manifest and latent tensions. *Journal of Higher Education, 68*(4), 363–397.

Garand, J. C., & Hendrick, R. M. (1991). Expenditure tradeoffs in the American States: A longitudinal test, 1948–1984. *Western Political Quarterly, 44*(4), 915–940.

Geddes, B. (1994). *Politician's dilemma: Building state capacity in Latin America.* Berkeley, CA: University of California Press.

Geddes, B. (1996). Initiation of new democratic institutions in Eastern Europe and Latin America. In A. Lijphart & C. H. Waisman (Eds.), *Institutional design in new democracies: Eastern Europe and Latin America.* Boulder, CO: Westview Press.

Goldin, C., & Katz, L. F. (1998). The origins of state-level differences in the public provision of higher education: 1890–1940. *American Economic Review, 88*(2), 303–308.

Grafstein, R. (1992). *Institutional realism: Social and political constraints on rational actors.* New Haven, CT: Yale University Press.

Grapevine System. (2011). *An annual compilation of data on state tax appropriations for the general operation of higher education*. Normal, IL: Center for the Study of Education Policy Illinois State University. http://www.coe.ilstu.edu/grapevine/

Gray, V., & Lowery, D. (1996). *The population ecology of interest representation: Lobbying communities in the American States*. Ann Arbor, MI: University of Michigan Press.

Gray, V., & Lowery, D. (2001). The expression of density dependence in state communities of organized interests. *American Politics Research, 29*(4), 374–391.

Hearn, J. C., & Griswold, C. P. (1994). State-level centralization and policy innovation in U.S. postsecondary education. *Educational Evaluation and Policy Analysis, 16*(2), 161–190.

Heller, D. E. (1999). The effects of tuition and state financial aid on public college enrollment. *The Review of Higher Education, 23*(1), 65–89.

Hero, R. E., & Tolbert, C. J. (1996). A racial/ethnic diversity interpretation of politics and policy in the states of the U.S. *American Journal of Political Science, 40*(3), 851–871.

Hoenack, S., & Pierro, D. (1990, January). An econometric model of a public university's income and enrollments. *The Journal of Economic Behaviour and Organization, 14*, 403–423.

Holcombe, R. G. (1989). *Economic models and methodology*. New York: Greenwood.

Hossler, D., Lund, J. P., Ramin, J., Westfall, S., & Irish, S. (1997). State funding for higher education: The Sisyphean Task. *Journal of Higher Education, 68*(2), 160–190.

Humphreys, B. R. (2000). Do business cycles affect state appropriations to higher education? *Southern Economic Journal, 67*(2), 398–413.

Jacoby, W. G., & Schneider, S. K. (2001). Variability in state policy priorities: An empirical analysis. *The Journal of Politics, 63*(2), 544–568.

Kane, T. J., & Orszag, P. R. (2003). *Funding restrictions at public universities: Effects and policy implications* (Brookings Institution Working Paper).

Kane, T. J., Orszag, P. R., Apostolov, E., Inman, R. P., & Reschovsky, A. (2005). Higher education appropriations and public universities: Role of Medicaid and the business cycle [with comments]. *Brookings-Wharton Papers on Urban Affairs, 6*, 99–146.

Kane, T. J., Orszag, P. R., & Gunter, D. L. (2003). *State fiscal constraints and higher education spending: The role of Medicaid and the business cycle* (Discussion Paper No. 11). Washington, DC: The Urban Institute.

Kiel, L. D., & Elliott, E. (1992). Budgets as dynamic systems: Change, variation, time, and budgetary heuristics. *Journal of Public Administration Research and Theory, 2*(2), 139–156.

Kingdon, J. W. (1984). *Agendas, alternatives, and public policies*. New York: HarperCollins.

Kingdon, J. W. (1995). *Alternatives, and public policies* (2nd ed.). Boston: Little, Brown.

Kiser, L., & Ostrom, E. (1982). The three worlds of action. In E. Ostrom (Ed.), *Strategies of political inquiry* (pp. 179–221). Beverly Hills, CA: Sage.

Kivisto, J. (2005). The government-higher education institution relationship: Theoretical considerations from the perspective of agency theory. *Tertiary Education and Management, 11*(1), 1–17.

Kivisto, J. A. (2007). *Agency theory as a framework for the government-university relationship*. Tampere, Finland: Higher Education Group/Tampere University Press.

Knott, J., & Payne, A. (2004). The impact of state governance structures on management and performance of public organizations: A study of higher education institutions. *Journal of Policy Analysis and Management, 23*(1), 13–30.

Koshal, R. K., & Koshal, M. (2000). State appropriation and higher education tuition: What is the relationship? *Education Economics, 8*(1), 81–89.

Lane, J. E. (2003). *State government oversight of public higher education: Police patrols and fire alarms*. Paper presented at the annual meeting of the Association for the Study of Higher Education, Portland, OR.

Lane, J. E. (2005). *State oversight of higher education: A theoretical review of agency problems with complex principals*. Paper presented at 2005 Annual Conference of the Association for the Study of Higher Education, Philadelphia.

Lane, J. E. (2007). The spider web of oversight: An analysis of external oversight of higher education. *Journal of Higher Education, 78*(6), 615–644.

Lane, J. E., & Kivisto, J. A. (2008). Interests, information, and incentives in higher education: Principal-agent theory and its potential application to the study of higher education governance. In J. Smart (Ed.), *Higher education: Handbook of theory and research* (Vol. XVIII, pp. 141–179). New York: Agathon Press.

Layzell, D. T., & Lyddon, J. W. (1990). *Budgeting for higher education at the state level: Enigma, paradox, and ritual* (ASHE-ERIC Higher Education Report 4, 1990, ERIC). Washington, DC: School of Education and Human Development, George Washington University.

Leslie, L. L., & Ramey, G. (1986). State appropriations and enrollments: Does enrollment growth still pay? *Journal of Higher Education, 57*(1), 1–19.

Lindeen, J. W., & Willis, G. L. (1975). Political, socioeconomic and demographic patterns of support for public higher education. *The Western Political Quarterly, 28*(3), 528–541.

Longanecker, D. (2006). A tale of two pities. *Change, 38*(1), 14.

Lowry, R. C. (2001). The effects of state political interests and campus outputs on public university revenues. *Economics of Education Review, 20*(2), 105–119.

March, J. G., & Olsen, J. P. (1984). The new institutionalism, organizational factors in political life. *American Political Science Review, 78*(3), 734–749.

McGuinness, A. C. (2003). *Models of postsecondary education and governance in the States*. Denver, CO: Education Commission of the States.

McLendon, M. K. (2003). The politics of higher education: Toward an expanded research agenda. *Educational Policy, 17*(1), 165–191.

McLendon, M. K., Deaton, R., & Hearn, J. C. (2007). The enactment of reforms in state governance of higher education: Testing the political instability hypothesis. *Journal of Higher Education, 78*(6), 645–675.

McLendon, M. K., Hearn, J. C., & Deaton, R. (2006). Called to account: Analyzing the origins and spread of state performance-accountability policies for higher education. *Educational Evaluation and Policy Analysis, 28*(1), 1–24.

McLendon, M. K., Hearn, J. C., & Mokher, C. G. (2009). Partisans, professionals, and power: The role of political factors in state higher education funding. *Journal of Higher Education, 80*(6), 686–713.

McLendon, M. K., Heller, D. E., & Young, S. P. (2005). State postsecondary policy innovation: Politics, competition, and the interstate migration of policy ideas. *Journal of Higher Education, 76*(4), 363–400.

McLendon, M. K., Mokher, C. G., & Doyle, W. (2009). "Privileging" public research universities: An empirical analysis of the distribution of state appropriations across research and non-research universities. *Journal of Education Finance, 34*(4), 372–401.

McLendon, M. K., Mokher, C. G., & Flores, S. M. (2011). Legislative agenda setting for in-state resident tuition policies: Immigration, representation, and educational access. *American Journal of Education, 117*(4), 563–602.

Moe, T. M. (1984). The new economics of organization. *American Journal of Political Science, 28*(4), 739–777.

Moe, T. M. (1987). An assessment of the positive theory of "congressional dominance". *Legislative Studies Quarterly, 12*, 475–520.

Morgan, D., Kickham, K., & LaPlant, J. (2001). State support for higher education: A political economy approach. *The Policy Studies Journal, 29*(3), 359–371.

Mortenson, T. G. (2005). *State tax fund appropriations for higher education FY1961 to FY2005*. Oskaloosa, IA: Postsecondary Education Opportunity. www.postsecondary.org

Ness, E. (2010). The politics of determining merit aid eligibility criteria: An analysis of the policy process. *Journal of Higher Education, 81*(1), 33–60.

Ness, E., Tandberg, D. A., & McLendon, M. (2008, April). *Interest groups and state policy for higher education: Toward new conceptual understandings and future research directions*. Presented at the Annual Meeting of the American Educational Research Association, San Diego, CA.

Nicholson-Crotty, J., & Meier, K. J. (2003). Politics, structure, and public policy: The case of higher education. *Educational Policy, 17*(1), 80–97.

North, D. (1990). *Institutions, institutional change, and economic performance*. New York: Cambridge University Press.

Nownes, A. J. (2006). *Total lobbying: What lobbyists want (and how they try to get it)*. Cambridge, UK: Cambridge University Press.

Nownes, A. J., Thomas, C., & Hrebenar, R. (2008). Interest groups in the states. In V. Gray & R. Hanson (Eds.), *Politics in the American States* (9th ed., pp. 98–126). Washington, DC: Congressional Quarterly Press.

Okunade, A. A. (2004). What factors influence state appropriations for public higher education in the United States? *Journal of Education Finance, 30*(2), 123–138.

Ostrom, E. (1992). *Crafting institutions for self-governing irrigation systems*. San Francisco: ICS. 111 pp.

Ostrom, E. (1999). Institutional rational choice: An assessment of the institutional analysis and development framework. In P. A. Sabatier (Ed.), *Theories of the policy process* (pp. 35–71). Boulder, CO: Westview.

Ostrom, E., Gardner, R., & Walker, J. (1994). *Rules, games, and common pool resources*. Ann Arbor, MI: University of Michigan Press.

Ostrom, V. (1991). *The meaning of American federalism: Constituting a self-governing society*. San Francisco: ICS Press.

Pascarella, E. T., & Terenzini, P. T. (2005). *How college affects students: A third decade of research*. San Francisco: Jossey-Bass.

Payne, A. A. (2003). The effects of congressional appropriation committee membership on the distribution of federal research funding to universities. *Economic Inquiry, 41*(2), 325–345.

Payne, A. A., & Roberts, J. (2004). *Government oversight of organizations engaged in multiple activities: Does centralized governance encourage quantity or quality?* Unpublished manuscript, McMaster University.

Peterson, R. G. (1976). Environmental and political determinants of state higher education appropriations policies. *Journal of Higher Education, 47*(5), 523–542.

Rabovsky, T. M. (2012). Accountability in Higher Education: Exploring Impacts on State Budgets and Institutional Spending Patterns. *Journal of Public Administration Research and Theory*.

Richardson, R., Shulock, N., & Teranishi, R. (2005). *Public policy and higher education performance in the state of California*. New York: Alliance for International Higher Education Policy Studies.

Rizzo, M. J. (2004). State preferences for higher education spending: A panel data analysis, 1977–2001. In *Federal Reserve Bank of Cleveland's conference on education and economic development*.

Ross, S. A. (1973). The economic theory of agency: The principal's problem. *American Economic Review, 63*(2), 134–139.

Sabatier, P. A. (1991). Toward better theories of the policy process. *PS: Political Science and Politics, 24*(2), 147–156.

Sabatier, P. A. (Ed.). (1999). *Theories of the policy process*. Boulder, CO: Westview.

Sabloff, P. L. (1997). Another reason why state legislatures will continue to restrict public university autonomy. *The Review of Higher Education, 20*(2), 141–162.

Shakespeare, C. (2008). Uncovering information's role in the state higher education policy-making process. *Educational Policy, 22*(6), 875–899.

Sharkansky, I. (1968). Agency requests, gubernatorial support, and budget success in state legislatures. *American Political Science review, 62*, 1220–1231.

Shepsle, K. A. (1979). Institutional arrangements and equilibrium in multidimensional voting models. *American Journal of Political Science, 23*(1), 27–59.

Shepsle, K. A. (1989). Studying institutions: Some lessons from the rational choice approach. *Journal of Theoretical Politics, 1*(2), 131–147.

Squire, P. (2000). Uncontested seats in state legislative elections. *Legislative Studies Quarterly, 25*(1), 131–146.

Squire, P., & Hamm, K. (2005). *101 chambers: Congress, state legislatures, and the future of legislative studies*. Columbus, OH: Ohio State University Press.

State Higher Education Executive Officers (SHEEO). (2011). *State higher education finance*. Boulder, CO: Author.

Strathman, J. G. (1994). Migration, benefit spillovers and state support of higher education. *Urban Studies, 31*(6), 913–920.

Tandberg, D. A. (2006). State-level higher education interest group alliances. *Higher Education Review, 3*, 25–49.

Tandberg, D. A. (2008). The politics of state higher education funding. *Higher Education Review, 5*, 1–36.

Tandberg, D. A. (2010a). Politics, interest groups and state funding of public higher education. *Research in Higher Education, 15*(5), 416–450.

Tandberg, D. A. (2010b). Interest groups and governmental institutions: The politics of state funding of public higher education. *Educational Policy, 24*(5), 735–778.

Tandberg, D. A. (2010c, November). *The conditioning role of state higher education governance structures*. Paper presented at the Annual Meeting of the Association for the Study of Higher Education, Indianapolis, IN.

Tandberg, D. A., & Ness, E. C. (2011). State capital expenditures for higher education: 'Where the real politics happens'. *Journal of Education Finance, 36*(4), 394–423.

Tankersley-Bankhead, E. A. (2009). *Student lobbyists' behavior and its perceived influence on state-level public higher education legislation: A case study*. Unpublished doctoral dissertation, University of Missouri, Columbia, MI.

Thomas, C., & Hrebenar, R. (1999). Interest groups in the states. In V. Gray & R. L. Hanson (Eds.), *Politics in the American States: A comparative analysis* (7th ed.). Washington, DC: Congressional Quarterly Press.

Thomas, C., & Hrebenar, R. (2004). Interest groups in the States. In V. Gray & R. L. Hanson (Eds.), *Politics in the American States: A comparative analysis* (8th ed., pp. 100–128). Washington, DC: CQ Press.

Thompson, J. A., & Felts, A. A. (1992). Politicians and professionals: The influence of state agency heads in budgetary success. *Western Political Quarterly, 45*, 153–168.

Toma, E. F., Berhane, I., & Curl, C. (2006). Political action committees at the state level: Contributions to education. *Public Choice, 126*, 465–484.

Toutkoushian, R. K., & Hollis, P. (1998). Using panel data to examine legislative demand for higher education. *Education Economics, 6*(2), 141–157.

Trostel, P. A., & Ronca, J. M. (2009). A simple unifying measure of state support for postsecondary education. *Research in Higher Education, 50*(3), 215–247.

Truman, D. (1951). *The governmental process.* Knopf: New York.

U.S. Bureau of the Census. (2011). *Statistical abstract of the United States.* Washington, DC: U.S. Bureau of the Census.

Volkwein, J. F. (1989). Changes in quality among public universities. *Journal of Higher Education, 60*(2), 136–151.

Weerts, D. J., & Ronca, J. M. (2006). Examining differences in state support for higher education: A comparative study of state appropriations for research universities. *Journal of Higher Education, 77*(6), 935–965.

Weerts, D. J., & Ronca, J. M. (2008). *Determinants of state appropriations for higher education from 1985–2005: An organizational theory analysis.* Madison, WI: Wisconsin Center for the Advanced of Postsecondary Education.

Zhang, L. (2010). The use of panel data models in higher education policy studies. In J. C. Smart (Ed.), *Higher education: Handbook of theory and research* (Vol. XXV, pp. 307–349). Dordrecht, The Netherlands: Springer.

Zumeta, W. (1992). State policies and private higher education: Policies, correlates, and linkages. *Journal of Higher Education, 63*, 363–417.

Zumeta, W. (1996). Meeting the demand for higher education without breaking the bank: A framework for design of state higher education policies for an era of increasing demand. *Journal of Higher Education, 67*(4), 367–425.

SECTION IV

INSTITUTIONAL RESOURCES AND FINANCIAL MANAGEMENT

Introduction to Section IV

Maureen W. McClure and Stuart E. Sutin
University of Pittsburgh

How is persistence successfully encouraged? The institutional effects on individual achievement in community colleges have not been studied very much, despite their importance. A more technical piece, Calcagno, et al ("Community College Student Success: What Institutional Characteristics Make a Difference?"), investigates the effects of institutional characteristics on community college outcomes, including degree attainment, transfer to another institution, or credit attainment. Institutional characteristics included location (urban, rural), tuition, enrollment size, share of part-time faculty, expenditures per student, distribution of expenditures across instruction, administration and student services, certificates versus associates degrees, and levels of financial aid. They analyzed individual-level data from the National Education Longitudinal Study of 1988 (NELS:88) and institutional-level data from the Integrated Postsecondary Education Data System (IPEDS), discovering an inverse relationship between school size and student's likelihood to graduate or transfer to a 4-year institution. Higher non-completion rates were found in schools with larger shares of minority populations. Finally, most expenditures were not correlated with graduation probabilities.

Linn ("Budget Systems Used in Allocating Resources to Libraries") comparatively analyzes different types of budgeting systems, assessing their strengths and weakness. For those without much experience in budgeting processes, this is a quick and easy guide. He first examines the pros and cons of the typical incremental budgets, those with same percentage raises or cuts across-the-board. In contrast, program-based models directly link budgeting and planning outputs, such as the number of students taught. Recently the accountability movement has focused on performance-based budgeting, linking budgets to perceived outcomes to verify what was taught was learned.

Lopez ("Towards Decentralized and Goal-Oriented Models of Institutional resource Allocation: The Spanish Case") compiles a helpful compendium of performance-based, results-oriented indicators in a variety of department planning and budgeting categories, e.g., teaching and learning resources, teaching activity, research activity, and administrative activity. Also included were center-based activity and production, regional models of funding, and decentralized budgeting and management practices. In a comprehensive descriptive analysis, Spanish universities were surveyed to see to what extent they had adopted these measures into their planning and budgeting policies. The paper concludes that only a few universities integrated performance-based measures into their quotidian resource allocation practices.

Santos ("Resource Allocation in Public Research Universities") used production functions to test two different theories of resource allocation for university departments at ten top public research universities, following state budgetary cutbacks in funding in the early 2000s. First, theories of the firm from conventional business management texts framed institutions as unitary, rational actors. Second, theories of resource dependency framed institutions as fragmented, populated by internally competing, coalition-building actors. His analysis supported both. Reductions in state budgets resulted in rational increases of teaching production. Even though returns to research productivity generated lower returns, undergraduate teaching appeared to have been "taxed" to fund it.

Sav's comparative analysis ("Funding Historically Black Colleges and Universities: Progress Toward Equality?") of state funding between 1995 and 2006 for both Historically Black Colleges and Universities (HBCUs) and Predominantly White Colleges and Universities (PWCUs) show both significant progress and residual problems. Using labor market theories of differential treatment, the discrimination indicator (intercept) declined from 16.7% to 12.5% during this period. Oddly, private endowments for HBCUs appeared to "crowd out" state funding; whereas, at PWCUs, both endowments and federal funding appeared to be rewarded. PWCUs were also more likely to receive additional state funding for professional schools. And PWCUs were more likely to have branch campuses.

This classic article by Volk, Slaughter, and Thomas ("Models of Institutional Resource Allocation: Mission, Market, and Gender") analyzed department resource allocations within a single public research university by testing two competing theories of resource allocation across departments. Findings included support for both, and findings also verified that departments, not just individuals matter. Rational/political theory was supported by grants and contracts production; by workflow variables, e.g. credit hours generated; and by strong support for high centrality, high quality departments. Critical/political theory was supported by apparent excessive allocations for graduate education at the expense of undergraduates. Higher undergraduate "exit salaries" were not matched by higher faculty salaries, suggesting segmented markets.

CHAPTER 20

COMMUNITY COLLEGE STUDENT SUCCESS: WHAT INSTITUTIONAL CHARACTERISTICS MAKE A DIFFERENCE?

JUAN CARLOS CALCAGNO, THOMAS BAILEY, DAVIS JENKINS,
GREGORY KIENZL, TIMOTHY LEINBACH

Most of the models developed to examine student persistence and attainment in postsecondary education largely fail to account for the influence of institutional factors, particularly when attendance is observed at multiple institutions. Multi-institutional attendance is common for students who begin at a community college, but until now an empirical framework to estimate the contribution of more than one institution's characteristics on students' educational outcomes has been largely absent in the literature. One of the goals of this study is to determine which institutional *characteristics are correlated with positive community college outcomes for students who attend one or more colleges as measured by* individual *student probability of completing a certificate or degree or transferring to a baccalaureate institution. Using individual-level data from the National Education Longitudinal Study of 1988 (NELS:88) and institutional-level data from the Integrated Postsecondary Education Data System (IPEDS), we find consistent results across different specifications; namely, a negative relationship between relatively large institutional size, proportion of part-time faculty and minority students on the attainment of community college students.*

1. Introduction

Community colleges are a crucial point of access to higher education for many individuals seeking additional education beyond high school. Previous research even suggests that if community colleges were not available, many of these individuals would not have enrolled in postsecondary education (Rouse, 1995). The community college access mission is built on low tuition, convenient location, flexible scheduling, an open-door admissions policy, and programs and services designed to support at-risk students with a variety of social and academic barriers to postsecondary success (Cohen & Brawer, 1996). Yet while community colleges continue to play a crucial role in providing further educational opportunities to a wide variety of students, access alone is not sufficient.

Many community college students who seek a postsecondary credential never finish a degree program. For example, in the 1995–96 academic year, only 36% of students who enrolled in a community college as their first postsecondary enrollment had completed either a certificate, associate's, or bachelor's degree within 6 years. Another 22% were still enrolled in college (about three-fifths of those were enrolled in a 4-year institution), leaving the remaining 42% of first-time community college students with varying amounts of postsecondary education but no formal degree or certificate. Low-income, minority, and first-generation college students all have even lower 6-year completion rates, and those who do complete among these populations tend to earn certificates rather than an associate's or bachelor's degree.[1] As policymakers, educators, accreditors, and scholars increasingly turn their attention to student persistence and completion, the most salient question now is: How can community colleges improve the completion rates of their students?

One strategy would be to establish more selective admissions criteria. Extensive research has shown that students who have stronger high school records, who come from higher income families, whose parents also went to college, who do not delay college entry after high school, who attend full time, and who do not interrupt their college studies are more likely to graduate

(Adelman, 1999, 2005, 2006; Bailey & Alfonso, 2005; Cabrera, Burkum, & La Nasa, 2005). Adopting this strategy, however, would defeat the primary purpose of these open-door institutions. In many states, students can attend community college even if they do not have a high school diploma or equivalent and in many colleges, a majority of students, after being assessed, are determined not to be prepared for college level coursework. The primary challenge facing community colleges then is not how to attract better students (although surely many would like to do that), but rather how to do a better job with the types of students they already have. Indeed, there is some evidence that colleges differ in their effectiveness in helping students to graduate since community college graduation rates vary significantly, even after controlling for characteristics of the student body (Bailey, Calcagno, Jenkins, Leinbach, & Kienzl, 2006).

The goal of the analysis presented here is to identify specific institutional characteristics of community colleges that are correlated with successful education outcomes, such as degree attainment, transfer to a 4-year institution, or credit accumulation. To this end, we examine several institutional characteristics that are controlled by the colleges or state policymakers. They include college size; tuition levels; the use of part-time faculty; overall expenditures per student; the distribution of those expenditures among possible functions such as instruction, administration, and student services; the extent to which the college focuses on certificates as opposed to associate's degrees; and the level of financial aid.

The structure of this article is as follows. Section 2 reviews the existing literature that has examined the factors that are associated with student success at both baccalaureate institutions and community colleges. In Section 3, we introduce the empirical model to estimate the institutional influence on the completion rate of community college students. The findings are presented in Section 4, and the results of several robustness tests are given in Section 5. The study concludes with a discussion of implications, limitations, and areas of future research.

2. Existing Research

Two of the most commonly used conceptual frameworks of persistence and completion are based on Tinto's Student Integration Model (1993) and Bean's Student Attrition Model (1985). The central institutional implication of the models is that administrators and faculty should try to foster the academic and social engagement of their students in and with the colleges. Drawing on the various studies that have emerged from these models, Titus (2004, 2006) developed a list of institutional characteristics of 4-year colleges that appear to influence student persistence, including control (public or private), whether the college is residential, college size, sources of revenue, and patterns of expenditure.[2] To test the influence o these characteristics, he merged two nationally representative datasets (BPS:96/98 and IPEDS 1995) and consolidated student data with the institutional information from the 4-year college where each student enrolled. He concluded that persistence is higher at more selective, residential, and larger institutions (Titus, 2004) and, in a subsequent paper, he found that higher expenditure per full-time equivalent student is associated with greater persistence, although within expenditures, college with relatively higher administrative expenditures tended to have lower persistence. Graduation rates were also higher at colleges in which a larger share of revenue came from tuition (Titus, 2006).

With these results in mind, this analysis contributes to the college persistence literature in three unique ways. First, we use a production function method with both college-level and individual variables to analyze the institutional correlates of persistence and completion (including transfer to a 4-year college) in community colleges. Education economists have used production functions for more than 30 years.[3] The method allows researchers to understand the influence of *individual* and *institutional* characteristics on educational outcomes, but they have not been widely used to examine higher education outcomes like persistence, completion, or credit accumulation.[4] Of the few studies that have explicitly analyzed the influence of institutional characteristics on individual-level higher education outcomes, all but one studied 4-year colleges.

Second, many students now attend more than one postsecondary institution (Adelman, 1999, 2005, 2006). Given the growth of multi-institutional attendance, particularly among students who enter higher education through community colleges, it is important to examine the entire undergraduate experience of students. This study incorporates institutional characteristic of *every* institution attended.

Third, unobserved institutional factors like leadership, faculty relations, and local political environment may have a bearing on students' outcomes. In order to estimate consistent coefficients for the observable variables, the unaccounted for variation in institutional-level factors is partitioned out using a random effects model, which will be discussed in more detail in the next section.

3. Empirical Model and Data

3.1 Econometric Models

Following the discussion in the last section, this study used a binary outcome and a continuous one to measure student success.[5] Taken in order, attainment of any degree (certificate, associate's, or bachelor's) or transfer to a 4-year institution is considered a successful outcome for our sample of community college students. This outcome takes the value of unity if any of the aforementioned outcomes are observed, and zero otherwise. The probability that a community college student will succeed is as follows:

$$y^*_{ic} = X'_{ic}\beta + v_{ic}, \quad i = 1, 2, \ldots, N \text{ and } c = 1, 2, \ldots, C \tag{1}$$

and

$$y_{ic} = 1 \text{ if } y^*_{ic} > 0; \text{ otherwise } y_{ic} = 0$$

where i denotes each student and c is the cluster, in this case, the community college, y^*, is the unobservable individual propensity to graduate, y is the observed outcome, **X** is a vector of exogenous *students* and *institutional* characteristics that affect the outcome and v_{ic} is the unobserved component. Under usual assumptions for the error component (mean zero, normalized variance σ^2_v equal to one), we could pool the data and use a standard probit model (henceforth, Model 1). Maximum Likelihood estimation guarantees asymptotically unbiased estimates, but the standard errors will be misleading. Therefore, a robust variance-covariance matrix is needed to account for serial correlation within institutions (Guilkey & Murphy, 1993).

Model 1 assumes that heterogeneity in students' probability to graduate is only affected by observable characteristics of the institution. However, unobserved institutional factors like students' academic preparedness, faculty and administration leadership and relations, and the local political environment may have a bearing on students' outcomes. Thus, Model 2 is designed to account for the institution-level unobserved factors that may affect the individual's propensity to graduate. We decompose the error term in Eq. (1) as follows:

$$v_{ic} = \alpha_c + u_{ic} \tag{2}$$

where α_c is the unobserved institution-specific effect and u_{ic} is the usual idiosyncratic error term. Both α_c and u_{ic} are assumed to be independent and identically distributed random variables with mean zero and variance σ^2_c and 1, respectively. The assumptions imply that $\text{Var}(v_{ic}) = \sigma^2_\alpha + 1$ and $r = \text{corr}(v_{ic}, v_{is}) = \sigma^2_\alpha/(\sigma^2_\alpha + 1)$, interpretable as the proportion of the total error variance contributed by the unobserved heterogeneity. Further, if error terms are independent of the vector of covariates **X** and we assume a standard normal distribution for u_{ic}, we obtain a random effect probit model for the outcome.[6] Maximum likelihood estimation with respect to β/σ^2_u and ρ provide asymptotically unbiased estimates.

For Models 1 and 2, only institutional data from the first year of student's enrollment in a community college is used. In so doing, the characteristics of subsequent institutions that student may have later enrolled in are ignored. According to the NELS:88 data, however, over 40% of community college students enroll in more than one institution during their time in postsecondary education. We contend that these institutions play a contributing role in students' outcomes, so an attendance weigh was created and applied to each institutional characteristic (Model 3). In each case, the attendance weight is proportional to the full-time equivalent (FTE) months enrolled in each institution relative to the FTE months enrolled at all institutions, prior to the student outcome event (certificate; degree; transfer; or last enrolled, if not outcome).[7]

In addition to the binary outcome measure, we conducted a parallel analysis using cumulative number of credits earned as a dependent variable (Model 4). The rationale for doing so is that a dummy variable as a measure of success of community college student outcomes can hide important individual and institutional information. This alternative measure of success has a methodological advantage in that common linear regression can be used. However, the distribution of this dependent variable is non-linear since community college students have a high propensity to drop out after earning fewer than 10 credits.[8] To normalize the distribution, the variable has been transformed into logs.

3.2 Dataset and Variables

We began with the National Education Longitudinal Study of 1988 (NELS:88) for student and enrollment information. NELS:88 follows a nationally representative sample of eighth graders in the spring of 1988.[9] The dataset contains rich demographic, standardized high school test scores, and socioeconomic (SES) measures of the respondents that allow us to control for the college sorting process.[10] The NELS:88 database also includes college transcripts of most individuals who enrolled in postsecondary education by 2000. With transcript data, the true enrollment patterns of college students, including the number and type of institutions attended, the intensity of the attendance at each institution, and the type of date of each credential earned, can be observed.

Institutional variables were drawn from the Integrated Postsecondary Education Data System (IPEDS), which contains information on aggregate student characteristics, faculty, enrollment, and finances. From these data, a file of institution's characteristics for each college over the span of NELS:88 was created and then merged with the student characteristics file using the institution identifier and school year of enrollment to assign the appropriate institutional characteristics.[11] The set of institutional characteristics can be divided in four groups: *general institutional characteristics*, which are under the control of the colleges or state policy makers; *compositional characteristics* of the student body; *financial variables* relating to revenue and expenditures; and *fixed location characteristics*.

3.2.1 General Institutional Characteristics

These factors are, at least in principle, under the control of the college or state policy makers are institution size, the proportion of the faculty working part time, and the balance between certificates and associate degrees awarded. Of these variables, institution size has been the most studied, but the direction of the relationship on student educational outcomes has been inconclusive. As mentioned earlier, Titus (2004) found that larger 4-year institutions have significant positive impacts on persistence, explained by the belief that larger institutions have stronger institutional socialization capabilities. On the other hand, it would seem easier to create a socially and academically engaged environment in a small institution, so a negative relationship between size and persistence would also be consistent with the engagement model (Bailey et al., 2006; Pascarella & Terenzini, 2005; Toutkoushian & Smart, 2001). We used a step function based on intervals of full-time-equivalent enrollments capture non-linear effects of institutional size.

The use of part-time faculty is a key cost saving strategy for community colleges, and indeed most 4-year colleges. The use of many adjuncts is generally considered a poor educational practice and accreditors set minimum percentages for full timers. However, the empirical evidence on the effectiveness of adjunct faculty is also mixed. Jacoby (2006) found a negative effect while Ehrenberg and Zhang (2005) found no effect.[12] We used the percentage of the faculty accounted for by part timers as our variable for this feature. A high proportion of part-time professors arguably make it difficult for colleges to develop the type of environment envisioned by the engagement model, part-time practitioners may be particularly effective in occupational fields, which are more important for community colleges than 4-year institutions.

Lastly, the mix of degrees (certificate versus associate's degree conferred by community colleges is a rough indication of the college's mission. Colleges that confer more certificates than associate's degrees are viewed as emphasizing short-term workforce development than more academic transfer-oriented programs, which implies a more occupational-oriented mission. Some researchers have argued that such a mission can lead to lower graduation and transfer rates (Bring & Karabel, 1989; Dougherty, 1994). We tested this hypothesis by including the ratio of certificate to associate's degrees in an analysis limited to students in associate's degree programs.

3.2.2. Student Compositional Characteristics

Institutional compositional variables are captured through indirect or peer effects. For example, full-time students would be less likely to persist if they attend a college dominated by part timers. Other compositional characteristics of the institution include the percent of part-time, female, and minority (comprising African American, Hispanic, and Native American) students. The expected relationship between these characteristics and student outcomes is as follows. Research on peer effects suggests that college students benefit when they take classes with or study with high-performing students (Winston & Zimmerman, 2004), but most of this work has focused on selective 4-year colleges. Assuming that this conclusion holds for community colleges, we would expect that colleges with high proportions of women, higher income students, and full-time students would have higher graduation rates, even after controlling for individual characteristics, since members all of these groups tend to be more successful students (Toutkoushian & Smart, 2001). Research on 4-year colleges that does not control for individual characteristics tends to confirm these relationships, although Titus (2004), who did control for individual characteristics, found no effect.

The engagement model would also predict that a prevalence of part-time students would weaken persistence, since many part-time students make it more difficult to develop the socially and academically engaged environment called for by this perspective. On campuses with a highly heterogeneous population it might also be more difficult to establish an environment conductive to engagement. Titus (2004) tested the effect of a measure of racial diversity and found no effect for 4-year colleges.

3.2.3. Financial Characteristics

These characteristics include federal student aid per FTE; average undergraduate in-state tuition; and average expenditures per FTE in instruction, academic support,[13] student services,[14] and administration.[15] The federal aid measure, which is primarily comprised of Pell Grants awarded to low- and middle-income students, also acts as a proxy for the relative income level of the student body.[16] Based on the findings of previous research, we expected expenditures in instruction and academic support to have a positive effect on the probability of success of community college students. Titus (2004) and Ryan (2004) found negative effects for administrative expenditures in 4-year institutions and argued that, although these expenses are necessary for day-to-day work, they might divert funds from more effective expenditures like instruction. Finally, we expected important effects if institutions spending large amounts on student services succeeded in compensating for the deficiencies that their students face (Astin, 1993). However, it is possible that colleges may spend more on student services and still not be able to help their students overcome the multiple barriers to success that they face (Ryan, 2004).

3.2.4. Fixed Location Characteristics

Our fourth category consist of just one variable: the college's location in an urban, suburban, or rural area. There is no strong argument for expecting any particular effect here. Perhaps suburban colleges might be expected to have more resources, especially in states where colleges collect revenue from local taxes, but this possibility ought to be accounted for by our expenditure variables. We included this variable to control for any factors that might be captured by a college's location.[17]

3.2.5. Individual Variables

The primary focus of this analysis is the effect of institutional factors, but selected individual characteristics were added to control for differences in the college sorting and completion processes. Individual-level characteristics were chosen based on studies that have shown that students who have stronger high school records, who come from higher income families, and whose parents when also went to college are more likely to graduate (Adelman, 1999, 2005, 2006; Bailey & Alfonso, 2005; Cabrera et al., 2005). To start, basic controls for gender and race/ethnicity were included in the models. Also, to control for the college sorting process—better students attending higher quality community colleges—measures of SES and cognitive ability were added. To measure SES, we used a composite variable in NELS:88 that included parental education, parental occupation, and total household income. Academic readiness was approximated using 10th grade composite test scores. Lastly, findings from previous research also indicate that students who delay their college entry after high school have lower levels of academic integration which, in turn, decreases the likelihood of persisting and attaining a degree (Pascarella & Terenzini, 2005; Tinto, 1993). To test for this, dummy variables were added to the models indicating delayed college attendance.

3.2.6. Sample

Our initial NELS:88 sample contained 2438 students whose initial postsecondary education was in one of 686 community colleges. However, regressions with full information included only 2196 students in 536 community colleges. Missing values corresponded mainly to high school tracking variables like test scores (173 observations), but also resulted from missing values in institutional variables merged from IPEDS (69 observations).[18]

We estimated our four models on two different samples. The first comprised all students whose initial postsecondary education was at a community college. The second was a subset containing community college students enrolled initially in an associate's degree program. In the latter case, we excluded a certificate as a successful outcome since students in an associate's degree program generally do not have earning a certificate as their goal. While the purpose of this research is to better understand the effect of institutional characteristics on community college student outcomes, we recognize that community college students are quite heterogeneous, especially in terms of their educational goals.[19] Conducting a separate analysis for associate's degree program students is a way to circumvent the problem.

4. Findings

Descriptive statistics for each sample group are provided in Table 20.1. A majority of community college students in the sample were enrolled in urban institutions and 43% were enrolled in large (more than 5000 full-time equivalent or FTE undergraduates) institutions. The student body in the average public, 2-year institution was composed of 21% minority students (black, Hispanic, and Native American), 56% female students, and 37% part-time students. Also, the average community college student enrolled at an institution were students received, on average, $1073 dollars in Pell Grants and were charged $1327 in tuition. Similarly, the average institution spent $2925 on instruction, $472 on academic support, $608 on student services, and $1329 on administrative expenses per FET student. Note also that the institutional-level variable means are reasonably similar for the associate's degree sample. In terms of student characteristics, the sample was overrepresented by racial/ethnic minorities (28%). Students in the sample are also more likely to come from disadvantaged backgrounds as measured by SES and academic readiness. Similar to the institutional-level characteristics, the subset of students in associate's degree programs shows comparable statistics.

Table 20.2 shows the distribution of completion rates by each type of degree attainment or transfer status across both samples. Overall, 48% of all community college students attained some outcome between 1992 and 2000. Interestingly, 5% of community college students in the sample received a certificate degree as their *highest* outcome, 11% received an associate's degree, 15% transferred to a 4-year institution, and 18% received a bachelor or post-baccalaureate degree before 2000. Recall that the NELS:88 sample contains mostly students who entered college soon after high school graduation, following the traditional pattern of postsecondary enrollment. Therefore, the sample is not a representative cross-section of all community college students, but by design is representative of a cohort of young adults.

TABLE 20.1

Descriptive Statistics for Institutional Characteristics

Variable	Percentage by Sample Type	
	All	**Associate's Degree**
General Institutional Characteristics		
1001–2500 FTE undergraduates	25.73%	25.04%
2501–5000 FTE undergraduates	24.96%	24.93%
More than 5000 FTE undergraduates	42.80%	42.79%
Proportion part-time faculty	51.55%	52.61%
Institution awards more certificates than associate degrees	10.59%	9.67%
Student Compositional Characteristics		
Proportion FTE minority	21.24%	21.63%
Proportion FTE female	56.25%	56.43%
Proportion FTE part-time	37.14%	36.42%
Financial Characteristics		
Federal aid (Pell Grants)[b]	1.073	1.085
In-state tuition[a]	1.327	1.371
Instructional expenditures[b]	2.925	2.840
Academic support[b]	0.472	0.466
Student services[b]	0.608	0.609
Administrative expenditures[b]	1.329	1.328
Fixed Locational Characteristics		
College is located in urban area	51.35%	47.67%
College is located in suburban area	45.89%	49.53%
College is located in rural area	2.76%	2.80%
Student Characteristics		
Female	49.66%	50.36%
White	71.71%	68.44%
Black	8.63%	10.61%
Hispanic	15.66%	17.92%
Asian	3.17%	2.40%
Delayed enrollment	32.20%	23.93%
SES: lowest quartile	17.24%	20.10%
SES: second quartile	28.97%	30.29%
SES: third quartile	32.55%	27.59%
SES: highest quartile	21.25%	22.01%
Test scores: lowest quartile	19.20%	18.38%
Test scores: second quartile	31.03%	31.78%
Test scores: third quartile	32.47%	34.68%
Test scores: highest quartile	17.30%	15.16%
Observations	2196	1188

Source: Estimates based on NELS:88 and IPEDS.
[a]In $1000s.
[b]In $1000s per FTE undergraduate

TABLE 20.2

Degree Completion of Community College Students by Highest Outcome

	Percentage by sample type	
Variable	**All**	**Associate's Degree**
Dropout	45.4	44.2
Still enrolled	6.5	4.6
Certificate	4.8	3.6
Associate's	10.6	14.7
Transfer	15.2	15.5
Bachelor's or post-baccalaureate	17.5	17.5
Positive outcome	48.0	47.7
Observations	2196	1188

Source: Estimates based on NELS:88.
Notes: A positive outcome for all students includes any certificate or degree earned or transfer to a 4-year institution with or without a credential. We excluded a certificate as a positive outcome for associate's degree students since these students generally do not have earning a certificate as their goal.

Estimates from the regression models applied on the entire sample of community college students and the subset of associate's degree students are shown in Tables 20.3 and 20.4, respectively.[20] The second column of Table 20.3 presents results of Model 1, the pooled probit regression (Eq. (1)). We used a robust variance-covariance matrix to account for serial correlation within clusters. Consistent with previous research (Bailey et al., 2006; Pascarella & Terenzini, 2005), we found that students enrolled in medium- and large-sized community colleges (1001–5000 FTE undergraduates and more than 5000 FTE undergraduates, respectively) were between 15% and 18% less likely to have a successful outcome than the reference students in small institutions (fewer than 1000 FTE undergraduates). Similarly, students enrolled in institutions with large proportions of part-time faculty and minority populations were less likely to attain a degree. A $1000 increase in academic support per FTE decreases the probability of graduating by 12% among NELS:88 students, although the result was statistically weak.

When unobservable institution-specific effects were accounted for in Model 2, the effect of medium- and large-sized institutions and the percentages of part-time faculty and minority students remained negatively associated with the probability of completing or transferring. However, the magnitude of the relationship was somewhat smaller than before. For instance, students enrolled in medium-size institutions (1000–5000 FTE) were now between 12% and 14% less likely to have a successful outcome than students in small institutions. Similarly, students enrolled in an institution with student body comprised 75% minority students were 9% less likely to succeed than are students enrolled in situations only with 25% minority students, compared to 13% less likely in Model 1.[21] However, the statistical association between academic support and the probability of graduating found in Model 1 has vanished.

The third column of Table 20.3 presents results for Model 3. After accounting for multiple institutional attendance by the students, the pattern of significant institutional covariates remained, but the size of the coefficients were larger than those from the previous two models. Nevertheless, across specifications, institutional size and the proportions of part-time faculty and minority students were negatively associated with our binary measure of educational success.

The fourth column of Table 20.3 shows the results of the re-estimated Model 2 (random effects model with multiple institutions) on the log number of credits earned. Consistent with previous

TABLE 20.3

Marginal Effects of Institutional Variables on Community College Student Outcomes

	Model 1		Model 2		Model 3		Model 4	
	Pooled Probit		Random Effect Probit		Pooled Probit Multiple Institutions		Random Effect Linear Model	
Variable	**dy/dx**	**S.E.**	**dy/dx**	**S.E.**	**dy/dx**	**S.E.**	**dy/dx**	**S.E.**
1001–2500 FTE undergraduates	–0.157**	0.061	–0.122**	0.056	–0.176***	0.064	–0.209*	0.112
2501–5000 FTE undergraduates	–0.176***	0.063	–0.139**	0.057	–0.200***	0.064	–0.250**	0.114
More than 5000 FTE undergraduates	–0.153**	0.064	–0.150***	0.057	–0.180***	0.063	–0.123	0.110
Proportion part-time faculty	–0.220**	0.092	–0.155***	0.058	–0.237**	0.102	–0.307**	0.135
Certificate degree oriented	0.001	0.056	–0.054	0.046	–0.002	0.057	–0.052	0.104
Proportion FTE minority	–0.269**	0.123	–0.186**	0.087	–0.293**	0.14	0.076	0.194
Proportion FTE female	0.351	0.267	–0.011	0.257	–0.237	0.26	–0.605	0.544
Proportion FTE part-time	–0.237	0.224	–0.018	0.121	–0.093	0.258	–0.606**	0.274
Federal aid (Pell Grants)[a]	0.054	0.064	0.041	0.05	0.112	0.083	–0.160	0.120
In-state tuition[b]	–0.026	0.019	–0.004	0.017	–0.019	0.018	0.029	0.036
Instructional expenditures[a]	0.004	0.02	0.000	0.016	–0.007	0.02	–0.031	0.036
Academic support[a]	–0.119*	0.068	0.013	0.056	–0.125*	0.068	–0.097	0.117
Student services[a]	–0.057	0.066	–0.030	0.049	–0.018	0.052	0.037	0.122
Administrative expenditures[a]	0.024	0.034	–0.032	0.028	0.025	0.046	–0.027	0.061
College is located in urban area	–0.044	0.041	–0.054	0.039	–0.057	0.041	–0.093	0.066
College is located in rural area	0.043	0.066	0.059	0.081	0.016	0.08	–0.101	0.208
Individual-level characteristics[c]	Yes		Yes		Yes		Yes	
Unweighted observations	2196		2196		2117		2196	
Number of institutions	536		536		—		536	
Log-likelihood	–1310.20		–1331.55		–1266.44		—	
Pseudo-R^2	0.137		0.139		0.139		0.089	
Estimated rho			0.117				0.072	

Source: Authors' estimates based on NELS:88 and IPEDS, various years.

Notes: The dependent variable in Models 1–3 is attainment of any degree (certificate, associate's, or bachelor's) or transfer to a 4-year institution, while in Model 4 the dependent variable is the logarithm of cumulative number of credits earned. (***), (**), (*), indicate statistically significance at 1%, 5% and 10% level.

[a]In \$1000s per FTE undergraduate.

[b]In \$1000s.

[c]Models include individual-level controls for gender, race, SES, availability and delay enrollment.

TABLE 20.4

Marginal Effects of Institutional Variables on Associate's Degree Student Outcomes

	Model 1		Model 2		Model 3		Model 4	
	Pooled Probit		Random Effect Probit		Pooled Probit Multiple Institutions		Random Effect Linear Model	
Variable	***dy/dx***	**S.E.**	***dy/dx***	**S.E.**	***dy/dx***	**S.E.**	***dy/dx***	**S.E.**
1001–2500 FTE undergraduates	−0.15*	0.08	−0.126*	0.073	−0.046	0.045	−0.252*	0.145
2501–5000 FTE undergraduates	−0.232***	0.081	−0.191***	0.074	−0.097**	0.049	−0.306**	0.147
More than 5000 FTE undergraduates	−0.197**	0.078	−0.152**	0.074	−0.129**	0.058	−0.232	0.148
Proportion part-time faculty	−0.180**	0.077	−0.118*	0.074	−0.113*	0.073	−0.229*	0.126
Certificate degree oriented	0.022	0.08	−0.011	0.067	−0.001	0.043	0.012	0.129
Proportion FTE minority	−0.308*	0.158	−0.289**	0.116	−0.387***	0.124	−0.003	0.239
Proportion FTE female	0.294	0.371	0.256	0.352	−0.245	0.226	0.029	0.661
Proportion FTE part-time	−0.420*	0.223	−0.329*	0.171	−0.227	0.168	−0.693**	0.341
Federal aid (Pell Grants)[a]	0.005	0.075	−0.002	0.07	−0.020	0.057	−0.334**	0.137
In-state tuition[b]	−0.014	0.027	−0.007	0.022	0.006	0.014	0.044	0.044
Instructional expenditures[a]	0.003	0.018	−0.019	0.024	0.014	0.017	0.032	0.046
Academic support[a]	−0.178**	0.089	−0.097	0.074	−0.115**	0.065	−0.036	0.135
Student services[a]	−0.042	0.08	0.061	0.069	−0.015	0.047	0.223	0.143
Administrative expenditures[a]	0.017	0.042	−0.036	0.039	−0.011	0.033	−0.130*	0.071
College is located in urban area	−0.018	0.051	−0.009	0.038	−0.010	0.03	0.009	0.077
College is located in rural area	0.123	0.086	0.181	0.108	0.064	0.065	0.208	0.21
Individual-level characteristics[c]	Yes		Yes		Yes		Yes	
Unweighted observations	1188		1188		1114		1188	
Number of institutions	423		423		—		423	
Log-likelihood	−682.75		−692.03		−625.36		—	
Pseudo-R^2	0.171		0.173		0.191		0.079	
Estimated rho			0.134				0.045	

Source: Authors' estimates based on NELS:88 and IPEDS, various years.

Notes: The dependent variable in Models 1–3 is attainment of any degree (certificate, associate's, or bachelor's) or transfer to a 4-year institution, while in Model 4 the dependent variable is the logarithm of cumulative number of credits earned. (***), (**), (*), indicate statistically significance at 1%, 5% and 10% level.

[a] In $1000s per FTE undergraduate.

[b] In $1000s.

[c] Models include individual-level controls for gender, race, SES, availability and delay enrollment.

estimates, institutional size and part-time faculty were negatively associated with the outcome, but the proportion of minority students was no longer statistically associated with cumulative credits earned. In addition, unlike the other three models previously discussed, there was evidence of a negative relationship between the proportion of part-time students and cumulative credits earned.

We now focus our attention on a more homogeneous population: students initially enrolled in an associate's degree program (Table 20.4). Examining the effects of the first institution only, the results generally mirror the patterns for the entire sample of community college students. Model 1 indicates that institutional size, part-time faculty, and minority student population were negatively associated with the probability of completion or transfer for associate's degree students. Interestingly, relatively large expenditures on academic support by community colleges were also negatively associated with the probability of completing a degree or transferring to a 4-year college. Perhaps academic support at community colleges is ineffective or instead reflects recognizable effort on behalf of colleges to address the academic deficiencies of their students that has not been captured by the test score variable. Regardless of the cause, the irregular pattern significance of this finance-related factor across the various models suggests a weak association with students' educational outcomes.

The second column in Table 20.4 controls for unobservable institution-specific effects (Model 2). Again, the results are similar to those from all community college students. For example, increases in institutional size have a strong and negative relationship on student success—students enrolled in medium-sized institutions are between 13% and 19% less likely to graduate than those enrolled in community colleges with 1000 FTE students or less. Note also that for students enrolled in associate's degree program having more part-time faculty has a negative influence on their educational success, although the result was statistically weak.

The results from Model 3 are shown in the third column of Table 20.4. The statistical significance of institution size remains, but the degree of association was less than the previous two models. Students in associate's degree programs were also negatively affected by increases in the proportion of part-time faculty, but as above the relationship has diminished when characteristics of all the institutions attended are controlled for. On the other hand, an increase in the percentage of minority students at the institution was associated with an even lower probability of completing or transferring. For example, students enrolled in an institution with a student body that is 75% minority are almost 19% less likely to succeed than are students enrolled in an institution with only 25% minority students (see footnote 15).[22]

Finally, the fourth column of Table 20.4 reports the results from the continuous measure—log of the total number of credits earned—after accounting for multiple institutional attendance. For the most part, the findings are similar to those from Table 20.3. There are, however, two key differences. First, an increase in Pell Grants was negatively associated with the (log) number of credits earned by students in associate's degree programs. Second, there was a weak relationship between administrative expenditures per FTE undergraduate and student success. Any importance placed on this finding is nominal given its level of significance and uniqueness among the other results.

The relative effects of individual student characteristics compared with institutional characteristics are shown in Table 20.5. Although measures of fit in limited dependent variable models do not have the same interpretation as with a linear regression model, they do provide some signal about the accuracy with which the model fits the data (Maddala, 1983). We fitted each model with a constant term, and then added sequentially the individual characteristics (Block 1) and the institutional variables (Block 2) to compute pseudo-R^2 using the log-likelihood values in each model. The results suggest that the addition of 16 institutional covariates improves the fit of the model, although the impact is relatively small. This finding indicates that individual student characteristic have a greater bearing on individual graduation rates than do institutional characteristics, or at least the institutional characteristics that are measured by IPEDS. Data on more specific institutional policies, practices, and programs may show these characteristics to be more influential than the more macro characteristics such as institutional size, student composition and overall expenditures that were used in this study.

TABLE 20.5

Measures of Fit Analysis: Individual versus Institutional Characteristics[a]

	Community College Students		Associate's Degree Students	
Model	**Block 1**[b]	**Block 2**[c]	**Block 1**[b]	**Block 2**[c]
Model 1	0.113	0.139	0.129	0.171
Model 2	0.121	0.132	0.148	0.173
Model 3	0.115	0.139	0.141	0.191

Source: Authors' estimates based on NELS:88 and IPEDS, various years.
[a]Fit of the model is measured as pseudo-R^2.
[b]Block 1 corresponds to models only with individual-level characteristics.
[c]Block 2 adds to Block 1 the institutional-level variables.

5. Robustness and Limitations of the Results

The first robustness test examines whether the pooled probit is a more appropriate specification than the random effect probit model. For this test, rho (ρ), which represents the proportion of the total variance contributed by the unobserved heterogeneity at the institution level, is reported in last row of the second columns of Tables 20.3 and 20.4 for Model 2. Taken in order, 12% of the variance in the unexplained outcome of all community college students can be explained by the unobserved institution-specific effect. Similarly, 13% of the unexplained variance in the outcomes of students in the associate's degree student sub-sample can be attributed to unobserved institutional-level effects. After estimating ρ, we compared the pooled probit and the random effect probit models using a likelihood ratio test ($\rho = 0$). The likelihood ratio test was distributed Chi-square with one degree of freedom. The estimated values of 16.43 for the community college students and 7.11 for the associate's degree sub-sample provide strong statistical evidence at the 1% level that the random effect probit model is the most appropriate model.

A second important sensitivity analysis is to demonstrate the value added by including NELS:88 data on individual students in the regressions. We conduct a series of regressions, as shown in Table 20.6, that first correlate student outcomes with only institutional factors (Model 1), and then sequentially add student demographics (Model 2), SES (Model 3) and test scores (Model 4). For this example, we re-estimate the random effect model to the entire student sample (Table 20.3, column 3). Results for Model 1, without any individual-level variables, suggest that institutional size is not statistically correlated with community college student outcomes, but it becomes statistically significant after controlling for students demographic characteristics. Overall, the coefficients on institutional size dummies and part-time faculty increase in absolute value after controlling for the full set of individual-level factors suggesting a bias towards zero. On the other hand, the coefficient on the proportion of minority students' increase after adding 10th grade test scores, suggesting that the former was capturing some negative influence of student ability.

One of the limitations of the analysis is the use of aggregate institutional measures to capture the variation in multiple educational outcomes—attainment of a certificate or associate's degree or transfer to a 4-year college. We recognize that these outcomes may be the result of different institutional priorities or realities, but most community college are often evaluated on their combined performance on these outcomes rather than singly or a subset. Thus, since the main objective of the study is to determine the institutional contribution to individual completion, we use the most generous definition of student success.

Also, some analytic problems remain. For example, we still must rely on the crude institutional measures available in IPEDS. So, while we may know that an individual is from a low-income family, we have no reliable information on the economic background of the typical student at that

TABLE 20.6

Marginal Effects from Random Effects Model with Stepwise Inclusion of Individual Characteristics

Variable	Model 1 dy/dx	Model 1 S.E.	Model 2 dy/dx	Model 2 S.E.	Model 3 dy/dx	Model 3 S.E.	Model 4 dy/dx	Model 4 S.E.
1001–2500 FTE undergraduates	–0.078	0.048	–0.131***	0.044	–0.126***	0.049	–0.122**	0.056
2501–5000 FTE undergraduates	–0.091*	0.054	–0.152***	0.045	–0.161***	0.051	–0.139**	0.057
More than 5000 FTE undergraduates	–0.080	0.049	–0.148***	0.045	–0.169***	0.051	–0.150***	0.057
Proportion part-time faculty	–0.141***	0.051	–0.096**	0.044	–0.100**	0.05	–0.155***	0.058
Certificate degree oriented	–0.063	0.042	–0.061	0.038	–0.060	0.042	–0.054	0.046
Proportion FTE minority undergraduates	–0.239***	0.071	–0.081	0.066	–0.087	0.075	–0.186**	0.087
Proportion FTE female undergraduates	–0.196	0.225	–0.214	0.198	–0.180	0.225	–0.011	0.257
Proportion FTE part-time undergraduates	–0.152	0.105	–0.083	0.092	–0.101	0.105	–0.018	0.121
Federal aid (Pell Grants)[a]	0.045	0.044	0.027	0.038	0.030	0.044	0.041	0.05
In-state tuition[b]	0.006	0.015	0.001	0.013	0.001	0.014	–0.004	0.017
Instructional expenditures[a]	–0.014	0.014	–0.006	0.012	–0.007	0.014	0.000	0.016
Academic support[a]	–0.047	0.049	–0.045	0.042	–0.046	0.048	0.013	0.056
Student services[a]	–0.013	0.042	–0.002	0.036	0.003	0.041	–0.030	0.049
Administrative expenditures[a]	–0.012	0.025	–0.012	0.022	–0.013	0.025	–0.032	0.028
College is located in urban area	–0.058*	0.026	–0.039*	0.023	–0.040	0.026	–0.054	0.039
College is located in rural area	–0.019	0.072	–0.018	0.064	–0.013	0.072	0.059	0.081
Student demographics[c]	No		Yes		Yes		Yes	
Student SES	No		No		Yes		Yes	
Student test scores	No		No		No		Yes	
Unweighted observations	2389		2381		2368		2196	
Number of institutions	548		548		547		536	

Source: Authors' estimates based on NELS:88 and IPEDS, various years.
Notes: The dependent variable in all Models is attainment of any degree (certificate, associate's, or bachelor's) or transfer to a 4-year institution. (***), (**), (*), indicate statistically significance at 1%, 5% and 10% level.
[a]In $1000s per FTE undergraduate.
[b]In $1000s.
[c]Demographic variables include controls for gender, race, and delay enrollment.

individual's college. In addition, we do not have measures of specific institutional policies, such as the types of student services or pedagogic strategies used to improve retention and completion. Finally, the NELS:88 sample is made up almost entirely of traditional-age college students, and therefore provides no information on older students, who comprise an important part of community college enrollments.

Alternatively, the magnitude of some variables may reflect a response to perceived student need as well as to some exogenously determined institutional policy. For example, as noted earlier, colleges whose students face multiple barriers may spend more on student services. While we add student characteristics to control for the college sorting process, there may be important factors that are not measured in our datasets. In this case, even if student services are effective in increasing retention, the negative effect of the initial student characteristics may offset the positive program effect resulting in a coefficient that suggests no effect. The reader is also cautioned that some unobservable student heterogeneity may be determining both the choice of community college and type of community college, i.e., large or urban or occupationally-oriented, which may affect the influence of the institutional measures included in the models on student completion.

6. Discussion

The overarching goal of this study is to measure the institutional characteristics that affect the success of individual community college students, which is acutely lacking in the literature. We estimate the institutional effect on a student's likelihood of completing a postsecondary credential or transferring to a 4-year college while controlling for individual characteristics such as a student's socioeconomic background and scores on standardized tests administered in high school. Our estimation strategy addressed two methodological challenges: unobserved institutional effects and multiple institution attendance.

Our results are generally consistent across both population and specifications. What do these findings imply about the policy, compositional, and financial variables that we analyzed? First, we observe an inverse relationship between school size and students' likelihood of completing or transferring to a 4-year college. This finding contrasts with some findings about 4-year colleges, but is consistent with other institutional analyses of 2-year colleges. Our finding is also consistent with the notion that a more professional atmosphere and personalized services, such as having a greater proportion of full-time faculty rather than part-time and expanding academic support services, seem to benefit the traditional-age student population in the NELS:88 sample.

Second, compositional factors have some influence as well. The findings from this study provides some support for the hypothesis that colleges with a larger share of minority students have lower graduation rates, a result that is consistent with research using institutional data at both community colleges and 4-year colleges. Given that we are controlling for race, test scores, and socioeconomic status, this is a result worth further examination.

Lastly, with the exception of academic support, selected expenditure and tuition levels are generally not related to differences in the graduation probabilities. This finding, however, stands in contrast to most of the findings for 4-year college students and is also a candidate for further study.

Ultimately, we find that individual characteristics are more strongly related to the completion probabilities than are institutional factors. There may be several explanations for the apparent greater importance of individual characteristics. First, the findings suggest that well-prepared students with economic resources are likely to survive and do well in a variety of institutions. On the other hand, students with many challenges, including personal and financial responsibilities, may have trouble even in strong colleges. Second, individual variables are measured with much more precision than institutional variables, especially with respect to the influence of factors on individuals. Students' individual characteristics obviously influence their experience, but colleges often comprised subcultures that are probably more important to individual students than average characteristics of the whole institution. Finally, our institutional characteristics are not able to capture effective institutional policies. Pedagogic strategies, successful guidance and academic counseling efforts, faculty culture, organizational characteristics, and many other factors are probably more influential than the broad characteristics measured by IPEDS.

Research on the relationship between institutional characteristics and institutional effectiveness is crucial to understanding how community colleges can increase their very low completion and transfer rates. There are several possible directions for future research. Certainly additional refinements of the type of analysis presented here using IPEDS and national longitudinal data, such as NELS:88 or the BPS:96/2001, will be important. State unit record data systems can provide much larger samples, including significant samples within individual institutions, although clearly the number of institutions will be much smaller. But within states it will be easier to have more comprehensive measures of institutional features. Evaluations of individual programs, such as particular strategies for remediation, can also play a role. Finally, additional insights can be gained by conducting qualitative research that searches for institutional features and policies that seem to be related to differences in institutional effectiveness.

Acknowledgements

This research was funded by the Ford Foundation. The work reported here has also benefited from research funded by the Lumina Foundation for Education (as part of the Achieving the Dream: Community Colleges Count initiative) and the US Department of Education (as part of the National Assessment of Vocational Education). The Community College Research Center was founded as a result of a generous grant from the Alfred P. Sloan Foundation, which continues to support our work. An earlier version of this paper was presented at the 2005 American Educational Research Association Annual Meeting and at the Council for the Study of Community Colleges, 47th Annual Conference. We also wish to thank Mariana Alfonso, Clive Belfield, Lauren O'Gara, Lisa Rothman, and Wendy Schwartz and three referees for their comments on an earlier draft.

Notes

1. Authors' calculations from the Beginning Postsecondary Student Longitudinal Study of 1995–1996.
2. According to Titus (2004, 2006), the other variables that are significantly correlated to student persistence are individual-level characteristics, such as degree goals, academic performance in high school, and the behavior of students' peers.
3. As summarized by Hanushek (1986), this strand of research typically focuses on the following two fundamental questions: "Do schools make a difference?" and "Does money matter?"
4. When this approach is used, the institution is typically treated as the unit of analysis and the influence of institutional characteristics (including average student characteristics) on the college's graduation rate are estimated (Austin, Tsui, & Avalos, 1996; Ryan, 2004; Scott, Bailey, & Kienzl, 2006). Only one study has conducted this type of analysis for community colleges (Bailey et al., 2006), and it concluded that institutions with a larger enrollment and a high share of minority students, part-time students, and women have lower graduation rates. Their results also confirm that greater instructional expenditures are related to a greater graduation rates.
5. In the discussion that follows, we use the terms *graduate*, *complete*, and *success* interchangeably for readability—in this context they all refer to earning a certificate or degree or transferring to a baccalaureate institution.
6. Wooldridge (2002) provide excellent reviews of the model and its properties.
7. Model 3 allows students to change institution; hence we expect the effect of the unobserved heterogeneity to be small. Nonetheless, results should be compared with Model 1.
8. Excellent examples of these distrbutions and a detailed analysis can be found in Kane and Rouse (1995).
9. The NELS:88 sample contains mostly students who entered college soon after high school graduation, following the traditional pattern of postsecondary enrollment. Therefore, the sample is not a representative cross-section of all community college students, but by design (of the survey) includes only cohorts of younger postsecondary students.
10. The NELS:88 sample design involved stratification and clustered probability sampling. We used the survey design correction included with Stata statistical software for estimating the models. However,

we were not able to account for stratification of the survey in our Model 2. Although we obtained the proper design-based point estimates, our standard errors might be misleading.

11. NELS:88 reports students' colleges by IPEDS ID number, so we were able to associate the characteristics of the college, reported in IPEDS, with the individuals in the NELS:88 sample.
12. Ehrenberg and Zhang (2005) found no evidence that increasing the percentage of part-time faculty members at 2-year colleges adversely influence institutional graduation rates. However, the authors used College Board data and included only those community colleges that report average SAT scores.
13. Academic support includes expenses for activities and services that support the institution's primary mission of instruction, research and public service, like display of educational materials in libraries, museums, or galleries.
14. Student services include expenses for admissions, registrar activities, and activities whose primary purpose is to contribute to students' emotional and physical well-being and to their intellectual, cultural, and social development outside the context of the formal instructional program.
15. Administration includes expenses for the day-to-day operational support of the institution.
16. Ehrenberg and Zhang (2005) also used the percentage of college students receiving a Pell Grant at the institution.
17. We also estimated our models with state dummies to capture any unobserved factor shared by institutions in the same state. However, results did not change after controlling for state fixed effects.
18. Compared with the final sample presented in Table 20.2, students with missing data are, on average, more likely to be Hispanic (22%), low SES (24%) and to delay enrollment after high school (45%). They are less likely to be white (59%).
19. A survey question asking first-time beginning community college students their primary reason for enrolling produced the following response distribution: job skills: 23%; degree or certificate: 21%; transfer: 39%; personal enrichment: 17% (Source: Beginning Postsecondary Students Longitudinal Study 1996–2001, authors' calculations).
20. Individual-level characteristics were included as covariates. Results are not shown here, but are available upon request from authors.
21. For variables originally expressed as a proportion, like part-time faculty, and minority, female, part-time students, the marginal effects represent a unit change from 0 to 1.
22. At the suggestion of a referee, we included a new explanatory variable in all models that measures the number of transitions between community colleges a student made during the 8-year window of observation. The goal is to capture the impact of transferring between community colleges. When added to regressions for all community college students (as in Table 20.3), the new variable was not statistically significant and the size and statistical significance of all other coefficients remained the same. However, when the new variable was added to the regressions for the subset of associate's degree students (Table 20.4), we found a positive and statistically significant effect, but small changes in the institutional variables. Although these results suggests that more transitions are associated with positive outcomes, it cannot necessarily be assumed that the transitions are occurring for academic reasons. Further research is necessary to determine the causes of these shifts between colleges.

References

Adelman, C. (1999). *Answers in the tool box: Academic intensity, attendance patterns, and bachelor's degree attainment.* Washington, DC: National Center for Education Statistics.

Adelman, C. (2005). *Moving into town and moving one. The community college in the lives of traditional-age students.* Washington, DC: National Center for Education Statistics.

Adelman, C. (2006). *Replicating the tool box hypotheses: Path the degree completion from high school through college.* Washington, DC: National Center for Education Statistics.

Astin, A. (1993). *What matters in college: Four critical years revisited.* San Francisco: Jossey-Bass.

Astin, A., Tsui, L., & Avalos, J. (1996). *Degree attainment rates at American colleges and universities: Effects of race, gender, and institutional type.* Los Angeles: Higher Education Research Institute, UCLA.

Bailey, T., & Alfonso, M. (2005). *Paths to persistence: An analysis of research on program effectiveness at community colleges.* Indianapolis: Lumina Foundation for Education.

Bailey, T., Calcagno, J., Jenkins, D., Leinbach, D., & Kienzl G. (2006). Is Student-Right-to-Know all you should know? An analysis of community college graduation rates. *Research in Higher Education*, 47, 5.

Bean, J. P. (1985). Interaction effects based on class level in an explanatory model of college student dropout syndrome. *American Educational Research Journal*, 22(1), 35-64.

Brint, S., & Karabel, J. (1989). *The diverted dream: Community colleges and the promise of educational opportunity in America, 1900–1985*. New York: Oxford University Press.

Cabrera, A., Burkum, K., & La Nasa, S. (2005). Pathways to a four-year degree: Determinants of transfer and degree completion. In A. Seidman, (Ed.), *College student retention: A formula for student success*. Westport: ACE/Praeger Series on Higher Education.

Cohen, A., & Brawer, F. (1996). *The American community college*. San Francisco: Jossey-Bass.

Dougherty, K. (1994). *The contradictory college: The conflicting origins, impacts, and futures of the community college*. Albany: State University of New York Press.

Ehrenberg, R., & Zhang, L. (2005). Do tenured and tenure-track faculty matter? *Journal of Human Resources*, 40(3), 647–659.

Guilkey, D., & Murphy, J. (1993). Estimation and testing in the random effects probit model. *Journal of Econometrics*, 59(3), 301–17.

Hanushek, E. (1986). The economics of schooling: Production and efficiency in public schools. *Journal of Economic Literature*, 24(3), 1142–1177.

Jacoby, D. (2006). Effects of part-time faculty employment on community college graduation rates. *Journal of Higher Education*, 77(6), 1081–1103.

Kane, T., & Rouse, C. (1995). Labor-market returns to two- and four-year college. *American Economic Review*, 85(3), 600–614.

Maddala, G. (1983). *Limited dependent and qualitative variables in econometrics*. New York: Cambridge University Press.

Pascarella, E., & Terenzini, P. (2005). *How college affects students: A third decade of research*, Vol. 2. San Francisco: Jossey-Bass.

Rouse, C. (1995). Democratization or diversion? The effect of community colleges on educational attainment. *Journal of Business and Economic Statistics*, 13(2), 217–224.

Ryan, J. (2004). The relationship between institutional expenditures and degree attainment at baccalaureate institutions. *Research in Higher Education*, 45(2), 97–114.

Scott, M., Bailey, T., & Kienzl, G. (2006). Relative success? Determinants of college graduation rates in public and private colleges in the US. *Research in Higher Education* 47(3), 249–279.

Tinto, V. (1993). *Leaving college: Rethinking the causes and cures of student attrition*. Chicago: University of Chicago Press.

Titus, M. (2004). An examination of the influence of institutional context on student persistence at 4-year colleges and universities: A multilevel approach. *Research in Higher Education*, 45(7), 673–700.

Titus, M. (2006). Understanding the influence of financial context of institutions on student persistence at 4-year colleges and universities: A multilevel approach. *Journal of Higher Education*, 77(2), 353–375.

Toutkoushian, R., & Smart, J. (2001). Do institutional characteristics affect student gains from college? *Review of Higher Education*, 25(1), 39–61.

Winston, G, & Zimmerman, D. (2004). Peer effects in higher education. In C. Hoxby (Ed.), *College choice: The economics of where to go, when to go, and how to pay for it*. Chicago: University of Chicago Press.

Wooldridge, J. (2002). *Econometric analysis of cross section and panel data*. Cambridge: MIT Press.

CHAPTER 21

BUDGET SYSTEMS USED IN ALLOCATING RESOURCES TO LIBRARIES

MOTT LINN

Purpose—The purpose of this article is to provide information about many different budgeting systems that are used to allocate resources to libraries.

Design/methodology/approach—A number of methods of resource allocation are reviewed. The types of budgeting covered are incremental line-item, formula, mathematical, zero-based, program (including planning, programming, and budgeting systems), performance-based, responsibility center, block-incremental, and initiative-based.

Findings—There are numerous types of budgeting systems and each of them functions differently.

Research limitations/implications—There are many variations of each of these basic types of budgeting systems. As a result, this article reviews the most prominent ones.

Practical implications—This is a very useful source of finding out the fundamentals of each of the basic kinds of budgeting systems. In addition, the article gives many references for finding out more about each of these methods.

Originality/value—This paper covers the various types of budgeting systems. This allows librarians to better understand the budgeting system they deal with so that they might better work with it to maximize their library's funding.

It is through the budget-making process that the hopes and dreams of educators are adjusted to the cold realities of dollars and cents (Harold W. Dodds, President of Princeton University) (Dodds, 1962).

One does not need to be a long-time president of an Ivy League school to know that budgets are a critical part of the effective running of an institution. A budget is a method of accomplishing many managerial tasks. A budget is not only a means of planning for various revenue streams, a control mechanism for an administration to keep from spending too much, a procedure for controlling its units, a process to coordinate the many activities that an institution undertakes, and a way to communicate to all stakeholders a summarization of the activities that the various units will undertake, but it is also a technique for setting the organization's priorities by allocating scarce resources to those activities that officials deem to be the most important and rationing it to those areas deemed less vital. Following the priorities set in a budget is a key element in determining the direction of the organization and its future success or failure, which is why it should be based on a formal plan, such as a strategic plan, that the institution is supposed to be following. The creating and following of budgetary priorities is important, even during relatively favorable financial times, while a downturn in financial circumstances only makes this more difficult and even more crucial. Consequently, budgets are a key element in determining the direction of the organization and its future success or failure (Goldstein, 2005; Maddox, 1999; Martin, 1993; McCabe, 1984).

A budget is just as important for nonprofit organizations, which by their nature are not required to maximize their profits, as it is for businesses, which exist to bring the utmost return on the stockholders' investments. Kevin Guthrie's *The New-York Historical Society* documents an extreme example of how the administrators of a nonprofit can create a calamitous situation when they ignore their financial position and budgetary constraints. In this case, an important archives and museum came exceedingly close to financial collapse on a number of occasions, mostly because its managers neither stayed within the bounds of the budget nor followed the institution's priorities when acquiring items for the collection (Guthrie, 1996). The need to prioritize one's spending is just as important for all types of repositories, including libraries.

Because of the importance of budgeting, it is prudent for those with fiscal responsibilities to have a solid understanding of how their budgetary system works. There are, however, many types of budgetary systems that are used by nonprofit organizations and these can accomplish their fiscal tasks in very different ways. Some state-financed institutions must follow budget procedures and formats dictated by their legislatures. Conversely, few private repositories have any restrictions as to which budgetary system they use. In this case, there are many possible influences upon the type of system that is chosen, including the type that the institution has historically used, the procedures the president is accustomed to, the institution's mission, and the organization's culture. When considering these various types of systems, it is wise to keep in mind John Green and David Monical's observation that there "are probably as many different ways of allocating resources in institutions of higher education as there are presidents" of these institutions (Green and Monical, 1985). This is no doubt also true for the governing bodies of other types of libraries. With this many allocation systems, while it is difficult to classify some of them, many can be categorized.

Incremental Line-Item Budgeting

Incremental line-item budgeting is probably the most widely-used type of system. It makes all increases and decreases to the budget equal for all units on a percentile basis. Essentially, the previous budget is seen as having already been justified and it is used as a base upon which to make the changes for the next fiscal year. Thus, unless the budget creators go out of their way to change part of the budget, budget lines will be re-funded whether or not the activities that they finance are still supported by the strategic plan, are needed for any other reason, or are being used optimally.

This system, by locking into place the decisions of the past, guarantees that the units that won the budgetary battle when the incremental system was installed, whether because they were the most important to fund or received more than they deserved because of political influence, will continue to win in this budgetary process until the incremental system is replaced or side-stepped, either temporarily or permanently. This system, however, tends to create the least amount of conflict during the budgeting process because it just continues the status quo. It seems that unit heads are much more likely to complain when some other units get significant increases while theirs gets left behind, than when everybody's budget moves in lockstep even if it seems to be doing so in an inequitable way.

Advantages of an incremental budget are that it is relatively easy to create and to allocate money; however, because all of the budget lines are moving together, strategic changes cannot be made to the budget without breaking its incremental nature. In particular, this is clearly a poor system for an institution to use during a period of change, like that currently facing academia due to pressures such as great technological change, stakeholders' demands for greater accountability, and reduced governmental monetary support (Caruthers and Orwig, 1979; Goldstein, 2005; Phelps, 1996).

Formula Budgeting

Formula budgeting is typically employed by governmental bodies as a means of distributing its money to its various sub entities. Although most states use this system to distribute funds to elementary and secondary schools, its use for higher education is most common in Northeastern and Midwestern states.

A formula is essentially a decision rule that reduces the complexity of the budgetary process. Those who create them have deemed the factors that are incorporated in the formula to be important in the running of the organization. Although formula budgeting can be thought of as a relatively rational approach to budgeting because there seems to be little room for political influence in the allocation of funds, the creation of the formula can be the result of a political process. Indeed, the subject of Richard Meisinger's dissertation is the politics of formula budgeting, and it is full of examples of how politics influenced the formula creation process in three states. As a result, those who have power at the time of the formula's creation or revision may be able to have those elements at which their unit excels to be those that are rewarded the most. For example, public libraries serving small populations would want their state to allocate to all of its public libraries the same amount of money per library, while those serving large populations would want the state's funding formula to be based solely on a per capita basis. Once the formula is created, the winners of this political battle have a built in advantage for every funding allocation until the formula is changed.

When formula budgeting is used within a particular institution, different formulas are used for units that function differently. For example, the library and physical plant would probably have different formulas than the parts of the institution that mainly do instruction. These various formulas are created to estimate the money that the units will require. Some examples of factors that are included in some formulas are degrees conferred, credit hours taught, number of programs that award graduate degrees, students enrolled, and gross square footage of space in buildings. As a result, a library could get as part of its funding $200 for each member of the university's faculty, $25 per undergraduate student, $125 per masters student, and $250 per doctoral student.

An advantage of formula budgeting is that it makes it relatively easy for the director to predict the amount of money that will be allocated. However, its rigidity makes it unlikely to foster innovative practices or new programs. In addition, formulas lack the flexibility that is needed when changes are made to the organization's mission (Allen, 1977; Caruthers and Orwig, 1979; Goldstein, 2005; Hallam and Dalston, 2005; Rodas, 2001; Meisinger, 1975; Phelps, 1996; McKeown, 1996a, b). For example, if the governing body does not allow for the library director to move money from one line to another, it might take a great deal of effort to be allowed to stop purchasing microfilm with money from its line and be allowed to use those funds to buy more databases. As a result, to try to maximize one's flexibility in this system, the library director should attempt to get the budget lines to be defined as broadly as possible. In the previous example, if there had been one line for the purchasing of all types of materials for the library collection, one could easily stop buying microfilm and use that money to purchase more databases.

Mathematical Decisions Models Budgeting

Mathematical decisions models were developed during the 1970s. These were created to help college administrators allocate money more effectively by using complicated computer models to determine the resources required for various needs. The use of these models quickly dropped-off for many reasons, including the time that is needed to be invested (Rodas, 1998, 2001).

Zero-based Budgeting

Zero-based budgeting (ZBB) is a system that, when used in its purest form, essentially has the organization recreate its budget from scratch every year. Consequently, every dollar on every line of the budget must be justified every year. In addition, every unit has to rank its lines in order of priority before sending the list up to the central administrators who decide on the allocations. As a result, the decision makers have a ranking of what the directors of every unit think are the most and least important activities to fund. This facilitates their ability to decide which departments should receive reduced funds and which should have increased allocations. In this way it is the opposite of the incremental approach of adding a certain amount to the budget that had been justified the year before. ZBB is also very different in that it concentrates on whether or not individual activities are still justified to be funded. As a result, it is more likely to be instituted during a time of fiscal retrenchment, rather than growth.

A benefit of ZBB is that it points out those expenses that are no longer necessary, thus allowing the library to shift money to where it will be needed in the future. Because ZBB requires that every item be justified it takes a great deal of time to do the work that this system requires. This is why a much smaller number of organizations now use ZBB than did a few decades ago. Many that do still use it do so in conjunction with another system. When utilized in this way, ZBB is used in one part of the institution every year, but the unit that is doing the intense budgetary work rotates every year, so that any given unit has to do it only once every so many years (Caruthers and Orwig, 1979; Chen, 1980; Goldstein, 2005; Hallam and Dalston, 2005; Harvey, 1977; Pyhrr, 1970; Maddox, 1999; Phelps, 1996; Wildavsky, 1979).

Program Budgeting

Program budgeting is the general name for a few slightly different systems, all of which require not only that there should be specificity in how funds are to be spent, but also why they will be spent that way. Program budgets list costs by each type of output, rather than, or in addition to, each type of cost, as most budgets do. A principle of program budgets is to attach all spending to one program or another. Consequently, the focus is on the various categories of outputs and on determining as closely as possible all of the costs, even the indirect ones, which go into producing each. In addition, because this is like doing cost-benefit analysis, not just the costs, but also the outputs must be at least somewhat quantifiable. Moreover, program budgets tie the total costs of various programs to the objectives of the library. As a result, it is relatively easy to determine which programs are the least cost effective. Conversely, a program budget is a bit unrealistic, in that it requires library administrative costs to be spread throughout the various programs. As an example of how a program budget could work, it could state that for a certain amount of money that the budget will invest in the bibliographic instruction program one should expect that a particular number of classes should have attended instruction sessions. One should be aware that with this system the more interdependence that the different outputs have, the more difficult this system becomes. By more closely tracking the output statistics, a program budget becomes a type of performance budget (Hallam and Dalston, 2005; Hirsh, 1966; Robinson and Robinson, 1994; Wildavsky, 1966).

Planning, programming, and budgeting systems (PPBS), which is the most commonly used type of program budgeting system today, links the planning process with the one for budgeting. As a result, this system is more likely than most to create a budget by looking towards the future, rather than looking to the past, but it focuses on what will be done, rather than how it will be done.

PPBS has three parts: a systematic process of long-range planning, the creation of programs to meet the goals of the plan, and a budget that supports these plans and programs. For this system one must not only determine the costs and benefits of the various program options, but also their comparative importance. Consequently, those who make the budget must be in agreement on the institution's priorities. This can be a problem in academia, because of the trouble a faculty would have agreeing on a ranking of the importance of all of their university's programs. In addition, it is difficult for budget leaders to agree as to how to define and measure educational outcomes, which would be an important factor in determining the benefits of a program. An advantage of PPBS is that because it requires aggregating even indirect costs to the various outputs of the library, it allows one to easily determine facts about a particular library that other systems do not. For example, one might find out that it costs more per square foot to provide study space than to shelve books or that it would cost more to shelve books on-campus than to use off-site storage and to pay people to retrieve any needed books. However, PPBS does not factor into its analysis the quality of the services provided, such as whether or not students who attend bibliographic instruction sessions actually learn anything from them, which could be important considering stakeholders' recently increased interest in measuring outcomes (Caruthers and Orwig, 1979; Goldstein, 2005; Hallam and Dalston, 2005; Lee, 1973; Rodas, 1998; Phelps, 1996; Raffel and Shishko, 1969; Wildavsky, 1966).

Performance-based Budgeting

Performance-based budgeting focuses on outcomes, as opposed to outputs. The difference is that an output of a bibliographic instruction program would be the number of students that received instruction, while an outcome would be the skills that those students had learned. It seems that this system was created in reaction to calls from stakeholders for greater accountability for all the funding they provide and as a way to bring together the strategic planning process with the budget creation process, which some systems, such as incremental and formula budgeting, can easily separate. Because this system relates inputs (funding), activities, and results (outcomes or impacts), it is easy not only to track the cost of each library service, but also to determine its efficiency. There are several reasons why this system is not widely used in higher education. For one thing, not only is student learning, which is the principle outcome in academia, difficult to trace back to the individual units that helped to bring it about, but also there is disagreement as to what higher education outcomes should be. In addition, performance budgeting takes a great deal of time to implement. Furthermore, there is a danger that those carefully keeping track of the statistics will start to view the numbers as an end in itself rather than a means to an end. With stakeholders putting more emphasis on making educational institutions accountable for their outcomes, however, there could be a resurgence in the use of this and other budgeting systems that require the analysis of educational outcomes (Axford, 1971; Caruthers and Orwig, 1979; Goldstein, 2005; Hallam and Dalston, 2005; Rodas, 1998; Burke and Modarresi, 2000; Phelps, 1996).

Responsibility Center Budgeting

Responsibility center budgeting (RCB), which has been referred to in many ways, including value centered management, cost center budgeting, and "every tub on its own bottom," attempts to make every unit more accountable by forcing it to manage its own expenses and revenues. It has been noted that academic units often have the authority to make changes that can greatly affect the institution's spending or revenue, but are often not held financially responsible and, thus, do not have to experience the direct effects of their actions. In RCB, the central administration gives its units both academic authority and fiscal responsibility. This creates incentives to restrict the number of money-losing programs, which in other allocation systems would be allowed to exist because of subsidies from money-making departments.

Central administrations that institute RCB often do so with the expectation that this will result in a more entrepreneurial culture on campus. Every responsibility center is accountable for all of its expenses and revenues, from donations to tuition per student taught. Responsibility centers that are to be profit centers are expected to run surpluses. They can carry any surpluses or deficits into future budget years, thus inspiring managers to control costs, be efficient, and increase revenue. As a result, the profit center can fund its own initiatives from its accumulated surpluses. For example, if the library wanted to purchase a database with a huge up-front cost, but a manageable yearly cost, it could accumulate unspent money for many years until it had enough to purchase the database. If an unexpected event were to occur, however, it is unlikely that the library would be able to get funding from the central administration to cover the cost. For example, if the library owned its computer server and it suddenly stopped functioning, the library would have to find a way to pay for its replacement using surpluses it had accrued or creating deficits that it would have to pay off.

One should note that by better aligning the university's and the units' budgetary goals, RCM minimizes the classic economics quandary of the principal-agent problem. For instance, the rolling over of any leftover funds at the end of the fiscal year removes the incentives for dynamic inefficiency that commonly finds administrators hurriedly spending all remaining monies in the budget at the end of every fiscal year, sometimes on items of questionable importance.

In some cases, like Harvard's, the libraries are mainly a cost of the unit of which they are a part. Thus, the Harvard Business School is responsible for the budget of its Baker Library. At most RCB schools, however, libraries are cost centers. A cost center is not expected to break even and are supported through taxes on the profit centers, which is called subvention. However, departments that should be profit centers, but that are losing money, risk having their managers replaced or, in extreme cases, having the whole program be terminated. For instance, Harvard eliminated its geography department decades ago because it was neither profitable nor prestigious.

An advantage of RCB is that it forces units to pay for everything they use and to be paid for what they supply. One problem with this system is that it can hamper cross-disciplinary work since each unit is so independent. In addition, there is the definite risk that costly redundancies within the greater institution may develop. For example, Harvard's law school offers its own accounting courses instead of sending its students that want an accounting class, and their tuition, to the Harvard Business School (Bava, 2001; Goldstein, 2005; Hallam and Dalston, 2005; Harris, 1970; Maddox, 1999; Rodas, 1998; Phelps, 1996; Neal and Smith, 1995; Strauss and Curry, 2002; Whalen, 1991; Priest *et al.*, 2002; West *et al.*, 1997; Class, 2004).

Block-Incremental Budgeting

Block-incremental or lump-sum budgeting is an alternative to RCB, in that it is a partly decentralized method of budgeting. In this system, while the spending part of the budget is decentralized, the central administration more tightly controls the income. As a result, an advantage of this system, as it is for RCB, is that unit heads have the flexibility to shift spending to where they think it is needed most. Like the federal government's method of funding some spending programs by the states, the central administration allots a unit's money in a block that those administrators that are further down the hierarchy and, thus, more knowledgeable of the various needs of the units, can dole out as they see fit. For example, if the university librarian thinks that more funding is needed for audio-visual materials than for monographs, funds can be expended in this way without needing to ask to be allowed to do this. Essentially, as long as the library director does not spend more than the amount in the block of funding, how much the library overspends or underspends on a particular line does not matter. As a result, a unit's budget may grow incrementally, but its various budget lines may not (Hallam and Dalston, 2005; Rodas, 1998; Phelps, 1996).

Initiative-based Budgeting

Initiative-based budgeting, which is also called reallocation budgeting, is more an organized way of creating a pool of money for funding new initiatives than a comprehensive budget system. It is also not a system that can be used indefinitely. No matter which variant of this an institution uses, it forces units to give back a certain percentage of their base budget, which forces units to reevaluate their activities to make sure that all of them are still needed. The central administration then uses the pool of money that this process creates to fund initiatives that were given priority in the college's planning process (Goldstein, 2005).

Finally, these budgeting systems can, and often are, mixed. For example, a college could use ZBB with a different unit every year, while all the others get budgeted using an incremental approach. Furthermore, one should keep in mind that institutions will sometimes employ a different budgeting system internally to distribute resources to their various units than the one that their governing authority uses to give them money. For example, Indiana University receives its funding from the state via formula budgeting, but allocates money to its units using a form of responsibility center budgeting.

Conclusion

The allocation of money via budgets can be done in many ways. Librarians need to be aware of how the system that they deal with functions so that they can attempt to minimize any negatives and to take advantage of its benefits, such as ways of increasing funding and of maximizing fiscal flexibility.

References

Allen, K.S. (1977), "Washington State Library formula: a case study", in Lee, S.H. (Ed.), *Library Budgeting: Critical Challenges for the Future*, Pierian Press, Ann Arbor, MI, pp. 27-47.

Axford, H.W. (1971), "An approach to performance budgeting at the Florida Atlantic University library", *College and Research Libraries*, Vol. 32 No. 2, pp. 87-101.

Bava, D.J. (2001), "Responsibility center management: a financial paradigm and alternative to centralized budgeting", PhD dissertation, University of the Pacific, Stockton, CA.

Burke, J.C. and Modarresi, S. (2000), "To keep or not to keep performance funding? Signals from stakeholders", *The Journal of Higher Education*, Vol. 71 No. 4, pp. 432-53.

Caruthers, J.K. and Orwig, M.D. (1979), *Budgeting in Higher Education*, Vol. 3, American Association for Higher Education, Washington, DC.

Chen, C.-C. (1980), *Zero-Base Budgeting in Library Management: A Manual for Librarians*, Oryx Press, Phoenix, AZ.

Class, M.D. (2004), "Organizational culture change as a result of a change in budgeting systems", PhD dissertation, University of Pennsylvania, Philadelphia, PA.

Dodds, H.W. (1962), *The Academic President: Educator or Caretaker?*, McGraw-Hill, New York, NY.

Goldstein, L. (2005), *College and University Budgeting: An Introduction for Faculty and Academic Administrators*, 3rd ed., National Association of College and University Business Officers, Washington, DC.

Green, J.L. Jr and Monical, D.G. (1985), "Resource allocation in a decentralized environment", in Berg, D.J. and Skogley, G.M. (Eds), *Making the Budget Process Work*, Vol. 52, Jossey-Bass, San Francisco, CA, pp. 47-63.

Guthrie, K.M. (1996), *The New-York Historical Society: Lessons from One Nonprofit's Long Struggle for Survival*, Jossey-Bass, San Francisco, CA.

Hallam, A.W. and Dalston, T.R. (2005), *Managing Budgets and Finances: A How-To-Do-It Manual for Librarians*, Neal-Schuman, New York, NY.

Harris, S.E. (1970), *Economics of Harvard*, McGraw-Hill, New York, NY.

Harvey, L.J. (1977), *Zero-Base Budgeting in Colleges and Universities: A Concise Guide to Understanding and Implementing ZBB in Higher Education*, Ireland Educational, Littleton, CO.

Hirsh, W.Z. (1966), "Toward federal program budgeting", *Public Administration Review*, Vol. 26 No. 4, pp. 259-69.

Lee, S.H. (1973), *Planning-Programming-Budgeting System (PPBS): Implications for Library Management*, Pierian Press, Ann Arbor, MI.

McCabe, G.B. (1984), "Austerity budget management", in Harvey, J.F. and Spyers-Duran, P. (Eds), *Austerity Management in Academic Libraries*, Scarecrow Press, Metuchen, NJ, pp. 225-35.

McKeown, M.P. (1996a), *State Funding Formulas for Public Four-year Institutions, State Higher Education Executive Officers*, Denver, CO.

McKeown, M.P. (1996b), "State funding formulas: promise fulfilled?", in Honeyman, D.S., Wattenbarger, J.L. and Westbrook, K.C. (Eds), *A Struggle to Survive: Funding Higher Education in the Next Century*, Corwin Press, Thousand Oaks, CA, pp. 49-85.

Maddox, D. (1999), *Budgeting for Not-for-Profit Organizations*, John Wiley & Sons, New York, NY.

Martin, M.S. (1993), *Academic Library Budgets*, Vol. 28, JAI Press, Greenwich, CT.

Meisinger, R.J. (1975), "The politics of formula budgeting: the determination of tolerable levels of inequality through objective incrementalism in public higher education", PhD dissertation, University of California, Berkeley, CA.

Neal, J.G. and Smith, L. (1995), "Responsibility center management and the university library", *The Bottom Line*, Vol. 8 No. 4, pp. 17-20.

Phelps, K.A. (1996), "Integrated budget and planning processes in higher education: a case study", PhD dissertation, University of Nebraska, Lincoln, NE.

Priest, D.M., Becker, W.E., Hossler, D. and St John, E.P. (Eds) (2002), *Incentive-Based Budgeting Systems in Public Universities*, Edward Elgar, Northampton, MA.

Pyhrr, P.A. (1970), "Zero-base budgeting", *Harvard Business Review*, Vol. 48 No. 6, pp. 111-21.

Raffel, J.A. and Shishko, R. (1969), *Systematic Analysis of University Libraries: An Application of Cost-Benefit Analysis to the MIT Libraries*, MIT Press, Cambridge, MA.

Robinson, B.M. and Robinson, S. (1994), "Strategic planning and program budgeting for libraries", *Library Trends*, Vol. 42 No. 3, pp. 420-47.

Rodas, D. (1998), "Resource allocation in private research universities", PhD dissertation, Standford University, Palo Alto, CA.

Rodas, D. (2001), *Resource Allocation in Private Research Universities*, RoutledgeFalmer, New York, NY.

Strauss, J.C. and Curry, J.R. (2002), *Responsibility Center Management: Lessons from 25 Years of Decentralized Management*, National Association of College and University Business Officers, Washington, DC.

West, J.A., Seidita, V., Mattia, J.D. and Whalen, E. (1997), "RMC as a catalyst", *NACUBO Business Officer*, Vol. 31 No. 2, pp. 24-8.

Whalen, E. (1991), *Responsibility Center Budgeting: An Approach to Decentralized Management for Institutions of Higher Education*, Indiana University Press, Bloomington, IN.

Wildavsky, A.B. (1966), "The political economy of efficiency: cost-benefit analysis, systems analysis, and program budgeting", *Public Administration Review*, Vol. 26 No. 4, pp. 292-310.

Wildavsky, A.B. (1979), *The Politics of the Budgetary Process*, 3rd ed., Brown & Company, Boston, MA.

CHAPTER 22

TOWARDS DECENTRALIZED AND GOAL-ORIENTED MODELS OF INSTITUTIONAL RESOURCE ALLOCATION: THE SPANISH CASE

MARÍA JOSE GONZÁLEZ LÓPEZ

The search for more flexibility in financial management of public universities demands adjustments in budgeting strategies. International studies on this topic recommend wider financial autonomy for management units, the use of budgeting models based on performance, the implementation of formula systems for the determination of financial needs of units and the signing of management goal-oriented contracts between decentralized units and the central administration of each institution. In this article we present a descriptive study of processes of internal resource allocation in Spanish public universities, with the following aims: firstly, to know the degree of introduction of normative models of internal resource allocation, the type of mechanisms applied and the variables on which such schemes are based; secondly, to analyse the degree of influence of regional funding models of higher education on the allocation of resources within each university; and, finally, to estimate the degree of delegation in financial management. In general, this study reveals the embryonic state in which Spanish universities are regarding a more strategic distribution of funds within institutions, although we have come across some universities with more innovative approaches to management.

Introduction

Spanish University System has experienced a large number of legal and organizational changes since the mid-eighties. The 1983 University Reform Act characterized Spanish Public Universities as public institutions with their own legal entity providing a limited degree of academic, economic and financial autonomy. Although they were defined as self-governing bodies, they have been highly dependent on public funds (in the year 2002, 78% of their income came from public resources—Hernández Armenteros 2004). Therefore, in practice their degree of autonomy has been somewhat limited.

The relationship between universities and government has also been altered. Between 1985 and 1996 a decentralization process took place in which responsibility for public higher education passed from the central government to the governments of the 17 autonomous regions into which Spain is organized. This process produced a favourable climate for the reflection on the best funding mechanisms to introduce a more rational resource allocation. In this direction, in the year 2000, a comprehensive study on the Spanish University System, known as Bricall (2000) Report, was published, in which the need to improve funding mechanisms of higher education was reinforced and also, the new 2001 Law on Universities stated that these institutions could prepare long-term plans which could lead to the approval of agreements and contractual programmes by autonomous governments, in which objectives, funding and performance evaluation criteria were clearly established.

In this context, processes of resource allocation in higher education systems are experiencing important changes. As in many other countries, there is an increasing use of normative and contractual models for public funding of universities. Normative funding models make use of objective and standardized criteria to determine and distribute funds between universities in order to rationalize the process of resource allocation. Contractual models are agreements between the government with authority in higher education and universities about the definition of objectives to be reached by institutions, measures of achievement and resources attached to the improvement of quality. Both types of mechanisms are frequently combined in regional funding models of higher education (see González López 2003).

In the institutional level, internal resource allocation mechanisms are also changing. Many institutions of different developed countries are advancing towards more decentralized budgeting mechanisms (Mims 1980; Hackman 1985; Brown and Wolf 1993; Berry 1994; Otten 1996; Strauss 1996; Aceto et al. 1998; Jongbloed 1998; The University of Birmingham 1998; among others), so that identifiable decentralized units have greater autonomy in the management of their budgets in order to achieve certain goals. The purpose is to combine the strengthening of intrinsic values of institutions with the introduction of some signals to make management units more concerned about changes in the market (Massy 1996). The assumption behind these approaches is that a larger degree of delegation in management, as well as a greater orientation of funds towards results, can lead to an improvement in the quality of universities in the provision of social service of higher education—as it is stated, for example, in the report published by the Association of European Universities (Jongbloed et al. 2000).

Although this phenomenon has been studied in depth in the United States and in some European countries, the Spanish case has not been exhaustively dealt so far. The main motivation of this research is to contribute to fill this gap and study the implications of these trends towards decentralization in the control of resources. In this sense, we have analysed the mechanisms employed by Spanish public universities to allocate funds internally to their different decentralized management units. Decentralized units in this context are those units having their own structure and specific academic and administrative functions into which Spanish universities are legally organized (departments and centres—faculties, technical colleges and university schools).

We have structured the rest of this paper as follows: in the next section we present the theoretical framework of the study, the research questions and the sources of information we have used; in the three following sections we analyse the data, in relation to the objectives that we had set out. In the last section we present the main implications of the study.

Theoretical Approach and Data Sources

The reform of resource allocation mechanisms in public universities is part of a wider process of change in management in the search for a more efficient use of public funds. As it was stated by the O.E.C.D. (1990, p. 55), "there can be little doubt that the ways in which higher education institutions receive their funds affect their incentive, and hence influence their internal organizational behaviour and the composition of the academic services they provide". To this effect, educational policy-makers have been introducing new resource allocation mechanisms (to and within universities) which try to break with traditional ones (incremental funding, line item budgeting, etc.) and use funding as a way to guide educational systems in the desired direction, increase competitiveness and financial autonomy and introduce more market signals (see Williams 1992). Bearing this idea in mind and focusing our analysis in the distribution of funds within universities, the research questions studied in this paper are:

(1) What kind of internal resource allocation mechanisms are in use in Spanish universities and what can we expect from them in terms of improving management?

(2) Can we find evidence of an influence of regional funding models of Spanish universities on the internal mechanisms applied by them to allocate resources between their different academic units?

(3) Are academic units in Spanish universities increasing their financial autonomy through the decentralization of resource management?

(1) The first question is related to the elements of internal resource allocation mechanisms. As in funding models of universities, internal resource allocation methods tend to replace incremental line item budgeting, in which each single item of expenditure of the budget is increased (or decreased) with respect to the budget of the previous year, with models which can be classified into two main groups: formula models and contractual agreements.

First ones calculate and allocate funds according to formulae or procedures based on objective data. They usually determine the need of funds of an academic unit through a simple algorithm which is the product of the volume of inputs or outputs of teaching and/or research activities and a theoretical unitary cost. In the so-called input-oriented mechanisms funds are linked to the inputs used by academic units in their production process which are considered to comprise both resources used to provide the service—personnel, material equipments, etc.—and the collaborating agents—students. Models based on enrolment or the size of staff are the most frequently used. In output-oriented models funds are linked to the results achieved by academic units in their teaching and research activities. The main problem of this last type of models is that it is very difficult to identify and quantify educational outputs; in practice, indicators are used as proxies to assess performance.

In contractual agreements funds to be allocated are linked to the accomplishment of certain goals or requisites which are previously agreed between the university central administration and each academic unit. As in formula models, there are input-oriented contracts (such as those which pay a certain amount of money if the number of enrolled students is over a certain level) and output-oriented contracts (funds for each doctoral dissertation presented, for example).

Although there are differences of opinion about the effect of both formula and contractual models on the improvement of university management, in general, they both introduce elements which are supposed to improve university financial management: a clear identification of the elements of the production process, the definition of standardized costs which assume an efficient use of funds and more transparency in the allocation criteria so that units can approximate the amount of funds they will receive in the future (making financial planning possible, reducing political pressures and favouring accountability).

As regards the effects of introducing output-oriented mechanisms, although there are arguments to support a positive impact of their implementation on performance (see United States General Accounting Office 1997), there are not conclusive studies in this sense (see, for example, Ziderman 1994; Jongbloed 1998; Liefner 2003). Experiences in performance funding and budgeting lead to highlight the advantages of this kind of approaches, but they also warn of their complexity (Seppanen 1998) and the aspects to take into account to implement them successfully (Joyce 1993; Galther 1997; Aceto et al. 1998; Layzell 1998). In Spain, there has been an important movement towards quality and performance evaluation in the higher education sector, but output-oriented funding mechanisms are not so widely used. Only few regional funding models of universities have recently introduced financial incentives linked to improvements in results (those of the Autonomous Regions of Valencia, Canary Islands, Castile and Leon or Catalonia). Therefore, we do not expect that output indicators are included in university's internal allocation models, except for those cases in which the regional funding model of universities make use of them.

(2) This leads us to the second research question. One of the hypotheses usually considered when studying resource allocation mechanisms is that the introduction of a certain funding model by the government responsible for the financing of higher education will influence institutional behaviour and the way funds are internally allocated to decentralized units (see, for example, Taylor 1991, p. 209; Woodhall 1992, p. 147; and Jongbloed 1998, pp. 7–12). In this sense, a result-oriented funding model would encourage universities to pay special attention to performance with the aim of getting more public funds. In some countries, such as Finland, the impact has been evident (Rekilä, et al. 1999).

In Spain, most regional funding models of universities use formula funding to determine core funding and contractual funding to incentive quality and promote the achievement of objectives that are considered strategic. We suspect that a positive association can exist between these regional funding models and internal resource allocation mechanisms.

(3) And finally, we have analysed the degree of decentralization of financial decisions within universities. Decentralized resource management is a process that combines the delegation of more autonomy of management with a higher accountability over it. It is considered to be positive to increase flexibility, responsibility and transparency in the use of public funds (see Massy 1990; Commonwealth Higher Education Management Service 1998; Jongbloed, et al. 2000). And there

is also a decisive financial objective behind these decentralizing processes: the concern of management units about income generation would be higher. In spite of its doubtless advantages, and that most university systems of developed countries seem to be advancing in this direction, this type of approach is not free of critics, mainly related to its difficult practical implementation: the need for appropriate information systems, the problems of coordination of decentralized units or the difficulties in aligning units' objectives and university's aims, among others. In any case, the prevailing opinion seems to be that benefits of decentralization outweigh the disadvantages (see, for example, Flynn and Strehl 1996, pp. 263–265).

Although the configuration of universities in Spanish legislation confers their essential teaching and research functions to decentralized units, there are also legal constraints to the management of certain budgetary items, such as, for example, the costs of personnel. These limitations, together with a long tradition of bureaucratic control (with many of their elements still present) lead us to expect a low degree of financial devolution in Spanish universities. However, as the 2001 Law on Universities has opted for a model of university where self-government and entrepreneurial features are reinforced, it is possible to expect changes in financial and organizational arrangements within institutions in the future.

To answer these questions, we have carried out a survey among Spanish public universities. According to statistics of the Spanish Council of Universities for the academic year 2001/2002, the Spanish university system comprised 66 universities, 49 of them public (Consejo de Universidades 2002).

With respect to the data sources we have used, these have been secondary and, mainly, internal:

- Initial budgets of Spanish public universities, in which they usually define the criteria used for the determination and distribution of funds corresponding to decentralized management units.
- Any other documents, internal regulations or publications to which we have had access and that came to complement such information.

Although we considered the possibility of going to primary sources, the examination of existing ones gave us, in general, enough information to respond to the objectives of the study. However, where this was not possible, we contacted the people in charge of services of planning and budgeting of those universities, in order to ask for the suitable complementary information.

The detail of universities we have analysed in this study is shown in Table 22.1. We have excluded from it those universities whose initial budgets do not contain any information on the criteria of internal resource allocation and we could not have any additional document. Consequently, the sample used for the study of processes of allocation of funds to decentralized units is made up of 30 public universities out of the 49 of total sector (more than 60% of the entire population of public universities).

Criteria for the Allocation of Decentralized Funds and Financial Incentives in Spanish Public Universities

In this section we concentrate on the first research question. The analysis is focused on delegated funds assigned to decentralized units so they can manage them autonomously. In practice, these are funds to cover operating expenses and some small capital investments of decentralized management units, as personnel budget is usually centrally managed.[1]

We have distinguished between the three previously identified types of resource allocation models: incremental line item budgeting, formula budgeting and funding agreements. The study shows that Spanish public universities, in general, tend to determine a lump sum to assign to units in an incremental way from the previous budget, that is, the global amount of money to be given to decentralized units altogether is calculated by increasing/decreasing the budget of the previous year in a certain percentage (to reflect inflation, new programmes, etc); then, most universities distribute that money between different units according to objective variables, using formulaic approaches.

TABLE 22.1

Sample of Spanish Public Universities for the Descriptive Study

University	Abbreviation	University	Abbreviation
University of Castilla La Mancha	UCLM	University of Las Palmas de Gran Canaria	ULPGC
University Complutense of Madrid	UCM	University of Malaga	UMA
University of Balearic Islands	UIB	University of Murcia	UMU
Universidad of Alcala de Henares	UAH	University of Salamanca	USA
University of Alicante	UAL	University of Seville	USE
University of Almeria	UALM	University of Valencia	UVA
University of Cadiz	UCA	University of Valladolid	UVALL
University of Cantabria	UCAN	University of Vigo	UVI
University of Cordoba	UCO	University of Zaragoza	UZA
University of Extremadura	UEX	University Jaume I	UJI
University of Girona	UGI	University Pablo de Olavide	UPO
University of Granada	UGR	Technical University of Catalonia	UPC
University of Huelva	UHU	Technical University of Valencia	UPV
University of Jaen	UJA	Public University of Navarra	UPN
University of La Rioja	ULR	University Rovira i Virgili	URV

Only two universities use a mechanism which is different from the formula model. First one is the University of Cadiz, where the traditional form of line item budgeting is still used. The second case, the one of the University Jaume I, is very different, in as much it is an example of a more innovative management. This institution is involved in a process of strategic planning and part of the budget is assigned to units according to the targets and courses of action agreed between each one of them and the Rectorship. The initiative is quite new in Spanish universities where, though several experiences in the implantation of processes of strategic management already exist, in general they do not link internal resources to them. Even though there is a general consensus about the importance of information about the results that are reached by universities, this does not occur when it is to link public funds to such results.

As regards the variables used for the distribution of funds in formula models, we analyse next the case of departments and centres separately.

Criteria for Resource Allocation to Departments

The main functions of departments are the coordination of teaching activities of their discipline in one or more faculties/schools and the support of teaching and research initiatives of their staff. In approximately half of the budgets we have analysed, variables related both to teaching and research were considered. And just in one case variables related to management were also included. In the rest of universities they considered variables referring only to teaching.

Indicators Related to Teaching and Learning

Teaching and learning indicators considered in departments funding can be classified into two groups: those more related to teaching inputs and processes, and those related to outputs and outcomes of this activity. Regarding the first group, Table 22.2 details the information. The third column of this table indicates the number of institutions that use each type of indicator. The last one shows the percentage of the whole sample (26 institutions for the case of formula models in departments) that these universities represent.

As can be seen, most universities introduce some indicator related to enrolment of the department (enrolled students in 53.8% of universities and registered credits in 26.9% of them). In most institutions, such measures receive the highest weight in the resource allocation formula (between 30% and a 50% of total funds). Enrolment is heeded exclusively in its quantitative dimension, as no

TABLE 22.2

Types of Indicators of Teaching and Learning Resources and Processes of Departments Incorporated to Mechanisms of Internal Resource Allocation in Spanish Public Universities

Type of Indicator	Universities	Freq.	%
Number of enrolled students	UIB, UJA, ULPGC, UMA, ULR, USA, UHU, UVA, UZA, UAH, UALM, UAL, UCO, USE	14	53.8
Number of registered credits	UAH, UCO, UMU, UPO, UGR, URV, UVALL	7	26.9
Size of the teaching staff[a]	ULR, USA, UAH, UAL, UCLM, UGR, UHU, UIB, UJA, ULPGC, UMA, UMU, UPO, UPC, URV, UVI, UPN, UVALL, UALM, UCO, UGI, USE	22	84.6
Teaching workload of staff	UCAN, ULPGC, UPN, UZA, UHU, UPV, UVA	7	26.9
Number of subjects taught by the department	UPN, UJA, USE	3	11.5
Enrolment in postgraduate programmes	UCAN, UCO, UGR, ULPGC, UPC, UPN, UJA	7	26.9
Number of postgraduate programmes	UCO, UGR, UJA	3	11.5
Degree of interdepartamentality, interdisciplinarity, stability or interest of doctoral programmes	UGR, UPC	2	7.7
Practical lessons	ULPGC, UPN, UIB, UZA	4	15.4
Number and type of discipline areas	UAL, UJA, ULR, UPN, USA, USE, UVALL	7	26.9
Number of different campus in which the department teaches	USE, UVALL, UZA	3	11.5
Material resources or specific requirements	UPC, UPN	2	7.7

[a]Full time equivalent teaching staff in most of the cases.

indicator of initial characteristics of students is considered. However, it is usual to weigh this indicator according to the intensity of studies (6-month, annual), or to the experimental nature of them (or to both aspects), in order to reflect the different cost of teaching. The number of different tariffs for disciplinary fields is usually around 4 or 5 (although this number varies from one university to another) and, frequently, it is related to the number of different registration fees levels established by the regional government for different courses, although we must say that the fixing of these prices is quite arbitrary.[2] We have not come across any case in which scale economies are taken into account in the allocations to departments, that is, prices are the same regardless of the number of students enrolled in subjects of each department. Finally, some universities distinguish between theoretical and practical lessons. They determine the cost of practical ones, which is used as weighing factor.

In all the cases, an indicator regarding the size of the teaching and research staff of each department (84.6% of universities) or their teaching workload (26.9% of cases) is considered, with an average weight in fund allocation of, approximately, 36%. In principle, if the number of academics is proportional to those needed to meet the demand (measured through enrolment), we could think that this variable is somehow redundant as both measures, students enrolled and number of academic to provide the service to them, are related to the same variable: demand for access. However, the design of academic staff depends not only on the total number of students enrolled but also on the size of groups for different types of lessons (lectures, laboratory, workshops, etc.), which can affect the quality in the provision of the services. Besides, historical circumstances (as different levels of demand in previous years) or the political power of different departments, have determined the configuration of staffs which, some times, are not related to those necessary to attend the demand. In any case, most universities that incorporate both variables—enrolment and teaching staff—are considering implicitly that allocated resources are also going to cover the needs of funds derived from the research activities of the academics. Besides, three Universities take into consideration the academic category of staff, in order to adjust for the quality of this resource.

The indicator that follows in importance, as far as frequency of use is concerned, is the one related to the number of different disciplinary areas of departments, although its weight in the allocation formula is much lower. Many institutions also introduce measures related specifically to postgraduate programmes. The number of enrolments is the most widely used indicator and some universities also award the interdisciplinary nature of programmes and other variables that could have a positive effect on the quality of these courses. The rest of indicators related to inputs or to the productive process of universities are not very important in resource allocation in most institutions.

More briefly, as they are scarce and have a very low weight in the models (they are used to allocate, at best, 10% of resources), we can review indicators related to the results of the teaching activity of departments, which are illustrated in Table 22.3.

We can distinguish four types of result indicators: (i) those related to the achievements of students: repetition rates, percentage of exams passed over enrolments or number of project dissertations presented by students; (ii) those related to the teaching quality of academics; (iii) for postgraduate programmes, the recruitment of students is considered as a result, and not only an input indicator of the teaching process; (iv) finally, the University of Valencia, according to the priorities of its regional government, also rewards teaching activities in Valencian language.

We can conclude this part of the analysis by saying that Spanish universities, when funding the teaching activity of their departments, prefer to use criteria related to the needs of resources of these units according to the tasks they will develop; therefore, indicators of inputs or, in some cases, of the production process, are widely used.

Only in five of the universities of the sample have we been able to find some link of the budget to the results of the teaching activity. This type of indicators usually appears in those autonomous regions in which the government makes also use of an output-oriented funding model for the higher education sector. The indicators finally used in the internal allocation are not always the same to those of the model used to finance the university system; nevertheless, the influence is remarkable. In the next section we will go into this topic in greater depth.

TABLE 22.3

Indicators of Results of the Teaching Activity of Departments Incorporated to Mechanisms of Internal Resource Allocation in Spanish Public Universities

Indicator	Universities	Freq.	%
Number of students to be funded according to repetition rates	UALM	1	3.8
Passed credits/enrolled credits in the previous year	UVA	1	3.8
Research projects and dissertations	ULPGC	1	3.8
Quality of teaching (assessed by the Quality Commission)	UCO	1	3.8
Indicators of teaching results of academics	UPV	1	3.8
% of academics with a teaching assessment superior to the average	UVA	1	3.8
% of enrolled credits in doctoral programmes in the previous year	UPV	1	3.8
Number of enrolled students/credits in postgraduate programmes	UVA	1	3.8
Number of registered credits in valencian groups/total registered credits	UVA	1	3.8

Indicators Related to Research

As we have done with teaching, we have also analysed the indicators used for resource allocation to departments related to the means needed to develop the research activity. And we have found just one institution, the Technical University of Catalonia, in which an indicator of this type is used: that of full time equivalent academics. The same does not happen when we look for indicators related to the results of such activity. Half of the universities of the sample introduce some indicator of this type or link part of the resources to the assessment of the research activity by the institution. We have summarized this information in Table 22.4.

The diversity of indicators is so high that only one of them, the number of doctoral theses defended in the previous year, is repeated in two institutions. We can say, however, that Spanish universities, regardless of the specific definition of measurement indicators, reward research according to three basic aspects: number of dissertations and doctoral theses defended by members of each department; research production, externally or internally assessed; and income earned by research activities regarding projects, agreements, etc.

We can conclude that Spanish universities, when trying to implement more output-oriented internal resource allocation mechanisms, prefer to do it in the research field. It seems to be generally accepted that research has to be assessed and that only those departments which prove to be excellent in this activity, will deserve additional funding.

Indicators Related to Administrative Activities

Although these indicators have limited weight in the funding of departments, we refer, briefly, to some examples incorporated in some universities to stimulate the improvement of several aspects of their administrative management or, simply, to reflect the cost of carrying out these tasks. Only three institutions in the sample have established some indicators of this nature. Their descriptions are detailed in Table 22.5.

TABLE 22.4

Types of Indicators of Results of the Research Activity of Departments Incorporated to Mechanisms of Internal Resource Allocation in Spanish Public Universities

Type of Indicator	Universities	Freq.	%
Indicators related to the achievement of "research aptitude" by doctoral students[a]	UGR, UVA	2	7.7
Doctoral dissertations defended	UCO, ULPGC, UPC, UGR	4	15.4
Quantity and/or quality of the scientific production of the members of the department	UAL, UIB, UVALL, UJA, UAH, UCO, UPC, UVA, UVI	9	34.6
Income earned from external activities	UPC, ULPGC, UALM, ULR	4	15.4
Number of research studentships from the Ministry, the Autonomous Community or the University	ULPGC	1	3.8

[a] In Spain, when doctoral students finish doctoral courses, they usually have to pass a public exam in which they have to show their research abilities (and sometimes they also have to defend a research project) so they achieve the so-called "research aptitude", which is a prerequisite for the presentation of the doctoral dissertations.

TABLE 22.5

Indicators Related to Administrative Activities of Departments Incorporated to Mechanisms of Internal Resource Allocation in Spanish Public Universities

Indicator	University	Freq.	%
% of modification in credit for bibliographic purchases when the budget of the year comes into effect	UJA	1	3.8
% of budgetary credit for bibliographic purchases which has been used/total credit by the end of the year	UJA	1	3.8
Budget for bibliographic purchases committed/available budget before October	UPN	1	3.8
Budget for bibliographic purchases used/ available budget from the previous year	UPN	1	3.8
Dedication of academic staff to administrative activities	UPC	1	3.8
Number of academics per campus and distance between each campus and the department	UPC	1	3.8
Distance between the department and the Rector's offce or to the centre in which the head of department is assigned	UPC	1	3.8

Criteria for Resource Allocation to Centres

As the essential task of faculties, colleges and schools consists of organizing the teaching function, in this part of the analysis we do not distinguish between teaching and research variables. We have maintained the differentiation between indicators of means and results.

Table 22.6 summarizes the type of indicators related to the inputs and processes of centres which are applied by the universities we have examined. The sample for which this information was available was composed of 24 institutions.

Again, most frequent input indicators are enrolments (some times weighted to take scale effects and/or academic disciplines into account) and number of academics or their teaching workload. The average weight of these types of indicators is around 50% and 20% respectively. The third type of indicator in importance is that related to the size and age of centres, because of their maintenance and running costs. The weight that universities give to the indicator fluctuates around 10%. The number of different degrees taught, which results in greater complexity of the organization of studies, is also considered in some mechanisms. The rest of indicators are not relevant.

As regards indicators related to output of centres, only three universities introduce them, as it is shown in Table 22.7. The average weight of these indicators in the resource allocation to centres is, in these three institutions, near 20%.

There are two types of measures related to results repeated in more than one institution, although with different specific indicators. The first one is the number or percentage of graduates. These indicators are more significant in the resource allocation to centres than to departments, as the last ones are responsible for specific subjects, while centres are in charge of degrees. The drawing up of curricula, the conditions in which teaching service is delivered, the regulations of student selection, the size of groups, the cooperation in the organization of bibliographical funds, etc., have an important impact on the teaching-learning process and depend directly on centres; that is why it seems reasonable to link part of the resources to the rate of students' success. Secondly, there are some indicators which try to reflect the ability of centres to encourage and facilitate the participation of students in complementary activities, like those derived from mobilities within international programmes of exchange or practices in companies.

We can conclude by stressing the low weight that measures of results have at present in the budget allocation to faculties and schools in Spanish public universities. When this type of financial incentives is introduced, they are mainly related to teaching products. If we take into account that

TABLE 22.6

Types of Indicators of Resources and Production Process of Centres Incorporated to Mechanisms of Internal Resource Allocation in Spanish Public Universities

Type of Indicator	Universities	Freq.	%
Number of enrolled students	UAL, UCAN, UCLM, UCM, UCO, UEX, UGI, UGR, UHU, UJA, ULPGC, ULR, UMA, UPC, UPO, URV, USA, USE, UVA, UVALL, UVI, UZA	22	91.7
Number of registered credits	UCM, UMU, UPV, UVA, UVALL, UVI	6	25.0
Size of the teaching staff	UAL, UCM, UCO, UEX, UHU, UJA, ULR, URV, USE, UVI	10	41.7
Teaching workload of staff	UCO, ULPGC, UPV, UZA	4	16.7
Size and age of buildings	UCM, UCO, UEX, UGR, UVI, UZA	6	25.0
Number of degrees taught	UAL, UJA, ULPGC, ULR	4	16.7
Other types of indicators	UCM, UGI, ULPGC, UMU, UPC, UVALL, UVI, UZA	8	33.3

TABLE 22.7

Indicators of Results of Centres Incorporated to Mechanisms of Internal Resource Allocation in Spanish Public Universities

Indicator	University	Freq.	%
Number of graduates weighed by credits of the degree	UPC	1	4.2
Number of students who have studied all the credits of the degree	UPV	1	4.2
Number of graduates/number of students *n*[a] years before	UVA	1	4.2
Number of students in international programmes	UPC	1	4.2
Number of months spent by students in exchange programmes	UPV	1	4.2
Number of months spent by students in exchange programmes/number of full time equivalent students	UVA	1	4.2
Number of months spent by students in practical training	UPV	1	4.2
Number of students in practices/number of students that can apply for practices	UVA	1	4.2
Number of full time students/real number of students	UVA	1	4.2

[a]Being "n" the scheduled length of the degree.

centres are in charge of enrolments processes, among other administrative tasks, we think that indicators referring to results or quality in these services are missing.

Degree of Influence of Regional Funding Models of Higher Education

In order to answer the second research question, that is, to contrast for the Spanish case the hypothesis of the influence that external funding models of universities can have on internal resource allocation schemes, we have compared the criteria used by universities sited in autonomous regions whose governments have introduced normative or contractual funding models with those used by governments to allocate funds to universities. Although the description of different regional approaches exceeds the scope of this article, we will mention their general features to facilitate the understanding of this section.

As autonomous regions are responsible for higher education, we can not talk about a common model for the public funding of all Spanish universities. However, we can observe that different approaches tend to a similar scheme of formula to calculate basic funding (inspired in the one implemented in the Autonomous Region of Valencia), completed with contractual mechanisms to stimulate quality. In this sense, core funding is calculated through a formula which is a standardized average cost per full time equivalent student (FTS). These estimations are based on the costs that would be needed to provide the educational service to a FTS: personnel costs, other current expenditure and, in some cases, maintenance and amortization costs of capital investments. Specific assumptions about subjects of study, size of teaching groups, teaching workload of academics, staff salaries, number of credits to define a FTS or equipment needs per student are taken into account. And it is precisely in the values of the weights in each element of the formula where the models applied in each autonomous region usually differ.

As regards contractual funding, this is used in all the cases as a supplementary stream of funds which is conditioned to the achievement of previously set goals or programs (which can be the same for all the institutions of the region, or different for each university according to their strategic plans). The assessment of these contracts is made through indicators and in most cases output measures receive the highest weight.

Once we have presented the structure of these financial schemes, Table 22.8 illustrates the specific links we have found between internal and external funding models for different autonomous regions: Andalusia, Canary Islands, Catalonia, Valencia and Galicia.

If we begin with Andalusia, we can observe that only one of the eight universities we have analysed allocates part of funds to departments following one of the parameters introduced in the Andalusia distribution model; in particular, the normalization of the number of students to be funded. In the rest of institutions, although some concepts are common to those used by the regional government (number of credits, age of buildings, etc.), indicators and weights used are significantly different. Perhaps the main explanation of this low influence can be found in the limited implementation of the regional model of funding higher education, as the funds corresponding to each university have not been practically altered by its application so far.

In the Canary Autonomous Region, it is difficult to find a clear correlation between the allocation criteria to decentralized units used by the University of Las Palmas de Gran Canaria with the objectives of the first Contractual Agreement signed in 2001 by the government and this University. Only the financial incentive to departments related to income from projects of research and agreements is similar to one of the key points of the contract.

In the case of Catalonia, as contractual programmes for the improvement of quality in universities (which have been agreed between the regional government and each university) have been drawn up taking into account the strategic plans of each institution, we can find important links between the internal and external resource allocation criteria. Thus it happens, to a great extent, in the Technical University of Catalonia that, for the case of the resource allocation to departments, considers the credits registered in postgraduate programmes, the development of specific programs of doctorate and the number of theses defended, which are also goals in the contractual program; at the same time, it has set up a scoring system for research and technology transfer activities which makes use of many of the indicators formulated in the contract.

The University de Girona, on the other hand, ties 70% of allocation to centres to the funding coming from the General Office for Universities and to incomes from enrolment. This implies that the budget of these units depends partially on the funding that the University has received from the autonomous government because of the teaching activity of each centre.

As regards the third Catalan university considered, the University Rovira i Virgili, budgets for the year 2001 defined formula based allocations to centres and departments depending basically on the evolution of the number of enrolled students/credits and full time equivalent academics. These mechanisms are clearly different from those established in the contractual funding arrangement decided with the regional government. However, as it was signed in November of the year 2000, it is quite probable that there would be changes in internal allocation criteria in the future, as the objectives of the contract reflect largely those of the strategic planning in this University.

To sum up, we can say that, in the case of the Autonomous Region of Catalonia, influences between autonomic funding and internal resource allocation of universities are reciprocal since contractual agreements are being signed. Regional funding has been able to gather the strategic goals of universities, while these ones have also assumed in their management commits the objectives and priorities stated by the government.

The Valencian Community designed in 1994 a long-term financial framework for Valencian universities, whose influence on the mechanisms of internal allocation is clear in most institutions. This relationship is, however, irregular. In the University of Valencia the influence is, perhaps, more evident, as the structure of the model used to fund centres and departments is equivalent to that of the region, the variables used in formula funding are also similar and most of the indicators used for the goal-oriented funding are the same than those of the general model.

The University of Alicante also establishes an allocation formula for departments that follows the general criteria of the government public funding of higher education. However, one third of

TABLE 22.8

Degree of Influence of the Regional Models of Funding in the Internal Resource Allocation in Spanish Public Universities

Autonomous Region	University	Degree of Influence	Criteria
Andalusia	UALM	≅ 22.75% (departments)	Students to be funded according to the academic participation formula
Canary	ULPGC	–	Income earned from research projects in the previous year Income earned from agreements in the previous year
Catalonia	UPC	≅ 33% (centres) ≅ 69.5% + complementary funds + doctoral programmes improvement funds (departments)	Number of registered credits in postgraduate programmes Doctoral programmes of specific interest Research points obtained Technology transfer points obtained Resources earned from agreements, European projects and public funding Number of doctoral dissertations defended Number of graduates Number of students in international programmes
	UGI	–	Funding from grants of the General University Office
Valencian Community	UAL	≅ 75% (departments)	Full time equivalent students weighed by type of discipline Full time equivalent academic staff
	UJI	–	Registered credits
	UPV		Credits registered by students Number of enrolled students Credits taught in lectures and practical lessons Incentive for graduates Incentive for participation of students in exchange programmes Incentive for participation of students in business sector practices Incentive for favourable results in the academic staff assessment programme Incentive for students in doctoral programmes
	UVA	≅ 92.5% (centres) ≅ 87.5% (departments)	Full time equivalent students Registered credits weighed by type of discipline Teaching workload in credits of academic staff Incentive for passed credits Incentive for graduates Incentive for participation of students in exchange programmes Incentive for participation of students in business sector practices Incentive for credits taught in valencian language Incentive for favourable results in the academic staff assessment programme
Galicia	UVI	–	Experimentality (type of discipline)

funding is based on an indicator, the number of research awards, which is not considered in the regional model. The Technical University of Valencia also uses indicators related to activities and results of centres and departments, which are also similar to those used by the programme of funding of the Autonomous Region.

The degree of influence of the funding programme of the Autonomous Region on the University Jaume I depends on the specific agreements defined with each centre and department. In any case, part of the resources is allocated according to the registered credits that are, as we are saying, one of the essential variables of such programme.

In general, internal resource allocation in Valencian universities is very aware of the funding model of the Autonomous Region. This is leading to more complex and evolutionated resource allocation mechanisms. The possibility of obtaining more government funds according to the accomplishment of the goals defined in the regional model is taken into account in most cases when designing internal distribution criteria.

If we move on to analyse the case of the University of Vigo, the only clear reference in the criteria of internal allocation to the Agreement of Funding of the University System of Galicia, is made in the allocation of 40% of expenses for repairs, maintenance and conservation to centres in accordance with the coefficient of experimentality of degrees defined in such agreement. Apart from that, although some budgetary concepts are distributed according to the number of registered students or the number of full time equivalent academics, indicators used to quantify these variables are different.

This part of the study shows that, except for the comments we have made, the analysed Andalusian, Galician and Canary Islands Universities do not follow significantly the criteria defined in funding models used to allocate public funds in the university system level. In the case of the Catalan Autonomous Region, when a contractual funding programme between the government and the university exists, we can perceive a remarkable degree of connection between mechanisms of resource allocation in different levels of decentralization. Finally, in the Valencian Community, with more tradition in the use of normative models in the funding of universities, the influence of parameters of the autonomic model on internal financial management is noteworthy.

Therefore, it is possible to assume that the mechanisms used by regional governments to finance university systems have, in general, an effect on the internal allocation of institutions. This influence is stronger when the definition of parameters in such models is more transparent and clear, and when criteria remain stable in time. The greater influence of Catalan and Valencian models can also be due to the important participation of universities in the formulation of the regional funding model.

Decentralization in Resource Management

The first feature that determines the degree of decentralization of an institution comes from the treatment given to management units. Main alternatives, which evolve from a slight to a greater degree of financial delegation, are the following (Williams 1992, pp. 24–25; Bourn 1994; pp. 5–24; the Commonwealth Higher Education Management Service 1998, p. 3):

- Decentralized management units treated as cost centres. In this case, the part of the university budget to be allocated to management units would be distributed between them according to historical criteria, their objective needs or the goals to be achieved.
- Systems in which, after separating a determined amount to cover centralized expenses, each decentralized unit receives the income it clearly generates (fees, incomes from governmental grant which can be attributed, etc.), in order to cover the necessary expenses to obtain such income.
- Schemes in which all the income is assigned to decentralized management units, settling down a system of overheads to cover expenses of central and support services.
- A last step in this process would be that of establishing a system of internal markets, in which decentralized units pay a price for services provided by central or support units.

It is difficult to find models of resource allocation that follow exclusively one of these perspectives; in most cases, we can find services provided using a system of prices, or some concepts that give rise to an overhead to cover expenses of central services. Anyway, we can say that, in general, Spanish public universities tend to be positioned in the first type of decentralization styles, although without a delegation of most functions related to personnel.

Table 22.9 illustrates about this, as it is reflected in initial budgets of Spanish public universities (in this part of the study the sample was extended to 29 institutions for which this information was available). We have considered decentralized management items those that are assigned in block to centres and departments, so that they can spend them as they seem suitable. We have excluded those concepts for which, even though the expense or investment can be made by the department or centre, the evaluation of proposals and the quantification of costs in such item are centrally made.

As can be observed, all universities determine a global unconstrained budget to cover operating expenses of decentralized units (excluded those from personnel). When we analyse the number of universities in which investment management is decentralized, the percentage is reduced to less than half of them. And, in such cases, delegation refers only to certain types of investments: bibliographical, furniture and equipment, computer and audio-visual material, software for computer laboratories, equipment for teaching laboratories and, in some cases, funds for research obtained by departments. Investments in land and buildings are usually excluded as they are centrally managed.

As regards the decentralization of expenditure items related to current transfers, in general they are related to the management of scholarships and other financial aids to students; such funds can not be derived to other items.

Finally, in some cases, income generated by each decentralized unit are made explicit and allocated to them in the budget (from programmes with specific diploma from the University, publications and products sales, current transfers from companies, the use of facilities, administrative concessions, etc).

This first level of analysis of decentralized concepts shows the slight degree of delegation existing in Spanish universities. The budgetary allocation to departments and centres is made just to guarantee and facilitate operations of units, but there is no scope for action in more strategic decision-making. However, some universities are advancing towards greater decentralization of resource management through the determination of the global amount to be distributed to each unit (department or centre), according to fees income or governmental grants, or by delegating funds to cover personnel costs.

A second part of our analysis on the degree of financial delegation in Spanish universities has been oriented to the estimation of the percentage of expenses that are managed by centres and departments. Table 22.10 summarizes such estimations for those universities in which it has been possible to observe this percentage (22 universities for the analysis of current expenses in goods

TABLE 22.9

Budget Items with Decentralized Management in Spanish Public Universities

Concept	University	%
Expenditure budget Operating expenses (excluded personnel expenses)	UAH, UAM, UALM, UCAN, UCLM, UCM, UEX, UGI, UGR, UHU, UIB, UJA, UJI, ULPGC, ULR, UMA, UMH, UMU, UPC, UPN, UPO, UPV, URV, USAL, USC (centres), USE, UVA, UVI, UZA	100
Current transfers	UJI (centres), ULPGC, USC (centres)	10.3
Investments	UAM, UCM, UGI, UGR (depart.), UJI (centres), ULPGC, UPN, UPO (depart.), URV, USAL, USC, UVI, UZA	44.8
Revenues budget Income generated by centres	UPC (centres), UVA	6.9

TABLE 22.10

Percentage of Expenses with Decentralized Management (in Centres and Departments) in Spanish Public Universities

Unit	Percentage of	Mean	Standard Deviation
Centres	Current expenses	8.94%	7.13%
	Capital expenditure	4.47%	5.80%
	Total budget	1.23%	1.13%
Departments	Current expenses	11.19%	5.24%
	Capital expenditure	3.93%	2.96%
	Total budget	1.59%	0.49%
Centres and departments	Total budget	2.87%	1.05%

and services, 7 for capital expenditure and 24 for total). Average values reveal a decentralization of expenses with respect to total budget of, around, 3% (and we can add that there was not any University that distributed 5% or more of the budget to centres and departments). If we analyse these percentages for each type of expenditure, we can observe that financial delegation is larger for current expenses (9% of total budget for the centres and 11% for departments), although it exists a high degree of variability of this percentage, especially for centres.

Main Findings and Implications of the Study

This study on internal resource allocation in Spanish public universities allows us to characterize this process by the following basic features:

- As regards to the allocation model, most institutions use a formula scheme, based on inputs, specifically on the number of students or credits enrolled and the number of full time equivalent academics. The purpose is to break with traditional incremental and negotiated methods of resource allocation which have proved to be opaque, rigid and inefficient. Rationale behind formula approaches is to give the same funding to equivalent programs and equivalent students according to normative criteria. These criteria usually take into account the level of education, academic discipline and intensity of study to reflect the different costs of teaching. It can be expected that the use of these models will favour a more efficient and equitable resource allocation and a more transparent accountability.
- Few universities introduce indicators related to the results of the teaching activity. For the funding of departments, these result indicators are mainly related to the academic success of students and the teaching quality of academic staff. In centres, together with measures related to the number of graduates, indicators related to the participation of students in business practices or international programmes are also used. While most universities are aware of the importance of performance measurement and are inmerse in processes of quality assessment, the use of performance-based budgeting is not seen with enthusiasm. The main requirements for a successful implementation of this type of budgeting are not present in most Spanish universities: accounting and other information systems are not prepared to offer an accurate assessment of performance, the introduction of a 'quality culture' is relatively recent and the use of strategic planning and management tools is scarce. There seem to be many steps to be made before the debate about performance budgeting can be seriously considered.
- Nevertheless, variables of results related to the research activity (in the case of department allocation) carry more weight: indicators related to research projects and theses defended,

the research production or the income earned from research are some of the indicators more frequently used. As there is a longer tradition in the evaluation of research of academics and there is more consensus about research assessment criteria, the implementation of this type of measures is seen as less problematic.

- With less quantitative importance, and only in isolated cases, some incentives related to the administrative activity of departments are introduced. In the search for more efficienct administrative services the use of other management tools, such as quality evaluation or total quality management, seems to be more adequate than financial incentives.
- In those Autonomous Regions in which governments have defined normative funding models of higher education, there is a remarkable influence of these models on universities' internal allocation, provided that these approaches are transparent enough, stable in time and, specially, when they link funds to the accomplishment of previously set goals. Normative funding models are proving themselves not to be neutral. They are usually designed to reflect governments' priorities for higher education institutions. As universities aspire to maximize the funds they receive from the government, they try to respond to the criteria included in the external funding model, and one way to contribute to that target is to introduce some of the elements of the external model on internal resource allocation mechanism. Besides, the introduction of goal-oriented funding increases the demand for accountability for the results and this requires transparent and systematic mechanisms of resource allocation at the institutional level (see Heads of University Management and Administration Network in Europe 2000, pp. 5–7).
- The use of contractual funding is also having an effect on university resource allocation. The influence is different according to the type of contract. There are some experiences of contracts which have been designed to integrate the objectives of the strategic plans of each university. This procedure is reinforcing strategic management, quality assessment systems and other management tools of universities.
- The degree of financial devolution within Spanish universities is quite low, both in quantitative and qualitative terms. This contrasts with other international experiences, with arguments in support of the benefits of delegation and with the decentralized structure of Spanish universities. It is expected that the new legislation on universities will result in an increase of the financial autonomy and the freedom of spend of universities.

The aspects mentioned above have policy and management implications. Governments can use funding to influence higher education systems, as it is confirmed by the increasing use of resource allocation mechanisms within universities which are similar to those used by the government. This can result in a loss of autonomy in universities—as they highly depend on public funding, they should behave as governments expect in order to get the funds—unless both universities and governments work together in the design of such models. This study shows that, in those cases in which government funding takes into account strategic plans of universities, motivation increases and positive results are achieved. It is not just funding, but the combination of it with other management tools what produces changes in universities. Normative and contractual resource allocation mechanisms can favour that decision-making processes and negotiations focus on what is relevant, the objectives to be reached and the best ways to do it. But it is necessary to be aware of the practical difficulties for their implementation (related both to the correct identification of teaching and research outputs and to the availability of accurate information systems to evaluate costs and performance) and the possible unintended consequencies of their use (increased concentration of funds for the best universities and/or departments or centres and low motivation for the rest—see Massy 1996, pp. 321–322; Geuna 2001).

Acknowledgements

I am grateful to the anonymous referees for their many constructive and helpful comments. I also thank the administrators and finance department's staff of the universities examined in this study for their collaboration, and Professor Juan Antonio Rivas for the language revision.

Notes

1. Universities have the autonomy to design their staffs and to recruit personnel. Internal regulations of most Spanish Universities give the Rector the authority for staff recruitment; in these cases, decision making in personnel management can not be delegated to decentralized units. That is why personnel matters are centrally managed in most Spanish Universities.
2. The fixing of registration fees in the Spanish university system is competence of regional government within the limits established by the national Council for the Coordination of Universities. Different prices are set-up according to academic disciplines in order to account for the different cost of teaching, but these prices are different in each region and do not reflect a real knowledge of the cost of provision of the service in different universities (see Hernández Armenteros and Valverde Peña 1998, p. 11).

References

Aceto, V. et al. (1998). *A Proposal for Merit-Based Performance Funding for the State University of New York.* Albany: State University of New York, Office of the Provost and Vice Chancellor for Academic Affairs, June.

Berry, R.H., ed. (1994). *Management Accounting in Universities.* London: The Chartered Institute of Management Accountants.

Bourn, M. (1994). 'A long and winding road: The evolution of devolution in universities', in Berry, R.H. (ed.), *Management Accounting in Universities.* London: The Chartered Institute of Management Accountants, 5–24.

Bricall, J.M. et al. (2000). Informe Universidad 2000. Barcelona, March.

Brown, M.A. and Wolf, D.M. (1993). 'Allocating budgets using performance criteria', in Altbach, P.G. and Johnstone, D.B. (eds.), *The Funding of Higher Education. International Perspectives.* New York: Garland Publishing, pp. 173–187.

Commonwealth Higher Education Management Service, C.H.E.M.S. (1998). 'Principles of Delegated Budgeting Guidelines for Universities'. *Chems Paper 25.* London, June.

Consejo De Universidades (2002). *Estadística universitaria* 2001-2002. [http://www.mec.es/consejou/estadis/avan0102/311.html].

Flynn, N. and Strehl, F. (1996). *Public Sector Management in Europe.* Hertfordshire: Prentice Hall.

Galther, J. (1997). 'Development and Use of Performance Indicator Systems', *Presented at the 19th European Association for Institutional Research Forum,* University of Warwick, August.

Geuna, A. (2001). 'The changing rationale for European university research funding. are there negative unintended consequences?', *Journal of Economic Issues* 35(3), 607–632.

González López, M.J. (2003). 'Estudio comparativo de los modelos de financiaciación de los sistemas públicos universitarios españoles', *Presupuesto y gasto público* 33, 101–121.

Hackman, J.D. (1985). 'Power and centrality in the allocation of resources in colleges and universities', *Administrative Science Quarterly* 30, 61–77.

Heads of University Management and Administration Network in Europe, Humane (2000). *Resource Allocation Models,* Report of the HUMANE Working Party. [http://www.ao.bham.ac.uk/aps/planning/RAMReview/]. 16 October 2003.

Hernández Armenteros, J. (2004). *La Universidad española en cifras (2004).* Madrid: Conferencia de Rectores de las Universidades Españolas (CRUE).

Hernández Armenteros, J. and Valverde Peña, F. (1998). 'La participación del usuario en la financiación de la enseñanza pública universitaria: especial referencia a Andalucía', *Cuadernos de Trabajo de la Universidad de Jaén.* Jaén: Servicio de Publicaciones de la Universidad de Jaén.

Jongbloed, B. (1998). 'Internal resource allocation in universities'. *Presented at the 20th Annual European Association for Institutional Research Forum, and published in Higher Education Policy Studies,* **298.** Enschede: Center for Higher Education Policy Studies.

Jongbloed, B., Amaral, A., Kasanes, E. and Wilkin, L. (2000). *Final Report on Spending Strategies. Spending Strategies: A Closer Look at the Financial Management of the European Universities, CRE Guide 3.* Geneve: CRE.

Joyce, P.G. (1993). 'Using Performance Measures for Federal Budgeting: Proposals and Prospects', *Public Budgeting and Finance* 13(4), 3–17.

Layzell, D.T. (1998). 'Linking Performance to Funding Outcomes for Public Institutions of Higher Education: the US experience', *European Journal of Education* 33(1), 103–111.

Liefner, I. (2003). 'Funding, resource allocation, and performance in higher education systems', *Higher Education* 46(4), 469–489.

Massy, W.F. (1990). 'Budget decentralization at Stanford University', *Planning for Higher Education* 18(2), 39–55.

Massy, W.F. (1996). *Resource Allocation in Higher Education*. Michigan: The University of Michigan Press.

Mims, R.S. (1980). 'Resource allocation: stopgap or support for academic planning?', *New Directions for Institutional Research* 28, 57–72.

O.E.C.D. (1990). Financing Higher Education. Current Patterns. Paris: O.E.C.D.

Otten, C. (1996). 'Principles of budget allocation at the institutional level', *Higher Education Management* 8(1), 69–84.

Rekilä, E., Larimo, M. and Tauriainen, K. (1999). 'Do changing state steering mechanisms have an impact on academia leadership at universities', *Tertiary Education and Management* 5(3), 261–277.

Seppanen, L.J. (1998). 'Performance Funding on the Bleeding Edge: No Improvement, No Funding', *Association for Institutional Research (A.I.R.) Forum*, Minneapolis (Minnesota), May. [http://ir-server.willamette.edu/forum98/15-519/AIR9815-519.htm]. 19 June 2000.

Strauss, J., Curry, J. and Whalen, E. (1996). 'Revenue responsibility budgeting', in Massy, W.F. (ed.), *Resource Allocation in Higher Education*. Michigan: The University of Michigan Press, pp. 163–190.

Taylor, M.G. (1991). 'New financial models', *Higher Education Management* 3(3), 203–213.

The University of Birmingham (1998). *Strategy, Planning, Resource Allocation & Indirect Cost Allocation*. [http://bham.ac.uk/planning/resall.htm], 25 November 2000.

United States General Accounting Office (1997). *Performance Budgeting. Past Initiatives Offer Insights for GPRA (Government Performance and Results Act) Implementation*. General Accounting Office/Accounting and Information Management Division, Washington.

Williams, G. (1992). *Changing Patterns of Finance in Higher Education*. Buckingham: The Society for Research into Higher Education & Open University Press.

Woodhall, M. (1992). 'Changing sources and patterns of finance for higher education: A review of international trends', *Higher Education in Europe* 17(1), 141–149.

Ziderman, A. (1994). 'Enhancing the Financial Sustainability of Higher Education Institutions', in Salmi, J. and Verspoor, A.M. (ed.), *Revitalizing Higher Education*. Oxford: Pergamon.

CHAPTER 23

RESOURCE ALLOCATION IN PUBLIC RESEARCH UNIVERSITIES

JOSÉ L. SANTOS

A study of internal resource allocation in public Research I universities is particularly timely and important as the patterns of expenditures and revenues at public universities, after a period of substantial change, stabilized in 1999. After 1999, a period of new retrenchments ensued as a result of intensified budget cutting that, in some cases, resulted in budget rescissions for some universities in fiscal years 2001–2002 and 2002–2003.

An analysis of the revenue streams for public institutions of higher education over the 15 years from 1985 to 1999 reveals a decline in the proportion of current-fund revenue provided from the state from 45.1% to 35.8%, an absolute decrease of 21%. During the same period, tuition and fees rose sharply from 14.6% in 1985 to 18.5% in 1999, an absolute increase of 27% while private gifts, grants, and contracts rose from 3.1% in 1985 to 4.8% in 1999, an absolute increase of 55% (National Center for Education Statistics [NCES], 1993, p. 322; NCES, 1996, p. 4; NCES, 2003, p. 372). In the period between 1986 and 1999, institutional expenditures (measured in 1999 constant dollars, using the Higher Education Price Index [HEPI] deflator) increased by $38 billion, from $103 billion in 1986 to $141 billion in 1999, a 37% increase (inflation adjusted) while government funding increased by $11 billion, from $62 billion in 1986 to $73 billion in 1999, a 17% increase (inflation adjusted) (NCES, 1993, p. 332; NCES, 1996, pp. 4, 5; NCES, 2003, p. 391; Research Associates of Washington, 2003). In short, government investment in public universities has declined, resulting in institutions' search for new revenue streams led by tuition and fees (Mayhew, Ford, & Hubbard, 1990) and private gifts, grants, and contracts. It is therefore important to explore how this public financing shift plays out in the internal resource allocation function.

Internal resource allocation has been studied in a number of different ways. As early as the 1980s, resource allocation became an important research topic because of fiscal volatility and budget crises. Researchers typically studied departments housed in different colleges within universities (Ashar, 1987; Ashar & Shapiro, 1990; Hackman, 1985; Melchiori, 1982; Morgan, 1984). The next decade characterized by university restructuring brought about studies of resource allocation that shifted the emphasis to faculty performance on productivity measures within departments as the unit of analysis (Layzell, 1996; Levin, 1991; Massy, 1996). In the first decade of the 21st century, state and institutional budget crises have led to increased attention to how scarce institutional resources are distributed. The shift from the department to the individual faculty member has omitted some critical perspectives of how departments, rather than individuals, mediate faculty behavior (Volk, Slaughter, & Thomas, 2001). As a result, using the individual faculty member may be inadequate in furthering our understanding of internal resource allocation in the context of constrained institutional resources. Traditionally, studies on internal resource allocation have employed either rational/political or critical/political frameworks. Only one study (Volk, Slaughter, & Thomas, 2001) uses both conceptual frameworks; however, it focuses on only one public research institution. In this study, I build on the work of Volk, Slaughter, and Thomas by focusing on breadth—that is, I examine resource allocation using departments and fields of study at 10 public research universities to explore the returns to teaching and research productivity on departmental earnings between fields of science. My hope is that a focus on departments as key units of analysis will further our understanding of internal resource allocation.

The purpose of this study is to conduct an econometric analysis of internal resource allocation. I estimate the production (allocation) function of public research universities by modeling the income-production function of academic departments. The goal is to estimate the relative "rate of return" that universities assign to teaching and research productivity. The allocation function is modeled by estimating a revenue function that is part of the family of functions known as income production functions. These functions, commonly found in the human capital theory literature, are used to estimate the relative importance of variables in the production of income (Jehle & Reny, 2001; Ramanathan, 1995; Varian, 1999).

Theory

How universities are conceived is important in selecting competing decision-making theories that guide their resource allocation. Although multiple theories of universities as organizations exist, two theories are especially useful for this study of resource allocation in public research universities: the theory of the firm and resource dependency theory.

Theory of the Firm

The "theory of the firm" conceives of higher education units as rational economic actors. This theory has been extended to include multi-product, not-for-profit organizations, thus making its application to universities reasonable (James, 1978). It is based on the paradigm that an organization pursues a set of goals to maximize its satisfaction, subject to one or more constraints (Clotfelter, 1996; Garvin, 1980; James, 1990; Jehle & Reny, 2001; Jencks & Reisman, 1968; Leslie & Rhoades, 1995; Mayhew, 1970; Tuckman & Chang, 1990; Varian, 1999; Vladeck, 1976). In short, these and other studies have identified prestige maximization as a common goal that yields maximum utility to university decision-makers. Overall, the distinguishing characteristic of the theory of the firm, as it may apply to public higher education, is its rooted attributions in rational, direct connection of means to ends and in resource allocation processes based on achieving goals (i.e., prestige maximization).

Resource Dependency Theory

Resource dependency theory lends itself to the study of universities as complex organizations with often diverse constituents and competing goals by emphasizing the political dimension of these organizations and their relationship to the external resource environment (Pfeffer & Salancik, 1978). The importance of goals as a defining characteristic of organizations has been criticized on several grounds: (a) Goals presume a singularity of purpose (Pfeffer & Salancik, 1978); (b) Organizations assume that goal setting and choice have an influence over outcomes (Bollinger, 1990; Chaffee, 1983; Doris & Loizer, 1990; Drohan, 1997; Hardy, 1991; Liff, 1997; Migliore, 1991; Mintzberg, 1994; Myers, 1996; Redding & Catalanello, 1994; Swenk, 1999; Weimer & Jonas, 1995); and (c) The importance of forces external to the organization are neglected (Pfeffer & Salancik, 1978). Resource dependency theory conceives of organizations as coalitions that "alter their purposes and domains to accommodate new interests, sloughing off part of themselves to avoid some interests, and when necessary, becoming involved in activities far afield from their stated central purposes" (Pfeffer & Salancik, 1978, p. 24). Pfeffer and Salancik see the relationship between resource providers and the organization as a political relationship because the resource provider holds great power, if not formal authority, over the organization. Recognizing the plurality of goals that exists within organizations, this framework allows for the occurrence of conflict and bargaining when goals are divergent.

The process of competing for resources and determining who secures them is central to this theoretical framework. In this framework, vulnerability stems from the possibility of changes in resource supply. To ensure the organization's survival, it is the compulsory responsibility of the production units to minimize the possibility of resources becoming scarce, given that scarcity is central to driving economic behavior in any economic theory. Using this theoretical framework in the case of contemporary public universities, a rational response to the declining rate of state funds has been to increase the share of other revenues in their base and, in so doing, to protect their revenue supply.

While the theory of the firm is a relatively straightforward connection of means to ends, resource dependency theory conceives of a much more complex set of relationships. The theories are used as interpretive lenses in examining resource allocation and are not mutually exclusive. Those who have employed the theory of the firm as a basis for estimating university production functions do not assume that economic theory fully describes organizational behavior (Winston, 1999; Volk, Slaughter, & Thomas, 2001).

Using both theoretical frameworks as a foundational guide, I developed and pursued the following research questions and testable hypotheses:

1. Does the relative weight of research productivity exceed that of teaching productivity in the income production function of academic departments in public Research I universities?
2. What is the impact of departmental quality on the production of departmental income in public Research I universities?
3. Do structural differences exist across these fields of science: computing and mathematics, life science, engineering, social science, and physical science?

Data and Methods

Data

This study uses the American Association of Universities Data Exchange (AAUDE) database, an underutilized data source containing valid and reliable estimates of expenditures and enrollments for the leading research and doctoral-granting universities in the nation (Dundar & Lewis, 1995). I drew my data from the latest complete AAUDE set, Delaware Expenditure Data, academic year 1998–1999. I selected a sub-sample of 10 major public research universities and 152 of their departments from the AAUDE for which complete data were available for AY1999.

I gathered expenditures, proxies for institutional allocations, and student credit hour production data from 53 types of constituent departments across five departmental fields: computing and mathematics, engineering, life sciences, physical science, and social science.

Variables

The dependent measure or input variable for the income production model is the departmental expenditures that include all wages paid to support the instructional function: faculty, clerical support, and professional and graduate student stipends. In addition, it includes expenditures for benefits associated with these personnel.

The teaching and research outputs of higher education which make up the independent variables consist of student credit hours (SCH) at two teaching levels—undergraduate (USCH) and graduate (GSCH)—that are used as proxies for teaching output. This use of SCH as teaching output proxies is noteworthy because the SCH is produced by each department and accurately reflects the teaching outputs of departments (Dundar & Lewis, 1995). Although public service is an institutional output, the measure of public service for this dataset proved unreliable. I therefore excluded public service from the study. (It is almost always eliminated from production function analyses.)

Research outputs usually are specified as the number of articles published, the number of patents granted, or the number of technological innovations developed (Candor, 1995; Dundar & Lewis, 1995); however, no such outputs are available in the AAUDE. Instead, I used total research expenditures (TOTRESEXP) as a measure of research output.

It is generally believed that output quality should be considered in examining departmental production. Thus, I selected two measures of quality: (a) scholarly quality of the program faculty

(NRCFQ) and (b) effectiveness (NRCER) of the program in educating research scholars. The measures captured elements of both teaching and research outputs of the department, although the first relates more to research outcomes and the second more to teaching. I obtained these measures from a national study by the National Research Council (Goldberger, Maher, & Flattau, 1995).[1]

Data Analysis

I employed a simple OLS multiple regression model relating institutional resource allocation to measures of departmental output for academic units in the sciences. As noted earlier, the semi-log model is widely used in human capital literature, whose theory suggests that the logarithm of earnings or wages be used as the dependent variable. When I applied this model to higher education, I substituted the department for the individual as the unit of analysis and measured the natural log of earnings (Y) of the department by its expenditures of non-restricted research money.

$$\text{In}(Y) = \beta_0 + \beta_1 L + \beta_2 A + \beta_3 T + \beta_4 F + \beta_5 P + \epsilon \quad (1)$$

Data Transformation

I transformed the data in a number of different ways to meet the model's specification. To facilitate an accurate interpretation of the results, here is an overview of these transformations.

1. Transformation 1: Semi-log Transformation

The semi-log relationship is obtained between departmental earnings and student credit hours. The same relationship holds true for research. The coefficients in this model may be interpreted as the marginal effects of the independent variables X upon ln *E* (natural log of earnings). Differentiating both sides with respect to *n* yields:

$$\beta_2 = \frac{d(\ln E)}{dX} = \frac{1}{E}\frac{dE}{dX} \quad (2)$$

The term (*dE/E*) can be interpreted as the change in *E* divided by *E*. Multiplying it by 100 gives the percentage change in *E* per unit change in X. Therefore, β_2 multiplied by 100, gives the rate of return in earnings for a one unit increase in X.

2. Transformation 2: Per Full-Time Equivalent (FTE) Instructional Faculty Member

Brinkman (1981) delineates three categories of higher education cost factors: environment, decision, and volume. Operationalized as input prices, input levels, and output levels, these factors alone may account for the variation in non-restricted expenditures. Controlling for these measures across departments, therefore, is necessary to delimit their potential confounding effect. For example, if outputs to the production process vary, they will account for a greater share of the variance in the dependent variable to the degree that the levels of those outputs differ. I made this correction by scaling all quantitative measures by a factor of (1/FTE), a technique that strives to eliminate the potentially confounding results from differing output levels. Thus, the coefficients of the independent variables should be interpreted as the rate of return per FTE instructional faculty member.

3. Transformation 3: Variable Transformations

Based on a methodology employed by d'Sylva (1998), I decided to sum the various levels of SCH into two levels: undergraduate and graduate. Variables such as Lower Division Organized Credit Hours (LDOCH), Upper Division Organized Credit Hours (UDOCH), and Undergraduate Individual Credit Hours (UICH) to create the new variable Undergraduate Productivity (UGPROD). I also aggregated variables such as Graduate Organized Credit Hours (GOCH) and Graduate Instruction Student Credit Hours (GISCH) to create Graduate Productivity (GPROD).

I also transformed the National Research Council's (NRC) rankings measures. I computed the mean of NRC's Faculty Scholarly Quality (NRCFQ) and NRC's Program Effectiveness Ratings (NRCER) to create a new variable called Quality (QUALITY). The resulting model consists of four independent variables, including a disturbance term. Moreover, with respect to the various Fields of Science (FIELDS), I collapsed math and computing into physical science and omitted the field of life sciences because there were insufficient NRC ranking measures for its various disciplines. Consequently, this study examines only three fields of study: engineering, social science, and physical science.

4. Transformation 4: General Linear Model (GLM) to Test Between Fields of Science Effects

To test the between-field effects of the various Fields of Science (FIELDS), I used a general linear model technique. To carry out the proper analysis it was important to recode the various values in (FIELDS) to test the individual coefficients per field of science. For example, in the first run I coded the various fields of science (the fixed factor) as 1 = "Engineering," 2 = "Social Science," and 3 = "Physical Science." "Physical Science" in this case was the control group against which the other two coefficients were contrasted. For example, $a_{PhysicalScience} - ß_{SocialScience}$ yields the difference between the two coefficients. I then tested such differences for their statistical significance. I ran separate regressions comparing the various fields using the GLM approach.

The resulting model, after all of the various transformations, has as the dependent measure the natural log of earnings (E) of the department. The independent variables consist of UGPROD (U), GPROD (G), TOTRESEXP (R), QUALITY (Q), and an individual disturbance term. Thus, the transformed model is expressed as follows:

$$\ln(E) = a_0 + a_1U + a_2G + a_3R + a_4Q + \mu \tag{3}$$

In summary, the semi-log model employed in this study is widely used in human capital theory literature to specify the earning functions of individuals, a common feature in cost studies. This study substituted the department for the individual and estimated the income production function for the department. I generated a system of three equations, excluding life sciences from the analysis that generated unbiased estimates of the coefficients. I specified an OLS model treating the size of an institution with respect to its FTE instructional faculty members. I also used tests that examined the effects between the three fields of science, using the general linear model (GLM) technique.

Results

I used OLS regression, controlling for FTE, to examine the returns to departmental earnings in fields of science. That is, I ran three separate models for each field of science. In addition, I employed a GLM technique to test the effects among the three fields of science: the overall goodness of fit statistics, significance of the independent variable coefficients, formal tests of multicollinearity using the Variance Inflation Factor (VIF), and between-field science effects.

Engineering (Model 1)

Within this model, engineering (n = 40), R^2 was 0.391, indicating that the model had fairly good explanatory power. The null hypothesis that all the coefficients in the engineering equation were jointly equal to zero was rejected $F(4,35) = 5.608$, $p < .001$, leading to the conclusion that at least one of the ßs was not zero. The coefficient for undergraduate productivity was statistically significant $t(39) - 1.661$, $p < .106$ and graduate productivity was statistically significant $t(39) = 3.059$, $p < .004$. Research productivity and quality were not statistically significant. (See Table 23.1.)

The rate of return on departmental earnings for an extra credit hour of graduate instruction per instructional faculty member (45.4%) was greater than the rate of return for an extra credit hour of undergraduate instruction (24.3%). The difference in this case was substantial; an additional unit

TABLE 23.1

Rate of Return on Earnings for Engineering, Social Science, and Physical Science

	Engineering (Model 1)			Social Science (Model 2)			Physical Science (Model 3)		
	Standardized beta	t-ratio	VIF	Standardized beta	t-ratio	VIF	Standardized beta	t-ratio	VIF
(Constant)		46.72			68.23			36.55	
Undergraduate productivity	0.24	1.66*	1.23	0.33	2.95***	1.09	0.01	0.07	1.03
Graduate productivity	0.45	3.06***	1.26	0.34	3.20***	1.00	0.29	2.24**	1.09
Research productivity	0.20	1.24	1.46	–0.01	–0.05	1.03	0.17	1.28	1.10
Quality	0.15	1.01	1.20	0.46	4.13	1.07	0.28	2.09**	1.13

*$p < 0.10$

**$p < 0.05$

***$p < 0.005$

of graduate teaching yields 21.1% more departmental earnings than an additional unit of undergraduate teaching. (See Table 23.1.)

All models were tested for multicollinearity using the formal test of Variance Inflation Factor (VIF). The null hypothesis for multicollinearity is as follows:

$$H_0 = \text{Multicollinearity exists if } VIF = \frac{1}{R^2} > 10 \tag{4}$$

The VIFs for all coefficients were substantially less than the threshold of 10 in all cases; therefore, the null hypotheses were rejected in all cases, and I determined that there is no multicollinearity in the models. (See Table 23.1.)

Social Science (Model 2)

Next we turn to the field of social science. In this field ($n = 40$), R^2 was 0.374, once again indicating that the model has fairly good explanatory power. The null hypothesis that all the coefficients in the social science equation were jointly equal to zero was rejected $F(4,55) = 8.226$, $p < .001$, leading to the conclusion that at least one of the βs was not zero. All coefficients were statistically significant save research productivity. Undergraduate productivity, graduate productivity, and quality were statistically significant $t(59) = 2.947$, $p < .005$; $t(39) = 3.202$, $p < .002$; and $t(39) = 4.128$, $p < .0001$, respectively. Although the variable of research productivity was not statistically significant, the direction of the coefficient is negative. (See Table 23.1.)

The rate of return on departmental earnings for an additional unit increase of quality (45.6%) was greater than both the returns for an extra credit hour of graduate instruction (34.2%) and the rate of return for an extra credit hour of undergraduate instruction (32.8%). The differences in this case were not substantial at all; an additional unit of quality yields 11.4% and 12.8% more departmental earnings than an additional unit of graduate teaching and an additional unit of undergraduate teaching respectively. An additional unit of graduate teaching yields 1.4% more departmental earnings than an additional unit of undergraduate teaching.

Physical Science (Model 3)

For the field of physical science ($n = 52$), R^2 was 0.270, once again indicating fairly good explanatory power for the model. (See Table 23.3.) The null hypothesis that all the coefficients in the physical science equation were jointly equal to zero was rejected $F(4,47) = 4.340$, $p < .005$, leading to the conclusion that at least one of the βs was not zero. The coefficient for graduate productivity was statistically significant $t(51) = 2.240$, $p < .030$, and quality was statistically significant $t(51) = 2.090$, $p < .042$. Undergraduate productivity and research productivity were not statistically significant. Although undergraduate productivity was not statistically significant, the magnitude of the coefficient is very small, approaching zero. (See Table 23.1.)

The rate of return on departmental earnings for an additional unit increase of graduate instruction (29.1%) was slightly greater than the return for an additional unit increase in quality (27.8%). Again, the differences in this case were not substantial; an additional unit of graduate instruction yields 1.3% more departmental earnings than an additional unit of quality.

Between-Fields Effects

In this model, I employed the GLM Univariate procedure, which provides regression analysis and analysis of variance for one dependent variable by one or more factors and/or variables. GLM uses a dummy variable approach that treats the three fields of science as the factor and the independent variables as the covariates in the model. I pooled the data to model the effects in the joint production of departmental earnings across the three various fields of science.

The null hypothesis for all fields is as follows:

$$H_0 = \beta_{PhysicalScience} = \beta_{SocialScience} = \beta_{Engineering} \tag{5}$$

When physical science was the control, the difference between the coefficients for social science and engineering are expressed with respect to the coefficient of physical science, that is, $\beta_{PhysicalScience} - \beta_{SocialScience}$ and $\beta_{PhysicalScience} - \beta_{Engineering}$. The contrasts between the coefficients of physical science and social science and physical science and engineering are both statistically significant. Therefore, the null hypothesis that $\beta_{PhysicalScience} = \beta_{SocialScience}$ is rejected, $\beta_{PhysicalScience} - \beta_{SocialScience} = .225$, $p < .0001$. Moreover, the null hypothesis that the coefficients for physical science and engineering are equal is rejected, $\beta_{PhysicalScience} - \beta_{Engineering}$, $p < .01$. (See Table 23.2.)

I ran a separate GLM in order to obtain the coefficient differences between social science and engineering. To do this, social science is now the control and the difference between the coefficients for engineering and social science. The difference between the coefficient of social science and engineering is statistically significant. Therefore, the null hypothesis that $\beta_{SocialScience} = \beta_{Engineering}$ is rejected, $\beta_{SocialScience} - \beta_{Engineering} = -.392$, $p < .0001$. (See Table 23.2.)

Summary

I estimated income production functions for departments in engineering, physical science, and social science for a sample of public, Research 1 universities, employing OLS regression models that controlled for instructional faculty FTE. I used GLM regressions to test for the effects between fields of science. Here is a brief discussion of the research questions and hypotheses.

1. Does the relative weight of research productivity exceed that of teaching productivity in the income production function of academic departments in public Research I universities?

To address this research question, I disaggregated teaching productivity into undergraduate and graduate productivity. There is no evidence that research exceeds the relative weight of teaching productivity. Instead, it is quite clear that, for all fields of science, the rate of returns for teaching productivity measures were greater than the rate of return for research productivity and were statistically significant. When teaching productivity is disaggregated, distinct differences emerge in the relative weight within teaching productivity itself. That is, engineering and physical science graduate productivity clearly exceed the weight of undergraduate productivity. Moreover, social science shows much more balance in the weights with respect to both undergraduate and graduate productivity. (See Table 23.3.)

2. What is the impact of departmental quality on the production of departmental income in public Research I universities?

Unit increases in departmental quality exhibited a consistent, positive, and statistically significant effect on the production of departmental income. Departmental quality was statistically significant for physical science and social science. Quality yielded the largest returns (45.6%) to departmental income in social science, exceeding physical science by 17.8% and engineering by

TABLE 23.2

Between Field of Science Effects

		Coefficient Difference
Contrast	$\beta_{PhysicalScience} - \beta_{SocialScience}$	–.225**
	$\beta_{PhysicalScience} - \beta_{Engineering}$	.167*
	$\beta_{SocialScience} - \beta_{Engineering}$	–.392**

*$p < .01$

**$p < .0001$

TABLE 23.3

The Rate of Return to Teaching Productivity versus the Rate of Return to Research Productivity by Fields of Science

	% Productivity		
Field	**Undergrad**	**Graduate**	**Research**
Engineering	24.3*	45.4****	19.8
Social science	32.8***	34.2***	–0.5
Physical science	0.9	29.1**	16.7

*$p < .10$
**$p < .05$
***$p < .01$
****$p < .001$

31%. From these results, we may conclude that departmental quality has a positive and significant effect on the production of departmental income. In addition, it is important to reiterate that quality is a proxy for research. (See Table 23.1.)

3. Do structural differences exist between the various academic fields of engineering, social science, and physical science? (I collapsed computing and mathematics with physical science.)

To address this research question, it was useful to examine the difference of the coefficients among all three fields of science. The rate of return for the joint production model of all fields, when physical science is the control, suggests that social science has an adverse effect on departmental earnings (–22.5%). The social sciences revealed a larger but still negative effect when contrasted with engineering (–39.2%). This result is indicative of the "halo effects" that engineering benefits from in perceived quality above and beyond that of social science. Moreover, social science has a negative and adverse effect on engineering and physical science and typically is disadvantaged in the allocation formula. (See Table 23.2.)

Discussion

I estimated the relative rate of return that universities assigned to teaching productivity and research productivity. In addition, I took the quality of the work into account in such estimation of returns by including a measure of departmental quality from the NRC rankings in the model. I modeled the allocation function by estimating the department's income production functions.

I will first discuss the major findings, then present the study's policy implications, and finally suggest needed research areas.

Major Findings

I used an econometric approach that employed OLS and GLM regressions to estimate the income production function for departments in engineering, social science, and physical science.

Teaching Productivity

Consistent with d'Sylva's (1998) findings, research has not displaced instruction as the chief priority in the allocation function of public research universities. I consistently found main effects to teaching productivity versus returns to research productivity across all fields of science.

So, what pays? Clearly, graduate education, quality, and engineering. Graduate education has a significant research component. Quality is a proxy for research, and engineering benefits from the "halo effects." Moreover, social science, the unit that has the largest returns to undergraduate education, is treated the worst in the institutional allocation. In other words, engineering is a clear winner and social science is a clear loser in the allocation "game."

How do these results converge with the alternative theoretical frameworks used in this study? As I reported in the introductory section, between 1988 and 1999 tuition, fees, private gifts, grants, and contracts increased dramatically to offset decreases in state appropriations, with tuition and fees showing the largest increases. Consequently, public research universities came to rely more heavily on student tuition and fee revenues as the rate of state support declined. As students became a more critical resource provider, institutions expected a concomitant increase in faculty attention to student instruction.

The results show clearly that teaching does matter in departments' revenue production function when aggregated by field type. Therefore, it appears that teaching also matters in the institution's allocation function. Specifically, undergraduate teaching matters, having yielded a consistently positive effect on the production of departmental income across fields of science. These results support the resource-dependency perspective that teaching is rewarded because resource shares from students and the state are great in their relative magnitude.

Engineering and physical science received significantly less return from the institution for teaching undergraduates. This result supports the theory of the firm hypothesis that profit-making undergraduate instruction is increasingly "taxed," presumably to support other revenue-losing endeavors that have greater utility to institutional decision makers. As suggested by the theory of the firm, endeavors that yield greater utility may be graduate instruction and departmental quality (i.e., research). The results support this hypothesis, for the rates of returns for graduate instruction across all levels are statistically significant and fairly large. Furthermore, the rate of return to departmental quality is more pronounced in social science and physical science and is statistically nonsignificant in engineering.

These results suggested that, for some fields, particularly engineering and physical science, undergraduate instruction, though still important in the revenue production function of departments, is increasingly being "taxed." As the "return" to undergraduate instruction has diminished, the "return" to graduate instruction and departmental quality has increased, at least in some cases. Undergraduate instruction, therefore, may have cross-subsidized graduate instruction and activities such as research that promote department quality. My findings support the argument that undergraduate instruction is being used to cross-subsidize research directly. The between-field effects clearly show that social science, which is large in undergraduate students, cross-subsidizes physical science, which is large in graduate students.

Research Productivity

The effect of teaching productivity on departmental earnings is greater than the effect of research productivity for all fields of science. However, this finding does not suggest that research is not important. Although the returns to research productivity were statistically insignificant across all fields of science, the direction and magnitude are important. Social science (–0.5%) shows a small negative return to departmental earnings, and engineering shows a positive (19.8%) return to departmental income. The hypotheses generated from both resource dependency theory and the theory of the firm suggest that research productivity would have a significant positive effect on generating departmental income. My study did not support this hypothesis, yet I would recommend caution in completely ruling it out, due to the limitations of the datatset.

Departmental Quality

The most important finding was that social science showed statistically significant, substantial, and the greatest returns to quality across fields and greater returns than physical science (but not engineering). The returns to quality in social science (45.6.%) were substantially greater than those in physical science (27.8%) and engineering (14.6%). These findings diverge from d'Sylva's (1998). It appears that none of the fields of science are being "penalized" for having relatively high national quality rankings. Most importantly, this result appears to support the theory of the firm's proposition that departmental quality is part of the institution's utility function.

Implications

Undergraduate instruction contributes significantly in the social sciences but less in engineering and physical science. Departmental quality contributes positively to the production of departmental income. Returns to research productivity were statistically nonsignificant but proved to be important with respect to the direction and the magnitude of its contribution when interpreting the results. Moreover, much caution is suggested when interpreting the returns to departmental earnings on research output because the research measures are conservative and may be underestimating the importance of such measure.

So what exactly are the implications of these results for major public research universities? If universities (and thereby departments) are rational economic actors, they certainly ought to continue to give major attention to instruction, especially undergraduate instruction, given its high returns. However, some departments in the social sciences may, in fact, be cross-subsidizing other departments, e.g., engineering and physical science. If this is the case, it has specific policy implications in that the undergraduate function of a research university is a core revenue-generating function but a less-valued function in the resource allocation game.

The implications for research productivity are mixed. While research productivity did not prove statistically significant, it certainly may be helpful. The direction and magnitude of the returns to research productivity shed light on how research is being favored, in what fields, and who is being penalized. Clearly, in the case of physical science, the rewards to research productivity are positive—but negative (although only slightly) in social science. Moreover, engineering benefits from a "halo effect" at the expense of other units, which are not only productive in undergraduate and graduate productivity but also in research productivity as measured by research quantity and quality, acting as a proxy for research. This finding has serious implications for whether administrators with budget authority are allocating internal funds fairly.

This study does not capture another serious implication which speaks volumes about the fact that how research really matters is not being counted. As this study demonstrates, such research measures, as a result, are underestimated. Research centers and institutes seem to be burgeoning. Such enterprises generate incredible amounts of external revenues that cannot be captured in a dataset like the AAUDE because they do not fit conveniently into traditional academic departments and fields. In short, it is almost certain that their research dollars are being seriously underestimated and so, consequently, are the nontraditional influence of such dollars. Moreover, if this is a trend, then it has significant implications for who is affiliated with such enterprises and to what end.

Quality plays a significant role in increasing departmental earnings and should correspondingly play an important role in the internal resource allocation function. As a result, the universities, departments, faculty, students, and public at large should strive to improve quality; even marginally improving quality will be rewarded significantly. These findings support Bowen's (1980) and Clotfelter's (1996) view that institutions of higher education essentially spend the most to be the best, and also support Leslie's (1995) findings of a connection between quality and financial resources.

Perhaps the major implication for the public and universities is that the undergraduate function is seen as an important function and that universities are, in fact, supporting it. However, this study's design limits its ability to examine whether undergraduate education is being allocated resources as a function of its mission or as a serendipitous result.

Recommendations for Future Research

The scope of work to be done in fully specifying the production function for higher education is just as colossal now as it was when other researchers examined resource allocation. This study added to the existing literature on internal resource allocation by focusing on departments and the aggregate fields of study and examining the effects between fields of science.

Analyzing data for departments in the humanities would be very insightful as this field employs large numbers of adjunct faculty (efficiency) and is typically high in student credit hours (instructional productivity). In other words, including humanities in a future study would permit the examination of a potentially "efficient" field that may be high in teaching productivity because it is minimizing operating costs: using adjunct faculty and low-cost technologies. Data for professional schools, such as education, law, and medicine, would also help to develop a broader view of these disciplines' production function. The effects of the interactions between these fields would also be instructive: Does adding or deleting certain types of departments significantly impact the overall production function of the university? Do complementarities exist—for example, between some physical science departments and engineering departments, between life science departments and medical departments? Also it would be important to understand how the allocation functions of public Research 1 universities compare to the allocation functions of private research universities.

The need exists to include an index for the proportion of women and minorities in any given department in these fields of science to test similar hypotheses that Volk, Slaughter, and Thomas (2001) explored for a single institution. Such a broadened study could be thought of as a sort of diversity index that would allow the specification of a single econometric model that estimates these types of parameters along with teaching and research productivity and quality.

It is important to disentangle further the relative importance of undergraduate and graduate levels (i.e., lower division, upper division, master's, and doctorates). Furthermore, to the extent possible, in the case of graduate student labor, it is important to tease out the extent to which their labor contributes to instruction versus research output.

Traditional academic departments may no longer be the best way to test external revenue generation—or even production functions—given that so much activity takes place in research centers and institutes whose members are separate from but related to traditional academic departments.

The need persists to define and understand the complex technologies of instruction and research and how certain revenues (e.g., tuition and fees) support the instruction-research nexus. As our understanding of such technologies and accounting for this significant revenue source improves, all stakeholders in the public research university will be able to make healthier and better-informed decisions about the allocation of constrained financial resources.

Finally, quantitative analysis is inherently limited in providing insights into the myriad complexities involved in resource allocation. Consequently, it would be helpful to explore how decision makers with budget authority conceive of key concepts in allocating resources. In short, any future study on resource allocation should take into account deep-seated beliefs held by resource allocators so that policy makers can fully appreciate the nuances of internal resource allocation consistent with suggestions from other scholars (Slaughter, 1993; Slaughter & Leslie, 1997; Slaughter & Rhoads, 2004).

Note

1. The 1993 National Research Council (NRC) rankings consist of 3,600 research doctoral programs at more than 279 institutions in 41 fields of study (Goldberger et al., 1995). Each program was evaluated by an average of 50 faculty respondents from the same field. The assessment of the "scholarly quality of program faculty" was based on measures of scholarly publication and peer review. Effectively, then, quality is a proxy for research. The study assessed "program effectiveness in educating research scholars and scientists" on measures of faculty accessibility, the department curricula, the instructional and research facilities, the quality of graduate students, the performance of graduates, and other departmental factors that were believed to contribute to a program's effectiveness. The values for "scholarly quality of program faculty" and "program effectiveness in educating research scholars and scientists" ranged from zero to five, with zero signifying "not sufficient for doctoral education" and five signifying "distinguished." Raters were required to designate no more than five programs as "distinguished." For each program, a mean rating was calculated; programs were then rank-ordered within fields on each of these two measures. My study uses the 1993 NRC rankings because the 2003 NRC rankings were not yet available.

References

Ashar, H. (1987). *Internal and external factors and their effect on a university's retrenchment decisions: Two theoretical perspectives.* Unpublished doctoral dissertation, University of Washington, Seattle.

Ashar, H., & Shapiro, J. W. (1990). Are retrenchment decisions rational? *Journal of Higher Education*, 61, 121–141.

Bollinger, J. (1990). Strategic planning in an academic environment. *Engineering Education*, 80(1), 19–22.

Bowen, H. (1980). *The costs of higher education: How much do colleges and universities spend per student and how much should they spend?* San Francisco: Jossey-Bass.

Brinkman, P. (1981). Factors affecting instructional costs at major research universities. *Journal of Higher Education*, 52(3), 265–278.

Chaffee, E. E. (1983). *Rational decision-making in higher education.* Boulder, CO: National Center for Higher Education Management Systems.

Clotfelter, C. (1996). *Buying the best: Cost escalation in elite higher education.* Princeton, NJ: Princeton University Press.

Cohn, E., Rhine, S., & Santos, M. (1989). Institutions of higher education as multi-product firms: Economies of scale and scope. *Review of Economics and Statistics*, 71, 284–290.

Doris, M. J., & Lozier, G. G. (1990). Adapting formal planning approaches: The Pennsylvania State University. *New Directions for Institutional Research*, 65, 5–21.

Drohan, W. (1997). Principles of strategic planning: A step by step approach. *Association Management*, 49(1), 85–88.

Dundar, H., & Lewis, D. (1995). Departmental productivity in American universities: Economies of scale and scope. *Economics of Education Review*, 14(2), 119–144.

d'Sylva, P. (1998). *Examining resource allocation within U.S. public Research 1 universities: An income production approach.* Unpublished doctoral dissertation, University of Arizona, Tucson.

Gander, J. (1995). Academic research and teaching productivities: A case study. *Technological Forecasting and Social Change* 49, 311–319.

Garvin, D. (1980). *The economics of university behavior.* New York: Academic Press.

Goldberger, M., Maher, B., & Flattau, P. (1995). *Research-doctorate programs in the United States: Continuity and change.* Washington, DC: National Academy Press.

Hackman, J. (1985). Power and centrality in the allocation of resources in colleges and universities. *Administrative Science Quarterly*, 30, 61–77.

Hardy, C. (1991). Configuration and strategy making in universities. *Journal of Higher Education*, 62(4), 363–393.

James, E. (1978). Product mix and cost disaggregation: A reinterpretation of the economics of higher education economics. *Journal of Human Resources*, 13(2), 157–185.

James, E. (1990). Decision processes and priorities in higher education. In S. H. Hoenack & E. L. Collins (Eds.), *The economics of American universities: Management, operations, and fiscal environment* (pp. 77–106). Albany, NY: SUNY Press.

Jehle, G. A., & Reny, P. J. (2001). *Advanced microeconomic theory* (2nd ed.). New York: Addison Wesley.

Jencks, C., & Reisman, D. (1968). *The academic revolution.* New York: Doubleday.

Kerr, C. (1994). *Troubled times for American higher education: The 1990's and beyond.* Albany, NY: SUNY Press.

Layzell, D. T. (1996). Faculty workload and productivity: Recurrent issues and new imperatives. *Review of Higher Education*, 19, 267–281.

Leslie, L. (1995). What drives higher education financial management in the 1990's and beyond? The new era in financial support. *Journal for Higher Education Management*, 10(2), 5–16.

Leslie, L., & Rhoades, G. (1995). Rising administrative costs: On seeking explanations. *Journal of Higher Education*, 66(2), 187–212.

Levin, H. M. (1991). Raising productivity in higher education. *Journal of Higher Education*, 62, 241–262.

Liff, A. (1997). Avoiding eight pitfalls of strategic planning. *Association Management*, 49(1), 120–25.

Massy, W. (1996). *Resource allocation in higher education.* Ann Arbor: University of Michigan Press.

Mayhew, L. (1970). *Graduate and professional education, 1980: A survey of institutional plans.* New York: McGraw-Hill.

Mayhew, L., Ford, P., & Hubbard, D. (1990). *The quest for quality.* San Francisco: Jossey-Bass.

Melchiori, G. (1982). Smaller and better: The University of Michigan experience. *Research in Higher Education*, 16, 55–69.

Migliore, R. H. (1991). Strategic planning/MBO with a human resources emphasis in educational administration. *CUPA Journal*, 42(4), 15–19.

Mintzberg, H. (1994). *The rise and fall of strategic planning*. New York: Free Press.

Morgan, A. W. (1984, September). The new strategies: Roots, context and overview. In L. Leslie (Ed.), *New Directions in Institutional Research* (No. 43, pp. 5–19). San Francisco: Jossey-Bass.

Myers, R. S. (1996, Summer). Restructuring to sustain excellence. *New Directions for Higher Education*, 94, 69–82.

National Center for Education Statistics (1993). *Digest of Education Statistics*. Washington, DC: U.S. Department of Education.

National Center for Education Statistics (1996). *Digest of Education Statistics*. Washington, DC: U.S. Department of Education.

National Center for Education Statistics (2003). *Digest of Education Statistics*. Washington, DC: U.S. Department of Education.

Pfeffer, J., & Salancik, G. (1978). *The external control of organizations: A resource-dependence perspective*. New York: Harper & Row.

Ramanathan, R. (1995). *Introductory econometrics with applications*. San Diego, CA: Harcourt Brace College.

Redding, J. C., & Catalanello, R. F. (1994). *Strategic readiness*. San Francisco: Jossey-Bass.

Research Associates of Washington. (2003). *Inflation measures for schools, colleges & libraries: 2003 update*. Arlington, VA: Research Associates of Washington.

Slaughter, S. (1993). Retrenchment in the 1980s: The politics of prestige and gender. *Journal of Higher Education*, 64, 250–282.

Slaughter, S., & Leslie, L. (1997). *Academic capitalism: Politics, policies, and the entrepreneurial university*. Baltimore: Johns Hopkins University Press.

Slaughter, S., & Rhoades, G. (2004). *Academic capitalism and the new economy: Markets, state, and higher education*. Baltimore: Johns Hopkins University Press.

Swenk, J. (1999). Planning failures: Decision cultural clashes. *Review of Higher Education*, 23(1), 1–21.

Tuckman, H., & Chang, C. (1990). Participant goals, institutional goals, and university resource allocation decisions. In S. H. Hoenack & E. L. Collins (Eds.), *The economics of American universities: Management, operations, and fiscal environment* (pp. 53–76). Albany, NY: SUNY Press.

Varian, H. R. (1999). *Intermediate microeconomics: A modern approach*. New York: W. W. Norton.

Vladeck, B. (1976). Why nonprofits go broke. *Public Interest* 42(4), 86–101.

Volk, C., Slaughter, S., & Thomas, S. L. (2001). Models of institutional resource allocation: Mission, market and gender. *Journal of Higher Education*, 72(4), 387–413.

Weimer, D., & Jonas, P. (1995). *Strategic planning: A participative model*. East Lansing, MI: National Center for Research on Teacher Learning. (ERIC Document Reproduction Service No. ED 390 324)

CHAPTER 24

FUNDING HISTORICALLY BLACK COLLEGES AND UNIVERSITIES: PROGRESS TOWARD EQUALITY?

G. THOMAS SAV

For decades, state funding of public historically black colleges and universities (HBCU) has been shown to be de facto discriminatory relative to the funding of their predominately white counterparts. Although the dual system has been legally dismantled, the disparate funding has remained in place in a number of ways. For example, recent research shows that in 1995 approximately 17% of the fewer state funding dollars allocated to historically black institutions (HBI) relative to predominately white institutions (PWI) could be attributed to fiscal discrimination. After more than a decade, the present research uses 2006 finance data to provide tests as to the extent of progress in moving HBI toward greater funding equality.

Introduction

It has long been more than suspect that in the public sector of higher education, HBI have been on a different and less generous financial footing in comparison to their predominately white counterparts. The disparate funding of the past is captured in decades of legal challenges brought forth under the U.S. Supreme Court "separate but equal" doctrine of *Plessy v. Ferguson* (1896).[1] That doctrine established the constitutionality of a racially separate and dual system of publicly provided education.[2] But the absence of equality in college and university facilities, libraries, program offerings, and the financing of such that arose at the outset of the separate higher education system was seriously documented by campus visits and several independent studies.[3] Equality continued to be challenged in the post *Brown v. Board of Education* (1954) era and after the Civil Rights Act of 1964. The 1980s witnessed lawsuits claiming that higher education funding allocations by state legislators and agencies were in violation of Title VI mandates and discriminatory against HBI. Moving into the later 1990s, cases continued to emerge—for example, Ohio lawmakers scrambled to develop financial plans for the state's historically black public university so as to ward off federal discriminatory lawsuits by the U.S. Department of Education's (USDE) Office for Civil Rights.[4]

When we turn our attention away from higher education to the notion of differential treatment in the labor market, many studies have focused on attempting to produce a single quantitative measure of the extent of racial or gender wage discrimination.[5] Using the same methodology employed in labor market studies, empirical evidence presented in this *Journal* suggests that approximately 17% of the lower state funding support of publicly controlled HBCU compared to predominately white state institutions could be attributed to fiscal discrimination in the allocation of state funds.[6] That evidence was based on college and university 1995 financial data reported to the USDE. More than a decade of finances has now passed and as with other research uncovering discriminatory treatment, the natural question arises as to whether or not the passage of time has narrowed or removed those funding inequalities. Therein is the purpose of this research. Using the currently available financial releases of the USDE data for 2006, the present article takes note to empirically test for the continued existence or disappearance of disparate funding treatment of HBCU with the hope that progress has been achieved in moving toward or attaining equality.[2]

Methodology

The main thrust of the methodology rests with state funding allocated to publicly controlled institutions of higher education, that is, predominately white colleges and universities (PWCU) and HBCU, depending upon specific funding measures that are tied to institutional performance and characteristics. However, it is recognized that not all state funding is allocated to public colleges and universities based on sets of rigid rules. There are discretionary monies that flow to institutions from the state bureaucratic machinery including state agencies and political committees. The latter, of course, can lead to funding imbalances that when uncounted for by financial funding rules appear as fiscally discriminatory. To empirically capture that possibility, a common empirical specification employs a dummy variable as follows:

$$STATEFUND = X\beta + HBCU + \varepsilon \tag{1}$$

where the annual state funding, *STATEFUND*, received by institutions varies depending upon a host of funding performance measures, X, and whether or not the receiving institution is a historically black college or university (HBCU).

If funding rules are strictly adhered to or legally enforced so that the funding effects with respect to performance measures as captured by the β's are thereby identical across all institutions, regardless of white or black, then any funding differentials due perhaps to discriminatory treatment would appear as a shift parameter in the intercept of equation (1). After accounting for funding measures X, for example, credit hour production, physical plant, etc., disparate funding of HBI would be attached to a negative coefficient on the HBCU variable. However, when it is suspected that differential funding treatment exists between groups with respect to the same performance measures, then the dummy variable approach must (out of necessity) be largely abandoned. In the present formulation of equation (1), the β's would differ for historically black compared to predominately white colleges and therefore, the dummy variable would fail in capturing the full differential treatment. A more complete specification in studying outcome differences between groups arises from the works of Blinder (1973) and Oaxaca (1973) and has had wide application including the analysis of wage differentials between males and females and whites and blacks.[7] In the present context, the Blinder-Oaxaca approach would estimate funding for PWI separately from HBI, thereby allowing any differences in funding treatment to be exposed in a shift parameter as well as additionally in the marginal effects of funding measures.

Applying the same set of funding measures X to PWCU and HBCU, the Blinder-Oaxaca methodology produces the following:

$$STATEFUND^{PW} = X^{PW}\beta^{PW} + \varepsilon^{PW} \tag{2}$$

$$STATEFUND^{HB} = X^{HB}\beta^{HB} + \varepsilon^{HB} \tag{3}$$

where the superscripts are used to identify the separate university and college groups, that is, *PW* for predominately white and *HB* for historically black. The approach allows the empirical results from (2) and (3) to be employed for decomposing an existence of differential funding into that which is due to legitimate differences and that which is due to say discrimination.

The decomposition proceeds as follows:

$$\overline{STATEFUND}^{PW} - \overline{STATEFUND}^{HB} = (\overline{X}^{PW} - \overline{X}^{HB})\hat{\beta}^{PW} + (\hat{\beta}^{PW} - \hat{\beta}^{HB})\overline{X}^{HB} \tag{4}$$

where the bars "—" denote the means and the hats "^" are the estimated coefficients for the predominately white *PW* and historically black *HB* colleges and universities, respectively. Thus, the average group funding difference on the left side of (4) is broken down into two parts. The first right hand term captures funding differences due to institutional performance measures, that is, the state funding rules that allocate monies to public colleges and universities based on the X funding factors such as credit hour production. It treats PWI as the advantaged group and therefore takes the estimated coefficients of funding for that group and evaluates the outcome of HBI, as if they received the same funding treatment as white institutions. The second right hand term is the accepted measure of discrimination in labor market studies. Here, it receives the same interpretation. Differences in marginal funding effects weighted by the mean performance characteristics of HBI potentially produce greater funding for PWCU compared to HBCU.

Empirically, we will investigate both the dummy variable approach and the decomposition approach in an attempt to determine whether and to what extent there are any remnants of fiscally discriminatory funding of HBCU. However, the more restrictive dummy variable approach will have to give way to the more powerful ability of the decomposition methodology and its widely accepted use throughout the literature.

Data

Data for individual colleges and universities are drawn from the Integrated Postsecondary Education Data System (IPEDS).[8] Under the auspices of the USDE, National Center for Education Statistics (NCES), IPEDS is an annual survey made available on a preliminary and final release basis. The most recent final release is for 2006 and establishes the data set used in this article.[9]

From IPEDS the selection of the dependent variable, *STATEFUND*, is quite straightforward and consists of all fiscal year legislated state appropriations allocated to each institution. What those appropriations are tied to is not so straightforward and defines the task at hand in constructing an empirically workable set of funding measures. The problem, of course, is that state funds flowing to individual institutions are in some instances tied to fairly rigid funding rules that result in automatic subsidies while in other instances there may result funding that flows from political-maneuvering and vote-gathering behavior. Yet, the available institutional financial data do not enable us to separate the two so that a given institutional characteristic or funding factor can drive, be responsible for, and influence both funding sources and, therefore, the resulting *STATEFUND*.

One would not likely get arguments that publicly supported state colleges and universities receive state financial support based on enrollment characteristics and more specifically on the production of credit hours. But all credit hours not being equal, state subsidies differ for undergraduate compared to graduate education and professional education, for example, law school. In IPEDS, it is not possible to separately account for institutionally generated graduate versus professional credit hours. The post baccalaureate credit hours are aggregated. Thus, we have two direct measures of production—(1) total undergraduate credit hour production (*UNDERGRAD*) and (2) total graduate and professional credit hour production (*GRADPRO*). Both *UNDERGRAD* and *GRADPRO* are directly tied to state supported subsidies and thus *STATEFUND*.

State support of public colleges and universities vary widely and vary with respect to the institution's ability to be somewhat private, that is, to rely on market forces rather than state tax revenues. The greater the ability to provide educational services based on direct charges, the less need there is for the public provision via the tax mechanism of higher education services.[10] Therefore, while there is public provision of higher education, the publicness of institutions varies inversely with the dependence on market generated revenues. A reasonable proxy to such would be the percent of total revenues produced from tuition charges (*TUITION*) and is included here as a funding measure with the expectation that it negatively correlates with an institution's state funding, *STATEFUND*.

Similar to this notion is a body of literature contending that one funding source tends to crowd out another funding source.[11] Specifically, increases in private giving so as to enable or enhance an activity or service, tends to crowd out and reduce government funding of the same activity or service. In the present inquiry, if publicly established colleges and universities can provide the publicly demanded level and quality of higher education in part from private donor dollars, then the state political machinery is for the same part potentially left off the hook to use state revenue tax dollars for the same educational service. Elected politicians and their state agency appointees in the vote-gathering process for reelection or party support are positioned to reallocate tax dollars to other publicly demanded activities, services, or projects in an attempt to maximize vote gathering. There are various channels of private giving that flow into colleges and universities and appear on the accounting books. In IPEDS there are two sources of private giving that we can turn to for modeling the crowding-out argument. One is the change in the institution's private endowments (*PRIVATE*) and the other is the institutionally provided scholarships and fellowships from restricted and unrestricted private giving (*SCHOLAR*). The first is private giving that is adding to the stock of the institution's private pool of wealth, while the second is private giving that is used for the provision of current educational services. From the crowding-out literature, both would be expected to negatively impact institutional funding received through state channels *STATEFUND*.

Still, there exists another level of government funding source to contend with—that is, the federal government and the dollars that flow from it to higher education. Here, the economic argument is that state politicians are keenly aware of the extent of federal government funding of their state-supported colleges and universities and, therefore, can engage in substituting through reallocation some of the federal monies for like state tax revenue dollars. Thus, the crowding-out hypothesis is applicable but now pertaining to, instead of private giving, another source of government funding (federal) reducing or crowding-out state funding. However, it is also the case that federal monies may come with tie-ins that require at least a portion of matching state dollars. Hence, it would be equally plausible to expect state funding to increase directly with federal support. Whether or not one effect rules or dominates the other is not clear a priori and, therefore, must remain an empirical issue. For this purpose then, we expect the IPEDS constructed measure of institutional revenues received through federal channels (*FEDERAL*) to produce either reductions in or increases in state funding, *STATEFUND*.

Two remaining funding measures are drawn from IPEDS. First, there are nonacademic revenues garnered from campus auxiliary enterprises (*AUXILIARY*) that provide internal and external community benefits. Campus housing, wellness centers, and healthcare facilities are services offered to students and, in some cases, faculty and staff. Arenas and theaters, for example, also produce external benefits that are enjoyed by the community at large. While these are usually fee driven, the prices are generally below market value and the service ends up being partially subsidized by the taxpayer—state funding. Taxpayer state funding additionally supports, in part, the infrastructure needs, including roads and buildings or more generally the physical plant of the campus community. From IPEDS, the value of the institution's physical plant assets (*ASSETS*) provides a means of comparing campus facilities among institutions. Both *AUXILIARY* and *ASSETS* are expected to generate larger amounts of state funding.

In sum, the state funding measures created from IPEDS that are to be employed in the empirical implementation of the methodology are as follows:

UNDERGRAD = total undergraduate credit-hour production
GRADPRO = total graduate and professional credit-hour production
TUITION = percent of total revenues produced from tuition charges
PRIVATE = change in private endowments
SCHOLAR = scholarships and fellowships
FEDERAL = revenues received through federal channels
AUXILIARY = revenues generated from auxiliary enterprise operations
ASSETS = physical plant assets

After eliminating non-reporting institutions—public institutions that failed to comply with reporting requirements and, in particular, state funding or enrollment responses, the final data set comprised 33 HBCU and 211 PWI.

Empirical Results

Descriptive statistics are summarized in Table 24.1. For the most part, all is as expected except interestingly the change in private endowment funds on average declined during the fiscal year, indicating that either private philanthropy slowed relative to institutional endowment spending needs or the latter accelerated beyond normal. Of course, simultaneously, higher education institutions were not likely to escape a decline in endowment investment yields that were borne by other sectors of the economy. Aside from that, larger institutions by any measure such as enrollments, physical plant size, etc. prevail in the predominately white group and therefore receive more state funding in

TABLE 24.1

Predominately White and Historically Black Colleges and Universities Group Means and Standard Deviations

Variable Description	Variable Symbol	Predominately White Mean	Predominately White Std. Dev.	Historically Black Mean	Historically Black Std. Dev.
State Funding, $1,000,000	STATEFUND	95.51	11.78	42.22	2.61
Undergraduate Credit Hours, 10,000	UNDERGRAD	29.90	25.06	12.60	6.48
Graduate and Professional Credit Hours, 1,000	GRADPRO	43.66	57.98	11.95	9.92
Tuition Revenue as % of Total Revenue	TUITION	25.20	10.52	16.30	5.89
Private Endowment, $1,000,000	PRIVATE	−1.3	4.1	−0.83	0.017
Institutional Scholarships/ Fellowships, $1,000,000	SCHOLAR	7.17	1.11	6.5	0.95
Federal Grants and Contracts, $1,000,000	FEDERAL	36.27	69.32	18.78	12.95
Auxiliary Enterprise Revenue, $1,000,000	AUXILIARY	13.05	27.37	2.89	3.84
Physical Plant Assets, $1,000,000	ASSETS	283.33	374.24	128.23	75.58
N Observations		211		33	

absolute amounts. However, there is substantially more funding variability among PWI compared to HBCU.

Table 24.2 presents the regression results for both the dummy variable model and the separate group estimates that are needed for the Blinder-Oaxaca decomposition model.

First turning to the dummy variable results, holding all our state funding measures constant, HBCU receive less state dollars. Those fewer dollars are allocated upon our assumption in the pooled model that both PWI and HBI receive the same per unit performance-based subsidies. Under that assumption, the expected larger credit hour (*UNDERGRAD* and *GRADPRO*) producing colleges and universities receive more state funding. Also, graduate and professional education carries greater per credit hour subsidies than undergraduate education. But the more consumers are willing to pay market prices for higher education (*TUITION*), the less willingness or need is present on the part of the state tax machinery to support higher education.

From a public finance policy perspective, the crowding-out hypothesis gets partial but important empirical support. Increasing private endowment funding (*PRIVATE*) tends to decrease state funding support. And although it was expected that the awarding of scholarships and fellowships (*SCHOLAR*) that come from private giving would likewise have that type of crowding-out effect, empirically it turns out to be of the opposite effect but of questionable significance. On the other hand, statistically significant is the positive effect that federal (*FEDERAL*) dollars have on state funding. It implies that the matching fund argument holds and state policy or decision makers are willing to allocate additional state funds to universities and colleges that succeed in increasing the federal portion of their revenue pie. Actual practice may require, in some instances, that at least a portion of state contributions are promised as a path to the award of federal funds and, therefore, the observed positive effect.

TABLE 24.2

State Funding Regressions Predominately White and Historically Black Colleges and Universities

	Pooled White-Black		Predominately White		Historically Black	
Independent Variable	β_i (s_β)	α*	β_i (s_β)	α*	β_i (s_β)	α*
INTERCEPT	9.59 (20.62)	87%	28.979 (23.498)	95%	0.454 (18.075)	90%
UNDERGRAD	0.155 (0.021)	1%	0.156 (0.022)	1%	0.189 (0.071)	10%
GRADPRO	0.446 (0.108)	1%	0.453 (0.116)	1%	0.092 (0.431)	10%
TUITION	–1.223 (0.277)	1%	–1.364 (0.304)	1%	–0.733 (0.420)	10%
PRIVATE	–0.001 (0.0003)	1%	0.002 (0.001)	1%	-0.003 (0.001)	1%
SCHOLAR	0.324 (0.687)	30%	0.353 (0.328)	20%	0.0430 (0.263)	85%
FEDERAL	0.597 (0.094)	1%	0.612 (0.102)	1%	0.222 (0.219)	1%
AUXILIARY	0.007 (0.004)	10%	0.009 (0.001)	1%	0.004 (0.002)	5%
ASSETS	0.001 (0.00002)	1%	0.017 (0.002)	2%	0.003 (0.0004)	1%
HBCU	–0.512 (0.216)	10%				
N Observations	244		211		33	
Probability>F Value	0.001		0.001		0.001	
Adjusted R2	0.861		0.872		0.814	

*α = minimum level of significance or better for a two-tailed test.

As predicted, the presence of auxiliary enterprises (*AUXILIARY*) on public campuses, whether they produce direct benefits for students and employees or also external community benefits, is partially subsidized through state funding. The same effect was expected with respect to the size of the campus physical plant as measured by ASSESTS and is here borne out empirically.

Moving from the pooled to the separate group modeling, Table 24.2 reveals that PWCU and HBCU are on par for state funding subsidies connected to undergraduate (*UNDERGRAD*) education. The smaller and weaker marginal effect of post-baccalaureate education (*GRADPRO*) at HBI is probably attributed to the problem that IPEDS combines professional and graduate credit hour education and relatively little to none of the former occurs at HBI. Thus, what arises in the predominately white group effect is the greater presence and state funding subsidization of law, medical, veterinarian, etc. schools.

Mimicking the public finance results of the dummy variable model, within each of the separate sectors, state funding dollars trail off the better the institution is at relying on market forces via tuition dependence (*TUITION*) as a relative revenue source. That does not hold with endowment fund raising and the proposition of crowding out. While growing the institutional endowment

(*PRIVATE*) decreases state funding for HBCU, it tends to get larger state funding rewards in the predominately white sector. This intersector imbalance is in contrast to previous research where crowding out was empirically present in both sectors. The sign flipping for the predominately white sector is likely created by the mandated changes in federal survey reporting requirements. That is, the IPEDS "parent/child" reporting method changed so that presently branch campuses are separate entities whereby previously they were combined with the finances of their main "parent" campus. Treated separately, the relatively small endowments of branch campuses are insignificant in reducing state funding and, therefore, correlate positively with state funding increases. With respect to the historically black sector, the empirical consistency with previous research that is herein observed can be attributed to the fact that branch campuses are relatively non-existent in that sector and thus the IPEDS reporting change did not alter the statistical result.

Given the empirical results of the pooled dummy variable model with respect to *SCHOLAR*, we would not expect much if any better statistically significant effect when institutions are separated by white and historically black. That expectation is confirmed by the results presented in Table 24.2. But with strong statistical significance within both sectors, state and federal dollars go hand-in-hand with somewhat of a more powerful marginal effect for PWI. Again, that is likely to be due to the presence of professional schools and more state federal-matched funding specific to professional education within the predominately white university sector. A similar effect exists with respect to auxiliary run campus enterprises (*AUXILIARY*) that are fewer and smaller at HBI and sector wise do not produce as much external benefit. Thus, while the enterprises generate positive amounts of state funding or subsidy, the effect tends to be less and more insignificant. Regardless of the sector, colleges and universities get state financial help with the physical plant (*ASSESTS*) and get more help the larger the plant.

Turning to the empirical interest of the Blinder-Oaxaca decomposition, Table 24.3 presents the results of equation (4) expressed, for convenience, as percentages. For comparison the 1995 decomposition results are reproduced.[12] Encouragingly, funding differences between PWCU and HBCU that are attributable to what we attempt to measure as discriminatory treatment, declined from

TABLE 24.3

Decomposition of Predominately White vs. Historically Black State Funding Differences

	Attributable to Institutional Characteristics (%)		**Attributable to Differential Treatment (%)**	
	1995	**2006**	**1995**	**2006**
TOTAL FUNDING DIFFERENCE DUE TO:	83.3	87.5	16.7	12.5
UNDERGRAD	49.1	50.7	49.3	–7.9
GRADPRO	17.4	26.9	–6.3	12.2
TUITION	–13.0	–22.8	–31.3	–19.3
PRIVATE	–3.7	–10.7	1.5	–5.2
SCHOLAR	n.a.	4.4	n.a.	13.7
CORPORATE	6.0	n.a.	0.0	n.a.
FEDERAL	12.0	20.1	–2.1	40.0
AUXILIARY	7.0	18.3	–5.8	3.0
ASSETS	8.5	0.5	–3.3	–37.9
INTERCEPT			14.7	16.0

16.7% to 12.5%. On average, that amounts to a 2006 average $6.7 million state funding differential that is absent from the institutional budgets of HBCU compared to PWCU. However, if the treatment had remained at its 1995 level of 16.7%, then that would have instead produced a $8.9 million funding differential for the 2006 fiscal year.

Decomposing the overall treatment into individual funding components, the bulk (50.7%) of state funding differences tied to institutional performance is due to lower undergraduate credit hour production (*UNDERGRAD*) among HBI. Still, the most dramatic 1995–2006 funding change occurs here. On sub-setting the 12.5% differential treatment effect, HBI receive an extra 7.9% state appropriated dollar per undergraduate credit hour. Of course, as noted above, they produce fewer credit hours on average but still that favored 7.9% compares to the reverse and negative treatment of 49.3% in 1995. Not as dramatic of a change, but some of the differential treatment effects appear to have shifted toward *UNDERGRAD* and away from *GRADPRO* as the latter went from a 1995 favorable 6.3% treatment to an unfavorable 2006 12.2%.

Summarizing the remaining results, if one assumes a fixed-state budget and a reallocation of that budget to achieve funding parity, then based on the differential treatment effects, HBCU would be due greater funding per graduate and professional credit hour produced (*GRADPRO*), scholarship monies raised (*SCHOLAR*), federal government dollars received (*FEDERAL*), and revenues to run campus auxiliary enterprises (*AUXILIARY*). Of course, funding cuts would have to be shouldered with respect to undergraduate credit hour production (*UNDERGRAD*), tuition revenue (*TUITION*), and endowment growth (*PRIVATE*) along with increases in the campus infrastructure (*ASSETS*). With those adjustments in place there would remain the need to remove the disparate funding effect that is unrelated to any of the institutional characteristics and is therefore discretionary as measured by the *INTERCEPT* and accounts for 16% of the differential funding.

Over the decade of attempted comparison presented here, higher education as an industry has experienced and struggled with many funding changes. Those funding changes are evident in the current empirical results and show that neither PWCU nor HBCU escaped them.

Conclusions

In any area where discrimination is found to exist, it behooves us to keep our fingers on the equality pulse to be sure it is alive and working to narrow and hopefully remove such discrimination. Based on the present data and statistical analysis, one would conclude that progress has been achieved in narrowing the gap in the state funding treatment of HBCU compared to PWCU. That gap has been noted and challenged at various levels in the legal system since the 1896 landmark Supreme Court decision legislated the higher education dual system. Recent research paralleling the present estimated that in 1995 16.7% of the fewer state dollars allocated to HBI was attributed to discriminatory treatment. The present article suggests that has decreased to 12.5% in 2006. If we tended to label this as progress, then simple trend analysis would lead us to believe that it would take three decades to achieve funding parity. But the methodology employed allows for a finer decomposition of the overall funding that reveals very substantial progress in narrowing and in some cases reversing the differential funding treatment, so as to favor HBI with respect to certain performance measures.

Thus, both positive and negative funding effects work in opposing directions to produce an overall disparity. That some of these statistical results produce contradictory evidence leads to the usual caveats. In this case, that resides in the quality of the survey data and its potential inability to accurately capture the complex performance of individual colleges and universities and the public-funding formulas that are tied to different performance measures. And while this research uses the most recently released financial data from the NCES, it has over time changed its survey methodology and reporting requirements. Those changes, as they potentially affect our statistical results, are indeed difficult to untangle. In addition, the current 2006 financial data undoubtedly holds some of the post 2005 devastating economic effects of Hurricane Katrina on the southern portions of the U.S. and its higher education industry. Perhaps to augment our current survey data, it is necessary to follow a future research path that returns in part to the 1916 methodology employing direct observation through comparable on-site visits to both predominately white and historically black campuses.

Notes

1. A'Lelis Robinson Henry, "Perpetuating Inequality: Plessy v. Ferguson and the Dilemma of Black Access to Public Higher Education," *Journal of Law and Education*, January 1998.
2. A legal historical account is provided in *Black-White Colleges: Dismantling the Dual System of Higher Education*, United States Commission on Civil Rights, Clearing House Publication 66, April 1981.
3. "*A Study of the Private and Higher Education Schools*," prepared for the U.S. Department of the Interior, Bureau of Education, 1916.
4. "Civil-Rights Office Reviews Ohio Plan to Improve Central State," *The Chronicle of Higher Education*, June 14, 1996.
5. For example, see Ernst R. Berndt, *The Practice of Econometrics: Classic and Contemporary*, Chapter 5, "Analyzing Determinants of Wages and Measuring Wage Discrimination," Addison-Wesley: Massachusetts, 1991.
6. Thomas Sav, "Tests of Fiscal Discrimination in Higher Education Finance: Funding Historically Black Colleges and Universities," *Journal of Education Finance*, 26:2, Fall 2000: 157-172.
7. Alan S. Blinder, "Wage Discrimination: Reduced Form and Structural Estimates," *Journal of Human Resources*, 18:3, Fall 1973: 436-455 and Ronald Oaxaca, "Male Female Wage Differentials in Urban Labor Markets," *International Economic Review*, 14:3 October 1973: 693-709.
8. United States Department of Education, National Center for Education Statistics, Integrated Postsecondary Education Data System, *Finance Survey FY 2006*.
9. A few nuances can arise in constructing identically consistent across time data sets from IPEDS. For one, the National Center for Education Statistics has changed the "parent/child" reporting method so that unlike that in 1995, main campuses are no longer to report combined data for their own (parent) campus and their branch (child) campuses, therefore making branch campuses separate reporting entities. In addition, survey changes have resulted in some previously collected data being dropped.
10. See, for example, Theodore Bergstrom, Lawrence Blume, and Hal Varian. "On the Private Provision of Public Goods." *Journal of Public Economics*, 29, February 1986, 25-50.
11. Elizabeth Becker and Cotton M. Lindsay. "Does the Government Free Ride?" *Journal of Law and Economics*, 37, April 1994, 277-296.
12. The 1995 decomposition results are presented here as a baseline for comparison to the present 2006 fiscal year results. However, as noted, the IPEDS survey changes have created data problems that render impossible exact comparisons. The "corporate" giving variable was available in the 1995 survey data and not the 2006 survey data. The variable "scholar" is in the 2006 analysis.

CHAPTER 25

MODELS OF INSTITUTIONAL RESOURCE ALLOCATION: MISSION, MARKET, AND GENDER

CINDY S. VOLK, SHEILA SLAUGHTER, AND SCOTT L. THOMAS

In an era when expansion is no longer the obvious solution for dealing with curricular change in research universities, the question of how and why institutions allocate resources among departments, the organizational units that deliver curricula, should become increasingly important. Resource constraint has caused widespread restructuring in public research universities, but few studies examine its effects on departments, although the broad goals of restructuring are to redesign institutions to lower costs, achieve greater student learning, give more attention to teaching, and contribute to regional economic development (Guskin, 1994; Gumport & Pusser, 1996; Massey & Zemsky, 1994), all efforts that depend on departmental cooperation. Institutional resource allocation affects departments in a number of ways. The resources available to departments shape who is hired, how much and whom they teach. Quality of faculty and work load, in turn, influence research norms and productivity. Changes in patterns of resource allocation among departments are critical to understanding the shape of knowledge in the twenty-first century.

In the 1980s, prompted by periodic state and institutional budget crises, researchers began to study internal resource allocation among departments within colleges and universities (Ashar, 1987; Ashar & Shapiro, 1990; Hackman, 1985; Melchiori, 1982; Morgan, 1983). But in the 1990s, questions about internal resource allocation among departments generally were put in the broader context of restructuring. This shift meant that attention turned away from departments as units that created and delivered particular kinds of knowledge and curricula efficiently and effectively and toward individual faculty performance on productivity measures as well as individual faculty response to institutional incentives (Layzell, 1996; Levin, 1991). If departments were considered at all, they were treated as generic departments that reacted to institutional and professional incentives rather than as departments organized around concrete kinds of knowledge, peopled by faculty with similar characteristics who trained students for specific careers (Fairweather, 1996; Massy & Wilger, 1992; Massy & Zemsky, 1994). Costing studies were the exceptions, but these used econometric models to identify abstract cost structures among departments aggregated in broad fields of study, a process that reified rather than explained patterns of difference in institutional investment (Brinkman, 1990; Dundar & Lewis, 1994).

Along with a relatively small number of researchers using critical theory and feminist perspectives, we see this shift from department to individual, or, conversely, broad field of study (science and engineering, humanities, social sciences) as the unit of analysis, as masking increasing stratification between departments and within universities (Bellas, 1994, 1997; Gumport, 1993; Kerlin & Dunlap, 1993; McElrath, 1992; Slaughter, 1993; Volk, 1995). Critical researchers view faculty and the curricula they deliver as organized in departments that powerfully mediate individual faculty performance. Faculty delivering some curricula may not receive the same resources as faculty associated with other curricula, just as faculty in departments preparing students for certain careers may not be given the same support as faculty in other, more favored departments. Department, rather than individual faculty performance, may be a powerful explanatory variable. Faculty located in under-resourced, overextended departments may not be able to respond fully to the complex array of institutional incentives and disincentives that characterize multimission public research universities.

We think that understanding which departments receive resources and why is critical to understanding the far-reaching reorganization and revaluing of knowledge that is presently occurring.

To explore our questions about resource allocation among departments, we reviewed the several theories that purport to explain variance in allocation. We identified two major perspectives, the rational/political and the critical/political. We decided to see which of the theories best explained resource allocation at a single public Research I university (Carnegie Foundation for the Advancement of Teaching, 1994), examining all departments except those located in the medical and law schools.[1] We identified a total of 30 independent variables that represented key components of the explanations offered by the two theories. We looked at standard variables researchers have traditionally used to explain variation in resource allocation among departments such as salary, size, grant dollars, and student FTE. Because we looked at critical/political as well as rational/political factors, we incorporated variables not usually used in departmental resource allocation studies, for example, variables for ascribed characteristics such as gender and minority status of faculty and students. We also developed variables that were proxies for closeness of departments to external markets, for example, assistant professor faculty entry salaries. Finally, we examined variables indicative of internal stratification such as lower division, upper division, and graduate student credit hours. We used multiple regression models to assess the effects of our independent variables on the dependent variable, internal allocation of state dollars to departments. After presenting our results, we discuss what our findings from the final model mean for the two theories and for the restructuring of universities, the reorganization of knowledge, and the stratification of academic work within public research universities.

Theory

The theories that guide researchers who study internal institutional resource allocation among departments generally fall into one of two frames: rational/political or critical/political. Rational/political theorists highlight the role of a small number of decision makers at the apex of the institution and emphasize the functional use of resources to maintain and enhance institutional efficiency and effectiveness (Morgan, 1983). Although they emphasize rationality, rational/political theorists are sensitive to political dimensions of internal budgetary processes and allow for interest group bargaining, acknowledge power differentials among departments, especially in the ability to win external grants and contracts, and recognize that groups external to the university can sometimes intervene to influence allocation (Ashar, 1987; Ashar & Shapiro, 1990; Hackman, 1985; Morgan, 1983). However, rational/political theorists generally explain resource allocation among departments by productivity and meritocratic criteria: funds flow to departments that are central to mission and workload, are productive in terms of student credit hours, grants and contracts and faculty scholarship, and are high in quality. Rational/political theorists acknowledge politics as an important factor, but never see politics as determining resource allocation to the point where they overwhelm institutional economy and efficiency.

The rational/political model initially drew heavily on organizational theory that treated institutions as self-contained and was concerned primarily with internal priority setting. As higher education continued to restructure (but not downsize, see Leslie & Rhoades, 1995) and economics became the preferred social science idiom, the market was incorporated into rational/political models in the form of human capital theory (Breneman, 1988; Slaughter & Leslie, 1997; Youn, 1989). This purportedly linked external labor markets for individual professional skills more closely to internal academic reward systems. Because human capital theory assumed markets to be free, rational and impartial, they were invoked by rational/political theorists to explain and justify increasing differences in salaries by department (Lee, Leslie, & Olswang, 1987).

In contrast, critical/political[2] theorists see resource allocation to departments as shaped by gender, race, power and service to external constituencies dominant in the broader political economy (Bellas, 1994,1997; Gumport, 1993; Kerlin & Dunlap, 1993; McElrath, 1992; Slaughter, 1993, 1998; Volk, 1995). Like rational/political theorists, critical/political theorists see politics and power as playing a part, but critical/political theorists foreground politics and power, arguing that differentials in political economic power among departments explain the majority of variance in resource allocation among departments. They read political power as patterned by gender, race, and relation of departments to federal and corporate research markets, high-end private sector markets for professionals, and the social welfare function of the state (Slaughter, 1997, 1998). Critical/political theorists make the case that concentrating institutional resources on departments close to federal and corporate research markets as well as high-end private sector markets for professionals loads institutional resources on departments where there are many graduate students and few undergraduates, creating systemic productivity problems for public research universities (Volk, 1995). They argue that marked inequities in resources among departments place faculty in some departments—particularly those with heavy lower-division teaching loads—at a disadvantage in responding to the complex array of institutional incentives and disincentives characteristic of multimission public research universities. Because the departments with the least resources and the highest undergraduate teaching loads are often departments with a relatively high number of women and minority faculty, critical/political theorists point out that this pattern of resource allocation undermines some institutional missions and goals, for example, the undergraduate teaching mission and the goal of equity.

Data and Methods

Our study included all departments (72) within a public research university, excluding the medical school and law school. The amount of state appropriated dollars to each department was the dependent measure.[3] We developed various measures on each of the 70 remaining departments. Data defining these variables were gathered from departmental profiles developed and maintained by the Office of Institutional Research, from the Sponsored Projects Office, from the Office of Student Affairs, from the Affirmative Action/Equal Opportunity Office, and from a 1992 University-Wide Quality Review, commissioned by the provost, of the centrality and quality of all departments.

Rational/Political Variables

Like Ashar (1987), Ashar & Shapiro (1990), and Hackman (1985), we did not focus on full professor salaries, a measure that traditionally explains most of the differences among departments with regard to state dollar allocations. We wanted to avoid having our analysis dominated by "pipeline" issues that suggest women and minorities are in the system, moving up, and in time and without intervention will receive salaries similar to men. To address this we treated the salaries of assistant professors as a control, allowing us to concentrate on variables that explained differences among departments, net of the primary cost driver, academic salary. Although we acknowledge the predictive value of full professor salaries, including the salaries of professors at different academic ranks in our model is statistically problematic, forcing us to choose one level over another for inclusion. We chose to include salaries at the assistant as opposed to full level to better capture departments' closeness to market. The rationale for this choice is discussed in a subsequent section. This control allowed us to then focus on the four areas commonly used by rational/political theorists to measure the rational decision-making processes in resource allocation: centrality, workflow, grant and contract productivity, and quality (Ashar 1987; Ashar & Shapiro, 1990; Hackman, 1985).

Centrality

In the literature, centrality usually refers to the importance of departments to university mission or the criticality of departments to maintaining institutional workflow. Centrality to mission (Hackman, 1985) foregrounds departments that teach large numbers of students yet also captures departments that teach few students but are critical to our substantive understanding of the educational task of universities. For example, English departments are central because they teach large numbers of undergraduates, but so are philosophy and classics departments, because faculty commonly agree that a university would not be a university without philosophy and classics departments even though these departments do not have large numbers of students. Centrality (CENTRAL) was measured by using the centrality score assigned to departments by the 1992 University-Wide

Quality Review Committee. Faculty committees explicitly charged with judging centrality to mission reviewed extensive documentation submitted by the various departments and assigned them scores of 0 (fails to meet criteria), 1 (meets criteria), and 2 (exceeds criteria).

Workflow

A second rational/political variable was departmental workflow productivity or workflow centrality (Ashar, 1987; Ashar & Shapiro, 1990). Workflow productivity sees departments as central even if they graduate few students, so long as they have a service function through which they offer courses to large numbers of students. For example, mathematics departments often do not graduate large numbers of majors but offer service courses such as introductory mathematics, calculus, and trigonometry. We measured departmental workflow productivity six ways: total student credit hours (TOTALSCH), the proportion of student credit hours taught at the lower division (PCTLDSCH), the proportion of student credit hours taught at the upper division (PCTUDSCH), the proportion of student credit hours taught at the graduate level (PCTGRSCH), number of full-time equivalent (STUFTE) students, and number of full time equivalent faculty (FACFTE).

Grants and Contracts

A third rational/political variable was grant and contract productivity (Ashar, 1987; Hackman, 1985) as measured by numbers of external dollars generated by the various departments (GRANTS). Grants and contracts comprised roughly one-third of the budgets of research universities and accounted for 34% of the annual operating budget of the institution under study. Researchers working from a rational/political frame saw departments with strong grants and contracts records as a rational choice for resource allocation because such investment strengthens departments' abilities to keep institutional operating budgets afloat. Institutions value departments' abilities to secure grants and contracts, especially in an era of federal decline in Research and Development (R&D) and volatility within federal R&D programs. However, critical theorists point out that not all departments have the same rich array of external resources available to them; those in science, math, engineering, and the health sciences are favored by federal grant and contract programs (Slaughter, 1997).

Department Quality

Departmental quality, a fourth rational/political variable, utilized two proxy measures. We again used external dollars in grants (GRANTS), which were generally highly competitive and peer reviewed, as one measure. The other measure was the quality score (QUALITY) assigned to each department by the 1992 University-Wide Institutional Resource Allocation 393 Quality Review Committee. As in the case of the centrality variable, faculty committees reviewed departmental materials and then rated departments with scores of 0 (does not meet criteria), 1 (meets criteria), and 2 (exceeds criteria). Like the grants and contract variable, the quality score is also a research productivity score. Number of publications and awards was the primary indicator in determination of quality rankings. The quality score is our only publication indicator because the university did not keep data on departmental or individual publication records.

Critical/Political Variables

Diversity

The primary critical/political variable was diversity of department. Diversity was measured four ways: numbers of male and female students (MALESTU and FEMSTU) by major, which we converted to departments; faculty gender (FEMFAC), using only full time equivalent faculty; ethnicity ("white" or other) of students by major (MINFAC), converted to departments; ethnicity ("white" or other) of faculty. For each measure, we calculated percentages (PCTFFAC and PCTMFAC) as well as raw numbers. Critical/political theorists argue that ascribed characteristics such as race or gender are reflective of economic and power divisions in the wider society and that they also play a part in determining who gets what in academe. They would expect departments with high numbers of women and minority faculty to receive fewer resources than others. Contrarily, rational/political theorists would make the case that resource allocation patterns are gender neutral because economy and efficiency are value-free and/or more important than ascribed characteristics.

Faculty and Student Resources

Secondary critical/political variables were the ratio of faculty to FTE faculty lines (FTERATIO) and an FTE student to FTE faculty line ratio (STUFACFT). The FTERATIO captures the use of off-track faculty, adjuncts, and departments' use of faculty from other departments in relation to full-time faculty within the department. Critical/political theorists would expect "have-not" or low-resourced departments to make use of large numbers of adjuncts or off-track faculty as cheap labor to produce SCH and argue that high use of adjunct faculty penalized departments by creating a heavier work load for-full time faculty who have correspondingly increased supervisory roles and committee assignments, reducing their ability to engage in other, more highly rewarded activities, such as research and grant and contract writing. Similarly, critical/political theories would expect high student to faculty ratios (STUFACFT) to result in decreased institutional resource allocations, because faculty in departments with high student to faculty ratios would not have time to engage in graduate education, research, and grant and contract activity.

Other Independent Variables

Closeness to Market

Because rational/political theorists are beginning to incorporate elements of human capital and labor market theory into their explanations of resource allocation to departments, we wanted to include variables that measured departments' closeness to the market. Human capital theorists take the position that the greater the market demand for particular types of expertise embodied in graduates, the higher their market value (Thurow, 1995). Therefore, the higher the salary for graduates, the greater the market demands for them, the higher the salary for the faculty who teach them, and the greater the resource allocation to the departments who teach them. Unpacked, the logic of this sequence of argument is as follows. Greater market demand for particular types of expertise drives up salaries in these fields. Graduates of such fields—for example, graduates in advanced computing—are offered many jobs at high starting salaries. To compete for candidates with these skills, universities must offer high salaries, especially for entry level positions. Given that salaries constitute the greatest share of departmental resources, departments that have to compete for faculty in fields with high external market demand need more resources.

Academic labor market theories offer[4] a somewhat different approach to market demand for expertise. Because they see demand for expertise as mediated by organizations, labor market theorists try to explain how organizational preferences order and shape supply and demand in specific markets (Spaeth, 1979; Stolzenberg, 1975; Tolbert, Patrick, & Beck, 1980). Their focus on market segmentation offers a challenge to human capital and rational/political theories. However, research on labor markets for academics looks neither at departments nor the concrete persons who work in departments, but instead focuses on allocation of faculty among various sectors (research universities, comprehensive universities, four-year colleges, community colleges), type of control (private versus public), and strata (elite versus non-elite) (Breneman & Youn, 1988; Tolbert, 1986; Youn, 1989). Nor does academic labor market theory examine empirically competition between universities and corporations for faculty who possess high-demand expertise, the crux of the rational/political and human capital arguments for differential salaries and, by extension, differential institutional resource allocation to departments.

Although feminist theorists concerned with academic labor deal with the same problems as labor market theorists, their work on faculty rarely intersects. Feminists, who are committed to understanding the salience of ascribed characteristics such as gender and ethnicity, include these variables in their approach to academic labor markets (Bellas, 1994, 1997; Tolbert, 1986), while academic labor market theorists generally do not (Youn, 1989).[5] Generally, feminist theorists found, all else equal, that "faculty in fields where women concentrate are paid less than comparable faculty in fields with comparable labor market conditions but with few women employees, . . . indicating discipline level discrimination" (Bellas, 1994, p. 816; see also Bellas, 1997). However, the Bellas studies, by far the most comprehensive to date, did not look at labor market segmentation, specifically at markets for research university faculty, nor did they look at institutional allocation to departments, which included more than salaries, nor at what we call "closeness to the market," which we take to be departments' position relative to the dynamic, high technology, private sector of the market, position relative to which usually predicts the highest salaries (Brint, 1994).

Although we were unable to look at competition among universities for research faculty because we studied only a single institution, we did develop variables for closeness to the market. Because we could locate no direct measures of closeness to the market, we used three proxy measures. The first was the average salary of baccalaureate recipients in their first jobs by department, which we refer to as student exit salary. We reasoned that high salaries would indicate high market demand. We could not find institutional data on exit salary, so we turned to the College Placement Council's national, annual salary summary of initial salary offers by curriculum area. We converted curriculum area to departments and used this information to calculate the average exit salaries of undergraduates by department (GRADSAL). The second proxy measure was initial salary of assistant professors (SALASST). In most studies of faculty compensation, seniority and stints in administration are the variables that most strongly predict high professorial salaries (Konrad & Pfeffer, 1990). These variables are internal to the institution and do not reflect free market competition. Assistant professor salaries are most likely to capture the value of professors on the open market because new PhDs have the option of taking a faculty or private sector position. We collected assistant professor salary data and computed average salaries for assistant professors by department. As a third measure we again used the number of grant and contract dollars generated by the various departments (GRANTS). We thought successful competition for grants and contracts measured the proximity of departments to federal research markets, which, in turn, might signal market competitiveness of departments in relation to research intensive corporations.

Many of the variables—grants, closeness to the market, student credit hours—are used to measure multiple constructs and figure in both rational/political and critical/political theories. For example, rational/political theorists argue that grants are measures of economic viability, scholarly productivity, and quality. They are an economic measure in that they bring external resources to the department, a productivity measure in that they indicate scholarly output, and a quality measure in that they are competitive and refereed. Critical/political theorists do not necessarily disagree with the rational/political theorists' line of argument, but would offer a different interpretation. They view grants as measures of economic productivity and quality but also see them as indicators of departmental closeness to federal research markets, proximity to which provides departments greater power in negotiating for internal resource allocations. Critical/political theorists also make the case that grants are only one of an array of quality measures and perhaps not the one that should be most heavily weighted, particularly if institutions are concerned with teaching and the production of undergraduate student credit hours or degrees. Because these variables are polyvalent, they acquire meaning only in the context of other variables deployed in complex arguments, which we hope to make in our subsequent discussion.

The data were gathered in Academic Year 1992–93. At that time, state allocations to the research university under study mirrored broad national trends, which were characterized by cut-backs at the state level (El Khawas, 1992; Gumport, 1993). We specified a multiple regression model to test the relationships implicit in the aforementioned theoretical perspectives; state allocation per department was the dependent measure. Because many of the measures used in the model exhibited relatively high intercorrelations (see appendix A) and the population being analyzed is relatively small ($N = 70$), special attention was paid to potentially problematic collinearity among the variables and to outliers that might be unduly influencing the parameters we report here. Parameter tolerances were assessed using a variance inflation factor (VIF) test derived from auxiliary regressions, condition indices were calculated, and the parameter variance was decomposed across each index. These tests indicated that collinearity was not a serious problem and that the data matrix was adequately conditioned for the analysis.[6] A residual analysis from the final model revealed four cases with absolute standardized residuals ranging from 2.23 to 2.79. Further analysis of these cases led us to conclude that they were not a threat to the estimates yielded by our final model.

Results

Our results are presented in four tables. Table 25.1 presents descriptive statistics on 14 key variables. Table 25.2 presents the OLS regression results from our final model. Table 25.3 displays key characteristics of the campus's 9 high quality-high centrality departments, while Table 25.4 presents key characteristics of the bottom and top 5 departments (non-high quality—non-high centrality), sorted by state dollar allocations.

Discussion

The OLS regression results in Table 25.2 do not fully support either the rational/political model or the critical/political model. Instead, they suggest that a rational/political interpretation works for some institutional missions and a critical/political model for others. When market variables are introduced, both interpretations become more complex.

Generally, the positive slopes reported in Table 25.2 support the rational/political model. The relatively small standard errors associated with most of these slopes suggest, except in the case of undergraduate degrees, that there is not a great deal of variance among departments on these variables. On average, for every $1000 in grants a department brings in, a department receives an extra $222 in state dollars, all else equal. Given that approximately one-third of the annual operating budgets of the top public research universities are comprised of federal grants and contracts, these are substantial multipliers of departmental resources. The grants variable is rational/political in that the institution provides resource allocations to units that bring in external funds and, because most grants are competitive and peer reviewed, rewards research quality as well. High centrality-high quality[7] units enjoyed substantial rewards relative to other units. On average, those departments viewed by the faculty as central to the university mission and as being of high quality received an extra $628,490, all else equal. Although this is the largest effect we have, the reward for quality as a lump sum, unmultiplied, so it is in most cases a smaller allocation than those for grants, graduate student credit hours, and the like. The high centrality-high quality variable fits well with the rational/political model in that the departments seen as most important to the university's mission and the departments highest in quality receive greater state resource allocations than others. The small proportion of departments meeting the high quality-high centrality criteria (13% or 9 departments) clearly enjoy substantial financial benefits.

Workflow, at least in terms of SCH and degrees granted, to some extent supports a rational/political model. Net of other variables in the final model, departments receive $82 for every SCH generated, which, given the approximately 35,000 students at the institution in question, is a substantial multiplier. A premium is placed on lower division SCH, however. The $82 per SCH return is adjusted downward $9,646 for each 1% increase in upper-division SCH. Although the concentration of state dollars at the lower division runs counter to the rational/political conception of educational costs increasing as subject matter complexity increases as students move from the freshman year though graduate school, a rational/political case could certainly be made for allocating more institutional resources to departments with large numbers of lower division students. Such a rational/political interpretation would probably stress that: (1) lower-division students are least likely to persist, so concentrating resources on departments that teach them would serve the retention function, ultimately increasing graduation rates; (2) lower-division students take the most service courses, and the departments that provide these need the resources to do the job. Moreover, such a reward structure could also be seen as an incentive to streamline student course-taking within the department (i.e., for undergraduate majors and graduate students) while creating multiple lower-division course-taking opportunities for students from outside the department.

TABLE 25.1

Mean, Standard Deviation, and Descriptions of Variables

Description of Variable	Mean	SD	Minimum	Maximum	Variable Names
Dependent Variable (N = 70 departments)					
State dollar allocation	$1,693,338.90	$1,068,092.10	$135,812.00	$5,149,621.00	STATEDOL
Rational/Political Variables					
High quality–High centrality department	0.13	0.34	0	1	HICNTQAL
Number of grad degrees awarded	20.02	22.01	0	106	GRADDEG
Number of undergrad degrees awarded	64.72	75.49	0	330	UGRADDEG
Total student credit hours (SCH) generated	5310.86	4968.61	183	26227	TOTALSCH
Percent SCH at lower division	43.11	24.87	0	92.29	PCTLDSCH
Percent SCH at upper division	36.32	21.24	1	100	PCTUDSCH
Percent SCH at graduate level	20.57	18.67	0	88	PCTGRSCH
Grants & contracts / 1000	$1,184.34	$1,538.74	0	$8,714.52	GRANTS
Critical/Political Variables					
Percent faculty that are female	29.32	23.14	0	100	PCTFFAC
Percent faculty that are non-white	10.89	11.80	0	56	PCTMFAC
FTE lines to department faculty	1.04	0.43	0.15	2.53	PTERATIO
FTE student to faculty ratio	18.93	8.20	6	41	STUFACFT
Other Variables					
Average assistant professor salary / 1000	$40.38	$7.39	$31.49	$65.94	SALASST
Average baccalaureate graduate salary / 1000	$24.81	$5.52	$18.58	$43.75	GRADSAL

TABLE 25.2

OLS Slopes of Rational & Critical Variables on Allocation of State Dollars

Variable	Unstandardized Slope	Standard Error	Standardized Slope	VIF Score
HICNTQAL	628490	199266	0.20	1.29
GRADDEG	17469	4309	0.36	2.58
UGRADDEG	1368	1161	0.10	2.20
TOTALSCH	82	20	0.38	2.86
PCTUDSCH	–9646	4261	–0.19	2.35
PCTGRSCH	–20836	5870	–0.36	3.44
GRANTS	222	51	0.32	1.77
PCTFFAC	– 1872	2909	–0.04	1.30
PCTMFAC	– 5241	5457	–0.06	1.19
FTERATIO	– 257922	154501	–0.10	1.29
STUFACFT	– 43110	10587	–0.33	2.16
SALASST	42351	11661	0.29	2.13
GRADSAL	– 29870	14730	–0.15	1.89
Intercept	1481990	550348		
Adjusted R^2	0.789			

However, conferring institutional resources on departments that teach large numbers of undergraduate students does not seem to translate in a straightforward way to undergraduate degree completion. On average, departments receive $1,368 for every undergraduate degree completed, a relatively modest amount compared to resources for lower division SCH.

The institutional resource allocation pattern is focused more on lower-division SCH than on undergraduate degree completion. This suggests, although does not explain, systemic productivity problems if undergraduate degree completion is the paramount institutional mission. This resource allocation pattern does not fit perfectly either the rational/political model or the critical/political model, because neither model specifies what is expected to occur at the lower and upper divisions, but it is perhaps closer to the critical/political in that process (course-taking) is rewarded rather than product (degree completion). Emphasis on course taking benefits faculty and institution by generating SCH, rather than benefitting students or their parents, who would presumably value undergraduate degree completion most highly. However, this view is somewhat tempered by the earlier observation concerning incentives for efficiencies in upper-division SCH production that are undoubtedly linked to degree production.

Graduate school involves departmental allocation processes that are quite different than those of undergraduate school. Departments generating larger proportions of their SCH at the graduate level find they experience an offset of $20,836 per 1% increase in graduate SCH. The penalty to graduate SCH is, of course, relative to lower division SCH and due in large part to the nature of graduate education. Unlike under-graduate SCH, especially at the lower division, most graduate SCH are within the department or program in which the graduate student has matriculated. Nor is there a large SCH multiplier at the graduate level. The penalty to graduate SCH is partially offset by the return to graduate degrees, which is approximately 12 times greater than the return to under-graduate degrees. Graduate education is product centered, emphasizing completed degrees

TABLE 25.3

Detailed Description of High Centrality–High Quality Departments (sorted by total state dollars received)

Department	Allocation	Grad. Degrees	UG Degrees	Asst. Prof. Salaries	Grants	% Female Faculty	% Min. Faculty	Total SCH	% SCH Upper Div	% SCH Lower Div	Students to Faculty	Faculty FTE Ratio
Pharmic. Sci.	$725,010	4	0	$50,032	$522,140	38	4	883	78	22	8	2.53
Hydrology	$1,293,609	20	9	$45,044	$2,769,984	7	21	1676	11	59	11	1.00
Art	$2,460,583	28	139	$31,486	$12,270	48	10	9186	34	11	17	1.14
Nursing	$2,693,291	35	85	$38,000	$1,867,531	100	8	3891	57	25	7	1.14
Psychology	$2,725,326	27	298	$36,000	$3,515,027	37	5	14515	42	8	26	0.96
Anthropology	$3,104,915	26	89	$35,667	$1,549,983	32	8	8779	37	15	18	0.98
Geological Sci.	$3,349,032	19	16	$36,680	$2,430,678	9	9	3808	14	23	9	0.97
Music	$3,705,301	31	46	$32,034	$160,079	30	12	9467	29	17	13	0.99
Astronomy	$4,313,180	37	8	$37,220	$8,714,516	0	0	5917	3	5	36	0.61

TABLE 25.4

Detailed Description of Non-High Centrality–Non-High Quality Departments (sorted by total state dollars received)

Department	Allocation	Grad. Degrees	UG Degrees	Asst. Prof. Salaries	Grants	% Female Faculty	% Min. Faculty	Total SCH	% SCH Upper Div	% SCH Lower Div	Students to Faculty	Faculty FTE Ratio
Bottom 5 in Terms of Dollar Allocation												
Judaic St.	$135,812	0	5	$40,370	$14,449	25	0	579	61	0	17	1.57
Med. Tech.	$263,764	0	3	$41,370	$0	100	0	327	100	0	7	1.00
Agric. Educ.	$395,600	6	9	$44,510	$332,854	0	0	596	73	16	20	1.60
Statistics	$449,067	3	0	$38,000	$40,000	29	29	2986	12	14	35	1.12
Journalism	$558,058	16	66	$33,690	$91,716	29	10	2628	38	12	22	2.26
Top 5 in Terms of Dollar Allocation												
Chemistry	$3,234,861	31	21	$36,329	$5,570,259	8	8	14014	9	7	15	0.56
Physics	$3,308,575	21	25	$39,363	$2,948,320	2	12	8672	11	10	13	0.91
Math	$4,053,120	26	42	$39,378	$2,410,747	26	14	26227	10	6	22	1.25
ECE	$4,162,881	83	138	$46,325	$4,585,782	9	11	7001	41	32	13	0.93
English	$5,149,621	82	160	$33,071	$639,148	45	8	24681	30	8	19	0.98

and the winning of federal grants and contracts. Undergraduate education, as we noted previously, is process-oriented: SCH is accumulated without degrees and grants.

There is a marked contrast between the resources allocated for completion of undergraduate and graduate degrees. While for every under-graduate degree granted a department receives $1,368, on average, departments receive $17,469 for every graduate degree they award. The rational/political model would expect the difference between undergraduate and graduate degrees because graduate education is more expensive due to greater subject matter complexity and greater student performance demands, which call for closer supervision of graduate students, all of which demands lower student to faculty ratios, which, of course, greatly increase costs. However, the rational/political model might not expect the very high dollar difference between graduate and undergraduate education that we found in Table 25.2. The differences in resource allocation to graduate and undergraduate degrees suggests that large public research universities have multiple and perhaps conflicting missions.

Like the rational/political model, the critical/political model predicts a difference between undergraduate and graduate degrees, but it would offer an alternative explanation. Rather than seeing graduate education as more expensive and the substantial dollar amount given for graduate students as functional, the critical/political model would see the high state dollar allocations of our model as excessive, unduly benefitting graduate students at the expense of undergraduates. The very large dollar difference between undergraduate and graduate degree completion may fit better with a critical/political than a rational/political interpretation.

Average assistant professor salaries, which we took to be a variable representing closeness of department to external markets, were consistent with market models. On average, for every $1000 increase is assistant professor salary, a department received an extra $42,351. Departments with high assistant professor salaries may be sufficiently resourced to put together more attractive packages to attract "hot" young professors, packages which include computers, laboratories and equipment, research assistants, and research support.

The negative slopes in Table 25.2 tell a somewhat different story, one that to some degree supports a critical/political model. We took the average salary of undergraduates on their first job after graduation, which we call student exit salary, as a variable indicating closeness of departments to external labor markets. Counterintuitive to market models, for every increase of $1000 to salary received by students on their first jobs, departments lost $29,870. When taken in conjunction with salary of assistant professor, another measure of closeness to external markets, institutions seem to be rewarding markets for faculty rather than markets for students. This suggests that institutions do not have a single market but multiple, and perhaps competing markets.

The variables associated with the critical/political model, percentage of female and minority faculty, confirm the expectation that departments with large numbers of women and large numbers of minorities receive less resources than other departments. This observation must be qualified by the large standard errors associated with these slopes which suggests that across departments there exists substantial variance in this association. For every increase in percentage of faculty who are female, departments lose $1,872. For every increase in the percentage of faculty who are racial minorities, departments lose $5,241. As noted above, there is great variation among departments on this measure.

The FTE ratio is the ratio of faculty headcount to the lines held by a department. This compares number of total faculty to the number of lines a department has, letting us see how the departments are rewarded when they use other than full-time, tenure-track faculty. For every line not held by a full-time, tenure-track faculty, departments lose $257,922. This finding suggests that departments that make heavy use of adjunct, part-time or off-track faculty or that are interdisciplinary, drawing heavily on faculty from other departments, are penalized in terms of state resource allocations.

The rational/political model does not specify use of nontrack faculty. The critical/political model sees the use of nontrack faculty as undercutting organizational stability, increasing the work load of track faculty, and generally substituting cheap labor for (appropriately) high salaried professional work. Contrarily, market theorists would interpret nontrack faculty, adjuncts and part-timers as a way of containing the costs and (appropriately) lowering resources to departments because the largest fixed cost within universities are faculty salaries.

The student FTE to faculty line ratio tells us that for every additional student per faculty line a department has, the department loses $43,110. In other words, the larger the faculty's student load, the fewer resources a department receives. As with the FTE faculty to line ratio, critical and market theorists would expect high faculty teaching loads to be unrewarded: these departments contain labor costs by hiring relatively few faculty relative to their student numbers and make heavy use of inexpensive adjunct faculty. However, critical/political theorists would condemn these practices as exploiting both faculty and students. Labor market theorists would see high student to faculty ratios as economies of scale. Conversely, rational/political models would expect departments with large student loads to receive more resources to facilitate workflow, an expectation our data do not confirm.

Overall, Table 25.2 suggests that there are at least two patterns for departmental resource allocation. One pattern generally fits the rational/political model in that departments that generate external funds, are central to SCH workflow, are high centrality-high quality, and confer a substantial number of graduate degrees receive high allocations of state dollars. The anomalies are concentration of resources at the lower division level and relatively low rewards for undergraduate degree completion, net of all other factors in the model. The other pattern is closer to the critical/political model, in which departments that have high percentages of female or minority faculty, use large numbers of off-track faculty, and have high student to faculty ratios receive lower state dollar allocations. However, there are a number of findings—such as loss of resources for upper-division student credit hours—that fit neither model and can be interpreted variously, depending on their relation to other variables.

Tables 25.3 and 25.4 allow us to see how the regression results in Table 25.2 play out in specific departments. Table 25.3 describes the 9 high quality-high centrality departments (recall that these departments enjoyed an average allocation premium of $624,490). Table 25.4 considers only those departments that failed to meet the campuses high quality-high centrality criteria and describes the 5 departments that receive the fewest state dollar allocations as well as the 5 departments that receive the most, allowing us to see the extremes.

Because Tables 25.3 and 25.4 are descriptive rather than analytic, we can use them only for illustrative purposes. We comment briefly on two departmental "Fat Cats" and then look at two departmental "Cash Cows" that are relatively unrewarded for their undergraduate labor.

The first of our Fat Cats is Astronomy, the last department ($4,313,180 in state dollars) in Table 25.3. Astronomy illustrates the (male) rational political model that rewards use of full time faculty, relatively large numbers of graduate students and high grant and contract dollars. Although the department teaches few upper division students and produces few undergraduate degrees, it nonetheless contributes to undergraduate education, producing large numbers of lower division student credit hours by teaching large service courses taken by students in the first few years. Indeed, this department may have a strategy of leveraging state dollars through large, nonfaculty intensive undergraduate courses while simultaneously leveraging federal grant and contract dollars through faculty intensive research and graduate education.

Our second Fat Cat is Chemistry ($3,234,861 in state resource allocations), which appears fifth among the top 5 departments. Much like Astronomy, Chemistry capitalizes on the rational political model that rewards the use of full-time faculty, relatively large numbers of graduate students, and high grant and contract dollars. Chemistry generates a relatively large number of SCH with the vast majority (84%) at the lower division level. A notable difference between Chemistry and Astronomy is the former's low student to faculty ratio—something we would expect to see from a laboratory intensive department. While obviously larger than Astronomy, Chemistry generates about 1/3 less extramural grant and contract dollars. This amount is, however, still quite large and may also be used as leverage for state dollars for the department. It is quite clear from the large proportion of graduate degrees awarded and the significant extramural funding received that, despite the large proportion of lower division SCH produced, the Chemistry department prizes research and graduate programs.

Our first Cash Cow is Psychology ($2,725,326 in state allocations), the sixth department in Table 25.3. Psychology is in many ways a model, hard working but relatively underresourced department. From our model in Table 25.2 it is clear how Psychology's emphasis on undergraduate degrees (which also entails a commitment to less well rewarded upper division SCH) is a less lucrative enterprise than the graduate degree and lower-division SCH emphasis of the "Fat Cats" considered above. Psychology also loses money for its relatively high percentage of female faculty. And of course, it loses due to its high student to faculty ratio. Its grants and contracts are at best a wash, considering its other liabilities. Yet, as we noted, Psychology produces more undergraduate degrees than any other displayed department.

Our second Cash Cow is Journalism ($558,058), the fifth of the bottom 5 departments. Journalism is very much like Psychology, except that is has fewer grants, and makes much greater use of adjunct faculty. Like Psychology, Journalism loses money for its relatively high percentage of female faculty and also for its relatively high percentage of minority faculty.

Our Fat Cats and Cash Cows suggest that some departments are better able than others to develop strategies for accruing resources. (Male) Fat Cat departments close to federal research markets (Astronomy, Chemistry) appear to be able to use grant funds to leverage state funds for more institutional resources. These departments serve lower division undergraduate students in service courses, for which they also receive relatively large amounts of institutional resources. Apparently these departments use their institutional resources to build their graduate programs, for which they then receive a premium for degrees completed. (Female) Cash Cows show that departments that award more undergraduate than graduate degrees (Psychology, Journalism), are far from federal grant and contract markets, and have high percentages of upper-division SCH are not as able to accrue institutional resources. Departments powerfully mediate individual academics' chances to receive institutional resources.

Conclusion

Looking at departments rather than at individuals or broad fields of study lets us see more clearly how state resources are associated with a range of variables used to explain institutional resource allocation. Looking at state resources rather than all resources was important because we were able to separate funds earmarked for research from moneys that traditionally have funded the core instructional mission (Gladieux, Hauptman, & Knapp, 1994). Departments were an appropriate unit of analysis because they are the organizational unit where the work of teaching, research and service are done, and they capture the way knowledge is organized.[8] We showed that departments powerfully mediate individuals' ability to accrue institutional resources. Funding for departments characterized by (male), full-time faculty, graduate degrees, grants, and contracts tend to be more highly resourced than departments characterized by (female) faculty, high (female) adjunct use, undergraduate SCH, particularly at the upper division level, and undergraduate degree granting.

None of the current models of resource allocation to departments—rational/political, critical/political, and market—fully explains resource allocation patterns. These models rely on underlying concepts of mission and market that may no longer be appropriate. Our conception of mission, first formulated in the last quarter of the nineteenth century, is rigid, unexamined, simplistic, and probably unsuited to the large, complex, bureaucratic organizations public research universities have become. Then, mission was conceived of as teaching, research, and service, the proportion of graduate to undergraduate students was very small, and most faculty were teachers who lacked PhDs and seldom engaged in research. Now, the numbers of graduate students have increased, most faculty have PhDs, and the time faculty devote to research has increased. (We never had measures for service, which also points to problems in our resource allocation models: how can we allocate rationally without performance measures?) Our study points to differentiation and conflict between undergraduate and graduate missions and points to why public research universities may have systemic productivity problems in undergraduate degree production.

Colleges and universities often try to clarify missions by focusing on markets. But markets are, like missions, multiple, complex and sometimes conflicting. As our study points out, the market(s) for newly degreed students may be very different from the market(s) for faculty, even when those faculty are assistant professors and are themselves relatively newly degreed. Instead, there are district and separate markets for faculty and for undergraduate students with newly completed degrees. Sometimes the markets for faculty are shaped by departmental proximity to federal research markets. There is not a linear market logic that dictates how state dollars are allocated to departments, so we cannot rely exclusively on market models.

We need to rethink our models of resource allocation as well as our ideas about mission and market. To do this, we will have to refine the categories we now use: for example, rather than teaching, we need to reconceptualize around lower-division teaching, upper-division teaching, and graduate education. We need to think about how teaching relates to degree completion and how that should be rewarded. Degree completion probably needs further refinement. For example, we did not distinguish between Master's degrees and PhDs, even though we suspect Master's degrees may be the Cash Cows of graduate education. When we think about research, we have to factor in how close departments are to federal research markets—in other words, are there substantial federal programs that can support research in the field—and if not, we have to decide whether to compensate such departments rather than penalize them. We have to conceptualize and operationalize service, something that has not yet been done. We also have to explore the growing resource gaps among departments and colleges, to understand how great they are and how we want to manage internal disparities by field. Finally, we have to include social justice measures: race, class, gender.

In other words, we need to break open the models of resource allocation we have used in the past because these are no longer adequate to complex, bureaucratic institutions with multiple missions and multiple markets. Faculty from various departments—whether in senates, or other forums—need to participate with institutional researchers and administrators in building these new models. Only by including faculty grounded in departments, which powerfully mediate resource allocation, will we be able to create understanding and commitment on the part of the university community to resource allocation processes.

APPENDIX A

Correlation Matrix ($N = 70$)

	STATEDOL	GRADDEG	UGRADDEG	GRADSAL	SALASST	GRANTS	PCTFFAC	PCTMFAC	TOTALSCH	PCTUDSCH	PCTGRSCH	HICNTQAL	STUFACFT
STATEDOL	1.0000												
GRADDEG	0.3770	1.0000											
UGRADDEG	0.2594	0.0753	1.0000										
GRADSAL2	–0.0334	–0.0496	–0.1557	1.0000									
SALASST2	–0.0201	–0.2609	0.0530	0.4878	1.0000								
GRANTS2	0.56[illegible]8	0.2558	–0.1151	0.2238	0.0895	1.0000							
PCTFFAC	–0.1795	0.1431	0.0477	–0.1713	–0.2274	–0.2869	1.0000						
PCTMFAC	0.0031	0.0265	0.1280	0.0835	0.2264	–0.1462	–0.0215	1.0000					
TOTALSCH	0.6635	0.3501	0.4980	–0.2507	–0.2412	0.1241	–0.0224	0.1023	1.0000				
PCTUDSCH	–0.2243	–0.1689	0.3245	0.1491	0.3077	–0.2595	0.1849	–0.0138	–0.1703	1.0000			
PCTGRSCH	–0.2235	0.4046	–0.3582	0.2939	0.1415	0.0885	0.0345	0.0045	–0.4368	–0.2281			
HICNTQAL	0.3675	0.0914	0.0612	0.0744	–0.1238	0.3040	0.0686	–0.0715	0.0893	–0.0447	–0.0004	1.0000	
STUFACFT	0.0058	0.0019	0.4071	–0.4901	–0.1348	–0.0444	0.0300	–0.0065	0.3256	–0.0903	–0.4437	–0.1401	1.0000
FTERATIO	–0.2911	0.1456	–0.0571	0.0758	–0.0883	–0.1684	0.1105	–0.0319	–0.1766	0.1861	0.1556	0.0929	–0.0069

Notes

1. The one exception to this was the Women's Studies Department, which was excluded because it was in its first year as a department and had only one faculty FTE allocated to it. We chose not to include departments within the medical school for several reasons. First, many public Research I universities, the category of institution we are examining, do not have medical schools. Second, medical schools have a disproportionate share of grant and contract dollars, given the great increases in funding by the National Institutes of Health in recent years, and we thought this would distort the effects of grants and contracts. Third, medical schools have an anomalous faculty-student ratio, often as low as one to one, which would again distort effects for the sample as a whole. Departments within the law school were also excluded, for no undergraduates are taught within this college.
2. These scholars generally draw on that body of theory that focuses on race, class, and gender but often do not attend to day-to-day organizational politics, nor do they often employ quantitative data. For the political and quantitative dimension of the critical/political model, we draw heavily on feminist theorists who deal with issues of women and work, usually through quantitative data. (See Bellas, 1994, 1997; Bellas & Reskin, 1994; England, 1992; Pfeffer & Davis-Blake, 1987; Reskin, 1988; Reskin & Roos, 1990; Tolbert, 1986.)
3. Our measure of state allocation per department is extremely conservative. We excluded overhead from federal grants and contracts from state dollars because the source was federal, not state. A substantial portion of the federal overheads, of course, accrue to the departments that win the grants and contracts, greatly increasing their departmental resources. The university central administration retains a portion of the overhead derived from each federal grant and spends the monies without restriction. The central administration's share of overheads may be reinvested in the very same departments or like departments that initially generated the grants, further concentrating resources on these departments.
4. Academic labor market theories attempt to bring together human capital theories from economics and status attainment theories from sociology, but as Breneman (1988) points out, the two are as yet uneasily married, and neither inspects the linkages between academic labor markets and markets for scientists and professionals in the wider society (Breneman & Youn, 1988).
5. In the Breneman and Youn (1988) volume, the most recent and comprehensive treatment of academic labor markets, gender is examined in only one article other than the single piece that addresses gender specifically. The Barbezat article, in that volume, focuses on and finds salary discrimination, as do all studies of salary differences between men and women in academe, but is cautiously optimistic about the reduction of discrimination over time (1968–1977), an interpretation not supported by more recent data (Bellas & Reskin, 1994). As Barbezat herself notes, her models examined only differences in relation of rewards to faculty characteristics, and as specified, cannot include gender differences in publication rates, nor institutional and departmental affiliations, all of which mediate the relation between faculty characteristics and rewards. Barbezat uses econometric models derived from the Oaxaca decompositions, which place a different set of constraints on the data than do the regression equations used by feminist researchers such as England (1992), Bellas (1994, 1997), and others. The implications of the differences between these approaches deserve further exploration.
6. All VIF scores were below 5, and no condition index exceeded 30. These thresholds are shown to be viable in Belsey, Kuh, and Welsch (1980).
7. Because quality and centrality were highly collinear in our preliminary models we combined these two variables in our final analysis.
8. The role of centers and institutes in relation to departmental workload remains unclear. The few studies that separate centers and institutes from departments suggest they are much more closely associated with research than with teaching (Brooks, 1996).

References

Ashar, H. (1987). *Internal and external factors and their effect on a university's retrenchment decisions: Two theoretical perspectives*. Unpublished doctoral dissertation, University of Washington, Seattle.

Ashar, H., & Shapiro, J. W. (1990). Are retrenchment decisions rational? *Journal of Higher Education*, 61, 121–141.

Barbezat, D. (1988). Gender differences in the academic reward system. In D. W. Breneman & T. I. K. Youn (Eds.), *Academic labor markets and careers* (pp. 138–164). New York: The Falmer Press.

Bellas, M. L. (1994). Comparable worth in academia: The effects of faculty salaries on the sex composition and labor market conditions of academic disciplines. *American Sociology Review*, 59, 807–821.

Bellas, M. L. (1997). Disciplinary differences in faculty salaries: Does gender bias play a role? *Journal of Higher Education*, 68, 299–321.

Bellas, M. L., & Reskin, B. F. (1994, September-October). On comparable worth. *Academe*, 83–85.

Belsey, D. A., Kuh, E., & Welsch, R. E. (1980). *Regression diagnostics: Identifying influential data and sources of multicollinearity*. New York: Wiley.

Breneman, D. W. (1988). Research on academic labor markets: Past and future. In D. W. Breneman & T. I. K. Youn (Eds.), *Academic labor markets and careers* (pp. 200–208). New York: The Falmer Press.

Breneman, D. W., & Youn, T. I. K. (Eds). (1988). *Academic labor markets and careers*. Philadelphia: The Falmer Press.

Brinkman, P. (1990). Higher education cost function. In S. A. Hoenack & E. I. Collins (Eds.), *The economics of American universities*. Albany, NY: SUNY Press.

Brint, S. G. (1994). *In an age of experts: The changing role of professionals in politics and public life*. Princeton, NJ: Princeton University Press.

Brooks, H. (1996). Evolution of U.S. science policy. In Bruce Smith & Claude Barfield (Eds.), *Technology, R&D, and the economy* (pp, 15–48). Washington, DC: The Brookings Institution and the American Enterprise Institute for Public Policy Research.

Carnegie Foundation for the Advancement of Teaching. (1994). *A classification of institutions of higher education*. Princeton, NJ: Author.

Chickering, A., & Gamson, Z. (1987). Seven principles for good practice in undergraduate education. *AAHE Bulletin*, 39, 3–7.

Dundar, H., & Lewis, D. R. (1994). Departmental productivity in American universities: Economies of scale and scope. *Economics of Education Review*, 14(2), 119–144.

El-Khawas, E. (1992). *Campus trends: 1992*. Washington, DC: American Council on Education.

England, P. (1992). *Comparable worth: Theories and evidence*. New York: Aldine de Gruyter.

Fairweather, J. S. (1996). *Faculty work and the public trust: Restoring the value of teaching and public service in American academic life*. Boston: Allyn and Bacon.

Gladieux, L. E., Hauptman, A. M., & Knapp, L. G. (1994). The federal government and higher education. In P. G. Altbach, R. O. Berdahl, & P. J. Gumport, *Higher education in American society* (3rd ed., pp. 125–154). Amherst, NY: Prometheus Books.

Gumport, P. J. (1993). The contested terrain of academic program reduction. *Journal of Higher Education*, 64, 283–31 1.

Gumport, P. J., & Pusser, B. (1996). Academic restructuring: Contemporary adaptation in higher education. In M. Peterson, D. Dill, & L. Mets (Eds.), *Planning strategies for the new millennium*. San Francisco: Jossey-Bass.

Guskin, A. (1994). Part II: Restructuring the role of faculty. *Change*, 26, 23–29.

Hackman, J. (1985). Power and centrality in the allocation of resources in colleges and universities. *Administrative Science Quarterly*, 30, 61–77.

Kerlin, S., & Dunlap, D. (1993). For richer, for poorer: Faculty morale in periods of austerity and retrenchment. *Journal of Higher Education*, 64, 348–377.

Konrad, A. M., & Pfeffer, J. (1990). Do you get what you deserve? Factors affecting the relationship between productivity and pay. *Administrative Science Quarterly*, 35(2), 258–85.

Layzell, D. T. (1996). Faculty workload and productivity: Recurrent issues and new imperatives. *Review of Higher Education*, 19, 267–281.

Lee, B. A., Leslie, D. W., & Olswang, S. G. (1987). Implications of comparable worth for academe. *Journal of Higher Education*, 58, 609–628.

Leslie, L. L., & Rhoades, G. (1995). Rising administrative costs: Seeking explanations. *Journal of Higher Education*, 66, 187–212.

Leslie, S. (1993). *The Cold War and American science: The military-industrial-academic complex at MIT and Stanford*. New York: Columbia.

Levin, H. M. (1991). Raising productivity in higher education. *Journal of Higher Education*, 62, 241–262.

McElrath, K. (1992). Gender, career disruption, and academic rewards. *Journal of Higher Education*, 63, 269–281.

Massy, W. F., Wilger, A. (1992, Winter). Productivity in postsecondary education: A new approach. *Educational Evaluation and Policy Analysis*, 14, 361–76.

Massy, W. F., & Zemsky, R. (1994). Faculty discretionary time: Departments and the 'academic rachet.' *Journal of Higher Education*, 65, 1–22.

Melchiori, G. (1982). Smaller and better: The University of Michigan experience. *Research in Higher Education*, 16, 55–69.

Morgan, A. W. (1983). The new strategies: Roots, context and overview. In A. W. Morgan (Ed.), *Responding to new realities in funding*. San Francisco: Jossey-Bass.

Pfeffer, J., & Davis-Blake, A. (1987). The effect of the proportion of women on salaries: The case of college administrators. *Administrative Science Quarterly*, 32, 1–24.

Reskin, B. F. (1988). Bringing the men back in: Sex differentiation and the devaluing of women's work. *Gender and Society*, 2, 58–81.

Reskin, B. F., & Roos, P. A. (1990). *Job queues, gender queues*. Philadelphia: Temple University Press.

Slaughter, S. (1993). Retrenchment in the 1980s: The politics of prestige and gender. *Journal of Higher Education*, 64, 250–282.

Slaughter, S. (1997). Class, race, gender, and the construction of postsecondary curricula in the Unites States: Social movement, professionalization, and political economic theories of curricular change. *Journal of Curriculum Studies*, 29(1), 1–30.

Slaughter, S. (1998). Federal policy and supply-side institutional resource allocation at public research universities. *Review of Higher Education*, 21, 209–244.

Slaughter, S., & Leslie, L. L. (1997). *Academic capitalism: Politics, policies and the entrepreneurial university*. Baltimore: The Johns Hopkins University Press.

Spaeth, J. L. (1979). Vertical differentiation among occupations. *American Sociological Review*, 49, 746–762.

Stolzenberg, R. M. (1975). Occupations, labor markets, and the process of wage attainments. *American Sociological Review*, 40, 645–665.

Thurow, L. (1995). *The future of capitalism*. New York: W. Morrow & Co.

Tolbert, C. M., Patrick, M., & Beck, E. M. (1980). The structure of economic segmentation: A dual economy approach. *American Journal of Sociology*, 80, 1–10.

Tolbert, P. (1986). Organizations and inequality: Sources of earnings differences between male and female faculty. *Sociology of Education*, 59, 227–235.

Volk, C. (1995). *Assessing competing models of resource allocation at a public research university through multivariate analysis of state financing*. Unpublished doctoral dissertation, Center for the Study of Higher Education, University of Arizona, Tucson, AZ.

Youn, T. I. K. (1989). Effects of academic labor markets on academic career. In J. C. Smart (Ed.), *Higher education: Handbook of theory and research* (Vol. 5, pp. 134–154). New York: Agathon.

SECTION V

HIGHER EDUCATION EXPENDITURES

Introduction to Section V

Stewart E. Sutin, John L. Yeager, and Kristin M. DeLuca
University of Pittsburgh

Cost containment, budget management, and resource allocation are among the major and most visible challenges faced by higher education. The articles contained in this section offer valuable insights into the inner sanctum of operations management. Perhaps no area of higher education is the source of more contested ideas and conjecture. The articles included in this section should help restore a measure of reason and observations based upon bodies of evidence.

Cunningham and Merisotis ("National Models for College Costs and Prices") build from the work of the 1998 National Commission on the Cost of Higher Education. The structure of higher education finance is distinctly different from that of a private for-profit firm and is not widely understood outside the education sector. This current study examines relationships among college prices, expenditures, and revenue streams within various groups of colleges and universities that are all degree granting and Title IV participating institutions with the goal of addressing the extent to which spending patterns contribute to tuition increases.

Derrico ("Budget Development Process for Community Colleges") was an accomplished senior administrator in community colleges, having served Miami Dade for many years before assuming the position of Vice Chancellor for Administration and Finance at Alamo Community College (San Antonio), where he also served as Interim Chancellor. He offers the practitioner a sound guide to budget preparation, content, and the review and approval processes. Derrico includes practical considerations for creating a budget that serves as a critical institutional financial planning and management instrument.

Guckert and King ("The High Cost of Building a Better University") received an award from the APPA Leadership in Educational Facilities organization for their article. The authors, senior leadership in facilities at the University of Iowa, explain the various elements and decisions involved in building higher education facilities. They argue that higher education facilities come at a premium cost due to appropriate and strategic high aspirations that stem from an institution's vision and strategic plan.

Laband and Lentz ("Do Costs Differ between For-Profit and Not-for-Profit Producers of Higher Education?") argue that, in theory, not-for-profit organizations will be characterized by higher production costs per unit of output than for-profit producers of otherwise-identical goods/services, since profit maximization implies cost minimization per unit of output. Using 1996 data, these authors estimate multi-product cost functions for 1,450 public, 1,316 private, not-for-profit, and 176 private, for-profit institutions of higher education in the United States. They find that publics produce more cheaply than private, not-for-profit institutions, but no statistically significant difference occurs between costs of for-profit and not-for-profit private providers.

McPherson and Shulenburger ("Understanding the Cost of Public Higher Education") assert that, in the case of higher education costs, diametrically opposed views have persisted over time. They describe the public research university as having two sectors: 1) a business-like, self-supporting set of activities whose costs must be covered by their revenues (auxiliaries, clinics, athletics, technology transfer, externally funded research, and similar activities), and 2) an education sector (state appropriations, tuition, gifts, and endowment earnings). Generally, state funds either are not appropriated to support the business sector or are appropriated only for a specific purpose (e.g., to fund a research-related economic development activity). States clearly have an interest in cost increases in the education sector. Through presentation of federal data, the authors show that educational costs have been stable over time and any increases that have occurred are largely a reflection of decreasing state appropriations. Further, those cost increases cannot be covered fully by generating additional revenues from the business side.

With costs increasing faster that per capita income, many institutions are increasingly relying on endowment funds to meet their needs. Michael ("The Cost of Excellence: The Financial Implications of Institutional Rankings") examines the relationship between endowment funds and variables associated with institutional rankings as determined by the *U.S. News & World Report*. The author argues that it is important for institutions to be careful about engaging in a pursuit of rankings, as the variables are cost-inducing factors.

A careful examination of higher education cost and price dynamics is provided by Middaugh ("Understanding Higher Education Costs"). The author, then an assistant vice president for institutional research and planning, presents an article that addresses the misunderstood concepts of cost versus price in higher education. The analysis supports a finding that higher education has been fiscally responsible, but that institutions need to be more proactive and transparent about their fiscal and human resources, as well as how they are utilized.

CHAPTER 26

NATIONAL MODELS FOR COLLEGE COSTS AND PRICES

ALISA F. CUNNINGHAM AND JAMIE P. MERISOTIS

In 1998, the National Commission on the Cost of Higher Education reported on an intensive six-month study of the trends and causes of tuition increases, which included a review of national research in addition to the commission's own investigation information. The commission explained that published tuition and fees had been increasing faster than inflation in both the public and private not-for-profit sectors and that expenditures were also increasing, but generally at a lower rate than prices. It was, however, unable to reach definitive conclusions about the root causes for the price increases due to the limited time frame for the study and the lack of available data to allow these questions to be addressed. The issue of the relationships among costs, revenues, and prices remains a salient one.

The goal of this study was to build on the commission's work by examining various relationships in order to address the extent to which spending patterns are contributing to tuition increases in higher education. The study, conducted for the National Center for Education Statistics, had two broad components: (1) a series of commissioned expert papers, discussed at a national invitational meeting and (2) empirical analyses of costs and prices in both the public and the private not-for-profit sectors.[1]

The commissioned papers and national meeting set the framework for the subsequent empirical analyses by reaching several conclusions about the structure of higher education finance, which differs substantially from the economics of a private for-profit firm. Most higher education institutions receive revenue from many sources, allowing them to supplement revenue from tuition. As a result, the price that most students pay does not cover the average costs of their education, and costs are generally only one of the factors influencing pricing decisions. At the same time, public and private not-for-profit institutions operate differently in terms of their revenue sources and the amount of political influence on decisions about tuition and enrollment levels: state and local government policies have far greater influence on decisions at public institutions than at private not-for-profit institutions. Thus, the factors associated with pricing decisions in the two sectors can be quite different. Given the complexity of the issue, it is important to keep these characteristics in mind when trying to understand college costs and prices.

The empirical analyses of costs and prices, conducted separately for public and private not-for-profit institutions, are the focus of this article and are explained below in greater detail. Broadly, the first step in the analyses was to compile aggregate trends in tuition, enrollment, revenues, and expenditures in order to provide some context. Subsequently, these data were examined in more detail through the use of statistical modeling techniques. Rather than breaking new ground, the analyses relied upon current knowledge of appropriate models. Therefore, previously developed models for the public and private not-for-profit sectors were identified and updated with more recent data. In each of these models, the associations between "sticker prices" (published tuition levels) and costs, revenues, and other factors were explored to expand upon previous studies and provide some insight into the nature of higher education finance.

Design and Methodology

The statistical analyses described here target tuition levels for full-time undergraduate students and focus on higher education institutions that are both degree granting and Title IV participating. To an extent, this focus is necessitated by limited information on non-degree-granting postsecondary institutions, particularly in the private for-profit and corporate sectors, and the difficulty of breaking down revenue and expenditure data by level of student. In addition, it is standard practice in cost studies to construct comparable groups of institutions for analysis; therefore, the criteria used in this report are consistent with those used in prior studies. All analyses were performed separately for seven groups of higher education institutions, based on public/private control of the institution and, for four-year institutions, Carnegie classification. The final groups include three categories of private not-for-profit institutions (research/doctoral, comprehensive, and bachelor's institutions) and four categories of public institutions (research/doctoral, comprehensive, bachelor's, and two-year institutions).[2]

To provide context for the statistical modeling and explore the comparative changes of categories over time, trend data on expenditures, revenues, enrollment, and prices were calculated for the period 1988–89 to 1995–96 (to 1997–98 for public institutions) for each group of institutions. These data include average, inflation-adjusted dollar changes over the whole period, average annual percentage changes, and shifts in the composition of revenues and expenditures.

In examining the relationships between variables, different statistical models were used for the public and private not-for-profit sectors, because research has consistently documented fundamental differences in the financing structures, enrollment markets, and tuition decision-making processes between the sectors.[3] Public institutions are heavily subsidized with state (and sometimes local) tax dollars, and pricing decisions are policy decisions shared between state governments and institutional governing boards, with tuition revenues often treated as offsets to state appropriation levels. For many public institutions, decisions about student enrollment also are made at the state level, with the individual institutions responsible for developing admissions policies that are consistent with these goals. As a result, enrollment demand at public institutions is determined less by market conditions, including price, than are enrollments at private not-for-profit institutions. At private not-for-profit institutions, price-setting decisions are influenced by internal budget considerations. However, they are more likely than at public institutions to be influenced by external market factors of the environments in which they operate, including competition from other institutions, the income levels of potential consumers, perceptions of quality and institutional reputation, and other factors. In addition, private not-for-profit institutions tend to have substantial control over their admissions policies. Given the differences in the models and the theories behind them, the variables included in the models for the two sectors differ slightly.

It is important to keep in mind that the analyses in this report use census data of a population, making the interpretation of the results (especially tests of statistical significance) slightly different than if the data were from a sample. Specifically, tests of statistical significance on census data do not measure the probability of whether sample results can be generalized to a population but can be used to judge the strength of relationships between the independent variables and the dependent variable in the population or to gauge the explanatory power of the model as a whole.

Model: Public four-year and two-year institutions. The model that was updated for public institutions is a single-equation correlational model developed by the U.S. General Accounting Office (GAO) in a 1998 report. This model describes the statistical associations between changes in institutional revenue and expenditure categories and changes in prices over time. The model is based on the theory that various categories of expenditures—such as instruction, administrative expenses, research expenditures, and operations and maintenance—are associated with changes in prices over time. The model also takes into account research suggesting that sources of revenue, especially from state and local governments, are relevant to tuition levels charged at public institutions. The model therefore focuses on factors internal to the institutions (expenditures and revenues) and captures external influences only indirectly—for example, state policy decisions on support for higher education are indirectly measured through the level of government appropriations revenue.

The GAO examined changes in undergraduate tuition and fees over the five-year period of 1989–90 to 1994–95 for public four-year institutions. Linear regression analysis was used to identify relationships between the dollar change in tuition over this period (the dependent variable) and the dollar changes in various revenue and expenditure categories per student (the independent variables). The model thus identified variables associated with larger or smaller tuition increases, i.e., the characteristics of institutions with larger or smaller tuition increases.

The updated regression model reproduced the GAO model with a few minor modifications. For four-year institutions, the dependent variable was the same: the dollar change in the tuition and required fees charged to the typical full-time, full-year, in-state, undergraduate student.[4] (For two-year institutions, in-district undergraduate tuition is used as the dependent variable.) The updated model includes public two-year institutions, whereas the GAO confined its study to four-year institutions. In addition, the updated model covers a longer time period—1988–89 to 1997–98—than in the GAO report.[5]

The updated model included the following 12 independent variables, some of which differed slightly from the GAO study due to clarifications or data issues. (Except where otherwise noted, changes are in terms of constant dollars per FTE student.)

- The level of in-state undergraduate tuition in the base year
- Change in instruction expenditures
- Change in research expenditures
- Change in student services expenditures
- Change in other student-related expenditures, including prorated portions of academic and institutional support, physical plant maintenance, and transfers
- Change in non-student-related expenditures, including public service and prorated portions of academic and institutional support, physical plant maintenance, and transfers
- Change in philanthropic revenue, including revenue from endowment income as well as revenue from private gifts, grants, and contracts
- Change in revenue from government appropriations from federal, state, and local sources
- Change in revenue from government grants and contracts from federal, state, and local sources, less federal, state, and local scholarships and fellowships
- Change in the amount by which educational and general (E&G) revenues exceed or fall short of E&G expenditures, where E&G revenues and expenditures are those categories that are most directly related to the missions of the institutions[6]
- Change in institutional scholarships and fellowships
- Percentage point change in the ratio of graduate FTE enrollment to total FTE enrollment (only for four-year institutions)

Regression analyses were run for each type of public institution. Independent variables were identified as "important" if the decline in the portion of variation accounted for (R-squared) by omitting the variable from the model was 10 percentage points or greater.

Model: Private not-for-profit four-year institutions. The model that was updated for private not-for-profit institutions is a simultaneous equation model of college enrollments and prices, jointly developed in a 1994 study by Westat and Pelavin Associates. The model assumes that prices and new enrollments simultaneously determine each other and are "endogenous" (jointly dependent), while other factors included in the model were assumed to be "exogenous" (predetermined or derived externally).[7] Based on the theory that various factors influence the supply of and demand for college placements, the structure of the model allows observed levels of tuition to be viewed as equilibrium prices at a specific point in time, while controlling for various factors that may influence institutions' and students' decisions regarding enrollment through two separate equations.[8]

One equation in the model tried to capture students' perspectives of prices given certain characteristics of the institutions and the market in which they operate (in other words, measures of the external environment). In this equation, prices (tuition levels) were assumed to be a function of new enrollments, plus other factors such as instructional quality, prestige, the provision of ancillary services and resources, the cost of attending alternative institutions, and the availability of financial aid.[9] In order to model the equation, the general factors had to be represented by specific, measurable variables, many of which were proxies.[10] The measures for the "external" equation reflected the fact that much of the information available to prospective students is from the previous year. The second equation in the model tried to capture institutions' internal perspectives on prices charged, given their costs of production and other internal factors. From this perspective, institutions must raise tuition to the level at which it will cover their current budgets (alternatively, they can only spend what they raise). In this equation, prices also were assumed to be a function of new enrollments, plus other factors, including the cost of inputs needed to educate students and other revenue that may offset the costs incurred in educating students.

Natural logarithms were taken of the variables on both sides of the equations, so that the results would express "elasticities," or the percentage change in the independent variables associated with a 1 percent change in the dependent variable (price), adjusting statistically for the covariation of all other independent variables. The model also tried to identify the extent of tuition increases that were not accounted for by other factors in the equation, by including dummy variables for each year (other than the base year).[11] The estimates for these dummy variables can be interpreted as representing factors not included in the model but associated with prices over time. Three-stage least squares regression was used to estimate simultaneously the coefficients of both equations for each group of private not-for-profit institutions.[12]

Westat-Pelavin applied the model to four-year private not-for-profit institutions over the period 1984 to 1989. The updated model reproduces the Westat-Pelavin model, with a few minor modifications, using data for a later time period, 1989–90 to 1995–96. Two of the three proxy measures of institutional reputation/prestige were eliminated from the first equation due to unavailability of data. Conversely, a few independent variables were added to the model to capture additional "external" and "internal" factors that were expected to be associated with prices. The updated model included the following variables:

Equation 1 (External Factors)

- Dependent variable: Undergraduate tuition and required fees[13]
- First-time freshmen FTE students[14]
- Indicators of the competitive environment:
  - Average in-state undergraduate tuition at public institutions in the state[15]
  - Proportion of undergraduates in the state enrolled at private not-for-profit four-year institutions
- Proxies for quality of instruction:
  - Previous year's instruction expenditures
  - Previous year's expenditures on plant maintenance, plus transfers
  - Previous year's research expenditures
  - Previous year's student-faculty ratio
- Proxy for institutional prestige/recognition: Philanthropic revenue (endowment income plus private gifts, grants, and contracts)[16]
- Availability of financial aid: Expenditures on institutional aid[17]
- Indicator of ancillary services: Previous year's expenditures on student services
- Measure of in-state consumer purchasing power: Average per capita income in the state
- Measures of change over time in the relationship between price and enrollment, not accounted for by other independent variables in the equation: Dummy variables for 1991, 1992, 1993, 1994, 1995, 1996 (base year = 1990)

Equation 2 (Internal Factors)

- Dependent variable: Undergraduate tuition and required fees
- First-time freshmen FTE students
- Proxies for price of inputs:
  - — Instruction expenditures
  - — Institutional aid expenditures
  - — Average faculty compensation
  - — Academic support expenditures
  - — Institutional support expenditures
  - — Student services expenditures
  - — Ratio of graduate to total FTE enrollment
- Measures of available nontuition revenue:
  - — Philanthropic revenue (endowment income plus private gifts, grants, and contracts)
  - — Federal grants and contracts, less federal aid funds
  - — Revenue from state and local sources, less state/local aid
- Measures of change over time in the relationship between price and enrollment, not accounted for by other independent variables in the equation: Dummy variables for 1991, 1992, 1993, 1994, 1995, 1996 (base year = 1990)

As in the 1994 model, many of these variables are proxies, assumed to measure certain external and internal factors that were expected to be associated with tuition levels.[18] Three-stage least squares regression was used to estimate the model coefficients simultaneously within each institutional type.

Data and institutional universe. The primary source of data for the analyses was the Integrated Postsecondary Education Data System (IPEDS), an annual series of national surveys of postsecondary education institutions that collect information on finances, enrollment, degree completions, faculty salaries and benefits, and other institutional characteristics. Most of the trend analyses and statistical models used panels of institutions constructed from IPEDS data, over the period 1988–89 to 1997–98 for public institutions and 1988–89 to 1995–96 for private not-for-profit institutions.[19] Revenue and expenditure variables were calculated on an FTE student basis, where FTE was generated from reported or estimated fall instructional activity (credit/contact hours).[20] All financial variables in all of the models were adjusted for inflation using the Consumer Price Index (CPI-U, 1982–84 = 100), adjusted to 1999 dollars.[21]

To create the panels, institutional characteristics data were used to define and measure selection criteria. Institutions were drawn from all Title IV participating, degree-granting institutions located in the 50 states and the District of Columbia. The following were excluded from the universe: institutions that enrolled less than 200 FTE students, four-year institutions with less than 50 percent undergraduate fall headcount enrollment, and four-year institutions with less than 25 percent full-time fall headcount enrollment. For remaining institutions, it was important to impute for missing data so that the panel institutions had data for all years. Institutions that had missing data in key variables for a certain number of years were eliminated from the universe; for institutions remaining in the universe after this cutoff, a simple interpolation procedure based on previous and subsequent years was used to impute missing data. For the public institutions only, cases with extreme outliers in specific variables were removed from the analysis.

For the panels of private not-for-profit institutions, the final data set was rearranged so that the structure included seven records for each institution, one for each year. Natural logarithms were taken of the model variables.[22] In cases in which variables contained missing, zero, or negative values (for which logarithms return no value), zero values were inserted into the logged variables and separate dummy variables were created to identify these cases.

The final data set comprised four panels of public institutions with data for all years of the 10-year period and three panels of private not-for-profit four-year institutions with data for all years of the eight-year period. The total number of public institutions remaining in the panels was 1,235 (research/doctoral = 135, comprehensive = 221, bachelor's = 66, two-year = 813). The total number of private not-for-profit institutions remaining in the panels was 690 (research/doctoral = 47, comprehensive = 192, bachelor's = 451). Although the final universe includes 64 percent of the original number of public four- and two-year institutions with data, the institutions remaining in the panels accounted for 84 percent of undergraduate enrollment at all public four-year institutions and 81 percent of undergraduate enrollment at all two-year institutions in 1997–98. The final universe of private not-for-profit four-year institutions includes 34 percent of the original number but captures 63 percent of the total undergraduate enrollment within these institutions.[23]

Findings

The trend analyses and model results found differences in the nature and the strength of relationships between costs and prices across types of institutions and within types of institutions over time.

In both the public and private not-for-profit sectors, average tuition charges increased at a faster rate than inflation over the period of the analyses, and tuition charges also increased faster than most expenditure categories within the institutions. The share of overall revenue coming from tuition has increased on average for all institutional types in both sectors, compared with relative decreases in other revenue sources (see Figures 26.1 and 26.2).

- Across all types of public institutions, in-state undergraduate tuition and fees increased annually between 1988–89 and 1997–98. On average, gross tuition revenue accounted for increasing proportions of total E&G revenue over this period, while revenue from state appropriations declined as a proportion of the total.
- Across all types of private not-for-profit institutions, undergraduate tuition and fees increased annually between 1988–89 and 1995–96. On average, gross tuition revenue accounted for increasing proportions of total E&G revenue over this period. At the same time, the proportion of E&G revenue from endowment income and private gifts, grants, and contracts decreased.

On the expenditure side for both public and private not-for-profit institutions, instruction expenditures continued to constitute the largest proportion of total E&G expenditures but remained flat or decreased as a proportion of E&G expenditures. Meanwhile, institutional scholarships and fellowships constituted one of the fastest growing expenditure categories and made up an increasing proportion of total E&G expenditures.

Public institutions. For public four-year institutions, revenue from state appropriations remains the largest source of revenue and is the single most important factor associated with changes in tuition, a finding that was not surprising given the results of prior research, including the original GAO study. The results of the updated model include the following (see Figure 26.3):

- State appropriations revenue decreased relative to other sources of revenue for all types of public four-year institutions and, in fact, experienced real annual decreases for research/doctoral and comprehensive institutions over the time period examined.
- Decreasing revenue from government appropriations (in which state appropriations make up the majority) was the most important factor associated with tuition increases at public four-year institutions over the period of analysis. Changes in revenue from government appropriations were a greater predictor of changes in tuition than other factors included in the models.
- Although increases in instruction expenditures were associated with increases in tuition at public four-year institutions, they did not explain as much of the variation in tuition changes as decreases in state appropriations revenue did. In addition, the proportion of total E&G expenditures for instruction for these groups of institutions declined slightly over the time period examined.

FIGURE 26.1

Summary of Selected Inflation-Adjusted Trends in Tuition and Selected Revenue and Expenditure Categories at Public Institutions, 1988–89 to 1997–98

	Research/ Doctoral	Comprehensive	Bachelor's	Two-Year
Average annual percentage change in in-state undergraduate tuition for FY, FT students	4.1	4.2	4.3	3.4
Tuition revenue				
Average annual percentage change	4.4	4.8	4.9	2.9
Average proportion of total E&G revenue	21.9	28.3	28.9	19.9
Percentage point change as a proportion of total E&G revenue	5.4	8.4	8.0	5.6
State appropriations revenue				
Average annual percentage change	−1.0	−1.2	0.0	−1.2
Average proportion of total E&G revenue	42.6	50.9	47.1	41.7
Percentage point change as a proportion of total E&G revenue	−9.8	−11.3	−6.9	−3.2
Instruction expenditures				
Average annual percentage change	1.0	0.6	1.1	−0.9
Average proportion of total E&G expenditures	35.6	42.1	38.5	44.1
Percentage point change as a proportion of total E&G expenditures	−1.9	−2.5	−1.6	−4.1
Scholarship and fellowship expenditures				
Average annual percentage change	4.5	3.6	2.5	4.3
Average proportion of total E&G expenditures	6.9	11.0	14.2	11.2
Percentage point change as a proportion of total E&G expenditures	1.7	2.2	1.0	3.9
Average annual percentage change in institutional scholarships and fellowships	8.1	7.7	8.0	6.8

Source: U.S. Department of Education, National Center for Education Statistics, Integrated Postsecondary Education Data System (IPEDS), Full Collections Years 1989 to 1996.

Note: Dollar amounts were converted to constant 1999 dollars using the CPI-U (1982–84 = 100) before annual changes were calculated. Average percentage changes were calculated as averages of the actual changes. All revenue and expenditure categories are per FTE student. Shares of total revenues and expenditures were calculated as averages over the 10-year period.

FIGURE 26.2

Summary of Selected Inflation-Adjusted Trends in Tuition and Selected Revenue and Expenditure Categories at Private Not-for-Profit Institutions, 1988–89 to 1995–96

	Research/ Doctoral	Comprehensive	Bachelor's
Average annual percentage change in in-state undergraduate tuition for FY, FT students	3.6	4.1	3.7
Tuition revenue			
Average annual percentage change	3.5	3.8	3.4
Average proportion of total E&G revenue	49.0	72.0	64.1
Percentage point change as a proportion of total E&G revenue	1.3	5.1	4.2
Revenue from endowment and private gifts			
Average annual percentage change, endowment income	1.4	−1.0	1.5
Average annual percentage change, private gifts	1.8	−0.2	1.1
Average proportion of total E&G revenue, both sources	18.1	11.6	21.7
Percentage point change as a proportion of total E&G revenue, both sources	−2.0	−3.1	−2.2
Instruction expenditures			
Average annual percentage change	3.3	1.9	2.0
Average proportion of total E&G expenditures	36.0	32.7	28.7
Percentage point change as a proportion of total E&G expenditures	0.3	−1.9	−0.8
Scholarship and fellowship expenditures			
Average annual percentage change	6.7	6.6	5.4
Average proportion of total E&G expenditures	12.8	20.4	23.4
Percentage point change as a proportion of total E&G expenditures	3.0	5.0	4.5
Average annual percentage change in institutional scholarships and fellowships	8.7	10.2	8.5

Source: U.S. Department of Education, National Center for Education Statistics, Integrated Postsecondary Education Data System (IPEDS), Full Collections Years 1989 to 1996.

Note: Dollar amounts were converted to constant 1999 dollars using the CPI-U (1982–84 = 100) before annual changes were calculated. Average percentage changes were calculated as averages of the actual changes. All revenue and expenditure categories are per FTE student. Shares of total revenues and expenditures were calculated as averages over the eight-year period.

For research/doctoral and comprehensive institutions, more of the variance in tuition changes remains unexplained than explained by the variables included in the models. It is likely that tuition policies at public institutions are influenced by state and local policy decisions that were outside the parameters of this model, such as limits on enrollment and student aid practices.

For public two-year institutions, the model found that changes in revenue and expenditure categories explained a very low percentage of the variation in tuition changes in comparison with the public four-year sector. This suggests there are some important differences between public two-year and four-year institutions that were not captured in this model.

FIGURE 26.3

Coefficients for the Regression of the Change in In-State Undergraduate Tuition on Selected Revenue and Expenditure Variables for Public Institutions, 1988–89 to 1997–98

	Research/ Doctoral	Comprehensive	Bachelor's	Two-Year
Constant	415.584	256.345	329.513	274.308
Level of in-state undergraduate tuition in base year	0.045	0.081	0.100*	0.058*
Change in instruction expenditures	0.161*	0.370**	0.380**	0.036*
Change in research expenditures	0.104	0.160	–0.081	–0.438
Change in student services expenditures	0.484*	0.639*	0.160	0.140*
Change in other student-related expenditures	0.209*	0.204*	0.187*	0.037*
Change in non-student-related expenditures	0.164*	0.459*	0.464**	0.060
Change in philanthropic revenue	–0.155*	–0.477*	0.408*	0.160
Change in revenue from government appropriations	–0.241**	–0.403**	–0.380**	–0.063*
Change in revenue from government grants and contracts	–0.046	–0.244**	–0.259*	–0.048*
Change in the amount by which E&G revenues exceed/fall short of E&G expenditures	0.068	0.321**	0.337**	0.033
Change in institutional scholarships and fellowships	0.349*	0.308*	–0.406*	0.081
Change in ratio of graduate to total enrollment	-203.935	1572.873*	-1670.457	—
R-squared	0.391	0.424	0.613	0.073
Adjusted R-squared	0.329	0.390	0.515	0.058
N	131	213	60	736

— Not applicable

*Relatively strong relationship

**Identified as "important"

Source: U.S. Department of Education, National Center for Education Statistics, Integrated Postsecondary Education Data System (IPEDS), Full Collection Years 1989 to 1998.

Private not-for-profit institutions. The results suggest that prices at private not-for-profit four-year institutions were related to both internal institutional budget constraints and external market conditions, as indicated in the original Westat-Pelavin study. In the private not-for-profit sector, no single overriding factor is as strongly related to tuition as state appropriations revenue is in the public four-year sector (see Figure 26.4).

- For all types of private not-for-profit four-year institutions, certain internal factors—higher costs in two areas (institutional aid and average faculty compensation levels) and lower levels of revenue from two nontuition sources (endowment income and private gifts, grants, and contracts)—were associated with higher levels of undergraduate tuition.

FIGURE 26.4

Coefficients for the Simultaneous Equations Estimation of Undergraduate Tuition on Selected Institutional and External Characteristics for Private Not-for-Profit Institutions, 1989–90 to 1995–96

	Research/Doctoral	Comprehensive	Bachelor's
Equation 1 (external factors)			
Log of first-time freshmen FTE students	0.095*	0.076*	0.154*
Log of previous year's instruction expenditures	0.048	0.148*	0.198*
Log of average tuition at public four-year institutions in the state	0.106*	0.032*	0.058*
Log of previous year's expenditures on plant maintenance transfers	–0.020	0.005	–0.015
Log of the proportion of undergraduates enrolled in the state attending private not-for-profit four-year institutions	0.004	–0.002	–0.022*
Log of previous year's research expenditures	0.048*	–0.012*	0.001
Log of previous year's student services expenditures	0.103*	0.032*	0.050*
Log of expenditures on institutional aid	0.286*	0.245*	0.256*
Log of previous year's student/faculty ratio	0.220*	0.037*	0.032*
Log of philanthropic revenue	–0.034*	–0.068*	–0.077*
Log of per capita income in the state	0.182*	0.124*	0.196*
Dummy variable for 1996	–0.008	0.037*	0.022
Constant	2.281*	4.402*	2.560*
R-squared	0.815	0.595	0.475
N	329	1344	3157
Equation 2 (internal institutional factors)			
Log of first-time freshmen FTE students	–0.210*	0.022	0.074*
Log of instruction expenditures	0.005	0.083*	0.158*
Log of expenditures on institutional aid	0.284*	0.252*	0.252*
Log of average faculty compensation	0.684*	0.226*	0.281*
Log of institutional support expenditures	0.079*	–0.005	–0.001
Log of academic support expenditures	–0.003	–0.004	–0.001
Log of student services expenditures	–0.051	0.025*	0.038*
Log of philanthropic revenue	–0.120*	–0.079*	–0.099*
Log of federal grants and contracts	0.083*	0.000	0.001
Log of revenue from state and local sources	–0.018*	0.001	0.001
Ratio of graduate FTE enrollment to total FTE enrollment	–0.369*	–0.017	–0.051
Dummy variable for 1996	0.052	0.049*	0.049*
Constant	1.410	4.540*	3.028*
R-squared	0.620	0.589	0.499
N	329	1344	3157

*Relatively strong relationship

Source: U.S. Department of Education, National Center for Education Statistics, Integrated Postsecondary Education Data (IPEDS), Full Collections Years 1989 to 1996; Bureau of Economic Analysis, Regional Accounts Data, Personal Income for States: 1958–98, released July 1999.

Notes: "N" refers to the number of observations, not the number of institutions; each institution has one observation for each year. The coefficients of the logged variables can be interpreted as the percentage change in tuition (dependent variable) associated with a 1 percent change in the independent variable. The coefficients of the dummy variables or the years can be interpreted as the change in tuition since the base year (1990), adjusting statistically for the covariation of the independent variables, by taking the inverse log into base e) of the estimated coefficient and subtracting 1 from it. Dummy variables for missing data and for the years 1991, 1992, 1993, 1994, and 1005 were not included in this summary table.

- For all types of private not-for-profit four-year institutions, certain external factors—such as the availability of institutional aid for students, the price of attending public institutions in the same state, and per capita income in the state—also were associated with tuition levels.
- Some differences were found regarding whether and the extent to which other factors—for example, instruction expenditures—were related to tuition, suggesting that the three types of private not-for-profit four-year institutions face different competitive environments and institutional budgeting decisions. For example, nontuition revenue was related to prices at research/doctoral institutions, where nontuition revenue makes up a higher proportion of total E&G revenue on average. Institutional aid was related to tuition levels at all three groups of institutions but made up higher proportions of total E&G expenditures at comprehensive and bachelor's institutions, which may face more competitive environments.

In considering these findings, it is important to keep in mind that many of the variables included in the models for private not-for-profit institutions were acting as proxies for expected relationships. In some cases, the proxies might not have measured the factor accurately. For example, the results for philanthropic revenue and student/faculty ratios were contrary to those expected; it is possible that these variables are weak proxies for institutional reputation and quality, and students' perceptions of institutional quality may be relevant in this regard.[24] Nonetheless, the results of the models are generally consistent with theoretical expectations regarding the institutional budget constraints and external, competitive environments faced by private not-for-profit institutions.

Conclusions

In general, these results show that available national data can be used to explore aggregate trends in revenues, costs, and prices for broad groups of institutions. Models using these data also can point out associations between revenue and expenditure variables and tuition—for example, as state appropriations for public four-year institutions decrease, the average undergraduate tuition at this type of institution tends to increase. Although this research improves and expands upon previous studies of costs and prices, the analyses have certain limitations.

Some, but not all, of the limitations are caused by the reliance on previously collected national data, reflecting the fact that institutions often do not collect the data required to answer questions about the relationships among prices, revenues, and expenditures. Several changes to national data collection systems (and the underlying financial reporting standards at postsecondary education institutions) would be needed to better approach these issues, including: more detailed institutional classification systems, comparable financial accounting standards between the public and private not-for-profit sectors, detailed net price data, information on sources of revenue for institutional aid, standard definitions for items such as merit aid and technology costs, isolation of revenue and expenditure data by level of student, and information on marketing bands/peer groups, especially for sectors in which competition heavily influences institutional decision making. Beyond data issues, the analyses were limited by the use of existing statistical models. These models cannot lead to definitive conclusions regarding the underlying relationships among changes in variables over time because they do not take into account all of the simultaneous direct and indirect effects of costs, revenues, financial aid, market conditions and other external influences, family resources, and college prices.

Even with future improvements in definitions, prospective data collection, and models, however, the technique of cost analysis will always provide only partial answers to questions about the reasons for price increases at colleges and universities. Given the distinctive characteristics of higher education—such as the availability of nontuition sources of revenue—there is little reason to expect a consistent relationship between costs and prices across all institutions or groups of institutions, even though a specific relationship may be present at one particular institution.[25] Nevertheless, the analyses presented in this article highlight trends and point to associations between variables that can lead to a better understanding of the nature of higher education finance.

Notes

1. This study was conducted in response to a congressional mandate in the 1998 amendments to the Higher Education Act of 1965. The National Center for Education Statistics (NCES) published the final report in December 2001 and submitted it to Congress in January 2002. Much of this article is excerpted from the final report.
2. In addition to private for-profit institutions, two-year private not-for-profit institutions were excluded from the analysis due to the small size of this sector as well as problems with data availability.
3. See, for instance, Winston 1998; McPherson and Schapiro 1991 and 1998; and Davis 1997.
4. In using in-state tuition as the dependent variable, this model may not reflect public institutions' pricing policies regarding out-of-state students; it is plausible that public institutions' behavior with regard to out-of-state students is more similar to the behavior of private not-for-profit institutions. Also note that this measure of tuition does not take into account tuition discounts, which are accounted for as expenditures on institutional scholarships and fellowships.
5. In addition, separate analyses were performed for three subperiods to see if there were differences within the period examined: 1988–89 to 1990–91, 1990–91 to 1994–95, and 1994–95 to 1997–98. In these subperiods, the average annual rate of increase in undergraduate tuition differed markedly, with the highest rate occurring in the middle subperiod for all four groups of public institutions.
6. E&G revenues include tuition and fees, government appropriations, government grants and contracts, private gifts, endowment income, sales and services, and other revenue. E&G expenditures include instruction, research, public service, academic support, student services, institutional support, plant operations and maintenance, scholarships and fellowships, and transfers. Both exclude revenue and expenditures for auxiliary enterprises, hospitals, and independent operations.
7. Another way of describing these terms is that "endogenous" variables are determined within the economic model, while "exogenous" variables are taken as a given by the model.
8. "Equilibrium" prices occur at the point at which the demand and supply curves intersect and where the quantity demanded is equal to the quantity supplied. The standard formulation of demand/supply curve equations places the quantity demanded/supplied (new enrollments in this case) on the left side of the equations and price (tuition) on the right, where the quantity demanded/supplied is a function of price plus other factors. In order to focus on prices, the Westat/Pelavin model reexpressed the equations' functional forms so that price is a function of enrollment plus other factors, leading to inverse demand/supply curves.
9. More accurately, prices and new enrollments are a function of each other; however, this characterization describes the functional form of the equations, which set price on the left side of the equations.
10. The proxies might or might not accurately capture the influences they attempt to represent; this is likely to be particularly true for instructional quality and institutional prestige, which are extremely difficult to measure. See Bradburd and Mann 1990.
11. Each dummy variable was defined so that it was equal to 1 if an observation was for a specific year (e.g., 1987) and 0 if the observation was for another year (e.g., any year but 1987). Because observations for the base year were coded 0 in all of the dummy variables, each dummy variable year is measured relative to the base year (1984). Note that each institution has multiple observations, one for each year of data included in the model.
12. The three-stage least squares procedure allows estimation of systems of structural equations where some equations contain endogenous variables among the explanatory variables. Reduced form regressions also were performed to see if the results supported the structural model results. Reduced form regressions incorporate all exogenous variables from both equations into one model, with tuition as the dependent variable (enrollment is excluded because it is endogenous, in other words, jointly determined with the dependent variable).
13. In general, in-state tuition does not differ much, if at all, from out-of-state tuition at private not-for-profit institutions. In fact, in 1995–96, in-state differed from out-of-state undergraduate tuition at only five of the 690 private not-for-profit institutions in the panel, and the average tuition levels differed by less than one-half of one percent. Therefore, although the variable for in-state tuition was used in the analysis, it is referred to here simply as undergraduate tuition.
14. For simplification, first-time freshmen were chosen as the enrollment measure. It is possible that total undergraduate enrollment is also associated with price.
15. This indicator represents competition for students within the state; however, competition with public institutions for out-of-state students may also be relevant, especially for private not-for-profit insti-

tutions that draw from a national base. According to data from the National Postsecondary Student Aid Study (NPSAS: 96), in 1995–96, almost 65 percent of undergraduates at all private not-for-profit four-year institutions were attending an institution in the state of their legal residence; for private not-for-profit research/doctoral institutions, the rate was about 48 percent, while for comprehensive and bachelor's institutions, the rate was more than 70 percent.

16. Note that the other two indicators of prestige from the Westat-Pelavin model, SAT scores and the percentage of applicants admitted, had to be dropped due to the lack of data. Endowment income was combined with private gifts revenue on the premise that both were associated with institutional prestige. Note that some revenue from private grants and contracts also is included.
17. Other forms of student aid, such as aid from federal, state, or local governments, were not captured in the original Westat-Pelavin model and are not included in the updated model. This is partly due to the limitations of the Integrated Postsecondary Education Data System (IPEDS), as it does not fully account for aid; for example, revenue from federal student loans generally shows up in revenue from tuition and fees.
18. It is important to note that in this model, some variables were used in both equations but as proxies for different aspects of the relationships characterized by the two equations. For example, institutional aid expenditures represent the availability of financial aid from the student perspective (which reduces the price they must pay) in one equation but represent part of an institution's cost of educating students from the internal perspective in the other equation.
19. The difference in time periods is a result of the changes in Financial Accounting Standards Board guidelines for private not-for-profit institutions, which were incorporated into the IPEDS finance survey beginning in fiscal year 1997.
20. Because IPEDS revenue and expenditure data cannot be broken down by level of student, per FTE variables were calculated using total FTE rather than undergraduate FTE. It is important to note that matching these variables with undergraduate tuition levels is not ideal. Nevertheless, this analysis was limited to the use of available data. Attempts were made to address this issue by limiting the universe of institutions to those with primarily undergraduate enrollment and by adding variables to the models to reflect the proportions of graduate students.
21. The Consumer Price Index for All Urban Consumers (CPI-U) measures changes in relation to a base period, in this case the average index level for a 36-month period covering 1982, 1983, and 1984, which is set equal to 100.
22. Logs were not taken of the ratio of graduate to total enrollment due to the large number of zero values, especially for comprehensive and bachelor's institutions.
23. The technical appendix in the final NCES report (2001) provides additional details on the institution selection process, imputation procedures, and statistical procedures. It also includes a bias analysis.
24. In this model, the measure of price is published tuition and fees, which indicates "sticker price" rather than net price (institutional aid is represented as an expenditure rather than as a discount in the price). Issues of institutional reputation and the so-called "Chivas Regal" effect may be incorporated into the relationship between enrollment and sticker price; in the absence of good information about quality or prestige, price may act as a signal to students of an institution's elite status.
25. For an overview of higher education finance and the relationship between costs and prices, see Stringer et al. 1999.

References

Bradburd, Ralph M., and Duncan P. Mann. 1991. The Market for Higher Education: An Economic Analysis. In Background Papers Prepared for the "Study of the Escalating Costs of Higher Education," edited by Pelavin Associates, Inc. Prepared under contract for the U.S. Education Department.

Davis, Jerry S. 1997. College Affordability: A Closer Look at the Crisis. Washington, D.C.: Sallie Mae Education Institute.

McPherson, Michael S., and Morton Owen Schapiro. 1991. Keeping College Affordable: Government and Educational Opportunity. Washington, D.C.: The Brookings Institution.

. 1998. The Student Aid Game: Meeting Need and Rewarding Talent in American Higher Education. Princeton, N.J.: Princeton University Press.

National Commission on the Cost of Higher Education. 1998. Straight Talk About College Costs and Prices. Phoenix: Oryx Press.

Stringer, William L., and Alisa F. Cunningham with colleagues. 1999. Cost, Price, and Public Policy: Peering into the Higher Education Black Box. USA Group Foundation New Agenda Series, vol. 1, no. 3. Indianapolis: USA Group Foundation.

U.S. Department of Education, National Center for Education Statistics. 1995–96. National Postsecondary Student Aid Study (NPSAS:96), Undergraduate Data Analysis System. Washington, D.C.: U.S. Department of Education, National Center for Education Statistics.

———. 2001. Study of College Costs and Prices, 1988-89 to 1997-98. NCES 2002-157 and 2002-158, vols. 1 and 2. Washington, D.C.: Government Printing Office.

U.S. General Accounting Office. 1998. Higher Education: Tuition Increases and Colleges' Efforts to Contain Costs. GAO/HEHS-98-227. Washington, D.C.: Government Printing Office.

Westat and Pelavin Associates. 1994. An Analysis of Institutional Decision Making—Final Report on Estimation Results. Prepared for the U.S. Education Department, Office of the Under Secretary. Washington, D.C.: Westat and Pelavin Associates.

Winston, Gordon C. 1998. College Costs: Subsidies, Intuition, and Policy. In Straight Talk About College Costs and Prices: The Final Report and Supplemental Material from the National Commission on the Cost of Higher Education. Phoenix: Oryx Press.

CHAPTER 27

BUDGET DEVELOPMENT PROCESS FOR COMMUNITY COLLEGES

DANIEL DERRICO

Introduction: An Experience-Based Pragmatic Approach

This chapter is intended to describe a practical approach for the practitioner—community college chief executive officer (CEO), or chief financial officer (CFO), and other administrators who have major responsibilities for creating and monitoring operating budgets and financial operations. Properly deployed, budget development and management is an indispensable component of an improved financial model. These ideas are being presented for now, and for the future, as colleges are increasingly challenged to balance their operating budgets while serving the needs of their students and community. It is also written for many others who are involved in, or are interested in budget and financial decisions. It presents common errors of current budget planning models, with a practical approach of how to avoid these mistakes, and what is required for a new model. An attempt is made to answer questions of what to do, when, by whom, how it should be done, and why. This approach emphasizes annual and multiyear budget planning models, multiyear revenue and expenditure forecasting, assumptions that lead to decisions, and the need to monitor revenues and expenses, evaluate results, and reexamine the accuracy of your assumptions on which your financial projections are based. The chapter is presented in a manner that would be applicable to any public community college of any size or location.

This method will require integrity, transparency, competence, planning, projecting and analyzing data, measuring results, accountability for results, and for the administration to work cooperatively with the board of trustees and the faculty and staff to achieve stated goals. Primary goals are to balance the annual operating budget, preferably to include an end-of-year budget surplus to add to the unencumbered fund balance, while maintaining or increasing quality, and achieving stated priority goals of the college's strategic plan. This chapter is not based upon research or a literature review. Rather, my observations and recommendations come from extensive experience with community college budget planning and implementation, as well as from lessons learned from other community college CEOs and CFOs with whom I have communicated over many years.

This chapter deals with the operating budget, consisting of all revenues and expenses except for grants, student scholarships and financial aid, foundation accounts, construction bonds, or other separately funded capital improvement projects. Operating budgets include revenues from state and local governments, student tuition and fees, contract for services rendered income, investment interest income, and auxiliary income from services such as cafeteria and bookstore operations. The budget plan is a summary of all projected operating revenues and expenses.

In these increasingly difficult financial circumstances that all public colleges and community colleges are now experiencing, it is more important than ever to supplement declining tax support with other revenues, to contain operating expenses, and to align the budget with the institutional mission, strategic plan, and priority goals. The budget should be aligned to the community college's mission statement, multiyear strategic plan, stated values, and priority goals. The main driver for all of this planning should be higher levels of student success, as measured by such factors as graduation and program completion rates, demonstrated skills, and job placements. Annual and multiyear budget planning should be done, reviewed, monitored, and revised as necessary, based on budget assumptions and projections of enrollment, student fees, state and local tax revenues, and auxiliary income. The budget development process is not an accounting tool. It should be used as a management tool to promote the mission and priority goals, and to create an improved financial model for the community college.

Common Operating Errors in Budget Development and Implementation

Some of the current community college budget development models do not have consistent, rational, or well-defined processes for developing their operating budgets. In this context, there are 14 common errors that have been made by community colleges. These errors must be avoided to develop and implement realistic operating budgets in order to support institutional mission and goals.

Planning

There may be little or no planning of projected revenues, expenses, or unit appropriations beyond the next single fiscal year budget. Longer-term enrollment projections and fee revenue must be projected, monitored, and revised every year, and budget allocations revised accordingly. Specific expense projections should be done for projected enrollment, new facilities, inflation, and proposed salary and fringe benefit increases. Planning should include improved purchasing processes such as bulk purchasing, obtaining bids for products and services, negotiated state-wide purchasing discount prices with venders for computers and other equipment, and energy-efficient systems.

Incremental Appropriations and Zero-Based Budgeting Models

In incremental models, staffing and funding resource allocation planning processes for the coming fiscal year start with the same base budget appropriation as the current year, and consider only marginal modifications with whatever total revenue increases or decreases are projected for only the coming fiscal year. This is often done with little or no regard to shifting enrollments, revenues, and costs among the various campuses or programs throughout the entire institution. On the other extreme is the zero-based budgeting concept that has been borrowed from the private sector. Our experience is that this model is not well suited for community colleges, except in the limited application of cost and revenue projections for entirely new academic and support programs.

Inflation Impact

Does the college project the annual and the multiyear impact of general inflation, or for above average specific cost increases such as energy or health care employee benefits? This requires constant revenue increases, improved operational efficiencies, and priority adjustments.

New Facilities

Budget allocations do not adequately account for the immediate impact of new facilities expenses or new academic or support programs, and the lag time to achieve the later revenue that results from the enrollment increases in student fees, and the even later revenue increases that come from state support that these new facilities or academic programs may generate. Costs and revenues must be projected for new facilities, locations, or campuses. For example, a new academic building will require additional faculty, support staff, administration, furniture, equipment, utilities, and custodial and other facilities maintenance. How will this be funded?

Strategic Planning

Budgets tend to be appropriation driven, with no apparent alignment with the priority institutional goals, and with insufficient accountability for results. These priority goals should be stipulated in the institution's strategic plan, which should place an emphasis on student success as measured by retention and completion. They may include new academic or workforce programs, and new facilities or campus locations.

Stakeholder Needs

Budget development does not always adequately reflect the various roles and differing needs of the board, the administration, the faculty, the staff, the students, and the external constituents such as the community, local political leaders, and local business community.

Evaluation and Consequences

The budget planning process often has inadequate year-to-year evaluation of the cost-benefit analysis of academic and support programs for which there is a declining enrollment or need, and there is extreme reluctance to eliminate low-enrollment or cost-ineffective programs. The administration often has inadequate mechanisms for rewarding program or departmental effectiveness and efficiency, or for addressing program ineffectiveness and inefficiency.

Budget Monitoring

Budget data analysis and monitoring during the fiscal year is often inadequate, which does not allow the administration to identify fiscal problems and make in-year budget adjustments in a timely manner.

Communication

Budget planning details and rationale are not well communicated, nor well understood within or outside of the institution.

Instructional Costs

Though direct instruction is the largest expense, there is insufficient or even nonexistent planning and modeling of class size, faculty staffing formulas based on department and course enrollment projections, and faculty ratios for the numbers of class sections to be taught by fulltime faculty, and class sections to be taught by less expensive adjunct faculty.

Special Fees

Specific "special fees" for student support services or for high-cost academic programs, and lab fees for specific courses, are often not adequately cost examined, projected, monitored, or allocated to the impacted departments to balance budget appropriations with expenses. They should be charged at real cost levels and monitored for accuracy each year. The process for charging and allocating special fees should be clearly written, well justified, and specifically audited.

Staffing Levels

There are often no staffing formulas, or peer institution staffing comparison data, for nonfaculty staff and administrative positions, complicating the decision and approval process for creating new positions in the budget, or for filling existing position vacancies when they occur, or for the next operating budget planning cycle.

Auxiliary Revenue

Operating budget revenues consist almost entirely of a combination of tuition and student fees, and state funding in all states, and local tax revenues in some states, with very little other revenue from either auxiliary enterprises such as bookstore, cafeteria, among others, private or publicly funded grants, donations from alumni, and other private donors.

Redundancy of Services

In large multicampus colleges or multicollege districts, there is duplication and overlap of operations and staff responsibilities that is cost-ineffective and even counterproductive. This duplication may also occur in smaller community colleges. Examples of this tendency for duplication include: information technology, research, promotions, media contact and public relations, academic program planning, data collection and reporting, fund-raising, business contacts, and workforce development. Miami Dade College centralized each of these functions at the district level many years ago, with very good results.

Successful Budget Planning: Who, When, What, and How

Who (Major Players)

The planning, development, monitoring, and adjusting (when appropriate) of the community college's operating budget is a team effort, requiring the involvement of many people. The CEO must initiate and lead this process, and establish the roles of others. Various guidelines have been delineated for the role and authority of the board of trustees, whether elected or appointed, by the regional accrediting associations, and by some state departments of education. The role of the board is very important but must be limited. We maintain that the board should set policy; provide direction for long-term priorities; set goals for unencumbered fund balances; hire and evaluate the CEO; set the example for integrity, service, and transparency; lobby for the college with public officials and the private sector to increase revenues; and help with fund-raising and with business partnerships. The board and the CEO should have ongoing dialogue concerning long-range strategic planning, and the need for new facilities and new service locations, to serve community needs. These matters will impact budget planning and development. The board should provide input, and then should review and approve (not initiate or determine in detail) the annual operating budget. The board should never "manage" much less try to "micromanage" the budget. They should avoid directing or interfering with the work of staff.

The budget development process should start with a discussion between the chancellor and the board, based on established priorities, current institutional mission statement and goals, and the considerations of the long-range strategic plan of the institution. All of these things are dynamic concepts, the current versions of which should all be in written form, and communicated widely throughout the institution, and on the college's website. The mission and goals of a comprehensive community college, with a large and diverse service area, must be broad enough to encompass transfer education, workforce development, adult education, and remedial education. However, it must be remembered that the institutional scope and mission must have limits. It cannot aspire to be "all things to all people" and difficult priority choices must be made due to the very real budgetary restraints of limitations of available resources (people, financial revenues, physical facilities, human energy, equipment, and expertise). These realities must be reflected in the budget development process, and priorities have to be established as to what can be funded in any budget cycle. The successful budget development process at the Alamo Community College District (ACCD) in San Antonio, a five-college district now with over 60,000 fall term credit students and an annual operating budget now in excess of $270 million was made possible by recent chancellors, and by a board of trustees that understood and observed these concepts.

Each community college should have a CFO, reporting directly co the CEO, and as a member of the college's executive committee, which should also include the campus presidents and other high-level district administrators. The role of these and other major administrators are further described in the Derrico-Sutin. This group should meet regularly, with special meetings on budget development, under the direction of the CEO. The CFO should have the major responsibility for budget development, recommending staffing and resource allocation formulas, projecting revenues from student fees and state, local, and other sources, developing and presenting data comparisons for past years and for peer institutions, and leading the effort to identify and project expenditures for a list of nondiscretionary items (examples: utilities, mandated employee benefits, debt service) that must be funded before any discretionary budget allocations can be made.

While not always included in the traditional model, there is a trend for a role for the faculty to play in a shared governance decision-making model, which is now practiced by many community colleges. We strongly endorse this concept. Faculty unions of faculty senates should be involved in meetings and discussions, directly with the CEO and the CFO, and as members of or participants in executive committee discussions. Everyone throughout the organization should have the opportunity to receive information and to provide input. Student input concerning their priority needs and budget concerns are best channeled through student government organizations, recommending at the campus level, for consideration and response from the campus president.

External expert consultants should be used to provide input and analysis and peer institution comparisons into the budget development process. This is a very cost-effective way to get valuable expertise, a different set of experiences and viewpoints, and external advice by those with no internal biases to affect their observations and recommendations. These external consultants should include individuals from other community colleges, but also those from the world of business or public sector agencies that may have relevant perspectives to share. While a public community college has important differences from a private business, it can and should adapt suitable and sound business budgeting concepts including setting priorities, determining cost-benefit analysis of all operations and programs, projecting short- and long-term revenues and expenses, emphasizing positive results, rewarding effectiveness and efficiency, and holding budget managers and others accountable for performance.

A useful role for the public in general should be exercised through the process of open board meetings, with announced agendas, inviting comments, observations, and recommendations from the public to the board, which may be taken under advisement by the board and the CEO. The CEO should be a member of local chambers of commerce, and other appropriate community groups. The CEO should arrange meetings with local business, community, and political leaders to obtain their input, educate them as to what the college is doing and what it needs to better serve their community. This level of communication and cooperation can have a very positive impact on the budget.

Most community colleges will have an internal auditor, probably reporting directly to the board of trustees. This should be the only person, other than the CEO who reports directly to the board, for purposes of fiscal checks and balances, and due to the board's special responsibility for the institution's finances. Ideally, the internal auditor will also communicate directly with the CEO and with the CFO. He or she can be an additional pair of eyes for the CEO and the CFO to monitor financial data and the efficiency of internal procedures and processes, and for compliance with board policies. The internal auditor, in coordination with an external auditing firm contracted by the community college, will audit the budget after the fact each fiscal year. After consultation with the CEO and the CFO, the internal auditor should report his or her findings and recommendations to the board. However, the internal auditor should not play a direct role in the budget preparation process, unless in response to specific technical questions from the chancellor or the CFO.

In summary, the board of trustees, the CEO, the CFO, the campus presidents, the faculty organization, staff, and external expert consultants should be involved in the budget development process. The internal auditor reviews (audits) the budget after the fact, and reports his or her findings to the board.

As with any important endeavor in a large organization, budget planning and administration is indeed a team effort, requiring the skills, knowledge, talents, and hard work of many individuals. Such efforts best succeed if we care more about achieving a good result than we care about who gets the credit. There will be ample credit to share if all goes well. To sustain this success over time, the CEO and the CFO must distribute this credit widely and very publicly.

When

At a special board meeting, there should be a budget presentation by the CEO and the CFO. A report should be prepared to include data, comparisons, graphs, and charts. This budget report should be widely distributed to all board members and major college administrators, and to faculty and staff group leaders, in advance of this meeting. This budget report should include the proposed annual operating budget for the next fiscal year. For example, do a June board meeting presentation for the fiscal year that would start on September 1. This presentation, additional support data and peer institution comparisons, data comparisons to recent previous years, the college's mission statement, core values, and strategic plan documents, and a five-year model of annual budget projections should also be placed on the college's website for anyone to see. Working backward from this date of the June board meeting, a calendar should be developed for the annual budget planning process.

Assuming a September 1 start to your fiscal year (or adjust accordingly), you will need to start the initial data gathering during the preceding fall term. Start in October with a discussion at a board budget workshop to discuss any possible modifications or additions to board policy, priorities, mission statement, core values, and the long-range strategic plan. Draft an initial outline of the next year's revenues and unavoidable expense increases, such as utilities cost increases, health care cost increases, commitments already made, funding trends, and the like. Schedule the discussion, and input meetings first with administrators, and then with faculty and staff leaders. Have continuous presentations and discussions at the executive committee meetings. Hold open presentations, with questions and answers, for faculty and staff at each of your college campuses. Use the external consultants alluded to earlier. Update your five-year revenue and expense model in March, but revise this dynamic document (a one-page spreadsheet) as needed as new information becomes available on enrollment, and receipt of state and local funding.

The first draft prepared should be prepared of the next fiscal year operating budget for an executive committee presentation, and then for a board workshop. Finalize the budget for a board presentation and approval for the June board meeting. If necessary, as a result of the board's direction at the June board meeting, revise the budget for a special meeting of the board by late June or early July to get final board approval of the annual operating budget that will begin on September 1. Adjust these dates accordingly if your fiscal year is on a different calendar than my example of September 1 through August 31 each year.

What and How

A useful starting point to annual operating budget preparation is the development of a five-year budget model that is based on certain relevant assumptions, to project revenues and expense estimates each year. The assumptions should start with enrollment projections, followed by an annual assumption of cost inflation, tuition and fee increases, state funding support, local tax collections where applicable for tax base, rate, and yield, cost impact of new planned facilities or campuses, and other revenue sources such as auxiliary income, interest income, and contract for services rendered income from business or other clients. During the budget planning process each year, you should review the most recent five-year budget model, confirm or modify the actual data for the current year compared to the projected totals, and reconsider each one of the assumptions that were made, as specified in the preceding sentence above. Make whatever changes to the assumptions and to the data that are appropriate.

Convert the first-year projections to the actual numbers, or to updated projections prior to the final actual numbers being available, modify each of the next years' projections as may be required by new information, and project out the next year at the end of the five-year model. While there can be much backup data, the model can and should be printed and widely distributed on a one-page data spreadsheet with the criteria as the left column showing projections for enrollment, facilities capacity, total expenditures, and projected revenues from the various sources of tuition and student fees, state funding, local tax support, and other revenue. The next five columns of numbers from left to right would be the current fiscal year, followed by the next four fiscal years. The footnotes at the bottom of the page should be your assumptions, such as annual enrollment growth of X percent, an annual general cost percentage inflation factor, facilities growth of X square feet and associated costs, tuition and fee increases, state funding support projections, local tax collections, and other funding revenues. An actual example of this five-year budget development projection model is shown as Table 27.1, and is described below.

The 2007–2008 opening fiscal year operating budget for the ACCD was $245.2 million. An assumption of a 4 percent per year general cost inflation would add approximately $10 million dollars per year, each year, to a budget of that size. This inflation increase alone would add over $50 million of expenses to the fifth budget year ahead, just to pay for the same items at inflated prices and salaries in the operating budget. Inflation will require periodic increases in tuition and student fee schedules. Local tax revenue increases will be required to cover inflation expenses, and must come from either increases in the local tax base, or the tax rate, or both. When the tax base is expanding tax rate increases will probably not be necessary. When tax bases are static or decreasing, tax rate increases must be considered to increase revenues. Future year state funding is difficult to project. In all states, state funding as a proportion of the total community college operating budget has decreased dramatically over the past 20 years or more. In Texas, that percentage decreased over that period of time from approximately 60 percent to approximately 30 percent. This decline is similar for Florida and many other states. This has required community college administrators and boards to significantly increase tuition and student fees, and in Texas to shift much more of the funding burden to the local taxpayers, requiring greater revenues from property taxes. Community colleges in most of the larger states, including Texas, California, New York, and Illinois, receive significant local funding, but many, including in Florida, receive little or no local tax support. In the current economic recession, when both state and local tax revenues are in decline, it is especially important to create additional auxiliary revenue from sources such as grants, interest income, and food service and bookstore income.

TABLE 27.1

Alamo Community Colleges: District Operating Budget Projection

	2006–2007	2007–2008	2008–2009	2009–2010	2010–2011
Square footage	2,747,930	3,648,712	4,058,879	4,058,879	4,058,879
Enrollment[a]	51,672	54,252	61,934	63,112	64,292
Operating budget[b]	220,121,423	238,896,933	275,483,884	284,928,284	295,927,817
Tuition & fees[c]	73,670,796	81,216,663	97,352,659	104,164,548	111,417,709
Continuing education	6,926,452	7,293,043	8,387,687	8,556,795	8,726,380
Tax revenue[d]	67,520,210	72,823,377	78,469,475	84,478,206	90,870,618
State funding[e]	65,368,636	72,814,547	73,962,054	86,040,941	86,040,941
Other[f]	10,232,501	11,049,960	13,553,412	13,965,875	14,383,665
Total projected revenue	223,718,595	245,197,590	271,725,287	297,206,365	311,439,313
Net revenue	3,597,172	6,300,657	(3,758,597)	12,278,081	15,511,496

[a]Enrollment is for the fall term credit hour headcount and includes exempted/waived enrollment. Enrollment information provided by the office of Student Outcomes Assessment and Research as of 20 February 2007.

[b]Operating budget will increase based on enrollment growth rate, annual inflation of 2.0 percent, and a surcharge of 20 percent of US$6.00 per square foot on new construction. Construction management and accounting costs for the CIP is included at a fixed annual amount of U5$680,000.

[c]Tuition and fees will increase with enrollment plus an anticipated annual Tuition & Fees increase of 5.0 percent in FY06/07 through FY10/11.

[d]Tax revenue projections are based on an increase in net taxable value of 6.0 percent annually. No tax rate increases are projected. Tax revenue projections have been adjusted for the impact of Proposition 13.

[e]State funding is projected on biennial increases in enrollment and an increase in the funding rate of 6.0 percent per biennial for each full-time student equivalent (FTSE).

[f]Other funding is projected to grow at 60.0 percent of the enrollment growth rate.

Nondiscretionary Items

Nondiscretionary items should be listed in your current budget, which should be reviewed again, with estimated costs of what you regard as nondiscretionary items that must be funded in the budget. These items, and their estimated cost increases, include debt service on capital bonds and other debt items, utilities, board elections (where applicable), employee health care and other mandated fringe benefits, insurance premiums, vehicle replacement, computer and technology replacements, and other multiyear replacement programs, which should be in place and funded in annual operating budgets at a fixed dollar amount or percentage of inventory value each year. This list, with expenses, should be published and distributed, and subject to continuous review.

Historical Data

Leaders need to use college historical data on enrollment, revenues, and expenses, and charts and graphs of peer community college comparisons should include past year actual and coming year proposed category summaries of how much funding is allocated to the different functional categories that are required for state reporting. While varying somewhat from state to state, they are very similar, consisting in Texas of eight functional categories: direct instruction, academic support, student services, public service, institutional support, plant operations and maintenance, scholarships and exemptions, and auxiliary expenses. Direct instruction should be the largest expense category.

Staffing and Dollar Appropriation Formulas

Staffing and functionally targeted dollar appropriation formulas can be helpful guides in the budget development process. There are a wide variety of such allocation formulas that have been implemented by different colleges, and others suggested in the literature on community colleges. Miami Dade College had staffing formulas for offices based on general enrollment, and some specific to function, such as the number of financial aid awards for their various campus financial aid offices, or to the number of custodians per square footage of buildings. Miami Dade, a very large multicampus college, has an excellent formula for budgeting the number of faculty positions and the cost of faculty salaries. It is based on average class size targets for different courses, then a ratio of sections to be taught in-load, overload, and by part-time adjunct faculty. In-load faculty salaries are at the highest rate, faculty overload (separate per class) is less expensive than in-load, and the adjunct faculty rate (set at two-third of the per-course overload rate) is the least expensive per class. Their departmental enrollment projections, in combination with class size goals, calculate the staffing formulas that tell them how many full-time faculty they need, and the dollar amount that they expect to spend on full-time faculty salaries and overloads and on adjunct faculty.

In multicampus colleges or districts you could have such staffing formulas. You might also use an allocation model to each campus that includes all of the tuition and student fee revenue and the state student contact hour funding. The college presidents, with input from each of their administration, faculty, and staff, could have much discretion in allocating these appropriations to their departments and to meet their internal priority needs and goals.

Unencumbered Fund Balance

Most states allow for an annual end-of-year unencumbered fund balance after the annual budget has been balanced. This fund balance is an excellent thing to have as a contingency fund to balance annual budgets in tough economic years, to support new programs, facilities, or campuses until they can become self-sufficient, and for special "one-time" expenses, such as purchasing land for future college growth. At ACCD, we had a board policy to maintain a minimum fund balance of 15 percent of the last year's operating budget, which for 2007 was a target fund balance of $36,000,000. We exceeded that target. That is a good place to be, and it also allows you to obtain substantial interest revenue for the operating budget each year.

CEOs Contingency Reserve Account

The CEO's contingency reserve account should be budgeted, which is not always specified in traditional budget models. From my experience, 1 percent of the operating budget should be so set aside in the CEO's contingency account of the operating budget. At ACCD this was US$2.5 million. We called this account the Chancellor's Reserve Account, which was to be allocated as the year progressed. No money should be spent directly from this account. Budget transfers should be done after the start of the fiscal year. They may be requested by the college or campus presidents or the district vice chancellors, and reviewed by the CFO. However, they should require the approval of the CEO, to meet emergencies, underfunded priorities, and other one-time needs. They are budget allocation transfers for the current year only, with the new annual appropriation starting again in the chancellor's contingency account at the start of the next fiscal year. Another method of funding this contingency account is to start the year with a smaller appropriation, and then to accrue monies from salary residuals from open (vacant) positions during the fiscal year. The CEO must have some method to access funds for such contingencies, to meet the unanticipated or underbudgeted needs of either the district offices or of the college or campus presidents. This contingency chancellor's reserve is in effect a reserve for the priority needs of the entire institution. To demonstrate transparency and accountability, a specific list should be maintained of all budget transfers funded from the chancellor's reserve account. This list (when, what, amount) should be revised and dated with each appropriation, with a running free balance, and made available to high-level administrators and others.

Salary Residuals

Salary residuals need a method for accumulating and distributing the unpaid salaries of positions that become temporarily or permanently vacant during the fiscal year. Each and every approved position in the budget should be assigned a unique position control number, and should be fully funded in the budget. Salary residuals are created as a result of vacant lines after termination salaries have been fully paid. These budgeted salary residuals can be left to accumulate for the year-end fund balance, or they may be budget-transferred for other purposes, either where they are, or preferably to a central salary residual account where they can be reprogrammed for other high-priority needs, or for new positions elsewhere that were not in the initial budget, bur have now been approved.

Direct Instruction and Other Functional Categories

Direct instruction, consisting mainly of the salaries and overloads (for teaching additional courses beyond their base workload) of full-time faculty, and for the salaries of adjunct faculty, is generally about 50 percent of the entire operating budget expense of a community college. This has been consistently confirmed by various national studies, and by data comparisons of peer institutions in recent years, including for the ACCD and the other five largest community colleges in Texas in 2006. The ACCD spent another 10 percent or so on academic support, another 10 percent or so on student services, and most of the remaining 30 percent of the operating budget on the categories of institutional support and plant operation and maintenance.

It is therefore very important to have a staffing and budget plan for this expense, based on average class size targets for different courses. Cost ratios can be computed and budgeted for average faculty costs per class for faculty overload and adjunct faculty instruction. Develop faculty staffing formulas based on those class sizes and the departmental enrollment projections, and a ratio of the numbers of class sections to be taught by full-time faculty in-load, faculty overloads, and by part-time adjunct faculty. While some community colleges have had higher percentages of fulltime faculty in the past, there is a clear trend toward more use of part-time adjunct faculty, who are less expensive to employ. Some colleges have gone below 50 percent for full-time faculty, but many faculty and administrators believe that lower levels would compromise the quality of instruction. My recommendation for the mix of teaching (by percentage of classes) that is cost-effective while maintaining quality instruction is as follows: Full-time faculty in-load, 50 percent; faculty overload, 10 percent; and part-time adjunct faculty, 40 percent.

Ratio of Compensation to Total Budget

Many community colleges target a ratio that is an appropriate guide for community colleges today. The total expenditures for all compensation costs for salaries and fringe benefits, including health care premiums, FICA (Federal Insurance Contributions Act), etc., should not be allowed to exceed 80 percent of your total operating expenses. This remaining 20 percent of budget appropriations is about the minimum required to purchase supplies and equipment, pay utilities bills, and all other noncompensation expenses. Before new staff can be approved, or salary increases can be provided, or fringe benefits increases can be funded, your annual and long-range budget planning models must take into account projected cost increases in all noncompensation expenses, and attempt to maintain this 20 percent noncompensation ratio. There is always pressure from faculty and staff for most or even for all of revenue increases to go for higher salaries or fringe benefits. There is always pressure from administrators for more staffing. These requests must be balanced against budget constraints and limited fiscal resources. Adhering to the 80 percent/20 percent ratio is a good guideline to follow in budget planning and preparation.

Lessons Learned Concerning the Budget Planning Process

The five-year budget model does allow us to plan and project revenues and expenses for the coming budget year and in outline for the next three years, while updating the data for the current fiscal year. While reviewing the current year budget, we do not simply add or subtract *incrementally* around the margins to prepare the next budget. We would revisit assumptions, projections, and priorities, and annually calculate staffing and allocation formulas based on new realities. We would account for *inflation*, and for the cost and impact of new facilities and programs. A "CEO's Contingency" account is created, funded, and monitored. A healthy unrestricted fund balance is maintained, as a matter of board policy. All of the key *stakeholders* are given a meaningful role to play. Information is gathered, compared with peers, discussed, and widely distributed. External expert *consultants* are used. A budget preparation *calendar* is developed and implemented. New programs are subject to *cost-benefit* analysis before they are approved and implemented. Academic or support programs of declining enrollment, or with significantly increasing costs, are similarly analyzed as part of each fiscal year's resource allocation process.

Class Size and Faculty Staffing Models

Class size and faculty staffing models should be continuously analyzed, refined as necessary, implemented, and monitored in an open and accountable process of enrollment management. As a reward mechanism, an academic department that exceeds their budgeted class size average is allowed to keep, to reallocate, and to spend the savings in adjunct faculty salaries for the lower number of courses required for their student enrollment, as they are allowed to keep and to spend the course student lab fees and other generated revenues. Budget-projected enrollments, revenues, and expenses are monitored throughout the year and are compared to the actual enrollment and revenue data to make the necessary plus or minus adjustments. If at the end of the fall term, enrollment and therefore student tuition and fee revenue is above projections on any campus, then they will be allocated that additional student fees revenue generated by that enrollment in order to offset the additional delivery expenses that are related to those same enrollment increases. Many people underestimate the large cost savings that can be realized by even moderate increases to average class size. When enrollment increases moderately, there is an opportunity to increase class size, thus increasing revenue while not increasing faculty cost. Conversely, when enrollment declines, it is very important to reduce the numbers of class sections, so that you do not have the same instructional expense with less offsetting revenue from student tuition and fees. If the target average class size is 20 students in each of 20 English classes, then a 10 percent enrollment decrease from projection should not result in 20 English classes of 18 students each. Two classes should be cancelled during registration and have 18 classes of 20 students each. At the ACCD, we had more than 15,000 individual credit course class sections each year. An increase in average class size of one student, from 20 to 21, was a 5 percent increase in faculty productivity, producing 750 fewer class sections (5 percent of 15,000), and a cost savings of more than $1,700,000 (750 sections at the average adjunct faculty rate of $2,300 per section). Academic deans and department chairpersons must add, cancel, or combine class sections to meet their assigned class size targets. This requires decisions as to which classes can be increased by one, two, or more students, and which classes cannot be increased for academic or facilities limitation reasons. These decisions are best made at the campus and academic department level by academic administrators.

Budget Committees

There should be academic committees who review and recommend budget-related decisions including class size, student lab fees, potential new academic and student support programs, and the possible elimination of low enrollment programs. However, budget preparation should be initiated each year by a budget preparation team, under the direction of the CEO and chaired by the CFO, including business office staff. This committee should do the data collection and analysis, past history, peer community college comparisons, revenue and expense projections, and staffing and allocation formula data runs to prepare the initial draft of the next annual operating budget. The enrollment projections are best provided by a district office of institutional research, with input from, but not directed by, the campus presidents and their staffs. The budget committee to review the work of this budget preparation team should be the executive committee of the community college, chaired by the CEO, and consisting of the campus presidents, district vice chancellors, and other high-level district administrators, and perhaps one representative of the faculty union or senate. For a board that has board subcommittees, one of those subcommittees could be the board committee on audit, budget, and finance. Reports can be made to, and workshops can be held with this subcommittee, and then with the entire board of trustees. This can be done prior to the final presentation to the board for their review and final approval of the annual operating budget, which must be done at an announced open meeting of the full board of trustees.

Funding Anticipated Future Enrollment Growth

There has been a decades-long trend of community college enrollment growth, which is expected to continue. How can community colleges project and plan for their budget growth to accommodate their enrollment growth over time? The general answer to that increasing annual expense problem is as follows.

Fund Enrollment Growth Expenses

Fund enrollment growth expenses with the corresponding enrollment growth revenue of the increase in student tuition and other fees that generates an immediate increase in total collections from the greater volume of student credits at the same per-credit rates, and the increase in state funding for the greater volume of student contact hours that comes later in the next state funding cycle. It must be remembered that community college boards mostly have control over student tuition and fee rates, control (with voter support) over local tax rates, but no control (hopefully some influence) over their state funding support.

Fund Inflation

Fund inflation (annual consumer price index [CPI] increases for goods, services, and salaries) from the inflation-created larger sales tax and local property tax revenues at the same tax rates, during those economic growth periods in the business cycle

Partially Fund Annual Movement through Salary Schedules

Partially fund annual movement through salary schedules and periodic general salary increases with the differences between the higher salaries of retiring and otherwise terminating faculty and staff with the lower salaries of their entry-level replacements. All jobs should have a salary schedule with minimums and maximums for each pay level. Employees should be allowed to progress through their pay ranges toward the maximum, but not beyond, unless they are promoted into a higher pay level (or faculty academic rank) position, with a higher salary maximum. There are many such community college salary schedules available for review. Consider implementing a model that has a 50 percent spread for each pay level, except for faculty positions, for which there could be a 100 percent spread for the four commonly used academic rank pay "'levels" of instructor, assistant professor, associate professor, and full professor. One full professor retirement at the top of that pay schedule, at say $80,000, who is replaced by an entry level instructor at say $40,000, will provide for a reasonable salary increase for each of the remaining faculty in that department. The same is generally true of staff turnover throughout the institution. The remaining part of your annual salary increases comes from the same inflation factors that in most years will provide additional state and local sales and property tax base growth, and tax revenue growth, without the need to increase tax rates.

Conclusion

The proposed approach for an effective budget and planning model will be of use to practitioners seeking to improve upon budget creation, while avoiding common errors of traditional models. The planning, developing, implementing, monitoring, and adjusting of the annual and longer-term operational budget is a critical piece of the success of any community college. Community colleges are viral to the success of the United States, and to the education of our people. They are in the forefront of the United Stares' commitment to the concept of quality education for the many, not just for the few.

It is now many years ago, in his seminal work *The Outline of History*, H. G. Wells wisely observed that: "History becomes more and more a race between education and catastrophe." It is the job of the community colleges, and of America's other educational institutions, to make certain that catastrophe does not win!

Reference

Wells, Herbert G. 1920. *The Outline of History*. New York: Doubleday and Company, Inc.

CHAPTER 28

THE HIGH COST OF BUILDING A BETTER UNIVERSITY

DONALD J. GUCKERT AND JERI RIPLEY KING

Higher education facilities seem to come at premium cost, even taking into account that educational facilities tend to cost more. The authors argue that this is due to appropriate and strategic high aspirations.

Higher education design and construction project managers perform their work on the forward-edge of an ever-changing world. We face increasingly complex facilities, shortening time lines, proliferating code and regulatory requirements, emerging technologies, and growing concerns for indoor air quality and environmental sustainability. As we strive to keep abreast of these changes, we continue to hear one question from governing boards, administrators, and customers: Why does it cost so much?

We cannot deny that educational facilities cost more to build than many other types of construction. Even in the realm of education, there is a hierarchy ranging from sophisticated research facilities to parking structures. Yet, all our facilities seem to come at a premium cost. Lower cost alternatives are always available, but our institutions choose, instead, to build to a quality level that is above the baseline. These choices flow from the institution's vision and strategic plan. The facilities we construct reflect the values and aspirations of our institutions.

A Sense of Place

Many universities are vying for national and international recognition. To do this, they compete for students, faculty, and research funding. More than ever before, university building designs are viewed as enhancing and preserving our institutional heritage while creating an attractive environment in which to learn, discover, and live. We do not just build or renovate structures; we create a "sense of place."

Clearly, this sense of place plays an important role in marketing the institution. In a 2001 study of college-bound high school seniors by Noel-Levitz, a market research firm, the most notable experiences seniors encountered on their best college visit had to do with the appearance of the campus and its facilities (Noel-Levitz 2002). This study confirmed the 1986 report by the Carnegie Foundation for the Advancement of Teaching that found that for 62 percent of prospective students, the most influential factor during a campus visit was the appearance of the buildings and grounds (Carnegie Foundation for the Advancement of Teaching 1986).

We do not just build or renovate structures; we create a 'sense of place.'

The attractive appearance of the grounds and buildings comes at a cost. In constructing a new building for a campus environment, we seek elaborate designs that convey emotions and reactions that range from stimulating debates over architecture to communicating notions of continuity and timelessness. Often the little extras add a lot to the quality of the built campus environment: prominent building entrances, buried utilities in tunnels and chases, hidden downspouts in interior walls, screened waste receptacles, underground cooling towers, discrete access for service vehicles, and extensive landscaping and courtyards.

Land must be used carefully, with attention to gathering places and circulation. The need for green space must balance the need for building space. This drives us to optimize building footprints by building skyward and below grade to conserve precious campus real estate. Multiple stories require more costly foundations and structures designed to withstand seismic and wind loading standards. Stair towers and elevators consume project resources and decrease the percentage of assignable space. All these factors lead to a higher cost per square foot.

Codes, Regulations, and Standards

The type of occupancy determines the applicable building code requirements. The large assemblies found in most university facilities dictate the highest level of life safety design. These code requirements have a tremendous impact on cost by requiring stair towers, fire-rated corridors, fireproofing on structural members, fire alarm systems, sprinklers, and smoke evacuation systems. Even the grade of carpeting in a university facility is selected to minimize concerns about flame spread.

In addition to codes, building design and construction must meet a myriad of legislative mandates and regulations. The list reads like alphabet soup: ADA, EPA, OSHA, and more. These laws and agencies govern building accessibility, removal of hazardous waste, asbestos, light ballasts, lead paint, storm water runoff, construction dust control, noise control, and more. Then, there are the state permits, local permits, contracts, agreements, and requirements by donors and funding agencies that must be managed.

The type of facility and occupancy also drives ventilation requirements. Labs require more ventilation than classrooms; classrooms require more ventilation than offices. Increased ventilation leads to upsizing HVAC systems, because outside air must be heated or cooled before it is delivered to the finished space. In a trend toward thwarting indoor air quality problems, building mechanical codes have increased ventilation requirements far beyond the infrastructure capacities in many buildings built before the 1990s. The impact is profound on renovation projects where HVAC costs alone can consume the majority of the project budget.

Institutional and Statutory Requirements

Institutional and statutory requirements can drive up costs too. Contractors must provide the highest industry coverage for insurance and bonding and construct in accordance with the highest industry standards. Architects may be required to furnish professional liability insurance. Public owners must follow state procurement statutes, which increase design and bidding costs and constrain the use of more cost-effective delivery approaches. Many institutions require contractors to pay prevailing wages to their workers, equating to union-scale.

An often overlooked impact on cost is the expectation that construction activities will be conducted with minimal disruption to campus life. The campus is a protected environment that accommodates learning, social interaction, discovery, living, dining, recreation, and public service. As invited guests into this haven, contractors are required to conduct their activities in a manner that minimizes the impact on the institution's primary missions. This is not a typical construction site. Project costs go up dramatically when universities restrict access to building sites; limit space for staging; require off-campus parking; enforce jobsite cleanliness; add fencing and protection; route construction vehicles around, rather than through, the campus; limit noise and hours of operation; and impose complex phasing schemes to accommodate academic calendars.

Time Is Money

Demanding schedules are an inherent part of higher education design and construction efforts. In general, shortening the time line will drive up costs, lengthening the schedule will drive them down. An aggressive three-month renovation will be unaffordable if we only allow six weeks for completion of the work. Conversely, easing the schedule to six months will yield savings.

Contractors, when bidding a shortened schedule, will increase their bids to reflect overtime payments to workers, incentive payments to vendors, reduced worker productivity, and contingencies to cover the risks of falling behind schedule or completing late. On the other hand, extra time in the schedule reduces the contractor's risk, facilitates effective coordination among subcontractors, and provides sufficient time for fabrication and delivery of materials and equipment and other accommodations that result in a more cost-effective project delivery.

More often than not, we aggressively work toward inflexible milestones, such as semester starts and athletic event schedules. In research environments, the need to be up-and-running is paramount. When the higher education environment demands design and construction projects delivered on increasingly shorter time lines, this drives up the cost of university projects.

Complexity

The facilities we build are among the most challenging in the building construction industry. We build state-of-the-art research facilities, high-occupancy performance and athletic venues, heavily trafficked and technological learning environments, and living and social environments that must appeal to a new generation. In short, we are constructing complex communities.

Program activities often dictate the need for a combination of classrooms, laboratories, meeting rooms, and offices. Although grouping one type of activity in a facility would reduce costs, our buildings rarely house only one type of activity. In addition, they must meet the functional requirements of the campus environment.

For example, classrooms and auditoriums are usually on the lower levels of a building and demand larger, column-free spans. The lower levels may then have to support upper floors designed to accommodate floor loadings for bookshelves and lab equipment. Inverting these spaces, by placing the column-free classrooms on the upper floors and the heavy load-bearing spaces on the lower floors, would be more cost-effective but less functional in a campus setting.

Our facilities must accommodate a mix of functions and heavy traffic. To manage this, we install complex building systems. Mechanical systems are designed for extreme conditions: hottest and coldest temperatures, humidity extremes, strictest climate control, and highest occupancy. We recognize that the design of a mechanical system represents the greatest opportunity for energy conservation in the future. Investments in energy-efficient mechanical systems will yield a lower stream of future utility costs.

Maintainability, Sustainability, and Longevity

Good stewardship involves constructing buildings that will last, buildings that can be easily maintained, and buildings that can be converted to other programmatic or technologic uses in the future.

With many people using university facilities in frequent cycles throughout the course of a day, not only do the structures need to be able to handle this, but also the components of these facilities must be of a quality to withstand constant heavy use and abuse. Because of the campus building boom in the 1960s, we know all too well the consequences of cheaper designed and constructed facilities that were not built to survive the test of time. Our requirement for durability raises the price of doors, door hardware, carpeting, entrance mats, floor tile, and restroom fixtures, but it lowers the future costs of maintaining and replacing the lower quality products. We are resolved not to repeat the shortsighted mistakes that were made by a previous generation of campus administrators and facilities managers.

Environmental sustainability is another factor having an increasing impact on construction costs within higher education.

The way we use our facilities demands that we construct utility systems within the building to high reliability standards. This often results in paying for system redundancies, generators,

Your House on Campus

by Donald J. Guckert and Jeri Ripley King

"You've got to be kidding! I could build a nice house for that amount!"

How many times have we heard that the cost of a "simple" renovation would buy a high-end home in a nice neighborhood? Customers typically react with sticker shock over the cost of a campus renovation when they receive the initial project estimate. This is the point at which worlds collide; where the institutional construction world of the project manager meets the customer's residential construction frame of reference.

Trying to justify the costs of institutional construction within a residential frame of reference is not easy. These two types of construction are a world apart. However, just for the fun of it, we wondered, what would it take to renovate your house into a campus facility? Suppose you request that we renovate the living room into a classroom, the kitchen into a lab, and the bedroom into an office. In addition, you request that this facility is located on campus. Let's take a walk through your house (Figure 28.1) to see what we will need to do.

To begin with, we'll need to make the facility safe and accessible. We'll add an elevator to the second floor, and an exit stair tower connecting all floors to the outside. To make this building look like it belongs on our campus, we'll arrange for matching towers and give the building an identifiable look. Unfortunately, this will add considerable cost and space to the building while not adding any space for program needs. After we widen the interior hallways and stairways for increased traffic and install a utility chase from the basement to the attic, we will actually reduce the amount of assignable space.

As a university facility, the house will fall under a different classification as far as building codes are concerned. This means we'll need to replace the $15 battery-operated smoke detectors

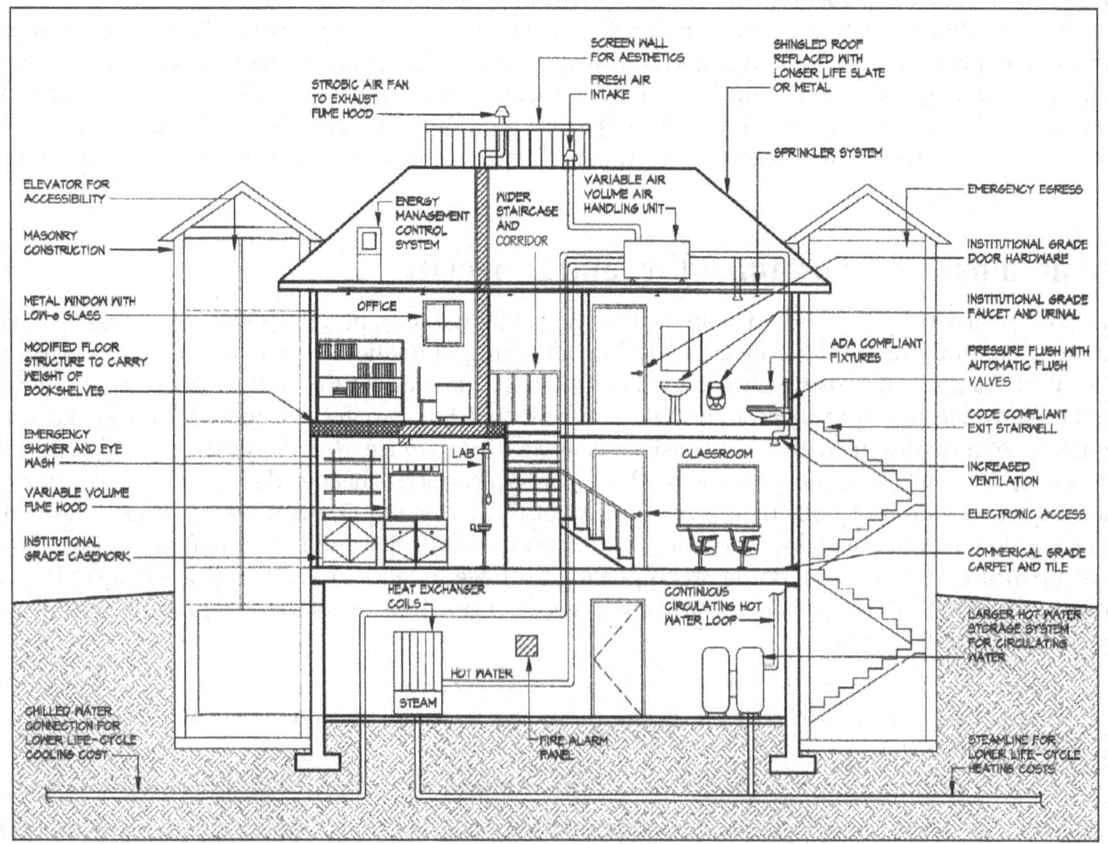

Figure 28.1 Your house on campus.

with a $15,000 fire protection system. This system, which includes a fire alarm panel, wired sensors, and sprinkler system, meets all of the requirements of the local fire marshal. To inhibit the spread of flames and smoke from one room to another, we will have to reconstruct the walls that separate the rooms from the hallway and make them "fire-rated walls." This is not cheap! The solid doors mounted to the metal doorframes that we'll use to replace the house's hollow doors and wooden frames are also not cheap.

We know the budget for this renovation is limited. Before the money runs out, we need to look at the mechanical systems. By code, our lab, classroom, office, and restroom require outside ventilation that your house doesn't have. The small air-conditioning unit and gas furnace will have to go. With the big increase in airflow, it wouldn't keep up after the first five minutes. We'll connect to chilled water and steam from our central plant. Our campus building will need redundant, dependable, code-compliant, and cost-effective mechanical systems.

Finally, we move to the kitchen. To convert it to a lab, we'll take out the $600 kitchen stove and hood and replace it with a $25,000 variable flow fume hood. Let's hope we won't need a strobic air fan for that hood; you don't even want to think about that cost. Those kitchen cabinets will come out to allow for the built-in lab casework. The refrigerator will have to go, too. In its place will be a $10,000 environmental chamber. We'll open up the walls when we install the lab gases, electrical conduits, and corrosion-resistant plumbing. While we are in the walls, let's replace the wooden studs with metal studs. Then, to complete this "kitchen remodeling," we'll replace the linoleum with an $8,000 epoxy floor, and the Formica counters with epoxy resin.

We're going to need to remove the ceiling above the kitchen to increase the structural support necessary to handle the small library in the office above. The anticipated weight of books will stress the existing floor joists. While the ceiling is open, we'll install the circulating hot water system, designed to serve the lab and restroom, and we'll upsize the mechanical ductwork to meet the new airflow requirements. Speaking of airflow, that "whooshing" sound will be distracting in the classroom next door, so we will need to put in sound attenuation devices.

To meet institutional standards, the wooden windows will need to be replaced with metal, commercial-grade windows that have energy-efficient glazing. Similarly, the roof shingles will need to be replaced with slate, due to concerns about life-cycle maintenance and architectural consistency. While we're on the roof, let's screen the unsightly mechanical systems. Oh yeah, we can't forget to do something about the pigeons.

Let's look at the outside again, just for a minute. Only the front facade was bricked when your house was originally constructed, so we'll need to install bricks on three sides. After all, our university is trying to project a certain image, and your house is now on campus.

At this point, we have more scope than budget. Money is running out, and there are more things we need to do to bring your house into compliance with our institutional standards.

What happened here? In trying to meet the more stringent codes, efforts to reduce future operating costs, aesthetic requirements, and programmatic needs, we exceeded the funds available for this renovation. For the money this renovation will cost, you really could build a nice house. But not on our campus!

uninterruptible power supply systems, harmonics reduction, and central utility systems. In addition, telecommunication/computer wiring and pathways are often overbuilt to enable user flexibility and save the expense of rewiring and reconstructing walls or ceilings in the near future. We have learned that planning for tomorrow can cut down on the costs of retrofitting existing buildings.

Higher education constructs buildings to last beyond our lifetimes.

Environmental sustainability is another factor having an increasing impact on construction costs within higher education. Facilities are being constructed with recyclable materials, materials that are certified as manufactured from renewable sources, and building and system designs that use progressive methods and technologies to conserve energy and reduce the waste stream. Pursuing Leadership in Energy and Environmental Design (LEED™) certification, developed by the U.S. Green Building Council, brings the prestige and positive publicity sought by many institutions seeking a progressive and environmentally sensitive image. However, this comes at a higher cost.

Making these long-term, sound, investment choices is what separates higher education from the vast array of other building environments. Higher education, more than any other built community and commercial environment, constructs buildings to last beyond our lifetimes. Every institution with an active building program envisions itself in existence into perpetuity. We make the choice to invest in higher quality construction of our campus, in part, because we have so many years ahead of us to reap the benefits on these initial investments.

Why Does It Cost So Much?

It is said that excellence is in the details. Thousands of details go into the construction of a university building. Rarely can we point to one item as driving the high project cost. The high cost of university construction is caused by the accumulation of investments in all of the details that go into building a quality facility. If we are to compete with the best institutions, we must meet the demands for higher quality facilities.

Construction costs mirror the values and aspirations of the institution. Our universities choose to provide stimulating, enriching environments that will serve our students, faculty, and researchers well into the future. We are building a better university, one that is built on the traditions of the past and constructed to compete for faculty and students into the next century.

References

Carnegie Foundation for the Advancement of Teaching. 1986. How Do Students Choose a College? *Change* (January/February): 29–32.

Noel-Levitz. 2002. *After 9/11: Campus Visit Expectations, Experiences, and Impact on Enrollment*. Retrieved October 2, 2003, from the World Wide Web: www.noellevitz.com/library/research/campus_visit/index.asp.

CHAPTER 29

DO COSTS DIFFER BETWEEN FOR-PROFIT AND NOT-FOR-PROFIT PRODUCERS OF HIGHER EDUCATION?

DAVID N. LABAND AND BERNARD F. LENTZ

In theory, not-for-profit organizations will be characterized by higher production costs per unit of output than for-profit producers of otherwise-identical goods/services, since profit maximization implies cost minimization per unit of output; breaking even does not imply cost minimization and, indeed, may imply inflated costs. We explore the empirical validity of this hypothesis in the context of higher education. Using 1996 data, we estimate multiproduct cost functions for 1,450 public, 1,316 private, not-for-profit, and 176 private, for-profit institutions of higher education in the United States. We fail to find a statistically significant difference between for-profit and not-for-profit private providers, but do find a statistically significant difference between private, not-for-profit institutions and public institutions.

Introduction

> Competition at the top is heavily positional. "Excellence" and "prestige" drive colleges, but these goals can be judged only with respect to others. Essentially the players become trapped in a sort of upward spiral, an arms race, seeking relative position; in the case of education, it may, in the extreme, involve expensive 'competitive amenities' that do not produce sufficient benefit to justify their cost directly, but are important to an individual school because others are offering these same amenities. (Winston, 1999, p. 30)

There is a slowly developing literature in which researchers investigate the relationship between costs and outputs in higher education. Although it has been established that there are significant differences in the cost functions between public and private institutions of higher education (IHEs; Cohn, Rhine, and Santos, 1989; Laband and Lentz, 2003), there has been no empirical analysis of possible cost differences between private for-profit IHEs and private not-for-profit IHEs. In theory, at least, not-for-profit IHEs arguably will be characterized by higher production costs per unit of output (e.g., per student) than the for-profit IHEs, since profit maximization implies cost minimization per unit of output; breaking even does not imply cost minimization and, indeed, may imply inflated costs.

Both Winston (1999) and Ehrenberg (2000) have suggested that competition between not-for-profit IHEs is "positional" in nature. In terms of both the internal and external reward structures, university administrators are (at least partial) residual claimants to how well their college or university stacks up relative to others. Thus, an IHE administrator behaves in ways that maximize his/her institution's position relative to other institutions against which it competes (for high-quality students, endowment funds, etc.). Such competition takes the form of trying to be the best at everything, with obvious implications for total costs.

The straightforward implication of such positional competition among not-for-profit IHEs is that they should be characterized by higher costs of production than for-profit IHEs. To our knowledge, this hypothesis has not been subjected to empirical testing. Using 1996 data, we estimate multi-product cost functions for 1,450 public, 1,316 private, not-for-profit, and 176 private, for-profit institutions of higher education in the United States. To our great surprise, we fail to find a statistically significant difference between for-profit and not-for-profit private providers of educational services, but do find a statistically significant difference between private, not-for-profit institutions and public institutions.

Data

Our data come from the National Center for Education Statistics (NCES) 1995–1996 fiscal year surveys on IHE finances, enrollments, and compensation. These surveys are part of the Integrated Postsecondary Education Data System (IPEDS), developed by and for the NCES. Prior to 1986, these institutions were surveyed under the Higher Education General Information Survey (HEGIS). However, the IPEDS data are more extensive than HEGIS, as they not only include the schools surveyed under HEGIS, they also include any other institutions that grant a bachelor's, master's, doctoral, or first professional degree and are eligible to participate in Title IV financial aid programs. Moreover, an institution that consists of multiple campuses is treated as a single entity under HEGIS, but treated as separate institutions in the IPEDS data. The latter is more consistent with our notion that economies of scale and scope reflect on production at a single location. Responses were received from 3,520 of the 3,965 IHEs surveyed. After omitting institutions with missing data on variables critical to our analysis, we had usable samples of 1,450 public IHEs and 1,492 private IHEs, of which 176 were for-profit and 1,316 were not-for-profit. While we acknowledge that data from 1995–1996 might be regarded as dated, this is the last year for which comparable data across sectors exists, due to changes in financial reporting by private IHEs beginning in the 1996–1997 fiscal year. Definitions and sample statistics for the variables used in our analysis are reported in Table 29.1.

As revealed in Table 29.1, there are truly stark differences between the three types of IHE with respect to their production of educational services. For example, only 4% of the private, for-profit IHEs produced externally funded grant research, whereas the comparable percentages for private, not-for-profit IHEs and public IHEs were 27.7 and 42.4, respectively. The average amount of externally funded grant research was $3,000 for the private, for-profit IHEs, $2.93 million for the private, not-for-profit IHEs, and $7.89 million for public IHEs. It seems abundantly clear that production of externally funded grant research is just not an activity in which the private, for-profit IHEs engage. Only one in eight private, for-profit IHEs has a graduate program, and the average number of graduate students across all 176 for-profit IHEs was 34. In contrast, one third of the public IHEs offered graduate education, with an average of 509 full-time equivalent (FTE) graduate students enrolled, and nearly 60% of the private, not-for-profit IHEs offered graduate programs, with an average enrollment of 343. Note also the differences in compensation paid to faculty: in 1995–1996, the average annual compensation paid by private, not-for-profit IHEs was $47,384—nearly 50% greater than the $31,976 paid by private, for-profit IHEs. This was exceeded in both cases by the faculty compensation paid at public IHEs, which averaged $53,247.[1] Bottom line: total costs are 10 (5) times greater at public (private, not-for-profit) IHEs than at private, for-profit IHEs, an artifact in large measure of scale effects.

In Table 29.2, we identify sizable differences between these three types of institutions with regard to instructional costs and degree production. During the 1995–1996 academic year, the average instructional cost per FTE student was nearly twice as high at private not-for-profit IHEs ($19,186) as at private, for-profit IHEs ($9,935). The average instructional cost at public IHEs ($11,032) also was considerably below the average instructional cost at private, not-for-profit IHEs. We observe that private, for-profit IHEs awarded fewer degrees than private, not-for-profit IHEs, which, in turn, awarded fewer degrees than public IHEs. Private, for-profit IHEs had the fewest degree programs; public IHEs had the most. Relatedly, there was significantly greater degree program concentration of students in the private, for-profit IHEs than in the private, not-for-profit IHEs. Public IHEs were characterized by the least degree program concentration.[2]

We now turn to the question of whether public IHEs, private, not-for-profit IHEs, and private, for-profit IHEs are characterized by significantly different cost structures once differences in the production of educational outputs are controlled for.

TABLE 29.1

Variable Descriptions and Sample Statistics

Variable Symbol	Description	Public		Private for-Profit		Private Not-for-Profit	
		Mean	**Std. Dev.**	**Mean**	**Std. Dev.**	**Mean**	**Std. Dev.**
TC	Total IHE expenditures (millions of $)	65.843	131.223	6.643	7.991	34.840	102.122
AVECOMP	average annual salary plus fringe benefits for non-medical faculty	53,247	11,955	31,976	12,798	47,384	17,166
RESDUM	= 1 if research > 0; = 0 otherwise	.424	.494	.040	.196	.277	.448
UGDUM	= 1 if undergraduate enrollment > 0; = 0 otherwise	.995	.069	.943	.232	.883	.322
GRADDUM	= 1 if graduate enrollment > 0; = 0 otherwise	.335	.479	.125	.332	.592	.492
RES	research output (millions of federal, state, local and private grant $)	7.890	32.639	0.003	0.023	2.930	21.509
UG	full-time equivalent undergraduate student enrollment (thousands)	4.413	4.733	0.644	0.704	1.228	1.710
GRAD	full-time equivalent graduate student enrollment (thousands)	0.509	1.332	0.034	0.150	0.343	1.011
RESUG	FTE undergraduate enrollment × research output (billions)	126.317	0.003	0.028	140.914	17.535	149.927
RESGRAD	FTE graduate enrollment × research output (billions)	39.650	247.544	0.000	0.000	16.267	169.009
GRADUG	FTE undergraduate enrollment × FTE graduate enrollment (millions)	6.961	27.801	0.041	0.397	1.453	8.867
COMPRES	faculty compensation × research output (billions)	571.868	2501.853	0.106	0.788	256.543	2115.840
COMPUG	faculty compensation × FTE undergraduate enrollment (millions)	262.376	335.593	24.387	36.925	262.376	335.593
COMPGRAD	faculty compensation × FTE graduate enrollment (millions)	34.832	98.673	1.723	8.879	34.832	98.673
Sample Size		1,450		176		1,314	

TABLE 29.2

Tests of Differences in Instructional Characteristics

	Instructional Costs ($ million)	Degree Concentration	Total Degrees Awarded	Total Degree Programs
(a) Private, for-profit	9.9354 (5.4101)	0.1549 (0.1712)	283.3239 (298.8104)	8.1420 (5.5680)
(b) Private, not-for-profit	19.1860 (27.0090)	0.1260 (0.1540)	445.9932 (736.7627)	27.6431 (31.9778)
(c) Public	11.0320 (15.3720)	0.0936 (0.1137)	1072.1400 (1320.8500)	53.9564 (49.0114)
t statistic for (a) ≠ (b)	10.34***	−2.22**	5.36***	19.96***
t statistic for (a) ≠ (c)	3.12***	4.46***	−19.05***	−33.78***
t statistic for (b) ≠ (c)	8.34***	6.08***	−15.55***	−16.84***

Note: Standard errors are in parentheses.

***Significant at 0.01 level; **significant at 0.05 level.

Empirical Methodology

Koshal and Koshal (1995) analyzed average total cost at 204 Ph.D.-granting institutions during the 1990–1991 academic year. Controlling for FTE enrollment, freshman SAT scores, and Carnegie classifications, they found that costs drop as the student/faculty ratio (taken as a measure of class size) increases. In their subsequent analysis of 158 private and 171 public comprehensive IHEs, Koshal and Koshal (1999) also found evidence of cost economies related to increasing class size. McLaughlin, Montgomery, Smith, Mahan, and Broomall (1980) estimated a total cost function for 1,347 public, 4-year IHEs using data from the 1975–1976 academic year and found economies of scale with respect to student enrollment. Using data from 1983 for 147 doctoral programs, de Groot, McMahon, and Volkwein (1991) estimated a 3-output translog cost function and found evidence of economies of scale at the mean levels of their outputs. Nelson and Hevert (1992) analyzed departmental expenditures on instruction and research in 31 academic departments at the same university, for the period 1979–1983. Based on their translog model estimation, they found no evidence of economies of scale with respect to student enrollments once class size was controlled for.

We follow the lead of Cohn et al. (1989) and Toutkoushian (1999) in treating producers of higher education as multiproduct "firms." Building on the methodology developed by Baumol, Panzar, and Willig (1982), we estimate a multiproduct cost function for IHEs, with measures of the research and teaching outputs entered directly. Our model is specified as a flexible fixed cost cubic function, with a dummy variable F_i that assumes a value of 1 (0) for (non)positive amounts of the output Y_i:

$$\text{Cost}_i = a_0 + \sum_i a_i F_i + \sum_i b_i Y_i + \sum_i c_i Y_i^2 + \sum_i d_i Y_i^3 + \sum_i \sum_j e_{ij} Y_i Y_j + \eta_i \tag{1}$$

Total cost refers to total expenditures by IHE I in 1996, a_0 and the a_is, b_is, c_is, d_is, and e_{ij}s are scalars, and η_i is the error term, which is assumed to be i.i.d. Output produced includes undergraduate education (measured as the number of FTE undergraduate students in a 12-month period), graduate education (the total number of FTE graduate students in a 12-month period), and externally funded research (measured as the sum of federal, state, local, and private grant dollars).[3] The F_i variables reflect differences across IHEs with respect to the fixed costs of producing different product sets.

We estimated the same equation for each of the three types of producers of educational services; our ordinary least squares (OLS) estimation results are reported in Table 29.3. To represent the classic textbook cost function that can show (dis)economies of scale, we estimated a total cost function that included squared and cubic measures of the three outputs in the model. Given the nonlinear structure of the model and the interaction terms, it is difficult to draw conclusions about

TABLE 29.3

Three-Output Cubic Cost Function Estimates

Variable	Public Institutions	For-Profit Private Institutions	Not-for-Profit Private Institutions
Intercept	–15.3021 (13.4149)	–0.7174 (2.5375)	–1.5871 (2.9344)
RESDUM	5.7039*** (1.7827)	0.1235 (6.9028)	3.7305*** (1.1250)
GRADDUM	1.6187 (2.3165)	1.3085 (1.8962)	0.4378 (1.0611)
AVECOMP	–0.3188 (0.3630)	0.0692 (0.0834)	0.0868 (0.0992)
COMPSQ	0.0046 (0.0034)	–0.0013 (0.0013)	–0.0003 (0.0010)
RES	2.8732*** (0.3353)	146.2721 (1259.9615)	6.0348*** (0.2980)
RES^2	–0.0004 (0.0011)	–547.8706 (9379.6030)	–0.0009 (0.0014)
RES^3	–5.12E-6** (2.19E-6)	2589.6499 (23190.6482)	–3.12E-6 (2.02E-6)
UG	1.3746 (1.2756)	8.1980*** (2.6202)	3.0975** (1.5516)
UG^2	0.0301 (0.0844)	–3.4924 (2.1867)	–1.5915*** (0.2158)
UG^3	0.0030 (0.0023)	0.6277 (0.4426)	0.0357*** (0.0064)
GRAD	–7.7252 (8.0202)	–18.2669 (28.9665)	–14.3899*** (4.1587)
$GRAD^2$	0.3844 (0.9324)	79.6094 (59.9915)	2.3632*** (0.6184)
$GRAD^3$	–0.1244** (0.0594)	–79.4194** (32.9265)	–0.2485*** (0.0370)
RESUG	–0.0526*** (0.0065)	63.1420 (930.9561)	0.0222 (0.0223)
RESGRAD	0.1741*** (0.313)	@	0.1804*** (0.0235)
GRADUG	–0.3490* (0.2050)	16.9209*** (4.6676)	2.3250*** (0.3615)
COMPRES	–0.0050 (0.0050)	–5.9052 (49.4198)	–0.0417*** (0.0045)
COMPUG	0.0726*** (0.0202)	0.1331*** (0.0378)	0.2629*** (0.0236)
COMPGRAD	0.4882*** (0.1201)	0.3208** (0.1640)	0.2994*** (0.0648)
N	1,450	176	1,316
Adjusted R^2	.9683	.8395	.9778
Modal F-statistic	2217.47***	49.18***	2901.96***

Note: Numbers in parentheses are standard errors.

@No observations.

***Significant at the 1 percent level or better, 2-tailed test; **significant at the 5 percent level or better, 2-tailed test; *significant at the 10 percent level or better, 2-tailed test.

the relationship between costs and outputs based on individual coefficients.[4] The method used by Cohn et al. (1989) of varying one output while holding the other two constant at their respective sample means, does not accurately reflect the observed output mixes of contemporary colleges and universities, which tend to produce more or less of all outputs, not just a single output. This speaks most strongly to the importance of economies of scope in public and private, not-for-profit institutions. Thus, in Fig. 29.1 we present a graph that depicts that impact of varying the scale of production on average costs at public and private, not-for-profit IHEs. To construct this diagram, we identified a representative institution as having 1,000 undergraduate students enrolled, 100 graduate students enrolled, and $250,000 in externally funded research. We standardized the graduate student enrollment output and externally funded research output against the undergraduate enrollment output by dividing the former two outputs by undergraduate enrollment (in thousands). For example, instead of externally funded research *per se*, our constructed variable reflects externally funded research dollars per thousand undergraduate students enrolled. This permits us to increase the scale of all three output variables simultaneously (in fixed proportion) while couching the scale changes in terms of undergraduate enrollments only. In Fig. 29.1, we observe that scale average cost for both public IHEs and private, not-for-profit IHEs is minimized (at just over $10,000) at an undergraduate enrollment level of approximately 18,000 students (with the associated graduate student enrollment of approximately 1,800 and externally funded research of $4.5 million). At output levels greater than this, scale average costs escalate much more rapidly for private, not-for-profit IHEs than for public IHEs.

We treat the private, for-profit IHEs separately, because almost none of these schools produce all three of the outputs simultaneously. Only 4% produce externally funded research, and only 12.5% have a graduate program. That is, the for-profit IHEs tend to specialize in producing undergraduate education. Accordingly, rather than showing average costs varying with all outputs, as we did for public and private, not-for-profit IHEs in Fig. 29.1, we show (Fig. 29.2) how average cost at the private, for-profit IHEs varies with the level of production of undergraduate enrollment only. Average cost is minimized at an undergraduate enrollment of approximately 3,000 students and escalates rapidly thereafter.

In pooled models with dummy variables for private, for-profit IHEs and public IHEs, as well as relevant interaction terms, we found no statistically significant cost difference between the private, for-profit IHEs and the private, not-for-profit IHEs ($F = 0.78$), or between the private, for-profit IHEs and public IHEs ($F = 0.75$), but a statistically significant cost difference between public IHEs and private, not-for-profit IHEs ($F = 26.96$). We do not report these regression results because the pooled

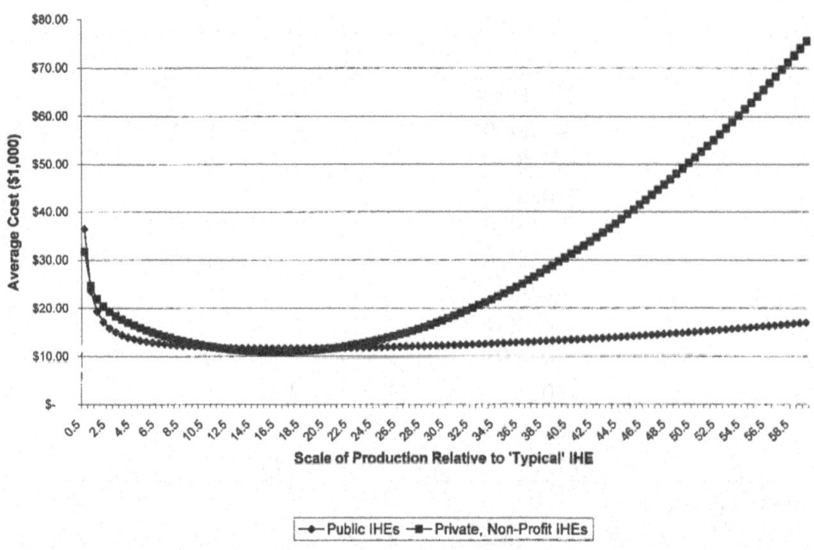

Figure 29.1 Scale effects on average cost of public and private, Not-for-Profit IHEs.

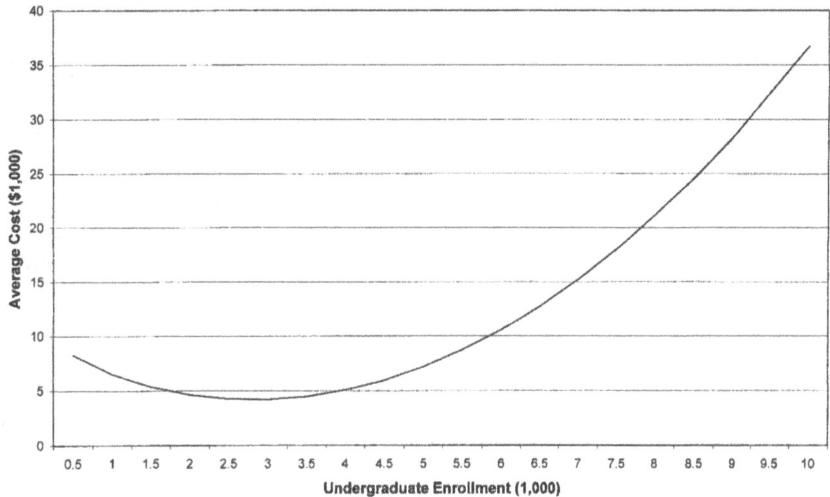

Figure 29.2 Undergraduate enrollment effects on average cost of private, for-profit IHEs.

model estimates are identical to the separate regression estimates after appropriate summation of coefficients.

Discussion

Previously, both Cohn et al. (1989) and Laband and Lentz (2003) found evidence of significant cost differences between public and private IHEs. By splitting the private institutions into for-profit IHEs and not-for-profit IHEs, we have determined that this previously reported cost difference stems from differences between private, not-for-profit IHEs and public IHEs. Although neither type of institution is characterized by an imperative to maximize profits (minimize costs), we find that the public IHEs produce more cheaply than the private, not-for-profit IHEs at almost all scales of output.

Our finding of no statistically significant difference in the cost structure of production between private, for-profit IHEs and private, not-for-profit IHEs is really quite striking. If it holds up under scrutiny, it calls into question the validity of the Winston/Ehrenberg theory of positional competition between not-for-profit IHEs. In this regard, it is worth noting that our finding is consistent with results reported by Mocan (1995), who estimated a translog cost function for 399 day care centers in four states and found no difference in cost between for-profit and not-for-profit providers. But, at least in theory, positional competition should characterize not-for-profit providers of day care services in much the same manner that it would characterize college and university administrators, although perhaps to a lesser extent given the difference in national/regional profile. Taken together, the Mocan and Laband/Lentz findings cast empirical doubt on the theory of positional competition.

Having made that point, it should be noted that there are at least two plausible explanations of our findings that do not jeopardize the theory of positional competition. The fact that we find no evidence of cost differences may not, in fact, mean that no cost differences exist in reality. How so? In the IPEDS data, the outputs produced by for-profit IHEs are considered to be identical to the outputs produced by not-for-profits IHEs. That is, all that is recorded in the IPEDS data is the number of FTE undergraduate and graduate students and the dollar amount of externally funded research. It is possible that this treatment obscures real differences in production between for-profit and not-for-profit IHEs.

Suppose, for example, that for-profit IHEs tend to specialize in production of relatively high-cost undergraduate education in the business and sciences disciplines, whereas not-for-profit IHEs produce a mix of undergraduate degree offerings that includes some business and sciences education but also a substantial amount of relatively low-cost undergraduate education in the liberal arts and humanities.[5] Suppose further that for-profit IHEs enjoy a real cost advantage over not-for-profit

IHEs with respect to provision of business and sciences education. Because all undergraduate students are treated identically in the IPEDS data, we cannot distinguish the fact that the two types of institutions produce markedly different undergraduate outputs. In this case, which we have hypothesized only, real cost and output differences between the two types of institutions would be obscured by data aggregation, resulting in an empirical finding of no differences in costs between for-profit and not-for-profit producers of higher education services.

A second possibility is that positional competition among IHEs occurs principally and with greatest effect (on costs) among a relatively small set of the most elite academic institutions. By implication, then, there is not much in the way of positional competition between most of the nearly 1,500 IHEs in our IPEDS sample, for even *U.S. News and World Report* only identifies direct positional comparisons for the top 50 institutions. So, while positional competition may drive up costs for some number of "elite" institutions, in our analysis this effect is swamped by the sheer number of "nonelite" institutions in our sample, which generates the empirical finding of no differences in costs between for-profit and not-for-profit institutions.

Finally, we acknowledge the possibility that the standard assumptions about the behavior of administrative personnel in both private, for-profit and private, not-for-profit IHEs may not hold as strongly in an academic setting as in other markets.[6] It may be, for example, that the senior management of for-profit institutions does not, in fact, seek to maximize profits; there may be alternative managerial goals such as maximization of student enrollment (market share) or average quality of students enrolled, subject to a minimum profit constraint. Cast in this light, the implication is that for-profit institutions may not, in fact, act to minimize costs. Moreover, despite their not-for-profit status, not-for-profit institutions may face cost control pressures. For example, given their fiduciary responsibilities, Boards of Trustees of not-for-profit institutions may pay more-than-passing heed to costs and therefore monitor spending that occurs on their watch. To the extent that the actual behavior of the individuals who manage for-profit and not-for-profit IHEs deviates from standard economic assumptions, it would help explain our finding of no significant difference in the structure of costs between the for-profit and not-for-profit private IHEs.

Many research papers end with the authors declaring that further work is desirable. In our case, it seems clear that further work not only is desirable, it is of fundamental importance to resolving the question of whether there are, in fact, no cost differences between for-profit and not-for-profit producers of higher education (a finding that would perhaps fatally damage the theory of positional competition), or that for-profit IHEs produce more efficiently than not-for-profit producers (a finding that is consistent with the theory of positional competition). More detailed specification of the outputs produced by IHEs and estimation of the costs of producing those outputs is essential. So, too, is investigation of how appropriate our assumptions are about the cost-minimization behavior of the different types of institutions. Testing for differences in costs between elite and nonelite institutions, in a *ceteris paribus* context, would help to clarify the empirical validity of the theory of positional competition.

Acknowledgments

Laband's work was supported by a McIntire-Stennis grant awarded through Auburn University's School of Forestry and Wildlife Sciences. We appreciate the helpful comments of two anonymous reviewers. Remaining errors are our responsibility.

Notes

1. Our findings with respect to average annual compensation being greater in public IHEs than in private IHEs are consistent with the findings reported by Cohn et al. (1989). However, our sample means seemingly are at odds with the salary figures reported for that year in the March/April 1996 issue of *Academe*, which show average compensation at private independent institutions to be higher than at public institutions. However, this discrepancy almost certainly is due to differences in data aggregation in our sample as compared to the samples reported on in *Academe*. For example, in the *Academe* article, it is reported that average annual compensation for faculty at all ranks in 2-year public IHEs is greater than

the average annual compensation for faculty at 2-year private IHEs or 2-year church-related IHEs. For IHEs without academic rank, average faculty compensation at the public IHEs was 50% greater than at either the private independent or church-related IHEs. At all institutions—except those without academic ranks—average annual faculty compensation was greater at public IHEs than at church-related IHEs, at every faculty rank. In our samples, data for both the 2-year IHEs and the church-related IHEs are aggregated into the larger samples of public, private for-profit, and private not-for-profit IHEs. We are quite confident that this aggregation explains the disparity in relative compensation between public IHEs and private IHEs between our article and the *Academe* report. An attentive reviewer brought this to our attention.

2. Our concentration measure was a straight Herfindahl Index, calculated by summing degree program *i*'s squared fraction of total degrees awarded across the *i* degree programs for each institution. In the limit, an institution with a single degree program would have a Herfindahl Index equal to 1.0.
3. There is considerable precedent for using FTE students as the measure of both the undergraduate and graduate education outputs produced at an IHE (Cohn et al., 1989; de Groot et al., 1991; Koshal and Koshal, 1995, 1999; McLaughlin et al., 1980). Before us, both Koshal and Koshal (1999) and Cohn et al. used external grant dollars as their measure of research output; however, in their analysis of 147 doctoral institutions, de Groot et al. employed publications as a measure of research output.
4. As one referee pointed out, the cost equation for public IHEs seems "flat" with respect to undergraduate enrollments, since none of the regression coefficients for the linear, squared, and cubed undergraduate enrollment variables is statistically significant. In part, this is a statistical artifact that is driven by high variance inflation factors. However, the total impact of undergraduate enrollments on cost is properly gauged as an additive effect of both the direct and indirect impacts that are reflected in the interaction terms.
5. Our thinking in this regard dovetails with that of McLaughlin et al. (1980), who argue that curricular complexity (the number and mix of degree programs offered) affects costs.
6. This possibility was pointed out to us by an anonymous referee.

References

Baumol, W. J., Panzar, J. C., and Willig, R. D. (1982). *Contestable Markets and the Theory of Industry Structure*, Harcourt Brace Jovanovich, New York.

Cohn, E., Rhine, S. L. W., and Santos, M. C. (1989). Institutions of higher education as multi-product firms: Economies of scale and scope. *Review of Economics and Statistics* 71(2): 284–290.

de Groot, H., McMahon, W. W., and Volkwein, J. F. (1991). The cost structure of American research universities. *Review of Economics and Statistics* 73(3): 424–431.

Ehrenberg, R. G. (2000). *Tuition Rising: Why College Costs so Much*, Harvard University Press, Cambridge, MA.

Koshal, R. K., and Koshal, M. (1995). Quality and economies of scale in higher education. *Applied Economics* 27(8): 773–778.

Koshal, R. K., and Koshal, M. (1999). Economies of scale and scope in higher education: A case of comprehensive universities. *Economics of Education Review* 18(2): 269–277.

Laband, D. N., and Lentz, B. F. (2003). New estimates of economies of scale and scope in higher education. *Southern Economic Journal* 70(1): 172–183.

McLaughlin, G. W., Montgomery, J. R., Smith, A. W., Mahan, B. T., and Broomall, L. W. (1980). Size and efficiency. *Research in Higher Education* 12: 53–66.

Mocan, H. N. (1995). Quality-adjusted cost functions for child-care centers. *American Economic Review* 85(2): 409–413.

Nelson, R., and Hevert, K. T. (1992). Effect of class size on economies of scale and marginal costs in higher education. *Applied Economics* 24: 473–482.

Toutkoushian, R. K. (1999). The value of cost functions for policymaking and institutional research. *Research in Higher Education* 40: 1–15.

Winston, G. C. (1999). Subsidies, hierarchy and peers: The awkward economics of higher education. *Journal of Economic Perspectives* 13(1): 13–36.

CHAPTER 30

UNDERSTANDING THE COST OF PUBLIC HIGHER EDUCATION

PETER MCPHERSON AND DAVID SHULENBURGER

In the case of higher education costs, diametrically opposed views have persisted over time. Why?

Factual matters ought to be easily resolved by examining the facts, but in the case of higher education costs, diametrically opposed views have persisted over time. Consider this statement by a prominent legislator as reported in *The New York Times* in an article on public university tuition increases: "Colleges and universities have not shown a willingness to contain costs" (Arenson 2003, A8). In that same article, the legislator committed to introduce legislation that would withdraw federal money from big tuition raisers. Contrast that stance with the findings of a Delta Cost Project[1] study conducted under the leadership of noted higher education researcher Jane Wellman: Real full educational cost per student at public research universities increased at an average annual rate of only .2 percent from 1998 to 2005 (Wellman, Desrochers, and Lenihan 2008). The Delta Cost Project study found that universities did contain educational costs; what they were unable to contain was tuition increases. So, did cost increases lead to tuition increases, as the legislator maintained?

In general, the costs borne by public research universities are made up of two components: (1) the costs of student education, paid for by state appropriations, tuition, and some donations, and (2) the costs for research, clinical practices, student residence halls, athletics, and other activities that in general produce their own revenue. (We realize that there is some cross-subsidization, but this pattern generally holds.) Public policy makers are appropriately concerned about educational costs because state appropriations and students (through tuition) pay the bill. On the other hand, public policy makers generally encourage increased revenue from activities that substantially pay for themselves because they contribute to the economy of the community and state, despite any increased cost to do so. We hope this two-sector conceptual model will help public policy makers focus more clearly on the actual costs and needed revenues of each specific university function, rather than misunderstand the situation by looking only at universities as a whole.

Tuition Increases vs. Cost of Education Increases

Clearly, university tuition and fees have increased dramatically in recent years. Tuition and fees represent the price of higher education to students and parents. From 1996 to 2006, private[2] universities experienced average compounded annual tuition increases of 5.68 percent, while their public university counterparts experienced increases that averaged 5.98 percent. These rates are more than double the compounded annual 2.44 percent increase in the consumer price index (CPI) for that period. From 1980 to 1990, public university tuition increased at a 4.3 percent rate and private university tuition increased at a substantially greater 5.6 percent rate (Alsalam 1996).

Price changes are experienced by consumers, while cost changes are directly experienced by producers.[3] The mass media often confuse the two, especially in reporting on tuition increases. This confusion is frequently reinforced by elected officials who seem to assume that it must be cost increases that lead to tuition increases. Similar confusion is evident among some members of the current Congress; the Higher Education Reauthorization Act of 2008 includes mechanisms to compel or cajole the study and control of costs by universities whose tuition increases exceed certain thresholds.

This confusion may have its roots in the classical economics model of price and cost behavior in a competitive market. Long term, in a purely competitive market, cost increases and price increases tend to be precisely the same amount, and, at equilibrium, the market clearing price and the firm's per unit marginal costs are also the same. But the market for earning a baccalaureate degree is not the competitive market envisioned by Adam Smith and David Ricardo. The student shares the price of a college education with donors, governments, and others. Information flows are far from perfect. Prices are often set by government action rather than by the market. As a result, increases in the price (i.e., tuition) and cost of a college education have diverged significantly over time.

What University Costs Are Relevant to This Discussion?

In answering this question, a brief segue into the composition of the modern U.S. research university is helpful. Clark Kerr (1963) recognized the unique nature of the institution when he coined the descriptive term "multiversity." The multiversity has many dimensions. While they make a complex whole, when finances are concerned the parts of the university are most appropriately analyzed separately.

Failure to disaggregate leads to inappropriate analysis. For example, public research universities created confusion for themselves and others when they called attention to the ever-decreasing state-funded portion of their *total* budget without explaining that state funding of their *educational* budget had declined proportionately less.

What we describe in detail in this article is the two-sector research university. One of the sectors is generally comprised of a business-like, self-supporting set of activities whose costs must be covered by their revenues. Auxiliaries, clinics, athletics, technology transfer, externally funded research, and similar activities belong to this sector. Generally, state funds either are not appropriated to support this sector or are appropriated only for a specific purpose, e.g., to fund a research-related economic development activity. Because it is largely self-supporting, states should be pleased when revenues from this sector grow, just as they are pleased when private business revenues grow. States do not worry about cost increases in private business since those increases are ultimately governed by the business's revenues. Similarly, cost increases in the self-supporting sector of the university are governed by that sector's revenues, which do not come from the state.

The other sector is the education sector. Costs in this sector are covered by a mix of state appropriations, tuition, gifts, and endowment earnings. Because tuition covers only a portion of total cost, the link between the number of students served and revenue is not as rigid in the education sector as is the link between volume and revenue in the business-like sector. States clearly have an interest in cost increases in the education sector; they do not view total revenue increases in this sector positively, since that revenue is largely derived from state appropriations and charges paid by constituents.

Interestingly, what we call "educational revenue," i.e., the sum of state appropriations and tuition revenues, amounts to 121 percent of the full educational cost per student at Carnegie-classified very high public research universities, varying by less than two percentage points from that average over the period from 1987 to 2007 and exhibiting no upward or downward trend. Specifically, throughout this period real state appropriation per student as a percentage of full educational cost decreased and tuition increased; however, the multiple of full educational cost they together constitute remained at a constant 121 percent. Thus, a roughly constant percentage of educational revenue was available for funding other core university activities. These monies provide significant leveraging and support for activities such as research, technology transfer, and core university services.

In Carnegie-classified high research universities (as opposed to very high research universities), the sum of state appropriations and tuition revenues amounts to a slightly lower 114 percent of the full educational cost per student. This figure is reflective of the less intense research responsibilities of these institutions.

Thus, one might think of tuition as covering some part of the direct cost of educating students and state appropriations as covering another (decreasing) portion of that direct cost, along with some of the indirect cost embedded within the responsibilities of major universities. Despite a decline in state support, in 2006 nearly two-thirds of full educational cost, or $9,647 per student per academic year, came from state sources. Disaggregating university revenues makes it clear that the core education function of the average public research university remains financially dependent on state support. It is the other functions of the university that are now largely independent of that support.

That education is only one "product" of the public research university is illustrated in Figure 30.1. Public research universities are complex bundles of enterprises, each with unique funding sources. The revenue sources that are largely tied to funding educational programs are tuition and state appropriations, whim are summed into what we call "educational revenue." Educational revenue grew 20 percent over the period from 1987 to 2006, a compounded annual growth rate of .97 percent. The entire bundle of activities that is the research university saw its revenues (labeled "total revenue" in Figure 30.1) grow 41 percent during the same period, for a compounded annual growth rate of 1.84 percent.

In 1987, educational revenue was 54 percent of total public research university revenue; in 2006, it was only 46 percent. As noted, educational revenue grew only modestly during this period, even though one of its components, tuition, grew from a very small base by 132 percent. However, this increase only slightly more than offset the 17 percent decline in the other component of educational revenue, state appropriations, which fell from a much larger base. Research, clinical, and auxiliary revenues grew at a far greater rate than did educational revenues.

Unfortunately, particularly for those who see universities only as producers of education, revenues from these high growth lines of "business" generally cannot be used to support the core educational mission. Research, clinical, and auxiliary revenues generally must be spent on the research, clinical, and specific auxiliary activities from which they were raised. Only a very small fraction of gifts to endowments are unrestricted; most endowment contributions are directed by donors to support a specific activity or purpose. While it is too much to claim that one line of a university's business has no positive or negative financial effect on another, such effects generally are very small. Each line of business largely must be supported by the funding sources associated with it, perhaps in small part augmented by revenues contributed specifically for its support through the auspices of endowments or foundations.

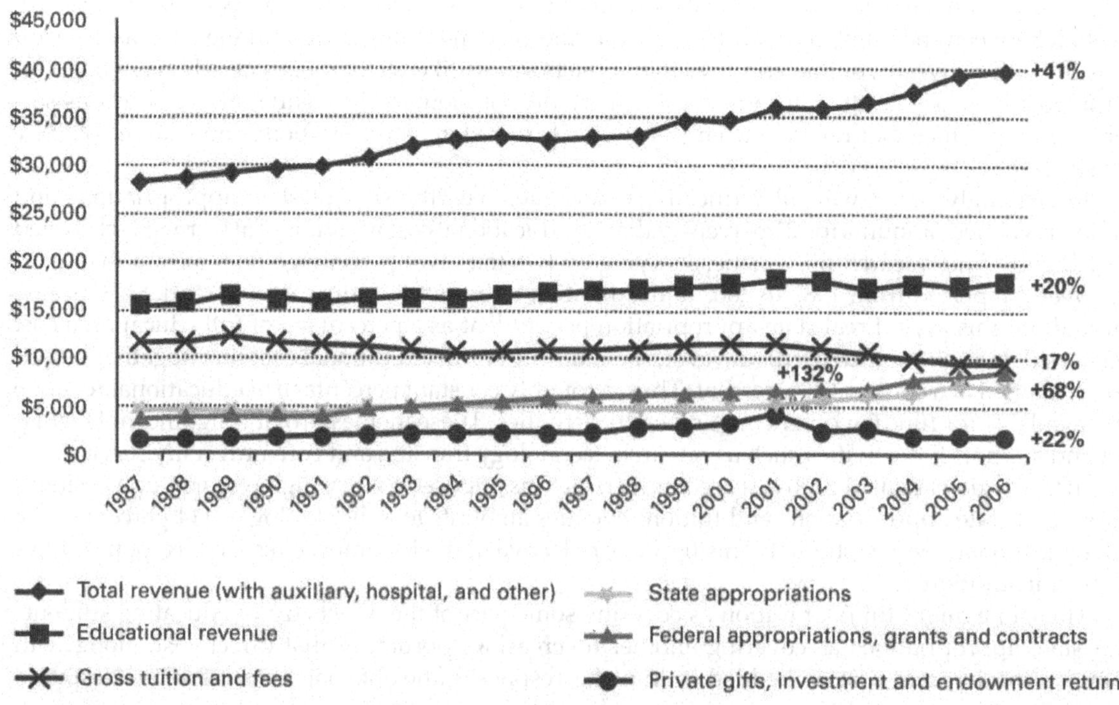

Figure 30.1 Per FTE student real revenues in very high research public universities.

To be meaningful, analysis of the cost of education in public research universities must disaggregate costs to match the disaggregation of revenues. The costs that are relevant to this analysis are educational costs. We turn now to a comparative analysis of those costs and their behavior over time.

Is Tuition Increasing Because Public Research University Educational Costs Are Out of Control?

What is the pattern of higher education cost increases? Jane Wellman of the Delta Cost Project and author of "Costs, Prices and Affordability" (Wellman 2006) and numerous other works on higher education economics and finance recently conducted a thorough examination of higher education finances. The data in Figure 30.2 are from the report of that study, titled *The Growing Imbalance* (Wellman, Desrochers, and Lenihan 2008). These data are presented by Carnegie Classification, based on data from the Integrated Postsecondary Educational Data System (IPEDS).

For reasons described previously, the column titled "Real Full Educational Spending/FTE" is the appropriate measure of the increase in expenditures required to provide educational services to students, including instruction. Over the period from 1998 to 2005, public universities increased per FTE student expenditures in CPI-adjusted real terms by only small amounts, ranging from 0.2 percent at research universities to 3.4 percent at master's universities. Private universities showed greater increases, with research universities increasing real expenditures by 4.5 percent and master's universities increasing real expenditures by 10.9 percent. The "Real Total Spending/FTE" column reveals a similar pattern: on the whole, private universities had substantially greater increases in expenditures than did their public counterparts.[4]

Figures 30.3 and 30.4 present detailed time series expenditure data for public high and very high research universities for the period from 1987 to 2006. The patterns evident in the Wellman data are repeated in these data for both categories of universities. Total expenditures increased at the most rapid rate. Full educational expenditures increased at a compounded annual rate of .84 percent for both high and very high public research universities. Total expenditures increased at a compounded annual rate of 1.44 percent for very high research private universities and 1.31 percent for high research private universities.

What accounts for the remarkably lower rate of increase in full educational expenditures at public universities as compared to private universities? It would not appear to be lack of tuition revenue. Net tuition revenue increased at a far faster pace at public universities during this period, although these data are deceptive. Because the base on which the increase is applied is much lower at public universities, the larger percentage increase in tuition revenue produces far fewer dollars for public universities than it would for private. Indeed, while public universities' real net tuition revenue rose at about double the rate of that at private universities, the actual per student increase in tuition revenue at public research universities was only $1.609, or 31 percent

FIGURE 30.2

Spending per FTE Student, 1998–99 to 2004–05

Sector	Real Full Educational Spending/FTE	Real Total Spending/FTE
Public research	+0.2%	+7.9%
Public master's	+3.4%	–3.0%
Public associate's	+0.3%	–3.4%
Private research	+4.5%	+17.8%
Private master's	+10.9%	+5.6%
Private bachelor's	+6.1%	+4.6%

Source: Data from Wellman, Desrochers, and Lenihan 2008, p. 32.

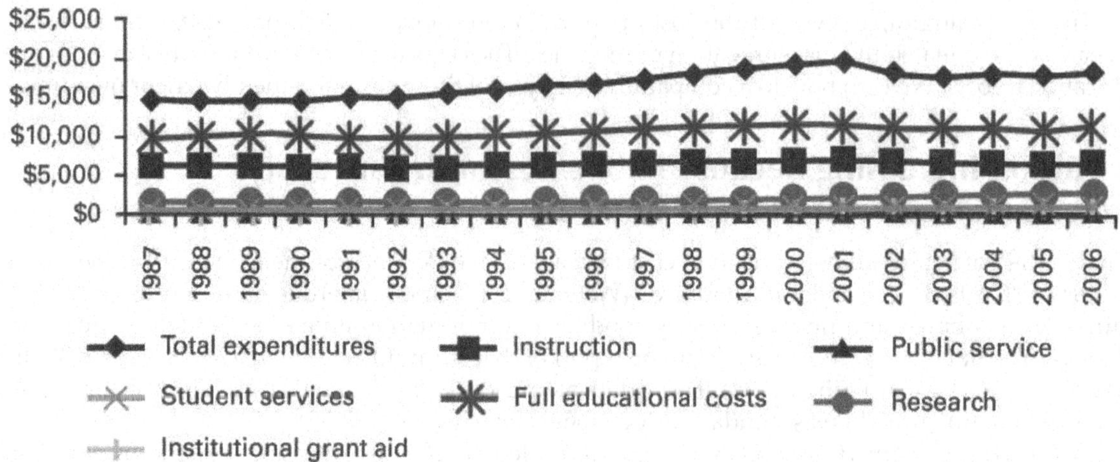

Figure 30.3 Public high research university expenditures per FTE (in 2006 $).

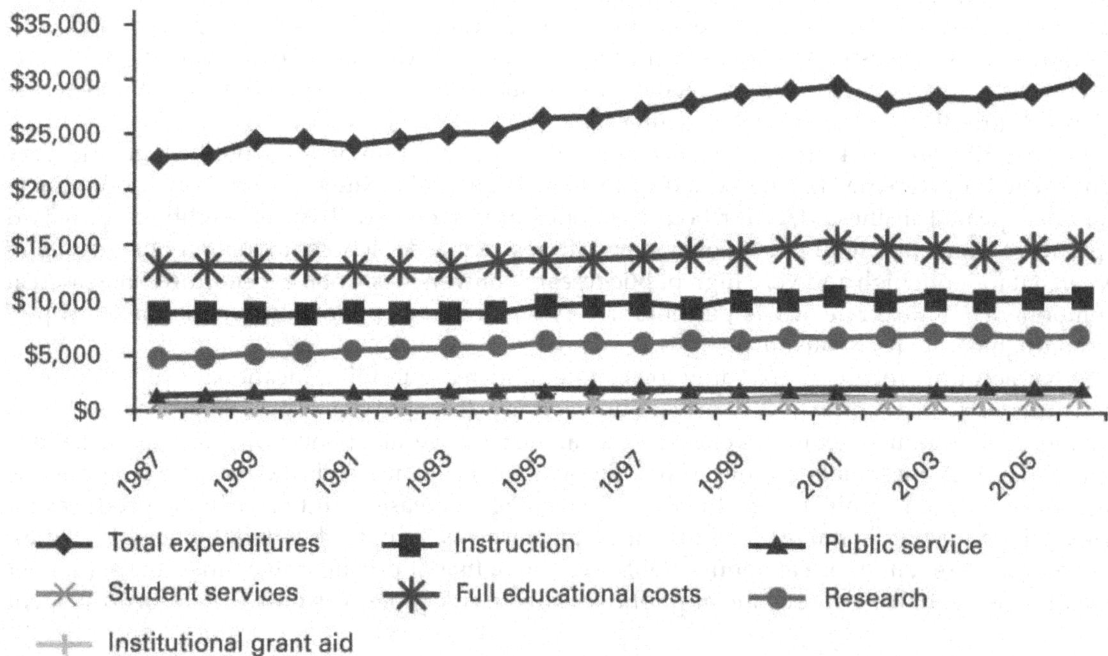

Figure 30.4 Public very high research university expenditures per FTE (in 2006 $).

of the actual dollar increase—$5,169—produced by the smaller percentage tuition rise at private research universities.

What appears to be most significant in accounting for the lower rate of increase in educational expenditures for public universities is the drop of 17 percent in real terms in direct state appropriations per FTE student between 1987 and 2006, a revenue source largely unavailable or only available in considerably smaller amounts to private universities.

For many years, the State Higher Education Executives Organization (SHEEO) has collected data on public higher education finances. Since 1986, these data have shown cyclical variability in the real value of state appropriations per student and have trended downward over time. The years we focus on in Figure 30.5, 1996 to 2007, are no exception. In 1996, real state appropriations per student were $6,896, dropping to $6,773 in 2007. While during this period net tuition increased as a proportion of real per student revenue, the increase barely made up for the drop in state revenues. In

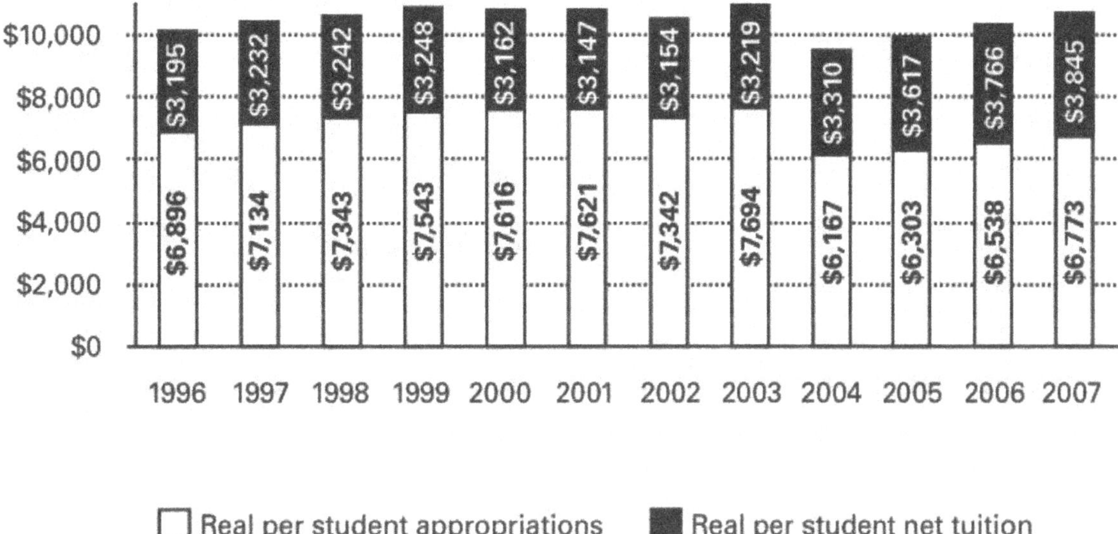

Figure 30.5 Real per student revenues of U.S. public higher education.
Source: State Higher Education Executive Officers 2008a.

1996, the sum of net tuition and state revenues per student (education revenue) was $10,091 and in 2007 it was $10,618, a scant $527 increase per student. Over the longer period from 1986 to 2007, the increase in real education revenue per FTE was only $954. That amounts to a 0.45 percent increase in real revenue per FTE student per year,[5] a rate of increase that is in no way "out of control."

The data are corrected for price changes by what we consider to be the best measure of inflation for universities, the higher education cost adjustment (HECA). If one uses the less appropriate CPI, the annual real increase is still just 0.84 percent per year.[6] To repeat, the substantial increase in tuition revenue over the last decade, and in fact over the last two decades, was only slightly more than the real revenue lost as real state appropriations were cut; total per student real revenue and, necessarily, total per student real expenditure barely increased in this period.

This conclusion is not novel. Analyses like this one typically conclude that in recent years, public university tuition increases have merely replaced revenues lost from state appropriations. D. Bruce Johnstone (2001) reaches this conclusion, as does Jane Wellman (Wellman, Desrochers, and Lenihan 2008). And, while not focused on revenue per student, the National Commission on the Cost of Higher Education (Harvey et al. 1998, p. 5) found that "in public four-year colleges and universities, the percentage of total student cost covered by the general subsidy declined from 79 percent to 68 percent" during the period from 1987 to 1996. The commission also noted periods when actual appropriations declined in a substantial number of states.

Tuition increases have merely replaced revenues lost from state appropriations.

Perhaps legislators are fixated on the absolute increases they have provided to higher education over time and do not clearly understand what has happened to real budgets on a per student basis. Figure 30.6, derived from SHEEO data, shows that enrollment increased rapidly during the period from 1986 to 2007. The growth from 7.1 million to 10.2 million FTEs over that period, a 43 percent increase, was not met by an equivalent percentage increase in real funding. Thus, real per FTE student funding actually declined. The rationalization that a few more students can be added to an existing class without additional cost may be true when a small number of students are added, but it breaks down completely when the increase is of this magnitude.

No matter how desirable it is to reduce tuition, it is clear that the economics of public universities depend on it. It is simply unrealistic to think that tuition and fee charges could be reduced significantly unless those funds are replaced from other sources.

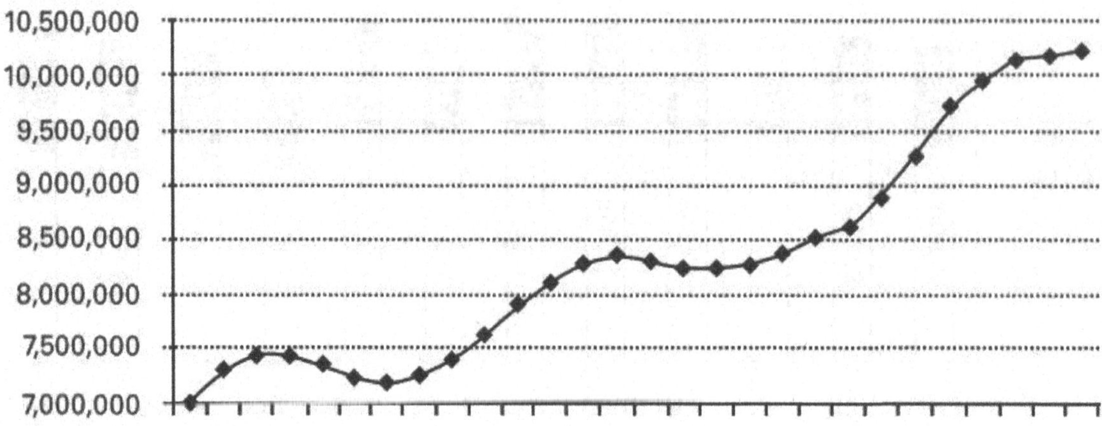

Figure 30.6 FTE enrollment in public universities, 1980–2007.
Source: State Higher Education Executive Officers 2008b, p. 18.

As we have shown, public universities have increased total expenditure per student by only a very small percentage. They have had little choice in the matter, as they have been constrained by the total revenues available. Because public universities generally must operate with balanced budgets, total operating expenditures may not exceed revenues. Ironically, private universities, having never had the advantage of relying on significant revenues from state appropriations, were saved the experience of real revenue decline. Put another way, private universities were able to put their tuition increases into educational expenditures while public universities had to use nearly all of their tuition increases to offset real decreases in state appropriations.

Therefore, while both private and public universities experienced cost increases, only private universities had sufficient resources to expand expenditures significantly beyond the rate of CPI growth. This situation is reflected in the recent Government Accountability Office (GAO) finding that between the 2001 and 2005 academic years, "increases in average tuition were matched or exceeded by increases in average institutional spending on education at private institutions, but not at public institutions" (U.S. Government Accountability Office 2007, p. 4).

That this discussion of public university budgets has not included private funds as a significant source of revenue is not an oversight. In recent years, private contributions to public universities have, on average, amounted to only a miniscule proportion of per student expenditures. *The Growing Imbalance* concludes that "private funds have not materially contributed to the bottom line in public institutions" (Wellman, Desrochers, and Lenihan 2008, p. 21). Data from this source demonstrate that private contributions to public master's institutions have not averaged as much as $300 per student during any year from 1987 to 2005; private contributions to public research universities averaged just over $700 per student per year. While these small amounts make a difference when used in well-targeted ways, their overall impact on public institutions is minimal. Since amounts per student from private contributions have remained at about the same level over the past two decades, they cannot be considered a revenue source for growing educational program budgets.

Students do not pay for even the variable cost of their education.

In addition, public universities subsidize their students; tuition and fees do not cover even the variable cost of educating them. In Figure 30.7, the variable cost of instructing students (i.e., the sum of instructional cost, academic support, and student services) is subtracted from tuition to yield the net operating subsidy to students. These figures must be seen for what they are, averages across all levels of students, since undergraduate instructional, academic, and student support services costs are neither accurately nor objectively assignable to each student level. In every public Carnegie category, students are subsidized. We make this point so that the reader understands that the

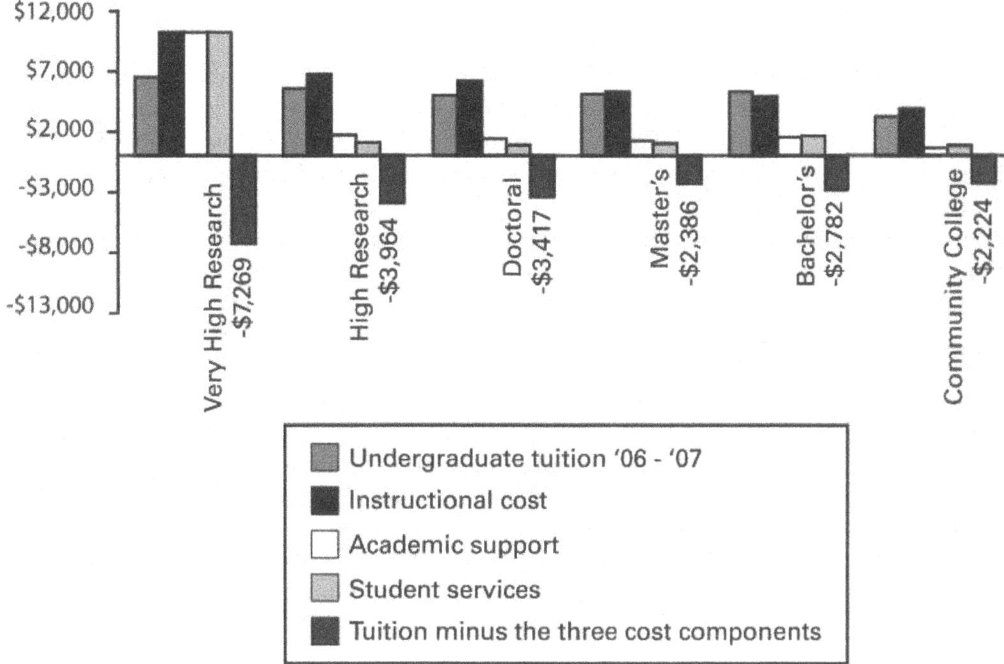

Figure 30.7 Public university subsidy to students.

immense cost pressures public universities have faced have not changed the basic fact that students in the public sector do not pay for even the variable cost of their education. *The Growing Imbalance* (Wellman, Desrochers, and Lenihan 2008) reports that average revenue from tuition is less than instructional costs for all categories of institutions, public and private. The report also finds that undiscounted tuition exceeds average instructional cost for only one category of university, the private master's university. Thus, student subsidies remain the rule at both public and most private universities.

Perceptions of runaway expenditures at public universities over the last 20 years are simply incorrect. Over the period for which we have consistent data, the real amounts spent by public universities per FTE student have increased only modestly. Public universities have had to make hard choices and to economize. They have not permitted overall levels of cost to rise in an uncontrolled, excessive fashion. With the consent of their governing boards and legislatures, they have increased tuition in an attempt to offset reductions in real state appropriations, not because cost increases forced them to do so.

Universities operate at a given tuition and cost level based on both the subsidy available to them and their mission to provide a specific type of education. A Carnegie-classified very high research university could choose to operate similarly to a Carnegie-classified master's institution and thereby reduce its cost of operation. Thus, for public institutions at least, it is the type of university they choose to be (i.e., the segment of the higher education market in which they choose to operate) that affects their cost of providing education. It is not an out-of-control cost environment that determines university costs and, hence, tuition.

Tuition level, then, is also a matter of choice. Clearly, in the long run the total revenue a university receives must cover its costs. Cost is determined by the type of education an institution offers or, most probably, by a series of choices made over decades by the institution and its governing board. As a result, the amount needed to balance the university budget after that cost choice is made essentially dictates the public institution's average tuition level. Thus, a given university ultimately has control over the type of institution it will be and over the tuition level it will charge. This choice, of course, may have consequences for the quality of education that university offers.

Students also have choices when it comes to the tuition they are willing to pay. The range of tuition and required fees is very large, ranging in 2007 from $34,965 per academic year at the average private, not-for-profit very high research university to an average of $7,063 at its public counterpart to an average of $2,812 at a public community college. These list prices do not reflect the prices most students actually pay for a year of attendance, since tuition discounting is common. Discounting ranges from an average reduction of 32.8 percent at private four-year schools to 15.7 percent at public four-year schools to 7.4 percent at public two-year schools. Discounts vary by income levels, demographic characteristics, and student academic abilities (Baum and Lapovsky 2006). Just as the choice of the type of institution a university wishes to be affects its cost of operation, so too is the educational experience of students affected by their choice of institution and the price they pay to attend.

Summary and Conclusions

Public research universities are complex entities that deliver two primary products: educational programs and a bundle of self-financed activities that includes auxiliaries, clinics, athletics, technology transfer, externally funded research, and the like. This latter set of activities is largely self-funded and should be analyzed as most private sector economic entities are analyzed; growth is highly desirable so long as the revenue produced by the activity covers its cost. Conversely, educational program costs are paid primarily by revenue generated from tuition and state appropriations; hence, public scrutiny of tax dollars and tuition levels is understandably great.

Educational cost has been constant on a per student basis for over 20 years.

When we examine educational program cost in public research universities, we find that it essentially has been constant in real terms on a per FTE student basis for over 20 years. Public university presidents and provosts have produced this constant-cost result because they must; during the last decade the real per student revenue available to pay for educational programs has remained essentially constant as state government appropriations per student have declined.

Public universities provide students with educational programs in exchange for tuition payments that are less than the cost of providing those programs. State appropriations still supply a substantial, although diminishing, subsidy to students. Public universities have managed to keep educational cost increases modest. Tuition has increased to fill the gap left when real per student appropriations declined. Were real per student state subsidies for education to stabilize, the benefit to students of careful public university cost management would be magnified.

Notes

1. The authors thank the Delta Cost Project for making available to researchers the Delta Cost Project-IPEDS Data Base 20-year matched set. That data set is the source from which most of the detailed information on university costs and revenues in this article is derived.
2. "Private," when used in this article as the sole descriptor of a university or group of universities, always refers to "private, not-for-profit" universities. It never refers to "private, for-profit" or proprietary institutions.
3. For a discussion of "cost" and "price," see page 4 of *Straight Talk About College Costs and Prices* (Harvey et al. 1998). This document is a report of the National Commission on the Cost of Higher Education, an independent advisory board created by an act of Congress.
4. A word of explanation is in order. Total spending includes more than educational expenditures; thus, it behaved differently in this period than did the narrower measure of full educational spending. From 1998 to 2005, private and public research universities increased total spending per FTE beyond inflation by 178 percent and 79 percent respectively. As regards public university spending in general, this appears to be an anomaly; although this spending increase is less than half that of their private counterparts, public research universities still increased their spending substantially. What accounts for this anomaly? Much of the increase occurred during a period of rapid growth in federal research expenditures, notably during the period in which the National Institutes of Health research budget was

doubled. Total spending is inflated by this and other factors whose origins are not rooted in increased cost for instruction or the purchase of goods and services required to generate instruction.

5. The SHEEO data series for 1986 to 1995 shows that real public higher education revenues differed little from those in 1996 or 2006 (State Higher Education Executive Officers 2008a). Total real per FTE revenue in 1986 was $9,663, with $2,220 from tuition and $7,443 from state appropriations. Thus, real per FTE revenue increased only $428 between 1986 and 2006. Note that SHEEO data include both four- and two-year schools, and the increase in enrollment in favor of two-year schools masks a slightly larger per student increase at four-year schools.
6. Note that SHEEO and Wellman use two different methods of adjusting figures to account for inflation. Wellman uses the consumer price index (CPI), while SHEEO uses its own cost index, the higher education cost adjustment (HECA). The SHEEO index is a combination of the Bureau of Labor Statistics' employment cost index (75 percent weight) and the gross domestic product (GDP) implicit price deflator (25 percent weight). SHEEO uses this combination because university expenses are roughly 75 percent personnel-related and 25 percent related to the purchase of a mix of items that approximates the mix in the GDP. Between 1997 and 2007, the CPI increased at a compounded annual rate of 2.58 percent, while the HECA increased at a rate of 3.38 percent. For a full explanation of CPI and HECA, see Appendix III, pages 86–87, of *University Tuition, Consumer Choice and College Affordably* (McPherson and Shulenburger 2008).

References

Alsalam, N. 1996. *The Cost of Higher Education.* Findings from the Condition of Education, 1995. no. 6. NCES 96-769. Washington, DC: U.S. Department of Education.

Arenson, K. W. 2003. Public College Tuition Increases Prompt Concern, Anguish and Legislation. *New York Times,* August 30, AS.

Baum, S., and L. Lapovsky. 2006. *Tuition Discounting: Not Just a Private College Practice.* New York: The College Board.

Harvey, J., R. M. Williams, R. J. Kirshstein, A. J. O'Malley, and J. V. Wellman. 1998. *Straight Talk About College Costs and Prices. Report of the National Commission on the Cost of Higher Education.* Phoenix: Oryx Press.

Johnstone, D. B. 2001. Higher Education and Those "Out of Control" Costs. In *In Defense of American Higher Education,* ed. P. G. Altbach, P. J. Gumport, and D. B. Johnstone, 144–78. Baltimore: Johns Hopkins University Press.

Kerr, C. 1963. *The Uses of the University.* Cambridge, MA: Harvard University Press.

McPherson, P., and D. Shulenburger. 2008. *University Tuition, Consumer Choice and College Affordability.* Washington, DC: National Association of State Universities and Land-Grant Colleges. Retrieved December 15, 2009, from the World Wide Web: www.aplu.org/NetCommunity/Document.Doc?id=1296.

State Higher Education Executive Officers. 2008a. Public FTE Enrollment. Educational Appropriations, and Total Education Revenue per FTE, United States, Fiscal 1983–2008. Retrieved December 15, 2009, from the World Wide Web: www.sheeo.org/finance/shef/she_data.htm.

——. 2008b. *State Higher Education Finance,* FY 2007. Boulder, CO: State Higher Education Executive Officers. Retrieved December 15, 2009, from the World Wide Web: www.sheeo.org/finance/shef_fy07pdf.

U. S. Government Accountability Office. 2007. *Tuition Continues to Rise, but Patterns Vary by Institution Type, Enrollment, and Educational Expenditures. Report to the Chairman, Committee on Education and Labor.* House of Representatives. Washington, DC: Government Accountability Office.

Wellman, J. V. 2006. Costs, Prices and Affordability. Issue Paper 13, Secretary of Education's Commission on the Future of Higher Education.

Wellman, J. V., D. M. Desrochers, and C. M. Lenihan. 2008. *The Growing Imbalance: Recent Trends in U.S. Postsecondary Education. Report of the Delta Cost Project.* Washington, DC: Delta Project on Postsecondary Education Costs, Productivity and Accountability.

CHAPTER 31

THE COST OF EXCELLENCE: THE FINANCIAL IMPLICATIONS OF INSTITUTIONAL RANKINGS

STEVE O. MICHAEL

Purpose—To examine the relationship between financial resources and variables associated with institutional rankings in the USA.

Design/methodology/approach—Pearson product moment correlation coefficient was used to investigate the relationship between endowment funds and variables associated with rankings as determined by the *U.S. News & World Report*.

Findings—College costs continue to increase faster than per capita income. Institutions are relying more on endowment funds to meet their needs. Endowment was positively associated with almost all the variables used for ranking top national doctoral universities with the largest endowment amounts. When endowment per student was used, the association became even stronger with these ranking variables. Endowment was weakly associated with almost all the variables used for ranking top national doctoral universities with the lowest endowment amounts. Relationships of endowment and ranking variables were stronger at medical research schools, business schools, and weaker at engineering schools.

Originality/value—Higher education administrators must realize that these variables are cost-inducing factors that cannot be fully satisfied. Unbridled pursuit of ranking variables will increase cost without commensurate increase in educational quality. Therefore, leaders must decide what rankings their resources allow and what position within the ranks is acceptable to them. Ranking agencies interested in quality should realize that money plays a significant role in how an institution is ranked. Therefore, institutions should be grouped according to the available resources before comparative analysis of ranking variables is made.

Two issues of major concern to governments, students, public policy makers, and higher education leaders worldwide are finance and quality of higher education. Although the level of public concern and agitation with respect to these issues have waxed and waned at different times in different countries, the implications for institutional management as we are witnessing across the globe have never been this severe. From Great Britain to Australia, Voronezh to Vancouver, there is a growing interest among higher education leaders for accountability measures and assessment as a way of ensuring quality improvement in higher education.

However, discussion about academic quality almost always takes place in absence or in separation from discussion about finance. There are many reasons for this. A widely recognized predicament in higher education is the inability to succinctly link finance to production level. This predicament makes public higher education particularly vulnerable in the hands of politicians who are eager to cut higher education budgets with a righteous indignation that says "show me where it bleeds?" Also, many higher education leaders and faculty accept their "calling" to educate with a sense of sacrifice and a demonstration of a pious and impecunious lifestyle—a lifestyle that is inimical to any visible, aggressive agitation for and pursuit of money. Ewell (2004) observed that:

> Money matters. Of course it does. We knew that. Yet when it comes to money matters, the academy has always exhibited a curious collection of attitudes and behaviors. On the one hand, we profess

> detachment. Collectively as a calling, we carefully (and sometimes disdainfully) distinguish ourselves from the vast majority of other ways to make a living, all of which emphatically revolve around money. We are above all that (p. 4).

Intuitively we know that money has something to do with the wide range of services (including the wide range of curricular offerings) available on campuses. While higher education leaders are quick to boast of improved offerings that is possible with additional infusion of new funds, few if any would make the reverse claim should equal amount of funds be cut from the budget. The resultant effects of this phenomenon are murky arguments that associate money with higher education quality. Admittedly, higher education differs significantly from business industry where fixed cost, variable cost, unit cost, and marginal cost are determinable with precise accuracy. However, the difference has in no way reduced the questions on the minds of the curious. For example, does financial strength have anything to do with quality as suggested by institutional rankings?

The thesis of this paper is that while it is possible for wealthy institutions to produce shoddy quality outcomes, it is practically impossible in today's environment for poorly endowed (in terms of financial resources) institutions to rank high on cost-intensive institutional variables employed by ranking agencies. For example, economies of scale result in lower unit cost and higher output similarly to how large class sizes result in greater credit hours. Hence, institutions would only reduce class size to the extent allowed by resource availability.

This paper describes several agencies whose roles are to rate and rank higher education institutions with the hope that the exercise will compel institutions to enhance institutional quality, examines the criteria they use, and discuss the financial implications of each criterion employed.

Quality Issues in US Higher Education

In a market economy, a wide range of market types exists for different products and services—a range which includes perfect market on the one side of the continuum and monopoly on the other end of the continuum. Duolopoly, oligopoly, and monopolistic competitions are different market types within the continuum. Market types have implications for quality and price of goods and services. For example, quality range is limited in a monopolistic condition. In essence, the monopolist determines the quality and since, by definition, the product or service has no close substitute, the range of quality options is often limited.

The lack of options and the freedom to decide among options are the main criticism of a totalitarian system, be it in politics or in economics. A country where higher education is provided and tightly regulated for efficiency solely by the state, without the option of institutional competition has, in fact, created a monopolistic higher education system. Under this condition, the state becomes the sole determinator of the higher education quality.

A perfect market condition, albeit an utopian condition, presents the best economic scenario for product variability. The diversity of product quality and the freedom to choose among many substitutable products and services make quality consideration particularly interesting. Under this market condition, producers compete among themselves on the basis of price, services, and most importantly, quality of offerings. Consumers have the opportunity to compare the quality of products before purchases are made. For example, one who is interested in a car may look at the consumer reports on Lexus, BMW, Cadillac, Mercedes Benz, etc. and focusing on quality indicators of interest, decide on which automobile to purchase.

Products differ from services in terms of quality consideration. While the quality of a product can be determined before hand, the quality of service on the other hand is usually determined at the point of experience. Education is a service; hence, the challenge in determining its quality. Also, education is a special type of service because the recipients of the service are usually not in a position to determine the quality even at the point of experience. For example, a student may not be able to tell that a professor has not covered all the materials in a curriculum or that the materials covered are the most important part of the knowledge that should be gained. By the time a student is able to comment competently on the quality of his or her education, it is usually too late!

Quality Actors

Given the condition described above, who should protect students from unscrupulous for-profit educators whose goals are to enrich themselves at the expense of the innocent students? The market-oriented higher education system runs a risk of having unaccredited diploma mills taking advantage of students. For this and other reasons, politicians have found education to be a popular political issue in the USA. At every election campaign we hear of individuals wanting to be known as "education governor," "education president," and "education congressman and woman." All campaign speeches are full of debates and declarations on how to improve the quality of education. Ridiculous politicians desire to take over the control of schools, ambitious ones design programs to force accountability, and reasonable ones are relatively temperate in their pronouncements and actions. Usually these politicians use financial strategies to attempt to accomplish their goals. Often, these financial strategies, which are usually financial cuts, redirection of funds toward institutions and programs that toll the line, or generous funding of programs of choice, leave higher education worse.

Consequently, academicians have always been wary about politicians or government attempts to control education. After all, one only needs to look at the management and effectiveness of government parastatals to have a sense of how successful government will be in protecting and promoting quality in higher education. In addition, academicians perceive any external attempt to foist quality upon the academy as an infringement of their academic freedom.

However, as Moberly in Brubacher (1990) noted, "universities are academic guilds, and history reminds us that guilds, left to themselves, are subject to certain faults: lethargy, prejudiced conservatism, and intolerance of innovation" (p. 29). Judging from the many popular publications criticizing higher education, American society seems to lay the blames of perceived poor quality of higher education graduates squarely on the educators (Sykes, 1989; Anderson, 1992). The Council on Competitiveness (1996) reported that:

> Universities have been even slower to incorporate quality practices into the operation of schools. Although a growing number of institutions of higher education are beginning to apply quality practices in academic and administrative areas, for many universities, quality is a foreign concept and few models exist in higher education for other schools to follow. Yet just as business-driven quality programs can increase customer satisfaction, quality practices can help universities meet the needs of their students and staff more effectively, while lowering costs (p. 29).

Critics of higher education maintain that the traditional accreditation amounts to nothing but a useless tally of library books and a jolly pat on the back of academic peers.

Perhaps it is for the reason mentioned above or for the "temptatious" pecuniary reward that private agencies or organizations have embarked upon the business of assessing colleges and universities and selling their reports to consumers. Prominent among these agencies are the *U.S. News & World Report*, *The Princeton Review*, and the *Kaplinger*. The most elaborate and perhaps the most popular among them is the *U.S. News &World Report* whose publication of college rankings is often either reviled or revered, jeered or cheered by academicians. Because the *U.S. News & World Report* provides an elaborate statistical information for ranking colleges and universities, this study utilizes data obtained from the agency.

Conceptual Framework

Figure 31.1 provides an illustration of various forces that are currently influencing the renewed focus on institutional quality. Prominent among these forces is the growing criticism of higher education, a phenomenon whose origin is popularly attributed to Sputnik and President Kennedy's subsequent effort to use the nation higher education research as a weapon of international politics. Since then, government's interest in higher education has continued to grow steadily. Although government's interest continues to shift among competing needs such as a push to increase access, a push to broaden access for minority groups, a push toward vocationalization of higher education, a push toward applied research, a push toward homogenization of curricula to mention but a few, the

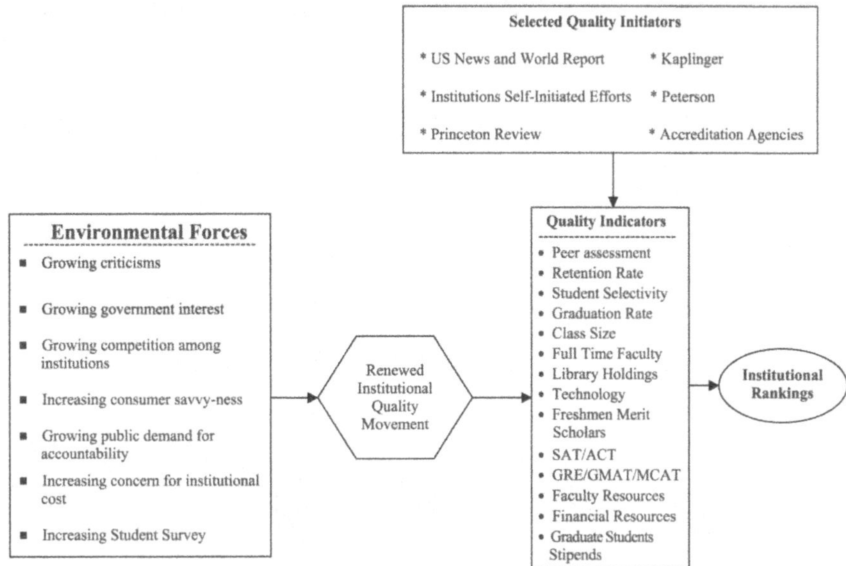

Figure 31.1 A conceptual framework for higher education institutional quality/ranking efforts.

resultant effects of increased government's interest are to force institution to do more with less and to compel institutions to become more responsive to societal needs.

For years, higher education in the USA operated under a monopolistic competition (many providers with real or perceived differentiated products/services), but the growing homogenization and vocationalization of curricula are pushing higher education toward perfect market condition—a condition that is characterized by many providers, many buyers, open entry, free exit, highly substitutable products and services, and a reasonable high level of market knowledge. The emergence and the rising number of for-profit institutions in the USA have taken institutional competition to a new level—a level that, in a pretty short time, will produce a mega university-network starting with the University of Phoenix that currently boasts of over 200,000 students (Noone, 2004) and over 17,000 instructors (www.uopxonline.com/aboutus.asp).

Students and their parents are becoming savvy buyers of higher education. Those who are informed about the internal workings of higher education scrutinize the college catalogs, visit schools for first hand information, carefully review scholarship packages, and examine all quality indicators before deciding on their selection. Many of those who are less informed about the internal workings of higher education are willing to hire consultants who will work them through the maze of financial aid and navigate through the plethora of institutional marketing. The consequence of all these is a growing sophisticated student body, individuals who are quick to vote with their feet and voice out their displeasures.

Along with the growing criticisms came public cry for accountability—accountability for educational outcomes and accountability for educational process. More than ever before, institutions are being compelled to demonstrate value added from one stage of education to another. In addition, both time and resource efficiencies are demanded of higher education institutions. Demand for accountability has resulted in experimentation with various business strategies from total quality management to strategic planning (Michael, 2004a, b; Seymour and Collett, 1991; Cornesky *et al.*, 1990).

The growing educational costs have added another impetus for a renewed attention to quality issues in higher education. With tuition as high as US$30,000 in some private institutions, both students and parents have the right to ask what they are getting for their money. Students' and parents' attention to cost will continue to increase as long as tuition continues to increase faster than inflation rates. Figure 31.2 illustrates the relationship between disposable income per capita and tuition both at the private and public higher education sectors.

The narrowing of the gap between college costs and disposable per capita income is clearly observable in the private higher education sector. Although, there is a comparatively big gap

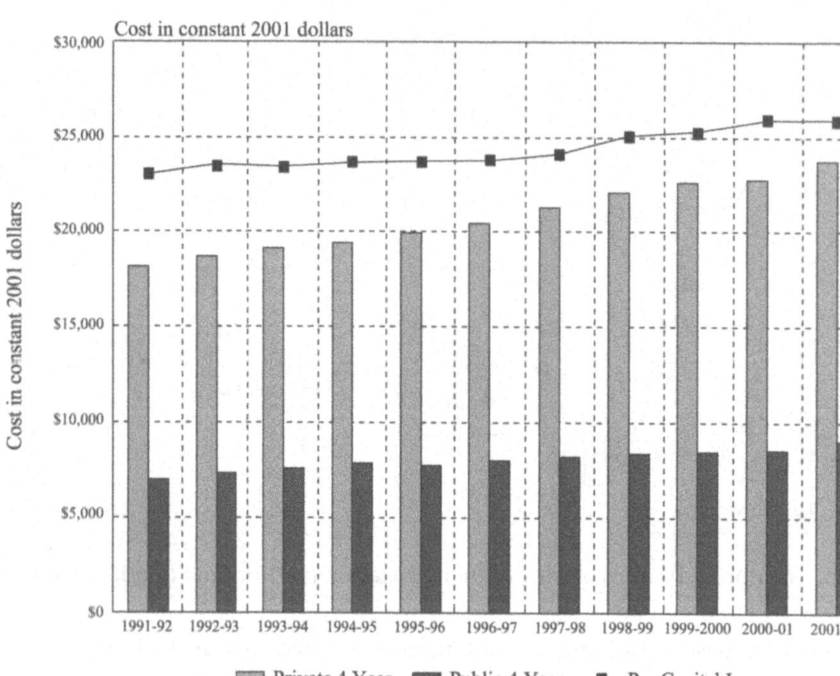

Figure 31.2 College costs and disposable per capital income.
Source: The College Board (www.collegeboard.com/highered/res/hel/hel.html#costs).

between college costs and disposable per capita income in the public higher education sector, this gap continues to narrow since 1991. As illustrated in Figure 31.2, increase in per capita income is happening at a lower rate than the increase of college costs at both the private and public higher education sectors.

Every year, *The Chronicle of Higher Education* conducts survey of students' opinions regarding several aspects of institutional life. Other agencies such as *The Princeton Review* also conduct annual student survey. In addition, almost every higher education institution in the nation conducts multiple student surveys annually. The result of these survey exercises is increase awareness on the part of students of the importance of their opinions to their institution. Also, every survey has the potential of educating respondents about what matters or what should matter; hence, colleges and universities are beginning to experience student populations with growing sophisticated tastes and demands.

These environmental forces rekindled the thrust for quality in higher education and business and non-profit organizations are responding to this pressure by initiating quality drive. A host of quality indicators are used by different agencies all for one or two purposes: assessing an acceptable level of quality and/or establishing the rank of an institution among the nation institutions. The list of quality indicators provided in Figure 31.1 is not exhaustive. However, they represent the most common variables published by commercial ranking agencies perhaps because they are easy to quantify even though their operational definitions may be somewhat debatable.

Methodology

The hypothesis of this study is that financial resources play a significant role in how institutions perform on these quality variables. For example, the number and amount of graduate stipends offered depend very much on the financial resources available to the institutions. If this hypothesis is valid, it means, therefore, that institutional rankings using these variables are a function of financial resources.

Defining financial resources of an institution presents a challenge because institutional total budget does not reflect the differences in internal allocations. The proportion of the total budget that is allocated to academic affairs differs based on the mission and priorities of institutions. However, for the purpose of this study, an institution's endowment size or amount is used to indicate the institution's financial resources. The proportions of endowment incomes at both the public and the private higher education sectors are illustrated in Figures 31.3 and 31.4.

Note that in the public higher education sector, endowment income represents only 0.7 percent of the 1999–2000 total revenues for the sector. However, as indicated on Figure 31.4, the share of the endowment income at the private higher education sector is over 31 percent (investment returns). Endowment income should not be confused with the size of endowment because the income represents the returns generated from endowment investment or activities in 1999–2000.

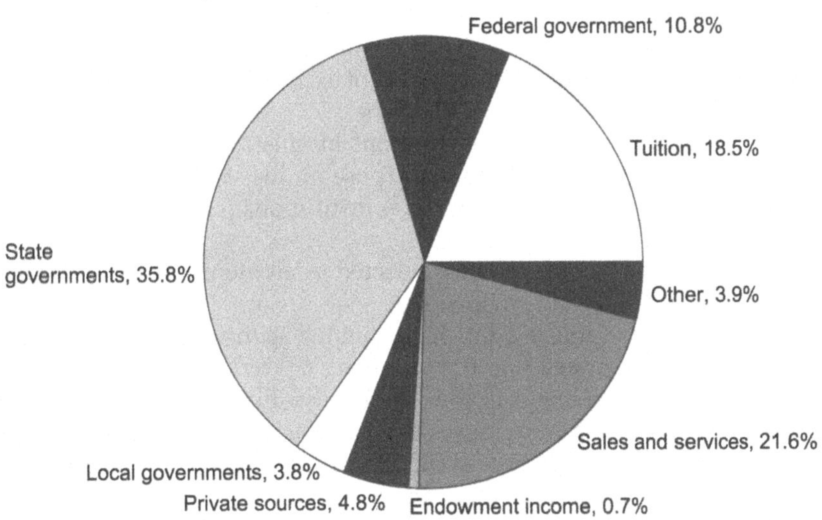

Current-fund revenues = $157.3 billion

Figure 31.3 Sources of current-fund revenue for public degree-granting institutions: 1999–2000.
Source: National Center for Education Statistics (2000).

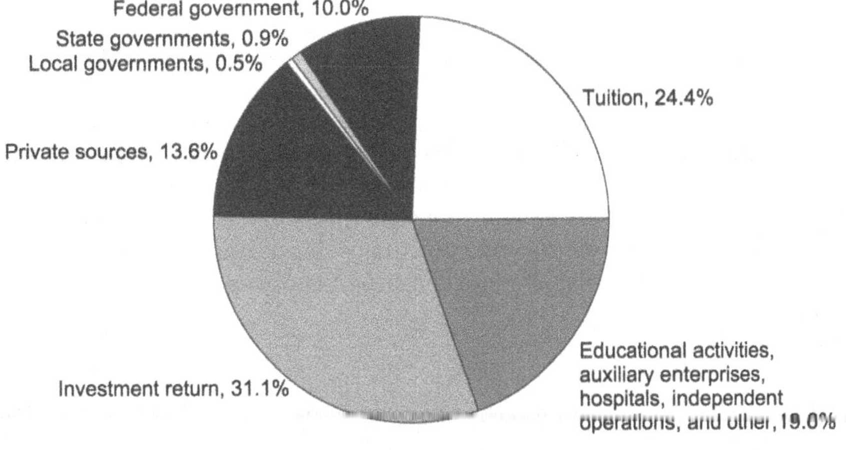

Total revenues = $121.5 billion

Figure 31.4 Sources of total revenue for private not-for-profit degree-granting institutions: 1999–2000.
Source: National Center for Education Statistics (2000).

Also note that out of the total higher education revenue of US$278.8 billion, the private higher education sector's share is 44 percent, while the public higher education sector's share is 56 percent in spite of the fact that 77 percent of students (i.e. 12,233,156) attend the public higher education sector and only 23 percent of students (i.e. 3,694,831) attend the private higher education sector in the USA (http://chronicle.com/prm/weekly/almanac/2004/nation/nation.htm). It is little wonder, therefore, that disproportionate number of private higher education institutions are among the top ranking institutions.

The hypothesis of this study is that there is a positive association between institutional financial resources and institutional rankings based on quantifiable variables popularly used by various institutional quality initiators. Using the Pearson product moment coefficient r, the relationship between financial resources and selected quality variables was determined. For the purpose of this study, financial resources are defined as the institution's total endowment. Endowment is preferred over institutional budget, which includes government appropriations in the public higher education sector, because, presumably, endowment represents that segment of financial resources that enable good institutions to freely pursue a higher level of excellence. In short, endowment is money available to make a good institution become a better one.

The *U.S. News & World Report* classifies institutions by mission; hence, there are top national institutions, tier 3, and tier 4 institutions. For the purpose of this study, r-coefficients were run for both the top national institutions as well as for tier 4 institutions (representing the lowest ranked national institutions).

A separate set of calculations were made for selected graduate programs. Graduate programs selected include business, medicine, and engineering.

One might criticize this study for using data from ranking agencies given that some of their data treatments are suspect. It can be argued that the *U.S. News & World Report* capriciously distributes weights on quality variables and changes in the weight distribution will result in changes in the outcome. It can also be argued that these agencies as well as accreditation agencies have inclination to use quantifiable data rather than the more difficult but more reliable qualitative data. Irrespective of the data integrity and the authenticity of the analyses conducted by ranking agencies, the products of their ranking exercise are out there having influence on student choices for institutions and given the number of institutions that are voluntarily submitting information to these agencies, non-participation may be worse than low ranking. In addition, the importance of this study does not depend on the veracity of ranking data, but on the influence of financial resources on how institutions are ranked.

A study of this nature, important as it is, has several limitations. First, as discussed above, higher education community is aware of the limitations inherent in the data used by ranking agencies. Second, an establishment of relationship does not suggest causation. The primary intent of the study is to establish an association with endowment and quality variables. Third, what is called quality variable in this study is, in fact, ranking variable and the two are not necessarily the same. However, since the criteria used for ranking portend to measure quality, the two are used interchangeably. Although negative relationships are reported on some variables, care must be exercised in interpreting them because while endowments represent continuous data, some quality variables are ordinal data such as rankings. Lastly, some may question the wisdom of using endowment amount rather than endowment income. The simple response to this is that endowment income is not readily available. Nevertheless, endowment income fluctuates depending on market performance and, one can reasonably assume that on the average, the size of endowment income will reflect the size of endowment amount.

Findings

Institutions with the Largest Endowment and Quality Variables

Table 31.1 presents data of top ten national institutions with the largest endowment as published by *The Chronicle of Higher Education.*

With over US$18 billion, Harvard continues to lead the nation in the size of endowment, followed by Yale (US$11 billion), Princeton and Stanford with over US$8 billion in 2003. Little wonders then that these institutions have continued to lead the nation on almost all the quality indicators used by ranking agencies.

Table 31.2 provides the summary of coefficients describing the relationships between endowment and quality variables.

As indicated on Table 31.2, the relationship between endowment and the number of merit scholars attracted to each institution ($r = 0.798$) is significant at 0.01 alpha level with a coefficient of

TABLE 31.1

Ten Top National Universities with the Largest Endowments

Rank	Institution	Amount (US$)[a]
1	Harvard University	18,849,491,000
2	Yale University	11,034,600,000
3	Princeton University	8,730,100,000
4	Stanford University	8,614,000,000
5	Massachusetts Institute of Technology	5,133,613,000
6	University of California	4,368,911,000
7	Columbia University	4,350,000,000
8	Emory University	4,019,766,000
9	University of Pennsylvania	3,547,473,000
10	University of Michigan	3,464,515,000

Source: The Chronicle of Higher Education (2004).

Notes: Endowments of university systems were excluded from this list.

[a]Amount as reported on June 30, 2003.

TABLE 31.2

The Relationship of Total Endowment with Selected Quality Indicators of Top National Doctoral Universities with the Largest Endowment

Quality Variables	n	r-coefficient	R^2 (percent)	Significance	α Level
Merit scholars	34	0.798	64	0.000	0.01
Alumni giving rate	38	0.559	31	0.000	0.01
Peer assessment	38	0.547	30	0.000	0.01
SAT/ACT	38	0.529	28	0.001	0.01
Six-year graduation	38	0.493	24	0.002	0.01
Freshmen retention	38	0.456	21	0.004	0.01
Class size	38	0.470	22	0.003	0.01
Top 10 percent of high school	38	0.453	21	0.005	0.01
Financial resources	38	–0.328	11	0.045	0.05
Faculty resources	38	–0.327	11	0.045	0.05
Student-faculty ratio	38	–0.316	10	0.053	NS
Full-time faculty	38	–0.037	0	0.826	NS

Source: Data used for this study were obtained from *The Chronicle of Higher Education, U.S. News & World Report, The Princeton Review* and *Kaplinger.*

determination of 64 percent. This pattern was observed with respect to the relationships of endowment and alumni giving rate ($r = 0.559$, $\alpha = 0.00$, $R^2 = 31$ percent), peer assessment peer ($r = 0.547$, $\alpha = 0.00$, $R^2 = 30$ percent), SAT/ACT scores ($r = 0.529$, $\alpha = 0.01$, $R^2 = 28$ percent), six year graduation rate ($r = 0.493$, $\alpha = 0.01$, $R^2 = 24$ percent), freshmen retention ($r = 0.456$, $\alpha = 0.01$, $R^2 = 21$ percent), class size ($r = 0.470$, $\alpha = 0.01$, $R^2 = 22$ percent), Top 10 percent of High School ($r = 0.453$, $\alpha = 0.01$, $R^2 = 21$ percent). The relationship between endowment and faculty resources ($r = -0.327$, $R^2 = 11$ percent) and financial resources ($r = -0328$, $R^2 = 31$ percent) were significant at alpha level of 0.05. Note that the negative coefficients do not reflect negative relationships between rankings and faculty resources and financial resources because these two items were ranked data before the coefficients were calculated.

Rather than using total endowment, Table 31.3 provides the results of analysis using endowment per student (total endowment divided by the total number of students). Participating institutions were randomly selected and the results indicate a much stronger relationships between endowment per student and quality variables. The strongest of all the relationships is that of endowment per student and alumni giving rate with $r = 0.967$, $R^2 = 93$ percent. This was followed by SAT/ACT scores and class size both with $r = 0.810$ and with coefficient of determination of 66 percent. Equally strong are the relationships between endowment per student and faculty resources as well as financial resources both with $r = -0.694$, $R^2 = 48$ percent and $r = -0.672$, $R^2 = 45$ percent respectively. These variables were followed by peer assessment and freshmen retention both with $r = -0.647$, $R^2 = 42$ percent and $r = -0.647$, $R^2 = 42$ percent respectively. The top 10 percent of high school graduates shows a moderate relationship of $r = -0.591$, $R^2 = 35$ percent, while the relationship between endowment and the percentage of full time faculty shows a weak relationship with $r = -0.218$, $R^2 = 0.05$ percent. All the relationships between endowment per student and quality indicators were significant at either the alpha level 0.01 (the majority of them) or 0.05 with the exception of the percentage of full time faculty.

Institutions with the Lowest Endowments and Quality Variables

As provided by *The Chronicle of Higher Education* (2004), the lowest endowment reported as of June 30, 2003 was US$14,274,000 from Andrews University. Table 31.4 contains the names of ten top national institutions and their reported endowments. The endowments of the ten top national

TABLE 31.3

The Relationship of Total Endowment per Student and Selected Institutions

Quality Variables	*n*	*r*-coefficient	R^2 (percent)	Significance	α Level
Alumni giving rate	35	0.967	93	0.000	0.01
SAT/ACT	35	0.810	66	0.001	0.01
Class size	35	0.810	66	0.001	0.01
Student-faculty ratio	34	0.787	62	0.001	0.01
Six-year graduation	35	0.731	53	0.002	0.01
Faculty resources	35	–0.694	48	0.004	0.01
Financial resources	35	–0.672	45	0.006	0.01
Peer assessment	35	0.647	42	0.009	0.01
Freshmen retention	35	0.647	42	0.009	0.01
Top 10 percent of high school	35	0.591	35	0.020	0.05
Full-time faculty	35	–0.218	0.05	0.434	NS

Source: Data used for this study were obtained from *The Chronicle of Higher Education, U.S. News & World Report, The Princeton Review* and *Kaplinger*

institutions with the least endowment amounts range from US$42,301,000 (University of Nevada, Las Vargas) to US$14,274,000 (Andrews University).

Table 31.5 presents an interesting observation. Of all the ranking variables examined, only the relationship between endowment and peer assessment and the relationship between endowment and the percentage of full time faculty are significantly different from zero at alpha levels 0.01 and 0.05 respectively. All but peer assessment ($r = 0.563$) showed a very weak relationship.

Selected Academic Programs

Apart from institutional rankings, there is a growing trend to rank schools or programs within an institution. The number of quality variables on which these programs are ranked are fewer, but

TABLE 31.4

Ten Top National Universities with the Smallest Endowments

Rank	Institution	Amount (US$)[a]
1	University of Nevada, Las Vegas	42,301,000
2	South Dakota State University	42,548,000
3	Illinois State University	38,882,000
4	Indiana State University	38,080,000
5	Widener University	37,421,000
6	Wright State University	33,999,000
7	Florida Institute of Technology	27,961,000
8	Oakland University	21,133,000
9	Middle Tennessee State University	19,712,000
10	Andrews University	14,274,000

Source: The Chronicle of Higher Education

Notes: Endowments of university systems were excluded from this list.

[a]Amount as reported on June 30, 2003

TABLE 31.5

The Relationship of Total Endowment with Selected Quality Indicators of Top National Doctoral Universities with the Lowest Endowment

Quality Variables	n	r-coefficient	R^2 (percent)	Significance	α Level
Peer assessment	40	0.563	32	0.000	0.01
Full-time faculty	40	−0.385	15	0.140	0.05
Six-year graduation	40	0.288	8	0.072	NS
Top 10 percent of high school	36	0.250	6	0.885	NS
SAT/ACT	40	−0.222	5	0.168	NS
Freshmen retention	40	0.201	4	0.214	NS
Class size	40	0.183	3	0.258	NS
Alumni giving rate	40	0.090	—	0.582	NS
Acceptance rate	40	−0.040	—	0.804	NS

Source: Data used for this study were obtained from *The Chronicle of Higher Education, U.S. News & World Report, The Princeton Review* and *Kaplinger*

they seem to be narrowly focused to each program. For example, MCAT scores are used for medical schools, while GRE scores are used for engineering programs.

Table 31.6 provides a summary of analysis of total endowment and quality variables for medical research schools. Of the five quality variables, three are significantly different from zero with the relationship between total endowment and National Health Research Grants having the strongest association ($r = 0.64$, $R^2 = 41$ percent, $\alpha = 0.01$), followed by the relationship between total endowment and peer assessment ($r = 0.477$, $R^2 = 23$ percent, $\alpha = 0.01$). Although significant at alpha level of 0.05, the relationship between total endowment and the average undergraduate grade point average (GPA) was relatively weak ($r = 0.36$).

In the business schools, the relationship between total endowments and quality variables presented were significant at alpha level of 0.01 with the exception of the percentage employed after graduation and undergraduate grade point average (GPA). The strongest associations (moderately strong relationships) were those of endowment and average starting salary of MBA graduates, peer assessment, and average GMAT scores with $r = 0.46$, $R^2 = 21$ percent, $r = 0.46$, $R^2 = 21$ percent, $r = 0.45$, $R^2 = 20$ percent respectively (see Table 31.7).

The schools of engineering presented a different scenario. With the exception of the relationship between total endowment and faculty members in the National Academy of Engineers with an $r = 0.572$, $R^2 = 33$ percent, none of the relationships with quality variables showed a significant difference from zero (see Table 31.8).

TABLE 31.6

The Relationship of Total Endowment with Selected Quality Indicators of Top Medical Research Schools

Quality Variables	*n*	*r*-coefficient	R^2 (percent)	Significance	α Level
National Health Research Grant	46	0.640	41	0.000	0.01
Peer assessment	46	0.477	23	0.001	0.01
Average undergraduate GPA	46	0.364	13	0.013	0.05
Acceptance rate	46	–0.225	5	0.087	NS
MCAT score	46	–0.002	—	0.989	NS

Source: Data used for this study were obtained from *The Chronicle of Higher Education, U.S. News & World Report, The Princeton Review* and *Kaplinger*

TABLE 31.7

The Relationship of Total Endowment with Selected Quality Indicators of Top Business Schools

Quality Variables	*n*	*r*-coefficient	R^2 (percent)	Significance	α Level
Average starting salary	47	0.460	21	0.001	0.01
Peer assessment	47	0.455	21	0.001	0.01
Average GMAT scores	47	0.452	20	0.001	0.01
Acceptance rate	47	–0.389	15	0.007	0.01
Percentage employed after graduation	47	0.167	—	0.261	NS
Average undergraduate GPA	47	0.093	—	0.533	NS

Source: Data used for this study were obtained from *The Chronicle of Higher Education, U.S. News & World Report, The Princeton Review* and *Kaplinger*

TABLE 31.8

The Relationship of Total Endowment with Selected Quality Indicators of Top Engineering Schools

Quality Variables	*n*	*r*-coefficient	R^2 (percent)	Significance	α Level
Faculty membership NAE	51	0.572	33	0.000	0.01
Research exp. by faculty	51	0.274	—	0.051	NS
Peer assessment	51	0.182	—	0.201	NS
Average GRE scores	51	0.170	—	0.239	NS
Acceptance rate	51	0.143	—	0.318	NS
Research expenditures	51	0.031	—	0.881	NS
PhD granted	51	0.023	—	0.875	NS

Source: Data used for this study were obtained from *The Chronicle of Higher Education, U.S. News & World Report, The Princeton Review* and *Kaplinger*

Discussion

There is no doubt that endowments are beginning to play an important role in higher education affairs. At the public university sector where government appropriations continue to either decline or increase less than the increase in education costs, institutions are turning to private sources for funds at a greater number. Of all the sources of institutional funds, endowment was chosen for this study because of the relative freedom and ease that institution leadership has to use the funds to accomplish institution's mission. The assumption is that where institution leaders have the freedom to expend funds, they will expend them to pursue quality variables in order to attain a better ranking for the institution, although many higher education leaders may not publicly admit to this.

While endowment is generally available to institution leaders to use in pursuit of institution's mission, almost all endowments have some restrictions. In some cases, donors specify conditions on which endowments or their proceeds may be expended. In other cases, the leadership of an institution sets these conditions. In addition, forecast of investment market conditions also exert some limitations on the latitude that institution leaders have to spend these moneys. Be that as it may, government appropriations in today's environment are almost always barely adequate to keep institutions alive, only private support of which endowment is a major part turns good institutions into great institutions, only private support provides the lever to lift an institution from one level of excellence to another.

If endowment funds provide institutional leadership with the freedom to pursue a wide range of policy options, it stands to reason that Harvard University with over US$18 billion endowment is perhaps the freest institution in the nation, a point that was recently demonstrated by the relative ease at which the leadership of the institution decided on a policy to offer free tuition to admitted low income students. Attractive as this gesture is, few institutions can emulate it and public institutions are even more restricted by their governments with respect to policy options.

Although this study reveals that total endowments have, on the whole, moderate relationships with quality or ranking variables, very strong relationships were the original expectations of the study. With respect to the top national doctoral universities with the largest endowments, the strongest relationship was between total endowments and the number of freshmen merit scholars enrolled. Freshmen merit scholars are the nation top students with the best credentials and scholarships to shop for the best education the nation offers. In addition, institutional financial strength determines the number and size of scholarships available to recruit this group of students. The second strongest relationship was between endowments and alumni giving rate. The most important determinants of alumni giving are the quality of experience alumni had when they were students as well as the institution's investment in alumni cultivation. To the extent that an institution has surplus funds to invest in these two determinants, to that extent the institution may reap the benefit of increased alumni giving. On the other hand, institutions with large endowment are often those that benefit from significant alumni giving and vice versa. Therefore, one can reasonably conclude that endowment size is a function of alumni giving. Peer Assessment also reveals a moderate strong relationship with total endowments—institutional wealth does create some positive impression. Of course, it is to be expected that institutions with resources to attract top scholars and to provide attractive conditions to retain them will enjoy better reputation among scholars.

At the low end of relationships are the percentage of full-time faculty and student faculty ratio. Institution's size of endowment may not have influence on an institution's policy to utilize part-time faculty and similarly, an institution's student-faculty ratio may have nothing to do with the endowment size. This too can be explained by the fact that there are many small colleges with very small endowments, but with a policy of high percentage of full-time faculty and small student-faculty ratio. These two quality variables indicate institution's policy more than endowment size.

An interesting observation was made when endowment per student statistics were used instead of the total endowment. First, there is an increase in the strength of relationships between endowment and quality variables. Second, the relationships between endowment and all the quality variables became significant at the alpha level of 0.01, with one (the proportion of the top 10 percent of high school graduates) at the alpha level of 0.05 and with one exception, ie, the percentage of full-time faculty. Third, the strongest relationship was between endowment and alumni giving rate, followed by the SAT/ACT scores and class size. Even the student-faculty ratio became significantly strong and so also was the proportion of students who graduated within six years and the level of faculty and financial resources. The observation with respect to endowment per student reveals that the absolute size of endowment has lower association with quality and ranking variables. This observation suggests that institutional wealth cannot or should not be discussed in absence of student population size. Therefore, endowment per student provides a more accurate data on institutional wealth. Many of the top flagship institutions are small to medium size institutions, but with large endowment. Therefore, small institutions with large endowments tend to perform better on ranking variables than large institutions with equally large endowments.

Apart from the top national universities with the largest endowments, this study also examined the relationships between total endowments and quality variables among top national universities with the smallest endowments. The *U.S. News & World Report* provided data on top national universities, while *The Chronicle of Higher Education* provided data on endowments. Again, another interesting observation was made with this exercise. None of the relationships between total endowment and quality variables were significant with the exception of two: peer assessment and the percentage of the full time faculty with alpha levels of 0.01 and 0.05 respectively. Perhaps the only explanation for this is that institutions' behaviors differ at different sizes of endowment or resources. If this holds true, institutions ought to be classified as small, medium, and large, and very large endowed institutions. Chances are that institution's policy with regards to how endowment income is spent differs based on these categories. Even more perplexing is the fact that at top universities with the smallest endowments there may be no predictable relationships between endowments and alumni giving and acceptance rates. An alternative explanation of this finding could be that institutions with relatively small endowments tend to be more conservative in spending. Perhaps many do not even spend their endowment income, but rather reinvest the income with the hope of growing their endowments.

Further probe was made into the relationships between endowments and quality variables specific to three academic programs: medical, business, and engineering. With respect to the top medical research schools, the relationships between endowments and National Health Research Grants (absolute amounts received), peer assessment, and undergraduate grade point average were found significant at alpha levels of 0.01, 0.01, and 0.05 respectively. The strongest of all the relationships was that of the National Health Research Grants. Many of these large institutions have large research offices and a number of research faculty whose sole responsibilities are to seek grants and conduct research.

With respect to the top business schools, the relationships between endowments and average starting salaries of graduates, peer assessment, average GMAT scores, and acceptance rates were significant at alpha level of 0.01. Institutions with the largest endowments are the top ranking institutions. It is little surprise then that their graduates command top most salaries upon graduation. For the business schools, the relationship between endowments and undergraduate grade point average was not established.

There was no significant relationships between endowments and quality variables found at the top engineering schools with the exception of the number of faculty members who hold membership at the National Academy of Engineers.

Conclusion and Implications

Do the ranking criteria actually demonstrate the quality of an institution? This study has not suggested either way. That is not the goal. Do ranking agencies suggest that ranking criteria speak to the quality of an institution? Yes, they do and both consumers and education providers are finding rankings difficult to neglect. In themselves, few academics will argue against these criteria. The number of merit scholars made sense because they represent what is attractive to and the presence of the best students. Both SAT/ACT scores and the proportion of top 10 per cent of high school graduates also speak to the issue of where the best students attend school. But the question remains, are they flocking to these schools because of the quality promised or because of the dollars offered? It is hard to conclude that both have no influence on students' decisions. As Wood (2004) observed, "stipends are key in competition to land top graduate students" (p. 1).

Peer assessment makes a good sense in determining institutional quality. After all, these are academic experts with good knowledge of research, publications, and to some extent, teaching taking place in one another's institutions. It is not impossible though that institution's popularity, age, and size may influence peer assessment more than the quality of an institution. The proportion of undergraduate students who graduate within six years and the proportion of freshmen retained make sense because first, they suggest that the students who came are academically prepared and two, that the institution has resources and programs to assist students in the most efficient and effective manner. However, retention and graduation rates may reflect differences in institution's mission and clientele rather than endowment size. For example, urban, non-residential institutions may have students with different academic behaviors from suburban, residential institutions. Therefore, there may be other forces at work other than the quality of students and institutional efficiency.

Class size, the percentage of full-time faculty, faculty resources, and financial resources also make sense at least on the surface. The smaller the class size, the greater the personal attention a student receives from the class instructor, all things being equal; the higher the percentage of the full-time faculty, the more students will be taught by experienced faculty who can be held accountable, assuming these faculty members are not preoccupied with research; the greater the faculty and financial resources, the more effective faculty will be—perhaps. It can be argued, however, that these are mere conjectures, unsubstantiated speculations. There are many sectarian institutions with meager resources, but with dedicated faculty with missionary zeal who continue to make significant difference in the lives of their students. These institutions, few as they may be, continue to prove that money, important as it is, may not be everything after all.

Nevertheless, in a market economy where there are many providers, buyers search for information to help sort through the myriad items of information from these providers. Buyers seek for easy answers to complex questions and, in many cases, would settle for surrogate quality facts in the absence of real facts. The more informed students and parents become, the more they will seek for basis to discriminate among institutions.

The implications of this study are many. Those interested in a follow up study should be advised to use endowment income per student rather than the absolute amount of endowment. This seems to suggest stronger associations than the size of endowment. Also, it should be possible to disaggregate some of the ranking data provided by agencies. For example, while a single ranking number is provided for financial resources, this variable contains average spending on instruction, research, student services, and educational expenditures. Differences in rankings may not capture the differences in spending policy regarding these areas.

Although an assumption was made at the beginning of this study that endowment represents "free" or surplus money for leaders to use in pursuit of quality agenda, it could be that an institution's total budget may provide richer information regarding the association between money and quality. Future researchers should continue to explore how different sources of funds interact to influence institutional behaviors. State administrators should be aware that how they fund public institutions have bearing on the kind of quality variables institutions pursue. As Johnstone (1988) observed, "it is difficult to contemplate radical changes in patterns of finance that do not either arise from, or cause, profound changes in the substance of the higher education enterprise" (p. 247).

In conclusion, Peterson's web site contains a caveat issued to those who rely unduly on commercial rankings of higher education institutions:

> Despite many people's attempts to quantify colleges according to certain characteristics, many educators agree that those characteristics do not add up to any meaningful measures of quality. Further, publishing such misleading information and making a national event of it encourages colleges to shade the truth and to focus on the wrong factors in accepting students (www.petersons.com/about/ranking.html).

Therefore, what ranking agencies are measuring may be nothing more than resource available to higher education institutions. Unfortunately, their ranking methodologies may not capture the hard work, dedication, and sacrifice taking place in many impressive institutions across the nation that are ranked low.

In addition, to the extent that ranking criteria represent cost-intensive variables, to that extent they represent another externally induced cost escalation factor. Institutional leaders must be careful in selecting ranking or quality criteria appropriate to their missions and within their resources. Unbridled chase after the reputation that rankings promise will result in unbridled cost escalations without necessarily adding values to student learning or values to society.

References

Anderson, M. (1992), *Impostors in the Temple: The Decline of the American University*, Simon & Schuster, New York, NY.

Brubacher, J.S. (1990), *On the Philosophy of Higher Education*, 3rd ed., Jossey-Bass, San Francisco, CA.

(The) Chronicle of Higher Education (2004), available at: http://chronicle.com/free/almanac/2003/nation/nation_index.htm#resources

Cornesky, R.A., Baker, R., Cavanaugh, C., Etling, W., Lukart, M., McCool, S., McKay, B., Min, A., Paul, C., Thomas, P., Wagner, D. and Darling, J.R. (1990), *W. Edwards Deming: Improving Quality in Colleges and Universities*, Magna Publications, Inc., Madison, WI.

Council on Competitiveness (1996), "A higher standard of quality in the '90s", *Quality Observer*, March, pp. 28–31.

Ewell, P.T. (2004), "Money matters", Editorial, *Change—The Magazine of Higher Education*, Vol. 36 No. 4, pp. 4–5.

Johnstone, B. (1988), "Revolution, evolution, or more of the same?", *The Review of Higher Education*, Vol. 21 No. 3, pp. 245–55.

Michael, S.O. (2004a), *Financing Higher Education for the 21st Century: An International Perspective*, Fall, Kent State University Press, Kent, OH.

Michael, S.O. (2004b), "In search of universal principles of higher education management and applicability to Moldavian higher education system", *International Journal of Educational Management*, Vol. 18 No. 2, pp. 118–37.

National Center for Education Statistics (2000), *Finance FY2000*, Integrated Postsecondary Education Data Systems (IPEDS), National Center for Education Statistics, US Department of Education, Washington, DC.

Noone, L.P. (2004), "Markets, customers, and products of higher education: a view from the dark side", paper presented at the Council of Fellows Weekend, Washington, DC, 5–6 June.

Seymour, D. and Collett, C. (1991), *Total Quality Management in Higher Education: A Critical Assessment*, Goal/QPC, Methuen, MA.

Sykes, C. (1989), *Profscam: Professors and the Demise of Higher Education*, St Martin's Press, New York, NY.

Wood, S.S. (2004), "Stipends are key in competition to land top graduate students", available at: http://chronicle.com/free/v48/i05/05a02401/htm

Further Reading

Winston, G.C. (1999), "Subsidies, hierarchy, and peers: the awkward economics of higher education", *Journal of Economic Perspectives*, Vol. 13 No. 1, pp. 13–36.

CHAPTER 32

UNDERSTANDING HIGHER EDUCATION COSTS

MICHAEL F. MIDDAUGH

Colleges and universities must be more proactive in describing to a wider public their of fiscal and human resources because, among other reasons, a careful analysis reveals counterintuitive results that support a finding that higher education has been fiscally responsible.

Introduction

For more than a decade, higher education has come under intense criticism for what is perceived to be a lack of fiscal discipline that has resulted in geometric growth of higher education costs. Robert Zemsky and William Massy, in developing the notion of the "academic ratchet," argued in 1990 that

> [the academic ratchet is] a term to describe the steady, irreversible shift of faculty allegiance away from the goals of a given institution, toward those of an academic specialty. The ratchet denotes the advance of an independent, entrepreneurial spirit among faculty nationwide, leading to increased emphasis on research and publication and on teaching one's specialty in favor of general introduction courses, often at the expense of coherence in an academic curriculum. Institutions seeking to enhance their own prestige may contribute to the ratchet effect by reducing faculty teaching and advising responsibilities across the board, thus enabling faculty to pursue their individual research and publication with fewer distractions. The academic ratchet raises an institution's costs, and it results in undergraduates paying more to attend institutions in which they receive less faculty attention than in previous decades. (Zemsky and Massy 1990, p. 22)

This position was reinforced in 1998 by the Boyer Commission on Educating Undergraduates in the Research University:

> To an overwhelming degree, they [American research universities] have furnished the cultural, intellectual, economic, and political leadership of the nation. Nevertheless, the research universities have too often failed, and continue to fail, their undergraduate populations. . . . Again and again, universities are guilty of an advertising practice they would condemn in the commercial world. Recruitment materials display proudly the world-famous professors, the splendid facilities and the ground-breaking research that goes on within them, but thousands of students graduate without ever seeing the world-famous professors or tasting genuine research. Some of their instructors are likely to be badly trained or untrained teaching assistants who are groping their way toward a teaching technique; some others may be tenured drones who deliver set lectures from yellowed notes, making no effort to engage the bored minds of the students in front of them. (Boyer Commission on Educating Undergraduates in the Research University 1998, pp. 5–6)

Even popular media such as *U.S. News & World Report* have weighed in:

> The trouble is that higher education remains a labor-intensive service industry made up of thousands of stubbornly independent and mutually jealous units that must support expensive and vastly underused facilities. It is a more than $200 billion-a-year economic enterprise—many of whose leaders oddly disdain economic enterprise and often regard efficiency, productivity, and commercial opportunity with the same hauteur with which Victorian aristocrats viewed those in "trade" . . . The net result: a hideously inefficient system that, for all its tax advantages and public and private subsidies, still extracts a larger share of family income. . . than almost anywhere else on the planet. (Elfin 1996, p. 91)

Finally, consider the following statements from Congressman Howard P. "Buck" McKeon that opened the September 23, 2003, congressional hearing on *The College Cost Crisis Report: Are Institutions Accountable Enough to Students and Parents?*:

> A few weeks ago Chairman [of the House Committee on Education and the Workforce] Boehner and I released a report called *The College Cost Crisis*, which declared that the nation's higher education system is in crisis as a result of exploding cost increases that threaten to put college out of reach for low and middle income students and families. The report concluded that decades of cost increases, in both good economic times and bad, have caused America's higher education system to reach a crisis point. It also concluded that students and parents are losing patience with higher education "sticker shock" and that institutions of higher education are not accountable enough to parents, students, and taxpayers—the consumers of higher education. . . .
>
> The following statistic is one I've repeated many times, and I will continue to repeat it until we can find a solution and interested parties start taking this issue seriously. The fact is, according to the Advisory Committee on Student Financial Assistance, cost factors prevent 48 percent of all college-qualified, low-income high-school graduates from attending a four-year college and 22 percent from pursuing any college at all. The statistics are similarly bleak for moderate income families. At the rate we are going, by the end of the decade, more than two million college-qualified students will miss out on the opportunity to go to college. (McKeon 2003)

It is evident from this spectrum of criticism that the term "cost" is being used to reflect both what students and their families pay for a college degree (price) and what a higher education institution expends to deliver that degree (cost). It is important to clarify what we know about both price and cost, and the relationship between the two.

Price

The 1998 reauthorization of the Higher Education Act included a mandate requiring the U.S. Department of Education's National Center for Education Statistics (NCES) to conduct a study of higher education expenditures. The study was to include an evaluation of expenditure patterns over time, an evaluation of the relationship of expenditures to the price charged for a college education, and an assessment of the effect of tuition discounting and federal financial aid on tuition-setting policy. NCES responded to the congressional mandate by commissioning three reports: *Study of College Costs and Prices, 1988–89 to 1997–98* (Cunningham et al. 2001), *What Students Pay for College: Changes in Net Price of College Attendance Between 1992–93 and 1999–2000* (Horn et al. 2002), and *A Study of Higher Education Instructional Expenditures: The Delaware Study of Instructional Costs and Productivity* (Middaugh et al. 2003). The findings from the first two studies concerning price were conclusive and somewhat contrary to the tone of criticisms leveled against higher education, typified by *U.S. News & World Report* and Congressman McKeon. It should be recalled that higher education institutions were under fire in the 1990s for extraordinary tuition increases in light of increases in the amount of available financial aid.

Specifically, the analysis of tuition increases in the *Study of College Costs and Prices, 1988–89 to 1997–98* (Cunningham et al. 2001) concluded that at both public and private institutions, tuition increased at a rate greater than the increase in the consumer price index over the period of time studied, and that tuition growth exceeded most other expenditure categories at most institutions. However, the study found virtually no relationship between financial aid and tuition increases at either public or private institutions across the Carnegie institutional classification spectrum. The sole exceptions were very weak correlations (0.103 at public comprehensive colleges and 0.188 at private comprehensive colleges) between availability of institutional aid and tuition increases. The study found that other, nonfinancial aid variables were more closely associated with increases in tuition:

- Decreasing revenue from government appropriations—in particular, state appropriations—was the single most important variable associated with tuition increases at public four-year institutions during the time frame studied. Although increases in instructional expenditures were associated with tuition increases at those institutions, that correlation was far weaker than the correlation with the decline in state support for higher education.

- Multiple factors at private four-year institutions were more strongly associated with tuition increases than was an infusion of federal financial aid. Among the internal factors were the availability of institutional aid and faculty compensation levels, as well as return on endowment, gift income, and contract/grant revenue. A number of external factors were also strongly associated with the magnitude of tuition increases, including competitor tuition rates, particularly at neighboring public institutions, and per capita income in the state where the institution was located.

While it is important to know that the rate of tuition increase is not as strongly associated with financial aid—particularly federal financial aid—as it is with other, non-aid factors, what additional information about college prices can help address the concerns of critics? The study *What Students Pay for College: Changes in Net Price of College Attendance Between 1992–93 and 1999–2000* (Horn et al. 2002) offers some very useful conclusions:

- It is important to clearly distinguish between "sticker price," i.e., the published schedule of tuition and fees that appears in a college or university catalog, and "net price," i.e., what a student actually pays for a college education after financial aid is factored in.
- After adjusting for inflation, there is a perceptible increase in average total tuition and average total cost of attending a college or university from 1992–93 to 1999–2000. However, when grant aid is subtracted from tuition to arrive at "net tuition," there is no change in the average amount paid by full-time undergraduates during the time frame under analysis.
- When housing, food, books, and other nontuition living expenses are added to tuition, grants are insufficient to cover the increase in the total cost of attending a college or university over time. However, not all students are affected by the increase in total cost in comparable ways. Grant aid does, in fact, cover total cost for students from the lowest income brackets, i.e., those who can least afford an increase. Students in higher income brackets borrowed to meet the increase.

These are important findings, considering that the average loan indebtedness for an undergraduate student following graduation typically approximates the price of a new car. While that automobile begins immediate depreciation after purchase, the effects of a college education, measured in terms of earning power, appreciate substantially over time. The foregoing findings with respect to what students actually pay for college over time indicate that higher education is an investment that is approachable by all income brackets.

There is no pure cause and effect relationship between price (tuition) and cost (what institutions expend in delivering a college education).

A final word about price: There is no pure cause and effect relationship between price (tuition) and cost (what institutions expend in delivering a college education). This is due in no small measure to the fact that institutions have multiple revenue streams available to them, and each revenue stream contributes to varying degrees to meeting institutional costs. Moreover, colleges and universities make choices about how they spend revenues. The balance between and among teaching, research, and service reflect an institution's mission and values. It would be foolish to suggest that tuition dollars contribute only to instructional expenditures at a college or university. That said, it is demonstrable that higher education institutions have been responsible fiscal stewards in containing instructional costs and, to the extent that tuition dollars contribute to the creation of knowledge through pure and applied research or extension and other service activity, the common good of society is served.

Cost

Instructional expenditures constitute the single largest cost category at colleges and universities, accounting for approximately 40 percent of education and general expenditures. Unlike some institutional expenditures such as health care costs, energy costs, unfunded governmental mandates, etc., that are beyond institutional control, instructional costs are within the domain of variables over which an institution can exert measures of containment, The question is, are colleges and universities doing so?

To answer this question, we will focus on data from the 1998, 2000, 2001, 2002, and 2003 data collection cycles of the Delaware Study of Instructional Costs and Productivity. (The 1999 Delaware Study data collection cycle was restricted to research and doctoral universities while a secure server was tested at the host institution. Hence, the 1999 sample is not comparable to other years.) The Delaware Study is a consortium of four-year colleges and universities that share detailed data on faculty teaching loads, direct instructional costs, and separately budgeted research and service expenditures, all at the academic discipline level of analysis. Since its inception in 1992, the Delaware Study has embraced over 400 participating institutions, with at least 200 participating in any given year. Participants run the gamut from research universities to baccalaureate colleges. Two-thirds of the participants are public, state-assisted institutions; one-third are private, independently chartered institutions. More detailed information on the Delaware Study can be found at www.udel.edu/ir/cost.

Let us first consider what we know about the nature of direct instructional expenditures—why do they vary from institution to institution, and which variables are most closely associated with the magnitude of those expenditures? In responding to the 1998 congressional mandate for an analysis of instructional expenditures, the NCES contracted with the Office of Institutional Research and Planning at the University of Delaware to examine multiple cycles of Delaware Study data to attempt to answer these questions. In the 2003 NCES research and development report *A Study of Higher Education Instructional Expenditures: The Delaware Study of Instructional Costs and Productivity* (Middaugh 2003), three cycles were examined—1998, 2000, and 2001.

In approaching the issue of variance in instructional expenditures across institutions, one might reasonably expect Carnegie institutional classification to explain much of the variation. Specifically, one might expect research universities to teach less at a higher cost than doctoral universities, which in turn teach less at a higher cost than comprehensive/master's institutions, which teach less at a higher cost than baccalaureate colleges. (Note: The Delaware Study continues to employ the 1995 Carnegie institutional taxonomy for analysis of instructional expenditures since, for purposes of this project, those institutional distinctions are more meaningful than the current version.) The results of the analyses are instructive:

- The single most important variable in explaining variation in the cost of instruction across four-year institutions that participate in the Delaware Study is the mix of academic disciplines at those institutions. The relative variance explained by this variable ranged from 76.0 to 82.6 percent in the three data collection cycles examined.
- While Carnegie institutional classification could be expected to account for some of the variance, its Understanding Higher Education Costs explanatory power does not approach that of the disciplinary mix within the institutional curriculum. When Carnegie institutional classification is taken into account, the relative variance due to disciplinary mix ranges from 81.0 to 88.0 percent in the three cycles under examination.

A graphic illustration underscores these findings (see Figure 32.1).

Figure 32.1 looks at direct instructional expenditures for five disciplines typically found at four-year institutions across the United States. The figure examines direct expense by institution type within each discipline and specifically shows the spread in cost per student credit hour taught within each of the five disciplines—chemistry, English, foreign languages, mechanical engineering, and sociology—for each of the four Carnegie institution types—research universities, doctoral universities, comprehensive institutions, and baccalaureate colleges. While there are differences in direct instructional expenditure per student credit hour taught within each of the disciplines, they are fairly small. The spread between the highest and lowest value for cost per student credit hour taught in chemistry is $83 (i.e., $264 at research universities versus $181 at comprehensive institutions). The spread is $28 in English, $71 in foreign languages. $63 in mechanical engineering, and $38 in sociology.

However, when direct instructional cost per student credit hour taught is arrayed by discipline within institution type, the picture is quite different, as is evident in Figure 32.2.

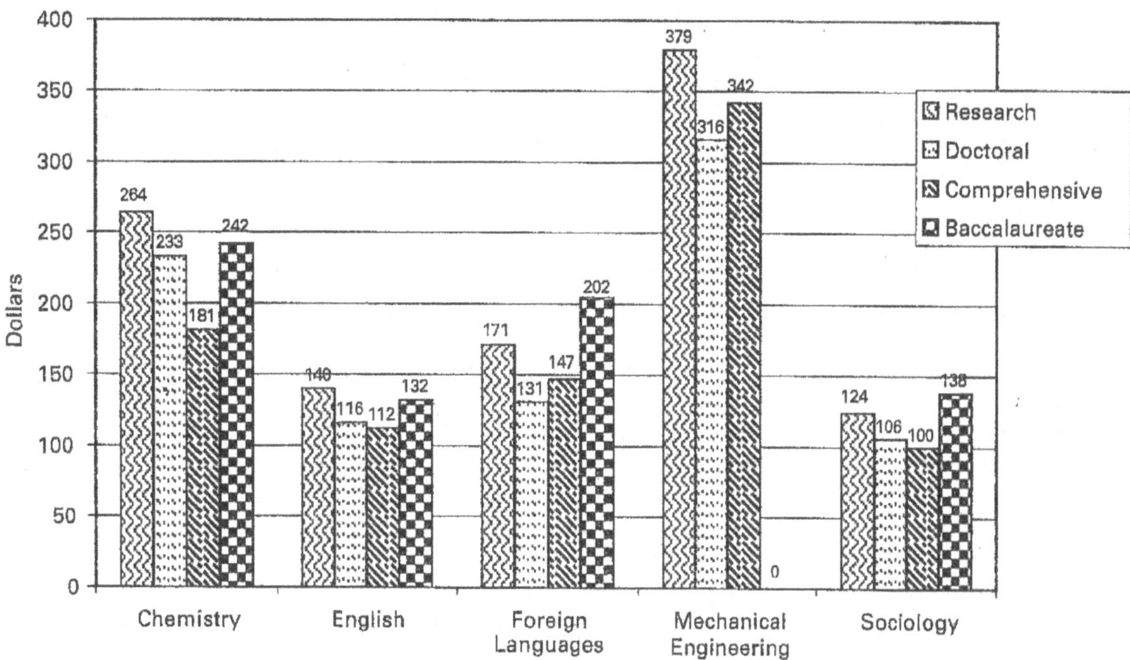

Figure 32.1 Direct expense per student credit hour taught: Institution type within discipline—academic year 2001.

Source: Middaugh et al. 2003, ix.

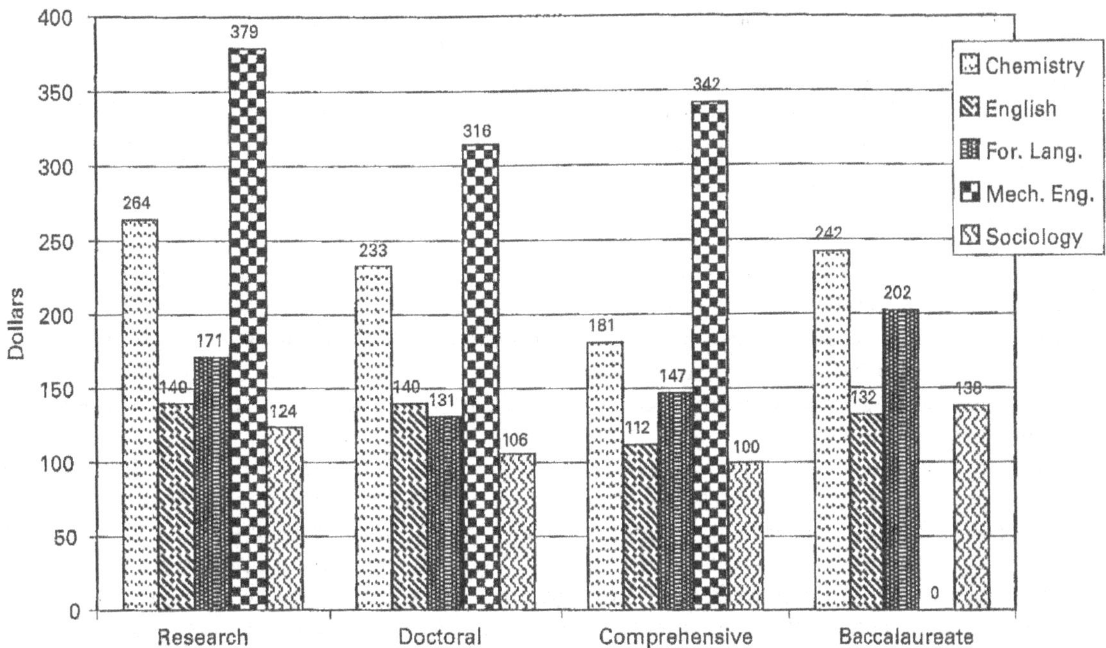

Figure 32.2 Direct expense per student credit hour taught: Discipline within institution type—academic year 2001.

Source: Middaugh et al. 2003, ix.

At research universities, the spread in expense per student credit hour taught between English and mechanical engineering is $239; the range between sociology and chemistry is $140. Similar ranges are apparent at doctoral, comprehensive, and baccalaureate institutions. These differences are far larger than those in Figure 32.1. Figures 32.1 and 32.2 taken together clearly illustrate that the Carnegie classification of a college or university is less important in determining overall direct instructional expenditures than the disciplines that the institution chooses to include in its curriculum. While Figures 32.1 and 32.2 reflect the 2001 Delaware Study data collection cycle, comparable patterns were evident in 1998 and 2000.

If disciplinary mix plays such an important role in determining overall instructional expense at an institution, have instructional costs within specific disciplines grown inordinately over time, and is it possible to identify those factors that are statistically most closely associated with direct instructional expenditures? The Delaware Study data set again helps to provide answers to these questions.

Figures 32.3, 32.4, and 32.5 examine data from 24 disciplines typically found at four-year colleges and universities in the United States. The data reflect average direct instruction cost per student credit hour taught within those disciplines for the 2000, 2001, 2002, and 2003 data collection cycles. Using 2000 as a base year, the figures also display annual changes in direct cost per student credit hour taught. To smooth out the fluctuation in costs over the four data cycles, a three-year weighted average cost per student credit hour taught is calculated for 2001 through 2003 and that weighted average is also compared with the 2000 base year. Figures 32.3, 32.4, and 32.5 reflect research universities, doctoral universities, and comprehensive institutions, respectively; there is no figure for baccalaureate colleges because of insufficient data points.

Although the cost data on all three figures vary considerably, there are a number of consistencies that cut across Carnegie institution types. Disciplines that are typically characterized as "service departments," i.e., those disciplines that are heavily subscribed by students attempting to satisfy general education requirements, tend to show minimal and, in a number of instances, negative growth in direct cost per student credit hour taught over the time frame under analysis. Examples of such disciplines include English, philosophy, history, and political science.

Other disciplines such as computer science and biological sciences are typical of those that have to compete with business and industry for newly minted Ph.D.s. As a result of this competition, entry-level salaries are generally substantially higher than those in less competitive disciplines, thereby driving up instructional expense. Within research universities, where faculty scholarship often mirrors industrial activity, this salary competitiveness is extended to disciplines such as business administration and financial management.

Disciplines such as visual and performing arts, which embrace components such as studio art and music and theater performance, rely heavily on individualized and small group instruction by definition and tend to be expensive. During a strong economic downturn such as that experienced from 2000 through 2003, the number of students majoring or enrolling in arts courses often declines, thereby exacerbating this expense pattern. On the other hand, disciplines such as engineering and nursing, equipment-intensive in nature and requiring small group instruction, are expensive to start with, so the magnitude of cost increases will appear relatively modest although the actual dollar expense is substantial.

Despite the vagaries of expenditure patterns within the disciplines, which are subject to a host of intervening variables (these variables will be discussed shortly), it is nonetheless demonstrable that higher education institutions, in general, have been responsible fiscal stewards. In looking at the overall percentage increase of the three-year weighted average cost per student credit hour taught for the 24 disciplines from 2001 through 2003 compared with the base year of 2000, we find that increase is 5.2 percent at research universities, 0.5 percent at doctoral universities, and 3.5 percent at comprehensive institutions. This compares with a 6.9 percent increase in the consumer price index for the same period, according to the U.S. Department of Labor. While these cost increases do not reflect an individual institution's increase (which will be a function of department size, enrollment, and other factors within the respective disciplines), they do provide a useful general barometer for thinking about instructional expense. As the data clearly suggest, those

FIGURE 32.3

Direct Instructional Cost per Student Credit HourTaught: Delaware Study Benchmarks for Research Universities

	2000	2001		2002		2003		2001 to 2003 3 Yr Wghtd Average	% Increase
	Cost/SCH	Cost/SCH	% Increase	Cost/SCH	% Increase	Cost/SCH	% Increase	Cost?SCH	from 2000
Communications	164	164	0.0	157	–4.3	161	2.5	160	–2.3
Computer Science	203	204	0.5	242	18.6	293	21.1	261	28.7
Education	268	260	–3.0	275	5.8	282	2.5	276	3.0
Engineering	415	417	0.5	438	5.0	453	3.4	442	6.5
Foreign Language	169	171	1.2	175	2.3	176	0.6	175	3.5
English	138	140	1.4	133	–5.0	141	6.0	138	0.1
Biological Sciences	286	276	–3.5	316	14.5	331	4.7	317	10.8
Mathematics	147	160	8.8	163	1.9	152	–6.7	157	6.8
Philosophy	134	132	–1.5	132	0.0	128	–3.0	130	–3.0
Chemistry	255	264	3.5	263	–0.4	246	–6.8	254	–0.3
Geology	223	211	–5.4	226	7.1	240	6.2	231	3.4
Physics	284	263	–7.4	292	11.0	253	–13.4	268	5.8
Psychology	150	150	0.0	167	11.3	172	3.0	167	11.1
Anthropology	148	157	6.1	157	0.0	171	8.9	164	10.8
Economics	145	154	6.2	144	–6.5	144	0.0	146	0.5
Geography	155	164	5.8	16S	3.0	165	–2.4	166	7.2
History	142	149	4.9	141	–5.4	148	5.0.	146	2.7
Political Science	168	164	–2.4	160	–2.4	161	0.6	161	–4.1
Sociology	130	124	–4.6	123	–0.8	120	–2.4	122	–6.4
Visual & Performing Arts	214	228	6.5	224	–1.8	239	6.7	232	8.5
Nursing	368	388	5.4	394	1.5	376	–4.6	384	4.3
Business Administration	175	199	13.7	208	4.5	209	0.5	207	18.3
Accounting	162	158	–2.5	164	3.8	176	7.3	169	4.3
Financial Management	184	187	1.6	201	7.5	215	7.0	206	11.8
Average	201	204	1.5	211	3.0	215	1.9	212	5.2

Source: Data from Delaware Study of Instructional Costs and Productivity for cited years.

FIGURE 32.4

Direct Instructional Cost per Student Credit HourTaught: Delaware Study Benchmarks for Doctoral Universities

	2000	2001		2002		2003		2001 to 2003 3 Yr Wghtd Average	% Increase
	Cost/SCH	Cost/SCH	% Increase	Cost/SCH	% Increase	Cost/SCH	% Increase	Cost?SCH	from 2000
Communications	143	130	9.1	138	6.2	141	2.2	138	−3.4
Computer Science	165	142	−13.9	171	20.4	190	11.1	176	6.5
Education	184	198	7.6	198	0.0	196	−1.0	197	7.1
Engineering	375	356	−5.1	390	9.6	392	0.5	386	2.8
Foreign Language	127	131	3.1	146	11.5	147	0.7	144	13.4
English	118	116	−1.7	118	1.7	121	2.5	119	1.0
Biological Sciences	201	191	−5.0	200	4.7	198	1.0	198	−1.7
Mathematics	122	116	−4.9	131	12.9	120	−8.4	123	0.8
Philosophy	129	120	−7.0	126	5.0	118	−6.3	121	−6.2
Chemistry	229	233	1.7	227	−2.6	219	−3.5	224	−2.2
Geology	201	197	−2.0	187	−5.1	175	−6.4	183	−9.1
Physics	191	203	6.3	209	3.0	190	−9.1	199	3.9
Psychology	135	131	−3.0	136	3.8	144	5.9	139	3.1
Anthropology	127	126	−0.8	133	5.6	141	6.0	136	7.0
Economics	139	144	3.6	145	0.7	147	1.4	146	4.9
Geography	137	125	−8.8	130	4.0	117	−10.0	123	−10.5
History	125	124	−0.8	131	5.6	121	−7.6	125	−0.1
Political Science	151	152	0.7	146	−3.9	134	−8.2	141	−6.6
Sociology	105	106	1.0	120	13.2	113	−5.8	114	−8.7
Visual & Performing Arts	200	199	−0.5	212	6.5	210	−0.9	209	4.4
Nursing	354	332	−6.2	359	8.1	337	−6.1	344	−3.0
Business Administration	161	137	−14.9	162	10.9	158	3.9	153	−5.3
Accounting	178	169	−5.1	170	0.6	175	2.9	172	−3.2
Financial Management	174	174	0.0	175	0.6	170	−2.9	172	−1.0
Average	174	169	−2.7	177	5.1	174	−1.7	174	0.5

Source: Data from Delaware Study of Instructional Costs and Productivity for cited years.

FIGURE 32.5

Direct Instructional Cost per Student Credit HourTaught: Delaware Study Benchmarks for Comprehensive Colleges and Universities

	2000	2001		2002		2003		2001 to 2003 3 Yr Wghtd Average	% Increase
	Cost/SCH	Cost/SCH	% Increase	Cost/SCH	% Increase	Cost/SCH	% Increase	Cost?SCH	from 2000
Communications	134	138	3.0	138	0.0	130	–5.8	134	0.0
Computer Science	135	155	14.8	165	6.5	195	18.2	178	32.1
Education	185	180	–2.7	188	4.4	184	–2.1	185	–0.2
Engineering	339	320	–5.6	358	11.9	383	7.0	364	7.4
Foreign Language	139	147	5.8	139	–504	140	0.7	141	1.3
English	109	112	2.8	115	2.7	112	–2.6	113	3.7
Biological Sciences	135	149	10.4	162	8.7	154	–4.9	156	15.4
Mathematics	105	106	1.0	111	4.7	113	1.8	111	5.9
Philosophy	124	118	–4.8	127	7.6	111	–12.6	118	–5.2
Chemistry	168	181	7.7	174	–3.9	179	2.9	178	5.8
Geology	160	144	10.0	149	3.5	155	4.0	151	–5.5
Physics	165	167	1.2	181	8.4	173	–4.4	175	5.9
Psychology	113	115	1.8	108	–6.1	111	2.8	111	–2.1
Anthropology	106	132	24.5	110	–16.7	91	–17.3	104	–1.7
Economics	112	126	12.5	111	–11.9	124	11.7	120	7.1
Geography	121	103	–14.9	118	14.6	118	0.0	116	–4.5
History	99	103	4.0	106	2.9	95	–10.4	100	1.0
Political Science	129	131	1.6	131	0.0	118	–9.9	125	–3.5
Sociology	99	100	1.0	105	5.0	103	–1.9	103	4.2
Visual & Performing Arts	174	180	3.4	199	10.6	192	–3.5	192	10.5
Nursing	316	318	0.6	326	2.6	310	–4.9	317	0.2
Business Administration	145	144	–0.7	142	–1.4	147	3.5	145	–0.1
Accounting	169	176	4.1	175	–0.6	173	–1.1	174	3.1
Financial Management	157	174	10.8	163	–6.3	158	–3.1	162	3.4
Average	152	155	3.0	158	1.7	157	–1.3	157	3.5

Source: Data from Delaware Study of Instructional Costs and Productivity for cited years.

disciplines that are most heavily subscribed and generate the major portion of student credit hours taught—service units—are the least expensive. Those disciplines that tend to be expensive—e.g., professional disciplines such as engineering and nursing—are often smaller units with lower teaching loads.

With a basic sense of the dynamics of cost growth over three years within 24 specific disciplines, the question then becomes: Which variables within disciplines are most closely associated with the magnitude of instructional expenditures? Once again, data from the Delaware Study provide some direction. Multiple data collection cycles were examined and it was found that between 60 and 75 percent of the variation in direct instructional expense *within* a given discipline or groups of related disciplines is associated with identifiable cost factors. Specifically, in looking at direct instructional expenditures per student credit hour taught:

- The volume of teaching activity, as measured by student credit hours taught, is a major expense factor. As one might expect, given a relatively constant faculty size, expense decreases as the volume of teaching increases.
- Department size, as measured in terms of total number of faculty, is consistently associated with expense. The larger the department, the higher the cost.
- The proportion of a department's faculty holding tenure is associated with expense. Since tenured faculty are "fixed costs," it is not surprising that the higher the proportion of tenured faculty, the higher the cost.
- A surprising finding was that, while the presence of graduate level instruction is associated with higher expense, the measured effect of this variable on the magnitude of cost is smaller than teaching volume, department size, or tenure rate.
- It is frequently assumed that disciplines such as engineering and the physical sciences are expensive, in part because of their equipment-intensive nature. While measurable, the extent to which expense is associated with equipment cost (as opposed to personnel cost) has less impact on the magnitude of expense than teaching volume, department size, or tenure rate.

A cost containment zealot might assume that the solution to restraining the growth in an institution's direct instructional expense rests with having fewer faculty teach more courses and with eliminating tenure. Before taking such draconian measures, clearly predicated on the assumption that faculty do nothing but teach, it must be recalled that institutional expenditure patterns are a function of institutional choices that are typically rooted in a college's or university's mission. These choices include a broader definition of instruction than simply teaching, one that includes both faculty scholarship that expands the body of knowledge and academic support activity—including faculty advising—directed at enhancing prospects for student success. Institutional choices also include pure and applied research and public service activities that contribute to the good of the region and the nation. To the extent that faculty engage in out-of-classroom activity, teaching loads may be reduced and concomitant instructional expenses may increase.

Institutional expenditure patterns are a function of choices that are typically rooted in an institutions mission.

Are faculty truly engaged in activity related to departmental and institutional missions when they are not engaged in teaching students? In 2001, the Delaware Study, under the auspices of a grant from the Fund for Improvement of Post Secondary Education (FIPSE), expanded its data collection activity to include selected measures of out-of-classroom faculty activity. Data on 38 measures of faculty activity were collected at the academic discipline level of analysis. These include activities related to academic advising, curriculum development, publication and other types of faculty scholarship, research, professional development, and public and institutional service. The full scope of this data collection effort, the results of which were published in *Understanding Faculty Productivity: Standards and Benchmarks for Colleges and Universities* (Middaugh 2001), can be ascertained by visiting the Delaware Study Web site at wwwudel.edu/ir/fipse.

For purposes of discussion, we will examine overall results from two distinctly different academic disciplines as they were reported in the initial data collection cycle of the "Out-of-Classroom Faculty Activity" portion of the Delaware Study. The data collection instrument tallies the number of instances recorded within 38 different measures of faculty activity, such as the number of courses wherein the curriculum was redesigned, number of advisees, number of publications, and number of professional presentations. The current discussion will focus on selected measures of faculty activity in English and chemistry. Because these data reflect the initial data collection cycle, the number of reporting institutions (N = 57) is smaller than the "Teaching Load/Cost" portion of the Delaware Study. Consequently, the benchmarks reflect medians rather than means, since medians better represent a measure of central tendency for this smaller group of respondents.

Figure 32.6 displays median benchmark data for English, arrayed by Carnegie institution type. This figure indicates that, at baccalaureate colleges, 1.5 courses were redesigned per full-time equivalent (FTE) faculty during the academic year, 9.12 undergraduate students were advised per FTE faculty during the academic year, 0.40 refereed publications and 0.33 nonrefereed publications were produced per FTE faculty during the academic year, and so on. The data yield some important findings with respect to faculty activity in English:

- Faculty at all institutions are engaged in curriculum redesign intended to keep courses current with the latest developments in the field with respect to both content knowledge and pedagogy.

FIGURE 32.6

Selected Measures of Non-Classroom Faculty Activity—English

	Redesign Curriculum	Ugrad Research	Grad Research	Ugrad Advisees	Grad Advisees
Teaching					
Baccalaureate	1.50	0.00	0.00	9.12	0.00
Comprehensive	1.25	0.21	0.00	7.97	0.87
Doctoral	1.72	0.59	0.36	11.10	2.24
Research	0.72	0.71	1.40	8.75	1.61
	Juried Shows, Exhibitions	**Refer Pubs**	**Nonref Pubs**	**External Grant Proposals**	**External Grants Awarded**
Scholarship					
Baccalaureate	0.23	0.40	0.33	0.00	0.00
Comprehensive	0.33	0.66	0.33	0.14	0.07
Doctoral	0.72	0.90	0.57	0.15	0.15
Research	0.45	0.72	0.72	0.11	0.16
	Leadership in Prof Assoc	**Prof Service**	**Ext/Outreach**	**Inst Service**	
Service					
Baccalaureate	0.25	0.50	2.00	4.25	
Comprehensive	0.58	0.37	1.25	3.66	
Doctoral	0.32	0.98	1.50	3.85	
Research	0.54	1.17	1.42	4.28	

Source: Data from Delaware Study of Instructional Costs and Productivity (2001).

- Despite the prevailing myth that baccalaureate and comprehensive colleges are purely teaching institutions, faculty scholarship is alive and well as evidenced by the presence of both refereed and nonrefereed publications as scholarly output. This may well be a function of implicit, if not explicit, expectations for promotion and tenure at these institutions. It is not surprising that there is more of this type of activity—as well as contract and grant activity—at doctoral and research universities, where this is an explicit condition for promotion and tenure.
- At comprehensive, doctoral, and research institutions, there is clear evidence of faculty working with undergraduate students on formal research. This activity occurs outside of a scheduled class (e.g., senior theses) and is intended to prepare students for research at the graduate level. The volume of non-thesis/dissertation research in which graduate students engage with faculty is heaviest at research universities, but is evident at doctoral institutions as well.
- Faculty at all institution types are involved with approximately four committees related to institutional service (e.g., Faculty Senate, Promotion and Tenure Committee) and at least one activity related to extension or outreach. They also report substantial involvement in both leadership in professional associations and professional service therein.

Figure 32.7 looks at comparable data from a decidedly different discipline—chemistry. Faculty are involved in curriculum redesign as was the case with English. The number of students engaged

FIGURE 32.7

Selected Measures of Non-Classroom Faculty Activity—Chemistry

	Redesign Curriculum	Ugrad Research	Grad Research	Ugrad Advisees	Grad Advisees
Teaching					
Baccalaureate	1.00	0.88	0.00	7.58	0.00
Comprehensive	0.80	1.40	0.00	10.46	0.64
Doctoral	0.77	1.85	1.27	3.51	2.76
Research	0.64	1.00	2.81	4.04	3.57
	Juried Shows, Exhibitions	**Refer Pubs**	**Nonref Pubs**	**External Grant Proposals**	**External Grants Awarded**
Scholarship					
Baccalaureate	0.00	0.00	0.00	0.00	0.00
Comprehensive	0.00	0.57	0.04	0.43	0.43
Doctoral	0.00	2.42	0.24	1.99	1.11
Research	0.14	4.00	0.68	3.30	1.60
	Leadership in Prof Assoc	**Prof Service**	**Ext/Outreach**	**Inst Service**	
Service					
Baccalaureate	0.00	0.00	0.53	3.10	
Comprehensive	0.50	1.07	2.19	4.17	
Doctoral	0.64	2.96	0.79	3.88	
Research	1.14	2.51	1.34	4.64	

Source: Data from Delaware Study of Instructional Costs and Productivity (2001).

in both undergraduate and graduate research with faculty is larger than with English, likely due to the analytical nature of chemistry. The volume of refereed publications and contract and grant activity is larger than with English because of the manner in which scientific information is communicated and the far greater availability of external funding in the physical sciences than in the humanities. Service activity, especially institutional service, is extensive. Where faculty in English appear to be more active in outreach, chemistry faculty appear more involved in service to the profession.

Summarizing the Research

The various studies described thus far lead us to the following conclusions with respect to higher education costs:

- There is a need for clarity in discussing higher education cost as opposed to higher education price. Research found no cause and effect relationship between cost and price. External factors (such as state appropriations and market pressures) tend to drive price, while internal factors (such as magnitude of teaching loads and department size) drive cost.
- While there has been a measurable increase in the *sticker price* of a college education, the *net price* after aid has seen minimal growth for most students and no growth for students from the lowest family income levels.
- While direct expenditures for instruction at four-year colleges and universities increased from 2000 to 2003, the average rate of increase across 24 disciplines typically found at those institutions was less than the increase in the consumer price index for the same period.
- Certain factors are associated with the magnitude of direct instructional cost. These include volume of student credit hours taught, department size in terms of full-time equivalent faculty, and tenure rate. However, before manipulating these factors in any draconian fashion to contain costs, it must be underscored that faculty engage in activities other than teaching that have significant value to students, the institution, and the larger society.
- Faculty are typically involved in out-of-classroom activities such as curriculum redesign, academic advising, thesis/dissertation supervision, academic scholarship, and service to the profession/institution/community.
- Emphasis on various types of out-of-classroom faculty activity generally reflects institutional choices related to mission and to the balance between and among teaching, research, and service.

It is clear from the research that, contrary to the criticisms cited earlier, colleges and universities have not instituted pricing structures that exclude significant numbers of students from access to higher education. While price has increased over the past decade, students who could least afford that increase have benefited from financial aid programs at colleges and universities. However, colleges and universities are not insulated from factors that have the potential to drive price increases. Aside from price drivers already discussed—declining state appropriations, endowment performance, etc.—other factors over which institutions have little control have the potential to significantly affect price. A dramatic increase in the cost of employee health insurance is one such factor, as is the current escalation in the cost of oil. In addition, colleges and universities have administrative structures in place to deal with issues that were not present in years past, such as access to facilities and education for disabled students, gender equity in athletics, and occupational health and safety issues. While these are important issues that should be addressed by postsecondary institutions, they are the product of what has become a pattern of unfunded mandates from governmental agencies that increase operating costs.

Colleges and universities must understand and monitor those costs over which they have internal control.

It is therefore imperative that colleges and universities understand and monitor those costs over which they have internal control. Institutions should not shrink from choices with respect to faculty activity that relate to institutional mission. It is crucial that faculty engage in research and scholarship to add to the body of knowledge in their academic fields. It is equally important that faculty have adequate time to advise students, redesign curriculum, and engage in professional development activity. That said, it is also incumbent upon institutions to manage their resources, including faculty teaching loads. Benchmarking tools such as the Delaware Study of Instructional Costs and Productivity aid provosts and department chairs in assessing their resources in comparison with peer departments and with other departments they would like to emulate.

In summary, colleges and universities must be more proactive in describing how and why they deploy fiscal and human resources as they do. The studies described in this article suggest that resource deployment has been quite responsible, and that planning and management tools are available for enhancing economy and efficiency without sacrificing mission (Middaugh 2001).

References

Boyer Commission on Educating Undergraduates in the Research University. 1998. *Reinventing Undergraduate Education*. Stony Brook, NY: State University of New York at Stony Brook.

Cunningham, A. F., J. V. Wellman, M. F. Clinedinst, and J. P. Merisotis. 2001. *Study of College Costs and Prices, 1988–89 to 1997–98* (NCES 2002157). Washington, DC: U.S. Department of Education, National Center for Education Statistics.

Elfin, M. 1996. The High Cost of Higher Education. From the America's Best Colleges issue. *U.S. News & World Report* September 16: 90–94.

Horn, L., C. C. Wei, and A. Berker. 2002. *What Students Pay for College: Changes in Net Price of College Attendance Between 1992–93 and 1999–2000* (NCES 20021741. Washington, DC: U.S. Department of Education, National Center for Education Statistics.

McKeon, H. P. 2003. Remarks opening September 23, 2003, congressional hearing on *The College Cost Crisis Report: Are Institutions Accountable Enough to Students and Parents?* Retrieved February 7, 2005, from the World Wide Web: www.edworkforce.house.gov/hearings/108th/21st/collegecost092303/osmckeon.htm.

Middaugh, M. F. 2001. *Understanding Faculty Productivity: Standards and Benchmarks for Colleges and Universities.* San Francisco: Jossey-Bass.

Middaugh, M. F., R. Graham, and A. Shahid. 2003. *A Study of Higher Education Instructional Expenditures: The Delaware Study of Instructional Costs and Productivity* (NCES 2003161). Washington, DC: U.S. Department of Education, National Center for Education Statistics.

Zemsky, R., and W. Massy. 1990. Cost Containment: Committing to a New Economic Reality. *Change* 22 (6): 16–22.

SECTION VI

STRATEGIC PLANNING AND RESOURCE ALLOCATION

Introduction to Section VI

W. James Jacob and Stewart E. Sutin
University of Pittsburgh

Strategic planning is central to realizing effective and sustainable higher education management of financial planning processes. Institutional vision, mission, and strategic plans underpin successful strategic planning initiatives. With increasingly stretched institutional budgets, resource allocation, and re-allocation decisions should be guided by sound strategic planning principles. Linking financial goals and resource allocations to institutional strategic plans and strategic planning processes provides enhanced management and quality control of these limited resources. Too often institutions lack definitive strategic plans that contain annual financial allocation plans (including financial goals and accountability mechanisms). This section includes a set of publications that examine the centrality of strategic planning processes for establishing and sustaining financial success and optimal resource management.

Achampong ("Integrating Risk Management and Strategic Planning: Integrated Risk Management and Strategic Planning Leverages the Benefits of Both Processes and Makes them Mutually Reinforcing") addresses a timely topic—risk management. The issue of institutions being risk driven versus risk aware in an "enterprise risk management" environment is significant. His emphasis on "enterprise" approaches and solutions is novel to public higher education. It is very useful to have him explain how "risk management," generally marginalized as a business service, is a key function in strategic planning. He suggests that higher education administrators should pursue an integrated approach incorporating both risk management and strategic planning with the end result ideally yielding maximum financial performance results.

Bresciani ("Aligning Values with Resources and Assessment Results") outlines how many challenges higher education leaders face in the accreditation process is related in one degree or another to financial budgeting and limited resources. She advocates an outcomes-based program review (OBPR) approach to overcome these challenges, noting how limited resources need to be managed according to values-based principles of good governance. She proposes a set of key steps for a higher education institution that include the following: 1) identifying the leadership values, 2) prioritizing values, 3) aligning desired outcomes with values, 4) defining criteria for quality, 5) identifying the capacity necessary for attaining quality, 6) determining the level at which decisions are to be made, and 7) implementing necessary resource reallocation.

Brinkman and Morgan's article ("Changing Fiscal Strategies for Planning") assists readers with understanding the comprehensive context surrounding the financial planning processes within higher education institutions (HEIs). The article is especially helpful for academic administrators who have had little or no prior management experience. The authors describe the strategic financial planning process, including issues such as budgeting, institutional strategic planning, and general resource development.

Hearn, et al. ("Incentives for Managed Growth: A Case Study of Incentives-based Planning and Budgeting in a Large Public Research University") discuss how administrators can delegate decision-making authority to individual cost centers within HEIs through the implementation of incentives-based budget systems (IBBS). This trend to decentralize decision-making authority is increasing in many HEIs. The authors identify several of the strengths and weaknesses of this IBBS trend. They also identify specific incentives that can help facilitate and manage financial resource allocation, depending on the strategic focus of the IBBS implemented. Some of the most obvious strengths are that academic departments and research, action, and outreach centers are not only responsible for their costs but also for raising institutional funds. The autonomy granted to cost center administrators also shift the primary locus of financial responsibility away from central administrative leaders to the particular functional unit (e.g., center, institute, department, etc). This study draws from case study data obtained from a university-wide IBBS program at the University of Minnesota.

Liefner ("Funding, Resource Allocation, and Performance in Higher Education") recognizes the many different funding and resource allocation models that exist globally as well as within countries. Based on a study of six elite research universities in the Netherlands, Switzerland, the United Kingdom, and the United States, Liefner identifies how these six HEIs differ in their resource allocation approaches, funding streams, and incentives required from faculty members and administrators. Liefner argues that higher education performance is often based on required accountability and evaluation measures. If higher education funding streams are secured regardless of individual performance, there is little incentive for individual faculty members and administrators to excel. When resource allocations are based predominantly on performance, activity tends to be higher among higher education personnel. Liefner concludes that while resource allocation changes provide incentives that can change faculty member performance, they do not have a sustainable impact on the long-term success of HEIs.

Trettel and Yeager ("Linking Strategic Planning, Priorities, Resource Allocation, and Assessment") draw upon their years as practitioners to examine resource allocation decisions in the context of institutional strategic planning. They elaborate upon the use of sound process management practices in which priorities are defined, an institutional mission is articulated, and financial and other resources are aligned with both. In doing so, these authors manage to integrate research and practice into a coherent narrative reminiscent of the Baldrige criteria for educational excellence (http://www.nist.gov/baldrige/enter/education.cfm).

CHAPTER 33

INTEGRATING RISK MANAGEMENT AND STRATEGIC PLANNING

FRANCIS K. ACHAMPONG

Introduction[1]

Strategic planning is one of the most critical means of fostering the success of an institution and the achievement of its vision, mission, and strategic goals. Strategic planning has been defined as "the process of developing and maintaining a strategic fit between the organization and its changing market opportunities" (Kotler and Murphy 1981, p. 471). This definition suggests environmental and resource analyses that allow goals to be set, followed by strategy formulation and systems improvements that lead to better performance. Thus, through the strategic planning process, institutions of every kind—public and private; for profit and non-profit; small, medium, and large—define or refine their visions and missions, set strategic goals and objectives, identify strategies for achieving them, and determine how they will measure the success of their efforts and implement improvements. Subsequent budget processes should then result in resource allocation decisions tied to these strategic imperatives in order to move the institution toward its vision.

There are many external and internal risk factors that, if not carefully managed, can impede the successful accomplishment of an institution's strategic goals, including changing demographics that pose enrollment challenges, developments in the general economy, shifting priorities in state and federal educational policy, natural disasters, and poor planning and management. Further, failure to strategically manage an institution's risks can actually compromise its continued financial viability. In risk management terms, "strategically managing risk" means identifying and planning to manage those uncertainties that could result in financial losses to the institution.

Risk management has been described as a managerial process involving the executive functions of planning, organizing, leading, and controlling activities in a firm relative to specified risks with a view to reducing their cost to the firm in order to maximize the firm's value (Trieschmann and Gustavson 1998). The process further involves systematic identification and evaluation of risks, selection and implementation of strategies for managing them, and continuous monitoring and improvement of the risk management program (Trieschmann and Gustavson 1998).

The process of managing all of an institution's risks from a holistic perspective is known as enterprise risk management.[2] A decade ago, Cassidy and others noted that the management of risk in higher education has traditionally been equated with crisis management or regulatory compliance and suggested that institutions should develop a balanced view of risk, one that tries to minimize hazards, influence and control uncertainties, and manage opportunities (Cassidy et al. 2001). Regrettably, in a recent study conducted by the Association of Governing Boards of Universities and Colleges and United Educators (2009), 60 percent of the 606 college administrators responding to a risk management survey said they are still not engaged in a comprehensive strategic assessment to identify risks that would negatively impact the success of their missions. The study found that fewer than 40 percent of all institutions use such an assessment. Only 5 percent of the study's respondents felt their institutions have exemplary practices that promote the success of their missions.

> Integrating risk management and strategic planning leverages the benefits of both processes and makes them mutually reinforcing.

In the final analysis, the ultimate goal of efforts to maximize an institution's value (through risk management) and set its strategic goals and objectives (through strategic planning) is the achievement of the institution's expressed vision. In light of that, it is both logical and desirable to integrate risk management and strategic planning into one coordinated, holistic process to create a synergistic effect that leverages the benefits of both processes and makes them mutually reinforcing. Also, since nearly all institutions engage in strategic planning to some degree, incorporating risk management into the strategic planning process will likely increase the number of institutions practicing enterprise risk management.

Unfortunately, strategic planning and risk management now appear to be mostly undertaken as separate activities, something seemingly borne out by the plethora of writing on the disparate subjects and the dearth of writing on their integration.[3] This article discusses how to integrate risk management and strategic planning into a coordinated, holistic process by sharing the experience of Penn State's Mont Alto campus as a potential best practice.

The Strategic Planning Process at the Pennsylvania State University

Institutions may have strategic planning processes that are unique to them in various ways. In general, however, strategic planning involves articulating strategic goals and objectives; defining tactics or strategies for their accomplishment, time frames for their completion, and metrics for measuring their success; and designating personnel accountable for achieving specific objectives.

To understand the strategic planning process at Penn State Mont Alto, one must also understand the complex organizational structure within which it exists. Penn State Mont Alto is one of the 24 campuses of the Pennsylvania State University, a geographically dispersed land-grant university in the state of Pennsylvania. The University Park campus, the largest of the 24 campuses, houses central administrative functions and academic colleges that provide both undergraduate and graduate education. Nineteen other campuses, known as the "Commonwealth Campuses," primarily deliver undergraduate education, while several campuses such as the Hershey Medical Center and the Dickinson School of Law have specialized missions.

In this complex structure, planning activities are "top down–bottom up" processes: the central university administration, led by the president and provost, sets the key targeted priorities for planning, and the campuses determine how to implement these priorities and other planning objectives in ways that will effectuate their specific missions.

For the 2008–13 planning period, as for previous planning periods, the Office of the Executive Vice President and Provost sent guidelines for strategic planning to the entire university in June 2007. These guidelines articulated the university's vision and mission and reaffirmed six general goals that were to be addressed over the planning period. Campuses, colleges, and administrative units were charged to work through their strategic planning committees to include and adapt these goals to their unique situations (such as the unit-specific mission, priorities, and organizational culture); articulate their visions; and develop objectives, strategies, and measures of success for their strategic planning efforts in pursuit of those visions. The completed plans for each campus, college, and administrative unit were then submitted to the provost's office for review by the end of the spring semester of 2008. These plans, in turn, served to inform the university's overall strategic plan.

In the spring of 2006, prior to the dissemination of the provost's guidelines for the 2008–13 strategic planning period and in the wake of the Hurricane Katrina disaster (with its still-evolving aftermath), Penn State's Risk Management Office, located on the University Park campus, began an initiative to have all campuses assess their risks using a questionnaire the office had developed. The questionnaire asked about major risks facing each unit and measures being taken to reduce or eliminate them, whether there were external or internal pressures negatively impacting the success of the unit, and whether the unit was aware of any other risks of physical damage or bodily injury that had not been effectively managed that could impact the university financially or by reputation.

Holistic Integration of Strategic Planning and Risk Management at Penn State Mont Alto

Laying the Ground Work

In response to these university-wide strategic planning and risk management initiatives, the Mont Alto campus began to take steps that would lead to the integration of these usually separate activities into one holistic process. The administrative council (the campus's governing body) discussed the formation of a campus risk management committee (RMC) as an integral part of the work of the campus's strategic planning committee, known as the policy and planning advisory committee (PPAC). Members of PPAC included all the members of the administrative council, those faculty members who served on the campus faculty senate planning committee, the chair-elect of the campus faculty senate (who co-chaired the PPAC with the chancellor), two representatives of the student government association, and selected members of the campus advisory board (the members of which are primarily community, government, and business leaders).

The chancellor commissioned the RMC in 2006. RMC members were selected because of their campus roles and their knowledge of critical care, public safety, environmental health and safety, disaster preparedness, crisis communications, information technology, and legal and risk management issues. Seven of the nine RMC members also served as members of the PPAC, thus allowing for a high degree of seamlessness in integrating the work of both committees. The chancellor served as an ex-officio member of the RMC.

The Integrative Planning Process in Motion

The following is an account of the integrative process whereby the PPAC developed a strategic plan that included risk management objectives, tactics, and metrics, and charged the RMC with the responsibility of executing the risk management component of the plan.

- *SWOT analysis.* The strategic planning process began with the PPAC conducting a SWOT analysis for the campus to develop goals, objectives, tactics, metrics, and time lines and to identify responsible people or groups accountable for facilitating the accomplishment of designated objectives.
- *Strategic goals.* The PPAC assigned various subcommittees to work on particular goals under the plan and then to report back to the committee for discussion. The committee eventually agreed upon language for six draft goals. This process was followed by a series of three focus groups held with various constituencies, including faculty, administrators, staff, students, the advisory board, and community leaders. The groups discussed and weighed in on the proposed goals and objectives, identifying what they saw as the campus's strengths, weaknesses, opportunities, and threats. The PPAC also sought input and feedback on the draft strategic plan from the executive committee of the Penn State Mont Alto alumni board. The committee then finalized the plan after taking into account the input and feedback from each group.

One of the six goals adopted in the 2008–13 strategic plan dealt with enhancing the financial stability of the campus. As with all the other goals, the institution identified a number of related objectives. These objectives included increasing existing revenue streams and identifying new sources of income, using new technologies to reduce costs, increasing total enrollment to a designated number, developing a capital purchasing plan, increasing the scholarship endowment to a designated value, increasing the endowment for program support by a certain sum, increasing the number of summer camps and conferences by a specified percentage, and identifying and managing campus risks.

Thus, the integration that began with the formation of the RMC continued with the inclusion of risk identification and risk management as key strategic planning objectives in the goal of enhancing the financial stability of the campus. The next steps involved identifying tactics, metrics, time lines, and responsible people or groups accountable for overseeing the accomplishment of the risk management objectives.

- *Tactics.* A key tactic in the strategic plan involved charging the RMC with the task of executing the risk management component of the plan, which involved identifying, managing, and monitoring the campus's risks, as well as training the campus community in crisis management and disaster preparedness. RMC members themselves received training in the fundamentals of risk management, including the nature of risk, risk identification and risk management techniques, incident management (under the U.S. Department of Homeland Security's National Incident Management System [NIMS]), and the importance of monitoring the risk management program and effecting continuous improvements. The training was provided by those members of the RMC with the necessary expertise.

The RMC used three simultaneous strategies to identify the campus's risks. The first was to administer the risk assessment questionnaire developed by the university to every campus department or unit to help it identify the risks it faced. A second strategy was to develop flowcharts of various aspects of campus operations (such as the flow of students from admission to graduation, the flow of employees from hiring to retirement or separation, and the flow of visitors or renters of campus facilities) and to identify the myriad risks associated with these flows. The third strategy involved physical inspections of the campus's facilities and physical plant. The RMC then analyzed all identified risks based on their likelihood of occurring (frequency) and their potential severity. Next, the committee categorized the risks into property, liability, worker's compensation, information technology, catastrophe, reputational, fidelity, and business interruption risks.[4] The culmination of this work was a 55-page risk management report that was disseminated to appropriate personnel.

The RMC made tactical decisions regarding which risk management strategies were most suitable for handling specific risks. These strategies included preventing and reducing losses, transferring them through insurance and bonds (surety and fidelity), retaining them, or avoiding certain activities that posed risks the campus did not want to assume. To achieve the strategic plan's goal of enhancing campus financial stability, the committee then took remedial measures to prevent potential loss. Finally, the RMC met monthly to monitor the risk management program and discuss necessary improvements.

- *Metrics.* The PPAC established metrics for all goals and objectives in the strategic plan in order to measure the success of the institution in accomplishing them. For the goal of enhancing campus financial stability, these metrics included reaching targeted amounts of scholarship and program support endowments and targeted numbers of new baccalaureate programs, summer camps and conferences held to generate revenue, and crisis management and disaster preparedness training sessions for the campus community as a whole. The metrics also included the creation of an ongoing risk management program to minimize the negative impact of risk on campus finances.

    1. To prepare for a possible crisis as part of the metric of having an ongoing risk management program, the campus collaborated with over 60 borough, county, and state emergency preparedness personnel and local police and fire departments during the 2008 spring break to simulate a live shooting emergency in a classroom. Faculty and staff volunteered to play various roles during the simulation. The RMC set up an emergency operations center and made crisis-management decisions based on reports from the chief of police (who was part of the incident command on the scene) about shooting victims and other developments in the evolving simulation. The exercise included crafting messages to be delivered, determining which methods should be used to communicate with particular constituencies (e.g., public address messages, text messages, e-mail messages, telephone broadcast messages), and handling communications with the press. In addition, to prepare for the threat of a pandemic, the institution held a town hall meeting to share the pandemic flu plan developed by the RMC with the campus community.[5] A variety of communications have also been sent to inform and educate the campus com-

munity as developments with the H1N1 (swine) flu virus have evolved. Seventy percent of full-time faculty attended training sessions in fall 2009 on continuing to teach with technology in the event of a temporary campus closure.

- *Time lines.* As a five-year strategic plan, the 2008–13 plan uses the year 2013 as a time line for a number of metrics. Other metrics, such as revenues from conferences and camps and the number of enrollments in off-campus credit programs, have annual time lines. Although ongoing risk management metrics have no particular time frame, the RMC set its own time frames for completing risk identification and analysis and implementing strategies to manage identified risks and met monthly until those processes were completed. The RMC then devoted subsequent monthly meetings to conducting tabletop exercises (simulating a hazardous materials spill, a tornado, and the pandemic flu) and staying on top of evolving risks, as in the case of the swine flu.

Risk management is an ongoing process in which efforts must be continually monitored and necessary improvements made. The PPAC will assess the progress made in achieving all the goals of the strategic plan midway through the five-year planning period. As a result, the progress on all objectives, including the risk management objectives, will also be assessed so that any deficiencies can be addressed. The loop will be closed at the end of the strategic planning period in 2013 with another review before the next planning period begins.

- *Responsible personnel.* The PPAC charged various personnel with responsibility for specified objectives in the strategic plan. The RMC was charged with responsibility for the risk management objectives. In annual personnel evaluations, those who have been assigned responsibility for particular strategic planning objectives must indicate how their accomplishments tie in with the strategic plan and thereby promote the achievement of the campus's mission and vision.

Conclusions

Integrating the activities of strategic planning and risk management into one coordinated and holistic process is both logical and desirable in order to create a synergistic effect that leverages the benefits of both processes and makes them mutually reinforcing. This integration also aligns the efforts of strategic planning and risk management committees in the accomplishment of strategic planning goals that relate to promoting the financial strength of an institution and, ultimately, to the achievement of its expressed vision.

Integration also aligns efforts to promote an institution's financial strength and achieve its expressed vision.

The following are notable lessons from the experience of Penn State Mont Alto in what is hoped will become a best practice in higher education planning:

- The integration of risk management and strategic planning must be supported and championed by top administration. At Penn State Mont Alto, the RMC was commissioned by the chancellor and staffed by many top administrators who were also assigned major responsibilities under the strategic plan.
- The committee or group charged with risk management responsibilities must consist of personnel with appropriate knowledge and experience. The Mont Alto campus experience shows that such expertise can be found among existing personnel, thus addressing concerns about bureaucratic bloat.
- An institution can incorporate its risk management program into its strategic plan by including it under appropriate planning goals and objectives, identifying appropriate tactics and metrics, and assigning responsibility for the risk management objectives to appropriate personnel.

- Members of the entire campus community must be involved in the strategic planning and risk management processes through committees, subcommittees, focus groups, and town hall meetings so that the plan can benefit from broad input and general buy-in.
- Appropriate training must be offered to members of the committee or group charged with risk management—and to the campus community in general—to effectively design and implement the risk management component of the strategic plan.
- Strategic planning and risk management are ongoing activities that require a not-insignificant investment of time, energy, and resources.

Sharing the experience of Penn State Mont Alto will, it is hoped, help inform efforts at other higher education institutions regarding the integration of risk management and strategic planning, as well as help increase the number of institutions engaging in enterprise risk management.

Notes

1. I would like to thank Dr. David Gnage, chancellor of Penn State Mont Alto, and Dr. Sandra Gleason, associate dean for faculty and research at Penn State's University College, for their helpful comments on an earlier draft. My sincerest thanks also go to the referees and editors of *Planning for Higher Education* for comments and feedback that helped me refocus and rewrite this article.
2. See National Association of College and University Business Officers and the Association of Governing Boards of Colleges and Universities (2007), in which these organizations sought to develop an enterprise risk management model for private and public colleges and universities of all sizes and to identify what roles top officials and trustees should play in the process.
3. Numerous books, journals, monographs, online resources, organizations, and associations are devoted to some aspect of planning, crisis management, or risk management. In higher education, the Society for College and University Planning and its journal, *Planning for Higher Education*, are valuable resources on planning. Similarly, the University Risk Management and Insurance Association and its URMIA *Journal* serve as excellent resources on risk management.
4. See Cassidy et al. (2001, p. 4), in which the authors discuss the "new language of risk" and categorize risk into five types: strategic, financial, operational, compliance, and reputational. The Mont Alto campus's risk management report cross-references these terms in its categorization of risks.
5. For an account of the Mont Alto campus's efforts in planning for an avian flu pandemic, please see Achampong (2007).

References

Achampong, F. 2007. Preparing for the Pandemic Flu from a Risk Management Perspective. *CPCU eJournal* 60 (1): 1–8.

Association of Governing Boards of Universities and Colleges and United Educators. 2009. *The State of Enterprise Risk Management at Colleges and Universities Today.* Washington, DC: Association of Governing Boards of Universities and Colleges and United Educators.

Cassidy, D., L. Goldstein, S. L. Johnson, J. A. Mattie, and J. E. Morley, Jr. 2001. *Developing a Strategy to Manage Enterprisewide Risk in Higher Education.* Washington, DC: National Association of College and University Business Officers and PricewaterhouseCoopers.

Kotler, P., and P. E. Murphy. 1981. Strategic Planning for Higher Education. *Journal of Higher Education* 52 (5) 470–89.

National Association of College and University Business Officers and the Association of Governing Boards of Colleges and Universities. 2007. *Meeting the Challenges of Enterprise Risk Management in Higher Education.* Washington, DC: National Association of College and University Business Officers and the Association of Governing Boards of Colleges and Universities.

Trieschmann, J. S., and S. G. Gustavson. 1998. *Risk Management & Insurance.* 10th ed. Cincinnati, OH: South-Western.

CHAPTER 34

ALIGNING VALUES WITH RESOURCES AND ASSESSMENT RESULTS

MARILEE J. BRESCIANI, PHD

Many regional accreditors now require that institutional leadership demonstrate the ability to use outcomes-based program review (OBPR) results to inform resource allocations. However, the reports from regional accreditation leadership reveal that many institutional leaders are facing challenges in doing this. The reasons for not engaging in this process typically have little to do with timing of the institutional budgeting process; rather, the institutional leaders either have not established a practice of using evidence to inform resource allocations or are unsure of the priorities that inform such resource allocations.

Regardless of whether there are new resources to allocate or existing resources to reallocate, and regardless of whether an institution's actual dollar allocation is tied to a biennial or an annual legislated budgeting process, the following framework can help an organization's leadership use outcomes-based results to inform resource decisions.

In order to begin this conversation, I encourage you to select the context that is most meaningful to you. For example, would you prefer to approach this conversation from the perspective of an institution, a division, a department, or a program? The framework can be applied regardless of the level you choose. Thus, after choosing your context, ask yourself the following questions:

1. What does your institution, college, division, department, or program value?
2. Are those values clearly articulated?
3. If so, are they prioritized?
4. How are those values made evident in your
   - decision making?
   - program planning?
   - outcomes-based assessment program review process?
   - resource reallocation?
   - hiring process?
   - personnel evaluations?

For many of us, while we may believe that we communicate clearly the values of our program, department, college/division, or institution, we may soon discover that those values are not prioritized. We may also discover that there is no evidence of those values in our daily practices, and therefore, we would not be surprised to discover that our values are not informing the way we allocate and reallocate resources. In particular, we would not see evidence that our prioritized values inform the way in which we spend our time. And we certainly would not see the results gathered from outcomes-based assessment being used in informing resource allocations.

The framework developed to address this challenge assists organizations in taking the steps needed to use OBPR results to inform resource allocations. This framework makes the bold assumption that institutional leaders do allocate resources according to what they value, even if those values are not publicly expressed. *Thus, the first step requires the organization to identify and clearly articulate what the leadership values.* This process can be done at any level in the organization.

The second step is to prioritize those values. Again, this can be done at any level in the organization. However, if it is not done at all levels, then it is not clear how varying priorities at various levels may impact the flow of resource allocation or reallocation. In other words, if I have different values at the program level than the vice president has at the division level, then it becomes clearer to me why another program—one that, according to the supporting evidence, is more aligned with what the vice president values—would be receiving a larger slice of the proverbial pie.

The third step is the alignment of outcomes to the values that have been expressed and, subsequently, the implementation of the OBPR. This allows for evidence generated from the OBPR process to be used in discussions that inform resource reallocation. In other words, if you don't articulate outcomes and align them to the various levels of values, the data generated from the OBPR process will be detached from any sort ot decision-making process that could inform allocation of resources, simply because it is detached from the values of the organization. In order to align the data derived from OBPR with organizational values, the outcomes themselves must be aligned with organizational values.

The fourth and fifth steps are inherent in the design of the outcomes-based program review process. They require that leadership *define the criteria for quality within the context of the values* as well as *identify the capacity for meeting the criteria of quality.* It is important for a program to define clearly what is meant by quality and to determine how well the criteria for that quality are aligned with the expressed value. The other part of this step is to determine whether there truly is organizational capacity to meet the expected level of quality within the expected context of the value.

For example, an institutional value might be diversity. In order to connect with that institutional value, one program has set outcomes for diversity and defines the criteria for diversity as being the successful education and graduation of Mexican-Americans. Yet another program has determined outcomes for and defines diversity as the expectation that all students participate in an international exchange. In both cases, when each program looks at its capacity to meet its stated criteria, it makes a discovery: One realizes that its applicant pool for Mexican-Americans is large, yet there are no support services for Mexican-American families; therefore, the outcome may not be realized and the value never expressed unless resources are allocated accordingly. The other program realizes that because the institution draws its students from a population with a lower socioeconomic status, the program may never reach its expected outcome without proper financial aid allocations.

The *sixth step* includes *gathering results generated from the OBPR process and determining at which level (e.g., program, department, college/division, or institution) the decision resides.* In many cases, programs can be improved by simply reallocating resources at the program level; that might mean reallocating time for one professional to invest more of herself in planning and evaluating a set of programs, or it could mean determining that certain programs can be cut to fund the improvement of another set of programs that align more directly with institutional priorities. In some cases, however, the program might need to request additional resources that it does not have the power to allocate, and therefore, that request, along with the evidence that informs such a request, needs to proceed to a higher level of the organization.

The final step embodies the whole purpose for implementing this framework: to *reallocate resources in order to improve your outcomes within your context and capacity for quality and in alignment with your values.* This entire process is all for naught if no actual reallocation of resources is made to improve whatever it is that the organization values.

CHAPTER 35

FINANCIAL PLANNING: STRATEGIES AND LESSONS LEARNED

PAUL T. BRINKMAN AND ANTHONY W. MORGAN

Financial planning is more important than ever as colleges and universities face serious if not unprecedented financial challenges.

Introduction

As the United States and U.S. higher education look ahead to a relatively austere future, the financial planning function within higher education institutions will become increasingly critical. Our purpose in this article is to describe this multifaceted function and to distill lessons learned from decades of practice as to how best to execute it. Although our experience is broader, our perspective is colored by the many years we have spent engaged in financial planning at the University of Utah, a public research university. We trust that our reflections can be usefully generalized, given that the issues we discuss are not necessarily unique to that type of institution.

We start by noting several environmental trends, both external and internal, that have implications for higher education financial planning in the future. We then provide a brief overview of the role of financial planning within a typical university; that is, the many ways in which financial planning can add value in the decision-making process. We next offer suggestions on how to make financial planning work well, describe how organizational context influences financial planning, and discuss how the focus of financial planning may need to change in the future. We have chosen to focus on organizational dynamics regarding financial planning rather than on analytic models or other more technical issues.

Environmental Factors Influencing Financial Planning

External Trends

Clark Kerr, former president of the University of California and former chair of the Carnegie Commission on Higher Education, often commented that the most significant changes in higher education have resulted from external forces (pers. comm.). Although there are many factors now affecting financial planning in higher education, we have chosen here to focus briefly on only five since most readers will be generally familiar with this topic.

First is the powerful force of shifting demographics. In earlier years. enrollment growth was, for the most part, the dominant demographic factor in financial planning. More recently (and especially looking to the future), the variability by state in the 18-year-old population and the low participation and completion rates of rapidly growing but underrepresented groups such as Hispanics loom large in thinking about enrollment and tuition, institutionally based financial aid, and net tuition revenue. Unless there are changes in the high school completion rates and college preparedness levels of underrepresented groups, the validity of the enrollment and financial planning assumptions commonly used in the past will be in some jeopardy.

Second, underlying philosophical assumptions about higher education have changed considerably during our professional careers and have greatly influenced financial planning. The tenants of "new public management," most notably the focus on output measures, have increasingly forced us to think about the connections among revenues, expenditures, and outcomes. We will comment more on this issue in the final section of the article.

Third is the shift in perception from higher education as a public good to higher education as a private good. This shift has been accompanied by a significant change in who pays for higher education (from government to students and their families), the continuing rise of tuition as a critical source of marginal revenue growth, and the growth of financial aid as an expenditure. As measured in constant dollars, state and local appropriations per $1.00 in tuition have declined from $2.65 in 1991 to $1.27 in 2006 (Wellman 2008). "High tuition/high aid" has become an increasingly dominant philosophy that now challenges financial planners to assess the elasticity of rising tuition levels, project net tuition income, and focus on the strategic use of scholarships.

Fourth are other significant changes in the relative importance of various revenue streams. While state and local appropriations for public colleges and universities have been essentially level in terms of constant dollars over the past 20 years, other revenue streams, including but not limited to tuition, have increased at many institutions. These other revenue streams include contracts and grants, private giving, auxiliaries, endowment and interest earnings, earnings from technology transfer (royalties and licenses), hospitals, and other sources. For the financial planner, this has meant learning how to predict changes in these revenues and understand the part they play in the institution's overall financial picture. The former is no easy task, as demonstrated by the dramatic swings in the stock market. The same can be said for predicting the potential impact of health care reform on academic medical centers and the effect of the post-stimulus environment on federally sponsored research.

Fifth, state governments have increasingly adopted the arguments of human capital theory and have pressured colleges and universities to increase participation and completion rates as a base for state economic development, although typically without commensurate state funding. (We acknowledge that this somewhat contradicts the third trend.)

Internal Trends

When we look internally at higher education, we see an aging campus in which deferred maintenance continues to grow, not only with respect to buildings but also electrical transmission lines, high-temperature water pipes, and other infrastructure issues. We see the need for extensive remodeling and equipment replacement, stunningly large start-up costs for experimental scientists, an insatiable demand for information technology resources, and a keen interest in sustainability efforts that require up-front investment.

We also see growing disparities in the amount and type of revenue flowing to individual academic units based not so much on winning or losing in the annual budget cycle as on access to alternate revenue sources. Units differ with respect to private fund-raising, endowments, funded research, opportunities for technology transfer revenue, and possibilities for differential tuition. These differences lead not only to "haves and have nots," but also to particular vulnerabilities (think of the unit heavily dependent on endowment earnings in fiscal 2007 versus fiscal 2009). How should an institution cope with these growing disparities and evolving vulnerabilities?

Finally, as our institutional strategic plans call for more interdisciplinary teaching and research, increased internationalization, greater efforts to engage students in the community, and more on-line courses and programs, we have seen the complexity of our funding needs grow, something likely to be true for other universities as well. While all these are worthy endeavors, they also create funding challenges as departmental silos come down, more partners and different entities become involved, and new cost and production functions come into play.

An Overview of the Role of Financial Planning

Financial planning in higher education no doubt means different things to different people, reflecting variations in personal experience and institutional configuration. Our focus in this article is on financial planning as a function that brings a coherent and integrative financial perspective to strategic planning, analyzes the environment from a financial perspective, guides the regular resource acquisition and allocation process, and develops the resources required to meet strategic objectives and address extraordinary situations. We distinguish financial planning from what one might call "financial analysis" or "financial assessment," the kind of activity that focuses, for example, on financial health ratios, even though "financial planning" is sometimes used to refer to these activities as well (e.g., Salluzzo et al. 1999; Townsley 2004). Some British colleagues writing on financial management take a somewhat broader view of financial planning, perhaps a bit closer to what we have in mind. by focusing on revenue generation as much as on financial strength (e.g., Prowle and Morgan 2005; Thomas 2001).

The focus is on revenue generation as much as on financial strength.

We conceive of the role of the financial planner as consisting of four activities: (1) interacting with strategic planning, (2) analyzing trends, (3) guiding the annual budget cycle, and (4) coordinating the development and use of strategic financial resources (see Figure 35.1). As described below, each activity is designed to add value by helping the institution achieve its goals, take advantage of opportunities, allocate its resources wisely, and cope with financial challenges.

Interacting with Strategic Planning

We need not dwell on the importance of either strategic planning or the necessity of including financial considerations in strategic plan development. That is a given for readers of this journal. We simply note that the financial planner is obligated both to know the financial implications of the various plans and to inform and interact with the planners so that the financial components of their plans are realistic in and of themselves and with respect to institutional capabilities and predilections. As Rowley and Sherman (2002, p. 9) note, "to ensure a successful strategic plan, those who are involved with the budget must also be involved in the strategic planning process."

Analyzing Trends

As is true for most planners, the financial planner must monitor both the external and internal environments. The financial planner is specifically obligated to assess the impact of environmental developments on the institution's overall financial prospects and to offer specific guidance regarding resource acquisition and allocation and the accumulation of strategic resources.

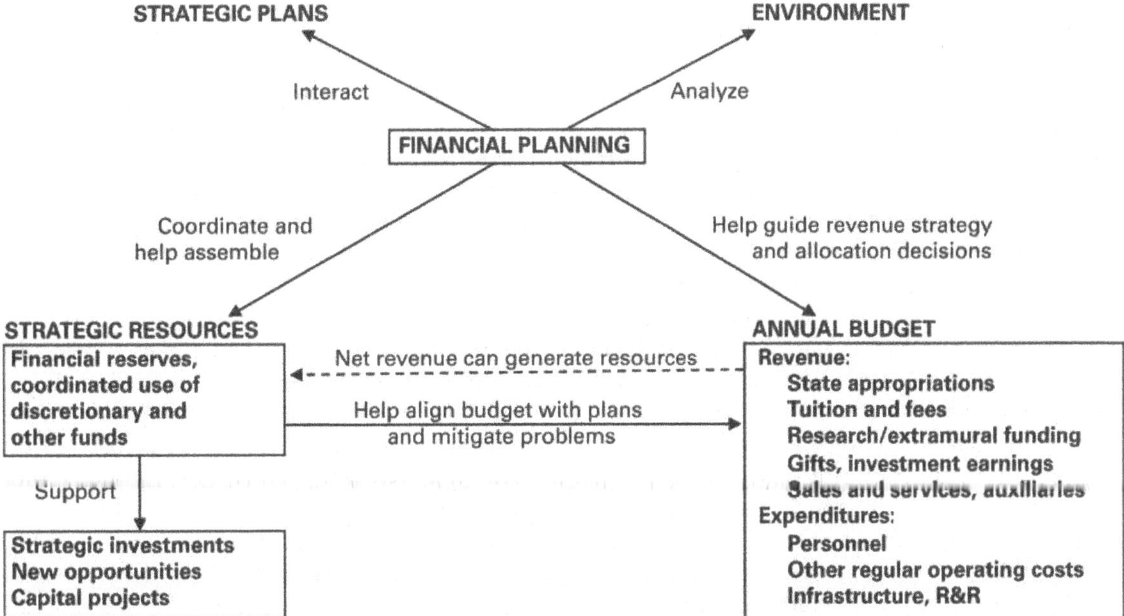

Figure 35.1 Where and how financial planning adds value.

Guiding the Annual Budget Cycle

The financial planner can assist in the achievement of institutional goals and objectives by helping to guide the annual revenue generation and budget allocation processes. The latitude that an institution has in crafting its revenue generation and resource allocation strategies will vary by both circumstance and types of funds available. There are many constraints, of course, both internal and external. Nonetheless, all institutions will have some room to maneuver, and the financial planner must find these spaces and exploit them.

Coordinating the Development and Use of Strategic Financial Resources

The financial planner should be an advocate for, and able to assist in, assembling strategic financial resources (in the form of financial reserves or calls on financial resources) that can be used to help fund the implementation of strategic plans, invest in new programs, seize unplanned opportunities, deal with emergencies, help start or complete capital projects, and help maintain the ongoing operations of the enterprise when it is under duress (Wellington 2007). Without readily mobilized strategic resources, the institution will likely be left with unpalatable alternatives, such as reneging on prior commitments or failing to do what needs to be done.

Making Financial Planning Work

Here we suggest a variety of approaches and tactics that we believe are effective for the financial planner in carrying out the four activities previously described. Examples are included to show how these efforts have worked for us.

Interacting with Strategic Planning

The financial planner should look to interact with strategic planning at both the institutional and unit levels. While the nature of the interaction will depend on the planning process and the financial planner's position in the organization, it is critical that the resulting plans include a financial component that is both thorough and realistic with respect to funds available and well integrated with institutional finances. Such plans include not only a determination of financial requirements, but also the timing and source of funding. Agreements reamed with central administration should be duly recorded on a master list so that the totality of commitments is clear to those providing the support.

On occasion, what is available is not so much a plan as it is a direction or vision. In this case, the financial planner supports the implementation of the vision by first advocating for and participating in the accumulation of needed resources and then helping to guide the allocation of these resources when concrete initiatives are undertaken on behalf of the vision. For example, our strategic plan calls for further internationalizing the campus but provides few specifics as to how this is to occur. Over the past few years, various campus groups have proposed ideas that have attracted financial support as part of the internationalization vision, such as a scholarship program to help students pay for study-abroad experiences, enhanced efforts to increase the number of international internships, and tuition waivers to recruit more Fulbright students from overseas. In our role as financial planners, we have not supplied resources for these programs directly, of course, but we have played a role by identifying sources of support and helping to set an agenda that connects resources and plans.

Regarding strategic plans at the unit level, the institutional financial planner can be helpful in several ways. One is to assist unit-level faculty and staff in assessing the financial realities of proposed initiatives by using the planner's knowledge of how the institution's budget and finances work. Another is to compile information about the various commitments made by central administration in support of unit plans to ensure that the combined weight, nature, and timing of those commitments is understood centrally and can be provisioned as promised. Finally, the financial planner can be an advocate for funding regular budget cycle requests that are tied to strategic plans. Giving those requests favored treatment, other things being equal, will both allow the plans to be implemented and help build a culture in which faculty and staff are willing to invest time and energy in planning because they see that it pays off.

Analyzing Trends

It is easy, at least conceptually, to know what trails to follow in scanning the external environment. First, the sources of the various revenue streams should be traced back to their origins. With respect to tuition, for example, what do the demographics suggest about enrollment prospects? What about pressure from Congress or the state legislature to suppress tuition increases? What are the prospects for different types of student aid? What are competitors doing? Someone needs to ask these questions and develop a range of possible outcomes using simulations and scenarios (as demonstrated, for example, in McIntyre 2004). Prospects for state support, research funding, long- and short-term investments, and other revenue streams must also be reviewed. It is unlikely that financial planners will be knowledgeable in all of these areas, so they must connect regularly with those who are.

Second, the sources of major expenditures should also be traced back to their foundations. Will competition for faculty likely increase or decrease over the near term? What about possible changes in health insurance premiums or the cost of utilities? Based on these investigations, again by tapping into expertise across the campus, the planner can assess the institution's overall financial prospects and their implications for strategic resources and then offer specific guidance on resource acquisition and allocation. For example, because utility costs are likely to continue to increase, we have worked hard to ensure that our state funding formula takes those increases into account.

There is much to monitor internally as well. We suggest at least three focal points. One, what is the condition of the physical plant? Is the institution keeping up with preventive maintenance? If there were a major failure in, for example, the electrical transmission system, what might be the cost and how would it be handled? What is the prioritized plan for major remodeling projects and how will those projects be funded?

Two, if it becomes necessary to cut budgets further, what is the history of past cuts? What cuts would most impair achievement of strategic planning objectives? What programs might reach critical levels of sustainability or thresholds in terms of faculty and students or accreditation if their budgets are cut? What reserves are in place at the unit level? What opportunities, if any, do the various units have for generating non-general-fund support?

Three, with respect to instructional programs, are there content or delivery developments that have significant implications for funding? These developments may be captured in strategic plans and addressed through that mechanism or they may not, or at least not in their full scope. For example, on our campus only some of the increase in on-line courses can be linked to formal plans. The rest has come about in an unplanned, organic manner. Both have serious implications for resources.

We have found that some version of scenario planning can be helpful in analyzing the potential impacts of events in the external and internal environments. Scenario planning models can range from quite formal to more simplified (Morrison and Wilson 1997); however, nearly any model can assist financial planners and their colleagues in thinking about and quantifying environmental impacts. Scenario planning can also serve as a useful discussion tool and learning vehicle for institutional leadership. One tool we often use is simulation modeling; our approach uses spreadsheets rather than specialized software.

Guiding the Annual Budget Cycle

Exploiting multiple sources of revenue is a hallmark of U.S. higher education, nowhere more so than at research universities. Institutions in the public sector must consider ways to ensure adequate state support, establish appropriate tuition levels, garner ever-greater amounts of philanthropic support, secure federal and private funding for research projects, cope with the vagaries of financial markets, find ways to benefit monetarily from their intellectual property (without "selling the farm"), and deal with a myriad of market and bureaucratic issues if health care is among the services they provide. The financial planner's ability to influence the revenue generation strategy in these respective areas will likely vary considerably from some to none; however, being at least a party to the discussions is important in gathering an overall understanding of the institution's finances.

Revenue from tuition is one area in which financial planners are likely to play a central role; this has been the case for us. It is an interesting area, rife with complex, even conflicting, institutional interests.

One must pay attention to price elasticities and revenue maximization goals while remaining attuned to expectations regarding the composition of the entering class across income, ethnic, and academic achievement dimensions, all the while looking beyond immediate needs. It is important to consider tuition from a comprehensive, multiyear, and strategic perspective. A narrow, one-year-at-a-time, strictly tactical approach is risky. Financial planners should be uniquely positioned to assist in this regard; scenarios can help demonstrate the risks of relying too heavily on short-term decision making.

Guiding or influencing resource allocation is conceptually straightforward. Ideally, marginal increments of funding would be allocated to those units whose requests for funding are in accord with institutional goals and objectives as well as with their own plans. In practice, this process can be hindered or facilitated by an institution's underlying approach to resource allocation. For example, an institution that relies entirely on an incremental approach, i.e., the new budget is the prior version plus a proportional share of any new money, will have a tough time steering the budget allocation process. In this approach, the process is essentially on autopilot and just a matter of the amount of fuel available. At the other end of the continuum, in theory a zero-based approach leaves plenty of room (too much perhaps) to redirect resources, but few institutions are willing to take on the work involved year after year.

In our experience, some combination of incremental, program, and formula budgeting operating simultaneously works reasonably well to balance the impact of different incentives over time. The prevalence and benefits of mixed model approaches worldwide are confirmed by Salmi and Hauptman (2006). Academic units at the University of Utah receive the bulk of their funding on an incremental basis, but they can also request funding for programmatic enhancements in accord with their strategic plans. These units also have access to so-called "productivity funding," wherein funds are provided in a formulaic manner depending on changes in the number of credit hours generated by the unit. This approach serves to allocate new money when enrollment increases and to reallocate money when enrollment decreases or student demand shifts internally. It is a means, in other words, of incentivizing academic departments to pay attention to students' instructional needs and interests. In addition, by adjusting the rates paid per credit hour, the university has been able to use this funding mechanism to further the achievement of other objectives, such as providing full degree programs at remote sites and enhancing interdisciplinary offerings. Financial planning has been critical in managing the budgeting process by keeping it focused on serving institutional interests and ensuring that resources are adequate to provision it.

Coordinating the Development and Use of Strategic Financial Resources

Creating a significant quantity of strategic resources will likely take time, particularly if it is to be done without causing disruption or paying a heavy political price. It may also require stitching together funds from multiple sources and assembling different types of money, including general funds, research overhead reimbursements, unrestricted gifts, cash management interest earnings, the yield on investments centrally held, bond payment reserves, proceeds from technology transfer activities, and, in some instances, patient care revenues and proceeds from businesses that the institution operates.

A workable process for assembling strategic resources will vary by institutional context, of course, but three levels of "assembling" can be distinguished: (1) literally accumulating reserve funds under central control to use for strategic purposes, (2) establishing levels of understanding and commitment across multiple revenue streams for the use of resources when needed, and (3) simply having knowledge of those streams (quantities, flows, restrictions, typical demands, reserves, persons responsible, etc.) so that capabilities are understood and negotiations can begin quickly when needed. We have found that a combination of these three approaches works reasonably well over time as institutional fortunes (by revenue stream) wax and wane, challenges and opportunities evolve, and players turn over. In our view, all major revenue streams should at least occasionally have a planned unallocated component so that reserves gradually accumulate. Additional opportunities to build reserve funds should be taken advantage of; for example, when some centrally managed funds happen to be unspent at year's end. A year-end sweep of unspent balances in the operating units is another workable approach, although not one we have used since our practice is to encourage units to accumulate their own reserves.

Funds should not be set aside in ways that will put the institution at odds with the legislature or other constituencies. We recognize that states differ in allowing institutions to carry forward positive balances. Where this is possible, a connection between reserves and plans or other specific purposes will help justify the targeted amounts. Being careful where and how the funds are "stored" will also help. If the ultimate use of reserve funds is known, then it may be possible to restrict their use and thus protect them (although the attendant loss of flexibility must be considered).

For an institution that is serious about developing strategic resources as a financial planning tool, at a minimum someone or some group must know where resources can be found, their respective quantities, the demands upon them, and the plans for their use. While this may seem obvious, such cross-campus knowledge may not exist or may not exist in sufficiently detailed and integrated terms to be useful. It has taken us some time to develop this knowledge, and an ongoing effort is required to maintain it. We live in a world of moving targets, it seems. In any case, a conscious, deliberate effort to develop such knowledge is highly recommended; we see it as a crucial element of effective financial planning.

If our experience is any guide, there will be many opportunities to use reserve funds. In the past few years, we have used reserves to buy and build out a data center, purchase facilities near the campus, undertake major remodeling projects, take down old buildings, address a host of infrastructure issues, purchase major equipment, support programmatic initiatives, and soften the effects of significant reductions in state support. These efforts required the application of various "colors of money." The data center project alone involved major contributions from research overhead funds, patient care earnings, technology transfer earnings, and business earnings, as well as general funds. Our institution would be a noticeably different place in the absence of these efforts and the reserve funds that made them possible.

Context Makes a Difference

We have sketched the basic tasks confronting the financial planner and offered some suggestions on how to accomplish them. We turn now to several other considerations that affect how financial planning is undertaken and its chances for success. Broadly speaking, these considerations relate to "context;" that is, the history and culture of the institution, interpersonal relationships, and the nuances or subtleties of organizational design and organizational life.

Organizational Structure

In our experience, the viability and success of financial planning depends in part on its location in the organization. We recognize that there is no one best model and that, in general, people matter more than structure. Traditionally, financial planning, rooted in accounting, budgeting, and financial reporting, has been located in a business vice president's office, just as other types of planning are typically dispersed by function (e.g., physical master planning by architects under a business vice president, academic planning under a provost or academic vice president). However, our experience suggests that financial planning is more likely to be successful if it is embedded organizationally in the president's or provost's office and connected tightly to the budgeting function.

Our primary experience has been with an organizational model that David Gardner brought to the University of Utah in 1983, in which he pulled planning and budgeting together in the Office of the President. This model, at the time common at many University of California campuses, was later modified when these functions were moved into what is essentially a provost's office. We have found that operating a financial planning and budgeting function from a presidential or provost base is highly advantageous. First, it enhances access to a greater variety of data and to people who know the meaning of the data. Second, it improves the chances that academic planning will drive financial and capital planning and that there will be a greater degree of planning integration. Third, it forces the integration of planning and budgeting organizationally—a normative mandate in the management literature, but one that is often weak in practice. (We acknowledge that this marriage may engender some role conflict in that planners tend to be "spenders" and those responsible for the budget tend to be "cutters.") Finally, it eliminates at least some of what Vandament (1989) refers to as "the ambiguities that can occur when the chief financial officer attempts to coordinate the financial activities of many departments and offices without direct line authority or responsibility for their general operation" (p. 18), and it overcomes the "lack of knowledge about the specific educational issues involved in the many academic programs of the campus" (p. 19) and other facets of campus life. Of course, in our planning and budgeting roles we work closely with the chief financial officer and his staff in mutually supportive ways.

This structure has been helpful in facilitating coherent responses to budget crises. For example, as we work through the massive reductions in state support triggered by the severe recession that began in 2008, the financial planning tool box contains a budget-reduction model (budget cuts net of incremental support by academic and administrative unit) connected to a multiyear plan for getting through the downturn (summary of cuts, incremental revenues, use of reserves) further connected to a strategic resources model (a series of multiyear, pro-forma-like plans detailing, among other things, the availability of reserves). Knowledge of institutional priorities (by the provost and planner) and unit-level finances (by the provost and budget officer/planner) guide the budget model. Assessments of external conditions (based on senior administration and planner input) and knowledge of internal strategic resources (by the provost and planner) guide the multiyear recovery plan. The budget model, the recovery plan, and the strategic resources model interact with each other. Collectively, they help us deal with the budget problem in an orderly fashion, one that we hope will limit the damage and keep the institution on target.

Organizational Culture of Research Universities

Organizational culture also greatly influences the chances of successful financial planning. Research universities tend to be highly decentralized organizations due in part to their size and high degree of specialization. The tendency toward decentralization is strengthened by the presence of multiple and sizeable revenue streams developed and largely controlled by various units ranging from medical schools and hospitals to colleges or departments that are highly successful in securing external research funding and private support.

Therefore, one of the challenges in establishing a strong financial planning function is gaining access to the needed financial data generated by these units and to the information on the variables and trends that will inform the meaningful use of these data. Of particular sensitivity are balances and reserves, commitments or claims on those balances, and degrees of flexibility. While accounting systems can provide data on balances, understanding what lies behind these data depends on a culture of trust and openness between decentralized units and the central administration. If the long-standing organizational culture of an institution is one of decentralization and autonomy, as is the case at the University of Utah, then development of a more centralized financial planning function can encounter organizational resistance. As noted previously, we have had to work long and hard to create a situation in which most if not all of the data are available centrally in a timely, usable fashion.

However, there is an inherent paradox in developing a culture of openness and transparency on one hand and developing strategic financial reserves on the other. Complete transparency of financial reserves inevitably generates internal demand to tap those reserves and external scrutiny that may result in losses or the discounting of institutional requests. While both internal and external audiences acknowledge, in theory, the need for reserves, institutional leaders sometimes find themselves in difficult circumstances. We have found that building long-term personal relationships of trust is the key to preserving these funds.

This paradox is exemplified in the nexus between strategic planning and financial planning. In our experience, formal institutional-level strategic plans are typically very public documents often produced through a relatively open planning process. To gain consensus and satisfy a wide variety of constituents, these plans are typically quite general and comprehensive in nature. Their value as a template for financial planning and resource allocation is limited by both their comprehensiveness and level of generality. To be realistic, strategic thinking and prioritization by institutional leadership must necessarily be more limited in scope and more specific in detail. This typically results in a more "private" version of the public strategic plan, i.e., an operational version. How widely shared or public this private version should be is a delicate issue.

In financial planning, context really does matter.

Organizational Dynamics

Financial planning is embedded in the realities of organizational dynamics and therefore depends on a culture of cooperation and strong presidential leadership. Context really does matter, in that both formal and informal powers vested and invested in the central administration vary considerably. In our experience, the effectiveness of a president operating in this changing environment depends heavily on what Hardy (1996) has called "the politics of collegiality"—how power and collegiality interact in the context of research universities. Institutional collegiality (shared organizational purpose and direction and collaborative processes) is joined with instrumental power (centralized information, budgets, and procedures) and symbolic power (the management of meaning). As the number and magnitude of revenue streams grows and as potentially decentralizing resource allocation models (such as "responsibility-centered budgeting" or the instance in which individual academic units reap the benefits of program-based or differential tuition) become more common, the normal budget-related leverage of the central administration may decrease or at least become more difficult to exercise. In this case, even greater attention to collegiality and collaborative processes will be required if central financial planning is to be done effectively.

Conclusion

If Clark Kerr was right in attributing the most significant changes in higher education to external forces, then perhaps considerable shifts in the role of the financial planner can also be expected. While major disruptions in U.S. financial markets have already taken their toll on endowments, interest earnings, and the wealth of foundations and individual donors, there may be more to come. Similarly, reforms in health care may have significant impacts on health care education and university hospitals. Our concluding comments focus on two trends that, taken together, may significantly change financial planning in universities and colleges.

Rising Costs and Limits on Revenue Growth

As it does with health care expenditures per capita, the United States spends about twice as much per higher education student as compared to other developed nations (OECD 2006). Similarly, we spend more than double the percentage of our GOP on tertiary education as compared to other developed nations (OECD 2006). Over the past 25 years, growth in higher education prices (tuition) has increased significantly faster than median family income and substantially faster than even health insurance premiums (Wellman 2007). The current trajectory of these trends cannot continue indefinitely and most likely will generate increasing political pressure for change. While public perceptions of costs differ substantially from the reality, cost concerns are always at the top of public opinion polls about higher education issues. As we know, politicians respond to widespread public perceptions.

Colleges and universities in the United States have been enormously successful in diversifying revenues, thereby lessening pressures on public sources. Yet, despite our success in revenue generation, we seem to live in a world in which costs outrun available revenues or in what Johnstone (2006) calls a time of "austerity." Johnstone has long stressed the limits on revenue diversification: "Austerity is endemic to higher education as the natural trajectory of higher education costs over time outpaces the likely trajectory of available revenue" (2006, p. 49). Given these political and economic realities, it seems likely that higher education costs will take center stage in the future, just as health care costs have today.

We seem to live in a world in which costs outrun available revenues.

Financial Planning on the Expenditure Side

Rising concerns over the cost of higher education, particularly at public research universities, coupled with the possibility of reaching a limit on the growth of new sources of revenue and tuition increases, will likely cause financial planning to move from its historic preoccupation with revenue planning to focus more on expenditure and cost patterns. Financial planners will then have to become much more familiar with cost modeling, identifying and experimenting with cost drivers (e.g., see Vandament 1989, chapter 6), benchmarking to gain better information on norms among peer institutions, and other modes of inquiry. If these trends are combined with continuing and increasing pressures to adopt the "output paradigm" of new public management, financial planners may also find themselves joining forces with institutional assessment specialists to learn about measuring output and tying expenditure patterns to outcomes.

Higher education has had the luxury of long-term revenue growth, which has allowed the continued expansion of services and programs over time. While we have certainly had to deal with severe but short-term revenue constraints in the form of one-time and base budget cuts, we have always been drawn back to focus on revenue generation and continued expansion at varying rates. Long-term or even permanent revenue constraints, should they occur, will have profound effects on the culture of research universities and the nature of financial planning.

References

Hardy. C. 1996. *The Politics of Collegiality: Retrenchment Strategies in Canadian Universities*. Montreal: McGill-Queen's University Press.

Johnstone, D. B. 2006. In Response to Austerity: The Imperatives and Limitations of Revenue Diversification in Higher Education. In *Financing Higher Education: Cost-Sharing in International Perspective*. ed. D B. Johnstone. 33–54. Rotterdam: Sense Publishers.

McIntyre, C. 2004. Using Scenarios and Simulations to Plan Colleges. *Planning for Higher Education* 33 (1): 18–29.

Morrison, J. L. and I. Wilson. 1997. Analyzing Environments and Developing Scenarios for Uncertain Times. In *Planning and Management for a Changing Environment*, ed. M. W. Peterson, D. D. Dill, and L. A. Mets, 203–229. San Francisco: Jossey-Bass.

OECD. *See* Organisation for Economic Co-Operation and Development.

Organisation for Economic Co-Operation and Development. 2006. *Education at a Glance: OECD Indicators 2006*. Paris: Organisation for Economic Co-Operation and Development.

Prowle, M., and E. Morgan. 2005. *Financial Management and Control in Higher Education*. New York and London: RoutledgeFalmer.

Rowley, D. J., and H. Sherman. 2002. Implementing the Strategic Plan. *Planning for Higher Education* 30 (4): 5–14.

Salluzzo, R. E., P. Tahey, F. J. Prager, and C. J. Cowen. 1999. *Ratio Analysis in Higher Education: Measuring Past Performance to Chart Future Direction*, 4th ed. New York: KPMG and Prager, McCarthy & Sealy, LLC.

Salmi, J., and A. M. Hauptman, 2006. Resource Allocation Mechanisms in Tertiary Education: A Typology and an Assessment. In *Higher Education in the World 2006*, 60-83. Global University Network for Innovation Series on the Social Commitment of Universities. New York: Palgrave Macmillan.

Thomas, H. G. 2001. *Managing Financial Resources*. Buckingham and Philadelphia: Open University Press.

Townsley, M. K. 2004. *Financial Planning Toolbox: A Companion to the Small College Guide to Financial Health*. Washington, DC: National Association of College and University Business Officers.

Vandament, W. E. 1989. *Managing Money in Higher Education: A Guide to the Financial Process and Effective Participation Within It*. San Francisco Jossey-Bass.

Wellington, S. 2007. The Financial Security of UK HE Institutions. *Perspectives: Policy and Practice in Higher Education* 11 (4): 103–106.

Wellman, J. V. 2007. The Issue is Cost, Presentation at the annual meeting of the Association of Governing Boards, Phoenix. Retrieved December 15, 2009, from the World Wide Web: www.deltacostproject.org/resources/ppt/wellman_az_2007—03-05.ppt,

——. 2008. The Higher Education Funding Disconnect: Spending More, Getting Less. *Change* 40 (6): 18–25.

CHAPTER 36

"INCENTIVES FOR MANAGED GROWTH" A CASE STUDY OF INCENTIVES-BASED PLANNING AND BUDGETING IN A LARGE PUBLIC RESEARCH UNIVERSITY

JAMES C. HEARN, DARRELL R. LEWIS, LINCOLN KALLSEN, JANET M. HOLDSWORTH, AND LISA M. JONES

In recent years, changing financial and political conditions have prompted many colleges and universities to revise their internal management processes. Especially notable is the increased implementation of incentives-based budget systems (IBBS), which place greater authority but also greater accountability at the level of individual academic units (Lang, 2001; Massy, 1996a; Priest, Becker, Hossler, & St. John, 2002). Although the terminology varies across campuses (other popular titles include Responsibility Center Management [RCM] and Value Centered Management [VCM]), the general aim of all such approaches is to integrate budgeting and management decision-making more fully at the level of individual cost centers within institutions. The move to IBBS reflects the higher-education community's interest in more decentralized management approaches. Unfortunately, little empirical research has been conducted on the benefits and challenges of the IBBS approach.

This article uses a variety of data sources and lenses to examine the strengths and challenges of the recent IBBS implementation at the University of Minnesota, an institution with one of the largest enrollments in the nation and the largest thus far to implement the IBBS approach. The institution has elected to integrate its version of IBBS into its planning efforts. It terms this process "Incentives for Managed Growth," or IMG for short. Using financial data covering 8 years, this study presents revenue flows (both pre- and post-implementation), the correlation of revenues to performance, and patterns in interdisciplinary activity and student enrollment behavior among institutional units. Raw data are supplemented with findings from targeted interviews with deans of three colleges at the university. Although the analysis is limited to the early years of the implementation, the findings do provide a glimpse of how business has changed—or not changed—in the IBBS environment at this particular university. We close the article with a discussion of the study's implications for research and practice.

Overview of Incentives-Based Budgeting Systems

Pursuing improved organizational flexibility, adaptability, and efficiency in the face of difficult fiscal conditions, many colleges and universities have begun to rethink their planning and management practices (Lewis & Dundar, 1999; Priest et al., 2002; Yudof, 2002). To that end, they are increasingly using tools borrowed from other kinds of organizations. While some of these efforts have proven beneficial, others are best characterized as passing "management fads"—approaches that enjoy brief popularity but are not diffused widely or deeply (Birnbaum, 2000). In this context, one may question whether IBBS, academe's own version of corporate "profit centers," will endure or simply join the graveyard of failed imports from the for-profit sector. To explore that question, it is particularly important to focus on the research university, arguably the most logical and frequent site of IBBS reform (see Whalen, 1991).

The idea of academic units being responsible for revenue production as well as certain associated costs has been around since tuition was first charged to students. In recent decades, institutions have increasingly come to see the advantages of highlighting this connection. Early versions of IBBS emerged in the 1970s and 1980s, mainly in private institutions, including Cornell, Harvard, Southern California, Vanderbilt, and Pennsylvania (Lasher & Greene, 1993; Rodas, 2001). Public institutions were slower to experiment with the approach, preferring instead their well-established "general-fund" approach—that is, a budgeting model directing revenue streams to central administrators who then redistribute funds to academic and support units according to institutional priorities. Now, however, increasing numbers of public institutions are adopting the IBBS approach, most of them in a form integrated with traditional centralized systems (West, Seidita, DiMattia, & Whalen, 1997; Priest et al., 2002).[1]

Leslie and Slaughter note that this trend should surprise no one:

> Within universities, during periods of fiscal stress, the press for decentralization of power to the operating units is relentless. Incentives and disincentives must be structured properly to ensure revenue maximization, and it is the operating units in the end that are responsible for achieving most revenue growth. . . . [G]etting the incentives and disincentives right will mean devolution of budgets, so that units are stimulated to increase competitive revenues and to control their expenditures. . . . Budget devolution may . . . be inevitable under conditions of resource scarcity and competition. (1997, p. 249)

In contrast to the general-fund approach, IBBS approaches attribute costs and revenues on a unit-by-unit basis, allowing colleges to benefit directly and immediately from their own revenue increases and cost savings. The goal is to grant each unit a degree of fiscal autonomy for deciding how revenues will be acquired and spent and how expenditures will be chosen and managed (Lang, 2001; Leslie, 1984; Massy, 1989–1990; Priest et al., 2002; Whalen, 1991, 2002). This approach marks a distinct shift away from centralized, incremental budgeting methods toward a program-performance emphasis in which local units' academic decisions have direct financial consequences for the unit (Meisinger, 1994). Ideally, decision quality is improved because better information is available at the unit level and because there is a direct, consequential link between decisions and unit outcomes (Massy, 1989–1990).[2]

Whalen (1991, pp. 10–17) characterized the primary emphases of the IBBS approach as (a) proximity—the closer the decision maker is to the implementation point, the better the decision will be; (b) proportionality—the larger an organization, the more it can benefit from decentralization of authority and accountability; and (c) knowledge—decisions will be better in an environment that has accurate and timely information. Whalen notes that, to succeed, incentive-based approaches require clear understanding of roles and responsibilities, a stable environment, and clear rewards and sanctions for performance at the unit level.

Academic units generate revenue from enrollments in the form of tuition, fees, and, in public institutions, state appropriations. They generate additional revenue from grants, contracts, and endowments. In the pure form of IBBS, all units that generate their own revenue also manage their own expenses. The growth and development of an academic unit depends upon its ability to control its costs while delivering value and quality to its stakeholders. An important focus in IBBS is on finding the appropriate cost center within the institution, which may be defined as the school, college, or department. Although some implementations on university campuses allow funds to flow back to individual departments, most systems send money back to the colleges housing the generating departments. This latter approach enables deans to move funds within their colleges from one academic or non-academic unit's budget to another, depending on the unit's needs and goals (Stocum & Rooney, 1997).

The decisions made by the leaders of each cost center under IBBS clearly affect not only the local unit but also the larger organization. Organizational relationships become more complex as local academic units come to understand the need to assess and evaluate how they are connected to other units and to various support centers (Whalen, 1991). When costs seem to outweigh returns, units may decide to sever ties with certain other units. In this environment, good coordination is essential—to succeed, IBBS must not only allow legitimate local-level decisions and responsibilities but also reward cooperation among units and encourage integration between academic and administrative strategies and planning (Whalen, 1991). Ideally, matching costs and revenues with their point of origin in the institution constrains deleterious bureaucratic and political tendencies, but effective central design and oversight are required (Adams, 1997; Johnson & St. John, 2002).

Because they generate fewer revenues, support units and central-administration units require special treatment under an incentives-based system. Usually, institutions impose a "taxation" system in which (a) central overhead costs are recovered from revenues before funds are available to individual units, and (b) transfers are made to support strategically critical but fiscally less self-supporting activities, e.g., larger colleges fund smaller units with a more service-oriented mission (Meisinger, 1994). Without close attention to designing appropriate cost-sharing mechanisms to fund non-revenue-generating units, an IBBS system may not function as intended (Whalen, 1991).

Because of such concerns, no institution has adopted a "pure" IBBS. Striking an appropriate balance is critical to any system's efficiency and effectiveness. Too much centralization may lead to missed local opportunities. Too much decentralization, however, may bring inefficient duplication of internal activities and externally offered services, as well as inattention to critical institutional goals (Cantor & Courant, 2003).

The Debate over IBBS

IBBS approaches have stimulated controversy. The two sides each merit attention here. Proponents mainly stress that IBBS principles place financial decisions closer to those with local authority and responsibility, and thus help leaders more effectively recognize performance (both positive and negative) and more efficiently allocate resources (Lasher & Greene, 1993; Whalen, 1991, 2002). Ideally, IBBS practices acknowledge market forces, encourage efficient management of resources, and make program subsidies a matter of choice rather than routine. IBBS proponents reject the view of economist and former college president Howard Bowen (1982) and others that, when a campus is facing difficult fiscal conditions, all units should share equally in the pain. To the contrary, proponents argue, the differential funding produced by interunit competition can preserve and nurture institutional strengths and bring enhanced efficiency in trying times.

Cogan (1980) warned that traditional budget processes "underestimate the resistance to change inherent in the tenure and seniority systems," and noted that institutions can best create change by implementing a decentralized resource policy reliant on internal market systems. That is, institutions can use budgeting policy to drive home the inherent connection between tuition, fees, and unit allocations, on the one hand, and educational services delivered, on the other. Put more bluntly, incentives-based systems encourage attention to students and other revenue providers as customers to be served (Gros Louis & Thompson, 2002).

By creating more autonomy at the unit level but pairing that autonomy with accountability for results, incentives-based systems can bring the push for efficiency and effectiveness to those most involved in academic productivity. The budget processes used in universities typically feature "repeated back-and-forth communication between the central administration" and other units within the organization (Cogan, 1980, p. 557). Central administrations provide the budget instructions, guidelines, and deadlines while academic units complete the requirements and submit their budget requests for the upcoming year. Ultimate responsibility for efficient and effective use of university resources rests with central management. Academic units compete for centrally administered funds but have limited flexibility in the way they use these funds (Stocum & Rooney, 1997). In contrast, decentralized budgeting can create "street-level" incentives to operate efficiently, respond to market pressures, and plan effectively.

Academic productivity is not always a straightforward concept, but it is central to the IBBS approach and its putative advantages. Universities are reluctant to cut underperforming or less productive programs, and Levin (1991) has proposed that productivity would increase if universities would establish clear organizational goals and priorities, along with measurable performance indicators, to communicate which activities central administrators value. From this perspective, IBBS proponents argue, central administration should employ incentive structures (e.g., cost- and revenue-sharing protocols) that reward unit performance in activities supporting the institutional mission.

As appreciation of the institution's overall costs and revenues grows, local cost centers may increasingly recognize the short- and long-term revenue and cost implications of their actions (Stocum & Rooney, 1997). Under systems in which central administrators "tax" for space-related costs, for example, the necessity of efficient space management may become more evident (Meisinger, 1994). A similar point applies to decisions on course offerings (Gros Louis & Thompson, 2002). Whalen (1991) provides an example: Under a traditional budgeting system, the local units of the organization may not even be aware of, or concerned about, the consequences of deleting a summer-session course from their program because of a faculty member's leave. Under an IBBS system, however, a local unit must decide whether and how to make up the lost revenue associated with dropping a course.

Proponents also note the clarity and adaptability an IBBS approach can bring. Under decentralized approaches, fund flows may be easier to track and redirect in the face of organizational change (Whalen, 1991). Traditional modes of budgeting do not easily accommodate the development of a new function within an organizational unit or the transfer of a function between units. Flexibility at the local level may be enhanced under IBBS as units have the "ability to autonomously shift funds between spending categories to meet unanticipated shortfalls or needs in one area or to take advantage of immediate opportunities in another." Units are also able to move funds from revenue-generating programs or carry-forward accounts into new initiatives (Stocum & Rooney, 1997, p. 57).

Interestingly, proponents argue that IBBS, although decentralized in orientation, may provide superior support for central-administration efforts to shape institutional objectives, establish priorities and policies, pursue long-term planning and strategy, and coordinate activities among organizational units (Gros Louis & Thompson, 2002; Massy, 1989–1990; Whalen, 1991). In other words, IBBS can allow for local decision-making and participation in the allocation of funds, yet it can also provide an opportunity for central leaders to direct the organization's overall efforts, via incentives and encouragement for each unit to perform effectively and efficiently.

Critics of IBBS proffer a variety of counterpoints. At its worst, they suggest, the "every tub on its own bottom" approach can be ruinous to the academic fabric of an institution. A local unit may create and offer academic programs and courses that generate revenue but compromise the unit's mission or purpose (Gros Louis & Thompson, 2002; Kirp & Roberts, 2002; Lasher & Greene, 1993; Whalen, 1991, 2002). Similarly, IBBS can lower incentives for collaborations across units (Cantor & Courant, 1997). Most dramatically, the quest for students and resources under IBBS can pit academic units against one another and encourage inefficient service delivery (Massy, 1989–1990; Meisinger, 1994). For example, duplication can arise when a course typically offered in one unit to robust and efficient class sizes is subsequently developed and offered simultaneously by other units. Units may be tempted by the incentive system to develop program requirements and advise students in such a way that students remain in that unit's courses and programs rather than venturing elsewhere for specific courses or minor program (Adams, 1997). Such self-protective logic may not only waste institutional resources but also slight the educational benefits of students taking courses in other units (Meisinger, 1994). Concern for the bottom line may thus mean sacrificing academic quality as well as efficiency.

Several angles of critique of IBBS involve academic culture. Some critics argue that such systems favor corporate over academic values. Adams, for example, says "the university has the responsibility to preserve, to correct, to integrate, and to advance the culture on all fronts," but the responsibility-centered approach "places at the heart of the university a mode of rationality in decision-making that subverts educational policy and weakens still more the university's ability for corrective cultural criticism" (1997, p. 59). All else equal, certain programs in the arts and humanities in universities can be disadvantaged by IBBS's focus on generating revenues via enrollments (Hearn & Gorbunov, in press). From this perspective, IBBS propels universities toward production-oriented logic, favoring such outcomes as reducing the number of professors, increasing professors' teaching loads, and eliminating majors and programs with low enrollment numbers (Adams, 1997; Wilms, Teruya, & Walpole, 1997).

What is more, incentives-based thinking, once implemented and embedded in the organizational culture, may grow beyond healthy bounds. A "perversion of principles" may occur in which unit leaders overestimate their autonomy (Whalen, 1991, p. 150). Once interunit competition is established, it can become difficult for units to see beyond their immediate local goals and extend their focus to larger organizational goals (Stocum & Rooney, 1997). A central administration may find it hard to redirect a local unit optimizing at the cost of larger organizational goals (Massy, 1989–1990).

Critics have also complained that units without instructional missions can find themselves disadvantaged under certain IBBS formulas; units with instructional missions may find themselves paying for non-instructional services without substantial influence over the quality and direction of those services; management and financial information systems may require substantially increased attention; temptations may rise to impose new service fees on students; grade inflation may be encouraged as units struggle for enrollment; central administrations may be pressed to find ways to preserve mission-critical resources in the face of unit resistance to taxation; and pressures may build to lower admission standards and program quality to facilitate enrollment-driven revenue-generation (see especially Gros Louis & Thompson, 2002, and Lang, 2002).

Much of the debate about IBBS concerns language and its implications. IBBS can stimulate a cultural clash between the use of management concepts and terms (customers, products, outputs) and academic concepts and terms (students, courses, completion rates). Reflecting on their experiences as high-level leaders under responsibility-centered management at the University of Michigan, Cantor and Courant (1997) argue that language can be the real culprit when faculty, staff, and students criticize incentives-based budget systems. They suggest that critics often infer that the language implies that central administrators see faculty as employees of a firm engaged in profit maximization. In reality, Cantor and Courant argue, "bottom-line" behavior would be a disaster for the university. Thus, what seems a fundamental problem to critics may in fact be a misunderstanding. Critics, however, are reluctant to cede the point.

Most fundamentally, opponents of IBBS have noted that there is little evidence of the benefits of the approach for learning and educational performance on campuses. Empirical research thus far has not provided clear evidence on the effects of incentivized budgeting systems on educational quality.[3] Beyond purely instructional outcomes, IBBS may raise the broader threat of "underproduction of public goods" (Cantor & Courant, 1997). The measurement of such goods is a dicey enterprise at best, but the growth of incentives-based systems should spur parallel growth in analyses of their implications for universities serving their larger social responsibilities.

Some contrarian opponents have even argued that IBBS approaches fail on the very grounds for which they have been designed and lauded. For example, Adams (1997) suggests that IBBS is yet another way for central administrators to ensure control of the budget, via the value-laden process of setting distributive formulas for resource allocations among programs (e.g., setting the central "taxation" rate, and units' local "return" rate, for various kinds of unit-generated instructional and research revenues). Thus, the idea of decentralized responsibility may itself be illusory, in that the value premises and incentive contexts of decisions remain under the control of high-level leaders. Along these lines, Leslie, Oaxaca, and Rhoades (2002) report that some academic department leaders are hostile to IBBS approaches on grounds of lost local control as well as high hidden costs. These striking findings (especially the perceived loss of unit power under IBBS) merit serious research attention.

Some proponents of incentivized approaches have acknowledged these and other concerns. For example, Zemsky, Porter, and Oedel note:

> The vulnerability of the subvention pool, the rivalries and jealousies fed by the sudden release of detailed budget data, the damage a weak dean might do, and the difficulty of translating income incentives into new programs and strategies mark the limits of responsibility center management. (1978, p. 252)

Another proponent, Whalen (1991, p. 149), suggests that responsibility-oriented approaches be carefully monitored to ensure that information produced will be as timely and accurate as needed for decision-makers to be efficient and effective; to achieve organizational balance among small and large units and units with varying missions[4]; to defeat attempts by units to beat the system; and to avoid external interference. In a similar vein, more recent analyses by Gros Louis & Thompson (2002) and Lang (2002) suggest that IBBS approaches require sensitivity to interconnections between public funding formulas and IBBS; awareness of the approaches' limitations; awareness of the impossibility of "quick fixes" via the approach; sensitivity to the varying appropriateness of IBBS across units; awareness of the difficulties of the approach for some administrators; and awareness of the need for attention to ongoing mechanical improvements.

Despite efforts on both sides to reconcile differences, disagreements over the merits of IBBS on campuses are often heated. Too often, these arguments are not grounded in empirical institutional data (Kallsen, Oju, Baylor, & Bruininks, 2001). For example, although the hortatory, critical, and conceptual literature is ripe with cautions about the potential dangers of IBBS approaches to cooperation and collegiality on campus, two recent analyses (Gros Louis & Thompson, 2002; Lang, 2002) present data suggesting that intraunit efforts may actually be facilitated by IBBS approaches, at least under certain conditions.[5] Clearly, this arena is in need of more such evidence, and more of the "Aha!" moments that only empirical research can deliver. The ratio of rhetoric to actual findings on the performance of IBBS is too high. This article represents a modest attempt to address this problem in the literature. It provides results from the implementation of IBBS at the University of Minnesota in the late 1990s.

Initiating IBBS at the University of Minnesota: The IMG Story

The University of Minnesota is a large, public, research, land-grant university. Its four campuses combined enroll approximately 50,000 students in 370 degree programs within 21 colleges. The university's total non-sponsored operating budget, including all expenditures, exceeds two billion dollars annually, making it the third largest of any public American university (University of Minnesota, 2000). Several characteristics of the university, including its relative autonomy derived through the state's constitution, its administrative culture, and its organizational structure, create a climate conducive for implementing a version of IBBS. The university's constitutionally granted autonomy allows the institution to maintain greater control of its internal budget compared to many other public institutions. The university was an early leader in market-driven reforms in tuitions and enrollment (Berg & Hoenack, 1987). The university invested in a data-warehouse strategy in the early 1990s, providing access to the types of management information needed to implement IBBS principles. Finally, the university has a long history of rather decentralized planning and decision-making, albeit within a context of centralized allocations.[6]

Development of IMG

Like many public institutions around the country, since the early 1990s, the University of Minnesota has experienced declining state funding as a percent of total state spending, a growing reliance on tuition revenues, and stagnation in public financial support (Hovey, 1999; Sundquist, 1997; University of Minnesota, 1999; Yudof, 2002). In the late 1990s, this fiscal and political climate forced the university to "shift from temporary budget-balancing measures to agonizing reappraisals of institutional missions and of the units that carry them out" (University of Minnesota, 1999, p. 2). The university restructured itself and revamped accounting, purchasing, and budgeting systems. In addition, stressing the desirability of unit subsidies becoming "a matter of conscious choice rather than of inadvertent outcomes or historical accidents," the university began to develop its own IBBS principles in 1995 (Bruininks & Kvavik, 1999; Kallsen et al., 2001; University of Minnesota, 1997).

The result was "Incentives for Managed Growth" (IMG), the University's distinctive version of IBBS. The underlying assumption was that IMG would support and stimulate institutional growth by aligning performance with resources, allowing academic units to ensure their own financial health, holding units more accountable for their activities, linking planning with budgeting, and, most generally, "creating incentives to enhance revenues and control costs" (Bruininks & Kvavik,

1999, p. 1). Structurally, the desired result was a flattened management structure with decentralized decision making its central feature.

IMG was a new initiative, but it was designed from the beginning to fit directly into the university's longstanding commitment to strategic planning. The university had long been noted nationally for its innovative strategic planning efforts (Hearn & Heydinger, 1985; Heydinger, 1982; Keller, 1983), but by the mid-1990s, those efforts had encountered strong external and internal challenges (Simsek & Louis, 1994). IMG represented an effort to update and advance the university's aggressive pursuit of long-term efficiency and effectiveness.

Implementation of IMG

IMG has three elements. The first involves the development of performance indicators for each of its constituent colleges. In some colleges, performance indicators are developed for individual departments and centers as well. The second part involves the formulaic remission of all tuition generated in the university, along with several other sources of external revenue flows, back to the generating colleges. The third part is the development of agreements (termed "compacts") between the provost and each of the constituent colleges on strategic plans and goals, programs, all-funds budgets, and evaluation procedures. In the development of these compacts, each of the deans meet on several occasions with the provost and his staff both to review current performance against previous compacts and to develop new understandings about the forthcoming year. All of these mutual understandings are transmitted through signed "compact" agreements. Several colleges develop similar compacts with their constituent departments, centers, and institutes. Following the periodic review of these agreements, rewards and sanctions are implemented.

The university formally implemented IMG during fiscal year 1997–1998, applying it to specific revenues generated by academic units' tuition, indirect cost recovery (ICR), and certain fees. State support remains managed and allocated by central administration, but tuition, ICR, and fee revenues are returned to the academic units generating them. The university employs an allocation approach, dividing student tuition between the college teaching the course (75%) and the college in which the student is majoring (25%). ICR revenue is allocated in proportion to how it is collected through the institution's negotiated ICR rate. State support was used to fund units to their "revenue neutral" starting point. Instead of receiving allocations from one general, central fund, colleges at the university receive under IMG a combination of state support, tuition revenue, and ICR. Typically, an administrative unit that generates no tuition or ICR operates only on state support (Kallsen et al., 2001).

Although units may keep newly generated revenue from tuition or ICR, units are responsible for revenue shortfalls, and the central administration's allocation of state support is discretionary. The use of discretionary funds must be for purposes that not only fulfill collegiate units' strategic investments but also fund any increases in academic support and administrative units. Thus, the university has created and implemented a system that is concerned primarily with incentives for the production of enrollment, instruction, and sponsored research. IMG is a hybrid system that decentralizes decision making to collegiate units, yet maintains central-administration control over the allocation of some funds.

This hybrid model was chosen in part to balance the university's long-standing, broad, and sometimes conflicting program-evaluation criteria: quality, demand, centrality to mission, comparative advantage, and efficiency/effectiveness (see Heydinger, 1982). For example, while there were arguments that, for efficiency's sake, funds should flow quickly to high-demand programs, concerns were expressed that maintaining some budgetary control in the hands of leadership was essential to conserving quality and respecting centrality to mission. The creation of the hybrid system was an attempt to address such trade-offs.[7]

IMG's design and implementation were explicitly aimed at linking budgeting to planning. Many of the performance indicators used in the compact agreements were related directly to the incentives for performance created under IMG. Table 36.1 provides examples of the general domains considered and some specific associated performance indicators.

TABLE 36.1

Examples of Specific Performance Indicators for IMG at the University of Minnesota

General Category	Specific Performance Indicators
Tuition Revenue Management	Cross-College Student and Course Activity
Instructional Cost Management	Marginal Cost/Revenue by Course and Instructor
Curricular Management	Course Control Size vs. Average Section Size
Enrollment and Tuition Management	Net Tuition Yield by Admission Score
Faculty Course Management	Courses and SCH by Instructor
	FTE/Demographics
	Tuition Revenue Cost by Course Release

Source: Kallsen et al, 2001; adapted from Moloney & Grotevant, 1997.

Early Evaluation of IMG's Performance

In 1999, an internal oversight committee provided the first evaluation of the IMG system (as reported in Kallsen et al., 2001). The report summarized comments by deans and department heads and made several recommendations: (a) the compact-planning process should be used to address historical patterns of funding inequities; (b) the compact-planning process should occur during alternate years; (c) the institution should establish an effective mechanism to soften the effects of tuition and ICR revenue variations; (d) central administration should provide collegiate units with the resources to perform better tracking, budgeting, and planning procedures; and (e) central administration should be more forthcoming and public about how centralized revenues are spent under IMG.

In 2001, Kallsen et al. evaluated IMG by examining evidence on some central IBBS principles. In the period after IMG was implemented, where were incremental new resources flowing? Specifically, were new resources indeed flowing toward units that increased research and teaching activity? Also, had IMG created a disincentive for interdisciplinary study and an incentive to "hoard" students to raise revenue?

This formal, quantitative, and systematic evaluation revealed that slightly less than 20% of the institution's budget was allocated in a new way under IMG. Although this may seem small, institutional planning initiatives seldom result in changes of such magnitude. The evaluation noted that professional colleges such as Agriculture, Public Affairs, Management, and Education were relative "winners" (i.e., experienced substantially increased revenues) under IMG, while academic units associated with the academic health center fared less well. Interestingly, non-revenue-generating units experienced a growth in funding despite their initial fear that their budgets would stagnate under IMG. The authors concluded that, with the exception of the continuing-education unit, academic or academic support units experienced no discernible negative financial effect under IMG.

Kallsen et al. (2001) examined whether there was a discernible rise in correlations, at the unit level, between enrollment and general operating/maintenance revenues and between sponsored awards and revenues from indirect-cost recovery. If so, the principles of IBBS would have been successfully followed, in that units would be receiving direct rewards for their successes in generating enrollments and research revenues. Over the period 1993–1994 to 1996–1997, the bivariate correlation between FYE students and operating/maintenance revenue averaged .92 for academic units at the University of Minnesota. Over the period 1997–1998 to 1999–2000, after the initiation of IMG, that correlation averaged .95, suggesting that units were indeed more directly rewarded for their efforts in enrollment management. Similarly, over the period 1993–1994 to 1996–1997, the bivariate correlation between sponsored awards and indirect-cost recovery averaged .90 for academic units. Over the period 1997–1998 to 1999–2000, after the initiation of IMG, that correlation averaged .99. It clearly appears that the initiation of an IBBS approach at the University of Minnesota meant units' enrollment and research performance more directly affected their financial status than they did in earlier years.

The initial evaluation by Kallsen et al. (2001) also addressed the hypothesis that colleges would purposefully hoard students and manipulate their course-taking behavior through curricular requirements, to maximize revenues for their units. Analyzing course-taking behavior of students university-wide, Kallsen et al. (2001) compared the percentage of student credit hours (SCH) taken by students within their home college in 1997–1998 (before IMG was implemented) with similar data collected in 2000–2001. The results, presented in Table 36.2, suggest that even with the financial incentives associated with IMG, the increase in the number of students concentrated in courses within their home colleges was only 0.5%. As noted by the researchers, this "represents a movement of 5000 student credit hours—less than 200 full-year equivalent undergraduate students" (Kallsen et al., 2001, p. 10).

An intriguing finding from Kallsen et al.'s evaluation involved units' credit-hour generation (see Table 36.3). The two units with the largest growth in credit-hour generation, Biological Sciences

TABLE 36.2

Percent of Student Credit Hours Taken within the Student's Home College, 1997–1998 and 2000–2001

	07–08	00–01	Change
Freshman Admitting/Undergraduate Colleges:			
College of Agric., Food, and Envir. Science	51.8%	51.3%	–0.5%
College of Biological Sciences	41.3%	31.6%	–9.7%
General College	61.2%	62.3%	1.1%
College of Human Ecology	51.6%	57.8%	6.3%
College of Liberal Arts	70.3%	70.7%	0.4%
College of Natural Resources	37.2%	36.4%	–0.7%
Institute of Technology	76.7%	79.1%	2.5%
Professional Schools:			
College of Architecture/Landscape Arch.	93.8%	78.7%	–15.1%
School of Management	71.2%	73.6%	2.5%
College of Education	79.8%	81.4%	1.5%
Institute of Public Affairs	76.0%	81.3%	5.3%
Law School	97.8%	98.4%	0.5%
Health Sciences:			
Medical School	95.0%	91.4%	–3.6%
School of Nursing	83.7%	91.9%	8.2%
School of Pharmacy	86.7%	88.8%	2.2%
School of Public Health	83.7%	87.8%	4.1%
School of Dentistry	85.9%	87.4%	1.5%
College of Veterinary Medicine	98.1%	97.9%	–0.1%
Other:			
College of Continuing Education	3.0%	6.2%	3.2%
Institutional TOTAL	70.8%	71.3%	0.5%

TABLE 36.3

Student Credit Hours Generated by Unit, 1997–1998 and 2000–2001

	07–08	00–01	Difference	Percent Change
Freshman Admitting/Undergraduate Colleges:				
College of Agric., Food, and Envir. Science	29,682	33,252	3,569	12.0%
College of Biological Sciences	21,760	32,103	10,343	47.5%
General College	33,387	40,561	7,174	21.5%
College of Human Ecology	28,139	30,430	2,291	8.1%
College of Liberal Arts	377,732	379,741	2,009	0.5%
College of Natural Resources	15,718	15,261	–457	–2.9%
Institute of Technology	138,756	139,989	1,233	0.9%
Professional Schools:				
College of Architecture/Landscape Arch.	5,039	9,963	4,923	97.7%
School of Management	64,583	74,655	10,072	15.6%
College of Education and Human Dev.	48,831	51,770	2,939	6.0%
Institute of Public Affairs	4,030	4,022	–9	–0.2%
Law School	15,293	20,724	5,431	35.5%
Health Sciences:				
Medical School	67,548	55,636	–11,913	–17.6%
School of Nursing	9,822	10,045	223	2.3%
School of Pharmacy	10,989	14,583	3,594	32.7%
School of Public Health	6,419	6,977	558	8.7%
School of Dentistry	20,797	22,160	1,363	6.6%
College of Veterinary Medicine	14,583	18,132	3,549	24.3%
Other:				
College of Continuing Education	93,232	63,734	–29,498	–31.6%
Institutional TOTAL	1,006,339	1,023,735	17,396	1.7%

and Architecture, were also the units that allowed their students to take the most courses outside their home unit. Kallsen et al. note:

> In both cases these colleges chose to admit more undergraduate students, liberalized the curriculum for majors, and began offering unique (as opposed to duplicative) service courses available to the entire university community. These colleges have attempted to grow the enrollment pie, instead of dividing it, and have been two of the most financially successful colleges under RCM practices. (2001, p. 11)

Of course, the data presented here are on the course-taking patterns of students, rather than on changes in requirements for the hundreds of majors at the university, but the data do suggest that conventional hypotheses about which behaviors will be "winners" under IMG were not always upheld by post-implementation findings.

The overall impacts of IMG have been mixed across the individual units of the university, but it is possible to generalize about the kinds of units gaining and losing under the system. Tuition-generating units were faring poorly relative to administrative units in the years before and immediately after implementation of IMG. Three years after implementation, however, those units had substantially closed the gap. It is impossible to state with certainty what would have happened had the university not elected to implement an IBBS approach, but it seems that the direct attribution of tuition neither advantaged nor disadvantaged specific kinds of units.

Kallsen et al. (2001) drew the following conclusions from the data. First, there is no evidence that academic or academic-support units at the University of Minnesota have been harmed financially by IBBS principles. Second, indirect-cost-recovery revenue, while proportionally a small amount of the total budget, has become more closely aligned with actual sponsored activity under IMG. Third, there is little empirical evidence that colleges have attempted to shape student enrollment patterns (e.g., via credit and prerequisite requirements for majors) to maximize their revenues under IMG. Fourth, although IMG does provide winners and losers, its rules have become well known to all parties, a clearly positive aspect of the new system. Fifth, continuing education as an organized unit has been the most negatively affected unit in the transition to IBBS principles, a finding perhaps indicative of larger trends for such units.

Interviews with Deans Working under the New IMG System

To supplement the largely quantitative data collected by Kallsen et al. (2001), we interviewed three collegiate deans on the university's Twin Cities campus in late 2001 and early 2002. We asked them to discuss their experiences as administrative leaders under the IMG system, with particular attention to the benefits and challenges associated with the new approach.

Before covering benefits and challenges, the deans emphasized what IMG was not as well as what it is. For them, IMG did not mean an abandonment of politics and power struggles on campus, or a foregoing of the need for strategic thinking and planning. As one dean noted,

> What IMG does is it simply controls in round numbers 270 million of a two billion dollar budget. It controls nothing about where state support is going to go. It controls nothing about what new academic initiatives involving central resources are going to do. It does nothing about [what] university priorities are going to be on the academic side.

The fact that the massive base state allocations to individual colleges on campus are still determined *a priori* at the central-administration level, as they were for many years before the implementation of IMG, is a particularly telling example of the independence of IMG from some fundamental and ongoing strategic and budget issues on this campus.[8]

Among the benefits of IMG suggested by the deans were: (a) providing a clear accounting of tuition and budget issues—"changing the way we do business"; (b) "fostering innovations"; (c) facilitating the implementation of needed academic reforms; (d) provoking an examination of student enrollments; and (e) creating an awareness of cost implications of actions—helping everyone to "recognize the finances of the place." One dean stressed this last point in particular: "The thing that IMG does is it allows you to put on the table what the accounting is so I know well what I am getting back from my investment."

In further discussing the benefits of IMG, one dean acknowledged that his unit must "fight harder to get money than we used to," suggesting that although this competition for funds may not necessarily be "fun," it is "appropriate" under IBBS principles. Another dean, speaking about the university moving to a new credit-minimum policy, noted:

> That's going to place some real demands on colleges and if we did not have IMG in place, this university would screw up in a major way on the implementation of a 13-credit minimum. Because, what's the incentive for me to surplus students unless I have the knowledge that if I open more classes to serve those students, [then] I'm going to get the revenue to cover my costs.

The deans also noted several challenges, including the oft-cited dangers of mission creep and duplication. Along these lines, one dean acknowledged the potential abuses of the system, noting its potential to create an unregulated marketplace insensitive to the larger good:

> The provost has to be a watchdog under IMG. If the provost isn't a watchdog for the bad incentives that IMG creates and doesn't stop that, you've got a stock exchange without a Securities and Exchange Commission—it just doesn't work.

A professional school dean raised the idea that unanticipated costs or unexpected events can create challenges for annual budget planning under IMG. The IMG system was described as one that shifts "under our feet year after year" whether through taxing and assessment (costs) or unanticipated events. In parallel terms, another dean raised doubts about the openness of IMG as conditions change:

> There is some sense that all of the costs should be a bit more transparent and they're not necessarily all put on the table or all managed. Suddenly you need to hire a bunch of additional people in the legal counsel's office; what did that cost you? Suddenly you decide you're going to bail out the athletic department and you didn't know about that; what did that cost you? Suddenly you realize that the costs of some of the new buildings are going online are higher than you expected, so there are some additional costs there. And when you put them all on the table, what are you doing as a university? There is some sensitivity among the deans because of that—because decisions are made in isolation of one another so that we don't see the whole picture of what is going on.

Another dean made a parallel observation, remarking:

> Part of the problem right now is that we have, as I put it, this moving target about what IMG is. . . . [I]f every single year there's a new way of doing it or a new little clue or a new little adjustment thing we made so that the thing doesn't collapse, then, what good is the thing that's undermining the incentives it is supposed to provide? [W]hat makes everybody crazy is that every two years or every year the rules change. How do you perform under that? How do you act responsibly under that? How do you trust the incentives under a system where the world is changing on you?

Deans noted another challenge: the variability among unit heads in their ability to function well within IMG. Faculty who come to serve as administrators are not necessarily savvy about financial management, so "they're doing it [IMG] intuitively and they're doing it by leaning a lot on people who do have the skill." The nature of the system encourages unit administrators to monitor closely all revenues and costs, but one dean cautioned about the inclination of some unit heads to be cautious, stating: "You can't lose sight of the opportunities that are out there simply because the dollars are staring you in front of the face and you're even more aware of what you have and what you don't have."

The deans to whom we spoke were unresolved on whether IMG had improved efficiency. As to the question of whether IMG increased bureaucracy in units, however, they were more sanguine. One dean noted that any increase in bureaucracy because of IMG implementation would be a relatively small cost compared to the larger benefit of units managing their own money. Another expressed concern over his own inability to assess whether IMG had affected bureaucracy in the college, acknowledging the unit's inability to date "to make full use of the information systems that the university has." The third dean interviewed noted that he saw no additional bureaucracy created by the adoption of IMG.

One dean called attention to the diverse IMG implementation styles across the various colleges on campus. Some colleges have decentralized most of the financial management and decision-making to individual departments within the college, while others maintain more centralized control of budgets and allocations in the dean's office.

The deans had different perspectives on the connection between IMG and the university's compact-planning process. Initially, one dean spoke of a disconnect between the two systems and processes. Later, though, that dean emphasized the idea that if the institution implemented IMG without the compact process, IMG "might neglect some entities that are of broad value to the place. . . . [there's] not enough to look out for the whole of the entity." This dean spoke of the interdisciplinary work and relationships that are created through the compact process that might otherwise be avoided if the university implemented only the IMG system. The compact process enables cooperation among colleges to serve a larger public good (e.g., pooling money to hire a librarian).

The compact process was seen by one dean as a mechanism for maintaining strategic academic priorities and thereby counterbalancing potential problems in a market model's incentives context:

> Incentives for mission creep, incentives for units that never talk about undergraduates before suddenly getting into the business of teaching undergraduates. Incentives for going after liberal education courses because they bring in . . . incentives for holding your own students in your own college

> rather than letting them flip into another college incentives for advertising. Your courses against other people's courses and trying to pick off students. . . . What ought to happen in a compact process [is that] a provost ought to blow the whistle and say, "No, you cannot do that. It violates principles about what the university is."

The deans provided several recommendations for improving the IMG approach at the university. Two deans pointed to a need to examine more closely the base allocation in the IMG formula, noting it remained largely unchanged after being set when the IMG process began for each college. The deans, while confessing self-interest, expressed concern that not changing the base institutionalized certain across-college inequities.

Thinking about the larger contexts of the IMG system, a dean remarked that there is a need for all involved to understand core costs at the university and a need to have the system reflect those costs. All colleges contribute to the institution's infrastructure via the "tax" the system imposes from their tuition returns, and this dean stressed that it would be helpful to have a "stable model" of what those infrastructure costs are over time. With this information, college leaders could make better-informed decisions and would better understand areas of concern in the overall IMG system.

One dean stressed that an IBBS system may tend to overlook certain public goods produced by the university. For example, if indirect costs are a critical element in the unit revenues generated under an IBBS approach, and if the unit is one that does substantial "land-grant" work for the state or other public agencies without the promise of indirect-cost returns, that unit may be penalized relative to units that are able to generate substantial indirect-cost revenues but without the returns to the larger public good:

> As we've been looking at our sponsored profile, we're doing a lot of charity work. We're bringing in indirect cost returns on the average of about 14%. You could say, "Well, you're stupid. Why don't you go after grants and contracts that actually return more indirect cost dollars?" Well, the answer is, we're doing an awful lot of work for the state of Minnesota. An argument could be made that because of the large number of students that we have and this large profile of research and contract activity, a lot of which is for the state, that we ought to be getting a larger portion of that state dollar.

Questions of service to the larger community and the public good were a consistent theme among our respondent deans. One said that it was important for units to look beyond the immediate bottom line to discern the costs and returns associated with the larger good. Another raised the same issue, noting, "It [IMG] hurts the ability of the university to fund collective goods. . . . That's the favorite argument of the libraries." Our respondents indicated that maintaining and fostering this sense of broader purpose may temper the competition inherent in IMG.

In all, it is striking that the three deans did not differ more in their perspectives on the importance, benefits, challenges, and possible improvements in IMG. Although our sample of deans was not large, it does appear from the limited evidence here that shared views do arise among those with similar leadership positions on a campus, despite their sometimes-competing internal budgetary interests.

Implications

This analysis cannot be considered a thoroughgoing evaluation of the effects of the implementation of an IBBS approach at Minnesota. The data are for only the early years of the new system. More importantly, because the budget reform was implemented across all units of the institution, we have no evidence of what would have happened in the focal period in the absence of the reform. We thus cannot definitively infer that the reform itself caused any outcome or prevented anything from happening. We just do not know. Yet, what evidence we do have is instructive. We can draw several tentative conclusions regarding the IBBS approach to campus budgeting and resource allocation. Each conclusion suggests empirical questions for research as well as directions for institutional leaders interested in pursuing incentive-based budgeting.

First, practitioners and analysts should question some of the conventional wisdom regarding the likely effects of IBBS in a given setting. At the University of Minnesota, there were several surprises, and some early worries appear to have been unwarranted. These results may not be paralleled elsewhere, but evidence for assumed outcomes should always be pursued.

Second, it is important to bear in mind that an IBBS system, no matter how aggressive, may not radically change budgetary outcomes or knowledgability. At Minnesota, only about 20% of the budget seems to have been redirected as a result of this reform. An IBBS by itself is unlikely to fully correct significant historical inequities in budgets, nor can it somehow ensure that everyone fully understands and agrees to the core budgeting assumptions of the institution.

Third, and somewhat conversely to the second point, IBBS reform can have significant effects at the margin. The 20% shift at Minnesota is significant and "large" compared with changes of less than 10% found in some IBBS implementations in the past. Veteran observers of university budgets tend to doubt the power of individual reforms, based on their past experiences with "zero-based budgeting," PPBS, and other long since-discarded ideas (Meisinger, 1994). IBBS seems to have somewhat more potential for reshaping allocations. At Minnesota, it appears that IMG is building organized capacity to adapt efficiently and productively to environmental changes. Revenue maximizing and cost minimizing appear to be occurring, and this is largely being done by creating more autonomy at the unit level accompanied by greater degrees of both internal and external accountability.

Fourth, successfully implementing IBBS requires full commitment from top leadership, open communication, and adequate information flows (Strauss, Curry, & Whalen, 1996). Critics have noted that the implementation of IBBS and the use of language borrowed from the for-profit world may cause faculty to reject the approach before they fully understand the system (Wilms, Teruya, & Walpole, 1997). The faculty may be concerned that market-driven forces and the drive for revenue among local units may obstruct higher educational goals such as quality, reducing the academic organization to a business with different goals (Cantor & Courant, 1997). Honest, open communication seems critical to avoiding faculty distrust and misunderstandings. The evidence from our respondents does not suggest major problems at that level, but deans did stress a need for greater clarity and transparency on how revenue streams are calculated and allocated, and we did not explore perceptions at the faculty level.

Importantly, local units need appropriate data and information for effective decision-making under IBBS. Whalen (1991) argues that, ideally, local units under IBBS will have increasing awareness about the implications of their decisions. At Minnesota, individual units demanded more and better information than planners anticipated when IMG was implemented. Locally specific and centrally dispersed information with format flexibility was needed, and web-based management-information systems became imperative. Even after an institution implements improved information systems, demands can persist. One of our interviewed deans noted that he did not really know enough about the effects of IMG on his college because of a lack of adequate centrally provided information. Those interested in the implementation of IBBS need to ask whether adequate information-management systems are in place to provide local units with data relevant to the decision-making at their level.

Fifth, and related to the above point, effective measurement of results is critical to the success of an IBBS system. Work at Minnesota suggests that it is critical to consider measurement methods for IBBS during development of the new budgeting system, as adjustments may be difficult to make later. There should be goals, rewards, and consequences for academic units as they seek to make decisions meeting institutional expectations, and measuring performance appropriately is critical to that process. IBBS and responsibility-centered management systems have emerged as a way to rationalize planning and budgets in higher education institutions, and institutions need to make sure that there are effective ways of evaluating IBBS's effects not only on the finances of institutions and their units but also on educational quality (Toutkoushian & Danielsen, 2002). As Massy (1996b) has noted, when institutions design decentralized systems in which the returns to improved performance and the penalties for poor performance are unclear, incentives are ineffective and investments may inadvertently flow to inappropriate activities.

In this context, it is important not to underestimate the challenges of effectively measuring results. As Toutkoushian and Danielson (2002) argue, it is dauntingly difficult to assess the effectiveness of incentive-based systems because solid measures of performance are rare and because simple correlations between IBBS and specific factors ignore the possible effects of other factors on those same metrics. At the institution these authors studied, the University of New Hampshire, confounding factors could not be dismissed in evaluating the institution's new responsibility-center management system:

> [S]uppose that UNH observes that the graduation rate declines in the years following the adoption of RCM. Without information on all of the other factors that might also have affected graduation rates, as well as an analysis of their impact, the university will not be able to determine if RCM also contributed the decline. Because the same caveats would apply to . . . other indicators [as well], it is questionable whether the data will be useful for examining the impact of RCM on even these measures. (p. 220)

Toutkoushian and Danielson suggest that effective assessment of any new system requires not only an array of quantitative indicators but also qualitative evidence, such as that to be acquired through reviews of faculty reports and discussions with deans and faculty. In accord with that perspective, the present analysis of the University of Minnesota system employs both quantitative and qualitative data. At the same time, it would be foolhardy to consider the evidence provided by this analysis comprehensive or definitive.

Sixth, our respondents and data suggest that it is critical for all parties to understand that an IBBS approach will inevitably evolve in any institutional context. It is probably impossible to "get it right" from the start. That said, there is a fine line between stakeholders perceiving a climate of incomprehensible instability and their perceiving a climate of ongoing appropriate refinements. Therein lies a major challenge for leaders. Importantly, measurement and evaluation systems must be evolving in harmony with the IBBS system, with the goal of ensuring that the currently implemented approach is well documented and open to empirical examination.

Seventh, the implementation of IBBS should be accompanied by re-examination of the nature of oversight and control of the university. Our interviews at Minnesota showed that base state allocations to colleges within the university have not been reexamined since IMG was implemented. Periodic reexamination and adjustments of state allocations seems imperative. This would strengthen the internal accountability measures IBBS inherently maintains and, ideally, might lessen pressures for expanded external accountability measures in an institution's internal budgetary process. As Whalen has observed, "If responsibility center budgeting makes communication and accountability easier, fewer rather than more constraints should result" (1991, p. 151). Of course, this result is likely only when the incentives in the budgeting system are congruent with the outcomes desired by both internal and external stakeholders.

Eighth, the ultimate effects of IBBS on efficiency and effectiveness are thus far unclear. At least, that certainly seems to be the case at the University of Minnesota. Efficiency may or may not increase, depending on how local decision-makers behave in response to the new system and how the central administration balances the need to decentralize fiscal decision-making with centralized direction.[9] IBBS may offer a credible response to historical inefficiencies in college and university budgeting, but an institution implementing an IBBS approach may still face obstacles rooted at the heart of academic organizations. As Massy put it:

> Few in higher education question the need for efficiency; the problem is that other forces constrain our ability to achieve and demonstrate it in the ways that have become familiar in business. The first arises from the intangible nature of academic outputs and the opacity and fragility of the production process, especially for the highest quality education and research. Budget cuts that ravage quality hardly improve efficiency. (1989–1990, p. 54)

It seems essential to define and assess efficiency and effectiveness at both the local and overall organizational level. Obviously, local units cannot survive without a healthy home institution. Efficiency and effectiveness at any specific institution may extend further than narrowly defined productivity (Cameron & Whetton, 1983). Unless a new budgeting approach is widely embraced by all members in the organization, unless all constituencies are involved in its creation and implementation, and unless it becomes an embraced part of the organizational culture top to bottom, success may be illusive.

Ninth, the effects of IBBS on innovation appear to depend heavily on the designed infrastructure and on local leadership. Regarding across-unit innovation, a professional-school dean complained about the paperwork and effort that go into just bringing a faculty member from another cost center to teach a course in his unit—something that isn't even all that "innovative." That dean commented that, if that takes extra effort, bureaucracy, and maybe even some negotiation to move ahead on cooperative teaching, the effects of IBBS on innovation may be negative. This suggests a researchable question of importance for the understanding and evaluation of IBBS. Beyond the structural conditions influencing innovation efforts, local units must also have in place the leadership to take advantage of the context for innovation provided by an IBBS approach. Stocum and Rooney (1997) have suggested that, under IBBS, units can move funds around to initiate new programs, but one of our interviewed deans suggested that department heads may not have the administrative capability or knowledge in financial management to take full advantage of incentives to be innovative. Might department heads need financial training to best implement IMG and understand its potential for improved innovation?

Tenth, the parallel adoption of the "compact" process at the University of Minnesota may have helped buffer the institution from retreat from units' commitments to the institutional community and mission, as well as to the larger public good. In some settings, leaders may need to explore sanctions for units pursuing behavior overtly contrary to broad campus agendas (Adams, 1997; Stocum & Rooney, 1997; Whalen, 1991). Massy (1989–1990) warns that when an IBBS mentality becomes embedded in the organizational culture, it may be difficult for central administrators to intervene when a local unit is optimizing at the cost of larger organizational goals. The recent onset of truly difficult financial circumstances at the University of Minnesota and many other large public institutions only heightens the need for vigilance on this front. It is therefore striking that such untoward behaviors as "hoarding" did not seem to be occurring in the early years of IMG at the University of Minnesota. The "compact process," tying IMG directly to strategic planning in units and overall, may have provided incentives for cooperative ventures and innovation in the university, countering the potential for excessive "profit" orientation at unit levels there. Implementing a parallel and complementary planning system at the same time as IBBS may represent an effective administrative choice.

Eleventh, while it may seem self-evident, it is important to note that implementations of IBBS must be integrated with the local organizational culture. At Minnesota, there was little appetite for devising complex formulas for attributing central support costs and administrative costs to academic units. At other institutions, such formulas may be financially necessary and culturally acceptable. It seems best to attune budgeting systems to local culture rather than to force local culture to adapt to budgeting systems.[10]

Finally, the organizational politics of IBBS are a topic little explored thus far in the literature, and this topic is well worth attention. One of our interviewed deans commented that deans and faculty need to understand who is involved in the decision-making process setting the grounds for the IMG approach at Minnesota, and how those decisions are made. Just because there has been a shift from traditional, central, incremental budgeting to IBBS does not at all mean that the politics of the budgetary process vanish. An administrator noted to us that, at Minnesota, the discourse around annual central-administration budget cycles has shifted somewhat from "who got what" to how to finance common goods like academic technology, or to how dependent individual colleges should be on tuition revenues. This might be taken to mean a decline in political wrangling but, of course, as debates arise concerning such general matters, all colleges offer perspectives that inevitably support their college's interests. Thus, one might even argue that, with budget rules more clearly understood on campus under the new system, there are more players and more politics in the budget cycle than under previous systems.

In this vein, it seems important to recall that power and politics on campus relate importantly to fields of study. As Volk, Slaughter, and Thomas have astutely pointed out, most past empirical studies of resource allocations among departments treat those units "as generic departments that reacted to institutional and professional incentives rather than as departments organized around concrete kinds of knowledge, peopled by faculty with similar characteristics who trained students for specific careers" (2001, p. 388). Although the putatively neutral workings of internal markets (i.e., the competition for student credit hours) might seem more linked to the "rational/political" rather than to the "critical/political" aspects of institutions, such an assumption downplays the distinctive grounding of each field and department in a variety of preexisting systems of stratification (see Gumport, 1993; Slaughter, 1993; Volk et al., 2001). The intersection of incentive-based models such as IBBS with critical resource-allocation theory such as that pursued so persuasively by Slaughter and her colleagues is beyond the scope of this article. Clearly, however, the question is of paramount importance for those interested in the equity implications of IBBS implementations.

Conclusion

Incentives-based budgeting systems bring to the forefront public institutions' difficult pursuit of the concurrent goals of access, quality, and efficiency. Deans interviewed for this project repeatedly referred to IMG's influences on these three domains of their colleges' operations and of the operations of the university as a whole. Of course, this "iron triangle" is difficult to manage and balance under any budgeting system (Hearn & Holdsworth, 2002). It may be that the great strength as well as the major vulnerability of incentives-based systems in the relatively open environments of public institutions is their potential to clarify and make more widely visible institutions' investment patterns, budgets, cross-subsidies, management strengths and weaknesses, and operational values.[11] To the extent institutions and their leaders at all levels can accept that transparency and deal effectively with it, through appropriately designed and implemented incentives and information systems, IBBS approaches may ultimately contribute to the success of the enterprise.

The evidence reported here suggests that IBBS, when well integrated with a responsive, participatory planning system, can indeed contribute to institutional efficiency and productivity. Of course, there is still much to learn about the outcomes of the IMG reform at the University of Minnesota. More broadly, there is much to learn about the implications of this kind of budgeting system on large public campuses. As Priest, St. John, and Tobin (2002) have noted, incentives-based systems are evolving and are very much a work in progress. Ideally, this analysis of recent developments at one institution will contribute to a growing empirical literature on an increasingly significant topic in higher-education organization and finance.

Epilogue

Since this article was written and accepted for publication, the University of Minnesota has continued to evaluate and reform its IBBS approach. Working throughout 2005 and into 2006, a system-wide committee of faculty and financial staff recommended that the university move further toward allocating revenues and costs directly to academic units. On the basis of these recommendations, the university approach is now evolving toward a "purer" IBBS system. In concert, the university is expanding the cost and productivity information it provides units and is developing new strategies to encourage interdisciplinary research and education, including novel systems for providing multi-unit allocations of tuition and funds from indirect-cost recovery.

Notes

1. In the 1990s, Indiana University became the first public research university to implement RCB, with the Universities of Michigan, Minnesota, and Virginia, UCLA, and others following (West et al., 1997).
2. Geiger has noted that "The widely recognized managerial revolution in higher education has either weakened or narrowed the sphere in which traditional collegial decision-making occurred. . . . [T]he new managerialism is a pervasive fact, and academic stewardship oversees a considerably smaller purview than it did just a generation ago" (2002, p. 46). Interestingly, the movement to incentivized budgeting appears to go in the opposite direction. Both observations are arguably "true," suggesting a focus for further analysis.
3. In fact, this uncertainty characterizes the broader literature on the relationships between educational costs and learning (Levin, 1991).
4. See also Lasher and Greene (1993).
5. In early conceptual work, Hoenack (1977) pointed to the potential of incentive-based budgeting systems for increasing, rather than threatening, cooperation.
6. For example, individual colleges have long been allowed to carry forward surpluses from year to year.
7. For an informative and spirited defense of hybrid models in action, see Cantor and Courant (2003).

8. This dean commented that, for real change to occur, "[S]tate dollars need to be moved around where they're needed. Where the best ideas are. Where the best possible return for students and academic excellence lie."
9. The barriers to achieving efficiency may be formidable. Boulding warns against an illusion of ever achieving efficiency in higher education and doubts the value of that pursuit, wryly noting that, "However carefully we refine our techniques, we must never desert the great tradition of muddling through" (1978, p. 418).
10. A similar point is stressed by Johnson and St. John (2002).
11. Mingle has noted that, "In the past, many institutions were reluctant to make explicit the cross-subsidies out of fear that they would be unpopular with powerful legislators. The question is, which strategy—stealth budgeting or more explicit commitment to unprofitable activities—will most likely sustain and encourage the institution to run counter to market forces?" (2000, p. 11).

References

Adams, E. M. (1997, September/October). Rationality in the academy: Why responsibility center budgeting is a wrong step down the wrong road. *Change*, 29, 58–61.

Berg, D. J., & Hoenack, S. A. (1987). The concept of cost-related tuition and its implementation at the University of Minnesota. *Journal of Higher Education*, 58, 276–305.

Birnbaum, R. (2000). The life cycle of academic management fads. *The Journal of Higher Education*, 71(1), 1–17.

Boulding, K. (1978, January/February). In praise of inefficiency. *AGB Reports*, 44–48.

Bowen, H. R. (1982, September). Sharing the effects: The art of retrenchment. *AAHE Bulletin*, 10–13.

Bruininks, R. H., & Kvavik, R. B. (1999, February 1). *Incentives for managed growth: A paper for discussion with the university community*. Minneapolis, MN: University of Minnesota. Retrieved from http://www.evpp.umn.edu/rcm/imgupd.htm.

Cameron, K. S., & Whetten, D. A. (1983). *Organizational effectiveness: A comparison of multiple models*. New York: Academic Press.

Cantor, N. E., & Courant, P. N. (1997, November 26). *Budgets and budgeting at the University of Michigan—A work in progress*. Ann Arbor, MI: The University Record. Retrieved from http://www.umich.edu/%7Eurecord/9798/Nov26_97/budget.htm.

Cantor, N. E., & Courant, P. N. (2003). Scrounging for resources: Reflections on the whys and wherefores of higher education finance. In F. K. Alexander & R. G. Ehrenberg (Eds.), *Maximizing revenue in higher education* (pp. 3–12). New Directions for Institutional Research, Vol. 119. San Francisco: Jossey-Bass.

Cogan, R. (1980). The design of budgeting processes for state-funded higher education organizations. *The Journal of Higher Education*, 51, 556–565.

Geiger, R. L. (2002). The American university at the beginning of the twenty-first century: Signposts on the path to privatization. In R. M. Adams (Ed.), *Trends in American and German higher education* (pp. 33–84). Cambridge, MA: American Academy of Arts and Sciences.

Gros Louis, K. R. R., & Thompson, M. (2002). Responsibility center budgeting and management at Indiana University. In D. M. Priest, W. E. Becker, D. Hossler, & E. P. St. John (Eds.), *Incentive-based budgeting systems in public universities* (pp. 93–107). Northampton, MA: Edward Elgar.

Gumport, P. J. (1993). The contested terrain of academic program reduction. *Journal of Higher Education*, 64, 283–311.

Hearn, J. C., & Gorbunov, A. V. (in press). *Funding the core: Understanding the financial contexts of academic departments in the humanities* (Occasional paper of the American Academy of Arts and Sciences). Cambridge, MA: American Academy of the Arts and Sciences.

Heam, J. C., & Heydinger, R. B. (1985). Scanning the external environment of a university: Objectives, constraints, and possibilities. *Journal of Higher Education*, 56(4), 419–445.

Hearn, J. C., & Holdsworth, J. M. (2002). The societally responsive university: Public ideals, organizational realities, and the possibility of engagement. *Tertiary Education and Management*, 80(2), 127–144.

Heydinger, R. B. (1982). *Using program priorities to make retrenchment decisions: The case of the University of Minnesota*. Atlanta, GA: Southern Regional Education Board.

Hoenack, S. A. (1977). Direct and incentive planning within a university. *Socio-economic Planning Sciences*, 11, 191–204.

Hovey, H. A. (1999). *State spending for higher education in the next decade: The battle to sustain current support* (National Center Report 99-3). Washington, DC: National Center for Public Policy and Higher Education.

Johnson, J., & St. John, E. P. (2002, June). The impact of incentives-based budgeting on planning: Understanding the structural and political aspects of budget reform. Paper presented at the Annual Forum of the Association for Institutional Research, Toronto, ON.

Kallsen, L. A., Oju, E. C., Baylor, L. M., & Bruininks, R. H. (2001, June). An RCM Success Story? Empirical Results of Responsibility Centered Management Principles. Paper presented at the annual meeting of the Association for Institutional Research, Long Beach, CA.

Keller, G. (1983). *Academic strategy: The management revolution in American higher education*. Baltimore, MD: Johns Hopkins University Press.

Kirp, D. L., & Roberts, P. S. (2002, Summer). Mr. Jefferson's university breaks up. *The Public Interest*, 70–84.

Lang, D. W. (2001). A primer on responsibility centre budgeting and responsibility center management. In J. L. Yeager, G. M. Nelson, E. A. Potter, J. C. Weidman, & T. G. Zullo (Eds.), *ASHE reader on finance in higher education* (2nd ed., pp. 568–590). Boston: Pearson Custom Publishing. (Reprinted from the CSSHE Professional File #117, Winter 1999, No. 17.)

Lang, D. W. (2002). Responsibility center budgeting at the University of Toronto. In D. M. Priest, W. E. Becker, D. Hossler, & E. P. St. John (Eds.), *Incentive-based budgeting systems in public universities* (pp. 111–135). Northampton, MA: Edward Elgar.

Lasher, W. F., & Greene, D. L. (1993). College and university budgeting: What do we know? What do we need to know? In J. C. Smart (Ed.), *Higher education: Handbook of theory and research* (pp. 428–469). New York: Agathon Press.

Leslie, L. L. (1984). Responding to new realities in funding. *New Directions in Institutional Research*, 43, 5–20.

Leslie, L. L., Oaxaca, R. L., & Rhoades, G. (2002). Revenue flux and university behavior. In D. M. Priest, W. E. Becker, D. Hossler, & E. P. St. John (Eds.), *Incentive-based budgeting systems in public universities* (pp. 111–135). Northhampton, MA: Edward Elgar.

Leslie, L. L., & Slaughter, S. A. (1997). The development and current status of market mechanisms in United States postsecondary education. *Higher Education Policy*, 10, 239–252.

Levin, H. M. (1991). Raising productivity in higher education. *The Journal of Higher Education*, 62, 241–262.

Lewis, D. R., & Dundar, H. (1999). Costs and productivity in higher education: Theory, evidence and policy implications. In J. C. Smart (Ed.), *Higher education Handbook of theory and research* (pp. 39–102). New York: Agathon Press.

Massy, W. F. (1989–90). Budget decentralization at Stanford University. *Planning for Higher Education*, 18, 39–55.

Massy, W. F. (1996a). Reengineering resource allocation systems. In W. F. Massy (Ed.), *Resource allocation in higher education* (pp. 15–48). Ann Arbor, MI: The University of Michigan Press.

Massy, W. F. (1996b). Value responsibility budgeting. In W. F. Massy (Ed.), *Resource allocation in higher education* (pp. 293–323). Ann Arbor, MI: The University of Michigan Press.

Meisinger, R. J. (1994). *College and university budgeting: An introduction for faculty and academic administrators*. Washington, DC: National Association of College and University Business Officers.

Mingle, J. R. (2000). *Higher education's future in "corporatized" economy* (Occasional Paper No. 44). Washington, DC: Association of Governing Boards of Universities and Colleges.

Moloney, D. P., & Grotevant, S. M. (1997, May). Collegiate and departmental performance indicators: The measures that matter! Paper presented at the 37th Annual Association for Institutional Research Forum, Lake Buena Vista, FL.

Priest, D. M., Becker, W. E., Hossler, D., & St. John, E. P. (Eds.). (2002). *Incentive-based budgeting systems in public universities*. Northampton, MA: Edward Elgar.

Priest, D. M., St. John, E. P., & Tobin, W. (2002). Incentive-based budgeting: An evolving approach. In D. M. Priest, W. E. Becker, D. Hossler, & E. P. St. John, (Eds.), *Incentive-based budgeting systems in public universities* (pp. 227–235). Northhampton, MA: Edward Elgar.

Rodas, D. (2001). *Resource allocation in private research universities*. New York: Routledge-Falmer.

Simsek, H., & Louis, K. S. (1994). Organizational change as paradigm shift: Analysis of the change process in a large, public university. *Journal of Higher Education*, 65(6), 670–695.

Slaughter, S. (1993). Retrenchment in the 1980's: The politics of prestige and gender. *Journal of Higher Education*, 64, 250–282.

Stocum, D. L., & Rooney, P. M. (1997, September/October). Responding to resource constraints: A departmentally based system of responsibility center management. *Change*, 29(5), 51–57.

Strauss, J., Curry, J., & Whalen, E. (1996). Revenue responsibility budgeting. In W. F. Massy (Ed.), *Resource allocation in higher education* (pp. 163–190). Ann Arbor, MI: The University of Michigan Press.

Sundquist, J. E. (1997). Uncertainty in a time of constrained resources. In P. M. Callan & J. E. Finney (Eds.), *Public and private financing of higher education* (pp. 169–197). Phoenix, AZ: American Council on Education and The Oryx Press.

Toutkoushian, R. K., & Danielsen, C. (2002). Using performance indicators to evaluate decentralized budgeting systems and institutional performance. In D. M. Priest, W. E. Becker, D. Hossler, & E. P. St. John (Eds.), *Incentive-based budgeting systems in public universities* (pp. 205–226). Northampton, MA: Edward Elgar.

University of Minnesota. (1997, December 11). *Institutional Performance Report*. Minneapolis, MN: Author.

University of Minnesota. (1999). *Responsibility center management: Report of the Responsibility Center Management Working Committee*. Minneapolis, MN: Author. Retrieved from www.evpp.umn/rcm/rptl.html.

University of Minnesota. (2000, January 21). *Report of the University of Minnesota Budget Management Task Force*. Minneapolis, MN: University of Minnesota.

Volk, C. S., Slaughter, S., & Thomas, S. L. (2001). Models of institutional resource allocation: Mission, market, and gender. *Journal of Higher Education*, 72, 387–413.

West, J. A., Seidita, V., DiMattia, J., & Whalen, E. L. (1997). RCM as catalyst: Study examines use of responsibility center management on campus. *NACUBO Business Officer*, August, 24–28.

Whalen, E. L. (1991). *Responsibility center budgeting: An approach to decentralized management for institutions of higher education*. Bloomington, IN: Indiana University Press.

Whalen, E. L. (2002). The case, if any, for responsibility center budgeting. In D. M. Priest, W. E. Becker, D. Hossler, & E. P. St. John (Eds.), *Incentive-based Budgeting systems in public universities* (pp. 111–135). Northampton, MA: Edward Elgar.

Wilms, W. W., Teruya, C., & Walpole, M. (1997, September/October). Fiscal reform at UCLA: The clash of accountability and academic freedom. *Change*, 29, 41–49.

Yudof, M. G. (2002, January 11). Point of view: Is the public research university dead? *The Chronicle of Higher Education*, 48, p. B24.

Zemsky, R., Porter, R., & Oedel, L. P. (1978). Decentralized planning: To share responsibility. *Educational Record*, 59, 229–253.

CHAPTER 37

FUNDING, RESOURCE ALLOCATION, AND PERFORMANCE IN HIGHER EDUCATION SYSTEMS

INGO LIEFNER

This article analyzes forms of resource allocation in university systems and their effects on performance in institutions of higher education. Internationally, higher education systems differ substantially with regard to research and education funding sources and to ways that resources are allocated. European universities receive the majority of their funding from public sources, but private funding plays a more important role in Anglo-American systems of higher education. Many governments use competitive elements in the process of allocating public funds to institutions of higher education. Examples include the implementation of performance measures through "formula funding", or resource allocation on the basis of evaluated project proposals. Corresponding forms of performance-based resource allocation can be found within most higher education institutions. This article analyzes how various forms of funding and resource allocation affect universities at the macro-level and individual behavior at the micro-level. A theoretical approach to this problem suggests that performance-based funding tends to bring about positive changes but is also a factor in unintended side effects. Forms of resource allocation influence the behavior of academics and managers in higher education, particularly their levels of activity as well as the kinds of activities they engage in and their ways of dealing with risks. Empirical analyses partly confirm these hypotheses. It can be shown that changes in resource allocation have an impact on the level and type of activity academics concentrate on but not on the long-term success of universities.

Introduction

Burton R. Clark (1983) classified national higher education systems (HES) into systems that are primarily coordinated by market interactions, "*market-oriented systems*", and systems that are coordinated by governmental planning, "*state-oriented systems*" (Clark 1983, p. 143). Other authors have used similar frameworks to categorize differences between national HES (see for example Massen and van Vught 1994; Trow 1997; McDaniel 1997). Most of them agree on several common features of market-oriented systems (see for example Clark 1983, pp. 161–169; Dill 1997, pp. 168–172; Ewers 1996, pp. 5–11): A high proportion of funding for higher education institutions is provided by private actors, for example, in the form of tuition and fees, gifts, grants, or research contracts. Their demand drives many activities of universities, faculty, and staff. Competitiveness is necessary for obtaining high levels of funding, and universities have to offer high-quality teaching and research and foster educational and organizational innovations. In traditional state-coordinated systems, programs of teaching and research offered by institutions of higher education are strongly managed by government directives. Moreover, these systems receive funding exclusively from their government (Clark 1983, pp. 125–127; Flitner 1989, pp. 145–158). The government allocates funds on the basis of the previous years' budgets and adds or deducts incremental changes (Ewers 1996, pp. 8–9). State-oriented systems have the tendency to conserve structures and be less innovative and less responsive to changes in demand. The higher education system in the United States is a prototype of a structure in which market-driven competition exists for both education and research. In traditional European systems governmental planning coordinates teaching and research activities as well as organizational structures. However, most national higher education systems employ features of both market-oriented and state-oriented control (Clark 1983, pp. 138–140; Trow 1997).

Over the last three decades public pressure has forced governments in many western countries to look for ways to meet society's needs without spending too much taxpayer-generated money. One way to respond to these pressures is to link funding to performance (Williams 1997; van Vught 1997; Layzell 1998, p. 108). Changes in funding methods, that is, shifts in income sources, or in the forms of resource allocation will likely have a major impact on the behavior of universities as well as their internal process of resource allocation. Research has shown that higher education administrators and institutions respond to changing mechanisms of resource allocation (for example, Mace 1995, pp. 62–69; Wagner 1996, p. 15; Schmidtlein and Taylor 1996, pp. 297–305). But changes in resource allocation also affect individual faculty, who are directly responsible for carrying out teaching and research duties. A detailed examination of approaches to the management of research and teaching, and academics' reactions to those approaches can provide insights into the impacts of performance-based and other methods of university budgeting.

Key research questions of this paper are:

(1) How does resource allocation vary among the higher education systems of several nations?
(2) What methods do universities employ to allocate their internal resources?
(3) How does performance-based budgeting affect individual faculty behavior?
(4) Does the national tradition of funding universities influence the applicability/outcome of performance-based methods of budgeting and the impact of monetary incentives?
(5) Does the method of resource allocation directly affect the long-term success of a university?

The Data

The empirical research for this project was conducted at the Department of Economic Geography at the University of Hannover, Germany. The investigation has been funded with the help of the German Science Foundation (DFG). It was based on case studies of universities and in-depth interviews with higher education administrators and professors. The universities selected for the case studies are regarded as prestigious research universities within their national system and are internationally recognized. Because the universities chosen for this study belong to different national systems, a wide spectrum ranging from market-oriented systems to state-oriented systems will be analyzed. The investigation includes universities from the United States (Massachusetts Institute of Technology [MIT], University of Texas at Austin [UT Austin]), Switzerland (Swiss Federal Institute of Technology [ETH Zurich], University of Basel), the Netherlands (University of Twente), and Great Britain (University of Bristol). In order to avoid the problem of defining and measuring "success" with respect to research universities, institutions generally acknowledged as having an outstanding reputation were chosen. The achievements in education and research of these selected institutions are widely recognized, and they serve as role models for other higher education institutions. Analyzing the behavior of these selected universities should provide some insights about how higher education institutions can be managed successfully.

The case studies were carried out between July 1998 and October 1999 and included visits, varying from two to four weeks, to each university campus. During the visits documents and publications were gathered, and in-depth interviews were conducted. At each campus administrators as well as experienced professors from the major academic disciplines were interviewed. The data provide distinct pictures of the selected universities but are not necessarily representative of national higher education systems in these four countries. However, the large number of interviews conducted (117) in these case studies allows descriptive methods of analysis to be applied. A detailed description of the data and methods can be found in Liefner (2001).

Concept

The article is divided into three sections. First the sources of funding and the internal budget allocation of the six universities are described to demonstrate international differences in funding and resource allocation. This section is followed by a discussion of the principal-agent theory, a concept that leads to hypotheses about the effects of performance-based budgeting on individual behavior. The theoretical hypotheses are then compared with empirical findings. The final section examines additional factors that may influence the long-term success of universities and ends with a brief discussion of implications relevant to university administrators.

International Differences in Funding Sources and Resource Allocation

The following description of the funding regimes of the universities analyzed concentrates on monetary sources that support these universities, allocation of public funds to universities, and internal resource allocation. The goals are (1) to demonstrate the enormous differences in how universities obtain funds from external sources (see Figure 37.1) and (2) to show how these differences are reflected in the internal budgeting and allocation process. Figure 37.1 shows that the importance of private funding and market-driven or performance-based public funding varies to a great extent.

(1) Swiss Universities: ETH Zurich and University of Basel

The Swiss Federal Institute of Technology in Zurich (ETH Zurich) is the largest and most prominent higher education institution for engineering and science in Switzerland. It has an annual budget of 1 billion Swiss francs, equivalent to 690 million US dollars[1] (ETH Zurich 1998a, pp. 48–64). Among the sources of income the federal government plays a dominant role as about 85 percent

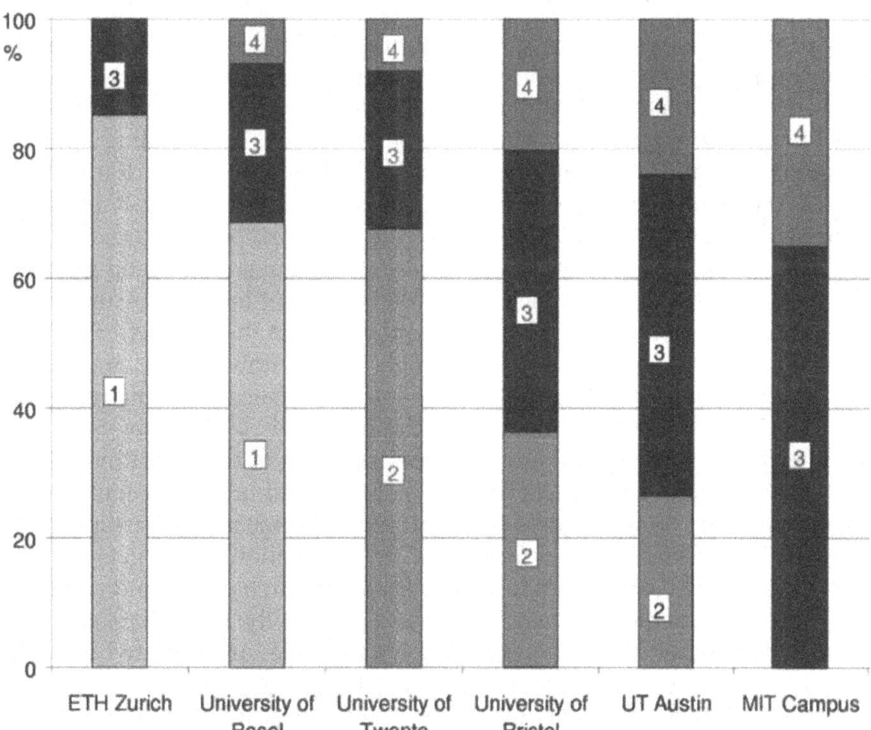

Figure 37.1 Differences in funding sources of the six universities.

Notes: 1) direct public funding, not performance-based; 2) direct public funding, partly performance-based; 3) private and public research grants and contracts, tuition; 4) endowment income, gifts and other income, not classified.

Source: ETH Zurich 1998a; University of Basel 1998; University of Twente 1998a; University of Bristol 1998b; MIT 1998; UT Austin 1998.

of the university's budget stems from it. This dominant income flow is not linked to performance. The federal government decides upon incremental changes from year to year. The administration of the ETH views the high and relatively stable funding from public sources as a factor ensuring academic freedom. Such freedom itself is regarded as a precondition for curiosity-driven research and successful long-term development (ETH Zurich 1998a, p. 32). This philosophy is reflected in the internal budget allocation. The driving force of this allocation is the number of professorships and faculty positions in the departments. A professorship is generally endowed with an average of nearly 13 faculty slots (ETH Zurich 1998b). The initial number of slots allocated to a full professor generally does not change. Hence, the resource allocation to the departments is stable, and incremental changes only occur when professors retire and their positions no longer seem necessary.

The University of Basel has a budget of 300 million Swiss francs, equivalent to 210 million US dollars[1] (University of Basel 1998, pp. 76–77, 106–110). Two regional governments jointly fund the institution and provide annual funding of 160 million francs. Some additional funds come from the federal government (35 million francs) and from other regional governments as a payment for the education of students residing in their regions (18 million francs). Despite this last portion of public income a link between performance indicators and public funding does not exist. The university's budget is a part of the legislature, and changes occur incrementally on an annual basis. The internal allocation of financial resources reflects the way the funds are obtained from the outside (University of Basel 1998, pp. 74–77). The allocation to the departments is largely stable and changes only marginally from year to year. Long-term changes are not driven by performance but by the decision of the board on how the organization should develop and fulfill its role as an innovative stimulator for regional development (University of Basel 1999).

(2) University of Twente, The Netherlands, and University of Bristol, Great Britain

The University of Twente views itself as an "Entrepreneurial University" that emphasizes organizational restructuring as well as active participation in industrial activities (Clark 1998, pp. 39–51). The annual budget of the university is 350 million Dutch guilders, equivalent to 180 million US dollars[1] (University of Twente 1998a, pp. 10, 45). The university receives direct funding from the Dutch government through the so-called "first income stream", which quantitatively dominates two-thirds of the budget and is partly related to performance (University of Twente 1998b, pp. 1–12). Under the current system of resource allocation, one-third of the funds of the first stream is labeled "teaching money". These funds are calculated on the basis of entering students and graduates and some historically fixed portions. The remaining two-thirds of the first income stream is called "research money". This part of the allocation is calculated on the basis of the number of Ph.D. dissertations, engineering certificates, recognized research schools at the universities, and again historically fixed portions. With regard to the large fixed portions in the calculation of "first income stream", 33.5 percent of the university's direct allocation of public funds to the university is linked to performance, 66.5 percent is fixed. Internal distribution is similar to the allocation of the first income stream from the government. Differences between external and internal resource allocation reflect the university's aim to act more business-like than most European universities do (University of Twente 1998b, p. 32). It uses additional factors for the calculation of budgets (numbers of exams passed after the second year, employees funded through research grants and contracts, employees funded through programs of the European Union) and reduces the fixed share of allocation in favor of performance-driven shares. Half of the institution's resources are allocated due to performance; the other half are allocated in fixed portions (see also Schutte 1998, pp. 3–5).

The University of Bristol belongs to a small group of successful British universities that combine high-quality teaching with high-quality research throughout the whole spectrum of the university's academic disciplines. It has a budget of 150 million pounds, equivalent to 245 million US dollars[1] (University of Bristol 1999). The University of Bristol receives 36 percent of its annual budget directly from the government through governmental organizations, so-called funding councils. Three fifths of that budget is spent on teaching, and two fifths on research. Other important sources of income are public and private research grants and contracts, and tuition (University of Bristol 1998a, pp. 8–14; 1999). The funding councils allocate funds for teaching depending on the number of students at a university as agreed upon with the national ministry. Research activities are funded on the basis of the result of a nationwide evaluation process (HEFCE 1998, pp. 4–16). Therefore, direct public funding involves competition in the fields of education and research. Competition is also a driving force behind all other sources of income as these involve private or public money that is paid in exchange for a specialized service or on the basis of reviewed project proposals. Internally the university does not alter this allocation system (University of Bristol 1998b). Instead it allocates all money to the departments that have "earned" the money through teaching, enrollment figures, project proposals, or high-quality research. The re-allocation of funds between departments is very moderate.

(3) Universities in the United States: MIT and UT Austin

MIT is one of the most prestigious private universities in the United States. For many years its engineering programs have been rated number one in the rankings published by US News (US News 2000a). The MIT campus has an annual budget of 920 million US dollars (MIT 1998, p. 20). As a private university, MIT does not receive direct public funding, but rather it relies on research grants and contracts (430 million US dollars per year), tuition and fees (235 million US dollars per year), and endowment income of up to 300 million US dollars per year as its principle sources of income (MIT 1998, p. 20). Competitiveness is a necessary precondition for obtaining these funds. Internally, resources that are allocated to the schools, as well as to departments and laboratories are not linked to performance indicators but to the previous year's budgets and the number of faculty slots in each department. Hence, there is no internal allocation of university funds due to performance. But the decisive function of grants and contracts as well as tuition income forces faculty, researchers, and staff to be active in obtaining external funding. Therefore the stable and incremental allocation of institutional funds complements the uncertainties connected with external funding.

The University of Texas at Austin has an annual budget of 940 million US dollars (UT Austin 1999, pp. 43–44, 95–123; 1998). The university is regarded as a successful research institution, and its growing reputation is shown in national rankings (US News 2000b). Grants and contracts, as well as tuition and endowment income make up two-thirds of the budget. About one-quarter is obtained from the state of Texas. This money is allocated according to a formula on the basis of current teaching activities of universities in the UT system (The State of Texas 1998). The determining factor for allocation is the number of semester credit hours weighted by discipline, the number of students, and the level of the courses offered. Therefore all major income sources are either market driven or linked to performance. The internal allocation of funds is organized in a way similar to MIT's. This is true despite the fact that UT Austin receives its public funding depending on its educational activities. The administration of UT Austin allocates money according to needs and not according to performance.

Table 37.1 summarizes this section. Funding sources and ways of budgeting differ enormously between different higher education systems. The above discussion has also shown that universities—at least the six universities analyzed—tend to react based on the way they receive external resources. This is true for the "traditional European system" represented by the Swiss universities. The bulk of their funding is not directly linked to performance. Internally they allocate most of the funds in the form of fixed budgets. Universities in the Netherlands and Britain both receive a large part of public funding through a system that contains competitive elements. Internally they, too, use a market-like approach. The two US-American universities obtain the majority of their funding in a competitive way. Competition is also a key factor for the amount of money available for individual departments and groups as many activities are directly funded by grants and contracts. Some stability in the allocation of the institutional funds to the schools and colleges is necessary to meet fixed operational costs in the form of faculty salaries and to maintain the university infrastructure.

Despite the fact that pronounced differences in funding sources and resource allocation between these universities exist, all of them are regarded as successful institutions within their national HES. Therefore a close link between the means of funding and success cannot be identified on the university level. Similar results have been discussed by Jongbloed (1998, pp. 12–13) with an

TABLE 37.1

Differences in External and Internal Resource Allocation

	ETH Zurich, University of Basel	University of Twente, University of Bristol	MIT, UT Austin
External funding and resource allocation	Public funding dominates, allocation not based on performance	Public funding dominates, allocation partly based on performance	Private funding important, allocation of public funds based on performance
Internal resource allocation	Allocation largely stable, not based on performance	Internal allocation similar to external allocation, partly based on performance	Stable allocation of limited university funds, dominance of other competitive funding sources

analysis of Dutch universities. In order to examine the effects of performance-based resource allocation more closely, the following section analyzes the level of individual behavior.

Resource Allocation and Behavior

This section analyzes the effects of different forms of resource allocation on individual behavior from a theoretical and an empirical perspective. The analyses in this section are derived from the principal-agent theory that seeks to explain the relationship between a principal and an agent (see for example, Arrow 1991, pp. 37–45; Pratt and Zeckhauser 1991, pp. 15–22). The focus of this theory is to find a payment structure that motivates the agent to work according to the goals of the principal. The following discussion does not use the restrictive and formalized framework of the principal-agent theory but similar arguments (see also Reichwald and Koller 1998). The basic assumptions and arguments of this theory are explained in Laux (1990).

The theory deals with the relationship of a principal who employs an agent or sets up a temporary contract with him/her; this agent can then be paid in different ways. In higher education the principal can be a ministry of science and education, the management board of a university, a president, dean, or department chair. The agents are those actors in higher education who receive assignments, funds, and salaries from the principals. Therefore a number of higher education managers, for example, heads of departments, are simultaneously principals and agents, whereas most of the professors, researchers, and lecturers can be viewed primarily as agents.

In the context of the principal-agent theory, the terms "level of activity", "success", and "risk" have to be defined. First, the level of activity means the amount of time and effort an agent puts into activities that are directly related to the goals of the principal. In higher education the achievement of high quality in teaching and research can generally be taken as the central goals of the principals. Second, in the strict sense of the principal-agent theory success has to be expressed in the form of monetary profits. In considering research universities, activities that do not necessarily directly produce monetary income, for example, teaching students or advancing knowledge, also have to be included. Third, risk can be understood as the possibility that some activities in teaching and research may fail to be successful.

Universities are complex organizations in which the agents have specialized knowledge about their activities that administrators do not share (Clark 1983, p. 25). Therefore activity is difficult to monitor, particularly on the level of research groups and individual scholars but also on the level of institutions. In order to avoid a situation where agents take advantage of the fact that their effort is hard to control and reduce their activity, a principal can link funding to performance (success). Examples include governments that allocate money to universities according to how successfully they meet certain goals, such as producing a certain number of graduates or publications per year (Williams 1997, pp. 276–279). Corresponding ways of performance-based budgeting can be observed within universities. The creation of incentives to work hard and according to the principal's assignments goes hand-in-hand with this form of funding. If universities or departments or individual academics perform well, they will enlarge their future budgets. If they are less successful, they will receive a lower level of funding. The many different forms of performance-based resource allocation like formula funding, funding through review processes, contracts, etc., employ this mechanism to maximize performance.

The effects of a change in the principal's behavior can be described as follows (see also Laux and Liermann 1993, p. 583): In a HES without private funding or performance-based budget allocation, the institution bears the risk of unsuccessful projects because it guarantees funding and salaries regardless of performance. All agents enjoy the flexibility to operate in any manner they wish because they need not be concerned about possible failure. Some departments or individuals will take advantage of this situation and be rather inactive or concentrate on activities that do not meet the interest of the principal. With the introduction of performance-based resource allocation, less-motivated agents must work harder and according to the given criteria. The motivated agents, too, will have to bear the risk of failure and lose some flexibility (see also Jongbloed and Vossensteyn 1999, p. 3). Therefore they will either reduce activities that have a high chance of failure or put away some funds as a reserve in the event of a future funding loss. Table 37.2 summarizes these effects.

Hence, the effect of introducing competitive elements or performance-based funding into HES depends on the motivation of individuals and their way of dealing with risks. The main hypotheses that can be drawn from the theory are:

(1) Agents that have been rather inactive before the introduction of performance-based resource allocation will have to work harder.

(2) With performance-based resource allocation agents will tend to avoid projects with a high chance of failure. Departments and individuals will concentrate on activities where success can be expected because they will have to meet a formula's criteria or market demand.

The theory relies on the assumption of uniform human behavior, and it disregards the national systems and traditions of funding universities. In order to analyze whether the theory can predict the real impact of competition and performance-based budgeting on behavior, the theoretical hypotheses mentioned above will be contrasted with empirical results. This part of the article summarizes findings from interviews conducted with 53 professors, who are active in teaching and research, from the selected universities. The study covered all major academic departments of the six universities in order to get a complete view on the institutions and to avoid a bias towards certain academic disciplines. The interviewees were all very familiar with their departments, mostly being

TABLE 37.2

Theoretical Effects of Different Forms of Resource Allocation on Behavior

Form of Resource Allocation	Effects on Level of Activity	Effects on Type of Activity
Non-competitive conditions of allocation:	– Levels of activity depend on motivation of actors	– Types of activity depend on motivation and interest of agents
Fixed budgets or stable allocation not linked to performance	– Low level of activity and low performance possible	– Mismatch between interests of university and academics possible
		– High flexibility to carry out projects with high risk of failure
Competitive conditions of allocation:	– Levels of activity depend on incentives connected with resource allocation system	– Types of activity have to be consistent with interests of university or meet market demand
Performance-based allocation or allocation through markets	– High level of activity necessary to maintain level of funding	– Projects that have a higher possibility of failure will not be carried out

either active or former chairpersons. They were asked to comment on the impact of the current resource allocation system expressing their faculty's view wherever possible. But of course, their answers also reflect individual preferences and experience as well as their national and cultural backgrounds. Thus, the sample reveals the influence of national traditions and culture, but it is not representative for national higher education systems. Nevertheless, the study was designed to differentiate between nations and universities as well as between disciplines (see Liefner 2001). A detailed analysis of national differences is only applied when the arguments underlying the answers given show that differences are not random but based on national characteristics and tendencies. The following section summarizes (1) comments on reactions to different systems of funding, (2) comments on the likely effects of a funding arrangement based solely on competition and (3) differences in the interviewees opinions due their national or university culture.

(1) The answers concerning the effects of performance-based funding can be summarized as follows: Sixteen professors state that the link between funding and performance leads to increased activity among their colleagues. "People work harder" was the most frequent reply of professors whose departments had undergone a shift towards performance-based resource allocation in recent years. The majority of the interviewees attribute this result to the fact that with performance-based funding an open discussion about the performance of groups and individuals emerges. This seems to be stimulating activity as poor performance becomes obvious and threatens to lead to a loss of funding, reputation, income, and prestige. Fewer of the scholars who are familiar with competitive bidding for funds or performance-based allocation point out that a shift in the manner of resource allocation changed people's attitude toward risks. Ten of them have experienced that people tend to stay within their academic fields and avoid projects with uncertain outcome. A professor illustrates his statement with the example of the scientific indicators: "publications" and "citations". The use of both indicators for the evaluation of research puts pressure on scholars to publish frequently in prestigious journals. Once they have established a reputation within a certain scientific field, their knowledge in this field and about the prospective developments within this field enables them to acquire funding for research projects, to produce new knowledge, and to get access to the top journals in the future. Hence, if continuous publication is crucial for sustaining the funding base, scholars are unlikely to take the risk of changing their fields of research.

Whereas these comments on effects of performance-based budgeting are mainly from US-American, British or Dutch professors, the following comments on the effects of stable funding arrangements draw basically on the experiences of Swiss interviewees. According to their comments, the main negative effect of a stable budget that grows incrementally and that is not linked to performance is the opportunity to be relatively inactive. Eighteen of the scholars who are familiar with the effects of fixed budgets report that they have observed this kind of behavior among their colleagues. The main positive aspect of fixed budgets is flexibility to follow new ideas and concentrate on pure research. Fourteen scholars explicitly state that a guaranteed basic budget that covers the costs of infrastructure and the salaries of some faculty and staff provides favorable conditions for curiosity-driven research.

Hence the theoretically expected effects of different ways of funding can be shown empirically. Performance-based funding produces incentives to work hard but also to concentrate on fields in which the scholar's expertise is well known. The absence of performance orientation allows scholars to work on projects that might have a high chance of failure. On the other hand it allows them to be rather inactive (for similar results see for example, Williams 1997, p. 288). If these statements of the interviewees not only reflect individual experiences but also effects that are generally connected with the different forms of funding—if the theoretically derived hypotheses are correct—performance-based funding should have specific effects on the activities of scholars.

(2) In order to confirm this result and get a more detailed impression of likely changes connected with performance-based funding, the professors were asked their opinions about the possible effects of a funding regime completely based on market forces and performance-driven allocation. Table 37.3 summarizes the results. The expectations are transformed into scores from "1" to "5", with a "5" indicating that professors expect a strong positive impact of completely performance-based

TABLE 37.3

Effects of Completely Performance-Based Resource Allocation

	Expectations of Interviewees . . .		
Impact of Completely Performance-Based Resource Allocation on . . .	**Who Favor Performance-Based Allocation**	**Who Oppose Performance-Based Allocation**	**Who are Undecided**
Quantity of pure research activities	3.1	2.6	2.7
Quality of pure research activities	3.6	2.1	2.3
Quantity of applied research activities	3.9	3.9	3.9
Quality of applied research activities	4.0	3.1	3.4
Number of scientific publications	3.8	3.1	3.4
Quality of scientific publications	3.8	1.9	2.6
Proximity to market application	4.5	4.0	4.1
Public acceptance of universities	4.1	3.8	4.0
Efficiency of internal organization	4.0	1.8	2.8
Motivation of faculty and staff	4.0	1.8	2.8

allocation, a "3" indicating that no changes are likely, and a "1" indicating the expectation of a strong negative impact. Table 37.3 shows arithmetic means of the marks given by the interviewees who generally favor performance-based resource allocation (group 1 [n = 9]), those who oppose a high degree of performance-orientation and competition (group 2 [n = 19]), and those who are undecided (group 3 [n = 17]). The table concentrates on activities that should be affected.

If the hypotheses are correct, a shift to completely performance-oriented funding and resource allocation should be connected with a reduction of pure research as this type of research has a relatively high chance of failure. Applied research in which the prospective outcome can be clearly defined in advance should increase. The table shows that all interviewees expect a large increase in the quantity of applied research carried out. They also expect the quality of these projects to be higher although professors who favor performance-oriented funding (group 1) are generally more optimistic than the others. In contrast, the quantity of pure research carried out would slightly decrease or remain stable. The opinions about likely changes in the quality of pure research differ. The scholars generally opposing a high degree of performance orientation (group 2) as well as the undecided ones (group 3) expect decreasing quality, whereas group 1 expects increasing quality.

A high degree of performance orientation should theoretically lead to increasing numbers of publications as this is an indicator of scientific performance which is easy to monitor. The quality of publications is not directly measurable; therefore, the quality of publications should go down. Again, the interviewees widely agree about changes in quantity but disagree about effects on quality. With performance orientation publishing activities will rise. In the view of group 1 positive changes in the quality of publications can be expected, yet the majority of the interviewees expect a negative influence.

Another aspect of scientific activity that should be affected by a completely competitive funding system is the transformation of new knowledge into marketable products. An additional benefit of accelerated technology transfer could be growing public acceptance of universities. The interviewees agree that the transformation of new knowledge into products will dramatically increase. Public opinion about universities will change positively as well. Furthermore the efficiency of universities and the motivation of personnel could be affected. Efficiency should be improved by the use of market coordination, whereas the effects on motivation depend on the individuals' attitudes toward competition. In these respects the expectations are totally split. Depending on their general attitude towards competition and performance orientation, the professors expect dramatic increases or decreases in efficiency and motivation.

This analysis shows two lines of argumentation that explain the results shown in Table 37.3. First, the professors interviewed argue that people will react to changes in the environment of their workplace. This argument—which is consistent with the theoretical hypotheses—explains the expected changes in quantities as well as an increasing proximity to the market. A shift toward applied research as well as a drive toward the creation of new products would be the likely outcome of increasing the importance of market forces and performance measures in university funding. The interviewees largely agree with this conclusion. Second, the arguments about changes in quality and working conditions depend on the general attitudes of the interviewees toward competition and performance orientation. The professors who favor a highly competitive funding and resource allocation system expect positive impacts on the quality of research and publications as well as positive changes in efficiency and motivation. The opposite is true for the majority of professors interviewed who are skeptical about a high degree of competition at universities.

Empirical studies either confirm these results or provide additional insight. Examples include the studies of Geuna (1999, p. 103), Mace (1995, p. 62) and Slaughter and Leslie (1997, pp. 180–184), who analyze changes in the relation between pure and applied research, or Owlia and Aspinwall, who focus on the application of knowledge to marketable products.

(3) So far, the analysis focused on differences between people favoring or opposing a high degree of competition in the funding of higher education and research. In terms of the large differences between national university systems with respect to the overall coordination and the funding arrangements, the opinions of professors could be influenced by their national backgrounds. This section addresses the question whether national or university culture determines the interviewees' expectations about the likely impact of competition and performance-based funding.

The following analysis looks at relations between the national background of the interviewees and the scores given. A table need not be shown here as there is no evidence for a connection between national background and expectations, except for two cases. First, Swiss professors tend to expect a more negative impact of competition on quantities compared to the other interviewees. They do not agree with the expectations of the majority of the interviewees that competitive funding arrangements will lead to a higher number of publications. Furthermore, they expect a strong negative impact on the number of projects of pure research, whereas the majority expects only a limited negative influence. Second, unlike the majority of the interviewees, British professors expect a positive impact of competitive funding arrangements not only on applied research but also on the quality of pure research and publications. These findings can be explained by the basic arguments underlying the interviewees' expectations. Some of the Swiss professors lack personal experience with performance-based funding and competition for resources. This is one factor that explains their skepticism. Some of them mention as a second factor that the Swiss culture is more based on consensus than on competition. This general, not university-specific feature also explains why many Swiss interviewees do not favor a dominant role of competitive elements in university funding. The strong positive expectations of British professors may be due to the recent positive experiences with the introduction of performance-based funding and quality assessments. Furthermore, the British (and Dutch) funding systems that combine stability and competition may also combine the advantages of both ways of funding. The expectations of the US-American professors are neither positively nor negatively pronounced. That may be due to the fact that universities in the United States have a longer tradition of being funded under competitive conditions. The professors know the advantages and the disadvantages of that funding arrangement, but as the system is generally accepted, there is less debate compared to European HES.

Hence, the differences in national or university cultures and funding arrangements are reflected in the expectations connected to performance-based resource allocation. But, these differences in expectations are relatively small compared to the common views of the interviewees on the prospective outcome of a strongly competitive funding system (e.g., more applied research, an increased number of publications, market application).

Discussion: What Determines the Success of Universities?

The analysis of interviews has shown that the impact of performance-based budgeting or at least the expectations about the impact of competition are similar in all six universities investigated; only minor differences exist. Instruments of performance-based budgeting work largely as predicted in theory. The first section of this article has shown that the application of performance-based resource allocation varies to a great extent between universities and national HES. Therefore, the link between performance-based resource allocation and the success of universities must be weak; otherwise, not all of the six universities could be successful institutions.

In order to assess the importance of resource allocation strategies for the long-term success of higher education institutions, the professors were asked which factors determine the educational and scientific potential of universities. "Importance" is expressed with marks ranging from "1" (unimportant) to "4" (extremely important). Figure 37.2 shows the median marks and the 95-percent confidence interval.

The figure shows that the only factor classified as decisive for long-term success by more than 90 percent of the interviewees is the quality of academics. The majority of the interviewees stress that this factor is far more important than all others. The second factor that has a significant impact on the long-term development prospects of universities is the ability (qualification and motivation) of students. The form of resource allocation is less important. The majority of the interviewees view resource allocation as a means of developing an innovative and performance-oriented culture within systems and institutions of higher education. Its direct effects on success are very limited. This ranking of factors looks exactly the same at all universities in the study.

These findings can help to explain why universities that work under various funding systems and apply different resource allocation mechanisms show considerably fewer differences with respect to their success in teaching and research. Obviously the six universities examined in this study manage to attract highly qualified faculty. This may be a result of their institutional

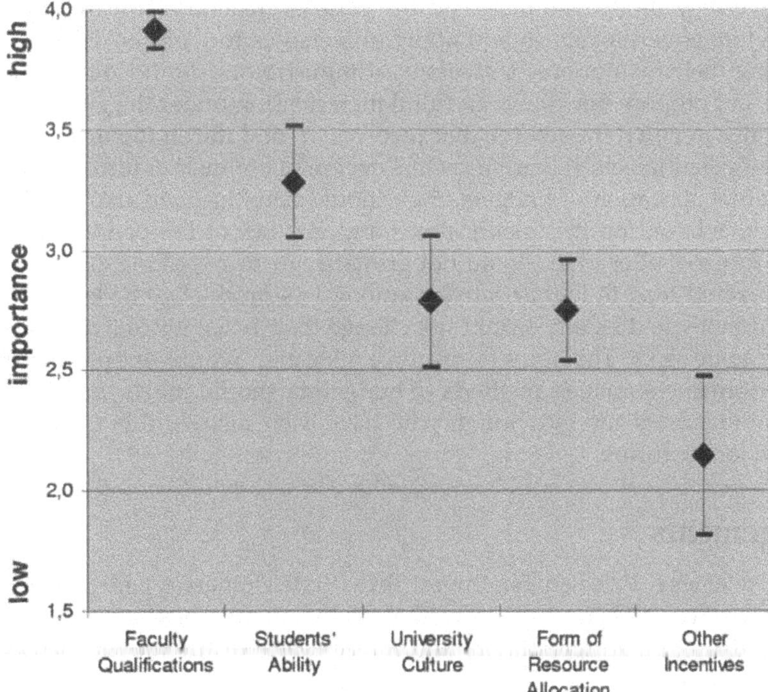

Figure 37.2 Importance of different factors for the long-term success of universities.

Source: Own investigation.

reputation and/or of the environment they offer for research and education. The majority of interviewees argue that a creative environment and a basic infrastructure are essential for attracting qualified people. Hence, existing reputation and success in the past as well as clear institutional goals will have a positive impact on future development. This explains why all six universities are successful institutions despite the enormous differences in the available budget and the form of resource allocation.

The result that the quality of faculty is a crucial factor for success can also be combined with the results of the hypotheses and the findings of the second empirical section. The majority of the interviewees agree that well-qualified people tend to respond less to monetary incentives. Instead they work according to their individual motivation and scientific interests. As they are confident of their scientific capabilities, they need not avoid risks. Faculty that are less motivated might respond to the pressures created with performance-based budgeting, but as they are not highly qualified, the outcome of rising activity will be small. This can explain why the existing effects of performance-based resource allocation on behavior do not lead to obvious differences on the university level. The hypotheses about changes in individual behavior are correct, but the factor "quality of personnel" is decisive for success and dominates the other effects. Universities with a large number of highly motivated and qualified faculty will be successful regardless of the form of resource allocation.

As the form of resource allocation cannot directly influence the long-term success of universities, what else can its function be? First, it can force institutions and individuals to pay attention to the governments and taxpayers who support the institution. Second it can help to adjust the organizational structures of universities more quickly to emerging needs and opportunities. Third it can be used to re-allocate funds to those groups and scholars that have proved to be successful and to reduce the budgets of those who are not performing in an acceptable way.

Policy Implications

This paper has shown that there is obviously no a priori superior approach to successful resource allocation in education and research. Furthermore, the culture and tradition of universities and national HES have only limited influence on the peoples' reactions towards performance-based budgeting. Therefore governments should allow universities to look for different and individual ways of managing their institutions. University administrators should define the basic goals of their institutions and propose how they can fulfill their mission under the given, historically developed, and culturally accepted framework that revolves around the endowment, the reputation, the regional industrial potential, etc. If administrators decide to use market forces or performance measures for the internal allocation of budgets, they should keep in mind that the long-term success of their institution is based on the qualifications and abilities of the people they employ. Therefore the internal forms of allocation should not primarily focus on giving all scholars incentives to work hard. This would lead to higher activity among less-productive or less-motivated scholars. The qualified and motivated faculty would not change their behavior or avoid projects that might be professionally more risky. This form of resource allocation would not produce better results in the long run. Performance-oriented methods of budgeting should make sure that resources could be reallocated to those units and individuals who have been successful in the past or demonstrate excellent promise for the future.

Acknowledgements

I am grateful to Dr. James F. Petersen (Southwest Texas State University), Jill Schneller and Dr. Javier Revilla Diez (University of Hannover), as well as to the anonymous referees for making helpful comments. I also thank the administrators and interviewees of the universities examined in this study for their cooperation.

Note

1. Calculation based on the average 1997 exchange rate of the Frankfurt stock exchange.

References

Arrow, K.J. (1991). 'The economics of agency', in Pratt, J.W. and Zeckhauser, R.J. (eds.), *Principals and Agents: The Structure of Business*, 2nd ed. Boston, pp. 37–51.

Clark, B.R. (1983). *The Higher Education System. Academic Organization in Cross-National Perspective*. Berkeley.

Clark, B.R. (1998). *Creating Entrepreneurial Universities: Organizational Pathways of Transformation*. Pergamon.

Dill, D.D. (1997). 'Higher education markets and public policy', *Higher Education Policy* 10(3/4), 167–185.

Ewers, H.-J. (1996). *Das Elend der Hochschulen—Eine oekonomische Analyse der Organisation und Finanzierung deutscher Universitaeten*. Diskussionspapier, Wirtschaftswissenschaftliche Dokumentation, Fachbereich 14, TU Berlin.

ETH Zurich (1998a). *Jahresbericht* 1997. Zurich.

ETH Zurich (1998b). *Mehrjahresplan 2000–2003 der ETH Zurich*. Zurich.

Flitner, H. (1989). 'Budgetierung', in Karpen, U. (ed.), *Hochschulfinanzierung in der Bundesrepublik Deutschland*. Eine Einfuehrung. Baden-Baden, pp. 145–184.

Geuna, A. (1999). *The Economics of Knowledge Production. Funding and the Structure of University Research*. Cheltenham.

HEFCE (Higher Education Funding Council for England) (1998). *Funding Higher Education in England. How the HEFCE Allocates Its Funds*. November 98/67 Guide, Bristol.

Jongbloed, B. (1998). 'Internal Resource Allocation in Universities', *Presented at the 20th EAIR Forum*, San Sebastian.

Jongbloed, B. and Vossensteyn, H. (1999). 'Performance based research funding. An international comparative perspective'. CHEPS Working Paper for the 12th CHER conference, Oslo.

Laux, H. (1990). *Risiko, Anreiz und Kontrolle. Principal-Agent-Theorie. Einfuehrung und Verbindung mit dem Delegationswert-Konzept*. Heidelberg.

Laux, H. and Liermann, F. (1993). *Grundlagen der Organisation. Die Steuerung von Entscheidungen als Grundproblem der Betriebswirtschaftslehre*, 3rd ed. Berlin.

Layzell, D.T. (1998). 'Linking performance to funding outcomes for public institutions of higher education: The US experience', *European Journal of Education* 33(1), 103–111.

Liefner, I. (2001). *Leistungsorientierte Ressourcensteuerung in Hochschulsystemen. Ein internationaler Vergleich*. Abhandlungen zu Bildungsforschung und Bildungsrecht, Berlin.

Maassen, P. and v. Vught, F. (1994). 'Alternative Models of Governmental Steering in Higher Education', in Goedegebuure, L. and v. Vught, F. (eds.), *Comparative Policy Studies in Higher Education*. Utrecht, pp. 35–63.

Mace, J. (1995). 'Funding matters: A case study of two universities' response to recent funding changes', *Journal of Education Policy* 10(1), 57–74.

McDaniel, O.C. (1997). 'Alternatives to government interference in higher education?', *Higher Education Management* 9(2), 15–133.

MIT (Massachusetts Institute of Technology) (1998). *Budget Book. Fiscal 1999*. Cambridge.

Owlia, M.S. and Aspinwall, E.M. (1996). 'Quality in higher education—a survey', *Total Quality Management* 7(2), 161–171.

Pratt, J.W. and Zeckhauser, R.J. (1991). 'Principals and agents: An overview', in Pratt, J.W. and Zeckhauser, R.J. (eds.), *Principals and Agents: The Structure of Business*. Boston, pp. 1–35.

Reichwald, R. and Koller, H. (1998). 'Zur Organisation der Universitaet der Zukunft. Eine oekonomische Betrachtung aus Sicht der Principal-Agent-Theorie', *Wissenschaftsmanagement* (1), 39–49.

Schmidtlein, F.A. and Taylor, A.L. (1996). 'Responses of American research universities to issues posed by the changing environment of higher education', *Minerva* 34, 291–308.

Schutte, F. (1998). 'Financial resources management'. *Established for the 16th Conference on University Management*, University of Valladolid.

Slaughter, S. and Leslie, L.L. (1997). *Academic Capitalism. Politics, Policies, and the Entrepreneurial University*. Baltimore.

The State of Texas. The Coordinating Board (1998). *General Appropriations Act, 75th Legislature, Article III (Education), Special Provisions*. http://www.thecb.state.tx.us/divisions/finance/uac/formulas9899.htm. 6 August 1999.

Trow, M. (1997). 'Reflections on diversity in higher education', in Herbst, M., Latzel, G. and Lutz, L. (eds.), *Wandel im tertiaeren Bildungssektor. Zur Position der Schweiz im internationalen Vergleich*. Zurich, pp. 15–36.

University of Basel (1998). *Jahresbericht* 1997. Basel.

University of Basel (1999). *Makroschwerpunkte der Forschung. Bericht der Konzeptkommission. Januar* 1999. http://www.zuv.unibas.ch/forschung/makro/bericht_konzkomm.html. 31 December 1999.

University of Bristol (1998a). *Financial Statements 1997–1998*. Bristol.

University of Bristol (1998b). *Resource Allocation Model*. Bristol.

University of Bristol (1999). Bristol University Resource Allocation Model 1999/00 Budget (unpublished).

University of Twente (1998a). *Annual Report 1997*. Enschede: University of Twente.

University of Twente (1998b). *Begroting 1999*. Enschede: Universiteit Twente.

US News (2000a). *2000 College Rankings*. http://www.usnews.com/usnews/edu/beyond/gradrank/eng/gdengt1.htm. 19 October 2000.

US News (2000b). *2000 College Rankings*. http://www.usnews.com/usnews/edu/college/rankings/natunivs/natu_a2.htm. 19 October 2000.

UT Austin (The University of Texas at Austin) (1998). *Financial Statements* (unpublished).

UT Austin (The University of Texas at Austin. Office of Institutional Studies) (1999). *Statistical Handbook 1998–1999*. Austin.

van Vught, F.A. (1997). 'Combining planning and the market: An analysis of the Government strategy towards higher education in the Netherlands', *Higher Education Policy* 10(3/4), 211–224.

Wagner, A. (1996). 'Financing higher education: New approaches, new issues', *Higher Education Management* 8(1), 7–17.

Williams, G. (1997). 'The market route to mass higher education: British experience 1979–1996', *Higher Education Policy* 10(3/4), 275–289.

Chapter 38

Linking Strategic Planning, Priorities, Resource Allocation, and Assessment

Brenda S. Trettel and John L. Yeager

Introduction

During the second half of the twentieth century, community college missions have expanded and changed. Today's community college missions require its leaders to understand the changes in their complex work environment, including the symbiotic relationship that exists between the college and the community that it serves. Such an understanding allows leaders to continuously change and adapt to external and internal challenges (American Association of Community Colleges [AACC] 2009). At the same time, the state and sometimes local government have direct influence and interest in the colleges' financing and an indirect influence on governance structures and operations. It is this consortium of interests of state, local community, and business and industry that contribute to uniqueness, strength, and challenges of these institutions.

This chapter examines strategic and financial management best practices while offering insights that may help community colleges to better align their missions, programs, and resources through the integration of select management functions. It should be noted that many community colleges operate under various organizational and governance systems. We recognize that no single model that fits all situations, and there is a need for modification of our approach to fit each college's realities.

Community College Management

As these institutions grew in size and complexity, they required an increased administrative sophistication in order to successfully manage their operations. This represented an additional challenge at the outset. Many colleges were initially under the leadership of administrators and faculty who were not specifically trained to lead or operate these new organizations. Many of the professional staff came from public schools, two-year institutions, four-year institutions, the public sector, and business and industry. Naturally, they used tools and skills they found to work in their previous positions and to the degree possible, and modified them to fit the challenges encountered in the community college setting. This presented a situation where some of the major institutional decision-makers had a mixture of management training and many different individual perspectives as to how a community college should be administered. Finally, each institution was embedded in the culture of its immediate community and operated under the legal and political systems in the state that they resided.

The Institutional Planning and Budget Management Process

Institutional management partially links the five components of the management process: (1) strategic planning, (2) resource allocation, (3) implementation, (4) assessment, and (5) dissemination of information. In many cases, these functions have been treated as separate and almost discrete functions or *silos*. For some leaders the silos mentality is an intentional choice but nonetheless represents a lack of conceptual integration that has led institutions to develop inefficient and ineffective management practices resulting in suboptimization of their resources in support of program activities.

Silo orientation of management functions often inhibit an institution from achieving its desired outcomes and prohibiting the transparency of operations. While conceptually it is a relatively simplistic task to link the several functions in practice, in reality, it is a major challenge. The evolution of enterprise financial management software systems create opportunities to integrate partially connected silos. Under conditions of restricted resources, competition for resources becomes a major distracter in the procurement and allocation of program funds.

Institutional Strategic Planning

Strategic planning provides the foundation and direction for other organizational activities. Mintzenberg (1994, 109) states: "strategic thinking is about synthesis." The outcome of strategic thinking is an integrated perspective of the enterprise, and vision of direction. It does not happen just because a meeting was held titled with that label. To the contrary, designing a strategy is a process interwoven with all the pieces needed to manage an organization. Strategy-making offers exceptional potential as a silo buster at the enterprise level. It is essential that the strategic planning be successfully completed as a basis for all functional areas to design their goals and implementation plans.

The strategic plan does not represent a blueprint cast in concrete but rather an interactive baseline that can respond to both external and internal changes through clarifying institutional priorities and as a foundation for ascertaining and measuring the degree of success in meeting intended outcomes. The development of a community college strategic plan represents three particular institutional challenges. First, strategic plans usually cover a multiyear time period ranging from three to five years. This time period does not coincide with the many community college programs that are a mixture of diplomas, certificates, and two-year programs, resulting in shorter planning periods and implementation. Hence, it is important that faculty be involved in the planning process. This is a difficult proposition since a large number of community college faculty and students are part-time, reducing available planning time and causing possible interruptions in faculty input year on year. The second challenge is that due to the multiplicity of sponsorships and stakeholders, consensus at the program level is often difficult to achieve although collegial efforts help reconcile divergent perspectives. Finally, communications and buy-in of the strategic plan is important especially in multicampus community colleges because of logistics, culture, busy schedules, and faculty governance systems.

Organization

Most institutional strategic planning, while conducted under the direction of the president with the approval of the board of directors, involves an active steering committee that includes key faculty, staff, and administrators. This offers an additional dimension of involvement. The steering committee is responsible for the oversight of the planning process including the appointment of working committees, such as student affairs, workforce development, facilities, finance emphasis, among others, which approve timeframes, components of the plan and make recommendations to the president. Often the planning forums are open to the public and actively engage a variety of stakeholders.

Size

These committees typically range in size from between 10 and 20 individuals. While the size of these committees often reflects the desire of the institution's leadership to insure a sufficient degree of institutional representation, we recommend that committees consist of approximately 15 members (Rowley and Sherman 2001). Larger committees are often difficult to manage and the representation of a multiplicity of agendas makes it difficult to reach consensus. The literature, however, does not have consensus on this issue as illustrated by the Planning Advisory Council at Carroll Community College, which had 27 members and was able to successfully lead their planning process (Clagett 2004, 114).

Plan-to-Plan

The plan-to-plan remains the primary function and is a road map for the development of specific timelines and directives for plan coordination. This includes the rationale for developing the plan, planning assumptions, organizational units to be included, timeframe, and tasks of the roles and responsibilities of institutional participants, committee structure, a communication plan, and specification of resources for developing the plan. At a minimum, this plan contains a number of components such as (1) background/context for planning; (2) situational analysis that includes external scan, internal analysis, and competitor analysis; (3) vision and mission statements; (4) goals and objectives; (5) strategic initiatives; (6) resource availability; (7) implementation guidelines; and (8) plan assessment. The plan-to-plan can be developed at both the institutional and suborganizational levels such as departments or administrative units. The resulting plan therefore consists of a set of interrelated planning and processing components with each level contributing to the total plan.

Key resources such as past accreditation studies, college reports to the board of directors, and specialized academic and management reports from the institutional research offices inform the plan-to-plan. Further, both the institutional research and the budget offices have detailed longitudinal enrollment, student, and financial information available that is important for development of the plan. Finally, previous strategic plans as well as plans from leading community colleges should be examined.

Positions the Institution within Its Operating Environment

The strategic plan identifies and evaluates external and internal events and trends that might impact the institution within "situational analysis." Environmental scans, internal reviews and competitor analysis should include assessments of probability and the degree of impact that each trend or perception of reality might have on the institution's mission and operations. This process is usually conducted within a framework that permits each trend or event to be categorized into predetermined groups. A typical system is referred to by the acronym, political, economic, social, and technology or in an expanded version, social, technical, economic, educational, and political and assists the college in organizing trends and events that are identified in the external environment.

Of high importance is the review of the college's vision, mission, goals, and values and when appropriate to update them to reflect the information obtained from the situational analysis where there is agreement and support among the stakeholders since missions change due to limited or decreasing resources. The American Productivity and Quality Center (1996) recommends several best practices that are important for community colleges to consider when developing strategic plans. The following six best practices have provided guidance in the development of institutional strategic plans for almost 15 years, and remain relevant: (1) stretch goals that drive strategic out-of-the-box thinking, (2) keep planning processes flexibility to reflect a continuous improvement philosophy, (3) formalize the communication process, (4) emphasize action plans and strategic thinking, (5) explicitly recognize strategic planning as a key element in the management system, and (6) document the strategic thinking process.

Therefore, the strategic planning process can serve as a framework for several specialized institutional subplans such as technology, facilities, enrollment, human resources, financial, and development plans. An important aspect of this process is to have the strategic plan be aligned with the budget.

The Resource Allocation Process

The strategic plan identifies priorities that are required to implement an appropriate resource allocation program based upon the institution's vision and mission. This becomes a key connection between the institution's strategic plan and the allocation process. The specification of a hierarchy of priorities offers a basis upon which to embark upon a resource allocation process.

Institutions that do not systematically define these important priorities, except in general terms, leave room for misinterpretations or misallocation of resources. Community colleges may elect to place programs or activities in general categories such as imperative, important, and highly desirable rather than in specific rank order. These assessments and assignments are determined based on perceived institutional mission relevance, previous or continuing commitment, current outcome attainment, and contribution to institutional prestige. This process is important in assisting to differentiate for funding purposes between the various program activities. It is typical that departments are requested to submit resource requests to the central administration in terms of the programs to be supported and their intended outcomes as well as a justification of the amount of funds requested. Too often the amount of funds requested are not in close alignment with the activities to be supported or the intended outcomes are approximations of the department head's or dean's requirements, which can be overly ambitious. In too many instances, little effort is made to examine program need requests in a comprehensive manner in terms of costs and relative outcomes.

Regular and periodic program review information can be used to augment or inform resource allocation decision. The resource decision process becomes even more complicated when both new programs and existing programs are considered in the same mix. While in many cases, institutions have made decisions concerning the relative merits of existing programs utilizing separate executive committees or specially appointed faculty/administrative resource allocation program committees. A more inclusive process to such decisions should be considered when choosing program trade-offs among new and existing programs.

One such process would apply a type of a decision tree model to assist in establishing relative program trade-offs considering program characteristics such as mission alignment, perceived program quality, costs, and competitive advantage. One example is the multiple attribute decision model, which proposes a methodology of assessing programs through the use of both qualitative and quantitative measures and provides a mechanism for comparing programs based on a framework of predetermined dimensions and weightings (Lasher and Greene 1993). This process assists the institution in determining the relative priorities of programs to serve as a basis for resource assignment. With this information, it is then possible to consider program allocation of funds.

Most institutions of higher education focus the majority of their "budgetary" attention on the distribution of funds among the several activities of the institution that may not be linked to the strategic plan or reflect institutional priorities. Hence, focus on "fund distribution" can actively distract from the important consideration of how the institution should maintain each of its major assets such as the faculty and staff, facilities, grounds, equipment, libraries, and image and reputation (Jones 1993, 8). Several of the most common methodologies for institutional resource allocation are incremental, formula, cost/revenue center, zero-base budgeting, and performance budgeting (Lasher and Greene 1993). In most cases, these methodologies have been borrowed from the business and industry sector, and are not usually applied in isolation but in combination with other methods and characteristics attempting to meet specific institutional needs. Of these approaches, the incremental process is the most widely used. This method in general assumes that the previous base budget of the entities is an appropriate allocation and adjustments are made incrementally to that base budget. For example, an institution might increase all budgets by a fixed amount or percentage. The focus of this process is on the increment or decrement and not on the unit's base budget. Colleges often reduce the previous year's expenditures by a fixed percentage that is used to establish a reserve fund to support new initiatives or to provide for areas of extraordinary need after which budgets are then adjusted on an incremental basis. A major advantage of this process is that it is easily understood and provides a significant amount of flexibility and discretion to the administrative decision process. A major disadvantage is that almost all the attention is focused on the size of the increment and not on the total amount being allocated. Often times once the budget increment has been announced, there is a tendency to give the increment without a careful analysis of exactly how the increment will be spent. In addition and most important, there is often only little attention given to how the base budget will be expended and the degree to which it is needed and to support the institution's mission.

Zero-based budgeting is an alternative process that requires the annual rebuilding and justification of each aspect of a specific unit budget. While this is an appropriate procedure, it is a difficult and time-consuming process since each section of the budget requires justification. Because of the potential benefits that can be derived by using zero-based budgeting, many colleges only examine selected areas on alternate years or the documentation process is truncated and not all costing and outcome estimates are provided in detail. Although not perfect, other factors such as tenure make the application of zero-based budgeting more difficult. These modifications provide important information in terms of the resource allocation process.

While many states distribute funding to community colleges based on various types of formulas, such as the number of students or credit hours generated, faculty positions, among others, community colleges do not internally disburse funds in a similar manner unless stipulated to do so by specific regulations. Internal allocation decisions are typically done based on demonstrated need for activities such as number of classes and sections to be offered, support services to be offered, previous commitments, and program continuations. These decisions consider previous plans and agreed upon initiatives as well as the feedback of performance information. While many states use formula-based budget allocation practices, formulas are used as method of distributing funding and not as a method of determining the amount of program funding required by a community college. While the stated needs of the institution, funding line item weightings, and the availability of state funds drive the format, there are many others that are unique to each state.

The college operating budget allocation process is done on an annual basis and represents a carefully orchestrated process since multiple revenue streams and changing expenditures must be comingled and integrated into an overall institutional budget plan within a specified time frame. While the process is usually annual, many institutions develop multiyear budget plans to more adequately assess current and future years of budget commitment although those budgets after the first year are for planning purposes only. Institutions have a number of revenue streams such as tuition, awarded contracts and grant allocations, state support, and local support from municipal governments, local businesses, alumni, and foundations. While many of the funding streams have restrictions, in total they provide a significant degree of latitude in terms of expenditures to permit management flexibility. Therefore to maximize allocations and program flexibility to any specific budget unit, the allocation must carefully consider and specify not only the amount of funds but the source of funding in terms of restricted and unrestricted funds.

While tuition is a critical source of funding, it is subject to the variability associated with enrollment levels. Some institutions have attempted to stabilize the estimated tuition portion of the budget through the implementation of a deregistration process. This process requires students to pay their tuition by a predetermined date before the semester starts to hold their class selections. The payment can be made through cash or a credit card by a student signing up for a payment plan and applying for financial aid and grants. If a student does not arrange some type of payment plan, they lose their class schedule after a date predetermined by the college. This permits the institution to monitor enrollments and tuition income immediately prior to the beginning of classes. The Community College of Allegheny County (CCAC) employs such a practice (CCAC 2009).

Plan Implementation and Monitoring

It is critical that the faculty and staff must be actively engaged in the development of the strategic plan and its implementation. To ensure faculty and staff input, community colleges should establish advisory committees with representation from faculty, staff, and administration to assist in the planning and allocation processes. This input is valuable in providing user feedback on decisions and to obtain information to assess the impact that various decisions might have on schools, departments, and individuals. Often frontline managers, faculty, and staff have a much clearer understanding of where the application of additional resources may have the greatest benefits or where reductions can be made without adversely affecting operations. This makes it imperative that the college administration, in order to make the best possible decisions, involves institutional-wide participation in the budget and plan implementation process. Therefore, it is important the institution members have a substantial understanding of why certain decisions were made. It is only through participation in the budget development process that individuals can gain understanding of both the decision process supporting budget development and program plan implementation.

Administrators and faculty are key planners and implementers of any program plan and have intimate knowledge as to the potential relative success and failure of programs. This information is particularly valuable when a college is confronted with fiscal difficulties and must reduce or eliminate programs.

Once program and resource decisions have been implemented, the monitoring process becomes critical to achieving key institutional outcomes. This requires the operating unit conducting the purposed activity to provide a monitoring system to assess progress and monitor program outcomes. One tool that has been found to be of assistance in performing this function is the creation of an institutional *performance dashboard*, which provides senior management with frequent timely snapshots of institutional performance data. These systems can be institutionally developed or commercially purchased. One partial shortcoming for the implementation of an assessment system is the fact that many community colleges do not have operational institutional research offices and college staff are often not trained to develop and maintain monitoring programs.

In a similar manner, monitoring processes have to be established for the institution's various financial income and expenditures. The institution's various income streams must be carefully estimated and charted throughout the course of the budget year and based on new information adjusted in terms of budget availability and program expenditures. One difficulty in establishing a monitoring process is that readily available operational data is not collected in a timely manner. Additionally, information support of identifying program performance and executive decision-making are often not available. It is important that most monitoring data show planned status versus operating status. For example, it is important that the college carefully projects and monitors its end-of-year fund balance. Colleges must be aware both as to potential budget surpluses as well as deficits since to only through such actions can sustain its short-term and long-term fiscal viability. Institutions should monitor planned revenue and expenditures on a monthly or quarterly basis using percentage estimates as benchmarks while a few use a composite of past year averages to develop benchmarks of patterns of revenues and expenditures. The purpose of these actions is to determine the amount of variances that are occurring between planned fiscal projections and actual expenditure (Capone 1991). The monitoring process can be done both at the college level as well as the department level. Finally, many colleges use the annual budget process, which oftentimes commences approximately half way through the fiscal year to collect monitoring data on program performance. It becomes essential information in the preparation of next year's budget.

Plan Assessment

A final function of the financial management process is evaluation/assessment. There are a variety of forms, each with their own unique characteristics. While this is a critical function, it is often not performed in a rigorous manner, and it is also not practiced by all community colleges. Hence, this section will identify processes to strengthen this element and to connect program outcomes to mission and goals. Measurement at this level is often difficult to formulate and successfully complete. The information that can be obtained from this process is essential for determining the degree the strategic plan is being successfully implemented. If the plan is not appropriately implemented, there is little chance that it can be successful. Once the strategic plan has been completed but before it is implemented, it is important to development an assessment plan. The assessment plan should include the frequency of assessment, what is to be assessed, who will conduct the assessment, the type of information to be collected, and what will be done with the result. Since strategic plans are multiyear in construction, assessments need not be conducted on an annual basis. These assessments are summative in nature since the organization has other processes in place to obtain formative assessment information such as budget reviews, accreditations, and specialized studies.

Outcome measures, as defined by key performance indicators (KPIs), represent one approach that could provide both quantitative and qualitative information, thereby providing critical information concerning the achievement of several of the most important institutional areas. Too often the resources required to obtain this information are considered low priority in relationships to other institutional needs and often times unorganized subjective information substitutes for formal evaluation. This information is collected only when a major review is conducted such as an accreditation or a program review to determine whether or not a program should be discontinued (Aloi 2005).

Since the 1970s, all institutions of higher education are facing increased scrutiny in terms of program outcomes and fiscal accountability. Community colleges have not escaped this accountability. In fact, because of their multiple missions and funding, programs and all of their activities have increasingly been questioned in terms of their financial stewardship and their program effectiveness and efficiency. There is a great deal of interest by the general public, state and regional governments, business and accreditation agencies in community college accountability. Programs are being reviewed and evidence sought as to the degree they achieve their stated mission particularly in terms of student access, retention, and graduation rates.

Dissemination of Information

Dissemination of information is critical to the success of the institutional strategic management process. This provides a holistic interpretation that we profile as important for all future management plans. All institutional members, faculty, staff, and administrators need to be fully aware and informed of the mission and direction of the community college for the college to be successful. It is essential that the resulting outcomes be widely disseminated and discussed—the pursuit of the college's mission is everyone's responsibility. There are many ways to disseminate information. Mailings, email, posters, newsletters, presentations, and other formal and informal means of communication are all appropriate to provide information to faculty and staff

Further at the end of the fiscal year and/or the planning period, the results should be reviewed and disseminated and where necessary plans should be revised. This is also an appropriate time to review planned goals and activities. These results should then be directed back into the fiscal and program management system and where necessary appropriate revisions made. As a final step, the results of the previous planning period and the revised plans should be discussed with institutional constituents and a revised strategic plan prepared.

Examples of Fiscal Management Systems

There are numerous examples of effective community college management systems that have been developed and implemented. One such institution, the Collin County Community College District located in North Texas, was able to successfully address several fiscal challenges through a disciplined implementation of an integrated management system (Tambrino 2001). Its strategic planning scanning process permitted them to identify potential fiscal problems in time to make adjustments and to develop a multiyear response plan. This awareness was accomplished through the addition of tracking such new factors as the volume of food stamps being distributed in the county along with home foreclosures, appraised property tax growth, and indigent health care claims. This new scanning information was then used to inform resource planning activities, which led to analysis and changes in instructional costs and reductions in a timely manner that permitted the college to make appropriate budgetary reductions. In addition to reducing costs, scanning assisted the institution in developing new funding streams such as charging for the use of college facilities by outside organizations. Also the college as a result of its revised planning process reexamined its budgeting process and decided that its previous incremental process needed to be replaced, one that clearly placed greater responsibility on budget managers. To that end, a form of zero-based budgeting was implemented coupled with open hearings that assisted in breaking down the silo effect through the sharing of budgetary information. This revised process helped to identify duplication of funding support that permitted greater institutional flexibility of program funding and provided broader and better information to the budget managers, a valuable educational process. A major lesson learned was the power of communication and the importance of focusing on the college's mission, goals, and strategic plan were of high importance in the financial and program management of the institution. The Collin Community College financial and program management system is an excellent example of an institution gaining greater efficiency and effectiveness through the integration of key management functions.

Another example is Iowa Valley Community College District, which consists of three separate operating units—two colleges, a continuing education unit, and a central office (Israel and Kihl 2006). This institution had previously experienced near fiscal bankruptcy in the early 1990s and implemented a contribution margin budget (CMB) system, which is a modification of a more generic responsibility central budgeting process. Under the CMB system, an institution empowers a unit budget manager to more actively manage institutional and program matters by making them responsible for all income and expenditures for their units. As a result of using a CMB system, the deans, division chairs, and faculty members of the colleges and schools are vested with fiscal responsibility in line with their academic authority. Each unit is responsible for developing and establishing their own budget. As a result of these efforts, Iowa Valley Community College ranks first in the state's community colleges with regards to fund balance as a percentage of operating expenditures (Israel and Kihl 2006).

Conclusion

Community college performance can be enhanced and assets maintained through the implementation of a comprehensive planning and management system that links strategic planning, resource allocation, plan implementation, and assessment. Each of these processes plays a significant role in the effective management of the institution. Strategic planning sets the baseline, describes the future directions of the institution, compares resource allocation trade-offs, and enables community colleges to evaluate progress towards mission achievement. However, to maximize the benefits of this process, it is important that all community college stakeholders—trustees, administrators, faculty, staff, students, and the general public they serve—be included in the planning and development of the process. All aspects of the four major functions and their associate linkages must be public and transparent, since it is only with such inclusion that the community college can achieve its mission. It is through the coupling of these processes a college has the ability to better understand and manage its various programs and resources through a comprehensive linking and selective integration of its management functions. This chapter has offered an enhanced model that is supportive of a rational system for aligning financial and other resources with college priorities embedded in the plan.

References

Aloi, Susan L. 2005. "Best Practices in Linking Assessment and Planning." *Assessment Update* 17 (3): 4–6.

American Association of Community Colleges (AACC). 2009. *Community College Past to Present*. Washington. DC: AACC. Available online at: http://www.aacc.nche.edu.

AACC. 2009. *Fast Facts*. Washington, DC: AACC. Available online at: http://www.aacc.nche.edu/AboutCC/Pages/fastfacts.aspx

American Productivity and Quality Center. 1996. *Strategic Planning: Final Report*. Houston: American Productivity and Quality Center.

Capone, F. W. Hendricks, and Ray Pohlman. 1991. *Building Budget Skills*, ed. rev. Shawnee Mission, KS: National Press Publications.

Clagett, Craig A. 2004. "Strategic Planning Carroll Community College." *New Directions for Institutional Research* 123: 114–120.

Community College of Allegheny County (CCAC). 2009. *Payment Due Dates for Credit Courses*. Pittsburgh: CCAC. Available online at: http://www.ccac.edu.

Israel, Carr A., and Brenda Kihl. 2006. "Using Strategic Planning to Transform a Budgeting Process." *New Directions for Community Colleges* 2006 (132): 77–86.

Jones, Dennis P. 1993. "Strategic Budgeting." In *Financial Management: Progress and Challenges (No. 83)*, ed. W. E. Vandament and D. P. Jones. San Francisco, CA: Jossey-Bass.

Lasher, William F., and Deborah L. Greene. 1993. "College and University Budgeting: What Do We Know? What Do We Need to Know?" In *Higher Education Handbook of Theory and Research (No. 9)*, ed. J. Smart. New York: Agathon Press.

Mitzenberg, Henry. 1994. "The Rise and Fall of Strategic Planning: *Harvard Business Review* 72 (1): 107–114.

Rowley, Daniel J., and Herbert Sherman. 2001. *From Strategy to Change: Implementing the Plan in Higher Education*. San Francisco. CA: Jossey-Bass.

Tambrino, Paul A. 2001. "Contribution Margin Budgeting." *Community College Journal of Research and Practice* 25 (1): 29–36.

SECTION VII

ETHICS AND HIGHER EDUCATION FINANCING

Introduction to Section VII

Michael G. Gunzenhauser and Laurie Cohen
University of Pittsburgh

Several years after the most recent global economic recession, institutions of higher education continue to face new financial challenges, among them rising costs, tighter competition, and declining budgetary support from state and federal governments. College and university personnel are called upon to be frugal stewards of public resources and entrepreneurial in the pursuit of new funding sources. Calls for accountability in all forms drive new fiscal practices and governance arrangements.

Higher education officials are expected to act ethically in light of all these challenges and to protect their institutions from all manner of financial exigencies—lawsuits, risky investments, and deep cuts in support from legislatures, just to name a few. As the articles in this section suggest, college and university officials may not be as prepared as they need to be for the moral and ethical challenges ahead. Changing financial times and the complexity of today's higher education institutions make ethical guidance now more important than ever. The works of the selected authors also tell us that changing times also have implications for the aims and values served by higher education.

The work in this section addresses two complementary considerations: ethical practices in areas related to higher education finance and moral implications of changing financial times. Renewed interest from higher education scholars and practitioners in ethical theory and standards of professional practice have provided the editors of the Third Edition with a wide array of scholarship to consider for the section. The editorial team began with a broad consideration of the issues and concerns that contribute to finance in higher education, to include fundraising, enrollment management, competition, globalization, public support for education, entrepreneurialism, and professional integrity. In each of the selections, authors present perspectives on the moral and ethical implications of one or more of these current challenges. All have implications for the financial well being of the university. The selections represent a range of scholarly approaches, with empirical studies, philosophical essays, and original reviews of research literature included.

Drawing from philosophical traditions in ethics and taking a social psychological perspective, Batson ("Why Act for the Public Good? Four Answers") sets the tone for this section by defining the concept of the public good and how it relates to the workings of institutions. He explains four varied justifications for the public good: egoism, collectivism, altruism, and principalism, as ways of thinking about the benefits and dangers associated with philosophically distinct motivations for acting in the public interest. The practitioner who can appreciate multiple motivations for acting in the public interest may be a more effective collaborator with various constituents, Batson suggests, particularly when motivations come into conflict. This essay was also included in the Second Edition of the *ASHE Reader on Finance in Higher Education*.

The next selection reports from a survey of financial officers in higher education institutions on the prevalence and use of ethical codes. Rezaee, Elmore, and Szendi ("Ethical Behavior in Higher Educational Institutions: The Role of the Code of Conduct") find that while many institutions have codes of conduct, rarely are the codes systematically enforced. The authors analyze codes of ethics in terms of how they follow a "high road" or "low road" and whether they are directly or indirectly related to specific practices. Implementation is generally rare, and the researchers found that codes of ethics in practice have very limited content intended to prevent particular financial indiscretions.

Caboni ("The Normative Structure of College and University Fundraising Behaviors"), a scholar and administrator, focuses on fundraising. Drawing from the sociology of professions, Caboni addresses fundraising as an emerging profession, evident in its lack of previously determined categories of inviolable norms. Caboni seeks to identify both inviolable and admonitory norms currently at work in the profession by surveying members of the Council for the Advancement and Support of Education (CASE) and analyzing their responses in relation to the standards CASE published in 2005. The three resulting inviolable norms—exploitation of resources, institutional disregard, and misappropriation of gifts—exemplify a recurring ethical concern among fundraisers to respect the needs and interests of both institutions and donors simultaneously.

The remaining articles address various moral implications of changing contexts in higher education finance. Eastman ("Revenue Generation and Its Consequences for Academic Capital, Values and Autonomy: Insights from Canada") addresses new contexts in higher education: the decreased public funding for higher education, the decentralization of educational resources within units, and the turn to responsibility-centered budgeting. In a comparative case study at four Canadian universities, Eastman studies how seeking alternate revenue streams has affected the internal values of institutions and the conflict between academic values and commercial considerations. She focuses on the ways in which institutions have adjusted to this phenomenon and placed academic values in relation to externally derived values, such as in the research-focused universities in her study, seeking entrepreneurial ways to generate revenue that support the cultural production of research faculty.

African-American students are the focus of the next selection, as students confront the rising cost of college and the changing dynamics of affirmative action in college admissions. St. John, Paulsen, and Carter ("Diversity, College Costs, and Postsecondary Opportunity: An Examination of the Financial Nexus between College Choice and Persistence for African Americans and Whites") develop a financial-nexus model to explain how students respond to costs, particularly how it affects their decision of where to attend college and the extent to which they will persist. They show how these processes vary across groups, with a main finding that cost and aid strongly affect choice and persistence for African-American students, leading to implications for policy and higher education finance.

Giroux ("Neoliberalism, Corporate Culture, and the Promise of Higher Education: The University as a Democratic Public Sphere") critiques the ideology of neo-liberalism at play in universities in his contribution. Giroux begins with an argument for the public good of universities and goes on to argue for the democratic contributions of higher education and how neo-liberalism and corporate culture influence practices that alter notions of citizenship along lines of consumption and private gain. Giroux identifies the dangers of public goals derived from appeal to egoistic, individualistic interests. Drawing from philosophy, social theory, and cultural studies, Giroux's scholarship uses examples from U.S. universities and addresses implications for students, faculty, and administrators in higher education.

Similarly concerned with the interaction of academic and corporate interests, the final selection is a case study of a single university department with significant connections to industry. Mendoza and Berger ("Academic Capitalism and Academic Culture: A Case Study") describe academic capitalism as a phenomenon that Eastman describes as "the generation of revenue through market-oriented partnerships and ventures." Mendoza and Berger selected the materials science department for this case study for the apparent ability of its faculty to embrace multiple logics—among them distinct academic and industrial logics—through carefully negotiated grants and contracts. Significant to the case are conditions of the particular department that enable faculty to protect their graduate students from industrial influence. Because of their strong reputation, their cohesive academic culture, and enough funding opportunities to be discriminating, faculty are able to reject grants or contracts that do not serve the academic mission of the department. Conflicts actually come into play when universities see grant-seeking as a money-making venture that conflicts with faculty academic goals. The authors note trends that may complicate conditions, especially elsewhere in less-ideal situations, and suggest policy implications.

CHAPTER 39

WHY ACT FOR THE PUBLIC GOOD? FOUR ANSWERS

C. DANIEL BATSON

A conceptual analysis is offered that differentiates four motives for acting for the public good: egoism, collectivism, altruism, and principlism. Differentiation is based on identification of a unique ultimate goal for each motive. For egoism, the ultimate goal is self-benefit; for collectivism, it is to increase group welfare; for altruism, to increase one or more other individuals' welfare; for principlism, to uphold one or more moral principles. Advocates claim that these last three motives cannot be reduced to egoism. Evidence for this claim is limited, however, especially for collectivism and principlism. It is hoped that the conceptual distinctions proposed will permit broader, more precise empirical study of nonegoistic motives for acting for the public good.

Failure to act for the public good has created major social problems. As the population continues to explode, acting in ways that suit our own self-interests—or whims—without considering the consequences for others has led to crisis after crisis: trash-littered public parks, streets, and highways; polluted rivers and streams; dropping water tables and shrinking reservoirs; vanishing rain forests; the continuing slaughter of whales; reduced social services and underfunded schools; free riders who enjoy public TV but do not ante up.

Yet these crises are only half the picture. There are times when we do act for the public good. We do, at times, pick up litter; we do recycle, carpool, and vote; we do contribute to public TV and the United Fund. We do help one another, and we do serve as volunteers in hospitals, nursing homes, AIDS hospices, fire departments, and rescue squads.

Acting for the public good, as I am using the phrase, means acting to increase the welfare of some person or persons other than oneself, thereby increasing the total welfare in society. In this sense, the public good includes not only economists' *public goods,* goods that can be used by more than one person (roads, parks, information, clean air, etc.), but also *private goods,* goods that can be used by only one person (food, clothing, shelter, rescue from danger, a comforting hug, etc.), if provided to others (Sen, 1977). Helping another individual is included within the present conception of the public good, or not, depending on whether, on balance, this help increases the total welfare in society, or not. One might argue that increasing one's own personal good increases the total welfare in society and therefore should also be considered acting for the public good. So it does; but the reason for speaking of public good is precisely to contrast it with exclusive regard for one's own personal good.

If not acting for the public good has created major problems for society, then acting for the public good has also created major problems—for behavioral and social scientists. The problems concern why people do it. It seems to violate an assumption about human motivation that has been foundational for virtually all major accounts of human action in psychology, sociology, economics, and political science. The assumption is that all human action is ultimately directed toward self-interest (Campbell, 1975; Mansbridge, 1990). Ecologist and social-policy analyst Garrett Hardin (1977) elevated this assumption to what he called the Cardinal Rule of Policy: "Never ask a person to act against his own self-interest" (p. 27).

Why Act for the Public Good?

If self-interest motivates all human action, then why do people act for the public good? Over the last decade or so, this question has been asked with increasing frequency and acuity by a small number of behavioral and social scientists (see Mansbridge, 1990, for a useful sampling). In general, those asking this question all agree on two points: (a) Self-interest is an important motivator of human action, including action for the public good; (b) self-interest is not the only motive for acting for the public good. There is far less agreement, however, on what the motive or motives other than self-interest are.

One might think that social psychologists could clarify matters, that we could speak with authority on the nature and scope of motives for acting for the public good. Unfortunately, we have had relatively little to say. Unable as yet to speak with clarity, this essay is more at the stage of clearing one's throat.

Four Answers

Reflection on the research and writings of others, as well as on some of my own research on empathy and altruism (Batson, 1991), leads me to suggest four answers to why we act for the public good. Each of these answers is based on a different motive. Following Lewin (1951), I am thinking of motives as goal-directed forces, and in this context it is important to distinguish among instrumental goals, ultimate goals, and unintended consequences. An *instrumental goal* is sought as a means to reach some other goal; an *ultimate goal* is sought as an end in itself; an *unintended consequence* is a result of acting to reach a goal but is not itself sought as a goal. It is the ultimate goal that defines a motive; each different motive has a unique ultimate goal.

The four different motives for acting for the public good that I wish to consider are egoism, collectivism, altruism, and what—for lack of an existing term—I shall call principlism. I wish to suggest that each of these motives is possible, even plausible, and that each has its own unique ultimate goal, as well as its own distinct promise and problems as a source of action for the public good. I believe that an adequate answer to the question of why we act for the public good needs to consider all four. It needs to consider not only the existence of each but also their interplay.

Egoism: Serving the Public Good to Benefit Oneself

The most obvious and parsimonious answer to why we act for the public good, given the pervasive assumption that all human action is motivated by self-interest, is *egoism*. A motive is egoistic if the ultimate goal is to increase the actor's own welfare. Action that serves the public good can be egoistically motivated if this action serves either as an instrumental goal on the way to or as an unintended consequence of reaching the ultimate goal of self-benefit. A philanthropist may endow a hospital or university to gain recognition and a form of immortality; a capitalist, nudged by the Invisible Hand, may create jobs and enhance the standard of living by relentless pursuit of personal fortune. Both are egoistically motivated.

Self-Benefits That Can Be the Ultimate Goal of Acting for the Public Good

A number of self-benefits can be the ultimate goal of acting for the public good. Most obvious, perhaps, are material, social, and self-rewards (e.g., monetary reward, praise, esteem enhancement) and avoidance of material, social, and self-punishments (e.g., fines, censure, guilt, shame).

When one looks beyond the immediate situation to consider long-term consequences and intangible benefits of one's action, self-interest becomes *enlightened*. From an enlightened perspective, one may see that headlong pursuit of self-interest will lead to less long-term personal gain than will acting for the public good, and so one may decide to act for the public good as a means of reaching the ultimate goal of maximizing self-benefit. Appeals to enlightened self-interest are often used by politicians and social activists trying to encourage action for the public good: They warn us of the eventual consequences for ourselves and our children of pollution or of squandering natural resources; they remind us that if the plight of the poor becomes too severe, we may face revolution. The motive they seek to evoke is egoism, our enlightened self-interest.

Nontangible self-benefits of acting for the public good have sometimes been called *side payments*. Most side payments involve an appeal to social pressure or to conscience. As John Stuart Mill (1861/1987) put it in his defense of utilitarianism: "Why am I bound to promote the general happiness? If my own happiness lies in something else, why may I not give that the preference?" (p. 299). Mill's answer was that we *will* give our own happiness preference until, through education, we learn the sanctions for doing so. These include external sanctions stemming from social censure (including divine censure) and internal sanctions stemming from conscience. Freud (1930/1961) presented a very similar view, as have most social learning and norm theorists since.

Promise and Problems of Egoism as a Source of Action for the Public Good

Egoistic motives offer promise for promoting public good because they are easily aroused and potent. They also offer problems because they are fickle. If the egoistically motivated individual finds that self-interest can be served as well or better without enhancing the public good, then the public good be damned. If he or she can break free from Mill's external and internal sanctions, from the constraint of social and self-censure, from anticipated guilt and shame over norm violation, then narrow self-interest reigns supreme.

As noted, a number of behavioral and social scientists have begun to doubt that all action for the public good can be explained by egoism. Three alternatives have been suggested (though, as far as I know, never by one person—except perhaps Jenks, 1990). The first alternative is collectivism.

Collectivism: Serving the Public Good to Benefit a Group

Collectivism is motivation with the ultimate goal of increasing the welfare of a group or collective. The group may be large or small, from two to over 2 billion. It may be a marriage or a partnership; it may be a sports team, a university, a community, a nation; it may be all humanity. The group may be one's race, religion, sex, political party, or social class. One need not even be a member of the group. One may, for example, act to increase the welfare of a racial or ethnic minority, of the homeless, of gays and lesbians, without being a member of these groups.

Explanations of action for the public good in terms of collectivism have at times been linked to social identity theory, with its emphasis on acting for the group rather than for oneself (Tajfel, 1978; Tajfel &Turner, 1986). More recently, however, self-categorization theory (Turner, 1987) has recast group identity in terms of self-definition at the group level; one sees oneself as partner, team member, male, European, New Yorker, and so on. With self-definition recast in this way, acting for the group becomes another form of acting for the self. So, to the extent that group-level self-definition occurs, collectivism becomes a special case of egoism.

If, however, independent of group-level self-definition, one values a group's welfare and this welfare is threatened or can be enhanced in some way, then collectivist motivation may be aroused, promoting action to benefit the group. At times, we may act in a way that benefits the group as a whole; more often, we may benefit only some members, perhaps only a single person. Still, if enhancing the group's welfare is the ultimate goal, then the motive for benefiting this person is collectivism. From the Lewinian perspective adopted here, it is the ultimate goal, not the number of people benefited, that determines the nature of the motive.

To illustrate, the person who supports and comforts a spouse, not out of concern for the spouse per se or for the self-benefits imagined but "for the sake of the marriage," is displaying collectivist motivation. So is the person who contributes to the local United Way because in enriches the community. So is the senator who supports building shelters with the ultimate goal of easing the plight of the homeless. So is the rescuer of a Jewish family in Nazi Europe whose ultimate goal is to benefit humanity in whatever way possible. If the ultimate goal is to benefit some group, whether large or small, inclusive or exclusive, the motive is collectivism.

Problems

Collectivist motives are not problem free as a source of action for the public good. Typically, we care about collectives of which we are members, an *us*. Identifying with a group or collective in this way usually involves recognition of an out-group; an *us* implies a *them* who is not us. Indeed, a them-us comparison is often used to define a collective, as Henri Tajfel (1978) and John Turner (1987) have pointed out. When this occurs, harming *them* may be one way to enhance the comparative welfare of *us*. We rejoice at their difficulties and defeats, even if we do not directly benefit as a result (Tajfel & Turner, 1986). We scapegoat. Dawes, van de Kragt, and Orbell (1990) remind us that Rudolf Hoess, the commandant at Auschwitz, systematically murdered 2.9 million members of an out-group to benefit his National Socialist in-group.

Promise

In addition to this very real danger, collectivist motivation has some virtues that egoism does not. Egoism is directed toward our own self-interest. Yet many needs in the world are far removed from our self-interest, even our enlightened self-interest, and from worry about norm violation or the prick of conscience, each of which can be anesthetized with excuses and diffusion of responsibility.

Think, for example, of the plight of the homeless in the United States, of poverty and illiteracy in Central America, of pollution, global warming, overpopulation, energy conservation, endangered species—the list goes on and on. These problems are particularly difficult to address because they are *social dilemmas*. A social dilemma arises when (a) individuals in a group or collective have a choice about how to allocate personally held scarce resources (e.g., money, time, energy) and (b) allocation to the group provides more benefit for the group as a whole than does allocation to oneself, but allocation to oneself provides more self-benefit than does allocation to the group as a whole (Dawes, 1980). In such a situation, the action that is best for me is to allocate resources to meet my needs, ignoring the needs of the group as a whole. But if everyone tries thus to maximize his or her own welfare, the attempt will backfire. Everyone, including me, is worse off. Unilateral pursuit of what is best for each individual creates a situation in which everyone suffers more.

If we rely on straightforward egoistic motivation to address the pressing social dilemmas we face, the prognosis looks bleak. Like lemmings heading for the sea, we will find ourselves racing pell-mell toward destruction. But the situation is not that grim. There is considerable evidence that when faced with a social dilemma, whether in a research laboratory or in real life, many people do not seek to maximize only their own welfare. Under certain conditions, people seek also to enhance the group welfare (Alfano & Marwell, 1980; Brewer & Kramer, 1986; Dawes, McTavish, & Shaklee, 1977; Kramer & Brewer, 1984; Orbell, van de Kragt, & Dawes, 1988; Yamagishi & Sato, 1986). The most common explanation for this attention to group welfare is in terms of collectivist motivation based on social or group identity (e.g., Brewer & Kramer, 1986; Dawes et al., 1990).

Does Collectivism Really Exist?

Still, it is important to consider the possibility that what looks like collectivism is actually a subtle form of individual egoism. Perhaps attention to group welfare in a social dilemma is simply a result of enlightened self-interest or side payments.

The most direct evidence that collectivism is independent of egoism comes from research by Dawes and his colleagues (Dawes et al., 1990; Orbell et al., 1988). The research indicates that if individuals are placed in a social dilemma after discussing the dilemma with other members of the group, they give more to the group than if they had no prior discussion. Moreover, this effect is specific to the in-group with whom the discussion occurred; allocation to an out-group is not enhanced by discussion.

On the basis of this research, Dawes et al. (1990) claim evidence for collectivist motivation independent of egoism. They claim that participants acted to enhance the welfare of the group "in the absence of any expectation of future reciprocity, current reward or punishment, or even reputational consequences among other group members" (p. 99). They also claim that this action was independent of the dictates of conscience.

These are bold claims, perhaps too bold. Dawes et al. (1990) believe they eliminated all forms of enlightened self- interest and side payments from their experiments by having participants make a single, anonymous allocation decision. They believe they tested the effects of conscience by providing some participants with a choice between allocating to themselves and to the no-prior-discussion out-group, whereas others chose between themselves and the prior-discussion in-group. Dawes et al. reasoned that a socially instilled norm to cooperate would dictate allocation to the out-group just as much as to the in-group. Yet this seems doubtful; the operative norm could easily be "Share with your buddies" rather than simply "Share."

Consistent with this suggestion, Dawes et al. (1990) found that, during the discussion period in their experiments, participants made lots of promises to cooperate. Promises were, of course, made only to members of the in-group with whom participants discussed, one's buddies, not to members of the out-group. Reneging on such a promise to gain a few dollars may be no small side cost for most people. Even if others will not know that you reneged, you will. Also consistent, in an earlier experiment, Dawes et al. (1977) found that prior discussion did not increase cooperative responses when subjects were not allowed to discuss the dilemma or possible strategies. This lack of increase seems hard to explain if the personalizing contact of discussion evoked group identity and collectivist motivation.

To discount these interpretative problems, Dawes et al. (1990) turned to research participants' self-reports of why they cooperated. When there was no prior discussion, most cooperators cited "doing the right thing" as their major motive; when there was discussion, most cited "group welfare." These self-reports are certainly of interest and are suggestive; yet are they enough to justify the conclusion that collectivist motivation is not reducible to egoism? Participants may not have known or, if they knew, may not have accurately reported their true reasons for acting. This seems especially likely given the multiplicity of potential motives and the value-laden decision.

The possibility that collectivism exists as a pro social motive independent of egoism is certainly intriguing and worthy of pursuit. Before conclusions are drawn, however, more and better evidence is needed.

Altruism: Serving the Public Good to Benefit One or More Others

Altruism is motivation with the ultimate goal of increasing the welfare of one or more individuals other than oneself. If these individuals are members of a collective or if their welfare is linked to the welfare of the collective, then pursuit of this ultimate goal may increase the welfare of the collective. It increases the welfare of the collective not as an ultimate goal but as an instrumental goal or unintended consequence. Thus, although altruism is most often contrasted with egoism, it can be contrasted with collectivism as well.

Note that altruism is a form of possible motivation. As such, it should not be confused with *helping behavior*, which is one possible form of action for the public good. Helping may or may not be altruistically motivated. Nor should altruism be confused with self- sacrifice, which concerns cost to self, not benefit to the other (see Batson, 1991, for a discussion of conceptions and definitions of altruism).

The most commonly proposed source of altruistic motivation is empathic emotion. By *empathy* I mean other-oriented feelings congruent with the perceived welfare of another person. If the other is perceived to be in need, empathy includes feelings of sympathy, compassion, tenderness, and the like. Empathy is usually considered to be a product not only of perceiving the other as in need but also of adopting the perspective of the other, which means imagining how the other is affected by his or her situation (Stotland, 1969). It is for this reason that empathic feelings are called other oriented. Such feelings have been named as a source—if not *the* source—of altruism by Thomas Aquinas, David Hume, Adam Smith, Charles Darwin, Herbert Spencer, and William McDougall and, in contemporary psychology, by Martin Hoffman (1976), Dennis Krebs (1975), and myself (Batson, 1987, 1991). I have called the proposal that feeling empathy for a person in need evokes altruistic motivation the *empathy-altruism hypothesis.*

Does Altruism Really Exist?

There is considerable evidence that feeling empathy for a person in need leads to increased helping of that person (see Eisenberg & Miller, 1987, for a review). Yet the motivation behind this relationship could be egoistic rather than altruistic. Obvious self-benefits result from helping a person for whom we feel empathy: We reduce our empathic arousal, which may be experienced as aversive; we avoid social and self-punishments for failing to help when we or others feel we should; and we gain social and self-rewards for doing what we or others feel is good and right. The empathy-altruism hypothesis does not deny that these self-benefits exist, but it claims that they are unintended consequences of the empathic ally aroused helper's reaching the ultimate goal of reducing the other's suffering. Egoistic explanations disagree; they claim that one or more of the self-benefits is the ultimate goal.

Over the past 15 years, other social psychologists and I have conducted more than 25 experiments designed to test the nature of the motivation to help evoked by empathy (see Batson, 1991, for a review). Results of these experiments have provided remarkably consistent support for the empathy-altruism hypothesis. None of the egoistic explanations proposed has received more than scattered support (see Cialdini et al., 1987; Schaller & Cialdini, 1988; Smith, Keating, & Stotland, 1989). This evidence has led me tentatively to accept the validity of the empathy-altruism hypothesis (Batson, 1991).

Problems

Even if empathy-induced altruistic motivation exists, is it a plausible source of motivation to act for the public good? Altruism, especially empathy-induced altruism, appears to be directed toward the interest of specific other individuals. It may not be possible to feel empathy for an abstract social category like *women*, *humanity*, or *the homeless*. Further, the likelihood that needs of different individuals will evoke empathic feelings is not equal; these feelings are more likely to be felt for those (a) who are friends, kin, or similar to us, (b) to whom we are emotionally attached, (c) for whom we feel responsible, or (d) whose perspective we adopt (Batson, 1991; Krebs, 1975; Stotland, 1969).

These observations suggest that many of our most pressing social problems may evoke little empathy. The people in need are too remote or the problems too abstract. For this reason Hardin (1977) dismissed altruism as a potential solution to our environmental and population crises: "Is pure altruism possible? Yes, of course it is—on a small scale, over the short term, in certain circumstances, and within small, intimate groups. . . . But only the most naive hope to adhere to a non-calculating policy in a group that numbers in the thousands (or millions!), and in which many preexisting antagonisms are known and many more suspected" (p. 26). Hardin quickly returned to his cardinal rule of never asking a person to act against his own self-interest.

More generally, as a source of motivation for public good, altruism may be limited in much the same way as egoism. If benefiting the person or persons for whom empathy is felt leads to increased public good as an instrumental means or an unintended consequence, then altruism may enhance the public good. If benefiting the person or persons is in conflict with the larger public good, then altruism may diminish it. Consistent with this reasoning, colleagues and I recently found that inducing empathy for one of the other individuals in a social dilemma increased allocation of scarce resources to this individual to the detriment of the group as a whole, much as increased egoistic motivation might (Batson, Batson, & Todd, 1993).

Promise

Still, in certain circumstances the potential of empathy-evoked altruism to serve the public good may be quite powerful. A careful look at data collected by Oliner and Oliner (1988) and their colleagues on rescuers of Jews in Nazi Europe suggests that involvement in rescue activity frequently began with concern for a specific individual or individuals for whom compassion was felt—often an individual known previously. This initial involvement sometimes led to further contacts and rescue activity that extended well beyond the bounds of the initial empathic concern.

Attempting to induce empathy for an individual who is an exemplar of a larger group seems to be a key strategy of many fund-raising campaigns, whether for children with disabilities, starving refugees, or harp seals, spotted owls, and whales; it also seems effective (Shelton & Rogers, 1981). Isaacson (1992) suggested that empathy was a potent factor in the 1992 decision to send the Marines into Somalia, so potent that he raises the question of whether the world will ignore the Sudan but rescue Somalia mainly because photographic footage of the latter evokes more compassion.

Even the needs of the physical environment may not lie beyond the reach of empathy. Think of the tendency to personalize these needs by using metaphors such as Mother Earth, the rape of the landscape, or dying rivers. Could it be that these metaphors are used to evoke empathy—and so altruistic motivation—by personalizing the natural environment?

Principlism: Serving the Public Good to Uphold a Principle

Principlism is motivation with the ultimate goal of upholding some moral principle, such as justice or the utilitarian principle of the greatest good for the greatest number. Once again, this motive could easily increase the public good as an instrumental means or an unintended consequence.

It is not surprising that most moral philosophers have argued for the importance of a motive to act for the public good other than egoism. But most since Kant (1724–1804) have also argued for a motive other than collectivism or altruism. Moral philosophers reject appeals to collectivism because it is bounded by the limits of the collective; they reject appeals to altruism based on feelings of empathy, sympathy, and compassion because they find these emotions too fickle and circumscribed. Moral philosophers typically call for motivation with an ultimate goal of upholding some universal and impartial moral principle.

For example, Kant argued that the Judeo-Christian commandment to love one's neighbor as oneself should be understood as a moral principle to be upheld rather than as an expression of social identity or personal compassion (1785/1889, sec. 1, paragraph 13). Tolstoy echoed Kant's view, calling the law of love "the highest principle of life" and asserting that love should be "free from anything personal, from the smallest drop of personal bias towards its object. And such love can only be felt for one's enemy, for those who hate and offend" (1908/1987, p. 230). Similarly, the utilitarian principle of the greatest good for the greatest number is universal and impartial; it affirms that one should give no more weight to what is good for oneself than to what is good for someone else (Mill, 1861/1987).

More recently, John Rawls (1971) has argued for a principle of justice based on the allocation of goods to the members of society from an initial position behind the veil of ignorance, where no one knows his or her place in society—prince or pauper, laborer or lawyer, male or female, Black or White. Why does Rawls require such a stance? Because it eliminates partiality and seduction by special interest. A universal, impartial principle of justice much like Rawls's is the basis for Lawrence Kohlberg's (1976) postconventional, or principled, moral reasoning, the highest level in his stage model of moral development.

Universalist, impartial views of morality have not gone unchallenged. Writers like Lawrence Blum (1980), Carol Gilligan (1982), Thomas Nagel (1991), Nel Noddings (1984), Joan Tronto (1987), and Bernard Williams (1981) call for recognition of forms of morality that allow for special interest in the welfare of certain others or certain relationships. In opposition to an ethic based on justice and fairness, these writers propose an ethic of care. Sometimes, it seems that these writers are proposing care as an alternative principle to justice, either as a substitute for justice or in dynamic tension with it; at other times, it seems that they are proposing care as an alternative to principled morality altogether. If care is an alternative principle, then it too might be an expression of principlism; one might act for the public good as a means of upholding the principle of care. If, however, care is a special feeling (a) for another individual, (b) for oneself, or (c) for a relationship that inclines one to act, then care would seem to be a form of altruism, egoism, or collectivism, respectively.

Does Principlism Really Exist?

Is acting with an ultimate goal of upholding some moral principle really possible? When Kant briefly shifted his focus from an analysis of what ought to be to what is, he was ready to admit that even when the concern we show for others appears to be prompted by duty to principle, it may really be prompted by self-love (1785/1889, sec. 2, paragraph 2). The goal of upholding a moral principle may be only an instrumental goal, a means of reaching the ultimate goal of self-benefit. If so, the motivation is actually egoistic.

To date, I do not think anyone knows whether principlism is a distinct form of motivation or only a subtle and sophisticated form of egoism. We have empirical evidence, limited and weak, that espousal of at least some moral principles, such as Kohlberg's (1976) principle of universal justice, can lead to increased prosocial behavior (Eisenberg, 1991; Emler, Renwick, & Malone, 1983; Erkut, Jaquette, & Staub, 1981; Sparks & Durkin, 1987). To the best of my knowledge, however, there is no empirical evidence that upholding justice (or any other moral principle) can be an ultimate goal. Nor is there empirical evidence that rules this possibility out.

Problems and Promise

The major problem with principlism as a source of motivation to act for the public good is knowing when and how a given principle applies. It may seem that moral principles, at least universal ones, always apply. But it is not that simple.

Most of us are adept at rationalization, at justifying to ourselves, if not to others, why a situation that benefits us or those we care about does not violate our moral principles—why, for example, the inequities in the public school systems of rich and poor communities in the United States are not really unjust (Kozol, 1991); why storing our nuclear waste in someone else's backyard is fair; why terrorist attacks by our side are regrettable but necessary evils, whereas terrorist attacks by the other side are atrocities; why we must obey orders even if it means killing innocents. The abstractness of most moral principles, and their multiplicity, makes rationalization all too easy. Skill in dodging the thrust of the moral principles we espouse may explain the weak empirical relation between principled morality and prosocial action. Perhaps moral principles serve more to censure or extol others' actions then to motivate our own.

However, if upholding moral principles can serve as an ultimate goal, defining a form of motivation independent of egoism, then perhaps these principles can provide a rational basis for acting for the public good that transcends reliance on self-interest or on vested interest in and feeling for the welfare of certain other individuals or groups. Quite an "if," but it seems well worth conducting research to find out.

Interplay and Conflict

What difference does it make why we act for the public good, as long as we do? Thinking about the different effects of the four proposed motives—egoism, collectivism, altruism, and principlism—suggests that it makes a lot of difference. Each motive has its own limiting conditions.

These different limiting conditions suggest that it is important to know which motives are operating in a given situation. It is also important to know what evokes each motive and how they interact. Sometimes, these motives may combine additively; at other times, they may be in conflict, one inhibiting or undermining another. The latter seems especially likely when self-benefits are made salient for behavior actually motivated by collectivism, altruism, or principlism. The self-benefits may lead to an interpretation of the motivation as egoistic, which may undermine the other motive, much as Lepper, Greene, and Nisbett (1973) found that extrinsic incentives can undermine the intrinsic motivation of children at play. In this way, the assumption that there is only one answer to the question of why we act for the public good—egoism—may become a self-fulfilling prophecy (Batson, Fultz, Schoenrade, & Paduano, 1987).

Conclusion

Obviously, there is much we do not know about the nature and function of motives for acting for the public good. The questions are subtle and difficult, and the stakes are high. But, building on the Lewinian tradition—both Lewin's rich conceptual framework for understanding motivation and his use of laboratory experimentation to isolate and identify complex social motives—social psychologists seem ideally situated to provide some answers. Perhaps we too can contribute to the public good.

Acknowledgments

Preparation of this article was supported by National Science Foundation Grant BNS-8906723, C. Daniel Batson, Principal Investigator, and by a Laurance S. Rockefeller Fellowship from the University Center for Human Values, Princeton University. Thanks to Diane Kobrynowicz for helpful comments on an earlier draft.

References

Alfano, G., & Marwell, G. (1980). Experiments on the provision of public goods by groups III: Non-divisibility and free riding in "real" groups. *Social Psychology Quarterly*, 43, 300–309.

Batson, C. D. (1987). Prosocial motivation: Is it ever truly altruistic? In L. Berkowitz (Ed.), *Advances in experimental social psychology* (Vol. 20, pp. 65–122). New York: Academic Press.

Batson, C. D. (1991). *The altruism question: Toward a social-psychological answer*. Hillsdale, NJ: Lawrence Erlbaum.

Batson, C. D., Batson, J. G., & Todd, R M. (1993). *Empathy and the collective good: Caring for one of the others in a social dilemma*. Unpublished manuscript, University of Kansas.

Batson, C. D., Fultz, J., Schoenrade, P. A, & Paduano, A (1987). Critical self-reflection and self-perceived altruism: When self-reward fails. *Journal of Personality and Social Psychology*, 53, 594–602.

Blum, L. A. (1980). *Friendship, altruism, and morality*. London: Routledge.

Brewer, M. B., & Kramer, R M. (1986). Choice behavior in social dilemmas: Effects of social identity, group size, and decision framing. *Journal of Personality and Social Psychology*, 50, 543–549.

Campbell, D. T. (1975). On the conflicts between biological and social evolution and between psychology and moral tradition. *American Psychologist*, 30, 1103–1126.

Cialdini, R. B., Schaller, M., Houlihan, D., Arps, K., Fultz, J., & Beaman, A L. (1987). Empathy-based helping: Is it selflessly or selfishly motivated? *Journal of Personality and Social Psychology*, 52, 749–758.

Dawes, R. M. (1980). Social dilemmas. *Annual Review of Psychology*, 31, 169–193.

Dawes, R M., McTavish, J., & Shaklee, H. (1977). Behavior, communication, and assumptions about other people's behavior in a commons dilemma situation. *Journal of Personality and Social Psychology*, 35,1–11.

Dawes, R, van de Kragt, A. J. C., & Orbell, J. M. (1990). Cooperation for the benefit of us—not me, or my conscience. In J. J. Mansbridge (Ed.), *Beyond self-interest* (pp. 97–110). Chicago: University of Chicago Press.

Eisenberg, N. (1991). Meta-analytic contributions to the literature on prosocial behavior. *Personality and Social Psychology Bulletin*, 17, 273–282.

Eisenberg, N., & Miller, P. (1987). Empathy and prosocial behavior. *Psychological Bulletin*, 101,91–119.

Emler, N., Renwick, S., & Malone, B. (1983). The relationship between moral reasoning and political orientation. *Journal of Personality and Social Psychology*, 45, 1073–1080.

Erkut, S., Jaquette, D. S., & Staub, E. (1981). Moral judgment-situation interaction as a basis for predicting prosocial behavior. *Journal of Personality*, 49, 1–14.

Freud, S. (1961). *Civilization and its discontents* (J. Strachey, Trans.). New York: W. W. Norton. (Original work published 1930)

Gilligan, C. (1982). *In a different voice: Psychological theory and women's development*. Cambridge, MA: Harvard University Press.

Hardin, G. (1977). *The limits of altruism: An ecologist's view of survival*. Bloomington: Indiana University Press.

Hoffman, M. L. (1976). Empathy, role-taking, guilt, and development of altruistic motives. In T. Lickona (Ed.), *Moral development and behavior: Theory, research, and social issues* (pp. 124–143). New York: Holt, Rinehart & Winston.

Isaacson, W. (1992, December 21). Sometimes, right makes might. *Time*, p. 82.

Jenks, C. (1990). Varieties of altruism. In J.J. Mansbridge (Ed.), *Beyond self-interest* (pp. 53–67). Chicago: University of Chicago Press.

Kant, I. (1889). *Kant's Critique of Practical Reason and other works on the theory of ethics* (4th ed.) (T. K Abbott, Trans.). New York: Longmans, Green. (Original work published 1785)

Kohlberg, L. (1976). Moral stages and moralization: The cognitive-developmental approach. In T. Lickona (Ed.), *Moral development and behavior: Theory, research, and social issues* (pp. 31–53). New York: Holt, Rinehart & Winston.

Kozol, J. (1991). *Savage inequalities: Children in America's schools.* New York: Crown.

Kramer, R M., & Brewer, M. B. (1984). Effects of group identity on resource use in a simulated commons dilemma. *Journal of Personality and Social Psychology*, 46, 1044–1057.

Krebs, D. L. (1975). Empathy and altruism. *Journal of Personality and Social Psychology*, 32, 1134–1146.

Lepper, M. R, Greene, D., & Nisbett, R E. (1973). Undermining children's intrinsic interest with extrinsic reward: A test of the "overjustification" hypothesis. *Journal of Personality and Social Psychology*, 28, 129–137.

Lewin, K (1951). *Field theory in social science.* New York: Harper.

Mansbridge, J. J. (Ed.). (1990). *Beyond self-interest.* Chicago: University of Chicago Press.

Mill, J. S. (1987). Utilitarianism. In J. S. Mill & Jeremy Bentham (Eds.), *Utilitarianism and other essays* (pp. 272–338). London: Penguin. (Original work published 1861)

Nagel, T. (1991). *Equality and partiality.* New York: Oxford University Press.

Noddings, N. (1984). *Caring: A feminine approach to ethics and moral education.* Berkeley: University of California Press.

Oliner, S. P., & Oliner, P. M. (1988). *The altruistic personality: Rescuers of Jews in Nazi Europe.* New York: Free Press.

Orbell, J. M., van de Kragt, A. J., & Dawes, R M. (1988). Explaining discussion-induced cooperation. *Journal of Personality and Social Psychology*, 54,811–819.

Rawls, J. (1971). *A theory of justice.* Cambridge, MA: Harvard University Press.

Schaller, M., & Cialdini, R. B. (1988). The economics of empathic helping: Support for a mood management motive. *Journal of Experimental Social Psychology*, 24, 163–181.

Sen, A. K. (1977). Rational fools. *Philosophy and Public Affairs*, 6, 317–344.

Shelton, M. L., & Rogers, R. W. (1981). Fear-arousing and empathy-arousing appeals to help: The pathos of persuasion. *Journal of Applied Social Psychology*, 11, 366–378.

Smith, K. D., Keating, J. P., & Stotland, E. (1989). Altruism reconsidered: The effect of denying feedback on a victim's status to empathic witnesses. *Journal of Personality and Social Psychology*, 57, 641–650.

Sparks, P., & Durkin, K. (1987). Moral reasoning and political orientation: The context sensitivity of individual rights and democratic principles. *Journal of Personality and Social Psychology*, 52, 931–936.

Stotland, E. (1969). Exploratory investigations of empathy. In L. Berkowitz (Ed.), *Advances in experimental social psychology* (Vol. 4, pp. 271–313). New York: Academic Press.

Tajfel, H. (1978). *Differentiation between social groups: Studies in the social psychology of intergroup relations.* London: Academic Press.

Tajfel, H., & Turner, J. C. (1986). The social identity theory of intergroup behavior. In S. Worchel & W. Austin (Eds.), *Psychology of intergroup relations* (pp. 7–24). Chicago: Nelson-Hall.

Tolstoy, L. (1987). The law of love and the law of violence. In *A confession and other religious writings* (J. Kentish, Trans.). London: Penguin. (Original work published 1908)

Tronto, J. (1987). Beyond gender differences to a theory of care. *Signs*, 12, 644–663.

Turner, J. C. (1987). *Rediscovering the social group: A self-categorization theory.* London: Basil Blackwell.

Williams, B. (1981). Persons, character, and morality. In B. Williams (Ed.), *Moral luck: Philosophical papers 1973–1980* (pp. 1–19). Cambridge: Cambridge University Press.

Yamagishi, T., & Sato, K. (1986). Motivational bases of the public goods problem. *Journal of Personality and Social Psychology*, 50, 67–73.

CHAPTER 40

ETHICAL BEHAVIOR IN HIGHER EDUCATIONAL INSTITUTIONS: THE ROLE OF THE CODE OF CONDUCT

ZABIHOLLAH REZAEE, ROBERT C. ELMORE, AND JOSEPH Z. SZENDI

The report of the Treadway Commission suggests that all public companies should establish effective written codes of conduct in promoting honorable behavior by corporations. The need for written "codes of conduct" for businesses is evident in the current literature. However, there is not sufficient evidence regarding the implication of codes of conduct in a college. Academic dishonesty has become an important issue in institutions of higher education. Codes of conduct can also provide a basis for ethical behavior in colleges and universities. Survey respondents were generally supportive of the concept of codes of ethical conduct in colleges and universities. The results of this study indicate that college codes of conduct tend to follow a "low road" approach. The results also suggest the following needed improvements in college and university codes of conduct: (1) greater emphasis on preventing financial, scientific, and academic fraud; (2) more inclusion of the faculty in the process; and (3) establishment of a proper process for implementation of the code.

Introduction

Increased organization governance and accountability appear to be a national trend. The public, regulators, and the accounting profession are taking a closer look at colleges and universities (hereafter C&U) that use public resources and trying to find ways to hold these institutions more accountable. The need for increased organizational governance and accountability is reflected in the new accounting standards requiring C&U to present their financial statements in similar form as for-profit organizations (FASB, 1993a, 1993b; GASB, 1999). Another aspect of this focus on increased accountability and governance for C&U is the establishment of codes of conduct. Prior research has investigated the importance of codes of conduct in C&U and their impact on the behavior of administrators, faculty, and students (e.g.; Engle and Smith, 1990; Kibler, 1994).

There is no empirical evidence regarding the status, nature of, and procedure for establishing codes of conduct in C&U. Thus the primary purposes of this study are to: (1) examine C&U codes of conduct; (2) identify the person(s) responsible for preparing the C&U code of conduct; (3) identify the procedures followed in implementing and monitoring the C&U code of conduct; and (4) provide guidance in establishing appropriate codes of conduct. These objectives are accomplished by conducting a survey of C&U administrators (vice-presidents of finance). Insights from those surveyed administrators are relevant to all institutions of higher education in establishing or revising their code of conduct.

Motivation for the Study

An important aspect of the trend toward increased corporate governance and accountability as well as greater emphasis on honorable behavior is reflected in the need for written codes of conduct. Situation ethics theory supports the relevance of the use of written codes of conduct (McCarthy, 1997). This approach suggests that because of the variety of value systems in a pluralistic society, it is impossible to achieve a consensus of opinion regarding morals and ethics.

However, it is easier to achieve a consensus on appropriate ethical practices. This consensus of opinion will provide the input for a code of conduct that will promote the appropriate ethical behavior (Baumhart, 1968).

There is considerable debate about the nature, scope, and effect of codes of conduct. Codes of conduct are seen as making a clear distinction as to what is permissible and what is not, and informing employees of actions that will land them in trouble (Gellerman, 1989). They also can help restore public trust, provide guidance, and be a source of professional identity and reference (Dobel, 1993). Codes of conduct, on the other hand are criticized as ". . . becoming a panacea for problems that they cannot solve . . ." which ". . . could contribute to the cynicism and distrust they are supposed to address (Dobel, 1993, p. 158)". Despite their proliferation, very little is known about how ethics codes are implemented or how they function (Dobel, 1993). This study gathers expert opinions regarding the status, nature, and content of codes of conduct for C&U and how they can be implemented and their functions. The C&U survey results can also be used by other profit oriented and not-for-profit organizations in establishing and implementing their codes of conduct.

Corporate Codes of Conduct

Corporations have been establishing codes of conduct throughout this century, so the concept is not a new one (Baumhart, 1968). However, the topic has received more attention since the 1970s. The National Commission on Fraudulent Financial Reporting (Treadway Commission, 1987) suggests that all public companies should establish effective written codes of conduct in promoting honorable behavior by corporations. Corporations perceive the establishment of corporate codes of conduct as achieving the following goals: (1) fostering their corporate moral principles and values; (2) communicating and monitoring their ethical expectations to employees; (3) demonstrating their commitment to ethical values; (4) providing legitimacy for possible legal actions; and (5) helping individuals resolve ethical dilemmas (Brenner and Molander, 1971; Montoya and Richard, 1994).

Stevens (1994) argues that this increase is the result of corporate self-protection, even though there is no solid evidence that corporate codes are effective. There are no appropriate evaluation standards to assess the effectiveness of corporate codes. Brenner and Molander (1976) found in a survey of corporate executives that while 75 percent of the respondents agreed that organizations should have ethical codes, they believed that ethical codes will not substantially improve business conduct. Montoya and Richard (1994), in a survey of 20 companies found no process in place to determine if the codes were known and were used. Neither the employees nor management knew what to expect from the codes.

An issue is why would an individual be willing to follow a code of conduct. Molander (1987) suggests that codes are followed for two reasons: the individual subjects himself to ethical standards above and beyond his personal beliefs, or they feel there are provisions for enforcement of such standards. Ultimately, there must be some type of enforcement or sanctions. Codes of conduct do not always provide the power or process for enforcement. Codes also may be ineffective because they have too many limitations, impede the flow of information, or restrict entry and competition (Molander, 1987). Organizations, personal beliefs, and the ethical dilemmas of society as a whole also have an impact upon the effectiveness of any code of conduct (Lawrence, 1975; Brenner and Molander, 1976; Mayer-Sommer, 1981; Molander, 1987; and Tyson, 1992).

Related Research

"High Road" vs. "Low Road" Codes of Conduct

Codes of conduct typically have been conceptualized as either "high road" or "low road" (Rohr, 1989; Bowman, 1990; Blake et al., 1998). High-road codes of conduct are proactive social ethics with a focus on doing the right thing. This consists of an ". . . emphasis on personal and organizational behaviors that stress self-respect, respect for others, love of people, responsiveness to people, and matters pertaining to equality, freedom, justice, and the truth (Rohr, 1989, p. 60)." The low road approach ". . . addresses ethical issues almost exclusively in terms of adherence to agency rules (Rohr, 1989, p. 60)." Low road codes are reactive, emphasizing legal and administrative controls to avoid wrongdoing. They often are created in response to scandal and as a result are punitive and negative with laundry lists of prohibitions (Dobel, 1993). The focus is upon conflict of interest definitions while breaking down barriers between private and public life.

Direct vs. Indirect Approaches

The usual approach to the encouragement of ethical behavior is a direct approach (Brien, 1998). The direct approach involves measures to ". . . focus on unethical behavior . . . make it clear what unethical behavior is, prescribe it, and attempt to deter and punish it by imposing or threatening to impose sanctions (Brien, 1998, p. 392)." On the other hand, indirect approaches ". . . aim for ethics indirectly by aiming for some proximate and attainable goal (Brien, 1998, p. 392)." This approach suggests actions that focus upon adherence to ethical conduct and promotion of desired goals. Brien (1998) contends that the goal of any professional should be trust and that this focus upon trust will generate ethical behavior.

Codes of conduct can be a part of either a direct or indirect approach. In a direct approach typically codes of conduct assume a central role. Unethical behavior is typically "identified and proscribed" by maintaining a code of conduct. The indirect approach assumes that beliefs, norms, and values must focus on and exemplify trust. An indirect approach requires that the people believe that trust is important and understand that what they do is right and good.

Codes of Conduct for Colleges and Universities

Academic dishonesty has become an important issue for C&Us. Kibler (1994) surveyed C&U regarding academic dishonesty, concluding that academic policies were legalistic and more concerned with "a legal/due process perspective rather than a student development perspective." This would suggest a low road perspective. Kibler found little evidence of any "systematic, comprehensive programs" promoting awareness of academic dishonesty for faculty or students. This legalistic approach is evidenced by the fact that universities have replaced honor codes with administrative disciplinary systems that handle dishonesty on a case-by-case basis.

It is assumed that if faculty is to teach ethics, then they must provide an ethical example (Callahan, 1980; Vincent and Monville, 1993). Engle and Smith (1990) surveyed faculty regarding their views on ethics. They found ". . . that a minority of faculty were plagiarizing research, falsifying research data, and accepting sex for grades . . ." while ". . . a sizeable number of faculty appear to be involved with cancelling office hours excessively, utilizing outdated lecture notes, and allowing students to grade nonobjective exams" (Engle and Smith, 1990, p. 28). Lewellyn (1996, p. 567) in a similar study also found evidence of ". . . padding expense accounts, attending professional meetings without substantive participation, using university equipment for personal activities, selling complementary copies of textbooks, allowing lecture notes to become outdated, or copying software in violation of licensing agreements." This has lead to the suggestion that there exists a need for a code of conduct for academics or the teaching of ethics to doctoral students (Loeb, 1990, 1994).

Previous research generally indicates that codes of conduct have a role in the promotion of ethical behavior in corporations, professions, and the government. However, there is little evidence regarding the use of codes of conduct in C&U. Our study seeks to determine the extent to which codes of conduct are currently used in C&U and to examine persons involved in procedures followed in establishing college and university codes of conduct. Rohr's (1989) "high road" and "low road" and Brien's (1998) "direct" and "indirect" dimensions will provide the conceptual framework for analysis. Insights into the set of elements of codes of conduct and procedures used for their formation should be of great interest and benefit to all C&U in establishing or revising their codes of conduct.

Methodology

This study surveyed 1000 financial administrators (vice presidents of finance) of C&U randomly selected from the 1996 membership rolls of the National Association of College and University Business Officers (NACUBO, 1997). There was a choice of whether to send the questionnaire to financial administrators (vice presidents of finance) or to deans, vice presidents of academic affairs, and vice presidents of research. The questionnaires were sent to vice presidents of finance, the principal reason being that they would have sufficient knowledge of their institutions' ethical codes. Furthermore, Frederickson (1993) concluded that codes of conduct at C&U tend to focus on financial indiscretions.

A two-page questionnaire was designed, pretested, revised, and then mailed to subjects. The questionnaire contained the following sections: (1) the existence of a code of conduct (ethical policy) at colleges and universities; (2) the guidelines included in the ethical policies; (3) the person(s) responsible in preparing the university code of conduct; (4) the procedures followed in implementing and monitoring the university code of conduct; (5) the need for adoption of a code of conduct; and (6) general demographic data.[1]

The questionnaire was accompanied by a cover letter stating the survey objectives, assuring confidentiality of the responses, agreeing to share the findings, giving the approximate time needed to complete the questionnaire, and providing a pre-addressed postage-paid return envelope. After six weeks, a second mailing was sent to all institutions that did not return a questionnaire in which they revealed their identity. The responses of both groups were compared, and no statistical differences between the two groups were found. Usable completed questionnaires were received from 292 vice-presidents of finance resulting in a response rate of 29.2 percent.

A *t*-test was used to test for significant differences in mean responses between public and private C&U of the level of agreement or disagreement about a series of statements regarding the need for adoption of a code of ethics. Bartlett's Box-F test was used to test for any violation of the heteroscedasticity assumption and, accordingly, any questions violating this assumption were eliminated. Levene's test was used to test for equality of variances. Responses were tested for non-response bias using an accumulated ANOVA test and found to be free of non-response bias.

The respondents were asked for demographic and background information, which was used for classification purposes. More than 60 percent of responding institutions were private schools, and the remainder was state supported universities. The majority of universities were primarily noncommuting (54.3 percent). Ninety-nine percent of the respondents' universities have been in operation more than 20 years. More than one-half have been in operation more than 100 years. Public universities are generally larger in all measures of size including students, faculty, and budget. Accordingly, classification as public vs. private provided the most significant explanatory variable of the demographic data. Table 40.1 provides the size characteristics in terms of students, faculty, and budget. The majority of respondents also reported having two to five colleges or schools. More than 32 percent of the responding universities have an annual budget of 21 to 50 million dollars, about 38 percent reported a total budget of over 50 million dollars, and approximately thirty percent indicated that their annual operating budget is less than 20 million dollars.

Results

The results are presented in the following sections: (1) the current status of codes of conduct; (2) persons involved in the preparation of the university code of conduct; (3) implementing and monitoring the university code of conduct; and (4) attitudes toward the need for adoption of a code of conduct.

The Current Status of College Codes of Conduct

Over 70 percent of the respondents (71.4 percent) indicated that their colleges had codes of conduct (ethics policies). Respondents having codes of conduct were then asked what was included in their codes of conduct. The results are presented in Table 40.2. The guidelines most commonly included in the ethics policy include conflict of interest (69 percent) and compliance with

TABLE 40.1

Characteristics of Respondents

	Number	Percent of Respondents
A. State supported or private		
State supported	115	39.7
Private	175	60.3
B. Commuting or non-commuting		
Commuting	122	45.7
Non-commuting	145	54.3
C. Number of years in operation		
Less than 20	2	1.0
20–50	62	21.4
51–100	76	26.2
Over 100	149	51.4
D. Student population		
Less than 2000	120	41.4
2001–5000	72	24.8
5001–10,000	43	14.8
10,001–20,000	26	9.0
20,000–35,000	19	6.6
Greater than 35,000	10	3.4
E. Number of faculty		
Less than 100	163	5.9
101–300	94	2.8
301–500	27	9.4
501–1000	27	9.4
1001–2000	23	8.0
2001–5000	10	3.5
Greater than 5000	3	1.0
F. Number of colleges (schools)		
5 or less	163	66.8
6 to 10	60	24.6
11 to 20	16	6.6
Greater than 20	5	2.0
G. Total budget in millions		
Less than 5 million	11	3.8
5 to 10	25	8.6
11 to 20	51	17.5
21 to 50	95	32.6
51 to 100	37	12.7
101 to 500	50	17.2
Greater than 500	22	7.6

TABLE 40.2

Guidelines for Ethical Policies

1. Does your university have a code of conduct (ethics policy)?

Yes	No
71.4%	21.6%

2. Which of the following guidelines are included in your ethical policy?

	Percent
Conflict of interest	69
Compliance with university policies	61
Compliance with applicable external rules and regulations including athletics	47
Faculty grievances	46
Administrators, faculty, and staff performance	45
Confidentiality of proprietary information	41
Tenure and promotion policies and procedures	40
Financial fraud	40
Allegation of fraudulent conduct in research or scholarly activities	39

university policies (61 percent). Less than half of the respondents indicated the following: compliance with applicable external rules and regulations including athletics (47 percent); faculty grievances (46 percent); administrators, faculty, and staff performance (45 percent); confidentiality of proprietary information; (41 percent); tenure and promotion policies and procedures (40 percent); financial fraud (40 percent); and allegation of fraudulent conduct in research or scholarly activities (39 percent).

Preparation of the Code of Conduct

Respondents were asked who was involved in preparing their university code of conduct. The results are presented in Table 40.3. Generally, codes of conduct are generated internally in the university. In a majority of the situations, the president of the university was involved (57 percent). To a lesser extent, other administrators or the faculty senate are involved. The provost and vice-president of academic affairs was involved 49 percent of the time, while the faculty senate was involved 46 percent of the time. Outside parties such as the board of regents, governmental and state authorities, and accreditation bodies are less likely to be involved in the process.

Implementing and Monitoring the University Code of Conduct

Respondents were asked which of the following procedure(s) is (are) followed in implementing and monitoring the university code of conduct. The results presented in Table 40.4 indicate that the majority of respondents (59 percent) distributed a copy of the code to administrators, faculty, and staff. The faculty senate, president, and board of regents approved nearly half of the codes of conduct (49 percent). Little interest was shown in compliance with the code, as only 19 percent of the respondents indicated that non-compliance is investigated and corrected. Only seven percent of respondents' institutions required a certificate of compliance with the code from administrators, faculty, and staff.

TABLE 40.3

Preparation of Codes of Conduct

Who was (were) involved in preparing your university code of conduct? Please check all that apply and place an asterisk (*) next to the person who approved the final draft.	**Percent**
President	57
Provost and vice-president of academic affairs	49
Faculty senate and/or union	46
Board of regents	39
Governmental and state authorities	19
Accreditation bodies	8

TABLE 40.4

Procedures in Implementing or Monitoring University Codes of Conduct

Which of the following procedures is (are) followed in implementing and monitoring your university code of conduct?	**Percent**
1. A copy of the code is distributed to administrators faculty, and staff	59
2. The code is approved by faculty senate, president, and Board of Regents	49
3. Non-compliance with the code is being investigated and corrected	19
4. A certificate of compliance with the code is annually received from administrators, faculty, and staff	7

Attitudes Toward the Need for Adoption of a Code of Conduct

Table 40.5 provides the attitudes of financial vice-presidents toward the need for codes of ethical conduct. Respondents were asked to indicate the extent of their agreement with several statements pertaining to codes of conduct, using a five-point Likert Scale, ranging from 1 = strongly disagree to 5 = strongly agree. Respondents strongly agreed that codes of ethical conduct could demonstrate the university's commitment to a set of standards that society expects them to meet (mean response of 4.211). They also strongly agreed that a set of ethical standards is needed to resolve ethical dilemmas in academic institutions (mean response of 4.085. Respondents also agreed that C&U should be required to have codes of ethical conduct and that a recognized set of standards will raise the stature of academia (mean responses of 3.873 and 3.606, respectively. They disagreed that the diversity of the academic milieu makes the adoption of a code of ethical conduct difficult (mean response of 2.718).

Public and Private Universities

A *t*-test test was performed to examine statistical differences in the mean responses between public and private universities. Table 40.6 shows the only significant difference is that private C&U

TABLE 40.5

Attitudes toward Codes of Conduct

Please indicate the extent to which you agree with the following statements regarding the need for adoption of a code of ethics for colleges and universities.

	Mean Response
a. Codes of ethics can demonstrate the university's commitment to a set of standards that society expects them to meet.	4.211
b. A set of ethical standards is needed to resolve ethical dilemmas in academic institutions.	4.085
c. Recognized set of standards will raise the stature of academia.	3.606
d. Colleges and universities should be required to have codes of ethics.	3.873
e. The diversity of the academic milieu makes the adoption of a code of ethics difficult.	2.718

TABLE 40.6

***T*-Test for Equality of Means Differences between Private and Public Universities' Attitudes toward Codes of Conduct**

Please indicate the extent to which you agree with the following statements regarding the need for adoption of a code of ethics for colleges and universities.

	Mean	Std. Deviation	*T*-Value	DF	Sig. (2-Tailed)
a. A set of ethicalstandards is needed to resolve ethical dilemmas in academic institutions.					
Public	4.0875	1.3239	0.691	162	0.490
Private	4.0000	1.2173			
b. Codes of ethics can demonstrate the university's commitment to a set of standards that society expects them to meet.					
Public	4.2750	0.7627	0.692	162	0.490
Private	4.1095	0.7987			
c. A recognized set of standards will raise the stature of academia.					
Public	3.5000	0.9808	–0.320	162	0.749
Private	3.5476	0.9236			
d. Colleges and universities should be required to have codes of ethics.					
Public	4.0625	0.9188	4.095	162	0.000
Private	3.3452	1.2847			
e. The diversity of the academic milieu makes the adoption of a code of ethics difficult.					
Public	2.6962	1.3239	–0.496	160	0.621
Private	2.7952	1.2173			

had less agreement with the statement that "C&U should be required to have codes of ethics." Responses on the other questions were not statistically different, indicating there is a general agreement between private and public colleges and universities regarding the adoption, implementation, monitoring, and need for the establishment of codes of conduct in institutions of higher education.

Discussion

The majority of respondents favored a code of ethical conduct. Similar to such cases in corporations, these codes of ethics are legalistic in nature. The guidelines most commonly included in the ethics policy include conflict of interest and compliance with university policies. These results are consistent with Rohr's (1989) "low road approach" in that the respondents favored a code of conduct that is more concerned with legal and administrative control. It appears that the "high road approach" may also exist in colleges in the form of behavioral expectations communicated in other ways. These expectations would be communicated through other means, including faculty handbooks, quality programs, seminars, performance evaluation, membership in professional organizations, and promotion or tenure policies. Low road codes of ethics could actually cause high-road efforts to be ignored by suggesting that, if the law is not broken, conduct is ethical (Blake et al., 1998; Loverd, 1989).

In a majority of the situations, the president or the vice-president of academic affairs of the university was involved in the preparation of the code of conduct. The faculty seems less likely to be involved in the process. The majority of respondents distributed a copy of the code to administrators, faculty, and staff, but less than half of the respondents indicate approval by the faculty senate. These results indicate lack of participation and possibly consensus by affected individuals in the preparation of C&Us' codes of conduct. Consensus of participants is a major consideration in assuring effectiveness of any code of conduct (Loeb, 1971; Brenner and Molander, 1974).

The results of this study provides little evidence of interest in compliance, as only 19 percent of the respondents indicated noncompliance with the code was investigated and corrected. Only seven percent of respondents' institutions required a certificate of compliance with the code of conduct. A comprehensive indirect approach would require a focus on these areas. This is similar to the problem of lack of standards of assessment for effectiveness of corporate codes (Molander, 1987; Montoya and Richards, 1994; Stevens, 1994).

Institutions of higher education must promote an environment of academic integrity to strengthen public trust in their effectiveness and ethics. This must be proven by all forms of written and verbal communication, evidence of practice, and the extent to which integrity is a priority in the leadership of the institution. Faculty must provide an ethical example (Callahan, 1980; Vincent and Monville, 1993). Although a majority of the schools communicated codes of conduct to administrators and faculty, there was little involvement with the faculty and very little follow-up on the code. Many faculty members tend to be isolated from the policies and procedures of their institutions, either by choice or through the unwillingness of administrators to foster faculty involvement. The faculty is in the best position to enforce standards and effectiveness and yet are seldom utilized in this role (Kibler, 1994).

The results show that university ethics policies are least likely to deal with financial fraud or fraud in research or scholarly activities. Based on surveys of faculty, these should be major areas of concern (Engle and Smith, 1990; Lewellyn, 1996). This would suggest that promotion and tenure policies are not adequately dealing with fraud in research and in scholarly activities. Financial fraud typically is the focus of governmental codes of ethics, despite the fact that most ethical violations are political rather than financial (Frederickson, 1993). Other than conflict of interest, there is no interest in any other type of financial fraud.

Conclusions

The new millennium will provide a great challenge for C&U. This challenge is centered on the C&Us' need to strengthen public trust. In this study respondents generally were supportive of the concept of codes of ethical conduct in C&U. This is understandable in the sense that colleges were more likely to follow a "low road" approach, and, within that approach, codes of conduct are considered appropriate and adequate. There seems to be little indication of an indirect approach in that there is little evidence of a comprehensive, proactive approach with the goal of generating trust. This is especially evident with little faculty involvement in the process and little concern for reviewing compliance with the codes of conduct. Consensus and enforcement are important factors in a proactive indirect approach. A college code of conduct can help eliminate unethical practices, relieve ethical dilemmas, and demonstrate a commitment to ethical conduct. Nevertheless, it must be fairly enforced and have a consensus of participants as to what is acceptable behavior and what should be the punishment of deviations from that behavior.

The findings of this study are subject to several limitations. First, the participants were all vice presidents of finance at the C&U, which may limit generalizability of the findings beyond that population. The apparently homogeneous sample of financial administrators may have systematic biases in their perceptions as to the nature, content, function and implementation of codes of conduct because of their role in dealing primarily with financial and human resources as aspects of codes of conduct. Second, despite the attempt made to compare late responses with early responses, a nonresponse bias may be present in the results. Third, the results are dependent on the nature of the responses. The sensitive aspect of codes of ethical conduct and ethical behavior may have inhibited some respondents from answering truthfully. Finally, this study gathered opinions regarding the status, nature, function of, and procedures for establishing codes of conduct in C&U, despite the differences that may exist among different colleges within the university (e.g., college of liberal arts and college of business). Future studies should examine the existence of codes of conducts for faculty and students in different colleges. Further research is also needed to determine whether the procedures of promotion and tenure, seminars, professional membership, quality programs, performance evaluation, and faculty handbooks can work with a code of conduct to support a goal of ethical conduct and public trust, or whether they are limited by their multiple goals and purposes.

APPENDIX

College and University Questionnaire

This questionnaire seeks your opinion regarding, the status, nature and procedures following in establishing codes of conduct at college and universities. Your response will be anonymous. If you enclose a business card for a copy of the results, it will be separated from the questionnaire when the envelope is opened.

PART I: CODE OF CONDUCT

1. Does your university have a code of conduct (ethical policy)? Yes _______ No _______

IF YOU ANSWERED NO TO QUESTION 1, PLEASE SKIP TO PART II.

2. Which ofthe following guidelines are included in your ethical policy (please check all that supply)?

 ____ Conflict of interest
 ____ Compliance with university policies
 ____ Compliance with external rules and regulations including athletics
 ____ Allegation of fraudulent conduct in research or scholarly activity
 ____ Faculty grievances
 ____ Tenure and promotion policies and procedures
 ____ Confidentiahty of proprietary information
 ____ Administrators, faculty, and stafF performance
 ____ Financial fraud
 ____ Others (please specify) ______________________________

3. Who was (were) involved in preparing your university code of conduct? Please check all that apply and place an asterisk (*) next to the person(s) who approved the final draft.

 ____ President
 ____ Provost and Vice President of Academic Affairs
 ____ Board of Regents
 ____ Faculty senate and/or union
 ____ Government and State authorities
 ____ Accreditation bodies
 ____ Others (please specify) ______________________________

4. Which of the following procedures is (are) followed in implementing and monitoring your university code of conduct (please check all that apply?

 ____ The code is approved by faculty senate. President, and Board of Regents
 ____ A copy of the code is distributed to administrators, faculty, and staff
 ____ A certificate of compliance with the code is annually received from administrators, faculty, and staff
 ____ Non-compliance with the code is being investigated and corrected
 ____ Others (please specify) ______________________________

(continued)

APPENDIX

College and University Questionnaire *(continued)*

5. Please indicate the extent to which you **agree** with the following statements regarding the need for adoption of a code of ethics for colleges and universities by circling one number.

	Strongly disagree				Strongly agree
a. A set of ethical standards is needed to resolve ethical dilemmas in academic environments.	1	2	3	4	5
b. Code of ethics can demonstrate the university's commitment to a set of standards that society expects them to meet.	1	2	3	4	5
c. A recognized set of standards will raise the stature of academia.	1	2	3	4	5
d. Colleges and universities should be required to have codes of ethics.	1	2	3	4	5
e. The diversity of the academic milieu makes the adoption of a code of ethics difficult.	1	2	3	4	5

PART II: GENERAL INFORMATION

1. Please provide the following information for your university. (Please circle the appropriate number for each category)

   a 1. State Supported (Public) 2. Private

   b. 1. Primarily commuting 2. Primarily non-commuting

   c. Number of Years in Operation

< 5	5–10	11–20	21–50
51–100	> 100		

   d. Student Population

< 2,000	2,001–5,000	5,001–10,000	10,001–20,000
20,001–35,000	>35,000		

   e. Number of Faculty

< 100	100–300	301–500	501–1,000
1,001–2,000	2,001–5000	> 5,000	

   f. Number of Colleges (Schools)

2–5	6–10	11–20	> 20

   g. Total Budget in Millions

< 5	5–10	11–20	21–50
51–100	101–500	> 500	

2. Would you like a copy of the summary of results? If yes, please check below and enclose your business card in the envelope. Yes ______ No ______

3. Please write any **comments** you may have on all four parts of the questionnaire and please do not hesitate to provide us with additional related information or materials.

Thank you again for your assistance. Please send the complete questionnaire along with additional related information or materials to Dr. Zabi Rezaee, MTSU, PO. Box 50, Murfreesboro, TN 37132.

Note

1. The initial questionnaire was pre-tested by 15 participants known by the authors and considered to be knowledgeable in financial reporting and administration of colleges and universities. Suggestions and comments of these participants were incorporated into the final version of the questionnaire. A copy of this questionnaire is available from the authors.

References

Baumhart, R.: 1968, *An Honest Profit* (Holt, Rinehart, and Winston, New York).

Beets, S. D.: 1992, 'The Revised AICPA Code of Professional Conduct: Current Considerations', *The CPA Journal* 62 (April), 26–32.

Blake, R., J. A. Grob, D. H. Potenski, P Reed and P Walsh: 1998, 'The Nature and Scope of State Government Ethics Codes', *Public Productivity & Management Review* 21 (June), 453–459.

Bowman, J. S.: 1990, 'Ethics in Government: A National Survey of Public Administrators', *Public Administration Review* 50(3), 345–353.

Brenner, S. N. and E. A. Molander: 1971, 'Is the Ethics of Business Changing?', *Harvard Business Review* (January–February), 57–71.

Brien, A.: 1998, 'Professional Ethics and the Culture of Trust', *Journal of Business Ethics* 17 (March), 391–410.

Callahan, D.: 1980, 'Goals in the Teaching of Ethics', *Ethics Teaching in Higher Education* (Plenum Press, New York), 61–80.

Carey, J. L.: 1965, *The CPA Plans for the Future* (American Institute of CPA's, AICPA, New York).

Committee of Sponsoring Organizations of the Treadway Commission (COSO): 1992, *Internal Control-Integrated Framework* (Coopers and Lybrand, New York).

Davis, R. R.: 1984, 'Ethical Behavior Reexamined', *The CPA Journal* 54 (December), 32–36.

Dobel, J. P: 1993, 'The Realpolitik of Ethics Codes: An Implementation Approach to Public Ethics', in H. George Frederickson (ed.). *Ethics and Public Administration* (M.E. Sharpe, New York), pp. 158–171.

Engle T. and J. Smith: 1990, 'The Ethical Standards of Accounting Academics', *Issues in Accounting Education* 5 (Spring), 7–28.

Financial Accounting Standards Board (FASB): 1993a, *SFAS No. 116: Accounting for Contributions Received and Contributions Made* (FASB, Norwalk CT).

Financial Accounting Standards Board (FASB): 1993b, *SFAS No. 117: Financial Statements of Not-For-Profit Organizations* (FASB, Norwalk CT).

Frederickson, H. G.: 1993, 'Ethics and Public Administration: Some Assertions', in H. George Frederickson (ed.). *Ethics and Public Administration* (M.E. Sharpe, New York), pp. 243–259.

Gellerman, S. W: 1989, 'Managing Ethics from the Top Down', *Sloan Management Review* 2 (Winter), 73–79.

Government Accounting Standards Board (GASB): 1999, *GASB No. 35: Basic Financial Statements and Management's Discussion and Analysis for Public Colleges and Universities* (GASB, Norwalk CT).

Kibler, W. L.: 1994, 'Addressing Academic Dishonesty: What are Institutions of Higher Education Doing and Not Doing', *NASPA Journal* 31 (Winter), 92–101.

Lawrence, F B.: 1975, 'Whose Ethics Guide Business?', *Industry Week* 27 (October), 25.

Lewellyn, P. A. G.: 1996, 'Academic Perceptions: Ethics in the Information Discipline', *Journal of Business Ethics* 15 (May), 559–569.

Loeb, S. E.: 1971, 'A survey of Ethical Behavior in the Accounting Profession', *Journal of Accounting Research* 9 (Autumn), 287–306.

Loeb, S. E.: 1990, 'A Code of Ethics of Academic Accountants?', *Issues in Accounting Education* 5 (Spring), 123–128.

Loeb, S. E.: 1994, 'Ethics and Accounting Doctoral Education', *Journal of Business Ethics* 13 (October), 817–827.

Loverd, R. A.: 1989, 'The Challenge of a More Responsible, Productive Public Workplace', *Public Productivity & Management Review* XIII (Fall), 43–58.

Mayer-Sommer, A. P. and S. P. Loeb: 1981, 'Fostering More Successful Professional Socialization among Accounting Students', *The Accounting Review* 56 (Winter), 125–136.

McCarthy, I. N.: 1997, 'Professional Ethics Code Conflict Situations: Ethical and Value Orientation of Collegiate Accounting Students', *Journal of Business Ethics* 16 (Sept.), 1467–1474.

Molander, E. A.: 1987, 'A Paradigm for Design, Promulgation and Enforcement of Ethical Codes', *Journal of Business Ethics* 6 (November), 619–626.

Montoya, I. D. and A. J. Richard: 1994, 'A Comparative Study of Codes of Ethics in Health Care Facilities and Energy Companies', *Journal of Business Ethics* 13 (September), 713–718.

National Association of Colleges and University Business Officers (NACUBO): 1996, *Membership Roll* (NACUBO, Washington, DC).

National Committee of Fraudulent Financial Reporting (Treadway Commission): 1987, *Report on the National Commission on Fraudulent Financial Reporting* (Treadway Commission, Washington, DC).

Rohr, J. A.: 1989, *Ethics for Bureaucrats. An Essay on Law and Values* (Marcel Dekker, Inc., New York), pp. 60–65.

Sellers, J. H. and E, E, Milam: 1979, 'Ethical Perceptions of Accounting Students', *Collected Papers of the American Association's Annual Meeting*, 635 644.

Stevens, B.: 1994, 'An Analysis of Corporate Ethical Code Studies: Where Do We Go from Here?', *Journal of Business Ethics* 13 (January), 63–70.

Touche-Ross: 1988, *Ethics in Business: An Opinion Survey of Key Business leaders on Ethical Standards and Behavior* (Touche-Ross, New York).

Tyson, T.: 1992, 'Does Believing that Everyone Else is Less Ethical Have an Impact on Work Behavior?', *Journal of Business Ethics* 11 (September), 707–17.

Vincent, V. C. and W D. Monville: 1993, 'Ethical Considerations for Streaming Business Publications', *Journal of Business Ethics* 12 (January), 37–43.

CHAPTER 41

THE NORMATIVE STRUCTURE OF COLLEGE AND UNIVERSITY FUNDRAISING BEHAVIORS

TIMOTHY C. CABONI

Within the fundraising community, there has been a drive toward professionalization. Carbone (1989) argues that the issue of whether or not fundraising is a profession is best studied by examining the occupation upon a continuum of professionalism. Sociologists who study the professions suggest that an occupational group's level of professionalization depends upon how many characteristics of a profession these occupations possess (Barber, 1962; Carr-Saunders & Wilson, 1933; Greenwood, 1957; Haries-Jenkins, 1970; Millerson, 1964; Moore, 1970). By comparing fundraising to other "true-professions," Carbone (1989) concluded that fundraising is "*an emerging profession*—an occupation that has moved steadily along the professional continuum; a profession with the potential to attain greater professional stature" (p. 46).

Bloland (2002) concludes that fundraising has reached professional status, but not on the basis of the five criteria of professions. Yet he later argues (Bloland & Temple, 2004) that the professional ideal, with true professions achieving each criteria to some degree, is an ideal status which can never be obtained precisely because it is an ideal.

Core Traits of Professions

Goode (1969) suggests that the mastery of a basic body of abstract knowledge and the ideal of service to clients are the two core traits which define professions. Those occupations which possess these two traits may legitimately claim professional status (Goode, 1969).

Mastery of Knowledge and Fundraising

One of the challenges for fundraising as it progresses toward professional status is the lack of inquiry into the fundraising function within the college and university environment. One of the markers of professionalism is the existence of a knowledge base in which practitioners are well versed. Typically, this knowledge is mastered through an extended period of training.

However, Kelly (1991) comments that "there are few, if any studies on basic research or theory building" (p. 114) in the literature of the profession. The research which does exist is limited, fragmented, and of marginal quality (Brittingham & Pezzulo, 1990).

Carbone (1986) writes that fundraisers themselves report that the knowledge they use in doing their duties as development officers is primarily general knowledge which is possessed by anyone. They also believe that such knowledge is best learned on the job rather than in formal education.

The fundraising profession lacks a substantial knowledge base from which to derive professional status.

However, the introduction of a journal focused entirely on institutional advancement and fundraising in higher education in 2000 (*International Journal of Educational Advancement*), the creation of research awards designed to reward and encourage outstanding doctoral research on fundraising, along with a recently published ASHE reader including advancement as a topical area have increased the number of higher education fundraising articles in the scholarly literature. Recently higher education fundraising topics explored in the literature include historical examinations of fundraising (Cash, 2005; Cohen 2008; Gasman, 2004); the president's role in fundraising (Nesbit, Rooney, Bouse, & Tempel, 2006; Nicholson, 2007) advancement as a community engagement strategy (Weerts, 2007); econometric analyses of large-scale data sets (Gottfried & Johnson, 2006); fundraising in an international context (Lee & Chang, 2008); and human resources strategies for fundraising programs (Iarrobino, 2006).

Even with the recent increase in the number of articles this characteristic of a profession remains tenuous at best. Additionally, no study has examined fundraiser behaviors or perceptions of these behaviors. If fundraising is to lay claim to status as a profession, focus must be placed upon the professional characteristic of the ideal of service.

Ideal of Service and Fundraising

Goode (1969) suggests that members of a profession must base their individual decisions on what will serve the needs and protect the welfare of their clients. If viewed through this lens, the fundraising profession has two separate clients for whom it is responsible: the institution and the donor.

First, professional fundraisers are responsible for the welfare of their institutional clients. Development officers are charged with providing necessary capital for the operations of their institutions and for raising money to create endowed funds to provide support for specific projects, programs, scholarships, and professorships in perpetuity (Worth, 2002). Along with this responsibility comes the potential for causing great harm to the institution. This harm may be caused in a number of ways.

Because there is great latitude afforded to development officers in soliciting gifts, a development officer might be tempted to enter into an agreement with a donor to create a specific program for which the university has no need or want. While accepting such a donation might help the institution reach its capital campaign, or yearly fundraising goals, it may move the college or university in an academic direction in which its leaders had not intended. The task of crafting academic policy is best left to provosts, deans, and department chairs not donors and development officers.

A second possible way in which the institutional client might be harmed is through inappropriate behavior on the part of the fund raiser. Because the role of fund raiser is one of boundary spanner, the development officer represents the organization to individuals who are outside of the organization and in the community. Because the development officer is the embodiment of the university, her actions will reflect directly on the institution's reputation. This is another instance where a fund raiser may cause harm to an institutional client.

Second, fundraisers must protect the individuals who provide funds to their institutions. In order to know as much as possible about potential donors, college and university development offices conduct research into the financial and personal backgrounds of these individual donors (Worth, 2002). Much of this information could be potentially damaging if revealed to the general public. Some donors also desire some degree of confidentiality about their gifts. Development officers are responsible for ensuring that this information is protected.

One area of fundraising that poses a potential threat to the welfare of the donor client is planned giving. Planned gifts are structured toward the later years of a prospect's life and in many cases provide income for that person until the time of his or her death. This type of gift can be potentially damaging to the donor if the amount of income guaranteed by the institution is not enough for the donor to meet expenses. Additionally, with uncertain health, a problem in elderly donors, those individuals who tie up a large percentage of their capital in a structured gift may run into problems taking care of themselves when unforeseen health problems arise.

Because of the potential financial and reputational damage which may be inflicted on a potential donor through a development officer's behavior, fundraisers do bear a responsibility for the welfare of their donor clients.

Professional Self-Regulation

Professions ensure that members adhere to the ideal of service through the use of formal and informal social control mechanisms (Braxton, 1986; Braxton, Bayer, & Finkelstein, 1992; Bucher & Strauss, 1961; Goode, 1957). Goode (1957) suggests these rules are taught to new members of a profession through the socialization process. These social control mechanisms define what behaviors by members of a profession are appropriate and inappropriate.

Formal Social Control Mechanisms

One marker of the degree of professionalism an occupation has attained is the existence of a code of conduct (Abbott, 1983; Barber, 1962; Carr-Saunders & Wilson, 1933; Harries-Jenkins, 1970). Published codes of ethics by which professionals are expected to abide are an example of a formal social control mechanism. These codes assist a profession in attaining professional autonomy and self-regulation (Cohen & Pant, 1991). They also serve as a measuring stick against which members of a profession may judge the relative impropriety of certain demands (Frankel, 1989). "Through its ethical code, a profession's commitment to the social welfare becomes a matter of public record, thereby insuring for itself the continued confidence of the community" (Greenwood, 1966, p. 14).

Both of the major professional organizations to which college and university fundraisers belong (Council for Advancement and Support of Education and National Society of Fundraising Executives) have explicitly stated codes of ethics for their members.

However, Kelly (1995) found that less than half (44%) of the organizations represented in NSFRE had policies regarding the acquisition of gifts and 50% count on professional fundraisers to abide by a code of professional ethics when receiving gifts or to judge gifts on an individual basis. Lombardo (1991) found that only four of the twelve charitable institutions she studied had formal guidelines to deal with cases of conflict of interest between fundraisers and donors. In his study of fundraisers who are members of CASE, Carbone (1989) found that 30% of them were unsure if their national organization played a role in setting standards and protecting the right to practice. Additionally, he found that "28% are unsure if this function is important and 10% thought it was unimportant for the organization to do this" (Carbone, 1989, p. 32).

Informal Social Control Mechanisms

In the absence of formal social control mechanisms, fundraisers must rely upon informal mechanisms to ensure that members of the profession are conforming to what are considered appropriate behaviors. Carlin (1966) and Friedson (1975) found that informal rules are more important social control mechanisms than formal controls.

Norms are one mechanism through which professions self regulate using informal social controls. Norms are shared beliefs about how an individual should act in a particular situation (Merton, 1968, 1973). Merton (1957, 1968) suggests that norms function as mechanisms of social control because they consist of prescribed and proscribed patterns of behavior. This concept is derived from Durkheim's (1951) statement that the natural human condition is unregulated passion, whereas conforming requires social regulation. Without a normative structure, individuals in the profession would be free to act as they saw fit, with individuals deciding for themselves what behaviors constituted appropriate and inappropriate behavior.

Additionally, "norms assure that professional choices adhere to the ideal of service" (Braxton & Bayer, 1999, p. 4). By self-regulating, a profession communicates to its members the necessity of stewarding the welfare of its clients.

The degree of moral outrage that accompanies the violation of a norm indicates the social significance of the norm (Durkheim, 1995). Those norms which individuals view as highly inappropriate carry a higher penalty and increased social significance when violated as compared to those behaviors which are not as inappropriate.

Morris (1956) writes that "norms are generally accepted, sanctioned prescriptions for or prohibitions against, others' behavior, belief or feeling, i.e. what others *ought* to do, believe, feel—or *else*" (p. 610). He goes on to state that violation of accepted norms always involve sanctions (Morris, 1956). Norms serve as a guide to how fundraisers perform the roles associated with the fundraising profession. They represent the "collective conscience" of the profession and dictate what is appropriate and inappropriate behavior for its members (Durkheim, 1951). Violation of these norms by development officers may result in sanctioning by peers, institutions, and the government.

Thus, if a normative structure for fundraising exists for practitioners within higher education, it would be a sign as to the degree of the occupation's progress toward professionalization.

Purpose of the Study

This study examines the environment in which college and university development officers operate. Specifically it attempts to answer the research question:

> Does a normative structure for college and university fundraising exist?

By examining those behaviors which fundraisers believe are highly inappropriate, we may more fully understand how the behavior of individuals within the profession is regulated by norms. These findings may suggest ways in which members of the fundraising profession could be socialized to adhere to ethical principals espoused by both professional organizations (CASE and NSFRE). Additionally, the absence of social controls may provide guidance to institutional advancement managers as to what areas of ethical behavior need to be more fully addressed.

Subjects

A two-stage sampling design was used for this study. The subjects for this study were drawn from the membership roster of CASE (the professional organization for college and university fundraisers). First, all individuals whose primary job function is raising money for their college or university were selected for a total population of 10,183 fundraisers. Then, of those individuals, 1,047 subjects (10% of the total population), were selected at random using the SPSS sample selector. After examination of the list and the titles of those individuals selected, those individuals whose jobs did not entail direct solicitation of prospects were culled from the list for a final sample size of 803 (7.7%). The sample drawn mirrored the CASE district representation.

Questionnaire Development

The data for this study were gathered by means of a mailed questionnaire which was completed by the selected fundraising professionals. The "College Fundraising Behaviors Inventory (CFRBI)," a four-page instrument composed of 84 behaviors and fund raiser characteristics which may meet normative criteria was designed and constructed for this study. These behaviors were worded negatively so that those behaviors which evoked strong negative responses from respondents would emerge. This use of negatively worded items follows the method employed by Braxton and Bayer (1999) in their study of the normative structure of college teaching. The use of negatively worded questions is derived from Durkheim's (1995) proposition that the degree of outrage which accompanies the violation of a norm indicates the level of social significance associated with that normative orientation. Specifically, the questionnaire is comprised of 71 six-point Likert-type questions and 13 questions requiring categorical-type responses.

Normative behaviors were created for the following broad categories of values in fundraising behavior: honesty, integrity, promise-keeping, fidelity/loyalty, fairness, caring for others, respect for others, responsible citizenship, pursuit of excellence, accountability, safeguarding the public trust, and duty. These twelve areas of fundraising behavior were derived from Marion's (1994) suggested framework for incorporating ethical values into fundraising activities. They are a modification of the Josephson Institute for the Advancement of Ethics' core values for nonprofit organizations and their development professionals (Josephson, 1988).

Variables

Because of the exploratory nature of this study, normative clusters of fundraising behaviors were not known a priori. They emerged as a result of the analyses performed on collected data. However, broad categories of important fund raiser values have been suggested and were used in the creation of the questionnaire. These broad categories included: honesty, integrity, fidelity/loyalty, fairness, caring for others, respect for others, responsible citizenship, pursuit of excellence, accountability, safeguarding the public trust, and duty (Marion, 1994).

Coding of Fundraising Behaviors

Each of the 71 behaviors constructed for this study were coded on a six-point Likert scale. Response categories were 1 = very inappropriate behavior, the fundraiser should be dismissed from the institution, 2 = very inappropriate behavior, requires formal administrative intervention, 3 = inappropriate behavior, should be handled informally by colleagues or administrators suggesting change or improvement, 4 = mildly inappropriate behavior, generally to be ignored, 5 = behavior which is neither appropriate nor inappropriate, 6 = behavior is appropriate.

Data Collected

Of the 803 questionnaires mailed to potential respondents, 313 questionnaires were returned. Of those 313, 18 respondents returned blank surveys as an indication that they were unwilling to participate in the study. A total of 295 useable questionnaires were returned for an overall response rate of 36.7%.

Leslie (1972) recommends a method for testing response bias in mail surveys. The procedure assumes that those individuals who answer in later mailing waves are more like nonrespondents than the individuals who returned questionnaires in the first mailing wave. By comparing the responses of those individuals from the first wave to those who respond to the second wave, it can be ascertained whether major bias exists in the data.

T tests were used to compare respondents from the first wave to respondents from the second mailing wave on inviolable and admonitory norms, as well as on the number of years they had been in fundraising and the number of years they had been employed by their current institution (Table 41.4). Some bias was found for the admonitory proscriptive norm of donor manipulation. Later respondents (mean = 2.73) voice less disdain for this pattern of behaviors than do those individuals who returned the survey initially (mean = 2.43). The difference is statistically significant at the 0.05 level.

Consequently, there is a high degree of confidence in the representativeness of the response group because of the mailing wave bias analysis demonstrated that the second wave of respondents were more like the first wave of respondents rather than sharing similarities with non-respondents.

Confidence in the representative nature of the respondents would have been strengthened further if a comparison were able to be made between respondents and case membership. Unfortunately, the author was unable to compare the response sample to those of the membership of case in the year in which the survey was conducted.

Respondents' Individual Characteristics

A majority of the fundraisers participating in this study have been fundraisers for over 10 years, reflecting a range of 1 to 43 years with a sample mean of 11 years (SD 7.81, see Table 41.1). Additionally, more than half of the respondents have been employed at their current institution for over 6 years (SD 5.69, see Table 41.1).

Of the fundraisers who returned a questionnaire, 53.9% were male, 53.2% were responsible for other professional fundraisers at their institution, and 52.8% previously had managerial responsibility for fundraisers. Respondents were predominantly engaged in major gift solicitations (74.8%). Only 8.5% or those participating in the study had a degree in nonprofit management or institutional advancement, and 21.1% had taken a course for credit focused on nonprofit management or institutional advancement. A majority of the subjects in this study were familiar with both the *Donor Bill of Rights* (80.3%) and the *Code of Ethical Principles and Standards of Professional Practice* (77.9%).

TABLE 41.1

Fundraisers' Years as Fundraiser and Years at Current Institution

Category	*N*	Range	X	*SD*
# of years as a fundraiser	295	1–43	11.08	7.81
# of years at current institution	295	1–30	6.04	5.69

TABLE 41.2

Individual Fundraiser Characteristics of Study Participants (Total # of Respondents = 295)

Variables	No.	%
Individual Fundraiser Characteristics		
Gender		
Male	159	53.9%
Female	136	48.8%
Conference attendance		
Yes	268	90.8%
No	27	9.2%
Managerial responsibility		
Yes	157	53.4%
No	137	46.6%
Previous managerial responsibility		
Yes	152	52.8%
No	136	47.2%
Primary solicitation type		
Annual	73	24.7%
Major	217	74.8%
I. A. degree		
Yes	25	8.5%
No	268	91.5%
I. A. course		
Yes	62	21.1%
No	232	78.9%
Familiar with *Donor Bill of Rights*		
Yes	237	80.3%
No	58	19.7%
Familiar with *Code of Ethical Principles*		
Yes	229	77.9%
No	65	22.1%

Respondents' Organizational Characteristics

Of those fundraisers who returned questionnaires, the majority were employed by public institutions (51.2%). Individuals employed by research institutions were the largest group of respondents (40.1%) followed by those employed by comprehensive institutions (22.8%), baccalaureate institutions (21.3%), doctoral institutions (12.7%), and associate institutions (3.0%). Respondents worked primarily in a centralized development office (64.8%) and were involved in a capital campaign (64.6%).

Because such a small number of respondents were employed by associate level institutions (8), those respondents were not included in analyses involving Carnegie Classification. This low response rate makes generalizing results to those individuals who are responsible for fundraising at associate institutions impossible.

Results

Inviolable Norms

Specific behaviors are defined as inviolable if their mean values were 2.00 or lower on the sanctioning scale following the procedures outlined by Braxton and Bayer (1999). Norms are considered inviolable when they require the strictest of sanctions when they are violated (Braxton & Bayer, 1999). Of the 71 behaviors on the instrument, 10 met the criterion of 2.00 or lower for inviolable norms. These 10 items were then subjected to factor analysis using the principal components method. This method was used because no a priori theory existed about the factors which were derived from the analysis. A three-factor solution was chosen using the scree test. The three factors were then rotated using the varimax method to determine the normative pattern underlying the specific fundraising behaviors and alpha levels were computed. Once these alpha levels were computed, composite scores were created for each construct by totaling the responses for each individual behavior and dividing the total by the number of behaviors in the construct.

From this analysis, three inviolable normative patterns emerged. The three inviolable norms in alphabetical order are: *Exploitation of Institutional Resources, Institutional Disregard*, and *Misappropriation of Gifts*.

TABLE 41.3

Organizational Characteristics of Study Participants (Total # of Respondents = 295)

Variables	No.	%
Carnegie classification		
Research	107	40.1%
Doctoral	34	12.7%
Comprehensive	61	22.8%
Baccalaureate	57	21.3%
Associate	8	3.0%
Public or private institution		
Public	146	51.2%
Private	139	48.8%
Centralized or decentralized office		
Centralized	188	64.8%
Decentralized	102	35.2%
Capital campaign		
Yes	190	64.6%
No	104	35.4%

Exploitation of institutional resources proscribes behaviors by fundraisers which take advantage of an institution's funds, or other things of value which the institution possesses (including offers of admission), for personal gain. While the alpha level of this norm is below 0.60 it is included because of the exploratory nature of the study. However, its purpose is primarily heuristic.

The normative pattern of institutional disregard proscribes behaviors by fundraisers which would damage the reputation of the fund raiser's employing institution. As discussed earlier, the institution for which a fund raiser works is a client of the fund raiser. Violating this norm puts at risk the welfare of the fund raiser's institutional client.

Finally, the inviolable norm regarding misappropriation of gifts includes transgressions by fundraisers in which donations are used for purposes which were not intended by the donor. Violation of this normative pattern could cause damage both to the donor client relationship (by misusing the funds given by the individual) and the institutional client (if the donor relationship is compromised because the donation was not used for its intended purpose, the donor might never make another gift to the college).

Admonitory Norms

Specific behaviors are defined as admonitory if their mean values were less than 3.00 and greater than 2.00 on the sanctioning scale. Braxton and Bayer (1999) define norms as admonitory when they "invoke less indignation when violated than inviolable norms" (p. 44). Of the 71 fundraising behaviors on the instrument, 23 met the criterion for admonitory norms. These 23 items were factor analyzed using the principal components method. This method was used because no a priori theory existed about the factors which were derived from the analysis. A six-factor solution was chosen using the scree test. The six factors were then rotated using the varimax method to determine the normative pattern underlying the specific fundraising behaviors and alpha reliabilities were calculated. Once these alpha levels were computed, composite scores were created for each construct by totaling the responses for each individual behavior and dividing the total by the number of behaviors in the construct.

From this analysis, six admonitory normative patterns emerged. The six admonitory norms in alphabetical order are: *Commission-Based Compensation, Dishonest Solicitation, Donor Manipulation, Exaggeration of Professional Experience, Institutional Mission Abandonment*, and *Unreasonable Enforcement of Pledges*.

The admonitory norm regarding commission based compensation includes transgressions by fundraisers in which an individual's salary is paid in-part, or in-full as a percentage of the dollar total raised by that fund raiser. Violation of this normative pattern is in direct conflict with the code of ethical standards for fundraisers at educational institutions approved by CASE in 2005 which state that fundraisers must "not accept commission-based compensation or compensation based on a percentage of funds raised; not accept external compensation for the receipt of a gift or information leading to a gift; [and] not agree to pay compensation to individuals in respect of a gift or information leading to a gift" (CASE, 2005).

The purpose of discouraging these types of compensation packages is to ensure that an individual raising funds for an institution does not take advantage of a donor for financial gain (e.g., pushing a donor to make a gift which will do harm to the individual's financial standing because a large gift will result in a large commission).

The normative pattern of dishonest solicitation proscribes behaviors by fundraisers which involve untruthfulness while a fund raiser asks a prospect for a gift. By violating this norm, a fund raiser takes advantage of the autonomy granted to development officers in the conduct of their professional duties. By lying or bending the truth, the fund raiser puts at risk the relationship with the potential donor.

The normative factor dealing with donor manipulation involves a fund raiser's handling of delicate relationships with a donor. Individuals who have lost or are losing the capacity to make sound decisions for themselves should not be solicited for gifts. By exploiting these individuals, a fund raiser is potentially causing harm to the donor client.

TABLE 41.4

Factor Loadings of Specific Behaviors of Inviolable and Admonitory Norms

Inviolable Normative Pattern/Item	Mean	*SD*	Loading
Exploitation of Institutional Resources			
Q8. A fundraiser makes personal charges on an institutional credit card and submits them as business expenses	1.44	0.55	0.81
Q15. A fundraiser agrees to get a student admitted to the institution if a gift is made	1.75	0.67	0.60
Q6. A fundraiser pads a call report with visits he/she did not make	1.95	0.68	0.71
Chronbach alpha = 0.58			
Institutional Disregard			
Q20. A fundraiser tells someone outside of the institution private information about a donor	1.72	0.75	0.64
Q50. A fundraiser gets drunk at an official institution function	1.89	0.79	0.63
Q55. A fundraiser speaks poorly about the institution to a prospect	2.00	0.73	0.75
Q25. A fundraiser provides a copy of a prospect list to another institution	1.97	1.09	0.67
Chronbach alpha = 0.63			
Misappropriation of Gifts			
Q19. A fundraiser allows the income from a restricted scholarship fund to be used for a purpose other than scholarships	1.73	0.62	0.83
Q18. A fundraiser uses restricted funds to support an institution's operating budget	1.82	0.84	0.78
Q17. A fundraiser allows a donors gift to be used for something other than what it was intended	1.86	0.69	0.81
Chronbach alpha = 0.77			
Admonitory Normative Pattern/Item	**Mean**	***SD***	**Loading**
Commission Based Compensation			
Q48. A fundraiser works on a commission basis	2.41	1.58	0.93
Q49. A fundraiser agrees to base a part of his/her annual salary as a percentage of total dollars raised	2.64	1.61	0.94
Chronbach alpha = 0.92			
Dishonest Solicitation			
Q62. A fundraiser allows a scholarship designated for minority students to be awarded to a non-minority student	2.10	0.74	0.64
Q56. A fundraiser says negative things about other staff members to a prospect	2.09	0.63	0.62
Q60. A fundraiser knows that a donor received double credit for a gift, but does not tell anyone	2.41	0.84	0.70
Q70. A fundraiser intentionally uses confusing language when describing the details of a planned gift to a donor	2.46	0.84	0.62

(continued)

TABLE 41.4

Factor Loadings of Specific Behaviors of Inviolable and Admonitory Norms *(continued)*

Admonitory Normative Pattern/Item	Mean	*SD*	Loading
Q46. A fundraiser tells a donor their gift will solve a particular institutional problem when, in reality, the gift will not solve the problem	2.64	0.95	0.56
Q59. A fundraiser makes a mistake and blames an administrative assistant	2.65	0.78	0.60
Q67. A fundraiser makes negative comments about another organization to which a prospect is considering making a gift	2.80	0.85	0.48
Chronbach alpha = 0.78			
Donor Manipulation			
Q34. A fundraiser attempts to solicit a planned gift from a prospect, even though it is not in the prospect's best interest	2.73	1.00	0.76
Q32. A fundraiser asks a prospect whose mental faculties are in question to make a gift because it would be of benefit to the institution	2.26	1.01	0.74
Chronbach alpha = 0.70			
Exaggeration of Professional Experience			
Q3. A fundraiser inflates his/her dollar raised totals in a previous position	2.36	0.82	0.80
Q10. A fundraiser misrepresents the amount of money raised by the institution to a potential donor	2.52	0.81	0.50
Q2. A fundraiser exaggerates his/her professional experience	2.49	0.82	0.78
Q1. A fundraiser takes credit for a gift brought in by another development officer	2.57	0.70	0.58
Q4. A fundraiser blames someone else for his/her not making yearly goals for dollar totals	2.75	0.75	0.63
Q7. A fundraiser takes credit for another staff member's idea	2.78	0.69	0.64
Chronbach alpha = 0.77			
Institutional Mission Abandonment			
Q13. A fundraiser allows a donor to make a gift which creates a program the institution does not need or want	2.74	1.11	0.87
Q14. A fundraiser agrees to accept a gift from a donor, the use of which is too narrowly defined to be of use to the institution	2.80	0.99	0.83
Q26. A fundraiser accepts a gift because it adds to fundraising totals, even though the institution has no need for the program the gift will fund	2.94	1.14	0.78
Chronbach alpha = 0.84			
Unreasonable Enforcement of Pledges			
Q37. A fundraiser refuses to return a gift to a donor who is upset with how the funds are being used and has asked for the gift to be returned	2.53	1.34	0.84
Q38. A fundraiser takes a deceased donor's family to court to force them to fulfill the donor's pledge	2.87	1.63	0.78
Chronbach alpha = 0.55			

The normative array with respect to exaggeration of professional experience centers on fundraisers who embellish the fundraising work they have done either at a previous institution or for their current employer.

The behaviors associated with institutional mission abandonment are centered around fundraisers attracting gifts for things and programs for which the institution has no need. Because fundraisers are not involved directly in the academic enterprise of the institution, they should not create or change academic programs according to the whim of donors. Doing so infringes upon the institution's autonomy to make programmatic decisions based upon the best interest of enrolled students.

The admonitory norm which proscribes the unreasonable enforcement of pledges is the final admonitory norm which emerged from the data. With an alpha level below 0.60, this norm also should be taken as heuristic. This norm prohibits fundraisers from taking legal action against a donor or their families in the pursuit of gifts promised to an institution, or from refusing to return a gift made by a donor who is unhappy with how the gift is being used. While a pledge may be considered a legally binding document, this norm advises fundraisers (and in turn their institutions) from pursuing legal action against donors and their families.

Respondent Characteristics and Norm Espousal

Capital Campaign Environment

Fundraisers in those institutions currently engaged in a capital campaign espouse levels of disdain for the three inviolable norms and the six admonitory norms similar to their counterparts in institutions not currently engaged in a campaign. The results of the t tests exhibited in Tables 41.5 and 41.6 support this statement. There is no statistically significant relationship between the capital campaign environment in which a fund raiser is operating and the espousal of inviolable or admonitory norms.

Familiarity with the Donor Bill of Rights

Statistically significant differences between fundraisers who are familiar with the *Donor Bill of Rights* and those not familiar with the *Donor Bill of Rights* was observed on all of the three inviolable patterns, and on three of the six admonitory patterns. Tables 41.7 and 41.8 exhibit the results of the bivariate relationships between the individual characteristic fundraiser familiarity with the *Donor Bill of Rights* and the level of espousal for each of the three inviolable (Table 41.7) and six admonitory (Table 41.8) normative arrays. As the tables illustrate, there are statistically significant relationships between familiarity with the *Donor Bill of Rights* and the espousal of all three inviolable norms and for three admonitory norms: Exploitation of institutional resources ($t = 2.17, p < 0.05$), institutional

TABLE 41.5

Bivariate Relationships Between the Three Inviolable Proscribed Normative Patterns and the Fundraiser Characteristic: Capital Campaign Environment

Normative Pattern	Mean In Campaign	Mean Non-Campaign	t value
Exploitation of institutional resources	1.71	1.71	0.16
Institutional disregard	1.90	1.86	0.51
Misappropriation of gifts	1.82	1.75	0.98

TABLE 41.6

Bivariate Relationships Between the Six Admonitory Proscribed Normative Patterns and the Fundraiser Characteristic: Capital Campaign Environment

Normative Pattern	Mean In Campaign	Mean Non-Campaign	*t* value
Commission-based compensation	2.48	2.61	–0.68
Dishonest solicitation	2.44	2.45	0.11
Donor manipulation	2.48	2.49	–0.02
Exaggeration of professional experience	2.58	2.56	0.24
Institutional mission abandonment	2.77	2.92	–1.33
Unreasonable pledge enforcement	2.76	2.54	1.38

TABLE 41.7

Bivariate Relationships Between the Three Inviolable Proscribed Normative Patterns and the Fundraiser Characteristic: Donor Bill of Rights Familiarity

Normative Pattern	Mean Familiar	Mean Not Familiar	*t* value
Exploitation of institutional resources	1.68	1.83	–2.17*
Institutional disregard	1.85	2.10	–2.84**
Misappropriation of gifts	1.76	1.95	–2.23*

* $p < 0.05$, ** $p < 0.01$

TABLE 41.8

Bivariate Relationships Between the Six Admonitory Proscribed Normative Patterns and the Fundraiser Characteristic: Donor Bill of Rights Familiarity

Normative Pattern	Mean Familiar	Mean Not Familiar	*t* value
Commission-based compensation	2.42	2.96	–2.40*
Dishonest solicitation	2.43	2.53	–1.11
Donor manipulation	2.48	2.50	–0.16
Exaggeration of professional experience	2.54	2.72	–2.28*
Institutional mission abandonment	2.77	3.09	–2.32*

* $p < 0.05$, ** $p < 0.01$

disregard ($t = 2.84$, $p < 0.01$), misappropriation of gifts ($t = 2.3$, $p < 0.05$), commission based compensation ($t = 2.40$, $p < 0.05$), exaggeration of professional experience ($t = 2.28$, $p < 0.05$), and institutional mission abandonment ($t = 2.32$, $p < 0.05$).

Those individuals participating in the study who are familiar with the *Donor Bill of Rights* (mean = 1.68) view the normative behavioral pattern concerning exploitation of institutional resources as requiring more severe sanctions than those who are not familiar with the document (mean = 1.83). Those with a familiarity with the *Donor Bill of Rights* (mean = 1.85) also express greater disdain for fundraisers who engage in institutional disregard than those who are not familiar with the *Donor Bill of Rights* (mean = 2.10). Also, the norm against institutional disregard does not meet inviolable normative criteria for those who are unfamiliar with the *Donor Bill of Rights*. However, it does warrant admonitory status. Finally, the inviolable norm misappropriation of gifts is perceived as more egregious by those who are familiar with the *Donor Bill of Rights* (mean = 1.76) than those who are not (mean = 1.95).

Respondents to the CFRBI who are familiar with the *Donor Bill of Rights* (mean = 2.42) express more disapproval of the admonitory norm commission based compensation than do respondents who are not (mean = 2.96). Fundraisers who are familiar with the *Donor Bill of Rights* (mean = 2.54) also disapprove more strongly than those who are not familiar (mean = 2.72) of the behaviors associated with the admonitory normative pattern regarding exaggeration of professional experience. Finally, participants in the study who are familiar with the *Donor Bill of Rights* (mean = 2.77) express more disdain for colleagues who engage in institutional mission abandonment than those participants who are not familiar with the *Donor Bill of Rights* (mean = 3.09).

Number of Years as a Fundraiser

Analyses of variance were conducted on each of the normative patterns to determine the influence of time in the profession on each pattern. The homogeneity of variance assumption was tested for each of the nine analyses of variance. Heterogeneous variances were not found. Post hoc Scheffe tests were then performed on those analyses in which there was a significant difference between measured groups. The Scheffe test is the most conservative of the post hoc tests and reduces the potential for making Type I errors in an ANOVA (Gravetter & Wallnau, 2006). Statistically significant differences between fundraisers who have been in the profession for longer and shorter periods of time were not found on each of the three inviolable patterns. However, differences in the number of years as a fundraiser exist on three of the six admonitory patterns.

Three admonitory norms (Table 41.9) are differentiated by the number of years an individual has been a fund raiser: those concerning commission based compensation, donor manipulation, and institutional mission abandonment. More specifically, fundraisers who have been in the profession for 0–3 years espouse significantly less outrage at the violation of the normative array associated with commission-based compensation (mean = 3.08) than those who have been in the profession for 15+ years (mean = 2.09). Statistically reliable differences between the various categories of years in the profession were also found for the norm of donor manipulation. Fundraisers who have been members of the profession for 0–3 years exhibit a lesser degree of disdain (mean = 2.88) for behaviors associated with donor manipulation than their colleagues who have been in the profession for 7–10 years (mean = 2.28) and 15+ years (mean = 2.34). Finally, respondents who have been fundraisers for 0–3 years (mean = 3.20) ascribe a statistically significant lesser distaste for institutional mission abandonment than those respondents who have been in the profession for 15+ years (mean = 2.54).

Limitations

This study is limited by several issues that must be addressed. First, while the list of fundraising behaviors on the CFRBI are representative of many of the things fundraisers do in the course of performing their jobs, the list is by no means exhaustive. There may be other behaviors which would be perceived as inappropriate which were not included on the instrument.

TABLE 41.9

Results of Analysis of Variance of the Three Inviolable and Six Admonitory Normative Patterns by Years as Fundraiser

Normative Pattern	*F* Ratio	Normative Pattern Means by Years as Fundraiser					Post Hoc Mean Comparisons
		0–3	4–6	7–10	11–15	15+	
Inviolable							
Exploitation of institutional resources	0.34	1.76	1.74	1.68	1.72	1.67	
Institutional disregard	0.52	1.94	1.84	1.97	1.89	1.84	
Misappropriation of gifts	1.10	1.94	1.82	1.79	1.72	1.74	
Admonitory							
Commission-based compensation	3.40**	3.08	2.73	2.53	2.36	2.09	0–3 years > 15+ years*
Dishonest solicitation	0.95	2.46	2.46	2.42	2.49	2.42	
Donor manipulation	3.61**	2.88	2.54	2.28	2.48	2.34	0–3 years > 7–10 & 15+ years*
Exaggeration of professional experience	0.59	2.63	2.65	2.54	2.57	2.53	
Institutional mission abandonment	3.99**	3.20	2.95	2.84	2.74	2.54	0–3 years > 15+ years*
Unreasonable pledge enforcement	0.67	2.47	2.73	2.88	2.61	2.71	

* $p < 0.05$, ** $p < 0.01$

Second, the number of respondents employed at community colleges was too small to be of any use in this study. Because so few community college fundraisers returned the survey, no generalizations can be made to community colleges, as fundraising is a recent arrival in the community college setting. Because of its infancy, few fundraisers within community colleges are members of CASE.

Third, only members of CASE were included in the sample. One of the challenges in surveying members of the fundraising profession is that they are highly mobile. The average tenure of the fundraisers in this study at their current institution is six years. Because they change positions so frequently, getting a sample of CASE members was the most efficient manner to draw the sample. However, this eliminated those individuals who raise money for colleges and universities who are not members of CASE. Non-members of CASE may have different criteria for what they perceive as inappropriate behaviors.

Fourth, the author was unable to compare the individual and organizational characteristics of respondents and the population of CASE. Confidence in the representativeness of the respondents would have been strengthened had this analysis been possible.

Fifth, the Cronbach alpha reliabilities for the norms institutional resources and unreasonable enforcement of pledges we too low to consider them as anything other than heuristic. While included because they add depth to the study, replication of these findings with a higher alpha level would increase the value of these two patterns.

Finally, a response rate of 36.7% was reached for this project. While this was dealt with through response-bias analysis, there is a small chance that respondents are different from those individuals who chose not to participate in the study. Perhaps additional steps could be taken in the future to increase the response rate if this study is replicated for other populations. Another possibility would be to confirm the results of this study and add to its richness by conducting interviews with fundraisers to confirm the norms which emerged in this analysis.

Discussion

This study set out to answer the research question: *Does a normative structure for college and university fundraising exist?*

The results of this study demonstrate that a normative structure does exist for college and university fundraising behavior. This section outlines two sets of proscriptive normative patterns which emerged from this study. The first set includes those proscriptions which evoke the most severe sanctions when violated. Braxton and Bayer (1999) named these norms inviolable. The three inviolable normative patterns which emerged in this study are: exploitation of institutional resources, institutional disregard, and misappropriation of gifts. Two of these clusters of behaviors, exploitation of institutional resources, and institutional disregard, prohibit fund raiser behaviors which would harm the institution. The third inviolable normative array, misappropriation of gifts, involves a donor's funds which have been given to the institution and used for purpose other than what they were intended. This is also a danger to the fund raiser's institutional client, because the misuse could negatively influence other individuals' decisions to make gifts, as well as potential problems if university records were ever audited. The welfare of a fund raiser's institutional client is included in all three of these inviolable normative patterns. As outlined above, fundraisers have two clients whose welfare they must protect. First, the fund raiser must protect the welfare of their donor clients. Second, development officers must also protect the welfare of the institutions for which they raise money. It is important to note that while there are two clients for fundraisers, the inviolable normative patterns which emerged in this study primarily serve to protect a fund raiser's institutional client.

The second set includes those proscriptions which meet admonitory criteria. Admonitory proscriptions evoke less indignation than inviolable norms (Braxton & Bayer, 1999). The six admonitory norms patterns which were found include: commission-based compensation, dishonest solicitation, donor manipulation, exaggeration of professional experience, institutional mission abandonment, and unreasonable enforcement of pledges. Five of these six are primarily concerned with the welfare of donor clients. The only admonitory normative pattern not focused on the welfare of the donor client is institutional mission abandonment which encompasses the receipt of gifts which the institution does not need or want. The most severe norms which emerged protect the fund raiser's institutional client, the next most serious protect the donor client.

Of the three respondent characteristics used to examine individual differences on each normative pattern, familiarity with the *Donor Bill of Rights* and years in the profession both demonstrated significant differences on some normative patterns. There was no significant difference in norm espousal between those individuals engaged in a campaign and those not.

Suggestions for Future Research

This study has identified three inviolable and six admonitory normative patterns of behavior for college and university fundraisers. The results of this study suggest several areas for research which should be explored in the future. These seven suggested areas are explored below.

First, the research described in this study should be extended into the community college. Because of a low response rate, no generalization can be made about the normative structure of college and university fundraising behaviors within community colleges. There may be important differences in how individuals in community colleges perceive fundraising behaviors. Because they have challenges which are very different from those fundraisers at the institutions which were the primary focus of this study, their attitudes toward fundraising transgressions may also be different.

Second, the current study should be expanded to include other fundraisers. Only fundraisers who are members of the Council for Advancement and Support of Education were included in the sample for this study. While this facilitated collecting the data for this project, it excluded those fundraisers who do not belong to CASE. There may be differences in the way non-CASE members perceive fundraising behaviors. Because they are not exposed to the educational materials and conferences designed for members of CASE, they may not be as familiar with the formal codes of ethics adopted by CASE. Additionally, being a CASE member provides opportunities to develop relationships with many individuals who have been in the fundraising profession for long periods of time, and who work for different types of educational institutions. Lacking these opportunities may influence the espousal of fundraising norms.

Third, other sources of social control should be examined which go beyond the variables studied in this project. Personal sources of social control should include ethnic/racial background of individuals participating in the study. Social controls should include the influence of department on the espousal of fundraising norms. The prevailing notion of what behaviors are inappropriate in a specific development department may wield greater influence on the behavior of an individual development officer than the institutional type or other sources of social control included in this study.

Fourth, other fundraisers should be asked about their perceptions of inappropriate behavior within the profession. Only individuals whose primary responsibility was raising money for a college and university were included in this study. There are many other nonprofit and charitable organizations which employ individuals in the endeavor of seeking voluntary support for their institutions. Churches, museums, recreational organizations, hospitals, social service organizations, and disease-related organizations are some examples of those groups who rely on the generosity of others for their continued support. Those in these organizations face very different challenges than college and university fundraisers. They have different constituencies and are frequently less well funded than higher education organizations. Perhaps these major differences will have some impact on fundraising norms within these types of groups. However, this research might support the argument that there is a set of common core values for all fundraisers, regardless of organizational affiliation.

Fifth, while this study examined perceptions of what fundraisers see as those behaviors which evoke disdain among colleagues if committed, we do not know how often these transgressions occur. One avenue for additional study would be to determine how often fundraisers engage in these proscribed behaviors. Merton (1948) suggests that a "painful contrast" exists between normative expectations and actual behavior (p. 40). By examining the areas in which fundraisers are most likely to violate their peers' normative proscriptions, the need for increased attention to these norms will become evident. This would also add to the research detailing the incongruence between attitudes and behaviors (Merton, 1948).

Sixth, one could examine the relationship between fundraising norms and the law. Laws can be perceived as codified social control (Horowitz, 1990). It would be interesting to examine those laws and regulations pertaining to fundraising, and to determine if they parallel or support the informal norms identified in this study.

Finally, the subjects of this study were all affiliated with colleges and universities within the United States. It would be interesting to see what differences exist between individuals who are engaged in fundraising in this country and those who are fundraisers in other countries. Development officers in other countries must overcome a lack of a philanthropic history, or culture of giving within those countries. This cultural difference between the U.S. and other countries may influence fund raiser espousal of proscribed norms.

Conclusions

From the findings listed above, the following six conclusions may be drawn. First, moral boundaries for the practice of fundraising in colleges and universities do exist. Braxton and Bayer (1999) suggest that normative patterns establish moral boundaries for members of a profession. These normative patterns espoused by members of the fundraising profession establish boundaries which should not be crossed in the conduct of their duties. These boundaries restrict the autonomy they have in how they solicit donors (unreasonable enforcement of pledges and dishonest solicitation), how they represent their institutions (institutional disregard), how they steward university funds (exploitation of institutional resources and misappropriation of gifts), how they persuade prospects to make donations (commission-based compensation and donor manipulation), how they decide for what individuals should be solicited (institutional mission abandonment), and how they represent themselves professionally (exaggeration of professional experience).

Second, because fundraisers within higher education presumably use norms to self-regulate, it is a marker of additional professionalism for the fundraising profession. The study's results support the assertion that fundraising is an emerging profession (Bloland, 2002; Carbone, 1989). College and university development officers enjoy latitude in the approaches they use to solicit individuals for gifts to their institutions. This professional autonomy is granted to a profession with the expectation that that profession's members will regulate their own behavior and the behavior of their colleagues (Goode, 1969). One way a profession ensures that its members behave appropriately is through the use of informal social control mechanisms. Norms are one device used by members of a profession to self-regulate. Because a normative structure does exist for college and university fundraisers, it suggests that fundraising is maturing as a profession.

Third, the identified normative patterns protect the welfare of both institutional clients and donor clients. Goode (1969) suggests that members of a profession must base their individual decisions on what will serve the needs and protect the welfare of their clients. The inviolable and admonitory norms which emerged from this study serve to protect the interests of both sets of clients for fundraising professionals. Although, the institutional client receives more protection, because the inviolable norms tend not to prohibit behaviors which might cause harm to the fund raiser's donor client. The donor client is protected through five of the six the admonitory norms.

Fourth, because there were no significant differences on any of the normative patterns for those engaged in a capital campaign, this may be evidence of the stability of the norms even with increased pressure to raise funds. During campaigns, there is an increased set of expectations for fundraisers to generate substantial gifts for an institution. Even in the face of these pressures, fundraisers still perceive these patterns of behaviors (which if engaged in might increase the likelihood or ease of a successful solicitation) as inappropriate.

Fifth, the difference between those who are familiar with the *Donor Bill of Rights* (who perceive some normative patterns as more inappropriate) and those not familiar with the document; and the difference between those new to the profession (who perceive several normative patterns as less disdainful) and those who have been in the profession for longer periods of time suggest that socialization to the profession is key for inculcating norms. Senior fundraisers, professional organizations, and leaders in the field should consider the benefit of establishing formal mentorships for those individuals who are entering the profession. By developing relationships between neophyte fundraisers and those who have been practicing members of the profession for many years, the profession will increase the chance that those behaviors which are perceived as inappropriate by those in the profession will be adopted by those who are new. Mentors could be assigned as individuals are hired into an organization. Professional organizations may also engage in this practice.

Sixth, the ethical code for CASE should have more specific language added to describe fundraiser responsibility to the institutional client. The focus of the *Donor Bill of Rights* is obviously on the welfare of the donor client. Specific responsibilities are not delineated for the institutional client. However, it is interesting to note that although an entire document exists outlining the rights of a donor, the normative patterns prohibiting behaviors which might cause harm to a donor are almost exclusively in the admonitory category. Those norms which proscribe behaviors which place the institution in jeopardy are primarily inviolable.

This study adds to the knowledge base informing the practice of fundraising at educational institutions. Additionally, it outlines an area of inquiry which would enhance the understanding of the fundraising profession, specifically how the profession self-regulates the behaviors of members and how that compares to formal social control mechanisms. Finally, it has utility for practitioners interested in understanding more fully the implications of perceived inappropriate behaviors of development officers, and how colleges and universities generate voluntary support.

References

Abbott, A. (1983). Professional Ethics. *American Journal of Sociology*, 88(5), 855–885.

Barber, B. (1962). *Science and the social order*. New York: Collier.

Bloland, H. G. (2002). No longer emerging, fundraising is a profession. *The CASE International Journal of Education Advancement*, 3(1), 7–21.

Bloland, H. G., & Tempel, E. R. (2004, Spring). Measuring professionalism. In L. Wagner & J. P. Ryan (Eds.), *Fundraising as a profession: Advancements and challenges in the field* (pp. 5–20). San Francisco: Jossey-Bass.

Braxton, J. M. (1986). The normative structure of science: Social control in the academic profession. In J. C. Smart (Ed.), *Higher education: Handbook of theory and research*. (Vol. 2., pp. 309–357). New York: Agathon Press.

Braxton, J. M., & Bayer, A. E. (1999). *Faculty misconduct in collegiate teaching*. Baltimore: John Hopkins University Press.

Braxton, J. M., Bayer, A. E., & Finkelstein, M. J. (1992, October). Teaching performance norms in academia. *Research in Higher Education*, 33, 553–569.

Brittingham, B. E., & Pezzullo, T. R. (1990). *The campus green: Fundraising in higher education*. Washington, DC: ERIC Clearinghouse on Higher Education.

Bucher, R., & Strauss, A. (1961, November). Professions in process. *American Journal of Sociology*, 66, 325–334.

Carbone, R. F. (1986). *An Agenda for Research on Fundraising*. College Park: University of Maryland, Clearinghouse for Research on Fundraising.

Carbone, R. F. (1989). *Fundraising as a profession*. (Monograph No. 3). College Park: University of Maryland, Clearinghouse for Research on Fundraising.

Carlin, J. (1966). *Lawyer's ethics*. New York: Sage.

Carr-Saunders, A. M., & Wilson, P. A. (1933). *The professions*. Oxford: Clarendon.

Cash, S. (2005). Private voluntary support to public universities in the United States: Late nineteenth-century developments. *International Journal of Educational Advancement*, 5(4), 343–356.

Cohen, J. R., & Pant, L. W. (1991). Beyond bean counting: Establishing high ethical standards in the accounting profession. *Journal of Business Ethics*, 10, 45–46.

Cohen, R. (2008). Alumni to the rescue: Black college alumni and their historical impact on alma mater. *International Journal of Educational Advancement*, 8(1), 25–33.

Durkheim, E. (1951). *Suicide* (J. H. Saulding & G. Simpson, trans.). New York: Free Press.

Durkheim, E. (1995). *The elementary forms of religious life* (K. E. Fields, trans.). New York: Free Press.

Frankel, M. S. (1989). Professional codes: Why, how and with what impact? *Journal of Business Ethics*, 8, 109–115.

Friedson, E. (1975). *Doctoring together: A study of professional social control*. New York: Elsevier.

Gasman, M. (2005). The role of faculty in fundraising at black colleges: What is it and what can it become? *International Journal of Educational Advancement*, 5(2), 171–179.

Goode, W. J. (1957). Community within a community: The professions. *American Sociological Review*, 22, 194–200.

Goode, W. J. (1969). The theoretical limits of professionalization. In A. Etzoni (Ed.), *The semi-professions and their organization*. New York: Free Press.

Gottfried, M., & Johnson, E. (2006). Solicitation and donation: An econometric evaluation of alumni generosity in higher education. *International Journal of Educational Advancement*, 6(4), 268–281.

Gravetter, F. J., & Wallnau, L. B. (2006). *Statistics for the behavioral sciences*. Florence, KY: Wadsworth.

Greenwood, E. (1957). Attributes of a Profession. *Social Work*, 2, 44–55.

Harries-Jenkins, G. (1970). Professionals in organizations. In J. A. Jackson (Ed.), *Professions and professionalization*. (pp. 53–107). New York: Cambridge University Press.

Iarrobino, J. (2006). Turnover in the advancement profession. *International Journal of Educational Advancement*, 6(2), 141–169.

Josephson, M. (1988). Ethical obligations and opportunities in philanthropy and fundraising. Paper presented at the National Forum on Fund-Raising Ethics, National Society of Fundraising Executives, Alexandria, VA, Dec. 11–13.

Kelly, K. S. (1991). *Fundraising and public relations: A critical analysis*. Hillsdale, NJ: Lawrence Erlbaum Associates.

Kelly, K. S. (1995). The fund-raising behavior of U.S. charitable organizations. *Journal of Public Relations Research*, 7(2), 111–137.

Lee, Y., & Chang, C. (2008). Intrinsic or extrinsic? Determinants affecting donation behaviors. *International Journal of Educational Advancement*, 8(1), 13–24.

Leslie, L. L. (1972). Are high response rates essential to valid surveys? *Social Science Research*, 1, 323–334.

Lombardo, B. J. (1991). Conflicts of interest between nonprofits and corporate donors. In D. F. Burlingame & L. J. Hulse (Eds.), *Taking fund-raising seriously: Advancing the profession and practice of raising money* (pp. 83–99). San Francisco: Jossey-Bass.

Marion, B. H. (1994). Decision making in ethics. In M. G. Briscoe (Ed.), *Ethics in fundraising: Putting values into practice: New Directions for philanthropic fundraising, No. 6* (pp. 49–61). San Francisco: Jossey Bass.

Merton, R. K. (1957). Priorities in scientific discovery. *American Sociological Review*, 2, 635–659.

Merton, R. K. (1968). *Social theory and social structure*. New York: Free Press.

Merton, R. K. (1973). *The sociology of science: Theoretical and empirical investigations*. Chicago: University of Chicago Press.

Millerson, G. (1964). *The qualifying associations*. London: Routledge.

Moore, W. E. (1970). *The professions: Roles and rules*. New York: Russell Sage Foundation.

Morris, R. T. (1956). A typology of norms. *American Sociological Review*, 21(5), 610–613.

Nesbit, B., Rooney, P., Bouse, G., & Tempel, E. (2006). Presidential satisfaction with development programs in research and doctoral universities: A comparison of results from surveys in 1990 and 2000. *International Journal of Educational Advancement*, 6(3), 182–199.

Nicholson,W. (2007). Leading where it counts: An investigation of the leadership styles and behaviors that define college and university presidents as successful fundraisers. *International Journal of Educational Advancement*, 7(4), 256–270.

Principals of Practice for Fundraisers at Educational Institutions. (2005). Retrieved on July 20, 2007, from http://www.case.org/Content/AboutCASE/Display.cfm?contentItemID=5715

Weerts, D. (2007). Toward an engagement model of institutional advancement at public colleges and universities. *International Journal of Educational Advancement*, 7(2), 79–103.

Worth, M. J. (2002). *New strategies for educational fundraising*. Phoenix, AZ: American Council on Education and Oryx Press.

CHAPTER 42

REVENUE GENERATION AND ITS CONSEQUENCES FOR ACADEMIC CAPITAL, VALUES AND AUTONOMY: INSIGHTS FROM CANADA

JULIA ANTONIA EASTMAN

The greatest challenge for institutions of higher education in most OECD countries since the 1970s has arguably been to cope with reduced public support. Many institutions responded to reductions in funding, first, by cutting costs and lobbying governments to reverse cutbacks, and then—when it became clear that funding levels would not be restored—by seeking out new sources of revenue. Some institutions decentralised resource allocation in order to encourage units to generate non-government revenue. Recent research into the revenue generation strategies of Canadian universities suggests, drawing upon the work of Pierre Bourdieu, that such measures, while potentially effective in stimulating resource acquisition—and beneficial in other important respects—change internal values and conditions in ways that may ultimately undermine universities' autonomy, public credibility and capacity to create knowledge. Can leaders and managers enable their institutions to secure vital revenue, without diluting the values and conditions that have made universities unique and valuable to society? Can decision makers in government foster entrepreneurialism and responsiveness on the part of higher education institutions without compromising their raison d'êhre? This paper sheds light upon these questions.

The late 20th century witnessed a decrease in public funding for higher education, relative to private funding, in most parts of the world (World Bank, 2002). In many OECD countries, the proportion of institutional funding received from the state declined; in some jurisdictions, this translated into reduced public funding per student (OECD, 2004). Many publicly funded universities responded, first, by cutting costs and, then—when it became clear that a return to the *status quo ante* was not in the cards—by seeking out new sources of revenue.

The flavour of universities' revenue generation strategies varied from country to country. Whereas short courses, overseas students and consultancy featured prominently in the revenue generation strategies of universities in the United Kingdom late in the 20th century, for example, fundraising and institutional marketing were central in the United States. In spite of these differences—largely attributable to differences in the regulatory regimes to which the universities were subject—there seem to have been commonalities in the internal management reforms introduced in order to survive in the new funding environment. One appears to have been decentralisation of resource allocation: movement away from central line-item budgeting to arrangements (such as block, responsibility centre or breakeven cost centre budgeting) that give faculties and other units greater incentive to control costs and/or generate revenue.

Recent research into the revenue generation strategies of four major Canadian universities suggests that decentralisation of resource allocation in a context of scarcity also changes values and behaviour. Although such measures may be necessary for financial survival—and, in important respects, beneficial—if carried too far, they may jeopardise universities' capacity to fulfill an independent role in society, the trust in which universities are held by the public and their claim on the public purse.

The Research

The research was a theory-building comparative case study of the revenue generation strategies of four major Canadian universities and their faculties of arts, business, dentistry and science. Conducted between 2002 and 2004, it involved semi-structured interviews with university leaders and deans, analysis of financial data, and extensive archival research. Although the study set out to investigate revenue generation strategies, its findings suggested that a focus on revenue is too narrow. A fuller understanding of the interview results and other data emerged when it was recognised that, as Pierre Bourdieu suggested, there are multiple forms of capital, for which individuals and organisations compete. The value of a particular type of capital is a function of its scarcity. The first and most familiar form is economic capital, i.e. capital "which is immediately and directly convertible into money" (Bourdieu, 1986, p. 243). A second is cultural capital, i.e. capital based on knowledge or culture. The type of cultural capital most relevant here consists of the knowledge, skills and cultural attainments of individuals. Cultural capital can be converted—with varying degrees of ease, time and risk—into economic capital, but cannot be reduced to it. Indeed, cultural capital that is seen to be too economically motivated loses its legitimacy and, hence, value.

Fields of Restricted and Mass Production

Bourdieu conceived of organisational fields (e.g. the literary community, the business community) as hierarchically structured networks of social relations. Fields differ in the forms of capital at stake within them. Individuals and organisations compete continuously for control of the capital at play in their fields, in their quests to get ahead.

The interview data obtained in the course of this research confirmed that universities comprise a field, thus defined. Asked about the aspirations of their universities or faculties, most interviewees described the latters' desired positions in a hierarchy ("to be in the first rank of public research universities in North America", "to be in the top five faculties . . . in the country", to be "among the major research universities of the country"). In other words, the most common institutional aspiration was to move up or to maintain one's position in one's field. Such aspirations are typical of not-for-profit institutions. As Winston and many others have noted, such institutions typically seek to move up in their reputational hierarchies, to emulate top institutions, to be "Harvard-in-the-small" (Winston, 1999, p. 10).

Bourdieu distinguished between fields of restricted cultural production and fields of large-scale or mass production. In the former, producers create cultural goods for other producers (e.g. poets write to be read by other poets). Such fields are governed by norms and sanctions specific to them. They are relatively self-contained communities, in which an individual's position depends principally on the esteem in which he or she is held by peers (Bourdieu, 1993). They are gift economies, in which products are given away in return for recognition. Cultural capital is valued highly, relative to economic capital. Indeed, in fields that are far removed from the market, financial and commercial success are scorned and interpreted as evidence of lack of merit.

In contrast, fields of large-scale production feature production for "the public at large". Investment is driven by the quest for markets and profits. Producers are subordinate to those who control the mechanisms of production and diffusion. Their work serves pre-existing external needs. Their performance is regulated by management control mechanisms and measured in terms of commercial success. Insofar as production is for existing market needs and demands, it is much less economically risky than restricted cultural production, which is driven by producers without reference to others' interests or needs.

How does the distinction between restricted and mass production apply to higher education? Academic disciplines are fields of restricted cultural production, in which producers create goods for each other (e.g. professors write for scholarly audiences). An individual's position within his or her discipline is a function of peer recognition and esteem. The value of an academic work is not reducible to its economic value or its public importance. To the extent that research is curiosity-driven, it is without reference to external needs or markets. The more autonomous the discipline, the more works derive value, not from readership or commercial success or public acclaim, but from conformity to what is regarded as legitimate and valuable in the field.

For the purposes of this paper, the cultural capital valued within academic disciplines will be referred to as academic capital. (Note that the term has a different meaning here than that given to it by Slaughter and Leslie, for example. They used "academic capital" to refer to a "commodity . . . which is no more than the particular human capital possessed by academics" (1997, p. 11)—in other words, to capital, the value of which is defined in economic terms. In contrast, academic capital as defined here derives its value from the discipline or profession in question.)

At the other end of the higher education spectrum, for-profit providers of higher education engage in mass production. Whether proprietary institutions or publicly traded companies, their mission is not—as for public universities and private not-for-profits—to advance and disseminate knowledge, but rather to generate profit. Their governance structures and processes are corporate in nature. Faculty power is greatly diminished. Unlike their counterparts in the not-for-profit sector, faculty members in the for-profit sector lack tenure and control over the curriculum. "In a real sense", Ruch observed, "faculty in the for-profits are viewed by the business side as being delivery people, as in delivery of the curriculum" (2001, p. 115).

For-profit providers are very responsive to student and employer demand. They take their cues from the market, rather than seeking to persuade the market of the value of what they offer. Unlike not-for-profit universities—known for adding new activities onto existing ones and consequent inability to control costs—for-profits are focused, quick to move out of unprofitable activities, efficient in the use of faculty and space, and rigorous in cost accounting and control (Ruch, 2001; Tooley, 2001). In Ruch's memorable words, "the academic side of the house becomes a tightly managed service operation" (2001, p. 17).

Insights from the Canadian Context

Canada is a federation in which higher education is a matter of provincial jurisdiction and in which the university sector consists overwhelmingly of "public" institutions—more precisely, not-for-profit corporations, established by acts of provincial legislatures and sustained by a combination of provincial operating funding, federal research funding, fees and other private funding. The four universities studied were all of this type. They were also similar in offering degrees from the baccalaureate to the doctoral level in a wide range of fields including medicine and dentistry. Nevertheless, owing to differences in age, location, size, history and funding, they and their faculties occupied different positions in the university hierarchy. The two largest were at or near the top and saw themselves as international players; the smaller universities were further down the hierarchy and sought to compete in the domestic realm.

The proportions of the four universities' operating income derived from government had declined by 33%, 26%, 16% and 4%, respectively, between 1990/91 and 2001/02 (CAUBO, Annual). Three had decentralised resource allocation as the operating funding they received from government had declined, in order to encourage faculties and other units to engage in revenue-generating activities. Were they behaving like profit-seeking corporations? Far from it. All four continued to subsidise activities they deemed to be central to their missions. That which they subsidised varied with their conceptions of their missions, but all four subsidised grant-funded research. This was necessary because Canadian governments were not funding fully the indirect and overhead costs involved. Contrary to the suggestions of much of the literature on academic capitalism, these universities did not do research in order to obtain revenue; they scrambled to secure revenue in order to fund research. Three of the four also appeared to be increasing the extent to which graduate education was subsidised (i.e. increasing the ratio of operating funding to fee revenue and other private funding).

Nevertheless, it appeared that two universities and numerous faculties had moved to varying degrees toward the field of mass production. One indication of such movement was increased responsiveness to the interests of students and other clients. Senior officials at the university that had experienced the most dramatic percentage reduction in government funding during the 1990s—and had become correspondingly more dependent on fee revenue—reported that it had become significantly more attentive to students. One interviewee observed that the university was "gradually moving from what I would call a faculty-centred university . . . to a more student-centred university". A leader of a second university said that its approach to students had changed a great deal as a result of its efforts to recruit international students: "We were an old, traditional university. People came to us; we didn't have to go after them. There was a lot of that [attitude] throughout the whole university. That's changed dramatically!"

Increased attentiveness to student satisfaction was reported by deans, as well, particularly within professional schools. Many of the business and dental schools had or were in the process of increasing fees for some programmes dramatically. The dean of a dental school, that had begun several years previously to charge full cost recovery fees to many of the students in its first professional programme, noted that students' expectations had risen with the fees they paid and that the faculty was having to change to meet them.

In order to continue to attract and retain full cost fee-paying students, the school was devoting much more attention to monitoring student satisfaction and responding to their feedback than it had in the past. The dean also wished to establish a career stream for individuals who were excellent teachers, but not active in research. In undertaking increasingly detailed evaluation of instruction and developing a teaching-only stream, the school was adopting some of the practices typical of for-profit higher educational organisations.

Rapid programme development and change appeared to be another characteristic of schools that were moving into mass production and charging fees approaching or exceeding costs for some programmes. Interviews with deans of business suggested that rapid change is the norm for executive development programmes and full cost recovery/premium fee degrees.

Research in some faculties appeared to be increasingly externally-driven as well.

A dean of science, whose faculty's revenue generation strategy consisted principally, not of the provision of education at full cost, but of securing externally funded research chairs, noted that the faculty's success in that endeavour had resulted in closer alignment of its research capacity with the needs and interests of industry. He remarked that "the areas of research the faculty engage in have become shifted towards things that are, sort of, imposed on us by outside".

A further indication of movement toward the field of mass production was that numerous deans reported increasing tension between teaching and research. This tension took various forms. Faculties, the financial survival of which depended on teaching large numbers of students, and which were constrained in the use of part-time and sessional faculty, struggled to protect faculty members' time for research. In several research-intensive faculties, deans described developments including: divergence between areas in which positions had been funded by external research sponsors and areas in which teaching capacity was needed; progressive separation of researchers from teaching and teachers—and disparity between the rewards accorded the two groups; and increasing reliance on practitioners and other part-time teachers to deliver instruction. Resurgence in federal funding for research and in rewards for top researchers was increasing the disparity between the salaries of researchers and those of teachers. Good teaching professors—people who "love the science and love teaching and love the university"—were said not to be well rewarded financially, nor to be receiving the praise and recognition that researchers got for their work.

These reports suggest that education and research are pulled in different directions as universities move into mass production in either or both realms. This is unsurprising insofar as "clients" for the two types of activity have different areas of interest and types of need. The complexity of the activities necessary to meet their needs—and the roles of regular faculty, sessional faculty and staff in carrying out those activities—differ as well. The evidence of divergence in demand, conditions and rewards for education and research also makes sense in light of the fact that for-profit providers of higher education tend not to do research (other than curriculum- or instructional technology related research and development). That in part explains their capacity to generate profits, even while competing with institutions that are subsidised by governments and/or private sources (Ortmann, 2001). As noted elsewhere (Eastman, 2006), the absence of research from their missions also explains why for-profits are able to manage their faculty and their costs tightly, dispensing with the less orderly, more expensive arrangements typical of creative organisations, including universities. Research-intensive universities have, to a great degree, traditionally favoured creativity and innovation over co-ordination and focus. Serving clients, however, requires co-ordination and focus, which is why management hierarchy and controls are pronounced in institutions of higher education and/or research engaged in mass production.

The universities involved in this study were far from behaving like commercial laboratories, on one hand, and educational companies, on the other. (Indeed, owing to federal reinvestment in university research, it appeared that, overall, they were moving toward mass production in education, while moving away from it in research.) It nevertheless appeared that teaching and research were bifurcating and that the teacher-scholar model was under great stress.

A final indication that some of the faculties studied were moving toward mass production lay in the economic philosophies espoused by their deans. The views expressed by one dental dean exemplified those of the leadership of a faculty engaged in restricted cultural production. The assumptions were that: good academic work deserves to be funded adequately; it is the responsibility of government to fund universities adequately and of universities, in turn, to fund their faculties properly; when funding is insufficient to meet the university's needs, resources should be allocated on the basis of academic priorities. This dean thus expressed concern about mechanisms whereby universities match private donations, the result of which is to direct university resources to activities favoured by external donors or funders, i.e. to skew the allocation of resources from that which is academically- to that which is externally-valued.

Most of the 14 deans interviewed were less insistent that academic, rather than financial, considerations should drive resource allocation and activity. Their view appeared to be that it is legitimate—indeed necessary—to generate revenue by meeting external needs in order to sustain one's faculty's activities—i.e. to subsidise restricted cultural production by means of mass production. A dean who held this view explained that, in designing a revenue generation strategy, one starts with the school's mission and vision and develops a business plan for generating the revenue required from sources including "tuition, [other fees], entrepreneurial activities, intellectual property spin-offs, and so on and so forth".

An even more radical perspective—for an academic leader at a publicly supported university—was voiced by two deans of business. In this view, there is no such thing as generating revenue; it's all about delivering value. One dean explained that universities and faculties can no longer look to governments to meet their financial needs, because governments are relinquishing responsibility for paying for post-secondary education. Henceforth, "the needs will have to be financed by where you[r faculty] add[s] value". The real question is therefore: "[W]here do you deliver value and how do you fund delivering that value? [Y]ou need to share in the value that you deliver. So, that would be my point: identify the points where you're adding value, where you should add value, and understand how some of that value is to be shared in order to fund your operation for delivering that value."

Whereas university leaders and members engaged in restricted cultural production, such as the dental dean quoted above, feared the corrupting effect of revenue generation, those engaged in "delivering value" reported that the quest for revenue forces one to improve quality. The business dean quoted above explained that revenue generation is not separate from a business school's mission, it is part of that mission. One's success in generating revenue is thus a reflection of one's success as a school. In this view, there is no such thing as autonomous academic capital; economic capital is the measure of value within and outside the university.

Conditions for Mass Production

When Bourdieu first wrote about the different types of cultural production, the exemplar of mass production in higher education—the publicly traded higher education company—did not yet exist. Bourdieu nevertheless witnessed and noted, decades ago, elements of mass production within state-sponsored higher education. He observed in *Homo Academicus* that the research-oriented social scientific groups and institutes that emerged in France in the 1960s behaved much like firms. Their heads represented "a new kind of cultural producer, whose presence in the academic field . . . constitutes a decisive break with the fundamental principles of academic autonomy, and with the values of disinterestedness, magnanimity and indifference to the sanctions and demands of practice. These academic managers [were] busy seeking funds for their 'laboratories', frequenting committees and commissions to pick up the contracts, information and subsidies necessary for the good running of their enterprise, and organising symposia designed to publicise their productions . . . " (1988, p. 124). In the intervening decades, entrepreneurial activities of many kinds have been undertaken by institutes, centres, schools of continuing education and other bodies, located upon the peripheries of universities. As noted above, such structures are much better equipped to respond to clients and markets than are faculties and departments. Marginson and Considine have indeed suggested that the development of centres and cross-disciplinary schools was fostered within Australian higher education during the late 20th century in order to circumvent academic departments and weaken the power of academic disciplines (2000, p. 10).

This research suggests that, as this century dawned, mass production was taking place in Canada, not only within peripheral bodies, but also at the core of some universities. Although only deans of business articulated economic philosophies consistent with mass production—i.e. argued that value is as determined by the customer, rather than in the academy—signs of mass production, such as increased service orientation and tension between teaching and research, were seen in other types of faculty as well.

Canadian universities are obviously not alone in moving toward mass production in higher education. What factors account for this? Derek Bok, reflecting on the American scene, suggested that two major developments have led universities to become more engaged in the marketplace: financial cutbacks and the "rapid growth of opportunities to supply education, expert advice, and scientific knowledge in return for handsome sums of money" associated with the rise of the knowledge economy (2003, p. 10); in other words, scarcity of economic capital, coupled with opportunities to transform academic capital into economic capital.

What happened to universities in most OECD countries late in the 20th century was that academic capital depreciated relative to economic capital, as a result of cutbacks in public funding. The relative economic value of academic capital in different fields of study also changed with the advent of the "knowledge economy", as revolutions in information technology and biotechnology increased the economic value of academic capital in these and related fields. In the 1960s and early 1970s, large-scale public investment in higher education had meant that academic capital was scarce relative to economic capital and, indeed, physical capital. There was great competition amongst universities for faculty members. For a short period, funding for education and research was plentiful. A "good department" (i.e. one with a lot of academic capital) had no difficulty securing resources from its university. By the 1980s, however, universities' administrations were handing out cuts. Academic capital no longer commanded resources. Although a reputation for excellence would probably stave off closure, it would not enable a faculty or department to expand its activities. Economic capital was necessary for that—and its scarcity raised its value, to differing extents within different fields of study, relative to academic capital.

As Bok suggests, financial scarcity is necessary, but not in itself sufficient to engender mass production: there must also be opportunities and incentives for serving markets. Universities must be able to charge tuition fees, negotiate contracts and reap financial benefits from serving clients in other ways. They in turn must decentralise resource allocation sufficiently to enable, indeed to require, faculties and other units to provide services and goods that are valued by clients and to share in that value. As Massy observed with respect to responsibility-centre budgeting, such decentralisation "extends the sensitivity to market forces down through the institution" (2001, p. 455). In its absence, faculties are likely to respond to academic over economic considerations. The vice-president finance of one of the universities involved in this research explained that the dire financial predicament in which it had found itself during the 1980s had been caused in part by the absence of incentives for enrolment growth:

> "I have a fixed piece of revenue", each dean and each faculty said, "and that won't change if I take less students". So enrolments actually declined [during the 1980s]. And, if you think about it, that was totally logical behaviour . . . [If my unit will] continue [getting its] cheque every month, [and] I can do less teaching for it, [I will] therefore have more time to do my scholarly work. Any sane person would do that! They acted appropriately, given the structures they were presented with. So we had to change the structures and change the behaviour.

Benefits and Costs of Moving into Mass Production

So, what are the pros and cons of decentralising resource allocation to expose faculties to the conditions of scarcity and opportunity that will "change the behaviour"?

The first and most obvious benefit is increased non-government revenue. The number of universities studied in the course of this research was small. Higher education being a provincial responsibility in Canada, the institutions were also subject to different constraints. That said, it may be noted that the university that had decentralised its budget earliest and to the greatest degree had achieved an increase in non-government operating income of 335% between 1990/91 and 2001/02, compared to between 197% and 80% for the other three institutions (CAUBO, Annual).

A second benefit of decentralising resource allocation appeared to be that it empowers faculties, which are no longer as dependent on institutional decisions, and thus fosters a sense—if not the reality—of self-reliance.

A third benefit is simplicity. For a university, making decisions and allocating resources based on a faculty or programme's capacity to generate revenue is liberatingly easy, compared to doing so on an academic basis. As one dean said about attempts to close faculties on other than financial grounds, academic decision making is "very messy; [politics] gets involved and there is no right or wrong at the end of the day". In a university in which academic capital prevails, all intellectual pursuits are equally worthy. It is difficult to discriminate amongst disciplines and professions. That is fundamentally why universities engaged in restricted cultural production tend to have myriad goals, to be unable to set priorities and to be beset by academic "property rights". Owing to the catholic character of the academic outlook, decisions about priorities are much more readily made when market or other external considerations are brought to bear.

Fourth, the research suggested that decentralisation of resource allocation may reduce some forms of internal conflict. In centralised budget systems, a faculty's leaders and members tend to assume that if their budget is inadequate, it is because the university does not fully appreciate them and what they do. In other words, the budget a faculty receives tends to be seen as a reflection of its perceived academic value. When resource allocation is decentralised, deans and other faculty leaders appear to accept at least partial responsibility for the adequacy of the resources available to them. Those deans who regarded their universities as sources of investment capital naturally appeared to be more positively disposed toward institutional leaders than those who expected their universities to be sources of adequate operating funding.

A final, very important benefit of moving toward mass production is, as noted above, that it increases institutional responsiveness to students, clients, donors and other sources of funding.

There are, of course, also important costs. One is, naturally, that as faculties gain autonomy from universities and lose autonomy from the various markets they serve, administrators, faculty and staff identify less with the university as a whole. A vice-president of the university that had moved furthest toward mass production said:

> I think that a consequence of decentralisation and every-ship-on-its-own-bottom is that there's less sense of [this university] and of being part of a university than there used to be, even when I came here . . . It's not like we're all one institution and we're proud of the one institution and we're all willing to pull together. [It's more,] "I'll pull with you, if you can help me with this joint programme, and we can both make money on it" sort of thing.

This and other suggestions that budgetary decentralisation unleashes centrifugal forces and focuses attention on the bottom line at the expense of institutional and academic considerations echo much literature on responsibility-centre budgeting (see, for examples: Lang, 2001; Strauss *et al.*, 2001).

A second major cost of moving into mass production is separation of teaching from research. As noted above, the extent and nature of this development varied from university to university and faculty to faculty. In some faculties, it appeared that research was being squeezed out by the demands of instruction; in others, separate classes of researchers and of teachers were emerging; in yet others, some departments were becoming more research-oriented while others were increasingly preoccupied with instruction.

Although bifurcation of teaching and research is listed here as a cost of mass production, it can also be seen as an opportunity. The five-year plan of one of the business schools featured in this research anticipated that:

> [O]ver the next decade, market evolution and segmentation will reduce the number of internationally successful schools and relegate others to niche roles or less distinctive status. In the past, there have been numerous "players" and few "winners". Going forward, there will continue to be opportunities to "win", but those who just stay to "play" will end up losing. [. . .] Losers, unable to produce new content and integrative thinkers, will be relegated to the position of "licensees", focused primarily on providing delivery mechanisms for the content the winners create. (University of Toronto, Rotman School of Management, 2000, pp. 10–11.)

The school's dean predicted that top business faculties will license entire curricula to other schools, earning royalties that will enable them "to pay more and more money and to provide better and better environments for real content-creating professors. They are going to congregate at fewer and fewer schools and those schools are going to aggressively market their content". The dean stressed during the interview for this research that the goal of [this] school is to be one of those end-game players. In other words, rather than bemoaning increasing separation of teaching from research, the school anticipated it and was preparing to be a creator of content, the delivery of which would be licensed to others.

Perhaps the greatest risk associated with movement toward mass production is that devaluation of academic capital will lessen universities' autonomy and hence their value to society and claim upon public support. Society has traditionally looked to universities for knowledge that is not only current, but disinterested, Why such confidence in academics' independence? Not because professors are more ethical than others, but because they have ascribed to values other than those that prevail within society and the economy at large, values reflecting the traditional primacy of academic capital. Furthermore, professors enjoy freedoms and powers within their institutions that enable them to speak their minds. If academic capital becomes devalued, universities will behave much more like corporations—those who teach will no longer subscribe to autonomous academic values, and/or management hierarchy will have developed to the point that faculty members are constrained in expressing views contrary to the institutional interest. Universities' capacity to provide disinterested information and perspectives on issues and events would wither and, along with it, the repute in which they are held and hence their claim on society's resources.

Implications for Policy and Practice

What are the implications for the way university leaders manage issues involving values and ethics? University leaders should be aware that, in decentralising resource allocation to promote revenue generation, they themselves may change internal values, roles and control systems in ways that increase institutional responsiveness to students and clients but ultimately lessen universities' capacities to play unique and autonomous roles in society.

Can this be avoided? That is not at all clear. The revenue generation strategies studied in the course of this research were prompted by funding cuts. The great majority of those interviewed had encouraged their institutions or faculties to generate revenue, not because they were enamored by the private sector, but because their institutions had first responded to cuts in public funding by cutting budgets and it had ended up crippling them. The alternative to revenue generation was, as one interviewee put it, a "death spiral". If the impetus for revenue generation is beyond their control, what insights can university leaders glean from this research about how to encourage it while sustaining the academic core?

First, although the generosity or scarcity of public financing is largely beyond university leaders' control—as are ebbs and flows in the economic capital of disciplines and professions—insofar as university leaders allocate unrestricted public funding to units and decide whether and how to share other revenues, they influence that which is valued within faculties and the extent to which the latter engage in mass production. This research suggests that those decisions are best informed by understanding of the portfolios of capital the university and each of its faculties possesses and can exchange with individuals and other organisations. The extent to which a faculty will move into mass production in response to a given budgetary requirement or incentive is a function of its market opportunities, its academic, reputational and other forms of capital, and its internal flexibility. As noted above, different faculties have different opportunities. Dental education in Canada had many of the features of oligopoly: a small number of producers with a highly sought after, relatively homogeneous good. Dental schools in provinces where professional tuition fees were unregulated therefore had much greater capacity to raise fees in response to budget cuts than did faculties of arts or science, for example. In response to budget pressure, the latter were more likely to increase enrolments, thereby running down their academic capital, particularly if constrained in the use of part-time and sessional faculty and unable to attract substantial private funding. Taking into account all the forms of capital faculties possess will sensitise university leaders to the broader consequences of the latters' quests for revenue. It will enable them to assess and compare the consequences of alternative strategies, not only for the bottom line, but also for the university's academic, reputational and physical assets.

A second suggestion is to maintain boundaries between not-for-profit higher education and the for-profit realm. One of the features of social and cultural capital identified by Bourdieu is that they risk evaporating if those who possess them are perceived to be economically motivated. Thus, for example, a university that permits an academic or other unit to compete with local business is likely to lose far more in reputation and future donations than it gains from the exchange. One of the universities involved in this study had encountered some "rough spots" in its fundraising endeavours, as a result of which it had developed guidelines to ensure that all donations were consistent with its commitment to academic freedom and its academic policies and priorities. In doing so, it shored up its reputational capital and its capacity to attract resources and faculty. A more subtle example of boundary maintenance was provided by the academic vice-president of a university, the revenue generation strategy of which consisted largely of enrolment growth. Asked if he perceived that the university's mission had been or might be skewed in any way by the need to generate revenue, he said:

> I don't see it as mission-skewing in any particular way. At the moment, I think we're able to attend to this as much as an educational question as a financial question. The goal here is not revenue generation. And, as long as we can avoid the goal being revenue generation—I mean, clearly, one of the outcomes is revenue generation, [but that's not the goal. T]he goal fundamentally is to maintain and enhance a first-rate educational institution.

Just as Oakes *et al.* (1998) found that the introduction of business planning in a public service context transformed a field of restricted cultural production into one of mass production, it may be possible to avoid or delay that transformation by keeping the focus on education, research or public service.

Finally, university leaders should resist the temptation to circumvent bodies and structures through which academic capital is built and sustained. As noted above, academic departments, rooted as they are in the disciplines, are less than optimally equipped for responsiveness to students and research clients. A university in financial duress might be inclined, as Marginson and Considine suggest happened in Australia, to weaken departments' power in order to improve service and generate revenue. Whereas some structures dedicated to mass production (e.g. continuing education units) can, by insulating departments and schools from such activity, protect them and their academic capital, others can weaken them, potentially jeopardising a university's capacity to make decisions on other than an economic basis in the longer run.

Asked whether he perceived any risk to his university's mission from the need to generate revenue, one provost said:

> I think it's a risk all the time. And I think you have to keep coming back to the fundamental values of the university. It's absolutely essential that you ask yourself, "What are we here for?" We're here to educate and to advance knowledge—and we're here to do that in a way that's not hampered, not restricted and not tied to anybody's special interests. [. . .] [O]ur whole credibility, our whole position in society, our position in the larger community, is built upon trust that we are the independent brokers, that we are that group which can look at things—not necessarily dispassionately—but in a way that looks at all sides of the issue. That's a fundamental principle and we've got to be there. And, that's where senates are important. It can be easy to get carried away with something. And you need to be brought back and answer those questions.

If reductions in public relative to private funding of higher education continue to require universities to move into mass production, conflicts between academic values and commercial considerations are inevitable. University leaders might be forgiven for preferring to avoid forums in which tough questions are asked. That said, how do they respond when, for example, a corporate partner objects to a research finding, confirms or subverts espoused values? The weight carried by academic capital in departmental, faculty and university governance forums may account in large part for universities' inability to set priorities, but it is also the source of their independence.

What, if any, insights emerge for decision makers in government? First, if public financing were to fall to such an extent that universities were forced wholly into mass production, they would be unable to fulfill their traditional functions in society. Responsiveness to clients and markets can, if taken to extremes, be inconsistent with responsiveness to the interests of society. Responsiveness in this larger sense requires some autonomy from clients and markets. Academic capital is the source of universities' autonomy and capacity to provide disinterested knowledge, information and comment. Continued devaluation of that capital would reduce their ability to serve society in this way, as well as their capacity to create knowledge.

Mass production of education is by no means a bad thing. Privately funded mass production fills needs that the publicly funded sector does not. Furthermore, it extends access to tertiary education in countries in which the public purse cannot afford to do so.

For-profit providers of higher education are not, however, universities. University education is intimately connected to the disciplines and professions, as well as to students' needs and market demands. For-profit providers have important roles to play in many countries, but allowing them to describe themselves as universities obscures the fact that their missions are fundamentally different. In doing so, it does a disservice to universities and to the public.

The appropriate mix of not-for-profit and for-profit institutions—and of public and private funding for the former—will vary from country to country. That said, an appropriate public policy goal for most societies is to foster universities that are entrepreneurial and responsive, but not so much so as to lose their essence. Achieving that goal merits and requires sustained public block funding. What if the demands upon government and the size of the publicly funded higher education sector are such that government cannot afford to enable universities to remain autonomous? A smaller, more independent public sector may be preferable to a larger sector, subservient to the demands of the market.

References

Bok, D. (2003), *Universities in the Marketplace*, Princeton University Press, Princeton.

Bourdieu, P. (1986), "The Forms of Capital", in J.G. Richardson (ed.), *Handbook of Theory and Research for the Sociology of Education*, Greenwood Press, New York.

Bourdieu, P. (1988), *Homo Academicus*, Stanford University Press, Stanford California.

Bourdieu, P. (1993), "The Market of Symbolic Goods", in P. Bourdieu, *The Field of Cultural Production: Essays on Art and Literature*, Columbia University Press, New York, pp. 112–293.

CAUBO (Canadian Association of University Business Officers) (Annual), *Financial Statistics of Universities and Colleges*, CAUBO, Ottawa.

Eastman, J. A. (2006), "Revenue Generation and Organisational Change in Higher Education", *Higher Education Management and Policy*, Vol. 18, No.3, OECD, Paris.

Lang, D. W. (2001), "A Primer on Responsibility Centre Budgeting and Responsibility Centre Management", in J. Yeager et al. (eds.), *The ASHE Reader on Finance in Higher Education*, second edition, Pearson Custom Publishing, Boston, pp. 568–590.

Marginson, S. and M. Considine (2000), *The Enterprise University. Power, Governance and Reinvention in Australia*, Cambridge University Press, Cambridge.

Massy, W. F. (2001), "Reengineering Resource Allocation Systems", in J. L. Yeager et al. (eds.), *ASHE Reader on Finance in Higher Education*, second edition, Pearson Custom Publishing, Boston.

Oakes, L., B. Townley and D. Cooper (1998), "Business Planning as Pedagogy: Language and Control in a Changing Institutional Field", *Administrative Science Quarterly*, Vol. 43, No.2, pp. 257–292.

OECD (2004), *On the Edge: Securing a Sustainable Future for Higher Education*, report of the OECD/IMHE-HEFCE project on financial management and governance of higher education institutions, OECD, Paris.

Ortmann, A. (2001), "Capital Romance: Why Wall Street Fell in Love With Higher Education", *Education Economics*, Vol. 9, No.3, pp. 293–311.

Ruch, R.S. (2001), *"Higher Education, Inc.: The Rise of the For-Profit University"*, The Johns Hopkins University Press, Baltimore.

Slaughter, S. and L. Leslie (1997), *Academic Capitalism: Politics, Policies and the Entrepreneurial University*, The Johns Hopkins University Press, Baltimore.

Strauss J., J. Curry and E. Whalen (2001), "Revenue Responsibility Budgeting", in J. Yeager et al. (eds.), *The ASHE Reader on Finance in Higher Education*, second edition, Pearson Custom Publishing, Boston, pp. 591–607.

Tooley, J. (2001), *The Global Education Industry*, second edition, Institute of Economic Affairs, London.

University of Toronto, Rotman School of Management (2000), *Raising Our Sights: A Five-Year Plan for the Joseph L. Rotman School of Management, 1999–2004*, Rotman School of Management, University of Toronto, Toronto.

Winston, G. C. (1999), "For-Profit Higher Education: Godzilla or Chicken Little?", *Change*, Vol. 31, January–February.

World Bank (2002), Constructing Knowledge Societies: New Challenges for Tertiary Education, The World Bank, Washington, DC.

CHAPTER 43

DIVERSITY, COLLEGE COSTS, AND POSTSECONDARY OPPORTUNITY: AN EXAMINATION OF THE FINANCIAL NEXUS BETWEEN COLLEGE CHOICE AND PERSISTENCE FOR AFRICAN AMERICANS AND WHITES

EDWARD P. ST. JOHN, MICHAEL B. PAULSEN, AND DEBORAH FAYE CARTER

Questions about how student financial aid and the costs of attending college influence educational opportunity for diverse racial groups have lurked beneath the surface of the policy debates about higher education for decades. When the Higher Education Act (HEA) was passed in 1965, there was a general acceptance that the federal government had a role to play in equalizing educational opportunity. At that time, the civil rights of African Americans were a concern of the majority of Americans, as evidenced by the many Great Society programs of the period. However, since 1980, the federal commitment to need-based grants has contracted as a result of shifting political priorities (McPherson & Schapiro, 1991), if not as a result of a breakdown in the old consensus about equal opportunity. More recently, the federal courts have narrowed the acceptable remedies in desegregation litigation (St. John & Hossler, 1998) and have brought race into question as an explicit consideration in the awarding of student aid (Strope & Wells, 1998). In this context, it is vital that we begin to build a better understanding of the relationship between the costs of college, student financial aid, and the postsecondary opportunities for racially diverse groups.

However, the analysis of the effects of prices and student aid is complicated by a broad critique of the old progressive assumptions. On the one hand, some economists continue to raise questions about the efficacy of student aid (Kane, 1995). Indeed, this line of inquiry has led some to question whether states and the federal government should invest more in student financial aid, even after decades of decline in grant aid (Heller, 1997; St. John, 2003b). In contrast, other economists and higher education researchers, along with cultural-capital theorists, have begun to question some of the basic assumptions behind this position (McDonough, Korn, & Yamasaki, 1997; Paulsen, 2001a, 2001b; St. John & Paulsen, 2001). These newer perspectives offer a different vantage point from which to critique the new direction of public policy in higher education (e.g., decline in affirmative action, merit-based over need-based aid, loans over grant aid), but they do little to combat the decline in federal and state student aid.

This article examines the role of the costs of college and student financial aid in promoting postsecondary opportunity for diverse groups. First, we examine theory and research that might inform an assessment of the effects of student financial aid on the educational opportunities for diverse racial groups. Then we describe our methods and present the findings. We used the financial-nexus model (Paulsen & St. John, 2002; St. John, Paulsen, & Starkey, 1996) to assess the effects of student financial aid on college choice and persistence by African Americans and Whites. Finally, based on these analyses, we consider the understanding of the relationship between financial aid and the educational opportunities of diverse racial groups that emerges from this study.

Background

Previous studies of the financial nexus have examined all students enrolled as undergraduates (St. John, Paulsen, & Starkey, 1996), students enrolled in public colleges compared to students in private colleges (Paulsen & St. John, 1997), and students across income groups (Paulsen & St. John, 2002). This study completes the full set of nexus studies on diverse groups of students enrolled in 1986–1987, by comparing how financial choices made by Whites and African Americans influenced their persistence. Given the age of this data, it is important to reconsider persistence by these populations, an issue we discuss after reviewing our logical approach.

The Logical Approach

Researchers have started examining the ways perceptions of financial factors (i.e., college costs and student aid) formed in the enrollment process influence eventual persistence decisions. One approach involves assessing the impact of students' attitudes about their ability to pay for college as a variable that can influence academic integration and persistence decisions (Cabrera, Nora, & Castañeda, 1992). Research using this "role of finances" approach has revealed that early perceptions of financial problems can influence how students experience college. More recently, the nexus approach (St. John, Paulsen, & Starkey, 1996) has examined how the financial reasons for choosing a college relate to college experiences as well as how these financial expectations and actual prices and subsidies influence persistence. This approach argued that there was a "nexus" between the financial reasons for choosing to attend a college and the ways students responded to prices—that is, actual amounts of costs and aid. These analyses have confirmed this proposition, which provides insights into the ways students respond to student aid in different settings (Paulsen & St. John, 1997).

The nexus approach integrates analysis of the influences of perceptions of finances with the analysis of the effects of costs and aid, using a differentiated price-response model that overcomes the limitations of the net price approach. However, questions remain about whether an understanding of the role of finances can help inform policy deliberations on equal opportunity. Berger (2000) argues that the financial nexus should be extended to examine diverse groups:

> Student choices regarding whether or not to attend college, which college to attend, whether to go full-time or part-time, what to study, whether to drop out, stop out, transfer, or complete their studies are all examples of important choices that individuals make regarding their postsecondary educational attendance. These are examples of what St. John, Paulsen, and Starkey (1996) identify as patterns of decision-making behavior. These patterns might also be defined in terms of an individual's habitus, and it stands to reason that students with similar habitus would be likely to continue to make similar choices once they enter college. Hence, we expect students with similar levels of capital resources to make similar types of decisions and act in similar ways while in college. (p. 103)

This argument, that there are diverse sets of patterns of choice, is vitally important given the changes in finance policy during the last two decades. A recent analysis of class differences related to the financial nexus (Paulsen & St. John, 2002) discovered marked differences in the ways students from lower-income groups and those from higher-income groups responded to finances. Poor students were more negatively influenced by grant inadequacy, and, compared to higher-income students, working-class students were more negatively affected by inadequate loan and work-study aid. In this study, we extend the nexus approach by analyzing racial differences in persistence. We examine how well the nexus model illuminates the differences in educational choices made by students of different racial groups.

Earlier analyses of differences among racial groups in their responses to student aid have indicated that African Americans are more responsive to student aid (Kaltenbaugh, St. John, & Starkey, 1999; St. John & Noell, 1989). However, these initial analyses did not fully deal with the complexity of racial differences in college choice. Recent research has indicated that students' college choices are constrained by their social circumstances. For instance, lower socio-economic status (SES) students tend to be constrained by their financial circumstances in that they attend less expensive institutions closer to their homes (Carter, 1999).

In addition, researchers have frequently studied the degree to which race and social class affect student access to college. Researchers often conclude that class, more than race, affects student college-going opportunities (Hanson, 1994; Hearn, 1984). However, there are also important racial differences in college access. For instance, Kao and Tienda (1998) have discussed an "aspirations-achievement paradox" where African Americans have high aspirations but underachieve relative to their aspirations. Kao and Tienda believe that African American students' social segregation in school can help explain why the students maintain high aspirations since African American students may be more likely to compare their performance in school to that of other African Americans and to see themselves favorably in the comparison.

Students' (and parents') lack of information about higher educational options is not restricted to the African American population. An American Council on Education (ACE) study of the "public's knowledge and attitudes about financing higher education" showed that people do not understand the differences between public and private institutions or 2- year and 4-year colleges (Hartle, 1998). Seventy-one percent of the people surveyed believed that college is not affordable for most families; 83% of the African American respondents believed so. Most people surveyed overestimated the price of college by several thousand dollars, and most did not realize how much financial aid is available for families to help pay college costs (Hartle, 1998). These analyses convey a message that college is affordable for all groups, and that increased information about financing options is the main barrier. The current study further explores the proposition of affordability.

However, recent analyses have raised doubts that more information will solve the access problem. The Advisory Committee on Student Financial Assistance [ACSFA] (2002) estimates that 4 million college-qualified low-income and middle-income students will be left behind in the next decade. Other analyses confirm there is a financial access problem (St. John, 2003b). If finances are a problem in enrollment and persistence, then it is even more important to examine these differences for diverse racial and ethnic groups.

This article adapts the financial nexus model to examine the role of perceptions about college costs in the responses by African American and White students to student financial aid in their college choices and enrollment decisions. African Americans and Whites have differing perceptions of college costs before going to college. These differing perceptions may also affect the groups' persistence once in college. It is crucial that evaluation research consider both the role of early expectations, formed as a consequence of financial opportunities, and the direct effects of costs and aid, especially when research considers diverse groups.

Situating This Study

The late 1980s was a turning point in the history of American higher education that went largely unnoticed. Between the Supreme Court's *Brown* decision in 1954 and about 1980, there had been an overt effort to equalize educational opportunity in the U.S. for African Americans compared to Whites. In the middle 1970s, African American high school graduates attended college at about the same rate as Whites (St. John, 2003b), but a gap in enrollment opportunity emerged after the 1980s. The college participation rate for African American high school graduates actually declined in the years after 1980, while the enrollment rate for Whites increased substantially, as did the overall enrollment rate. Therefore, the participation gap that is now the focal point of public policy (Ruppert, 2003) is relatively recent.

Starting in the late 1980s, analysts working for the federal government began to focus on differences in high school curriculum as the explanation for the recently emergent disparity in opportunity (Pelavin & Kane, 1988, 1990). While some researchers focused on the role of the decline in federal grant aid as the explanation of the new disparity (St. John, 1991, 1994), the academic explanation grew in popularity among analysts representing different constituents and points of view (Choy, 2002; Gladieux & Swail, 1999; Greene & Foster, 2003; King, 1999; NCES, 1997). And while the methodological error in some of the basic studies (e.g., NCES, 1997) have gained the attention of researchers in economics and higher education policy (Becker, in press; Fitzgerald, in press; Heller, in press), the explanation for the downturn in opportunity for African Americans has not been sufficiently examined.

The nexus model provides a proven methodology that can be used to reexamine the educational choices made by college students during this important transitional period. Previous studies have explained some of the economic disparity that emerged in the late 1980s (Paulsen & St. John, 2002), an area of inquiry that has informed recent efforts to reexamine student aid policy (ACSFA, 2002; Fitzgerald, in press; St. John, 2002, 2003b). By extending nexus research to explicitly consider persistence by African Americans and Whites, this article focuses on the ways federal policy on student aid—the increased emphasis on loans and the decline in grants that took shape in the late 1980s and that continues to present—influenced the disparity in opportunity for African Americans versus Whites that emerged during this period.

Research Approach

The nexus model examines how student background, finance-related reasons for choosing a college, college experience, current aspirations, prices and subsidies, and living costs influence persistence. This section describes the statistical methods, model specifications, and study limitations.

Statistical Methods

Consistent with prior analyses using the nexus model, the current study uses sequential sets of logistic regression analyses of the National Postsecondary Student Aid Survey of 1987 (NPSAS-87) (Paulsen & St. John, 2002; St. John, Paulsen, & Starkey, 1996). Logistic regression is an appropriate approach for analyzing models with dichotomous outcomes, such as the decision to persist (Cabrera, 1994). We also converted beta coefficients to delta-p statistics using a method recommended by Cabrera (1994). Further, the systematic uses of sequential logistic analyses provide a means of examining the confounding relationships between different sets of variables in the persistence-decision process. In the nexus model, we examine the influence of variables related to student background, college choice, college experience, current aspirations, and financial support on persistence.

Model Specifications

First, we included 16 variables related to student background (see Table 43.1). Most of these variables were included in design sets of dichotomous variables. Students whose mothers had less than a high school education, some college, college degrees, master's degrees, or doctoral degrees were compared to students whose mothers had completed high school. Students who completed GEDs and who did not complete high school were compared to students who had completed high school. Students from lower-, upper-middle-, and upper-income families were compared to students from lower-middle-income families. Four variables used conventional dichotomous coding: males were compared to females; married students were compared to students who were not married; working students were compared to non-working students; and independent students were compared to others (dependent aid applicants and non-aid applicants). In addition, one variable (age) used continuous coding.

Second, two design sets of dichotomous variables were added related to the financial reasons for choosing a college. First, students who gave the highest possible ratings to student aid, low tuition, and both tuition and student aid were compared to students who did not give these variables the highest ratings. These variables represent costs that were essentially fixed at the time students entered college and that were set by the college. Second, students who gave the highest rating to low living costs, to being able to work and attend school, or to both of these variables were compared to students who did not give any of these variables the highest rating. These cost-related considerations were considered "controllable" because students can constrain these costs by making financially astute choices about residences and employment opportunities. The inclusion of these choice-related variables represents the most distinctive feature of the nexus model since they assess the role of perceptions about college costs and aid in the persistence process.

Third, 10 variables related to college experience were included in the analysis. These included three dichotomous variables related to the college attended: students attending 4-year colleges were

TABLE 43.1

Coding of Variables

Variable	Coding	Variable	Coding
Student background		Controllable costs	
Gender		Low living cost	1,0
Male	1,0	Could work	1,0
Mother's education		Living cost & work	1,0
Less than H.S	1,0	College experience	
High school	Uncoded	Four-year	1,0
Some college	1,0	On campus	1,0
College	1,0	Full time	1,0
Master's	1,0	Years in college	
Advanced	1,0	Freshman	Uncoded
Age	Year of age	Sophomore	1,0
Marital status		Junior	1,0
Married	1,0	Senior	1,0
High school graduate status		Grades	
GED	1,0	Below C	1,0
No H.S. diploma	1,0	Mostly C	1,0
H.S. diploma	Uncoded	B average	Uncoded
Employment		Mostly A	1,0
Working	1,0	Not reported	1,0
Dependency status		Aspirations	
Independent	1,0	Vocational	1,0
Income		Some college	1,0
Lower	1,0	College	Uncoded
Lower middle	Uncoded	Master's	1,0
Upper middle	1,0	Advanced	1,0
Upper	1,0	Financial	
College choice		Fixed costs	
Fixed costs		Grant $	Actual $/1,000
Financial aid	1,0	Loan $	Actual $/1,000
Low tuition cost	1,0	Work $	Actual $/1,000
Tuition & fin. aid	1,0	Tuition $	Actual $/1,000
		Food/housing $	Actual $/1,000

compared to students attending 2-year colleges[1]; students living on campus were compared to other students; and full-time students were compared to others. Year in college was recoded as a design set of dichotomous variables, with sophomores, juniors, and seniors being compared to freshmen. Further, college grades were coded as a design set, with students with below C grades, mostly Cs, mostly As, and no reported grades[2] being compared to students with mostly B grades.[3]

Fourth, aspirations were coded as a design set of dichotomous variables. Students who aspired to complete vocational certificates, some college, master's degrees, and advanced degrees were compared to students who aspired to complete bachelor's degrees.

Fifth, four price-related variables were added: grant amount, loan amount, work-study amount, and tuition charges. These variables were divided by 1,000 because this coding of dollar amounts is easier to interpret. This approach to assessing the impact of financial aid variables provides a more reliable approach to assessing the impact of student aid than other commonly used approaches (St. John, Andrieu, Oescher, & Starkey, 1994).

Finally, annual food and housing costs[4] were used as indicators of living costs. This variable was also divided by 1,000 so that all dollar amounts would be comparable. Living costs were treated separately from price-related variables because it is easier for students to "control" their living costs (St. John, Paulsen, & Starkey, 1996).

The statistical analyses have two further distinctive features. First, we present change of probability measures (delta-p statistics) for each of the independent variables. This allows us to assess the impact of a unit change in the independent variable on the probability of persisting. Second, we use sets of design variables for categorical variables that have proven not to have a linear relationship with persistence (e.g., grades and year in college). This improves the predictive ability of the logistic models. While this model represents a refinement over prior nexus models,[5] this approach does have a few limitations (St. John, Paulsen, & Starkey, 1996), discussed in the next section.

Limitations

First, while the NPSAS-87 database is well suited for the analysis of within-year persistence, it does not include a full sample of all college students. The survey sampled all students enrolled in the fall term and followed up with a survey in the spring term. Students who enrolled in the spring but not in the fall were not included in the sample. Given our focus on continuous enrollment, this limitation is not a problem for this study.

Second, NPSAS-87 does not include a complete set of variables related to high school experience. Thus, the influences of high school grades and high school courses were not considered. However, because there is a high correlation between high school grades and college grades, this limitation is not a serious problem for this study.

Third, NPSAS-87 is more than a decade old. However, it merits further analysis because it is uniquely suited for the analysis of within-year persistence,[6] an outcome that is directly linked to equal opportunity.[7] Furthermore, the financial conditions of the late 1980s—including the growing emphasis on loans relative to grants—remain largely in place, and federal student grant aid has declined substantially since the late 1980s (College Board, 1998). Therefore while there have been changes in institutions' policies during the past decade, the analysis remains relevant to the current policy context.

Findings

There were substantial differences in the characteristics of the four populations (Table 43.2). A larger percentage of African American college students was female, had mothers with high school educations or some college, was financially independent, and was from low- and lower-middle-income families. In addition, African Americans had lower grades, and a higher percentage aspired to complete master's degrees. Higher percentages of Whites had parents who had completed master's degrees, had completed high school, were from upper-middle- and upper-income families, and received B grades.

There were also differences in the ways financial considerations influenced the college-choice process. Larger percentages of African Americans chose college because of financial aid offers and because of financial aid and low tuition. A larger percentage of African Americans were also concerned about finances when they made their college choices. Given these differences, there is good reason to use the nexus model to examine persistence decisions by these four distinct populations of undergraduates.

Finally, there were also notable differences in the financial situations facing both populations. African Americans had higher grants and loans as well as lower tuition charges. This means they had greater financial need and could still only afford to attend less expensive colleges. Whites attended colleges that were more expensive. Thus, there were marked contrasts in the relative

TABLE 43.2

Comparison of Populations

	African Am. % / ave.	White % / ave.		African Am. % / ave.	White % / ave.
Student background			Controllable costs		
Gender			Low living cost	14.4	10.0
Male	38.4	47.2	Could work	26.9	25.0
Mother's education			Living cost & work	14.9	10.6
Less/H.S	22.7	10.4	College experience		
High school	33.4	32.3	Four-year	80.2	82.2
Some college	25.6	24.4	On campus	34.4	35.9
College	10.6	19.2	Full time	75.2	78.2
Master's	5.1	8.8	Freshman	30.7	28.9
Advanced	2.6	5.0	Sophomore	27.7	25.6
Age			Junior	21.8	21.5
Years old	23.8	23.0	Senior	19.8	24.0
Marital status			Grades		
Married	11.4	16.8	Below C	13.4	5.8
High school			Mostly C	40.2	33.1
GED	4.2	2.0	B average	16.4	31.5
No H.S. diploma	3.5	2.0	Mostly A	1.3	3.4
H.S. diploma	92.4	96.0	Not reported	28.7	26.1
Employment			Aspirations		
Working	57.9	58.6	Vocational	1.6	1.7
Dependency status			Some college	7.9	7.3
Independent	27.0	22.5	College	35.3	42.2
Income			Master's	37.0	34.4
Lower	36.0	15.0	Advanced	18.1	14.3
Lower middle	37.3	27.3	Financial		
Upper middle	21.8	40.2	Grant $	2,002	1,165
Upper	4.9	16.8	Loan $	1,032	855
College choice			Work $	197	98
Fixed costs			Tuition $	2,595	3,038
Financial aid	25.3	15.9	Food/housing $	1,466	1,598
Low tuition cost	17.2	19.8	Sample N	1,967	22,304
Tuition & fin. aid	22.7	11.5			

financial situations of the two populations, which is a further indicator that the nexus model could reveal differences in how students in different racial groups experience college costs and make persistence decisions.

African Americans

First, for African Americans, five background variables were significant in at least one of the steps of the logistic analysis (Table 43.3). Three of these variables had consistent effects across all three

TABLE 43.3

Sequential Logistic Analysis of Within-Year Persistence by African American Undergraduate Students

Factor/Variable	Step 1 Initial Model Delta P	Step 2 Tuit & Aid Delta P	Step 3 Housing & Food Delta P
Student background			
Gender			
Male	0.0008	−0.0054	−0.0055
Mother's education			
Less than HS	−0.0304	−0.0054	−0.0349
Some college	−0.0463*	−0.0374*	−0.0513*
College degree	0.0128	0.0531	0.0027
Master's	−0.0348	−0.0438	−0.0411
Advanced	−0.0055	0.0167	0.0185
Age			
Years old	0.0042**	0.0036**	0.0032**
Marital status			
Married	0.0272	0.0031	0.0378*
High school			
GED	−0.0045	−0.0097	−0.0251
No H.S. deg.	0.0771**	0.0756**	0.0785**
Employment			
Working	0.0226	0.0154	0.0173
Dependency status			
Independent	−0.0647**	−0.0458*	−0.0379
Total income			
Lower	−0.0029	0.0009	0.0101
Upper-middle	−0.0025	−0.0188	−0.0198
Upper	0.0229	0.0211	0.0232
College choice			
Fixed costs			
Fin. aid	0.0331**	0.0555**	0.0556**
Low tuition	−0.0115	−0.0167	−0.0146
Tuition & aid	0.0126	0.0280	0.0245
Controllable costs			
Low living costs	0.0221	0.0165	0.0270
Could work	−0.0095	−0.0210	−0.0149
Living & work	0.0118	−0.0034	−0.0013
College experience			
Four year	−0.0619**	0.0241	0.0246
On campus	−0.0688*	−0.0115	−0.0279
Full time	−0.1585**	−0.0672**	−0.0609**

Year in college			
Sophomore	0.0106	0.0098	0.0088
Junior	−0.0213	−0.0290	−0.0196
Senior	0.0072	−0.0047	0.0010
Grades			
Below C	0.0626**	0.0531**	0.0535**
C ave.	0.0065	−0.0018	0.0022
A ave.	0.0768**	0.0678*	0.0751**
None rep.	0.0527*	0.0414*	0.0436*
Aspirations			
Vocational	0.0666**	0.0621*	0.0619*
Some coll.	0.0344*	0.0361*	0.0360*
Master's	−0.0336	−0.0262	−0.0200
Advanced	−0.0946**	−0.0714*	−0.0500
Financial			
Grant $		−0.0330**	−0.0327**
Loan $		−0.0133	−0.0114
Work $		−0.0213	−0.0219
Tuition $		−0.1201**	−0.1170**
Housing/food $			−0.0454**
Baseline P			
Model "N"	1,967	1,967	1,967
Somer's D	0.520	0.624	0.645
au-a	0.106	0.127	0.131
−2 LOG L	1490.409	1398.914	1369.835
DF	35	39	40

*p ≤ .05; **p ≤ .01; ***p ≤ .001

steps. Students whose mothers had some college were about 5% less likely to persist, while each year of age increased the probability of persistence by about 2%, and having no high school degree increased the probability of persistence by about 8%.[8] These findings suggest that the influence of parents' education, age, prior educational attainment, and prior education experience do not have a relationship with finances for African American students.

However, two background variables do change in significance across the steps in the model. Married students were more likely to persist only when housing and food costs were considered in the last step of the model. This suggests that students who were married had lower additional living costs associated with college attendance. In addition, financially independent students were less likely to persist in the first two steps, but not when living costs were also considered. It is possible that the federal need analysis criteria underestimate the costs associated with attendance by independent students. Thus, not only do both of these variables change in significance when housing costs are considered, but there also are logical reasons for these changes in significance.

Second, only one of the college choice variables was significant. African Americans who chose to attend their colleges because of financial aid offers were about 5% more likely to persist. Further, choosing a college because of low tuition or low living costs was not significantly associated with persistence. For African Americans, the offer of student aid appeared to have a substantial intrinsic value independent of the direct effects of student aid or other financial variables.

Third, several variables related to the college experience were significant for African Americans, four of which had consistent effects across the three steps. Attending full-time was negatively associated with persistence across all three steps. In addition, having below C grades, having A grades, and having no reported grades were all significant and positively associated with persistence across all three models. This suggests that the positive effects of attending full-time and the direct effects of grades on persistence do not interact with finances for African Americans.[9]

However, two college-experience variables did change in significance. Attending 4-year colleges and living on campus were negatively associated with persistence before financial aid was considered (step 1), but not in the final two steps. Both of these variables were logically related to college costs: Four-year colleges tend to charge higher tuition than 2-year colleges do, and residential colleges tend to charge more than locally situated campuses.

Fourth, three variables related to current aspirations were significant in at least one step. Aspiring to complete some college or to attain vocational certification consistently increased the probability of persistence. Having short-term goals made it easier to persist in the face of inadequate financial support.[10] However, students who aspired to attain an advanced degree were less likely to persist before living costs were considered. This means that some students with long-term aspirations were forced to put off their enrollment to contend with short-term financial needs, another indicator of the inadequacy of federal student aid. While this is consistent with prior analyses of persistence by all undergraduates (St. John, Andrieu, Oescher, & Starkey, 1994; St. John, Paulsen, & Starkey, 1996), it is distinctive to African Americans in this analysis of the two distinct populations.[11] Thus, it appears that African Americans were more likely to be faced with difficult choices due to the inadequacy of student aid.

In the second step, financial aid and tuition were added. The amount of grant awarded was significant and negatively associated with persistence across the two steps, indicating that grant aid was insufficient even after living costs were controlled for. Further, tuition was negatively associated with persistence across both models. Each thousand dollars of tuition differential decreased the probability of persistence by about 12%. Not only were African Americans more responsive to tuition than the other populations, but they also attended colleges with lower costs (see Table 43.2). Therefore, it seems that the greater the tuition the less likely African American students would receive enough aid to offset costs. Further, living costs were negatively associated with persistence (see Table 43.2). Each thousand dollars of differential in living costs decreased the probability of persistence by 4.5% for African Americans.

It should also be noted that there was substantial economic diversity among African American college students. While the majority were low-income and highly price sensitive, approximately one quarter were in the upper-middle- or upper-income groups (see Table 43.2). Interestingly, 18% of all African Americans had mothers with college degrees or higher attainment. Further, more than one quarter did not consider low tuition or student aid to be very important in their college choice. In sum, even though this study focuses on differences between racial groups, it is important to note that there is evidence of substantial diversity among individuals within each group as well. Furthermore, this economic diversity is reflected in the significant effects of college choice and cost and aid variables.

Whites

First, five background variables were significant for Whites (Table 43.4). Students with GEDs and working students were more likely to persist in all three analyses. Therefore, the effects of these factors on persistence were unrelated to college costs. However, males were less likely to persist, and students whose mothers had a master's degree were more likely to persist only in the final step, after living costs were considered; and older White students were more likely to persist before prices were considered. Thus, there were several confounding relationships between financial variables and background characteristics.

Second, three college choice variables were significant. Choosing a college because of the financial aid offer was significant and positively associated with persistence only after tuition and aid were considered. This indicates an inadequacy of student aid relative to tuition. Similarly, those choosing a college because of low tuition were less likely to persist after price-related variables were considered, indicating that even though such students might have attended colleges with lower tuition, students' tuition-sensitivity could have had offsetting effects. Further, Whites who chose

TABLE 43.4

Sequential Logistic Analysis of Within-Year Persistence by White Undergraduate Students

Factor/Variable	Step 1 Initial Model Delta P	Step 2 Tuit & Aid Delta P	Step 3 Housing & Food Delta P
Student background			
Gender			
Male	0.0375	0.0057	−0.0084*
Mother's education			
Less than HS	−0.0073	−0.0083	−0.0080
Some college	0.0030	0.0001	0.0017
College degree	0.0101	0.0075	0.0090
Master's	0.0133	0.0109	0.0156*
Advanced	0.0084	0.0123	0.0134
Age			
Years old	0.0008**	0.0005	0.0004
Marital status			
Married	0.0072	0.0018	−0.0006
High school			
GED	0.0218**	0.0206**	0.0223**
No H.S. deg.	0.0025	0.0011	0.0014
Employment			
Working	0.0200**	0.0190**	0.0167**
Dependency status			
Independent	0.0032	0.0604	0.0089
Total income			
Lower	0.0020	0.0051	0.0056
Upper-middle	−0.0062	−0.0827	−0.0086
Upper	0.0013	0.0230	0.0051
College choice			
Fixed costs			
Fin. aid	−0.0118	0.0188**	0.0218**
Low tuition	−0.0072	−0.0140**	−0.0132**
Tuition & aid	−0.0044	0.0079	0.0085
Controllable costs			
Low living costs	0.0017	−0.0048	−0.0036
Could work	0.0151**	0.0108*	0.0062
Living & work	0.0058	0.0008	−0.0012
College experience			
Four year	−0.0314**	0.0215**	0.0231**
On campus	−0.0445**	0.0057	0.0432**
Full time	−0.1213**	−0.0563**	−0.0490**

(continued)

TABLE 43.4

Sequential Logistic Analysis of Within-Year Persistence by White Undergraduate Students *(continued)*

Factor/Variable	Step 1 Initial Model Delta P	Step 2 Tuit & Aid Delta P	Step 3 Housing & Food Delta P
Year in college			
Sophomore	−0.0210**	−0.0063**	−0.0126**
Junior	0.0020	0.0059	0.0092**
Senior	−0.0344**	−0.0375**	−0.0337
Grades			
Below C	0.0583**	0.0550**	0.0557**
C ave.	0.0234**	0.0200**	0.0221**
A ave.	0.0189**	0.0156*	0.0152*
None rep.	0.0421**	0.0419**	0.0422**
Aspirations			
Vocational	0.0320**	0.0318**	0.0306**
Some coll.	0.0194**	0.0211**	0.0193**
Master's	−0.0300**	−0.0229**	−0.0186**
Advanced	−0.0534**	−0.0331**	−0.0297**
Financial			
Grant $		−0.0135**	−0.0131**
Loan $		−0.0089**	−0.0044
Work $		−0.0389*	−0.0385*
Tuition $		−0.1090**	−0.1042**
Housing/food $			−0.0495**
Baseline P	0.913	0.913	0.913
Model "N"	22,304	22,304	22,304
Somer's D	0.546	0.641	0.666
Tau-a	0.087	0.102	0.106
−2 LOG L	14555.422	13702.51	13430.221
DF	35	39	40

*p ≤ .05; **p ≤ .01; ***p ≤ .001

their colleges so they could work were more likely to persist before living costs were considered, indicating that these students either had lower living costs or were able to efficiently manage living costs with work-related income. In combination, these findings indicate direct relationships between financial reasons for choosing college and college costs for Whites.

Third, all of the variables related to college experience were significant for Whites. Attending a 4-year college and living on campus were negatively associated with persistence before price-related variables were considered (step 1) and positively associated with persistence after the effects of both prices and living costs were considered (step 3). In addition, even though attending full-time was consistently negatively associated with persistence, the effects became less negative as prices (step 2) and living costs (step 3) were added to the model. In combination, these findings indicate that 4-year, on-campus, and full-time college attendance are all associated with higher college costs. However, when costs are controlled for, results indicate that 4-year and on-campus attendance increase the probability of persistence, due to greater academic and social aspects of the college experience related to living on campus.[12] Interestingly, sophomores and seniors were consistently less likely to persist than freshmen were, while juniors were more likely than freshmen were to persist only after living costs were considered.

Fourth, there was an association between grades and persistence for some groups and not others. Including non-reported grades helped clarify the role of grades compared to earlier analyses. Students with low grades (C average or below C), as well as those with very high grades (A average), were consistently more likely to persist than those with B average grades. This means that the relationship between college achievement and grades does not have a linear association with persistence.

Fifth, all of the aspirations variables were significant and associated with persistence. Aspiring to complete a vocational qualification or some college consistently had a positive association with persistence compared to aspiring to complete a college degree, while aspiring to attain a master's or advanced degree consistently had a negative association with persistence. This again suggests that students with more immediate goals were more likely to continue their enrollment because of those goals.

Sixth, all of the price-related variables were significant for Whites. Grants, work-study, and tuition differentials were negatively associated with persistence in both models, indicating that aid was insufficient. Further, loan amounts were negatively associated with persistence when prices were first considered (step 2), but not when living costs were considered (step 3). This finding illustrates that loans were inadequate to contend fully with living costs. Conversely, borrowing money to pay for living costs could have an adverse impact on persistence. Further, there is a negative association between living costs and persistence. Each thousand dollars of differential in living costs decreased the probability of persistence by about 5%.

While there was economic diversity among White students, the majority was from upper-middle- or upper-income families. Further, a smaller percentage chose their colleges because of low tuition or student aid. Thus, while grants, loans, and work-study aid were influential in students' persistence decisions by Whites, a percentage of this group was adversely affected by aid inadequacy.

Conclusions and Implications

These analyses provide insight into the role financial aid played in the emergence of the new equality. As a conclusion, we first examine patterns of choice among diverse racial groups, and then we consider the implications for public policy and higher education finance.

Patterns of Student Choice

Our primary conclusion is that there were diverse patterns of educational choice both across and within both racial groups. Further, there is a continuity of choice patterns within each group, suggesting that habitus is reinforced as a result of the confluence of family backgrounds and public policies. Distinctive patterns were evident for the two groups examined.

African Americans were highly sensitive to finances in their college choices and in their persistence decisions. Tuition and student aid played a substantial role in the college choice process for African Americans, while grants and tuition had a substantial and direct influence on persistence. Further, choosing a college because of student aid was positively associated with persistence even when the direct effects of tuition and student aid were considered. This majority pattern among African Americans was similar, in some respects, to the pattern of college choice by students from low-income families observed in a recent analysis of social class and college costs (Paulsen & St. John, 2002).

However, a substantial percentage of African Americans were from high-earning families with high levels of education. Further, levels of parents' education, as well as students' aspirations, were associated with persistence for African Americans, indicating that those with cultural capital may have aspired to reproduce this capital in their families, albeit with mixed success. Thus, within the African American population there is clearly a pattern of economic diversity that accentuates the role of finance in college choice and persistence for African Americans.

In contrast, on average, Whites were more economically advantaged than were African American students, as evidenced by the distribution of students across income categories. Yet there was considerable economic diversity among the White population, which would explain why Whites were quite responsive to tuition and student grants. However, while loans were negatively associated with persistence by Whites, they ceased being significant when living costs were controlled for, indicating that loans were more effective for Whites than for other groups.

Policy Implications

First, student grants and tuition levels play more substantial roles in college choices and persistence by African Americans than for Whites. Thus, reductions in federal grants, and concomitant rapid growth in tuition, during the past two decades have had a more substantial influence on African Americans than on Whites, because grants and tuition play more substantial roles in choice processes for African Americans than for Whites. Further, institutional policies that use grants to offset tuition increases and to promote diversity would seem an especially viable approach to encouraging African American enrollment.

In contrast, the emphasis on loans seems to favor Whites. Not only was a larger percentage of Whites from high-income families, but Whites used loan capital to pay living costs associated with college attendance. Thus, the new loan policy environment accentuates the privileges of Whites and increases inequities between Whites and African Americans.

On a positive note, this study confirms arguments that student aid can be used to reduce the inequalities in higher education, as was the case in the 1970s. The challenge facing policymakers on campuses, in state houses, and in Washington, DC, is to figure out strategies for using aid that are fair and just for all groups. Clearly, the current policy environment accentuates differences in ways that simply are not just for all. At the very least, there is a need to reexamine arguments for need-based grant aid, an approach that would increase equity for African Americans, if not to also reconsider low tuition policies, approaches that seem especially important for African Americans given their high tuition sensitivity.

More generally, these findings have implications for admissions and retention efforts aimed at improving diversity. The recent Supreme Court decision in the Michigan case constrained the use of race in admission. However, it is still possible to design admission and retention programs in ways that target students with high needs or students who have achieved in spite of their disadvantages. Specially, it is important to provide academic support for all students. Financial aid is linked to the opportunity to be engaged in faculty research for high achieving students of color (St. John, 2003a). It is important that the research community continue to seek better ways of directing need-based aid and merit aid to students who need this support to become engaged as learners in their colleges and universities. It is equally important to intervene to make sure there are opportunities for such engagement. This article reinforces the emergent understanding that opportunities for engagement are limited for high achieving, low-income students—including students of color—who must work excessive hours to pay for college.

Notes

1. This represents an adaptation of the nexus model. Prior analyses examined only students in 4-year colleges. The population was expanded to capture sufficient cases for separate analyses of each ethnic group. Further, in the initial analysis, students attending private colleges were compared to students in public colleges (St. John, Paulsen, & Starkey, 1996). This variable was dropped from the current analyses because of a high correlation between attending a private college and tuition charges.
2. In previous persistence studies using variations of this model, students with reported grades remained uncoded and thus were combined with students with mostly B grades (e.g., St. John, Andrieu, Oescher, & Starkey, 1994; St. John, Paulsen & Starkey, 1996). Treating no reported grades as a distinct variable represents a further refinement of the nexus model.
3. High school and college grades are generally highly correlated. Therefore, a potential limitation due to the absence of data on high school achievement (i.e., test scores and grades) is somewhat mitigated.
4. Housing and food represents a further refinement over prior models. This variable was constructed by the National Center for Educational Statistics and included fewer missing cases than the housing and other-living-costs variables used in prior analyses (e.g., St. John, Paulsen, & Starkey, 1996).
5. We described these refinements in the footnotes above.

6. NPSAS-87 included a fall sample of all students enrolled in postsecondary institutions and a spring follow-up survey. In subsequent years, this sampling approach was replaced with a revolving sample to get a better approximation of full-year enrollment.
7. It provides a measure of whether students can actually afford to complete the academic year, a basic measure of affordability.
8. We expect that students with no high school degrees were more likely to persist because these students were more committed, possibly because they have fewer options to fall back on.
9. In fact, in looking across the results for each racial/ethnic group, these variables did not change in significance across any of the populations.
10. This is a consistent pattern across populations and is consistent with prior analyses (St. John, Paulsen, & Starkey 1996).
11. We base this interpretation on a comparison of the significance of this variable across the analyses of the different populations (see Tables 43.3 and 43.4).
12. We agree with the reviewers of this paper that this interpretation is supported by research on college students by Astin (1975), Tinto (1987, 2000), and others who have examined integration processes for students who live on campus.

References

Advisory Committee on Student Financial Assistance. (2002). *Empty promises: The myth of college access in America. Washington*, DC: Author.

Astin, A. W. (1975). *Preventing students from dropping out.* San Francisco: Jossey-Bass.

Becker, W. E. (in press). Omitted variables and sample selection problems in studies of college-going decisions. In C. Teddlie & E. A. Kemper (Series Eds.) & E. P. St. John (Vol. Ed.), *Readings on equal education: Vol. 19. Public policy and college access: Investigating the federal and state roles in equalizing postsecondary opportunity.* New York: AMS Press, Inc.

Berger, J. B. (2000). Optimizing capital, social reproduction, and undergraduate persistence: A sociological perspective. In J. M. Braxton (Ed.), *Reworking the student departure puzzle* (pp. 95–124). Nashville, TN: Vanderbilt University Press.

Cabrera, A. F. (1994). Logistic regression analysis in higher education: An applied perspective. In J. C. Smart (Ed.), *Higher education: Handbook of theory and research* (Vol. 10, pp. 225–256). New York: Agathon Press.

Cabrera, A. F., Nora, A., & Castañeda, M. B. (1992). The role of finances in the persistence process: A structural model. *Research in Higher Education*, 33, 571–593.

Carter, D. F. (1999). The impact of institutional choice and environments on African American and White students' degree expectations. *Research in Higher Education*, 40, 17–41.

Choy, S. P. (2002). *Access & persistence: Findings from 10 years of longitudinal research on students.* Washington, DC: American Council on Education.

College Board. (1998). *Trends in student aid.* Washington, DC: Author.

Fitzgerald, B. (in press). Federal financial aid and college access. In C. Teddlie & E. A. Kemper (Series Eds.) & E. P. St. John (Vol. Ed.), *Readings on equal education: Vol. 19. Public policy and college access: Investigating the federal and state roles in equalizing postsecondary opportunity.* New York: AMS Press, Inc.

Gladieux, L. G., & Swail,W. S. (1999). Financial aid is not enough: Improving the odds for minority and low-income students. In J. E. King (Ed.), *Financing a college education: How it works, how it's changing* (pp. 177–197). Westport, CT: Oryx Press.

Greene, J. P., & Foster, G. (2003). *Public school graduation and college readiness rates in the United States.* (Education working paper #3). New York: Center for Civic Innovation at the Manhattan Institute.

Hanson, S. L. (1994, July). Lost talent: Unrealized educational aspirations and expectations among U.S. youths. *Sociology of Education*, 67, 159–183.

Hartle, T. W. (1998). Clueless about college costs. *Presidency*, 1(1), 20–27.

Hearn, J. C. (1984, January). The relative roles of academic, ascribed, and socioeconomic characteristics in college destinations. *Sociology of Education*, 57, 22–30.

Heller, D. (1997). Student price response in higher education: An update of Leslie and Brinkman. *Journal of Higher Education*, 68, 624–659.

Heller, D. E. (in press). NCES research on college participation: A critical analysis. In C. Teddlie & E. A. Kemper (Series Eds.) & E. P. St. John (Vol. Ed.), *Readings on equal education, Vol. 19. Public policy and college access: Investigating the federal and state roles in equalizing postsecondary opportunity.* New York: AMS Press, Inc.

Kaltenbaugh, L. S., St. John, E. P., & Starkey, J. B. (1999). What difference does tuition make? An analysis of ethnic differences in persistence. *Journal of Student Financial Aid*, 29(2), 21–31.

Kane, T. J. (1995). *Rising public college tuition and college entry: How well do public subsidies promote access to college?* (Working paper series No. 5146). Cambridge, MA: National Bureau of Economic Research.

Kao, G., & Tienda, M. (1998). Educational aspirations of minority youth. *American Journal of Education*, 106(5), 349–384.

King, J. E. (1999). Crisis or convenience: Why are students borrowing more? In J. E. King (Ed.), *Financing a college education: How it works, how it's changing* (pp. 165 –176). Westport, CT: Oryx Press.

McDonough, P. M., Korn, J., & Yamasaki, E. (1997). Access, equity, and the privatization of college counseling. *The Review of Higher Education*, 20(3), 297–317.

McPherson, M. S., & Schapiro, M. O. (1991). *Keeping colleges affordable*. Washington, DC: Brookings Institution.

National Center for Education Statistics. 1997. *Confronting the odds: Students at risk and the pipeline to higher education*. (NCES 98-094). By Laura J. Horn. Project officer: C. Dennis Carroll. Washington, DC: Author.

Paulsen, M. B. (2001a). The economics of human capital and investment in higher education. In M. B. Paulsen & J .C. Smart (Eds.), *The finance of higher education: Theory, research, policy and practice* (pp. 55–94). New York: Agathon Press.

Paulsen, M. B. (2001b). The economics of the public sector: The nature and role of public policy in the finance of higher education. In M. B. Paulsen & J. C. Smart (Eds.), *The finance of higher education: Theory, research, policy and practice* (pp. 95–132). New York: Agathon Press.

Paulsen, M. B., & St. John, E. P. (1997). The financial nexus between college choice and persistence. In R. A. Voorhees (Ed.), *Researching student aid: Creating an action agenda* (pp. 65–82). San Francisco: Jossey-Bass.

Paulsen, M. B., & St. John, E. P. (2002). Social class and college costs: Examining the financial nexus between college choice and persistence. *Journal of Higher Education*, 73(3), 189–236.

Pelavin, S. H., & Kane, M. B. (1988). *Minority participation in higher education*. Washington, DC: Pelavin Associates.

Pelavin, S. H., & Kane, M. B. (1990). *Changing the odds: Factors increasing access to college*. New York: College Board.

Ruppert, S. S. (2003). *Closing the college participation gap: A national summary*. Denver: Education Commission of the States.

St. John, E. P. (1991). What really influences minority student attendance? An analysis of the High School and Beyond sophomore cohort. *Research in Higher Education*, 32(2), 141–158.

St. John, E. P. (1994). *Prices, productivity and investment: Assessing financial strategies in higher education* (ASHE/ ERIC Higher Education Report, No. 3). Washington, DC: George Washington University.

St. John, E. P. (2002). *The access challenge: Rethinking the causes of the new inequality* (Policy Issue Report # 2002-01). Bloomington, IN: Indiana Education Policy Center.

St. John, E. P. (2003a). *Diverse pathways: The roles of financial aid and student involvement in expanding educational opportunity*. Prepared for the Bill & Melinda Gates Foundation.

St. John, E. P. (2003b). *Refinancing the college dream: Access, equal opportunity, and justice for taxpayers*. Baltimore: Johns Hopkins University Press.

St. John, E. P., Andrieu, S. C., Oescher, J., & Starkey, J. B. (1994). The influence of student aid on within-year persistence by traditional college-age students in four-year colleges. *Research in Higher Education*, 35, 301–334.

St. John, E. P., & Hossler, D. (1998). Higher education desegregation in the post-Fordice legal environment: A critical-empirical perspective. In R. Fossey (Ed.), *Readings in equal education* (pp. 123–156). New York: AMS Press, Inc.

St. John, E. P., & Noell, J. (1989). The effects of student financial aid on access to higher education: An analysis of progress with special consideration of minority enrollment. *Research in Higher Education*, 30, 563–581.

St. John, E. P., & Paulsen, M. B. (2001). The finance of higher education: Implications for theory, research, policy and practice. In M. B. Paulsen & J. C. Smart (Eds.), *The finance of higher education: Theory, research, policy and practice* (pp. 545–568). New York: Agathon Press.

St. John, E. P., Paulsen, M. B., & Starkey, J. B. (1996). The nexus between college choice and persistence. *Research in Higher Education*, 37, 175–220.

Strope, J. L., Jr., & Wells, J. A. (1998). The Podberesky Case and race-based financial aid. *Readings in Equal Education*, 15, 157–172.

Tinto, V. (1987). *Leaving college: Rethinking causes and links of student attrition*. Chicago: University of Chicago Press.

Tinto, V. (2000). Linking learning and leaving. In J. M. Braxton (Ed.), *Reworking the student departure puzzle* (pp. 81–94). Nashville, TN: Vanderbilt University Press.

CHAPTER 44

NEOLIBERALISM, CORPORATE CULTURE, AND THE PROMISE OF HIGHER EDUCATION: THE UNIVERSITY AS A DEMOCRATIC PUBLIC SPHERE

HENRY A. GIROUX

In this article, Henry Giroux addresses the corrosive effects of corporate culture on the academy and recent attempts by faculty and students to resist the corporatization of higher education. Giroux argues that neoliberalism is the most dangerous ideology of the current historical moment. He shows that civic discourse has given way to the language of commercialization, privatization, and deregulation and that, within the language and images of corporate culture, citizenship is portrayed as an utterly privatized affair that produces self-interested individuals. He maintains that corporate culture functions largely to either ignore or cancel out social injustices in the existing social order by overriding the democratic impulses and practices of civil society through an emphasis on the unbridled workings of market relations. Giroux suggests that these trends mark a hazardous turn in U.S. society, one that threatens our understanding of democracy and affects the ways we address the meaning and purpose of higher education.

> *Neoliberalism is the defining political economic paradigm of our time—it refers to the policies and processes whereby a relative handful of private interests are permitted to control as much as possible of social life in order to maximize their personal profit. Associated initially with Reagan and Thatcher, for the past two decades neoliberalism has been the dominant global political economic trend adopted by political parties of the center and much of the traditional left as well as the right. These parties and the policies they enact represent the immediate interests of extremely wealthy investors and less than one thousand large corporations.*
>
> —Robert W. McChesney[1]

> *The task in theory no less than in practice is . . . to reilluminate public space for a civil society in collapse. . . . Societies that pretend that market liberty is the same thing as civic liberty and depend on consumers to do the work of citizens are likely to achieve not unity but a plastic homogeneity—and . . . to give up democracy. . . . We seem fated to enter an era in which in the space where our public voice should be heard will be a raucous babble that leaves the civic souls of nations forever mute.*
>
> —Benjamin R. Barber[2]

The Dystopian Culture of Neoliberalism

As the forces of neoliberalism and corporate culture gain ascendancy in the United States, there is an increasing call for people either to surrender or narrow their capacities for engaged politics in exchange for market-based values, relationships, and identities. Market forces have radically altered the language we use in both representing and evaluating human behavior and action.

One consequence is that civic discourse has given way to the language of commercialism, privatization, and deregulation. In addition, individual and social agency are defined largely through market-driven notions of individualism, competition, and consumption. Celebrities such as Martha Stewart, Jane Pratt, George Foreman, and Michael Jordan now market themselves as brand names. The widely read business magazine *Fast Company* devoted an entire issue to the theme "The Brand Called You."[3] No longer defined as a form of self-development, individuality is reduced to the endless pursuit of mass-mediated interests, pleasures, and commercially produced lifestyles.

One egregious example of self-marketing can be observed in two recent high school graduates' successful attempt to secure corporate sponsorship to pay for their college tuition and expenses. Just before graduating from high school in June 2001, Chris Barrett and Luke McCabe created a website, *ChrisandLuke.com*, offering themselves up as "walking billboards for companies" willing to both sponsor them and pay for their college tuition, room, and board. Claiming that they "would put corporate logos on their clothes, wear a company's sunglasses, use their golf clubs, eat their pizza, drink their soda, listen to their music or drive their cars," these two young men appeared impervious to the implications of defining themselves exclusively through those market values in which buying and selling appears to be the primary marker of one's relationship to the larger social order.[4] Eventually, First USA, a subsidiary of Bank One Corporation and a leader in issuing Visa credit cards to students, agreed to sponsor Chris and Luke, thus providing them with the dubious distinction of becoming the first fully corporate sponsored university students.

Once the deal was sealed, Chris and Luke were featured in most of the major media, including *USA Today*, the *New York Times*, and *Teen Newsweek*. Hailed in the press as a heartwarming story about individual ingenuity, business acumen, and resourcefulness, there was little criticism of the individual and social implications of what it meant for these young people to both define their identities as commodities and present themselves simply as objects to be advertised and consumed. And, of course, nothing was said about spiraling tuition costs coupled with evaporating financial aid that increasingly puts higher education out of reach for working-class and middle-class youth. In a media-saturated society, it appears perfectly legitimate to assume that young people can define themselves almost exclusively through the aesthetic pleasures of consumerism and the dictates of commercialism rather than through a notion of publicness based on ethical norms and democratic values.[5] In short, it appears that a story in which students give up their voices to promote a corporate ideology is viewed in the public media less as a threat to democratic norms and civic courage than as an ode to the triumphant wisdom of market ingenuity. Equally disturbing is the assumption on the part of the two students that their identities as corporate logos is neither at odds with their role as university students nor incompatible with the role the university should play as a site of critical thinking, democratic leadership, and public engagement. Undaunted by blurring the line between their role as corporate pitchmen and their role as students, or for that matter about the encroachment of advertising into higher education, Chris and Luke defended their position by claiming, "We want to be role models for other kids to show that you don't have to wake up every day and be like everybody else."[6]

After Chris and Luke's story ran in the *New York Times*, a related incident gained widespread public attention, perhaps inspired by Chris and Luke's inventive entrepeneurialism. A young couple in Mount Kisco, New York, attempted to auction off on Ebay and Yahoo the naming rights of their soon-to-be-born child to the highest corporate bidder. These are more than oddball stories. As William Powers, a writer for the *Atlantic Monthly*, observes, these public narratives represent "dark fables about what we are becoming as a culture."[7] One wonders where this type of madness is going to end. But one thing is clear: As society is defined through the culture and values of neoliberalism, the relationship between a critical education, public morality, and civic responsibility as conditions for creating thoughtful and engaged citizens are sacrificed all too willingly to the interest of financial capital and the logic of profit-making.

This sad and tragic narrative suggests that citizens lose their public voice as market liberties replace civic freedoms and society increasingly depends on "consumers to do the work of citizens."[8] Similarly, as corporate culture extends even deeper into the basic institutions of civil and political society, there is a simultaneous diminishing of noncommodified public spheres—those institutions such as public schools, churches, noncommercial public broadcasting, libraries, trade unions, and various voluntary institutions engaged in dialogue, education, and learning—that address the relationship of the self to public life and social responsibility to the broader demands of citizenship, as well as provide a robust vehicle for public participation and democratic citizenship. As media theorists Edward Herman and Robert McChesney observe, such noncommodified public spheres have played an invaluable role historically "as places and forums where issues of importance to a political community are discussed and debated, and where information is presented that is essential to citizen participation in community life."[9] Without these critical public spheres, corporate power often goes unchecked and politics becomes dull, cynical, and oppressive.[10] But more importantly, in the absence of such public spheres it becomes more difficult for citizens to challenge the neoliberal myth that citizens are *merely* consumers and that "wholly unregulated markets are the sole means by which we can produce and distribute everything we care about, from durable goods to spiritual values, from capital development to social justice, from profitability to sustainable environments, from private wealth to essential commonweal."[11] As democratic values give way to commercial values, intellectual ambitions are often reduced to an instrument of the entrepreneurial self and social visions are dismissed as hopelessly out of date.[12] Public space is portrayed exclusively as an investment opportunity, and the public good increasingly becomes a metaphor for public disorder. That is, any notion of the public—for example, public schools, public transportation, or public parks—becomes synonymous with disrepair, danger, and risk. Within this discourse, anyone who does not believe that rapacious capitalism is the only road to freedom and the good life is dismissed as a crank. Hence, it is not surprising that Joseph Kahn, writing in the *New York Times*, argues without irony, "These days, it seems, only wild-eyed anarchists and Third World dictators believe capitalism is not the high road to a better life."[13]

Neoliberalism has become the most dangerous ideology of the current historical moment.[14] It assaults all things public, mystifies the basic contradiction between democratic values and market fundamentalism, and weakens any viable notion of political agency by offering no language capable of connecting private considerations to public issues. Similarly, as Jean and John Comaroff, distinguished professors of anthropology at the University of Chicago, point out in "Millennial Capitalism: First Thoughts on a Second Coming," neoliberalism works to "displace political sovereignty with the sovereignty of 'the market,' as if the latter had a mind and morality of its own."[15]

Under the rule of neoliberalism, politics are market driven and the claims of democratic citizenship are subordinated to market values. What becomes troubling under such circumstances is not simply that ideas associated with freedom and agency are defined through the prevailing ideology and principles of the market, but that neoliberalism wraps itself in what appears to be an unassailable appeal to common sense. As Zygmunt Bauman notes, "What . . . makes the neo-liberal world-view sharply different from other ideologies—indeed, a phenomenon of a separate class—is precisely the absence of questioning; its surrender to what is seen as the implacable and irreversible logic of social reality."[16] Also lost is the very viability of politics itself. As the Comaroffs observe, "There is a strong argument to be made that neoliberal capitalism in its millennial moment portends the death of politics by hiding its own ideological underpinnings in the dictates of economic efficiency."[17]

Defined as the paragon of all social relations by Friedrich von Hayek, Milton Friedman, Robert Nozick, Francis Fukuyama, and other market fundamentalists, neoliberalism attempts to eliminate an engaged critique about its most basic principles and social consequences by embracing the "market as the arbiter of social destiny."[18] In this instance, neoliberalism empties the public treasury, hollows out public services, and limits the vocabulary and imagery available to recognize noncommercialized public space, antidemocratic forms of power, and narrow models of individual agency. It also undermines the translating functions of any viable democracy by undercutting the ability of individuals to engage in the continuous translation between public considerations and the private interests by collapsing the public into the realm of the private. As Bauman observes, "It is no longer true that the 'public' is set on colonizing the 'private.' The opposite is the case: it is the private that colonizes the public space, squeezing out and chasing away everything which cannot be fully, without residue, translated into the vocabulary of private interests and pursuits."[19] Divested of its political possibilities and social underpinnings, freedom finds few opportunities for translating private worries into public concerns or individual discontent into collective struggle.[20]

Within neoliberalism's market-driven discourse, corporate culture becomes both the model for the good life and the paradigmatic sphere for defining individual success and fulfillment. I use the term *corporate culture* to refer to an ensemble of ideological and institutional forces that functions politically and pedagogically both to govern organizational life through senior managerial control and to fashion compliant workers, depoliticized consumers, and passive citizens.[21] Within the language and images of corporate culture, citizenship is portrayed as an utterly privatized affair whose aim is to produce competitive self-interested individuals vying for their own material and ideological gain.[22] Reformulating social issues as strictly private concerns, corporate culture functions largely to either cancel out or devalue social, class-specific, and racial injustices of the existing social order by absorbing the democratic impulses and practices of civil society within narrow economic relations. Corporate culture becomes an all-encompassing horizon for producing market identities, values, and practices. The good life, in this discourse, "is construed in terms of our identities as consumers—we are what we buy."[23] The good life now means living inside the world of corporate brands.

Accountable only to the bottom line of profitability, corporate culture, and its growing influence in U.S. life has signaled a radical shift in both the notion of public culture and what constitutes the meaning of citizenship and the defense of the public good. For example, the rapid resurgence of corporate power in the last twenty years and the attendant reorientation of culture to the demands of commerce and regulation have substituted the language of personal responsibility and private initiative for the discourses of social responsibility and public service. This can be seen in the enactment of government policies designed to dismantle state protections for the poor, the environment, working people, and people of color.[24] This includes not only President George W. Bush's proposed welfare bill, which imposes harsh working requirements on the poor without the benefits of child-care subsidies, but also the dismantling of race-based programs such as the California Civil Rights Initiative and the landmark affirmative action case, *Hopwood vs. Texas*, both designed to eliminate affirmative action in higher education; the reduction of federal monies for urban development, such as HUD's housing program;[25] the weakening of federal legislation to protect the environment; and a massive increase in state funds for building prisons at the expense of funding for public higher education.[26] According to Terrance Ball, professor of political theory at Arizona State University, corporate culture rests on a dystopian notion of what he calls marketopia and is characterized by a massive violation of equity and justice. He argues:

> The main shortcoming of marketopia is its massive and systematic violation of a fundamental sense of fairness. Marketopians who cannot afford health care, education, police protection, and other of life's necessities are denied a fair (or even minimally sufficient) share of social goods. Indeed, they are destitute of every good, excluded from a just share of society's benefits and advantages, pushed to the margins, rendered invisible. They are excluded because they lack the resources to purchase goods and services that ought to be theirs by right.[27]

As a result of the corporate takeover of public life, the maintenance of democratic public spheres from which to organize the energies of a moral vision loses all relevance. State and civil society are limited in their ability to impose or make corporate power accountable. As a result, politics as an expression of democratic struggle is deflated, and it becomes more difficult, if not impossible, to address pressing social and moral issues in systemic and political terms. This suggests a hazardous turn in U.S. society, one that both threatens our understanding of democracy as fundamental to our freedom and the ways in which we address the meaning and purpose of public and higher education.

Unchecked by traditional forms of state power and removed from any sense of place-based allegiance, neoliberal capitalism appears more detached than ever from traditional forms of political power and ethical considerations. Public sector activities such as transportation (in spite of the recent Amtrak bailout, an exception to the rule), health care, and education are no longer safeguarded from incursions by the buying and selling logic of the market, and the consequences are evident everywhere as the language of the corporate commercial paradigm describes doctors and nurses as "selling" medical services, students as customers, admitting college students as "closing a deal," and university presidents as CEOS.[28] But there is more at stake here than simply the commodification of language. There is, as Pierre Bourdieu has argued, the emergence of a Darwinian world marked by the progressive removal of autonomous spheres of cultural production such as journalism, publishing, and film; the destruction of collective structures capable of counteracting the widespread imposition of commercial values and effects of the pure market; the creation of a global reserve army of the unemployed; and the subordination of nation states to the masters of the economy. Bourdieu is worth quoting at length on the effects of this dystopian world of neoliberalism:

> First is the destruction of all the collective institutions capable of counteracting the effects of the infernal machine, primarily those of the state, repository of all of the universal values associated with the idea of the public realm. Second is the imposition everywhere, in the upper spheres of the economy and the state as at the heart of corporations, of that sort of moral Darwinism that, with the cult of the winner, schooled in higher mathematics and bungee jumping, institutes the struggle of all against all and cynicism as the norm of all action and behaviour.[29]

I am not suggesting that neoliberal capitalism is the enemy of democracy or that market investments cannot at times serve the public good, but that in the absence of vibrant, democratic public spheres, corporate power, when left on its own, appears to respect few boundaries based on self-restraint and the public good, and is increasingly unresponsive to those broader human values that are central to a democratic civic culture. I believe that in the current historical moment neoliberal capitalism is not simply too overpowering but that "democracy is too weak."[30] Hence, the increasing influence of money over politics, corporate interests over public concerns, and the growing tyranny of unchecked corporate power and avarice. Increasing evidence of the shameless "greed-is-good" mantra can be found in the corruption and scandals that have rocked giant corporations such as Enron, WorldCom, Xerox, Tyco, Walmart, and Adelphia. The fallout suggests a widening crisis of confidence in the United States' economic leadership in the world and reflects comments such as those by Guido Rossi, a former Italian telecom chairman, who points out that "what is lacking in the U.S. is a culture of shame. No C.E.O. in the U.S. is considered a thief if he does something wrong. It is a kind of moral cancer."[31] Clearly, there is more at stake in this crisis than simply the greed of a few high-profile CEOs. More importantly, there is the historic challenge neoliberalism and market fundamentalism pose to democracy, citizenship, social justice, and civic education.

Such commentary reflects a fundamental shift regarding how we think about the relationship between corporate culture and democracy.[32] In what follows, I argue that one of the most important indications of such a change can be seen in the ways in which educators are currently being asked to rethink the role of higher education. Underlying this analysis is the assumption that the struggle to reclaim higher education must be seen as part of a broader battle over the defense of public goods and that at the heart of such a struggle is the need to challenge the ever-growing discourse and influence of neoliberalism, corporate power, and corporate politics. I conclude by offering some suggestions as to what educators can do to reassert the primacy of higher education as an essential sphere for expanding and deepening the processes of democracy and civil society. I also offer some ideas for new places and spaces of resistance in which individuals and groups can affirm and act on the values of critical engagement and civic responsibility to deepen and expand the values and practices of a substantive democratic society.

Incorporating Higher Education

Struggling for democracy is both a political and an educational task. Fundamental to the rise of a vibrant democratic culture is the recognition that education must be treated as a public good—as a crucial site where students gain a public voice and come to grips with their own power as individual and social agents. Public and higher education cannot be viewed merely as sites for commercial investment or for affirming a notion of the private good based exclusively on the fulfillment of individual needs. Reducing higher education to the handmaiden of corporate culture works against the critical social imperative of educating citizens who can sustain and develop inclusive democratic public spheres. A long tradition extending from Thomas Jefferson to John Dewey and

C. Wright Mills extols the importance of education as essential for a democratic public life. Sheila Slaughter has argued persuasively that at the close of the nineteenth century "professors made it clear that they did not want to be part of a cutthroat capitalism. . . . Instead, they tried to create a space between capital and labor where [they] could support a common intellectual project directed toward the public good."[33]

The legacy of public discourse appears to have faded as the U.S. university reinvents itself by giving in to the demands of the marketplace. Venture capitalists now scour colleges and universities in search of big profits made through licensing agreements, the control of intellectual property rights, and promoting and investing in university spin-off companies.[34] In the age of money and profit, academic disciplines gain stature almost exclusively through their exchange value on the market, and students now rush to take courses and receive professional credentials that provide them with the cachet they need to sell themselves to the highest bidder. Michael M. Crow, president of Arizona State University, echoes this shift in the role of higher education by proclaiming, without irony, that professors should be labeled as "academic entrepreneurs." In light of his view of the role of academic labor, it is not surprising that he views knowledge strictly as a form of financial capital. He states, "We are expanding what it means to be a knowledge enterprise. We use knowledge as a form of venture capital."[35]

The current debate over the reform of higher education appears indifferent both to the historic function of U.S. universities and to the broader ideological, economic, and political issues that have shaped it. Against the encroaching demands of a market-driven logic, a number of educators have argued forcefully that higher education should be defended as both a public good and an autonomous sphere for the development of a critical and productive democratic citizenry.[36] For many educators, higher education represents a central site for keeping alive the tension between market values and those values representative of civil society that cannot be measured in narrow commercial terms but are crucial to a substantive democracy. Central to defending the university as a public good and site of critical learning is the recognition that education must not be confused with job training, suggesting all the more that educators must resist allowing commercial values to shape the purpose and mission of higher education. Richard Hoftstadter, the renowned American historian, understood the threat that corporate values posed to education and once argued that the best reason for supporting higher education "lies not in the services they perform . . . but in the values they represent."[37] For Hoftstadter, it was the values of justice, freedom, equality, and the rights of citizens as equal and free human beings that were at the heart of what it meant for higher education to fulfill its role in educating students for the demands of leadership, social citizenship, and democratic public life.

The ascendancy of corporate culture in all facets of life in the United States has tended to uproot the legacy of democratic concerns and rights that has historically defined the stated mission of higher education.[38] Moreover, the growing influence of corporate culture on university life in the United States has served to largely undermine the distinction between higher education and business that educators such as Hoftstadter wanted to preserve. As universities become increasingly strapped for money, corporations are more than willing to provide the needed resources, but the costs are troubling and come with strings attached. Corporations increasingly dictate the very research they sponsor, and in some universities, such as the University of California, Berkeley, business representatives are actually appointed to sit on faculty committees that determine how research funds are to be spent and allocated. Equally disturbing is the emergence of a number of academics that either hold stocks or other financial incentives in the very companies sponsoring their research. As the boundaries between public values and commercial interests become blurred, many academics appear less as disinterested truth seekers than as operatives for business interests.

But there is more at stake than academics selling out to the highest corporate bidder. In some cases, academic research is compromised, and corporations routinely censor research results that are at odds with their commercial interests. For instance, Eyal Press and Jennifer Washburn reported that "in a 1996 study published in the *Annals of Internal Medicine* . . . a senior research scholar at Stanford's Center for Biomedical Ethics, . . . Mildred Cho, found that 98 percent of papers based on industry-sponsored research reflected favorably on the drugs being examined, as compared with 79 percent of papers based on research not funded by the industry."[39] Press and Washburn also provided examples of companies that have censored corporate-sponsored research papers by removing passages that highlighted unfavorable results or negative outcomes.[40]

It gets worse. As large amounts of corporate capital flow into the universities, those areas of study in the university that don't translate into substantial profits get either marginalized, underfunded, or eliminated. Hence, we are witnessing both a downsizing in the humanities and the increasing refusal on the part of universities to fund research in services such as public health that are largely used by people who can't pay for them. Moreover, programs and courses that focus on areas such as critical theory, literature, feminism, ethics, environmentalism, postcolonialism, philosophy, and sociology suggest an intellectual cosmopolitanism or a concern with social issues that will be either eliminated or technicized because their role in the market will be judged as ornamental. Similarly, those working conditions that allow professors and graduate assistants to comment extensively on student work, teach small classes, take on student advising, conduct independent studies, and engage in collaborative research will be further weakened or eliminated, since they do not appear consistent with the imperatives of downsizing, efficiency, and cost accounting.[41]

The new corporate university values profit, control, and efficiency, all hallmark values of the neoliberal corporate ethic. These far outweigh considerations about pedagogy or the role of the faculty in maintaining some control over what they teach. For example, Patricia Brodsky, a professor of foreign language and literature, tells the story of an enterprising dean at the University of Missouri at Kansas City who informed the faculty of the Department of Foreign Languages and Literatures that he wanted them to offer a series of beginning language courses in German and Spanish. To save money, he proposed that the courses be taught by computer in the language laboratory rather than be taught in a classroom by a traditional teacher. The word spread quickly among the students that the course was an easy way to get ten hours' credit, and at one point over five hundred students enrolled in first and second-semester Spanish. There were only two part-time instructors to handle these students, and their role was limited to performing the technical task of assigning grades produced by computer-graded exams. It soon became clear that the computer-driven course was a disaster. As Brodsky points out:

> The method employed was totally passive. Students didn't speak at all and rarely wrote. They looked at pictures and listened to voices say words and sentences. Nor were any grammatical concepts presented. Exercises were not interactive, nor did they take advantage of other possibilities offered by computer technology. The only plus for the student was that they didn't have to show up for class at regularly scheduled times. The problems worsened when students attempted to transfer from these courses into the mainstream curriculum at the third semester level, for they had learned virtually nothing. This caused havoc for instructors in the third semester courses as well as hardship for the students. Their graduation dates sometimes had to be delayed, and they were justifiably angry at having wasted their time and money. It also necessitated our teaching additional remedial courses so that the students could fulfill their requirement.[42]

From the dean's perspective, the course was a great success. He only had to pay the salaries of two part-time faculty while a huge number of students paid full tuition. When the faculty voted to cancel the course because of its obvious problems and failures, the dean responded by claiming the faculty didn't know how to teach and continued the courses by offering them under a different program.[43]

Within the neoliberal era of deregulation and the triumph of the market, many students and their families no longer believe that higher education is about higher learning, but about gaining a better foothold in the job market. Colleges and universities are perceived—and perceive themselves—as training grounds for corporate berths. Jeff Williams, editor of *The Minnesota Review*, goes even further, arguing that universities have become licensed storefronts for brand-name corporations. He writes:

> Universities are now being conscripted as a latter kind of franchise, directly as training grounds for the corporate workforce; this is most obvious in the growth of business departments but impacts English, too, in the proliferation of more "practical" degrees in technical writing and the like. In fact, not only has university work been redirected to serve corporate-profit agendas via its grant-supplicant status, but universities have become franchises in their own right, reconfigured according to corporate management, labor, and consumer models and delivering a name brand product.[44]

The "brand naming" of the university is also evident in the increasing number of endowed chairs funded by major corporations and rich corporate donors. For example, Nike CEO Phil Knight has donated $15 million to the University of Oregon for the creation of a number of endowed chairs across the campus, seven of which have been established, including the Knight Chair for University Librarian and a Knight Chair designated for the dean of the School of Law. The Knight Chair endowment coupled with matching contributions "are expected to eventually support at least 30 new endowed chairs."[45] In addition, the Knight family name will appear on a new law school building named the William W. Knight Law Center, after Phil Knight's father. The Lego company not only endowed a chair at the MIT Media Laboratory, it also funds a $5 million LEGO Learning Lab. Academic titles not only signal wealthy corporate donors' influence on universities, but have also served as billboards for corporations. Some of the more well known include the General Mills Chair of Cereal Chemistry and Technology at the University of Minnesota, Stanford University's Yahoo! Chair of Information Management Systems, and the University of Memphis' FedEx Chair of Information-Management Systems.

Corporate giving through the funding of endowed chairs also, in some instances, gives business an opportunity to play a significant role in selecting a faculty member. In this way, they can influence what kind of research actually takes place under the aegis of the endowment. For instance, Kmart approved the appointment of J. Patrick Kelly for its chair at Wayne State University. Kelly worked for years on joint projects with Kmart and, not surprisingly, once he occupied the chair he engaged in research projects that not only benefited Kmart but also saved the company millions of dollars. In response to criticisms of his role as a Kmart researcher, Kelly argues in an article in the *Chronicle of Higher Education* that "Kmart's attitude always has been: What did we get from you this year? Some professors would say they don't like that position, but for me, it's kept me involved with a major retailer, and it's been a good thing." Kmart defends their influence over the chair by claiming, "We continue to use Dr. Kelly for consulting as well as training. It's certainly an investment, and one that we do tap into."[46] The tragedy here is not simply that Kelly defines himself less as an independent researcher and critical educator than as a Kmart employee, but he seems to have no clue whatsoever about the implications of this type of encroachment by corporate power and values upon academic freedom, responsible scholarly research, or faculty governance.

In the name of efficiency, educational consultants all over the United States advise their clients to act like corporations selling products and to seek "market niches" to save themselves. The increased traffic between the world of venture capitalism and higher education is captured in a recent issue of the *Chronicle of Higher Education*.[47] Goldie Blumstyk, a *Chronicle* reporter, followed business consultant and venture capitalist Jonah Schnel of ITU Ventures for four days as he traveled between Southern California and Pittsburgh, Pennsylvania. In the course of his travels, Schnel met with deans and a number of promising professors at the University of California, Los Angeles, and Carnegie-Mellon University in order to explore the possibility of creating spin-off companies capable of producing lucrative profits for both the involved faculty and the university. Within this discourse, the lure of profit is the only cachet that seems to matter. Research projects are discussed not in terms of their contribution to the public good or for their potential intellectual breakthroughs, but for what they produce and the potential profits they may make in the commercial sector.

The consequences of transforming university research into a commercially driven enterprise can be seen most clearly in the profitable bioscience and pharmaceutical industries. As David Trend points out, "The overwhelming majority of research investment [in the pharmaceutical industry] has gone not to saving the lives of millions of people in the developing world, but to what have been called 'lifestyle drugs' [that treat] such maladies as impotence, obesity, baldness and wrinkles . . . [even though] malaria, tuberculosis, and respiratory infections killed 6.1 million people last year."[48] Research investment for finding new drugs to combat these diseases is miniscule. While pharmaceutical companies will spend more than $24 billion in research working with universities to develop high-profit drugs such as Viagra, only $2 billion will be spent on drugs used to combat deadly diseases such as malaria, even though the disease is expected to kill more than forty million Africans alone in the next twenty years.[49] The corrosive effects of the influence of corporate power on higher education can also be seen in the complex connections between universities and corporations that are developing over intellectual property rights, licensing income, and patenting agreements.

Online courses also raise important issues about higher education and intellectual property, such as who owns the rights for course materials developed for online use. Because of the market potential of online lectures and course materials, various universities have attempted to claim ownership of such knowledge. The passing of the 1980 Bayh-Dole Act and the 1984 Public Law 98-620 by the U.S. Congress enabled "universities and professors to own patents on discoveries or inventions made as a result of federally supported research."[50] These laws accorded universities intellectual property rights, with specific rights to own, license, and sell their patents to firms for commercial profits. The results have been far from unproblematic.[51] Julia Porter Liebeskind points to three specific areas of concern that are worth mentioning.

First, the growth of patenting by universities has provided a strong incentive "for researchers to pursue commercial projects," especially in light of the large profits that can be made by faculty.[52] For instance, in 1995 five faculty members in the University of California system and an equal number at Stanford University earned a total of $69 million in licensing income. And while it is true that the probability of faculty earning large profits is small, the possibility for high-powered financial rewards cannot be discounted in shaping the production of knowledge and research at the university.

Second, patenting agreements can place undue restraints on faculty, especially with respect to keeping their research secret and delaying publication, or even prohibiting "publication of research altogether if it is found to have commercial value."[53] Such secrecy not only undermines faculty collegiality and limits a faculty member's willingness to work collectively with others, it can also damage faculty careers and, most important, prevent valuable research from becoming part of public knowledge.

Finally, the ongoing commercialization of research places undue pressure on faculty to pursue research that can raise revenue and poses a threat to faculty intellectual property rights. For example, at UCLA, an agreement was signed in 1994 that allowed an outside vendor, OnlineLearning.net, to create and copyright online versions of UCLA courses. The agreement was eventually "amended in 1999 to affirm professors' rights to the basic content of their courses . . . [but] under the amended contract, OnlineLearning retain[ed] their right to market and distribute those courses online, which is the crux of the copyright dispute."[54]

The debate over intellectual property rights calls into question not only the increasing influence of neoliberal and corporate values on the university, but also the vital issue of academic freedom. As universities make more and more claims on owning the content of faculty notes, lectures, books, computer files, and media for classroom use, the first casualty is, as UCLA professor Ed Condren points out, "the legal protection that enables faculty to freely express their views without fear of censorship or appropriation of their ideas."[55] At the same time, by appropriating property rights to courses, even for a fee, universities infringe on the ownership rights of faculty members by taking from them any control over how their courses might be used in the public domain.

Within this corporatized regime, management models of decisionmaking replace faculty governance. Once constrained by the concept of "shared" governance, administrations in the past decade have taken more power and reduced faculty-controlled governance institutions to advisory status. Given the narrow nature of corporate concerns, it is not surprising that when matters of accountability become part of the language of educational reform, they are divorced from broader considerations of social responsibility. As corporate culture and values shape university life, corporate planning replaces social planning, management becomes a substitute for leadership, and the private domain of individual achievement replaces the discourse of public politics and social responsibility. As the power of higher education is reduced in its ability to make corporate power accountable, it becomes more difficult within the logic of the bottom line for faculty, students, and administrators to address pressing social and ethical issues.[56] This suggests a perilous turn in U.S. society, one that threatens both our understanding of democracy as fundamental to our basic rights and freedoms and the ways in which we can rethink and re-appropriate the meaning, purpose, and future of higher education.

Higher Education, Corporate Leadership, and the Rise of the Academic Manager

As corporate governance becomes a central feature of U.S. higher education, leadership is being transformed to model the highest reaches of corporate culture. In a widely read article, "Its Lowly at the Top: What Became of the Great College Presidents," Jay Mathews argues that it has become increasingly difficult to find models of academic leadership in higher education that emulate the great college presidents of the past, many of whom played an esteemed and pronounced role in the drama of intellectual and political life. Pointing to such national luminaries as Charles Eliot, James Conant, Robert M. Hutchins, Theodore Hesburgh, Clark Kerr, and, more recently, Kingman Brewster, Mathews argues that the latter were powerful intellectuals whose ideas and publications provoked national debates, shaped public policy, and contributed to the intellectual culture of both their respective universities and the larger social order. Leadership has taken a different turn under the model of the corporate university. Mathews argues, and rightly so, that today's college presidents are known less for their intellectual leadership than for their role "as fundraisers and ribbon cutters and coat holders, filling a slot rather than changing the world."[57]

Academic administrators today do not have to display intellectual reach and civic courage. Instead, they are expected to bridge the world of academe and business. Sought after by professional headhunters who want candidates that are both safe and "most likely to shine in corporate boardrooms," the new breed of university presidents are characterized less by their ability to take risks, think critically, engage important progressive social issues, and provoke national debates than they are for raising money, producing media-grabbing public relations, and looking good for photo shoots.[58] As reported recently in *USA Today*, "more and more colleges and universities are hiring presidents straight from the business world."[59] To prove the point, *USA Today* provided three high-profile examples: Babson College named a Wall Street veteran as its president, Bowdoin College gave the job to a corporate lawyer and, in the most famous case of all, Harvard University picked former U.S. Treasury Secretary Lawrence Summers as its president. Admittedly, the neoliberal Summers seems to be equally concerned with engaging ideas and asking unsettling questions as with the more mundane task of fundraising.[60] The overt corporatization of university leadership makes clear that what was once part of the hidden curriculum of higher education—the creeping vocationalization and subordination of learning to the dictates of the market—has become an open and defining principle of education at all levels of learning.[61]

In the aftermath of the U.S. recession and the terrorist attacks of September 11, 2001, many colleges and universities are experiencing financial hard times. These events have exacerbated a downturn in economic conditions brought on by the end of the Cold War and the dwindling of government-financed defense projects, coupled with a sharp reduction of state aid to higher education. As a result, many colleges and universities are all too happy to allow corporate leaders to run their institutions, form business partnerships, establish cushy relationships with business-oriented legislators, and develop curricular programs tailored to the needs of corporate interests.[62] I am not suggesting that corporate funding is any less reprehensible than military funding as much as I am noting how the changing fiscal nature of universities underscores their growing reliance on corporate models of leadership. One crucial example of this is the increasing willingness on the part of legislators, government representatives, and higher education officials to rely on corporate leaders to establish the terms of the debate in the media regarding the meaning and purpose of higher education. Bill Gates, Jack Welch, Michael Milken, Warren Buffet, and other members of the Fortune 500 "club" continue to be viewed as educational prophets—in spite of the smirched reputation of former CEOs such as Kenneth Lay of Enron, Al Dunlap of Sunbeam, and Dennis Kozlowski of Tyco.[63] Yet, the only qualifications they seem to have is that they have been successful in earning huge profits for themselves and their shareholders, while at the same time laying off thousands of workers in order to cut costs and raise profits. While Gates, Milken, and others couch their concerns about education in the rhetoric of public service, corporate organizations such as the Committee for Economic Development, an organization of about 250 corporations, have been more blunt about their interest in education.[64] Not only has the group argued that social goals and services get in the way of learning basic skills, but also that many employers in the business community feel dissatisfied because "a large majority of their new hires lack adequate writing and problem-solving skills."[65]

Matters of leadership and accountability within neoliberalism and corporate culture in general rarely include broader considerations of ethics, equity, and justice, and it is precisely this element of market fundamentalism that corporate leaders often bring to academic leadership roles. Corporate culture lacks a vision beyond its own pragmatic interests and seldom provides a self-critical inventory about its own ideology and its effects on society. It is difficult to imagine such concerns arising within corporations where questions of consequence begin and end with the bottom line. For instance, it is clear that advocates of neoliberalism, in their drive to create wealth for a limited few, have no incentives for taking care of basic social needs. This is obvious not only in their attempts to render the welfare state obsolete, privatize all public goods, and destroy traditional state-protected safety nets, but also in their disregard of the environment, their misallocation of resources between the private and public sectors, and their relentless pursuit of profits. It is precisely this lack of emphasis on being a public servant and an academic citizen that is lacking in the leadership models that corporate executives often bring with them to their roles as academic administrators. Unfortunately, it often pays off.

Neoliberalism taints any civic-inspired notion of educational leadership because it represents a kind of market fundamentalism based on the untrammeled pursuit of self-interest—often wrapped up in the post–September 11 language of patriotism. Consequently, its corporate executives and market professionals may not be the best qualified to assume roles of leadership in higher education. As market-fund mogul George Soros has pointed out, the distinguishing feature of market fundamentalism is that "morality does not enter into [its] calculations" and does not necessarily serve the common interest, nor is such fundamentalism capable of taking care of collective needs and ensuring social justice.[66] It is highly unlikely that corporations such as Disney, IBM, Microsoft, or General Motors will seriously address the political and social consequences regarding policies they implement that have resulted in downsizing, deindustrialization, and the "trend toward more low-paid, temporary, benefit-free, blue- and white-collar jobs and fewer decent permanent factory and office jobs."[67] Rather, the onus of responsibility is placed on educated citizens to recognize that corporate principles of efficiency, accountability, and profit maximization have not created new jobs but in most cases have eliminated them (over 75 million jobs have been lost since 1973).[68] It is our responsibility to recognize that the world presented to them through allegedly objective reporting is mediated—and manipulated by—a handful of global media industries. My point, of course, is that such absences in public discourse constitute a defining principal of corporate ideology, which refuses to address—and must be made to address—the scarcity of moral vision that inspires such calls for educational reform modeled after corporate reforms implemented in the last decade.

Absent from corporate culture's investment in higher education is any analysis of how power works in shaping knowledge in the interest of public morality, how the teaching of broader social values provides safeguards against turning citizen skills into training skills for the workplace, or how schooling can help students reconcile the seemingly opposing needs of freedom and solidarity in order to forge a new conception of civic courage and democratic public life. Knowledge as capital in the corporate model is privileged as a form of investment in the economy, but appears to have little value when linked to the power of self-definition, social responsibility, or the capacities of individuals to expand the scope of freedom, justice, and the operations of democracy.[59] Knowledge stripped of ethical and political considerations offers limited, if any, insights into how universities should educate students to push against the oppressive boundaries of gender, class, race, and age domination. Nor does such a language provide the pedagogical conditions for students to critically engage knowledge as an ideology deeply implicated in issues and struggles concerning the production of identities, culture, power, and history. Education is a moral and political practice and always presupposes an introduction to and preparation for particular forms of social life, a particular rendering of what community is, and what the future might hold. If higher education is in part about the production of knowledge, values, and identities, then curricula modeled after corporate culture have been enormously successful in preparing students for low-skilled service work in a society that has little to offer in the way of meaningful employment for the vast majority of its graduates. If CEOs are going to provide some insight into how education should be reformed, they will have to reverse their tendency to collapse the boundaries between corporate culture and civic culture, between a society that defines itself through the interests of corporate power and one that defines itself through more democratic considerations regarding what constitutes substantive citizenship and social responsibility. Moreover, they will have to recognize that the problems with U.S. schools cannot be reduced to matters of accountability or cost-effectiveness. Nor can the solution to such problems be reduced to the spheres of management, economics, and technological quick fixes such as distance education. The problems of higher education must be addressed in the realms of values and politics, while engaging critically the most fundamental beliefs U.S. citizens have regarding the meaning and purpose of education and its relationship to democracy.

Corporate Culture's Threat to Faculty

As universities increasingly model themselves after corporations, it becomes crucial to understand how the principles of corporate culture intersect with the meaning and purpose of the university, the role of knowledge production for the twenty-first century, and the social practices inscribed within teacher-student relationships. The signs are not encouraging. In many ways, the cost accounting principles of efficiency, calculability, predictability, and control of the corporate order have restructured the meaning and purpose of education. In the never-ending search for new sources of revenue, the intense competition for more students, and the ongoing need to cut costs, many colleges and university presidents are actively pursuing ways to establish closer ties between their respective institutions and the business community. For example, in what has become a typical story, *USA Today* approvingly reports that Brian Barefoot, the new president of Babson College, has thirty years of experience at Paine Webber and Merrill Lynch and will "use his business contacts to get graduates jobs, and he'll make sure the curriculum reflects employer needs."[70] The message here is clear: Knowledge with a high exchange value in the market is what counts, while those fields such as the liberal arts and humanities that cannot be quantified in such terms will either be underfunded or allowed to become largely irrelevant in the hierarchy of academic knowledge.

David L. Kirp suggests that hiring part-time workers is a form of outsourcing, "the academic equivalent of temp agency fill-ins," and as a practice undermines the intellectual culture and the academic energy of higher education.[71] He supports this charge by claiming:

> From a purely financial perspective, it's a no-brainer to outsource teaching, because it saves so much money. . . . But the true costs to higher education—even if hard to quantify—are very high. To rely on contract labor in the classroom creates a cadre of interchangeable instructors with no sustained responsibility for their students, scholars with no attachment to the intellectual life of the institution through which they are passing.[72]

Unfortunately, Kirp seems to suggest that the part-time workers are as deficient as the conditions that create them. It is one thing to be the victim of a system built on greed and scandalous labor practices, and another thing to take the heat for trying to make a living under such conditions—as if all efforts can be measured simply by the nature of the job. The real issue here is that such conditions are exploitative and that the solutions to fixing the problem lie not simply in hiring more full-time faculty, but, as Cary Nelson points out, in reforming "the entire complex of economic, social and political forces operating on higher education."[73]

In other quarters of higher education, the results of the emergence of the corporate university appear even more ominous. One telling example that proved prescient took place in 1998 when James Carlin, a multimillionaire and former successful insurance executive who had been appointed as the chairman of the Massachusetts State Board of Education, gave a speech to the Greater Boston Chamber of Commerce.[74] Signaling corporate culture's dislike of organized labor and its obsession with cost cutting, Carlin launched a four-fold attack against the academic professoriate. First, he argued that higher education has to model itself after successful corporations, which means that colleges and universities have to be downsized. Second, he echoed the now familiar call on the part of corporate culture to abolish tenure. Third, he made it clear that democratic governance is not suitable for the corporate model of the university and that faculty have too much power in shaping decisions in the university. Finally, he explicitly condemned those forms of knowledge whose value lies outside of the instrumental sphere of commodification. More specifically, Carlin argued that "at least 50 percent of all non-hard sciences research on American campuses is a lot of foolishness" and should be banned.[75] He further predicted that "there's going to be a revolution in higher education. Whether you like it or not, it's going to be broken apart and put back together differently. It won't be the same. Why should it be? Why should everything change except for higher education?"[76] Carlin's "revolution" was spelled out in his call for increasing the workload of professors to four, three-credit courses a semester, effectively reducing the time educators might have to do research or shape institutional power.

Carlin's anti-intellectualism and animosity toward educators and students alike is simply a more extreme example of the forces at work in the corporate world that would like to take advantage of the profits to be made in higher education, while simultaneously refashioning colleges and universities in the image of the new multiconglomerate landscape. Missing from this corporate model of leadership is the recognition that academic freedom implies that knowledge has a critical function, that unpopular and critical intellectual inquiry should be safeguarded and treated as an important social asset, and that faculty in higher education are more than mere functionaries of the corporate order. Such ideals are at odds with the vocational function that corporate culture wants to assign to higher education.

While the call to downsize higher education appears to have caught the public's imagination at the moment, it belies the fact that such "reorganization" has been going on for some time. In fact, more professors are working part-time and at two-year community colleges than at any other time in the country's recent history. A 2001 report by the National Study of Postsecondary Faculty recently pointed out that "in 1998–1999, less than one-third of all faculty members were tenured . . . [and that] in 1992–1993, 40 percent of the faculty was classified as part-time and in 1998–1999, the share had risen to 45 percent."[77] Creating a permanent underclass of part-time professional workers in higher education is not only demoralizing and exploitative for many faculty who had such jobs, but such policies increasingly deskill both partial and full-time faculty by increasing the amount of work they have to do. With less time to prepare, larger class loads, almost no time for research, and excessive grading demands, many adjuncts run the risk of becoming either demoralized, ineffective, or both. Michael Dubson, writing as an adjunct, captures the process in the following comment:

> I am an adjunct. . . . I believed caring, working hard, doing a good job mattered and would add up to something concrete. Instead, I find myself on a wheel that turns but goes nowhere. I don't expect this situation to change. . . . I have watched my self-esteem drop, drop, drop from doing work that is, theoretically, enhancing the self-esteem of my students. I have seen the tired eyes, the worn clothes, the ancient eyes of long-term adjuncts. I have looked into their eyes as they have failed to look back into mine. . . . I have known thirty year old men living at home with their parents, forty year old women teaching college and going hungry, uninsured fifty year aids with serious illnesses. I have known adjunct teachers who hand out As and Bs like vitamins and help students cheat on their exams so they'll get good course evaluations. . . . I am a dreamer. I am an idealist. I am a victim. I am a whore. I am a fool. I am an adjunct.[78]

There is more at work here than despair; there are the harsh lessons of financial deprivation, heavy workloads, and powerlessness. As power shifts away from the faculty to the managerial sectors of the university, adjunct faculty increase in number while effectively being removed from the faculty governance process. In short, the hiring of part-time faculty to minimize costs simultaneously maximizes managerial control over faculty and the educational process itself. As their ranks are depleted, full-time faculty live under the constant threat of either being given heavier workloads or simply having their tenure contracts eliminated or drastically redefined through "post-tenure reviews." These structural and ideological factors not only send a chilling effect through higher education faculty, they also undermine the collective power faculty need to challenge the increasing corporate-based, top-down administrative structures that are becoming commonplace in many colleges and universities.

Corporate Culture's Threat to Students

Corporate culture's threat to students will also bear the burden of privatization as higher education joins hands with the corporate banking world. Lacking adequate financial aid, students, especially poor students, will increasingly finance the high costs of their education through private corporations such as Citibank, Chase Manhattan, Marine Midland, and other sanctioned lenders. Given the huge debt such students accumulate, it is reasonable to assume, as Jeff Williams points out, that loans "effectively indenture students for ten to twenty years after graduation and intractably reduce their career choices, funneling them into the corporate workforce in order to pay their loans."[79]

Of course, for many young people caught in the margins of poverty, low-paying jobs, and the casualties of the recession, the potential costs of higher education, regardless of its status or availability, will dissuade them from even thinking about the possibilities of going to college. Unfortunately, as state and federal agencies and university systems direct more and more of their resources such as state tax credits and scholarship programs toward middle- and upper-income students, the growing gap in college enrollments between high-income students (95% enrollment rate) and low-income students (75% enrollment rate) with comparable academic abilities will widen even further.[80] In fact, a recent report by a federal advisory committee claimed that nearly 48 percent of qualified students from low-income families will not be attending college in the fall of 2002 because of rising tuition charges and a shortfall in federal and state grants for low- and moderate-income students. The report claims that "nearly 170,000 of the top high-school graduates from low- and moderate-income families are not enrolling in college this year because they cannot afford to do so."[81] Those students who do go on to higher education will often find themselves in courses being taught by an increasing army of part-time and adjunct faculty. Not only do such policies harm faculty, they also cheat students. Too many undergraduates throughout the nation's colleges and universities often find themselves in oversized classes taught by faculty who are overburdened by heavy teaching. Moreover, those professors who are rewarded for bringing in outside money will be more heavily represented in fields such as science and engineering, which attract corporate and government research funding. As Sheila Slaughter observes, "Professors in fields other than science and engineering who attract funds usually do so from foundations which account for a relatively small proportion of overall research funding."[82]

Neoliberalism's obsession with spreading the gospel of the market and the value of corporate culture through privatization and commercialization has restructured those spaces and places outside of classrooms in which students spend a great deal of time. Corporations are increasingly joining up with universities to privatize a seemingly endless array of services that universities used to handle by themselves. For example, bookstores are now run by corporate conglomerates such as Barnes & Noble, while companies such as Sodexho-Marriott (also a large investor in the U.S. private prison industry) run a large percentage of college dining halls, and McDonald's and Starbucks occupy prominent locations on the student commons. In addition, housing, alumni relations, health care, and a vast array of other campus services are leased out to private interests. One consequence is that spaces once marked as public and noncommodified now have the appearance of shopping malls. David Trend points out that as university services were privatized,

> student union buildings and cafeterias took on the appearance—or were conceptualized from the beginning—as shopping malls or food courts, as vendors competed to place university logos on caps, mugs, and credit cards. This is a larger pattern in what has been termed the "Disneyfication" of college life . . . a pervasive impulse toward infotainment . . . where learning is "fun," the staff "perky," where consumer considerations dictate the curriculum, where presentation takes precedence over substance, and where students become "consumers."[83]

The message to students is clear: customer satisfaction is offered as a surrogate for learning, and "to be a citizen is to be a consumer, and nothing more. Freedom means freedom to purchase."[84]

Everywhere students turn outside of the university classroom, they are confronted with vendors and commercial sponsors who are hawking credit cards, athletic goods, and other commodities that one associates with the local shopping mall. Universities and colleges compound this marriage of commercial and educational values by signing exclusive contracts with Pepsi, Nike, Starbucks, and other companies, further blurring the distinction between student and consumer. Colleges and universities do not simply produce knowledge and values for students, they also play an influential role in shaping their identities. If colleges and universities are going to define themselves as centers of teaching and learning vital to the democratic life of the nation, they are going to have to acknowledge the danger of becoming corporate or simply adjuncts to big business. At the very least, this demands that they exercise the political, civic, and ethical courage needed to refuse the commercial rewards that would reduce them to becoming simply another brand name or corporate logo.

Corporate Culture, Pedagogy, and the Politics of Online Education

The turn to downsizing and deskilling faculty is also exacerbated by the attempt by many universities to expand into the profitable market of distance education. Such a market is all the more lucrative since it is being underwritten by the combined armed services, which in August 2000 pledged almost $1 billion to "provide taxpayer-subsidized university-based distance education for active-duty personnel and their families."[85] David Noble has written extensively on the restructuring of higher education under the imperatives of the new digital technologies and the move into distance education. If he is correct, the news is not good.

According to Noble, online learning largely functions through pedagogical models and methods of delivery that not only rely on standardized, prepackaged curriculum and methodological efficiency, but also reinforce the commercial penchant toward training, deskilling, and deprofessionalization. With the deskilling of the professoriate there will also be a rise in the use of part-time faculty, who will be "perfectly suited to the investor-imagined university of the future."[86] According to Noble, the growing influence of these ideological and methodological tendencies in higher education will be exacerbated by the powerful influence of the military.[87] As Noble observes, an education subsidized by the military

> is likely to entail familiar patterns of command, control, and precisely specified performance, in accordance with the hallmark military procurement principles of uniformity, standardization, modularization, capital intensiveness, system compatibility, interchangeability, measurability, and accountability—in short, *a model of education as a machine*, with standardized products and prescribed process.[88] (emphasis added)

Teachers College president Arthur Levine has predicted that the new information technology may soon make the traditional college and university obsolete. He is hardly alone in believing that online education will either radically alter or replace traditional education. As Eyal Press and Jennifer Washburn point out, "In recent years academic institutions and a growing number of Internet companies have been racing to tap into the booming market in virtual learning, which financial analysts like Merrill Lynch estimate will reach $7 billion by 2003."[89] The marriage of corporate culture, higher education, and the new high-speed technologies also offers universities big opportunities to cut back on maintenance expenses, eliminate entire buildings such as libraries and classrooms, and trim labor costs. Education scholars William Massy and Robert Zemsky claim that universities must take advantage of the new technologies to cut back on teaching expenditures. As they put it, "With labor accounting for 70 percent or more of current operating cost, there is simply no other way."[90]

Reporting on the coming restructuring of the university around online and distance education, the *Chronicle of Higher Education* claims that this new type of education will produce a new breed of faculty "who hails not from academia but from the corporate world." Hired more for their "business savvy than their degree, a focus on the bottom line is normal; tenure isn't." This alleged celebration of faculty as social entrepreneurs appears to offer no apologies for turning education into a commercial enterprise and teaching into a sales pitch for profits. As one enthusiastic distance educator put it for the *Chronicle*, "I love not only the teaching but the selling of it."[91]

Universities and colleges across the country are flocking to the online bandwagon. As Press and Washburn point out, "More than a half of the nation's colleges and universities deliver some courses over the Internet."[92] Mass-marketed degrees and courses are not only being offered by prestigious universities such as Seton Hall, Stanford University, Harvard University, New School University, and the University of Chicago, they are also giving rise to cyber-backed colleges such as the Western Governors University and for-profit, stand-alone virtual institutions such as the University of Phoenix.

This is not to suggest that online distance education is the most important or only way in which computer-based technologies can be used in higher education, or that the new electronic technologies by default produce oppressive modes of pedagogy. Many educators use email, networking, and web resources in very productive ways in their classrooms. The real issue is whether such a technology in its various pedagogical uses undermines human freedom and development. As Herbert Marcuse has argued, when the rationality that drives technology is instrumentalized and "transformed into standardized efficiency . . . liberty is confined to the selection of the most adequate means for reaching a goal which [the individual] did not set."[93] The consequence of the substitution of technology for pedagogy is that instrumental goals replace ethical and political considerations, result in a loss of classroom control by teachers, make greater demands on faculty time, and emphasize standardization and rationalization of course materials. Zygmunt Bauman underscores the threat of this danger by arguing that when technology is coupled with calls for efficiency, modeled on instrumental rationality, it almost always leads to forms of social engineering that authorize actions that become increasingly "reasonable" and dehumanizing at the same time.[94] In other words, when the new computer technologies are tied to narrow forms of instrumental rationality, they serve as "moral sleeping pills" that are made increasingly available by corporate power and the modern bureaucracy of higher education. Of the greatest importance here is how the culture of instrumental rationality shapes intellectual practices in ways that undermine the free exchange of ideas, mediate relations in ways that do not require the physical relations of either students or other faculty, and support a form of hyper-individualism that downplays forms of collegiality and social relations amenable to public service.[95]

The issue here is that such technologies, when not shaped by ethical considerations, collective dialogue, and dialogical approaches, lose whatever possibilities they might have for linking education to critical thinking and learning to democratic social change.[96] In fact, when business values replace the imperatives of critical learning, a class-specific divide begins to appear in which poor and marginalized students will get low-cost, low-skilled knowledge and second-rate degrees from online sources, while those students being educated for leadership positions in the elite schools will be versed in personal and socially interactive pedagogies in which high-powered knowledge, critical thinking, and problem-solving will be a priority, coupled with a high-status degree. Under such circumstances, traditional modes of class and racial tracking will be reinforced and updated within the proliferation of what David Noble calls "digital diploma mills."[97] Noble underemphasizes, in his otherwise excellent analysis, all indications that the drive toward corporatizing the university will take its biggest toll on those second- and third-tier institutions that are increasingly defined as serving no other function than to train semiskilled and obedient workers for the new postindustrialized order. The role slotted for these institutions is driven less by the imperatives of the new digital technologies than by the need to reproduce a gender and class division of labor that supports the neoliberal global market revolution and its relentless search for bigger profits.

Held up to the profit standard, universities and colleges will increasingly calibrate supply to demand, and the results look ominous with regard to what forms of knowledge, pedagogy, and research will be rewarded and legitimated. As colleges and corporations collaborate over the content of degree programs, particularly with regard to online graduate programs, college curricula run the risk of being narrowly tailored to the needs of specific businesses. For example, Babson College developed a master's degree program in business administration specifically for Intel workers. Similarly, the University of Texas at Austin is developing an online master of science degree in science, technology, and commercialization that caters only to students who work at IBM. Moreover, the program will only orient its knowledge, skills, and research to focus exclusively on IBM projects.[98] Not only do such courses run the risk of becoming company training workshops, they also open up higher education to powerful corporate interests that have little regard for knowledge tied to the cultivation of an informed, critical citizenry capable of actively participating in and governing a democratic society.

As crucial as it is to recognize the dangers inherent in online learning and the instructional use of information technology, it is also important to recognize that there are many thoughtful and intelligent people who harness the use of such technologies in ways that can be pedagogically useful. Moreover, not everyone who uses these technologies can be simply dismissed as living in a middle-class world of techno-euphoria in which computers are viewed as a panacea. Andrew Feenberg, a professor at San Diego State University and former disciple of Herbert Marcuse, rejects the essentialist view that technology reduces everything to functions, efficiency, and raw materials, "while threatening both spiritual and material survival."[99] Feenberg argues that the use of technology in both higher education and other spheres has to be taken up as part of a larger project to extend democracy and that under such conditions it can be used "to open up new possibilities for intervention."[100]

Higher Education as a Democratic Public Sphere

Higher education should be viewed as a resource vital to the democratic and civic life of the nation against the current onslaught to corporatize higher education. Higher education needs to be safeguarded as a public good against the ongoing attempts to organize and run it like a corporation, because, as Ellen Willis points out, the university "is the only institution of any size that still provides cultural dissidents with a platform."[101] But more importantly, higher education must be embraced as a democratic sphere because it is one of the few public spaces left where students can learn the power of questioning authority, recover the ideals of engaged citizenship, reaffirm the importance of the public good, and expand their capacities to make a difference. Central to such a task for the university is the challenge to resist becoming a consumer-oriented corporation more concerned about accounting than accountability, and whose mission, defined largely through an appeal to excellence, is comprehended almost exclusively in terms of a purely instrumental efficiency.[102]

Higher education can be removed from its narrow instrumental justification by encouraging students to think beyond what it means to simply get a job or be an adroit consumer. Moreover, the crisis of higher education needs to be analyzed in terms of wider configurations of economic, political, and social forces that exacerbate tensions between those who value such institutions as public goods and those advocates of neoliberalism who see market culture as a master design for all human affairs. Educators must challenge all attempts on the part of conservatives and liberals to drain democracy of its substantive ideals by reducing it to the imperatives of hypercapitalism and the glorification of financial markets.

Challenging the encroachment of corporate power is essential if democracy is to remain a defining principle of education and everyday life. Part of such a challenge requires educators, students, and others to create organizations capable of mobilizing civic dialogue, provide an alternative conception of the meaning and purpose of higher education, and develop political organizations that can influence legislation to challenge corporate power's ascendancy over the institutions and mechanisms of civil society. In strategic terms, revitalizing public dialogue suggests that faculty, students, and administrators need to take seriously the importance of defending higher education as an institution of civic culture whose purpose is to educate students for active and critical citizenship.[103] Such a project suggests that educators, students, and others will have to provide the rationale and mobilize efforts toward creating enclaves of resistance, new public spaces to counter official forms of public pedagogy, and institutional spaces that highlight, nourish, and evaluate the tension between civil society and corporate power while simultaneously struggling to prioritize citizen rights over consumer rights.

Situated within a broader context of issues concerned with social responsibility, politics, and the dignity of human life, higher education should be engaged as a site that offers students the opportunity to involve themselves in the deepest problems of society, to acquire the knowledge, skills, and ethical vocabulary necessary for modes of critical dialogue and forms of broadened civic participation. This suggests developing pedagogical conditions for students to come to terms with their own sense of power and public voice as individual and social agents by enabling them to examine and frame critically what they learn in the classroom "within a more political or social or intellectual understanding of what's going on" in the interface between their lives and the world at large.[104] At the very least, students need to learn how to take responsibility for their own ideas, take intellectual risks, develop a sense of respect for others different from themselves, and learn how to think critically in order to function in a wider democratic culture. At issue here is providing students with an education that allows them to recognize the dream and promise of a substantive democracy, particularly the idea that as citizens they are "entitled to public services, decent housing, safety, security, support during hard times, and most importantly, some power over decision making."[105]

But more is needed than defending higher education as a vital sphere in which to develop and nourish the proper balance between democratic values and market fundamentalism, between identities founded on democratic principles and identities steeped in forms of competitive, self-interested individualism that celebrate their own material and ideological advantages. Given the current assault by politicians, conservative foundations, and the media on educators who spoke critically about U.S. foreign policy in light of the tragic events of September 11, it is politically crucial that educators at all levels of involvement in the academy be defended as public intellectuals who provide an indispensable service to the nation.[106] Such an appeal cannot be made in the name of professionalism, but in terms of the civic duty such intellectuals provide. Too many academics have retreated into narrow specialties that serve largely to consolidate authority rather than critique its abuses. Refusing to take positions on controversial issues or to examine the role they might play in lessening human suffering, such academics become models of moral indifference and unfortunate examples of what it means to disconnect learning from public life.

On the other hand, many leftist and liberal academics have retreated into arcane discourses that offer them mostly the safe ground of the professional recluse. Making almost no connections to audiences outside of the academy or to the issues that bear down on their lives, such academics have become largely irrelevant. This is not to suggest that they do not publish or speak at symposiums, but that they often do so to limited audiences and in a language that is often overly abstract, highly aestheticized, rarely takes an overt political position, and seems largely indifferent to broader public issues. I am reminded of a story about one rising "left-wing" public relations intellectual, who berated one of his colleagues for raising some political concerns about an author that the newly arrived "left" professor had read. According to our young celebrity, political discourse was not "cool," thus affirming the separation of scholarship from commitment, while justifying a form of anti-intellectualism that parades under the banner of cleverness that threatens no one but clearly sells on the market. This is more than academic fluff or the mark of an impoverished imagination; it is irrelevance by design.

Engaged intellectuals such as Arundhati Roy, Noam Chomsky, Edward Said, and the late Pierre Bourdieu have offered a different and more committed role for academics. Mocking those intellectuals for whom irony and cleverness appear to be the last refuge of academic scoundrels who disdain any form of commitment, Roy defends the link between scholarship and commitment as precisely "uncool," as if being fashionable is the most important factor for shaping the identity and work of engaged intellectuals. She writes:

> I take sides. I take a position. I have a point of view. What's worse, I make it clear that I think it's right and moral to take that position, and what's even worse, I use everything in my power to flagrantly solicit support for that position. Now, for a writer of the twenty-first century, that's considered a pretty uncool, unsophisticated thing to do. . . . Isn't it true, or at least theoretically possible, that there are times in the life of a people or a nation when the political climate demands that we—even the most sophisticated of us—overtly take sides?[107]

Noam Chomsky claims that "the social and intellectual role of the university should be subversive in a healthy society . . . [and that] individuals and society at large benefit to the extent that these liberatory ideals extend throughout the educational system—in fact, far beyond."[108] Postcolonial and literary critic Edward Said takes a similar position and argues that academics should engage in ongoing forms of permanent critique of all abuses of power and authority—"to enter into sustained and vigorous exchange with the outside world"—as part of a larger project of helping "to create the social conditions for the collective production of realist utopias."[109]

Following Bourdieu and others, I believe that intellectuals who inhabit our nation's universities should represent the conscience of this society not only because they shape the conditions under which future generations learn about themselves and their relations to others and the outside world, but also because they engage pedagogical practices that are by their very nature moral and political, rather than simply cost-effective and technical. Such pedagogy bears witness to the ethical and political dilemmas that animate the broader social landscape and are important because they provide spaces that are both comforting and unsettling, spaces that both disturb and enlighten. Pedagogy in this instance not only works to shift how students think about the issues affecting their lives and the world at large, but potentially energizes them to seize such moments as possibilities for acting on and engaging in the world. The appeal here is not merely ethical; it is also an appeal that addresses the materiality of resources, access, and politics, while viewing power as generative and crucial to any viable notion of individual and social agency.

Organizing against the corporate takeover of higher education also suggests fighting to protect the jobs of full-time faculty, turning adjunct jobs into full-time positions, expanding benefits to part-time workers, and putting power into the hands of faculty and students. Moreover, such struggles must address the exploitative conditions under which many graduate students work, constituting a de facto army of service workers who are underpaid, overworked, and shorn of any real power or benefits.[110] Similarly, programs in many universities that offer remedial courses, affirmative action, and other crucial pedagogical resources are under massive assault, often by conservative trustees who want to eliminate from the university any attempt to address the deep inequities in society, while simultaneously denying a decent education to minorities of color and class. For example, the City University of New York, as a result of a decision made by a board of trustees, has decided to end

> its commitment to provide remedial courses for academically unprepared students, many of whom are immigrants requiring language training before or concurrent with entering the ordinary academic curriculum. . . . Consequently . . . a growing number of prospective college students are forced on an already overburdened job market.[111]

Educators and students need to join with community people and social movements around a common platform that resists the corporatizing of schools, the roll-back in basic services, and the exploitation of teaching assistants and adjunct faculty. But resistance to neoliberalism and its ongoing onslaught against public goods, services, and civic freedoms cannot be limited either to the sphere of higher education or to outraged faculty. There are several important lessons that faculty can learn from the growing number of broad-based student movements that are protesting neoliberal global policies and the ongoing commercialization of the university and everyday life. As far back as 1998, students from about one hundred colleges across the United States and Canada "held a series of 'teach-ins' challenging the increasing involvement of corporations in higher education."[112] Students from Yale University, Harvard University, Florida State University, and the University of Minnesota, among other schools, organized debates, lectures, films, and speakers to examine the multifaceted ways in which corporations are affecting all aspects of higher education. Within the last few years, the pace of such protests on and off campuses has grown and spawned a number of student protest groups, including the United Students Against Sweatshops (USAS), with over 180 North American campus groups, the nationwide 180/Movement for Democracy and Education, and a multitude of groups protesting the policies of the World Trade Organization (WTO) and the International Monetary Fund.[113]

Students have occupied the offices of university presidents, held hunger strikes, blocked traffic in protests of the brand-name society, conducted mass demonstrations against the WTO in Seattle, and protested the working conditions and use of child labor in the $2.5 billion dollar collegiate apparel industry. In January 2000, students from the conservative Virginia Commonwealth University joined the rising tide of anticorporate protest by organizing a sleep-in "outside of the vice president's office for two nights to protest the university's contract with McDonald's (the school promised the fast-food behemoth a twenty-year monopoly over the Student Commons)."[114] As diverse as these struggles might appear, one of the common threads is their resistance to the increasing incursion of corporate power over higher education. As Liza Featherstone observes:

> Almost all of the current student struggles—whether over tuition increases, apparel licenses, socially responsible investing, McDonald's in the student union, the rights of university laundry workers, a dining-hall contractor's investment in private prisons or solidarity with striking students in Mexico—focus on the reality of the university as corporate actor.[115]

Many students reject the model of the university as a business, which increasingly views students as consumers, the classroom as a marketplace, and the public space of the university as an investment opportunity. Students recognize that the corporate model of leadership shaping higher education fosters a narrow sense of responsibility, agency, and public values because it lacks a vocabulary for providing guidance on matters of justice, equality, fairness, equity, and freedom, values that are crucial to the functioning of a vibrant, democratic culture. Students are refusing to be treated as consumers rather than as members of a university community in which they have a voice in helping to shape the conditions under which they learn and how the university is organized and run. The alienation and powerlessness that ignited student resistance in the 1960s appears to be alive and well today on college campuses across the country. Featherstone, once again, captures this rising anticorporate sentiment. She writes:

> "Campus democracy" is an increasingly common rallying cry (just as, at major off campus protests, demonstrators chant "this is what democracy looks like"). . . . Like the idealists who wrote the Port Huron Statement, students are being politicized by disappointment.[116]

Student resistance to corporate power has also manifested off campus in struggles for global justice that have taken place in cities such as Seattle, Davos, Porto Alegre, Prague, Melbourne, Quebec, Gothenburg, Genoa, and New York. These anticorporate struggles not only include students, but also labor unions, community activists, environmental groups, and other social movements. The importance of these struggles is in part that they offer students alliances with nonstudent groups, both within and outside of the United States, and point to the promise of linking a university-based public pedagogy of resistance to broader pedagogical struggles and social movements that can collectively fight to change neoliberal policies. Equally important is that these movements link learning to social change by making visible alternative models of radical democratic relations in a wide variety of sites that extend from the art gallery to alternative media to the university. Such movements offer instances of collective resistance to the glaring material inequities and the growing cynical belief that today's culture of investment and finance makes it *impossible* to address many of the major social problems facing both the United States and the larger world. These new forms of politics perform an important theoretical service by recognizing the link between civic education, critical pedagogy, and oppositional political agency as pivotal to modes of organizing that challenge the depoliticization of politics and open up the possibilities for promoting autonomy and democratic social transformation.

Students protesting the corporatization of the university and neoliberalism's assault on public institutions and civil society both understand how dominant pedagogies work within the various formations and sites of capital—particularly corporate capital's use of the global media and the schools'—and refuse to rely on dominant sources of information. Such strategies point to an alternative form of politics outside of the party machines, a politics that astutely recognizes both the world of material inequality and the landscape of symbolic inequality.[117] In part, this has resulted in what Imre Szeman calls "a new public space of pedagogy" that employs a variety of old and new media including computers, theater, digital video, magazines, the Internet, and photography as a tool for both learning and organizing.[118] While employing many of the technologies used in online learning and other computer-based educational programs, these technologies operate out of a different political and pedagogical context designed to link learning to social change and challenge the often hierarchical relationships in higher education.

Higher education and the larger culture are too corporatized to become the only sites of learning and struggle. New spaces and places of resistance have to be developed, and this demands new forms of pedagogy and new sites in which to conduct it while not abandoning traditional spheres of learning. The challenge for faculty in higher education is, in part, to find ways to contribute their knowledge and skills to understanding how neoliberal pedagogies create the conditions for devaluing critical learning and undermining viable forms of political agency. Academics, as Imre Szeman puts it, need to figure out how neoliberalism and corporate culture "constitute a problem of and for pedagogy."[119] Academics need to be attentive to the oppositional pedagogies put into place by various student movements in order to judge their "significance . . . for the shape and function of the university curricula today."[120]

The challenge here is for faculty to learn as much as possible from student movements about pedagogical approaches and how these movements mediate the fundamental tension between the public values of higher education and the commercial values of corporate culture. If the forces of corporate culture are to be challenged, educators must also enlist the help of diverse communities, foundations, and social movements to ensure that public institutions of higher learning are adequately funded so that they will not have to rely on corporate sponsorship and advertising revenues.

Jacques Derrida has suggested in another context that any viable notion of higher education should be grounded in a vibrant politics, which makes the promise of democracy a matter of concrete urgency. For Derrida, making visible a democracy that is to come, as opposed to that which presents itself in its name, provides a referent for both criticizing everywhere what parades as democracy and critically assessing the conditions and possibilities for democratic transformation. Derrida sees the promise of democracy as the proper articulation of a political ethics and by implication suggests that when higher education is engaged and articulated through the project of democratic social transformation it can function as a vital public sphere for critical learning, ethical deliberation, and civic engagement. Toni Morrison understands something about the fragile nature of the relationship between higher education and democratic public life, and she rightly suggests, given the urgency of the times, the need for all members of academia to rethink the meaning and purpose of higher education. She writes:

> If the university does not take seriously and rigorously its role as a guardian of wider civic freedoms, as interrogator of more and more complex ethical problems, as servant and preserver of deeper democratic practices, then some other regime or menage of regimes will do it for us, in spite of us, and without us.[121]

Both Derrida and Morrison recognize that the present crisis represents a historical opportunity to refuse the commonsense assumption that democracy is synonymous with capitalism and critical citizenship is limited to being an unquestioning consumer. Markets need to be questioned not simply through economic considerations but as a matter of ethical and political concerns. The language of neoliberalism and the emerging corporate university radically alters the vocabulary available for appraising the meaning of citizenship, agency, and civic virtue. Within this discourse everything is for sale, and what is not has no value as a public good or practice. It is in the spirit of such a critique and act of resistance that educators need to break with the "new faith in the historical inevitability professed by the theorists of [neo-] liberalism [in order] to invent new forms of collective political work" to confront the march of corporate power.[122] This will not be an easy task, but it is a necessary one if democracy is to be won back from the reign of financial markets and the Darwinian values of an unbridled capitalism. Academics can contribute to such a struggle by, among other things, defending higher education for the contribution it makes to the quality of public life, fighting for the crucial role it plays pedagogically in asserting the primacy of democratic values over commercial interests, and struggling collectively to preserve its political responsibility to provide students with the capacities they need for civic courage and engaged critical citizenship.

The current regime of neoliberalism and the incursion of corporate power into higher education present difficult problems and demand a profoundly committed sense of collective resistance. Unfortunately, it is not a matter of exaggeration to suggest that collective cynicism has become a powerful fixture of everyday life. But rather than make despair convincing, I think it is all the more crucial to take seriously Meghan Morris' argument that "things are too urgent now to be giving up on our imagination."[123] Or, more specifically, to take up the challenge of Jacques Derrida's recent provocation that "we must do and think the impossible. If only the possible happened, nothing more would happen. If I only did what I can do, I wouldn't do anything."[124]

Notes

1. Robert W. McChesney, "Introduction," in Noam Chomsky, *Profit over People: Neoliberalism and Global Order* (New York: Seven Stories Press, 1999), p. 7.
2. Benjamin R. Barber, "Blood Brothers, Consumers, or Citizens? Three Models of Identity—Ethnic, Commercial, and Civic," in Carol Gould and Pasquale Pasquino, eds., *Cultural Identity and the Nation State* (Lanham, MD: Rowman and Littlefield, 2001), p. 65.
3. See Tom Peters, "The Brand Called You," *Fast Company* (August/September 1997), 83–94.

4. This quote is taken from the ChrisandLuke.com website. Retrieved July 2002, from http://www.ChrisandLukc.com/ap.html
5. For a classic critique of the brand-name society, see Naomi Klein, *No Logo: Taking Aim at the Brand Bullies* (New York: Picador, 1999).
6. Cited in Dawn Kessler, "What Would You Do for a Free Ride to College?" Retrieved July 2, 2002, from http://www.collegeboundmag.com/side/quickconnect
7. William Powers, "The Art of Exploitation," *Atlantic Monthly,* Retrieved July 2002, from http://www.theatlantic/politic/nj/ powers2001-08-08.html
8. These ideas are taken from Barber, "Blood Brothers, Consumers, or Citizens?" p. 65.
9. Edward S. Herman and Robert W. McChesney, *The Global Media: The New Missionaries of Global Capitalism* (Washington, DC: Cassell, 1997), p. 3.
10. I address this issue in Henry A. Giroux, *Public Spaces, Private Lives: Beyond the Culture of Cynicism* (Lanham, MD: Rowman and Littlefield, 2001).
11. Barber, "Blood Brothers, Consumers, or Citizens?" p. 59.
12. I take up this issue of cynicism in great detail in Giroux, *Public Spaces, Private Lives.*
13. Joseph Kahn, "Redrawing the Map," *New York Times,* June 25, 2000, p. 5.
14. This is a position shared by a number of influential social and political theorists. For example, see Robert W. McChesney, *Corporate Media and the Threat to Democracy* (New York: Seven Stories Press, 1997); Pierre Bourdieu, *Acts of Resistance against the Tyranny of the Market* (New York: New Press, 1998); Chomsky, *Profit over People;* Colin Leys, *Market Driven Politics* (London: Verso, 2001).
15. Jean Comaroff and John L. Comaroff, eds., *Millennial Capitalism and the Culture of Neoliberalism* (Durham, NC: Duke University Press, 2001), p. 333.
16. Zygmunt Bauman, *In Search of Politics* (Stanford, CA: Stanford University Press, 1999), p. 127.
17. Comaroff and Comaroff, "Millennial Capitalism," p. 322.
18. James Rule, "Markets, in Their Place," *Dissent* (Winter 1998), 31.
19. Zygmunt Bauman, *The Individualized Society* (London: Polity Press, 2001).
20. Bauman, *The Individualized Society.*
21. The classic dominant texts on corporate culture are Terrance Deal and Alan Kennedy, *Corporate Culture: The Rites and Rituals of Corporate Life* (Reading, MA: Addison-Wesley, 1982) and Thomas Peterson and Robert Waterman, *In Search of Excellence* (New York: Harper and Row, 1982). I also want to point out that corporate culture is a dynamic, ever-changing force. But in spite of its innovations and changes, it rarely if ever challenges the centrality of the profit motive, or fails to prioritize commercial considerations over a set of values that would call the class-based system of capitalism into question. For a brilliant discussion of the changing nature of corporate culture in light of the cultural revolution of the 1960s, see Thomas Frank, *The Conquest of Cool* (Chicago: University of Chicago Press, 1997).
22. Gary Becker captures this sentiment in his book, *The Economic Approach to Human Behavior.* He argues, "We not only ought to think and act as self-interested agents, but we are already acting (if not yet thinking) in precisely those ways. We are each of us self-interested calculators of our own advantage, however much we might wish to hide that fact from others and even (or perhaps especially) from ourselves." Cited in Terrance Ball, "Imagining Marketopia," *Dissent* (Summer 2001), 78.
23. Alan Bryman, *Disney and His Worlds* (New York: Routledge, 1995), p. 154.
24. Robin D. G. Kelley, *Yo' Mama's Disfunktional: Fighting the Culture War in Urban America* (Boston: Beacon Press, 1997).
25. HUD refers to the Department of Housing and Urban Development created as a cabinet-level agency in 1965. Its stated purpose is to create opportunities for home ownership, provide housing assistance for low-income persons, create affordable housing, enforce the nation's housing laws, promote economic growth in economically disadvantaged neighborhoods, and alleviate homelessness.
26. For a context from which to judge the effects of such cuts on the poor and on children, see *The State of America's Children: A Report from the Children's Defense Fund* (Boston, MA: Beacon Press, 1998). On the emergence of the prison-industrial complex and how it diverts money from higher education, see Giroux, *Public Spaces, Private Lives;* Christian Parenti, *Lockdown America: Police and Prisons in the Age of Crisis* (London: Verso Press, 1999).
27. Ball, "Imagining Marketopia," p. 78.
28. CEO refers to Chief Executive Officer, a term designating the primary head of an organization. This example is taken from Leys, *Market Driven Politics,* pp. 212–213.
29. Pierre Bourdieu, "The Essence of Neoliberalism," *Le Alonde Diplomatique,* December 1998, p. 4. RetrievedJuly 1, 2002, from http://www.en.monde-diplomatique.fr/1988/12/08bourdieu
30. Benjamin R. Barber, "A Failure of Democracy, Not Capitalism," *New York Times,* July 29, 2002, p. A23.

31. Cited in Tom Turnipseed, "Crime in the Suites Enabled by Political Corruption Causes a Crisis in the Credibility of US Capitalism," *Common Dreams,* June 29, 2002, p. 1. Retrieved July 1, 2002, from www.commondreams.org/views02/0629-01.htm
32. Critical educators have provided a rich history of how both public and higher education have been shaped by the politics, ideologies, and images of industry. For example, see Samuel Bowles and Herbert Gintis, *Schooling in Capitalist America* (New York: Basic Books, 1976); Michael Apple, *Ideology and Curriculum* (New York: Routledge, 1977); Martin Carnoy and Henry Levin, *Schooling and Work in the Democratic State* (Stanford, CA: Stanford University Press, 1985); Stanley Aronowitz and Henry A. Giroux, *Education Still under Siege* (Westport, CT: Bergin & Garvey, 1993); Stanley Aronowitz and William DiFazio, *The Jobless Future* (Minneapolis: University of Minnesota Press, 1994); Cary Nelson, ed., *Will Teach for Food* (Minneapolis: University of Minnesota Press, 1997); D. W. Livingstone, *The Education-Jobs Gap* (Boulder, CO: Westview, 1998).
33. Sheila Slaughter, "Professional Values and the Allure of the Market," *Academe* (September/October 2001), l.
34. An example of how cozy the relationship between venture capitalism and the university has become can be seen in the story uncritically reported in *Chronicle of Higher Education.* See Goldie Blumenstyk, "Chasing the Rainbow: A Venture Capitalist on the Trail of University-Based Companies," *Chronicle of Higher Education,* March 15, 2002, pp. A28–A32.
35. Goldie Blumenstyk, "Knowledge Is a Form of Venture Capital for a Top Columbia Administrator," *Chronicle of Higher Education,* February 8, 2001, p. A29.
36. Some recent examples include: Aronowitz and Giroux, *Education Still under Siege;* Randy Martin, *Chalk Lines* (Minneapolis: University of Minnesota Press, 1998); Stanley Aronowitz, *The Knowledge Factory: Dismantling the Corporate University and Creating True Higher Learning* (Boston: Beacon Press, 2000); Henry A. Giroux, *Impure Acts: The Practical Politics of Cultural Studies* (New York: Routledge, 2000).
37. Richard Hoftstadter, cited in Eyal Press and Jennifer Washburn, "The Kept University," *Atlantic Monthly,* March 20, 2000, p. 54. Hoftstadter, with C. De Witt Hardy, expands on these views in *The Development and Scope of Higher Education in the United States* (New York: Columbia University Press, 1952); with Walter P. Metzger, *The Development of Academic Freedom in the United States* (New York: Columbia University Press, 1955); *Anti-Intellectualism in American Life* (New York: Vintage Books, 1963). A more complicated though ultimately distorting critique appears in Stephen Brier and Roy Rosenzweig, "The Keyboard Campus," *Nation,* April 22, 2002, pp. 29–32.
38. See Sheila Slaughter and Larry L. Leslie, *Academic Capitalism: Politics, Policies, and the Entrepreneurial University* (Baltimore: Johns Hopkins University Press, 1997).
39. Press and Washburn, "The Kept University," p. 42.
40. Press and Washburn, "The Kept University," pp. 39–54.
41. This issue is taken up in Michael Berube, "Why Inefficiency Is Good for Universities," *Chronicle of Higher Education,* March 27, 1998, pp. B4–B5.
42. Patricia P. Brodsky, "Shrunken Heads: The Humanities under the Corporate Model," p. 5. Retrieved July 1, 2002, from http://www.louisville.edu/journal/workplace/patbrodsky.html
43. Brodsky, "Shrunken Heads," p. 6. Retrieved July 1, 2002, from http://www.louisville.edu/journal/workplace/patbrodsky.html
44. Jeff Williams, "Brave New University," *College English* 61, No.6 (1999), 744.
45. Maureen Shine, "Knight, Matching Gifts Endow Record Number of UO Chairs," *University of Oregon News.* Retrieved July 1, 2002, from http://comm.uoregon.edu/newsreleases/latest/june98/006l198.html. It should be noted that "the Gates Foundation Minority Fellowship Program spends more on advertising than it does on the scholarships themselves." Cited in Jennifer L. Croissant, "Can This Campus Be Bought?" *Academe* (September/October 2001), 3. Retrieved July 1, 2002, from http://www.aaup.org/publications/AcademeOISO/soOlcro.html
46. Both quotes are cited in Julianne Basinger, "Increase in Number of Chairs Endowed by Corporations Prompt New Concerns," *Chronicle of Higher Education,* April 24, 1995, p. A53.
47. Blumenstyk, "Chasing the Rainbow."
48. David Trend, *Welcome to Cyberschool: Education at the Crossroads in the Information Age* (Lanham, MD: Rowman and Littlefield, 2001), p. 59.
49. Trend, *Welcome to Cyberschool,* p. 59.
50. Sheila Slaughter, "Professional Values," p. 3.
51. For an extensive analysis of the issue of intellectual property rights and the control over academic work in the university, see Corynne McSherry, *Who Owns Academic Work? Battling for Control of Intellectual Property* (Cambridge, MA: Harvard University Press, 2002).

52. Julia Porter Liebeskind, "Risky Business: Universities and Intellectual Property," *Academe* (September–October, 2001), 2. Retrieved July 1, 2002, from http://www.aaup.org/publications/Academe/01S0/s0011ie.htm
53. Liebeskind, "Risky Business."
54. Eyal Press and Jennifer Washburn, "Digital Diplomas," *Mother Jones*, January/February 2001, p. 8. Retrieved July 1, 2002, from http://www.motherjones.com/motherjones/JFOl/toc.html
55. Press and Washburn, "Digital Diplomas."
56. On this issue, see Bauman, *In Search of Politics.*
57. Jay Mathews, "It's Lowly at the Top: What Became of the Great College Presidents?" *Washington Post*, June 10, 2001, p. BO1.
58. Clara M. Lovett, "The Dumbing Down of College Presidents," *Chronicle of Higher Education: The Chronicle Review*, April 5, 2002, p. B20.
59. Jim Hopkins, "Universities Hire More Executives to Lead," *USA Today*, April 22, 2002, p. 1B.
60. Hopkins, "Universities Hire More Executives." See, for instance, the story on Summers by Martin Van Der Werf, "Lawrence Summers and His Tough Questions," *Chronicle of Higher Education*, April 26, 2002, pp. A29–A32.
61. There are a number of excellent texts that touch on this issue. Some of these include Aronowitz and Giroux, *Education Still under Siege;* Michael Berube and Cary Nelson, eds., *Higher Education under Fire* (New York: Routledge, 1995); Bill Readings, *The University in Ruins* (Cambridge, MA: Harvard University Press, 1996); Slaughter and Leslie, *Academic Capitalism;* Aronowitz, *The Knowledge Factory;* Geoffrey D. White, ed., *Campus, Inc.: Corporate Power in the Ivory Tower* (Amherst, NY: Prometheus Books, *2000).*
62. Stanley Aronowitz, "The New Corporate University," *Dollars and Sense*, March/April, 1995, pp. 32–35.
63. The many books extolling corporate CEOs as a model for leadership in any field is too extensive to cite, but one typical example can be found in Robert Heller, *Roads to Success: Put into Practice the Best Business Ideas of Eight Leading Gurus* (New York: Dorling Kindersley, 2001).
64. For an excellent analysis of Michael Milken's role in various education projects, see Robin Truth Goodman and Kenneth Saltman, *Strange Love: Or How We Learn to Stop Worrying and Love the Market* (Lanham, MD: Rowman and Littlefield, 2002).
65. Catherine S. Manegold, "Study Says Schools Must Stress Academics," *New York Times*, September 23, 1998, p. A22.
66. George Soros, *On Globalization* (New York: Public Affairs, 2002), p. 164.
67. Stanley Aronowitz and William De Fazio, "The New Knowledge Work," in A. H. Halsey, Hugh Lauder, Phillip Brown, and Amy Stuart Wells, eds., *Education: Culture, Economy, Society* (New York: Oxford, 1997), p. 193.
68. This is amply documented in Jeremy Rifkin, *The End of Work* (New York: G. Putnam Books, 1995); William Wolman and Anne Colamosca, *The Judas Economy: The Triumph of Capital and the Betrayal of Work* (Reading, MA: Addison-Wesley, 1997); Aronowitz and DiFazio, *The Jobless Future; The New York Times Report: The Downsizing of America* (New York: Times Books, 1996); Stanley Aronowitz and Jonathan Cutler, *Post-Work* (New York: Routledge, 1998).
69. Cornel West, "The New Cultural Politics of Difference," *October* 53 (Summer 1990), 35.
70. Jim Hopkins, "Universities Hire More Executives to Lead," *USA Today*, April 22, 2002, p. 1B.
71. David L. Kirp, "Higher Ed Inc.: Avoiding the Perils of Outsourcing," *Chronicle Review*, March 15, 2002, p. B14.
72. Kirp, "Higher Ed Inc.," p. B14.
73. Cary Nelson, *Manifesto of a Tenured Radical* (New York: New York University Press, 1997), p. 169.
74. I take up Carlin's position in much greater detail in Henry A. Giroux, *Impure Acts* (New York: Routledge, 2000), pp. 51–54.
75. Carlin, cited in William H. Honan, "The Ivory Tower under Siege," *New York Times*, January 4, 1998, p. 4A33.
76. Carlin, cited in Honan, "The Ivory Tower under Siege," p. 4A33.
77. Cited in NEA Higher Education Research Center, Update 7, No. 3 (June 2001), 1.
78. Michael Dubson, "Introduction," in *Ghosts in the Classroom: Stories of College Adjunct Faculty—and the Price We All Pay* (Boston: Camel's Back Books, 2001), pp. 9–10.
79. Jeff Williams, "Brave New University," *College English* 61, No. 6 (July 1999), 740.
80. This information is taken from, "Pricing the Poor Out of College," *New York Times*, March 27, 2002, p. A27.
81. Stephen Burd, "Lack of Aid Will Keep 170,000 Qualified, Needy Students Out of College This Year, Report Warns," *Chronicle of Higher Education* (June 27, 2002), p. 1. Retrieved July 1, 2002, from http://

chronicle.com/daily/2002/06/2002062701n.html. For a robust argument for making college free for all students, see Adolph L. Reed, Jr., "Free College for All," *The Progressive* (April 2002), 12–14.

82. Sheila Slaughter, "Professional Values and the Allure of the Market," *Academe* (September/October 2001), 3–4.
83. David Trend, *Welcome to Cyberschool: Education at the Crossroads in the Information Age* (Lanham, MD: Rowman and Littlefield, 2001), p. 55.
84. Croissant, "Can This Campus Be Bought?"
85. David F. Noble, 'The Future of the Digital Diploma Mill," *Academe* 87, No.5 (September–October 2001), 29. These arguments arc spelled out in greater detail in David F. Noble, *Digital Diploma Mills: The Automation of Higher Education* (New York: Monthly Review Press, 2002).
86. Noble, "The Future of the Digital Diploma Mill."
87. For an extensive commentary on the Army's distance-education program, see Michael Arnone, "Army's Huge Distance-Education Effort Wins Many Supporters in Its First Year," *Chronicle of Higher Education*, February 8, 2002, pp. A33–A35. This highly favorable, if not flattering, piece of reporting is accompanied by another commentary on David Noble in which his views are badly simplified and his professional integrity called into question. See Jeffrey R. Young, "Distance-Education Critic's Book Takes Aim at Army's Efforts," *Chronicle of Higher Education*, February 8, 2002, p. A34.
88. Noble, "The Future of the Digital Diploma Mill," pp. 29–30.
89. Both Levine's statement and the following quote can be found in Press and Washhurn, "Digital Diplomas."
90. Massy and Zemsky, cited in Press and Washburn, "Digital Diplomas," p. 8.
91. Noble, "The Future of the Digital Diploma Mill."
92. Press and Washburn, "Digital Diplomas."
93. Herbert Marcuse, "Some Social Implications of Modern Technology," in Douglas Kellner, ed., *Technology, War, and* Facism (New York: Routledge, 1998), p. 45.
94. Zygmunt Bauman, *Modernity and the Holocaust* (Ithaca, NY: Cornell University Press, 1989).
95. John Hinkson brilliantly explores this issue in "Perspectives on the Crisis of the University," in Simon Cooper, John Kinkson, and Geoff Sharp, eds., *Scholars and Entrepreneurs: The University in Crisis* (North Carlton, Australia: Arena, 2002), pp. 233–267.
96. For a critical analysis of the flaws and possibilities of such approaches in higher education, see: Trend, *Welcome to Cyberschool;* Andrew Feenberg, *Questioning Technology* (New York: Routledge, 1999); Hubert L. Dreyfus, *On the Internet* (New York: Routledge, 2001); Mark Poster, *What Is the Matter with the Internet?* (Minneapolis: University of Minnesota Press, 2001).
97. Noble, *Digital Diploma Mills.*
98. For more details on the creation of online degrees for corporations, see Dan Carnevale, "Colleges Tailor Online Degrees for Individual Companies," *Chronicle of Higher Education*, January 28, 2002. Retrieved July 1, 2002, from http://chronicle.com/cgi2-bin/printable.cgi
99. Andrew Feenberg, *Questioning Technology* (New York: Routledge, 1999), p. viii.
100. Feenberg, *Questioning Technology*, p. xv.
101. Ellen Willis, *Don't Think, Smile: Notes on a Decade of Denial* (Boston: Beacon Press, 1999), p. 27.
102. Bill Readings, *The University in Ruins* (Cambridge, MA: Harvard University Press, 1996). As Ronald Strickland points out, Readings has almost nothing to say about how the corporate university reproduces the academic and social division of labor between elite and second-tier universities that is so central to changing global economic landscape. See Ronald Strickland, "Gender, Class and the Humanities in the Corporate University," *Genders* 35 (2002), 1–16. Retrieved July 1, 2002, from http://www.genders.org/g35/g35_stricland.htm
103. There are a number of books that take up the relationship between schooling and democracy; some of the more important recent critical contributions include Elizabeth A. Kelly, *Education, Democracy, and Public Knowledge* (Boulder, CO: Westview, 1995); Wilfred Carr and Anthony Hartnett, *Education and the Struggle for Democracy* (Philadelphia: Open University Press, 1996); Henry A. Giroux, *Border Crossings: Cultural Workers and the Politics of Education* (New York: Routledge, 1993); Stanley Aronowitz and Henry A. Giroux, *Postmodern Education* (Minneapolis: University of Minnesota Press, 1991); Aronowitz and Giroux, *Education Still under Siege;* and Henry A. Giroux, *Pedagogy and the Politics of Hope* (Boulder, CO: Westview, 1997).
104. A conversation between Lani Guinier and Anna Deavere Smith, "Rethinking Power, Rethinking Theater," *Theater* 31, No. 1 (2002), 36.
105. Robin D. G. Kelley, "Neo-Cons of the Black Nation," *Black Renaissance Noire* 1, No. 2 (1997), 146.

106. For an analysis of such events, see David Glenn, "The War on Campus: Will Academic Freedom Survive?" *Nation,* December 3, 2001, pp. 11–14; also see Robin Wilson and Ana Marie Cox, "Terrorist Attacks Put Academic Freedom to the Test," *Chronicle of Higher Education,* October 5, 2001, p. A12.
107. Arundhati Roy, *Power Politics* (Cambridge, MA: South End Press, 2001), pp. 11–12.
108. Noam Chomsky, "Paths Taken, Tasks Ahead," *Profession* (2000), 35.
109. Pierre Bourdieu, "For a Scholarship of Commitment," *Profession* (2000), 42–43.
110. See Nelson, *Will Teach for Food.*
111. Cited in Aronowitz, *The Knowledge Factory,* pp. 63, 109–110.
112. Short Subjects, "Students Hold 'Teach-Ins' to Protest Corporate Influence in Higher Education," *Chronicle of Higher Education,* March 13, 1998, p. All. Also note Peter Dreier's commentary on student activism emerging in 1998, in "The Myth of Student Apathy," *Nation,* April 13, 1998, pp. 19–22.
113. For a commentary on students against sweatshops, see Liza Featherstone, "Sweatshops, Students, and the Corporate University," *Croonenbergh's Fly* No. 2 (2002), 107–117.
114. Liza Featherstone, "The New Student Movement" *Nation,* May 15, 2000, p. 12.
115. Featherstone, "The New Student Movement," p. 12.
116. Featherstone, "Sweatshops, Students, and the Corporate University," p. 112.
117. I have taken this idea from Nick Couldry, "A Way Out of the (Televised) Endgame?" *Open Democracy,* p. 1. Retrieved July 1, 2002, from http://www.opendemocracy.net/forum/strands_home .asp
118. Imre Szeman, "Introduction: Learning to Learn from Seattle," in Imre Szeman, ed., Special Double Issue, Learning from Seattle, *Review of Education, Pedagogy, and Cultural Studies* 24, No. 1–2 (2002), 5.
119. Szeman, "Introduction," p. 4.
120. Szeman, "Introduction," p. 5.
121. Toni Morrison. "How Can Values Be Taught in This University?" *Michigan Quarterly Review* (2001), 278.
122. Pierre Bourdieu, *Acts of Resistance* (New York: New Press, 1999), p. 26.
123. Cited in "Why Does Neo-Liberalism Hate Kids? The War on Youth and the Culture of Politics," *Review of Education/Pedagogy/Cultural Studies* 23, No.2 (2001), 114.
124. Jacques Derrida, "No One Is Innocent: A Discussion with Jacques about Philosophy in the Face of Terror," *The Information Technology, War and Peace Project,* p. 2. Retrieved July 1, 2002, from http://www.watsoninstitute.org/infopeace/911/derrida_innocence.html

CHAPTER 45

ACADEMIC CAPITALISM AND ACADEMIC CULTURE: A CASE STUDY

PILAR MENDOZA AND JOSEPH B. BERGER

This case study investigated the impact of academic capitalism on academic culture by examining the perspectives of faculty members in an American academic department with significant industrial funding. The results of this study indicate that faculty members believe that the broad integrity of the academic culture remains unaffected in this department and they consider industrial sponsorship as a highly effective vehicle for enhancing the quality of education of students and pursuing their scientific interests. This study provides valuable insights to federal and institutional policies created to foster industry-academia partnerships and commercialization of academic research.

The investment policies outlined in the *National Science Foundation (NSF) Strategic Plan* for the years 2003–2008 continue to emphasize research and development of technologies with commercial applications. This trend started in the 1980s when the U.S. government designed policies and laws to encourage the cooperation of industries with universities to bridge federal funding gaps for research and cope with global competitive markets (Campbell & Slaughter, 1999; Slaughter & Leslie, 1997; Slaughter and Rhoads, 2004). In the early 1980s, the National Science Foundation (NSF) established a program to enhance industry-academia interactions through the Industry/University Cooperative Research Centers (I/UCRCs) around industrially relevant research, education of scientists in new technologies, and transfer of university-developed research and technology to industry. Other examples include the creation of the Business-Higher Education Forum, the Government-University-Industry Research Roundtable, and the Advanced Technology Programs housed in the Department of Commerce (Slaughter & Rhoades, 1996). As a result of these initiatives, science and engineering fields became more entrepreneurial around new technologies developed in areas such as materials science, optics, cognitive science, and biomedical research (Gumport, 1999; Krimsky, 2003; Slaughter & Rhoades, 2004).

This pattern is a developing trend for universities throughout the world as the increasingly global environment has pushed shifts in governmental funding and policies, increased reliance on private and corporate funds, and administrative decision-making (Neave, 2001). One of the greatest concerns is that these policy changes are occurring rapidly with little attention paid to the effects of these shifts on academic culture, the relevance of academic work, the attractiveness of the academic profession, and the role of faculty in generating and disseminating knowledge (Duderstadt, 2001). Public universities are responding to these external forces by expanding revenues through market-like behaviors, a phenomenon called academic capitalism. Some of these market-oriented activities that are the subject of this study involve university partnerships with industry, commercialization of research through patents, and the formation of spin-off companies (Slaughter & Leslie, 1997; Slaughter & Rhoades, 2004).

This emerging trend described above has fueled concerns that academic capitalism might be harming traditional academic culture as faculty members engage in market-like behaviors such as partnering with companies and commercializing research (Gumport, 2002, 2005; Newman, Couturier, & Scurry, 2004). These concerns focus on the potential incongruence between market values and the values embedded in the various logic models that shape meaning and guide behavior of academic professionals, faculty who must increasingly respond to the complex demands of contemporary academic life. From an organizational culture perspective, the academic culture is driven by and manifested in multiple logic systems—including institutional, social, and industrial logic. The first two are found easily within a university. Institutional logic comprise the institutional practices and symbolic constructions that shape organizations' cultures (Friedland & Alford, 1991). The social logic of universities is based on a range of social expectations such as mass education, citizenship, and knowledge preservation and advancement.

In contrast to this social logic, and increasingly introduced into the academic workplace through academic capitalism, industrial logic is the contribution to society via economic growth, the training of a skillful workforce, and research with commercial applications, all promoted and gauged through market forces. This coexistence of multiple logics in today's academic institutions is generating tensions over conflicting practices (Gumport, 2002; Mendoza & Berger, 2005). For example, academics are expected to foster and disseminate basic knowledge as part of their social mission (Merton, 1957). However, some of the direct implications of industry-university partnerships documented in the literature include overemphasis in applied research and secrecy of knowledge (Campbell & Slaughter, 1999; Gladieux & King, 2005; Slaughter, Campbell, Hollernan, & Morgan, 2002). Reward structures constitute another area where major differences between industrial and academic cultures exist (Mendoza & Berger, 2005; Slaughter & Leslie, 1997). The academic profession is driven by intrinsic motivation and rewards that have historically been based on the fascination with research, the enchantments of teaching, and discipline-oriented prestige rather than on material or monetary incentives (Clark, 1987). Given fundamental differences among these logic systems, faculty members participating in academic capitalism might move away from values such as altruism and public service as they move toward market values (Slaughter and Leslie, 1997). This study tests this claim with empirical evidence regarding the impact of academic capitalism on academic culture, examining the perspectives of faculty members in a department with significant industrial funding.

Theoretical Framework

Drawing from the works of Allaire and Firsirotu (1984), Becher (1984), and Clark (1970), Kuh and Whitt (1986) provide a framework for analyzing culture in higher education. This framework has four layers of analysis that portrays culture in institutions of higher education as a dynamic system shaped by the interplay of these cultural layers. The four layers in question are the external environment that surrounds a given higher education institution, the institution itself, subcultures within the institution, and individual actors. The external environment layer is characterized by the continually evolving nature of colleges and universities according to the interactions between conditions in the external environment and the needs and concerns of groups within the institution (Tierney, 1988). The institutional layer refers to the different cultures present across types of higher education institutions. Some elements involved in institutional culture include size and type as well as the institutional mission, leadership, and symbols used to communicate values (Kuh & Whitt, 1986). For example, at major universities research is highly valued while the highest value in liberal arts colleges is the interaction between faculty and students (Clark, 1987).

Different subcultures operate within higher education institutions, which in themselves correspond to the third layer of Kuh and Whitt's framework (1986). Administrators, faculty, and students are the three most predominant subcultures in higher education. In addition, there are subcultures within these groups: discipline-based subcultures among faculty, professional ones among administrative staff, and minority associations among students (Tierney, 1988). Another example is the existence of subcultures within disciplines formed around people with different views about the discipline, as might be the case between clusters of professors who are more entrepreneurial and who hold values different from their colleagues (Slaughter & Leslie, 1997). Conflicts and tensions between subcultures are common, as is the case between administrators and faculty. Administrators tend to hold a managerial (Rice, 1986) or utilitarian (Etzioni, 1961) culture in opposition to faculty members' core values of discovery and dissemination of knowledge through autonomy and academic freedom (Peterson & Spencer, 1990). Finally, the fourth layer includes the role of individual actors as shapers of culture such as presidents, heads of departments, and individual faculty members. All agents participate in the construction of culture (Kuh & Whitt, 1986).

While the cultural framework proposed by Kuh and Whitt (1986) focuses on the cultural complexity of colleges and universities, Becher (1984) suggests that discipline-based subcultures are the primary source of faculty identity and expertise. Elements of disciplinary subcultures include a range of assumptions about what is to be known and how, the tasks to be performed, standards for effective performance, patterns of publication, professional interaction, and social and political status (Becher, 1984; Clark 1984). Some scholars assert that differences across disciplines have greater impact on faculty than do individual similarities among faculty members (Becher, 1989). Moreover, Bowen and Schuster (1986) found that differences among faculty members were related more to disciplines than to type of institution. In a similar vein, Clark (1987) illustrated the nature of the academic profession as a collection of academic tribes and territories with a widening array of disciplines and specialties. Nonetheless, departments are the main structure of higher education, and their culture is also a significant source of identity for faculty members (Becher, 1989). Finally, there is an overarching core culture of the academic profession based on concepts of academic freedom, individual autonomy, production and dissemination of knowledge, collegiality, collegial governance, service to society through the production of knowledge, and education of the young (Clark, 1980; Morril & Speed 1982, Ruscio, 1987). Given the multiple sources of influence and the complex nature of academic culture, this study uses a multi-layered approach for understanding academic culture as the basis for exploring how involvement in academic capitalism has impacted one academic department in an American research university.

Methods

This article reports on a case chosen for its ability to answer key questions about academic capitalism. Due to their revelatory nature, case studies that represent critical or unique cases are particularly useful to extend or challenge theories. More specifically, Denscombe (2002) notes,

> Social researchers can opt to focus on instances that are anything but representative or typical. Extreme instances may be selected deliberately because they have certain qualities that exaggerate the influence of a particular factor that is of interest to the researchers. (p. 147)

Guided by the approach described above and by other experts in the use of qualitative methodologies (e.g. Berg, 2004; Creswell, 1998; Denscombe, 2002; Yin, 1994), this study employs an embedded case study (Yin, 1994) as a strategy for studying a unique department that is heavily involved in academic capitalism and in which the faculty members themselves are the main source of empirical evidence. The primary focus is how industrial partnerships within a specific academic context influence the culture of an academic department.

The department selected for this study is a top-ranked materials science unit in a large Research I University that exhibits a series of unique circumstances, evidence of the impact of academic capitalism on academic culture. In particular, the department is considered one of the best centers in fundamental polymer science and the training of outstanding scholars, indicating high levels of academic achievement. In addition, the department is heavily involved in partnerships with industry and attracts significant funds from businesses. We selected this department because we were intrigued by the department's apparent ability to be successful at embracing institutional logics that some describe as inherently contradictory.

This department has close collaborations with industry given the natural proximity of the field of polymer science to industrial applications. Industry-funded research in the department comprises approximately 30% of the total research sponsorship. According to several faculty in the department, this level of industrial sponsorship is significant compared to peer departments in the field, which according to these faculty bring in 5% or less funding from industry. In the 1970s, the National Science Foundation (NSF) sponsored the establishment of a center in the department to promote interdisciplinary collaborations. Today, this NSF-supported center integrates efforts of more than 20 faculty from departments in science and engineering and supports research collaborations and outreach programs with more than 10 other academic institutions across the country. In the early 1980s, another center was established to enhance industrial interactions as part of the Industry/University Cooperative Research Centers (I/UCRCs) program sponsored by the NSF. NSF created the I/UCRC program to foster partnerships between universities and industry around industrially relevant fundamental research, the education of scientists with an industrially oriented perspective, and the transfer of university-developed research and technology to industry. An I/UCRC often begins with a small grant to seed partnered approaches to emerging research areas for five years to a university professor, a faculty member expected to form a team to run a successful center with industrial funding. After the initial five years, the center is expected to be self-sufficient and supported primarily by industrial funds. The I/UCRC center in this department is one of the few centers of this kind that has survived beyond NSF's initial support. Today, the center has more than 40 industrial partners and four basic programs of interactions with industry with specific guidelines and regulations. It operates mainly as a consortium where multiple companies invest in an area of common interest, but it also channels sponsorships to individual faculty members around specific projects.

To explore the culture of this department, we used semi-structured face-to-face interviews approximately one hour long with 10 faculty members, individuals who represent the vast majority of the department; field observations during numerous visits to the site throughout an academic year; and collection of relevant documentation and artifacts. The interview protocol was designed based on the cultural knowledge around academic capitalism identified in previous studies (e.g. Mendoza, 2007a; Mendoza & Berger, 2005; Slaughter, Archerd, & Campbell, 2004). The interview protocol included questions about the central topics in the interaction of institutional logic, social logic, and industrial logic: how departments balance conducting basic research and educating their students alongside working with industrial sponsors; the benefits and downsides of industry-university collaborations; the advantages and disadvantages of industrial versus governmental grants; the impact of industry-university collaborations to students, basic research, publications, and academic freedom; the motivations of industry and faculty to engage in industry-university alliances; and the ways industry-academia collaborations can be improved. All interviews were recorded and transcribed. Data analysis was based on a constant comparative method to identify and contrast analytical constructs to generate theoretical explanations of the phenomenon in question. Categorical analysis was conducted based on open coding techniques and the guidelines set forth by Rossman and Rallis (2003) and Lincoln and Guba (1985) to ensure the trustworthiness, validity, and authenticity of the study. Throughout the study, the researchers constantly searched for rival explanations or evidence, established a chain of evidence, and created a case database. These procedures and the multiple sources of data provide sufficient warrant for our claims about this department.

Results

Three main themes dominate our results and thus the presentation in this section. First, we describe participants' general description of the department's research and funding. Second, we discuss how faculty protect their academic values as they partner with industrial sponsors of research. Finally, we take a closer look at the implications of industrial funding to key components of the academic culture. Shared meaning was found among faculty, and very few differences were found among participants. Therefore, unless explicitly stated, the results described represent the shared view of faculty interviewed.

Participants' Descriptions of the Department's Research and Sponsorship

Faculty unanimously agree that the main goal of the department is training polymer scientists, followed by the production of fundamental polymer science. One department member said,

> If you think of the polymer science and engineering department, what is it that we sell? There are really two things that we offer: first of all the scholarship that we perform be it fundamental or applied, but equally or probably more important are the scholars we train.

This academically-oriented goal among faculty indicates the presence of a strong traditional academic culture despite the department's active engagement in academic capitalism.

Professors believe that the department has a good combination of both applied and fundamental research as well as a balance across types of funding (private and public). As one faculty described it, "The strength of this department has been the fact that we can marry the fundamental with the applied." Faculty participants explained that their research is related to the fundamental physical and chemical principles of polymers, but usually their research has clear technological applications if several steps away from the actual manufacturing of a product in an industrial setting. Several faculty members alluded to the erosion of boundaries between applied and basic research are very blurred in the field due to the nature of their work. However, they stated that the department is focused on fundamental science compared to other departments in the field, which they described as more product oriented or more interested in the development of new technologies. Despite the fact that faculty in this department are mainly involved with fundamental research, they have also discovered materials that are worthy to patent for future applications.

These views support findings from previous studies that have shown that faculty members in science and engineering have a clear sense that the boundary between academia and industry has changed (Mendoza, 2007a; Slaughter et al., 2004). For many faculty members in these fields, the "wall" between industry and academia is no longer present. This shift has open the possibility to a host of opportunities, but it also provides surprises and potentially compromising situations with implications for the integrity of the academic profession (Slaughter et al., 2004).

One faculty member indicated that faculty in the department are successful at obtaining both federal and industrial grants. Nonetheless, those faculty members who have been in industry for a number of years before becoming academics see differences between themselves and faculty who have not been in industry for extended periods of time. These faculty members recognize that faculty who have been in industry tend to think more about practical applications, a habit that might facilitate their ability to attract industrial funds. In addition, some of these industry-experienced faculty indicated that faculty who have been in industry are better at dealing with people, sharing equipment, and working collaboratively. In doing so, they said, they bring different perspectives to their teaching and advising by being able to talk about real past experiences in industry and understand the industrial world more accurately. These differences become clearer through students' positive teaching evaluations of those faculty who have been in industry.

Faculty believe that the department can afford to reject industrial funds at odds with their interests because of the reputation of its scientists and the large amount of overall funding it enjoys. These results suggest that there is sufficient funding available for these faculty members and that it is the responsibility of individual faculty members to shelter their students from industrial demands and provide students with training in basic science that lead to publications. One department member said,

> I think certainly, we're at a point to negotiate. We have the luxury of being able to say no, and we're not so absolutely destitute or desperate that we almost have to take anything to make it work. I think a lot of companies appreciate our being very frank.

Some faculty mentioned that there are other institutions that tend to serve industry and bend their mission more to please corporate sponsors. One professor mentioned that once a long-lasting collaboration has been established with a corporation, there might be cases where faculty will serve industry needs in very specific occasions. In these cases, an industrial sponsor usually provides support for a broader research program involving several students. Within that broader partnership, faculty in this department might agree to perform several measurements for the company. Faculty justify this activity by noting that these measures do not typically demand a lot of time and energy on the part of the students, who at the same time are learning how to conduct specific measurements with sophisticated instrumentation. Faculty insist that these types of short projects might be viewed as service to industry, but in reality they provide an educational experience for the students that is beneficial as long as it does not interfere with students' main dissertation research. Faculty members claim that they are well aware of and intentionally guard against the potential negative issues associated with such projects; for example one faculty member observed,

> Some of these company projects, if you're not careful, they can be really contract work. Maybe the university has an electron microscope and all they want is a technician to crank samples through those instruments and they can afford to give lots of money and it would be useful to train a student on those pieces of equipment in the short term. But that doesn't make science and it doesn't make a thesis, and so it's the job of the advisor to say, "OK, well, your thesis is going to be partly of running these samples, and while you may be entirely funded by doing this, we've got to find something that demonstrates your full capability as a researcher."

Department faculty believe they have the necessary autonomy to protect their shared values.

The Department's I/UCRC Center

Academic departments are affected in mixed ways by initiatives such as the I/UCRC centers; issues include potential conflicts over intellectual property, secrecy of knowledge, and exclusivity clauses against the formation of corporate-academia alliances. However, these organized research units (ORU) bring benefits such as encouragement of interdisciplinary research, exposure to current industrial research and needs, additional funds, and job opportunities for students (Anderson, 2001; Gumport, 2005; Slaughter & Rhoades, 2004). The faculty interviewed in this study strongly support initiatives such as the I/UCRC centers and believe that those concerns are manageable and minimal compared to the benefits that these initiatives bring to the department.

Several faculty talked about the uniqueness of the department's I/UCRC and the benefits it brings to the department, greatly enhancing the department's ability to obtain funds. According to many of the faculty, the success of this center begins with a full time director dedicated to collecting industrial funding and working on agreements attractive to both faculty and industry. The director handles all of the legal contracts, including timelines and identification of common objectives between potential sponsors and the department, organizes meetings with industry representatives, assists faculty in writing proposals that meet the demands and needs of industrial sponsors, and actively networks with potential sponsors. The following comment by a faculty member illustrates how the director of the center finds opportunities:

> Our director for the center looks at faculty and says, "What is this person going to be interested in? What companies should be supporting that? What companies are also interested in those things? There are a lot of companies out there, thousands of companies. Let's identify a few of them that are really going to be interested in his results. They should be supporting him."

Another advantage of the center is that it manages one-on-one research contracts that are normally handled through the university's office of grants and contracts. The arrangement is advantageous because the department's director can talk directly to industry sponsors about technical, administrative, and legal details, an arrangement that expedites the contract process. In addition, a small portion of the industrial funds channeled through the center are saved to create grants for junior faculty members in the department. Faculty mentioned that an important aspect of the center is that it provides a structure and consistency that allows the development of long lasting relationships with industry and long-term projects. Similarly, several studies have indicated that faculty members believe that the collaboration between government and industry through centers dedicated to fundamental research allows long-term projects, which is the preference of academics (Slaughter & Leslie, 1997; Slaughter et al., 2002; Slaughter & Rhoades, 2004).

Given the success of the department in partnering with industry, faculty offered the following advice to programs interested in developing productive collaborations with industry: conduct a critical assessment of what the department could offer to industry, find a niche according to what the department has to offer, devote substantial resources and planning, mentor junior faculty, develop a center similar to the one the department hosts, hire a full time staff administrator dedicated to the center, encourage individual faculty to actively develop one-on-one relationships with industry, actively network in conferences and other meetings, and be loyal and honest about the department's values and protect the department from corporate interests. One faculty member explained:

> You have to be loyal to the academic goals . . . to the university. And, you have to make sure that those goals can overlap with industrial [goals] . . . there can't be any conflicts. So, you go in and accept those things that are in line with what you want to do and you have to be honest with industry up front, not just take money and promise them stuff that you can't deliver because your reputation will kill you.

This last piece of advice reveals the way faculty approach industry and shows the existence of a strong academic culture in the department.

Federal versus Industrial Funding

Several faculty consider government grants more stable, competitive, longer term, and more closely related to the more fundamental science than industrial grants. (The exceptions include grants from the U. S. Department of Defense.) Faculty recognize that federal funds are more prestigious because they are awarded through a rigorous peer review process and thus competitive. The higher value of federal grants in the department agrees with the pillars of the academic culture related to the value of basic science and the peer review process. Moreover, one faculty member mentioned that national rankings are mainly based on federal grants rather than on industrial grants. However, senior faculty in this study recognized that industrial grants are valuable as well and that some industrial grants are as open-ended and competitive as federal grants (thus raising their prestige value). Another reason given by several faculty for the higher value of federal grants is related to the tenure review process. According to these faculty, to achieve tenure, a faculty member must have established a record of renewed federal grants as a measure of the quality of a faculty member's research. However, one faculty member mentioned that federal grants were starting to lose their value within tenure review because the renewal process is longer than a typical faculty member's probationary (tenure-track) period. In addition, another faculty mentioned that federal grants are being tailored towards large multidisciplinary projects involving several investigators, which diminishes the ability of individual junior faculty members to obtain federal grants. Overall, in agreement with what has been suggested by Slaughter et al. (2004), faculty believe that while it was prestigious in the past, federal funding is losing its value, and in part because federal grants have also become more difficult to obtain, faculty members have become more interested in funding from other sources.

According to the faculty in this study, industrial grants are also becoming more difficult to obtain. Several faculty mentioned that over the last 15 years, industry sponsorship in material sciences has been shrinking. These professors also report that industries once had unrestricted think tanks to support basic science. However, the internal research structure of companies has changed. Because company executives are more accountable and have to demonstrate global competitiveness, industry looks for research that is more product dependent and reliable for short-term results. Many of the scientists who worked in those think tanks migrated to academia as companies began cutting funds for those programs. Also, as one professor noted, many chemical and materials companies have moved overseas and no longer have central domestic research facilities.

Protecting the Core Values of the Academic Profession

Faculty interviewed for this study tended to define good research in line with traditional concepts of rigorous scientific research. None of the responses reflected industrial or business related values such as the idea that research should lead to useful applications competitive in the market or cost-efficient. On the contrary, faculty considered that good research should make an original contribution to knowledge or to a particular technological application, and good research has an impact on society or the scientific community. None of the faculty considered that good research should aim directly at the development or improvement of a specific application. In addition, some faculty members talked of the importance of scientific rigor and originality in any good research. Faculty believe that rigorous research is recognized through the peer review processes in the form of publications and by its capacity to attract funding. However, some faculty members mentioned that the best research is measured by its impact over time. Several interviewees also mentioned that in an academic setting, good research should lead to the proper education of students. Faculty believe that their department appropriately balances educating students, conducting research and working with industry. Some faculty members went further: they believe that these are not opposing forces that need to be balanced. In general, faculty are satisfied with industrial partnerships and have been able to successfully pursue both their scientific and educational objectives.

Protecting the Education of Students

All of the faculty interviewed for this project asserted that their main professional goal is to educate students through basic science and to conduct fundamental research. Therefore, faculty carefully partner with industry assuring that such traditional academic goals are preserved. Some faculty mentioned having to turn down offers from industry in cases where those partnerships had the potential to interfere with academic goals. Similarly, faculty believe that if partnerships with industry are conducted properly, it is a mutually beneficial arrangement in which faculty obtain funds to support research and students, students engage in meaningful projects and learn about the industrial world, and industry gains access to new knowledge, expertise, and facilities. The key is to carefully plan and craft the agreements with industry in ways that students' education is not harmed. To accomplish this, faculty adapt industrial projects into a meaningful educational experience for students. One department member said,

> A lot of what we look at when industries come to us is, "Is there a synergy and does this fit with mine?" The company could come to me and say, "We have all this money and we want to get this done in three months," and I look at the question and the problem and say, "Is this something I'm interested in, is this an area that I have expertise, that I personally feel I can contribute to?" But then I have to sit back and say, "Do I have a student who can contribute to this program where it's either directly in line with their thesis investigation? Involves a slight deviation? Or is the student at the point where we can take a detour for three months?" It's all timing and situational dependent . . . I'm not going to do every- and anything just to get a few thousand dollars or tens of thousands of dollars or even one hundred thousand dollars if it's not going to be a really good fit because it's a waste of money from the industrial sponsor's perspectives, it's a waste of time and energy and effort on my behalf and the student's behalf.

Another said,

> There are a number of companies that call us up wanting help on something very specific and whether it is fire-fighting type of research where they need something in the next three months or six months and we're very upfront, I often point them to other places that could help them better. We're real honest; we don't do that kind of research here. Now, we pick programs that fit with educating students and post-docs . . . with getting their thesis and that's paramount here. I mean, you have to look at the students . . . we train students, that is what we do.

A third said,

> I'm not in the business of providing some company their next product; it's just not part of the game. You know, the game is to educate students, and if it's done properly, everyone wins.

As illustrated in these comments, faculty in this department strive to balance industrial funding with the education of graduate students. Most of the faculty interviewed said that the department's main product is their students, who should be trained through basic research; therefore, industrial money must be used for education in basic research.

Most of the faculty in this department assert that the use of students in industrial projects that compromise students' education and ability to publish is unethical and exploitative. They believe faculty should avoid putting students in projects that are too applied without an educational component unless the student is about to graduate and the experience will help him or her get a job. One professor said that helping students obtain professional positions is not only rewarding for faculty, but placement is also more important to the university and the department than patents or funds. To this department member, a good education results in satisfied alumni, which is essential for an academic institution to succeed:

> I have a post-doc who is applying to Harvard; I hope I can get him into Harvard. . . . If I can get students and post-docs into these institutions, that's going to be far more important to this university than getting a patent or getting a bag of money . . . because these people go into these other institutions and are going to provide students to this university and students are what makes this university. What you want to be able to do is to get people into the institutions that provide feeders . . . if you increase the quality of students and grad students, everything else comes.

Department faculty believe that they safeguard their educational mission from the potential danger of industrial incentives' corrupting their academic principles.

Protecting Free Dissemination of Knowledge and Academic Freedom

Every interviewee asserted that the primary driver of projects is personal scientific interest and curiosity coupled with expertise. However, due to the blurred boundaries between basic and applied research in this field, scientific problems are related directly or indirectly to applications. Some faculty feel attracted by the intellectual challenge involved in coming up with original solutions to existing problems or improvements of technologies, while other faculty are more driven than others toward what are the present needs of industry, although with a focus on the fundamental science behind those applications. Significantly, faculty report they are able to obtain enough funding to pursue their scientific interests fully; they do not believe that sponsors have played a role in directing their research. This ability to find enough funding to pursue their research interests is associated with faculty members' success at selling their ideas properly to either government or industrial sponsors. Two faculty members highlighted the importance of writing large grant proposals and actively seeking funds to pursue their interests freely, rejecting grants that might undermine their professional interests.

The department faculty interviewed for this study feel strongly about the importance of publishing for their careers as the most important measure of good scholarship. Also, some faculty members highlighted the paramount importance of freedom in research. Therefore, these faculty members carefully design contracts with industry to ensure satisfying degrees of freedom and publications. These faculty members in general are very satisfied with their academic freedom and ability to publish despite their involvement with industrial sponsorship. In some cases, industry funds come without restrictions in the form of gifts or block grants. According to one faculty member, in some cases, industry values greatly publications as an effective vehicle to learn the basic science behind their products. Also, faculty argue, some government grants can be more restrictive than industrial grants, especially grants from the Department of Defense. One faculty member pointed out that the only difference between government agencies and companies is that the initial conversations with potential industrial sponsors tend to be more defined with a clearer goal in mind than with grants from the government. Moreover, some faculty members feel that they have had more freedom with industrial grants than with NSF grants, which demand publications for renewals. Interestingly, one faculty member mentioned that the bigger the scope of an industrial grant, the more control a company might have over a research group. Therefore, he prefers to set up contracts with industry around very specific and clear deliveries and expectations as a way to control the scope of control of the company on his research. On the other hand, he compensates for that restriction by having government grants and industrial gifts to purse his research interests more freely and educate students properly.

The Consequences of Industrial Sponsorship

Investment of Time and Human Resources

Several scholars have mentioned that faculty are spending considerable time in patenting and developing relationships with potential donors; in other words, market-like activities are absorbing faculty time that could be used for other purposes such as research or graduate education. Over time, faculty members spend significant time acquiring expertise in recognizing the commercial value of their science, locating commercial partners, and negotiating contracts (Clark, 1987; Gumport, 2005; Slaughter & Leslie, 1997). The faculty in this study recognized that healthy and productive collaborations with industry requires significant effort to develop. One department member noted the investment needed in networking inside individual companies:

> It takes a lot of legwork to go to these companies, and you are not always sure of whom the main contact person should be; who makes the decisions in the company . . . each company is very different so there is no set kind of strategy for getting industrial money.

Faculty also pointed out the networking role of presentations in this uncertain environment:

> Your point of contact may get reassigned, transferred to a new position, might even leave the company... you cannot rely on one person to maintain a relationship if it's going to be a long term relationship. So it's better to go once a year to the company, give a presentation, talk to hopefully 30 or 40 people every year where they get to know your face, once a year at least, and when one person gets reassigned, you know somebody else there.

On occasion, interviewees noted, there was a frustratingly low return on that investment in establishing relationships:

> A lot of times we spend you know, a year or two just in discussions with companies... I spend a lot of time talking to them and the dollar per hoop ratio is completely out of balance. You can often times spend six or eight months working on a company and maybe there'll be $20,000. . . . and a lot of it is just laying some future ground work in trying to build up a rapport, teaching them what you can do, having them develop some confidence. . . . And many times they test you: "We'll give you a small project on a short time frame. Can you deliver?"

Impact on Students

One opportunity cost of establishing relationships with industry is the time that could be spent with students. Findings from previous studies have raised concerns that time spent by faculty members engaging in academic capitalism might be taking professors away from their labs, students, and university service (Gumport, 2002; Kerr, 2002; Lee and Rhoads 2003; Milem, Berger & Dey, 2000; Slaughter & Leslie, 1997). Moreover, Gumport (2005) indicates that the training of graduate students has been tailored towards the needs of industrial sponsors, and that this tendency challenges the presumptions that faculty are interested in the disinterested pursuit of knowledge. However, faculty in this study strongly believe that industrial partnerships, a clear form of academic capitalism, enhances the quality of graduate education and does not undermine faculty desire and conduct of disinterested fundamental science. As noted earlier in the article, faculty defended the educational value of industry ties:

> I think that the industry funded program here is a huge opportunity for students; it's a wonderful, wonderful program. You know, 95% of what's going on there is very, very good from the projects they work on, to the contacts they make, to what it can be in the future, it's very, very good. And so the implications are mostly positive, mostly positive.

Another department member said,

> As an educator I think industry [is] a tremendous vehicle that can be used to show the students about life that you can't do inside the classroom.

The value of industrial involvement in the education of students inspired faculty to create an educational program in which students have an opportunity to learn about the industrial world in a structured fashion. Through this program, faculty invite outside speakers from industry to teach students about a variety of topics such as what industry thinks is important, patents, scaling up and manufacturing, safety issues, diversity in the work place, barriers for women's advancement, communication, and team research. In addition, some faculty mentioned that they intentionally structure opportunities to expose students to industry by arranging visits to companies with students, sending students to conduct research in industrial labs for a period or time, and encouraging companies to visit the department and meet students.

Faculty were convinced that the most positive effect of industrial sponsorship on students is the opportunity to learn about industrial enterprise through visits to companies, direct interactions with industry representatives, and work on industrial problems that might have a significant impact on society. One faculty member prefers industrial grants because students are usually attracted to a specific industrial need or problem. According to faculty, another positive experience is when students present their research to industrial representatives, an interaction that exposes students to different ways of communication with industry representatives as well as providing an opportunity for students to receive feedback on their research. Faculty believe that these are very powerful experiences that teach students about the industrial world including its culture, people, and research, experiences better than those available in any traditional academic setting. One professor alluded to the fact that usually alumni are very grateful about the quality of the education they obtained in the department and the opportunities they had to interact with industrial sponsors:

> The students who are working on a particular project are the ones that are actually doing the work. And when I have these meetings with these companies who come here to see their research, it's my students who present the results with me, so those students are the ones who are actually involved, so that gives them more opportunities to practice communication skills, presentation skills... learn how to organize a presentation or respond to a question in a succinct way or expand as necessary based on the type of questions.

Job and networking opportunities for students were also mentioned by several faculty as some of the positive aspects of industrial funding:

> It makes it easier for students to get a job, to share with prospective employers "I've worked on this application" or "I've worked on research toward this application." A lot of prospective employers can identify with that a little easier than they can with fundamental research and hire directly rather than tying in the fundamental research. Too, I think there is a difference in terms of culture between academia and industry in terms of what research takes place or how research takes place so the student can be exposed both to the advisor as well as a collaborator in industry to see what science in industry is like . . . to give them an idea.

When faculty were asked about the negative effects of industrial funding, they refer to possibilities that might harm students, but they asserted that normally there are no such issues in their program. Some faculty mentioned that there is the possibility that sponsors might withhold students' publications on rare occasions. One professor said that he has seen few instances in which students were unable to talk about their industry-sponsored research in job interviews; however, this professor stated that these conflicts could always be managed. Other professors mentioned that industrial funding has the potential to be restricted and constrained to meet specific demands. However, if a student is working in this kind of project, it is usually a small portion of his or her research. Another faculty member said that sometimes industry has hard deadlines and demand quick results that may jeopardize the quality of the science; but again, according to this professor, students are involved in other projects with sufficient basic science that fulfill the educational mission of the department.

Impact on Research

According to faculty in this study, there are also positive aspects of industrial sponsorship related to research—the opportunity to learn about new materials and technologies being developed as well as information that might be part of trade secrets. Other benefits of industrial sponsorship reported include faculty members' being connected to industrial research as well as to their needs and issues as sources of new research projects:

> Many of the positive aspects are just the exposure to new ideas and new materials... that are covered under patents . . . all the sort of knowledge and information that has been accumulated that is sort of hidden behind the veil of trade secrets. I think the other big positive is the fact that you get a feel for what modern industry is looking for and you can better prepare your students to go out and be competitive.

One faculty member argued for a positive interaction between basic and applied research:

> It keeps the department honest, because you have to do research that actually is going to move the frontier of polymer science forward. So even though you still may be doing stuff that is blue sky and exploratory using government funds or whatever, you're still able to push the boundaries of what is being applied and used out in the real world by having those industrial contacts.

Other benefits mentioned by faculty include the fact that industrial grants offer more flexibility in terms of travel money for conferences. Also, according to one professor, industry researchers tend to be very critical of the research being sponsored, and are willing to cut off funding if they are not satisfied, what this faculty member thought was a form of beneficial accountability nonexistent in federal research support:

> With a company you have to be 99% sure you can deliver what you say... they will hold you accountable. In a government proposal, unfortunately, there's no accountability... an outside committee reviews the quality of the proposals that might sound like they are feasible at the time, but whether the PI actually executes what they say they are going to do is not evaluated by that same committee three years later... it's up to the program manager to assess that, but they don't have that expertise or that level of interest in every single project that they're funding.

Faculty argued that disadvantages of industrial sponsorship are minimal compared to the benefits that these partnerships bring to the department, their academic careers, and students. In any case, the most commonly mentioned disadvantage of industrial funding was that it is subject to economic and market constraints, a fact that might force companies to cut funding suddenly. In those cases, faculty believe it is the job of the faculty member involved to continue funding students from other sources. Some faculty members expressed their frustration with industry's unwillingness to provide grants for at least three years, an uncertainty that makes it difficult to accommodate these grants with the curriculum of students. Faculty felt that this uncertainty was an obstacle to sponsoring students—the Ph.D. program requires at least five years of study. As one department member explained,

> To get that second year of funding up front is very difficult so you are always on a six month or one year kind of renewal basis, which makes it difficult to forecast for planning the growth of the group... whereas a government grant comes in for 3-5 years usually.

One faculty member pointed out the frustrations in a more vivid way:

> The biggest negative side is that you're a foster child. What I mean by that is, when companies go through cost-cutting, the best way to save costs are through the academic kinds of funding that are doing once a year. And so you have to be mature and have enough different programs going so that when one disappears, you have another one that is up and coming that can support your student and put together a thesis that has good sound science and a good focus. . . . So that's the biggest challenge, the time frame.

Finally, two faculty members mentioned that one barrier to industrial funding is corporate competition. Sometimes, a faculty member might be working on areas of interest to more than one company. As industry strives to keep their research confidential, a faculty member might face restrictions imposed by their industrial sponsors.

Intellectual Property

According to Slaughter et al. (2004), the three areas where the greatest disputes emerge between academia and industry are publishing versus patenting, secrecy versus access, and contested ownership over intellectual property. Findings from other studies demonstrate that faculty members consider publishing more valuable than patenting despite the pressure by university administrators to generate streams of revenues from commercialization of research (e.g. Campbell & Slaughter, 1999; Gladieux & King, 2005; Mendoza & Berger, 2005; Slaughter et al., 2004). One of the reasons for faculty members' reluctance to patent is the perception that any individual profit is unlikely to generate significant royalties (Slaughter et al., 2004). Moreover, younger professors cannot afford long delays in publishing their research. In the work by Slaughter et al. (2004), some professors thought industry was blocking the free flow of knowledge, including new discoveries. Sometimes the stakes are high when faculty members have developed long term and elaborate relationships with industry, forcing faculty members to maintain industrial secrets. However, professors in this study (in material sciences) believe it is possible to publish and patent simultaneously, especially among established faculty with long-term programs. In some cases, professors address intellectual-property concerns by removing confidential data from theses and publications. These professors are convinced this practice does not compromise the integrity of the science because the portion removed from publications is either very small or too applied to a specific product. This result suggests that despite industrial contracts and universities' policies to control faculty members' research, faculty are able to manipulate situations to protect their integrity as researchers. In great part this is possible because faculty members are experts, and their sponsors or employers do not know enough to regulate faculty in such a detailed fashion (Slaughter & Rhoades, 2004).

Faculty argued that generally there are no intellectual property issues (IP) with industrial sponsors because agreements are in place beforehand, and companies usually agree to these provisions. Such agreements are in line with the University's IP policy and generally provide industrial sponsors with a waiting period of three months in which sponsors can file a patent before publication. According to faculty, the waiting period of three months does not represent a significant delay because publication timelines are usually longer:

> I could simultaneously be writing a very prestigious publication, drafting a patent disclosure, take that patent disclosure and file that in a very short time frame, a week, and then, you know, 30 minutes after I knew the patent application had been filed in the U.S. Patent Office . . . [then] I'd submit it to the journal.

Several professors mentioned that industries are not interested in funding research that might lead to patents or too close to their products to avoid issues around IP:

> Industry generally doesn't want me to be involved in research that is related to the next product and the reason is, quite clearly, intellectual property. . . . Because if I discover something, then the intellectual property remains at the university or there has to be some special accommodations made between the university and industry.

Finally, one professor noted that he has had difficulty managing restrictions on information when he has worked for competitors simultaneously.

More prominent in intellectual property than a conflict with industry sponsors was a conflict with the institutional logic of patenting. Several faculty members expressed frustrations that the University sees faculty's research as a money maker, which in the minds of faculty is unrealistic; in their view, profitable research tends to stay within industries, and faculty are not interested in making money. Faculty find more (and more reliable) value in conducting basic science, publishing, and educating students:

> Universities still don't know what they're doing. They look at it as a money making venture and you know, it doesn't really work that way that well. . . . My main reason for being here is that I wanted to teach and I wanted to do the kind of research that I wanted to do . . . and I enjoy working with students . . . so when the university all of a sudden looks at you as a money-making entity, they want to make money off of patents, and they put all sorts of constraints on you... that's difficult. The thing is that the rules have changed a lot since many of us first came here and what I've seen over the years is that the university in some way is trying to become more and more like industry. . .

Several other professors argued that the university's administration should understand that educating students, conducting basic research, and publishing is the core mission of the university, a mission that should not be jeopardized to generate revenues through patents and partnerships with industry.

Discussion

Previous empirical studies have shown that faculty members in science and engineering believe collaboration between government, industry, and academia bring benefits to academia such as providing faculty with opportunities to do research, contracts to fund students, networking for future funding, equipment gains, recruitment opportunities of faculty and staff from clients, service contributed by project personnel, spillover to research and teaching, and employment opportunities for students (e.g. Blumenthal, Causino, Campbell, & Seashore Louis, 1996; Campbell & Slaughter, 1999; Mendoza, 2007a; Slaughter & Leslie, 1997; Slaughter et al., 2002; Slaughter & Rhoades, 2004). Although the results of this case study also highlight most of these benefits, the rich descriptions provided by the participants illustrate the interplay of factors involved in partnerships between industry and academia that illuminate additional insights and questions for future research as well as policy implications.

Powell and Owen-Smith (2002) portray the post-modern life scientist in research universities as an entrepreneur:

> The traditional view of the university researcher as a dedicated and disinterested, though passionate, searcher for truth is being replaced in the life sciences by a new model of the scientist-entrepreneur who balances university responsibilities and corporate activities in the development of new compounds and devices designed to both improve human health and generate revenues for the investigator, the university, and investors. (p 108)

The emergence of this new type of faculty members demonstrates the effect of what Kuh and Whitt (1986) call the environmental layer of their cultural framework. The neo-liberalist culture in our society of the last decades is the environmental layer that is pushing faculty members to turn to academic capitalism to maintain research resources and maximize prestige. Resource dependency theory offers a more detailed explanation of how this environmental layer affects the actions of individual faculty members (Slaughter and Leslie, 1997). Dependency theory is based on the premise that internal behaviors of organizational members are understood through the actions of external agents. In the case of higher education, the external agents are manifested in federal policies aimed to cope with global economic competition such as industry-academic collaborations forcing higher education to compete for the new sources of funds targeted to specific areas of R&D in applied fields. Since most faculty members teach and many perform public service but fewer win competitive research funds from government or industry, research is the activity that differentiates universities, where elite departments are defined in terms of excellence in scholarship and originality in research (Becher, 1989). Thus, research funds bring material gain and prestige to universities and push them to engage in academic capitalism. Departments in research intensive universities such as the one in this case study are particularly influenced by the environmental culture based on neo-liberalist ideologies due to the high value placed on research in this type of institution.

The second layer of the framework refers to institutional cultures. The department we studied belongs to a large top ranked research university. These universities are "citadels of the academic culture" (Kuh & Hu, 2001, p. 2) based on concepts such as academic freedom, production and dissemination of knowledge, and education of the young. The results of this study clearly demonstrate a culture among participants that strives to preserve these fundamental values despite their engagement with industry and entrepreneurial opportunities. In opposition to what has been suggested in previous research (Gumport, 2005; Slaughter and Leslie, 1997), the core academic culture in this department is not being consciously disrupted or altered in any significant way by academic capitalism. Moreover, the fact that very few differences where found among faculty members demonstrates that the department has a very strong homogeneous academic culture—even with the additional influences of industrial sponsors as external agents.

The results of this study clearly also suggest that significant clashes are occurring between faculty and administrators around intellectual property issues. These differences are explained by the tensions that usually occur among different subcultures in the third layer of Kuh and Whitt's framework. In this case, university administrators hold managerial values that are in sharp opposition to the academic culture of faculty. This study also discovered subcultures among faculty who have worked in industry and faculty who have followed traditional academic paths—although there were surprisingly few differences between these groups. Finally, the results of this study support the fourth layer of Kuh and Whitt's framework, in which individuality plays a significant role in shaping the culture of a given unit. On several occasions, faculty made clear that it was up to individuals how to respond and protect their academic interests as they became involved in partnerships with industry. However, this study found that individual differences were small when compared to a strong and cohesive academic culture in the department. The departmental academic culture in this case seems to be even stronger than the discipline-based cultures given that faculty believe other departments in the field respond differently to academic capitalism.

One of the most significant findings of this study is the high value that faculty place on education. This finding is particularly important given concerns raised in previous literature about the diminishing time and effort spent by faculty in the education of students due to academic capitalism (e.g., Gumport, 2002; Lee & Rhoads, 2003; Slaughter & Leslie, 1997). Although faculty in this study recognize that they spend considerable energy developing industry-academia relationships, they emphatically state that the education of students is one of the most important goals of their careers and the department. The results of this study suggest that faculty intentionally use industrial funding to enhance the quality of the education of their students and actively protect students from sponsors' demands, to the point of rejecting funding if it jeopardizes the education of their students. Moreover, faculty strongly believe that industrial funding brings significant benefits to the education of students. Also, faculty in this study believe that industry's main reason for funding research in the department is to support the training of a skillful workforce in basic science and provide the opportunity to know students comprehensively throughout the years in the program, to help recruit those students who best fit their needs. Therefore, according to faculty in this department, sponsorship benefits both industry and academia because the interests of industry do not necessarily conflict with faculty interests. These results support the findings of Mendoza's (2007a) case study on the positive effects of industry-academia collaboration on the socialization and education of graduate students.

Faculty in this study report that despite their significant involvement with industrial sponsors, they are able to maintain their academic freedom, conduct basic research, and publish in peer-reviewed journals. This result contradicts previous assertions about potential overemphasis on applied research, restrictions in research, and secrecy of knowledge as faculty engage in academic capitalism (e.g., Powell & Owen-Smith, 2002; Gumport, 2005; Slaughter et al., 2004). Nonetheless, recent studies have also indicated that these constraints are not necessarily the case and that faculty are able to publish, follow their scientific interests, and comply with sponsors' demands simultaneously (Mendoza, 2007a; Slaughter et al., 2004). Faculty in this study explain that this is possible because research sponsored by industry is several steps away from direct applications. In addition, given that the development of any technology must relay on basic science, there are always possibilities to conduct fundamental research and publish in applied projects.

This study contributes to our knowledge regarding the impact of academic capitalism on the academic profession by documenting a case in which the broad integrity of the academic culture of faculty members in a department remains purely Mertonian, even with significant industrial funding (Merton, 1957). Moreover, these faculty members consider industrial sponsorship a highly effective vehicle for enhancing the quality of education of students and pursuing their scientific interests. However, the results of these studies are highly context-dependent and may not transfer to other academic settings. Therefore, the implications of industrial partnerships to the academic culture await additional empirical research across different types of institutions and disciplines.

Despite the overall positive findings, this study suggests some areas of concern requiring careful investigation. One of these areas is the perception among faculty indicating that general support for basic research is becoming less favorable as both industry and federal funding for basic science continues to decrease (Mowery, 1998). This raises important questions about the fate of fundamental discoveries in basic research. Several faculty indicated that there are other institutions within their field less committed to fundamental science either by choice or necessity. In some cases, faculty mentioned that departments or individual faculty members might end up bending their core academic values to please industrial sponsors. This study suggests this department is in a position to negotiate with industrial sponsors to protect their interests as a result of their privileged position as a top-ranked department with outstanding scientists able to attract significant funding both from industry and government. This position of privilege combined with a strong Mertonian culture explains the department's ability to maintain its core values in light of academic capitalism. Future research should investigate other departments in less privileged positions and with less cohesive cultures to determine to what degree academic capitalism forces encourage these institutions to compromise their academic values.

Implications for Policy

This case study has several implications for both institutional and social policy. On the one hand, an area of tension clearly voiced in this study relates to faculty members' negative perceptions of the University's intellectual-property policy, which they characterize as the greatest obstacle to partnering with industrial sponsors. As suggested in other recent studies, faculty complained about the pressure they experience by university administrators to patent their research though faculty are not interested in pure monetary incentives (Mendoza & Berger, 2005; Slaughter et al., 2004). Moreover, faculty in this study believe it is not cost-effective for universities to adopt these policies. Institutions should reexamine their policies for ways to create support for faculty who negotiate industrial contracts. In particular, campus leaders may want to look at ways their intellectual property policies are structured to ensure they maximize material benefits from licensing and encourage collaborations with industry. In addition, these policies could enhance benefits by offering faculty adequate institutional support that enables them to maximize autonomy when negotiating external contracts, particularly with industrial partners (Mendoza & Berger, 2005). Campus leaders may also want to offer workshops that teach newer faculty members how to negotiate such contracts. These types of workshops could also be offered through disciplinary associations. More experienced faculty members could be encouraged to collaborate with and mentor newer colleagues to balance their work strategically in light of current market pressures and the particular position of their academic department within the larger competitive organizational field.

Findings from this study provide valuable insights into federal policies related to the distribution of research funding and the shaping of programs aimed to stimulate collaborations between industry and academia by presenting additional evidence about the impact of these policies and funding distribution on the traditional norms and values of the academic profession and on the training of doctoral students. In particular, this study provides empirical evidence in support of federal programs such as the Industry/University Cooperative Research Centers (I/UCRCs). However, the benefits of this type of federal programs can be maximized if other types of organizations are included to create networks of knowledge. For example, the Canadian Networks of Centers of Excellence (NCE) are a web of social, economic, legal and administrative relationships among different types of institutions such as companies, universities, hospitals, schools, nonprofit organizations and federal agencies around critical issues of scientific, technological, cultural, social national importance. The Canadian government directs funding primarily to the administration of these networks and infrastructure to host conferences, workshops, professional training, and publications. Mendoza (2007b) argues that the Canadian networks offer a wider variety of benefits and opportunities for participants than the American I/UCRC program, and policymakers might want to consider this model for future R&D national investments (Mendoza, 2007b).

The results of this study also suggest potential negative effects that can result from uneven distributions of federal funding across academic institutions. In short, this study suggests that if federal grants are concentrated in a few institutions, those departments in fields relevant to industry with less federal funding might be compromising their core values to service industrial sponsors in exchange for funds. The government and its various funding agencies could evaluate the types of grants they offer and the availability to different types of departments and institutions. Faculty members emphasized a strong preference for unrestricted grants to help them generate more cohesive and strategic research agendas that enable them to do better basic and applied research and properly train students. Therefore, increased funding for federal research would provide better opportunities for more faculty members to have their work supported in ways that do not require them to make short-term decisions to pursue more restrictive and less prestigious grants and contracts that are also lower in monetary support. Greater federal funding would also enable faculty members to be in stronger negotiating positions of industrial contracts which would better protect the ability of faculty members to drive their own research agendas and have more control over intellectual property.

Federal funding agencies should also consider ways to better support faculty members in less prestigious departments by continuing to expand initiatives such as the NSF EPSCOR program. This type of policy emphasis could strengthen the quality of research being conducted at a wider range of institutions, thereby increasing knowledge generated across the entire academy. The federal government may also want to broaden the impact of programs that fund cross-campus initiatives to better spread the wealth and to limit the effects of accumulative advantage. These recommendations come recognizing that the quality of research should still be the primary determinant for federal funding. However, the best ideas for future research may be limited by the quality of facilities in some departments and this issue should be examined closely as priorities for federal funding are considered in future funding cycles.

References

Agrawal, A., & Henderson, R. (2002). Putting patents in context: Exploring knowledge transfer from MIT. *Management Science*, 48(1), 44–60.

Allaire, Y., & Firsirotu, M. E. (1984). Theories of organizational culture. *Organization Studies*, 5, 193–226.

Altbach, P. G. (2005). Harsh realities: The professoriate faces a new century. In P. G. Altbach, R. O. Berdahl, & P. J Gumport (Eds.), *American higher education in the twenty-first century: Social, political, and economic challenges* (pp. 287–314). Baltimore, MD: Johns Hopkins University Press.

Anderson, M. S. (2001). Complex relations between the academy and industry. *Journal of Higher Education*, 72(2), 226–246.

Becher T. (1984). The cultural view. In B. Clark (Ed.), *Perspectives in higher education* (pp. 165–198). Berkeley: University of California Press.

Becher, T. (1989). *Academic tribes and territories: Intellectual enquiry and the culture of disciplines*. Bristol, PA: SRHE and Open University Press.

Berg, B. L. (2004). *Qualitative research methods* (5th ed.). Upper Saddle River, NJ: Pearson Education, Inc.

Blumenthal, D., Causino, N., Campbell, E., & Seashore Louis, K. (1996). Relationships between academic institutions and industry in the life sciences—and industry survey. *New England Journal of Medicine*, 334(6), 368–371.

Bowen, H. R., & Schuster, J. H. (1986). *American professors: A national resource imperiled*. New York: Oxford University Press.

Campbell, T., & Slaughter S. (1999). Faculty and administrators' attitudes towards potential conflicts of interests, commitment, and equity in university-industry relationships. *Journal of Higher Education*, 70(3), 309–352.

Clark, B. (1970). *The distinctive college*. Chicago: Aldine.

Clark, B. (1980). *Academic culture*. Working paper No. 42. New Heaven, CT: Yale University Higher Education Research Group.

Clark, B. (1984). *The higher education system: Academic organization in cross-national perspective*. Berkeley: University of California Press.

Clark, B. (1987). *The academic life: Small worlds, different worlds*. Princeton, NJ: Carnegie Foundation for the Advancement of Teaching.

Creswell, J. W. (1998). *Qualitative inquiry and research design: Choosing among five traditions*. Thousand Oaks, CA: Sage Publications.

Denscombe, M. (2002). *Ground rules for good research: A 10 point guide for social researchers*. Philadelphia, PA: Open University Press.

Duderstadt, J. J. (2001). Fire, ready, aim! University decision-making during an era of rapid change. In W. Z. Hirsch & L. E. Weber (Eds.), *Governance in higher education: The university in a state of flux* (pp. 26–51). London, UK: Economica.

Etzioni, A. A. (1961). *Comparative analysis of complex organizations: On power, involvement, and their correlates* (2nd ed.). New York: Free Press.

Friedland, R., & Alford, R. (1991). Bringing society back in: Symbols, practices and institutional contradictions. In W. Powell & P. DiMaggio (Eds.), *The new institutionalism in organizational analysis* (pp. 232–264). Chicago: University of Chicago Press.

Gladieux, L. E., & King, J. E. (2005). The federal government and higher education. In P. G. Altbach, R. O. Berdahl, & P. J. Gumport (Eds.), *American higher education in the twenty-first century: Social, political, and economic challenges* (2nd ed., pp. 163–197). Baltimore, MD: The Johns Hopkins University Press.

Gumport, P. J. (2005). Graduate education and research: Interdependence and strain. In P. G. Altbach, R. O. Berdahl, & P. J. Gumport (Eds.), *American higher education in the twenty-first century: Social, political, and economic challenges* (2nd ed., pp. 425–460) Baltimore, MD: The Johns Hopkins University Press.

Gumport, P. J. (2002). Universities and knowledge: Restructuring the city intellect. In S. Brint (Ed.), *The future of the city of intellect: The changing American university* (pp. 47–81). Stanford, CA: Stanford University Press.

Kerr, C. (2002). Shock wave II: an introduction to the twenty-first century. In S. Brint (Ed.), *The future of the city of intellect: The changing American university* (pp. 1–19). Stanford, CA: Stanford University Press.

Krimsky, S. (2003). *Science in the private interest: Has the lure of profits corrupted biomedical research?* Lanham, MD: Rowman & Littlefield Publishers, Inc.

Kuh, G. D., & Whitt, E. J. (1986). *The invisible tapestry: Culture in American colleges and universities.* ASHE-ERIC Higher Education Report No 1. Washington, DC: George Washington University.

Kuh, G. & Hu, S. (2001). Learning productivity at research universities. *Journal of Higher Education*, 72(1), 1–28.

Lee, J. J., & Rhoads, R. A. (2003). *Faculty entrepreneurialism and the challenge to undergraduate education at research universities.* Paper presented at the American Educational Research Association (AERA), Chicago, IL.

Mendoza, P., & Berger, J. B. (2005). Patenting productivity and intellectual property policies at Research I universities: An exploratory comparative study. *Education Policy Analysis Archives*, 13(5).

Mendoza, P. (2007a). Academic capitalism and doctoral student socialization: A case study. *Journal of Higher Education*, 78(1), 71–96.

Mendoza, P. (2007b). *Educating for the public good through comprehensive federal research & development policies.* ASHE/Lumina Policy Briefs and Critical Essays No. 3. Ames: Iowa State University, Department of Educational Leadership and Policy Studies.

Merton, R. K. (1957). *Social theory of science.* Chicago: University of Chicago Press.

Milem, J. F., Berger, J. B., & Dey E. L. (2000). Faculty time allocation: A study of change over twenty years. *Journal of Higher Education*, 71(4), 454–474.

Morril, P. H., & Speed, E. R. (1982). *The academic profession: Teaching in higher education.* New York: Human Sciences Press.

Mowery, D. C. (1998). The changing structure of the U.S. National Innovation System: Implications for international conflict and cooperation in R&D policy. *Research Policy*, 27, 639–654.

Newman, F., Couturier, L., & Scurry, J. (2004). *The future of higher education: Rhetoric, reality, and the risks of the market.* San Francisco, CA: Jossey-Bass.

Neave, G. (2001). Governance, change and the universities in western Europe. In W. Z. Hirsch & L. E. Weber (Eds.), *Governance in higher education: The university in a state of flux* (pp. 52–67). London, UK: Economica.

Peterson, M. W., & Spencer, M. G. (1990). Understanding academic culture and climate. *New Directions for Institutional Research*, 17(4), 3–18.

Powell, W. W., & Owen-Smith, J. (2002). The new world of knowledge production in the life sciences. In S. Brint (Ed.), *The future of the city of intellect: The changing American university* (pp. 107–130). Stanford, CA: Stanford University Press.

Rice, R. E. (1986). The academic profession in transition: Toward a new social fiction. *Teaching Sociology*, 14, 12–23.

Ruscio, K. P. (1987). Many sectors, many professions. In B. Clark (Ed.). *The academic profession* (pp. 331–368). Berkeley: University of California Press.

Slaughter, S., & Leslie, L. (1997). *Academic capitalism: Politics, policies, and the entrepreneurial university.* Baltimore: The Johns Hopkins University Press.

Slaughter, S., Campbell, T., Hollernan, M., & Morgan, E. (2002). The "traffic" in graduate students: Graduate students as tokens of exchange between academe and industry. *Science, Technology, and Human Values*, 27(2), 282–313.

Slaughter, S., & Rhoades, G. (2004) *Academic capitalism and the new economy: Markets, state, and higher education.* Baltimore: Johns Hopkins University Press.

Slaughter, S., Archerd, C. J., & Campbell, T. I. D. (2004). Boundaries and quandaries: How professors negotiate market relations. *Review of Higher Education*, 28(1), 129–165.

Smircich, L. (1983). Concepts of culture and organizational analysis. *Administrative Science Quarterly*, 28, 339–358.

Tierney, W. G. (1988). Organizational culture in higher education. *Journal of Higher Education*, 59(1), 2–21.

Tierney, W. G., & Rhoads, R. A. (1993). *Enhancing promotion, tenure and beyond: Faculty socialization as a cultural process.* Washington, DC: George Washington University.

Yin, R. K. (1994). *Case study research: Design and methods* (3rd ed.). Newbury Park, CA: Sage Publications.

SECTION VIII

INTERNATIONAL FINANCING OF HIGHER EDUCATION

Introduction to Section VIII

W. James Jacob and John C. Weidman
University of Pittsburgh

Multiple global financial shifts have significantly impacted higher education in recent years. The global financial crisis that began in 2007 and lasted for several years had long-lasting influence on how higher education institutions receive funding from their respective governments, students, and grant agencies. Increasingly governments are encouraging HEIs to diversify their funding schemes with a goal to become more self-sustaining and autonomous. In most country contexts, higher education administrators are forced now more than ever to be frugal and do much more with less financial resources.

The privatization of government HEIs is a trend that will continue well into the future. Government-supported higher education finance schemes differ depending on the context. Some countries have experienced significant stability and economic growth over the past decade that has helped their governments invest heavily in their higher education subsectors. Others have struggled during this same time period. This section highlights some of the disparities that exist between higher education systems in international contexts. We include articles from the world's largest higher education system as well as regional examples and trends of financing higher education.

Buckner ("Access to Higher Education in Egypt: Examining Trends by University Sector") finds that access to higher education in Egypt is expanding in both the public and private sectors. Using a nationally representative sample from the Survey of Young People in Egypt, she disaggregates patterns of access by both demographic group and university sector and explores their socio-economic implications. Access in the public sector is governed strongly by performance on exit exams and is growing most rapidly for women, rural youth, and middle-class Egyptians. In contrast, access to private universities is growing most rapidly for males, youth in Cairo, and the top wealth quintile. She concludes that continued expansion of the public sector is likely to promote greater inclusiveness, while expansion of the private sector may exacerbate wealth and regional inequalities.

Del Rey and Racionero ("Financing Schemes for Higher Education") address how many countries are dealing with covering the increasing costs of student tuition. They base their findings and analyses on four financing schemes for higher education: (1) traditional tax-subsidy, (2) pure loans, (3) income-contingent loans with risk-sharing, and (4) income-contingent loans with risk-pooling. Arguing that the latter scheme has the greatest potential for wide participation, the authors argue that students are willing to help finance higher education costs if the students attain desired outcomes. No funding scheme guarantees that students will be able to secure a job following graduation in a particular field.

The income-contingent loan with risk-pooling scheme enables successful students to cover the costs of their own schooling as well as the costs of students who are unsuccessful in obtaining employment. Drawing from a wide number of country case examples, Del Rey and Racionero base their findings on a theoretical model that assumes successful students will be willing to help pay for their own schooling as well as the higher education tuition costs of those starting college at the same time who did not succeed. The article has a strong introduction that is linked to many examples of countries that participate in one or more of the four funding schemes and follows with their optimal model for income-contingent loans with risk-pooling.

Devarajan, Monga, and Zongo ("Making Higher Education Finance Work for Africa") view the current status of higher education in Africa as a vicious cycle of insufficient resources and often poor management over and use of existing resources. The article builds upon a solid historical literature overview of higher education in Africa and then rightfully identifies the financing of higher education as among the many challenges facing this subsector continent wide. Other challenges the authors identify only exacerbate the financial challenge, including decades of overemphasis on the primary and more recently secondary subsectors of education; rigid curricula that are misaligned with local and global economic markets; demand for higher education that has increased dramatically in recent years, far outpacing the supply; and the quality of higher education offered, which is a global trend as well. Another financial factor that further exacerbates the quality of higher education is the inability of most African countries to keep many of their most accomplished and talented faculty members from remaining in country. Uncompetitive salaries, poor research facilities and support mechanisms, and dilapidated libraries and infrastructure often serve as push factors that encourage many faculty members who are able to look for alternative countries to establish and continue their careers.

The authors argue against the two traditional rationales for more government support in higher education—equity and efficiency—and instead provide two *principles* to help provide country-specific strategies for overcoming the higher education financial challenges unique to African countries. The first principle is that students should finance their own education and the second that governments should regulate both public and private higher education in terms of governance and quality assurance. They also conclude that HEIs should be re-conceptualized and organized in Africa to focus on generating and disseminating knowledge and better meeting market needs. In this way the curriculum and student graduates will be prepared for competitive employment opportunities and fill positions based on market demands.

Ngolovoi ("Cost Sharing in Higher Education in Kenya: Examining the Undesired Policy Outcomes") argues that the notion of cost sharing originally derived from a United States context and has since been used across international development education circles across the world. By definition, cost sharing denotes that the combined contributions of students, parents of students, local communities, and donors (including international donor agencies) should be shared to help supplement, or in some cases off-set, costs that exceed what governments are willing or able to pay for public schooling, and in the case of this article toward the higher education subsector. The government of Kenya has responded by establishing a Higher Education Loans Board to enable students to finance their higher education ambitions. While proponents argue that cost sharing leads to several long-term benefits to governments, including reducing financial obligations and increases equity in higher education, Ngolovoi highlights three equity challenges in the current national cost sharing program: weaknesses with the loan application process; loan amounts that are insufficient to finance all costs of a higher education degree; and a non-nuclear family context (i.e., a society based on a substantial proportion of polygamous family structures). Finally, she details the unique challenges of implementing a cost-sharing program in Kenya.

Stromquist's ("Internationalization as a Response to Globalization: Radical Shifts in University Environments") case study of a private research university looks at the phenomenon of internationalization, an economic and political response by universities to search for new markets in light of pressures from globalization. She contrasts this with an imagined alternative in which universities position themselves in service to areas of the world that are currently less advantaged. Operating in the context of declining value and articulation of public service and the liberal arts, Stromquist finds that in various units of the case study university, administrators have begun placing greater emphasis on skills acquisition and external relations that promote resource acquisition. She proposes the beginning of a dangerous cultural shift in the organization toward the more market-driven internationalization, even though the shift in priorities is couched in terms of internationalism (or a belief in the value of cross-cultural interconnections).

The final article in this section focuses on equity implications of China's higher education finance policy. Sun and Barrientos ("The Equity Challenge in China's Higher Education Finance Policy") discuss how the government has financed and currently finances higher education. The authors also provide a concluding section that presents some suggestions for how policymakers and government planners can help ensure more equitable higher education access in the future.

CHAPTER 46

ACCESS TO HIGHER EDUCATION IN EGYPT: EXAMINING TRENDS BY UNIVERSITY SECTOR

ELIZABETH BUCKNER

Access to higher education in Egypt is expanding in both the public and private sectors. Using a nationally representative sample from the Survey of Young People in Egypt, this article is able to disaggregate patterns of access by both demographic group and university sector. Findings suggest that access in the public sector is governed strongly by performance on exit exams and is growing most rapidly for women, rural youth, and middle-class Egyptians. In contrast, access to private universities is growing most rapidly for males, youth in Cairo, and the top wealth quintile. Although far from equal, continued expansion of the public sector will likely promote greater inclusiveness, while expansion of the private sector may exacerbate wealth and regional inequalities.

Introduction

Egypt's higher education landscape is currently transitioning from a predominantly elite system of public universities to a mass system with both public and private universities (Trow 1973, 2007; Fahim and Sami 2011). This shift has important implications for not only how many students attend higher education but also who these students are and what types of institutions they attend. This article conceptualizes these changes as occurring within two sectors, public and private, governed by fundamentally different logics: meritocracy and market demand.[1] While expansion in both sectors facilitates overall access, the two sectors have opposite implications for equity of access.

A number of studies on higher education in Egypt have argued that despite rhetoric of meritocracy, access to higher education is biased against the poor. In 2005, individuals from the highest quintile still occupied more than 40 percent of spaces in Egyptian universities, while those from the lowest wealth quintile represent less than 10 percent (Cupito and Langsten 2011, 192–93). Nonetheless, the policies pursued by Egypt since 2005 signal a desire to widen access to substantially more youth, in line with "massification" policies (Trow 1973, 2007). Egypt has established five new public universities since 2005 and has initiated income-generating programs to help offset costs of expansion. Quantitatively, enrollment in public universities rose from roughly 1.49 million in 2001 to 1.93 million in 2009, and continued expansion is planned (CAPMAS 2011).

Substantial research in the sociology of education finds that educational expansion does not necessarily reduce the effect of parental resources on educational attainment, a phenomenon known as "persistent inequality" (Shavit and Blossfeld 1993; Shavit et al. 2007; Pfeffer 2008). Yet research does suggest that once a saturation point has been reached among the upper classes at a given level of education, continued expansion of that level will increase access for traditionally excluded youth, a phenomenon known as "inclusiveness" (Shavit et al. 2007). Therefore, continued expansion of higher education in Egypt will likely be associated with more individuals from all backgrounds attending higher education in the long run (Cupito and Langsten 2011). However, to date, whether Egypt has reached its saturation point since implementing the 2005 reforms remains unclear.

In addition to public sector growth, privatization reforms initiated in 1992 and expanded in 2005 have created a separate university sector governed by market dynamics. The private university sector is highly controversial in Egypt, as privatization is associated with a larger project of neoliberalism and the dismantling of the public sector, encouraged by foreign donors, including the World Bank and the IMF (Mazawi 2010). New private universities charge tuition and are often targeted toward the elite and upper-middle classes, who are willing and able to pay substantial tuition. While private higher education serves 17 percent of all postsecondary students, private bachelor's degree-granting universities serve only 2.5 percent of all Egyptian university students, meaning they still play a small role in the higher education landscape. Nonetheless, enrollment in Egypt's private universities tripled between 2000 and 2005, and expansion of private universities is viewed as an integral part of Egypt's attempt to increase access to higher education (Fahim and Sami 2011).

In Egypt, the newly founded private universities have higher tuition and fees than public universities, and researchers have already expressed concern that private universities are only accessible to the upper and upper-middle classes (Fahim and Sami 2011). Yet private universities also have lower admissions standards and are considered by many to be of lower quality than the public universities. As such, the wealthy may use their considerable resources to help their children enroll in public universities by investing in both private tutors and paying for spots in new programs in public university tracks (Elbadawy et al. 2007; Sobhy 2012).

We know little about how student populations in public and private universities may differ in Egypt or whether family wealth plays a more important role in determining access to the public or private sectors. Nor do we know how Egypt's policies to privatize access to higher education have interacted with the many factors that shape families' decisions about investment in education. Given that women's labor force participation rates in Egypt are among the lowest in the world, it is possible that families are making different investment decisions for their female children than their male children.[2]

Additionally, we have little understanding of what the effects of increasing the number of private universities will be on equity of access. Despite a growing body of research on private higher education worldwide, the theoretical literature on the effects of the privatization of higher education is inconclusive. On the one hand, comparative education research consistently indicates that the tuition-dependent private sector is likely to serve students from more advantaged backgrounds, which would suggest that the expansion of private higher education exacerbates inequalities in access.[3] Nonetheless, in a cross-national study of access to higher education, Yossi Shavit, Richard Arum, and Adam Gamoran (2007) find that the effects of privatization on inequality are offset by the system-wide expansion and diversification of higher education providers, which are associated with expanded access, meaning that privatization has no net effect on inequality in access.

To shed light on how access to higher education in Egypt is changing in light of massification and privatization, this article provides a comprehensive view of recent trends in access to higher education in Egypt by disaggregating patterns of access by university sector. It takes a three-pronged approach: first, it examines demographic characteristics of students in each sector; second, it examines which factors affect eligibility and enrollment in higher education overall and by sector; and finally, it examines patterns in access to higher education across two cohorts of Egyptian youth to understand how the 2005 higher education reforms are influencing access and equity.

Research Significance

This article provides a baseline of information on access to higher education in the Arab world, where many have noted that we lack in-depth understanding.[4] Although a number of recent studies have examined the financing of higher education in Egypt (Fahim and Sami 2011) and demographics of university students (Megahed 2010; Cupito and Langsten 2011), these studies have not investigated the question of university sector with student-level data. The present study brings new and substantially more detailed data to the question of access to higher education in Egypt by using a nationally representative survey of youth that includes information on high school type and secondary exit exam score (Population Council 2010). As such, this article is able to examine how academic performance in secondary school interacts with other demographic characteristics to shape youth access to university. Moreover, to date, no study has examined differences in student demographics across educational sector (i.e., public or private universities) in the Arab world, which this article is able to do.

The larger question of inequality of educational opportunity in Egypt is an important concern for researchers and international observers alike. The explosion of youth-led protests throughout the Arab Middle East, known as the Arab Spring, cannot be divorced from larger discussions of youth education and employment (al-Momani 2011; Anderson 2011). In Egypt, worldwide attention has focused on the role that youth played in leading and organizing nearly 3 weeks of daily marches and protests in January 2011, which ultimately led to the ouster of former President Hosni Mubarak and the subsequent democratic transition. The most vocal protesters were discontent youth, angry over the lack of employment opportunities, widespread corruption, and exacerbating income inequalities. Thus, the question of persistent inequality in Egypt and the role of the higher education system in the differential structuring of young people's opportunities is one with very real geopolitical consequences. Unfortunately, despite the widespread concern over the quality of higher education in the Middle East and North Africa (MENA) and the ability of higher education institutions to prepare graduates for professional work (Rugh 2002; Dhillon and Yousef 2009; Labaki 2009), reforms to higher education in MENA are often suggested in line with global models of privatization, with little understanding of who goes to higher education and what the effects of privatization may be on dynamics of quality and inequality in this area (Sanyal 1998; Rugh 2002).

Higher Education in Egypt

In 1952, there were only three national universities in Egypt—Cairo University, Alexandria University, and Ain Shams. In addition, two religiously affiliated private universities were operating—Al-Azhar University and the American University in Cairo. After the national revolution in 1952, the Nasser regime instituted a number of higher education reforms, in line with revolution's goals of social justice and equity (Arabsheibani 1988). Major reforms included guaranteeing admission to higher education to all secondary school graduates, instituting a national secondary exit exam (known as the *thanawiya amma*) to determine one's placement in higher education, eliminating tuition fees, and guaranteeing all university graduates public sector employment (Howard-Merriam 1979; Rugh 2002; Cupito and Langsten 2011). These policies were specifically designed to counter the colonialist legacy of reserving higher education for the wealthy and well connected.

Egypt's current higher education system is largely a product of its original nationalist reforms. As in many Arab states, Egyptian students are sorted into secondary school tracks based on exit exams at the end of primary schooling. They either enter general (i.e., academic) or vocational secondary schools, where they can specialize in industrial, agricultural, or commercial studies. A small percentage of secondary students also study at high schools affiliated with Al-Azhar. In 2005–6, 56.4 percent of students attended vocational secondary school, 35.6 percent attended general secondary school, and 8 percent were in Al-Azhar secondary schools. In 2006–7 the transition rate from general secondary to postsecondary school was 80.7 percent, while the transition rate from vocational secondary was 8.9 percent (Hamid 2010). As such, admission to the general secondary track is an important determinant of university enrollment.

The Supreme Council of Universities determines the number of spaces available in each university program, and the Admission Office of Egyptian Universities is in charge of coordinating the application and admissions process (Helms 2008). Admissions decisions are based primarily on the *thanawiya amma* (Helms 2008). Performance on this secondary exit exam determines precisely which educational options are open to young people—generous government subsidies mean that attending public universities is nearly free for high academic achievers (Hargreaves 1997). In principle, access to higher education is meritocratic, as admission is granted to only the most academically gifted students, regardless of the family's ability to pay. In reality, however, the *thanawiya amma* requires extensive memorization and places a huge financial burden on families for private tutoring, which is thought to contribute to inequalities in access (Valverde 2005; Elbadawy et al. 2009; Sobhy 2012). Yet even when confronted with criticism of the higher education admissions process in 2001, Egypt's Minister of Higher Education, Mufid Shebab, remained a staunch advocate of the examination system on both logistical and ideological grounds, stating that "the application system still has one significant virtue: equal opportunity" (*Al-Ahram Weekly* 2001).

Egypt's higher education system is the largest in the region, and recent reforms have focused on expansion. In 2009–10, more than 2.4 million Egyptians were in some form of postsecondary institute or university, and of those 1.9 million were in government universities (CAPMAS 2011). The Strategic Planning Unit anticipates continued growth rates of 3 percent annually, from roughly 28 percent in 2006 to upward of 35 percent in 2021 (Helal 2007; World Bank 2010; Cupito and Langsten 2011). In recent years, the Ministry of Higher Education has actively expanded the number of universities. In 2005–6, five new universities were established, bringing the total to 17 public universities, in addition to Al-Azhar, a publicly funded Islamic university that operates within its own administrative and admissions structure.

In 2006, Egypt also instituted a number of reforms that garner additional funding for public universities, consistent with the global trend of cost sharing as a way of raising private revenues to offset costs (Johnstone and Marcucci 2010). The Egyptian government has "allowed public universities to charge nominal tuition fees for special academic programs that are perceived to be of high academic quality and for which there is high demand" (Fahim and Sami 2011, 61). Some universities charge small fees, and in recent years, students with lower exit exam scores have been allowed to pay tuition to enroll in the faculties of law, commerce, and the arts.[5] These cost-sharing reforms now allow students with lower scores to secure spots in public universities (World Bank and UNESCO 2000; Rugh 2002). However, this initiative is limited to certain programs, and the fees charged amount to only 33 percent of the total cost (Fahim and Sami 2011).

In addition to expansion in the public sector, the private university sector has also been growing. A major overhaul of higher education law was passed in 1992, which first permitted the establishment of new private universities, and the first private universities were licensed in 1996. In the year 1999, only four private universities were operating, serving roughly 6,000 students, compared to the 12 public institutions serving nearly 1.5 million students (Farag 2000). However, enrollments in private universities started growing rapidly in 2002, with 12 new private universities established between 2002 and 2010, and six of those founded in 2006–7 (Hamid 2010). The number of students enrolling in private universities also increased dramatically from 11,000 to 48,000 between 2000 and 2005 (Fahim and Sami 2011). As of 2009–10, private universities serve approximately 70,000 young people (World Bank 2010; CAPMAS 2011). The expansion of private universities suggests a shift in the logic of higher education admissions. Fundamentally, privatization suggests that access to higher education is no longer solely a matter of state planning but also operates within an open market for credentials governed by individual calculations of costs and benefits (Galal 2002).

Many Egyptians have expressed concern over the effect of privatization on equity and quality. Yasmine Fahim and Noha Sami (2011) argue that the transition to the private provision of higher education will most likely negatively affect equity of access to higher education, as tuition may prevent the poorest from attending university. The authors explain that "the main concern is equitable access to higher education and cream skimming . . . [as] less affluent students will not be able to enroll in these institutions, placing them at a disadvantage to the rich" (Fahim and Sami 2011, 60).

Additionally, the quality of the private universities remains highly debated. In 2001, the Egyptian Ministry of Education established a minimum score of 80 on the *thanawiya amma* for students specializing in scientific and technical fields, and a minimum of 65 for those in literature and the humanities (*Al-Ahram Weekly* 2001). Although this was a first attempt to regulate quality, these benchmarks are far below admissions requirements in the public sector. In the public sector, the minimum requirement is different for every major and every university, but science and engineering programs in major cities generally require upward of 85 percent, with many highly desired programs requiring 90 percent or more (El Sebai 2006; Mahmoud 2010). In fact, the majority of new private universities are widely perceived as "selling" their degrees, as many private universities reap a profit, excepting the older prestigious universities such as the American University of Cairo (ICHEFP 2011).

Access to Higher Education

This article draws on sociological research on inequality in access to higher education to understand recent trends in Egypt. Research consistently finds that the wealthy use their substantial resources to secure both qualitative and quantitative advantages in the formal education system (Buchmann and Hannum 2001). Samuel Lucas's (2001) "Effectively Maintained Inequality" thesis (EMI) argues that the wealthy use their financial resources both to disproportionately gain access to levels of education that are not universal and to obtain a qualitatively better education regardless of whether a level of education is universal or not. In the Egyptian case, scholars have consistently pointed out that despite the meritocratic claims of Egyptian educational rhetoric, higher education policies actually serve as a subsidy for the upper classes because the wealthy have access to higher-quality primary and secondary schooling, which help their children get into the academic secondary track (Cupito and Langsten 2011).

Parents also pay for extensive outside tutoring to improve their students' scores on secondary exit exams (Elbadawy et al. 2007; Hartmann 2007; Fahim and Sami 2011). Asmaa Elbadawy, Dennice Ahlburg, and Deborah Levinson (2009) report that 62 percent of secondary students pay for private tutoring. This finding is in line with substantial cross-national research on the rise of shadow education markets, which finds that families pay substantial out-of-pocket costs to help children perform better on standardized tests (Baker and LeTendre 2005; Bray and Silova 2006; Kuan 2011).

Nonetheless, substantial cross-national research has found that as youth move through the formal education system, the effect of parental resources tends to decline with each successive transition (Mare 1981; Shavit and Blossfeld 1993). If this is true in Egypt, it could mean that family wealth is a less significant predictor of access at the university level than at lower transitions. In particular, given Egypt's consequential secondary exit exams, family resources may matter more in helping students graduate from secondary school than in their decision to enroll in university. However, it is also possible that family resources matter more in facilitating access to the private sector than the public sector, given expensive tuition in the private sector. The relative role of wealth at each educational transition, and within each university sector, is still not yet well understood in Egypt and is a question this article addresses.

Expansion and Equity of Access

Research on access to education worldwide shows that expansion means greater inclusiveness—essentially, more young people and those from less advantaged backgrounds attend higher education (Trow 2007). Yet the empirical research is quite mixed as to whether expansion actually leads to greater equity of access. A wide body of cross-national research on educational opportunity has found that the effect of parental resources on educational attainment has remained relatively constant across time and across nations, despite massive educational expansion worldwide and varied nation-level educational policies (Shavit and Blossfeld 1993; Torche 2010). For example, Yossi Shavit and Hans-Peter Blossfeld (1993) find that expansion of the higher education system did not reduce relative inequality in educational attainment in 11 of 13 countries studied, although there are examples of expansion both increasing inequality (e.g., Russia) and decreasing inequality (e.g., Sweden).

Expansion of the higher education system exacerbates wealth inequalities if the upper classes are able to use their financial and cultural capital to disproportionately gain access to additional spots in higher education, which occurs when there is unmet demand prior to expansion (i.e., a bottleneck; Gerber and Hout 1995). In contexts where achievement on exit exams is an important factor, parental resources may have a large impact on students' ability to access the next level of schooling if family wealth is used to improve student achievement on exams (Baker and LeTendre 2005).

Indeed, expansion without equity befits the initial years of massification in Egypt. In examining Egypt's higher education policies since independence, Emily Cupito and Ray Langsten (2011) find that Egypt's long-standing policies to expand and democratize access to university have not equalized opportunity to Egyptians from lower class backgrounds. They argue that saturation had not been reached by 2005: "since demand by the wealthy was not saturated in 1988, the wealthiest groups seized the new higher education spaces first. In all likelihood, demand by the advantaged groups remains unsaturated in 2005" (Cupito and Langsten 2011, 194). Yet, their findings are also limited by their data—they cannot control for important factors such as high school track or academic achievement and, as such, cannot examine whether saturation has been reached among those in the academic track.

As the higher education system continues to expand, research suggests a saturation point will be reached. Once all upper-class youth who are interested and able to go to higher education are actually enrolled, the continued expansion of the system means that opportunities for enrollment "trickle down" to more students from lower classes (Raftery and Hout 1993). In a cross-national study of access to higher education over time, Shavit and colleagues (2007) argue that despite the fact that the wealthy may maintain their advantage in other ways, such as advanced credentials, greater inclusiveness is itself an important finding. The authors argue that the continued expansion of higher education ultimately increases access to that level for traditionally excluded youth, which has positive social benefits in and of itself. In Egypt, an important empirical question is whether a saturation point for university has been reached among the upper class since 2005.

Expansion of higher education is often facilitated by private higher education, yet the theoretical literature on the effects of the privatization is inconclusive. Comparative education research consistently finds that the tuition-dependent private higher education sector tends to serve students with lower academic qualifications and those from more advantaged backgrounds, which would suggest that the expansion of private higher education exacerbates inequalities in access (Altbach and Levy 2005; Levy 2006; Shavit et al. 2007). In analyzing the emergence of the private sector in Vietnam, Kimberly Goyette (2012) finds that the latter privileges more affluent students and those from urban centers (Goyette 2012).

Yet Shavit and colleagues (2007) find that the net effects of private funding of higher education on inequality are minimal because privatization is associated with system-wide expansion and diversification of higher education providers. As such, they argue that the tendency of privatization to exacerbate inequalities is counterbalanced by the greater overall inclusiveness. However, their findings are based on static correlations between the percentage of funding for higher education from private sources and the overall levels of inequality in access to higher education in a sample of nations. A limitation to their analysis, which the authors recognize, is that they do not analyze the effects of changing patterns of funding in the same country over time. Despite this limitation, their study makes it clear that national higher education systems that incorporate more private funding tend to be diversified and more inclusive than predominantly publically funded systems. However, it is also clear that greater reliance on private funding could also lead to greater inequality if privatization is not accompanied by greater inclusiveness. In Egypt, it is unclear whether the equalizing trends of massification—which are occurring contemporaneously—outweigh the expected inequalities introduced by expanding privatization. Additionally, their analysis relies on a measure of private funding of higher education, not the extent of private sector higher education; indeed, the growth of cost sharing (i.e., charging tuition) in the public sector may facilitate access to the public sector, independent of the effects in the tuition-dependent private sector. To understand how patterns of access to higher education in Egypt are affected by university sector, I now turn to empirical analyses of access to higher education across sector and cohort.

Data and Methods

Data come from the Survey of Young People in Egypt (SYPE), a nationally representative sample of Egyptian youth 12–29 years old, conducted by the Population Council, in collaboration with the Egyptian Cabinet Information and Decision Support Center. The survey is a multistage stratified cluster sample that drew on the 2006 Population Census to select a representative sample of young people. Data were collected in the first quarter of 2009. The final sample of interviewed households included 11,372 households yielding 15,029 young people ages 10–29 (Population Council 2010, 266). Household and individual weights are used in the analysis to accurately reproduce the structure of the population in the 2006 census.[6]

The population of interest is all surveyed youth ages 21–29. The minimum age is set at 21 to eliminate potential bias, as repetition rates in primary and secondary schooling are high (33.5 percent), and repetition is also negatively correlated with family wealth, meaning youth from poorer backgrounds are more likely to take longer to graduate from high school. For the majority of my analyses, I focus exclusively on university education because 75 percent of all youth in higher education enroll in university (Cupito and Langsten 2011). Additionally, university education is more comparable across sectors than are technical programs. University enrollment is defined as having ever attended university.

Descriptive Variables

Table 46.1 provides the means and number of observations for variables used in later analyses. Of all youth selected to participate in the survey, 6,798 were ages 21–29, and the survey sample is slightly more female than male (53 to 47 percent). Of those who had attended high school, 3,313 graduated (roughly 70 percent of those who attend high school), with 35.9 percent placed in the academic track. In the sample, 1,664 (24.5 percent) young people were either in some form of postsecondary schooling at the time of the survey or had graduated from higher education. Of those enrolled in university, 1,086 studied in public universities, 219 in private universities, and 103 in Al-Azhar.

TABLE 46.1

Descriptive Variables (Total = 6,798)

Variable (Ages 21–29)	Mean	*N*
Demographic characteristics:		
Female	.53	3,625
Age	24.71	6,798
Young cohort (ages 21–25)	.61	4,170
Residency:		
Urban	.34	2,312
Rural	.56	3,785
Unincorporated urban	.10	701
Governate:		
Greater Cairo (other = excluded)	.12	838
Wealth quintiles:		
Q1 (lowest)	.18	1,241
Q2 (second)	.21	1,409
Q3 (middle)	.21	1,452
Q4 (fourth)	.21	1,432
Q5 (highest)	.19	1,264
Secondary school:		
Ever attended secondary school	.69	4,712
Attended academic track	.24	1,458
Attended vocational track	.42	2,563
Graduated from secondary school	.54	3,313
Average secondary exit exam score	74.21	3,057
Postsecondary education:		
Ever enrolled in postsecondary	.25	1,664
Ever attended technical college or institute	.04	240
Ever attended 4-year university	.21	1,424
Public university	.16	1,086
Private university	.03	219
Al-Azhar	.02	103

Of the students in public postsecondary institutions, 87.4 percent were in 4-year programs, while 73.7 percent of students in private institutions were in 4-year programs, reflecting the fact that private institutions are more likely to offer 2-year vocational degrees.

The wealth index is calculated from household characteristics and assets. The specific variables used to construct the wealth index include family members per room (for sleeping arrangements), the materials of the floors, drinking water source, type of toilet facility, presence of a kitchen, type of cooking fuel, electricity, garbage disposal method, and ownership of various household assets and durable goods.[7]

Data Analysis Strategy

Data analysis is guided by the research questions and centers on three major topics: student demographics, factors affecting access to university, and the effects of recent expansion. The analytic focus of each section is whether differences in students' access exist across university sector. First, to understand who goes to higher education in Egypt and how student characteristics vary in Egypt's different higher education sectors, I run summary statistics on the demographic characteristics of students in each sector.

Second, to assess the role of family wealth in determining access to higher education, I carry out linear and logistic regressions to examine the relative effect of various demographic characteristics on Egyptian students' likelihood of making a given educational transition. In particular, I examine when, and to what extent, family resources positively influence students' educational transitions. To test whether these factors differ by sector, I carry out a multinomial logit that uses students in the public university as the baseline.

Third, because my data cover two cohorts of Egyptian youth, those entering higher education before and after the 2005 reforms, I examine changes in demographics across each sector and use binary logistic regression with cohort interaction to visualize how patterns of access to higher education vary by cohort and sector for different wealth quintiles.

Dimensions of Inequality

Four factors are expected to play an important role in shaping access to higher education: student academic achievement, family wealth, gender, and region.

Academic Achievement

Student performance on the *thanawiya amma* determines how numerous and prestigious students' options are for university. Assuming that public universities are still the most desirable options for the vast majority of Egyptians, *thanawiya amma* scores will likely be positively correlated with attending university overall and negatively correlated with the probability of attending a private university.

Family Wealth

Financial resources help students attain higher education, namely (*a*) the wealthy are more likely to attend general academic secondary schools than vocational secondary schools, (*b*) they are able to afford extensive private tutoring in order to score higher on the *thanawiya amma*, and (c) they can afford the direct and indirect costs of higher education (Fahim and Sami 2011). However, if we assume that scores on one's *thanawiya amma* embody the academic and cultural capital a family has devoted to its children's education, then by controlling for scores on the secondary exit exam, we can test whether family financial resources benefit the upper classes directly and how this effect is changing over time and by sector. Given that the private universities charge substantially higher tuitions, we expect that family wealth will be more important in determining access in private universities than in public universities.

Gender

Gender is an important predictor of university enrollment and may influence the choice of university sector. Recent statistics suggest a significant increase in females' access to higher education in Egypt. Fahim and Sami (2011) find that in 2006, university graduation rates are actually higher for females than males and that urban females have equal enrollment rates in higher education. Nonetheless, Cupito and Langesten (2011) find that although women have made substantial gains in access to higher education, they are still 70 percent less likely overall to be in university, holding other demographic variables constant. These statistics are consistent because women are less likely to make it to general high school. Yet, conditional on having attended secondary school, women are more likely than men to graduate from high school and attend public universities, presumably because they perform better on the secondary exit exam.

Nonetheless, researchers have also pointed out that the payoff to education differs by gender. Unemployment rates for Egyptian females are much higher than for males (Population Council 2010).[8] Egyptian women are also more likely to work in lower-status and lower-paid professions than men (Megahed and Lack 2011). Female employees also face discrimination in the private sector, where employers do not want to pay for mandated benefits such as maternity leave (Yousef 2004). If we adopt the perspective of the "economy of the family," whereby families make rational decisions about the payoff to education for their children, then we might expect that families will be less willing to pay expensive tuition at private universities for their daughters than their sons.

However, Carlo Barone (2011) finds that families are not choosing to "invest" differently in their children, but rather, young women may be opting into care professions as opposed to technical ones (Barone 2011). This certainly may be the case in Egypt; Nagwa Megahed (2010) finds that in 2006–7, women made up 72 percent of the humanities, 73 percent of the arts, and 72 percent of education enrollments, but only 28 percent of engineering. Because private universities tend to specialize in technical fields such as business or technology, women may choose not to enroll in them. Importantly, both mechanisms—the economy of the family and gendered preferences for major—suggest that gender differentials will be greater in private universities than in public universities.

Region

Prior research suggests that higher education in Egypt is biased in favor of urban areas and Lower Egypt (i.e., Cairo and surrounding areas). Approximately 70 percent of all Cairo youth enrolled in some form of higher education, while less than 10 percent of youth in Fayoum, Luxor, and Minya are enrolled in higher education (Fahim and Sami 2011). Geographic differences exist because graduation rates from primary and secondary schooling are much lower in rural areas, and, in general, rural Egyptians are still generally poorer and rely more on agricultural economies. Nonetheless, private universities are concentrated in and around Cairo, while public universities tend to be built in urban centers throughout the country. As such, geographic disparities may vary between the two sectors. In the following analyses, I examine how various factors shape young people's access to higher education and whether predictors differ by sector.

Findings

1. Who Goes to University in Egypt, and Do Demographic Characteristics Vary by Sector and Type of Postsecondary Institution?

Table 46.2 presents student demographics, distinguishing among three sectors: public, private, and Al-Azhar. It is clear that there are significant sector differences in student characteristics. Students at Al-Azhar are much more likely to come from rural areas and from lower socioeconomic backgrounds and slightly more likely to be female than those in public schools. Students in private universities exhibit the opposite trends—they are much less likely to be female and more likely to come from urban areas, specifically greater Cairo. The gender gap is quite substantial in private universities—only 38 percent of students in private universities are female, whereas more than 50 percent of students in the other two sectors are female.

TABLE 46.2

Demographics of Students by Sector

	All University	Al-Azhar	Public	Private
Female***	.52	.58	.54	.38
Age (years)***	24.31	24.52	24.42	23.63
Urban***	.53	.20	.53	.69
Rural***	.34	.69	.33	.19
Unincorporated urban	.13	.10	.14	.11
Q1 (lowest)	.03	.12	.03	.01
Q2 (second)	.07	.16	.07	.05
Q3 (middle)	.12	.25	.12	.09
Q4 (fourth)	.24	.31	.24	.20
Q5 (highest)**	.53	.16	.55	.65
Ages 21–25***	.68	.62	.66	.81
Exit exam score (0–100)***	80.37	77.69	82.15	73.02
Vocational high school***	.08	.00	.07	.19
Ever failed or repeated in secondary***	.22	.29	.16	.41
Greater Cairo (Cairo and Giza)***	.25	.05	.22	.48

Note: Public-private mean tests were conducted; null hypothesis is that group means are the same.

*$P < .05$.

**$P < .01$.

***$P < .001$.

There are also significant differences between public and private universities in the top wealth quintile. The top 20 percent of Egyptians make up approximately 55 percent of all youth in public universities and 65 percent of students in private universities. We also note that the mean age of students who studied in private universities is younger, and over 80 percent of youth in the sample who attend private universities are ages 21–25, which reflects the fact that private universities are newer and have only recently grown to be competitive players in the Egyptian higher education system.

Table 46.2 also indicates that students in private universities have lower mean scores on their secondary exit exams (73.0 to 82.15) and are more likely to have ever failed or repeated a grade in secondary school. Students in private universities are also much more likely to have attended vocational education (19 percent to 7 percent for students in public universities).

Given the strong, positive correlation between family wealth and academic achievement worldwide, the finding that Egypt's private universities serve both wealthier and less academically prepared students presents a puzzle. It suggests that private universities may not be a first choice but rather are viewed as a last resort for wealthy families who would prefer to send their children to the free public universities. This finding raises an important question of when and how family resources matter in helping students attend higher education, the question I turn to next.

2. What Student Characteristics Affect Access to Higher Education, and Do Determinants Differ by Sector?

Important predictors of student access to higher education, such as region, family wealth, and educational achievement, tend to co-vary. To isolate which factors facilitate access to higher education in Egypt, I carry out a set of multivariate regressions to predict the likelihood that a student will be enrolled in a given level or sector, given the student made the last transition. The multivariate analyses also allow us to compare how student characteristics matter at each educational stage. Drawing on Mood (2010), I model outcomes with both linear and logistic regressions. Mood (2010) contends that coefficients across logistic models cannot be compared, as the populations vary, and omitted variables affect the results of each model differently, regardless of whether coefficients are standardized or not. She advises using linear regressions when the models could plausibly be linear and the findings do not vary substantially from logistic models. The sign and significance of all variables are the same in both sets of models; I present standardized linear coefficients, which allow for comparison of coefficients across models.

In each model, the dependent variable is an indicator variable, coded 1 if the student (*a*) enrolled in the academic track, as compared to those in vocational, given ever enrolled in school (model 1); (*b*) ever graduated from high school, given enrollment in general secondary (model 2); (*c*) enrolled in a 4-year public university, compared to those who did not, given secondary graduation (model 3); and (*d*) enrolled in a 4-year private university, given secondary graduation (model 4). Table 46.3 presents the results.[9]

Independent variables include gender, wealth quintile, age cohort, urbanicity, high school type, and Cairo governate. Model 1 also includes a control variable for student scores on the nationalized middle school exam, which is used to track students into general or vocational high school. Models 2 and 3 include controls for school type and national exit exam score. Model 2 does not control for exit exam, as high school graduation is largely determined by exit exam score and therefore is collinear with the dependent variable. Greater Cairo and urban are both included

TABLE 46.3

Factors Predicting Eligibility and Access to Higher Education

	Model 1	**Model 2**	**Model 3**	**Model 4**
	Academic Track (if Ever School)	**HS Graduate (if General)**	**Public University (if HS Grad.)**	**Private University (if HS Grad.)**
Female	−.030**	.165***	−.001	−.071***
	(.010)	(.012)	(.011)	(.008)
Family wealth index	.228***	.203***	.071***	.084***
	(.004)	(.005)	(.005)	(.003)
Young cohort	.047***	.005	−.011	.085***
	(.010)	(.012)	(.011)	(.008)
Urban	.002	.005	.032*	.029
	(.012)	(.014)	(.013)	(.009)
Greater Cairo	.006	.004	−.036*	.169***
	(.016)	(.017)	(.020)	(.018)
Middle school exam score	.368***			
	(.001)			
Secondary exit exam score			.221***	−.194***
			(.001)	(.001)
Vocational high school			−.606***	−.157***
			(.016)	(.010)
Observations	5,359	4,103	3,311	3,311

Note: Coefficients are standardized. Models include an indicator variable for missing exit exam score data to control for nonrandom missing data. HS = high school. Standard errors are shown in parentheses.

*$P < .05$.

**$P < .01$.

***$P < .001$.

in the models, as they represent different phenomena. Roughly 9 percent of students in greater Cairo can live in the unincorporated parts of town (i.e., slums) and are not considered urban, while two thirds (67 percent) of Egyptian students living in urban centers are in cities other than Cairo. Therefore, both variables are included to capture the trends of urbanicity and geographical distribution around Cairo, separately.[10]

Table 46.3 indicates that certain student characteristics predict enrollment better at different stages of a student's education. Controlling for other factors, females are less likely than males to be enrolled in the academic track of high school. However, once enrolled, they are more likely to graduate from high school—most likely because they tend to perform better than their male counterparts on the *thanawiya amma*. At the university level, of all those who graduated from high school, females are less likely than males to enroll in private universities but not less likely to enroll in public universities.

Model 3 also shows that while being from an urban area generally increases the likelihood of enrollment in a public university, being from Cairo does not. In contrast, students in the private universities are much more likely to be from Cairo but not other urban areas in Egypt. This makes sense, as private universities are highly concentrated in greater Cairo, while Egypt's public universities are located in major urban areas throughout the country.

Family wealth is a statistically significant predictor of enrollment in each model. Of the specific transitions examined, results indicate that family wealth has a larger impact on helping students enroll in the general track and graduate from high school than determining which higher education sector they attend, suggesting that family resources matter more in determining eligibility for university than in determining university sector, by helping young people enroll in, and graduate from, the academic track of secondary schooling.

Models 3 and 4 also suggest that family resources may be a more significant predictor of enrollment in the private sector than the public sector, as the coefficient is quantitatively larger in model 3 than model 4. To test whether certain factors independently facilitate enrollment in the private sector more than in the public sector, and whether these differences are statistically significant, I run a multinomial logit model with public university enrollment as the base category. A multinomial model is the preferred technique because after graduation, students have many choices, including no postsecondary, a two-year vocational degree, the public university sector, private university sector, and Al-Azhar. Public university students are the baseline because the focus of interest is on whether student characteristics in public and private universities differ. Table 46.4 presents the results, comparing relative risk ratios of students in private universities and Al-Azhar to the baseline of students in the public sector.[11]

Table 46.4 indicates that a one-unit increase in wealth quintile increases the likelihood of enrollment in the private sector by roughly 33 percent more than the same increase in wealth brings in the public sector. And being from greater Cairo or from the younger cohort increases the likelihood of enrollment in the private sector more than twice as much as they impact enrollment in the public sector. Conversely, an increase in exit exam score has a weaker impact on enrollment in the private sector than the same increase would have on enrollment in the public sector. These findings suggest that while increases in wealth may facilitate access to the private sector slightly more than in the public sector, being from Cairo and of the younger cohort have a much stronger impact on enrollment in the private sector than they do on the public sector enrollment. In contrast, as is consistent with other findings, academic achievement is a larger predictor of enrollment in the public sector than in the private sector. Generally, these findings suggest that the factors that determine enrollment in private universities encompass both ability to pay and, perhaps more significantly, the ability to access private universities. In contrast, academic achievement remains a more significant factor in determining access in the public sector than in the private sector.

3. Have the 2005 Reforms Altered Patterns of Access to Higher Education, and Do Trends Differ by University Sector?

The percentage of young people attending higher education in Egypt is increasing. Among the younger cohort, 26.8 percent of Egyptian youth are attending some form of postsecondary schooling, up from 20.8 percent in the older cohort, and 23.2 percent of Egyptian youth are now enrolled

TABLE 46.4

Relative Risk Ratios from Multinomial Logistic Regression Predicting Postsecondary Choice (Public = Base)

	No Postsecondary	Vocational Degree	Private University	Al-Azhar
Female	1.608**	1.192	.571***	1.401
	(.275)	(.213)	(.094)	(.309)
Family wealth index	.560***	.849	1.322**	.622***
	(.044)	(.071)	(.133)	(.058)
Young cohort	.737	.919	2.358***	.737
	(.129)	(.167)	(.456)	(.166)
Urban	.541**	.681	1.110	.578
	(.109)	(.144)	(.239)	(.165)
Greater Cairo	.685	1.012	2.750***	.436
	(.162)	(.255)	(.544)	(.220)
Vocational high school	519.684***	24.411***	2.980***	.135*
	(118.981)	(4.961)	(.679)	(.137)
Exit exam score	.936***	.869***	.913***	.965**
	(.011)	(.010)	(.008)	(.011)
Constant	44.279***	6,572.751***	28.547***	13.785**
	(41.944)	(5,767.882)	(21.157)	(13.163)

Note: Models include an indicator variable for missing exit exam score data to control for nonrandom missing data. Standard errors are shown in parentheses.

*$P < .05$.

**$P < .01$.

***$P < .001$.

in a 4-year degree program, up from 17.4 percent. In this section, I investigate how recent expansion is affecting patterns of access. For this analysis, youth are grouped into two separate cohorts—21–25-year-olds, who came of university age after the 2005 reforms, and an older cohort of 26–29-year-olds, who graduated from high school before the implementation of the 2005 reforms.

Access to university is increasing across nearly all subgroups of demographics. Females have been one of the main beneficiaries of university expansion overall, with a 6 percent overall growth rate across cohorts. In the public sector, growth rates are quantitatively largest among students from unincorporated urban areas (0.08) and females (0.04), as well as the third and fourth wealth quintiles (0.04 and 0.06, respectively). This growth represents only a few percentage points more than growth among the top quintile (0.03), but we also find that access to higher education among the lowest quintile of Egyptians is equal to that of the wealthiest Egyptians (0.03 for both). Thus, expansion in the public sector is not exacerbating inequality between the top and bottom quintiles and does seem to be reducing the advantage of the wealthiest quintile to a small extent, as the middle and upper-middle classes catch up slightly. This contrasts with the patterns of growth in the private sector, where growth rates are much faster for urban youth (0.05), the wealthiest quintile (0.08), and particularly among youth from the wealthiest quintile with exit exam scores less than 65 (0.19). There has been no real increase in access to private universities among the poorest 40 percent of Egyptians, which suggests that private sector expansion is not benefiting the lower classes at all.

To understand how patterns of access are changing in the public and private sectors, we can predict the probability of students' enrollments in both public and private universities as these probabilities vary across quintiles of wealth.[12] We can then graph the likelihood that students from particular demographic groups would be enrolled in public or private universities. The goal of this procedure (shown in Fig. 46.1) is to understand how these likelihoods change across gender, wealth, and age groups. Figure 46.1*a* shows the predicted probability that a student will attend a public university, estimated at the mean academic achievement for all students (even though students attending public universities have scores higher than the mean). Similarly, Figure 46.1*b* shows the predicted probability of enrollment in the private sector by cohort and gender, also supposing achievement at the mean (even though students attending private universities have lower than average exit exam scores). Taken together, Figures 46.1*a* and 46.1*b* illustrate the changing likelihood of access to Egyptian universities across cohorts, by gender and sector.

Figure 46.1*a* shows the changing likelihood of enrollment in public universities, holding all students at the mean level of academic achievement (roughly 75 on the *thanawiya amma*). By comparing the probabilities of enrollment in the younger cohort to the older cohort, we see that expansion for both men and women is occurring more rapidly at the lower wealth quintiles than at the upper quintiles, where there seems to be some convergence. By contrast, at the upper wealth quintiles there seems to have been a "ceiling effect," a saturation of demand of eligible youth in public universities. Moreover, in looking at the role of wealth on likelihood of enrollment, we see that the relationship for younger males is weaker than older males, although still positive. This suggests that, for males, wealth may be a less important predictor of enrollment in the public sector among the youngest cohort. This shift could reflect many possible processes, including a saturation of demand among young wealthy males or declining preference for the public sector among the wealthy; this is an area in need of further research. In comparing men and women, it is also important to note that among youth from the wealthiest quintile, females in the younger cohort have a greater probability of enrolling in public universities than their male counterparts.

Figure 46.1*b* shows the predicted probabilities of enrollment in the private sector. This figure indicates that enrollment in the private sector is increasing substantially; growth is faster in the private sector than in the public sector. However, growth in the private sector is largest for the top wealth quintiles, while likelihood of enrollment has expanded much less among youth from the lowest two quintiles. This suggests that there has not been a saturation of demand or ceiling effect for the private sector and that the wealthiest quintiles are those most likely to benefit from recent expansion.

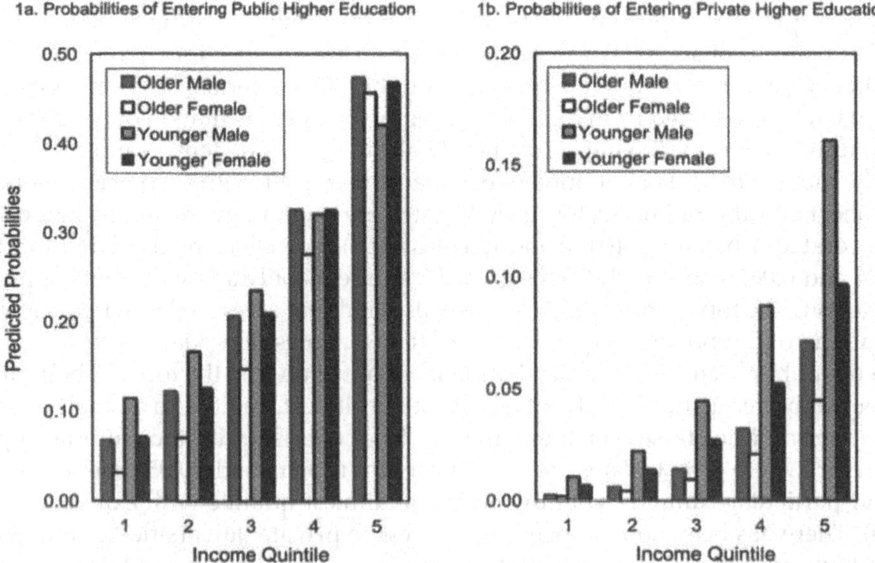

Figure 46.1 Probabilities of studying in a public and private university, by cohort, gender, and quintile of wealth.

Note: Predicted probability of enrollment at each wealth quintile, by gender and cohort, predicted at means academic achievement, controlling for urban and Cairo region.

Additionally, in comparing men and women, we note that access to private universities has increased most rapidly for males, and the gap between male and female enrollment in private universities is actually wider in the younger cohort than in the older cohort. This suggests that socioeconomic and gender inequalities in access to the private sector are actually exac in the younger cohort of Egyptians.

Discussion

Data analyses demonstrate that recent higher education policies in Egypt are contributing to an expansion of the higher education system, which is allowing a greater proportion of Egyptian students to attend university. Expansion in the public sector is benefiting some traditionally underrepresented groups, including females and some from the lower-middle classes, albeit to a small extent. While scholars have long argued that Egypt's admissions processes benefit the wealthy, recent growth rates in public sector universities are highest for youth from the third and fourth wealth quintiles, indicating a trickling down of access to those in lower quintiles. This finding is supported by Figure 46.1*b*, depicting a flattening of the role of wealth in facilitating access for males and an increase in females' access at all wealth quintiles. Together, these analyses suggest that continued expansion of the public sector will lead to greater inclusiveness, which likely means the continued trickling down of access to lower wealth quintiles.

However, despite the overall expansion of access to higher education, it is also clear that the poorest Egyptians are still much less likely to attend university than their peers, and, as such, even the equalizing tendencies found here do not represent an "equalization" of opportunity across wealth quintiles. Importantly, the source of inequalities seems to differ by sector. Academic achievement—and the ability of the upper classes to ensure their children enroll in the academic high school track and achieve higher scores on the secondary exam—seems to be the major source perpetuating inequalities in the public sector. In contrast, privatization is associated with an exacerbation of family wealth and geographical location in determining access. In particular, analyses suggest that the private sector may be serving a niche clientele—wealthy families whose children do not score high enough to enroll in their desired major in the public sector, particularly those concentrated primarily in Cairo.

Nonetheless, the role of family resources in predicting access is nuanced. The effect of family wealth is quantitatively largest as a predictor of high school type and likelihood of graduation. This finding is interpreted in light of substantial prior research on the role of private tutoring in Egypt. Although Tables 46.1 and 46.4 indicate that wealthy students are more likely to be found in private universities, Table 46.3 shows that family wealth is a more significant determinant of university eligibility than university sector. The ability of wealthy families to enroll in academic high schools and then achieve higher scores on the *thanawiya amma* maintains their advantage in the public sector. This suggests that family wealth plays a large role in students' early lives, by ensuring academic success at lower levels of schooling, which allows them to gain admission to the public sector. In contrast, the relationship between family wealth and enrollment in the private sector is the direct result of the ability to pay tuition fees and access campuses.

Findings also suggest that females are much less likely to attend private universities both before and after controlling for the fact that females tend to perform better on the exit exam overall. This finding could indicate an economic decision on the part of the family but could also suggest that female students are simply less interested in attending private universities, either because of their generally inferior reputations or their more limited selection of majors. More qualitative research on those factors that shape females' decisions about higher education is needed to parse out discrimination from preferences.

The analyses also raise many questions about the nature of inequality in Egyptian higher education and suggest important avenues for future research. Despite overall expansion, prior research on educational equity suggests that expansion of undergraduate higher education may actually worsen other inequalities, an outcome this analysis does not rule out (Lucas 2001). We may predict increasing inequalities in the postgraduate sector, as well as the potential for even greater concentration of the wealthy among elite universities, or in highly competitive career tracks, such as medicine. Currently, the findings suggest that the public sector still attracts the highest academic achievers, which may allay concerns, at least for the time being, that private universities are cream skimming the best students from public universities. However, this may change with time. Many private universities offer degrees targeted to the workforce and tend to offer better learning environments and resources to students; in contrast, there is widespread criticism of overcrowding at public universities, which some have called "unmanageable," and their facilities are generally found lacking (Lindsey 2012).[13] As such, future research must investigate the relative prestige of each sector and preferences of Egyptian youth and families in determining a higher education sector. Similarly, defining and understanding dimensions of quality in higher education will be an important area for future research.

Finally, the analyses suggest that the public and private sectors are experiencing countervailing trends. The real question is whether expansion in the public sector can actually occur without an accompanying private sector. Shavit et al. (2007) find that increased private funding of higher education is associated cross-nationally with larger and more expansive higher education systems. Private financing for higher education could hypothetically be increased in the public sector through increases in tuition fees. Although Egypt has begun to implement a variety of cost-sharing programs within the public sector, the fees are still relatively small. Moreover, higher education policies in Egypt are highly politicized, and charging higher tuition rates in the public sector remains controversial and is unlikely to be embraced politically in the foreseeable future (Lindsey 2012). Nonetheless, the findings from this study do indicate that, assuming a goal of greater equity, increasing public sector fees would be a preferable option to expanding the private university sector, particularly if tuition fees could be progressive in nature and graduated according to family wealth.

Conclusion

This article argues that access to higher education in contemporary Egypt is occurring within two separate sectors, founded on two distinct logics, and, as such, analyses of access should be disaggregated by sector. Although access to public universities is highly unequal and strongly biased in favor of urban and wealthy youth, its underlying logic of meritocracy is apparent in recent trends in access—females, rural students, and the upper-middle classes are gaining access to higher education at higher rates than the urban and very wealthy. Academic achievement is the main predictor of access in the public sector. In contrast, private universities are governed by the logic of private resources and individual preferences, which has tended to exacerbate inequalities in access.

Notes

1. This article recognizes that the definitions of "public" and "private" are far from agreed upon and that public regulation and tax incentives make a clear separation between public and private sectors impossible (see Levy 2006; Johnstone and Marcucci 2010). For the purposes of this article, the focus is on funding. Private universities henceforth refer to those universities not funded by the state; in Egypt this includes both for-profit and nonprofit universities.
2. According to the 2006 census, the unemployment rate for all women was 25 percent, which is substantially higher than that of the labor force as a whole (9.3 percent; Hamid 2010).
3. Altbach and Levy (2005), Torche (2005), Levy (2006), Goyette (2012).
4. Rugh (2002), Abi-Mershed (2010), Donn and Manthri (2010), El-Araby (2011).
5. Tuition at these programs varies. Nahla El Sebai (2006) reports that fees are approximately US$280 as annual tuition for a degree program in business that uses English as a medium of instruction, and a one-time admission fee of US$100 for programs in law, commerce, and the arts.
6. See Population Council (2010) for more details on the SYPE sampling frame and methodology.
7. The wealth index included in the SYPE data set provides little documentation; therefore, I carry out my own factor analysis to replicate the SYPE wealth index. A Kaiser-Meyer-Olkin (KMO) test of sampling adequacy was used to validate the factor analysis; the KMO statistic was 0.785. Any KMO statistic above 0.5 can be considered appropriate for factor analysis, although the higher the value, the more reliable it is (Ferguson and Cox 1993). The constructed index was highly correlated with the wealth index provided by SYPE (0.98) and with wealth index quintiles (0.96).

8. Findings from the SYPE indicate that average male youth unemployment is 12.6 percent, while female unemployment is 31.7 percent (Population Council 2010).
9. A one-unit change in the standard deviation of the independent variable is associated with *B* change in the standard deviation of the dependent variable, adjusted for the effects of the other variables.
10. The two variables have a correlation of 0.45.
11. For a one-unit change in the independent variables (e.g., gender, urban) the relative risk ratio of the given postsecondary choice, relative to public sector enrollment, is expected to change by *B*, given that other variables are held constant. A coefficient of one means that a change in the independent variable has the same anticipated effect in the public sector as in the target sector. Coefficients greater than one suggest that a change in independent variable increases has a stronger effect on enrollment in the target sector than in the public sector.
12. The focus of this analysis is on changing patterns of access, by cohort, so I do not include the regression estimates in this text.
13. For an overview of postrevolution issues in Egyptian higher education, see Lindsey (2012).

References

Abi-Mershed, Osama. 2010. "Introduction, the Politics of Arab Educational Reforms." In *Trajectories of Education in the Arab World*, ed. O. Abi-Mershed. New York: Routledge.

Al-Ahram Weekly. 2001. "Crunching the Numbers, Minister of Higher Education Mufid Shehab Talks to Al-Ahram Weekly about Making the Most of a Flawed System." *Al-Ahram Weekly*, August 9–15, 2001.

Al-Momani, Mohammad. 2011. "The Arab Youth Quake: Implications on Democratization and Stability." *Middle East Law and Governance* 3 (1–2): 159–70.

Altbach, Philip, and Daniel Levy. 2005. *Private Higher Education: A Global Revolution*. Rotterdam: Sense.

Anderson, Lisa. 2011. "Demystifying the Arab Spring." *Foreign Affairs* 90 (3): 2–7.

Arabsheibani, Gholamreza. 1988. "Educational Choice and Achievement: The Case of Secondary Schools in the Arab Republic of Egypt." *Higher Education* 17 (6): 37–46.

Baker, David, and Gerald LeTendre. 2005.National Differences, *Global Similarities: World Culture and the Future of Schooling*. Stanford, CA: Stanford University Press.

Barone, Carlo. 2011. "Some Things Never Change." *Sociology of Education* 84 (2): 157.

Bray, Mark, and Iveta Silova. 2006. "The Private Tutoring Phenomena: International Patterns and Perspectives." In *Education in a Hidden Marketplace: Monitoring of Private Tutoring*, ed. I. Silova, V. Budiene, and M. Bray. New York: Open Society Institute.

Buchmann, Claudia, and Emily Hannum. 2001. "Education and Stratification in Developing Countries: A Review of Theories and Research." *Annual Review of Sociology* 27 (2001): 77–102.

CAPMAS. 2011. *Education Indicators*. Central Agency for Public Mobilization and Statistics. http://www.capmas.gov.eg/pages_ar.aspx?pageidp1033.

Cupito, Emily, and Ray Langsten. 2011. "Inclusiveness in Higher Education in Egypt." *Higher Education* 62 (2): 1–15.

Dhillon, Navtej, and Tarik Yousef. 2009. *Generation in Waiting*. Washington, DC: Brookings Institution Press.

Donn, Gary, and Yahya Al Manthri. 2010. *Globalisation and Higher Education in the Arab Gulf States*. Oxford: Symposium.

El-Araby, Ashraf. 2011. "A Comparative Assessment of Higher Education Financing in Six Arab Countries." *Prospects* 41 (1): 9–21.

Elbadawy, Asmaa, Dennice Ahlburg, and Deborah Levison. 2009. *Private and Group Tutoring in Egypt: Where Is the Gender Inequality?* Washington, DC: Population Council. http://www.popcouncil.org/pdfs/2009IUSSP_posters/Elbadawy1.pdf.

Elbadawy, Asmaa, Ragui Assaad, Dennice Ahlburg, and Deborah Levison. 2007. "Private and Group Tutoring in Egypt: Where Is the Gender Inequality?" Working Paper series, Economic Research Forum, Cairo.

El Sebai, Nahla. 2006. "The Egyptian Higher Education System: Towards Better Quality in the Future." *Journal of Futures Studies* 11 (2): 75–92.

Fahim, Yasmine, and Noha Sami. 2011. "Adequacy, Efficiency and Equity of Higher Education Financing: The Case of Egypt." *Prospects* 41 (1): 47–67.

Farag, Iman. 2000. "Higher Education in Egypt: The Realpolitik of Privatization." *International Higher Education* 18 (Winter): 16–17.

Ferguson, Eamonn, and Tom Cox. 1993. "Exploratory Factor Analysis: A User's Guide." *International Journal of Selection and Assessment* 1 (2): 84–94.

Galal, Ahmed. 2002. "The Paradox of Education and Unemployment in Egypt." Report, Egyptian Center for Economic Studies, Cairo.

Gerber, Theodore, and Michael Hout. 1995. "Educational Stratification in Russia during the Soviet Period." *American Journal of Sociology* 101 (3): 611–60.

Goyette, Kimberly. 2012. "Stratification and the Emergence of the Postsecondary Private Education Sector in Vietnam." *Comparative Education Review* 56 (2): 197–222.

Hamid, Galal Abdel. 2010. "Higher Education in Egypt Country Review Report." Ministry of Higher Education Strategic Planning Unit, Cairo. http://s3.amazonaws.com/zanran_storage/mhe-spu.org/ContentPages/2473387763.pdf.

Hargreaves, Eleanore. 1997. "The Diploma Disease in Egypt: Learning, Teaching and the Monster of the Secondary Leaving Certificate." *Assessment in Education* 4 (1): 161–76.

Hartmann, Sarah. 2007. "The Informal Market of Education in Egypt: Private Tutoring and Its Implications." In *Youth, Gender and the City: Social Anthropological Explorations in Cairo*, ed. Thomas Hüsken. Mainz: Institut für Ethnologie und Afrikastudien, Johannes Gutenberg-Universität.

Helal, Hany. 2007. "Strategic Planning in Higher Education." Report, Egyptian Ministry of Higher Education. http://cairo.daad.de/imperia/md/content/kairo/tempus/saad_sharaf_higher_education_enhancement_strategy_in_egypt.pdf.

Helms, Robin. 2008. "University Admission Worldwide." In *Education Working Paper Series Number 15*. Washington, DC: World Bank Institute.

Howard-Merriam, Kathleen. 1979. "Women, Education, and the Professions in Egypt." *Comparative Education Review* 23 (2): 256–70.

ICHEFP (International Comparative Higher Education and Finance Project). 2011. "Higher Education Finance and Cost-Sharing in Egypt." International Comparative Higher Education and Finance Project. http://gse.buffalo.edu/org/inthigheredfinance/files/Country_Profiles/Africa/Egypt.pdf.

Johnstone, D. Bruce, and Pamela Marcucci. 2010. *Financing Higher Education Worldwide: Who Pays? Who Should Pay?* Baltimore: Johns Hopkins University Press.

Kuan, Ping-Yin. 2011. "Effects of Cram Schooling on Mathematics Performance: Evidence from Junior High Students in Taiwan." *Comparative Education Review* 55 (3): 342–68.

Labaki, Boutros, ed. 2009. *Enseignement supérieur et marché du travail dans le monde Arabe* [Higher education and the labor market in the Arab world]. Beirut: Institut Français du Proche-Orient.

Levy, Daniel. 2006. "The Unanticipated Explosion: Private Higher Education's Global Surge." *Comparative Education Review* 50 (2): 217–40.

Lindsey, Ursala. 2012. "Higher-Education Reform Stalls amid Egypt's Turmoil." *Chronicle of Higher Education*, June 19. http://chronicle.com/article/article-content/132405/.

Lucas, Samuel. 2001. "Effectively Maintained Inequality: Education Transitions, Track Mobility, and Social Background Effects." *American Journal of Sociology* 106 (6): 1642–90.

Mahmoud, Mohammed. 2010. "Low Exam Scores Force Egyptian Students to Give Up Dream of Enrolling at Top Colleges." *Al-Shorfa*, July 9.

Mare, Robert. 1981. "Change and Stability in Educational Stratification." *American Sociological Review* 46 (February): 72–87.

Mazawi, André Elias. 2010. "Naming the Imaginary." In *Trajectories of Education in the Arab World: Legacies and Challenges*, ed. O. Abi-Mershed. New York: Routledge.

Megahed, Nagwa. 2010. "Access to the University and Women's Participation in Higher Education in Egypt." In *Viewpoints Special Edition, Higher Education, and the Middle East: Empowering Under-served and Vulnerable Population*. Washington, DC: Middle East Institute. http://www.mei.edu/sites/default/files/publications/EducationVPVol.II_.pdf.

Megahed, Nagwa, and Stephen Lack. 2011. "Colonial Legacy, Women's Rights, and Gender-Educational Inequality in the Arab World with Particular Reference to Egypt and Tunisia." *International Review of Education* 57 (3–4): 397–418.

Mood, Carina. 2010. "Logistic Regression: Why We Cannot Do What We Think We Can Do, and What We Can Do about It." *European Sociological Review* 26 (1): 67–82.

Pfeffer, Fabian. 2008. "Persistent Inequality in Educational Attainment and Its Institutional Context." *European Sociological Review* 24 (5): 543–65.

Population Council. 2010. *Survey of Young People in Egypt*. Cairo: Population Council.

Raftery, Adrian, and Michael Hout. 1993. "Maximally Maintained Inequality: Expansion, Reform, and Opportunity in Irish Education, 1921–1975." *Sociology of Education* 66 (January): 41–62.

Rugh, William. 2002. "Arab Education: Tradition, Growth, and Reform." *Middle East Journal* 56 (3): 396–414.

Sanyal, Bikas. 1998. "Diversification of Sources and the Role of Privatization in Financing of Higher Education in the Arab States Region." Report, UNESCO International Institute for Education Planning, Paris.

Shavit, Yossi, Richard Arum, and Adam Gamoran. 2007. *Stratification in Higher Education: A Comparative Study*. Stanford, CA: Stanford University Press.

Shavit, Yossi, and Hans-Peter Blossfeld. 1993. *Persistent Inequality: Changing Educational Attainment in Thirteen Countries*. Social Inequality Series. Boulder, CO: Westview.

Sobhy, Hania. 2012. "The De-Facto Privatization of Secondary Education in Egypt: A Study of Private Tutoring in Technical and General Schools." *Compare: A Journal of Comparative and International Education* 42 (1): 47–67.

Torche, Florencia. 2005. "Privatization Reform and Inequality of Educational Opportunity: The Case of Chile." *Sociology of Education* 78 (4): 316–43.

Torche, Florencia. 2010. "Economic Crisis and Inequality of Educational Opportunity in Latin America." *Sociology of Education* 83 (2): 85–110.

Trow, Martin. 1973. *Problems in the Transition from Elite to Mass Higher Education*. Berkeley, CA: McGraw-Hill.

Trow, Martin. 2007. "Reflections on the Transition from Elite to Mass to Universal Access: Forms and Phases of Higher Education in Modern Societies since WWII." In *International Handbook of Higher Education*, ed. J. J. F. Forest and P. G. Altbach. Dordrecht: Springer.

Valverde, Gilbert. 2005. "Curriculum Policy Seen through High-Stakes Examinations: Mathematics and Biology in a Selection of School-Leaving Examinations from the Middle East and North Africa." *Peabody Journal of Education* 80 (1): 29–55.

World Bank. 2010. *Higher Education in Egypt*. Washington, DC: World Bank. http://siteresources.worldbank.org/INTEGYPT/Resources/REPORTHigherEducationinEgypt-2010FINAL-ENGLISH.pdf.

World Bank and UNESCO. 2000. *Higher Education in Developing Countries: Peril and Promise*. Washington, DC: World Bank Institute.

Yousef, Tarik. 2004. "Development, Growth, and Policy Reform in the Middle East and North Africa since 1950." *Journal of Economic Perspectives* 18 (3): 91–115.

CHAPTER 47

FINANCING SCHEMES FOR HIGHER EDUCATION

ELENA DEL REY AND MARÍA RACIONERO

Most industrial countries have traditionally subsidized the provision of higher education. Alternative financing schemes, which rely on larger contributions from students, are being increasingly adopted. Those based on income-contingent loans provide insurance against uncertain educational outcomes. We consider a unified framework where we analyze the following schemes: 1) the traditional tax-subsidy, 2) pure loans, 3) income-contingent loans with risk-sharing, and 4) income-contingent loans with risk-pooling. We focus on their insurance role and their effect on higher education participation. We show that an income-contingent loan with risk-pooling can induce the optimal level of participation provided that it covers both financial costs of education and forgone earnings.

1. Introduction

Most industrial countries have traditionally subsidized the provision of higher education. However, alternative financing schemes, which rely on larger contributions from students, are being increasingly adopted. The problem of cost-sharing with students is that some of them may be unable to contribute and, even if loans are made available to overcome their liquidity constraints, education is often viewed as a risky investment, which can further hinder participation. Funding schemes that rely on income-contingent loans (hereafter ICLs), like the Australian Higher Education Contribution Scheme or the funding arrangements resulting from recent reforms in the UK, provide insurance against uncertain educational outcomes. This paper analyzes several financing schemes for higher education, with particular emphasis on their insurance role and their effect on higher education participation.

Using the terminology from Chapman (2006), we consider the following schemes: 1) the traditional tax-subsidy system—where the cost of education is financed by general taxes, 2) pure loans—where each student pays for her own education, 3) ICLs with risk-sharing—where successful graduates pay the full cost of their education but the cost of the education of unsuccessful students is financed by general taxes and is, hence, shared by the whole population (including unsuccessful students themselves, a fact that is often forgotten when ICLs of this type are evaluated), and 4) ICLs with risk-pooling—where successful students pay the full cost of the education of their cohort. These schemes differ in the way educational costs and risks are shared among the population, but there is a clear link between costs and finance determined by the budget, which is always balanced.

Our paper builds on García-Peñalosa and Wälde (2000). In a model without uncertainty and with endogenous wages, they show that the traditional tax-subsidy scheme cannot simultaneously yield equity and efficiency. Then they consider an alternative setting with uncertainty and exogenous wages and analyze three alternative financial schemes, which they call pure loans, ICLs, and graduate taxes, but that correspond, in our terminology, to pure loans, ICLs with risk-sharing, and ICLs with risk-pooling, respectively.[1] García-Peñalosa and Wälde (2000) show that, when education outcomes are uncertain, and the degree of risk aversion is large enough, ICLs with risk-pooling are better than both pure loans, because they provide greater insurance, and ICLs with risk-sharing, because they do not involve any redistribution from non-students to students.

Our model departs from García-Peñalosa and Wälde's (2000) in several aspects. First, we consider a unified framework, where the investment in higher education is uncertain and wages are exogenously given, to analyze and compare, in efficiency terms, the aforementioned financing schemes for higher education, including the traditional tax-subsidy system. Second, in our model individuals differ in ability to accumulate human capital rather than inheritance. When individuals differ in inheritance, the social optimum implies that either none or all should study. When individuals differ in ability, we are able to compute an optimum threshold ability level (i.e. an optimal level of participation in higher education) and we can then analyze inefficiencies that may result in insufficient or excessive participation.

Like García-Peñalosa and Wälde (2000), we do not consider externalities. We also abstract from redistributional issues in order to focus exclusively on efficiency. We understand that externalities and redistributional considerations may be important in educational policy, and often provide a rationale for government intervention, particularly in primary and secondary education. We choose to ignore those in the present framework because the main purpose of this paper is to highlight the insurance role of the alternative higher education financing schemes, and characterize the nature of government intervention in the absence of externalities and redistributional considerations.

We show that when individuals are risk averse none of the schemes considered leads unambiguously to the optimal level of participation. As in García-Peñalosa and Wälde (2000) we find that the system that provides the largest insurance—i.e. the ICL with risk-pooling—is likely to yield higher participation when risk aversion is sufficiently large. However, participation remains inefficiently low. We propose an alternative financing scheme that, by fully insuring the lowest ability individual who should enroll in higher education, induces optimal participation. We show that this scheme is equivalent to an ICL with risk-pooling that covers both financial costs of education and forgone earnings.

There is some reticence to accept risk-pooling schemes in higher education finance. According to Johnstone (2005), "the weakness in the cohort mutualization concept has been the difficulty of demonstrating why the shortfalls from low earners, which admittedly have to be made up somehow, should have to be made up not just by high earners—which would be not unlike any other scheme of income redistribution—but by that particular class of high earners *who also had to borrow to finance their education.*"[2] In our framework, optimal participation can be achieved if it is precisely *that particular class of high earners* that pays and, as long as all students face the same probability of failure, it is not necessary to compel them to do so. Students are risk averse and they are willing to pay more than the cost of their education if successful in exchange of the assurance that their incomes do not fall below a certain level if unsuccessful. The scheme has the additional advantage that no general taxation is used to finance higher education.

In the main part of the paper we do assume that the probability of success is the same for all individuals. The expected contribution to the cost of education is then the same for all those who opt to study. We later explore the consequences of letting the probability of success depend positively on ability. The main difference is that, for the risk-pooling ICL, higher ability students expect to pay more, and lower ability students expect to pay less, than the student with the average probability of success. Students with relatively high ability would be willing to opt out of such a scheme. However, in order to do so, they would need access to alternative means of finance, such as personal wealth and/or pure loans. We do not allow the individual to switch from a scheme to another, and focus instead on the resulting participation (and how it compares with the optimal participation) when all individuals face the same scheme. We neither consider wealth heterogeneity, which is explored in detail in García-Peñalosa and Wälde (2000). The presence of personal wealth would allow some high ability students to opt out from the risk-pooling ICL. This type of adverse selection can be prevented if the scheme is made mandatory (i.e. a graduate tax with a balanced budget). Yet the fact that lower ability students end up paying relatively less, due to the cross-subsidization from higher ability students, has additional implications for participation. In particular, the risk-pooling ICL that covers the cost of education and forgone earnings now yields excessive participation. Optimal participation for such a scheme can be achieved by appropriately adjusting the repayment schedule.

ICLs that cover financial costs of education and provide students with a stipend for living costs are used in New Zealand since 1992, and are seriously considered in Australia. In Sweden, education is provided free of charge but students may receive grants and loans for their living expenses, where loans are repaid, with interest, in an income-contingent fashion. However, neither of these schemes, nor the ICLs used in Australia, UK and some developing countries to cover the financial costs of education, is of the risk-pooling type. To the best of our knowledge, only Hungary uses an ICL of the risk-pooling type. It does so since 2001 and it allows to partially fund living expenses.

The paper is organized as follows. We first present the model and describe each financing scheme in Section 2. In Section 3 we analyze participation in the benchmark case of risk neutrality. In Section 4 we consider risk aversion and its effect on participation. We also identify the insurance and subsidy components of the different schemes. In Section 5 we analyze optimal participation when individuals are risk averse, show that none of the schemes considered yields unambiguously the optimal participation, and propose alternatives that do so. We discuss the implications of allowing the probability of success to depend on ability in Section 6. We conclude in Section 7.

2. The Model

We consider a very simple economy in which a continuum of individuals of mass N live for 2 periods. Individuals differ in their ability $a \in [\underline{a}, \overline{a}]$, distributed according to the density function $f(a)$. In the first period they can either work for a low-skill wage or study. Education is tuition free or fully subsidized in the first period. E is the per capita cost of education (i.e. the size of the subsidy). Individuals who study forgo the low-skill wage.

In the second period all individuals work and some of them (maybe all) contribute to finance the education of their cohort. Nonstudents continue to receive the low-skill wage whereas students face uncertain educational outcomes. The uncertainty associated with the investment in higher education could in principle take different forms: a student might not be employed as a high-skill worker once graduated, or she might not graduate; this could depend on effort, ability, requirements of course undertaken, etc. As García-Peñalosa and Wälde (2000), we focus on the simplest form of uncertainty: an individual who invests in education is lucky with probability $p \in (0, 1)$. Successful graduates earn a high-skill wage which, in our framework, depends on their ability a, $w_H(a)$, whereas unsuccessful students earn the low-skill wage, w_L. Wages are assumed to be exogenously given, with $w_H(a) > w_L$ for all a.

The government subsidizes education and raises the necessary revenue in a manner that differs according to the financing scheme. A potentially different amount of individuals H^j, where j represents the funding scheme, enroll in higher education and receive the subsidy E in the first period.

In the tax-subsidy system (TS), the cost of education is financed by general taxation in the second period. Therefore each individual pays $H^{TS}E/N$ in present value terms, irrespective of her situation.

Recently, several countries have introduced ICLs in order to finance either newly introduced or increased tuition fees. The Higher Education Contribution Scheme (hereafter, HECS), established in Australia in 1989, was the first broadly based ICL policy adopted in the world. Several developed countries have implemented variations of the HECS—the most notable examples are New Zealand and the UK—and there is a current debate on adoption of ICLs in developing countries, such as Ethiopia, Namibia, Indonesia, among others. An ICL of the HECS type is a loan the student receives from the state with the following main characteristics: repayment only takes place in the event that the income after the period of education exceeds a pre-specified level, annual repayments do not constitute more than a certain proportion of her income, and repayment ceases once the loan plus interest, if applicable,[3] has been repaid. Successful graduates pay the amount of their loan plus interest while the cost of the education of unsuccessful students is financed out of general taxes and is, hence, shared by the whole population.

We model this type of ICL as in García-Peñalosa and Wälde (2000) but, following Chapman (2006), we refer to it as ICL with risk-sharing (RS). All individuals who want to study borrow E. Only those individuals who are successful have to repay the amount in full. However, a lump-sum tax, which amounts to $(1-p)H^{RS}E/N$ in present value terms, is levied on all individuals in order to raise the revenue needed to cover the education cost of unsuccessful students.

All ICL schemes contend with the fact that some participants in the scheme will default or have insufficient income to fully repay their loan balances. We have just seen how the risk-sharing type relies on general taxation to finance the amount defaulted. Instead, an ICL with risk-pooling (*RP*) consists of a mutual fund in which participants are grouped in a common repayment cohort with collective, rather than individual, repayment responsibilities over a certain period. The repayment deficit from lower earners is therefore compensated by the repayment surplus of higher earners. The Yale Tuition Postponement Option is the best known implementation of an ICL scheme as a mutual fund. For a few years in the 1970s, students at Yale could borrow from the University to fund their education with repayment being contingent on income earned in the years after graduation. All students graduating in any year with an outstanding debt were grouped in repayment cohorts with collective repayment responsibilities. An individual student's contractual obligation did not terminate upon repayment of her individual loan balance, instead her obligations concluded only when her cohort repaid the aggregate loan balance, or after 35 years. Nerlove (1975) explored the adverse selection consequences of the Yale plan and concluded that, for such a university, hoping to attract the highest quality students, the scheme had the perverse effect of encouraging those students who expected to be successful in the labour market to seek enrollment at universities offering non-ICL financial assistance. In fact, the Yale plan was soon discontinued. A universal ICL with risk-pooling is in place in Hungary since 2001.[4]

In this paper, with a universal risk-pooling income-contingent plan, all individuals who want to study borrow E, but only those individuals who are successful have to repay the amount in full. In addition, successful graduates have to pay the debt of the unsuccessful students. In present value terms, successful graduates pay E/p.

Finally, with a pure loan scheme (*L*) students pay back the cost of their education in the second period, whether they are successful or not (i.e. the penalty for default is extreme). In our framework, the pure loan scheme can be taken as a reference in which the only role of the government is to advance the necessary funds. It is worth noting that this is an ideal (hypothetical) situation as in reality it is often the case that student loans are guaranteed and a proportion of individuals, sometimes large, defaults (see, for instance, Harrison, 1995; Barr and Crawford, 1998). If default costs are paid by the government, this policy is akin to an ICL of the risk-sharing type.

3. Participation with Risk Neutrality

In this section we determine the threshold ability level above which an individual is willing to invest in higher education for the benchmark case of risk neutrality and for each financing scheme $j = L,TS,RS,RP$, where L stands for loan, TS for tax-subsidy, RS for risk-sharing ICL and RP for risk-pooling ICL.

For each financing scheme j, let y_N^j denote the net lifetime income of a non-student, y_U^j the net lifetime income of an unsuccessful student and $y_S^j(a)$ the net lifetime income of a successful graduate of ability a. An individual is indifferent between investing and not investing in higher education when the lifetime income as a student is equal to the lifetime income as a non-student. For each financing scheme j, the threshold ability level $\hat{a}^j$ above which a risk-neutral individual is willing to invest in higher education satisfies:

$$(1-p)y_U^j + py_S^j(\hat{a}^j) = y_N^j. \tag{1}$$

With a pure loan, any individual who studies pays the full education cost, E, irrespective of whether or not she succeeds in education. If R is the discount rate, the expected lifetime income of a student of ability a is $(1-p)Rw_L + pRw_H(a) - E$. The lifetime income of a non-student is in this case $(1+R)w_L$. The threshold ability level $\hat{a}^L$ satisfies:

$$(1-p)Rw_L + pRw_H(\hat{a}^L) - E = (1+R)w_L. \tag{2}$$

With the tax-subsidy system, each individual pays her share of higher education irrespective of whether she studies or not. The threshold ability level $\hat{a}^{TS}$ satisfies:

$$(1-p)Rw_L + pRw_H(\hat{a}^{TS}) = (1+R)w_L. \tag{3}$$

Clearly, $\hat{a}^{TS} < \hat{a}^L$.

With a risk-sharing ICL, all individuals who want to study borrow E but only those students who are successful have to repay the amount in full. A lump-sum tax is levied on all individuals in order to raise the revenue needed to cover the education cost of unsuccessful students, which is $(1-p)H^{RS}E$. The expected lifetime income of a student of ability a is:

$$R[(1-p)w_L + pw_H(a)] - E\left[\frac{(1-p)H^{RS}}{N} + p\right],$$

where:

$$(1-p)\frac{H^{RS}}{N} + p < 1,$$

since students do not expect to pay the full cost of education, which is partly subsidized by non-students. The threshold ability level $\hat{a}^{RS}$ satisfies:

$$(1-p)Rw_L + pRw_H(\hat{a}^{RS}) - pE = (1+R)w_L. \tag{4}$$

From (2) to (4), $\hat{a}^{TS} < \hat{a}^{RS} < \hat{a}^{L}$. Higher education participation is lower than with the tax-subsidy system. This is due to the fact that the cost of education is partly subsidized by non-students but to a lesser extent than in the tax-subsidy system. At the same time, more individuals get educated than with the pure loan since, in expected terms, students are only responsible for part of the cost of their education.

Finally, with a universal risk-pooling income-contingent plan, all individuals who want to study borrow E. Successful graduates have to repay the amount in full and, in addition, they have to pay the debt of the unsuccessful students:

$$E + \frac{(1-p)H^{RP}E}{pH^{RP}} = \frac{E}{p}.$$

The threshold ability level $\hat{a}^{RP}$ satisfies:

$$R[(1-p)w_L + pw_H(\hat{a}^{RP})] - E = (1+R)w_L. \tag{5}$$

The level of participation in higher education thus coincides with that resulting from the pure loan: $\hat{a}^{RP} = \hat{a}^{L}$.

What is the optimal level of participation? Individuals differ in ability, which affects the potential benefits of education. Focusing exclusively on efficiency, it is optimal that an individual studies when her expected earnings as a student net of the cost of her education exceed her earnings as a non-student. It is possible to determine a threshold ability level, $\hat{a}$, above which an individual should study and below which an individual should not study:

$$R[pw_H(\hat{a}) + (1-p)w_L] - E = (1+R)w_L. \tag{6}$$

The optimal amount of graduates is $H^* = \int_{\hat{a}}^{\bar{a}} f(a)da$.

If we compare the optimal ability threshold with the ability thresholds obtained above for the alternative financing schemes we get:

Proposition 1. With risk neutrality, $\hat{a}^{TS} < \hat{a}^{RS} < \hat{a} = \hat{a}^{RP} = \hat{a}^{L}$.

When individuals are risk neutral both the pure loan and the risk-pooling ICL induce the optimal level of participation. However, participation is excessive for both the risk-sharing ICL and the tax-subsidy scheme: individuals who do not study are worse-off under both schemes, since they have to pay taxes for a service from which they do not directly benefit, and some of them may be induced to invest in education. Among these schemes, the one with the largest contribution from non-students (i.e. the tax-subsidy system) results in the highest level of participation.

Obviously, referring to risk-sharing and risk-pooling when individuals are risk neutral may appear awkward. These results should just be taken as a benchmark that allows us to understand the effect of risk aversion on participation in higher education, and the insurance role of the alternative financing schemes, which is analyzed in the following section.

4. Effect of Risk Aversion on Participation

Let $G^j(a)$ denote the expected net utility gain from investing in higher education under scheme j for a risk-averse individual with ability a:

$$G^j(a) \equiv (1-p)U(y_U^j) + pU(y_S^j(a)) - U(y_N^j), \tag{7}$$

where $U(.)$ is assumed to be increasing and concave. The expected net utility gain from investing in higher education increases with ability:

$$\frac{dG^j(a)}{da} = pU'(y_S^j)Rw_H'(a) > 0.$$

More able individuals have higher expected utility from studying than less able individuals, and are hence more likely to choose higher education. When individuals are risk averse we denote by $\tilde{a}^j$ the threshold ability level (i.e. the ability level of an individual who is indifferent between studying and not studying associated with financing scheme j. Risk aversion reduces participation for all financing schemes considered above. To see this, it suffices to evaluate Eq. (7) at $\hat{a}^j$ (i.e. the threshold ability level associated with financing scheme j when individuals are risk neutral):

$$G^j(\hat{a}^j) = (1-p)U(y_U^j) + pU(y_S^j(\hat{a}^j)) - U((1-p)y_U^j + py_S^j(\hat{a}^j)) < 0.$$

Since $G^j(a)$ is increasing and $G^j(\tilde{a}^j) = 0$ participation falls with risk aversion for all j, as established in Proposition 2.

Proposition 2. $\tilde{a}^j > \hat{a}^j$ for all financing schemes j.

When individuals are risk neutral, participation increases with the subsidy from non-students to students. As risk aversion increases, the transfer from successful to unsuccessful students (degree of insurance) becomes more important in determining participation levels and it is no longer possible to rank all thresholds unambiguously. We can show that, for the schemes considered above, the degree of insurance is larger the lower the subsidy.

To see this, we represent in Fig. 47.1 the income obtained by a successful student, $y_S^j(a)$, against the income she obtains when unsuccessful, y_U^j, for each financing scheme j. The 45-degree line represents the certainty line. Iso-expected income lines, which are tangent to the indifference curves at the 45-degree line, have slope $-(1-p)/p$. Indifference curves are convex due to risk aversion.

In Fig. 47.1, the income combinations for the pure loan and the risk-pooling ICL, $(y_U^L, y_S^L(a))$ and $(y_U^{RP}, y_S^{RP}(a))$ respectively, are on the same iso-expected income line, but the income combination for the pure loan scheme is further from the certainty line. The risk-pooling scheme can be viewed as an actuarially fair pure insurance policy with incomplete coverage, where students receive an indemnity in case of failure that covers only a proportion of the total loss. Let the total loss suffered by an

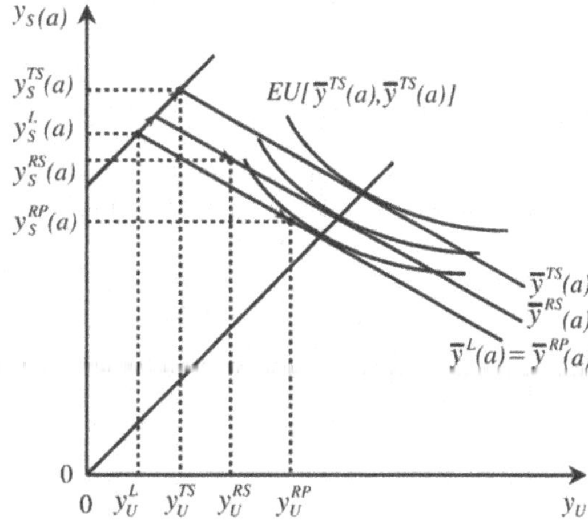

Figure 47.1 Subsidy and insurance components of the alternative financing schemes.

unsuccessful individual be the present value of the difference between what they would get if they were successful and what they get when unsuccessful: $R(w_H(a) - w_L)$. It is worth noting that the total loss in case of failure differs across individuals of different ability and is also different in general from the total cost of the investment in education, incurred both by successful and unsuccessful students, which amounts to $E + w_L$ (i.e. financial costs plus forgone earnings). Under the risk-pooling ICL, students pay a premium $(1-p)E/p$ in excess of the financial cost E in order to receive an indemnity E/p if unsuccessful. In other words, the risk-pooling scheme covers a fraction k^{RP} of the total loss, with $k^{RP} = \frac{E/p}{R(w_H(a) - w_L)}$. Successful students pay an extra amount of $(1-p)E/p$ above the cost of education in order to guarantee a minimum income of Rw_L in case of bad luck. As a result, for any a, the expected utility is greater with the risk-pooling ICL than with the pure loan, while the safe option (not to study) is the same for both. Therefore, $\tilde{a}^{RP} < \tilde{a}^L$. In both schemes, non-students do not contribute at all to education finance.

ICLs with risk-sharing provide both a subsidy and insurance. If we take the pure loan allocation as a reference point, the risk-sharing ICL includes a subsidy that provides both successful and unsuccessful students a higher level of expected income. The subsidy from non-students to students, whether successful or not, is $E(1 - p)(N - H^{RS})/N$. This subsidy encourages participation, although to a lesser extent than the larger subsidy in the tax-subsidy scheme. However, the risk-sharing ICL also provides some insurance, thus further enhancing participation. Students pay a premium $(1 - p)E$ that entitles them to receive an indemnity E when unsuccessful. The insurance cover provided by this scheme is however smaller than the insurance cover implicit in the risk-pooling ICL. The fraction of the loss $R(w_H(a)-w_L)$ that is covered is $k^{RS} = E/R(w_H(a) - w_L)$, and $k^{RS} = pk^{RP}$. The move from $(y_U^L, y_S^L(a))$ to $(y_U^{RS}, y_S^{RS}(a))$ can be decomposed into an upwards shift along a 45-degree line to an allocation that provides the same subsidy $E(1 - p)(N - H^{RS})/N$ to all students and the same expected income as that of the risk-sharing allocation, and a movement along the iso-expected income line, towards the certainty line, to reach the final allocation $(y_U^{RS}, y_S^{RS}(a))$. This last move could be viewed as stemming from an actuarially fair partial insurance policy, with lower coverage than that implicit in the risk-pooling scheme.

It can also be shown that $\tilde{a}^{TS}$ and $\tilde{a}^{RS}$ are both smaller than $\tilde{a}^L$ and, hence, a larger proportion of the population undertakes higher education. For both the tax-subsidy and risk-sharing ICL schemes, the expected utility with education is higher, and the utility without education is lower, than with the pure loan.

Finally, the relationship between $\tilde{a}^{TS}$, $\tilde{a}^{RS}$, and $\tilde{a}^{RP}$ depends on the degree of risk aversion. For low degrees of risk aversion, $\tilde{a}^{TS} < \tilde{a}^{RS} < \tilde{a}^{RP}$ and, hence, $H^{TS} > H^{RS} > H^{RP}$. When risk aversion increases the ability thresholds increase, reducing participation. However, the magnitudes of these increases may differ for each financing scheme, and for a sufficiently large level of risk aversion the ordering of participation levels across schemes could change. In Del Rey and Racionero (2006) we show that the ordering of these thresholds remains the same (i.e. $\tilde{a}^{TS} < \tilde{a}^{RS} < \tilde{a}^{RP}$) if the degree of risk aversion is sufficiently low: we identify a condition, which depends on the curvature of the indifference curves, for this to be the case.

5. Optimal Participation and Alternative Schemes

We now characterize the optimal level of participation when individuals are risk averse and compare it with the levels achieved with the financing schemes considered above. A risk-averse individual is willing to pay for full insurance more than it costs to insure her. As a result, welfare is maximized when each individual is fully insured, at an actuarially fair premium, against a bad outcome. An actuarially fair full insurance policy would cover the entirety of the total loss by providing a student with ability a an indemnity $R(w_H(a) - w_L)$ when unsuccessful in exchange for the premium $(1-p)R(w_H(a) - w_L)$. The fraction of the total loss covered is 1 for all a. This guarantees the maximum expected utility from education to all those who invest in education, who are precisely those for whom:

$$U(pRw_H(a) + (1-p)Rw_L - E) \geq U((1 + R)w_L). \tag{8}$$

Eq. (8) is satisfied with equality at $a = \hat{a}$. Thus, the optimal participation level with risk aversion coincides with the one obtained with risk neutrality (see Eq. (6)).

The ICL with risk-pooling and the pure loan yield the optimal level of participation in the benchmark case of risk neutrality. Since risk aversion reduces participation, it can then be easily concluded that participation fails to be optimal for both schemes when individuals are risk averse. Participation deviates from optimality less for the risk-pooling ICL than for the pure loan due to the fact that ICLs with risk-pooling provide more insurance although, as highlighted above, the insurance cover is incomplete. We have also shown that participation levels with the risk-sharing ICL and the tax-subsidy schemes remain higher than with the pure loan when individuals are risk averse. Unfortunately, it is not possible to show in general whether these two schemes, which rely fully or partially on general taxes, result in excessive or insufficient participation. This depends on the degree of risk aversion. Participation could be optimal with the risk-sharing ICL or the tax-subsidy in some circumstances. However, in general, none of the schemes considered yields the optimal level of participation unambiguously.

García-Peñalosa and Wälde (2000) argue that, if the degree of risk aversion is large enough, their graduate tax (a version of our risk-pooling ICL) is better than pure or (risk-sharing) IC loans. We obtain a similar result but, like them, we are unable to provide further insights without resorting to the use of specific functional forms. A relevant question that remains open in such a general setting is whether at the level of risk aversion required for the assertion to hold anyone remains interested in investing in higher education. In any case we have shown that participation under the risk-pooling scheme is inefficiently low due to incomplete coverage, and this makes worthwhile investigating alternative policies that have not been considered above.

We have already pointed out that the underlying reason for insufficient participation is risk aversion and that providing full insurance, at an actuarially fair premium, for all those individuals with ability $a > \hat{a}$, yields the optimal level of participation in higher education. However, fully insuring each student would require knowing her individual ability. An alternative scheme that yields the optimal level of participation with lower informational requirements consists in fully insuring the lowest ability individual who should gain access to higher education (i.e. individual with ability $\hat{a}$). The optimal threshold ability $\hat{a}$ is determined by Eq. (6) and depends on parameters of the model that we have assumed to be known. With this policy all students pay the same premium $(1 - p)R(w_H(\hat{a}) - w_L)$ and all unsuccessful students receive $R(w_H(\hat{a}) - w_L)$. There is no need to observe the ability level of each individual since they will apply for this insurance policy, and become students, if they find it attractive, and only those with $a \geq \hat{a}$ will do so. Note however that the greater simplicity is gained at some cost since individuals with ability $a > \hat{a}$ are just partially insured and are hence worse-off than under full insurance. For individual $a = \hat{a}$ the fraction of the total loss covered by this scheme is 1 whereas for individuals with $a > \hat{a}$ the fraction of the total loss covered is $R(w_H(\hat{a}) - w_L) \;/\; R(w_H(a) - w_L)$. The expected income of an individual of ability a is, as in the case of full insurance, $\bar{y}(a) = R(pw_H(a) + (1 - p)Rw_L) - E$, but there remains a gap $R(w_H(a) - w_H(\hat{a}))$ between success and failure. Yet, participation is optimal.

Using the optimality condition (6), the indemnity $R(w_H(\hat{a}) - w_L)$ is equal to $(E + wL)/p$. Thus, the lifetime income of unsuccessful students is:

$$y_U = Rw_L - E + \frac{w_L + E}{p} - (1 - p)\frac{w_L + E}{p} = (1 + R)w_L,$$

whereas the lifetime income of successful graduates is:

$$y_S(a) = Rw_H(a) - E - (1 - p)\frac{w_L + E}{p}.$$

In other words, fully insuring the lowest ability individual who should access higher education is equivalent to making successful graduates pay for the education of their cohort plus a compensation to unsuccessful students for their forgone earnings in the first period. As a result, unsuccessful students receive the same income as non-students. This is the minimum insurance required for participation to be optimal.

Proposition 3. A universal risk-pooling ICL that covers both the financial cost of education and the forgone earnings induces optimal participation in higher education.

Proof. The income of unsuccessful students and non-students is the same (i.e. $(1 + R)w_L$). Consequently, an individual would undertake higher education as long as the income when successful is larger than the income when unsuccessful. This is in fact the case for all $a > \hat{a}$. To see this note that, for $\hat{a}$, the expected return from education, $pR(w_H(\hat{a}) - w_L)$, equals its cost, $E + w_L$, and hence:

$$w_L + Rw_H(\hat{a}) - \frac{E + w_L}{p} = (1 + R)w_L,$$

where the LHS is the expected income of a successful graduate of ability $\hat{a}$ under a risk-pooling ICL that includes E and w_L. The individual with ability $\hat{a}$ is just indifferent between studying and not studying, but all individuals with higher abilities than $\hat{a}$ prefer to study, and there is optimal participation.

Although several countries provide ICLs to students for their living expenses, only the ICL currently in place in Hungary is of the risk-pooling type. It has been traditionally difficult to accept that only the high-income earners who completed higher education should be held responsible for the cost of education of those students who end up being low-income earners. As it turns out, it is in the interest of all risk-averse individuals to accept a deal under which they will pay more than the cost of their education when successful and nothing when unsuccessful. We have shown that an ICL of the risk-pooling type can achieve optimal participation provided that the loan covers both financial costs of education and forgone earnings. It is worth pointing out that in the framework considered so far such a scheme does not need to be compulsory but universal. A key assumption is that all individuals face the same probability of success. In the following section we discuss the implications of letting the probability of success, and not only the wage of a successful graduate, depend on ability.

6. On Adverse Selection

When all individuals face the same probability of success, all students contribute the same amount, in expected terms, to the cost of their education and no adverse selection takes place (i.e. no student is willing to opt out). In order to understand the implications of letting the probability of success depend on ability, we assume that $p(a) \in (0, 1)$, with $p'(a) > 0$ for all $a \in [\underline{a}, \bar{a})$.

As before, we focus first on the benchmark case of risk neutrality. The threshold ability levels for the different schemes satisfy, respectively:

$$p(\hat{a}^L)R(w_H(\hat{a}^L) - w_L) = w_L + E,$$

$$p(\hat{a}^{TS})R(w_H(\hat{a}^{TS}) - w_L) = w_L,$$

$$p(\hat{a}^{RS})R(w_H(\hat{a}^{RS}) - w_L) = w_L + p(\hat{a}^{RS})E,$$

and

$$p(\hat{a}^{RP})R(w_H(\hat{a}^{RP}) - w_L) = w_L + E\left[\frac{p(\hat{a}^{RP})}{\bar{p}(\hat{a}^{RP})}\right],$$

where $\bar{p}(\hat{a}^{RP})$ represents the average probability of success among all individuals who undertake education under the risk-pooling ICL scheme (i.e. all individuals with $a \geq \hat{a}^{RP}$):

$$\bar{p}(\hat{a}^{RP}) = \frac{\int_{\hat{a}^{RP}}^{\bar{a}} p(a)f(a)da}{\int_{\hat{a}^{RP}}^{\bar{a}} f(a)da} > p(\hat{a}^{RP}).$$

The optimal threshold ability level is given now by

$$p(\hat{a})R(w_H(\hat{a}) - w_L) = w_L + E. \tag{9}$$

Hence, $\hat{a}^{TS} < \hat{a}^{RS} < \hat{a}^{RP} < \hat{a}^L = \hat{a}$.

The main qualitative difference with respect to the results in Section 3 is that the risk-pooling ICL scheme yields now excessive participation. There is an individual with ability level $a' > \hat{a}^L$, with $p(a') = \overline{p}(\hat{a}^{RP})$, so that all individuals with $a \in [\hat{a}^{RP}, a')$ pay less, and all individuals with $a \in (a', \overline{a}]$ pay more, in expected terms, than the cost of their education. Lower ability students are partially subsidized by higher ability students and this induces an inefficiently large amount of individuals to undertake higher education. Some of the higher ability individuals, particularly those close to the highest ability level, might wish to opt out from such a scheme. In this model this is not possible because self-financing is not an option (i.e. there is no personal wealth and pure loans are not offered simultaneously).

As in Section 4, risk aversion decreases the level of participation for all schemes and the pure loan yields inefficiently low participation. However, it is not possible to determine whether participation is insufficient, excessive or optimal with the risk-pooling ICL with $p(a)$, whereas with p it was inefficiently low. In any case, and as before, it is not possible to unambiguously rank the participation levels for *TS*, *RS* and *RP* in general.

As in Section 5, a scheme that provides actuarially fair full insurance to all students yields optimal participation, and this is still the case of a scheme that fully insures the individual with threshold ability $\hat{a}$ that is offered to all. However, such a scheme no longer corresponds to the risk-pooling ICL that covers the cost of education and forgone earnings. The scheme that fully insures the individual with ability $\hat{a}$ provides the individual an indemnity $R(w_H(\hat{a}) - w_L)$ when unsuccessful in exchange for the premium $(1 - p(\hat{a}))R(w_H(\hat{a}) - w_L)$, where $R(w_H(\hat{a}) - w_L) = (w_L + E)/p(\hat{a})$ from (9). An individual with ability $\hat{a}$ gets the income of a nonstudent, $(1 + R)w_L$, regardless of success or failure, and all individuals with ability $a > \hat{a}$ obtain $(1 + R)w_L$ when unsuccessful and

$$y_S(a) = w_L + Rw_H(a) - \frac{E + w_L}{p(\hat{a})}$$

when successful, which, using (9), is strictly larger than $(1 + R)w_L$. A risk-pooling ICL that covers the cost of education and forgone earnings, hereafter denoted by RP^*, also provides $(1 + R)w_L$ when unsuccessful but

$$y_S(a) = w_L + Rw_H(a) - \frac{E + w_L}{\overline{p}(\hat{a}^{RP^*})}$$

when successful, where $\overline{p}(\hat{a}^{RP^*})$ represents the mean probability of success among those who study and $\hat{a}^{RP^*}$ satisfies

$$w_L + Rw_H(\hat{a}^{RP^*}) - \frac{E + w_L}{\overline{p}(\hat{a}^{RP^*})} = (1 + R)w_L.$$

It can be shown that $\hat{a}^{RP^*} < \hat{a}$: there is excessive participation because lower ability students are partially subsidized by higher ability students. In order to achieve optimal participation with a risk-pooling ICL that covers the cost of education and forgone earnings, the repayment of a successful student should be multiplied by a factor $\overline{p}(\hat{a}) \,/\, p(\hat{a})$ so that it becomes

$$\frac{\overline{p}(\hat{a})}{p(\hat{a})}(E + w_L)\left[1 + \frac{1 - \overline{p}(\hat{a}^{RP^{**}})}{\overline{p}(\hat{a}^{RP^{**}})}\right],$$

where RP^{**} stands for this modified scheme. Note that the scheme identified in Proposition 3 is a particular case of this when $p(\hat{a}) = \overline{p}(\hat{a}) = p$.

Both the insurance policy that fully insures the individual of ability $\hat{a}$ and the RP^{**} yield optimal participation. However, as in any scheme of the *RP* type when ability affects the probability of success, individuals of ability $a > \hat{a}$ would prefer to pay an actuarially fair premium for this partial coverage, since $(1 - p(a))R(w_H(\hat{a}) - w_L) < (1 - p(\hat{a}))R(w_H(\hat{a}) - w_L)$, and individuals with high enough ability may prefer to self-finance. However, in order to do so, they need access to alternative sources of finance.

As mentioned before, in this model students are not able to switch from an ICL to a pure loan, or to rely on personal wealth. In reality they might be able to do so. Self-financing effectively means forgoing the insurance that is implicit in the ICLs. Nevertheless, some students might be willing to do so if they find that the coverage provided by the ICL is relatively small and/or the price they pay for it relatively high. It is worth mentioning that self-financing is not a desirable option for students who are offered risk-sharing ICLs since all taxpayers, including themselves, are still required to share the cost of the education of unsuccessful students (however, recall that participation is generally not optimal under this kind of schemes). Only the risk-pooling ICLs considered above are prone to this adverse selection problem, which can be prevented if the scheme is made mandatory (i.e. a graduate tax).

7. Concluding Remarks

Higher education is a risky investment. We have studied several financing schemes that differ in the way educational costs and risks are shared among the population. In this model liquidity constraints have been ruled out, because the government overcomes the problem of incomplete capital markets by advancing the funds to those individuals willing to study. Yet, inefficiencies arise due to the fact that individuals are risk averse. In particular, participation is suboptimal if the role of the government is limited to advancing the funds in the first period (as in the pure loan). It is possible to increase participation levels by means of subsidies from non-students to students (as in the tax-subsidy system), from successful to unsuccessful students (as in the risk-pooling system), or both (as in the risk-sharing system).

For the schemes considered here, the larger is the subsidy from non-students to students, the lower is the insurance or transfer from successful to unsuccessful graduates. This is the reason why the participation levels resulting from each scheme cannot be relatively ranked in general. For a small degree of risk aversion, the subsidy effect is relatively more important and participation will be larger for those schemes that include the larger subsidies, as we showed in the benchmark case of risk neutrality. For a large degree of risk aversion, the result is ambiguous because the insurance component plays an increasingly important role.

Fully insuring all students would induce optimal participation, but implementing such a full insurance policy may imply non-negligible informational requirements. We have proposed an alternative insurance policy that, by fully insuring only the lowest ability individual who should access higher education, yields optimal participation. We have shown that this scheme is equivalent to a universal ICL with risk-pooling that covers both financial costs of education and forgone earnings when the probability of success is equal for all individuals. In this case such a scheme does not need to be compulsory but universal.

We have also explored the consequences of letting ability affect positively the probability of success. Most of the qualitative results remain valid. However, there are some differences worth mentioning. First, the risk-pooling ICL now yields excessive participation when individuals are risk neutral, and when individuals are risk averse participation can be excessive, insufficient or optimal depending on the degree of risk aversion. Second, even though the insurance policy that fully insures the lowest ability individual who should access higher education still yields optimal participation, such a scheme no longer corresponds to the risk-pooling ICL that covers the cost of education and forgone earnings, which now yields excessive participation. In order to achieve optimal participation, the repayments of successful students in such a risk-pooling ICL need to be appropriately adjusted and we have identified the adjustment ratio. It is also worth noticing that, when the probability of success depends on ability, the higher ability individuals expect to pay more than the cost of their education in a risk-pooling ICL scheme and, accordingly, some would be willing to opt out. However, to effectively be able to do so, they would need access to alternative means of finance (for instance, personal wealth and/or pure loans being offered simultaneously). This possibility has not been explicitly considered in this model. We briefly discuss the implications of allowing students to self-finance. Among the ICLs considered only those of the risk-pooling type are prone to adverse selection, which can be prevented by making these schemes compulsory. Then the risk-pooling ICL schemes become effectively graduate tax systems, which have also been advocated for by García-Peñalosa and Wälde (2000) and Cigno and Luporini (2009) for different reasons and in different frameworks.

Problems of moral hazard are also often associated with the provision of insurance. Although we have not explicitly considered moral hazard in the present paper, a natural way to do so would be to allow the probability of success to depend positively on student effort. Unfortunately, even though market insurance and self-insurance (effort that reduces the size of the loss) are often found to be substitutes, market insurance and self-protection (effort that reduces the probability of a loss) can be either complements or substitutes in general (Ehrlich and Becker, 1972). In addition, the relationship between risk aversion and self-protection is generally ambiguous (Dionne and Eeckhoudt, 1985).[5] Empirical evidence has not helped to resolve this theoretical ambiguity. It has proven particularly difficult to estimate the moral hazard effects of income-contingent loans,[6] unlike adverse selection effects, which Nerlove (1975) identified as the most likely reason why the Yale Plan was discontinued. To the best of our knowledge, Cigno and Luporini (2009) is the first theoretical model of higher education finance to explicitly deal with a moral hazard problem associated with the unobservability of study effort. They advocate for a graduate tax that redistributes from the better paid to the academically more successful and, in absence of externalities, generates sufficient revenue for the policy to break even. In our terminology, this would also be a mandatory ICL of the risk-pooling type, albeit more complex in design. As pointed out by Vandenberghe and Debande (2008), using such mandatory schemes may be unpopular amongst certain categories of graduates. Yet, unlike alternative schemes, ICLs of the risk-pooling type have the advantage that they do not rely on general tax revenues to finance the default. It should not be neglected that many schemes currently in place may be unpopular among taxpayers who never use higher education.

Acknowledgements

The first version of this paper was written during a visit of the first author to RSSS, Australian National University, and revised while she was visiting CORE, Université catholique de Louvain. She thanks both RSSS and CORE for their hospitality and, for financial support, the Spanish Ministry of Education (mobility program JC2008-00098 and project SEJ2007-60671), the Generalitat de Catalunya (grant 2003BEAI400325, contract 2009SGR189, and the XREPP). Both authors also gratefully acknowledge financial support from Fundación BBVA. We are grateful to Bruce Chapman, Louis Eeckhoudt, Andrew Leigh and Rhema Vaithianathan for their helpful comments. We have also benefited from comments of participants at the 23rd Australasian Economic Theory Workshop, the 1st Workshop in Public Policy Design at the University of Girona, the 6th Public Economic Theory Conference, the Higher Education Multijurisdictionality and Globalization Conference in Mons, the Workshop on Fairness and Education in Alicante, and seminars at the Research School of Social Sciences—ANU, the University of Antwerp, the Technical University of Dresden and IRES—Université catholique de Louvain. We also thank two anonymous referees for their useful feedback. The errors remain ours.

Notes

1. The student loan terminology is indeed not yet stabilized, as pointed out by Vandenberghe and Debande (2008), where "risk-shifting" is used instead of risk-sharing to stress the fact that the cost of default is shifted to taxpayers. Similarly, we choose to refer to ICLs with risk-pooling instead of graduate taxes to stress the fact that the cost of higher education is pooled among the graduates and general taxation is not used to subsidize education nor tax revenues from education are used to subsidize other expenses. Barr (2001), Chapman (2006) and Jacobs and Van der Ploeg (2006) argue that with what is generally understood as graduate taxes the higher education budget may not be necessarily balanced. However, it is worth noting that García-Peñalosa and Wälde (2000) define, and advocate for, graduate taxes that balance the higher education budget and in this sense we are considering exactly the same scheme.
2. www.gse.buffalo.edu/org/IntHigherEdFinance/textForSite/IncomContLoans.pdf, p. 3.
3. In New Zealand the loans initially carried a market rate of interest, however at present interest charges are subsidized and depend on the financial circumstances of debtors. In Australia the debt is indexed by the rate of inflation but there is no additional interest charged. When the real interest is zero, there

is an implicit subsidy for both high- and low-earning graduates. The magnitude of the implicit subsidy depends crucially on the rate of preference for time and the pattern of repayments.

4. See main features of the scheme on http://www.diakhitel.hu/en/. Universal means that it is available to all students, but it is not necessarily compulsory.
5. In our model if the probability depends on effort and the cost of effort is separable, we obtain a negative relationship between insurance and effort. However, additional assumptions are required in order to determine the effect of changes in the degree of risk aversion on effort, and even if these additional restrictions are imposed, once we account for the effect of different effort levels on the probability of success, and hence on the expected utility from education, we remain unable to order relative participation levels under the different schemes.
6. Chapman and Leigh (2009) come closest to doing this, by finding statistically significant evidence of bunching below the repayment threshold of the Higher Education Contribution Scheme (HECS) in Australia. However, this effect is shown to be economically trivial, as it affects around 0.3 percent of graduates with a HECS debt.

References

Barr, N., 2001. The Welfare State as Piggy Bank: Information, Risk, Uncertainty, and the Role of the State. Oxford University Press, Oxford.

Barr, N., Crawford, I., 1998. Funding higher education in an age of expansion. Educ. Econ. 6, 45–70.

Chapman, B., 2006. Income contingent loans for higher education: international reforms. In: Hanushek, E.A., Welch, F. (Eds.), Handbook on the Economics of Education, Vol. 2. North-Holland, Amsterdam, pp. 1435–1503.

Chapman, B., Leigh, A., 2009. Do very high tax rates induce bunching? Implications for the design of income contingent loan schemes. Econ. Rec. 86, 276–289.

Cigno, A., Luporini, A., 2009. Scholarships or student loans? Subsidizing higher education in the presence of moral hazard. J. Public Econ. Theory 11, 55–87.

Del Rey, E., Racionero, M., 2006. Financing Schemes for Higher Education. Working Papers in Economics and Econometrics No. 460, The Australian National University.

Dionne, G., Eeckhoudt, L., 1985. Self-insurance, self-protection and increased risk aversion. Econ. Lett. 17, 39–42.

Ehrlich, I., Becker, G., 1972. Market insurance, self-insurance, and self-protection. J. Polit. Econ. 80, 623–648.

García-Peñalosa, C., Wälde, K., 2000. Efficiency and equity effects of subsidies to higher education. Oxf. Econ. Pap. 52, 702–722.

Harrison, M., 1995. Default in guaranteed student loan programs. J. Stud. Financ. Aid 25, 25–42.

Jacobs, B., van der Ploeg, F., 2006. Guide to reform of higher education: a European perspective. Econ. Policy 47, 535–592.

Johnstone, B., 2005. The Economics and Politics of Income Contingent Repayment Plans. International Comparative Higher Education Finance and Accessibility Project WWW Publications Page.

Nerlove, M., 1975. Some problems in the use of income-contingent loans for the finance of higher education. J. Polit. Econ. 83, 157–183.

Vandenberghe, V., Debande, O., 2008. Refinancing Europe's higher education through deferred and income-contingent fees: an empirical assessment using Belgian, German & UK data. European Journal of Political Economy 24, 364–386.

CHAPTER 48

MAKING HIGHER EDUCATION FINANCE WORK FOR AFRICA

SHANTAYANAN DEVARAJAN, CÉLESTIN MONGA, AND TERTIUS ZONGO

This paper identifies the twin problems of higher education financing in Africa—inadequate resources and poor use of existing resources—and traces them to the preponderance of free, public tertiary education in most countries, despite a weak economic rationale for such an approach and unintended consequences of inequitable access and politicization of higher education. It proposes a reform of higher education finance based on principles of rationalizing government's role, taking into account the politics of such reforms and the institutional changes needed for a well-functioning system of tertiary education in Africa.

> *"The food in this restaurant is terrible," says one diner to her companion.*
> *"Yes, and the portions are too small," the companion replies.*
>
> Woody Allen

Higher education in Africa shares many of the characteristics of Woody Allen's oft-told story. Universities and colleges are under-staffed, under-financed and in poor operating condition. The quality of the education is poor, with outdated curricula and employers complaining that graduates lack the basic skills for doing their jobs. But the stakes for higher education in Africa are much greater than a restaurant meal. Quite simply, to compete in the global marketplace—the only way Africa will sustain growth and reduce poverty—the continent needs highly skilled and well-trained workers, and the current system of higher education does not seem to be fulfilling this objective. Furthermore, thanks to high fertility rates 15 years ago and increases in primary and secondary enrolment, the number of young Africans seeking higher education is growing by leaps and bounds. In addition to missing out on global competitiveness therefore, Africa may suffer a crisis of failed expectations.

This paper addresses one aspect of Africa's higher education problem, namely, the financing of universities and colleges. In Section 1, after a brief review of the history of higher education in Africa, we describe the current problems facing the sector and their links to financing. We then note that, if the current problems appear serious, they pale in comparison with any projection for the future when the sector will face a real crisis. Section 2 provides an analytical framework with which to approach a solution. We show that the two rationales for public intervention in higher education—efficiency and equity—are either weak or have been undermined by 'government failures'. We propose therefore in Section 3 a different way of approaching higher-education financing, one that provides an environment where public and private resources could jointly strengthen higher education in Africa.

1. The State of Higher Education in Africa

1.1 Historical Evolution

There is little documentation about pre-colonial institutions of higher education in Africa, which included training centres for rulers, priest, diviners and centres of Islamic education—the most famous being Al Azhar University (founded in the tenth century) and the University of Timbuktu, which flourished in the fifteenth century. The European colonial powers that ruled most of the continent after the sixteenth century did not consider education a priority. While some missionaries made attempts in the seventeenth and eighteenth centuries to establish schools in their stations in various parts of the continent, most of these efforts were short-lived. As Brydon observes, 'it was not until the era of mission expansion in the 19th century (and acceptance of the "scientific" belief that Africans were human and therefore had souls to be saved and practical abilities and intellects to develop) that more persistent efforts to educate West African were made' (1997, p. 1).

Missionaries needed some literate functionaries for their churches. With the expansion of colonial territories during the nineteenth centuries, the British and the French governments also needed some locally trained, low-level assistants. They gradually started providing basic education to limited groups of people—often carefully selected within specific social and ethnic groups. The purpose of the newly created 'modern' education systems was therefore not to produce a literate society but simply to create a small class of 'civilized' (*'évolués'*) members of intermediaries and to ensure that the colonial state had enough *'auxiliaires d'administration'*, as the French put it, to function. The schooling provided was generally along the lines of European primary education, with schools located either in colonial towns or near mission stations. Secondary education was restricted to a handful of schools. There were essentially no institutions of tertiary education.[1]

In the early twentieth century (especially after 1920), there were frequent debates among colonial policymakers about the type of education (practical, vocational or academic) that was appropriate for African territories. In Francophone Africa, many politicians feared that the diffusion of formal schooling would undermine colonial control. They imposed restrictions on the type and amount of education offered to 'natives'. 'Until 1944, metropolitan and colonial education systems were completely distinct. There was no institutional bridge (no examination or academic procedure) enabling African students to move upward from the latter to the former system' (Clignet, 1997). The fact that educational expenditures were mostly financed by local revenues further limited the availability of formal education.

After 1945, because of the intense participation of African soldiers in World War II, the massive human losses sustained by the colonies, and the emergence of decolonisation movements often supported by European trade unions, the French and British governments sought to adopt new education policies across the continent. Under the framework of 'modernization', they placed greater emphasis on enrolments, with the goal of creating a class of university-trained African bureaucrats able and willing to maintain Western influence. As a result, the first generation of African students was often sent to Europe with scholarships to attend metropolitan institutions of higher learning. However, these reforms were not uniformly carried out. Despite some successes, the postwar 'assimilationist' policies mostly yielded little results. It is well known that countries such as the Central African Republic and Chad had virtually no college graduates when they became independent in 1960.

Higher education only became a strategic priority for most African countries after independence. Nationalist leaders such as Kwame Nkrumah, Félix Houphouet-Boigny, Jomo Kenyatta and Julius Nyerere thought that their new nations needed a well-educated populace to reclaim their place on the world stage. Tertiary education was seen not just as key to economic development; it was also a matter of pride. At the 1962 Tananarive Conference on the Development of Higher Education in Africa, African leaders stated somewhat idealistically that universities should be 'key instruments for national development'. The newly independent countries needed to produce human resources necessary to run the public services hitherto under the charge of expatriate staff. Many countries adopted measures considered essential to develop the higher education they needed.[2] They invested heavily in education and training, which led to a rapid rise in enrolments in virtually all countries during the 1960 and 1970s. Whatever their shortcomings, African universities succeeded in providing personnel for the civil service, and local experts in various domains of national development—law, economics, medicine, agriculture, engineering etc.

However, following the first oil shock of the early 1970s, the collapse of African economies and increased corruption and poor governance, universities began to decline. Because of their very nature as intellectual centres, these universities also became strongholds for political opposition, especially under authoritarian, single-party regimes. This led to government intrusion into university matters, the bureaucratisation of the system of higher education and increased state control over the activities of students and teachers. The nature of colleges and universities changed gradually from 'the production of knowledge and skills to create wealth and modernize African societies' as stated at the 1972 Accra African Union Workshop, to training civil servants, mainly to provide employment and contribute to sociopolitical stability.

Even today, many state universities continue to perform these functions, with outdated curricula and over 80% of their funding spent on personnel and student costs, leaving little for research or maintenance. Approximately one-third of the 300 universities currently operating across Sub-Saharan Africa are privately funded, the majority established in the past decade. They have a mixed record. Many have done quite well and established themselves as credible alternatives to failing public institutions (like the Lagos Business School, Yaoundé Catholic University and Daystar University in Kenya). Others have become profit-driven businesses which offer low-quality education despite their high levels of tuition.

1.2 Current Challenges

The many problems of higher education in African countries are reflected in the still very low enrollments rates, by far the lowest in the world. Although they have increased from 1% in 1965 (TFHE, 2000) to about 5% according to the most recent estimates, gross enrolment rates in Africa today remain at the same levels observed in other developing regions more than 40 years ago.

Several interrelated factors explain this poor performance. First, the continent's demographic trends have worsened the imbalances of supply and demand in the higher education market: Africa's youth population, age 15–24, has quadrupled since independence, increasing from 52.3 million in 1960 to an estimated 209 million in 2010. Although, during the past quarter century, the number of tertiary students increased from 800,000 in 1985 to more than 3 million in 2002, and to 9.3 million in 2006 (Materu, 2007; World Bank, 2010), there continues to be a shortage of well-functioning colleges and universities—which partially explains the low enrollment rate.[3]

Second, public policies in the African context have long focused on primary and secondary education, to the detriment of tertiary education. Prior to the recent wave of empirical research on the rates of return of various levels of education (Bloom *et al.*, 2006), it was widely believed in policy circles that primary and secondary education are more important for economic development than tertiary education. Moreover, providing basic literacy to the largest groups of population was considered a primary social equity objective for poor countries. Furthermore, in countries with authoritarian regimes where colleges and universities were perceived to be the breeding grounds of political opposition and urban protest, shifting public resources from tertiary to primary education was also considered a good strategy to address political economy problems (Kom, 1996).

Third, higher education in Africa suffers from institutional rigidities that make it difficult for colleges and universities to adjust their curriculum and strategies to be more responsive to changes in global knowledge and labour market demands. In some countries—such as Cameroon, Tanzania and Madagascar—universities are highly centralised and under the strict control of ministries of education which select and appoint faculty members (often using political criteria), determine salaries, conditions for promotions etc. In other countries like Angola and Liberia, universities have considerable legal autonomy.

Fourth, there is increasing concern about the quality of higher education in Africa. Materu notes that quality is a challenging notion to grasp. 'Any statement about quality implies a certain relative measure against a common standard; in tertiary education, such a common standard does not exist. Various concepts have evolved to suit different contexts ranging from quality as a measure for excellence to quality as perfection, quality as value for money, quality as customer satisfaction, quality as fitness of purpose, and quality as transformation (in a learner).' (2007, p. 7) Still, perhaps because of the many challenges facing African institutions of higher learning, there is the perception that the quality of education has been deteriorating in recent years.

Despite all these challenges, there is wide consensus in policy and academic circles that Africa's higher education systems should be supported for at least two reasons. First, there are high rates of return on higher education and the potential contribution to economic and social development (mainly through knowledge diffusion and the accumulation of human capital) is very high.[4] Second, the widespread brain drain of graduates from African universities indicates that these institutions still offer training programmes that are valued outside the continent.[5]

1.3 The Looming Financing Crisis

Despite their low levels of revenue per capita, African countries have by and large managed to maintain a steady allocation of resources to higher education since the mid-1990s. On average, the continent has devoted 0.78% of its gross domestic product to tertiary education, compared with 0.66% on average for other developing countries and 1.21% for the OECD countries. This commitment is also reflected in the fact that African governments allocate about 20% of their current expenditures on education to higher education (Figure 48.1), a rate that is higher than non-African developing countries (18%).

As a recent World Bank study indicates, however, the priority given to tertiary education in the distribution of the overall budgetary envelop for public education varies considerably, from less than 5% in Cape Verde to almost 40% in Egypt and Lesotho (World Bank, 2010). Even in countries such as Burkina Faso, Côte d'Ivoire, Ethiopia and Rwanda that are still far from ensuring universal school enrolment at the primary level and where a balanced allocation rule would suggest a smaller share of public resources to post-primary education, this subsector still accounts for more than 20% of the education budget. Conversely, several countries such as South Africa, Kenya, Ghana, Cape Verde and Namibia—where universal primary school enrolment has already (or almost) been achieved and one would expect to find a larger share of the education budget devoted to higher education—show low ratios (Figure 48.2).

Because of demographic trends, the demand for higher education has been increasing faster than the funding capacity of African governments. The total number of higher education students has increased from 2.7 million in 1991 to 9.3 million in 2006 (16% annually), while aggregate current expenditures in this sub-sector have only increased at an average annual rate of 6%. The mean ratio between the average increase in the number of students and the increase in the resources available during the period was 1.45 (for a sample of 36 countries), again with wide variations from Lesotho (0.5%) to Mali (almost 8%).[6] Africa has therefore experienced a 30% decline in the volume of current public expenditure per student in the last 15 years.

While the quality of higher education is not a linear function of the resources available, there is some evidence that the decline in financing may have led to the deterioration in outcomes. Faced with economic crises and hard budget constraints—most notably in the 1980 and 1990s—many African governments reduced maintenance budgets and public wages, froze recruitment of

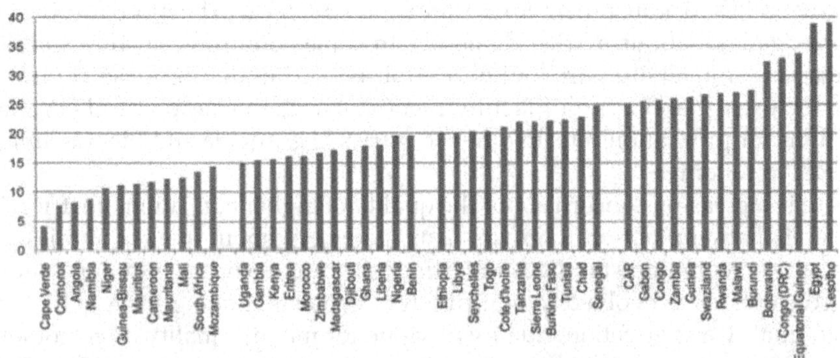

Figure 48.1 Higher education's share of current public expenditure on education, African countries, 2006 (or closest year), as a percent of total current expenditure.

Source: World Bank (2010).

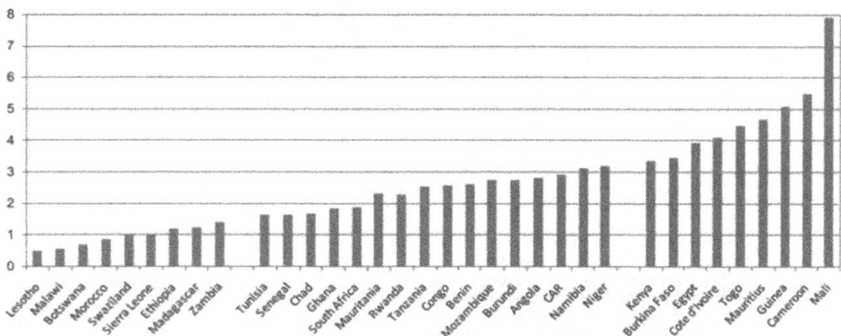

Figure 48.2 Ratio between change in the number of higher education students and change in public resources allocated to current expenditure on higher education, 1991–2006.*

*A ratio value above 1 indicates an increase in the number of higher education students greater than the increase in public resources allocated to current expenditure on higher education.

teaching staff and infrastructure investment, cut social aid and scholarships, eliminated expenditures on books and equipment, all of which resulted in overcrowded lecture halls and excessive student–teacher ratios. Student protests and teachers' strike often prevented the completion of the curriculum and weakened academic achievement. Limited funding and poor management are also associated with the low level of contributions from researchers based in African colleges and universities to international academic research.[7] Inadequate funding also worsens the existing problems and diminishes the incentives for good faculty members to stay in the academic or research field when other activities are more profitable and more valued.

The financing gaps are likely to worsen in the future and raise even more problems for Africa's higher education system. The ever increasing number of college and university students (directly related to progress achieved in primary and secondary school enrolment) suggests that the current trends may be financially unsustainable. It is conservatively projected that Africa will have between 18 and 20 million higher-education students by 2015, with about 10 countries (including Tanzania, Senegal, Mali, Ethiopia and Rwanda) recording at least triple the number of students they had in 2006 (Figure 48.3). Given the currently narrow tax base and fiscal constraints of most African economies, and their dependence on foreign aid for much of their investment budgets, it is critical that the challenge of accommodating a large number of students and providing them with high-quality education be carefully analysed.

A baseline scenario—which assumes the maintenance of African countries' macro capacity, no change in the current levels of public expenditure per student, same share of private education and similar budgetary allocations among education sub-sectors—projects that for a sample of 27 countries, public resources for recurrent expenditures on higher education (excluding studies abroad) would amount to $914 million (in 2004 dollars) in 2015, compared with $594 million actually spent in 2004, an increase in 54% (Figure 48.4). The cumulative virtual gap for the 27 countries would amount to $6.75 billion for the period 2004–2015 (World Bank, 2010). In fact, this scenario suggests that maintaining the current rates of expansion of higher education would lead to a cumulative level of current expenditures 75% higher than the volume of public resources that could be mobilised. Moreover, such a large increase in student enrolment would require a sizable number of new teachers whose training would require time and resources. In order to simply maintain the current student– teacher ratio (20 per instructor), the number of instructors would have to be increased from 456,000 in 2006 to 908,000 in 2015. With a rate of departures (mostly due to retirement) estimated at 20% during the period, 566,000 new instructors would have to be recruited and trained between 2006 and 2015 for the 27 countries in the sample.

In addition, expanding African higher education systems to meet the projected demand in 2015 would necessitate large infrastructure investment, which the World Bank estimates at $45 billion (in 2006 dollars). An assessment of the current capacity for public investment in higher education shows that it would only meet about one-third of total requirements; the implied investment

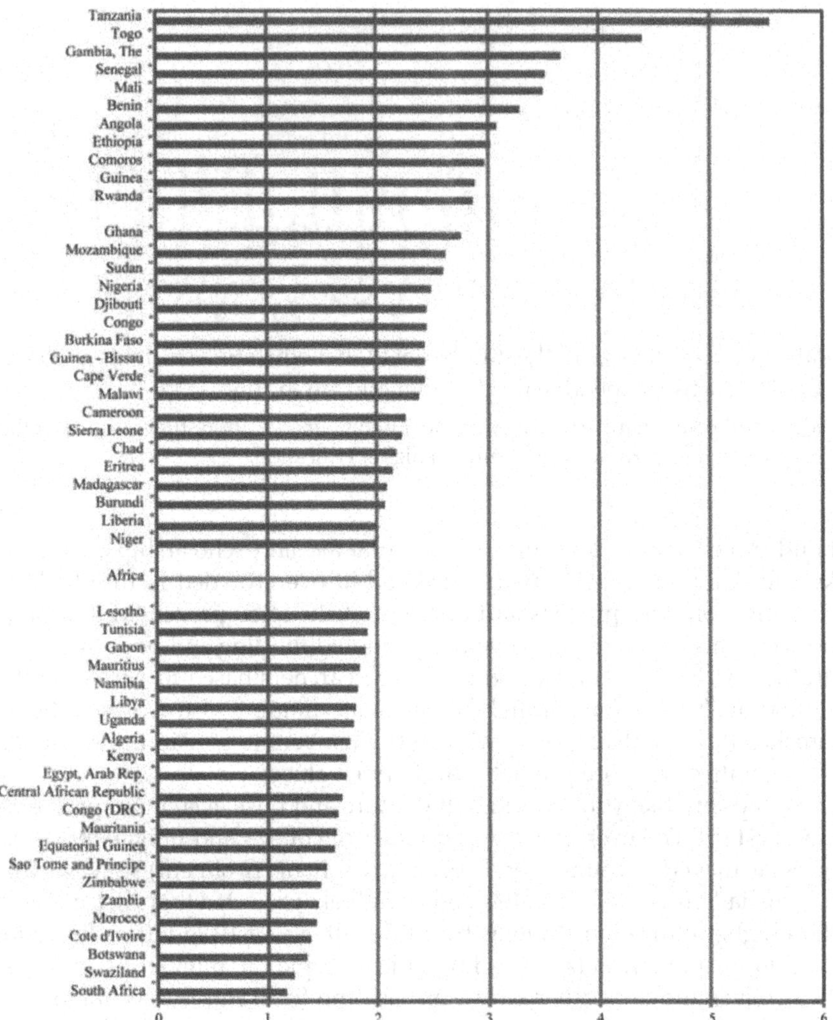

Figure 48.3 Number of students, expressed as a multiple of the 2006 level, expected in 2015 on the basis of current higher education growth trends.

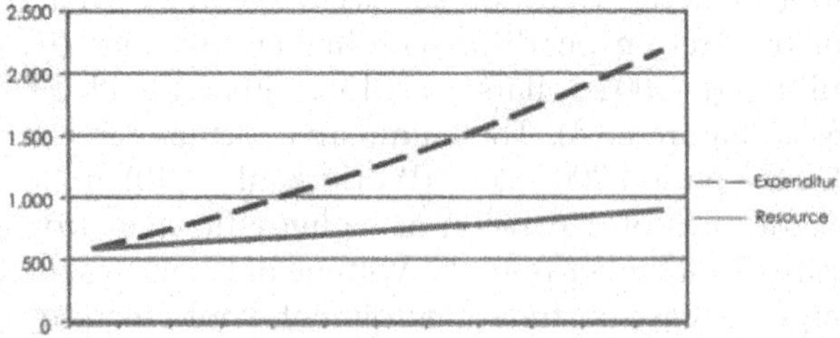

Figure 48.4 Current expenditure on higher education and public expenditure required for expansion of higher education at current rates and unit costs (annual expenditure per student in US dollars).

Source: World Bank (2010).

Note: This simulation concerns only 27 African countries.

financing deficit is therefore of the order of $30 billion in the years ahead (Bruns *et al.*, 2003). These projections highlight the need to rethink the financing framework of higher education in Africa.

2. An Analytical Framework for Addressing Higher Education Finance in Africa

As the previous section made clear, not only is the higher education system in Africa suffering from numerous weaknesses—many of which are tied to financing—but an extrapolation of current trends shows that the system is financially unsustainable. In this section, we begin the process of developing a solution to the problem by specifying an analytical framework for evaluating higher-education finance in Africa, and then assessing options relative to that framework.

Government intervention in tertiary education—or in any kind of economic activity for that matter—can be justified on two grounds. First, if there is an externality or public good, so that the market by itself will not achieve the socially desirable outcome. If a university education confers benefits to society over and above those that are enjoyed by the degree holder (where the latter is usually captured by higher lifetime wages), then there is an externality associated with tertiary education. Government intervention in the form of a subsidy to higher education would then be justified, as it will lead to a higher level of university graduates (and greater benefits to society) than the market-determined levels.

While this argument is compelling, empirical evidence showing that there is such an externality in higher education is quite thin. A number of studies associate tertiary education with economic growth, based on the traditional production function that links accumulation of factor inputs (including human capital) and total factor productivity growth with overall economic growth. For instance, Bloom *et al.* (2006) show that by raising the stock of tertiary education by 1 year, African economies could raise their growth by 0.24 percentage points from factor inputs and an additional 0.39 percentage points through an increase in productivity (World Bank, 2008). But this finding does not distinguish between the individual and collective benefits from tertiary education. Do individual graduates capture all those gains in growth, or do some of them accrue to the rest of society? Other studies estimate the rate of return to tertiary education by distinguishing between the 'private' and 'social' rate of return. Psacharopoulos and Patrinos (2004) review the worldwide estimates of the social rate of return to higher education and find the average of 10.8% to be *lower* than the private rate of return of 19%. At first blush, this sounds as if the externality is a negative one. The problem is that the social rate of return does not incorporate the social benefits to higher education, but it does take into account the social costs, which is mainly the subsidies given to universities to educate these students. The term 'social' is therefore somewhat misleading in this context. Psacharopoulos (2006), among others, has alluded to the social benefits of higher education—in terms of safety, democratisation and less corruption—but not provided any quantitative estimates of their magnitude.

Even if there were no externality, there is a second rationale for government intervention in higher education, namely, equity. The argument here is that the private returns to tertiary education are so high that it is a possible means for poor people to escape poverty. Yet, without some form of subsidies, the families of qualified, poor students would not be able to afford to send their children to university. To the extent that society would prefer to have a more equal distribution of wealth, subsidising higher education is a means of achieving this goal. Once again, the logic of the argument is compelling. The problem, however, is that the empirical evidence seems to indicate the opposite. Throughout the developing world, including in Africa, the lion's share of public spending on higher education accrues to the non-poor. The chart on Indonesia (Figure 48.5) in the early 1990s is typical of the distribution of higher education subsidies around the world.

The pattern is one where the distribution of primary education subsidies is mildly progressive (because poor people have more children and send them to public schools). The distribution of secondary education is increasing in income levels. And the distribution of tertiary education subsidies

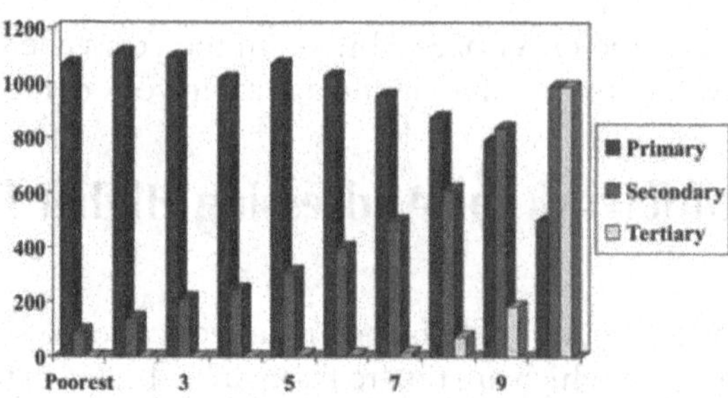

Figure 48.5 Distribution of education subsidies in Indonesia, early 1990s (in rupiah per month).

is concentrated in the top two deciles. This same pattern is found almost everywhere in Africa. In fact, when we consider the share of total public spending in education that goes to the 10% of the population that is most educated (also the wealthiest), we find that in Africa, the average is 43%, with some countries like Malawi and Rwanda exceeding 60% (Figure 48.6).

In short, if the rationale for public intervention in higher education were equity, the resulting distribution appears to be going in the opposite direction. The explanation for this seemingly paradoxical finding is the following: Given the high private rates of return to higher education, the existence of free, public universities represents a huge rent to those who are fortunate enough to get access. Universities ration the excess demand for places through competitive entrance exams. To increase their chances of scoring well in the competitive exams, the wealthier students enroll in high quality, private secondary schools. The net result is that these wealthy students get into universities and benefit from the free tuition, while only a small fraction of the poor gain access.

To sum up, the two rationales for public intervention in higher education are found to be lacking. One, the 'efficiency rationale' has very little empirical evidence behind it. The other, the 'equity rationale' has plenty of empirical evidence, but it all points in the opposite direction from the rationale. Nevertheless, as we saw in Section 1, governments intervene almost everywhere in higher education. And, as we also saw in Section 1, the state of higher education in Africa is extremely poor. We will now explore whether there is a connection between these two observations.

By providing free, public universities, governments have created a range of government failures that have come to characterise higher education in Africa. First, as mentioned above, given government budget constraints, the number of places at universities is severely rationed. While there are now almost 4 million tertiary education students in Africa, and the number is growing at about 8% a year (World Bank, 2008), the number of secondary school graduates in African countries is almost 10–20 times these numbers, implying that there is significant excess demand. As mentioned in Section 1, this excess demand will increase significantly over the next decade. Given the explosion in the numbers of private universities, there are enough Africans that are willing to pay more than the current price of public education.

Second, the universities themselves face financial difficulties (especially in fiscally constrained governments), resulting in low salaries, poor facilities and generally low quality of education. The staff to student ratio in West African universities rose from 1:14 in 1990 to 1:32 in 2002. The universities are subject to the vagaries of their governments' overall fiscal balance. By relying on public funds, universities are having to compromise on quality. Again, given the number of fee-paying universities and students studying abroad, it is apparent that there is a demand for quality that is not being satisfied.

Third, the choice of subjects at universities does not seem to be geared to the labour market. For example, engineering, science and health science are among the subjects with the highest salary for graduates; yet 47% of African university graduates had degrees in social sciences and humanities, and another 22% in education. It is possible that, when students do not pay for their education, their desire to enroll in high-return subjects is diminished.

Fourth, and most disturbingly, the universities have become politicised. Various political parties have taken over student governments in many universities and are using students as agents for their political purposes. While some of this is due to the fact that students are of an impressionable

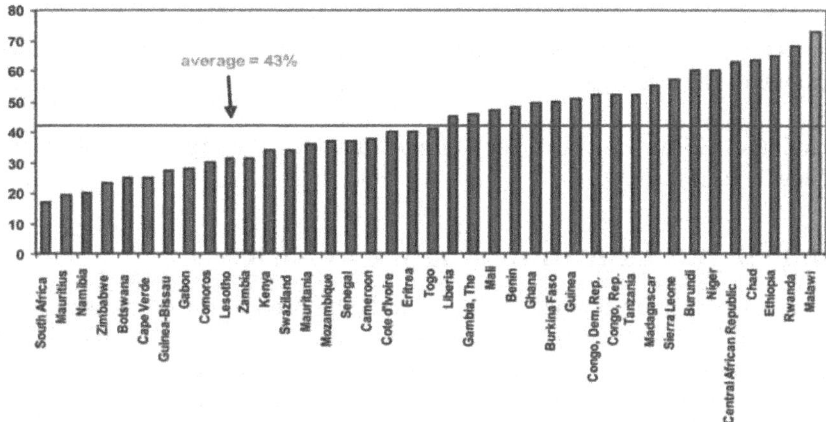

Figure 48.6 Share of public resources used for the 10% most educated, Africa region.

age, it is also a function of the fact that university education is free. Political activity in fee-paying private universities is much lower. Kapur and Crowley (2008) suggest that the growth of the non-university private tertiary institutions is due to the fact that they offer a 'safe haven' from staff strikes and student demonstrations.

It is clear therefore that the system of financing higher education needs to change. Not only is the current system not meeting its objectives, but it is unsustainable. At a minimum, the free public universities should introduce fees, with means-tested subsidies, for poor students. Furthermore, governments should provide a regulatory environment to allow private and public universities to compete on the same footing.

To be sure, there has been a virtual explosion of private universities in Africa. Whereas public universities doubled from 100 to 200 between 1990 and 2007, the number of private tertiary institutions in the same period went from 24 to 468. These private universities appear to be responding to the excess demand for university places. Their programmes emphasise social sciences, economics/business and law because of their low start-up costs (World Bank, 2008). Some of their teachers are moonlighting from public universities. And with some exceptions, they are neither regulated effectively nor is there much quality assurance. World Bank (2008) notes that the attempts to regulate private universities are 'overly restrictive or controlling; [including] cumbersome registration procedures that are less transparent than they should be' (p. 81). Importantly, the emergence of private universities does not appear to have had an effect on the quality or management of the public universities.

Likewise, many countries have attempted to increase cost-sharing in public universities. The East African universities have gone the furthest and have been able to reduce the share of tertiary education in their education budgets even as enrolments have increased. Southern Africa started off with a similar system but was not able to withstand the explosion in enrolments after 2000, resulting in an increase in tertiary education's share in the budget. While there has been some progress in West Africa, Central Africa has been unable to control its level of public spending on tertiary education. Brossard and Foko (2008) note that student welfare expenses constitute 45% of the tertiary education budget in Francophone countries.

The main reason for this mixed record, despite the compelling empirical evidence on the need for reform, is that entrenched interests will resist such reforms. The problem is compounded by the point made earlier about the politicisation of universities. During the early 1990s, Senegal put in place a consensus-based reform at the Université Cheikh Anta Diop, only to have it overturned when the opposition party won the national elections. Ghana, Mali, Nigeria and Senegal have all found that strong staff unions and student associations can stalemate reform efforts.

What we have here, therefore, is a low-level equilibrium trap. Thanks to weakly justified and poorly implemented government interventions in the tertiary education sector, public universities are under-performing. But attempts to reform the system are resisted by the few who are benefiting from the system. Private universities may try to work around the system and meet the excess demand but they cannot fulfill their potential unless there is a system-wide regulatory framework. And yet this framework is also driven by a desire to control rather than facilitate higher education in the countries.

The next section explores possible options for Africa's higher education institutions to emerge from this low-level equilibrium.

3. Reforming Higher Education Finance in Africa

Any reform of higher education finance will have to be tailored to the circumstances of individual countries. However, this review of the state of higher education finance in the continent, and the application of the market failures/government failures framework, suggests that there are certain principles that can guide the reform in each country. We provide below some of the principles and a discussion of how they may be implemented in what is clearly a highly politicised environment.

3.1 Principles

Given the weakness of the rationale for public intervention in higher education—in theory and in practice—a starting principle should be that the costs of higher education should be borne by the students unless there is a compelling reason for these costs to be subsidised. This principle may seem controversial, even radical, in light of the tradition of government-funded public universities in Africa. Yet, it is little more than a validation of what is actually happening in Africa today, with hundreds of thousands of students paying for higher education in the 400+ private universities on the continent, and the millions of students at public universities who have the ability to pay but do not have to because of the policy of free public tertiary education. The aim of this principle is to shift the presumption from free education to cost-sharing in higher education. The key word here is 'presumption', for it does not follow that everyone should pay to attend university. On the contrary, the application of this principle includes the possibility that students from poor families will receive subsidies so that qualified students are not prevented from gaining tertiary education for financial reasons. The revenues from fee-paying students will release funds to finance these scholarships. There is also the possibility that universities produce some externalities, such as through research by professors on various applied topics. If the externality is faculty research, then governments should subsidise this research directly rather than indirectly, through subsidised student tuitions (which are likely to have only a tenuous relationship with the research output).

The second principle is that governments should provide a regulatory environment for all institutions of higher education, public or private, to address some of the information market failures in the system. As with other private goods such as food, government has a role to play in ensuring that minimal standards of quality are met, and that consumers are informed about it. In the case of higher education, governments should provide certification of the curriculum and teaching standards of all universities and colleges by, for instance, regularly inspecting them, and making this information available to the public. Again, many countries have such bodies in place but they typically regulate only the private institutions (the regulation and quality certification is often done by faculty and administrators of the public university). As a result, the regulation becomes one of control of the private sector rather than the provision of a public good to the citizenry. To avoid this outcome, the regulatory bodies should be independent of any institutions of higher learning and should certify the quality of both public and private universities.

3.2 Politics

While both of these principles follow from the economic logic and empirical evidence presented in the paper and, as stated above, they do not deviate dramatically from the status quo, they will be seen as controversial and are likely to be resisted. They threaten the 'rents' of many of the participants in higher education today. For instance, the large number of students currently enrolled in public universities may oppose the imposition of fees. Similarly, faculty at public universities may not welcome being regulated and having the quality of their teaching certified, especially if they are in one of the most prestigious universities in the country (although it should be noted that the most prestigious universities in the world—such as Harvard, Oxford and Cambridge—subject themselves to the same scrutiny).

The application of these principles will therefore have to take into account these potential obstacles. The policies should be designed to build political support, or at least overcome political opposition, so that they have a chance of being implemented. While there are no clear rules for achieving this, a few simple ideas may be helpful.

One is to exempt the current generation of university students from cost-sharing, so that campus protests and the like may be diminished. It would be more difficult for prospective students to mobilise against a policy, so that pre-announcing the policy to take effect 4 years from now may dampen resistance.

A second approach would be to link increases in costs with improvements in quality. Most students would be willing to pay higher fees if they were assured that it would lead to better quality education (those who go to private universities are expressing this sentiment by voting with their feet). A programme where indicators of quality that can be monitored would be announced alongside the introduction of student fees may have a better chance of being accepted than one where students are being asked to pay more with a vague prospect of getting something in return.

Third, a system-wide regulatory framework that oversees public and private universities should be rolled out after an intense publicity campaign that informs the public about the potential benefits of quality standards for all institutions of higher learning. Otherwise, the public universities may launch a publicity campaign pointing to various drawbacks of such a system (including, possibly correctly, that it will become a witch-hunt of faculty who are critical of the present government).

3.3 Economics

The proposed shift in higher education financing is one of many reforms that are required for Africa's higher education system to fulfill its promise. As noted in Section 1, many institutions of higher education in Africa are still suffering from the intellectual and political legacy of colonialism and its aftermath, authoritarianism. As a result, their current function is primarily a sociopolitical one, as they essentially produce generation after generation of civil servants to run the state, or graduates whose final objective is not to create wealth and value in the private sector but rather to use their diplomas to position themselves either on the administrative scene or in the broader public sphere. The main goal of tertiary education should be re-centered to give priority to economic motives, and to ensure that colleges and universities are organised to generate and disseminate knowledge, and satisfy labour market needs.

In order to better perform these economic functions, African institutions of higher education should implement a series of reforms:

First, they should review their selection procedures and admission criteria. Many reputable African universities still follow the old European models of selecting students whom they consider the brightest. They generally do it through tests to determine the students' ability for mathematics or quantitative analysis. Those considered most talented are therefore selected, not on the basis of their overall application package—as is done in most top universities in the world—but on the basis of test results in mathematics. Because of the obsessive focus on selection, a 16-year-old high school student with average grades is almost certainly excluded from admissions to the top academic institutions. Yet, we know from experience and from history that if given the opportunity, some of these average high schools students can turn their life around and go on to achieve greatness (Albert Einstein was only one of many such students). Tertiary education should not focus on testing but on identifying potential leaders, training them, helping them explore, discover and develop their talents and providing them with good theoretical and applied knowledge so that they creatively respond to the challenges of a constantly changing economic environment.

Second, early specialisation, which is often required from undergraduates and even high school students (especially in Francophone Africa), should be dropped. The idea that students at age 14–18 should be forced to make definitive and sound decisions on their choice of academic specialisation (and career) is unrealistic. It has so far served African economies and societies poorly. Few people know at that young age where their real intellectual interests are—especially without prior exposure to the nuts and bolts of the discipline they are contemplating. Students should not be pushed to make career-path decisions until completing at least 2 or 3 years of tertiary education. The Anglo-Saxon model appears optimal, as it leaves some time to test the waters, investigate the quality of professors and courses and adjust academic choices consequently. The American model of maximum flexibility seems to be working quite well and should be considered by African universities. A student can obtain a Bachelor's degree in music history or chemical engineering (for which he does not have to select a major before his last year), and subsequently decide to pursue a Master's in business administration or a PhD in sociology. In fact, the majors that students choose in college do not set the course for the rest of their lives—they are usually the starting point. The academic system allows them to follow their interests and discover what they love.[8] It also offers second and third chances to students who may not get off to a good start. As Blanchard notes, a high school student with average performance can be initially rejected by top academic institutions and left only with the option of attending a small, unknown community college. Still, if he/she does well, he/she will automatically be accepted in a 4-year university, and could 1 day end up at Harvard University. 'If that is not the rule, it is certainly not the exception.' (1998). The moral of the story is clear: ensuring that there are intellectual bridges among academic paths is an essential ingredient for success.

Third, African institutions of higher education should revisit and update (or modernise) their academic curriculum. This is certainly true for most universities, whose structures, organisation and programmes often date back to colonial times. It is also true for many professional schools of administration, business and engineering in Francophone Africa (*Ecoles nationale d'administration* and *Ecoles nationales de magistrature*) that train most of the ruling elites.[9] Despite their claim to specialisation, many of these institutions produce graduates who are generalists—in the best of circumstances—and who lack the cutting-edge knowledge and the mastery of new techniques that would allow them to enter the labour force as anything else but civil servants. One way to induce the necessary changes in the curriculum and make African universities more responsive to the demands of the labour market could be to grant public universities more complete autonomy. Making them responsible for their own objectives, financial management and hiring and firing decisions would force them to become more competitive and to focus on the private and social benefits of their activities.

Fourth, it is important to change the current incentive system, which tends to assign the entire responsibility of the design and implementation of tertiary education policies to the states, with no (or very little) involvement by students, teachers, parents or the private sector. Charging fees to students (or graduates) who can afford it would change the dynamics by creating a more accountable system of mutual responsibility: students acting as investors for their own future would be more demanding on the quality and relevance of their education—they would choose fields with the highest probability of employment opportunities. Getting tertiary education would no longer appear like a handout with sociopolitical underpinnings from the states, but a transactional business with economic significance. Universities would receive higher revenues but would be forced to adjust their programmes to labour market dynamics, knowing that they would eventually go out of business if they produced graduates who could not find jobs. In order to ensure quality they would be forced to recruit qualified staff and develop solid systems for supporting study and research programmes that are of relevance to economic needs. The likelihood of mismatches and gaps in fields of study and graduate competence with job markets will be reduced. Teachers would be more accountable for results as they would understand the business rationale of generating knowledge and providing effective and good training to students. The business sector would be more willing to get involved in the design of the curriculum, in teaching and in the funding of research. In sum, all key stakeholders would feel the need—and obligation—to ensure that tertiary education serves its primary purpose, which is to satisfy the needs of the economic system.

Acknowledgments

The views in this paper are our own, and not necessarily those of the World Bank or the Government of Burkina Faso. We thank Ernest Aryeteey, Olivier Blanchard and Ambroise Kom for comments on an earlier draft, Peter Materu for providing us with some of the data, and Mapi Buitano for editorial assistance.

Notes

1. Fourah Bay College, founded in 1827 in Sierra Leone by the Church Missionary Society, provided the only tertiary education in British West Africa until the 1940s, apart from teacher training colleges that were often associated with missions.
2. In 1961–62 for instance, Nigeria established a second federal university in Lagos and three regional universities in Nsukka, Zaria and Ife. Around the same time, Ghana established two new universities of science and technology at Kumasi and Cape Coast. Similar trends were observed in French-speaking African countries with the creation of *grandes écoles* and *instituts* for specialist professional studies and *écoles nationales supérieures* that worked directly with government ministries to train technicians in administration, public works, agronomy etc.
3. This appears to be a worldwide trend: since the late 1980s, the global market for tertiary education has been growing at an average rate of 7% a year. Worldwide, more than 80 million tertiary students pursue their studies with the help of 3.5 million people employed in teaching and related work. Global annual spending on tertiary education amounts to about $300 billion or 1% of global economic output. Annual income from tuition fees is estimated to be over $30 billion, increasingly from private sources (Materu, 2007, p. 9).
4. Some empirical studies, such as Bennell (1996), have suggested that returns to education in Africa could be smaller than previously estimated. This may be due to methodological problems in earlier studies, especially the bias in OLS estimates caused by the endogenous nature of the schooling variable or the validity of some of the instrumental variables used for the analysis. Even in countries where average returns to education may be low, it has been shown that returns can be substantially increased with reforms (Oyelere, 2008).
5. It is estimated that about 30% of Africa's university-trained professionals—including some 50,000 PhDs—live outside the continent (InterAcademy Council, 2004).
6. A ratio value above 1 indicates an increase in the number of higher education students greater than the increase in public resources allocated to current expenditures on higher education. *Source:* World Bank (2010).
7. In 2002, Sub-Saharan Africa contributed 3,696 scientific publications (compared with 4,468 in the Middle East and North Africa and 16,789 in Latin America and the Caribbean), and its residents submitted only 101 patent applications (compared with 926 in the Middle East and North Africa and 40,003 in Latin America and the Caribbean). *Source:* World Bank (2010).
8. The majority of students in America change their major at least once during their college career and many others do it several times.
9. They were built on the model of the so-called Grandes Ecoles that even the French Government is now trying to reform completely (Lebègue and Walter, 2008).

References

Bennell, P. (1996) 'General versus Secondary Education in Developing Countries: A Review of the Rate of Return Evidence', *Journal of Development Studies*, 33: 230–48.

Blanchard, O. (1998) 'L'université malade', *Libération*, June 22.

Bloom, D.E., D. Canning and K. Chan (2006) 'Higher Education and Economic Development', World Bank Working Paper no. 102, Africa Region Human Development series. Washington, D.C.: World Bank.

Brossard, M. and B. Foko (2008) *Costs and Financing of Higher Education in Francophone Africa*. Africa Human Development Series, World Bank.

Bruns, B., A. Mingat and R. Rokotomala (2003) *Achieving Universal Primary Education by 2015: A Chance for Every Child*. Washington, D.C.: World Bank.

Brydon, L. (1997) 'Education: Anglophone West Africa', in J. Middleton (ed.), *Encyclopedia of Africa South of the Sahara*, vol. 1. New York: Charles Scribner's Sons, pp. 1–4.

Clignet, R. (1997) 'Education: Francophone Western Africa and Madagascar', in J. Middleton (ed.), *Encyclopedia of Africa South of the Sahara*, vol. 1. New York: Charles Scribner's Sons, pp. 9–12.

InterAcademy Council (2004) *Realizing the Promise and Potential of African Agriculture*. Amsterdam: InterAcademy Council.

Kapur, D. and M. Crowley (2008) 'Beyond the ABCs: Higher Education and Developing Countries', Center for Global Development Working Paper 139.

Kom, A. (1996) *Education et démocratie en Afrique : le temps des illusions*. Paris: Yaoundé: L'Harmattan, Editions du CRAC.

Lebégue, T. and E. Walter (2008) *Grandes écoles: la fin d'une exception française*. Paris: Calman-Lévy.

Materu, P. (2007) 'Higher Education Quality Assurance in Sub-Saharan Africa: Status, Challenges, Opportunities and Promising Practices', World Bank Working Paper no. 124. Washington, D.C.: Africa Region Human Development Department.

Oyelere, R.U. (2008) 'Understanding Low Average Returns to Education in Africa: The Role of Heterogeneity across Education Levels and the Importance of Political and Economic Reforms,' IZA Discussion Papers series no. 3766, Bonn: IZA.

Psacharopoulos, G. (2006) 'The value of investment in education: Theory, evidence and policy', *Journal of Education Finance* 32 (2): 113–36.

Psacharopoulos, G. and H. A. Patrinos (2004) 'Returns to investment in education: a further update', *Education Economics*, 12 (2): 111–34.

TFHE (Task Force on Higher Education and Society). (2000) *Higher Education in Developing Countries: Peril and Promise*. Washington, D.C.: World Bank.

World Bank (2008) *Accelerating Catch-up—Tertiary Education for Growth in Sub-Saharan Africa*. Washington, D.C.: World Bank.

World Bank (2010) *Financing Higher Education in Africa*. Washington, D.C.: World Bank.

CHAPTER 49

COST SHARING IN HIGHER EDUCATION IN KENYA: EXAMINING THE UNDESIRED POLICY OUTCOMES

MARY S. NGOLOVOI

Cost sharing in higher education is a policy that comes from the United States. The policy advocates that costs of higher education should be shared between the government, parents, students and/or donor organizations. Proponents of the policy (such as the World Bank) have over the years been advocating for its implementation in African countries. This is because the governments cannot afford to fully finance the increasing numbers of students pursuing higher education. This research study uses qualitative methods to reveal that this 'one size fits all approach' is particularly problematic within African societies for various reasons. The study furnishes recommendations, which are useful when implementing cost sharing in countries that are very different from the United States, in terms of the economy and family structure.

Introduction

Higher education is fundamentally crucial to any country or society that desires socioeconomic development, poverty reduction and stable democratic institutions (Bruns *et al.*, 2003). It is in the institutions of higher education, which serve as spaces for equipping students with advanced knowledge and skills, that students are prepared for positions in government, private enterprise, business and professions (Oketch, 2003).

Over the last two decades Kenya has experienced an increasing demand for higher education. Owing to the high demand for higher education the government of Kenya was forced to introduce cost sharing in higher education in the early 1990s, so as to allow the public purse to cater to health, infrastructure, primary education and eradicate poverty. Johnstone (2004) defines cost sharing as a shift of at least some of the costs that were once borne predominantly by the government or taxpayers, to being shared by (or borne partly by) parents, students and other non-governmental sources of revenue. With the introduction of cost sharing parents and students were to share in some of the costs of higher education that had been catered to by the government. Currently, a student loan programme that is administered by the Higher Education Loans Board (HELB) provides financial assistance to needy students who would otherwise be unable to access higher education.

Although cost sharing in higher education seems to be the only way forward for developing countries that have slow growing economies and various public needs (such as the eradication of HIV/AIDS, health and infrastructure) it is important to examine the undesired outcomes that have resulted from implementation of the policy. Proponents of cost sharing in higher education argue that cost sharing increases equity, reduces public expenditure on education from the government purse, generates revenue for universities, and solves the problem of academic malingering (Johnstone, 2004). Although more countries (especially in Africa) are turning to cost sharing in higher education for the aforementioned reasons it is pertinent to examine which undesired outcomes have emanated from the policy. The aim of this research study was to investigate these outcomes in Kenya.

Literature Review

The introduction of cost sharing has often been met with student resistance in African countries. When cost sharing was introduced in Kenya students responded by 'mobilizing a show down with the government and university in which they demanded that the previous system of financing university education be maintained' (Ngome, 2003, 363). There were also incidents of violence and destruction of property following the introduction of this policy. However, the idea of cost sharing has now been widely accepted owing to the means-tested student loan programme that is in place and the provision of bursaries, both of which aim to increase access to higher education by students from low-income families. Furthermore, because of the existence of financial aid, one can also argue that cost sharing is no longer a daunting phenomenon or one that is perceived as having the 'camel's nose in the tent'. Students today perceive the policy as one that is inevitable and is there to stay. A study by Ngolovoi (2007) showed that students in Kenya were not opposed to cost sharing. The students were aware of the extent of poverty experienced by the majority of Kenyans who live on less than US$2 a day. They articulated that they were cognizant and even sympathetic about critical issues such as fighting the HIV/AIDS pandemic, developing infrastructure, and the provision of free primary education that necessitated the use of funds from the public purse.

Uganda and Nigeria are other countries in Africa where cost sharing in higher education has been met with resistance. In Uganda it could be posited that students resisted the policy because of the absence of financial aid for needy students. In Nigeria, a study by Obassi (2002) showed that students would be more accepting of the policy if they were involved in decisions made regarding tuition and fees as well as financial aid. A study by Some (2006) that examined cost sharing in Burkina Faso, West Africa revealed that university students resisted the policy as paying for education had not improved the quality of teaching and other resources on campus, the loans were inadequate, and corrupt politicians were using the nation's meagre funds to line their own pockets.

There seems to be a common thread that runs through these countries with regard to cost sharing. It is evident that students are bitter about the misuse of government funding and the inadequate financial aid necessary for cost sharing. It can, therefore, be discerned from these studies that cost sharing is likely to be more acceptable if there is transparency in the use of public monies, student involvement in financing policies, and most important, the existence of sufficient means-tested loans available to all needy students who need to borrow to pursue higher education.

Methodology

In order to collect data, 30 second-year, undergraduate students were interviewed for the study. The participants attended both private and public universities in rural areas as well as in the cities. I obtained the participants' contact information from the HELB and interviewed those who wished to take part in the study. On meeting the students, I noticed that they seemed suspicious and nervous and they explained that this was because they had thought that I had been sent to interview them by the HELB because they had mistakenly been awarded loans. The students immediately relaxed when I assured them that I had no affiliation whatsoever to the HELB. The last vestiges of suspicion melted away when I explained to them that to ensure that their confidentiality was maintained, I would ascribe pseudonyms when using excerpts of their interviews in my research study and that it would be impossible for whatever they told me to be used against them at a later date.

In order to provide a comfortable and non-threatening space for loan applicants, all interviews were conducted at a rented office that was located within the city of Nairobi. This research site was convenient because it was easily accessible to the participants and also close to the public transportation areas.

After all the interviews were transcribed the data was analysed using open and focus coding (Bogdan and Biklen, 1998). This entailed sifting through and categorizing small segments of the interview data in order to identify and develop concepts that were important in providing analytic insights through close examination and reflection of the data (Emerson *et al.*, 1995). In other words, open coding was employed to the raw interviews in an effort to locate themes and assign initial codes in an attempt to compress the data into categories, while focus coding entailed linking up categories to develop analytic themes (Neuman, 2006). This process allowed me to develop three pertinent themes for discussing the findings of the study.

Findings

Three major themes were developed from the study. They are loan application difficulties, loan amounts: a portrait of students' experiences and legitimization of nuclear families.

Loan Application Difficulties

The HELB has designed a questionnaire, to be filled out by all students applying for loans, to gather information pertaining to their socioeconomic background and that of their families. The HELB has for some time now given chiefs the responsibility of verifying whether this information is accurate. The participants stated that they found the loan application process distressing as the local chiefs would demand bribes before signing their forms. This was particularly annoying to students who stated that it was preposterous to pay the chiefs to do their jobs. Other students articulated that the chiefs would also ask students unnecessary questions and if they were unable to answer them satisfactorily they would be turned away without having their forms signed.

> Syombua (grimacing): When I went to see the chief he asked me about the course content of my degree and I tried to explain to him what the Bachelor of Commerce entailed. He however told me that he did not know what I was saying and sent me away and told me to return when I was ready to ensure that he understood what my degree was all about. He turned me away three times and in the end I had to get my father to have my form signed for me.

Clearly, demanding bribes and making it difficult for students to obtain signatures is an unfortunate consequence of the cost sharing policy in higher education. Needy students have no choice but to borrow loans to access higher education. However, the chiefs are making it very difficult for students to apply for loans.

Loan Amounts: A Portrait of Students' Experiences

The other major theme that emerged from this study was related to the loan amounts. The HELB awards various loan amounts to the students after determining their levels of neediness. Hence, some loan applicants in this study did not receive any money while others were awarded loans because they were found to be incapable of accessing higher education without financial assistance. Although there were substantial differences in the costs of education (with private institutions charging more for tuition), students from both the private and public universities lamented that the loan amounts they were receiving from the HELB were not sufficient to cater to all their expenses.

> Musa: As engineering students we must purchase text books because they are not available in the libraries. The books in the library are outdated. One text book costs KES 9,000 (US$129). If I buy two textbooks about half my loan is gone. I am really suffering.
>
> * * *
>
> Kamau: (A student in a private university) My tuition is over KES 100,000 (US$1428) per semester. I got KES 35,000 (US$500) from the HELB and that is very little considering the fact that my parents have to pay the remaining balance for this semester and the next one. I wish the HELB had given me more money.

It appeared that students were spending a lot of money on photocopying reading assignments as they could not afford to purchase text books. They would borrow textbooks from their professors or classmates from wealthy families who were able to afford all the required learning resources. The participants also complained that the KES 18,000 (US$257) they received from the HELB for their practicum (which lasted over three months) was also not sufficient to meet their living expenses. During their practicum they were required to work for various companies or institutions, some of which were many miles away from their homes. This meant that they had to incur expenses such as rent, utilities, transportation, supplies, and meals. Therefore KES 18,000 (US$257) was not sufficient for many of the students whose parents could not contribute towards their expenses. The characteristic of inadequate loan funds is not unique to Kenya only. Some (2006) found that the loan amounts awarded to students in Burkina Faso were insufficient as the amounts had not increased although tuition fees and the rate of inflation had increased.

Survival Strategies

The participants who complained bitterly about the inadequate loan amounts discussed various survival strategies as well as alternative sources of funding they employed to supplement the loans from the HELB. They also explained how other students managed to cope with the shortfall of the student loans.

> Kimotho: I have learnt to skip meals so that I can be able to survive the whole semester. I survive on two meals a day. It is really tough but what else can I do? My parents are not able to support me. I come from a very poor family and my parents are hoping that I will finish my education and then help them to educate my siblings. So that is why I have to scale my finances very carefully.
>
> ***
>
> Angela: My parents buy me flour, rice, and beans at the beginning of the semester. I then buy vegetables and cook in my room. I find that I use less money this way than if I had to buy food in the dining hall or the cafeteria.
>
> ***
>
> MM: How do other students manage to survive if the loans are not adequate?
>
> George: I have a friend who brought two sacks each of maize and beans. He used to cook githeri[1] and eat it most of the time because he could not afford to eat in the dining hall, which is the cheapest place on campus. It saved him money. Many students these days cook in their rooms to save money. Others engage in crime. It is sad that some students have been forced to become criminals. You also find many girls with sugar daddies. I see them being picked up in nice cars by men that are older than their fathers.

It seemed like the best way to stretch the students' finances was by spending less money on food either by cooking in the university rooms, skipping meals or by eating meals that would be physically satisfying but not balanced. None of these strategies was appropriate as both skipping meals and eating food that was not nutritionally balanced is unhealthy. In addition, skipping meals is likely to impair the students' level of concentration on their studies and lead to poor grades. Cooking in the students' rooms is also risky due to the prevalence of fires that have occurred in the past as a result of overloading of electrical circuits. It was appalling that engaging in commercial sex for financial gain seemed to be prevalent among the female students. This was consistent with Mwinzi's (2002) study, which found that female students engaged in prostitution in order to generate additional funds needed to survive on campus. However, whereas in this particular study only the female students took part in commercial sex, Mwinzi's (2002) study showed that the male students also engaged in the same practice. By engaging in these activities (which are considered to be immoral in Kenyan society) students risk their lives by exposing themselves to sexually transmitted diseases. Furthermore, commercial sex could contribute to psychological problems among students such as low self-esteem levels and even depression, which could inhibit students from performing well in their studies.

A number of participants stated that they were involved in businesses. Through these small-scale businesses students were able to generate substantial income, which they used to supplement student loans. A few of them narrated that on some occasions they had been forced to miss classes; when presented with the choice between attending a class and making an extra KES 500 (US$7) the latter would always take precedence. Sometimes the businesses required the students to be away from their universities for more than five consecutive days in a week. This was either due to a problem with obtaining the merchandise or the businesses being located far away, hence requiring many hours of travel. The businesses nevertheless appeared to be profitable and worthwhile.

> MM: What type of business do you do?
>
> Timothy: I buy and sell maize for a sizeable profit. My business is located upcountry, five hours from my university. It is very difficult for me to balance my business with my studies because sometimes I have to travel at short notice and in doing so I miss my classes.
>
> * * *
>
> David: I run a Safaricom[2] dealership where I sell scratch cards.[3] My business is doing very well and I am making good money.

Owing to the demands of the businesses, the participants explained that they had to copy schoolwork from students who had attended lectures and expressed that on several occasions they had been unable to understand what had been taught during their absence, although they had tried to learn from their peers. One participant mentioned that she had asked a friend to take a test on her behalf to avoid getting into trouble with her lecturer. The friend took the test without the lecturer finding out. It is clearly impossible from these findings for students to maintain good grades while running these businesses.

The finding that there were university students who engaged in businesses to earn incomes to supplement the loans from the HELB was consistent with Mwinzi's (2002) study, which showed that students in two public universities engaged in income-generating activities to enable them to address their educational and living expenses. It was interesting to discover that although the student loan amounts had been increased since Mwinzi's (2002) study, from KShs.20,000 (US$285) to KShs.35,000 (US$500), the current study conducted five years later revealed that the loan amounts are still inadequate for most students. However, unlike Mwinzi's (2002) study, which also showed that other reasons for engaging in businesses included the need to support the students' families, unchallenging academic work, the lack of enjoyable recreational activities, and the desire to train for future entrepreneurship ventures, in this particular research study the only reason that participants articulated for engaging in businesses was to pay for their educational costs.

Johnstone (2004) argues that one of the limitations of cost sharing in higher education is that the ability of parents to contribute towards their children's education may be hampered as they lack financial resources. This is especially true in the Kenyan case, where although the HELB expects families to be able to contribute to their children's education, it may not be possible for all families to contribute any finances at all. The result of this is evidenced in the study through the students' engagement in businesses and other activities to cater to educational expenses when the HELB inaccurately presupposes that their families should contribute some financial amount towards their education. It is clear that the inadequate loan amounts arise from the fact that the HELB does not have adequate finances to cover all the loan applications.

It was also interesting to learn that a large number of participants in the study had part-time jobs during the school semester that were instrumental in generating extra money to meet their educational costs when the student loans were not enough. Some of these jobs included tutoring high-school students, teaching in commercial colleges, and data entry in various companies.

Other students sought funding from their constituencies from the Constituency Development Funds. Each constituency in Kenya has been allocated funds from the government for the purpose of development and with the aim of eradicating poverty at the constituency level. In order to receive these grants students are required to approach the members of parliament who are in charge of their constituencies for funding. The participants in the study received varied amounts, which ranged from KES 2,000 (US$29) to KES 20,000 (US$286). Those who received grants stated that they had found the money to be very useful in catering to their living expenses.

Some participants also stated that they had received funds from the student associations in their universities. Each public university in Kenya has a student association, which has funds allocated for use by the student population. Although the participants articulated that they did not receive much money from these associations, they were nevertheless grateful for the additional funding because they mused that any amount of money was better than nothing.

Work-study programmes were also sources of obtaining funds to supplement the loan programme. This concept has been borrowed from the United States. However, in comparison to the United States, the Kenyan work-study programmes are highly competitive and also pay very little. Moreover, they are available only in a few, mainly private institutions.

> MM: How would you describe the work-study programs in your university?
>
> Susan: They are highly competitive and the opportunities are few. The last time I checked, students were paid KES. 55 (US$0.78) an hour and were allowed to work for 10 hours a week. The maximum period a student can work is only two weeks. So in total students can work for 20 hours in two weeks for the whole semester and then the jobs are given to other needy students. This is really ridiculous! Also, most students actually are unable to get these jobs because they are very few. Over two thirds of the students apply for work-study jobs, which is demonstrative of the extent of neediness among the student population. We are also not sure about the criteria for those who get the jobs.

The work-study programme is not an instrumental method for supplementing the student loans because as indicated by the data, the jobs are highly competitive and the positions are very few. Furthermore, when the contracts run for short periods of time, there is not much money to be made by students. Although the jobs are supposed to be on the basis of need, many participants perceived that some students who got these jobs were friends or relatives of the faculty and administration staff.

Other alternative sources of funding revealed by the study came from *harambees*,[4] churches and relatives. The participants in the study who had held *harambees* explained that they had not managed to collect substantial amounts of money. It could be argued that the reason for this is that the money collected during *harambees* depends on the socioeconomic status of the people who attend these functions. As the students whose families held *harambees* were poor, it was likely that the people they invited to attend these events were from the same social network, thereby possessing similar economic backgrounds and as a result very little money was collected. The churches and relatives also did not give very much towards the participants' education for the same reasons.

A number of insights can be drawn from these interviews. First, the HELB is not disbursing loans in alignment with the demands of the students' educational majors. This finding is consistent with Otieno's (2004) observation that there is no equity in the way loans are awarded as students taking science majors such as medicine and engineering are likely to incur higher costs when purchasing textbooks and laboratory equipment compared to those who major in Fine Art and Home Economics. According to Otieno (2004), students majoring in the latter courses are likely to incur lower costs as their learning resources (such as chalk, writing materials and design supplies are cheaper in comparison). It therefore seems unfair to disburse blanket loan amounts without taking into consideration the majors of students.

Further scrutiny of the data also revealed that textbooks are essential for good academic performance. However, all the public university students stated that their university libraries lacked adequate textbooks and only a few copies were available to serve large numbers of students. Furthermore, students articulated that even when they were lucky enough to find the textbooks listed on their course outlines, they were often outdated editions. As a result, for students to work on their readings and assignments, they had to purchase the text books. The majority who found the costs to be prohibitive were forced to borrow the books from their wealthy peers and photocopy the chapters that were assigned by their lecturers. Hence, many students lamented that they had been forced to spend exorbitant amounts each semester on photocopies. The loan amounts were evidently still insufficient to cater to either the purchase of the text books or photocopies.

Second, Ziderman (2002) argues that one of the objectives of student loans is to assist students by easing their financial difficulties, increasing commitment to their studies, and achieving financial independence. He also posits that other objectives of the student loan schemes are to provide income to universities and for the expansion of the university system. In a country where the government budget is financially constrained, it has been difficult to successfully achieve all these objectives as the capital available for loans is very low. As a result some students have been forced to engage in businesses and part-time jobs which pull them away from their studies. This is likely to lead to poor grades as they do not put in the time required to attend classes, work on assignments and study for their examinations. Also, the constant worrying and struggling to obtain funds to address the financial shortfall from the loans is likely to lead to psychological stress that could adversely affect the academic performance of students. The inadequacy of the loan amounts stems from the fact that the funds are not commensurate with the cost of living as they had never been adjusted to reflect the rate of inflation.

Legitimization of Nuclear Families

As mentioned earlier, the HELB uses a questionnaire that is filled out by all students applying for loans, to gather information pertaining to their socioeconomic background as well as their families. The study showed that the loan application form that the HELB uses to collect information pertaining to the applicants' socioeconomic status is tailored for nuclear families. Using such an instrument in a country like Kenya where polygamy is widely practiced and culturally accepted is particularly problematic as the HELB does not factor in the household size when determining the level of need among loan applicants. Hence a number of participants whose families practiced polygamy were denied loans because the HELB found their fathers' incomes to be higher than the threshold they use to award loans. This raised major financial problems because although the family income appeared to be high, the total expenses were also high owing to the number of wives and children in the household. Hence the participants who did not get loans due to these reasons suffered greatly when trying to generate alternative resources. Cost sharing in higher education is a policy that comes from the Western countries. Proponents of the policy such as the World Bank have, over the years, been advocating for its implementation in African countries. The study shows that this 'one size fits all approach' is particularly problematic within African societies. Hence, legitimizing of nuclear families in a society that still practices polygamy is clearly an undesirable technical consequence of the cost sharing that remains problematic.

Policy Suggestions and Conclusion

The rationales for introducing the cost sharing policy in higher education in Kenya were mainly to address the declining governmental support to universities through tuition and to increase equity because students from the middle and upper income families can and will continue to afford to finance their education owing to its private benefits. It was expected that with the implementation of the policy and the introduction of the means-tested loan programme, more academically qualified students from low-income families would access and participate in higher education. Although the implementation of this policy still appears at the moment to be the most practical solution, given the government's declining financial support for higher education, it is important to critically examine the undesirable outcomes that have resulted due to technical reasons associated with the implementation of the policy.

As discussed in the findings there are three major problems associated with the technical aspects of implementing cost sharing in higher education in Kenya. These are: the difficulties in the loan application process, which stem from the chiefs demanding bribes and bullying students by turning them away for not satisfactorily answering unnecessary questions; inadequate loan amounts that take away the students' commitment to their studies by forcing them to generate additional finances; and lastly the legitimization of nuclear family structures in a polygamous society. Clearly all these outcomes of the policy are not what the proponents of cost sharing had in mind when they implemented the policy in Kenya.

The chiefs are doing a disservice to the needy students who apply for loans by demanding bribes and also bullying students before signing loan application forms. The HELB should find other ways of verifying the socioeconomic information of loan applicants. This will make the cost sharing policy work better by ensuring that needy students are not deterred from applying for loans, which they desperately need to access higher education.

The respondents in the study vehemently attested to the fact that the loan amounts they were receiving from the HELB were not adequate to meet all the costs of education. Students from both private and public universities expressed the hope that the HELB would increase the loan amounts as, for many of them, surviving on campus was difficult. The inadequate loan amounts could be attributed to the technical flaws of the means-testing system in failing to screen out the wealthy and awarding them loans, which should instead have been disbursed to the students from the low-income families. Moreover, the inadequate loan amounts also stem from the fact that the government has not been able to substantially increase the loan capital owing to the presence of other compelling public needs (such as health and elementary education). It could be further posited that for this reason the HELB is attempting to stretch the available funds as much as possible, so as to cater to more students rather than matching the levels of need with loan awards. Nonetheless, it is difficult to fathom the magnitude of student survival strategies, which include engaging in immoral activities (such as crime and prostitution), forgoing classes to work or run income-generating ventures and failing to meet basic needs. It is apparent that the students' physical wellbeing is threatened not only because they are eating unhealthily but also because they are engaging in crime and prostitution. It is therefore imperative to disburse adequate student loans commensurate with the standard of living. This can be achieved by adjusting the amounts each year to reflect the inflation rate.

One of the ways through which the HELB can increase its loan capital and subsequently loan amounts is through aggressive loan recovery. Over the last five years, the law (under Section 16(i)(b) of the HELB Act) has been enforced by the HELB for employers to ensure that a percentage of the salaries of loan beneficiaries are remitted to repay their debts. Employers have been forced to cooperate in the loan recovery process as they want to avoid paying fines as penalties for not remitting salaries of loan beneficiaries to the HELB. This has been highly instrumental in increasing the rate of loan recovery. However, more needs to be done to increase loan recovery as currently there are 60,000 loan beneficiaries owing over KES 7 billion (US$100,000,000) who have not remitted a single cent to the HELB (Otieno, 2007a). The HELB is currently holding discussions with the recently licensed Credit Reference Bureau (CRB) so that loan defaulters can be tracked down (Otieno, 2007b). The CRB keeps all the financial data on credit performance of individuals and banks, and can furnish information on borrowers who have a history of defaulting with other lenders (Otieno, 2007b). The HELB hopes to be incorporated with other credit institutions so that all the defaulters will be denied loans and mortgages (Otieno, 2007b). This is an excellent strategy, which will prompt loan beneficiaries to repay their debt so that they can appear credit-worthy to financial lenders. The other collection strategy that HELB recently announced was that all the names of parliamentary and civic aspirants who have not repaid their loans would be published in the national daily newspapers if they failed to contact the board and initiate payment arrangements (Ngetich and Ngare, 2007). The HELB hopes that all the parliamentary hopefuls who have not repaid their loans will immediately initiate repayments because they do not want to be shamed and appear as untrustworthy leaders who cannot be responsible for public affairs (Ngetich and Ngare, 2007).

Second, the HELB should start using co-signatories to increase the amounts recovered. However, the role of co-signatories should not be to serve as guarantors responsible for loan repayment in the event of defaults as not all students have families with sufficient assets that can be used as collateral when borrowing (Johnstone and Marcucci, 2007). Using co-signatories for this purpose would only appear threatening to many of the low-income students, which in turn would deter them from borrowing. Therefore, the HELB should use 'soft' co-signatories whose sole purpose would be to provide information about the whereabouts of loan defaulters for collection purposes (Johnstone and Marcucci, 2007).

Third, it is very difficult for the Kenyan diaspora to repay loans as they cannot make transactions over the internet, which would be the easiest method of loan repayment. This has hindered the repayment process as they have to contact the HELB to enquire about loan repayment procedures and often fail to receive feedback or perhaps find the process tedious due to global time differences. The HELB can remedy this problem by designing a website where repayments can be made over the internet, thus making the process easier and cheaper. Finally, the HELB can track down, through debt collectors, beneficiaries of loans and initiate payment plans. There are some loan beneficiaries who need to be traced and who had benefited from the loans under the previous loan programme. Hence debt collectors will certainly be useful in the collection of education loans.

It is also important for the HELB to recognize that polygamy is still very prevalent in many parts in Kenya. Therefore, loan application forms should be designed with such families in mind. This will prevent applicants from being turned down when they apply for loans in cases where their fathers' wives do not have jobs or businesses, thereby making it difficult to make ends meet.

Notes

1. An inexpensive Kenyan dish made by boiling maize and beans.
2. Safaricom is the leading mobile telephone company in Kenya.
3. Scratch cards are used for providing 'talk time' on mobile phones and all cards have various monetary values.
4. Harambee is a Swahili word coined by the first president of Kenya, Mzee Jomo Kenyatta, which refers to the act of pulling together to work towards a common goal. In this article harambee refers to the collective action of friends, families and the local community efforts in coming together to contribute money that is used to pay for educational costs.

References

Bogdan, R. and Biklen, S. (1998) *Fieldwork in Qualitative Research in Education: An Introduction to Theory and Methods*, Boston: Allyn and Bacon.

Bruns, B., Mingat, S. and Rakotomalala, R. (2003) *Achieving Universal Primary Education by 2015*, Washington, DC: The World Bank.

Emerson, R., Tretz, R. and Shaw, L. (1995) *Writing Ethnographic Field Notes*, Chicago: The University of Chicago Press.

Johnstone, D.B. (2004) 'Higher education finance and accessibility of tuition fees and student loans in sub-Saharan Africa', *Journal of Higher Education in Africa* 2(2): 11–36.

Johnstone, D.B. and Marcucci, P. (2007) *Financially Sustainable Student Loan Programs: The Management of Risk in the Quest for Private Capital*, Washington, DC: Educational Policy Institute, Global Center on Private Financing of Higher Education.

Mwinzi, D.C. (2002) 'The Impact of Cost-Sharing Policy on the Living Conditions of Students in Kenyan Public Universities: The Case of Nairobi and Moi Universities', Proceedings of the 28th Annual International Symposium; Dakar, Senegal.

Neuman, L. (2006) *Social Research Methods: Qualitative and Quantitative Approaches*, 6th edn, Boston: Pearson Education Inc.

Ngetich, P. and Ngare, P. (2007) 'Varsity loan defaulters told, pay up or elsey', *The Daily Nation* 10 August.

Ngolovoi, M. (2007) 'Cost sharing in Kenya: Implications on equity and access', *International Journal of Learning* 14(7): 65–70.

Ngome, C. (2003) 'Kenya', in D. Teffera and P. Altbach (eds.) *African Higher Education: An International Reference Handbook*, Bloomington, IN: Indiana University Press, pp. 359–371.

Obassi, I. (2002) 'An empirical study of the cost sharing crises in Nigeria University', AAU's Study Program on Higher Education Management in Africa, Research Paper Series.

Oketch, M.O. (2003) 'Affording the unaffordable: Cost sharing in higher education in sub-Saharan Africa', *Peabody Journal of Education* 78(3): 88–106.

Otieno, S. (2007a) 'HELB to give Sh 120 m loans to students next year', *The East African Standard*, 7 May.

Otieno, S. (2007b) 'HELB plans new way of netting defaulters', *The East African Standard*, 4 September.

Otieno, W. (2004) 'Student loans in Kenya: past experiences, current hurdles, and opportunities for the future', *Journal of Higher Education in Africa* 2(2): 75–99.

Some, T.H. (2006) 'Cost sharing and institutional instability in francophone West Africa: Student resistance at the University of Ouagadougou, Burkina Faso', Ph.D. dissertation, Department of Education, Leadership & Policy, State University of New York, University at Buffalo.

Ziderman, A. (2002) 'Alternative objectives of national student loan schemes: Implications for design, evaluation and policy', *The Welsh Journal of Education* 11(1): 37–39.

CHAPTER 50

INTERNATIONALIZATION AS A RESPONSE TO GLOBALIZATION: RADICAL SHIFTS IN UNIVERSITY ENVIRONMENTS

NELLY P. STROMQUIST

This case study probes recent developments in a number of academic and non-academic aspects of a private research university in response to current globalization trends. Under the name of internationalization, university administrators and external firms are emerging as powerful decision-makers shaping academic content and even academic governance. This is manifested in student recruitment and in the hiring of prestigious professors and researchers to increase university reputation and thus to appeal to more students and secure more research funds. Among disciplines central to economic and technological globalization, such as communication, business, and engineering, patterns of convergence are emerging. Rather than internationalism, internationalization is found to prevail, and internationalization is found to signify predominantly a search for student markets domestically and abroad rather than positioning the university's knowledge at the service of others in less advantaged parts of the world.

Introduction

As technological innovations relentlessly compress the world in space and time and our economies become rapidly impelled into the highly competitive environment of global markets, educational institutions are being challenged to follow suit. At the university level, globalization is manifested by what is termed by insiders as "internationalization," a subtle response that not only affects academic programs, faculty, and students, but also creates new administrative structures and privileges.

The majority of US research universities mention internalization in their current mission statements, and about half include it in their strategic plans (Siaya and Hayward 2003). The Association of American Colleges and Universities (AACU) endorses global education to prepare students for the global world of work as well as to bring about a shared future marked by justice, security, equality, human rights, and economic sustainability. Ideally, to meet this challenge universities will incorporate an international/intercultural dimension into their teaching, research, and service functions (de Wit 1999). In practice, internationalization covers a wide range of services, from study abroad and greater recruitment of international students, to distance education and combinations of partnerships abroad, internationalized curriculum, research and scholarly collaboration, and extracurricular programs to include an international and intercultural dimension (Altbach 1998; Biddle 2002; de Wit 2002).

According to Jones (2000), "internationalism" is different from "internationalization." He defines the former as: "Common sense notions of international community, international cooperation, international community of interests, and international dimensions of the common good," including promotion of global peace and well-being (p. 31). Husén offers a view of learning close to internationalism when he maintains that "global learning means a focus on global issues and the learning needs which are associated with them" (p. 160). In a related vein, concepts of global citizenship also point to the notion of internationalism. McIntosh (2005, p. 23) proposes as global citizenship, "the ability to see oneself and the world around one, the ability to make comparisons and contrasts, the ability to see 'plurality' as a result . . . and the ability to balance awareness of one's own realities with the realities of entities outside of the perceived self." For her part, Ladson-Billings (2005) holds that competent and responsible citizens are those with the capacity to think critically, are willing to dialogue with others, and are concerned for the rights and welfare of others. She finds that schools tend to be undemocratic spaces because, among several other traits, they focus on passive learning, emphasize compliance and obedience, and lack attention to global issues. Internationalization, in contrast, refers to greater international presence by the dominant economic and political powers, usually guided by principles of marketing and competition.

Are universities moving toward internationalism or rather internationalization? A study that represented a landmark in the examination of universities under market-led forces was that by Slaughter and Leslie (1997). Their study, which focused on public universities in four countries (US, Canada, UK, and Australia), covered institutional trends between 1970 and 1995[1] and documented the impact of competition for external funds upon university performance. In the years elapsed since then, there have been additional developments such as increased global economic competition and new information and communication technologies.

There is consensus that higher education is undergoing substantial change in the face of globalization, which brings a greater emphasis on market forces to the process of educational decision-making. However, universities experience pressures in different ways, depending on whether they are private or public institutions. Among the public universities, there are significant trends toward decentralization, mergers, privatization, and accountability. Among private institutions, there are considerable pressures to position themselves as the universities of choice for students and to be highly competitive in the procurement of research funds, both of which generate complex dynamics in their functioning. Since private institutions are more dependent on external support than public institutions, they are forced to monitor current trends in the economic environment and look for new opportunities; hence, private universities by the nature of their organization are likely to be more sensitive to globalization forces.

Interpretations of the changes going on in higher education under the influence of globalization are by no means uniform. While the majority asserts that we are increasingly facing homogenizing tendencies in the administration, teaching, and research practices of universities, others hold that we are experiencing more localized responses, because it is not only economic forces that are at work but also cultural and environmental processes that create differences in adoption of new ideas and practices. Thus, speaking for changes in the United Kingdom, Deem (2001) considers that, while teaching and research audits were brought in for finance-driven reasons, in some cases they were introduced to reassure the public that universities' academic standards remain high.

A mechanism that will further expand the globalization of education is the General Agreement on Trade in Services (GATS). This agreement includes tertiary education among the 12 trade-related sectors now being negotiated among countries. GATS will have major repercussions on the types of tertiary institutions that are created abroad and on the presence of private universities in many parts of the world. GATS functions through a set of "commitments," some general and some voluntary. Education is considered a voluntary commitment, so WTO member nations will decide the degree of access to provide for different education sectors, but once agreed upon, all members are to be treated equally (OECD 2004). The United States was a major actor in requesting free trade for education and health services. Education and training represents indeed its fifth largest service sector. Globally, education investments abroad resulted in capital flows of more than $30 billion in 2003 (Aviles 2005).

From a theoretical perspective, I explore two theses. One is that globalization gives rise not only to new economic dynamics but also to new social relations, and that these in turn have consequences for social and organizational structures. In education, the expanded economic and social forms that have come to dominate the landscape of many nations are creating "a master discourse informing policy decisions at all levels of education" (Gough 2000, p. 78). Technological innovations influence the dynamics of social relations, either by concentrating certain kinds of power in the hands of few or by dispersing it among the many and, while being constantly constructed, these "resources of power and differential knowledge about the working of institutions are implicated in the construction, manipulation, and maintenance of the social world, at both the national and international level" (Welton 2001, p. 16).

My second thesis asserts that the strong links developing between business firms and educational institutions produce a tendency for the latter to imitate the former, a phenomenon first detected between schools and the economy in the United States under the principle of "correspondence" (Bowles 1972; Bowles and Gintis c1977). Along the same lines, noting the substantial homogeneity of organizational forms and practices among a wide variety of institutions, Powell and DiMaggio (1991) ask: What causes the similarity? They identify two forms of isomorphism: competitive (present in fields that have free and open competition), and institutional (visible in organizations that compete not just for resources and customers but for political power and legitimacy). This second case would seem to apply to universities. Powell and DiMaggio use the term "institutional isomorphism" to explain the ways organizations develop similarities in methods, procedures, purposes, and outcomes, a convergence that they attribute primarily to the frequent movement of administrators from one organization to another. Agre (1999) highlights the influence of information technology in bringing standardization to courses as independent universities negotiate degrees. I modify the concept of "institutional isomorphism" by positing that new cultural practices—including those adopted by universities—derive from material conditions and thus are not totally independent innovations as the simple circulation of administrators would seem to imply. I further use the concept of institutional isomorphism to explore convergence among units within a single institution. Universities—long considered examples of loosely coupled sets of units and even taken as examples of "organized anarchies" (Weick 1976; Cohen and March c1986)—are irresistibly generating patterns of conformity in objectives, processes, and outcomes of disciplines touched by economic and technological globalization. Since universities are leaders in the process of knowledge production, they engage in practices with demonstrable positive consequences for recognition and access to financial resources. Universities, dependent on external resources acquired through competition, are evincing a rapid change from their immediate past as well as an increased similarity with each other.

Study Methodology

This article centers on a private university, which I will call Progressive University (PU hereafter). Located on the west coast of the United States, PU sees itself as uniquely positioned to develop ties with the Pacific Rim. Its brochures describe itself as ranking among top 10 private research universities in federal research and development support. Indeed, PU receives about $400 million annually in sponsored research, which situates it in the 9th position for research funding among all private university and in the 18th position among all universities. PU has also been quite successful in attracting private donations, averaging over $350 million annually in cash gifts. According to the *Philosophical Gourmet Report* and *US News & World Report*, PU is ranked among the top 50 research universities in the country.

To examine PU's internationalization efforts, I use the case study approach (Ragin and Becker 1992; Yin 1994), which fosters a holistic understanding of organizational processes by being attentive to a number of trends combine and reinforce each other to create particular impacts. The naturalistic method of the case study enables the researcher to present the points of view of the social actors involved, and to link these perceptions to their particular locations in academic units.

Deem argues that studies which do not offer full comparative and longitudinal data do not permit research to capture the substantial hybridity that is occurring; in particular, she maintains that case studies are not suitable tools to engage in local-global analysis. While comparative (and longitudinal) studies provide valuable data, one could argue, on the other hand, that case studies provide an in-depth look into phenomena that might easily be missed when using questionnaires that cover a large number of universities but minimize the particular context and location in which they operate. Case study approaches bring to life the interrelated parts of an organization while enabling us to see the interplay between the organization and its environment.

Understanding the details of key aspects of university functioning in a non-profit private institution—which despite the formal legal name status, is vulnerable to profit making—offers a window to useful knowledge and insight, as some of the transformations they undergo today may dramatically forecast patterns that public universities will evince tomorrow.

Universities comprise numerous fields of study. The intention here is not to represent the full university but rather to understand its internationalization dynamics. To do so, I focus on four key axes of university work: governance, research, teaching, and student and faculty selection. Since Slaughter and Leslie (1997) argue that business, vocational, and professional programs have benefited most from globalization, I have limited our study to these types of programs in order to update the nature of the globalizing influence. Focusing on three professional schools: engineering, communication, and business, I interviewed 12 professors, evenly distributed across each of the three selected schools, to explore their experiences and perspectives.[2] In addition, on two occasions I interviewed a top-level administrator in charge of advancing the university's strategic plan. The faculty interviewed in communications and business included prior experience as former deans and associate deans, program directors, and department and curriculum development chairs. Planning documents sketching PU strategies over mid- and long-term scenarios were also analyzed. Data analysis was sensitive to predetermined themes such as program offerings, curriculum, governance, university/industry ties, and the effect of all of these on faculty roles and hierarchies, but it was also alert to new themes. Among these, student recruitment and study abroad turned out to be unexpectedly vigorous.

PU's Definition of Internationalization

The first time internationalization is mentioned in PU's strategic planning discourse, it appears in the context of the growing importance of globalization, which it defined as the sharing of information across borders, developing international research collaboration, and enabling students to come from overseas or to work overseas (PU 1994a). Ten years later, PU's strategic plan of 2004 continues to refer to internationalization. It appears as one of its three strategic pillars, and the term is now translated as an "expanding global presence," which is defined as having two dimensions: "developing a global perspective and presence . . . to ensure that the work of our faculty is read and applied worldwide," and assuring that PU "will attract the most talented students in the world" (PU 2004a, p. 3). The internationalization section of the plan highlights the effectiveness that students will achieve by understanding the language and cultures of the people with whom they interact. However, it circumscribes involvement to the Pacific Rim and Latin America and states that connections are to be made with universities, communities, alumni, and corporations abroad to increase research collaboration, attract students, and develop opportunities in other countries for PU faculty and students (PU 2004a). The 2004 strategic plan ends stating, "We seek to become the university of choice for future leaders in all parts of the world" (PU 2004a, p. 3).

Competition with Other Universities for Faculty, Students, and Rankings

Interview data indicate that PU's faculty is on top of developments in other private universities. Faculty is also quite cognizant of the rankings academic units have in comparison to those in other elite universities (what PU faculty call their "reference" universities). They are knowledgeable as well of how other academic units within their own university are doing; namely, which departments are nationally known and therefore can be considered "major selling points" for PU.

To compare well with other universities, PU seeks to augment its research funding and to attract well-known and proven academics. It also engages in numerous less visible maneuvers: merging weak and strong departments to produce increased average reputation ratings, reallocating research funds to make a particular school appear more able to attract research grants/contracts, having researchers from peripheral units serve as "joint appointments" to decrease the faculty/student ratio, and pursuing a much higher number of student applications than it will ever admit in order to produce high student selectivity indices. These efforts are carried out at the departmental/school level, but they are fully known and supported by central administrators.

Shifts in Program Offerings

All three academic departments in the study engage in efforts to promote a greater global presence. This often means seeking what respondents call "multilateral collaboration" among universities, which implies the creation of worldwide university networks. Partnerships have therefore been achieved with foreign universities, carefully choosing reputable institutions with leading departments or schools. PU's school of communication has successfully secured a joint master's in communication management with the London School of Economics, while its business school has crafted a joint MBA with the University of Shanghai. In addition, both schools have study-abroad exchanges with universities in Amsterdam, Singapore, and Hong Kong. For its part, the school of engineering is now developing a new collaborative research program with a Korean institution. Faculty indicate that over the past five years, there has been a sizable growth in the number of international study programs in PU as a whole. There is also greater participation of PU faculty in international conferences.

Programs whose internationalization importance increases succeed also in augmenting the numbers of their faculty. Twenty years ago, the business communication department within the business school had only six faculty members; by 2004, it had 33 full-time faculty. The business school as a whole has 184 full-time faculty. Even larger is the school of engineering, with 202 full-time faculty (PU 2004b).[3] Specialization in fields that ensure a solid return on investment are allowed to grow; in contrast, other specializations that suffer from a lack of external funding—even though they may serve to address the important societal problems targeted by the university's strategic plan—are closed down gradually through non-replacement of faculty or abruptly by simply declaring them unproductive. Ironically, thus, the specialization on international and comparative education, which deals with the relevant issues of globalization and intercultural education, was summarily shut down.

Several new fields have been emerging in the past 10 years at PU. Some of this growth might be attributable to the competition frenzy that leads to the development of innovations, which in turn calls increasingly for interdisciplinary approaches. Three such fields making a solid appearance are bioengineering, neurobiological sciences, and the biosciences. These fields receive much attention and are favored with funding to hire "star" faculty, defined as those who both have attained national and worldwide reputation and are engaged in multi-million dollar research grants that will be brought to PU as they join the university.

Student Recruitment and Expectations

A number of PU administrators maintain regular contacts with heads of international schools abroad (which produce highly mobile high school graduates) to identify potential recruits. A large number of international faculty come to PU to teach on a short-term basis; they usually bring additional contacts and referrals with them.

As students come to PU with a job already in mind, professors are concerned with serving them. Seeing them as consumers, faculty members try to satisfy their expectations. Several business professors stated that, "a faculty member can forget the idea of [acquiring] tenure if he does not please the students who evaluate him." Faculty share the view that students are increasingly seeing university education as a path to job procurement rather than as an occasion to deepen their knowledge of the surrounding world. They note that, in many cases, the reputation of a particular university is shaped by its ability to place students in high-paying jobs when they graduate. In some programs, such as the master's in business administration, it is not uncommon for a student to invest $60,000 to $70,000 in student loans, obliging him or her to seek immediate placement after graduation.

The expectation of students in seeking skills for careers is also justified because in the competitive economic world climate there is less emphasis on well-rounded individuals. Practical experience has become more highly rewarded than the traditional broad-based knowledge. For students, this translates into getting good grades, not learning. According to several professors of engineering, many students do not learn what they need to know to succeed in life, and show attitudes very different from those of their parents, who went to college with a greater sense of scholarship and pursued knowledge for the sake of knowledge. The targeting of students as the new customers has also brought changes in the relationship between faculty and students. As tuition rates are high and rising, students expect higher levels of institutional responsiveness and professor responsiveness. In the view of one administrator, "Students are now very demanding consumers who perceive the university as a vendor. Conversely, the university looks at students as paychecks."

Students have changed in other significant ways. Professors with lengthy experience at PU recall that 20 years ago, several students could articulate what liberal arts education means. In their view, today, even faculty have difficulty understanding this concept. Hence, it seems that the idea of a liberal arts education is dying. An anthropologist professor working at PU for over 20 years, and normally very nuanced in his judgment, comments that the undergraduate students from engineering and business he encounters in his classes (which are part of the general education requirement) rarely have the ability to think abstractly and synthesize diverse pieces of information. He finds them skilled in solving problems within a narrow and predetermined range, and unwilling to learn subjects whose practical application is not immediately visible.

As with other institutions in a market-led economy, universities—including the non-profit—seek to accumulate capital. This is manifested in the recruitment of students who pay their tuition fully, although a few scholarships are available to them. For many years, PU has had one of the largest numbers and proportions of international students of any private US university. Some 20 years ago, most international students came to PU from the Middle East; today, most of them come from South and East Asia. The regions have changed but the common denominator is that these students come from countries that enable them to pay for their studies. PU is extremely interested in maintaining this advantage since higher education is seen as an export commodity; the recruitment of Asian students, at both undergraduate and graduate levels, from China, India, Hong Kong, Taiwan, Japan, and other Asian countries has therefore become aggressive.

The recruitment of international students by the business school is justified on multiple counts, some of which stand in contradiction to each other. The respondents argue that business schools today need to link to the international community and to remain competitive as a university requires greater recruitment of international students; here the assumption is that a global presence and recognition generates more students and connections that feed into an expanding cycle. Business schools throughout the US are indeed making significant efforts to reach overseas students. They do so through satellite schools abroad and by joint partnerships, as exemplified by the links between the University of Chicago and schools in Singapore and Spain, a joint program between the University of Texas at Austin and the Monterrey Institute of Technology and Higher Education Studies (ITESEM) in Mexico, and between PU and the University of Shanghai. Arguments are presented that "the international scope requires greater international sensitivity, more awareness of foreign cultures." Finally, related comments by the business faculty but focusing on US students state that, "because business has become more global, we have to educate more global-minded students." Contradictions emerge, however, because students from poorer regions such as those from Africa and many Latin American countries are not recruited. Contradictions surface only because, while recruitment has been intensified, the curriculum has not been adapted to global needs. Guided by the need to recruit more students as well as to develop more connections with other institutions, PU has now established four "development offices" in four Asian countries and one in Mexico. An important objective of these offices is to organize recruitment fairs, especially for prospective science and business students.

The search for international students is officially limited to students who can speak English well enough to take classes. A business professor assures that, "We use great caution to limit our recruitment to students who can speak English fluently." To this end, some Asian students are contacted by phone early in the morning in their homes to verify their English proficiency. However, instructors at PU's Language Institute serve yearly over 600 Asian students (mostly in engineering) whose

English is so incipient that they must take intensive language classes often for two semesters before joining regular classes.

International students have become more common in US universities as national boundaries have become more blurred: the increasing homogenization of cultures has made it psychologically easier to travel and to live and study in a foreign culture. It is surprising, however, to learn that in some cases PU does not seek to respond to students' needs and identities but rather to cater to those who already buy into US culture and society. This is evidenced in the following comment by a business professor:

> We limit our recruitment efforts to students who share an American market ideology because we don't have the resources or time to preprogram students to think like Americans. If they don't think like capitalists before they come to the States, they likely will not find jobs in the US when they graduate. We assume that all the students we recruit will stay in the country to work, even though some return back home. (Professor with 28 years at USC)[4]

Part of the students' practical experience, especially for US students, involves study abroad to become familiar with other contexts. In the case of the schools of communications and business, there are programs that take students for intensive tours of firms and institutions. Since all major firms today have international subsidiaries in all regions of the world, the business school seeks to "train our students to work for these firms." Its programs, therefore, have been redesigned so that business students may visit a foreign corporation to help solve problems the corporation is facing. Some professors assert, "We identify problems and then offer solutions on how to fix them." Others say, "The students become aware of international business and gain more awareness of international and global sourcing activities." Such experiences have already taken students to Thailand, Cuba, Mexico, and China. But since these are brief visits to the other country (about 10 days) and even briefer to the corporation involved, it is doubtful that considerable cultural or organizational knowledge is gained. Often, students go to these countries with a minimal understanding of the culture and even more frequently with no knowledge of the language spoken there. Students have greater exposure abroad, but such experience seems superficial since not only is their stay brief but they live in an English speaking cultural bubble.

Internationalization of program offerings and student recruitment have become today the new form of entrepreneurialism, moving into new conceptions of students and knowledge. In turn, this permeates faculty governance. The search for new student markets and attractive programs unleashes a need for more students, more faculty to teach them, and timely decisions based on constant scanning of the environment—both national and international. Globalization and internationalization therefore become entangled.

Faculty Governance

Although PU never had a very strong faculty participation in major decisions, there is ample consensus that decision-making by the faculty has been reduced greatly over the past 30 years, while that of the administration has grown considerably. Faculty assert most power resides with the PU board of trustees and the "Central administrators." Several factors are identified as contributing to the current situation: First, a decrease in tenured faculty has brought considerable increase in full-time and part-time adjuncts and clinical professors. While prestigious universities have more tenured or tenure/track professors than less prestigious ones, slightly less than half (49.6%) of the PU faculty is tenured or on tenure/track. However, the three schools in the study, whose fields are deeply involved in the globalization process, have a greater proportion of tenured or tenure-track faculty (62% for business, 66% for communication, and 81% for engineering) (PU 2004b).[5] It would seem, therefore, that powerful (i.e., wealthy) schools and departments are able to negotiate better conditions for their faculty and to address the "problem" of teaching by less secured faculty by enlarging their faculty, rather than by changing the faculty status.

Second, even though most research universities are run primarily by faculty, this is not so at PU, where deans have traditionally had more power than the faculty. This dominance is justified by the need to differentiate between governance and leadership. Presumably the latter calls for a greater visionary role and the ability to act within short windows of opportunity. According to the respondents, the deans' dominance in decision-making processes has often resulted in the promotion of managerial over intellectual interests, with budgetary and profit-seeking rationales prevailing over academic considerations.

Echoing a pattern detected at national level, in which faculty in doctoral institutions stated having substantial influence in general standards of promotion and tenure and for evaluating teaching, and in setting graduate education policy, but relatively little in setting strategic and budget priorities for the institution. For their part, administrators (academic vice presidents) acknowledged high influence in setting strategic priorities and slightly less so in setting graduate education policy. While there is an emergent bifurcation of decision making in the university, the majority of faculty in the study were in agreement with the current state of affairs as the large majority felt there was "sufficient trust" concerning actions on governance issues (Tierney and Minor 2003).

The faster rate of growth of administrators over professors, as well as the increasing rate of part-time faculty also noted by Rhoades (1998), who observed the phenomenon between 1977 and 1989. PU professors saw it as having accelerated significantly in the 1990s. Rhoades detected also a simultaneous stratification of faculty (into tenure and non-tenured track) and the solidification of university professors as merely university employees, whom he termed "managed professionals."

The contrast between governance and leadership is often made among the respondents, with leadership the dominant concept. University leaders are said to be much needed if an academic unit or university is to be competitive, for they are the ones with fundraising experience and the "business savvy required to perform the job." Because of the increased leadership role by administrators, the number of mid-level management positions has grown tremendously at PU and its structure is becoming more complex. In the voice of one engineering professor, "I cannot believe how many provosts and associate deans are hired today!" Explaining the situation, a communication professor makes the analogy, "Just as hospitals no longer hire the most talented doctors to head up administration, universities no longer credit the most talented professors to run them either." Corroborating this view, a professor from the school of engineering indicates that leaders today must be "marketers, politicians, and administrators." Some decisions based on funding rationale run into opposite consequences. For instance, in the school of engineering it would be impossible to hire as a faculty member someone who cannot raise a substantial amount of money for the university. Presumably, faculty who get external funding are addressing problems with major social implications, but this is not always the case.

Third, a number of fields have seen the formal incorporation of business firms into the governance of the academic unit. A recent development has been the formation of Corporate Advisory Boards (CAB), which provides an opportunity for the universities to invite the most generous donors to participate in them. According to a business school professor who served as curriculum coordinator for several years, once on the board, these influential figures shape course offerings.

Facing the current changes, some faculty express ambivalence. This is reflected by a communications professor, who states:

> The number of faculty involved in governance is down. But I do not believe this is a negative shift because faculty are not always known for having a positive influence on the direction of the university. They tend to think conservatively. But on the other hand, I am concerned that many deans today do not have a vested interest in academic life either. Often we hire administrators with little or no research experience. They come from outside of the university culture, often with little knowledge of the disciplines they oversee. (Faculty with 24 years at PU)

The Impact of Industrial Ties on the University

According to the administrator with key responsibilities for implementation of PU's strategic plan, there has been an "exponential increase each year in the degree of collaboration with industry."[6] Increased connections are reported by all three schools in the study. Longitudinal data on PU's funded research (Table 50.1) confirms a steady decline of federal research funds and, concomitantly,

TABLE 50.1

PU Sponsored Projects by Sponsor (in Thousands of Dollars), 1985–2004

Source	FY 1985	FY 1990	FY 1995	FY 2000	FY 2004
Federal	98,595	141,387	176,487	240,506	328,845
State/local	89%	81%	76%	74%	78%
Government	3059	4,474	10,777	16,975	12,203
	3%	3%	5%	5%	3%
Private	9215	28,593	44,053	67,875	80,014
	8%	16%	19%	21%	19%
Total	110,869	174,454	213,317	325,356	421,062

Source: PU Office of Contracts and Grants, June 2005.

an increase in private research funds, going from 8% of all sponsored projects in terms of amount in 1985 to 19% by 2004. The federal government remains the main source of research funds, but it is clear that competition for public and private funds is on the increase.

Although the link between academia and industry has always characterized journalism programs, the relationship has become even more pronounced in the school of communication because industrial leaders in the media industry expect universities to produced students with specific communicational skills. In engineering, some industries, such as aerospace, have long connected to PU, but now the links have expanded to cover electronics, media, and computers, resulting in significant contractual research. The school of engineering has a Board of Counselors made up of domestic and international advisors from industry; this board promotes connections especially with the Pacific Rim.[7] IBM and other industries have endowed several chairs in engineering, and these endowments have been used to hire specific faculty who have interests that align with the interests of those industries. The number of endowed chairs that industry finances within each department has also grown significantly over recent years. Respondents noted that though industry has traditionally supported endowed chairs across business school departments, the number of faculty in the PU business school who are sponsored by corporate donors has escalated.[8]

In describing the connection with industry, some engineering professors indicate that the relationship goes both ways. Thus, many professors often work for industrial firms before, after, or while they work as university professors. Also, many faculty have started their own companies. Communication professors consider that they have a say in industrial administrative matters as well because many boards of industry recruit academicians and thus professors have an increasingly important voice in corporate boardrooms. The links are not free of problems. Especially in engineering, it is noted that industry and the university have different timelines, with industry seeking quicker cutting-edge ideas than academia produces.

The links between PU and industry not only affect research and governance; they affect curriculum as well. The Accrediting Board for Engineering and Technology (ABET) has issued directives pressuring engineering schools to de-emphasize theory and promote application. ABET is shaped by the views of professional societies that are staffed by industry. Its views are strongly considered in determining undergraduate programs in engineering. Similar influences can be detected in business schools. Reportedly, a very small number of CPA firms influence what accounting schools should teach. These firms are known as the "Big Four"—large professional firms offering a wide array of services, such as "auditing, taxes, consultation, and an increasingly broader focus on international business." At PU the Big Four support the school of accounting by matching alumni donations. In return, these firms also expect to recruit from the universities they sponsor. To be responsive to industry, the school of communications established an entertainment track about five years ago for undergraduates. The influence of industry on the university is sometimes subtle. As one communication professor puts it, "Industrial sponsors cannot tell universities what to study, but they can chose to sponsor only programs that align to their interests" (Faculty with 26 years at PU). Yet another communication professor offers a sharper judgment: "Faculty are forced to become prostitutes, because today they are forced to recruit the support of industry. We, here at [PU's school of communication], are fortunate because of the endowment we have received. If faculty are the prostitutes, then administrators have become the pimps" (Faculty with 32 years at PU and six years as a former department chair).

Shifts in Faculty Roles and Hierarchies

As noted above, to move up in ranks compared to other universities, the hiring of "star" professors is a common strategy. These faculty instantly bring with them large research projects and the high probability of new research funds in the future. Often, "star" projects are allowed to create their own research centers. However, as these faculty take on research projects, they "buy out" their teaching responsibilities, a practice that results in hiring of adjuncts to teach classes at PU and seriously compromises the quality of instruction students receive, according to several professors.

The pressing need to engage in problem-solving research in certain areas is promoting an interdisciplinary approach by which entrepreneurial faculty seek partners in fields perceived to make contributions to a greater understanding of a given issue and its potential solution. PU itself is presently involved in efforts to increase interdisciplinary research and has shown willingness to make exceptions to its revenue center management, a practice which makes each academic unit exclusively and totally responsible for generating the revenues it needs to function. The interdisciplinary initiatives offer much promise; they are also creating a typology of faculty into the "old guard" (traditional academics who commit themselves to one disciplinary area) and the "new guard" (the growing number of faculty with interdisciplinary preferences).

With research given greater weight than teaching, and with the increasing need to serve the practical interests of industry, universities are changing their hiring practices. In the school of engineering, the tendency is to hire faculty who have real world experience, especially those who own their own business. Faculty across all engineering specializations are being hired for their potential to raise money for the school or to bring in research funds. As one engineering professor observes:

> The only way to improve the ranking of PU in the *US News and World Report* is to increase grant money from industry. We live and die by this ranking. We are now ranked [among the top ten] in the nation. Our graduate program is ranked by the quality of our faculty. Faculty who are affiliated with professional organizations, those who publish, and those who raise money for research increase the ranking of the school. (Faculty with 17 years at PU)

The recruitment of "star faculty" creates new dynamics and contradictions. PU's strategic planning officer states that the "compensation offered to hot faculty has skyrocketed in its lavishness, up to a half million [dollars] for the most desirable." Of course, this is not true of every discipline; business and law are identified as two fields that have the resources to pay these salaries. Some star faculty use agents today, especially if they publish frequently. Hiring the best means satisfying a whole array of demands. Usually an academic position has to be offered also to the spouse. Facilities for housing, labs, travel expenditures are part of the negotiations. "The amount of money we spend on labs and other perks to bring in the big guns would amaze you," asserted a former department chair.

The increased presence of international students is also creating pressure to hire professors from abroad. The majority of the respondents noted, however, that most of these international faculty are trained in the US or in the West because "foreign-trained academics do not command the same respect the American-trained academics do." In addition, some schools, such as business and engineering, seek recruitment of international faculty with both international teaching experience and business experience. According to a business professor with 20 years experience at PU, the university has a particular interest in hiring faculty with first-hand familiarity in Asian affairs to increase the number of students it can recruit from the Pacific and Asian mainland. Several external political events have also affected the internationalization of PU's faculty. Professors in the school of engineering report that the collapse of the Soviet Union led to an increase in hiring of Russian engineers for US industry and academic positions. Innovations in communications and transportation are also identified as having facilitated the intense exchange between academics abroad and those at PU.

Task-Focused Curricula

As a whole, the curricula emerging in all three fields investigated in this article show a marked tendency toward practical applications and job relevance. Many academicians observe that PU has shifted away from funding and supporting certain programs that promote a more comprehensive education while pushing more money into other programs that promote skills-based education. The influence of ABET in the field of engineering extends to selection of the kinds of courses that are preferred by industry. These are described as courses that teach skills like communications and how to be interdisciplinary team players. A professor of engineering exclaims, "Today, skills, skills, skills Nobody cares about anything other than skills. Education means hands-on engineering. Students learn computer programs and computer language." Engineering faculty are unanimous in expressing the view that today industrial leaders look for a workforce that is more broadly skilled; thus, there is a greater tendency toward general skills-related education as opposed to specialized knowledge at the undergraduate level.

Professors of engineering, a field notorious for emphasizing practical applications, consider that university education has become diluted, for, "If you ask a student today to conduct research on a topic, and I am not only talking about undergraduates, even a graduate student . . . he would enter his search on a Google or another popular Websearch engine. They do not even think about the authenticity of the research they undertake" (professor with 12 years at PU). Echoing opinions made by other faculty in the school of engineering, the same professor observes that the curriculum focus on skills has displaced the traditional emphasis on the science curricula the students should receive: "We promote jobs skills over life-long enduring knowledge. There are faculty who try to nurture students to become whole individuals, but most faculty today push students to develop marketable skills." PU's school of business has established a very extensive study-abroad program to promote global awareness and to make its students more competitive in international markets.

In the field of communication, the curriculum is now said to be much more sensitive to the international media, and thus courses are described as being more varied. The curriculum changes include globalization as a subject area, more coverage of cultural diversity, and introduction to new media forms to promote a range of technological competencies. On the other hand, the school of communications has decreased the number of mandatory coursework requirements in order to encourage students to pursue double majors or double minors, but with an emphasis on acquiring practical skills. For example, an English major might minor in communications, to gain some professional preparation. In addition, the school of communications has come up with the notion of tracks. This is explained thus by a former department chair: "Today we have tracks rather than majors. Our programs are geared toward careers as opposed to knowledge for the sake of knowledge. These tracks help students to develop focus in their concentration area." The need to connect university training to jobs is encouraging an interesting blurring of fields; thus, for instance, students in communication are moving into business track fields, such as advertising and media culture.

Faculty report changes in instructional methodologies, as there is an emphasis away from rote memorization of facts to skills that stress writing, working in groups, and communication. The curriculum, especially in engineering, is constantly changing because the US technology is said to undergo substantial change every five years. A trend that seems to be quite strong in all departments is the use and reliance on educational technology within the classroom. Industry grants have allowed these academic units to make technological renovations in every department and classroom. In addition, student research must involve technological resources, which make it possible for every student to incorporate the most current information, facts and figures in their presentation and papers.

Mutually reinforcing ties have developed between students, industry, and programs, as this business professor explains: "New alumni networks enable [PU] to connect with industry abroad to recruit more and more international students. These industrial firms conversely inform the new programs that we develop here. If we want international corporations to send their employees to PU to train, we need to formulate programs that meet their needs" (Faculty with 30 years in business and 10 years as a PU faculty member).

Conclusions

Dynamics linked to economic and technological features of globalization have led to university responses known collectively as internationalization. This term seems to be the new and more palatable term for the "entrepreneurialism" observed by Slaughter and Leslie (1997).

What we can see from the PU examination, is that: (1) there is a major effort to recruit more international students and faculty; (2) there is considerable shift toward convergence among schools in strategies and decisions affecting the issues of governance, curriculum, and selection of both faculty and students; (3) there is a growth of "star" faculty in the pursuit of higher institutional rankings and thus of higher number of student applicants; (4) there is a sustained increase in the proportion of administrative positions, as internationalization is based on "strategic planning" that requires knowledge of external forces and quicker response times; and (5) the expansion of the student markets leads to a dissociation between teaching and research, with increased numbers of professors in non-tenure, part-time, and clinical positions being reported. In all, notions of knowledge have been reshaped and become predicated on utility and narrowly focused problem-solving rather than on seeking broader understandings or an expanded vision of reality which might in the long term provide greater resilience and adaptability to the rapid and seemingly inexorable obsolescence of the transitory technologies that are the staple of these fields.

There are, nonetheless, different dynamics at work in the three schools investigated. Business and communications feel a stronger pressure to develop international contacts and expand their array of international experiences. Engineering is quite successful with its recruitment of international students, in part because the US is considered by most observers as the most technologically developed country. Communications puts the greatest weight on curricula that will give practical experience to students.

While it is still not clear how the new internationalization efforts of joint programs and study abroad will impact the university culture on a long-term basis, the hierarchies now being formed within PU are clearly giving greater salience to those fields that can be directly linked to growth in revenue. Among faculty who have been at PU for more than 15 years, there is consensus that significant changes have occurred. Behaviors analogous to those of business firms are increasingly evident, for now university rankings receive top priority, presumably because they give information as to the quality of the product. As knowledge becomes a product, then the market logic dominates. If customers are willing to buy the products in sufficient numbers for the projected class size to make a profit, then the product is offered. If not, courses and programs simply disappear. They risk disappearing also when the job market does not favor their alumni with salaries high enough to make them potential donors. As internal differentiation continues, the sense of common purpose that traditionally united different disciplines will decrease and the private university will emerge instead as a collection of economically productive units.

DiMaggio and Powell (1991) detected three mechanisms that secure institutional isomorphism: the coercive, the imitational, and the normative. At least the latter two would seem to apply to universities today as staff/faculty transfers are increasing due to constant raids by competitors to acquire the best people, and elite universities (those that supply most of the faculty) are characterized by training, academic practices, and professional norms that closely resemble each other. We find that the competition fueled by globalization increases turnover of faculty (and likely also administrators) and accelerates border-crossing between industry and the academic world. Competition for excellence also leads to standardized norms of performance, both in quality and quantity of academic production.

DiMaggio and Powell (1991) predict an alignment of organizations with successful models when technologies are not clear. Universities, especially private universities, consider imitating the business world a safe approach and thus introduce criteria of competitiveness, marketability, and profitability that have done well in the marketplace. A second reason for the imitation, however, is that universities feel compelled actually to join the market and its strategies. The translation of such features to the university signals the beginning of a process that has deeply transformed the conception of higher education and the disciplines it has traditionally housed. PU's case study did not reveal that at the faculty level any changes in the *purpose* of education had occurred, but students have now become more interested in practical training to succeed in the new economy, and industry is happy to help. Students and some of their funders are shaping academic programs to promote their economic potential not their intellectual growth. While faculty still hold on to the more expansive views of knowledge and would like to think of themselves as a community of scholars, they are becoming complicit in the ongoing transformations. The evidence from PU's priorities and activities is that internationalization reigns, with little contestation of its full-range, long-term consequences.

Contacts between PU and institutions in other countries are increasing. There is also greater recruitment of international students and greater exposure of US students to conditions abroad. This internationalization is an expression of economic and technological globalization in which university "entrepreneurs" are not merely looking for more contracts and contacts with industry but, ultimately, are concerned with establishing regular international sites and presence. The current pursuit of overseas expansion and recognition at PU is to a large extent internationalization and even though its own discourse refers to sensitivity and usefulness to other cultures, it is not *internationalism*. Finally, this case study sees internationalization from the perspective of an advanced industrial country's response to the process of globalization; it would be useful to examine whether private universities located at the periphery of globalization dynamics are experiencing a similar process.

Notes

1. Many scholars have described unprecedented changes in higher education (for a full set of references see Slaughter and Leslie 1997, p. 208) and several have linked the transformations to the global economy.
2. The sample consisted of 10 men and 4 women, all full professors with an average of 22 years at PU, and thus able to comment on perceived academic and organizational changes over time. Their length at USC ranged from 10 to 40 years. I sought to interview a larger number of women, but since women faculty were underrepresented in these disciplines, I could locate only these few respondents. The interviews with faculty and administrators lasted about one hour each; they were followed by additional communications to clarify points as needed. Data were conducted between 2002 and 2004. The meticulous and persistent research assistance of Carlos Cortez in the procurement of the interview data is gratefully acknowledged. Anthony Tambascia's help for some of the literature references is also acknowledged.
3. Another phenomenon, widespread in US universities, is the growth of part-time faculty, or what Kirp (2003) calls the "outsourcing of higher education" (2003, p. 114), which results in considerable reduction in teaching expenses. By 2004, 46% of PU's faculty was part-time.
4. Recent data indicate that doctoral recipients from other countries in science and engineering have firm plans to stay in the US; this is the case for about 55% of students in those fields from India, 53% from the UK, and 48% from China (Johnson and Regets 1998, p. 2).
5. PU statistics on the breakdown of faculty by full-time and part-time status or by tenure/tenure track and other full-time status could be obtained only for 2002 and 2003. Perhaps because this represents a very brief period, no shifts could be detected in the distribution of faculty in the three schools selected for this study.
6. Some connections between industry and the academy predate globalization. If industry leaders had never sponsored the construction of the first business schools, it is likely that Tier I universities would not have created MBA programs. Schools of communication were established after World War II, in the 1950s, with the impetus from the media industry.
7. Approximately 70% of the global economic growth is estimated to be produced by the 21 member countries of the Asia-Pacific Economic Cooperation (APEC). The attention to Asia, therefore, has a strong economic rationale.
8. Indicative of the increased importance of private firms is the change in the classification of research universities. The Carnegie Corporation, whose role it has been to develop classifications for higher education institutions, changed its classification in 2000. Whereas before the top segment of universities were classified as Research I universities and defined as those that granted 50 or more doctoral degrees and received $40 million in federal support per year, the 2004 definition dropped the federal research criterion and created instead the "research university—extensive" to refer to those that granted "50 or more doctoral degrees per year across at least 15 disciplines" (The Carnegie Foundation 2001, p. 10).

References

Agre, P. (1999). Information technology in higher education: the "global academic village" and intellectual standardization, *On the Horizon* 7(5), 8–11.

Altbach, P. (1998). *Comparative Higher Education: Knowledge, the University and Development.* Greenwich, CT: Ablex.

Aviles, K. Rectores de Latinoamerica, contra la mercantilización educativa. La Jornada. 21 June 2005. Retrieved 9 July 2005, http://www.journal.unam.mx/2005/jun05.

Biddle, S. (2002). Internationalization: Rhetoric or Reality. ALCS Occasional Paper no. 56. American Council of Learned Societies. New York.

Bowles, G. (1972). Unequal education and the reproduction of the social division of labor, in Carnoy, M. (ed.), *Schooling in a Corporate Society*. New York: David Mckay.

Bowles, S. and Gintis, H. (c1977). *Schooling in Capitalist America. Educational Reform and the Contradictions of Economic Life*. New York: Basic Books.

Cohen, M. and March, J. (c1986). *Leadership and Ambiguity: The American College President.* Boston: Harvard Business School Press.

de Wit, H. (1999). Changing rationales for the internationalization of higher education. International higher education (online), Spring 1999. http://www.bc.edu/bc-org/avp/soe/cihe/newsletter/New15/text.html.

de Witt, H. (2002). *Internationalization of Higher Education in the United States of America and Europe: A Historical, Comparative, and Conceptual Analysis*. Westport, CT: Greenwood.

Deem, R. (2001). Globalisation, new managerialism, academic capitalism and entrepreneurialism in universities. Is the local dimension still important? *Comparative Education*. 37(1), 7–20.

DiMaggio, P. and Powell, W. (1991). The iron cage revisited: institutional isomorphism and collective rationality in organizational fields, in Powell, W. and DiMaggio, P. (ed.), *The New Institutionalism in Organizational Analysis*. Chicago: The University of Chicago Press, pp. 63–82.

Gough, N. (2000). Globalization and curriculum inquiry: locating, representing, and performing a transnational imaginary, in Stromquist, N. and Monkman, K. (ed.), *Globalization and Education: Integration and Contestation Across Cultures*. Boulder: Rowman & Littlefield.

Green, M., Ackel, P. and Barblan, A. (2001). *The Brave New (and Smaller) World of Higher Education: A Transatlantic View*. Washington, DC: American Council on Education and European University Association.

Husén, T. (1990). *Education and the Global Concern*. Oxford: Pergamon Press.

Johnson, J. and Regets, M. (1998). International mobility of scientists and engineers in the United States—brain drain or brain circulation? Report No. NSF-98-316. Arlington, VA: National Science Foundation, Division of Science Resource Studies.

Jones, P. (2000). Globalization and internationalism: democratic prospects for world education, in Stromquist, N. and Monkman, K. (ed.), *Globalization and Education: Integration and Contestation Across Cultures*. Boulder: Rowman & Littlefield, pp. 27–42.

Ladson-Billings, G. (2005). Differing concepts of citizenship: schools and communities as sites of civic development, in Noddings, N. (ed.), *Educating Citizens for Global Awareness*. New York: Teachers College Press, pp. 69–80.

McIntosh, P. (2005). Gender perspectives on educating for global citizenship, in Noddings, N. (ed.), *Educating Citizens for Global Awareness*. New York: Teachers College Press, pp. 22–37.

OECD (2004). *Internalisation and Trade in Higher Education: Opportunities and Challenges*. Paris: Organization for Economic Cooperation and Development.

Powell, W. and DiMaggio, P. (eds.) (1991). *The New Institutionalism in Organizational Analysis*. Chicago: University of Chicago Press.

Press, E. and Washburn, J. (2000). The Kept University, *The Atlantic* 285(3), 39–54.

PU. Fall 2004 Data Portfolio. Faculty by Rank. Internal document, 2004a.

PU. *PU's Plan for Increasing Academic Excellence: Building Strategic Capabilities for the University of the 21st Century*. October 2004b.

PU. *The Strategic Plan of the PU*. Adopted by the PU Board of Trustees, 8 June 1994a.

PU. *University of PU. Four-Year Report on the 1994 Strategic Plan*. Adopted by the PU Board of Trustees, 7 October 1998.

Ragin, C. and Becker, H. (eds.) (1992). *What is a Case? Exploring the Foundations of Social Inquiry*. Cambridge: Cambridge University Press.

Rhoades, G. (1998). *Managed Professionals. Unionized Faculty and Restructuring Academic Labor*. Albany: State University of New York Press.

Siaya, L. and Hayward, F. (2003). *Mapping Internationalization on US Campuses*. Washington, DC: American Council on Education.

Slaughter, S. and Leslie, L. (1997). *Academic Capitalism: Politics, Policies, and the Entrepreneurial University*. Baltimore: John Hopkins University Press.

The Carnegie Foundation for the Advancement of Teaching (2001). *The Carnegie Classification of Institutions of Higher Education*. New York: The Carnegie Foundation for the Advancement of Teaching.

Tierney, W. and Minor, J. (2003). Challenges for governance: a national report. Los Angeles: Center for Higher Education Policy Analysis, Rossier School of Education, University of Southern California.

Weick, K. (1976). Educational organizations as loosely coupled systems, *Administrative Science Quarterly* 21(1), 1–19.

Welton, G. (2001). The Materialist Basis of a Socially Constructed World? Globalisation as a Political Project. Paper presented at the Center for International Studies, University of Southern California, Los Angeles, 16 October 2001.

Yin, R. (1994). *Case Study Research: Designs and Methods*, 2nd ed. Thousand Oaks: Sage.

CHAPTER 51

THE EQUITY CHALLENGE IN CHINA'S HIGHER EDUCATION FINANCE POLICY

FENGSHOU SUN AND ARMANDO BARRIENTOS

Sustaining China's rapid economic growth in the future will come to depend in large part on the quantity and quality of the human resources it can mobilize. The paper considers the prospects for higher education financing, and highlights the importance of improving equity in access to higher education as a precondition for a sustainable expansion in the higher education sector. The paper aims to throw light on two key questions: What are the links existing between current financing arrangements and equity in access to higher education? What kind of financing arrangements could ensure increasing access to higher education?

Introduction

Sustaining China's rapid economic growth in the future will come to depend in large part on the quantity and quality of the human resources it can mobilize. Education policy is fundamental to social and economic development in all countries, and this is especially the case with China at this juncture. Getting education policy right could unlock the enormous potential of its large population and spread the benefits from growth to all groups in society, but getting it wrong could place a stranglehold on development and reinforce existing inequalities in access across urban and rural areas. China faces significant challenges in terms of education provision and financing. The main purpose of this paper is to consider the prospects for higher education provision and financing, and in particular the importance of improving equity in access to higher education in conditioning these prospects. The paper aims to throw light on two key questions: What are the links existing between current financing arrangements and equity in access to higher education? What kind of financing arrangements could ensure increasing access to higher education?

Current levels of education spending in China are insufficient to meet the demand arising from rapid economic growth. Consolidated government expenditure in education reached only 2.79% of GDP in 1999, rising marginally to 2.82% in 2005 (Ministry of Education, Ministry of Finance and State Statistics Bureau, 2000; MoE, 2006; Heckman, 2002). This is significantly lower than the developing country average at 4.1% of GDP, and lower than the developed country average at 5.3% of GDP in the mid-1990s (World Bank, 1997). Education expenditure is skewed towards higher education. China spent almost a quarter of its education budget on higher education in 1998–1999 (UNESCO Institute for Statistics, 2004a), whereas participation rates in higher education remain low. Although China adopted the policy of rapid expansion of enrolment in higher education from 1999, participation rates in higher education were 21% of the relevant population group in 2005 (Zhou, 2006). The further expansion of enrolment has been slowed down in recent years following quality concern arising from resource constraints (Mohrman, 2008). There are large differences in access to education across urban and rural areas. It has been estimated that over 30% of eligible students in rural areas cannot go on to secondary school due to the lack of funding (Lin, 1999). And the proportion of university students from urban households is 84.43%, even though urban workers account for only 19.33% of the labour force.

Financial arrangements are an important factor in producing existing differentials in access to higher education. Decentralization in government finances has led to a reduction in the contribution of central government to higher education. For the higher education sector, revenue allocated from central government revenue have declined from 24.4% of GDP in 1985 to 13% in 1992 (State Administration of Taxation of China, 2000, www.chinaonline.com/refer/ministry_profiles/SAT.asp), and to between 10 and 11% of GDP at the end of the 1990s (Remick, 1999, cited in Norling, 2003). The decentralization of education finance has increased inequalities in access across regions, especially as the poor regions have reduced capacity to finance education at all levels. Increases in tuition fees make matters worse. The marketization of higher education since the 1980s, especially after 1992, has led to a one-third rise in higher education tuition fees across the board (Dahlman and Aubert, 2001). An average tuition fee of between 450 and 700 US dollars per year constitutes a large barrier preventing students from low-income households from entering university. Private financing of higher education, proposed by the World Bank, does not appear to provide a sustainable solution (Dahlman and Aubert, 2001). Borrowing by public universities in China is currently at 28.17 billion US$, a dangerous level for some universities (CASS, 2007).

There is considerable urgency in examining the options for financing a further expansion of higher education in China, taking on board equity considerations. Some attention has been paid to issues of financing and there has been some debate around issues of equity in the context of access, but few have connected these two issues satisfactorily. The present study aims to contribute to fill in this gap. It investigates the equity implications of current finance policy of higher education in China, and searches for more equal and efficient alternatives to the current financing mix.

The paper is organized as follows. The next section reviews the case for public financing of education in an international context. The subsequent section examines the main sources of financing of higher education in China and trends. It pays special attention to government financing and tuition fees. Then the further section outlines and discusses the ethical implications of the current financing mix. The penultimate section explores the available financing options and the final section gathers together the main conclusions.

Public Financing of Higher Education in an International Perspective

Public financing plays an important role in the financing of education across the world. There are both efficiency and equity considerations providing a strong justification for public financing of education (Colclough (1993) and Barr (2001) provide a good review of the literature). Within a human capital perspective, education is considered as an investment in future productive capacity. Investment in a project is justified whenever the returns on that project exceed the value of resources tied up in that project, and should be given priority relative to other investment opportunities when the rates of return exceed the returns on alternative projects. Empirical studies have demonstrated that rates of return to education are positive and substantial compared to alternative investment opportunities (Psacharopoulos, 1994).

This is especially the case in developing countries, but in the absence of public financing of education, investment will be largely determined by household resources. In this context, the likelihood of significant underinvestment in education is strong. Low-income households, the majority in developing countries, may not be able to afford the direct costs of sending children to school and the earnings foregone. Financial institutions are generally reluctant to lend for the purposes of education, and are scarce in developing countries (Palacios, 2004). Among poorest households, facing acute deficits in current consumption, potential income flows in the future are heavily discounted. In a developing country context, public subsidies to education could help overcome these constraints. In addition, public financing can be justified by the positive externalities generated by a more educated labour force and population. Public financing of education can help overcome these restrictions on human capital investment and successfully realize potential gains from positive externalities, by ensuring investment in education moves closer to the optimum level (Smith and Szymanski, 2003).

In addition to the 'market failure' and 'public goods' justifications of public financing of education discussed above, the latter can also be justified on the grounds that education is a 'merit good', reflecting strong social preferences (Creedy, 1995). Public financing of education can also be justified on pure equity grounds, as a response to the need to ensure equal opportunities for all in a fair society (Barr, 2001). The strong correlation between income and education, health and education and intergenerational mobility and education, to name a few, suggest that policies enhancing educational opportunities can be crucial to addressing inequality (World Bank, 2006).

Efficiency and equity considerations can support a strong justification for public investment in education at all levels, including investment in higher education. However, in a developing country context in which fiscal resources are insufficient to provide the full range of basic services needed, the extent of public financing at different levels of education provision will become an important policy variable. Fiscal constraints are binding where a rapid expansion of the higher education sector is needed. Barr (2001) holds that there are strong arguments for full public financing and provision in primary and secondary education, but suggests that where public finances are limited, a mix of financing in higher education could advance both efficiency and equity considerations. This mix would involve public and private financing. This echoes World Bank proposals for the introduction of user fee and private sector into the higher education finance to facilitate expansion enrolment (World Bank, 1986, 1997).

Several options are available for arranging partial public financing of higher education, including direct grants (Barr, 2001), subsidized loans (Colclough, 1990, 1993) and grants financed with a graduate tax (Creedy, 1995; Palacios, 2004). The US has achieved the higher participation rate in higher education, 62% of high school graduates reach higher education, through a mix of direct public spending and relatively high tuition fees. In UK, the reforms following the Dearing Report, published by National Committee of Inequity into Higher Education in 1997, introduced relatively low top-up fees of £1,000 per year per student irrespective of universities and discipline (Barr, 2001), with exemptions for low-income students. A top-up fee of £3,000 per year was introduced in England and Wales from September 2006. The direct grant system was replaced by subsidized loans, but there is concern that graduates will end up with debts as high as £17,500 (*The Independent*, 14 August 2007). Among the developing countries, Sri Lanka keeps its education free from primary to tertiary level. But the high rate of subsidy has been a heavy burden on public expenditure, while universities are underdeveloped due to insufficient funding. Its gross enrolment rate in 2001 was only 5.1% (World Bank, 2004), skewed towards students from urban areas (Tudawe, 2001).

The Financing of Higher Education in China

In China, the financing mix for higher education is dominated by government subsidies, but additional finance comes from civil society and tuition fees (Ministry of Education, Ministry of Finance and State Statistics Bureau, 2000). Table 51.1 provides summary information for the 1990s. Government subsidies have declined as a share of total financing from 64.6% in 1990 to 53.1% in 1998. At the same time, the share of financing contributed by tuition fee has risen rapidly since 1990, especially after 1997. Contributions from civil society, including funding from enterprises, increased in the first half of the period under examination, but at the end of the period they have returned to their 1990 level.

In common with many developing countries, public subsidies to education in China are many times larger for higher education students than for students in primary and secondary education. Table 51.2 illustrates this point by comparing China with other regions in the world. The figures in part reflect the fact that rates of participation in higher education in China are relatively low. In 1998–1999, public spending on higher education as percentage of total public education expenditure reached 24% (UNESCO Institute for Statistics, 2004b). While China's overall public spending in education is low at around 2% of GDP, spending on higher education grew by an annual average of 9.7% between 1978 and 1994 (World Bank, 1997, 41).

TABLE 51.1

Sources of Finance in Education Expenditure in the 1990s

Year	Total expenditure (100m. yuan)	Government budget (%)	Civil society contribution (%)	Tuitions and incidentals (%)
1990	659.4	64.6	33.1	2.3
1991	731.5	62.8	34.6	2.5
1992	867.1	62.1	35.0	2.9
1993	1059.9	60.8	36.2	3.0
1994	1488.8	59.4	36.7	4.0
1995	1878.0	54.8	40.9	4.4
1996	2262.3	53.6	41.3	5.1
1997	2531.7	53.6	40.8	5.6
1998	2949.1	53.1	34.4	12.5

Source: Adapted from Xiaobo Zhang and Ravi Kanbur, September 2003 (original data from China State Statistical Bureau, 2000, Table A-14 in *Comprehensive Statistical Data and Materials on 50 Years of New China*, 14).

Note: 1. 'Government budget' mainly comes from general tax and additional education fee. 2. 'Civil society contribution' includes the private sector funding, enterprise support, donation, etc. 3. US$=7.16Yuan

TABLE 51.2

Cross-Regional Comparison of Public Subsidies per Student as a Percentage of GNP per Capita by Level of Education, 1980–94

Region/Country (No. of Countries)	Year	Preschool and Primary	Secondary	Tertiary
China	1980	4	13	362
	1990	5	15	193
	1994	—	—	175
Latin America (19)	1980	8	14	56
	1990	11	13	80
East Asia (8)	1980	5	14	182
	1990	8	19	98
South Asia (4)	1980	15	27	84
	1990	10	20	76
Middle East and North Africa (9)	1980	—	—	63
	1990	—	—	81
Sub-Saharan Africa (23)	1980	13	46	796
	1990	14	51	481

Source: World Bank (1997, 48) (originally from UNESCO, World Education Report, 1995, Table 12, 104, 156–159).

These figures raise important issues regarding China's higher education policy. A sustained increase in participation rates in education at all levels, but higher education in particular, will require a significant injection of resources. Current trends imply that attention will need to be paid to the room for increases in public subsidies to higher education, and to the role of private financing, mainly through tuition fees. These will be discussed below. A significant constraint in raising additional financing lies in the distributional implications emerging from the current financing mix of higher education. This section examines the financing of higher education and its distributional implications. It focuses in particular on public financing and tuition fees.

Tax Revenues Are Broadly Regressive

Tax revenues in China can be classified mainly into five main categories: Consumption taxes are dominant, contributing 71% of total tax revenues; income taxes provide a further 12%; council taxes and other contribute a further 16% (Su, 2004).

Tax revenues are designed to support industrialization policies at the expense of agriculture. Under the urban/industry-biased economic policies in place since the 1960s, the government has imposed price control on agricultural products. However, the prices of the industrial products like farm tools and fertilizer have risen steadily and, as a result, the rural economy has generally slowed down during the Reform Era since 1980s (Norling, 2003). Price controls imply that rural producers pay higher rates of implicit taxes, as their products are artificially undervalued. The difficulty involved in determining income in rural areas has persuaded the authorities to rely on a flat rate of income tax, which ensure that taxation is regressive. The Tax Reform Act 1994 gave the local governments more discretion in fundraising, leading to the imposition of higher tax rates and user fees on residents, especially on rural producers. Since the mid-1990s, rural local governments have come to depend increasingly on user fees. On January 2006, agricultural taxes on farmers in many east provinces were abolished, leaving local government even more dependent on various fees.

In contrast, in the industrial sectors, liberalization has led to the abolition of many forms of taxation, which are considered a hindrance to trade and commerce, such as local taxes, quotas and licensing fees (Rozelle, 1996, cited in Norling, 2003). The revised Individual Income Tax Law of 1994 further lessened the burden on industrial sectors in general as enterprises are relieved from many social obligations that had been imposed on them in the past. Taxation on urban residents, especially employees in the formal sector, is mainly in the form of personal income tax based on self-declaration. The rate of income tax ranges progressively from 5 to 45% (Su, 2004), but it is poorly implemented and evasion is extensive. In sum, the urban-bias of economic policy has widened the income gap between rural and urban residents: the ratio of urban to rural per capita income increased from approximately 2:1 in 1985 to 3:1 in 2000 (Gilley, 2001, cited in Norling, 2003). The per capita urban income was 1,466US$ while the per capita rural income was only 454US$ in 2006 (China Statistical Year Book 2006, quoted in Mohrman, 2008). The implication from this discussion of tax revenues is that they take disproportionately from rural areas, and from low-income groups. In short, subsidies to higher education are financed from broadly regressive forms of taxation.

Rise in Higher Education Tuition Fees

Marketization, decentralization and privatization since the 1980s, but especially after 1992, have led to reforms in higher education, which have in turn reinforced the role of private financing. These policies and reforms have various equity implications.

Before 1985, access to higher education was free to qualified students, subject to government budget quotas (Tropical Research Group, cited in Yin and White, 1994). Only a small number of students were required to pay, including commissioned or self-supported students beyond the existing quotas. Commissioned students are sponsored by an enterprise and they agree to work for the enterprise after the graduation. During 1985–1989, there was an increase in the number of fee-paying students (Yin and White, 1994). From 1989, the policy of charging tuition fees for all students was adopted, although state-sponsored students pay much less than self-supporting and commissioned students.

The 14th congress of Communist Party of China in October 1992 agreed the policy of building up 'socialist market economy' (Yin and White, 1994). The policy also recognizes that it is necessary to introduce the non-state sectors into educational development to meet the people's pressing needs (Zha, 2001). In December 1992, higher education institutions were allowed by the State Education Commission to admit fee-paying students, with a ceiling of 30% of their total enrolment (Yin and White, 1994). The guidelines set out under the Educational Reform and Development policy (State Council of China, 1993, www.development.yangtzeu.edu.cn/jyfg/jyglzh/law_12_1202.htm) set the goal of recovering 20% of costs through the charging of tuition fees by 1997 (World Bank, 1997, 4). Starting from 1994, the fee levels of all students, including those financed by state, enterprises or self-financed, were unified at a rate of 20–25% of the total estimated higher education cost per student. By 1994, tuition fees had increased by 6 times since 1978. From 1997 onwards, all students in higher education had to pay tuition fees. All universities, except for normal and military universities, currently charge a fee of around 450–700US$ per year.

The 1993 guidelines also advocated the decentralization of university finance (World Bank, 1997, 4). As part of the decentralization, a new financial arrangement, referred to as 'joint establishment', required that local government provided partial funding for higher education institutions under central supervision (Zhong and Zhu, 1997), although central government funding retained a main role.

At the same time, the status of universities in China has changed. In 1956 all higher education institutions were publicly funded in China (Zha, 2001). In March 1982, China had its first private or '*Minban*' university—Zhonghua Zhehui University. In December 1982, the renewed Constitution of China encouraged 'collective economic organizations, governmental enterprises and other social groups to initiate and administer various kinds of legal educational activities' (Zha, 2001, 6). In 1993, and for the first time, a national policy was set aimed to provide 'active encouragement, strong support, proper guidelines and sound management' for non-state sectors to run education (Yuan, 2003). In 1995, the new Education Law confirmed this policy change (State Education Commission, 1995, cited in Zha, 2001). The Law on *Minban*/private Education Promotion of 2002 stated that *Minban*/private education institutions have the equal legal status with public ones (China Education and Research Net, 27-8-2003). The number of private higher education institutions in China has been growing very fast, from 800 in 1994 to 1,277 in 1999, with 37 of them fully authorized to grant degrees/diplomas (Hu, 1999; Yang, 2000, cited in Zha, 2001).

Equity Implications

In this section the equity implications of changes in higher education financing are explored.[1]

Public Subsidies to Higher Education Have Equity Implications

There is a strong and longstanding urban-bias in enrolment policy, and changes in public financing and increasing reliance on tuition fees will reinforce. Since 1962, a higher proportion of children from urban and better-off families go to university than among rural and low-income students. Table 51.3 compares the distribution of the working population and the distribution of university students in socioeconomic groups. The data on university students are based on the available statistics of the background of students in 34 universities in China in 2000. It can be seen from the table that the proportion of students from the urban families is 84.43%, although the urban population contributes only 19.33% of the working force. The share of university students from rural areas is 15.56%, but the rural population contributes as much as 80.77% of the working population.

The barriers in access to university faced by students from rural areas are set early on in their educational experience. According to Lin (1999), more than 30% of eligible rural students cannot go on to secondary school due to lack of funding, especially in the senior secondary school which

TABLE 51.3

Share of Working Population and Background of Higher Education Students by Socioeconomic Group in China (%)

	% of the Working Population	% of University Students
Rural workers	80.77	15.56
Blue-collar workers	8.3	32.86
Technicians	4.16	16.58
Government officials, military staff, enterprise managers and others	6.77	35
Total	100	100

Source: Adapted from Li (2002), Table 5.1.

is not compulsory. This reduces the chances of entering higher education for students in rural areas. Although in 2004 that the proportion of exam candidates from rural backgrounds exceeded that of candidates from urban backgrounds for the first time, reaching 55% of the total (News Release, MoE, 5 June 2004), the share is still less than merited by the share of population in urban and rural areas. According to the figures in Table 51.3, it can be roughly estimated that one in six urban students is able to enter higher education but that the rate for rural students is only one in twenty.

The decentralization of higher education finance has increased the gap between poor and rich regions, especially between the poor regions of the West and East.[2] Local governments in poor areas lack resources for education investment. Table 51.4 shows the differences of higher education investment by different levels of government in selected provinces. The investment in higher education per student in Beijing is double than that of Sichuan Province, although Sichuan is a relatively richer province in the West. This facilitates a significant underinvestment in higher education. In 1994, there were on average 43.3 university students per 10,000 in China. The figure for Beijing was 136, but that of Guizhou Province, a poor province in the remote west, was only 9 (World Bank, 1997). Decentralization in the financing of higher education will inevitably reinforce inequalities in access to the detriment of potential students from rural areas and low-income households.

The rise in tuition fees in higher education will restrict the participation rate, and could worsen inequalities in access. Table 51.1 shows the significant increase of out-of-pocket education expenses: the share of tuition and incidental fees rose from 2.3% in 1990 to 12.5% in 1998 (Zhang and Kanbur, 2003), and to 15.45% of total educational revenues in 2002 (MoE, 2002). Tuition fees for higher education, in addition to living expenses, constitute a huge burden to students from a rural background and low-income urban households. A survey carried out by the National Bureau of Statistics concluded that more than 50% of respondents believed they are unable to afford higher education for their children because of the excessive increase in the tuition and other fees (Huang, 2001).

Privatization of higher education is likely to exacerbate inequality in access. As the higher education enrolment rate is low in China, the demand for higher education is far from being met. At present, *Minban*/private higher education provides those who could pay some sort of higher education. Well-off households can afford for their children to enter private universities even at low levels of pre-university educational attainment. At the same time, the quality of the private education is deteriorating as institutions in the private sector exploit excess demand for places. Private institutions usually employ retired or part-time teachers from publicly funded universities and colleges, and provide lower quality facilities and support.

TABLE 51.4

Government Allocation of Funds per Student to Provincial Universities and Colleges in Selected Provinces, 1992 (Unit: yuan, 1 US$ = 7.16 yuan)

Provinces	Total Government Allocation per Student	Recurrent Allocation per Student	Capital Allocation per Student	Provincial GDP per Capita	Percentage of GDP for Higher Education
Beijing	7,007	5,309	1,698	6,434	2.9
Guangdong	6,630	5,157	1,473	3,514	1.5
Shanghai	5,341	4,707	634	7,925	2.4
Anhui	4,154	3,613	541	1,243	1.8
Sichuan	3,471	3,019	452	1,357	1.6

Source: World Bank (1997, 44).

Exploring the Options for Higher Education Financing

What are the available options for financing an expansion of access to higher education in China? This section explores existing schemes to support higher education students and assesses their effectiveness.

A scholarship scheme was established for all undergraduate candidates in 1986–1987, later extended to postgraduate candidates in 1991. At present, these reach only a small number of students. Around 20–30% of students in public universities get financial aid in China, and the level of support is too low. The academic scholarship, which is the main type of grants, provides 50$ per year to students securing a first prize (10% of all undergraduate students). Students securing the third prize, covering another 10% of all undergraduate students, receive only 25$ per year (China Education and Research Net, 2001). A relatively higher scholarship/grant is provided by the National Scholarship Scheme initiated in 2002. It provides up to 845$ per year per student. It is open to all types of students, but it only covers 45,000 students per year, about 0.6% of all higher education students (MoE, 2003; Xinhua Net, 2003). Scholarships are more accurately seen as a subsidy than a grant.

The loans system in higher education in China was piloted in 1996 and fully implemented in 1999 (China Education and Research Net, 2001). Students are expected to pay back within 4 years after graduation. Currently, the amount of money available for loans to students with financial difficulties is 140$ per person per year or more. However, since there is no comprehensive financial market or an effective credit system in place in China, the loans are least used by students from low-income households. Students from low-income households are not well informed about the loans, and the loans are not sufficient to cover their basic needs. Students are deterred by the high opportunity cost of future debt—this is particularly the case for students from a rural background. In addition, there have been serious problems in the implementation of the loans scheme because of the high default rate. Owing to high subsidy element of the loans and the resulting low profit for providers, the loans are poorly managed. In 2002, due to the high default rate of 50%, Xian Communication University became the first university to be suspended from applying for student loans by banks (Li and Cui, 2004). In Beijing, Zhengfa University was suspended from applying for student loans by Industrial and Commercial Bank of China for the 26% of default rate (Beijing News, 21 April 2004, Zhengfa University Suspended from Loans: students doubting the bank's credibility, www.thebeijingnews.com/). The year 2003–2004 is the peak year for student loans repayment, but the average default rate is nearly 20%, which is beyond the capacity of the banks to absorb. In 2004, the new system of student loans was initiated to guarantee the continuation of student loans. In the new loans system, the government will subsidize the interest before the student's graduation from university. Students will have to pay back the loans within 6 years after graduation but there is no threshold for repaying. To mitigate the risk of bad payment to the bank, the government and university jointly set up a Risk Compensation Fund for the bank, approximately 6% of the contract value. Government and university pay 50% of the compensation fund, respectively, to the contract bank (MoE, 2004). In July 2006, the Ministry of Education signed a memorandum of understanding with the Bank of China to finalize the financial arrangements between government, university and bank. However, there is a large financial risk for the government associated with the compensation fund provided.

A 'graduate tax' is defined as 'a tax that all graduates have to pay for a special period of time or as long as the individual pays taxes' (Palacios, 2004, 46). It is free at the point of consumption, and thus enables students from low-income backgrounds to enter university. The high private rate of return to education should ensure a basis for future repayments. As higher wage earners can subsidize lower earners, it can be a progressive tax. Providing it is incorporated within existing income tax collection, it is possible to avoid extra administration and costs. Therefore, a graduate tax can be fairer, easier to collect and offers sustainable funding for higher education.

However, the graduate tax is criticized by some commentators because the percentage of tax imposed by the government will depend on the political decision (Palacios, 2004); it can generate work disincentives, and future taxes may not reflect the cost of earlier education. It could be argued that these criticisms ignore distributional concerns. It can create a sustainable funding provision for both the rich and the poor, and ensures that the poor are able to attend university as it makes higher education free at the point of consumption. It is reasonable to require students to pay for part of their higher education by committing a share of their future earning because they are the direct beneficiaries. The argument that it is unfair for very successful graduates to pay a tax much higher than the cost of their education is not well founded. Fairness should be achieved through taxing the rich to subsidize the poor. It is the tax on the higher-earning graduates that makes the 'graduate tax' system fair and sustainable, especially as the Income Gini Coefficient in China has increased from 0.33 in 1980 to 0.45 in 2002 (Lu, cited in Yang, 2002). There is great advantage in a graduate tax as a means of securing funds for the extension of higher education while improving access to low-income groups. The only investment for government to provide is the start funds needed to get the scheme off the ground. It may be some kind of public subsidy but it only needs subsidy for the first 4 years' start-up period and will solve the financial problem in the long run.

It has been suggested that the private sector could take a large role in financing higher education. Financial support from enterprises has been lingering at around 1.69–1.83 billion US$ per year, but the contribution from donations has been declining (Luo, 2004). Cao and Levy (2005, quoted in Mohrman, 2008) also noted that the donations from society only happened in a very few cases. There is still a great potential to develop higher education funding from enterprises and civil society including alumni. Students are not the only beneficiaries of higher education (Palacios, 2004).

Conclusions

This paper has examined the financing of higher education in China. This is an important issue in the context of the rapid economic and social transformation of the Chinese economy and society. There is great urgency in facilitating an expansion of access to higher education in China, both to sustain the growth in the economy, and to support the extension of economic opportunity and social mobility. The paper considered the capacity of current sources of finance to enable an increase in the participation rate in higher education, and the equity implications. The two dimensions of efficiency and equity are closely interlinked. Inequality in access to higher education is becoming a problem for equal social and economic development, and a barrier to sustainable financial arrangements.

It will be useful to summarize the main findings emerging from the discussion in the paper. Public expenditure in education is low compared to countries at similar levels of development, at 2.79% of GDP. Higher education absorbs one quarter of total government expenditure on education, but despite recent growth in enrolment rates in tertiary education only 21% of the relevant age group access it.

Tax revenues constitute the main source of higher education financing. A brief discussion of government tax revenues identified urban and industrial bias to the extent that public expenditure on higher education is largely financed from general tax revenues, important equity and efficiency issues arise in the context of extending access.

The process of marketization of higher education in China has aimed to increase the role of tuition fees and private financing of higher education. Charging tuition fees directly to students attending universities further restricts access to higher education by students from rural and low-income households. Decentralization of education finance appears to increase inequality across regions, especially given differential capacity of local government in raising revenues. Access to higher education is limited in poorer regions. The privatization of higher education results in greater inequality in access to higher education. Private higher education institutions facilitate participation by the better off who are able to pay, even with lower pre-university qualifications than students from rural and low-income households. There is a danger that privatization will lower the quality of higher education as a whole.

Scholarships, grants and loans have only a limited role in promoting the development of higher education at present in China as only a small proportion of students are covered, and the level of support is low. Loans have not been successful in lifting constraints in university access, partly because comprehensive financial markets and an effective credit system are lacking, but also because of implementation issues. High default rates among students who have taken education loans undermine the effectiveness of loans as a means to increase access. The contribution of enterprises and other private sources of financing have remained marginal.

An expansion in higher education participation in China will require additional financing. However, sustainable financing will require financial arrangements that maximize access and opportunity for all. The equity implications of the new financial arrangements need urgent consideration. It will be important to ensure that support for improved primary and secondary education for rural and low-income households is forthcoming. Improving the educational opportunities of these groups is essential to extend access to higher education. Ensuring high educational achievement in primary and secondary education will raise the rate of university participation by the poor, and will promote the development of the rural and poor areas.

The decentralization of government revenue mobilization might need fine-tuning in the context of higher education financing. Central government financing can ensure redistribution across poor and better-off regions. This is essential to achieve equity and sustainability in the public financing of higher education. The decentralization in revenue mobilization and financing has made it harder for poor regions to make the necessary investment in education.

A graduate tax appears to be as fair and sustainable as it is progressive. A graduate tax is fairer because it plays some role of redistribution as higher earning graduates may subsidize the lower earners. It facilitates increased access to higher education as it makes higher education free at the point of consumption. It is sustainable as the rate of return of higher education provides a sound basis for future repayment, but government needs to provide the start funds needed to get the scheme off the ground.

As to other sources of finance, enterprise and alumni are some of the potential sources for higher education finance. Their contribution to supporting higher education is justified, as they are direct beneficiaries and stakeholders.

The equity challenge in China's higher education finance needs to be addressed urgently, especially as sustaining China's rapid economic growth in the future will come to depend in large part on the quantity and quality of its human resources.

Notes

1. An important issue is that subsidies to higher education crowd out the public support to primary and secondary education, but for reasons of space this is not covered in the paper.
2. The *west poor areas* include 12 provinces/municipalities/autonomous regions. They consist 18% of China's GDP, 29% of the population, 60% of the poor people, 72% of the minority population and 72% of the surface area of China (The World Bank Group for China, 22 January 2003, 17).

References

Barr, N. (2001) *Welfare State as Piggy Bank: Information, Risk Uncertainty and the Role of the State*, Oxford: Oxford University Press.

China Education and Research Net. (2001) 'Scholarship for whom?' http://www.cer.net/article/20010101/3039204.shtml.

Chinese Academy of Social Science (CASS). (2007) *Analysis and Forecast on China's Social Development 2006*, Beijing: Social Sciences Academic Press.

Colclough, C. (1990) 'Raising additional resources for education in developing countries: Are graduate payroll taxes superior to student loans?' *International Journal of Educational Development* 10(2–3): 169–180.

Colclough, C. (1993) 'Who should Learn to Pay? An Assessment of Neo-liberal Approaches to Education Policy', in C. Colclough and J. Manor (eds.) *States or Markets? Neo-liberalism and Development Policy Debate*, Oxford: Clarendon Press.

Creedy, J. (1995) *The Economics of Higher Education: An Analysis of Taxes Versus Fees*, Hants: Edward Elgar.

Dahlman, J.C. and Aubert, J.E. (2001) *China and the Knowledge Economy: Seizing the 21st Century*, Washington, DC: The World Bank, p. 71.

Garner, R. (2007) 'Generation debt', *The Independent*, 14 August.

Heckman (2002) 'China's investment in human capital', NBER Working Paper 9296, www.nber.org/papers/w9296.

Hu, W. (1999) 'China's non-governmental education development and the strategic framework', China Education Online, www.eol.com.cn/privateschool/private_school_expert_bbs/psl_gejia_0020.html.

Huang, Y. (2001) 'Half families cannot afford excessive high increase on education expenditure', *People Daily*, 15 October, www.edu.cn/20011015/3004972.shtml.

Li, W. (2002) 'On equality of access to higher education in China', unpublished doctoral dissertation, China Economics Studies Centre, Beijing University: Beijing.

Li, B. and Cui, L. (2004) 'NPC Representative: let those bad student debtor isolated from society', *China Youth Newspaper*. www.learning.sohu.com/20040726/n221193503.shtml.

Lin, J. (1999) *Social Transformation and Private Education in China*, Westport, CT: Praeger Publishers.

Luo, Y. (2004) 'Fund shortages frustrate development of higher education', in China Today report, www.chinatoday.com.cn/English/e2004/e200406/p18.htm.

Ministry of Education, Ministry of Finance and State Statistics Bureau. (2000) '1999 National report on the education expenditure', File No: JIAOCAI (2000) 22, 3 November 2000, www.legal.mof.gov.cn:8000/subject.asp.

MoE. (July 2002) 'Education in China', Report, Ministry of Education, Beijing.

MoE. (2003) 'Introduction to China national scholarship system', www.moe.edu.cn/jytouru/gjjiangxuejin/1.htm.

MoE. (2004) 'News Release', 31 August 2004, www.news.xinhuanet.com/edu/2004-08/30/content_1927555.htm.

MoE, National Bureau of Statistics, Ministry of Finance. (2006) 'Report on the implementation of 2005 education budget', Beijing.

Mohrman, K. (2008) 'The emerging global model with Chinese characteristics', *Higher Education Policy* 21(1): 29–48.

Norling, J. (2003) 'Their capacity to endure: taxation in China and its impact on the rural peasantry', www.focusanthro.org/essays/norling–03-04.html.

Palacios, M. (2004) *Investing In Human Capital: A Capital Market Approach to Student Funding*, Cambridge: Cambridge University Press.

Psacharopoulos, G. (1994) 'Returns to investment in education: A global update', Report, The World Bank, Washington, DC.

Smith, H.P. and Szymanski, S. (2003) 'Why political scientists should support free public higher education?' *PS: Political Science & Politics* 36: 399–703.

Su, S. (2004) 'An Introduction to taxation of China', unpublished lecture, May 2004, www.ifa.org.uk/Article on-Taxation-in-China.doc.

The World Bank Group for the People's Republic of China, Country Management Unit, East Asia and Pacific Region. (2003) 'Memorandum of the president of the international bank for reconstruction and development and the international finance corporation to the executive directors on a country assistance strategy', Report No. 25141,World Bank, Washington, DC January 22, p. 17.

Tudawe, I. (2001) 'Chronic poverty and development policy in Sri Lanka: Overview study', CPRC Working Paper No. 9, Chronic Poverty Research Centre (CPRC), Manchester University, Manchester.

UNESCO Institute for Statistics. (2004a) 'Gross enrolment rate in tertiary education', April 2004, www.uis.unesco.org/TEMPLATE/html/HTMLTables/education/ger_tertiary.html.

UNESCO Institute for Statistics. (2004b) 'Percentage distribution of public expenditure on education by level of education', April 2004, www.uis.unesco.org/ev.php?ID=5045_201&ID2=DO_TOPIC.

World Bank. (1986) *China: Management and Finance of Higher Education*, Washington, DC: World Bank.

World Bank. (1997) *China Higher Education Reform: A World Bank Country Study*, Washington, DC: World Bank.

World Bank. (2004) 'Summary education profile: Sri Lanka', www.devdata.worldbank.org/edstats/SummaryEducationProfiles/CountryData/GetShowData.asp?sCtry=LKA,Sri%20Lanka.

World Bank. (2006) *World Development Report 2006: Equity and Development*, Washington, DC: The World Bank.

Xinhua Net. (2003) 'Scholarship system of China higher education', 15 August, www.news.xinhuanet.com/school/2003-08/15/content_1028550.htm.

Yang, M. (2002) 'Income gap increasing in China', *VOA Business Scene Magazine* 1(1). Washington, DC, www.freexinwen.com/caijing/pages/june02/june6.HTM.

Yin, Q. and White, G. (1994) 'The marketization of Chinese higher education: A critical assessment', *Comparative Education* 30(3): 217–221.

Yuan, S. (2003) 'Private higher education in China: evolution, features and problems', www.gse.buffalo.edu/org/inthigheredfinance/PDF/Private%20Higher%20Ed%20in%20China%20edited.pdf.

Zha, Q. (2001) 'The resurgence and growth of private higher education in China', www.education.mcgill.ca/csshe/Conf/Archives/Papers_2001/CSSHE2001_Zha.pdf.

Zhang, X. and Kanbur, R. (2003) 'Spatial inequality in education and health care in China', Centre for Economic Policy Research, Discussion Papers No. 4136, September, www.cepr.org/pubs/dps/DP4136.asp.

Zhong, B. and Zhu, C. (1997) *Higher Education in Transition Economies in Asia*, The First Workshop on Strategies and Policies in Higher Education Reform in Transition Economies in Asia, Xi'an, China, 7–10 October, Source: www.unesco.org Documents.

Zhou, J. (2006) 'Speech on the inauguration of the Committee on Teaching Supervision 2006–2010', News Letter of Ministry of Education, Issue 7, www.jyb.com.cn/cm/jycm/beijing/jybgb/zh/t20061111_48376.htm.

Brief Biographies of Editors

John C. Weidman is professor of higher and international development education, Department of Administrative and Policy Studies, School of Education, University of Pittsburgh, where he teaches courses on education policy, planning, capacity building, and sector analysis. He has been director, Institute for International Studies in Education (IISE), and held distinguished visiting faculty appointments at the Graduate School of International Development, Nagoya University, Japan; Beijing Normal University, China; Maseno University, Kenya; and Augsburg University, Germany. He has published extensively in peer-reviewed journals, books, and research monographs and is co-editor of the Sense Publishers series, Pittsburgh Studies in Comparative and International Education.

John L. Yeager is an emeritus associate professor of higher education in the Department of Administrative and Policy Studies, School of Education, University of Pittsburgh, where he taught courses in budgeting and strategic planning. He is a former Vice Chancellor for Administration at the University of Pittsburgh and the former director of the Institute for Higher Education. He was the lead editor of the Second Edition of the *ASHE Reader on Finance in Higher Education.*

Laurie Cohen is liaison librarian for education, Jewish studies and religious studies at Hillman Library, University of Pittsburgh. She purchases library titles in her subject areas, answers chat reference and instant messages, and conducts in-person consultations. She serves on library and university committees, chairs the University Senate Community Relations Committee, and offers library instruction sessions for faculty and students.

Linda DeAngelo is an assistant professor of higher education in the Department of Administrative and Policy Studies, School of Education, University of Pittsburgh. She teaches courses on college student development and student affairs management. She studies social reproduction/stratification, equity, and diversity issues. She focuses on the differential effect of institutions on students, pipeline and educational transitions, outcomes for first-generation, low-income, and underrepresented students, and learning and change in diverse environments.

Kristin DeLuca is a higher education doctoral student in the Department of Administrative and Policy Studies, School of Education, University of Pittsburgh. Her research interests include single-sex education, student political behavior, and gender differences in college student development. She works in the University Honors College as an academic advisor and oversees living learning communities.

W. James Jacob is associate professor of higher and international development education in the Department of Administrative and Policy Studies, School of Education, University of Pittsburgh, and director, Institute for International Studies in Education (IISE). His research and consultancy experience focus on higher education management, governance, quality assurance, and organizational development; HIV/AIDS multi-sector prevention, policy, and capacity building; and indigenous education issues of culture, language, and identity. He is past chair of the Comparative and International Education Society's (CIES) Higher Education SIG and co-editor of book series by Palgrave Macmillan (International and Development Education) and Sense Publishers series (Pittsburgh Studies in Comparative and International Education).

Michael G. Gunzenhauser is associate professor of the philosophy of education in the Department of Administrative and Policy Studies, School of Education, University of Pittsburgh. He studies ethics and epistemology in education and research methods. He coordinated pre-college programs at Duke University and was a residential counselor at the North Carolina School of Science and Mathematics. He is author of a recent (2012) book, *The Active/Ethical Professional: A Framework for Responsible Educators.*

Maureen W. McClure is associate professor of educational leadership in the Department of Administrative and Policy Studies, School of Education, University of Pittsburgh. She is an education strategist interested in the design of institutional management and public policy for development, both domestically and internationally, especially in the presence of major crises. She teaches courses in resources management and strategic management, education and development debates, and economics of education with a special interest in international and domestic crisis response, broadly defined. She has consulted widely for international organizations, including USAID and UNESCO.

Stewart E. Sutin is clinical professor of higher education in the Department of Administrative and Policy Studies, School of Education, University of Pittsburgh. He is a former president of the Community College of Allegheny County, former senior vice president of Mellon Bank, and former president of Bank of Boston International. He has presented on transforming the financial model of community colleges for the American Association of Community Colleges, College Board, and New England College Council. He is senior editor of a recent (2011) book on community college finance, *Increasing effectiveness of the community college financial model: A global perspective for the global economy*.